W9-AZW-616

ScottForesman LITERATURE AND INTEGRATED STUDIES

Annotated Teacher's Edition
Volume One

English Literature

ScottForesman

Editorial Offices: Glenview, Illinois
Regional Offices: San Jose, California • Tucker, Georgia
Glenview, Illinois • Oakland, New Jersey • Dallas, Texas

Visit ScottForesman's Home Page at http://www.scottforesman.com

acknowledgments

Cover (detail): Dante Gabriel Rossetti, *The Beloved*/Tate Gallery, London/Bridgeman Art Library, London/Superstock, Inc. **T5(l)** © Tony Freeman/Photo Edit **T5(r)** © David Young-Wolff/Photo Edit **T20(t)** © Karen Holsinger Mullen/Unicorn Stock Photos **T20(c)** © David Young-Wolff/Photo Edit **T20(b)** © Robert Brenner/Photo Edit **T22(t)** © Steve Bourgeois/Unicorn Stock Photos **T22(b)** © Michael Newman/Photo Edit **T23** © Richard Hutchings/Photo Edit **T24(b)** © David Young-Wolff/PhotoEdit **T24(t)** © Dana White/PhotoEdit **T26(t)** © Superstock, Inc. **T27(b)** © Michael Newman/Photo Edit **T28** © Jeff Greenberg/Photo Edit **T29** © Superstock, Inc. **T30(b)** © Martin R. Joni/Unicorn Stock Photos **T31(t)** © Superstock, Inc. **T31(c)** © Superstock, Inc. **T31(b)** © Jeff Greenberg/Photo Edit **T32(c)** © Mary Kate Denny/PhotoEdit **T32(b)** © Billy E. Barnes/PhotoEdit **T32(t)** © David Young-Wolff/PhotoEdit **T34(t)** © Aneal Vohra/Unicorn Stock Photos **T34(b)** © Michael Newman/Photo Edit **T35** © David Young-Wolff/Photo Edit **T36(l)** © David Young-Wolff/PhotoEdit **T36(r)** Alinari/Art Resource **T38(t)** © Tony Freeman/Photo Edit **T38(b)** © Michael Newman/Photo Edit **T39** © Superstock, Inc. **e(t)** David Young-Wolff/PhotoEdit **e(b)** Werner Forman Archives/Art Resource **f(t)** Alcock-Camelot Research Committee **f(b)** British Library **103c(t)** Folger Shakespeare Library **103d(b)** Kobal Collection **219e(t)** Corbis-Bettmann **219f(t)** Ian Murphy/Tony Stone Images **289e(t)** Sidney Harris **289e(br)** Photofest **289f(t)** P. F. Bentley/Black Star

ISBN: 0-673-29466-8

1.800.554.4411
http://www.scottforesman.com

1 2 3 4 5 6 7 8 9 10 DR 03 02 01 00 99 98 97 96

contents

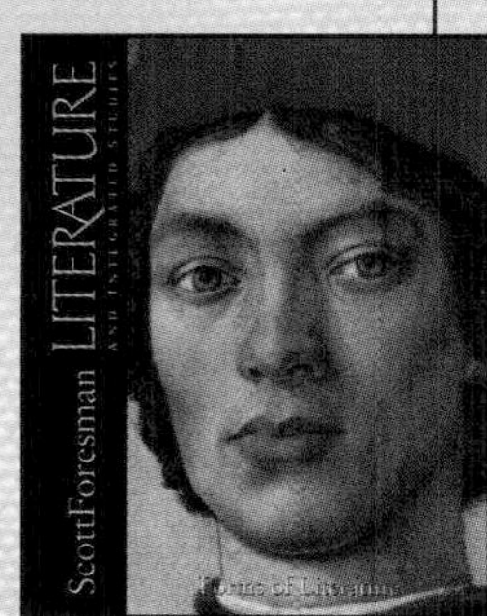

Forms of Literature

World Literature

American Literature

English Literature

a step ahead

ScottForesman Literature and Integrated Studies is a multi-dimensional program that is a step ahead of other literature series . . . from in-depth multicultural explorations to integration that includes interdisciplinary study to a strong new focus on media and visual literacy.

A step ahead . . .

- **In Literary Content** that combines thematic organization with an innovative blend of classic and modern literature.
- **In Integration** that blends outstanding literature with rich, structured writing assignments and solid skills instruction.
- **In Interdisciplinary Studies** that capture students' attention, command their interest, and explore the natural links between literature and other subject areas.
- **In Skills Focus** that introduces reading, vocabulary, literary, writing, and language skills in context plus special attention on the media and visual literacy skills students need in today's world.
- **In Achieving Success for All Students** with strong support for reading comprehension; extensive help for students with limited English proficiency; mini-lessons on vocabulary, spelling, grammar and mechanics, and strategic reading; suggestions for both at-risk and gifted students—plus a Teacher's Resource File with more than 1500 pages of additional materials.
- **In Useful, User-Friendly Technology** at every level and for every purpose . . . beginning with test generators and journal-writing software . . . moving on to 3 exciting new CD-ROM programs on custom publishing, Shakespeare, and in-depth research on more than 40 major authors . . . and,
- **In Unparalleled Support for Novels** with 36 literature kits for major literary works taught across the curriculum.

materials

A Pupil Book with Authentic Integration

- Integration begins with thematic groups of literature.
- Literature lessons incorporate reading, critical thinking, literary, and vocabulary skills.
- Interdisciplinary studies move beyond the language arts into other content areas.
- Scaffolded writing workshops present assignments based on the literature.
- Language skills are embedded in the writing workshops at point of use.

Innovative Materials to Support Student Lessons

- 2-volume Annotated Teacher's Editions provide traditional and non-traditional lesson support, a rich variety of mini-lessons, and abundant help for students who are less-proficient in English.
- Teacher's Resource Files are filled with a wealth of skill-building and enrichment materials that allow each teacher to adjust the program to meet class needs and teaching styles.

Useful, User-Friendly Technology and Supplemental Materials

- Software programs include discs for assessment, writing, and journal keeping.
- AuthorWorks™, a 7-disc CD-ROM research database with Project books, provides a wealth of author information.
- The ScottForesman Custom Literature Database CD-ROM holds over 1400 additional selections with lessons and correlations to student anthology.
- The top-rated BBC Shakespeare CD-ROM series presents 5 of the bard's best-loved plays.
- NovelWorks™ kits supply in-depth teaching materials for 36 popularly taught novels.
- Points of Departure—a supplemental literature series—includes 7 titles with focused coverage of specialized literary genres.

goals

To bring teachers and students these unique materials, ScottForesman sought the guidance and direction of America's premier educators in order to forge an exciting new pedagogy, ambitious and flexible enough to move easily into the next millennium. Two program goals guided the creation of these materials:

To assist students in becoming lifelong readers and critical thinkers

To help teachers renew the excitement of teaching and to revitalize their role as important professionals in today's society

literature-based integration

AN AUTHENTIC BLEND

Authentic integration occurs when the language arts — including literature, reading, vocabulary, writing, and language skills — are carefully woven together so that one flows naturally into another and students acquire **new information at point of use** rather than in isolation.

ScottForesman Literature and Integrated Studies provides a **tightly-crafted integration** of lessons in the pupil books as is illustrated by abbreviated tables of contents such as the one shown. These literature organizers appear at the beginning of each integrated grouping.

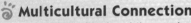

Part One

Romantic Truths and Terrors

The Romantic movement of the early 1800s optimistically proclaimed that any determined individual could better society. Yet, there was an ominous side to Romanticism as well—a fascination with death and an interest in the unknown, unpredictable parts of the human psyche.

Multicultural Connection **Individuality** may mean either accepting or rejecting cultural norms or group standards. How do the narrators and characters in the following selections express their individuality?

220 UNIT THREE: AMERICAN CLASSIC

Multicultural Connection
Authentic multicultural themes begin here and are woven throughout each unit.

Literature
Thematic groupings of classic and contemporary selections make literature relevant for students.

Interdisciplinary Study
Theme-related studies in other disciplines are part of a fresh approach to integration.

Writing Workshop
Writing process assignments include revising and editing lessons.

In 1845 Thoreau built a cabin in the woods by Walden Pond and lived there for two years. He wanted to simplify his life to the point where he could learn what the true essentials in life were. While there, he planned to write and study nature. Thoreau began his book, Walden, after he left the pond, and finished it in 1854. Modern photographer Elliot Porter, who took the photo on the right, has found inspiration for his work in Thoreau's writings.

Walden

HENRY DAVID THOREAU

When first I took up my abode in the woods, that is, began to spend my nights as well as days there, which, by accident, was on Independence Day, or the fourth of July, 1845, my house was not finished for winter, but was merely a defense against the rain, without plastering or chimney, the walls being of rough weather-stained boards, with wide chinks, which made it cool at night. The upright white hewn studs and freshly planed door and window casings gave it a clean and airy look, especially in the morning, when its timbers were saturated with dew, so that I fancied that by noon some sweet gum would exude from them. To my imagination it retained throughout the day more or less of this auroral character, reminding me of a certain house on a mountain which I had visited the year before. This was an airy and unplastered cabin, fit to entertain a traveling god, and where a goddess might trail her garments. The winds which passed over my dwelling were such as sweep over the ridges of mountains, bearing the broken strains, or celestial parts only, of terrestrial music. The morning wind forever blows, the poem of creation is uninterrupted; but few are the ears that hear it. Olympus[1] is but the outside of the earth everywhere. . . .

I was seated by the shore of a small pond, about a mile and a half south of the village of Concord and somewhat higher than it, in the midst of an extensive wood between that town and Lincoln, and about two miles south of that our only field known to fame, Concord Battle Ground; but I was so low in the woods that the opposite shore, half a mile off, like the rest, covered with wood, was my most distant horizon. For the first week, whenever I looked out on the pond it impressed me like a tarn high up on the side of a mountain, its bottom far above the surface of other lakes, and, as the sun arose, I saw it throwing off its nightly clothing of mist, and here and there, by degrees, its soft ripples or its smooth reflecting surface was revealed, while the mists, like ghosts, were stealthily[2] withdrawing in every direction into the woods, as at the breaking up of some nocturnal conventicle.

1. **Olympus** (ō lim′pəs), mountain home of the gods in Greek mythology.
2. stealthily (stelth′ə lē), *adv.* secretly; slyly.

The very dew seemed to hang upon the trees later into the day than usual, as on the sides of mountains. . . .

I went to the woods because I wished to live deliberately, to front only the essential facts of life, and see if I could not learn what it had to teach, and not, when I came to die, discover that I had not lived. I did not wish to live what was not life, living is so dear; nor did I wish to practice resignation, unless it was quite necessary. I wanted to live deep and suck out all the marrow of life, to live so sturdily and Spartanlike[3] as to put to rout all that was not life, to cut a broad swath and shave close, to drive life into a corner, and reduce it to its lowest terms, and, if it proved to be mean, why then to get the whole and genuine meanness of it, and publish its meanness to the world; or if it were sublime, to know it by experience, and be able to give a true account of it in my next excursion. For most men, it appears to me, are in a strange uncertainty about it, whether it is of the devil or of God, and have *somewhat hastily* concluded that it is the chief end of man here to "glorify God and enjoy him forever."

CLARIFY: What kind of life does Thoreau want to live?

Still we live meanly,[4] like ants; though the fable tells us that we were long ago changed into men; like pygmies we fight with cranes; it is error upon error, and clout upon clout, and our best virtue has for its occasion a superfluous[5] and evitable wretchedness. Our life is frittered away by detail. An honest man has hardly need to count more than his ten fingers, or in extreme cases he may add his ten toes, and lump the rest. Simplicity, simplicity, simplicity! I say, let your affairs be as two or three, and not a hundred or a thousand; instead of a million count half a dozen, and keep your accounts on your thumb nail. In the midst of this chopping sea of civilized life, such are the clouds and storms and quicksands and thousand-and-one items to be allowed for, that a man has to live, if he would not founder and go to the bottom and not make his port at all, by dead reckoning, and he must be a great calculator indeed who succeeds. Simplify, simplify. Instead of three meals a day, if it be necessary eat but one; instead of a hundred dishes, five; and reduce other things in proportion. Our life is like a German Confederacy, made up of petty states, with its boundary forever fluctuating, so that even a German cannot tell you how it is bounded at any moment. The nation itself, with all its so called internal improvements, which, by the way, are all external and superficial, is just such an unwieldy and overgrown establishment, cluttered with furniture and tripped up by its own traps, ruined by luxury and heedless expense, by want of calculation and a worthy aim, as the million households in the land; and the only cure for it as for them is in a rigid economy, a stern and more than Spartan simplicity of life and elevation of purpose. It lives too fast. Men think that it is essential that the *Nation* have commerce, and export ice, and talk through a telegraph, and ride thirty miles an hour, without a doubt, whether *they* do or not; but whether we should live like baboons or like men, is a little uncertain. If we do not get out sleepers, and forge rails, and devote days and nights to the work, but go to tinkering upon our *lives* to improve *them*, who will build railroads? And if railroads are not built, how shall we get to heaven in season? But if we stay at home and mind our business, who will want railroads? We do not ride on the railroad; it rides upon us. . . .

I left the woods for as good a reason as I went there. Perhaps it seemed to me that I had several more lives to live, and could not spare any more time for that one. It is remarkable how easily and

3. **Spartanlike,** *adj.* simply; without frills. In ancient Greece, the inhabitants of the city of Sparta were known for their simple and severe manner of living.
4. meanly (mēn′lē), *adv.* of a small-minded nature.
5. superfluous (sü pėr′flü əs), *adj.* more than is needed.

On-page vocabulary

Vocabulary study words are underlined and defined on the page where they appear.

Reading help

Interlinear questions are used to guide students through more difficult selections.

Informational art captions

Quality fine-art pieces are enhanced with provocative questions that often extend the multicultural focus.

How does the composition of this painting, *Men Are Square* (1919) by Gerrit A. Beneker, reflect the cultural values of **individuality** and **self-reliance**?

Self-Reliance

RALPH WALDO EMERSON

To believe your own thought, to believe that what is true for you in your private heart is true for all men,—that is genius. Speak your latent conviction, and it shall be the universal sense; for the inmost in due time becomes the outmost, and our first thought is rendered[1] back to us by the trumpets of the Last Judgment. Familiar as the voice of the mind is to each, the highest merit we ascribe to Moses, Plato and Milton is that they set at naught books and traditions, and spoke not what men, but what *they* thought. A man should learn to detect and watch that gleam of light which flashes across his mind from within, more than the lustre of the firmament[2] of bards and sages. Yet he dismisses without notice his thought, because it is his. In every work of genius we recognize our own rejected thoughts; they come back to us with a certain alienated majesty. . . .

1. render (ren′dər), *v.* give in return.
2. **firmament** (fėr′mə mənt), *n.* arch of the heavens; sky.

a step ahead

in total integration of all skills and disciplines

interdisciplinary studies

A NEW DIMENSION

For the first time in any series, integration moves beyond the language arts to include **other content areas.** *ScottForesman Literature and Integrated Studies* presents highly motivating, visually appealing interdisciplinary sections that generate student excitement, provide **informational reading** opportunities, and **connect literature to the real world.**

INTERDISCIPLINARY STUDY

Romantic Truths and Terrors

An Appetite for Fright

Pop Culture Connection
Eerie tales and horror stories like those of Irving, Poe, and Hawthorne have long been a popular form of entertainment. When motion pictures were invented in the 1890s, horror stories were among the first films to be produced. The films pictured here represent some of the types of horror that have thrilled movie goers. On pages 288-289, a modern master of the horror story, Stephen King, talks about why this type of fiction remains popular.

This house may seem innocent enough, but in Psycho (1960), nothing is as it first appears. In this classic thriller, like many other Hitchcock films, subtle details and plot twists keep audiences on the edge of their seats. When you take a closer look, what subtleties of the house and its surroundings contribute to its ominous atmosphere?

AN APPETITE FO

CENTURIES OF PASSION PENT UP IN HIS SAVAGE HEA

CREATU FROM BLACK LAG

Literary links

Interdisciplinary studies are based on unit themes.

a step ahead

in blending cross-curricular content with language arts

Making connections

Studies in history, sociology, psychology, science, math, geography, careers, and pop culture make literature come alive for students.

What's on the Other Side of the Door?

from **Danse Macabre**
STEPHEN KING

I want to say something about imagination purely as a tool in the art and science of scaring people. The idea isn't original with me; I heard it expressed by William F. Nolan at the 1979 World Fantasy Convention. Nothing is so frightening as what's behind the closed door, Nolan said. You approach the door in the old, deserted house, and you hear something scratching at it. The audience holds its breath along with the protagonist as she or he (more often she) approaches that door. The protagonist throws it open, and there is a ten-foot-tall bug. The audience screams, but this particular scream has an oddly relieved sound to it. "A bug ten feet tall is pretty horrible," the audience thinks, "but I can deal with a ten-foot-tall bug. I was afraid it might be a *hundred* feet tall." . . .

Bill Nolan was speaking as a screenwriter when he offered the example of the big bug behind the door, but the point applies to all media. What's behind the door or lurking at the top of the stairs is never as frightening as the door or the staircase itself. And because of this, comes the paradox: the artistic work of horror is almost always a disappointment. It is the classic no-win situation. You can scare people with the unknown for a long, long time (the classic example, as Bill Nolan also pointed out, is the Jacques Tourneur film with Dana Andrews, *Curse of the Demon*), but sooner or later, as in poker, you have to turn your down cards up. You have to open the door and show the audience what's behind it. And if what happens to be behind it is a bug, not ten but a hundred feet tall, the audience heaves a sigh of relief (or utters a scream of relief) and thinks, "A bug a hundred feet tall is pretty horrible, but I can deal with that. I was afraid it might be a *thousand* feet tall." . . .

The *danse macabre* is a waltz with death. This is a truth we cannot afford to shy away from. Like the rides in the amusement park which mimic violent death, the tale of horror is a chance to examine what's going on behind doors which we usually keep double-locked. Yet the human imagination is not content with locked doors. Somewhere there is another dancing partner, the imagination whispers in the night—a partner in a rotting ball gown, a partner with empty eye sockets, green mold growing on her elbow-length gloves, maggots squirming in the thin remains of her hair. To hold such a creature in our arms? Who, you ask me, would be so mad? Well . . . ?

"You will not want to open this door," Bluebeard tells his wife in the most horrible of all horror stories, "because your husband has forbidden it." But this, of course, only makes her all the more curious . . . and at last, her curiosity is satisfied.

"You may go anywhere you wish in the castle," Count Dracula tells Jonathan Harker, "except where the doors are locked, where of course you will not wish to go." But Harker goes soon enough.

And so do we all. Perhaps we go to the forbidden door or window willingly because we understand that a time comes when we must go whether we want to or not . . . and not just to look but to be pushed through. Forever.

The theme of horror is not limited to books and films—it also shows up in fine art, such as this painting,* That Which I Should Have Done I Did Not Do *(1931-41) by American artist Ivan Albright. What techniques does Albright use to create a feeling of dread?

Responding

1. How is reading a scary book different from watching a scary movie? Which do you prefer?
2. Which of the selections you read would translate best into a horror movie? Why?
3. Do you agree with King's explanation of the continuing appeal of horror in films and literature?

STEVEN McQUEEN
ANETA CORSEAUT · EARL ROWE
PRODUCED BY JACK H. HARRIS · DIRECTED BY IRVIN S. YEAWORTH, JR. · SCREENPLAY BY THEODORE SIMONSON · KATE

FRIGHT

Released in 1986, Friday the 13th Part VI was one in a long series of Friday the 13th movies that started in 1980. These extremely violent slasher films ushered in, along with others, what critics have called a "depressing trend in American films." How is the horror portrayed in these movies different from earlier films?

JASON LIVES
FRIDAY THE 13TH PART VI

This climactic scen... the gigantic gori... New York City. ... using a 16 inc... against spe... effects tric... to life on...

INTERDISCIPLINARY STUDY

Health Connection
Horror has a reputation of being somehow less than respectable. Yet some health experts believe that horror, in moderate doses, might actually be good for you! Read the following article, and decide whether you agree.

The Thrill of Chills

by Ellen Blum Barish

Does the idea of riding a roller coaster at an amusement park excite you or terrify you? How about watching Freddy Krueger in *Nightmare on Elm Street* in a dark theater? Do you ever pick up a Stephen King novel, or do you stick with drama and romance?

Lots of teens say there is nothing like a good scare from the thrill of an amusement park ride or a tense moment from a horror story. In fact, there are so many who think so, that the "chill industry" is doing very well, thank you.

According to a recent survey of young people age 10 to 13, 89 percent had seen at least one movie in the *Friday the 13th* or *Nightmare on Elm Street* series; 62 percent had seen at least four of them. *Friday the 13th* grossed a total of $200 million dollars. Horror fans have made horror writer Stephen King a millionaire many times over.

In spite of the evidence showing that the chill industry is anything but frozen, there are people who would rather stay far away from scary rides and hold-your-breath movies. But, is one approach better than the other? Is seeking chills a healthy pursuit for teens?

Experts say yes . . . and no. For example, going to a horror movie is experiencing a safe and sometimes much-needed escape, says horror critic Douglas E. Winter. "We love to see something so grotesque and unexpected that it makes us scream or laugh . . . secure in the knowledge that in the fun house of fear, such behavior is not only accepted but encouraged," Winter wrote in 1985, the year he published a book of interviews with horror writers called *The Faces of Fear.*

"Every horror story," Winter writes, "has a happy ending. We have a simple escape—we can just wake up and say it was all a dream."

The "dream" can also be a way of preparing for life, according to Dr. Lenore Terr, a San Francisco child psychologist. Dr. Terr says that going to a horror movie or riding a roller coaster can help us feel in control. "It is a way for us to confront our fears," Dr. Terr says, "and gain mastery over our feelings."

There is a feeling of reassurance, notes Dr. Terr, "when you come out (of the movie) alive." . . .

But there is a downside to too much chill seeking. Long-term viewing of the creep shows and horror flicks may lead to violent or aggressive behavior in some young people, says a 1990 American Academy of Pediatrics statement.

Other experts point out that too much horror movie watching or roller coaster riding is like too much of anything—unhealthy—and can keep a teen from experiencing a variety of other activities. . . . Chill seekers should keep in mind that the chill seeking is a temporary, fun, thrill-like experience. . . .

Almost everyone is afraid of something, even if it isn't ghostly. You may steer clear of roller coasters but enjoy in-line skating because it's fast. Or you may change the TV channel if a horror movie comes on but not fear jumping from the high diving board at the pool.

It's healthy to try new things every once in a while—like taking a well-thought-out risk. It's worth finding out what you like, what you dislike, and what you want to avoid. A good scare now and then can help you sort out those feelings.

Responding

1. Do you agree that reading or viewing horror stories can, in moderation, be healthy for you? Explain your answer.

Interdisciplinary ...

integrated writing

A SCAFFOLDED APPROACH

Students write about ideas, themes, and characters from the literature—often connecting these ideas to their own lives. To help each student experience **success in writing**, workshops are carefully **scaffolded** to provide support for writers who need it and flexibility for writers who are ready to try new strategies and techniques. Each workshop begins with a **Writer's Blueprint** that lists guidelines for creating a successful paper. In addition, the workshop includes Revising and Editing **(Grammar)** lessons integrated at point of use.

in providing students with a blueprint for writing success

Writing in Style

Assignment After reading stories by Poe and Hawthorne, you know that each author has his own distinctive style. Now see if you can imitate one of these author's styles.

WRITER'S BLUEPRINT

Product: A scene from a story

Purpose: To explore the ominous side of American Romanticism through the styles of Poe and Hawthorne

Audience: People who are familiar with Poe and Hawthorne

Specs: As the writer of a successful paper, you should:

- ❑ Analyze the style of "The Pit and the Pendulum" and "Dr. Heidegger's Experiment." Imitate the style of one of these authors in a scene from a story of your own. Set your scene in modern times with your own original plot and characters.
- ❑ Take care not to copy anything directly, but to imitate your author's style so skillfully that your audience will recognize your source.
- ❑ Use the technique of contrast to help develop mood.
- ❑ Follow the rules of grammar, usage, mechanics, and spelling. Take special care to avoid spelling mistakes in which you use too few letters.

STEP 1 PREWRITING

style (stīl), *n.* characteristic way in which a writer uses language.

Analyze style. To imitate Poe or Hawthorne, you'll first need to examine their work closely. To get started, look at the Literary Source.

292 UNIT THREE: AMERICAN CLASSIC

Clear guidelines

The Writer's Blueprint tells students exactly what to do to achieve a well-written paper.

Strategies

Literary and student models, plus a wide array of options and organizers, offer help to every student.

Notice how Poe uses a semicolon to combine sentences—he does this often. These and other observations about Poe's style are noted in the chart below. You'll find that they hold true for Poe's other stories as well.

Poe—"The Pit and the Pendulum"

Elements of Style	Observations	Examples
Sentence structure (length, variety)	—uses semicolons to combine sentences —likes exclamations	"My eyes followed its outward . . . unspeakable!"
Vocabulary	—lots of long, physical modifiers	—spasmodically,
Imagery	—shows people in the grip of terror	—"Still I quivered in every nerve . . ."
Figurative language		

LITERARY SOURCE
"My eyes followed its outward or upward whirls with the eagerness of the most unmeaning despair; they closed themselves spasmodically at the descent, although death would have been a relief, oh! how unspeakable! Still I quivered in every nerve . . ."
from "The Pit and the Pendulum" by Edgar Allan Poe

OR . . .
Look through more stories by these authors. Check to see that your observations hold true for them as well, and add new observations to your chart.

Use a chart like this one to analyze the Poe and Hawthorne selections. Then decide which author's style you'd rather work with.

Brainstorm scene ideas. With a group of people who've chosen the same author as you, discuss ideas for a scene. Remember that your scene will be set in today's world, and that the plot and characters will be your own original creations.

Plan your scene by making notes on the setting, characters, action, dialogue, and mood. For tips on creating a strong mood, see the Revising Strategy on page 294.

STEP 2 DRAFTING

Before you draft, review the Writer's Blueprint, your style chart, and writing plan.

As you draft, here are some things to keep in mind.

- Remember that you're imitating the author's style only. The plot and characters must be your own original creations.
- Use vivid verbs to make the action come alive for the reader.

STEP 3 REVISING

Ask a partner for comments on your draft before you revise it.

✔ Have I imitated the author's style successfully?

✔ Have I developed a strong mood?

LITERARY SOURCE
"Age, with its miserable train of cares and sorrows and diseases, was remembered only as the trouble of a dream, from which they had joyously awoke. The fresh gloss of the soul, so early lost . . . again threw its enchantment over all their prospects."
from "Dr. Heidegger's Experiment" by Nathaniel Hawthorne

Revising Strategy

Using Contrast to Develop Mood

Contrast is one technique that writers use to develop a mood. In the Literary Model, notice how Hawthorne contrasts images of old age with images of youth to create a mood of miraculous joy and exhilaration. In the Student Model below, notice how the writer used contrast to help develop a mood of doom. Can you tell which author this writer is imitating?

> Was this then to be my ironical fate? Was I, a fisherman, to be put to death in the depths of the very ocean from which I had made my living? My wrists wriggled and squirmed in the padlocked chains like nightcrawlers on a hook; in two parallel columns, bubbles from my nostrils, life! rose from the ~~depths~~ *black and murky* depths to which I had plummeted, escaping ever upward toward the *brilliant sunlit* surface of the sea.

STUDENT MODEL

STEP 4 EDITING

Ask a partner to review your revised draft before you edit. When you edit, look for errors in grammar, usage, spelling, and mechanics. In addition, check for spelling errors that come from leaving certain letters out of words.

Editing Strategy

Using Too Few Letters

If you don't hear certain letters when you pronounce a word, you may misspell it. Practice saying each word below carefully, being sure to pronounce the underlined part. Look for mistakes with words like these when you edit your work.

probably	favorite	desperate	different
aspirin	remembered	temperature	separate

STEP 5 PRESENTING

Here are some suggestions for presenting your narrative.

- Have a Poe/Hawthorne imitator contest. Appoint a panel of judges to decide who did the best job, and present the winners with certificates.
- Turn your scene into a radio play with music and sound effects.

STEP 6 LOOKING BACK

Self-evaluate. What grade would *you* give your paper? Look back at the Writer's Blueprint and give yourself a score for each point, from 6 (superior) down to 1 (inadequate).

Reflect. What have you learned about the ominous side of American Romanticism and about the writer's craft from doing this assignment? Write responses to these questions.

✔ From looking at the styles, characters, and plots of Poe and Hawthorne, what sorts of conclusions could you draw about the society in which they lived?

✔ In the future, when people look back on literature, movies, and television shows of the 1990s, what are some conclusions you think they will draw about our society?

For Your Working Portfolio Add your narrative and your reflection responses to your working portfolio.

Grammar

Editing strategy lessons are an important part of every workshop.

The last step

Each workshop ends with suggestions for self-evaluation and reflection.

annotated teacher's edition

Along with objectives, annotations, and lesson support, the two-volume Teacher's Edition includes three important features.

A focus on **mini-lessons** at the bottom of most left-hand pages. Mini-lesson subjects include grammar, study skills, spelling, vocabulary, visual literacy, technology, literary language, and speaking/listening.

Support for students of **all abilities and learning styles,** especially those who are less proficient in English. Specific teaching tips for these students have been provided by professional educators and can be found at the bottom of most right-hand pages.

Point-of-use cross-references to support materials and technology.

in a user-friendly, 2-volume teacher's edition with strategies for helping all students

A multitude of minis

Mini-lessons on a wide variety of skills are located at the bottom of most left pages.

During Reading

Selection Objectives

- To reflect on the consequences of conformity and nonconformity
- To identify examples of figurative language
- To analyze main and supporting ideas
- To recognize verb forms

Unit 3 Resource Book
Graphic Organizer, p. 1
Study Guide, p. 2

Theme Link

The theme of Romanticism and a search for truth is reflected in Emerson's uncompromising dedication to the value of an individual's convictions. He and many Romantics held an optimistic view of the world, unlike pessimistic Romantic writers, such as Nathaniel Hawthorne and Herman Melville.

Vocabulary Preview

render, give in return
bestow, give as a gift
hinder, get in the way; make difficult
importune, ask urgently or repeatedly
capitulate, surrender

Students can add the words and definitions to their word lists in the Writer's Notebook.

Art Study

Response to Caption Question
The man is depicted in a confident, self-contained pose.

Gerrit A. Beneker (1882–1934) painted portraits of industrial workers and people who worked at sea, such as fishermen.

222

How does the composition of this painting, *Men Are Square* (1919) by Gerrit A. Beneker, reflect the cultural values of **individuality** and self-reliance? ➤

Self-Reliance

RALPH WALDO EMERSON

To believe your own thought, to believe that what is true for you in your private heart is true for all men,—that is genius. Speak your latent conviction, and it shall be the universal sense; for the inmost in due time becomes the outmost, and our first thought is rendered[1] back to us by the trumpets of the Last Judgment. Familiar as the voice of the mind is to each, the highest merit we ascribe to Moses, Plato and Milton is that they set at naught books and traditions, and spoke not what men, but what *they* thought. A man should learn to detect and watch that gleam of light which flashes across his mind from within, more than the lustre of the firmament[2] of bards and sages. Yet he dismisses without notice his thought, because it is his. In every work of genius we recognize our own rejected thoughts; they come back to us with a certain alienated majesty. . . .

1. render (ren′dər), *v.* give in return.
2. firmament (fėr′mə mənt), *n.* arch of the heavens; sky.

222 UNIT THREE: AMERICAN CLASSIC

MINI-LESSON: GRAMMAR

Verb Forms

Teach Verbs such as *becomes, replied,* and *(have) done* illustrate **present, past,** and **past participle** forms. Another verb form, or part, is **present participle** (example: *betraying*). Review the forms of these and other verbs in "Self-Reliance," pointing out uses of past participles, such as passive voice *(is rendered)* and perfect tenses *(has tried).*

Activity Ideas

- Students can find verbs in present and future tense and in imperatives that use the present form. Examples include *speak* and *dismisses* (p. 222) and *can come* and *will live* (p. 223).
- Students can identify past participles, such as *(has) tried* and *(is) given* (p. 223).

Unit 3 Resource Book
Grammar, p. 4

*For summaries of the selection in Engl and other languages, see the **Building English Proficiency** book.*

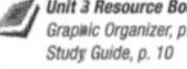

Selection Objectives

- To explore Romantic themes concerning what is important in life
- To analyze an argument
- To recognize allusions and their communicative value
- To understand affixes and parts of speech

Unit 3 Resource Book Graphic Organizer, p. 9 Study Guide, p. 10

Theme Link

Love of nature was part of Romanticism, and no one better expressed that love than Thoreau at Walden. This interlude and his act of civil disobedience exemplified his convictions about personal freedom.

Vocabulary Preview

stealthily, secretly, slyly
meanly, in a small-minded way
superfluous, more than is needed
enterprise, undertaking or project
garret, a space or room in a house just below a sloping roof
dissipation, a scattering in different directions
obsequious, polite or obedient, from hope of gain
abolitionist, person who advocates doing away with an institution or custom, such as slavery
hindrance, person or thing that hinders; an obstacle
abet, urge or assist, especially in doing wrong

Students can add the words and definitions to their word lists in the Writer's Notebook.

In 1845 Thoreau built a cabin in the woods by Walden Pond and lived there for two years. He wanted to simplify his life to the point where he could learn what the true essentials in life were. While there, he planned to write and study nature. Thoreau began his book, Walden, after he left the pond, and finished it in 1854. Modern photographer Eliot Porter, who took the photo on the right, has found inspiration for his work in Thoreau's writings.

Walden

HENRY DAVID THOREAU

When first I took up my abode in the woods, that is, began to spend my nights as well as days there, which, by accident, was on Independence Day, or the fourth of July, 1845, my house was not finished for winter, but was merely a defense against the rain, without plastering or chimney, the walls being of rough weather-stained boards, with wide chinks, which made it cool at night. The upright white hewn studs and freshly planed door and window casings gave it a clean and airy look, especially in the morning, when its timbers were saturated with dew, so that I fancied that by noon some sweet gum would exude from them. To my imagination it retained throughout the day more or less of this auroral character, reminding me of a certain house on a mountain which I had visited the year before. This was an airy and unplastered cabin, fit to entertain a traveling god, and where a goddess might trail her garments. The winds which passed over my dwelling were such as sweep over the ridges of mountains, bearing the broken strains, or celestial parts only, of terrestrial music. The morning wind forever blows, the poem of creation is
1 uninterrupted; but few are the ears that hear it. Olympus[1] is but the outside of the earth every where. . . .

I was seated by the shore of a small pond, about a mile and a half south of the village of Concord and somewhat higher than it, in the midst of an extensive wood between that town and Lincoln, and about two miles south of that our only field known to fame, Concord Battle Ground; but I was so low in the woods that the opposite shore, half a mile off, like the rest, covered with wood, was my most distant horizon. For the first week, whenever I looked out on the pond it impressed me like a tarn high up on the side of a mountain, its bottom far above the surface
2 of other lakes, and, as the sun arose, I saw it throwing off its nightly clothing of mist, and here and there, by degrees, its soft ripples or its smooth reflecting surface was revealed, while the mists, like ghosts were stealthily[2] withdrawing in every direction into the woods, as at the breaking up of some nocturnal conventicle.

1. Olympus (ō lim′pəs), mountain home of the gods in Greek mythology.
2. stealthily (stelth′ə lē), adv. secretly; slyly.

SELECTION SUMMARY

Walden, Civil Disobedience

Walden The selection from *Walden* gives Thoreau's account of life at Walden Pond, beginning in lyrical terms with a description of his cabin and its beautiful natural surroundings. Thoreau details his reasons for living at the pond; contrasts his simple life there with the complex and artificial life in society; and records philosophical reflections on solitude and the nature of human existence.

Civil Disobedience The passionate excerpt from "Civil Disobedience" focuses on the relationship between individuals and government, particularly on individual responsibility for actions taken by government in the name of its citizens. He recounts his short jail stay when he withheld tax payments to resist what he saw as immoral government actions.

For summaries in other languages, see the ***Building English Proficiency*** *book.*

BUILDING ENGLISH PROFICIENCY

ESL LEP ELD SAE LD

Building Vocabulary with Antonyms

Students can use Thoreau's descriptive language to increase their vocabularies. They can make a T-chart, like the one shown.

- List words from the selection, such as the ones from page 226, as shown.
- Explain that antonyms are words with opposite meanings. Provide examples of antonyms, such as *hot, cold, true,* and *false.*
- Have students write antonyms or words with contrasting meanings for the words in the left column of the chart; other words chosen from the selection.

first	(last)
began	(ended, stopped)
rough	(smooth)
stealthily	(open)

1 Literary Focus
Allusion

Olympus also is known as Mount Olympus.

Question What does Thoreau suggest about the whole outdoors by calling it Olympus? *(Possible response: that any outdoor place is a worthy residence for gods)*

2 Literary Element
Figurative Language

Questions What does Thoreau say Walden Pond "throws off" each morning? *(its nightly mists)*

To what human action does he compare this morning change? *(to taking off night clothes)*

Art Study

Photographer Eliot Porter, renowned for his images of New England, Appalachia, Baja California, Antarctica, Egypt, and other places, also is an expert on birds. His book *In Wilderness Is the Preservation of the World: From Henry David Thoreau* has been reprinted by the Sierra Club (1988, 1989).

There is a time in every man's education when he arrives at the conviction that envy is ignorance; that imitation is suicide; that he must take himself for better for worse as his portion; that though the wide universe is full of
1 good, no kernel of nourishing corn can come to him but through his toil bestowed[3] on that plot of ground which is given to him to till. The power which resides in him is new in nature, and none but he knows what that is which he can do, nor does he know until he has tried. . . .

Trust thyself: every heart vibrates to that iron string. Accept the place the divine providence has found for you, the society of your contemporaries, the connection of events. Great men have always done so, and confided themselves childlike to the genius of their age, betraying their perception that the absolutely trustworthy was seated at their heart, working through their hands, predominating in all their being. . . .

Whoso would be a man, must be a nonconformist.[4] He who would gather immortal palms must not be hindered[5] by the name of goodness, but must explore if it be goodness. Nothing is at last sacred but the integrity of your own mind. Absolve you to yourself, and you shall have the suffrage of the world. I remember an answer which when quite young I was prompted to make to a valued adviser who was wont to importune[6] me with the dear old doctrines of the church. On my saying, "What have I to do with the sacredness of traditions, if I live wholly from within?" my friend suggested,—"But these impulses may be from below, not from above." I replied, "They do not seem to me to be such; but if I am the Devil's child, I will live then from the Devil." No law can be sacred to me but that of my nature. Good and bad are but names very readily transferable to that or this; the only right is what is after my constitution; the only wrong what is against it. A man is to carry himself in the presence of all opposition as if every thing were titular[7] and ephemeral[8] but he. I am ashamed to think how easily we capitulate[9] to badges and names, to large societies and dead institutions. . . . 2

The other terror that scares us from self-trust is our consistency; a reverence for our past act or word because the eyes of others have no other data for computing our orbit than our past acts, and we are loath to disappoint them. . . .

A foolish consistency is the hobgoblin of little minds, adored by little statesmen and philosophers and divines. With consistency a great soul has simply nothing to do. He may as well concern himself with his shadow on the wall. Speak what you think now in hard words and tomorrow speak what tomorrow thinks in hard words again, though it contradict every thing you said today.—"Ah, so you shall be sure to be misunderstood."—Is it so bad then to be misunderstood? Pythagoras was misunderstood, and Socrates, and Jesus, and Luther, and Copernicus, and Galileo, and Newton, and every pure and wise spirit that ever took flesh. To be great is to be misunderstood. . . .

Insist on yourself; never imitate. Your own gift you can present every moment with the cumulative force of a whole life's cultivation; but of the adopted talent of another you have only an extemporaneous half possession . . .

A political victory, a rise of rents, the recovery of your sick or the return of your absent friend, or some other favorable event raises your spirits, and you think good days are preparing for you. Do not believe it. Nothing can bring you peace but yourself. Nothing can bring you peace but the triumph of principles.

3. bestow (bi stō′), *v.* give as a gift.
4. **nonconformist** (non′kən fôr′mist), *n.* person who refuses to be bound by established customs.
5. hinder (hin′dər), *v.* get in the way; make difficult.
6. importune (im′pôr tün′), *v.* ask urgently or repeatedly.
7. **titular** (tich′ə lər), *adj.* in title or name only.
8. **ephemeral** (i fem′ər əl), *adj.* lasting only for a very short time.
9. capitulate (kə pich′ə lāt), *v.* surrender.

1 Literary Focus
Figurative Language

Emerson uses an extended metaphor, comparing a person's intellectual and spiritual life to a farmer's cultivation of a plot of ground.

Questions How can someone till (farm) his or her plot of ground, or mind? *(Possible response: by carefully attending to one's experience and thoughts)*

What "corn" can be harvested from it? *(Possible response: understanding and insight)*

2 Reader's Response
Personal Connections

Question What "badges," names, societies, and institutions affect people today?

Check Test

1. According to Emerson, what do geniuses accept about themselves? *(their own thoughts or convictions)*
2. Does Emerson think it is better to be a conformist or a nonconformist? *(nonconformist)*
3. What does he think of being consistent in what a person says and thinks? *(Possible response: Consistency is not necessary; it's better to be true to what you believe at any time.)*
4. Why are great people often misunderstood? *(because they think differently from others or don't worry what others think)*
5. Whose principles are key in deciding how to live, according to this essay? *(Each person must live by her or his own principles.)*

Unit 3 Resource Book
Alternate Check Test, p. 5

BUILDING ENGLISH PROFICIENCY

ESL LEP ELD SAE LD

Making Personal Connections

To help students understand Emerson's philosophy, consider either of these talking or writing activities.

- Discuss whether Emerson's ideas are applicable only to adults. Ask whether—or to what extent—teenagers could follow his advice, if they should want to.
- Ask students in pairs to devise and write their own "rules for life" or "rules for thinking." These may be similar in format to Emerson's sentences. They may draw on proverbs and cultural ideas known to the students. The class might create a collage of the ideas.

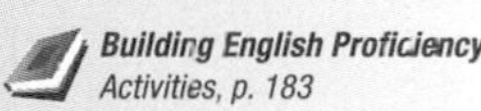

Building English Proficiency
Activities, p. 183

Easy on the eyes

Large type, as shown above, makes teacher notes easy to read.

Other Teacher's Edition Features

- Unit Planning Pages
- Selection Summaries
- Art Study Notes and Questions
- Historical Notes
- Suggestions for both At-Risk and Gifted students
- Check Tests
- Multicultural Notes
- Cross-Curricular Connections
- Writing Workshop Assessment Criteria

Building student success

Most right-hand pages contain special help for students who are less-proficient in English.

teacher's resource file

Flexibility and options are built into the Teacher's Resource File which contains **over 1500 pages of copy masters and transparencies** plus software and audio cassettes to support your teaching style and address each student's needs.

For ease of use, all copy masters that relate to an individual selection are located together in Unit Resource Books—one Resource Book for each unit in the student anthology.

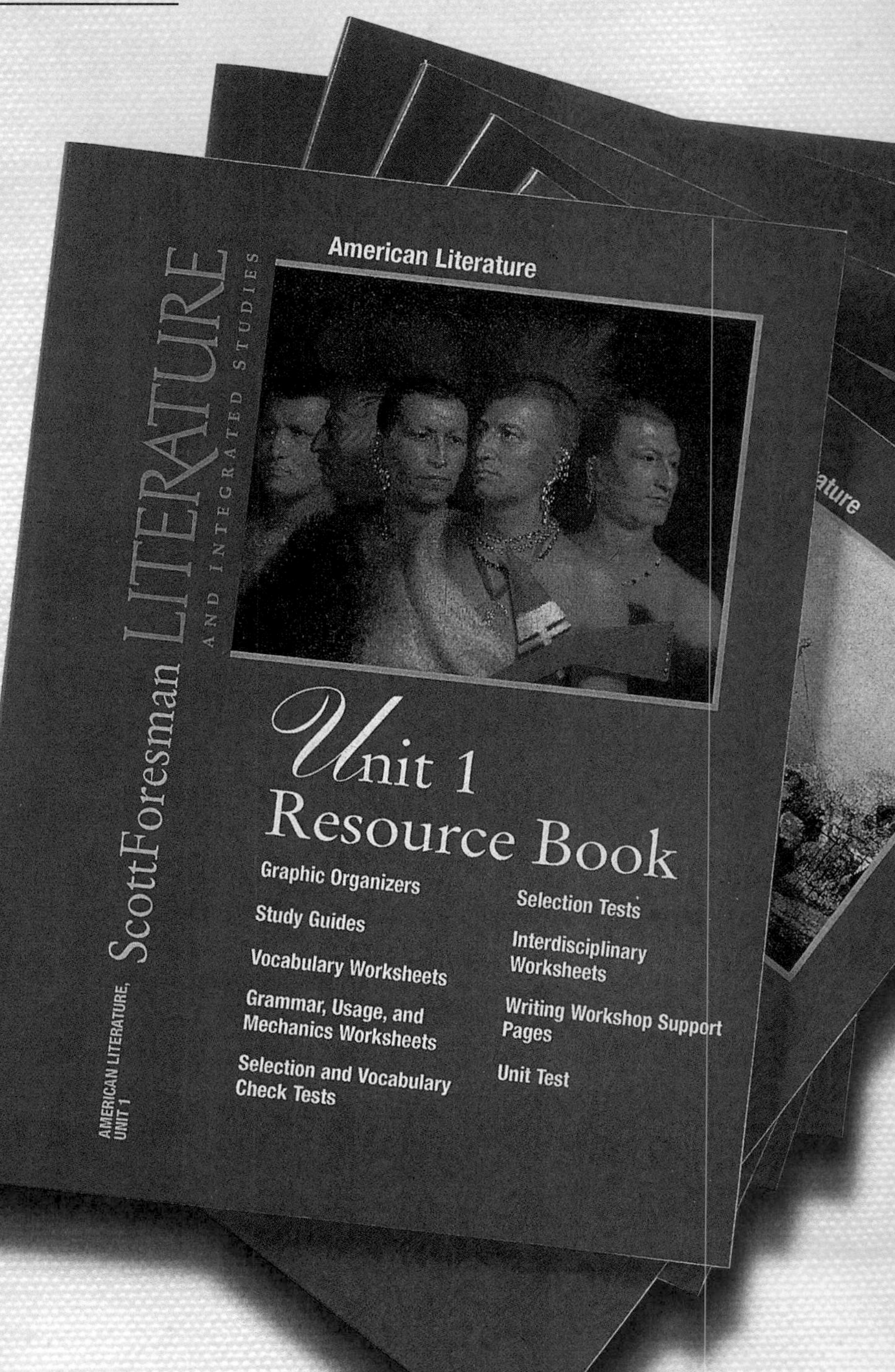

Unit Resource Books

Selection materials

- Graphic Organizers
- Study Guides
- Vocabulary Worksheets
- Grammar, Usage, and Mechanics Worksheets
- Selection and Vocabulary Check Tests
- Selection Tests

Unit materials

- Interdisciplinary Worksheets
- Writing Workshop Support Pages
- Unit Test

The Resource File Also Includes

- Program Overview
- Resources for Building English Proficiency
- Reading, Writing & Grammar SkillBook
- Transparency Collection
- The World of Work: Investigations and Activities
- Assessment Handbook
- Test Generator
- Writing Software
- Audio Cassettes (15-20 cassettes per grade)

in providing an abundance of quality enrichment materials

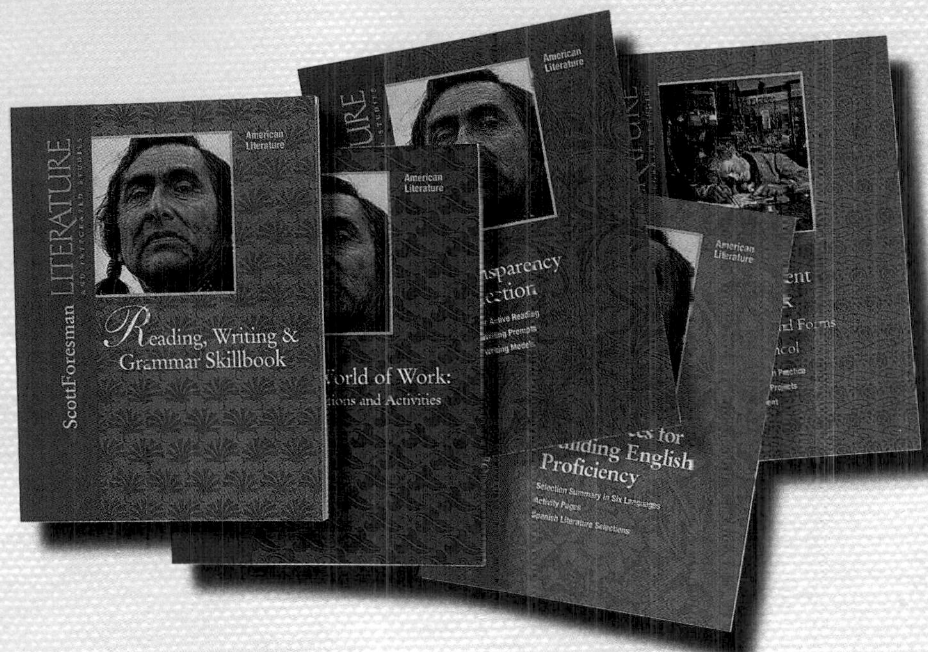

user friendly technology

CD-ROMS

AuthorWorks™ CD-Rom Series

A 7-disc CD-ROM series produced in cooperation with the Library of Congress offers fascinating, in-depth studies of a broad range of well-known authors. Writers' lives are accessed through a rich database of information about their personal lives, their writings, and their times. Material is presented through various media including slideshows, oral readings, movies, music, interviews, historical documents, maps, text screens, and so forth. Extensive project books for each grade level direct student research, which can be captured and transported into multimedia reports.

AuthorWorks™ Authors

Chinua Achebe
Isabel Allende
Jane Austen
William Blake
Emily & Charlotte Brontë
Gwendolyn Brooks
Albert Camus
Willa Cather
Anton Chekhov
Joseph Conrad
Robert Cormier
Stephen Crane
E. E. Cummings
Charles Dickens
Emily Dickinson
Rita Dove
F. Scott Fitzgerald
Robert Frost
Nadine Gordimer
Lorraine Hansberry
Thomas Hardy
Nathaniel Hawthorne
Ernest Hemingway
Langston Hughes
Zora Neale Hurston
Henrik Ibsen
D.H. Lawrence
Ursula Le Guin
Doris Lessing
Jack London
Guy de Maupassant
Arthur Miller
Flannery O'Connor
George Orwell
Alan Paton
Edgar Allan Poe
Cynthia Rylant
Bernard Shaw
Mary Shelley
Gary Soto
John Steinbeck
Henry David Thoreau
Leo Tolstoy
Mark Twain
Yoshiko Uchida
Derek Walcott
Walt Whitman
Elie Wiesel
William Wordsworth
Richard Wright
W.B. Yeats
Laurence Yep
Paul Zindel

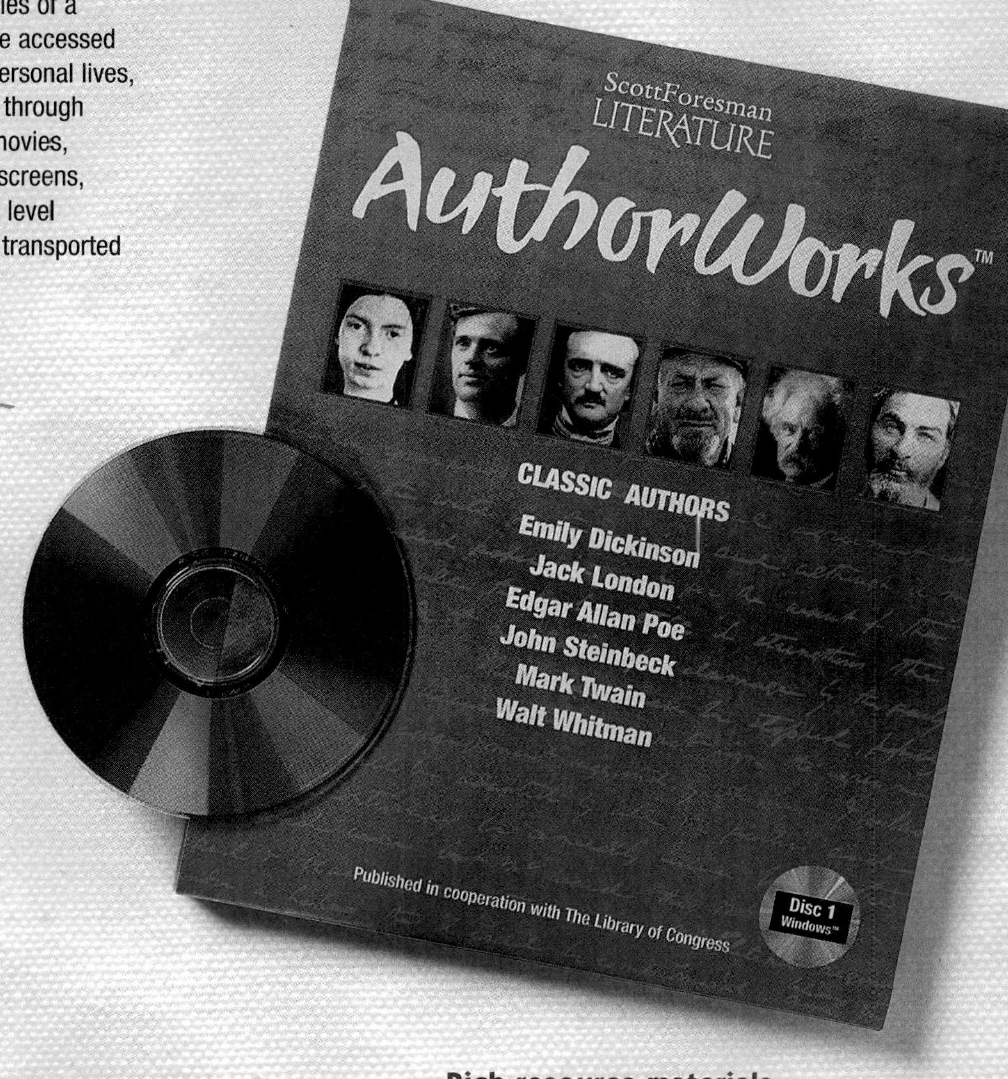

ScottForesman
LITERATURE
AuthorWorks™
CLASSIC AUTHORS
Emily Dickinson
Jack London
Edgar Allan Poe
John Steinbeck
Mark Twain
Walt Whitman
Published in cooperation with The Library of Congress
Disc 1
Windows™

Rich resource materials

Published in cooperation with the Library of Congress.

BBC Shakespeare CD-ROM Series

Bring favorite plays to life with this top-rated series produced by the BBC. Each disc includes the complete play script, scenes from professional productions, interviews with well-known drama and literary figures, plus extensive background on Shakespeare and the Globe Theater.

More Software

Test Generator allows teachers to customize assessment.

Writer's Resource supports pupil book assignments and provides grammar lessons and research paper instruction.

Writer's Notebook includes selection-based prompts; allows students to keep a personal journal on computer; provides opportunities for dialectical journal writing.

in making technology that works for you and your students

ScottForesman Custom Literature Database CD-ROM

Personalize your literature teaching with an additional 1400 contemporary and classic literary works. Selections are easily accessed through genre, author, title, ethnicity, literary themes, or grade level indexes and produce high quality reproducible prints. Special selections are keyed directly to the themes in the ScottForesman pupil anthologies and are accompanied by custom teaching materials.

novel works

NovelWorks™ is ScottForesman's answer to teaching novels and other longer works. Quality collections of resource materials in a convenient kit are available for 36 popular middle school and high school titles.

NovelWorks™ Titles

To Kill a Mockingbird
Johnny Tremain
The Call of the Wild
The Pearl
The Diary of Anne Frank
The Adventures of Tom Sawyer
Where the Red Fern Grows
The Clay Marble
The Outsiders
Hatchet
Eyes of Darkness
Roll of Thunder, Hear My Cry
Nilda
Their Eyes Were Watching God
Farewell to Manzanar
The Odyssey
Things Fall Apart
The Adventures of Huckleberry Finn
Great Expectations
Lord of the Flies
The Joy Luck Club
A Separate Peace
Like Water for Chocolate
The Great Gatsby
Black Boy
Lord Jim
The Scarlet Letter
Wuthering Heights
Jane Eyre
Animal Farm
The Mayor of Casterbridge
A Raisin in the Sun
Bless Me, Ultima
Cry, the Beloved Country
Cyrano de Bergerac
The Grapes of Wrath

Each Kit Contains

Teacher's Resource Book Over 80 pages of teaching support offers background, vocabulary, chapter-by-chapter support, literary themes and elements, maps, time lines, media resources, fine art studies, and assessment options.

Writing Options Book 4 complete writing lessons—one in each major mode—with grammar and punctuation mini-lessons and assessment rubrics.

Thematic Connections Book Additional literary selections further explore the work's major themes.

Audio Cassette 60-minute audio cassette offers dramatic readings, essential for students needing extra language support.

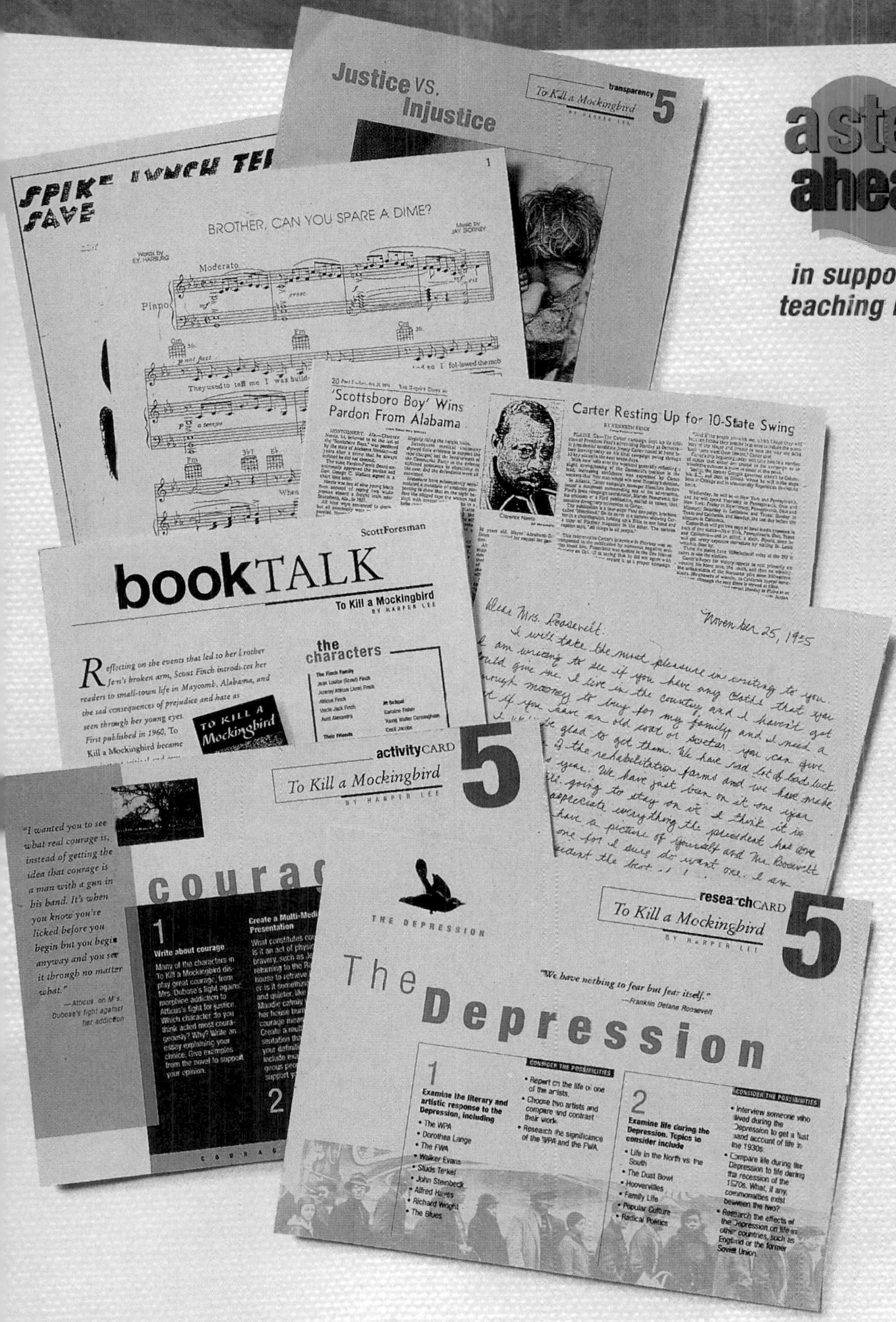

a step ahead

in support for teaching novels

Points of Departure

A low-cost, high-interest series of supplemental literature texts to accent the main anthology.

Titles include

- Crossroads (young adult literature)
- Multicultural Voices
- Reflections on a Gift of Watermelon Pickle (poetry)
- World Writers Today
- American Studies Album
- An Introduction to the Humanities
- The Bible as/in Literature

Activity Cards 4 cards, each with 8 activities, explore themes and develop cross-curricular connections.

Research Cards 4 cards with 4–5 suggested ideas per card focus on and develop research projects.

Fine Art Transparencies Full-color reproductions of fine art introduce and explore major themes.

BookTalk Reproducible newsletter engages students' interest and introduces them to the literary work and author. 60-minute audio cassette offers dramatic readings, essential for students needing extra language support.

Documents 5 historical items help build background and context for the work and provide unique bulletin board material.

Professional Commentary

Literature and Integration

Statement of Philosophy: ScottForesman Literature and Integrated Studies

by Alan C. Purves

Director of the Center for Writing and Literacy

State University of New York at Albany

Albany, New York

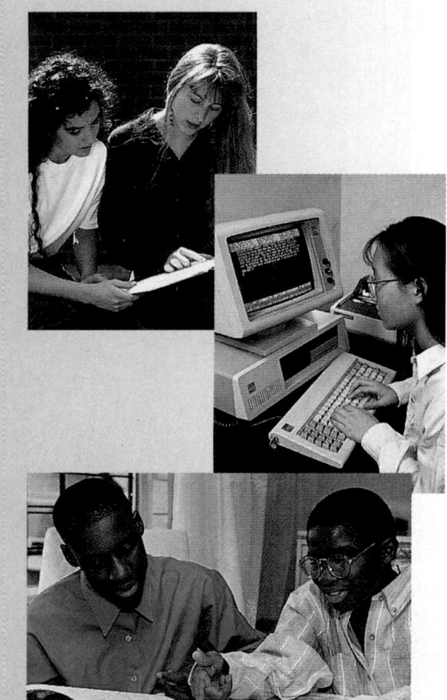

This collection of books, computer disks, CD-ROM's and other materials has the following purpose: to present literature of quality from around the world to a variety of students and to encourage them to become thoughtful readers, writers, and users of a variety of media.

In assembling these materials, the consultants, writers, and editors have a philosophy they would like to share. The philosophy involves beliefs about reading and responding to literature, about the role of the classroom and the teacher, and about the nature of learning in English.

Reading

For most people reading begins with looking. When we read, we use our eyes (or if we know Braille, our fingertips), and we see the shapes of letters, words, paragraphs, poems, stories, plays, and other kinds of text materials on the page or on the screen. As we look at these collections of marks in relation to the white space we begin to make sense of them, to connect them with ideas, arguments, events, feelings, and questions of one sort or another. When we do this we are responding to what we have read and understood.

We can't avoid having a response to our reading. Perhaps we stop reading, turn the page, scratch our head, nod, yawn, get ideas, make mental pictures, cry, laugh, or decide to do something as a result of our reading. Reading is reading in and between the lines and it is responding to what we see. Studies have shown that most people see similar things in a given text and that their responses are quite similar.

Our responses are generated partly by what we are reading now and partly by what we have read, seen, heard, or done in the past. When we read a story we tend to meet it halfway. We have ideas, images, and meanings of words in our head. They are often activated by what we read. We may identify with a particular character because she reminds us of what we were like at a particular time or because she seems like a person we know. These responses result from our past and present images and associations as they meet the words, images, characters, places, and ideas in the literature we read.

If our responses result from past experiences, why are they often so similar to one another when each of us has had quite distinct experiences? In part it is because all of us are sharing the same words, sentences, images, and events in the story. In part it is because we share attitudes and understandings concerning people, places, and events. We all tend to be sad when the villain menaces the girl or when the favorite dog dies. We all know the hero wears a white hat and doesn't smoke. We all tend to laugh at the same jokes. These are common emotions caused by years of association of the emotion to the event. A lot of what we read or watch uses these common scenes, images, and people. Literary people call them conventions, stereotypes, motifs, or archetypes. They work because they are consistent and expected. Where people's responses mainly differ lies in what they say or do about their responses. These differences depend on how each individual has learned to express his or her response. In school, teachers want students to think about what they have read and how they respond to what they have read. We want to push their responses into new dimensions.

Literature

As students go through school reading literature, talking and writing about it, and taking tests on it, they pick up ideas of what makes a good response. These ideas then become habits of reading, talking, and writing. Although scholars and critics of literature argue the fine points of criticism and theory, they generally agree that all of them are based on three broad sets of questions about a work of literature.

1. **How can we understand the work in light of the place and time in which it was written?**

2. How can we understand the work in terms of our own time?

3. What are the implications of the work?

These three broad questions are the heart of this series and its instructional program. We have placed them after the selections to shape students' responses to the literature in this anthology. The essential first step in this shaping is to ask students to describe what happened to them upon reading the selection, and we suggest a variety of means to get them to begin to shape their first responses. Then we build on this first step by moving to broader questions, which will help students become thoughtful readers and responders. Dealing with these questions will also help them see literature in terms of the author and the author's culture, explore themes in a cultural and historical context, see the relationship between the literature and other art forms, and relate the literature to their on-going lives as students and as creative, thoughtful people. In the classroom we can help students explore these questions.

In exploring the first broad question about understanding a literary work in its time, students need to deal with the big ideas, the major events, and the everyday concerns of the past or of countries or cultures. Students then come to see that the words on the page did not come there by magic; they were put there by someone who had a purpose, something to say, some desire to give readers pleasure, to excite them, to make them think.

In exploring the second question, students come to understand how the interpretation and judgment of a work of literature today can be different from what it might have been in the past. We read and look at things in terms of our contemporary concerns, and in doing so we make even ancient works come alive for us. The story of Macbeth is not just the story of some people in Scotland nearly a thousand years ago; nor is it a story geared only to the concerns of playgoers in Shakespeare's England; *Macbeth* deals with themes and issues that can be found on the nightly news—stories about political intrigue and domestic violence. How do people deal with these passions today? Are they like Macbeth?

The third question is equally important. In asking it we move beyond the work to look at the larger issues and concerns that reading and understanding the work bring to mind. Some students may see how the work can suggest other kinds of expression, a video, a set of poems, an animation, a dramatic reading. Others may be inspired to do further reading. Still others may be led to explore a variety of presentations of the work (film versions, for example), or another treatment of the themes and issues (in a history course). Some students may want to create a hypermedia production around the text and their response to it. The shaping of these extensions takes place in the classroom, and it is in the shaping that we help students explore new dimensions of themselves and the literature. An important outcome will be that the literature remains alive in the students' minds.

Although the order of these three questions may vary depending on which seems the most immediate or relevant to you and your students, they invite students to explore historical background, genre and literary form, authors and related arts, themes and major issues of past and current concern, and the nature of the creative process itself.

Integration

In creating this program, we do not see literature separate from writing or the study of language. Literature is made up of language which has a structure, a history. The structure and history of the language helped shape the way in which the selections were written and help shape the way your students write and make their attempts to become authors themselves.

Reading and writing are the two dimensions of literacy. In a literature program we begin by looking at the writing of others and turn to the writing of our students. The compositions that emerge from our students should receive as careful attention from us as we ask students to give to the works in the books we assign. In reading we ask the students to seek to know the author; in writing we ask them to seek to know their audience. The two activities are closely related. They are related to speaking and listening as well; after all, much literature was and still is performed orally, and talk and discussion are among the most valuable aspects of a classroom.

Ours is a world in which literature is not confined to words on a page.

Nor do we see the literature that is printed and bound in books or the writing of your students as separate from literature that is presented on the screen, on audio or video disks, or in one of the new multimedia or hypermedia versions. Ours is a world in which literature is not confined to words on a page. Just as your students are aware of the variety of media as an audience, so they should explore those media as creators and shapers. Many of the activities we suggest ask students to explore dimensions of composition beyond writing on the page. We hope they will have a chance to explore hypertext and hypermedia, drama, video, simulation gaming, theater, and many of the other ways by which people express and communicate their ideas and understandings. Learning in English goes far beyond reading and writing. It is indeed a way by which each student can master a variety of media and gain a further degree of independence as a user of all the power of language and literature.

Writing and Thinking Critically

Fostering Critical Thinking and Writing Through Writing Workshop

by Carol Booth Olson
University of California, Irvine
Irvine, California

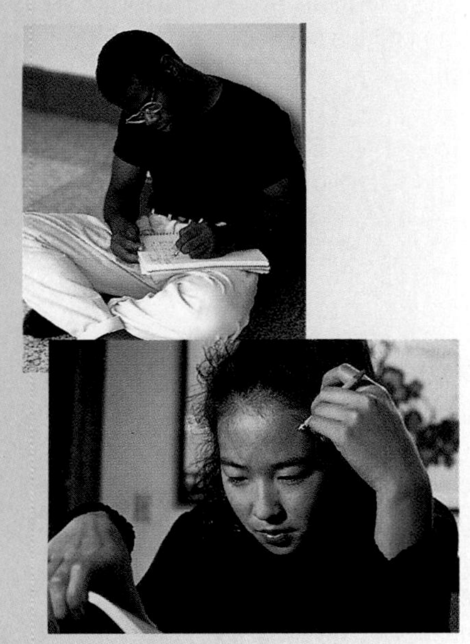

The lessons in the Writing Workshop section that concludes each group of literary selections blend learning theory, composing process research, and the practical strategies of the National Writing Project. They are designed to help students cope with the cognitive demands of two questions they juggle simultaneously: *What do I want to say?* and *How do I transform what I want to say into a written product?*

Underlying the way the lessons have been developed are a number of fundamental premises about thinking that inform the teaching of writing.

Writing is a mode of thinking. In order to produce a composition, writers must generate ideas, plan for both the process of writing and for the written product itself, translate thought into print, revise what they have articulated, and evaluate the effectiveness of their efforts. In short, in moving from conception to completion, writers tap all of the levels of Bloom's taxonomy of the cognitive domain (201–207).

Thinking is progressive. As Piaget observed, the mind is better able to make cognitive leaps when learning moves from the concrete to the abstract. Individual thinking/writing tasks should begin by focusing on something tangible and/or concrete. For example, students who observe a seashell are encouraged to think analogically by creating similes about the seashell. An overall writing curriculum should also *move progressively.* Such a *progression* might take the form of sequencing the domains of writing from descriptive to narrative to expository, or it might involve moving from known to unknown audiences.

Thinking is cumulative and recursive. All thinking experiences build upon one another. However, the pathway to more complex thought is not a linear one. Researchers have noted that writing, in particular, is a recursive process. Writers often go back in their thinking in order to move forward with their writing. Therefore, teachers who use a stage process model of composition which moves from prewriting to writing to revising and editing should continually invite students to think about their thinking and their writing by revisiting what they have written. So too, a writing curriculum should be scaffolded in such a way that students must go back to prior learning in order to move forward to the next task.

...students must go back to prior learning in order to move forward to the next task.

Thinking is not taught but fostered. Thinking is an innate capacity which can be enhanced through the act of writing. Hilda Taba concludes that "how people think may depend largely on the kinds of 'thinking experience' they have had" (12). The teacher, then, plays a crucial role by providing students with thinking experiences that facilitate cognitive growth. Writing is one of the most complex and challenging thinking experiences the teacher can provide.

The key to independent thinking and writing is practice. Teachers must provide students with the guided practice in a range of thinking and writing tasks that will enable them to develop and internalize a repertoire of problem-solving strategies that they can apply with confidence to future thinking/writing challenges.

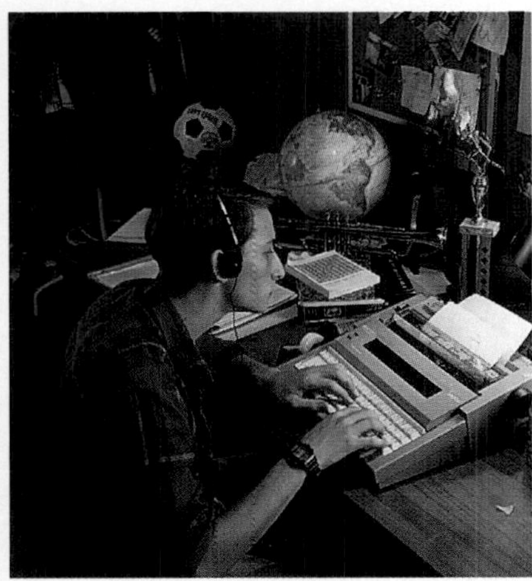

With these premises in mind, the designers of the Writing Workshop lessons selected a type of writing that was compatible with the themes and issues of the literary works (for example, a descriptive poem, an autobiographical incident, an interpretive essay, a persuasive letter, a reflective essay, and so forth) and then did a task analysis to determine how best to "scaffold" the lesson activities in a way that would give students practice in the key thinking and writing skills called for in the assignment.

> **...the ultimate goal of instructional scaffolding is to gradually withdraw the teacher-guided practice ...**

In a scaffolded approach, the teacher analyzes the language task to be carried out by the students, determines the difficulties that task is likely to pose, and then selects and provides guided practice in strategies that enable students to approach and complete the task successfully. Just as a real scaffold is a temporary structure that holds workers and materials while a building is under construction, the ultimate goal of instructional scaffolding is to gradually withdraw the teacher-guided practice when students demonstrate that they have internalized the strategies and can apply them independently.

The Writing Workshop lesson scaffolds provide a framework of thinking and writing activities to help students move from conception to completion. While there is no one description of the writing process, the format below uses a stage process model of composition to guide students from the prewriting or *generating* phase of writing to the *planning* phase, from drafting to revising, and then to editing and evaluation.

Writing Workshop Lesson Format:

Title of Lesson—Identifies the writing task students will focus on.

Assignment—Provides a brief abstract of the writing task.

Writer's Blueprint:

- **Product**—Identifies the type of writing called for in the assignment.
- **Audience**—Specifies the audience for whom the writing is intended.
- **Specs**—Lists the specific features of a successful written product.

Prewriting—Provides a sequence of activities that help the writer connect the writing task to the literary selections and generate ideas about what to write. Activities may include clustering, quick writes, drawing, mapping, role-playing, and so forth.

Plan your Product—Helps students focus on how to get their ideas down in written form. Students formulate a writing plan using charts, microtheme forms, outlines, time lines, storyboards, and so forth.

Drafting—Gives tips for how to get started, how to make the writing focused and/or lively, important elements of the writing task to highlight, and so forth.

Revising—Presents students with a mini-lesson on specific strategies to work on to enhance the written product—for example, how to show and not just tell or how to use the active rather than the passive voice.

Editing—Focuses on an element of correctness that is relevant to the writing task. For instance, a task that requires dialogue may focus on the rules for writing a dialogue.

Presenting—Gives students ideas regarding how to publish or disseminate their work via displays, read-arounds, creating class books, presenting their papers to another class, and so forth.

Looking Back—Invites students to reflect upon what they have written and the lessons learned—both about the craft of writing and about life.

Ultimately, the goal of the Writing Workshop lessons is to provide students with a range of options for writing about literature and life, to introduce them to specific writing types or products, and to help them to develop a repertoire of strategies they can internalize and apply as autonomous learners to future thinking and writing challenges.

References

Bloom, Benjamin, ed. *Taxonomy of Educational Objectives–Handbook I: Cognitive Domain.* New York: David McKay Company, Inc., 1956.

Taba Hilda. *Thinking in Elementary School Children.* Washington, D.C.: U.S. Dept. of Health, Education and Welfare, Cooperative Research Project No. 1574, 1964.

Interdisciplinary Studies

Making Connections: An Interdisciplinary Approach

by Catherine Porter Small
American Studies Teacher and Social Studies Coordinator
Nicolet High School
Glendale, Wisconsin

"The Winslow Homer film is in my room for the week. Sign up if you want it. Can we all go to West Bend together for that exhibit before it leaves?"

—Rick (English)

"Let's rename that course 'Gender in literature, history and art.' It reflects the curriculum of that elective more accurately."

—Julie (History and English)

"The symphony's fall performance for students is about the American Dream. There's even a selection from that opera about Malcolm X. Shall we do a field trip?"

—Lon (English)

"When do you want me to do the architecture slide lecture for your students? Next week will work for me."

—Kathy (History)

"Public television is running a special on American jazz this week. I'll tape it for our teamed class if you want."

—John (History)

"Has anyone got a tape on the Salem witch trials I can use? It's Crucible *time again."*

—Jan (English)

"Aren't you going to the NCSS? Please look in on the session on making connections between history and science. I've got a live one interested in the science department."

—Dennis (History)

The Interdisciplinary Inoculation for Teachers

Burn-out is a professional disease among teachers. Stressed out and overworked, veterans of the school wars are susceptible to digging in, doing it the old way, and preserving energy. After years of the paper burden, it may be that English teachers are most susceptible to the dreaded disease, with history teachers close behind. Yet the memos above are just a sampling of those I received from colleagues during the first quarter this year. One teacher has taught sixteen years and the rest between twenty and thirty. I teach American History and American Literature and taught my first classes in 1974, but I'm still fired up and so are they. We've received the interdisciplinary inoculation against burn-out. Our intellectual health has improved along with our students'.

However, when we began interdisciplinary courses at the freshman and junior years seven years ago, not all of these teachers initially embraced it with equal fervor.

"Is this just one more swing in the educational pendulum?"

"Will I lose coverage in a course that already contains too much material and too few days?"

"I don't know enough to teach this way! What do I know about the other disciplines?"

To make the connections necessary to establish a new curriculum of this kind, we had to begin to rely on the expertise of others in our school and community. History teachers wrote simple time lines of major events to jog the memory of the English teachers. English teachers reviewed the plots of novels read long ago by history teachers. We all invited each other to classes. Regular meetings revolved around ways to make linkages, sharing discoveries. We threw lesson plans and hand-outs in each others' mailboxes. Nobody minded much the extra time they were taking because they saw the possibilities of teaching in an expanded way from a wider understanding with a safety net of their fellows. Ultimately, we saved time as we worked with one another, and collegiality replaced the lonely, closed classroom.

The unexpected benefit of establishing, developing, and maintaining interdisciplinary connections has been in the professional growth of the faculty. We've attended workshops, institutes, concerts, and art exhibitions together, and we call upon one another's expertise on a regular basis.

Cooperative learning takes place at the faculty level. I suspect the interdisciplinary approach has been the inoculation that has prevented that dreaded burn-out that assaults too many veteran teachers. I've seen colleagues who were tired get reinspired, including myself. Perhaps it's not the inoculation as much as the mental exercise that produces the teaching fitness.

The Advantages for Students

I ran into Tanya at a restaurant a few years ago. She was in my history class before we used an interdisciplinary approach. She said, "I'm embarrassed that I only got a D in your class. But you'll be glad to know that I took History of American Art last year. I learned so much! Now I get it. I even read historical novels all the time." I should have offered the apology. She was a visual learner, and I was a print teacher. She brought interest and capability to class that I had not tapped. Now she would use the images of Paul Revere and Jacob Lawrence and George Caleb Bingham as text too. Now she would read Black Boy while studying the Great Migration. Now she would "get it."

The advantages for the students are clear. Interdisciplinary study provides a context for learning, a background for the figures of literature. When we learn anything in context, comprehension improves. When comprehension improves, interest increases. When interest increases and learning occurs in context, students retain what they learn better than they do when they learn subjects in isolation. Each of us has had the experience of making connections sloppily, and sadly too late. If only we'd taken that American history class at the same time we'd taken the American literature course, the literature would have made sense. If only we'd taken Western Civilization while we took Art Appreciation, or perhaps Philosophy, we would have understood.

Marshal McLuhan, the media guru of the sixties, warned us that we would be teaching a new breed of young people not as enamored with print media as their parents because they learned in an electronic environment of television, radio, and movies. They would be visual and aural learners in print-dominant schools. Our first attempt to meet this challenge was to expand technology and resources: audiotapes and videotapes flooded the classrooms. Newer technologies have followed, especially those linked to computers. What we frequently missed, however, was that the way we learn outside the classroom has less to do with technology and more to do with the way the world works: separating the disciplines is in itself artificial. Writers don't write isolated from their culture. They are informed by the intellectual ferment of their history and times. All literature has time and setting. Poets respond to their times. History is written from perspectives shaped by the artistic response to events. Visual artists create works of art that have symbolic content, real or imaginary, in styles shaped by the milieu of the American experience. To study these subjects separately is as limiting to students as studying from the printed page alone. Providing linkage provides real insight. And insight leads to wisdom.

In a meaningful way, an interdisciplinary approach can put to a consistent use the educational buzzwords and concepts that keep reemerging: cultural literacy upper-level thinking skills, writing across the curriculum, multiple intelligences, authentic assessment, cooperative learning, and so on. These are the natural tools of such a curriculum. The insights students gain are audible: "Aha! Now I get it."

Guidelines for Developing a Program

The following guidelines may assist you in starting or expanding a program:

1. If you make it a goal to look for connections, you will find them, either thematically or chronologically, or, best of all, both.
2. If your state has a humanities council, apply for a grant for workshop time.
3. Your goal is to give the students entry-level knowledge in disciplines that do not fall under the course headings. You don't have to be an expert.
4. Discover the strengths of your faculty. Much of what you want to include in your curriculum can be taught to you or your students by other teachers with expertise developed either inside or outside classrooms.
5. Document your linkages so they can be duplicated by other teachers or even next year.
6. Challenge the students to look for and articulate connections. Popular music lyrics sometimes contain strong references to arts and letters.
7. Teach new, test new. If you take twenty minutes to allow students to "read" Winslow Homer's painting, "Prisoners at the Front," while studying the Civil War, questions about it had better show on the next test.
8. Use your textbooks in new ways. Help students discover the assumptions their text was based on. Use the illustrations for developing context. Have the students look for connections in their other texts.

A Final Word

Thirty years ago, I entered college as an English major and met the New Criticism. As I understood it, each work should stand alone and be judged on its own merits. The author's life, the times he (of course) lived in, the "conversation" he was having with other artists who used other media of expression were to be ignored. How sterile. How threadbare. What unfortunate training for so many of us. For the future English majors in our classes, that old New Criticism might work. For the rest, and especially for the Tanyas in our classes, they deserve as rich a fabric as we can weave.

Professional Commentary

Multiculturalism

Developing Multicultural Understanding

by Carlos E. Cortés
Professor Emeritus of History
University of California, Riverside
Riverside, California

According to the futurist Alvin Toffler, "All education springs from some image of the future. If the image of the future held by a society is grossly inaccurate, its educational system will betray its youth."

This integrated language arts series is based upon an image of the future—that schools must strive to help young people prepare for life in our increasingly multicultural society and the rapidly shrinking globe. This means helping students develop better interpersonal and intergroup understanding—a sense of their own place on the map of humanity, a deeper insight into the similarities and differences that link them to others with whom they share our nation and planet, an ability to understand the roots of their own points of view and the perspectives of others, a capacity for making informed, considered choices in multicultural situations, and a facility for communicating effectively with those who may come from both similar backgrounds and significantly different cultural heritages.

In addressing the topic of multicultural understanding, each grade-level book includes a wide range of selections written by women and men of different ethnic, racial, religious, and (in most of the books) national backgrounds. These selections provide windows for examining varieties of human experience—varieties that often emerge from different cultures, traditions, and group experiences, as examined by both insiders (those who belong to those groups) and outsiders (external observers).

Some selections examine specific cultures, the manner in which they have established traditions, the ways they have changed, and the processes by which they have influenced and been influenced by individuals who are a part of those cultures. Other selections examine cultures as they operate within a large context, such as racial, ethnic, or religious groups within a nation. Still other selections examine multicultural interactions, whether between nations, among groups within nations, or among individuals of different racial, ethnic, cultural, religious, or gender identities.

But this series goes well beyond merely including different perspectives; it also encourages students to examine the basic relationship of commonality and diversity—similarities and differences—within the human experience, to engage a continuing set of fundamental multicultural themes, and to consider the implications of these themes for their own lives.

Underlying the entire multicultural approach are the three basic questions. What human similarities link people of all backgrounds? What group differences contribute to the uniqueness of each individual? What are the implications of those similarities and differences for successful and constructive living in a multicultural world that is shrinking by the day because of advances in communication and transportation?

Multicultural Themes

To explore these three increasingly critical questions, this series continuously addresses seven fundamental, inevitably overlapping and interacting multicultural themes—**Groups, Individuality, Perspective, Interactions, Change, Choice,** and **Communication**. While there are many themes that could be addressed when examining the topic of diversity, we have decided that these seven themes are so essential to multicultural understanding that all students will benefit from examining them.

1. GROUPS—the process by which groups come into existence and develop, including the ways by which groups of peoples—ranging from family units to globe-spanning cultures—have created group norms, values, codes, and behavioral guidelines (such as rules and laws), have developed internal diversity, and have interacted with, influenced, and been influenced by those who belong to those groups.

2. INDIVIDUALITY—the process by which an individual develops her or his own personal uniqueness, including relating to the multiple groups to which she or he belongs, by accepting and drawing upon group norms, values, and heritage; by challenging group or community expectations or pressures; and by dealing with the consequences of those decisions and actions.

3. PERSPECTIVE—the process by which individuals and groups, including cultures and nations, develop patterns of viewing and reacting to the world around them.

4. INTERACTIONS—the process by which people respond to each other, including the various types of interactions that occur when individuals or groups of people of different backgrounds come together, such as through cooperation, conflict, and efforts to build understanding and discover common ground.

5. CHANGE—the process by which groups and individuals undergo and respond to change over time.

6. CHOICE—the process by which individuals and sometimes groups make critical choices, such as when confronted with crises, significant changes, intergroup contact, or collisions between group expectations and individual desires.

7. COMMUNICATION—the process through which individuals and groups have managed or failed to communicate, as well as the process by which different cultures have developed their own languages, literatures, and other forms of expression.

Some of these themes are highlighted explicitly in individual selections; some are used to connect the discussion of various selections; all are used as basic themes for each book. Whether or not these themes are stated explicitly in connection with specific selections in either the student or teacher edition, all can be drawn upon whenever teachers or students find them appropriate and enriching. While each book explores the seven themes in different ways, the following suggested exploratory questions may be useful at any grade level.

(1) GROUPS—*How does group experience and culture emerge and develop?* This theme is examined within the frameworks of a variety of groups–for example, ethnic, racial, gender, age, and religious groups. How does a particular group's experience create common, uniting group bonds, traditions, worldviews, and shared connections—what we often call culture? In what respects have different groups' experiences led to internal diversity—comparing the experiences and cultures of different groups?

2. INDIVIDUALITY—*What are the relationships between an individual and the multiple groups to which she or he is connected?* How is an individual influenced by different types of group connections—for example, by his or her gender, or by coming from one or more ethnic, racial, religious or national heritages? What group pressures, norms, rules, expectations, or restrictions are sometimes imposed by groups on their members in an effort to create conformity or unity? How have some people accepted and embraced group norms and responsibilities, while others have challenged and struggled against group expectations and pressures? Why have some individuals attained special prominence within group cultural contexts? Why have some people become role models who transcend group boundaries?

How have history, heritage, culture, and experience influenced the varying ways that different individuals and groups have viewed the same events?

3. PERSPECTIVE—*How have different individuals and groups perceived various events and how have those perceptions influenced their actions?* How and why have group perspectives or worldviews emerged? How have history, heritage, culture, and experience influenced the varying ways that different individuals and groups have viewed the same events? How have differing, sometimes competing, perspectives divided people and caused conflict? How have some people learned to look beyond their own perspectives to understand the perspectives of others?

4. INTERACTIONS—*What happens when different groups or individuals of different group backgrounds come into contact?* How have different groups perceived each other? How have understanding or animosity developed? How have people erected, maintained, or destroyed barriers that separate or restrict groups or individuals? How have people built bridges to connect groups or individuals so that intergroup cooperation, harmony, equality, and justice can be created?

5. CHANGE—*How do individuals and groups react to change?* What happens as people grow older or move into new cultural situations? How have groups responded to change such as by modifying their cultures or struggling to preserve traditions?

6. CHOICE—*How do individuals and groups exercise choice in varying cultural or intercultural situations?* How does culture influence choice—for example, by encouraging or restricting certain choices? How do individuals exercise options despite cultural pressures or restraints?

7. COMMUNICATION—*What roles does communication play in intercultural living?* How have cultural experience, heritage identity and perceptions influenced communication, both in expression and reception? What opportunities, obstacles, and complications in communication have developed when individuals or groups of different backgrounds come into contact?

It is our hope that this series, in addition to providing students with a rich, diverse selection of literature, will further their understanding of the multicultural dimensions of the current world and the future in which they will live. We believe that our multicultural approach will both enrich their examination of the selections and help prepare them to become better and more constructive societal and global contributors.

Building English Proficiency

The Importance of Background Knowledge in Second-Language Learning

by Lily Wong Fillmore
University of California, Berkeley
Berkeley, California

Just as readers must apply their linguistic knowledge to the interpretation of the texts they read, so too must they make use of their knowledge of the world and their prior experiences in reading. Writers have in mind an "ideal reader," as Charles Fillmore (1982) has described it, when they construct any text. The "ideal reader" for the texts they are writing is one with just the language skills and background knowledge required to arrive at complete understandings of the texts the writers intended them to understand. However, no text contains every bit of information needed to understand it fully. Writers generally assume a level of prior knowledge and cultural and real world experience when they write, depending on the age and background of the intended readers of their texts. If they believe that the intended readers are unlikely to be familiar with certain words or concepts used in the text, they will define or discuss them in the text itself. Otherwise, they can simply presuppose that the readers will be able to apply their knowledge of language and of how it works to assist in the reading and interpretation of the text, and that they will draw on their knowledge of the world and on their experiences to fill in the gaps in the text. The ideal reader then is one who has the cultural background, experience and linguistic knowledge to do just what the writer hopes the intended readers of the text will be able to do when they read it.

That fact presents a special problem to educators who are concerned with finding or preparing appropriate instructional materials and texts for children from diverse cultural and linguistic backgrounds. Writers of educational materials in the U.S. generally assume that the readers of their materials will be English speakers with a mainstream, American cultural background, with the cognitive and linguistic development that is typical for students at whatever grade-level the materials are intended. But will such materials work for children from cultural and linguistic backgrounds that are different from those assumed by their writers? Is it necessary to provide materials that are specifically designed and prepared for them, or can these children be given the same materials that are available to other students? These are questions that are raised especially where English language learners are concerned. How, the question goes, can children deal with texts that are as complex as those used for mainstream students? How can they possibly comprehend materials that presuppose cultural background, knowledge and experiences that they don't already have? Shouldn't they be given materials that are culturally familiar, that deal with the world as they know and have experienced it?

It is by reading that children, particularly English learners, build up their store of cultural and background knowledge.

I will argue that the education of children irrespective of their background would be greatly diminished if educators were to choose materials for them that were in any way narrowed or lowered in level because of putative deficiencies in the children's backgrounds. Such decisions must take into account the role authentic and challenging materials play in building children's background and in supporting language development. Children also gain the very kind of background that they need to have to deal with materials they read in school from the literature and textbooks they have already read. This argument might seem rather circular at first glance. How do children get the background they needed in the first place?

If with each story they read, children were to encounter a few new thoughts, words, experiences, glimpses of other worlds, understandings of someone else's perspective, it would not take long for them to have the rich and varied experiences and background that are needed to deal with any piece of text they are likely to get in school. It is by reading that children, particularly English learners, build up their store of cultural and background knowledge. Perhaps that is how most English language learners eventually come to master not only English, but to have the kind of cultural background and schemata (Bartlett, 1932; Rumelhart, 1980) that the text writers assume readers have and can apply to the interpretation of the materials they are writing.

The Teacher's Role in Making Written Texts Work as English Input

I believe that written texts are perhaps the most reliable and consistent source of academic English input children can have. This is not to suggest that teachers do not have a role to play in providing help and access to this kind of English for children who are learning it as a second language. Even a short text can offer to children the grammar and vocabulary of written English. However, texts do not by themselves reveal how the language in them works, nor do they provide many clues as to what the words that appear in them mean or how they are used. Granted, when readers are quite proficient in the language used in the text, they are usually able to figure out the meaning of some of the words they don't know based on the contexts in which the unfamiliar words are used (Sternberg & Powell, 1983). But there is a limit on how many words in a text can be unfamiliar or new to a reader—perhaps 8 to 10 percent. When the percentage is that high, the reader will have much greater difficulty using context to figure out what new words mean. Until language learners are relatively proficient in English, there will be much that is new to them in any text. They will find it hard to use texts as input for language learning without help. This is especially true if the learners are insecure in their knowledge of the role played by the grammatical forms such as "from," "should," and "before" in indicating relationships and meanings in sentences and texts. Any text is pretty uninformative by itself, where language learners are concerned. To serve as input for language learning, not only does it have to be a well-formed text—which is to say, it must be coherent and cohesive, well constructed and interesting. It goes without saying that it must be a good example of grammatical English for it to work as English input. But the content has to be engaging, too—it has got to hold the attention of language learners, and be a great enough challenge to them to be worth the effort they have to make to read a text they can't easily understand. The best instances of such texts can be found in children's literature.

The question is, what role do teachers play in helping children make use of the written materials, especially authentic children's literature, as input for language learning? Such materials work as input —1) when teachers provide the support learners need for making sense of the text; 2) when they call attention to the way language is used in the text; 3) when they discuss the meaning and interpretation of sentences and phrases within the text with the learners; 4) when they help the learners notice that words they find in a text may have been encountered or used in other places; and 5) when they help them discover the grammatical cues that indicate relationships such as cause and effect, antecedent and consequence, comparison and contrast, and so on in the text.

In short, teachers help written texts become usable input—not only by helping children make sense of the text—but by drawing their attention, focusing it, in fact, on how language is used in the materials they read. Done consistently enough, the learners themselves will soon come to notice the way language is used in the materials they read. When they can do that, everything they read will be input for learning.

References

Bartlett, F. (1931) *Remembering.* Cambridge: Cambridge University Press.

Fillmore, C.J. (1982) Ideal readers and real readers. In D. Tannen (Ed.) *Analyzing Discourse: Text and Talk. Georgetown Round Table on Language and Linguistics 1981.* Georgetown University Press, 248-270.

Rumelhart, D.E. (1980) Schemata: The building blocks of cognition. In R.J. Spiro, B.C. Bruce & W.J. Brewer (Eds.) *Theoretical Issues in Reading Comprehension.* Hillsdale NJ: Erlbaum.

Sternberg, R.J. & Powell, J,S, (1983) Comprehending verbal comprehension. *American Psychologist,* 8, 878-893.

Building English Proficiency

Building English Proficiency among ESL Students: Theory and Practice

by Dr. Jim Cummins

Professor Modern Language Centre and Curriculum Department

Ontario Institute for Studies in Education
Ontario, Canada

In many urban centers across North America, the numbers of students who are learning English as a second language (ESL) have increased dramatically in recent years. These students face a formidable challenge in meeting the standards of academic English required to graduate from high school. Considerable research has shown that, although conversational fluency in English often is acquired fairly rapidly (within about two years), it normally takes between five and ten years for ESL students to catch up to grade expectations in academic aspects of the language. There are two reasons for this:

- Academic language is much more complex than conversational language in terms of vocabulary and syntax.
- ESL students must catch up with a moving target insofar as speakers of English as a first language (L1) continue to grow every year in academic language abilities, such as reading and writing skills, range of vocabulary, and command of complex syntax.

In order to promote academic language development among ESL students, it is important to provide abundant opportunities for students to develop their thinking abilities, to encourage them to read and write extensively, and, above all, to let them feel your support in the personal journeys they are taking into a new language and culture.

Keep up the Cognitive Challenge!

The flip side of this is "don't dumb down the content!" ESL students are as intellectually bright as the other students in your class; they just don't have full command of the language at this point in time. They need cognitive challenge to maintain their interest and motivation just as much as any other student.

Provide Contextual Support!

In order for ESL students to be able to participate in cognitively challenging activities, they usually will require more contextual support than English L1 students. This contextual support is provided in two basic ways:

- Activating students prior knowledge and sparking their interest and motivation to invest academic effort. Activating prior knowledge mobilizes relevant concepts and information that students already possess, thereby making the learning process more efficient.
- Present content through visual or graphic displays (maps, Venn diagrams, semantic webs, outlines of chronological or causal sequences, etc.) that allow concepts to be taught in concrete ways that all students can figure out.

Brain Power in Action!

Both of these approaches increase students' brain power by activating and/or building their conceptual knowledge. The more students already know, the more they can comprehend, and the more they comprehend, the more they learn. These approaches also free up brain power. Because students have grasped the concept, they have more brain power to focus on the language itself and extend their understanding of vocabulary and syntax.

Extending Personal Horizons Through Reading and Writing

The importance of providing ample opportunities and encouragement for students to read and write volumes (literally!) cannot be overstated. Academic language, the language of text, is found only in books. You don't find it in the playground or on the street, or on popular television. If ESL students are not reading a lot, and reading in a variety of genres, they are not getting access to the language they need for graduation.

Technology

The CD-ROM Research Environment

by Mary Cron
Rymel Multimedia
Rolling Hills Estates, California

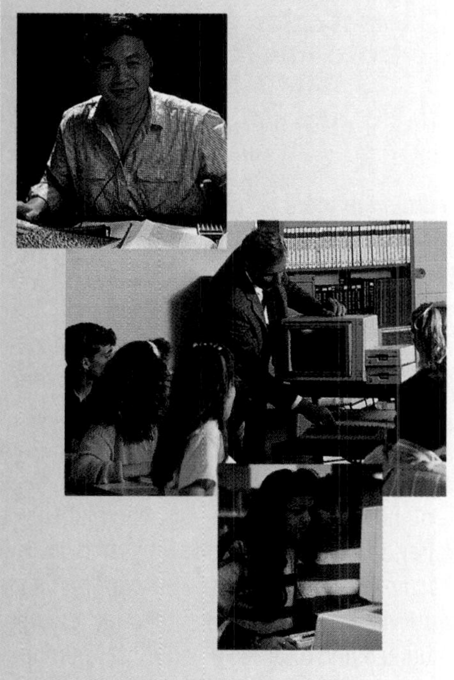

In the early 1980s, I was sitting with a group of teachers at one of the early educational technology conferences. With feet up in comfortable overstuffed lobby chairs, we fantasized about the future—*way* into the future—to a day when educational computer programs might be in color, present more than drill and practice options, have music and realistic sound effects instead of annoying beeps, and contain *much* more content. Conversation ended in laughter. Not in our lifetimes.

The Vision

Even in those early days, we were beginning to frame a vision of a multi-sensory on-line learning environment engaging to students of various learning styles and interests. We didn't just want students to be drilled and tested. In this information-rich, on-line world we envisioned, students could explore, hypothesize, gather information, analyze—in other words, use and develop their critical thinking skills. Happily, the future arrived much faster than any of the armchair visionaries anticipated. The CD-ROM format and accompanying developments in sound compression, video, and hardware capabilities have made it possible to include thousands of colorful images and pages of text.

Multimedia Research

A multimedia research environment presents information on a topic or set of related topics. Students can explore this information dynamically through a variety of inviting graphic navigational screens and sorting techniques.

In this CD-ROM environment students have more enthusiasm for research and spend more time working on their investigations than they do using print only.

The CD-ROM research environment also teaches important skills in media literacy that will prepare students for the learning tools they will use in higher education and in the workplace. These tools include mosaic thinking; analytical investigation of text, visual, and audio content; and the use of multimedia tools to create and present their own knowledge effectively.

Thinking Mosaically

One of the most difficult adjustments those of us from the print world have had to make when producing and using CD-ROM applications is to give up thinking only in linear terms. CD-ROM, with its quick sorting capabilities, is an amazing door opener to this mosaic world. In the CD-ROM research environment, students are able to make their own investigative choices connecting topics and ideas in a variety of ways. They can search for key words, type of media, topics, themes, and projects. Because the environment is highly interactive, their choices quickly activate new research paths.

Critical Analysis

Because the media is varied, the CD-ROM research environment requires students to go further than just analyzing text. They have photographs, audio, video, fine art, and illustrations both contemporary and archival to examine as potential sources of information. They have to weigh the viability, point of view, and usefulness of that information. They learn to observe and listen carefully and to question what they see and hear in any media. These are important critical-thinking skills in a media-driven society.

Using Multimedia Tools to Present Knowledge

Finally, in a multimedia research environment, student investigation results in the communication of new knowledge to others. Production tools are provided that enable students to enter their ideas, collect evidence of different media to support opinions, and prepare a sequenced presentation. The use of a multimedia bibliography and credits throughout the presentation discourages student plagiarism and reinforces the importance of accurate research to support hypotheses.

Professional Commentary

Ways of Learning

Learning Modalities and the Successful Teacher

by Dr. Jerry Hay
Director of Middle and High School Programs
Spalding University
Louisville, Kentucky

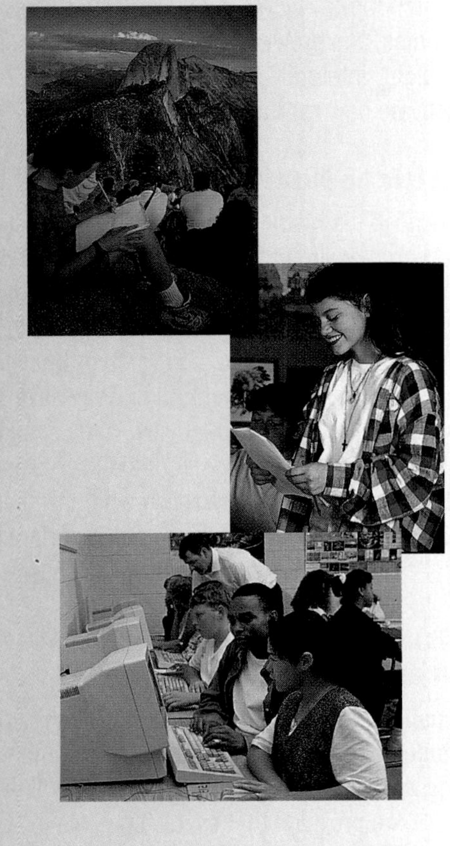

Imagine a conversation between two people of different cultures. The cultures need not be the cultures of different countries, but could even be the cultures of different socio-economic classes. During conversation, the speaker uses a word that the other does not understand. When the speaker recognizes the look of confusion on the other's face, the speaker begins to use all of the other words known to mean about the same thing. When these new words also fail to communicate, the speaker employs metaphors, similes, and analogies to help with the transfer of meaning. The speaker may eventually resort to a combination of grunts, facial expressions, body movements, and wild gestures to communicate. We have all experienced the frustration of failed communication from both ends of a conversation. This experience is in itself a rationale for using learning style theory in the teaching of literature.

Like the two conversationalists of different cultures, communication occurs only when meaning is transferred in a mode mutually understood. In a conversation, the speakers use a variety of words and gestures as needed only when stimulated by a lack of understanding. If one person in a conversation knew ahead of time that the other person best understood a particular language, vocabulary, or jargon, it would be possible to plan for the most effective and efficient conversation by taking that communication strength into account. Teachers face the same dilemma; they must communicate daily with a large group of students who may each have a particular communication or learning strength. Knowing about the learning strengths of students facilitates effective teaching.

How People Learn

A variety of theories deal with the differences in learning modalities. While each theory is unique, all contribute to an understanding of how people learn. These theories range from genetic to developmental and from broad to the very specific. One general theory considers the differences in function between the right and left lobes of the brain. This right brain–left brain theory, discussed in Betty Edward's' book, *Drawing on the Right Side of the Brain*, contends that the left side of the brain controls logical, linear thought while the right side of the brain controls the more general, global thought processes. Edwards also contends that teaching students to think or learn in only one lobe of the brain limits their perceptions of content. She advocates that teachers best serve students when they combine teaching strategies that incorporate both linear and global learning opportunities. Literature students benefit from not only the study of plot and character development, but also the study of global relationships. Walter Barbe and Raymond Swassing, in *Teaching Through Modality Strengths: Concepts and Practices*, support the need for teachers to recognize and address a variety of learning strengths in students. Learning modalities relate to strengths. It is logical for teachers to address these learning strengths and thus increase the rate or extent of learning by providing information through the most efficient channel for each student.

> **...teachers best serve students when they combine teaching strategies that incorporate both linear and global learning strategies.**

Recognizing the four learning modalities, teachers can arrange learning experiences for students that increase the rate of individual success by emphasizing the appropriate learning modality for each student. Teachers can also take the approach of systematically including all the learning strengths to ensure the greatest rate of student success. Students with a visual learning modality learn by seeing or watching demonstrations, think in pictures, and respond best to visual arts. Auditory-modality students learn through verbal instruction, think in sounds, and favor the musical arts. Kinesthetic learners learn by doing and by being physically involved, think with a physical memory, and react to all art in expressions of movement, touch, and physical involvement. Social learners respond best to learning situations within groups, think in terms of relationships within groups, and react to art as a social relationship.

Related to the realization that people can have different thought modalities, other researchers advance the belief that individuals have multiple intelligences or learning styles. Howard Gardner, in *Frames of Mind: The Theory of Multiple Intelligences*, contends that individuals have at least seven varieties of intelligences. He also feels students learn successfully when taught by teachers who incorporate learning opportunities that cater to the various intelligences. David Lazear, in *Seven Ways of Knowing: Teaching for Multiple Intelligences*, extends Gardner's approach by suggesting that teachers not only can incorporate learning based on the various intelligences but also can expand and develop their own multiple intelligences through a systematic program of intellectual exercises. These seven intelligences can easily be related to learning modality theory. Of the seven intelligences, verbal/linguistic is comparable to the auditory learning modality; visual/spatial intelligence is the visual learning modality; inter- and intra-personal intelligences relate directly to the social learning modality and rhythmic/musical and body/kinesthetic intelligences parallel the kinesthetic learning modality. The logical/mathematical intelligence can be equated either to visual or auditory learning modalities.

Effective Teaching

How do any or all of these different theories about how people learn affect the teaching of literature or any other content? These theories, which recognize that all people learn with different modalities or strengths, should influence how all content is taught. Literature students with any one of the four learning modalities will flourish in a classroom providing a combination of learning experiences that include opportunities for visual, auditory, kinesthetic, and social learning. To be effective, each lesson need not include all four learning modalities on any given day; but attention should be given to all four within a given unit of study. It is true that many teachers maintain excellent learning climates that, over the course of a term, may contain more than one of the learning modalities. There is a difference, however, between the accidental utilization of this approach, and deliberately planned teaching that recognizes and takes advantage of the learning modalities. The difference between the accidental and the planned utilization of learning modalities can be the difference between the occasionally successful and the consistently successful classroom. Without consistent application, theory is just speculation about possibilities.

Consider students in the 12–18 year age range. This age group presents the richest assortment of likes, dislikes, personalities, strengths, weaknesses, and learning preferences. These factors change on an almost daily basis and could change on an hourly basis for middle-school students. Flexibility and adaptability are the prerequisites for dealing with this age group. The use of modality learning theory to design, deliver, and assess instruction is one path to a consistent flexibility in meeting student needs.

Students benefit from instruction consistent with learning modality theory because this classroom will provide for the development and support of authentic self-esteem. Student success is the most effective source of student self-esteem. Too often, the activities planned for the development and support of student self-esteem are artificial, with little or no relationship to the content of the class. The self-esteem resulting from these "add-on" activities will usually last only for the duration of the activity. Teach to a student's learning strength and the positive feelings about education will last well beyond the moment. In addition to improved self-esteem developed through authentic learning success, the student should actually learn more in a classroom based on learning modalities. This is the most important outcome of the application of learning modalities in teaching. As teachers, we may actually be more successful, particularly with those students overlooked in the past because they did not learn as well in the dominant learning modality of our instruction.

Increased success in student learning, in addition to the boost any teacher would enjoy from this phenomenon, also carries the added bonus of better classroom management. That the successful, involved student is not a disruptive student is a universally held belief among experienced teachers. Ignore a student's learning strength and that student will be involved in activities other than those planned by the teacher. Students who experience success, and who come to expect to experience continued success, will likely be assets to the teacher and to the class.

Each of the theories regarding differentiated learning, or learning modalities, illustrates the basic concept that humans are different in many ways, including the way in which they most effectively learn. Many of our differences are superficial and easily identified; learning strengths are not as easily recognized. The interrelatedness of Edward's right brain–left brain theory, Gardner's seven intelligences, and Barbe's modality strengths all support a classroom that recognizes the differing learning strengths of the students. The successful teacher uses those learning differences to create a learning climate supportive of all students. The recognition of learning strengths will lead to a more successful student and a more successful teacher.

Professional Commentary

Media Literacy

Beyond Print: Media and Visual Literacy

by Dr. Harold M. Foster
Professor of English Education
The University of Akron
Akron, Ohio

The future is here and it is both an opportunity and a threat. The future offers unlimited information and entertainment. It offers an endless stream of choices and enticements. But it will take all your time if you let it.

The future is on your televisions and on your movie screens. Never before has television and film offered as many choices or technological advances. Every aspect of life may be affected by these media.

These media are neither good nor bad. They are powerful. Used with judgment and restraint, the media are an incredibly positive force. Used thoughtlessly and capriciously, the media can be dangerously manipulative. The key to productive engagement with the complex array of communication systems is education. And that is exactly the purpose of the *Beyond Print* feature of this text series. By engaging reflection and perception about the media, this section educates the young people who use this text.

> **These media are neither good nor bad. They are powerful.**

Television

Television is the most pervasive of all the media. It is ubiquitous like central heating. Many televisions sets are on whenever anybody is home, whether someone is actively watching or not. Most of the time television is a low-engagement medium. Viewers watch it with the lights on. Much of the time television is what people use to fall asleep. Thus, the images and values of television seep into the lives of people without their complete awareness.

However, there are moments of great intensity on television like the finish of an excitingly close sports event or the reporting of a devastating hurricane. During the moments of intensity, television becomes a national cathedral—as when John F. Kennedy was assassinated—or a global village square where everyone goes to hear the news or to dwell on the most earth shattering events. Think about the power of a medium which can engage the attention of almost the entire world at the same time. The Olympics do that in some ways. The election of a president certainly has most of the U.S. mesmerized. The Tienanmen Square uprising and the collapse of the Berlin Wall captured the attention of much of the world. The few voices that bring people all this information are amazingly powerful.

Television is good news for those intelligent enough to form their own opinions, who can see through the endless stream of commercials and fantasy lifestyles television portrays. Television is good news for those who turn TV off and read. Television is good news for those people who see television as a tool to enhance their lives, but also realize that television is not life. These are the citizens who use television wisely and understand the medium and the role it plays.

But there is the other scenario. What about the people who have television on all the time, who watch it but seldom think about what they see? What about those that watch anything? How about people who seldom talk to their families, and never read, and hardly ever engage with people unless they have to? What about people who unwittingly take on the ethos of television: money is everything; how you look is who you are; problems are solved in an hour; sex is easy and without emotional consequences; if you don't get your way, hit or shoot the guy; buy, buy, buy; if you are bored, change the channel?

Are there viewers out there like this—viewers who see their own lives through the distorted prism of TV? Most people who study television think so; most members of our government think so; most responsible mothers, fathers, and guardians of children think so; even many of the people who bring us television think so.

So in a free society what do you do about this? You educate and through education not only do you hope to eliminate the negative impact of television, you hope to help make television a wonderful part of the lives of young people. Television is a blessing. Let us use it wisely.

Movies

The *Beyond Print* feature in this anthology also concerns film. Film is different from television. It is a more intense medium. Film works by having light pass through a translucent celluloid cell and projecting a sharp image of the picture from the cell onto a screen. The sense of movement is created by flicking the cells past this bright, projected light at a rate of 24 pictures per second. This flicking creates an illusion of movement akin to the illusion found in children's toys where you flick cards or pages of a series of pictures and it appears that the objects are moving.

When you view a film these pictures on a screen have great emotional impact. Even though the technology is old, nothing yet comes close to the quality of a motion picture. A lighted room ruins the image so you watch films in the dark, eyes riveted to the screen. Your attention seldom wanders. Films are meant to be viewed without distraction, as if someone else was creating a dream for the viewer. These dreamlike qualities of movies make them potentially very powerful.

Most people love movies. They are a wonderful form of entertainment and escape, and truly great movies are so much more, a world-class art as lofty and sublime as any other art form. These qualities are why films need to be studied. The more a person knows about film, the more likely it is that the person will appreciate the best that film has to offer and will have critical viewing standards for all films.

Seeing, Speaking, and Listening

Beyond Print also deals with seeing, speaking, and listening—skills which are even more important now with modern communication technology. Both film and television require people to be perceptive about seeing. Film in particular can be like a moving painting where the more trained you are to see the better viewer you will be. *Beyond Print* broadens the scope of its young readers through activities which educate them to appreciate fine painting and photography.

Speaking and listening are ageless skills made even more important by a culture which rewards those who can move an audience. *Beyond Print* provides many opportunities to use oral skills to argue and persuade.

Perhaps even more important than speaking for a truly sensitive, caring culture are people with the ability to listen to each other. *Beyond Print* offers the opportunity to engage in active listening exercises. These exercises require careful and precise listening, a skill so often ignored in this society to its detriment.

Reading and Writing

Beyond Print provides student-friendly activities to promote reading and writing. All of the activities in *Beyond Print* come at the end of units or unit parts in the series. But, the ultimate goal of these texts is as it should be, to create good readers. Reading is still at the heart of society. Those who read well will write the television and movies which sadly keep so many others in the population barely literate. That is why so many of the *Beyond Print* activities involve reading and writing. Also, learning about the media creates more selective viewers who may have some time left over for reading. So *Beyond Print* not only promotes an understanding of the new literacies, but also promotes through that understanding a heightened awareness of the importance of reading and writing.

Goals

These are the educational goals of *Beyond Print*:

1. To transform students into discriminating TV and film viewers who can distinguish good from bad, exploitation from communication.
2. To sensitize students so they perceive how television and film are designed to influence and manipulate them.
3. To educate students to understand television and film visually and thematically so they can analyze and critique the media they watch.
4. To develop critical awareness so students will pass up at least the very worst of the electronic media and have time to read and study.
5. To develop in students an aesthetic appreciation for the finest the electronic media have to offer.
6. To educate students to see with perception and understanding all visual media including photography and painting.
7. To help students speak and listen with power and intelligence to prepare for a culture which rewards those who are effective public speakers and cherish those who listen with compassion and deep understanding to others.

(Adapted from Harold M. Foster's *Crossing Over: Whole Language for Secondary English Teachers*, Harcourt Brace, Fort Worth, Texas, 1994, p. 197.)

Professional Commentary

Visual Literacy

Art in the Literature Classroom

by Neil Anstead
Coordinator of the Humanitas Program
Cleveland Humanities Magnet School
Reseda, California

Students as visual learners

Many years ago when I started teaching literature, my goal was to hook kids with ideas. But it didn't take long for me to find out that many of my students didn't learn easily from words alone, and when they had to struggle with the language, they gave up before arriving at concepts. After a lot of struggle and failure, I started looking for other meaningful ways to supplement the use of words in order to gain understanding. My initial efforts were with music, lyrics, and even opera; these helped, but not enough. Next, I turned to the visual arts; the results were not a cure-all, but they were much better than before. In using art in the literature classroom, one can either begin with the literature or begin with the art.

Moving from the literature to the art

When studying *Macbeth*, I wanted my students to understand that individualism was a dominant force in the Renaissance, and that when carried to extreme, it could be very dangerous. Macbeth's career is a good example.

To introduce the concept of individualism, we first studied a well-known art work, Michelangelo's *Pietà*. If it had been sculpted in the Middle Ages, we might never have known the name of its creator. At that time, signing one's name to any creative effort was considered a sin of pride. God was the creator and the individual was simply his vehicle. But by the time of the Renaissance, artists were egotistical about their efforts, and when Michelangelo overheard his recently finished sculpture attributed to another artist, he boldly put his name across the Madonna's sash. He, not God, was the creator.

Next, we looked at the Florence Baptistery Doors, the so-called *Doors of Paradise*. Had they been made in the Middle Ages, artists would have worked cooperatively as they had on the great cathedrals. Not so in the Renaissance. The church held a competition for a single artist to create these magnificent portals. Students can identify with these concrete images of self-centeredness; indeed, it is one of the legacies of the Renaissance in their lives. These art works, together with others, became the background for the study of Shakespeare's *Macbeth*, and the experience proved helpful.

Another benefit of using art in conjunction with literature emerged as we worked together with images. It seemed to promote a holistic habit of mind. If *Macbeth*, the *Pietà*, and the *Doors of Paradise* reflect the spirit of individualism, and if individualism is a fundamental concept that pervades Renaissance culture, then we speculated that we would find this same characteristic elsewhere. And sure enough, we found it in Machiavelli, in the competition between city states, and in the development of mercantile capitalism.

Moving from the art to the literature

I started by saying that many of my students are finding it increasingly difficult to learn from words alone. At this point the reader might ask, "Then why not use art as a starting point and work toward literature?" My response is, "Indeed, why not?" Another example might prove instructive.

Although many of today's high school students were born after the Vietnam War, the war is still affecting their lives. Because it influenced all aspects of American society—economics, political philosophy, attitudes about war, the visual arts, film, literature, and more—it is best treated as an interdisciplinary topic. If starting with literary works proves difficult, try using the Vietnam War Memorial.

Students will be interested to know that Maya Lin designed the Memorial as a school project, and that even though it won in the design competition for a veterans' memorial, many politicians never dreamed it would be constructed. It was controversial from the very beginning. Memorials are normally imposing white marble monuments, not black granite walls sunk into the ground. Compare it to the Washington Monument that stands nearby. What does its color and location suggest? And why does it have a polished surface? When we see ourselves as we peruse the names of the dead, do we question our own part in the war? Was that the intent? And aren't the names on most war memorials arranged according to rank? On the Maya Lin memorial, they are listed according to date of death. Is it really an art work? and if so, are there any antecedents? Finally, why have two traditional monuments been added to it?

Experience has taught me that students will be engaged if there is controversy. Furthermore, I think they will identify with Maya Lin, a young Asian student who did her homework to the best of her ability, struggled, and eventually won out over powerful opponents.

Ours is a world in which literature is not confined to words on a page.

A transitional activity might be to read some short first-person narratives of Vietnam soldiers. Such accounts have frequently become the raw material for good literature. The actual books or stories you end up using depend on many things, the reading ability of your students, the time allotted, and the availability of textbooks to mention a few.

Students probably learn as much from pictures as they do from the printed words. I wish I had a dollar for every student who told me that he or she learned more history by studying art history than from a history textbook. Lovers of words may feel uncomfortable with this, but I think it's true. Therefore, I encourage you to use the images that have been carefully selected for this book. They do more than beautify the pages, they provide a point of entry. And in the process, students might end up appreciating art, which is a bonus.

Guidelines in evaluating art

The following are a few points to consider when you evaluate art for possible use in the literature classroom:

- *Will the artwork engage your students?* Some works—Dali's *Persistence of Memory* is a good example—immediately intrigue kids; others can be made interesting through a teacher's scholarship and enthusiasm.
- *Are the interdisciplinary links between the artwork and the literature clear and natural?* If students can grasp these connections easily, it will enhance both their cultural understanding and enthusiasm for learning.
- *Does the artwork, in conjunction with literature, serve as a springboard for interesting writing assignments and other projects?* The full value of art in the classroom is not realized unless students work with it creatively—in writing, in discussion, and in a broad range of creative projects.
- *Is there good, accessible critical literature about this artwork?* Don't make your preparation more difficult by focusing on obscure works that will be difficult to research. Museum curatorial and education staffs can be useful resources.

Professional Commentary

Assessing Student Learning

The Dimensions of Assessment

by Alan C. Purves
Director of the Center for Writing and Literacy
State University of New York at Albany
Albany, New York

We all know that what is important in any class is what is on the test. Although we provide a lot of questions and assignments which could be considered "The Test," we think they should be used in another way, one that will help students become more mature, self-confident, and independent learners. That is why there is an assessment strand—one that is as important as the instructional strand.

You are surrounded by assessment. You are asked "How am I doing?" by students, "How is my child doing?" by parents or caretakers, "How are they doing?" by administrators at the building, district, state, and national level. You are told by administrators that there are local, state, or national examinations that your students must take; you are asked by parents to help their students prepare for college entrance or scholarship examinations, and you may even be asked to take teaching examinations yourself. How do you work through that maze of demands?

Many people think that tests are the same as assessment, but tests are only a small part of today's whole assessment activity. When students ask, "How am I doing?" they may not be satisfied with a test score. One student may want to know if something about what she's reading is worth anything to you and to the class. Another may want to know if his class participation is valued and how and for what. A third might be concerned with your rating of her capacity to work with others. A fourth may be concerned with his progress towards a goal. Students usually want to know how well they are doing as part of their on-going work; for them assessment is a part of learning. Assessment therefore should be an integral part of your teaching.

Teaching literature and the language arts encourages a great variety of activities, including individual and collaborative projects, reading logs, writing about literature and its relation to other subjects, working on computers, taking quizzes, taking part in classroom discussion, creating and participating in drama, working on art projects, and much more. This variety does not lend itself to a single test. All these facets of what it means to learn English and literature need to be thought of as part of the assessment of your students' work and of your class. A comprehensive assessment package needs to match a complex subject matter, and assessment has many audiences, many questions, and many things to attend to. The audiences include you as the teacher, other teachers, the students, parents, and the school and community.

Assessment is not just an examination at the end of the quarter or the year. It begins before the first day of class.

Course Objectives

Assessment is not just an examination at the end of the quarter or the year. It begins before the first day of class. You need to look at your syllabus, the anthology, and other materials you are using. Start by defining your course objectives:

- What do you want students to know at the end of the quarter or the end of the year?
- What do you want students to do that they couldn't do before taking this course? To put it another way, what skills do you want them to develop?

• What habits of reading and writing do you want them to acquire? Knowledge, practice, and habits are the core of any curriculum and plan of instruction. As you look at the materials, the selections, and the activities you are going to use, it helps to keep these questions in mind. What sorts of products will tell you whether the students have gained in their knowledge, their skills, and their habits? These will form the evidence for the assessment of their learning. The list of products can be large:

final tests and examinations
unit tests
quizzes
short papers
on-going records
reading logs
tapes of discussions
projects
art works
musical performances or compositions
research papers
computer programs
dramatic presentations
videotapes
photographs
out-of-class publications
contest materials
cross-subject papers or projects

Some of these may be individual student work, some may be collaborative projects with one or more partners, and some may be whole class projects. You should plan which of these you are going to require and which you are going to suggest.

Developing a Sense of Independence

One of the ways you can develop a sense of independence in students' learning involves giving students responsibility for their own work by setting broad goals for their learning and then inviting them to set their own specific goals. By setting and monitoring their own progress, students take command of their own learning. For some students a goal might be to read a novel by Toni Morrison; for another student it might be to finish a chapter of a book. Both are worthy goals; each is right for a particular student at a particular time.

By setting and monitoring their own progress, students take command of their own learning.

A second way to make students' learning more independent is to provide students with opportunities to do projects that are complex and involve bringing together a number of sources of information and a number of skills. Many of these projects may be group projects such as the creation of a diorama, the presentation of a play, a debate, a video production of a class interpretation, or the like.

We have found that central to the setting and reaching of goals in literature and writing is the portfolio. During the course of the year students

keep a working portfolio of their reading logs, their drafts and papers, their projects and tapes. As they go through this portfolio periodically they look for signs of their growth in the ways in which they have met or exceeded their goals. At the end of the year, they prepare a presentation portfolio, a formal presentation of themselves as readers and writers. This is an important testimony to the worth of each student's efforts. Accomplishing a successful portfolio is a sign that students have gained maturity as readers and writers.

Teachers in all sorts of classrooms report that students do better when they become partners in their assessment rather than simply taking assigned tests. When they know what is expected of them and how they are going to be judged, students become more responsible and serious about their work. If this approach works in the world of business, sports, and the professions, there is no reason why it can't work in school as well. After all, school and life should not be separated.

Program Skill Development

Scope and Sequence

Literature	Grades 6	7	8	9	10	11	12
Literature Appreciation							
Appreciate literary selections representing various genres	X	X	X	X	X	X	X
Understand characteristics of major literary genres	X	X	X	X	X	X	X
Recognize universal themes in literature	X	X	X	X	X	X	X
Recognize the relationship of literary structure and/or devices to meaning	X	X	X	X	X	X	X
Appreciate literature representing a variety of cultures and traditions	X	X	X	X			
Appreciate selections from world literature					X		
Appreciate selections from the American literary heritage						X	
Appreciate selections from the British literary heritage							X
Recognize topics characteristic of major writers of the period						X	X
Value literature from various periods in history	X	X	X	X	X	X	X
Understand that literature selections reflect a cultural context	X	X	X	X	X	X	X
Understand that literature selections reflect a social context	X	X	X	X	X	X	X
Understand that literature selections may reflect a political context						X	X
Choose to read independently	X	X	X				
Genres							
Biography/Autobiography	X	X	X	X	X	X	X
Drama/Play (including Comedy, Tragedy)	X	X	X	X	X	X	X
Essay	X	X	X	X	X	X	X
Expository nonfiction	X	X		X	X		
Fable	X	X	X	X	X	X	X
Folk tale	X	X	X	X	X	X	X
Historical document		X	X		X	X	X
Legend	X	X	X	X	X	X	X
Literary criticism							X

Literature	Grades 6	7	8	9	10	11	12
Genres cont.							
Myth	X	X	X	X	X	X	X
Narrative nonfiction	X	X	X	X	X		
Parable							X
Novel	X	X	X	X	X	X	X
Poetry (include lyric, narrative, ballad, epic)	X	X	X	X	X	X	X
Short Story	X	X	X	X	X	X	X
Literary Terms and Techniques							
Allegory							X
Alliteration	X	X	X	X	X	X	X
Allusion						X	X
Archetype							X
Characterization	X	X	X	X	X	X	X
Denotative and connotative language						X	X
Dialect	X	X	X	X	X	X	X
Dialogue	X	X	X	X	X	X	X
Diction	X	X	X	X	X	X	X
Figurative language	X	X	X	X	X	X	X
Flashback		X	X	X			
Foreshadowing			X	X	X	X	X
Hyperbole	X	X	X	X	X	X	X
Idiom	X	X	X	X	X	X	X
Imagery	X	X	X	X	X	X	X
Irony (dramatic; situational)		X	X	X	X	X	X
Metaphor	X	X	X	X	X	X	X
Meter				X	X	X	X
Mood	X	X	X	X	X	X	X
Multiple narration							X
Onomatopoeia	X	X	X	X	X	X	X
Personification	X	X	X	X	X	X	X
Plot	X	X	X	X	X	X	X

Literature

Literary Terms and Techniques cont.

Literature	6	7	8	9	10	11	12
Point of view	X	X	X	X	X	X	X
Pun				X	X	X	X
Repetition	X	X	X	X	X	X	X
Rhythm	X	X	X	X	X	X	X
Rhyme	X	X	X	X	X	X	X
Satire						X	X
Setting	X	X	X	X	X	X	X
Simile	X	X	X	X	X	X	X
Sound devices	X	X	X	X	X	X	X
Stream of consciousness						X	X
Style	X	X	X	X	X	X	X
Symbolism	X	X	X	X	X	X	X
Theme	X	X	X	X	X	X	X
Tone	X	X	X	X	X	X	X

Writing

Use the Writing Process

Prewrite	6	7	8	9	10	11	12
Choose writing tools and/or equipment	X	X	X	X	X	X	X
Use technology	X	X	X	X	X	X	X
Choose topics of interest to self and others	X	X	X	X	X	X	X
Narrow topics	X	X	X	X	X	X	X
Set schedule and intermediate goals	X	X	X	X	X	X	X
Consider audience and purpose	X	X	X	X	X	X	X
Use sources such as personal experience and literature	X	X	X	X	X	X	X
Use strategies to generate ideas	X	X	X	X	X	X	X
Use aural and visual stimuli to generate ideas	X	X	X	X	X	X	X
Gather information and technical data	X	X	X	X	X	X	X
Organize ideas; outline	X	X	X	X	X	X	X

Writing

Use the Writing Process cont.

Develop Draft	6	7	8	9	10	11	12
Establish a thesis				X	X	X	X
Write supporting ideas	X	X	X	X	X	X	X
Include related paragraphs in longer papers				X	X	X	X
Provide examples, reasons, evidence	X	X	X	X	X	X	X
Provide incidents and anecdotes	X	X	X	X	X	X	X
Include information (facts, statistics) from variety of sources	X	X	X	X	X	X	X
Use sensory details	X	X	X	X	X	X	X
Use figurative language		X	X				
Use tone, point of view and style appropriate to topic and purpose	X	X	X				
Order ideas: time, importance, cause and effect, compare and contrast, spatial order	X	X	X	X	X	X	X
Use literary devices				X	X	X	X
Use introduction, middle, conclusion	X	X	X	X	X	X	X
Develop a personal voice/style				X	X	X	X
Revise							
Improve content by adding, deleting, reorganizing information	X	X	X	X	X	X	X
Alter mood, plot, characterization, or voice	X	X	X	X	X	X	X
Generalize from specific information	X	X	X	X	X	X	X
Analyze writing for reasoning				X	X	X	X
Examine word choice (vivid/specific nouns, active/concrete verbs)	X	X	X	X	X	X	X
Maintain consistent voice	X	X	X	X	X	X	X
Check appropriateness of formality/informality			X	X	X	X	X
Achieve precision in meaning				X	X	X	X
Choose vocabulary appropriate to intent	X	X	X	X	X	X	X
Combine sentences	X	X	X	X	X	X	X
Expand sentences	X	X	X	X	X	X	X

Scope and Sequence

Writing	Grades 6	7	8	9	10	11	12
Use the Writing Process cont.							
Improve sentences using parallel structure, details, a variety of sentence structures, and effective transitions	X	X	X	X	X	X	X
Proofread/Edit							
Interact with peers in editing	X	X	X	X	X	X	X
Use conferences in editing	X	X	X				
Develop analytic criteria for responding				X	X	X	X
Check for legibility	X	X	X	X	X	X	X
Edit for sentence fragments			X				
Edit for run-on sentences			X				
Use conventions of standard English	X	X	X	X	X	X	X
Cite sources appropriately						X	X
Present							
Use visuals, graphics	X	X	X	X	X	X	X
Produce oral discourse/composition	X	X	X	X	X	X	X
Keep portfolio	X	X	X	X	X	X	X
Share written discourse orally	X	X	X	X	X	X	X

Write in a Variety of Modes	6	7	8	9	10	11	12
Narrative	X	X	X	X	X	X	X
Descriptive	X	X	X	X	X	X	X
Expository/Informative	X	X	X	X	X	X	X
Persuasive/Argumentative	X	X	X	X	X	X	X
Personal Expression	X	X	X	X	X	X	X
Expressive/Creative/Imaginative	X	X	X	X	X	X	X

Use a Variety of Forms and Techniques	6	7	8	9	10	11	12
Advertisement	X	X	X	X	X	X	X
Analysis/speculation about effects (CA)	X	X	X	X	X	X	X
Answers to essay questions					X	X	X
Autobiographical incident (CA)	X	X	X	X	X	X	X

Writing	Grades 6	7	8	9	10	11	12
Use a Variety of Forms and Techniques cont.							
Bibliography			X	X	X	X	X
Biographical sketch	X	X	X	X	X	X	X
Business letter	X	X	X	X	X	X	X
Cause/effect	X	X	X	X	X	X	X
Character sketch/description/study	X	X	X	X	X	X	X
Cite information from primary and secondary sources				X	X	X	X
Clarification	X	X	X	X	X	X	X
Comparison/contrast	X	X	X	X	X	X	X
Controversial issue/position paper (CA)				X	X	X	X
Critique/review (book, play, movie, TV)	X	X	X	X	X	X	X
Definition/explanation	X	X	X	X	X	X	X
Develop criteria to evaluate research project							X
Develop visuals for oral presentation	X	X	X	X	X	X	X
Dialogue	X	X	X	X	X	X	X
Diary/journal/ log entry	X	X	X	X	X	X	X
Editorial/statement of opinion	X	X	X	X	X	X	X
Essay	X	X	X	X	X	X	X
Evaluation/evaluative writing (CA)	X	X	X	X	X	X	X
Friendly letter; thank you notes; invitations	X	X	X	X	X	X	X
I-Search paper	X	X	X	X	X	X	X
Imaginative writing	X	X	X	X	X	X	X
Interpretation (CA)	X	X	X	X	X	X	X
Letter of application (job, college, scholarship)						X	X
Letter of complaint						X	X
Memoir	X	X	X			X	X
News article;/feature story	X	X	X				
Observational writing/reflection (CA)	X	X	X	X	X	X	X
Personal narrative	X	X	X	X	X	X	X
Poem	X	X	X	X	X	X	X
Problem/solution	X	X	X	X	X	X	X

Writing

Use a Variety of Forms and Techniques cont.	Grades 6	7	8	9	10	11	12
Proposal				X	X	X	X
Questionnaire; interview; survey	X	X	X	X	X	X	X
Reflective Essay (CA)	X	X	X	X	X	X	X
Report based on conclusions from direct observation	X	X	X	X	X	X	X
Research paper that interprets and/or theorizes							X
Research report/ report of information (CA)	X	X	X	X	X	X	X
Resumé							X
Science fiction/fantasy					X	X	
Script or play	X	X	X	X	X	X	
Speculation about causes and effects (CA)				X	X	X	X
Speech/oral presentation		X	X	X	X	X	X
Story (include myth, tall tale, fable, etc.)	X	X	X	X	X	X	X
Summary	X	X	X	X	X	X	X
Support or refute a formal proposition							X
Synthesize information from several sources	X	X	X	X	X	X	X
Technical report in nontechnical language							X
Use documentation for sources					X	X	X
Use technical and statistical data				X	X	X	X
Writing about literature	X	X	X	X	X	X	X

Grammar

Grammar, Usage, Mechanics, Spelling	Grades 6	7	8	9	10	11	12
Understand sentence structure (syntax)	X	X	X	X	X	X	X
Analyze grammatical structures						X	X
Recognize the functions of all the parts of speech in sentences		X	X	X	X	X	X
Understand the origins and development of the English language							X
Recognize sentence fragments	X	X	X	X	X	X	X

Grammar

Grammar, Usage, Mechanics, Spelling cont.	Grades 6	7	8	9	10	11	12
Recognize run-on sentences	X	X	X	X	X	X	X
Produce simple, compound, and complex sentences	X	X	X	X	X	X	X
Produce compound-complex sentences				X	X	X	X
Apply knowledge of subordinate and coordinate clauses					X	X	X
Use the parts of speech effectively in sentences	X	X	X	X	X	X	X
Use parallel construction				X	X	X	X
Use affixes to change a word from one part of speech to another					X	X	
Apply standard usage in writing							
Noun and pronoun forms	X	X	X	X	X	X	X
Singular and plural nouns	X	X	X	X	X	X	X
Possessive nouns	X	X	X	X	X	X	X
Indefinite pronouns	X	X	X	X	X	X	X
Pronoun-antecedent agreement	X	X	X	X	X	X	X
Subject-verb agreement	X	X	X	X	X	X	X
Verb forms	X	X	X	X	X	X	X
Consistent verb tense	X	X	X	X	X	X	X
Recognize colloquialisms, slang, idioms, and jargon				X	X	X	X
Recognize American dialects						X	
Apply conventions of standard written English in writing							
Capitalization	X	X	X	X	X	X	X
Quotation marks and dialogue	X	X	X	X	X	X	X
Sentence punctuation	X	X	X	X	X	X	X
Comma	X	X	X	X	X	X	X
Semicolon			X	X	X	X	X
Colon	X	X	X	X	X	X	X
Hyphen			X	X	X	X	X
Apostrophe	X	X	X	X	X	X	X
Paragraph indention	X	X	X	X	X	X	X

Scope and Sequence

Grammar Grades	6	7	8	9	10	11	12
Grammar, Usage, Mechanics, Spelling cont.							
Word choice	X	X	X	X	X	X	X
Manuscript form	X	X	X	X	X	X	X
Apply the rules of spelling in writing	X	X	X	X	X	X	X
Avoid commonly misspelled words	X	X	X				
Adding endings	X	X	X				
Write legibly	X	X	X	X	X	X	X

Reading/Thinking Grades	6	7	8	9	10	11	12
Strategies							
Use prereading strategies	X	X	X	X	X	X	X
Predict outcomes	X	X	X	X	X	X	X
Set purposes for reading	X	X	X	X	X	X	X
Use prior knowledge	X	X	X	X	X	X	X
Preview	X	X	X	X	X	X	X
Set intermediate goals for reading						X	X
Comprehend	X	X	X	X	X	X	X
Recall details and facts	X	X	X	X	X		
Order events	X	X	X	X			
Understand sequence	X	X	X	X	X	X	X
Recognize cause and effect	X	X	X	X	X	X	X
Classify	X	X	X	X	X	X	X
Compare and contrast	X	X	X	X	X	X	X
Make judgments	X	X	X	X	X	X	X
Recognize main idea, supporting details	X	X	X	X	X	X	X
Generalize; draw conclusions	X	X	X	X	X	X	X
Visualize	X	X	X				
Distinguish between fact and nonfact, opinion	X	X	X	X	X	X	X
Connect ideas/see relationships	X	X	X				

Reading/Thinking Grades	6	7	8	9	10	11	12
Strategies cont.							
Respond critically to literature							
Question	X	X	X	X	X	X	X
Predict	X	X	X	X	X	X	X
Clarify (or Interpret)	X	X	X	X	X	X	X
Infer				X	X	X	X
Analyze				X	X	X	X
Evaluate	X	X	X	X	X	X	X
Connect	X	X	X	X	X	X	X
Summarize				X	X	X	X
Synthesize	X	X	X	X	X	X	X
Relate literature to personal experience	X	X	X	X	X	X	X
Relate literature to human concerns; recognize values	X	X	X	X	X	X	X
Respond creatively to literature in written, oral, dramatic, and graphic ways	X	X	X	X	X	X	X
Evaluate author's viewpoint; detect bias	X	X	X	X	X	X	X
Identify author's purpose	X	X	X	X	X	X	X
Identify author's qualification						X	X
Recognize the use of persuasion	X	X	X	X	X	X	X
Recognize propaganda	X	X	X	X	X	X	X
Recognize assumptions and implications						X	X
Use problem-solving techniques	X	X	X	X	X	X	X
Detect fallacies in reasoning						X	X
Understand that a literary selection may have more than one level of meaning					X	X	X
Adjust reading rate	X	X	X	X	X	X	X
Adapt reading strategies to different purposes (skim, scan)	X	X	X	X	X	X	X
Use fix-it strategies (reviewing, questioning)	X	X	X	X	X	X	X
Use self-questioning	X	X	X				
Apply reading strategies to content area material	X	X	X				
Apply the fundamentals of logic			X				

Speaking

Speaking, Listening, Media and Visual Literacy	6	7	8	9	10	11	12
Formal and informal situations							
Whole group discussion	X	X	X	X	X	X	X
Collaborative group discussion	X	X	X	X	X	X	X
Partner discussion	X	X	X				
Debate	X	X	X	X	X	X	X
Dramatization	X	X	X				
Speech/talk	X	X	X	X	X	X	X
Choral reading	X	X	X				
Interview	X	X	X	X	X	X	X
Interpretive reading	X	X	X	X	X	X	X
Readers theater	X						
Personal experience	X	X	X				
Parliamentary procedure	X	X	X				
Oral report	X	X	X	X	X	X	X
Use appropriate speaking behavior for a variety of purposes	X	X	X	X	X	X	X
To inform	X	X	X	X	X	X	X
To entertain	X	X	X	X	X	X	X
To persuade	X	X	X	X	X	X	X
To respond	X	X	X	X	X	X	X
To summarize	X	X	X	X	X	X	X
To give directions	X	X	X	X	X	X	X
To conduct a meeting	X	X	X	X	X	X	X
Social occasions	X	X	X	X	X	X	X
Use topic, vocabulary, tone, and style appropriate to audience, purpose, time, time limits, and place	X	X	X	X	X	X	X
Demonstrate poise and confidence	X	X	X	X	X	X	X
Communicate clearly and effectively							
Phrasing	X	X	X	X	X	X	X
Rate	X	X	X	X	X	X	X
Pitch, modulation, volume, inflection	X	X	X	X	X	X	X
Enunciation/pronunciation	X	X	X	X	X	X	X

Speaking

Speaking, Listening, Media and Visual Literacy cont.	6	7	8	9	10	11	12
Plan a speech/talk	X	X	X	X	X	X	X
Focus and limit topic	X	X	X	X	X	X	X
Gather and organize information	X	X	X	X	X	X	X
Outline	X	X	X	X	X	X	X
Draft the speech	X	X	X	X	X	X	X
Present a speech	X	X	X	X	X	X	X
Monitor audience reaction	X	X	X	X	X	X	X
Respond to audience questions	X	X	X	X	X	X	X
Be open to constructive criticism	X	X	X	X	X	X	X
Use multi-media or technology as appropriate	X	X	X	X	X	X	X
Understand nonverbal cues							
Eye contact	X	X	X	X	X	X	X
Gestures	X	X	X	X	X	X	X
Facial expression	X	X	X	X	X	X	X
Movement	X	X	X	X	X	X	X
Monitor audience reaction	X	X	X	X	X	X	X
Respond to audience questions	X	X	X	X	X	X	X
Use multimedia or technology as appropriate	X	X	X	X	X	X	X
Understand strategies used in discussion (contribute ideas; support contributions)	X	X	X	X	X	X	X

Listening

Formal and informal situations	6	7	8	9	10	11	12
Advertising/commercials			X	X	X	X	X
Discussion	X	X	X	X	X	X	X
Debate	X	X	X	X	X	X	X
Dramatization	X	X	X				
Speech/talk/oral report	X	X	X	X	X	X	X
News item	X	X	X	X	X	X	X
Interview	X	X	X	X	X	X	X
Interpretive (dramatic) reading	X	X	X	X	X	X	X

Scope and Sequence

Speaking	Grades 6	7	8	9	10	11	12
Listening cont.							
Listen for a variety of purposes, including information, entertainment, appreciation of literature and language, directions, understanding of cultural differences	X	X	X	X	X	X	X
Listening skills/responses/behaviors							
Realize purpose of speaker	X	X	X	X	X	X	X
Set purpose for listening	X	X	X				
Suspend judgment	X	X	X				
Detect transitional words	X						
Understand verbal and nonverbal cues	X	X	X				
Identify relevant information	X	X	X				
Take notes			X				
Focus attention				X	X	X	X
Identify patterns of organization	X	X	X			X	X
Recognize different speaking styles used for different purposes	X	X	X			X	X
Identify criteria for evaluating a speech	X	X	X	X	X	X	X
Identify a central theme or thesis			X			X	X
Monitor understanding	X	X	X	X	X	X	X
Detect bias and propaganda techniques	X	X	X	X	X	X	X
Recall/retell	X	X	X				
Elaborate	X	X	X				
Ask questions	X	X	X	X	X	X	X
Identify inferences	X	X	X	X	X	X	X
Analyze			X			X	X
Evaluate	X	X	X	X	X	X	X
Summarize/synthesize	X	X	X	X	X	X	X
Follow directions	X	X	X				
Write responsively	X	X	X				
Distinguish fact from opinion	X	X	X	X	X	X	X
Provide constructive criticism			X				
Respond to speakers in a variety of ways	X	X	X				
Express opinions	X	X	X	X	X	X	X

Speaking	Grades 6	7	8	9	10	11	12
Media and Visual Literacy							
Interact with non-print media (drama, film, TV, computers) for a variety of purposes	X	X	X	X	X	X	X
Use media for learning	X	X	X	X	X	X	X
Use technology and other media as a means of expression	X	X	X	X	X	X	X
Recognize different purposes of media							
Entertainment	X	X	X	X	X	X	X
Information	X	X	X	X	X	X	X
Communication	X	X	X	X	X	X	X
Compare and contrast print and non-print media	X	X	X	X	X	X	X
Respond critically to nonprint media (criticize, evaluate, analyze)	X	X	X	X	X	X	X
Recognize the effectiveness of nonverbal modes of communication	X	X	X	X	X	X	X
Recognize bias	X	X	X	X	X	X	X
Recognize propaganda	X	X	X	X	X	X	X
Distinguish between fact and opinion	X	X	X	X	X	X	X
Understand and evaluate impact of mass media					X		
Compare and contrast print and non-print media	X	X	X	X	X	X	X
Describe characteristics of the arts	X	X	X				
Identify processes and tools used to produce art	X	X	X				
Demonstrate skills in creating art	X	X	X				
Work with design, drawing, painting, printmaking, sculpture, and fiber arts		X	X				
Identify and appreciate significant works of art from major historical periods	X	X	X	X	X	X	X
Analyze how major works of art reflect societies, cultures, and civilizations	X	X	X	X	X	X	X
Draw conclusions about/evaluate art	X	X	X	X	X	X	X
Relate art to personal experience	X	X	X	X	X	X	X
Express experiences in visual form	X	X	X	X	X	X	X

Vocabulary

Vocabulary and Study Skills	6	7	8	9	10	11	12
Expand reading vocabulary	X	X	X	X	X	X	X
Use context clues for word meaning	X	X	X	X	X	X	X
Use dictionaries for word meaning	X	X	X	X	X	X	X
Use appropriate grade-level vocabulary	X	X	X	X	X	X	X
Read uncommon low-frequency words	X	X	X	X			
Recognize multimeaning words	X	X	X	X			
Expand vocabulary using structural analysis	X	X	X	X	X	X	X
Understand content area vocabulary	X	X	X	X	X	X	X
Recognize ambiguities and shades of meaning				X	X	X	
Understand antonyms, synonyms	X	X	X				
Understand homonyms	X	X	X				
Use etymologies/word origins		X	X	X	X	X	X
Understand connotations, denotations				X	X	X	X
Understand analogies					X	X	X
Recognize colloquialisms				X	X	X	X
Recognize idioms	X	X	X	X	X	X	X
Recognize dialect			X	X	X	X	X
Recognize root words	X	X	X				
Use affixes	X	X	X				
Recognize slang				X	X		
Recognize jargon				X	X		
Locate, use, and evaluate reference sources							
Almanac	X	X	X	X	X		
Bibliography	X	X	X	X	X	X	X
Card catalog; electronic retrieval system	X	X	X	X	X	X	X
Database	X	X	X	X	X	X	X
Dictionary/Glossary	X	X	X	X	X	X	X
Electronic Media	X	X	X	X	X	X	X
Encyclopedia	X	X	X	X	X	X	X
Handbook, style manual	X	X	X	X	X	X	X
Newspapers/periodicals	X	X	X	X			

Vocabulary

Vocabulary and Study Skills cont.	6	7	8	9	10	11	12
Reader's Guide	X	X	X	X			
Software	X	X	X	X	X	X	X
Telephone directory	X	X	X	X	X	X	X
Thesaurus	X	X	X	X	X	X	X
Interpret graphic sources	X	X	X	X	X	X	X
Charts/tables	X	X	X	X			
Graphs	X	X	X	X			
Schedules	X	X	X	X			
Diagrams	X	X		X			
Maps/atlases	X			X	X		
Apply reading strategies to content area reading	X	X	X	X	X	X	X
Create and use graphic organizers	X	X	X	X	X	X	X
Follow directions	X	X	X	X	X	X	X
Outline	X	X	X	X	X	X	X
Take notes	X	X	X	X	X	X	X
Use the parts of a book (footnotes, text features, appendices, etc.)	X	X	X	X	X	X	X
Use both primary and secondary sources			X			X	X
Use test taking stratiegies	X	X	X	X	X	X	X
Use text features	X						

Multicultural

Multicultural Awareness and Appreciation	6	7	8	9	10	11	12
Recognize, respect, and appreciate the similarities and differences in the literature and languages of diverse cultures	X	X	X	X	X	X	X
Learn about and appreciate the past and present contributions of diverse groups and individuals	X	X	X	X	X	X	X
Explore how people of diverse groups express similar values and goals	X	X	X	X	X	X	X
Respect, value, and appreciate diverse opinions	X	X	X	X	X	X	X

Scope and Sequence

Multicultural

Multicultural Awareness and Appreciation cont.	6	7	8	9	10	11	12
Develop sensitivity to discriminatory practices	X	X	X	X	X	X	X
Develop positive self-image based on one's own culture	X	X	X	X	X	X	X
Develop cultural awareness to aid in solving conflicts in school and community	X	X	X	X	X	X	X

Habits

Habits and Attitude	6	7	8	9	10	11	12
Integrate reading and writing into school, home, and leisure-time activities	X	X	X	X	X	X	X
Pursue ongoing personal reading and writing interests	X	X	X	X	X	X	X
Schedule reading and writing time	X	X	X				
Challenge self to expand reading and writing horizons	X	X	X	X	X	X	X
Read for enjoyment	X	X	X	X	X	X	X
Read to gather and clarify information	X	X	X	X	X	X	X
Read and write for purpose of discovery	X	X	X	X	X	X	X
Communicate with diverse audiences	X	X	X	X	X	X	X
Read in order to discover interrelationships of concepts/disciplines	X	X	X	X	X	X	X
Read and write to clarify personal thinking and understanding	X	X	X	X	X	X	X
Use reading and writing in decision-making and negotiating	X	X	X	X	X	X	X
Assess the suitability of materials	X	X	X	X	X	X	X
Work cooperatively with others toward a common goal	X	X	X	X	X	X	X
Work with others to discover meaning in literary selections	X	X	X	X	X	X	X
Work with others to develop and publish a piece of writing	X	X	X	X	X	X	X
Work cooperatively to solve problems	X	X	X	X	X	X	X

Life Skills

Life Skills	6	7	8	9	10	11	12
Change	X	X	X	X	X	X	X
Self-image/awareness/acceptance	X	X	X	X	X	X	X
Communications (conflict resolution)	X	X	X	X	X	X	X
Personal management (planning, energy, stress, etc.)	X	X	X	X	X	X	X
Team management	X	X	X	X	X	X	X
Service	X	X	X	X	X	X	X
Life cycles	X	X	X	X	X	X	X

Consumer and Job-Related Skills	6	7	8	9	10	11	12
Read product labels for information	X	X	X	X	X		
Find information in a warranty, policy, or contract	X	X	X	X	X	X	X
Job application	X	X	X	X	X	X	X
Multi-paragraph letter to apply for a job	X	X	X	X	X	X	X
Interviews	X	X	X	X	X	X	X
Resumé				X	X	X	X

Assessment Skills

Performance-based Assessment	6	7	8	9	10	11	12
Student portfolios	X	X	X	X	X	X	X
Teacher observation	X	X	X	X	X	X	X
Peer assessment	X	X	X	X	X	X	X
Self-assessment	X	X	X	X	X	X	X
Integration of writing, literature, and comprehension	X	X	X	X	X	X	X
Activities	X	X	X	X	X	X	X

ScottForesman

LITERATURE

AND INTEGRATED STUDIES

Middle School: Grade Six

Middle School: Grade Seven

Middle School: Grade Eight

Forms in Literature

World Literature

American Literature

English Literature

The cover features a detail of Dante Gabriel Rossetti's *The Beloved,* which also appears on this page. Rossetti (1828–1882), who achieved equal fame as a painter and a poet, is known for the sensuousness and exoticism of his works in both areas. *Tate Gallery, London*

ScottForesman LITERATURE AND INTEGRATED STUDIES

English Literature

Senior Consultants

Alan C. Purves
State University of New York at Albany

Carol Booth Olson
University of California, Irvine

Carlos E. Cortés
University of California, Riverside (Emeritus)

ScottForesman

Editorial Offices: Glenview, Illinois
Regional Offices: San Jose, California • Tucker, Georgia
Glenview, Illinois • Oakland, New Jersey • Dallas, Texas

Visit ScottForesman's Home Page at http://www.scottforesman.com

Acknowledgments

Texts

8 Reuse of abridgment of *Beowulf: The Oldest English Epic,* translated by Charles W. Kennedy from pages 3-101. Reprinted by permission. **35** From *Grendel,* by John Gardner. Copyright © 1971 by John Gardner. Reprinted by permission of Alfred A. Knopf Inc. **47–48** "The Prologue" and "The Pardoner's Prologue and Tale" from *The Canterbury Tales* by Geoffrey Chaucer, translated by Nevill Coghill (Penguin Classics 1951, Fourth revised edition, 1977). Copyright © 1951, 1958, 1960, 1975, 1977 by Nevill Coghill. Reproduced by permission of Penguin Books Ltd. **61** From *Sir Gawain And The Green Knight,* translated by M. R. Ridley. Reprinted by permission of Reed Consumer Books. **88** From *A Distant Mirror* by Barbara W. Tuchman. Copyright © 1978 by Barbara W. Tuchman. Reprinted by permission of Random House, Inc. **92** From *The Once and Future King* by T.H. White. Reprinted by permission. **192** From *Ancient Egyptian Literature, Three Volumes,* by Miriam Lichtheim, pp. 125-126. Copyright © 1973-1980 by The Regents of the University of California. Reprinted by permission of The University of California Press. **193** "Aeschylus" from *The Eumenides,* translated by Richmond Lattimore. Copyright © 1953 by The University of Chicago. Reprinted by permission. **194** From *Crime And Punishment* by Feodor Dostoevski. Reprinted by permission. **211** "Summer is Gone" from *A Book Of Ireland,* edited by Frank O'Connor. Reprinted by permission. **212** "Fern Hill" by Dylan Thomas from *The Poems Of Dylan Thomas.* Copyright 1952 by The Trustees for the Copyrights of Dylan Thomas. Reprinted by permission of New Directions Publishing Corporation and David Higham Associates Limited. **219** "Lineage" from *Crow* by Ted Hughes. Reprinted by permission. **239** From "David's Story" and "The Bubble Boy" by Carol Ann with Kent Demaret in *People Weekly,* October 29, 1984 and November 5, 1984. Copyright © 1984 by Time, Inc. Reprinted by permission. **241** From *Six Degrees* Of Separation by John Guare. Copyright © 1990 by John Guare. Reprinted by permission of Vintage Books, a Division of Random House Inc. **244** Lyrics only of "We Are The World" by Michael Jackson and Lionel Richie. Reprinted by permission. **280** "Postcard from Paradise" by Chris Williamson. Copyright ©1993 by Bird Ankles Music (BMI). Reprinted by permission of Chris Williamson. **369** Excerpts from *Fame In The 20th Century* by Clive James. Reprinted by permission. **389** Excerpt from A Room of One's Own by Virginia Woolf. Reprinted by permission. **394** Lyrics only of "London Pride" by Noel Coward. Reprinted by permission. **394** "October 10, 1940" from *This Is London* by Edward R. Murrow. Reprinted by permission. **434** Abridgment of "The Power Of Dreams" by George Howe Colt in *Life,* September 1995. Reprinted by permission. **507** From "The Monster's Human Nature" by Stephen Jay Gould in *Natural History,* July 1994. Copyright © 1994 by the American Museum of Natural History. Reprinted by permission.

continued on page 1017

ISBN: 0-673-29450-1

1.800.554.4411
http://www.scottforesman.com

1 2 3 4 5 6 7 8 9 10 DR 03 02 01 00 99 98 97 96

Senior Consultants

Alan C. Purves

Professor of Education and Humanities, State University of New York at Albany; Director of the Center for Writing and Literacy. Dr. Purves developed the concept and philosophy of the literature lessons for the series, consulted with editors, reviewed tables of contents and lesson manuscript, wrote the Assessment Handbooks, and oversaw the development and writing of the series testing strand.

Carol Booth Olson

Director, California Writing Project, Department of Education, University of California, Irvine. Dr. Olson conceptualized and developed the integrated writing strand of the program, consulted with editors, led a team of teachers in creating literature-based Writing Workshops, and reviewed final manuscript.

Carlos E. Cortés

Professor Emeritus, History, University of California, Riverside. Dr. Cortés designed and developed the multicultural strand embedded in each unit of the series and consulted with grade-level editors to implement the concepts.

Series Consultants

Visual and Media Literacy/Speaking and Listening/Critical Thinking

Harold M. Foster. Professor of English Education and Secondary Education, The University of Akron, Akron. Dr. Foster developed and wrote the Beyond Print features for all levels of the series.

ESL and LEP Strategies

James Cummins. Professor, Modern Language Centre and Curriculum Department, Ontario Institute for Studies in Education, Toronto.

Lily Wong Fillmore. Professor, Graduate School of Education, University of California at Berkeley.

Drs. Cummins and Fillmore advised on the needs of ESL and LEP students, helped develop the Building English Proficiency model for the program, and reviewed strategies and manuscript for this strand of the program.

Fine Arts/Humanities

Neil Anstead. Coordinator of the Humanitas Program, Cleveland Humanities Magnet School, Reseda, California. Mr. Anstead consulted on the fine art used in the program.

Reviewers and Contributors

Pupil and Teacher Edition

Jay Amberg, Glenbrook South High School, Glenview, Illinois **Edison Barber,** St. Anne Community High School, St. Anne, Illinois **Lois Barliant,** Albert G. Lane Technical High School, Chicago, Illinois **James Beasley,** Plant City Senior High School, Plant City, Florida **Linda Belpedio,** Oak Park/River Forest High School, Oak Park, Illinois **Richard Bruns,** Burges High School, El Paso, Texas **Kay Parks Bushman,** Ottawa High School, Ottawa, Kansas **Jesús Cardona,** John F. Kennedy High School, San Antonio, Texas **Marlene Carter,** Dorsey High School, Los Angeles, California **Patrick Cates,** Lubbock High School, Lubbock, Texas **Timothy Dohrer,** New Trier Township High School, Winnetka, Illinois **Margaret Doria,** Our Lady of Perpetual Help High School, Brooklyn, New York **Lucila Dypiangco,** Bell Senior High School, Bell, California **Judith Edminster,** Plant City High School, Plant City, Florida **Mary Alice Fite,** Columbus School for Girls, Columbus, Ohio **Montserrat Fontes,** Marshall High School, Los Angeles, California **Diane Fragos,** Turkey Creek Middle School, Plant City, Florida **Joan Greenwood,** Thornton Township High School, Harvey, Illinois **William Irvin,** Pittsfield Public Schools, Pittsfield, Massachusetts **Carleton Jordan,** Montclair High School, Montclair, New Jersey **Mark Kautz,** Chapel Hill High School, Chapel Hill, North Carolina **Elaine Kay,** Bartow High School, Bartow, Florida **Roslyn Kettering,** West Lafayette Junior/Senior High School, West Lafayette, Indiana **Kristina Kostopoulos,** Lincoln Park High School, Chicago, Illinois **Julia Lloyd,** Harwood Junior High School, Bedford, Texas **John Lord,** Ocean Township High School, Oakhurst, New Jersey **Dolores Mathews,** Bloomingdale High School, Valrico, Florida **Jim McCallum,** Milford High School, Milford, Massachusetts **Monette Mehalko,** Plant City Senior High School, Plant City, Florida **Lucia Podraza,** DuSable High School, Chicago, Illinois **Frank Pool,** Anderson High School, Austin, Texas **Alice Price,** Latin School, Chicago, Illinois **Anna J. Roseboro,** The Bishop's School, La Jolla, California **Peter Sebastian,** Granite Hills High School, El Cajon, California **Rob Slater,** East Forsyth High School, Winston Salem, North Carolina **Catherine Small,** Nicolet High School, Glendale, Wisconsin **Dennis Symkowiak,** Mundelein High School, Mundelein, Illinois **Rosetta Tetteh,** Senn High School, Chicago, Illinois **Pamela Vetters,** Harlandale High School, San Antonio, Texas **Polly Walwark,** Oak Park High School, Oak Park, Illinois **Karen Wrobleski,** San Diego High School, San Diego, California **Dru Zimmerman,** Chapel Hill High School, Chapel Hill, North Carolina

v

Multicultural Review Board

Duane BigEagle, writer and teacher, Tomales, California **Maria Campanario,** Raphael Hernandez School, Stoughton, Massachusetts **Pat Canty,** Beverly Woods Middle School, Charlotte, North Carolina **Jesús Cardona,** John F. Kennedy High School, San Antonio, Texas **Diego Davalos,** Chula Vista High School, Chula Vista, California **Sandra Dickerson,** Milwaukee Public Schools, Milwaukee, Wisconsin **Lucila Dypiangco,** Bell Senior High School, Bell, California **Marion Fleming,** Roselle Junior/Senior High School, Roselle, New York **Gloria Garcia,** Madero Middle School, Chicago, Illinois **Thelma Hernandez,** Edison Junior High School, San Antonio, Texas **Yvonne Hutchinson,** Markham Intermediate School, Los Angeles, California **Narva Jackson,** Roselle Junior/Senior High School, Roselle, New York **May Lee,** Baldwin Senior High School, Baldwin, New York **Dolores Mathews,** Bloomingdale High School, Valrico, Florida **Jack Matsumoto,** Edison Regional Gifted Center, Chicago, Illinois **James Masao Mitsui,** Hazen High School, Renton, Washington **Ed Ramirez,** Wang School, Derry, New Hampshire **Harolene Steele,** Hill Middle School, Winston-Salem, North Carolina **Suthinee Suktrakul,** Norcross High School, Norcross, Georgia **Jerry Tagami,** New Harbor High School, Newport Beach, California **Barbara Wheeler,** Harford County Public Schools, Bel Air, Maryland **Raymond Zamarippa,** Bowie Junior High School, Irving, Texas

English Language Development (ESL/LEP)

Kate Alvidrez, Newton High School, Newton, Iowa **Judy Bebelaar,** International Studies Academy, San Francisco, California **Rebecca Benjamin,** University of New Mexico, Albuquerque, New Mexico **Ioana Cummins,** Toronto, Ontario **Nancy Duke S. Lay,** City College of New York, New York, New York **Doti Foster,** Lubbock Independent School District, Lubbock, Texas **Bridget Hawthorne,** Oliver Hazard Perry Middle School, Providence, Rhode Island **Sandra Huezo,** Gompers Secondary School, San Diego, California **Nancy Hykel,** Harlandale High School, San Antonio, Texas **Mary Ann Jentel,** Madonna High School for Girls, Chicago, Illinois **Jose Lebron,** Julia De Burgos Middle School, Philadelphia, Pennsylvania **Mary Linnstaedter,** Nimitz High School, Houston, Texas **Mayra Menendez,** School Board of Broward County, Fort Lauderdale, Florida **Sharese Tisby,** Waukegan High School, Waukegan, Illinois **Sylvia Velazquez,** Braddock Senior High School, Miami, Florida **Greta Vollmer,** International Studies Academy, San Francisco, California **Shirley Wright,** Longview Independent School District, Longview, Texas **Suzanne Zweig,** Norwood Park School, Chicago, Illinois

Writer's Workshop Prompt Writers

Bill Burns, Sonora High School, LaHabra, California **Patricia Clark,** Century High School, Santa Ana, California **Glenn Patchell,** Irvine High School, Irvine, California **Maureen Rippee,** Woodrow Wilson High School, Long Beach, California **Julie Simpson,** Sunny Hills High School, Fullerton, California

Student Model Writers

Jennifer Biebel Susan Biebel Albert Chalegua Nicole Childers Alexander Walsh Cohn Courtenay Noelle Collins Alice Day Colleen Dunham Heath Fisher Allison Gumz Jamie Hindin Adam Kotlarczyk Katarzyna Kubiak Barbara A. Kurcz Michael Levy Julie Lynk Mohsen Mahani Cheryl S. Michaels Karen Peterson Sara Rashid Sheila Saltzman Robert L. Samuels, Jr. Merrick P. Schaefer Anna Sowle Tyler Stevenson Jeni Topliff Katherine Wengel Cindy Zay

Student Active Reading Panel

Andria Lopez Dean Tsilikas Leah Vaughn

Contents

Part 2: Codes of Honor

viii

Unit 2 The Elizabethan Era

The Lure of Ambition

ix

THEMES IN ENGLISH LITERATURE: NATURE: GARDEN OR WILDERNESS?

Unit 3 The Seventeenth Century

Part 1: The Meaning of Life

xi

Part 2: The Fall from Grace

xii

Unit 4 **The Age of Reason**

Part 1: A Focus on Society

Part 2: Other People's Lives

xiv

Unit 5 The Romantic Era

Part 1: Visions and Dreams

Part 2: The Outsider

Part 3: Exceeding Human Limits

xvi

Unit 6 The Victorians

Part 1: The Struggle to Understand

Part 2: Hope and Despair

xviii

Unit 7 The Early Twentieth Century

Part 1: Upward Mobility

Part 2: War and Aftermath

xix

Part 3: The Search for Identity

xx

Unit 8

The Later Twentieth Century

Part 1: The Passing of Empire

xxi

Part 2: The Slant View

xxii

Glossaries, Handbooks, and Indexes

Genre Overview

Short Stories

Novel Excerpts

Tales, Romances, and Narratives

Poetry

xxiii

Epic Poems

Folk Ballads

Plays

Essays

Biography, Autobiography, and Other Nonfiction

Feature Overview

Visual Overviews

xxiv

Interdisciplinary Studies

Language Histories

Writing Workshops

Beyond Print

Themes in English Literature

xxv

Before Reading

MODEL FOR ACTIVE READING

Introduce

Introduce students to the active readers identified on the page. You may want to point out the icons that are associated with each reader so that students will be able to follow their comments as they read.

Model for Active Reading

Good readers read actively. They become involved in what they read, relating the characters and situations to people and events in their own lives. They question, clarify, predict, and in other ways think about the story or article they are reading. These three students agreed to let us in on their thoughts as they read "The Lumber-Room." You might have different ideas and questions than they did about this story. However, their ways of responding will give you ideas for how you can get actively engaged as you read literature.

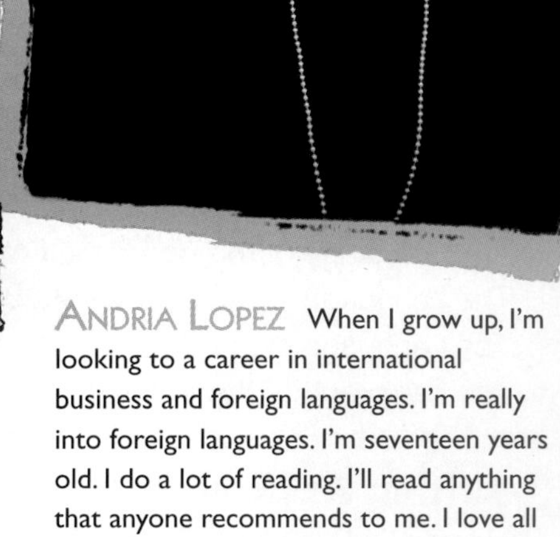

DEAN TSILIKAS I'm seventeen years old, and basically I'm interested in politics. Maybe I'll start out in law and then go into politics. What kinds of books are part of my library? I like mysteries a lot. And I also like to read magazines.

ANDRIA LOPEZ When I grow up, I'm looking to a career in international business and foreign languages. I'm really into foreign languages. I'm seventeen years old. I do a lot of reading. I'll read anything that anyone recommends to me. I love all kinds of poetry.

LEAH VAUGHN I'm seventeen. I want to be a criminal psychologist when I grow up. I like to read mysteries—that's all I've ever liked to read, ever since I was a little girl. Now that I'm in high school, I have a lot of schoolwork to do, and I don't read as much as I'd like to.

Six Reading Strategies

Following are some of the techniques that good readers use often without being aware of them.

Question Ask questions that arise as you read.

Example: Why doesn't the author ever tell us the aunt's name?

Predict Make reasoned guesses, based on what's happened so far, about what might happen next.

Example: I think Nicholas is going to be in real trouble once the aunt gets out of the rain-water tank.

Clarify Clear up confusion and answer questions.

Example: This woman is not really Nicholas's aunt—she only pretends to be.

Summarize Review some of the main ideas or events.

Example: Nicholas is delighted with the things he finds in the lumber-room. They fill him with a sense of awe and wonder.

Evaluate Reason from common sense, established guidelines, and evidence to arrive at sound opinions and valid conclusions.

Example: The aunt doesn't seem to like children very much. She even seems to take pleasure in punishing them.

Connect Compare the text with something in your own experience, with another text, or with ideas within the text.

Example: I've known some people who are like the aunt in this story—people who seem to find no joy in living and who don't want others to be happy, either.

Six Reading Terms Explained

Review with students the techniques used by good readers. Ask them to demonstrate examples of *question, predict, clarify, summarize, evaluate,* and *connect.*

During Reading

THE LUMBER-ROOM

Option 1

Read the story aloud in class, asking volunteers to play the role of the readers by reading their comments. Other students may want to make their own comments as the reading proceeds.

Option 2

Assign students to read the story silently in class or for homework. Suggest that they write down their own questions and comments as they read, in preparation for a class discussion of the story.

One of the elements that add to the eeriness and surrealism of P. J. Crook's paintings is her habit of extending the painting onto the frame, as in *Terrible Twins* (1989). Do you agree, as some people claim, that it is the duty of adults to provide limits for children? Might it then be the duty of children to test those limits?

The LUMBER-ROOM

SAKI (H. H. MUNRO)

The children were to be driven, as a special treat, to the sands at Jagborough. Nicholas was not to be of the party; he was in disgrace. Only that morning, he had refused to eat his wholesome bread-and-milk on the seemingly frivolous ground that there was a frog in it. Older and wiser and better people had told him that there could not possibly be a frog in his bread-and-milk and that he was not to talk nonsense; he continued, nevertheless, to talk what seemed the veriest nonsense, and described with much detail the coloration and markings of the alleged frog. The dramatic part of the incident was that there really was a frog in Nicholas's basin of bread-and-milk; he had put it there himself, so he felt entitled to know something about it. The sin of taking a frog from the garden and putting it into a bowl of wholesome bread-and-milk was enlarged on at great length, but the fact that stood out clearest in the whole affair, as it presented itself to the mind of Nicholas, was that the older, wiser, and better people had been proved to be profoundly in error in matters about which they had expressed the utmost assurance.

"You said there couldn't possibly be a frog in my bread-and-milk; there *was* a frog in my bread-and-milk," he repeated, with the insistence of a skilled tactician who does not intend to shift from favorable ground.

So his boy-cousin and girl-cousin and his quite uninteresting younger brother were to be taken to Jagborough sands that afternoon and he was to stay at home. His cousins' aunt, who insisted,

DEAN It says that Nicholas is "in disgrace." That seems pretty harsh, if all he did was put a frog in his bowl. (evaluate)

LEAH I think that Nicholas is trying to prove that the adults are wrong—that's why he put the frog in his bowl. (clarify)

ANDRIA So far, the attitude of the story seems to be very anti-adult. Maybe the adults won't turn out to be as smart as they think they are. (predict)

DEAN Nicholas's age isn't given, but I think he must be about seven or eight, maybe nine years old. Do you agree? (question)

ANDRIA I agree that he's young—and he also seems very intelligent. (evaluate)

by an unwarranted stretch of imagination, in styling herself his aunt also, had hastily invented the Jagborough expedition in order to impress on Nicholas the delights that he had justly forfeited by his disgraceful conduct at the breakfast-table. It was her habit, whenever one of the children fell from grace, to improvise something of a festival nature from which the offender would be rigorously debarred; if all the children sinned collectively they were suddenly informed of a circus in a neighboring town, a circus of unrivalled merit and uncounted elephants, to which, but for their depravity, they would have been taken that very day.

A few decent tears were looked for on the part of Nicholas when the moment for the departure of the expedition arrived. As a matter of fact, however, all the crying was done by his girl-cousin, who scraped her knee rather painfully against the step of the carriage as she was scrambling in.

"How she did howl," said Nicholas cheerfully, as the party drove off without any of the elation of high spirits that should have characterized it.

"She'll soon get over that," said the *soi-disant*[1] aunt; "it will be a glorious afternoon for racing about over those beautiful sands. How they will enjoy themselves!"

"Bobby won't enjoy himself much, and he won't race much either," said Nicholas with a grim chuckle; "his boots are hurting him. They're too tight."

"Why didn't he tell me they were hurting?" asked the aunt with some asperity.

"He told you twice, but you weren't listening. You often don't listen when we tell you important things."

"You are not to go into the gooseberry garden," said the aunt, changing the subject.

"Why not?" demanded Nicholas.

"Because you are in disgrace," said the aunt loftily.

Nicholas did not admit the flawlessness of the reasoning; he felt perfectly capable of being in disgrace and in a gooseberry garden at the same moment. His face took on an expression of considerable obstinacy. It was clear to his aunt that he was determined to get into the gooseberry garden, "only," as she remarked to herself, "because I have told him he is not to."

Now the gooseberry garden had two doors by which it might be entered, and once a small person like Nicholas could slip in there he could effectually disappear from view amid the masking growth of artichokes, raspberry canes, and fruit bushes. The aunt had many other things to do that afternoon, but she spent an hour or

1. **soi-disant** (swa dē zän), *adj.* calling oneself thus; self-styled; so-called.

DEAN Who exactly is this woman? In the story, she's referred to as "his cousins' aunt." Does that imply that she's not Nicholas's aunt also? (question)

ANDRIA It seems like the aunt does this often—she punishes the children by telling them where she would have taken them if they hadn't been so bad. (summarize)

DEAN The aunt is so mean—she reminds me of the wicked stepmother from Cinderella. (connect)

LEAH They're going to Jagborough in a carriage. This story must take place a long time ago. (evaluate)

LEAH The footnote says that *soi-disant* means "self-styled, so-called." So she's not his aunt after all—she just pretends that she is. (clarify)

DEAN Nicholas is expected to cry when the children leave for Jagborough. But he doesn't—instead, he seems to be in a good mood. That doesn't seem normal to me—most young children would cry, complain, throw a tantrum. (connect)

LEAH The aunt doesn't seem like a very caring person—she doesn't pay attention to the children's needs, like when Nicholas's cousin tells her that his boots are too tight. She seems small and petty—she's "a woman of few ideas." (evaluate) two in trivial gardening operations among flower beds and shrubberies, whence she could keep a watchful eye on the two doors that led to the forbidden paradise. She was a woman of few ideas, with immense powers of concentration.

Nicholas made one or two sorties into the front garden, wriggling his way with obvious stealth of purpose towards one or other of the doors, but never able for a moment to evade the aunt's watchful eye. As a matter of fact, he had no intention of trying to get into the gooseberry garden, but it was extremely convenient for him that his aunt should believe that he had; it was a belief that would keep her on self-imposed sentry-duty for the greater part of the afternoon. Having thoroughly confirmed and fortified her suspicions, Nicholas slipped back into the house and rapidly put into execution a plan of action that had long germinated in his brain. By standing on a chair in the library one could reach a shelf on which reposed a fat, important-looking key. The key was as important as it looked; it was the instrument which kept the mysteries of the lumber[2]-room secure from unauthorized intrusion, which opened a way only for aunts and such-like privileged persons. Nicholas had not had much experience of the art of fitting keys into keyholes and turning locks, but for some days past he had practised with the key of the schoolroom door; he did not believe in trusting too much to luck and accident. The key turned stiffly in the lock, but it turned. The door opened, and Nicholas was in an unknown land, compared with which the gooseberry garden was a stale delight, a mere material pleasure.

Often and often Nicholas had pictured to himself what the lumber-room might be like, that region that was so carefully sealed from youthful eyes and concerning which no questions were ever answered. It came up to his expectations. In the first place it was large and dimly lit, one high window opening on to the forbidden garden being its only source of illumination. In the second place it was a storehouse of unimagined treasures. The aunt-by-assertion was one of those people who think that things spoil by use and consign them to dust and damp by way of preserving them. Such parts of the house as Nicholas knew best were rather bare and cheerless, but here there were wonderful things for the eye to feast on. First and foremost there was a piece of framed tapestry that was evidently meant to be a fire-screen. To Nicholas it was a living, breathing story; he sat down on a roll of Indian hangings, glowing in wonderful colors beneath a layer of dust, and took in all the details of the tapestry picture. A man, dressed in the hunting costume of

2. **lumber,** old furniture and other household items no longer being used; useless bric-a-brac.

DEAN Even if she isn't really his aunt, I still think Nicholas's attitude toward her is not normal for a young child. He does seem twisted. He seems to like to toy with his aunt. (evaluate)

ANDRIA I don't think he's twisted. He's a tough little kid. He's playing her game—it's like a war between them. (evaluate)

LEAH It's almost like the aunt is a child too. She's toying with Nicholas also, but Nicholas is wise to his aunt's little tricks—she does things like this all the time. (evaluate)

ANDRIA What Nicholas does here shows that he's more intelligent than most kids his age. Look at the way he manipulates his aunt and carries out his plan for getting into the lumber-room. (connect)

LEAH Yes, Nicholas does seem really intelligent. He's already worked out a plan in his mind, practiced opening a lock with a key, etc. (evaluate)

DEAN The lumber-room seems to be a symbol of the forbidden—at least what's forbidden to the young. (connect)

ANDRIA Nicholas really appreciates the lumber-room, but his aunt doesn't. She has such a narrow-minded outlook—she thinks that things are spoiled by using them. (summarize) some remote period, had just transfixed a stag with an arrow; it could not have been a difficult shot because the stag was only one or two paces away from him; in the thickly growing vegetation that the picture suggested it would not have been difficult to creep up to a feeding stag, and the two spotted dogs that were springing forward to join in the chase had evidently been trained to keep to heel till the arrow was discharged. That part of the picture was simple, if interesting, but did the huntsman see, what Nicholas saw, that four galloping wolves were coming in his direction through the wood? There might be more than four of them hidden behind the trees, and in any case would the man and his dogs be able to cope with the four wolves if they made an attack? The man had only two arrows left in his quiver, and he might miss with one or both of them; all one knew about his skill in shooting was that he could hit a large stag at a ridiculously short range. Nicholas sat for many golden minutes revolving the possibilities of the scene; he was inclined to think that there were more than four wolves and that the man and his dogs were in a tight corner.

But there were other objects of delight and interest claiming his instant attention: there were quaint twisted candlesticks in the shape of snakes, and a teapot fashioned like a china duck, out of whose open beak the tea was supposed to come. How dull and shapeless the nursery teapot seemed in comparison! And there was a carved sandal-wood box packed tight with aromatic cotton-wool, and between the layers of cotton-wool were little brass figures, hump-necked bulls, and peacocks and goblins, delightful to see and to handle. Less promising in appearance was a large square book with plain black covers; Nicholas peeped into it, and, behold, it was full of colored pictures of birds. And such birds! In the garden, and in the lanes when he went for a walk, Nicholas came across a few birds, of which the largest were an occasional magpie or wood-pigeon; here were herons and bustards, kites, toucans, tiger-bitterns, brush turkeys, ibises, golden pheasants, a whole portrait gallery of undreamed-of creatures. And as he was admiring the coloring of the mandarin duck and assigning a life-history to it, the voice of his aunt in shrill vociferation of his name came from the gooseberry garden without. She had grown suspicious at his long disappearance, and had leapt to the conclusion that he had climbed over the wall behind the sheltering screen of the lilac bushes; she was now engaged in energetic and rather hopeless search for him among the artichokes and raspberry canes.

"Nicholas, Nicholas!" she screamed, "you are to come out of this at once. It's no use trying to hide there; I can see you all the time."

It was probably the first time for twenty years that any one had smiled in that lumber-room.

DEAN This whole thing about the tapestry—is it a symbol of Nicholas's fight against the adults? (question)

ANDRIA I think so. Nicholas has the role of the huntsman, and the wolves are the adults. (clarify, connect)

DEAN So if Nicholas is the huntsman, he's just trying to do his own thing, but the wolves—his aunt and the other adults—are trying to stop him from doing what he wants to do. (connect)

LEAH What do you think might happen? (question)

DEAN The outcome could be that the huntsman could escape and the wolves could feed on the stag. And maybe Nicholas will outwit the adults. (predict)

DEAN This room helps me understand why Nicholas has so much anger toward his aunt. His aunt has kept him away from all these beautiful things. Why should she hide this room from him? It's like she doesn't want him to enjoy his life. (clarify, evaluate)

ANDRIA Going back to the tapestry—I think the stag stands for bad things Nicholas does. He does bad things to distract people. The wolves could feast on the stag, paying no attention to the huntsman. In the same way, Nicholas distracts his aunt by making her think he will try to get into the gooseberry garden. (evaluate)

LEAH It's like the aunt is playing games with Nicholas. (evaluate)

Presently the angry repetitions of Nicholas's name gave way to a shriek, and a cry for somebody to come quickly. Nicholas shut the book, restored it carefully to its place in a corner, and shook some dust from a neighboring pile of newspapers over it. Then he crept from the room, locked the door, and replaced the key exactly where he had found it. His aunt was still calling his name when he sauntered into the front garden.

"Who's calling?" he asked.

"Me," came the answer from the other side of the wall; "didn't you hear me? I've been looking for you in the gooseberry garden, and I've slipped into the rain-water tank. Luckily there's no water in it, but the sides are slippery and I can't get out. Fetch the little ladder from under the cherry tree—"

"I was told I wasn't to go into the gooseberry garden," said Nicholas promptly.

"I told you not to, and now I tell you that you may," came the voice from the rain-water tank, rather impatiently.

"Your voice doesn't sound like aunt's," objected Nicholas; "you may be the Evil One tempting me to be disobedient. Aunt often tells me that the Evil One tempts me and that I always yield. This time I'm not going to yield."

"Don't talk nonsense," said the prisoner in the tank; "go and fetch the ladder."

"Will there be strawberry jam for tea?" asked Nicholas innocently.

"Certainly there will be," said the aunt, privately resolving that Nicholas should have none of it.

"Now I know that you are the Evil One and not aunt," shouted Nicholas gleefully; "when we asked aunt for strawberry jam yesterday she said there wasn't any. I know there are four jars of it in the store cupboard, because I looked, and of course you know it's there, but *she* doesn't, because she said there wasn't any. Oh, Devil, you *have* sold yourself!"

There was an unusual sense of luxury in being able to talk to an aunt as though one was talking to the Evil One, but Nicholas knew, with childish discernment, that such luxuries were not to be over-indulged in. He walked noisily away, and it was a kitchenmaid, in search of parsley, who eventually rescued the aunt from the rain-water tank.

Tea that evening was partaken of in a fearsome silence. The tide had been at its highest when the children had arrived at Jagborough Cove, so there had been no sands to play on—a circumstance that the aunt had overlooked in the haste of organizing her punitive expedition. The tightness of Bobby's boots had had disastrous effect on his temper the whole of the afternoon, and

DEAN I wonder what has happened to the aunt? She must be in some kind of trouble—she seems to need Nicholas's help. (question, predict)

DEAN The aunt is in dire need of help, all right. And what does Nicholas do? He plays games with her. (clarify)

ANDREA I don't think she's about to die. The aunt is a person who thinks way too much of herself. It's Nicholas's job to let her know this. (evaluate)

LEAH It's like Nicholas is saying: "Look, I tricked her." (clarify)

ANDREA I don't think the aunt's detention in the rain-water tank is unmerited. If I'd been insulted like that, I would have done the same thing. She deserves it. (evaluate)

LEAH Nicholas seems to really like to provoke his aunt. In that way he seems like a typical little kid. (connect)

DEAN Even if she does deserve it, I don't think it's normal for a child of Nicholas's age to want revenge, to want to teach his aunt a lesson. (evaluate)

DEAN It seems like the aunt now fears Nicholas, because of what happened with the rain-water tank. (evaluate)

ANDREA I don't think the aunt is scared of him—I think she now realizes how intelligent he is. I bet she won't play these childish games with Nicholas anymore. She knows he's beyond all that. (evaluate, predict)

altogether the children could not have been said to have enjoyed themselves. The aunt maintained the frozen muteness of one who has suffered undignified and unmerited detention in a rain-water tank for thirty-five minutes. As for Nicholas, he, too, was silent, in the absorption of one who has much to think about; it was just possible, he considered, that the huntsman would escape with his hounds while the wolves feasted on the stricken stag.

DEAN The tapestry seems to be a symbol of how Nicholas views the struggle between the adults and the children. (connect)

LEAH I think the tapestry is used to show us that Nicholas is the living, breathing story. (connect)

Discussion After Reading

General Comments

DEAN The whole story seems to be about what is going on in Nicholas's mind—what he sees and feels. The narrator favors Nicholas and is on his side. (summarize)

ANDRIA The narrator doesn't give the aunt much credit, so I wouldn't want to know what she thinks anyway. The way the narrator focuses on Nicholas makes the reader think he is smarter than the aunt. The whole story seems to downplay the role of adults and their intelligence. (evaluate)

DEAN It's true that it's the children versus the adults. But I still think that Nicholas's satirical or cynical view of his aunt just doesn't seem right for a child this young. (evaluate)

LEAH Well, we did agree that Nicholas seems a lot smarter and more advanced than other kids his age. (clarify)

ANDRIA If *lumber* means "useless bric-a-brac," I think they misnamed the room, because there's a lot of good stuff in there. (evaluate)

LEAH Well, the stuff is useless to the aunt. It's her useless stuff. (clarify)

DEAN To Nicholas, the room is beautiful. He's submerged in a world filled with things he's never seen before. (clarify)

ANDRIA Once Nicholas is in the lumber-room, that's where he finds his identity. (evaluate)

LEAH I agree. That's where you learn who Nicholas is. The other stuff is just superficial. Once he's in the lumber-room, he acts like other little kids. It's his aunt who forces him to be conniving. She makes him act more grown-up than he should. (evaluate)

Is it sometimes difficult for you to talk about literature once you've read it? Take some cues from active readers, who reflect and respond in a variety of ways. After reading "The Lumber-Room," these three students reveal their personal reactions (Shaping Your Response) and literary responses (Analyzing the Story), along with the connections they have made to their own experiences (Extending the Ideas). These are the types of questions you will find in this book.

Shaping Your Response

At the beginning of the story, Nicholas is "in disgrace." Do you think that he is really a wicked, sinful boy? Explain.

DEAN When I think of Nicholas, I have a picture in my mind of a wicked little kid, with horns sticking out of his head like the devil, just smiling at his aunt.

LEAH I don't think he's evil—that's too strong a word.

DEAN I agree. But you can't tell me Nicholas is a normal child.

ANDRIA I would not say that all children are as intelligent as Nicholas, who's able to plan ahead and manipulate others. When he's in the lumber room, looking at bird pictures in the book, you see that he's just as interesting and amazing as these birds. He's not an evil, wicked child—he's a good kid. It's just that his aunt never takes the time to open up his "book covers" and see who he is.

Analyzing the Story

How would you characterize the tone of this story? How does the tone contribute to the overall effect?

DEAN I think the tone is satirical.

ANDRIA I agree. The adults are being satirized. So many of the words that are used are directed against adults.

LEAH I agree that the tone is sarcastic and cynical throughout most of the story. But I think the tone changes when Nicholas is in the lumber-room. He's happier because he's focusing on the wonderful things that are locked up inside this room.

DEAN In the lumber-room, Nicholas has stepped into a world where there's no longer an aunt to deal with or worry about. That's why the tone changes.

Extending Your Ideas

Nicholas seems to be fascinated by what is forbidden. Suggest other stories or real-life situations in which characters have similar fascinations.

DEAN The depiction of the lumber-room as a forbidden paradise reminds me of the story of Adam and Eve, from the Bible.

LEAH The gooseberry garden in this story reminds me of *The Secret Garden.*

DEAN Kids in general are fascinated by the forbidden. When I was a little kid, if someone told me not to do something, of course I did it. I assume that a fascination with the forbidden is part of every child's life.

After Reading

DISCUSSION AFTER READING

Shaping Your Response

This question encourages students to respond personally to the story as they experienced it. Encourage as many students as possible to share their reactions. Ask them which of the readers most closely reflects their own responses.

Analyzing the Story

This question directs students back to the story to look for details that will help them understand the author's purpose in writing. You may want to explain literary terms and techniques as they apply to the story.

Extending the Ideas

This question asks students to make connections to their own experiences and to look at other works of art (books, movies, television programs, and so on) in comparison to the story. Are students familiar with the works mentioned by the readers? What other suggestions do they have?

Transparency Collection
Models for Active Reading
Short Story, 1A–1D
Nonfiction, 2A–2C
Poetry, 3A–3B

Part One: Getting Even

Planning Unit 1: Medieval Literature

Literature	Integrated Language Arts: Literary	Writing/Grammar, Usage and Mechanics	Reading, Thinking, Listening, Speaking	Vocabulary/Spelling
from Beowulf *translated by Charles W. Kennedy* Epic Poem *(challenging)* p. 9	Alliteration Style Figurative language Archetype, irony Allegory, symbolism	Paragraph on heroism Letter Describe Grendel Pronoun/antecedent agreement	Infer Draw conclusions Recognize values	Context clues
Lord Randal Folk Ballad *(average)* p. 24 **Edward** Folk Ballad *(average)* p. 26 **Get Up and Bar the Door** Folk Ballad *(average)* p. 28	Repetition	Story ideas Ballads Newspaper story Spelling changes over time and/or homophones	Compare and contrast Draw conclusions	Repetition

Meeting Individual Needs

Multi-modal Activities	Mini-Lessons
Research report Recorded music Exploring key concepts Analyzing alliteration Exploring key thoughts Making personal connections Interpreting events dramatically Appreciating language and imagery Summarizing a character	Alliteration Context clues Pronoun/antecedent agreement Listening to poetry
Performing or playing ballads Talk on early instruments Exploring dialect Analyzing humor	Spelling changes over time and/or homophones Repetition

Interdisciplinary Studies
Faces of Evil

Format	Content Area	Highlights	Skill
Collage: **Evil from East to West**	Multicultural	These pages show different cultural concepts of good and evil.	Compare and contrast
Essay: **from Grendel** *by John Gardner*	Multicultural	This essay relates the epic poem *Beowulf* from Grendel's point of view.	Scanning for information

Writing Workshop

Mode	Writing Format	Writing Focus	Proofreading Skills
Expository writing	An interpretive essay	Keeping to the main idea	Clarifying pronoun reference

Program Support Materials

For Every Selection

Unit Resource Book
Graphic Organizer
Study Guide
Vocabulary Worksheet
Grammar Worksheet
Spelling, Speaking and Listening, or Literary Language Worksheet
Alternate Check Test
Vocabulary Test
Selection Test

For Every Writing Workshop

Unit Resource Book
Prewriting Worksheet
Revising Strategy Worksheet
Editing Strategy Worksheet
Presentation Worksheet
Writing Rubric
Transparency Collection
Fine Art Transparency
Student Writing Model Transparencies

For Every Interdisciplinary Study

Unit Resource Book
Study Guide
Mini-Lesson Skill Worksheet

Assessment

Unit Resource Book
TE Check Tests
Alternate Check Test (blackline master)
Vocabulary Test (blackline master)
Selection Test (blackline master)
Test Generator Software
Assessment Handbook

Part Two: Codes of Honor

Planning Unit 1: Medieval Literature

Literature	Integrated Language Arts			
	Literary	Writing/Grammar, Usage and Mechanics	Reading, Thinking, Listening, Speaking	Vocabulary/Spelling
from The Prologue to the Canterbury Tales **from The Pardoner's Prologue and Tale** *by Geoffrey Chaucer* Narrative Poem *(average)* p. 46	Irony Literary criticism Connotation and denotation Characterization Personification	Character descriptions Plan a television series Misplaced modifiers	Draw conclusions Recognize values Analyze	Word analogy test Figures of speech that have endured Recognize slang
from Sir Gawain and the Green Knight Romance *(average)* p. 61	Foreshadowing Personification Allusion Characterization Simile, imagery Tone	Paragraph Character sketch Essay Poem/song/rap Recognize run-on sentences	Compare and contrast Make judgments Find the main idea Recognize values Make analogies	Matching Word choice
The Day of Destiny from Morte Darthur *by Sir Thomas Malory* Tale *(challenging)* p. 79	Protagonist/antagonist Foreshadowing Symbolism	List of challenges Write a narrative Description Origins and development of the English language	Recognize values	Define words and write a paragraph

Meeting Individual Needs

Multi-modal Activities	Mini-Lessons
Creating an illustration Poster Starting vocabulary notebooks Analyzing characters Relating key concepts Exploring characterization	Irony Figures of speech that have endured Misplaced modifiers Synthesize Recognize slang
Designing a coat of arms Interview Considering a key concept Expanding vocabulary notebook Making inferences Understanding causes and effects Making personal connections Responding to a character Exploring symbols	Recognize run-on sentences Cause and effect Word choice Identify alternatives Foreshadowing
Creating a skit Creating a picture essay Designing a wall hanging Exploring key statement Tracking story events Analyzing a conclusion	Protagonist/antagonist Origins and development of the English language

Interdisciplinary Studies
Legends of Arthur

Format	Content Area	Highlights	Skill
Article: **Chivalry** *by Barbara Tuckman*	Humanities	This article provides a look at chivalry and the life of a noble.	Locate, use, and evaluate reference sources
Collage: **Arthur and His Court**	Humanities	This selection shows various depictions of Arthur's story.	
Article: **The Once and Future King** *by T. H. White*	Humanities	This excerpt is of a conversation between King Arthur and a young page.	

Writing Workshop

Mode	Writing Format	Writing Focus	Proofreading Skills
Exposition/persuasive writing	An essay of opinion	Clarifying abstract terms	Making subjects and verbs agree

Program Support Materials

For Every Selection	For Every Writing Workshop
Unit Resource Book Graphic Organizer Study Guide Vocabulary Worksheet Grammar Worksheet Spelling, Speaking and Listening, or Literary Language Worksheet Alternate Check Test Vocabulary Test Selection Test	**Unit Resource Book** Prewriting Worksheet Revising Strategy Worksheet Editing Strategy Worksheet Presentation Worksheet Writing Rubric **Transparency Collection** Fine Art Transparency Student Writing Model Transparencies

For Every Interdisciplinary Study	Assessment
Unit Resource Book Study Guide Mini-Lesson Skill Worksheet	**Unit Resource Book** TE Check Tests Alternate Check Test (blackline master) Vocabulary Test (blackline master) Selection Test (blackline master) **Test Generator Software** **Assessment Handbook**

Unit 1 Supplemental Resources

Media and Technology

Part One Selections

from Beowulf

Computer Software *History of English Literature I* and *II,* CD-ROM for IBM, Macintosh, and Windows, Clearvue, 1996, explores literature from the Anglo-Saxon period to modern writers.

Videotape Students will appreciate the information in *Background to Beowulf,* 25 minutes, Educational Video Network, 1994. *Beowulf,* 38 minutes, Films for the Humanities & Sciences, is a journey into Celtic-British-Anglo-Saxon culture and the oral epic tradition.

Home Connection The monster Grendel is invulnerable to weapons so Beowulf must wrestle him. Students might ask a family member who competes in some form of wrestling—such as Olympic-style, judo, karate, and so on—to speak to the class describing rules, training, levels of expertise, tournaments, and other aspects of their sport.

Lord Randal/Edward/Get Up and Bar the Door

Audiotape *Early English Ballads,* Smithsonian/Folkways, includes "Lord Randal" and "Get Up and Bar the Door."

Videotape *England in the Middle Ages,* 30 minutes, Guidance Associates, explores the literature of the medieval era.

Community Resources You might invite someone interested in folk music—either as a performer or a scholar—to speak to the class about the traditional English ballads and how these songs were transplanted to America. If your community has someone familiar with another ballad tradition, like the Hispanic corrido or border ballad, you might ask them to discuss the similarities and differences between these songs and the English ballads.

Connections to
Custom Literature Database

For Part One "Getting Even" Selections with Lessons

- "The Conversion of Edwin" from *The Ecclesiastical History of the English People,* Book II, Chapters 9–13 by Bede
- "Sir Patrick Spens"

Additional theme-based selections can be accessed on the ScottForesman database.

Beowulf v Grendel

Background to Beowulf and *Beowulf* are two videos that give students background on Beowulf and his battles with Grendel.

Part 2 Selections

The Pardoner's Prologue and Tale

Videotape *A Prologue to Chaucer*, 29 minutes, and *Geoffrey Chaucer and Middle English Literature*, 35 minutes, both from Films for the Humanities & Sciences, are exciting portrayals of the man and his times.

Computer Software The CD-ROM program, *The Time, Life, and Works of Chaucer,* is a multimedia presentation from Society for Visual Education, 1995, for IBM, Macintosh, and Windows.

Community Resources Are there any religious or historical shrines in or near your community, such as the birthplaces or homes of famous people, battlefields, and places of worship? If so, students might be interested in researching their history or taking a field trip to visit such sites.

from Gawain and the Green Knight

Home Connection Both Gawain and his opponent the Green Knight have their origins in the Celtic mythological traditions of Wales and Ireland. Students might use the resources of the local library to research the backgrounds of these two figures.

Day of Destiny from Morte Darthur

Videotape A wealth of material is presented in the three video set, *Le Morte D'Arthur, The Making of the King,* and *The World of Sir Thomas Mallory*, 50 minutes each, Library Video Company.

Community Resources Students might use the resources of their local library to research places in Britain associated with Arthur, particularly Glastonbury, where some say the Isle of Avalon really existed. Ancient Welsh legends tell of a British general who fought in the area of Glastonbury around A.D. 500. Glastonbury is southwest of London in the county of Somerset.

Connections to
Custom Literature Database

For Part Two "Codes of Honor" Selections with Lessons

- "The Wife of Bath's Tale" from *The Canterbury Tales* by Geoffrey Chaucer
- "Sir Gawain and the Green Knight"

Additional theme-based selections can be accessed on the ScottForesman database.

The World of Geoffrey Chaucer

The Time, Life, and Works of Chaucer is available as a CD-ROM program for several different platforms.

Unit 1

Medieval Literature

Art Study

The Arming of the Knights, a detail of which is produced on pages xxxvi and 1 was designed by Sir Edward Coley Burne-Jones (1833–1898). A painter and designer born in Birmingham, he designed tapestry and stained glass for William Morris's design firm and the Kelmscott Press. Morris's design company produced furniture, textiles, and wallpapers, as well as tapestries and stained glass, and this tapestry was created by Morris weavers in the nineteenth century. It now hangs in the City Art Gallery in Birmingham.

Question Which details in the tapestry seem realistic? *(the horses and the armor)*

Question Which details seem unrealistic? *(the profusion of flowers, the quietness of the scene, the idea that the women would be handing weapons to the knights)*

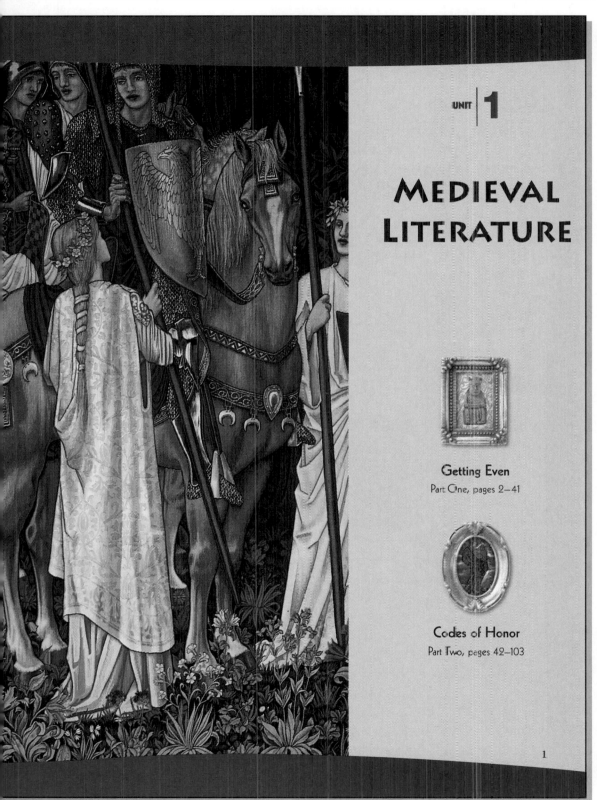

UNIT 1

MEDIEVAL LITERATURE

Getting Even

Codes of Honor

1

THEMATIC CONNECTIONS

Although the medieval period was frequently a time of bloodshed, there were rules about one's personal conduct. Wrongs were avenged, but loyalty, bravery, and courtesy were also important in feudal society.

Part One
Getting Even

Part One explores the ideas of evil, revenge, and punishment, as well as the epic hero.

Ideas to Explore

- What are our chief sources of information about early Britain?
- What is the nature of the epic hero?

Part Two
Codes of Honor

Part Two focuses on the Prologue and Tale of the greedy Pardoner in *The Canterbury Tales* and the chivalric ideals as represented in the romance of "Sir Gawain and the Green Knight" and the tale of King Arthur.

Ideas to Explore

- What are some codes of behavior today?
- What are the results of a failure to live up to these codes?

The walrus ivory chess piece representing a king is from the Viking era and was discovered in the Hebrides Islands. The figure of Sir Gawain is from an early fourteenth-century manuscript from northeastern France titled *Le Roman de Lancelot du Lac.*

Part One: Getting Even

Historical Overview

EXPLORING CONCEPTS

- Britain has been occupied by many different peoples.
- Evidence of several cultures are still visible in Britain.
- Some conquerors were absorbed into existing cultures, and new cultures were formed.

Research Activity Students might like to research Stonehenge or other stone circles in Britain, the Sutton Hoo treasure, or the Battle of Hastings.

Each illustration represents a group of inhabitants. 1. Stonehenge originally consisted of four concentric circles of stone. Most scientists think that Stonehenge was used for measuring solar movements. 2. This first century B.C. Celtic neck ornament or torque was fashioned from an alloy of gold and silver and was found at Snettisham in Norfolk. 3. The image of a centurion is from a Roman tombstone in Britain. 4. The purse lid was unearthed in 1939 with the Sutton Hoo treasure from the grave of an Anglo-Saxon king. 5. The post head from a Viking ship is preserved in an Oslo museum. 6. The Bayeux Tapestry (c.1077) recorded the entire 1066 Norman invasion, including the death of the English king, Harold (pictured here), in the Battle of Hastings.

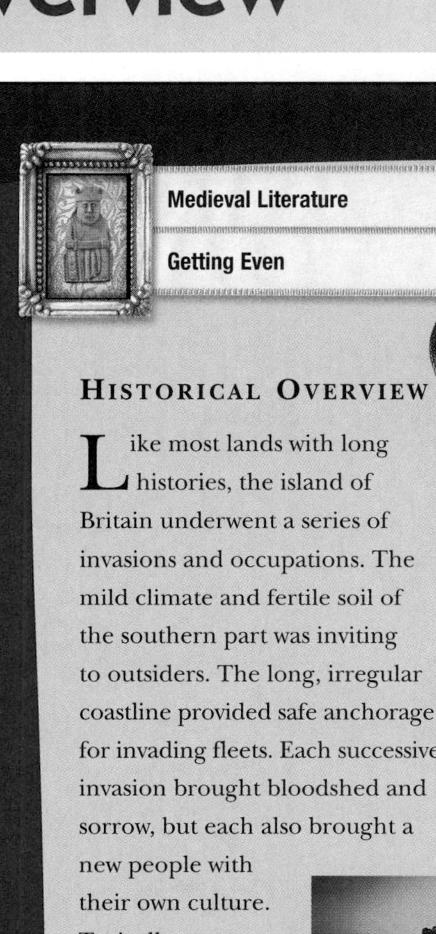

HISTORICAL OVERVIEW

Like most lands with long histories, the island of Britain underwent a series of invasions and occupations. The mild climate and fertile soil of the southern part was inviting to outsiders. The long, irregular coastline provided safe anchorage for invading fleets. Each successive invasion brought bloodshed and sorrow, but each also brought a new people with their own culture. Typically, new waves of immigrants came from the east and south, and the displaced refugees fled to the west and north, into what would become Wales, Ireland, and Scotland. But always some remained to blend with the newcomers and form a new culture that was a product of all its parts. Thus, through conflict and combination these different peoples created a nation.

2 CELTS

The Celts spread throughout Europe before reaching the British Isles. They built walled farms and hut villages and grew crops, using bronze and then iron tools. Separate tribes, each with its own king, warred with each other, erecting timber and stone fortresses and riding to battle in two-wheeled chariots. Their priests—called *druids*—conducted sacrifices in forest shrines.

INVASIONS

1 EARLY INHABITANTS

Cave dwellers lived on the island in prehistoric times. Invaders from what is now Spain and Portugal overcame their fragile culture, creating a society sophisticated enough to erect Stonehenge, the circle of huge upright stones on Salisbury Plain.

6 NORMANS

In a decisive battle at Hastings, William, Duke of Normandy (now northwest France) defeated the other claimants to the disputed English monarchy. During a lengthy struggle called the Norman Conquest, most of the Anglo-Saxon nobility was wiped out. William redistributed their lands and established a system of land ownership called *feudalism*.

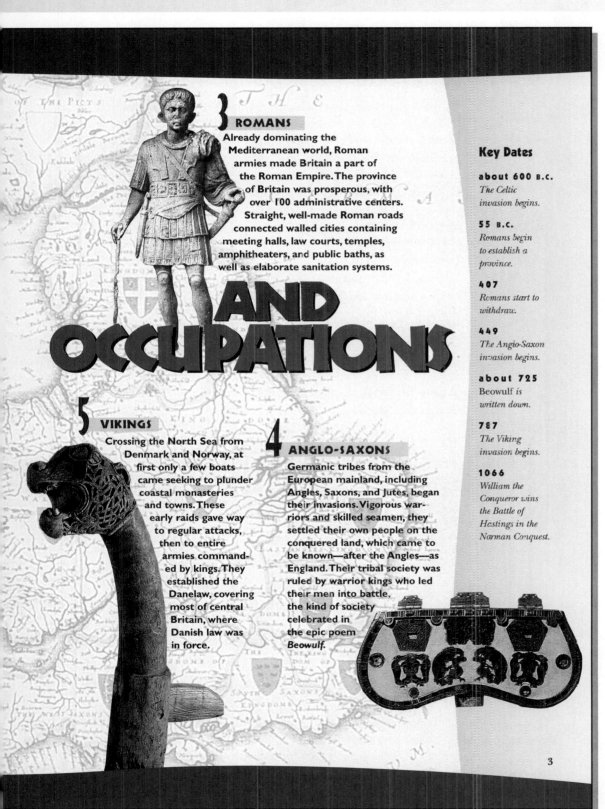

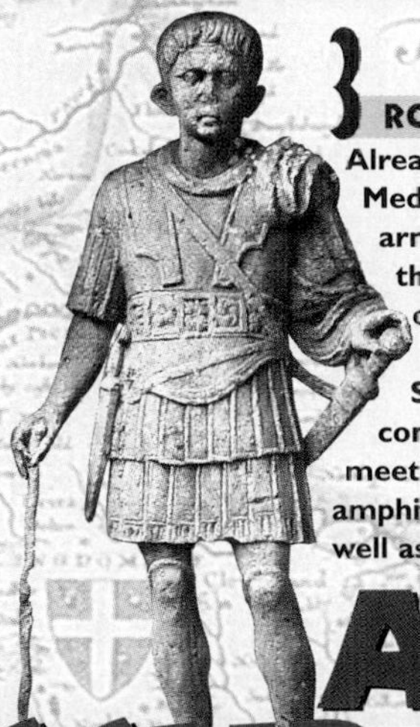

3 ROMANS

Already dominating the Mediterranean world, Roman armies made Britain a part of the Roman Empire. The province of Britain was prosperous, with over 100 administrative centers. Straight, well-made Roman roads connected walled cities containing meeting halls, law courts, temples, amphitheaters, and public baths, as well as elaborate sanitation systems.

AND OCCUPATIONS

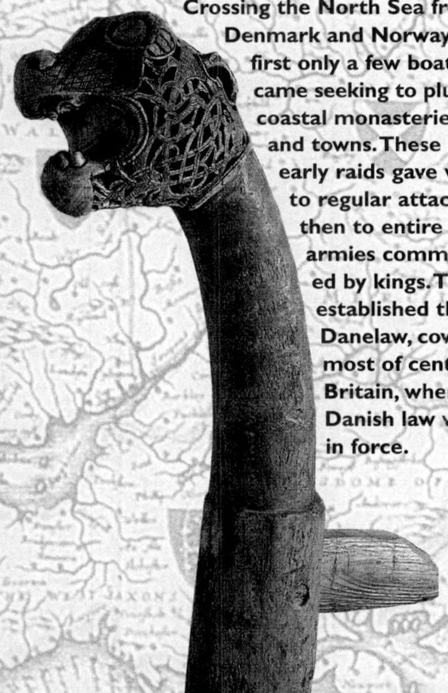

Key Dates

about 600 B.C.
The Celtic invasion begins.

55 B.C.
Romans begin to establish a province.

407
Romans start to withdraw.

449
The Anglo-Saxon invasion begins.

about 725
Beowulf *is written down.*

787
The Viking invasion begins.

1066
William the Conqueror wins the Battle of Hastings in the Norman Conquest.

5 VIKINGS

Crossing the North Sea from Denmark and Norway, at first only a few boats came seeking to plunder coastal monasteries and towns. These early raids gave way to regular attacks, then to entire armies commanded by kings. They established the Danelaw, covering most of central Britain, where Danish law was in force.

4 ANGLO-SAXONS

Germanic tribes from the European mainland, including Angles, Saxons, and Jutes, began their invasions. Vigorous warriors and skilled seamen, they settled their own people on the conquered land, which came to be known—after the Angles—as England. Their tribal society was ruled by warrior kings who led their men into battle, the kind of society celebrated in the epic poem *Beowulf.*

3

Key Dates

- In Britain, the Celts fiercely defended their island against invasion but were finally conquered by Rome in A.D. 43 during the reign of the Emperor Claudius.
- Tribal attacks over much of Europe weakened the Roman Empire, as did internal strife among its generals. By 500, the Romans had abandoned much of their vast empire, and tribes were setting up their own kingdoms in what is now Britain, France, and Germany.
- Vikings, a word meaning "sudden raider," staged numerous attacks on the British Isles between A. D. 700–1000.

MATERIALS OF INTEREST

Books

- *The Hero with a Thousand Faces* by Joseph Campbell (Princeton, 1973).
- *Stonehenge Complete* by Christopher Chippindale (Thames & Hudson, 1994).
- *The Golden Bough* by James George Frazer (Macmillan, 1950).
- *Grendel* by John Gardner (Knopf, 1971).

Multimedia

- *Beowulf and Old English Literature* [videotape]. 38 min., color, VHS. Films for the Humanities.
- *England at Bay* [videotape]. 29 min., color, VHS. PBS (Vikings! Series). Overview of the Danish Viking invasion of England and their defeat at the Battle of Edington.

Connections to **Custom Literature Database**

For further historical background, **Under Background Articles** see **Anglo-Saxon England 450–1066.**

Preview

Getting Even

FOR ALL STUDENTS

Use the first paragraph on page 4 and the following questions to spark a discussion on the theme of "Getting Even."

- What maxims or proverbs have you heard that deal with this theme or its converse? *(Possible responses: an eye for an eye, a tooth for a tooth, revenge is sweet, turn the other cheek)*
- To further explore the theme, use the Fine Art Transparency referenced below.

Transparency Collection
Fine Art Transparency 1

For At-Risk Students

Ask students to recall movies or television shows that dealt with the theme of revenge or getting even.

For Students Who Need Challenge

Students might read *Grendel* by John Gardner.

For Visual Learners

Preview the illustrations in Part One and ask students to discuss what they can learn about the ideals, beliefs, interests, and achievements of the people mentioned on pages 2 and 3.

MULTICULTURAL CONNECTION

Encourage students to give examples of how the cultural group(s) to which they belong influence various aspects of their lives, such as food, clothing, holidays, religion, marriage partner, and occupation. Such aspects must have been changed over and over again in Britain's early history as succeeding groups overran the existing population.

Part One

Getting Even

It's a theme that's almost as popular in human history as love or success: What do you do about people who have done something to you, and what do you do to them in return? Sometimes the answer is humorous, but more often it's serious—even bloody.

Multicultural Connection **Choice** is often influenced by the cultural values of the society in which we live. The so-called heroic values that emphasize bravery and loyalty to family or clan can sometimes cause people to act in certain ways; on the other hand, they can sometimes restrict the actions that people perform. In the following selections, to what extent do the cultural values of individuals either cause or restrict the choices they make?

IDEAS THAT WORK

Motivating with Meter

"This is a magnificent opportunity to teach the poetics of meter, stress-patterned speech. Students should perform and audio- or videotape major sections of *Beowulf,* assuming roles of various speakers in the epic, scoring the text for percussive performance, and thus learning scansion. Drums, wood blocks, chimes, cymbals, and keyboards can mark the beat of the recitation, and drone instruments may involve other participants.

As *Beowulf*'s concerns are centrally masculine, after trying to get students excited about heroism, I would ask female students to make a critical evaluation of the hero's role.

To generate writing I would assign a traditional five-paragraph in-class critical analytical composition."

Frank Pool
Austin, Texas

Reading an Epic Poem

The Germanic tribes who invaded Britain in the fifth century had a long literary tradition, carried on chiefly by wandering story tellers or musicians called *scops* who composed and recited or sang poems about past heroes and their brave deeds. These epic poems served warrior cultures by boosting tribal pride and teaching a code of values. The Anglo-Saxons (a term that came to refer to all the Germanic invaders of Britain, including Angles, Saxons, and Jutes) carried this oral tradition with them when they sailed westward to the place we now call England.

Understand Anglo-Saxon verse. Simple, direct, and relatively flexible, Anglo-Saxon verse is well fitted to oral composition and recitation. Here are a few lines from *Beowulf.* Written in the original Anglo-Saxon or Old English, it looks very different from the English we know. Nor does it sound like twentieth-century English.

The break in the middle of each line is called a *caesura* (si zhur′é); thus each line of verse divides into two half-lines. Each half-line contains two stressed syllables, making four strong beats to each line.

Alliteration, the repetition of initial sounds, is used, usually in the stressed syllables. Anglo-Saxon poetry is seldom rhymed.

The flexibility of the Anglo-Saxon language was a help to the scop, who at times must have composed his poetry on the spot. For example, if the first stressed syllable in a line started with an *h* sound, the scop could continue *on hranrade* ("on the whale-road"); if the line began with an *s* sound, he could use *on seglrade* ("on the sail-road"). To say "warrior," he could choose among *beorn, freca,* and *wiga,* which all mean the same but have different sounds and different connotations.

Alliterating words are in red.

Fyrst forð ġewāt; flota wæs on ȳðum,
bāt under beorge. Beornas ġearwe
on stefn stigon,— strēmas wundon,
sund wið sande;

Half line

Caesura

A literal translation is: "Time forth went; floater was on waves, / boat under cliff. Warriors eager / on prow climbed; streams eddied, / sea against sand."

READING AN EPIC POEM

Teaching Objectives

- to understand the characteristics of Anglo-Saxon verse
- to recognize the characteristics of the epic hero
- to identify and interpret epithets

Introduce

Ask students to look at the lines from the Old English version of *Beowulf* and have them study the literal translation at the bottom of the page. What words in the original are recognizable as the English we speak today? *(on, under)* What words are similar to the English we speak? *(bat, stremas, sande)* Point out the caesura and the half-line breaks. Then ask students to read the characteristics of an epic poem.

Follow Up

Students may work in small groups as they begin to read *Beowulf,* with each group responsible for finding examples of one of the characteristics of an epic poem. Group members may present their findings orally, in charts, or with annotated copies of the poem.

BUILDING ENGLISH PROFICIENCY

Alliteration

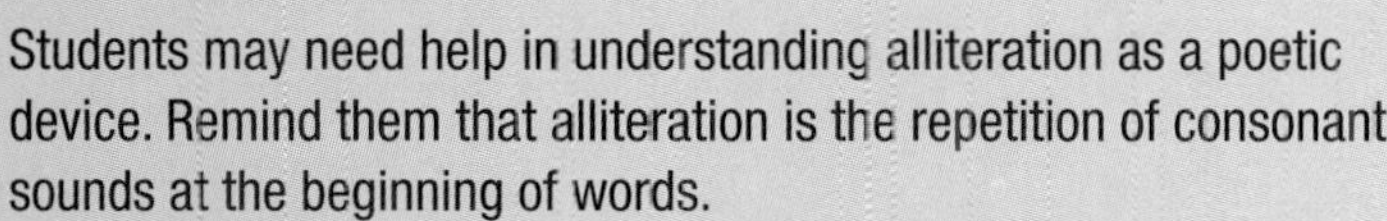

Students may need help in understanding alliteration as a poetic device. Remind them that alliteration is the repetition of consonant sounds at the beginning of words.

Ask students to think of people they know or have read about whose first and last names are alliterative. List these on the chalkboard. What products have they seen in stores that have alliterative names?

Activity Students can create tongue-twisters or advertising slogans that make use of alliteration. Display these around the classroom or tape-record the students as they read their examples aloud to the class. Then ask students to work in small groups to find examples of alliteration in the lines of *Beowulf.*

Activity Options

Activity 1 Students may want to make a "master" annotated version of *Beowulf* by collecting all the group information.

Activity 2 Students can compare and contrast the qualities of an epic hero such as Beowulf with those of modern-day heroes.

Activity 3 Ask students to prepare epithets for contemporary news figures. They can use newspaper photos and add phrases written on note cards or on self-adhesive notes.

Another characteristic of Anglo-Saxon poetry is its use of metaphorical compounds, called **kennings:** for example, "whale-road" and "sail-road" both mean "sea." "Peace-weaver" for woman and "candle of heaven" for the sun are further examples of these descriptive comparisons that add beauty and a certain mystery to Anglo-Saxon poetry.

Examine the sentence structure. The version of *Beowulf* that follows has been translated from the Old English, but the translator has conveyed the quality of the poetry as well as the actions. Read the lines as you would prose lines, looking for the subject and the verb. Recognize also that many phrases are repetitions of what has just been said, added for greater emphasis.

Be aware of the nature of the epic hero. The heroic actions described in epic poetry—perilous journeys, battles with monsters, and so on—may be familiar to you; however, concepts of heroes differ from culture to culture. As you read *Beowulf,* look for clues that tell what this hero is like. Winning always matters, but the epic focus is more on *how* the hero fights. Read to learn what strategies Beowulf uses and how he responds to challenges.

Understand the purpose of the speeches. Characters in epics rarely make casual conversation. Instead, they communicate through formal speeches, boasting of their own accomplishments, challenging hostile rivals, advising each other about how to act, and philosophizing about human destiny.

Notice parallelisms. The epic of *Beowulf* begins with the story of King Scyld, who does not play any part in what follows, but who is mentioned because his story parallels or is similar to the story of Beowulf. (Scyld does not appear in this excerpt.) This comparison of people and events from earlier times is meant to add to the stature of the hero; he is thus seen as part of a long heroic tradition. Characters further this comparison by recalling their own and each other's family histories and past deeds of glory.

Look for symbolic descriptions. The *Beowulf* poet does not spend much time describing the appearance of people and places, but when he does, it is for a specific purpose. He dwells upon the beauty of Hrothgar's mead-hall because it represents certain ideals: order, security, human closeness. Much description occurs in the form of **epithets**—descriptive phrases that often occur in a series and refer in different ways to the same person. For example, King Hrothgar is referred to as "Prince of the Danes, protector of Scyldings, Lord of nations, and leader of men."

Appreciate the pageantry. Ceremony plays an important part in Anglo-Saxon life. When Beowulf arrives in Hrothgar's kingdom, Hrothgar throws a banquet for him, complete with formal speeches and lavish gifts. Such ceremony figures heavily in the rest of the poem. King Hrothgar delivers a speech and formally presents the hero with gifts, which the poet lists in detail. The oratory and the rewards define what the poet considers the most important values in life: honor, loyalty, and perseverance.

Before Reading

from Beowulf

The Beowulf Poet

The identity of the person who wrote *Beowulf* is a mystery. Some think the poet was a **scop,** or singing poet, associated with an Anglo-Saxon court. Scops composed their poetry extemporaneously, recounting past history and present events and preserving a record of people's achievements. Although the poem is based in part on traditional Germanic tales and has many pagan elements, the author seems to have been acquainted with the Bible and with Christianity, to which the Anglo-Saxons began to convert in the 500s. The poem was first written down sometime between A.D. 650 and 850.

Building Background

Imagine the Scene In the large wooden meeting-hall, the king and his thanes, or knights, gather, along with their wives, children, and servants. It is the end of the day—a time for feasting and for listening to tales of heroes. As the sounds of the day give way to nighttime sounds, and the fearsome darkness closes in, they huddle more closely together before a ruddy fire, drawn by the warmth, by the sounds of the scop strumming his lyre, and by the desire to hear a good story. "Tell us," someone says eagerly, "about Grendel and about how Beowulf killed that gruesome monster."

Literary Focus

Alliteration The repetition of sounds, usually consonants, at the beginnings of words or accented syllables is called **alliteration** (ə lit ə rā′shən). Note the repeated sounds in these lines:

Grim and greedy the gruesome monster,
Fierce and furious, launched attack, . . .

In Anglo-Saxon verse, alliteration is used for emphasis and to provide a kind of verbal music. Alliteration also makes words and phrases easier to remember, and since a scop recited his poems from memory, a device that made lines easier to remember would have been welcome.

Writer's Notebook

Unlock Your Word-Hoard The hero, Beowulf, after being asked who he is and where he comes from and why, unlocks "his word-hoard"; that is, he begins to tell about himself. What makes Beowulf a hero—his own claims, other people's claims, or his own deeds? Before starting to read, write down in your notebook all the qualities you think a hero should have. As you read, check to see which ones Beowulf possesses.

Before Reading

Building Background

Students might discuss what they have learned about early medieval times from history or social studies courses.

Literary Focus

Beowulf and similar Old English poetry was originally recited aloud, often to the strum of a harp. Each line of *Beowulf* has four strong beats, like 4/4 time in music. Repeating sounds on accented beats adds to the internal rhythm. Suggest that students read some parts of *Beowulf* aloud, listening to how alliteration accents rhythm.

Writer's Notebook

Students might begin a chart to keep track of Beowulf's heroic qualities.

My Idea of a Hero	Beowulf's Traits
Fair	
Strong	
Kind	

More About Beowulf

The only surviving *Beowulf* manuscript, which dates from the 900s, is charred at the edges from a 1731 fire. Fortunately, the two pre-fire transcriptions that survive preserve passages now unintelligible in the original.

SUPPORT MATERIALS OVERVIEW

Unit 1 Resource Book
- Graphic Organizer, p. 1
- Study Guide, p. 2
- Vocabulary, p. 3
- Grammar, p. 4
- Alternate Check Test, p. 5
- Vocabulary Test, p. 6
- Selection Test, pp. 7–8

Building English Proficiency
- Selection Summaries
- Activities, p. 205

Reading, Writing & Grammar SkillBook
- Vocabulary, pp. 1–2, 3–4, 5–6
- Writing, pp. 123–124
- Grammar, Usage, and Mechanics, pp. 187–188, 209–210

The World of Work
- Police Officer, p. 1
- Activity, p. 2

Technology
- Audiotape
- Writer's Notebook Software
- Custom Literature Database: For other selections dealing with Getting Even, see "The Battle of Brunanburh" and "The Battle of Otterbourne" on the database.
- Test Generator Software

Art Study

Response to Caption Question Students may suggest that the detailed, intricate carving shows extraordinary skill. The depiction of a warrior at the entrance of a church indicates that the ability to fight well was important in this society. It also suggests that warriors asked God for protection and guidance.

Visual Literacy In the medieval period, churches and cathedrals were often repositories of art. Craftspeople produced their best work for the church in the hopes of pleasing God as well as powerful church leaders. Church art usually told a story and taught a lesson to an audience that was largely illiterate.

Question In what ways does this carving remind you of Beowulf? *(Like the tale, the carving captures action; both could be interpreted as a battle between good and evil.)*

SELECTION SUMMARY

Beowulf

This excerpt tells the story of the young hero Beowulf. At home in the land of the Geats (southern Sweden), Beowulf hears that a monster has been raiding the great hall of the Danish king, Hrothgar. Beowulf at once commands a ship to be fitted out and sails swiftly to Denmark. On the first night of his visit, he waits in Hrothgar's hall. When the monster, Grendel, comes for his nightly raid, Beowulf overpowers him; Grendel escapes only by leaving his arm behind. The monster runs to a hiding place, where he dies of his injuries. In the morning the Danes rejoice at Grendel's defeat; that night they celebrate Beowulf's victory.

For summaries in other languages, see the ***Building English Proficiency*** *book.*

The saga of Sigurd the Dragon-Slayer is depicted in a group of carvings that grace the entrance to a Norwegian church built in the 1100s. In this detail from one of the carvings, Sigurd is shown slaying the fearsome dragon Fáfnir. What does the style of this wood carving suggest to you about the artistic skills of these people? About what they consider important?

To Hrothgar was granted glory in war,
Success in battle; retainers bold
Obeyed him gladly; his band increased
To a mighty host. Then his mind was moved
To have men fashion a high-built hall,
A mightier mead-hall than man had known,
Wherein to portion to old and young
All goodly treasure that God had given,
Save only the folk-land, and lives of men.
His word was published to many a people
1 Far and wide o'er the ways of earth
To rear a folk-stead richly adorned;

Beowulf (bā′ō wulf).
1 **Hrothgar** (hrōth′gar), king of the Danes.

6 **mead** (mēd), *n.* an alcoholic drink made from fermented honey and water.

9 **folk-land,** common land owned by the community. Germanic tribal law reserved this land for grazing.
11 **o'er,** over.

During Reading

Selection Objectives

- to read an example of literature translated from Old English
- to identify alliteration
- to analyze the role of the hero in literature
- to analyze unfamiliar vocabulary through contextual clues

Unit 1 Resource Book
Graphic Organizer, p. 1
Study Guide, p. 2

Theme Link

In this Old English epic, Beowulf fights and kills Grendel, a monster who has murdered many men, reinforcing the theme Getting Even.

Vocabulary Preview

revelry, noisy partying
peerless, without equal; matchless
gallant, noble in spirit or in conduct
esteem, high regard
prudent, sensible; discreet
wrath, great anger
dissuade, persuade not to do something
compass, plot; scheme
grievous, causing great pain or suffering; severe
prowess, bravery; daring

Students can add the words and definitions to their Writer's Notebook.

1 Literary Element
Style

The translator uses medieval-sounding constructions and wording.

Question What does "To rear a folk-stead richly adorned" mean? *(to create a well-appointed home)*

EDITORIAL NOTE This excerpt has been shortened for length.

BUILDING ENGLISH PROFICIENCY

Exploring Key Concepts

The qualities of a leader, as embodied here in Hrothgar, are key to this saga but are rather abstract. Help students grasp this concept.

1. Ask students to think about a present-day leader that they admire. Have them think of three words or phrases that describe their leader and list those words on the left-hand side of a chart.

2. Then have students look in lines 1–9 for indications that Hrothgar is a worthy leader. On the right-hand side of their charts, have them list three relevant words or phrases.

WHAT QUALITIES MAKE A LEADER	
Words describing . . .	
My leader	Hrothgar

Building English Proficiency
Activities, p. 205

2 Historical Note
The Germanic Peoples

Beowulf is part of the oral tradition of the Germanic peoples. The poem describes an ancient heroic society of Danes and Geats in Scandinavia. These were Germanic tribes living near the European homeland from which the Anglo-Saxons, another Germanic people, had come to England. Interestingly enough, the poem is believed to be the longest and greatest poem extant in Old English, yet there is not one word about England or English people in the poem.

3 Reader's Response
Making Personal Connections

Response A seemingly rational creature, Grendel is described as a "monster" descended from the biblical Cain.

4 Literary Focus
Alliteration

Questions

- What sound is repeated in line 54? *("gr"—grim, greedy, gruesome)*
- What sound is repeated in line 56? *("s" and "sl"—slew, spearmen, asleep)*

The task was speeded, the time soon came
That the famous mead-hall was finished and done.
To distant nations its name was known,
2 The Hall of the Hart; and the king kept well
His pledge and promise to deal out gifts,
Rings at the banquet. The great hall rose
High and horn-gabled, holding its place. . . .
Then an evil spirit who dwelt in the darkness
Endured it ill that he heard each day
The din of revelry ring through the hall,
The sound of the harp, and the scop's sweet song.
A skillful bard sang the ancient story
Of man's creation; how the Maker wrought
The shining earth with its circling waters;
In splendor established the sun and moon
As lights to illumine the land of men;
Fairly adorning the fields of earth
With leaves and branches; creating life
In every creature that breathes and moves.
So the lordly warriors lived in gladness,
At ease and happy, till a fiend from hell
Began a series of savage crimes.
They called him Grendel, a demon grim
Haunting the fen-lands, holding the moors,
Ranging the wastes, where the wretched wight
Made his lair with the monster kin;
He bore the curse of the seed of Cain
Whereby God punished the grievous guilt
Of Abel's murder. Nor ever had Cain
Cause to boast of that deed of blood;
God banished him far from the fields of men;
Of his blood was begotten an evil brood,
Marauding monsters and menacing trolls,
Goblins and giants who battled with God
A long time. Grimly He gave them reward!
Then at the nightfall the fiend drew near
Where the timbered mead-hall towered on high,
To spy how the Danes fared after the feast.
Within the wine-hall he found the warriors
Fast in slumber, forgetting grief,
Forgetting the woe of the world of men.
4 Grim and greedy the gruesome monster,
Fierce and furious, launched attack,
Slew thirty spearmen asleep in the hall,
Sped away gloating, gripping the spoil,

16 Hall of the Hart, Hrothgar's mead-hall, or meeting hall. The hart or male deer was a symbol of Germanic kingship.
19 horn-gabled, perhaps with roof ornaments carved to resemble a stag's, or deer's, antlers.
22 revelry, (rev′əl rē) *n.* noisy partying.
23 scop's sweet song. The scop (skop) was the tribe's storyteller, chanting his tales to the sound of a harp.
25 wrought, (rôt), *adj.* made. *Wrought* is an archaic past tense of the verb *work.*

35 Grendel (gren′dl).

39 seed of Cain. In the Bible, Cain murders his brother Abel and is driven into the wilderness by God (Genesis 4:8–14). According to later legend his offspring included a variety of monsters.

45 maraud (mə rôd′), *v.* go about in search of plunder.

3 ■ What impression do you get of Grendel throughout this selection—that he is an animal behaving as an animal behaves or that he is a rational creature planning to murder humans and eat them?

MINI-LESSON: LITERARY FOCUS
Alliteration

Teach Alliteration is the repetition of sounds at the beginning of words or accented syllables. Students should note that even though the poet might choose the words that create alliteration for their sound effects, the words are also appropriate to the meanings conveyed by poetry. Have students find examples of alliteration on pages 10–11. Some examples are

- Line 16: "Hall of the Hart"
- Line 35: "Grendel, a demon grim"
- Line 76: "baldly blazoned in baleful signs"
- Line 79: "raided and ravaged the realm"
- Line 92: "Fitted and furnished; he fain would sail"

Question *Beowulf* was originally an oral poem. Why might an oral storyteller use alliteration? *(The repetition of sounds is appealing to the listener, especially when spoken aloud. Alliteration might also serve as a memory device, helping the storyteller to remember the lines of the poem.)*

Activity Ideas

For practice, each student might

- write a short poem using alliteration
- write a tongue-twister, a humorous version of alliteration

5 Dragging the dead men home to his den.
Then in the dawn with the coming of daybreak
The war-might of Grendel was widely known.
Mirth was stilled by the sound of weeping;
The wail of the mourner awoke with day.
And the peerless hero, the honored prince,
Weighted down with woe and heavy of heart,
Sat sorely grieving for slaughtered thanes,
As they traced the track of the cursed monster.
From that day onward the deadly feud
Was a long-enduring and loathsome strife.
Not longer was it than one night later
The fiend returning renewed attack
With heart firm-fixed in the hateful war,
Feeling no rue for the grievous wrong.
'Twas easy thereafter to mark the men
Who sought their slumber elsewhere afar,
Found beds in the bowers, since Grendel's hate
Was so baldly blazoned in baleful signs.
He held himself at a safer distance
Who escaped the clutch of the demon's claw.
So Grendel raided and ravaged the realm,
One against all, in an evil war
Till the best of buildings was empty and still.
'Twas a weary while! Twelve winters' time
The lord of the Scyldings had suffered woe,
Sore affliction and deep distress.
And the malice of Grendel, in mournful lays,
6 Was widely sung by the sons of men. . . .

The Coming of Beowulf

Then tales of the terrible deeds of Grendel
Reached Hygelac's thane in his home with the Geats;
Of living strong men he was the strongest,
Fearless and gallant and great of heart.
He gave command for a goodly vessel
Fitted and furnished; he fain would sail
Over the swan-road to seek the king
Who suffered so sorely for need of men.
And his bold retainers found little to blame
In his daring venture, dear though he was;
They viewed the omens, and urged him on.
Brave was the band he had gathered about him,
Fourteen stalwarts seasoned and bold,
Seeking the shore where the ship lay waiting. . . .

63 peerless (pir′lis), *adj.* without equal; matchless.
63 honored prince, Hrothgar.
65 thanes, warriors. A thane ranked between an earl (a nobleman) and an ordinary freeman.

72 rue (rü), *n.* regret.
73 'twas, it was.

83 lord of the Scyldings, Hrothgar. His grandfather, Scyld (shild), was founder of the Danish line of kings, the Scyldingas.
88 Hygelac's thane . . . Geats, Beowulf. Hygelac (hī′jə lak) was king of the Geats (yā′əts), a people who lived in southwestern Sweden. Hygelac actually lived and was famous for his unusual height. He died in battle in A.D. 521.
90 gallant (gal′ənt), *adj.* noble in spirit or in conduct.

■ Anglo-Saxon poetry often makes use of a poetic device known as **kenning.** The writer uses a compound word that names something in a metaphorical way. For example, line 93 refers to the "swan-road." What sort of "road" would swans travel on? 7

99 stalwart (stôl′wərt), *n.* strong, brave, and steadfast person.

5 Historical Note
The *Beowulf* Saga

No historic Beowulf is known to have existed. The hero's fight with Grendel, excerpted here, may be adapted from the folk tale "The Bear's Son," of which more than 200 variants exist. The name Beowulf probably means bear, although literally it means "bee-wolf." Scholars of Old English believe that the hero's name means: "This one is to bees as a wolf is to men," that is, a bear.

6 Reading/Thinking Skills
Infer

Questions

- Who is telling the Beowulf story? *(an unknown poet/storyteller)*
- What does the narrator think of Grendel? How do you know? *(Because the narrator describes Grendel as a monster, demon, creature of malice, we can infer that he believes Grendel is evil and without redeeming qualities.)*

7 Literary Element
Figurative Language

Response Swans generally live on water, so a "swan-road" is a body of water, such as a river.

BUILDING ENGLISH PROFICIENCY
Analyzing Alliteration

Introduce the Literary Focus, alliteration, early in this selection.

1. From page 10, read line 44 aloud. Ask students which consonant sound is repeated three times *(b)*. Explain that this repeating of beginning consonant sounds in nearby words is called *alliteration*. Explain that almost all languages use alliteration. Ask students why poets might use alliteration. *(It emphasizes the alliterated words and makes the line more rhymic and musical.)*
2. Ask students to find alliteration in lines 45–47 *(the* m *sound in line 45; the* g *sound in lines 46–47)*.
3. Divide students into small groups and ask each group to recall or create and then share three examples of alliteration in English or another language.

8 Literary Element
Archetype

Beowulf is in many ways an archetypal hero: someone larger than life, able to perform deeds beyond human capability.

Questions

- How is Beowulf described in line 108? in line 118? *(a "stalwart leader"; a man with "thirty men's strength")*
- What other literary figures does Beowulf remind you of? *(Possible responses: Hercules, Superman)*

9 Reader's Response
Making Personal Connections

Questions

- What do you think of Beowulf so far? *(Possible responses: loyal, adventurous, brave, strong)*
- Would he make a good friend? Why or why not? *(His courage and willingness to fight for his friends would make him a good friend; or his heroic spirit might be a bit much in every day life.)*

10 Historical Note
Family in Society

Response Family relationships were important in determining one's place in society.

Beowulf and his men sail from the valley of the Gota River in Sweden to the Danish island of Zealand to offer their services to King Hrothgar. They are greeted by Wulfgar, the king's herald, or official messenger, who carries their message to his king.

Beowulf's Welcome at Hrothgar's Court

Wulfgar saluted his lord and friend:
"Men from afar have fared to our land
Over ocean's margin—men of the Geats,
Their leader called Beowulf—seeking a boon,
The holding of parley, my prince, with thee.
O gracious Hrothgar, refuse not the favor!
In their splendid war-gear they merit well
8 The esteem of earls; he's a stalwart leader
Who led this troop to the land of the Danes."
Hrothgar spoke, the lord of the Scyldings:
"Their leader I knew when he still was a lad.
His father was Ecgtheow; Hrethel the Geat
Gave him in wedlock his only daughter.
Now is their son come, keen for adventure,
9 Finding his way to a faithful friend.
Sea-faring men who have voyaged to Geatland
With gifts of treasure as token of peace,
Say that his hand-grip has thirty men's strength.
God, in His mercy, has sent him to save us—
So springs my hope—from Grendel's assaults.
For his gallant courage I'll load him with gifts!
Make haste now, marshal the men to the hall,
And give them welcome to Danish ground."
Then to the door went the well-known warrior,
Spoke from the threshold welcoming words:
"The Danish leader, my lord, declares
That he knows your kinship; right welcome you come,
You stout sea-rovers, to Danish soil.
Enter now, in your shining armor
And vizored helmets, to Hrothgar's hall.
But leave your shields and the shafts of slaughter
To wait the issue and weighing of words."
Then the bold one rose with his band around him,
A splendid massing of mighty thanes;
A few stood guard as the Geat gave bidding
Over the weapons stacked by the wall.
They followed in haste on the heels of their leader
Under Heorot's roof. Full ready and bold
The helmeted warrior strode to the hearth;

101 Wulfgar (wulf′gar), Hrothgar's herald, an official who carries messages.

105 parley (pär′lē), *n.* conference.

108 esteem (e stēm′), *n.* high regard.

112 Ecgtheow (edj′thā ō), Beowulf's father.
112 Hrethel (hreth′l), Beowulf's mother's father.

10 ■ Many lines in Beowulf are devoted to tracing kinship, or family relationships. What does this tell you about the society of these people?

138 Heorot (hā′ə rot), Hrothgar's mead-hall, the "Hall of the Hart."

MINI-LESSON: VOCABULARY
Context Clues

Teach The use of context clues can help students decipher the meaning of the many unfamiliar words in *Beowulf.*

Activity Idea Divide students into groups, and assign one or more of these words from the selection to each group:

stalwart (line 108)	corselets (line 182)
wantonly (line 201)	ween (line 211)
nowise (line 285)	baleful (line 315)

Ask each group to

- read the line in which the word is found, as well as those above and below
- brainstorm possible meanings, based on context
- decide on a possible meaning and try replacing the word with the agreed-upon meaning to see if the sentence still makes sense
- if possible, find the word in a dictionary and check its meaning
- report the meaning to the class

Beowulf spoke; his byrny glittered,
11 His war-net woven by cunning of smith:
"Hail! King Hrothgar! I am Hygelac's thane,
Hygelac's kinsman. Many a deed
Of honor and daring I've done in my youth.
This business of Grendel was brought to my ears
On my native soil. The sea-farers say
This best of buildings, this boasted hall,
Stands dark and deserted when sun is set,
When darkening shadows gather with dusk.
The best of my people, prudent and brave,
Urged me, King Hrothgar, to seek you out;
They had in remembrance my courage and might.
Many had seen me come safe from the conflict,
Bloody from battle; five foes I bound
Of the giant kindred, and crushed their clan.
Hard-driven in danger and darkness of night
I slew the nicors that swam the sea,
Avenged the woe they had caused the Weders,
And ended their evil—they needed the lesson!
And now with Grendel, the fearful fiend,
Single-handed I'll settle the strife!
Prince of the Danes, protector of Scyldings,
Lord of nations, and leader of men,
I beg one favor—refuse me not,
Since I come thus faring from far-off lands—
That I may alone with my loyal earls,
With this hardy company, cleanse Hart-Hall.
I have heard that the demon in proud disdain
Spurns all weapons; and I too scorn—
May Hygelac's heart have joy of the deed—
To bear my sword, or sheltering shield,
Or yellow buckler, to battle the fiend.
With hand-grip only I'll grapple with Grendel;
Foe against foe I'll fight to the death,
And the one who is taken must trust to God's grace! . . .
If death shall call me, he'll carry away
My gory flesh to his fen-retreat
To gorge at leisure and gulp me down,
Soiling the marshes with stains of blood.
There'll be little need longer to care for my body!
If the battle slays me, to Hygelac send
This best of corselets that covers my breast . . .
Finest of byrnies. Fate goes as Fate must!"

140 byrny, shirt of chain mail.
150 prudent (prüd′nt), *adj.* sensible; discreet.
157 nicor (nik′ər), *n.* a water demon animal in shape.
158 Weders (wā′dərz), Beowulf's people, the Swedes.

12 ■ Notice that the poet often uses a series of descriptive names (called **epithets**) to refer to the same person, as in lines 162–163. What do you learn about Hrothgar in these lines?

13 ■ The Beowulf poet is fond of **understatement,** a statement that expresses a fact less emphatically than it should. What makes line 180 an example of understatement?

This iron warrior's helmet, with its cap covered by richly decorated bronze sheets, dates from Sweden of the 600s. What does the helmet's construction suggest about the dangers faced by the warrior who wore it? What does the helmet's rich ornamentation suggest about the warrior's status in his society?

11 Historical Note
Crafting Chain Mail

"War-net" was chain mail—a mesh of small, separately hand-forged links. An armorer hammered out an iron bar until it was long and thin. He then wound it around a slender rod to form a coil of rings; cut off one ring after another; and linked them with rivets. A full suit often took months to complete.

12 Reading/Thinking Skills
Draw Conclusions

Response It can be concluded that Hrothgar was an important leader.

13 Literary Element
Irony

Response The understatement is ironic in that if Beowulf dies, Grendel will devour his body.

Response to Caption Question He needed protection from head injuries; as he had the resources for a richly-decorated helmet; he was probably a nobleman.

BUILDING ENGLISH PROFICIENCY

Exploring Key Thoughts

In lines 140–183, Beowulf covers a variety of subjects. Students may identify key thoughts more easily with this chart.

1. Divide students into small groups assigned to one of the four topics covered by the chart. Working together, they can look for a statement or two on their topics.
2. Ask each group to summarize and share Beowulf's thoughts.

Beowulf's Thoughts About . . .	
Hrothgar:	Himself:
Past Dangers:	Facing Grendel:

14 Historical Note
The Old English *Scop*

Germanic kings of the medieval period kept professional poets, which were called "scops" in England. A scop composed and performed his own poems to harp accompaniment. He had two functions: to praise his patron; and to entertain at celebrations. Even after the advent of Christianity, the scop recited the old sagas, which kept alive customs, conventions, and ideals of conduct from pagan times.

15 Reader's Response
Challenging the Text

Possible Responses Students may wonder if Beowulf is more foolhardy than brave or if he is strong enough to slay Grendel.

Literary Criticism

"*Beowulf* has been [compared] to our historical novel, but for all its absorption with antiquity, [it] reflects the social realities of the Anglo-Saxon audience's world rather than a historian's reconstruction of an earlier society. . . . Swords, shields, coats of ring-mail, helmets with surmounted boar figures, drinking vessels, royal halls . . . , all [attest] to . . . Anglo-Saxon society."

George Clark
Beowulf

Hrothgar invites Beowulf and his men to a banquet in their honor.

Then in the beer-hall were benches made ready
For the Geatish heroes. Noble of heart,
Proud and stalwart, they sat them down
And a beer-thane served them; bore in his hands
The patterned ale-cup, pouring the mead,
14 While the scop's sweet singing was heard in the hall.
There was joy of heroes, a host at ease,
A welcome meeting of Weder and Dane.

Unferth Taunts Beowulf

Then out spoke Unferth, Ecglaf's son,
Who sat at the feet of the Scylding lord,
Picking a quarrel—for Beowulf's quest,
His bold sea-voyaging, irked him sore;
He bore it ill that any man other
In all the earth should ever achieve
More fame under heaven than he himself:
"Are you the Beowulf that strove with Breca
In a swimming match in the open sea,
Both of you wantonly tempting the waves,
Risking your lives on the lonely deep
For a silly boast? No man could dissuade you,
Nor friend nor foe, from the foolhardy venture
Of ocean-swimming; with outstretched arms
You clasped the sea-stream, measured her streets,
With plowing shoulders parted the waves.
The sea-flood boiled with its wintry surges,
Seven nights you toiled in the tossing sea;
His strength was the greater, his swimming the stronger! . . .
Therefore, I ween, worse fate shall befall,
Stout as you are in the struggle of war,
In deeds of battle, if you dare to abide
Encounter with Grendel at coming of night."
Beowulf spoke, the son of Ecgtheow:
"My good friend Unferth, addled with beer
Much have you made of the deeds of Breca!
I count it true that I had more courage,
More strength in swimming than any other man.
In our youth we boasted—we were both of us boys—
We would risk our lives in the raging sea.
And we made it good! We gripped in our hands
Naked swords, as we swam in the waves,

192 Unferth (un′fèrth), **Ecglaf's** (edj′lafs) **son.** Unferth's name can be interpreted as "Peacebreaker."

199 Breca (brek′ə), a friend of Beowulf's youth.

203 dissuade (di swād′), *v.* persuade not to do something.

15 ■ Unferth's role is a common one in epic poetry, that of the king's rude retainer who mocks the hero. What questions does this episode raise in your mind?

MINI-LESSON: GRAMMAR
Pronoun/Antecedent Agreement

Teach Remind students that pronouns must match or *agree with* their antecedents (the noun that the pronoun is replacing) in gender, (male, female, or neuter), person (first, second, or third), and number (one or many). In the sentence Joan did not expect anyone to beat her in the swim meet, *her* is a pronoun replacing the antecedent *Joan.* Point out that on page 9 of Beowulf there are four pronouns, but only one antecedent. What is the one antecedent? *(Hrothgar)* What is its gender? *(male)* What is its person? *(third)* What is its number? *(one)*

Activity Idea Have students fill in the following sentences with a pronoun to match its antecedent. Then ask them to identify the gender, person, and number of each.

- The members of the club proudly wore _______ epaulets. *(their)*
- "Helen and Anthony, _______ haven't got a chance to be voted 'most hard-working.'" *(you)*
- Gerald's hospitality was so ostentatious ____ made us feel that he was trying to prove something. *(he)*
- Amy admitted that _____ had hoped to get a full scholarship. *(she)*

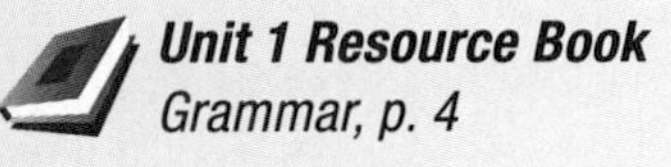

Unit 1 Resource Book
Grammar, p. 4

Guarding us well from the whales' assault.
In the breaking seas he could not outstrip me,
Nor would I leave him. For five nights long
16 Side by side we strove in the waters
Till racing combers wrenched us apart,
Freezing squalls, and the falling night,
And a bitter north wind's icy blast.
Rough were the waves; the wrath of the sea-fish
Was fiercely roused, but my firm-linked byrny,
The gold-adorned corselet that covered my breast,
Gave firm defense from the clutching foe.
Down to the bottom a savage sea-beast
Fiercely dragged me and held me fast
In a deadly grip; none the less it was granted me
To pierce the monster with point of steel.
Death swept it away with the swing of my sword.
"The grisly sea-beasts again and again
Beset me sore; but I served them home
With my faithful blade as was well-befitting. . . .
Fate often delivers an undoomed earl
If his spirit be gallant! And so I was granted
To slay with the sword-edge nine of the nicors.
I have never heard tell of more terrible strife
Under dome of heaven in darkness of night,
Nor of man harder pressed on the paths of ocean.
But I freed my life from the grip of the foe
Though spent with the struggle. The billows bore me,
The swirling currents and surging seas,
To the land of the Finns. And little I've heard
17 Of any such valiant adventures from you!" . . .

Beowulf Slays Grendel

In the hall as of old were brave words spoken,
There was noise of revel; happy the host
Till the son of Healfdene would go to his rest.
He knew that the monster would meet in the hall
Relentless struggle when light of the sun
Was dusky with gloom of the gathering night,
And shadow-shapes crept in the covering dark,
Dim under heaven. The host arose.
Hrothgar graciously greeted his guest,
Gave rule of the wine-hall, and wished him well,
Praised the warrior in parting words:
18 "Never to any man, early or late,
Since first I could brandish buckler and sword,

228 **combers,** waves.

231 **wrath,** (rath), *n.* great anger.

252 **Finns,** probably the Lapps, inhabitants of Finmarken, around the North Cape in the northern extremity of Norway and above the Arctic Circle.

256 **Healfdene** (hā′alf den ə), Hrothgar's father.

266 **brandish** (bran′dish), *v.* wave threateningly; flourish.

16 Literary Element
Archetype

Question How does the swimming match add to Beowulf's legend? *(No ordinary man could have stayed alive in the open sea, let alone kill fierce sea-beasts. Beowulf is again shown to possess attributes of the archetypal hero.)*

17 Reader's Response
Making Personal Connections

Question Who wins the battle of words—Beowulf or Unferth? *(Students will probably feel Beowulf bests Unferth: while his swimming match was youthful boasting, he did last seven nights in the open sea fighting off monsters. He finishes by taunting: "little I've heard of any such valiant adventure from you!")*

18 Reading/Thinking Skills
Recognize Values

Questions

- Does the poet/narrator approve of Beowulf? *(He describes Beowulf as brave and courageous.)*
- What values might the young in the poet's time have inferred from the epic? *(A man should be brave, adventurous, and despite dangers, help those in need.)*

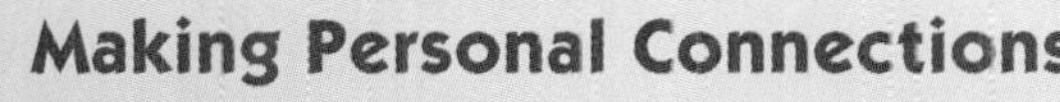

Making Personal Connections

Help students relate lines 192–253 to their own lives.

1. Review the situation: Unferth tries to make Beowulf look bad by bringing up an event from the past when Beowulf supposedly lost a swimming race.

2. Ask students how Beowulf beats Unferth at his own game. *(Beowulf adds to his reputation. After killing nine whales, he says, ocean currents carried him to Finland.)*

3. Ask students if they can think of a book, TV program, or movie in which a similar thing happened: when someone tried to make the hero look bad, the hero took advantage of the situation and looked better than ever. Students also might write or talk privately about a similar experience in their own life.

The World of Work

Police Officer

For a real-life struggle between good and evil, use the pages referenced below.

The World of Work
pp. 1–2

19 Reading/Thinking Skills
Draw Conclusions

Question Do you predict Beowulf will slay Grendel? Why or why not? *(Students may answer yes, based on Beowulf's heroic attributes and what they know of heroes. Others may answer no, considering that Grendel has slain many already, and Beowulf is going to fight with his bare hands.)*

20 Literary Element
Allegory

Some critics believe that *Beowulf* is an allegory—a narrative in which characters and actions represent abstract concepts—of the struggle between good and evil.

Questions

- Who or what represents evil? Why do you think so? *(Grendel—a vicious monster who eats his victims—about which the narrator has nothing good to say)*
- Who or what represents goodness? Why? *(Beowulf, who is fair, courageous, helpful, and ascribed with all the manly virtues)*

Have I trusted this ale-hall save only to you!
Be mindful of glory, show forth your strength,
Keep watch against foe! No wish of your heart
Shall go unfulfilled if you live through the fight."
Then Hrothgar withdrew with his host of retainers,
The prince of the Scyldings, seeking his queen,
The bed of his consort. The King of Glory
Had stablished a hall-watch, a guard against Grendel,
Dutifully serving the Danish lord,
The land defending from loathsome fiend.
The Geatish hero put all his hope
In his fearless might and the mercy of God!
He stripped from his shoulders the byrny of steel,
Doffed helmet from head; into hand of thane
Gave inlaid iron, the best of blades;
Bade him keep well the weapons of war.
Beowulf uttered a gallant boast,
The stalwart Geat, ere he sought his bed:
"I count myself nowise weaker in war
Or grapple of battle than Grendel himself.
Therefore I scorn to slay him with sword,
Deal deadly wound, as I well might do!
Nothing he knows of a noble fighting,
Of thrusting and hewing and hacking of shield,
Fierce as he is in the fury of war.
In the shades of darkness we'll spurn the sword
If he dares without weapon to do or to die.
And God in His wisdom shall glory assign,
The ruling Lord, as He deems it right."
Then the bold in battle bowed down to his rest,
Cheek pressed pillow; the peerless thanes
Were stretched in slumber around their lord. . . .
But the hero watched awaiting the foe,
19 Abiding in anger the issue of war.
From the stretching moors, from the misty hollows,
Grendel came creeping, accursed of God,
A murderous ravager minded to snare
Spoil of heroes in high-built hall.
20 Under clouded heavens he held his way
Till there rose before him the high-roofed house,
Wine-hall of warriors gleaming with gold.
Nor was it the first of his fierce assaults
On the home of Hrothgar; but never before
Had he found worse fate or hardier hall-thanes!
Storming the building he burst the portal,

284 ere, (er), *conj.* before.
303 ravager (rav′ij ər), *n.* destroyer.

Though fastened of iron, with fiendish strength;
Forced open the entrance in savage fury
And rushed in rage o'er the shining floor.
A baleful glare from his eyes was gleaming
Most like to a flame. He found in the hall
Many a warrior sealed in slumber,
A host of kinsmen. His heart rejoiced;
The savage monster was minded to sever
Lives from bodies ere break of day,
To feast his fill of the flesh of men.
But he was not fated to glut his greed
With more of mankind when the night was ended!
The hardy kinsman of Hygelac waited
To see how the monster would make his attack
The demon delayed not, but quickly clutched
A sleeping thane in his swift assault,
Tore him in pieces, bit through the bones,
Gulped the blood, and gobbled the flesh,
Greedily gorged on the lifeless corpse,
The hands and the feet. Then the fiend
stepped nearer,
Sprang on the Sea-Geat lying outstretched,
Clasping him close with his monstrous claw.
But Beowulf grappled and gripped him hard,
Struggled up on his elbow; the shepherd of sins
Soon found that never before had he felt
In any man other in all the earth
A mightier hand-grip; his mood was humbled,
His courage fled; but he found no escape!

21 ■ One unlucky thane is torn to pieces before Beowulf grapples with Grendel. Is this because of carelessness on Beowulf's part? If not, what might be the poet's intention here?

The Oseberg ship was a magnificent Viking vessel built in the 800s. It served as a royal barge before becoming the ship grave of a Norwegian queen. Before burial, the ship was loaded with elegant furniture, clothing, and other items that the queen would need in her royal afterlife. What does this Viking burial custom suggest about the Vikings' concept of life after death?

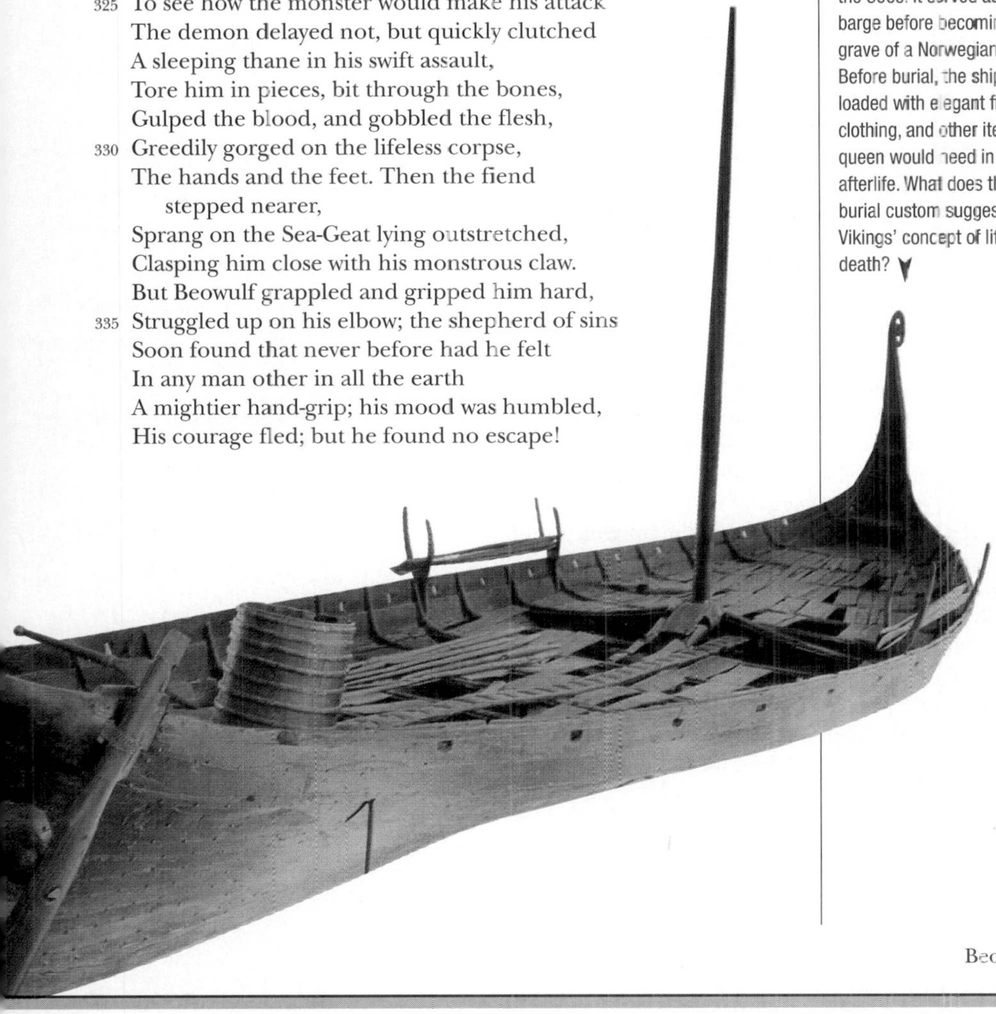

21 Reading/Thinking Skills
Infer

Response Students may feel that Beowulf was careless; his delay allowed Grendel to kill a thane. Others may feel that the narrator is building suspense, as well as showing the monster's speed and ferocity.

Art Study

Response to Caption Question The Vikings obviously believed in an afterlife in which earthly goods would come in handy. Otherwise they would not have buried a magnificent ship, furniture, clothing, and other items with the queen.

Between A.D. 700 and 1000, the Vikings (from the lands of present-day Norway, Sweden, and Denmark) were the most skilled boat builders and seamen in northern Europe. Their boats were built of overlapping wood planks and were double-ended: the stern looked the same as the bow. They were steered by an oar called a steerboard fixed to one side (hence our term "starboard").

BUILDING ENGLISH PROFICIENCY

ESL LEP ELD SAE LD

Interpreting Events Dramatically

This activity will help students visualize the confrontation between Beowulf and Grendel.

1. Invite volunteers to audition, in pairs, for the roles of Beowulf and Grendel.
2. Ask students to list Grendel's and Beowulf's actions on the chart at right. In the right column, have them list the student who, in their opinion, better performs each action.
3. Choose a student to direct the scene with the students who won the roles of Beowulf and Grendel.

Grendel	Beowulf	Better actor

22 Literary Focus
Alliteration

Questions

- Does the repeated "f" in lines 340–342 fall on accented or unaccented syllables? *(mainly on accented syllables)*
- How does the placement of the repeated "f" add to the sound of the poem? *(Possible response: The placement of f's on accented syllables give the lines a quality of being a pronouncement—Grendel is doomed and the listener hears it.)*

23 Historical Note
Hrothgar's Hall

Hrothgar's hall, Heorot, was a wooden, rectangular structure built somewhat like a barn. The walls were made of timber posts clamped with iron. Inside, around the walls were fixed benches, which by day served as seats and by night as beds. The entrance door was wide and high enough to admit a man on horseback. According to the poem, Heorot was "plated with gold"; tapestries woven with golden thread covered its walls. Archaeologists have uncovered a similar royal hall in present-day Northumberland, England.

22 He was fain to be gone; he would flee to the darkness,
The fellowship of devils. Far different his fate
From that which befell him in former days!
The hardy hero, Hygelac's kinsman,
Remembered the boast he had made at the banquet;
He sprang to his feet, clutched Grendel fast,
Though fingers were cracking, the fiend pulling free.
The earl pressed after; the monster was minded
To win his freedom and flee to the fens.
He knew that his fingers were fast in the grip
Of a savage foe. Sorry the venture,
23 The raid that the ravager made on the hall.
There was din in Heorot. For all the Danes,
The city-dwellers, the stalwart Scyldings,
That was a bitter spilling of beer!
The walls resounded, the fight was fierce,
Savage the strife as the warriors struggled.
The wonder was that the lofty wine-hall
Withstood the struggle, nor crashed to earth,
The house so fair; it was firmly fastened
Within and without with iron bands
Cunningly smithied; though men have said
That many a mead-bench gleaming with gold
Sprang from its sill as the warriors strove.
The Scylding wise men had never weened
That any ravage could wreck the building,
Firmly fashioned and finished with bone,
Or any cunning compass its fall,
Till the time when the swelter and surge of fire
Should swallow it up in a swirl of flame.
Continuous tumult filled the hall;
A terror fell on the Danish folk
As they heard through the wall the horrible wailing,
The groans of Grendel, the foe of God
Howling his hideous hymn of pain,
The hell-thane shrieking in sore defeat.
He was fast in the grip of the man who was greatest
Of mortal men in the strength of his might,
Who would never rest while the wretch was living,
Counting his life-days a menace to man.
Many an earl of Beowulf brandished
His ancient iron to guard his lord,
To shelter safely the peerless prince.
They had no knowledge, those daring thanes,
When they drew their weapons to hack and hew,

364 ween (wēn), *v.* suppose; believe.

367 compass (kum′pəs), *v.* plot; scheme.

369 swirl of flame, one of a number of references in the poem to the later burning of Heorot.

MINI-LESSON: SPEAKING AND LISTENING
Listening to Poetry

Teach *Beowulf* is part of an oral tradition; it was meant to be recited to a group of listeners. However, today's listeners don't often hear poetry recited aloud. Students may gain a greater appreciation and understanding of *Beowulf* by hearing parts of it read aloud.

Activity Idea Have students listen as you play the Audiotape or as you or a volunteer reads a section of the poem aloud. Ask students to compare and contrast the spoken and written versions:

- Do they hear rhythms they didn't notice when reading the poem silently?
- Do they hear repetition of phrases or epithets?
- Is the alliteration more noticeable?
- Is it easier or harder to follow the story?

Encourage students to continue to concentrate on the "sound" of the poem as they read the selection.

To thrust to the heart, that the sharpest sword,
The choicest iron in all the world,
Could work no harm to the hideous foe.
On every sword he had laid a spell,
On every blade; but a bitter death
Was to be his fate; far was the journey
The monster made to the home of fiends.
Then he who had wrought such wrong to men,
With grim delight as he warred with God,
Soon found that his strength was feeble and failing
In the crushing hold of Hygelac's thane.
Each loathed the other while life should last!
There Grendel suffered a grievous hurt,
A wound in the shoulder, gaping and wide;
Sinews snapped and bone-joints broke,
And Beowulf gained the glory of battle.
Grendel, fated, fled to the fens,
To his joyless dwelling, sick unto death.
He knew in his heart that his hours were numbered,
His days at an end. For all the Danes
Their wish was fulfilled in the fall of Grendel.
The stranger from far, the stalwart and strong,
Had purged of evil the hall of Hrothgar,
And cleansed of crime; the heart of the hero
Joyed in the deed his daring had done.
The lord of the Geats made good to the East-Danes
The boast he had uttered; he ended their ill,
And all the sorrow they suffered long
And needs must suffer—a foul offense.
The token was clear when the bold in battle
Laid down the shoulder and dripping claw—
Grendel's arm—in the gabled hall!

The Joy of the Danes

When morning came, as they tell the tale,
Many a warrior hastened to hall,
Folk-leaders faring from far and near
Over wide-running ways, to gaze at the wonder,
The trail of the demon. Nor seemed his death
A matter of sorrow to any man
Who viewed the tracks of the vanquished monster
As he slunk weary-hearted away from the hall,
Doomed and defeated and marking his flight
With bloody prints to the nicors' pool.
The crimson currents bubbled and heaved

24 Earlier (in lines 168–173 and again in lines 285–293), Beowulf has declared that he will use no weapons to fight Grendel. How does that **choice** contribute to his success and to his status as a hero among his people?

397 grievous (grē'vəs), *adj.* causing great pain or suffering; severe.

24 Multicultural Note
Heroic Stature

Response Although Beowulf was unaware of it, Grendel, under the protection of a spell, could not be slain by sword. Beowulf's decision to fight hand-to-hand allowed him to defeat Grendel and enhance his own stature as a great hero.

Literary Criticism

"The (governing theme of) *Beowulf* . . . is the old . . . heroic ideal . . . *sapientia et fortitudo* (wisdom and prowess). . . . His *fortitudo* [prowess] is obvious. His *sapientia* [wisdom] is variously illustrated by his skill and prudence in battle and a wisdom and foresight in the ways of violence generally; his skill in speech; his ability to predict accurately in his own and others' affairs; his respect for the counsels of the wise; his diplomatic ability; his realization of his dependence on higher powers; and by pagan Germanic standards, his properly high evaluation of glory."

R. E. Kaske
"The Governing Theme of Beowulf"
from Beowulf, *edited by Joseph F. Tuso*

BUILDING ENGLISH PROFICIENCY

Appreciating Language and Imagery

Staging a "Quaker reading" is one way to allow students to share phrases and word pictures that appeal to them.

1. As students read, ask them to jot down five to ten words, phrases, and images that catch their attention. There are no "right" or "wrong" choices; they may select anything that strikes them as interesting, vivid, or unusual. (Examples might include *woe of the world of men, gallant and great of heart,* and *swirling currents.*)

2. Afterward, ask students to stand and share their selections. Write responses on the chalkboard, especially responses that several students give. Point out that repeated choices indicate truly memorable language.

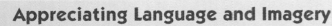

25 Literary Element
Symbolism

Response Grendel's hand has been hung from the roof as a battle trophy.

Question What might the cutting off of an evil character's hand suggest symbolically? *(Possible response: that evil, at least for the time being, had been "disarmed")*

26 Reading/Thinking Skills
Recognize Values

Questions

- How does Hrothgar reward Beowulf? What does this tell you about the values of the poet's era? *(Hrothgar states that he will treat Beowulf as a son and reward him with treasure. His speech indicates that family relationships were of great importance.)*
- To what power does Beowulf attribute his victory? What does this tell you about values during this era? *(Beowulf attributes his victory to "the favor of God," indicating that humility and reverence were important values.)*

In eddying reaches reddened with gore;
The surges boiled with the fiery blood.
But the monster had sunk from the sight of men.
In that fenny covert the cursed fiend
Not long thereafter laid down his life,
His heathen spirit; and hell received him.
        Then all the comrades, the old and young,
The brave of heart, in a blithesome band
Came riding their horses home from the mere.
Beowulf's prowess was praised in song;
And many men stated that south or north,
Over all the world, or between the seas,
Or under the heaven, no hero was greater,
More worthy of rule. But no whit they slighted
The gracious Hrothgar, their good old king. . . .
        Then spoke Hrothgar; hasting to hall
He stood at the steps, stared up at the roof
High and gold-gleaming; saw Grendel's hand:
"Thanks be to God for this glorious sight!
I have suffered much evil, much outrage from Grendel,
But the God of glory works wonder on wonder.
I had no hope of a haven from sorrow
While this best of houses stood badged with blood,
A woe far-reaching for all the wise
Who weened that they never could hold the hall
Against the assaults of devils and demons.
But now with God's help this hero has compassed
A deed our cunning could no way contrive.
Surely that woman may say with truth,
Who bore this son, if she still be living,
Our ancient God showed favor and grace
On her bringing-forth! O best of men,
I will keep you, Beowulf, close to my heart
In firm affection; as son to father
Hold fast henceforth to this foster-kinship.
You shall know not want of treasure or wealth
Or goodly gift that your wish may crave,
While I have power. For poorer deeds
I have granted guerdon, and graced with honor
Weaker warriors, feebler in fight.
You have done such deeds that your fame shall flourish
Through all the ages! God grant you still
All goodly grace as He gave before."
        Beowulf spoke, the son of Ecgtheow:
"By the favor of God we won the fight,

431 covert (kuv′ərt), *n.* hiding place.

435 blithsome (blīᴛʜ′səm), *adj.* happy and cheerful.

437 prowess (prou′is), *n.* bravery; daring.

25 ■ What happens to Grendel's hand?

466 guerdon (gėrd′n), *n.* reward.

Did the deed of valor, and boldly dared
The might of the monster. I would you could see
The fiend himself lying dead before you!
I thought to grip him in stubborn grasp
And bind him down on the bed of death,
There to lie straining in struggle for life,
While I gripped him fast lest he vanish away.
But I might not hold him or hinder his going
For God did not grant it, my fingers failed.
Too savage the strain of his fiendish strength!
To save his life he left shoulder and claw,
The arm of the monster, to mark his track. . . ."
Then slower of speech was the son of Ecglaf,
More wary of boasting of warlike deeds,
While the nobles gazed at the grisly claw,
The fiend's hand fastened by hero's might
On the lofty roof. Most like to steel
Were the hardened nails, the heathen's hand-spurs,
Horrible, monstrous; and many men said
No tempered sword, no excellent iron,
Could have harmed the monster or hacked away
The demon's battle-claw dripping with blood.
In joyful haste was Heorot decked
And a willing host of women and men
Gaily dressed and adorned the guest-hall.
Splendid hangings with sheen of gold
Shone on the walls, a glorious sight
To eyes that delight to behold such wonders.
The shining building was wholly shattered
Though braced and fastened with iron bands;
Hinges were riven; the roof alone
Remained unharmed when the horrid monster,
Foul with evil, slunk off in flight,
Hopeless of life. It is hard to flee
The touch of death, let him try who will;
Necessity urges the sons of men,
The dwellers on earth, to their destined place
Where the body, bound in its narrow bed,
After the feasting is fast in slumber.

This ferocious human mask is just one of the many intricate carvings that decorate a wooden cart found aboard the Oseberg ship (see pages 16–17). What might the mask suggest about the Viking view of human nature?

Art Study

Response to Caption Question
The mask suggests that the Vikings valued the more aggressive, warlike aspects of human nature.

Visual Literacy The Osberg cart, buried with the Osberg ship, may have been a hearse, a ceremonial carriage for carrying the dead; this usage suggests that the carved heads represented fierce warriors who would protect the person of the dead in an afterlife.

Check Test

1. Who is Grendel? *(a monster that has been attacking Hrothgar's people)*
2. Who is Beowulf? *(a hero who comes to fight Grendel)*
3. What happens at Heorot before Beowulf fights Grendel? *(Beowulf is welcomed by Hrothgar, and he and his men are honored with a feast.)*
4. How does Beowulf fight Grendel? *(with his bare hands)*
5. What is the outcome of the fight? *(Beowulf tears off Grendel's arm. The monster runs off and dies in a secret pool.)*

Unit 1 Resource Book
Alternate Check Test, p. 5

BUILDING ENGLISH PROFICIENCY

Summarizing a Character

Creating a "bio poem" will give students a summary of Beowulf's character and help them review the saga. Have them follow the pattern below.

Line 1: Hero's name
Line 2: Four words that describe him
Line 3: Three things that the hero enjoyed
Line 4: Three emotions that the hero felt
Line 5: One thing that the hero accomplished
Line 6: Hero's title (for example, Son of ________)

1. Beowulf
2. ________, ________, ________, ________
3. ________, ________, ________
4. ________, ________, ________
5. ________________________
6. Son of Ecgtheow

After Reading

MAKING CONNECTIONS

1. Students might say "yes," since Grendel is consistently portrayed as a demon, a monster, a man-eater. Those that disagree may feel that no creature, no matter how horrible, deserves to die.

2. Ratings should be based on examples of Beowulf's heroism or lack of heroism from the selection.

3. Due to a spell, no sword could harm Grendel. Thus, Beowulf's decision to use only his bare hands allows him to beat Grendel, as well as make his victory even more astonishing and heroic.

4. Possible response: The poet describes Grendel in horrible terms. He shows Grendel killing a man as Beowulf watches. He has Grendel and Beowulf struggle for awhile as other men jump into the fight before allowing Beowulf to triumph.

5. Possible responses: Grendel is called a "fiend from hell" and one of an evil brood of monsters. He can't be killed by a sword; he can bite through bones; and he has claws for hands.

6. Accept all reasonable responses. There are still many cultures that place a strong emphasis on family heritage and/or loyalty to a leader.

7. Possible responses: Some people like to be frightened; monsters represent some-thing universal to human beings, perhaps that we all have fears; over-coming the monster is a way of overcoming our fears.

After Reading

Making Connections

Shaping Your Response

1. Does Grendel get what he deserves? Does he deserve what he gets?
2. How heroic is Beowulf? Give him a heroism rating from 0% to 100%. Then explain your rating.

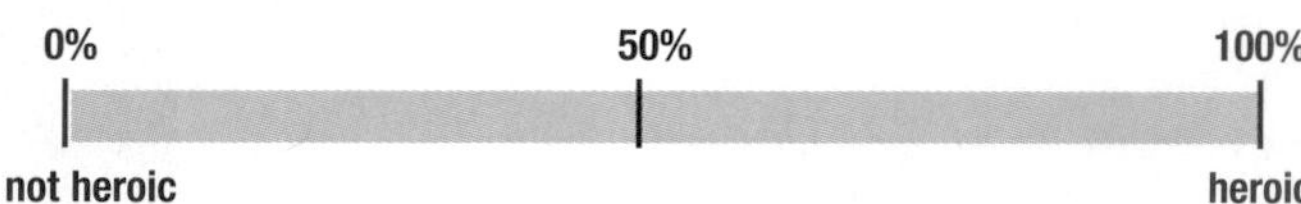

Analyzing the Epic Poem

3. Beowulf insists upon fighting Grendel without weapons. How does the way in which he fights the monster contribute to his success and increase his stature as a hero?
4. How does the poet build suspense throughout this episode?
5. Grendel has some traits that make him seem human, but in most respects he seems superhuman. What characteristics mark him as such?

Extending the Ideas

6. Throughout *Beowulf* there is emphasis on family heritage and on the importance of one's loyalties to a leader. Do the ancient Danes seem to be more concerned with these matters than other cultures you're familiar with—or less so?
7. Even today stories are told about monsters such as Big Foot and the Loch Ness monster that some people think might be real. What is it about monsters that is appealing? Do you find this appeal odd at the end of the 1900s? Why or why not?

Literary Focus: Alliteration

The repetition of sounds at the beginning of words or accented syllables is called **alliteration.** Which words alliterate in lines 87–90? in lines 150–155? Find some other alliterative passages in *Beowulf* and read them aloud. Do these passages make the lines more rhythmical? Do they make the meaning clearer?

Vocabulary Study

Match each lettered definition to the appropriate vocabulary word. You will not use all the definitions.

1. compass	a. persuade not to do something
2. dissuade	b. noisy partying
3. esteem	c. severe
4. gallant	d. great anger

LITERARY FOCUS: ALLITERATION

Responses Lines 87–90: tales/terrible; Grendel/great. Lines 150–155: courage/conflict; bloody/battle; five/foes; crushed/clan.

Students might focus on passages with a great deal of alliteration, such as lines 35–58. Review with students:

- Sounds repeat at the beginning of words or accented syllables.
- Alliteration creates rhythm in the poetry, giving it almost a musical feel.
- Alliteration also serves as a memory device for oral recitation.

As students read, they should keep in mind that the words were chosen not just to alliterate but to paint a picture in the listener's mind.

5.	grievous	**e.**	high regard
6.	peerless	**f.**	bravery
7.	prowess	**g.**	search for plunder
8.	prudent	**h.**	without equal
9.	revelry	**i.**	scheme
10.	wrath	**j.**	noble in spirit
		k.	sensible

Expressing Your Ideas

Writing Choices

Writer's Notebook Update Does Beowulf live up to the heroic qualities you recorded in your notebook before reading the selection? Make a list of the heroic traits Beowulf demonstrates and write a paragraph or two about his heroism. First define heroism and then describe Beowulf's different heroic characteristics. Support your ideas with examples from the poem.

A Night to Forget Imagine that you are a thane or a member of a thane's family in Hrothgar's court on a night when Grendel attacks. Write a **letter** to a friend or relative in another country about what happens. You might start by describing the mead-hall during the evening meal; next tell how you feel as you prepare for sleep. Then tell of Grendel's awful attack. How do you escape?

Reconstructing Grendel You're the person in charge of special effects for a filming of this first part of *Beowulf.* The poet is not very specific about what Grendel looks like, however. Write a **description** of the monster, taking into account where he lives, how he acts, and what descriptive details the poet does provide, to aid your crew in creating the creature. Don't forget to include colors and textures.

Other Options

Sutton Who? In 1939 archaeologists excavated a large burial mound on an English estate called Sutton Hoo. Here, in the hull of what had once been an eighty-five foot wooden ship, they uncovered the richest hoard of Anglo-Saxon objects ever found. No trace of a body was found, but the coins, silver, jewels, and other articles indicate that Anglo-Saxon culture was far more advanced than had previously been imagined. Do some **research** on this fabulous find at Sutton Hoo and **report** to the class.

Listen! Composers of music for films are skilled at creating mood. Find some **recorded music** that seems to suit at least part of the section of *Beowulf* that you have just read and play it for the class—perhaps as background music for an oral reading.

VOCABULARY STUDY

1. i. scheme
2. a. persuade not to do something
3. e. high regard
4. j. noble in spirit
5. c. severe
6. h. without equal
7. f. bravery
8. k. sensible
9. b. noisy partying
10. d. great anger

More Practice Students can suggest synonyms for each vocabulary word.

Unit 1 Resource Book
Vocabulary, p. 3
Vocabulary Test, p. 6

WRITING CHOICES

Writer's Notebook Update

Students might compare and contrast their ideas of a hero with Beowulf's heroic qualities in a chart such as this.

My Idea of a Hero	Beowulf's Traits
Fair	He only fights bad guys and monsters.
Strong	He stays afloat in the raging seas for a week; he is stronger than Grendel.
Kind	can't tell

Reconstructing Grendel

Visual learners might include a drawing or clay model of Grendel with their written descriptions.

OTHER OPTIONS

Sutton Who?

Suggest the following research tips:

- Many books on *Beowulf* include a description of Sutton Hoo.
- Sutton Hoo may be mentioned in books on medieval art and on archaeology in England.
- Post a question about Sutton Hoo on an Internet art or history board.

Listen!

Suggest that students

- locate early music recordings, especially music with a harp, such as a scop might have played
- find music that reflects the adventure and excitement in the poem

Selection Test

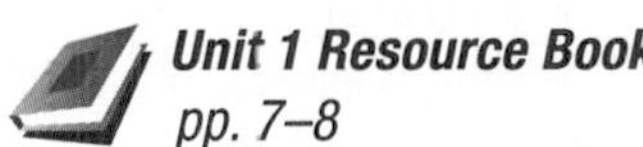

Unit 1 Resource Book
pp. 7–8

Before Reading

Building Background

Students might discuss what they know about ballads or folk songs and/or about musical lyrics.

Literary Focus

As students read the following ballads, suggest they

- watch for repeated lines and refrains, noticing how they affect each work
- compare and contrast the effect of repetition between the three ballads

Writer's Notebook

Students' ideas might include athletic feats, accidents, courageous acts, funny happenings, crimes, or exciting explorations or discoveries.

More About Ballads

- A ballad is a narrative song that usually contains a simple but dramatic story often told through dialogue.
- Literary ballads, written in the style of a folk ballad, include Keats's "La Belle Dame Sans Merci" (which students will read on page 423) and Coleridge's "The Rime of the Ancient Mariner."

Before Reading

Folk Ballads

Balladeers

Most early ballads were composed by anonymous musicians or entertainers. As generations of ballad singers passed their songs on, they added or dropped verses and changed details, such as names of people and places. Sometimes details were changed to please certain audiences and sometimes because a singer forgot or garbled some of the words. In the 1700s, hundreds of immigrants from the British Isles to America brought their ballads with them to Virginia, North Carolina, and the Appalachian Mountain region. They made further changes. For example, in the version of "Edward" included here, a hawk and a horse are mentioned. In an American version they have been changed to a grey mare and a coon dog. In the Scottish "Lord Randal," he bequeathes hell and fire to hislove. In one American version, he leaves a rope to hang her. In effect, then, anyone who sings (and alters) a ballad is a composer.

Building Background

Nobleman Poisoned! In many ways, folk ballads served as the tabloid newspapers of their day. Ballad content is usually sensational, frequently criminal, often romantic, and occasionally supernatural. Drownings, poisonings, hangings, and hauntings are standard ballad fare, and "Lord Randal" and "Edward" are both about murders. Outlaws such as Robin Hood and unhappy—often tragic—love affairs figure prominently. Comic ballads, although few in number, usually deal with domestic disagreements.

Literary Focus

Repetition Words, sounds, phrases, or whole lines are often repeated throughout a ballad. This **repetition** is used for melodic effect, to provide emphasis, to unify parts of the ballad, or to build suspense. For example, the first three lines of each stanza of "Lord Randal" are similar. The mother's question changes from "O where ha' you been?" in line 1 to "And wha met you there?" in line 5. This **incremental repetition,** the repetition of lines that contain some small additions or increments, is used to advance the story and build to a climax. The repetition of lines at the end of each stanza is called a **refrain.** Use a chart such as the following to help you analyze the repetition in these three ballads.

Ballad	Words and Phrases	Lines and Refrains
Lord Randal		
Edward		
Get Up and Bar the Door		

Writer's Notebook

Heard Any Good Stories? What makes a good topic for a ballad? Almost anything, provided there's a good story involved. Think of sensational stories you have read or heard about. Jot down a few ideas for ballads in your notebook.

SUPPORT MATERIALS OVERVIEW

Unit 1 Resource Book

- Graphic Organizer, p. 9
- Study Guide, p. 10
- Vocabulary, p. 11
- Grammar, p. 12
- Alternate Check Test, p. 13
- Vocabulary Test, p. 14
- Selection Test, pp. 15–16

Building English Proficiency

- Selection Summaries
- Activities, p. 206

Reading, Writing & Grammar SkillBook

- Reading, p. 22–25

Technology

- Audiotape
- Writer's Notebook Software
- Custom Literature Database: For other selections dealing with Getting Even, see "The Demon Lover" and "Clementine" on the database.
- Test Generator Software

Lord Randal

1

"O where ha' you been, Lord Randal my son?
And where ha' you been, my handsome young man?"
"I ha' been at the greenwood; Mother, make my bed soon,
For I'm wearied wi' hunting and fain wad lie down."

"And wha met you there, Lord Randal my son?
And wha met you there, my handsome young man?"
"O I met wi' my true-love; Mother, make my bed soon,
For I'm wearied wi' hunting and fain wad lie down."

"And what did she give you, Lord Randal my son?
And what did she give you, my handsome young man?"
"Eels fried in a pan; Mother, make my bed soon,
For I'm wearied wi' hunting and fain wad lie down."

"And wha gat your leavins, Lord Randal my son?
And wha gat your leavins, my handsome young man?"
"My hawks and my hounds; Mother, make my bed soon,
For I'm wearied wi' hunting and fain wad lie down."

"And what becam of them, Lord Randal my son?
And what becam of them, my handsome young man?"
"They stretched their legs out and died; Mother, make my bed soon,
For I'm wearied wi' hunting and fain wad lie down."

"O I fear you are poisoned, Lord Randal my son,
I fear you are poisoned, my handsome young man."
"O yes, I am poisoned; Mother, make my bed soon,
For I'm sick at the heart and fain wad lie down."

"What d'ye leave to your mother, Lord Randal my son?
What d'ye leave to your mother, my handsome young man?"
"Four and twenty milk kye; Mother, make my bed soon,
For I'm sick at the heart and fain wad lie down."

"What d'ye leave to your sister, Lord Randal my son?
What d'ye leave to your sister, my handsome young man?"
"My gold and my silver; Mother, make my bed soon,
For I'm sick at the heart and fain wad lie down."

"What d'ye leave to your brother, Lord Randal my son?
What d'ye leave to your brother, my handsome young man?"

1 ha', have.

4 wearied . . . down, wearied with hunting, and gladly would lie down. *Down* is pronounced in the Scottish manner (dūn) to rhyme with *soon.*

5 wha, who.

11 eels . . . pan, a method of poisoning that appears in many old ballads.

13 wha . . . leavins, who ate the food you didn't eat?

17 becam, became.

27 kye, cows.

During Reading

Selection Objectives

- to read, then compare and contrast, folk ballads
- to examine the poetic effects of repetition
- to examine the use of dialogue to explicate emotions and conflicts
- to analyze how spelling changes over time and examine homophones

Unit 1 Resource Book
Graphic Organizer, p. 9
Study Guide, p. 10

Theme Link

All three ballads reflect the Getting Even theme: on his death bed, Lord Randall curses his true love; Edward damns his own mother; the husband and wife in "Get Up and Bar the Door" go to extremes to get even.

1 Literary Focus
Repetition

Questions

- What phrases repeat in each stanza throughout the ballad? *(first line: "Lord Randal my son"; second line: "my handsome young man"; third line: "Mother, make my bed soon"; fourth line: "and fain wad lie down")*
- After Stanza 5, the last line changes to "For I'm sick at the heart and fain wad lie down." Why do you think this change occurs? *(He reveals that he has been poisoned; thus, he no longer acts as if he were merely tired from hunting.)*

SELECTION SUMMARY

Lord Randal; Edward; Get Up and Bar the Door

Lord Randal The first ballad relates a conversation between a nobleman and the mother to whom he has returned after being poisoned by his true love.

Edward The second ballad dramatizes another mother/son conversation; Edward has just slain his father, apparently after being manipulated into the act by his mother.

Get Up and Bar the Door This comic ballad tells of a couple who are willing to endure housebreakers rather than be the first to speak after a fight.

*For summaries in other languages, see the **Building English Proficiency** book.*

2 Literary Focus
Repetition

Question How is repetition used to build suspense in "Edward"? *(Possible response: Edward's mother questions him three times about the blood on his sword and his sadness. The first two times he puts her off by saying that he has killed first his hawk, then his horse. Finally he admits he has murdered his father. The mother's repeated questions build suspense regarding what or whom Edward really has killed.)*

3 Reading/Thinking Skills
Compare and Contrast

Suggest students make a Venn diagram to compare and contrast "Lord Randal" and "Edward."

Possible response

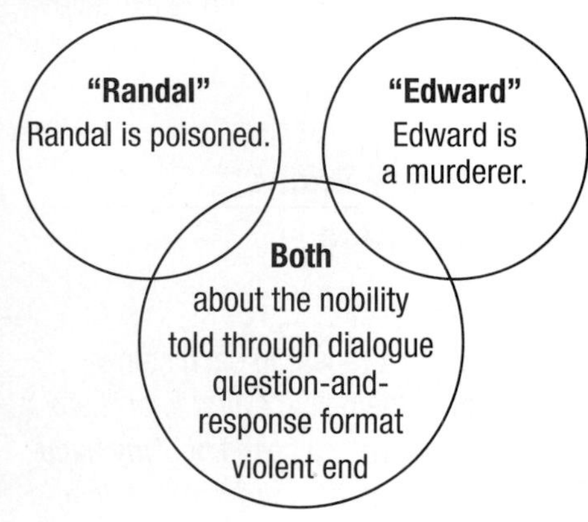

"My houses and my lands; Mother, make my bed soon,
For I'm sick at the heart and fain wad lie down."

"What d'ye leave to your true-love, Lord Randal my son?
What d'ye leave to your true-love, my handsome young man?"
"I leave her hell and fire; Mother, make my bed soon,
For I'm sick at the heart and fain wad lie down." 

During the medieval period, the hunt was an important and beloved pastime of the nobility. In this idyllic scene, serfs are shown grooming their lord's hunting dogs. How do the peace and tranquillity of this scene contrast with the events described in these three folk ballads? ➤

Edward

2 "Why dois your brand sae drap wi bluid,
Edward, Edward,
Why dois your brand sae drap wi bluid,
And why sae sad gang yee O?"
"O I hae killed my hauke sae guid,
Mither, mither,
O I hae killed my hauke sae guid,
And I had nae mair bot hee O."

"Your haukis bluid was nevir sae reid,
Edward, Edward,
Your haukis bluid was nevir sae reid,
My deir son I tell thee O."
"O I hae killed my reid-roan steid,
Mither, mither,
O I hae killed my reid-roan steid,
That erst was sae fair and frie O."

"Your steid was auld, and ye hae gat mair,
Edward, Edward,
Your steid was auld, and ye hae gat mair,
Sum other dule ye drie O."
"Oh I hae killed my fadir deir,
Mither, mither,
O I hae killed my fadir deir,
Alas, and wae is mee O!"

"And whatten penance wul ye drie for that,
Edward, Edward,
And whatten penance wul ye drie for that?
3 My deir son, now tell me O."

1 dois . . . bluid, does your sword so drip with blood.
4 gang yee, go you.
5 hae . . . guid, have killed my hawk so good.
6 Mither, Mother.
8 nae . . . hee, no more but him.
9 haukis . . . reid, hawk's blood was never so red.
12 deir, dear.
13 reid-roan steid, red-roan horse. "Red-roan" means a red coat mottled with white or grey.
16 erst . . . frie, once was so fair and free.
17 auld, old.
17 mair, more.
20 sum . . . drie, some other sorrow you suffer.
21 fadir, father.
24 wae, woe. "Woe is me" is a traditional expression for "I am greatly troubled or saddened."
25 whatten penance, what kind of penance. A penance is any act done to show that one is sorry for wrongdoing.

MINI-LESSON: GRAMMAR
Homophones

Teach Remind students that a ***homophone*** is one of two or more words that share the same sound but differ in meaning, spelling, and origin. For example, the words *sum* and *some* are homop hones.

Activity Idea Have students write the words that form homophones with the following. Answers are in italics.

adds *and* ________ (a tool) *(adz)*
born *and* ________ (carried, endured) *(borne)*
cruel *and* ________ (a handicraft) *(crewel)*
dyer *and* ________ (dreadful) *(dire)*
hear *and* ________ (at this place) *(here)*
four *and* ________ (toward the front) *(fore)*
gall *and* ________ (ancient name for France) *(Gaul)*
hail *and* ________ (healthy) *(hale)*
might *and* ________ (tiny amount) *(mite)*
knot *and* ________ (nothing) *(naught)*
laps *and* ________ (a slip or decline) *(lapse)*

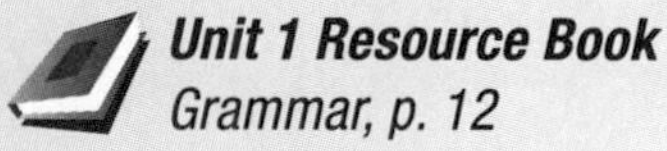
Unit 1 Resource Book
Grammar, p. 12

Art Study

Response to Caption Question The tranquil scene stands in stark contrast to the murderers and thieves that populate these three ballads.

Visual Literacy In medieval times, illuminated manuscripts, from which this detail is taken, were the leading form of painting in northern Europe. The Bible was the most frequently illustrated manuscript, but prayer books and calendars were hand-decorated for the nobility as well.

Question What settings come to mind as you look at this art? *(While responses will vary, settings will most likely be agrarian.)*

BUILDING ENGLISH PROFICIENCY

Exploring Dialect

Decoding the dialect in "Edward" will give some students a chance to share strategies that they have developed as they have grown in English.

1. Divide the class into small groups, making sure that each includes at least one English-proficient student.

2. Play the Audiotape to illustrate the dialect of "Edward." Then have each group decipher one verse.

3. Ask each group to share the strategies that helped them figure out the meaning. Encourage students to become "expert consultants" in decoding an unfamiliar language.

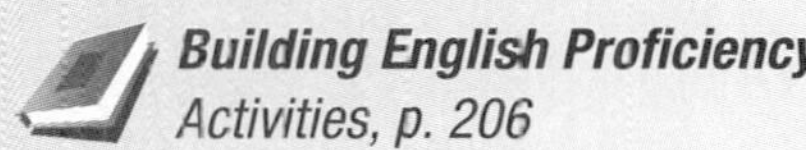

Building English Proficiency
Activities, p. 206

4 Reading/Thinking Skills
Draw Conclusions

Questions Why does Edward curse his mother in the last lines of the ballad? *(Either his mother urged him to kill his father, or she set his mind against his father so that he felt he had to kill him. In either case, he obviously hates her now that the deed is done.)*

5 Reader's Response
Making Personal Connections

In medieval poetry, time is often reckoned by intervals before, between, or after Christian holidays.

Invite students to share holidays they celebrate. Are these holidays cultural, political, religious, or personal in origin? *(Possible responses shown in chart.)*

Religious holidays	Christmas, All Souls' Day, Rosh Hashanah, Hanukkah, Easter
Cultural holidays	Thanksgiving, Kwanzaa, New Year's, Mother's Day, Halloween, Valentine's Day
Political holidays	Memorial Day, Fourth of July, el Cinqo de Mayo, Labor Day, Martin Luther King Day
Personal holidays	birthdays, anniversaries

"Ile set my feit in yonder boat,
Mither, mither,
Ile set my feit in yonder boat,
And Ile fare ovir the sea O."

"And what wul ye doe wi your towirs and your ha,
Edward, Edward,
And what wul ye doe wi your towirs and your ha,
That were sae fair to see O?"
"Ile let thame stand tul they doun fa,
Mither, mither,
Ile let thame stand tul they doun fa,
For here nevir mair maun I bee O."

"And what wul ye leive to your bairns and your wife,
Edward, Edward,
And what wul ye leive to your bairns and your wife,
Whan ye gang ovir the sea O?"
"The warldis room, late them beg thrae life,
Mither, mither,
The warldis room, late them beg thrae life,
For thame nevir mair wul I see O."

"And what wul ye leive to your ain mither deir,
Edward, Edward,
And what wul ye leive to your ain mither deir?
My deir son, now tell me O."
"The curse of hell frae me sall ye beir,
Mither, mither,
4 The curse of hell frae me sall ye beir,
Sic counseils ye gave to me O."

29 Ile . . . feit, I'll set my feet.

32 fare ovir, go over.

33 doe . . . ha, do with your towers and your hall.

37 thame . . . fa, them stand till they fall down.

40 maun, must.

41 leive . . . bairns, leave to your children.

45 warldis . . . life, world is room (large enough); let them beg through life.

49 ain, own.

53 frae . . . beir, from me shall you bear.

56 sic counseils, such counsels (advice).

Get Up and Bar the Door

5 It fell about the Martinmas time,
And a gay time it was then,
When our goodwife got puddings to make,
And she's boild them in the pan.

The wind sae cauld blew south and north,
And blew into the floor;
Quoth our goodman to our goodwife,
"Gae out and bar the door."

1 Martinmas time, Martinmas is a church festival that falls on November 11 and honors St. Martin.
3 puddings, sausages.
5 cauld, cold.
8 gae, go
8 bar the door, that is, set the wooden bar across the door so that it cannot blow open or be opened by anyone from outside.

MINI-LESSON: LITERARY FOCUS
Repetition

Teach Repetition is an important sound device in ballads. It serves to organize and structure lyrics, as well as increasing melodic effect. Repeated phrases or lines can build suspense and provide emphasis.

Question Folk ballads were sung and passed on orally; they were rarely written down until this century. How might repetition serve as a memory device for the singer? *(The repetition of refrains and other lines at given points in each stanza means the singer need only memorize the refrain and other repeated lines once. This greatly reduces the total amount the singer must commit to memory.)*

Activity Idea Divide students into three groups and assign a ballad to each group. Ask each group to

- find several examples of repetition in its assigned ballad
- analyze how the repetition adds to the ballad's effect
- report the group's findings to the class

"My hand is in my hussyfskap,
Goodman, as ye may see;
An it shoud nae be barrd this hundred year,
It's no be barrd for me."

They made a paction tween them twa,
They made it firm and sure,
That the first word whaeer shoud speak,
6 Shoud rise and bar the door.

Then by there came two gentlemen,
At twelve o clock at night,
And they could neither see house nor hall,
Nor coal nor candlelight.

"Now whether is this a rich man's house,
Or whether is it a poor?"
But neer a word wad ane o them speak,
For barring of the door.

And first they ate the white puddings,
And then they ate the black;
Tho muckle thought the goodwife to hersel,
Yet neer a word she spake.

Then said the one unto the other,
"Here, man, tak ye my knife;
Do ye tak aff the auld man's beard,
And I'll kiss the goodwife."

"But there's nae water in the house,
And what shall we do than?"
"What ails ye at the pudding-broo,
That boils into the pan?"

O up then started our goodman,
An angry man was he:
"Will ye kiss my wife before my een,
And scad me wi pudding-bree?"

Then up and started our goodwife,
Gied three skips on the floor:
"Goodman, you've spoken the foremost word,
7 Get up and bar the door."

9 hussyfskap (hus′if skap), *n.* housewife's work.
11 an . . . nae, if it should not.
12 no . . . for, not going to be barred by.
13 paction . . . twa, pact, or agreement, between the two of them.
15 whaeer, whoever.

23 neer . . . ane, never a word would any (either the goodwife or the goodman).

25 they, that is, the "two gentlemen."

27 tho muckle, though much.
28 spake, spoke.

31 aff, off.

35 ails . . . pudding-broo, why can't you use the hot broth in which the sausages are cooking.

39 een, eyes.
40 scad, scald.

42 gied, gave.

6 Literary Focus
Repetition

Question What examples of repetition can you find in "Get Up and Bar the Door"? *(The last line is frequently a variation on the title:*
- *line 8—Gae out and bar the door*
- *line 16—rise and bar the door*
- *line 24—for barring of the door*
- *line 44—Get up and bar the door)*

7 Reader's Response
Making Personal Connections

Encourage students to discuss the emotions and feelings these ballads evoke. Ask students to explain whether or not the ballads were what they expected and to describe their original expectations and how the ballads compared to these.

Check Test

1. What happened to Lord Randal? *(He was poisoned by his true love.)*
2. How does Edward's mother know something has happened? *(His sword is dripping with blood, and he seems sad.)*
3. What did Edward do? Why did he do it? *(He murdered his father, apparently because of his mother's advice.)*
4. Why don't the man and his wife speak to the two gentlemen? *(They're fighting and have agreed that whoever speaks first will have to bar the door.)*
5. Why is the wife so happy at the end of the ballad? *(Her husband has spoken first, so he must bar the door.)*

Unit 1 Resource Book
Alternate Check Test, p. 13

BUILDING ENGLISH PROFICIENCY

Analyzing Humor

Help students understand that this funny poem, like much comedy throughout the ages, derives some of its humor from an unfunny situation. You may want to discuss the following questions.

- What seems to be the poet's view of marriage? *(presumably negative)*
- What danger faces the couple just before the climax of the story? How does this make the poem funny? *(He is about to be scalded; she is to be kissed; each would rather face harm than give in to the other.)*
- Where have you seen this same "unfunny" view of marriage or danger used to make people laugh? *(movies and particularly situation comedy on TV)*

After Reading

MAKING CONNECTIONS

1. Students' responses will vary but will probably be based on emotions evoked by one of the works.

2. "Get Up and Bar the Door." Ballads told through dialogue, which read more like plays, have a more immediate effect. The narrated ballad, which reads more like an anecdote or short story, is more removed.

3. Possible response: The mother receives milk cows, which she could use for milk, food, or cash as she ages; the sister receives gold and silver, which she could use either as a dowry or for her family; the brother receives the house and land, since only men could inherit land at this time; the true-love is damned to the fires of hell, since she is a murderess.

4. Possible response: either Edward's mother either urged him to kill his father or set Edward's mind against his father so that he felt he had to kill him.

5. The wife and her husband are more concerned about winning the pact than in protecting themselves from intruders. When the man finally yells at the intruders, she is pleased only because he's lost the pact.

6. Possible responses: that his mother drove him to kill his father or that she made him temporarily insane with anger. Answers will vary as to whether or not Edward is guilty, based on how much credence they give his probable defense.

7. Students might point out that married couples (or anyone in a long-term relationship) continue to have silly arguments in which they lose sight of the big picture.

After Reading

Making Connections

Shaping Your Response

1. These ballads are fairly typical of the tragic and comic ballads of the British Isles. Which of these three ballads appeals to you most? Why?

Analyzing the Folk Ballads

2. The story in a ballad can be told through narration or through **dialogue.** In which ballad is the story told mainly through narration? Compare the effect with that of the ballads told through dialogue.
3. The legacies or "testaments" that Lord Randal leaves to various people are another element that appears in many folk ballads. Explain how each legacy seems appropriate to the person Lord Randal leaves it to.
4. The listener is not told what "counseils," or advice, Edward's mother gave him. What do you think it might have been, based on information in the ballad?
5. What is **ironic** about the situation and the ending in "Get Up and Bar the Door"?

Extending the Ideas

6. If Edward appeared today in a court of law, what do you think his defense might be? What are his chances at being judged guilty or not guilty?
7. Does the kind of argument the goodwife and goodman get into in "Get Up and Bar the Door" have any counterpart in today's culture? Explain.

Literary Focus: Repetition

Repetition is a literary technique in which words, lines, phrases, and sounds are repeated. Repetition of lines that contain some small additions or increments is called **incremental repetition;** repetition of whole lines at the end of stanzas is called **refrain.** Point out several examples of the use of repetition in "Get Up and Bar the Door" or "Edward." What is the chief effect of the repetition in each ballad? To provide emphasis? unity? suspense?

LITERARY FOCUS: REPETITION

If students made charts as they read the ballads, they might refer to them now (see p. 24). Suggest they focus on the refrain in "Get Up and Bar the Door" and the repetition of lines in "Edward." They will probably note that the incremental repetition in the refrain of "Get Up and Bar the Door" provides emphasis, unity, and suspense. The repetition of lines in "Edward" provides emphasis and suspense but doesn't add much to the unity, since the lines change each time.

Remind students that

- repetition creates a rhythmic effect, necessary for musical lyrics
- repetition, like alliteration, serves as a memory device for oral recitation

Expressing Your Ideas

Writing Choices

Writer's Notebook Update Choose one of the story ideas you jotted down and think about how the story could be developed. List the major characters, actions, secrets to be revealed, and so on.

I Write the Songs Try writing a **ballad** of from three to five stanzas based on a comic or a tragic story. Follow the style of one of the ballads you have just read. Before you start, it may help you to list some words, phrases, and lines that you want to repeat for various effects.

Inquiring Minds Want to Know If a tabloid newspaper story could be a ballad, why can't a ballad be a **newspaper story?** Take another look at "Lord Randal" and decide why he was poisoned by his true-love. Was he unfaithful? Was she? Was there another reason? Write the story in newspaper style, using your imagination to fill in names, places, and so on. Explain the reason for this crime and how you, as a reporter, found out the truth.

Other Options

Class Balladeer Find a book or a recording of old ballads and **perform** or **play** some of them for the class. There are hundreds of these old songs available; in addition to those imported from England and other countries, many were created by balladeers in the Appalachian mountains, on the western frontier, and in other parts of the country.

Instrumental Instruction In this painting by the Italian painter Simone Martini (1284–1344), the musicians are playing a double flute and a mandola, a larger variety of a mandolin. Find some drawings or paintings of other early musical instruments and show them as part of a **talk on early instruments.** You may not be able to bring any early instruments to class, but you might bring modern instruments and demonstrate how they differ.

WRITING CHOICES

Writer's Notebook Update

Students can refer to the entries they made while they were reading the three ballads. They might find it helpful to organize their ideas for stories on a simple story map such as this:

- main characters
- problem/secrets
- action
- resolution

I Write the Songs

Some students might find it easier to write a ballad if they set the lyrics to a melody they know.

Inquiring Minds Want to Know

Point out that the typical newspaper story is constructed in the shape of an upside-down pyramid:

Most Important Information
Next Most Important Information
Additional Information

Selection Test

Unit 1 Resource Book
pp. 15–16

Transparency Collection
Fine Art Writing Prompt 1

OTHER OPTIONS

Class Balladeer

To research folk ballads, students might look for the work of ethnomusicologists, such as Alan Lomax, who traveled the United States in the early part of this century recording and transcribing the music of the people.

Instrumental Instruction

Suggest the following research tips:

- Locate books on musical instruments, such as *Music* by Neil Ardley (Knopf, 1989), which provides photos and descriptions of many instruments, from 40,000-year-old whistles to the shawm, a reed instrument from medieval times.
- Call the music department of a local college and ask if they have specialists in early and/or Renaissance music on staff.

Interdisciplinary Study

Theme Link

Art is a way of expressing and dealing with reactions to a world both evil and good. In creating a face for the devil or other evil beings the artist may hope to evoke fear or dread, may try to explore some reasons for evil, or may make evil more human and therefore more able to be appeased, controlled, or avenged.

MULTICULTURAL CONNECTION

The world's peoples are generally agreed on what constitutes evil. According to one comparative study of religions, evil is basically pain and death. Pain can be experienced as disease, injury, fear, and so on. The causes of evil are sometimes attributed to divine action, sometimes to human sin, and sometimes to both.

Terms to Know

Kali, in Hinduism, a goddess personifying creation and destruction.

Medusa, in classical mythology, one of the three Gorgons, sisters who are all represented as having snakes for hair. Medusa was killed by Perseus, a son of Zeus.

Pegasus, in classical mythology, a winged horse created from Medusa's blood.

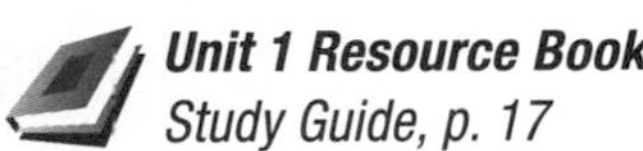

Unit 1 Resource Book
Study Guide, p. 17

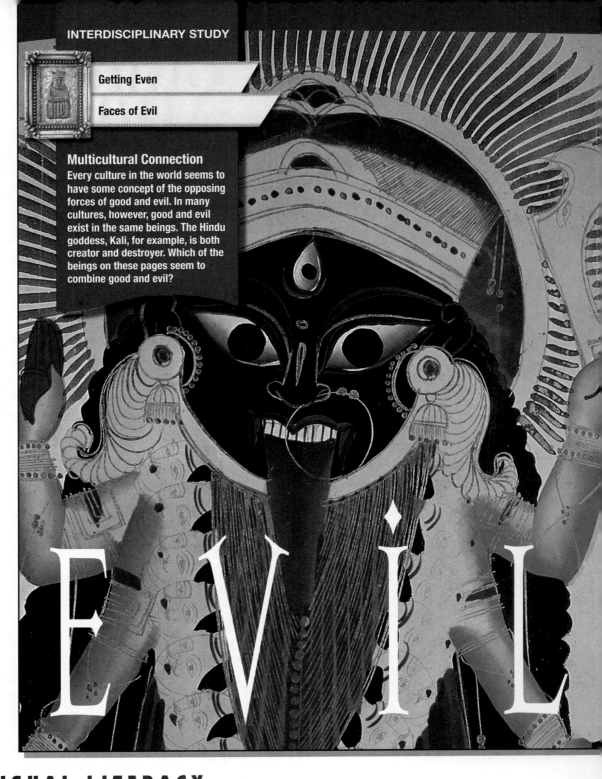

INTERDISCIPLINARY STUDY

Getting Even

Faces of Evil

Multicultural Connection

Every culture in the world seems to have some concept of the opposing forces of good and evil. In many cultures, however, good and evil exist in the same beings. The Hindu goddess, Kali, for example, is both creator and destroyer. Which of the beings on these pages seem to combine good and evil?

EVIL

MINI-LESSON: VISUAL LITERACY

Compare and Contrast

Teach Though the masks and sculptures on pages 32–33 were created by artists from widely separated cultures, they all depict a similar idea. Explain to students that a deeper understanding of cultural beliefs can sometimes come through comparing various artistic treatments of the same idea.

Apply Have students compare and contrast the three depictions of evil on pages 32–33.

Activity Ideas

- Have students brainstorm specific attributes that accompany images of evil, i.e., horns, cloven hooves, fangs.
- Lead a discussion as to how images of evil could be used to help ward off evil.

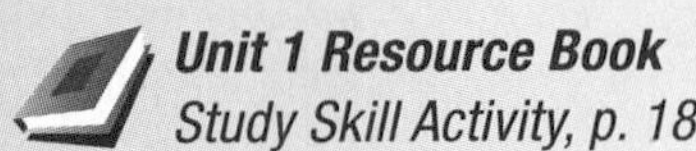

Unit 1 Resource Book
Study Skill Activity, p. 18

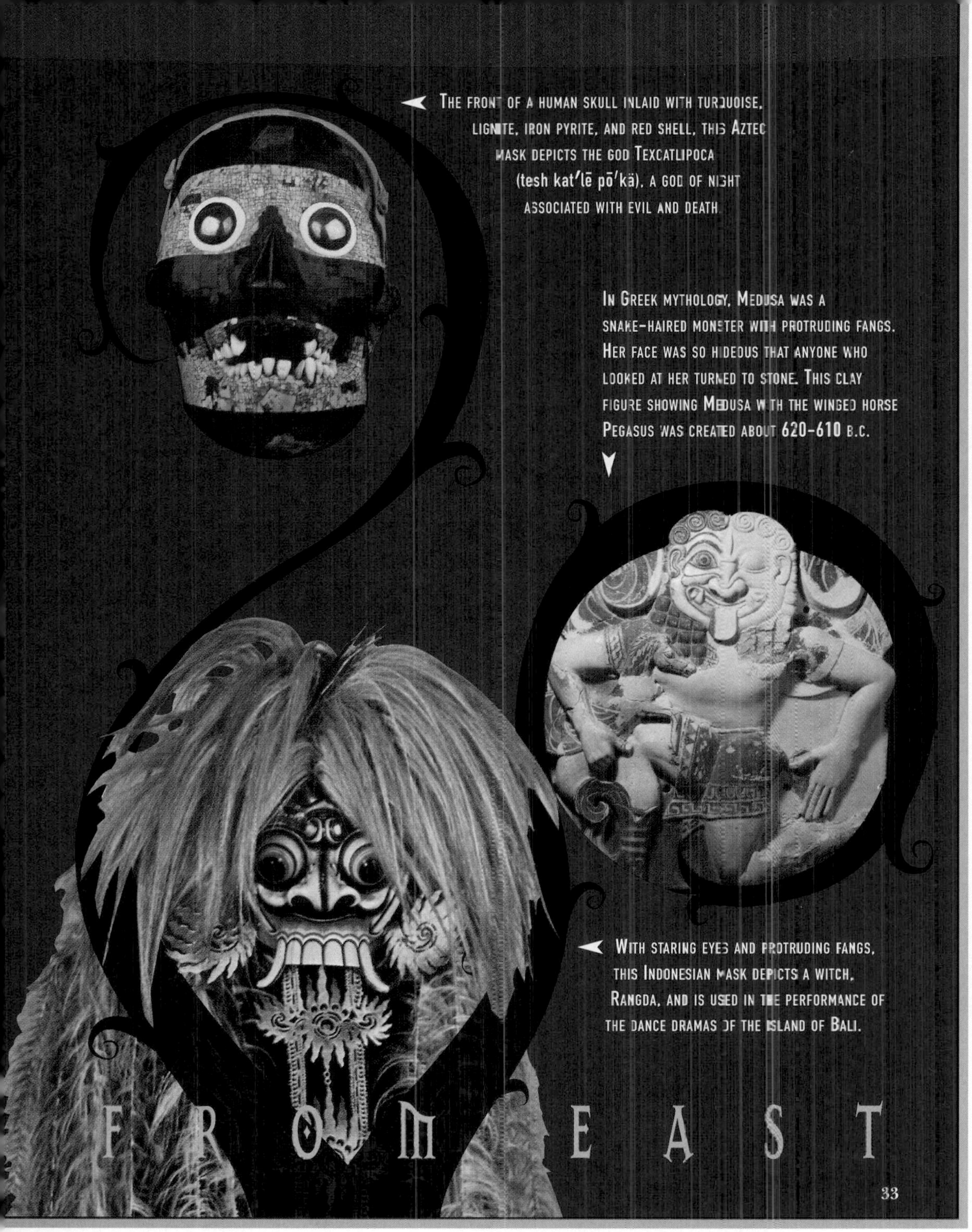

THE FRONT OF A HUMAN SKULL INLAID WITH TURQUOISE, LIGNITE, IRON PYRITE, AND RED SHELL, THIS AZTEC MASK DEPICTS THE GOD TEXCATLIPOCA (tesh kat'lē pō'kä), A GOD OF NIGHT ASSOCIATED WITH EVIL AND DEATH.

IN GREEK MYTHOLOGY, MEDUSA WAS A SNAKE-HAIRED MONSTER WITH PROTRUDING FANGS. HER FACE WAS SO HIDEOUS THAT ANYONE WHO LOOKED AT HER TURNED TO STONE. THIS CLAY FIGURE SHOWING MEDUSA WITH THE WINGED HORSE PEGASUS WAS CREATED ABOUT 620–610 B.C.

WITH STARING EYES AND PROTRUDING FANGS, THIS INDONESIAN MASK DEPICTS A WITCH, RANGDA, AND IS USED IN THE PERFORMANCE OF THE DANCE DRAMAS OF THE ISLAND OF BALI.

FROM EAST

33

Art Study

Masks of many types are found in cultures around the world. People often act out relations with the spirit world through dances and ceremonial rituals in which the dancer disguises him or herself with elaborate masks and costumes. The origin of these dance rituals goes back as far as 10,000 B.C., and there is evidence that animal disguises were worn then.

The image of the Hindu goddess is an eighteenth-century miniature painting.

The Aztec god Tezcatlipoca, one of the creator gods, was both a single god and four gods in one. Although he was associated with death and destruction, he was eternally young, omnipotent, and could give or take life.

Indonesian masks for dance drama are made of wood or painted leather. They usually have protruding fangs and staring eyes and are elaborately adorned. This Indonesian mask is from the nineteenth century.

Question What is the purpose of Halloween, Mardi Gras, or other types of masks in American culture? Is the purpose to frighten? disguise? cause laughter? *(Students can probably make a case for all three reasons.)*

BUILDING ENGLISH PROFICIENCY

Exploring Key Concepts

Throughout history, masks have been used to portray various emotions and feelings. Students who understand why and how masks are used will be more adept at deciphering their meanings.

Activity Ideas

- Bring in books that deal with masks and share with students.
- Have students draw rough sketches of masks that could be used to portray emotions such as fear, happiness, disappointment.
- Use actual masks to discuss figurative masks—that is, to explore ways in which people often present an appearance that disguises their true thoughts and feelings.

Art Study

The art of glass painting is very old, and there are stained glass cathedral windows in Germany and France dating from the eleventh and twelfth centuries. Most early ecclesiastical stained glass windows are pictorial and illustrate biblical stories, incidents involving saints, or a theological point. The subject matter evolved in part because most of the populace could not read.

Martin Schongauer (c. 1430–1491) was a German painter and engraver and a member of an Augsburg family of artists. He settled in Colmar, Alsace, where he worked as an engraver of religious scenes. St. Anthony (A.D. 251?–366?) was an Egyptian hermit.

Visual Literacy Since in most medieval thought, the universe was the scene of an endless duel between good and evil, medieval artists and craftsmen put a frightening face on evil, partly as a deterrent; images of the devil and hell were meant to keep believers on the narrow path.

Question How might the depiction of St. Anthony here be a lesson for the medieval viewer? *(Possible response: His calm resistance to the demons tormenting him might be seen as the ideal response to the temptations of daily life.)*

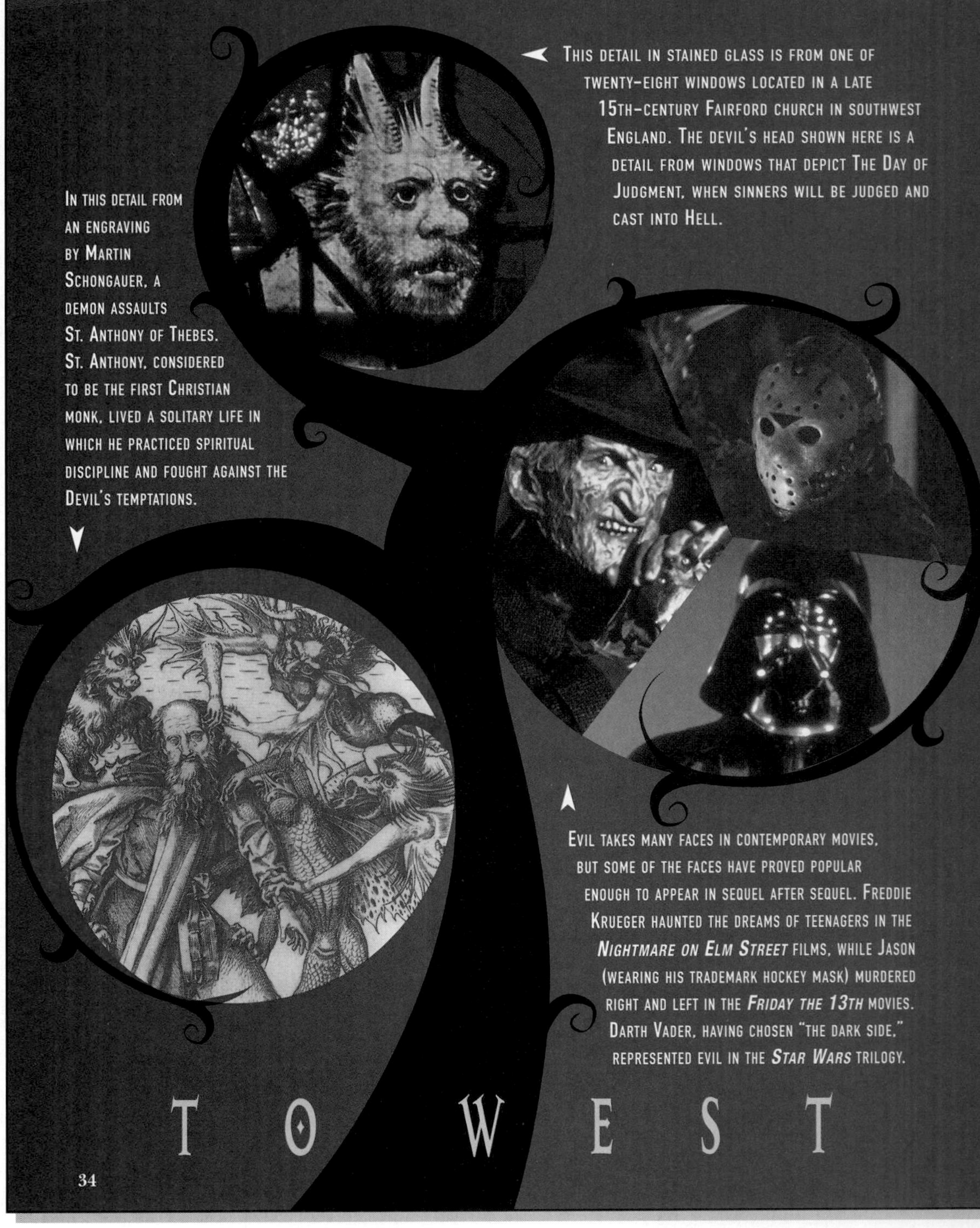

THIS DETAIL IN STAINED GLASS IS FROM ONE OF TWENTY-EIGHT WINDOWS LOCATED IN A LATE 15TH-CENTURY FAIRFORD CHURCH IN SOUTHWEST ENGLAND. THE DEVIL'S HEAD SHOWN HERE IS A DETAIL FROM WINDOWS THAT DEPICT THE DAY OF JUDGMENT, WHEN SINNERS WILL BE JUDGED AND CAST INTO HELL.

IN THIS DETAIL FROM AN ENGRAVING BY MARTIN SCHONGAUER, A DEMON ASSAULTS ST. ANTHONY OF THEBES. ST. ANTHONY, CONSIDERED TO BE THE FIRST CHRISTIAN MONK, LIVED A SOLITARY LIFE IN WHICH HE PRACTICED SPIRITUAL DISCIPLINE AND FOUGHT AGAINST THE DEVIL'S TEMPTATIONS.

EVIL TAKES MANY FACES IN CONTEMPORARY MOVIES, BUT SOME OF THE FACES HAVE PROVED POPULAR ENOUGH TO APPEAR IN SEQUEL AFTER SEQUEL. FREDDIE KRUEGER HAUNTED THE DREAMS OF TEENAGERS IN THE ***NIGHTMARE ON ELM STREET*** FILMS, WHILE JASON (WEARING HIS TRADEMARK HOCKEY MASK) MURDERED RIGHT AND LEFT IN THE ***FRIDAY THE 13TH*** MOVIES. DARTH VADER, HAVING CHOSEN "THE DARK SIDE," REPRESENTED EVIL IN THE ***STAR WARS*** TRILOGY.

T O W E S T

MINI-LESSON: STUDY SKILLS

Scanning for Information

Teach When researching a particular topic, such as demons in medieval art, students might need to read through a great deal of information to find the pertinent sections. Remind them that they can scan for the particular information in which they are interested. Scanning titles, heads, captions, words in italics or boldface type, and illustrations are all ways to zero in on specific information. Once they find a key word such as "demons," they should then stop and read the information.

Activity Idea Ask students to scan a book or magazine article for a particular piece of information. You might consider making this a timed activity, perhaps five or ten minutes. They can follow these steps:

- Narrow the search by using the index, chapter headings, or section headings.
- Scan for captions, words in italics or boldface, or illustrations related to the topic.
- Scan for particular words, names, or dates related to the topic.
- Read the relevant sections and jot down a few sentences about what they find.

What if the story of Beowulf were told from the point of view of the monster Grendel?

I touch the door with my fingertips and it bursts, for all its fire-forged bands—it jumps away like a terrified deer—and I plunge into the silent, hearth-lit hall with a laugh that I wouldn't much care to wake up to myself. I trample the planks that a moment before protected the hall like a hand raised in horror to a terrified mouth (sheer poetry, ah!) and the broken hinges rattle like swords down the timbered walls. The Geats are stones, and whether it's because they're numb with terror or stiff from too much mead, I cannot tell. I am swollen with excitement, bloodlust and joy and a strange fear that mingle in my chest like the twisting rage of a bone-fire. I step onto the brightly shining floor and angrily advance on them. They're all asleep, the whole company! I can hardly believe my luck and my wild heart laughs, but I let out no sound. Swiftly, softly, I will move from bed to bed and destroy them all, swallow every last man. I am blazing, half-crazy with joy. For pure, mad prank, I snatch a cloth from the nearest table and tie it around my neck to make a napkin. I delay no longer.

I seize up a sleeping man, tear at him hungrily, bite through his bone-locks and suck hot, slippery blood. He goes down in huge morsels, head, chest, hips, legs, even the hands and feet. My face and arms are wet, matted. The napkin is sopping. The dark floor steams, I move on at once and I reach for another one (whispering, whispering, chewing the universe down to words), and I seize a wrist. A shock goes through me. Mistake!

It's a trick! His eyes are open, were open all the time, cold-bloodedly watching to see how I work. The eyes nail me now as his hand nails down my arm. I jump back without thinking (whispering wildly: *jump back without thinking*). Now he's out of his bed, his hand still closed like a dragon's jaws on mine. Nowhere on middle-earth, I realize, have I encountered a grip like his. My whole arm's on fire, incredible, searing pain—it's as if his crushing fingers are charged like fangs with poison. I scream, facing him, grotesquely shaking hands—dear long-lost brother, kinsman-thane—and the timbered hall screams back at me. I feel the bones go, ground from their sockets, and I scream again. I am suddenly awake. The long pale dream, my history, falls away. The meadhall is alive, great cavernous belly, gold-adorned, bloodstained, howling back at me, lit by the flickering fire in the stranger's eyes. He has wings. Is it possible? And yet it's true: out of his shoulders come terrible fiery wings. I jerk my head, trying to drive out illusion. The world is what it is and always was. That's our hope, our chance. Yet even in times of catastrophe we people it with tricks. Grendel, Grendel, hold fast to what is true!

Suddenly, darkness. My sanity has won. He's only a man; I can escape him. I plan. I feel the plan moving inside me like thaw-time waters rising between cliffs. When I'm ready, I give a ferocious kick—but something's wrong: I am spinning—*Wa!*—falling through bottomless space—*Wa!*—snatching at the huge twisted roots of an oak...a blinding flash of fire...no, darkness. I concentrate. I have fallen! Slipped on blood. He viciously twists my arm behind my back. By accident, it comes to me, I have given him a greater advantage. I could laugh. *Woe, woe!*

And now something worse. He's whispering—spilling words like showers of sleet, his mouth three inches from my ear. I will not listen. I continue whispering. As long as I whisper myself I need not hear. His syllables lick at me, chilly fire. His syllables lick at me, chilly fire. His syllables lick at me, chilly fire. His syllables lick . . .

Responding

1. What details in the story change with this shift of point of view? Does Grendel seem to recognize how much a monster he appears to humans? How does he react to the humans' attitude?

2. Which of the faces on pages 32-34 seems to you most truly evil? Why?

Background Information

Grendel by John Gardner retells the Beowulf story, but from the monster's point of view. Grendel compares his values with those of human beings and suggests that his values are better. While both humans and monsters kill, Grendel at least eats his kill. He is sickened by "the waste of it all they killed—cows, horses, men—they left to rot or burn." The difference, according to Grendel, was that men such as Hrothgar had poets to turn their deeds into a story, which Grendel felt "was all lies."

Responding

1. Possible response Details reveal what it feels like to be Grendel; the monster considers Beowulf's strategies to be tricks; Grendel also describes the incredible pain of Beowulf's grasp.

2. Possible response No; he seems to look on the humans as prey and so does not consider how he appears to them. Too late, he realizes that one of the Geats was only pretending to sleep, which he considers a "trick."

BUILDING ENGLISH PROFICIENCY

Exploring Point of View

In this selection, part of *Beowulf* is retold from the point of view of the monster. Understanding this shift in perspective will help students with their reading and their own writing.

1. Have students pick a familiar story, fable, or fairy tale with several characters.

2. In small groups or pairs, have students rewrite the story using other possible points of view. For example, they might tell Little Red Riding Hood from the point of view of the wolf.

3. As volunteers read the stories aloud, analyze the changes that occur with each new point of view.

Writing Workshop

WRITER'S BLUEPRINT

Specs

The Specs in the Writer's Blueprint address these writing and thinking skills:

- comparing and contrasting
- using specific examples
- quoting from literature
- making generalizations
- keeping to the main idea
- clarifying pronoun references

These Specs serve as your lesson objectives, and they form the basis for the **Assessment Criteria Specs** for a superior paper, which appear on the final TE page for this lesson. You might want to read through the Assessment Criteria Specs with students when you begin the lesson.

Linking Literature to Writing

Discuss what it means to be heroic. Reading the blueprint together will help focus the discussion. Develop with students a working definition of heroism based on Beowulf's qualities. Encourage them to keep this definition in mind as they choose a modern hero and develop their own definition of heroism based on their ideas and experiences.

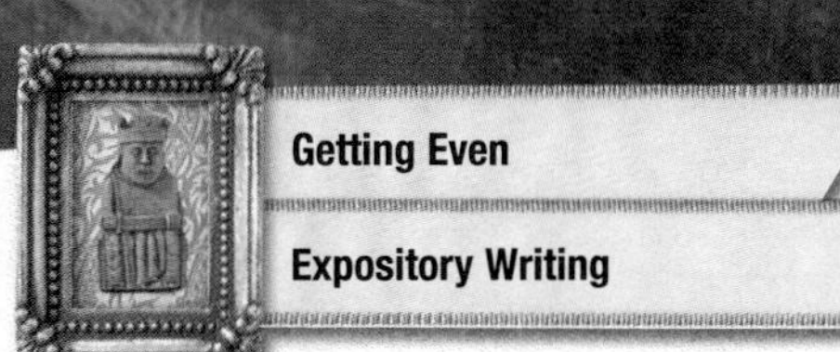

Writing Workshop

Heroes Old and New

Assignment How has the concept of the hero changed since the time when *Beowulf* was written? Write an essay in which you answer this question.

WRITER'S BLUEPRINT

Product	An interpretive essay
Purpose	To explore the concept of the hero
Audience	People who have read *Beowulf*
Specs	To write a successful, essay you should:

- ❑ Choose a modern fictional hero from books, movies, or television, or a real-life hero from recent history, to compare and contrast with Beowulf.
- ❑ Begin your essay in a dramatic manner that shows the two heroes in action and identifies your purpose for writing.
- ❑ Go on to compare and contrast your heroes in terms of three of the aspects of comparison listed below, using a clear comparison-contrast organization. Include specific examples of both heroes' words and actions to support your comparisons and contrasts, including quotations from literature where appropriate.

Aspects of comparison: —the worlds in which the heroes exist—the obstacles they must overcome—the resources, physical and mental, that they must rely on to overcome these obstacles—the weaknesses that make them vulnerable to their enemies—the qualities of character that make them heroes—other aspects of your own choosing

- ❑ Conclude by answering the question: How has the concept of the hero changed since the time when ***Beowulf*** was written?
- ❑ Write focused paragraphs that each keep to one main idea.
- ❑ Follow the rules of grammar, usage, spelling, and mechanics, including correct pronoun reference.

The instructions that follow are designed to lead you to a successful essay.

WRITING WORKSHOP OVERVIEW

Product
Expository writing: Interpretive Essay

Prewriting
Brainstorm to find fictional heroes—Diagram ideas for comparison—Choose the three best aspects—Plan your essay—Ask a partner
Unit 1 Resource Book
Prewriting Worksheets pp. 19–20

Drafting
Refer to your plan
Transparency Collection
Student Models for Writing Workshop 1, 2

Revising
Ask a partner—Strategy: Keeping to the Main Idea
Unit 1 Resource Book
Revising Worksheet p. 21

Editing
Ask a partner—Strategy: Clarifying Pronoun References
Unit 1 Resource Book
Grammar Worksheet p. 22
Grammar Check Test p. 23

Presenting
Videotape Presentation
Poster

Looking Back
Self-evaluate—Reflect—For Your Working Portfolio
Unit 1 Resource Book
Assessment Worksheet p. 24
Transparency Collection
Fine Art Writing Prompt 1

STEP 1 PREWRITING

Brainstorm to find fictional heroes to pair with Beowulf. Working with a group, make a list of modern characters that your group sees as heroic. Try to include a wide variety of characters from books, movies, and television. Then choose the person you'll be comparing and contrasting with Beowulf.

Diagram ideas for comparison. Draw a Venn diagram like the one that follows. Label each circle with the heroes' names. Then make notes about them based on the aspects of comparison listed in the Blueprint. Where the circles intersect, write about what the two heroes have in common. In the outer part of the two circles, write what is unique to Beowulf and to your modern hero.

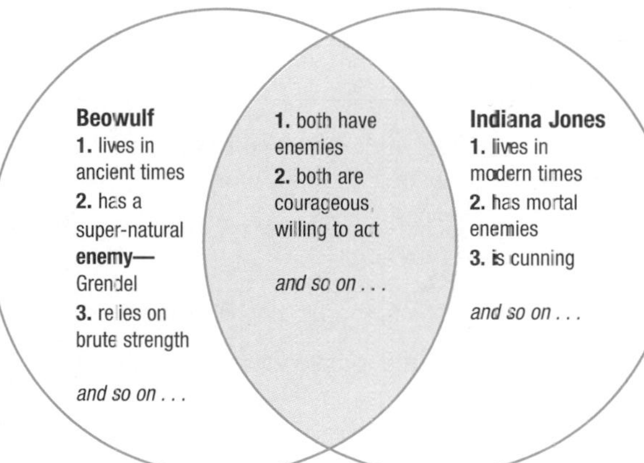

OR . . .
Instead of fictional heroes, use real people from recent history or someone you know personally whom you see as heroic. Consider moral courage and leadership as well as physical bravery.

LITERARY SOURCE
Grim and greedy the gruesome monster,
Fierce and furious, launched attack,
Slew thirty spearmen asleep in the hall,
Sped away gloating, gripping his spoil,
Dragging the dead men home to his den.
from Beowulf
(*lines* 54–58)

Choose the three best aspects for comparison from your Venn diagram—the aspects that best illustrate the similarities and differences between your two heroes. These are the aspects you'll use to compare and contrast them. Note specific examples of each aspect you chose. Look for specific things your heroes and their friends and foes do and say to illustrate each aspect.

Plan your essay. On the next page are two methods for organizing a comparison–contrast essay. Choose the method you feel more comfortable with. Use the information you gathered in prewriting to help you make notes on each bulleted point.

BUILDING ENGLISH PROFICIENCY

Exploring Key Concepts

As groups choose their heroes, they may find the following activities useful.

Activity Ideas

- Have the class brainstorm to complete a three-column chart. Ask them to consider heroic *Qualities* (for example, *brave* and *dedicated*), *Locations* where heroes are found (such as *battlefields* or *hospitals*), and *Careers* that might be considered heroic (*firefighting* or *surgery*, for example).
- Ask students to think of real-life heroes whom they admired while they were growing up or whom they still admire today. These might include famous people or people they have known personally.

STEP 1 PREWRITING

Brainstorm to find fictional heroes

Help students get off to a good start by asking the class for a few ideas about heroic characters. List their ideas on the board. Elicit a range of characters from movies, books, television, and real life. Ask for reasons why each character should be included on the list. For additional support, see the worksheet referenced below.

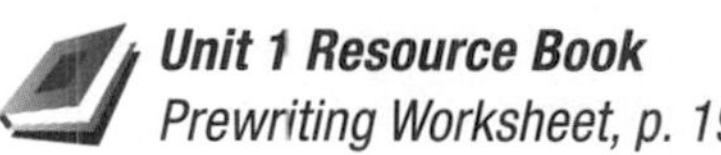

Unit 1 Resource Book
Prewriting Worksheet, p. 19

Diagram ideas for comparison

Remind students that they need to use three of the aspects of comparison as stated in the blueprint. Encourage them to address as many of these aspects as possible while developing their Venn diagrams.

Choose the three best aspects

Give students the following criteria to help them choose aspects for comparison:

1. the most striking difference or similarity
2. the most characteristic aspect of one or both heroes
3. the details that are the most relevant to heroism

For additional support, see the worksheet referenced below.

Unit 1 Resource Book
Prewriting Worksheet, p. 20

Plan your essay

Discuss the differences between Method 1 and Method 2 at the top of the next page. Help students see that Method 1 focuses on each character, and Method 2 focuses on the aspects. Encourage students to choose the method that they think will work best for their essay. Stress to students that time spent on this step will help the drafting stage go more smoothly.

Ask a partner (Peer assessment)

As students review one another's plans, suggest that they refer to the applicable organizational method (Method 1, Method 2, or one of their own) to check whether the organization is clear and consistent throughout.

Connections to **Writer's Notebook**

For selection-related prompts, refer to Writer's Notebook.

Connections to **Writer's Resource**

For additional writing prompts, refer to Writer's Resource.

STEP 2 DRAFTING

Refer to your plan

Have students review their organizational plans carefully before beginning. Have them return to the literature or their notes to fill in missing information or to supply supportive details. Point out that the drafting tips and comparison/contrast words will help them as they draft.

The Student Model

The **transparencies** referenced below are authentic student models. Review them with students before they draft. These questions will help:

1. Did the writer of model 1 begin by showing the heroes in action and stating a purpose for writing?
2. Did the writer of model 2 conclude by answering this question: How has the concept of the hero changed since the time when *Beowulf* was written?

Transparency Collection
Student Models for Writing Workshop 1, 2

OR . . .
Use your own method for planning, whatever works for you. Just make sure it addresses the points in the Writer's Blueprint.

Method 1	Method 2
Introduction • Beowulf in action • The modern hero in action • My purpose for writing	**Introduction** • Beowulf in action • The modern hero in action • My purpose for writing
Body: Discuss one at a time • Beowulf: Heroic aspect 1 . . . Examples . . . Heroic aspect 2 . . . Examples . . . Heroic aspect 3 . . . Examples . . . • Modern Hero: Heroic aspect 1 . . . Examples . . . Heroic aspect 2 . . . Examples . . . Heroic aspect 3 Examples . . .	**Body: Compare/contrast as you go** • Aspect 1 Beowulf . . . .Examples . . . Modern hero . . .Examples . . . • Aspect 2 Beowulf . . .Examples . . . Modern hero . . .Examples . . . • Aspect 3 Beowulf . . . .Examples . . . Modern hero . . .Examples . . .
Conclusion • How the concept of the hero has (has not) changed since Beowulf was written)	**Conclusion** • How the concept of the hero has (has not) changed since Beowulf was written

Ask a partner to look over your plan before you draft. Use these questions as a guide.

✔ Do I have enough specific examples of my heroes' words and actions to illustrate each aspect?

✔ Am I following the Specs in the Writer's Blueprint?

Use your partner's comments to help you revise your plan.

STEP 2 DRAFTING

Refer to your plan as you draft. Here are some drafting tips you might use.

- You don't have to draft the introductory paragraph first. Some writers prefer to write the body first, and then write the introduction and conclusion.
- When you draft the body, use words like these to help make your comparisons and contrasts:

  Comparison: both, and, like, same, similar, in the same way, alike
  Contrast: while, unlike, on the other hand, different, but, yet, instead

MINI-LESSON: WRITING STYLE

Keeping to the Main Idea

Teach Point out that the revised student model focuses on just one main idea: Both heroes were resourceful. Next, have students read the deleted sentences. Ask, *What might the topic sentence be in a new paragraph that uses the deleted information?* Have students write a new paragraph using the deleted information.

Activity Idea Write the sentence "Heroism does not necessarily mean physical bravery" on the board. Have students work in groups to write a paragraph that supports this main idea. Then ask a member of each group to read aloud his or her paragraph while other classmates listen for the information that successfully focuses on this single idea.

Apply Have students reread their essays and underline (or boldface on the computer) the main idea in each paragraph. If there are paragraphs for which the main idea is not clearly laid out, they should add a main idea sentence. Then have them reread to make sure that all sentences in each paragraph support the main idea.

STEP 3 REVISING

Ask a partner for comments on your draft before you revise it.

✔ Have I followed the Specs in the Writer's Blueprint?

✔ Have I begun in a dramatic way and made my purpose clear?

✔ Have I used specific examples for my three aspects of comparison?

Revising Strategy

Keeping to the Main Idea

An essay is usually more convincing when each paragraph is focused on a single idea. If a paragraph mixes up two main ideas—especially if the writer hasn't planned this—the result can be confusing.

In the Student Model the paragraph as first drafted mixes up two main ideas (resources and worlds). Based on a partner's comment, the writer revised the paragraph so that it now deals with resources only.

COMPUTER TIP
As you revise, **boldface the main idea** of each paragraph. Then you can easily glance back to the main idea to make sure each sentence focuses on it. Remove this boldface when you make your final copy.

Is this about worlds or resources?

Beowulf and Indiana Jones used the resources they had to get out of sticky situations. ~~They also existed in different worlds.~~ For example, Beowulf relied on his strength when he attacked Grendel to defend the innocent. Indiana Jones relied on his intelligence to find a way out of a sealed chamber full of poisonous snakes. ~~On the other hand, Beowulf existed in an ancient world while Indiana Jones lived in the early 1900s.~~

STEP 4 EDITING

Ask a partner to review your revised draft before you edit. When you edit, look for errors in grammar, usage, spelling, and mechanics. Look especially for unclear pronoun references.

MINI-LESSON: GRAMMAR

Clarifying Pronoun Reference

Write the following sentences on the board. Ask students to determine whether the referents of the pronouns are clear. If not, ask them to suggest corrections.

1. Sword in one hand and olive branch in the other, Stinger made a choice to defend the kingdom with it as best as he could. (*it* could be the sword or the olive branch)

2. The difference between heroes of today and heroes of long ago is that they have flaws in their characters. (*they* could be the heroes of today or of long ago)

3. When monsters outnumber heroes, they will no longer be a problem. (*they* could be the monsters or the heroes)

4. The virtues of a hero are his or her greatest asset. (clear)

Unit 1 Resource Book
Grammar Worksheet, p. 22
Grammar Check Test, p. 23

STEP 3 REVISING

Ask a partner (Peer assessment)

Tell students that as they review their partner's draft, their main role is to alert the writer to problems by giving clear, specific comments, and that they should not try to correct the problems themselves. Remind students to use the Specs at the beginning of this lesson as a checklist for reviewing the draft.

Revising Strategy: Keeping to the Main Idea

Have students close their eyes and listen as you read the student model aloud first without the revisions and then with the revisions. Discuss how removing irrelevant details improved the passage and helped the paragraph stick to a single, clear main idea. Ask students if this paragraph could have been revised any other way.

For additional support, see the mini-lesson at the bottom of page 38 and the worksheet referenced below.

Unit 1 Resource Book
Revising Worksheet, p. 00

Connections to **Writer's Resource**

Refer to the Grammar, Usage, and Mechanics Handbook on Writer's Resource.

STEP 4 EDITING

Ask a partner (Peer assessment)

Suggest that students review each other's drafts twice: first for general problems with grammar, usage, spelling, and mechanics; and secondly to look specifically at the clarity of pronoun references.

Editing Strategy: Clarifying Pronoun References

For additional support, see the mini-lesson at the bottom of page 39 and the worksheets referenced below.

Unit 1 Resource Book
Grammar Worksheet, p. 22
Grammar Check Test, p. 23

Connections to **Writer's Resource**

Refer to the Grammar, Usage, and Mechanics Handbook on Writer's Resource.

STEP 5 PRESENTING

Videotape Presentation

Have students choose a short, information-packed video clip to impress upon them how much visual and aural information is available in a brief amount of time.

Poster

Students might want to turn their Venn diagrams into posters.

STEP 6 LOOKING BACK

Self-evaluate

The *Assessment Criteria Specs* at the bottom of this page are for a superior paper. You might want to post these in the classroom. Students can then evaluate themselves based on these criteria. For a complete scoring rubric, use the *Assessment Worksheet* referenced below.

Unit 1 Resource Book
Assessment Worksheet, p. 24

Reflect

Suggest that students first brainstorm ideas that come to mind as they read each question, and then formulate responses based on one or several of these ideas.

To further explore the theme, use the Fine Art Transparency referenced below.

Transparency Collection
Fine Art Writing Prompt 1

Editing Strategy

FOR REFERENCE
For more help on pronoun reference, see the Language and Grammar Handbook at the back of this text.

Clarifying Pronoun References

Pronouns like *he, she, they,* and *it* can be confusing if you fail to make clear which person, object, or idea the pronoun refers to.

Reference unclear When the enemy faced the hero on the bridge *he* shook with terror.

Somebody shook, but was it the hero or the enemy? Here are two ways to clear up the problem.

Substitute a noun When the enemy faced the hero on the bridge, *the enemy* shook with terror.

Change the word order The enemy shook with terror as he faced the hero on the bridge.

Search your draft for these kinds of problems with pronouns.

STEP 5 PRESENTING

Try these ideas as you read your essay aloud:

- If you chose a hero from a television show or movie, show videotaped clips of her or him in action.
- Make a poster to illustrate the similarities and differences between your two heroes and use it as a graphic aid as you present.

STEP 6 LOOKING BACK

Self-evaluate. Rate your paper on each item in the Writer's Blueprint, from 6 (superior) to 1 (inadequate).

Reflect. Write your thoughts on these questions.

✔ Do all heroes make good role models for your own life? Explain.

✔ Review the ratings you gave yourself, and describe what you might do the next time you write to improve any rating that was less than superior.

For Your Working Portfolio Add your interpretive essay and your reflection responses to your working portfolio.

ASSESSMENT CRITERIA SPECS

Here are the criteria for a superior paper.

6 Superior The writer of a 6 paper impressively meets these criteria:

- Dramatically opens the essay by portraying two heroes in action.
- Organizes the essay clearly.
- Insightfully compares and contrasts the heroes through three or more aspects of comparison.
- Includes specific examples of the heroes' words and actions for each aspect.
- Effectively chooses quotations from the literature to amplify and support opinions.
- Clearly focuses each paragraph on a single main idea.
- Convincingly concludes with a discussion of how the concept of a hero has changed since Beowulf's time.
- Makes clear pronoun references and follows the conventions of standard written English.

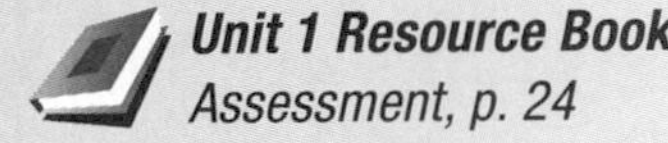

Unit 1 Resource Book
Assessment, p. 24

Beyond Print

Glossary of Technology Terms

As you use computers and other technologies, you need to understand certain terms. Here are some common technology terms.

Application A particular computer program or piece of software.

Bulletin Board Service (BBS) An individual or company that allows users to connect to their server to download or upload information.

CD ROM Compact Disc Read Only Memory; this is used to store information, such as text, sounds, pictures, and movies.

Database An organized collection of information.

Desktop The area on a computer screen that contains icons, menus, and windows.

Directory A particular area in the computer or storage that contains all applications and files.

Download To copy a file from a server or network.

Home Page The first screen that appears when you access a server on the World Wide Web; it can contain text, graphics, and sound.

Internet A series of computer servers connected together across the country and world, allowing a user who is connected to the Internet to access any information stored on those servers.

Menu A pull-down list of items at the top of the computer screen.

Multimedia Any combination of media types, including text, sound, pictures, and video.

Network Two or more computers connected together.

Server A computer that operates a network.

Upload To copy a file onto a server or network.

Activity

Create a glossary of your own with other Technology Terms. Keep this in your notebook and add to it as you come across new terms.

ANOTHER APPROACH

On Borrowed Terms

You might point out that many computer terms are comprised of words or combinations of words that have been borrowed from standard English. These words are chosen for their connotative relationship to a technological application. For example: *A Home Page* represents the "home base" or "shelter" of the company or individual who created that particular server. Have students review each featured technology term and identify its connotative relationship, if any, to the standard English words that comprise it.

Beyond Print

Teaching Objectives

- to introduce and define key technology terms
- to explore the practical application of sophisticated computer technology
- to explore the connection between language and technology

Curricular Connection: Technology Skills

Use the material on this page to give students a background in basic computer terminology and its applications towards research, communication, and data organization.

Introduce

- Discuss the importance of computer literacy in today's world, exploring the role of the computer in career and education opportunities.
- Ask students who have a computer at home to describe the challenges they faced as they learned how to use it. Ask these students, as well as students with access to school computers, to brainstorm a list of computer terminology that they already use.

Activity Options

Activity 1 Have students periodically compare their lists with other students to expand their vocabulary and share their knowledge.

Activity 2 You might suggest that students make flash cards for the computer terms and attempt to memorize them.

Activity 3 Inform students that if they are interested in technology terms and the application of computer technology, they can find more information in a computer magazine such as *Wired, MacUser, PCWorld,* and *Family PC.*

Historical Overview

EXPLORING CONCEPTS

- According to the Domesday Book (1086–1087), 90 percent of the people in England lived in the country, but cities soon began to grow. Townspeople during the feudal age were shopkeepers, craftsmen, and apprentices.
- One's clothing, carriage, and speech functioned as an immediate I.D. card—marking one's socioeconomic and religious status, means of livelihood, and place of residence.

Question What, if anything, is functional about the dress of the serf, the merchant, the cleric, the knight, and the noble? *(Students may note that the serf's apron-like overgarment might aid in carrying harvest or gleanings; the merchant's pockets can hold and therefore give him easy access to money; the cleric's raiment is simple so as not to distract him from spiritual matters; the knight's armor is designed to protect his body; the noblewomen's crown is symbolic of her rank.)*

Research Activity Have students pick the social class that interests them most and prepare a report on daily life within it.

The Serf, who is sowing winter grain, is a detail from October in *Les Très Riches Heures du Duc de Barry* (1413–1416) by the Limbourg Brothers. The three Limbourgs were Flemish but settled in France. The Duc de Barry was the wealthy brother of the French king.

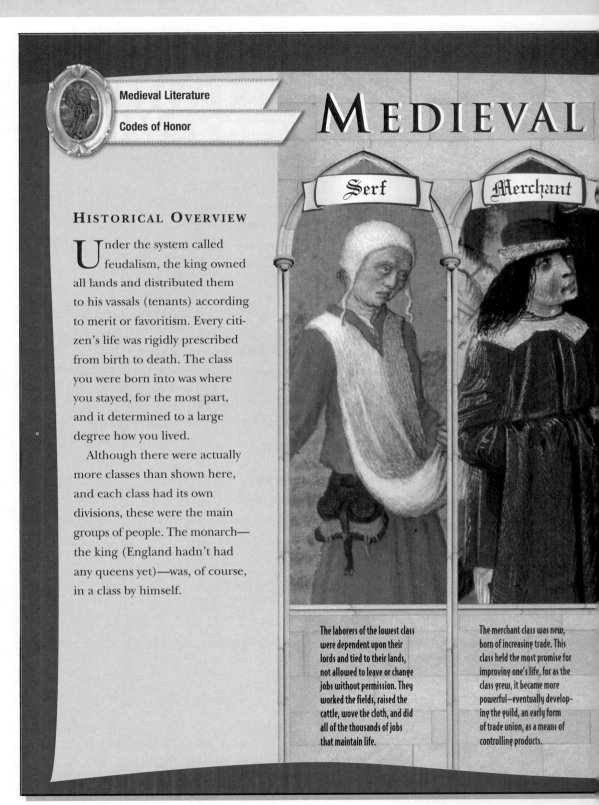

Medieval Literature

Codes of Honor

MEDIEVAL

HISTORICAL OVERVIEW

Under the system called feudalism, the king owned all lands and distributed them to his vassals (tenants) according to merit or favoritism. Every citizen's life was rigidly prescribed from birth to death. The class you were born into was where you stayed, for the most part, and it determined to a large degree how you lived.

Although there were actually more classes than shown here, and each class had its own divisions, these were the main groups of people. The monarch—the king (England hadn't had any queens yet)—was, of course, in a class by himself.

Serf

The laborers of the lowest class were dependent upon their lords and tied to their lands, not allowed to leave or change jobs without permission. They worked the fields, raised the cattle, wove the cloth, and did all of the thousands of jobs that maintain life.

Merchant

The merchant class was new, born of increasing trade. This class held the most promise for improving one's life, for as the class grew, it became more powerful—eventually developing the guild, an early form of trade union, as a means of controlling products.

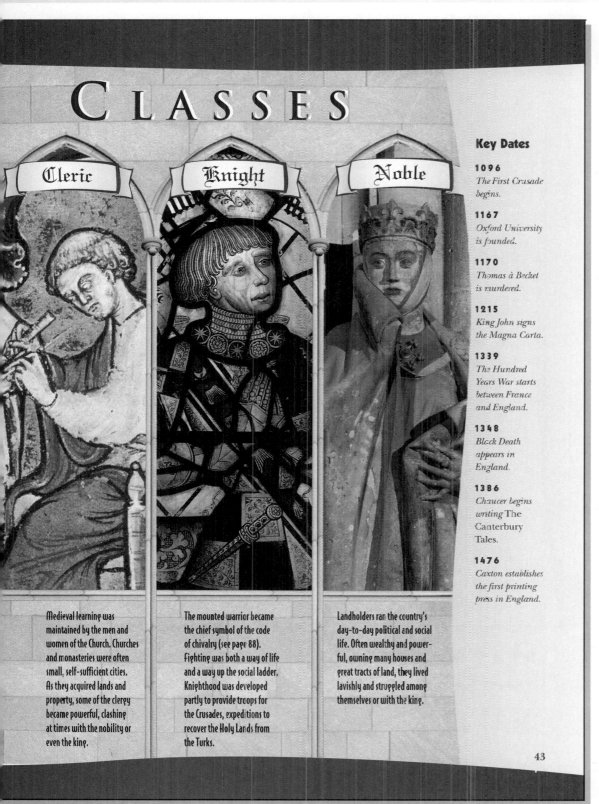

CLASSES

Cleric

Knight

Noble

Medieval learning was maintained by the men and women of the Church. Churches and monasteries were often small, self-sufficient cities. As they acquired lands and property, some of the clergy became powerful, clashing at times with the nobility or even the king.

The mounted warrior became the chief symbol of the code of chivalry (see page 88). Fighting was both a way of life and a way up the social ladder. Knighthood was developed partly to provide troops for the Crusades, expeditions to recover the Holy Lands from the Turks.

Landholders ran the country's day-to-day political and social life. Often wealthy and powerful, owning many houses and great tracts of land, they lived lavishly and struggled among themselves or with the king.

Key Dates

1096 *The First Crusade begins.*

1167 *Oxford University is founded.*

1170 *Thomas à Becket is murdered.*

1215 *King John signs the Magna Carta.*

1339 *The Hundred Years War starts between France and England.*

1348 *Black Death appears in England.*

1386 *Chaucer begins writing* The Canterbury Tales.

1476 *Caxton establishes the first printing press in England.*

43

Key Dates

1214 Roger Bacon, mathematician and intellectual, is born.

1215 Jews and Muslims are forced to wear an identifying badge.

1264 John Duns Scotus, leading theologian, is born.

1290 Jews are expelled from England.

1485 Henry VII, the first Tudor king, accedes to the throne.

MATERIALS OF INTEREST

Books

- *The Medieval Cookbook* by Maggie Black (Thames & Hudson, 1996).
- *The New Penguin Atlas of Medieval History* by Colin McEvedy (Viking Penguin, 1992).

Multimedia

- *England in the Middle Ages* [videotape]. 30 min., color, VHS. Britannica, 1982, Order #3714.
- *The Middle Ages* [videotape].40 min., color, VHS. Educational Audio Visual, order #J7VH0496. Depicts the daily life of kings, nobles, and peasants.

Connections to **Custom Literature Database**

For further historical background, under **Background Articles,** see **Medieval England 1066–1500.**

Art Study

The Knight is taken from a stained glass window in East Harling Church, Norfolk. The Noblewoman is the Countess Uta. She and her husband, Ekkehard, (c. 1250–1260) helped found the Romanesque cathedral in Naumburg.

Preview

Codes of Honor

FOR ALL STUDENTS

Have students read the two paragraphs on page 44 and then brainstorm a list of organizations, nations, or people who have set forth a system of beliefs to live by. Where are these beliefs stated, or in what forms have they been given?

To further explore the theme, use the transparency referenced below.

Transparency Collection
Fine Art Transparency 2

For At Risk Students

Ask students to think of movies, comic books, games, and television shows that involve the legend of King Arthur. You might remind students that Merlin and Lancelot are key figures of this mythology.

For Students Who Need Challenge

Students might read one or two other tales from *The Canterbury Tales* and retell the stories for the class.

For Visual Learners

Ask students to find pictures of medieval castles in Britain and bring them to show the class.

MULTICULTURAL CONNECTION

The Pardoner jokes about his dishonorable intentions, claiming that he doesn't really care about the souls of those he "pardons"; he is a con artist who manipulates the Christian code of honor for profit. Gawain and Arthur, on the other hand, risk their very lives to follow their court's codes of honor.

Part Two

Codes of Honor

Honor means different things to different people. It is a sense of what is right or proper; it is nobility of mind; it is integrity; it is respect or high regard. Some people live their lives trying to get around it; some die trying to uphold it.

Multicultural Focus Membership in a **group** involves the collective development of codes, rules for behavior that individuals are expected to follow. In this period of history, such group codes included loyalty, bravery, honesty, courtesy—and the honor to uphold these values even when no one else was watching. In what respects do the characters in these selections follow or depart from their codes of honor?

IDEAS THAT WORK

Motivating with Models

"Students like to personalize these stories by creating their own code of honor. Sometimes it's helpful to bring in samples of other familiar codes as examples (school honor codes, oaths of office, Hippocratic oath). I give a lot of flexibility for this activity, letting students use art, music, or poetry as possible forms of expression. It's also interesting to create codes of honor for the characters in the selections.

Students have fantastic imaginations, and I try to tap this creativity by encouraging them to model the forms of writing in this cluster. Their original Canterbury tale or Arthurian legend is not only fun to read but also to act out in front of the class. Making a video of their performance adds to the excitement."

Karen Wroblewski
Spring Valley, California

Before Reading

from The Canterbury Tales by Geoffrey Chaucer

translated by Nevill Coghill

Geoffrey Chaucer
1342?–1400

Throughout most of his life Geoffrey Chaucer (jef′rē chô′sər) was connected in some way with members of the royal family. In 1359 he was sent to France to fight in the Hundred Years' War. Chaucer was taken prisoner but was ransomed in the following year; King Edward III himself contributed toward his ransom. Some years later, he began undertaking diplomatic missions to France, Spain, and Italy for the king. In his later life as a customs official, he and his wife, Philippa Roet, who also had court connections, lived in free lodgings above Aldgate in London. There he liked to retire "as an hermyte," he says, after his working day was done. He lost or gave up his job in 1386 and probably began writing *The Canterbury Tales* soon thereafter.

Building Background

A Very Special Journey It's a fine spring morning. The air is soft, the birds are singing, and the earth is beginning to send forth green shoots. It's a perfect time to set out on a journey—say, to the cathedral at Canterbury, the shrine of the martyr Saint Thomas à Becket, murdered in 1170 for resisting the policies of King Henry II. Visiting a holy place was a popular pastime in the Middle Ages, not only for religious reasons, but because it was an adventure. And the journey there and back, known as a **pilgrimage,** is an ideal setting for presenting a varied group of travelers who tell stories to entertain each other. Thus, *The Canterbury Tales* is an ingenious concoction of character sketches, conversations, and stories—all set within the frame, or larger narrative, of this pilgrimage, undertaken by twenty-nine pilgrims (and Chaucer) who meet each other at the Tabard Inn in Southwark, across the Thames River from London. Representing a cross section of the population of England in the 1300s, Chaucer's pilgrims—also called *palmers*—range in rank from a knight to a poor plowman, and the tales they tell range from sermons to off-color jokes. Chaucer planned to include 120 stories, two told by each pilgrim each way on the journey, but he managed only twenty-four, some of these incomplete, before his death.

Literary Focus

Irony The contrast between what appears to be and what really is, is called **irony.** Different types of irony include *verbal, dramatic,* and *situational,* in which something occurs contrary to what is expected or intended. Irony can be bitter or humorous, and in the hands of a master storyteller it is highly effective. Look for instances of irony in *The Pardoner's Prologue* and *Tale.*

Writer's Notebook

A Modern Pilgrimage How would you update the idea of a group of travelers telling their stories to each other during a journey? What kinds of people might take a modern pilgrimage? Where would they go and for what purpose? How would they travel? In your notebook, jot down some answers to these questions.

Before Reading

Building Background

Ask students to recall books, plays, movies, or TV shows that provide a framework for presenting a wide range of dissimilar characters and their stories.

Literary Focus

- *Verbal irony* includes sarcasm and understatement.
- *Dramatic irony* exists when the reader or audience knows what a character does not know.
- *Situational irony* is the result of unexpected or unintended events.

Writer's Notebook

Students might make lists of memorable people, reasons for travel, means of transportation, and interesting destinations.

More About Geoffrey Chaucer

Chaucer, son of a wine merchant, spent much of his youth in London's wine-selling district, where he encountered people of all classes and character types.

SUPPORT MATERIALS OVERVIEW

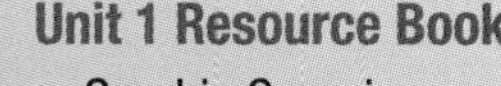

Unit 1 Resource Book
- Graphic Organizer, p. 25
- Study Guide, p. 26
- Vocabulary, p. 27
- Grammar, p. 28
- Alternate Check Test, p. 29
- Vocabulary Test, p. 30
- Selection Test, pp. 31–32

Building English Proficiency
- Selection Summaries
- Activities, p. 207
- "The Pardoner's Tale" in Spanish

Reading, Writing & Grammar SkillBook
- Reading, pp. 74–75
- Grammar, Usage, and Mechanics, pp. 147–148

The World of Work
- Pharmacist, p. 3
- Activity, p. 4

Technology
- Personal Journal Software
- Custom Literature Database: Additional selections by Chaucer can be found on the database.
- Test Generator Software

Art Study

Responses to Caption Questions
Responses will vary. People continue to make pilgrimages to a variety of shrines, both religious and secular, and for a variety of reasons. Thousands of Muslims from around the world annually make the *hajj,* or pilgrimage to Mecca. In France, pilgrims travel to Lourdes, and in Mexico thousands make pilgrimages to the Basilica of Our Lady of Guadalupe—both sites of purported miracles. People also make pilgrimages to such secular shrines as houses of former Presidents, battlefields, national monuments, and cemeteries.

Visual Literacy This book illustration from the 1400s furnishes a reliable picture of what an English city in the late-medieval period looked like. Notice that the city is still protected by castle-like walls and that the cathedral truly dominates the scene.

Questions What do the town walls suggest about life at the time? *(that walls were still necessary for protection)* What does the dominance of the cathedral suggest? *(that religion was a dominant force)*

The Canterbury Tales

Geoffrey Chaucer

In the General Prologue *to all the tales, Chaucer briefly introduces each pilgrim, who then tells a bit about himself or herself before relating a tale. The lines below are the opening of the General Prologue in Chaucer's English and in modern English.*

THE PROLOGUE

Whan that Aprille with hise shourės sote
The droghte of March hath percėd to
    the rote,
And bathėd every veyne in swich licour
Of which vertu engendrėd is the flour;
Whan Zephirus eek with his sweetė breeth
Inspirėd hath in every holt and heeth
The tendre croppės, and the yongė sonne
Hath in the Ram his halfė cours yronne,
And smalė fowlės maken melodye
That slepen al the night with open iye
(So priketh hem Nature in hir corages):
Thanne longen folk to goon on pilgrimages,
And palmeres for to seken straungė strondes,
To fernė halwės, couthe in sondry londes;
And specially from every shirės ende
Of Engėlond to Caunterbury they wende,
The holy blisful martir for to seeke,
That hem hath holpen whan that they were seke.
    Bifel that in that seson on a day,
In Southwerk at the Tabard as I lay
Redy to wenden on my pilgrimage
To Caunterbury with ful devout corage,
At nyght was come into that hostelrye
Wel nine and twenty in a companye
Of sondry folk, by aventure yfalle
In felawship, and pilgrimes were they alle
That toward Caunterbury wolden ryde.

THE PROLOGUE

When in April the sweet showers fall
And pierce the drought of March to the root,
    and all
The veins are bathed in liquor of such power
As brings about the engendering of the flower,
When also Zephyrus with his sweet breath
Exhales an air in every grove and heath
Upon the tender shoots, and the young sun
His half-course in the sign of the *Ram* has run,
And the small fowl are making melody
That sleep away the night with open eye
(So nature pricks them and their heart engages)
Then people long to go on pilgrimages
And palmers long to seek the stranger strands
Of far-off saints, hallowed in sundry lands,
And specially, from every shire's end
Of England, down to Canterbury they wend
To seek the holy blissful martyr, quick
To give his help to them when they were sick.
    It happened in that season that one day
In Southwark, at *The Tabard*, as I lay
Ready to go on pilgrimage and start
For Canterbury, most devout at heart,
At night there came into that hostelry
Some nine and twenty in a company
Of sundry folk happening then to fall
In fellowship, and they were pilgrims all
That towards Canterbury meant to ride.

◄ In this illustration from a manuscript of the 1400s, characters from *The Canterbury Tales* are shown on their pilgrimage to the shrine of St. Thomas à Becket. If you were to make a pilgrimage for religious or other reasons, where would you go? Why?

During Reading

Selection Objectives

- to read an example of Middle English literature
- to identify examples of irony
- to recognize misplaced modifiers
- to use simple sentences

Unit 1 Resource Book
Graphic Organizer, p. 25
Study Guide, p. 26

Theme Link

The theme, Codes of Honor, is explored through the character of a professional pardoner, whose self-admitted aim is to grow rich by exciting—and, for a price, relieving—people's fears about the consequences of their sins.

Vocabulary Preview

avarice, cupidity; a greed for wealth
adversary, opponent; enemy
publican, tavern keeper
absolution, a declaration that frees a person from guilt or punishment for sin
pique, anger; wounded pride

Students can add the words and definitions to their Writer's Notebooks.

SELECTION SUMMARY

General Prologue; The Pardoner's Prologue; The Pardoner's Tale

The Canterbury Tales excerpts begin with the "General Prologue" in which the narrator asserts that the revivifying powers of spring impel people to go on pilgrimages to seek God. "The Pardoner's Prologue" is an unabashed profession of greed and hypocrisy by one of the pilgrims, a professional pardoner of sin. In this brazen address, he pledges allegiance to his one god, wealth. His story, "The Pardoner's Tale," illustrates how he fleeces people with a parable of three men who seek to kill Death, but who through their own greed end up murdering each other.

*For summaries in other languages, see the **Building English Proficiency** book.*

1 Geographic Note
Medieval Canterbury

Canterbury, which means "borough of the folk of Kent," was the capital of Ethelbert, King of Kent and Overlord of Britain, from A.D. 560–616. During Ethelbert's reign, Saint Augustine arrived and established a monastery; when he was named bishop, Augustine built a cathedral—the same cathedral in which Thomas à Becket was later murdered. In Chaucer's time, the economy of Canterbury was based on the minting of coins and tourism from pilgrims.

2 Literary Focus
Irony

Question What is ironic about the Pardoner's sale of "relics" year after year? *(Possible response: It does not seem to occur to many people that it would be remarkable if even one of these ancient, highly sought-after objects were in the Pardoner's possession—let alone the steady supply that he proffers.)*

3 Reading/Thinking Skills
Draw Conclusions

Response The Pardoner profits handsomely by passing off bits of animal bone as holy relics.

Question What could you conclude about people who were so gullible about "bones and ragged bits of clout"? *(Possible response: At a time when there were few effective cures for disease and ordinary people had little control over their lives, "miraculous relics" offered hope.)*

One of the pilgrims is a Pardoner, a church official charged with the granting of indulgences (which were supposed to free believing Christians from punishment for their sins) in return for church offerings.

1

The Pardoner's Prologue

"My lords," he said, "in churches where I preach
I cultivate a haughty kind of speech
And ring it out as roundly as a bell;
I've got it all by heart, the tale I tell.
I have a text, it always is the same
And always has been, since I learnt the game,
Old as the hills and fresher than the grass,
Radix malorum est cupiditas.
"But first I make pronouncement whence I come,
Show them my bulls in detail and in sum,
And flaunt the papal seal for their inspection
As warrant for my bodily protection,
That none may have the impudence to irk
Or hinder me in Christ's most holy work.
Then I tell stories, as occasion calls,
Showing forth bulls from popes and cardinals,
From patriarchs and bishops; as I do,
I speak some words in Latin—just a few—
To put a saffron tinge upon my preaching
And stir devotion with a spice of teaching.
Then I bring all my long glass bottles out
Cram-full of bones and ragged bits of clout,
Relics they are, at least for such are known. 2
Then, cased in metal, I've a shoulder-bone,
Belonging to a sheep, a holy Jew's.
'Good men,' I say, 'take heed, for here is news.
Take but this bone and dip it in a well;
If cow or calf, if sheep or ox should swell
From eating snakes or that a snake has stung,
Take water from that well and wash its tongue,
And it will then recover. Furthermore,
Where there is pox or scab or other sore,
All animals that water at that well
Are cured at once. Take note of what I tell.
If the good man—the owner of the stock—
Goes once a week, before the crow of cock,
Fasting, and takes a draught of water too,
Why then, according to that holy Jew,
He'll find his cattle multiply and sell.

8 Radix . . . cupiditas. "Avarice (greed for wealth) is the root of all evil." *[Latin]*
10 bull, formal announcement or official decree from the pope.

19 saffron (saf′rən), *n.* an orange-yellow spice used to color and flavor certain dishes, such as rice.
22 clout, cloth.

25 sheep . . . Jew's, that is, he is claiming that the sheep's bone belonged to some biblical patriarch, such as Abraham, Isaac, or Jacob.

32 pox, any disease, such as chicken pox or small pox, characterized by skin eruptions.

3 ■ Why does the Pardoner carry these relics around with him?

MINI-LESSON: LITERARY FOCUS
Irony

Teach Remind students that they have studied three types of irony—verbal, dramatic, and situational. Suggest that irony is an important element in literature because people frequently perceive ironies in life. There are situations that evoke sarcasm or turn out in unanticipated ways, and people unknowingly act with incomplete information.

Activity Idea Suggest that students write three examples of each type of irony, either from their experience or from their imagination.

"'And it's a cure for jealousy as well;
For though a man be given to jealous wrath,
Use but this water when you make his broth,
And never again will he mistrust his wife,
Though he knew all about her sinful life,
Though two or three clergy had enjoyed her love.
"'Now look; I have a mitten here, a glove.
Whoever wears this mitten on his hand
Will multiply his grain. He sows his land
And up will come abundant wheat or oats,
Providing that he offers pence or groats.
"'Good men and women, here's a word of warning;
If there is anyone in church this morning
Guilty of sin, so far beyond expression
Horrible, that he dare not make confession,
Or any woman, whether young or old,
That's cuckolded her husband, be she told
That such as she shall have no power or grace
To offer to my relics in this place.
But those who can acquit themselves of blame
Can all come up and offer in God's name,
And I will shrive them by the authority
Committed in this papal bull to me.'
"That trick's been worth a hundred marks a year
Since I became a Pardoner, never fear.
Then, priestlike in my pulpit, with a frown,
4 I stand, and when the yokels have sat down,
I preach, as you have heard me say before,
And tell a hundred lying mockeries more.
I take great pains, and stretching out my neck
To east and west I crane about and peck
Just like a pigeon sitting on a barn.
My hands and tongue together spin the yarn
And all my antics are a joy to see.
The curse of avarice and cupidity
Is all my sermon, for it frees the pelf.
Out come the pence, and specially for myself,
For my exclusive purpose is to win
And not at all to castigate their sin.
Once dead what matter how their souls may fare?
They can go blackberrying, for all I care!
"Believe me, many a sermon or devotive
Exordium issues from an evil motive.
Some to give pleasure by their flattery
And gain promotion through hypocrisy,

50 pence or groats. *Pence* is the plural of *penny*; a groat is an old English coin worth four pence.

56 cuckold (kuk′əld), *v.* be unfaithful to.

61 shrive (shrīv), *v.* hear the confession of and grant forgivness to.

63 a hundred marks. A mark was a coin of much higher denomination than a groat. In other words, the Pardoner has been making good money from "that trick."

66 yokel (yō′kəl), *n.* a country person. It is often meant as an insult, as the Pardoner means it here.

74 avarice (av′ər is), *n.* . . . **cupidity** (kyü pid′ə tē), *n.* Avarice is greed for wealth; cupidity is the eager desire to possess something.

75 pelf, money.

78 castigate (kas′tə gāt), *v.* punish in order to correct.

82 exordium (eg zôr′dē əm), *n.* introductory part of a speech.

4 Reader's Response

Making Personal Conections

Question How do you interpret the Pardoner's open use of the derogatory term "yokels"? *(He is flaunting his disdain for people in his speech. By implication, he is flattering his audience, to set them up for his game.)*

Question How would you feel if you were in the Pardoner's audience and had been called a yokel? *(While most students will respond negatively, this kind of taunt has been used successfully for centuries as a selling tool; politician Huey Long called his constituents "hicks"; nightclub entertainer Texas Guinan called her patrons "suckers.")*

BUILDING ENGLISH PROFICIENCY

ESL LEP ELD SAE LD

Starting Vocabulary Notebooks

To promote vocabulary growth, have students start a vocabulary notebook. As they're reading, whenever students meet an unfamiliar word, have them look up its meaning in a dictionary or consult with an English-proficient classmate.

1. Instruct students to record the following information in their vocabulary notebook: the new word or phrase, a brief definition, and a sentence using it.

2. Model a sample entry, as shown. Other words that students might add from page 47 include *sundry, wend, hostelry,* and *fellowship.*

engendering	producing
The engendering of love from friendship may happen quickly.	

Building English Proficiency
Activities, p. 207
"The Pardoner's Tale" in Spanish

5 Literary Focus
Irony

Question What is ironic in "That's not the counsel of my inner voice"? *(Possible response: One's "inner voice" usually refers to one's conscience.)*

6 Reading/Thinking Skills
Recognize Values

Question Do you think that the Pardoner values something more than money? *(Possible response: He craves attention and needs to feel more clever than other people.)*

7 Literary Critcism
Style

"Chaucer, in his own time and ever since, has been recognized as one of the greatest English poets. His style ranges from a simple and earthy directness to elaborate splendour. His humor, occasionally broadly farcical, often of the subtlest delicacy, is all pervading, yet the feeling most frequently expressed is a tender pity. Perhaps the secret of his greatness lies in this capacity to behold and harmonize the contradictory nature of life's experiences."

Derek Stanley Brewer
Lecturer in English at Cambridge University

Some out of vanity, some out of hate;
Or when I dare not otherwise debate
I'll put my discourse into such a shape,
My tongue will be a dagger; no escape
For him from slandering falsehood shall there be
If he has hurt my brethren or me.
For though I never mention him by name
The congregation guesses all the same
From certain hints that everybody knows,
And so I take revenge upon our foes
And spit my venom forth, while I profess
Holy and true—or seeming holiness.
"But let me briefly make my purpose plain;
I preach for nothing but for greed of gain
And use the same old text, as bold as brass,
Radix malorum est cupiditas.
And thus I preach against the very vice
I make my living out of—avarice.
And yet however guilty of that sin
Myself, with others I have power to win
Them from it, I can bring them to repent;
But that is not my principal intent.
Covetousness is both the root and stuff
Of all I preach. That ought to be enough.
"Well, then I give examples thick and fast
From bygone times, old stories from the past.
A yokel mind loves stories from of old,
Being the kind it can repeat and hold.
What! Do you think, as long as I can preach
And get their silver for the things I teach,
That I will live in poverty, from choice?
5 That's not the counsel of my inner voice!
No! Let me preach and beg from kirk to kirk
And never do an honest job of work,
No, nor make baskets, like St. Paul, to gain
A livelihood. I do not preach in vain.
There's no apostle I would counterfeit;
6 I mean to have money, wool and cheese and wheat
Though it were given me by the poorest lad
Or poorest village widow, though she had
A string of starving children, all agape.
No, let me drink the liquor of the grape
And keep a jolly wench in every town!
"But listen, gentlemen; to bring things down
7 To a conclusion, would you like a tale?

90 brethren (breᴛʜ′rən), *n. pl.* the fellow members of a church.

107 covetousness (kuv′ə təs-nis), *n.* desire for things that belong to others.

117 kirk, church.

119 make baskets . . . St. Paul, a reference to St. Paul the Hermit, not the Apostle Paul.

125 agape (ə gāp′), *adj.* open-mouthed with wonder or surprise.

MINI-LESSON: GRAMMAR

Simple Sentences

Teach A simple sentence has a complete subject and a complete predicate; either the subject or the predicate or both may be compound, but a simple sentence has only one clause. (By contrast, two independent clauses in one sentence form a compound sentence; one independent and one dependent clause in one sentence form a complex sentence.)

Most sentences in this selection are complex or compound/complex sentences. However, write these examples of simple sentences on the board:

I do not preach in vain. (line 120)

He withdrew/And deftly poured the poison into two. (p. 55, lines 215–216)

Dearly beloved, God forgive your sin/And keep you from the vice of avarice! (p. 56, lines 248–249)

Have students tell the subject and the predicate of each simple sentence.

Activity Idea Have students pick a sentence at random from the selection, read it aloud, and tell whether or not it is a simple sentence and how they know.

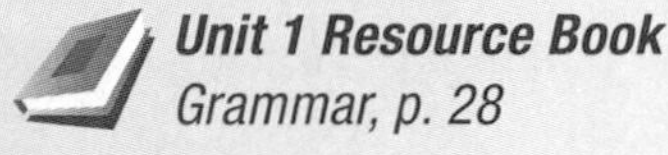

Unit 1 Resource Book
Grammar, p. 28

Now as I've drunk a draught of corn-ripe ale,
By God it stands to reason I can strike
On some good story that you all will like.
For though I am a wholly vicious man
Don't think I can't tell moral tales. I can!
Here's one I often preach when out for winning;
Now please be quiet. Here is the beginning."

THE PARDONER'S TALE

9 . . . It's of three rioters I have to tell
Who, long before the morning service bell,
Were sitting in a tavern for a drink.
And as they sat, they heard the hand-bell clink
Before a coffin going to the grave;
One of them called the little tavern-knave
And said "Go and find out at once—look spry!—
Whose corpse is in that coffin passing by;
And see you get the name correctly too."
"Sir," said the boy, "no need, I promise you;
Two hours before you came here I was told.
He was a friend of yours in days of old,
And suddenly, last night, the man was slain,
Upon his bench, face up, dead drunk again.
There came a privy thief, they call him Death,
Who kills us all round here, and in a breath
He speared him through the heart, he never stirred.
And then Death went his way without a word.
He's killed a thousand in the present plague,
And, sir, it doesn't do to be too vague
If you should meet him; you had best be wary.
Be on your guard with such an adversary,
Be primed to meet him everywhere you go,
That's what my mother said. It's all I know."
The publican joined in with, "By St. Mary,
What the child says is right; you'd best be wary.
This very year he killed, in a large village
A mile away, man, woman, serf at tillage,
Page in the household, children—all there were.
Yes, I imagine that he lives round there.
It's well to be prepared in these alarms,
He might do you dishonor." "Huh, God's arms!"
The rioter, said, "Is he so fierce to meet?
I'll search for him, by Jesus, street by street.
God's blessed bones! I'll register a vow!
Here, chaps! The three of us together now,

8 ■ The Pardoner admits to being "a wholly vicious man." What do you think of this confession?

6 **knave** (nāv), *n.* servant.
15 **privy** (priv′ē), *adj.* secret; hidden.
22 **adversary** (ad′vər ser′ē), *n.* opponent; enemy.
25 **publican** (pub′lə kən), *n.* tavern keeper.
28 **tillage** (til′ij), *n.* cultivation of land.

This pilgrim's badge from the 1300s shows Thomas à Becket riding in triumph as Archbishop of Canterbury. Pilgrims wore badges like this around their necks or pinned to their hats. What kind of souvenirs do pilgrims obtain today?

8 Literary Element
Connotation/Denotation

Response He may be "confessing" because he is a little drunk, but there may be another explanation. "Vicious" has taken on connotations—particularly those associated with certain animals or criminals. Suggest that students look up "vicious" in the dictionary, paying close attention to the etymology.

Question What might be the denotation of "vicious" as used by the Pardoner? *(Possible response: that he has all the vices and is proud of it)*

9 Literary Element
Characterization

Question In your own words, how does the Pardoner characterize the three men in the first sentence of the tale? *(riotous drunks)*

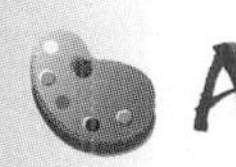

Art Study

Response to Caption Question
The variety is endless: crosses, icons, candles, reproductions of art, etc.

BUILDING ENGLISH PROFICIENCY

Analyzing Characters

To help students understand the Pardoner, have them collaborate on a character web.

1. Ask them to write the character's name—the Pardoner—in the center block.
2. On each line coming out of the center block, have them write one of the Pardoner's traits.
3. In the outer blocks, have them give examples that illustrate each trait.

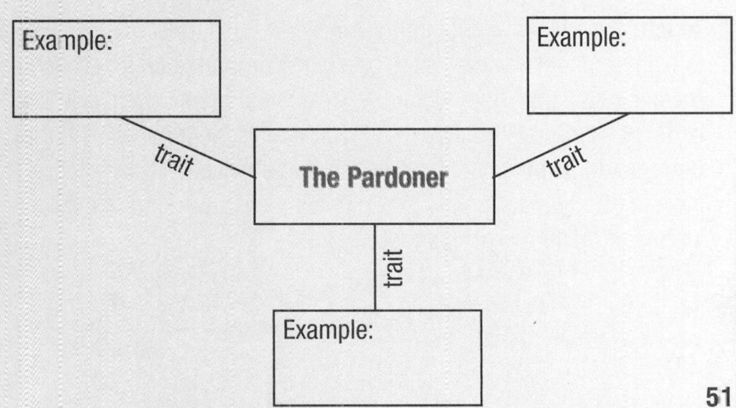

10 Multicultural Note
Group

Response The three rioters have formed a kind of brotherhood, like today's gangs. However, because they are drunk and their purpose—to kill Death—is absurd, they will probably not stay together.

11 Literary Element
Personification

Possible Responses Excited and worked up in their search for Death, the callow fellows are aggressive and unable to imagine they will ever be old.

Question If you were going to create personae for death and for youth unaware of its mortality, what would they be? *(While responses will vary, students should note Chaucer's personification of death and callow youth.)*

Hold up your hands, like me, and we'll be brothers
In this affair, and each defend the others,
And we will kill this traitor Death, I say!
Away with him as he has made away
With all our friends. God's dignity! Tonight!"
They made their bargain, swore with appetite,
These three, to live and die for one another
As brother-born might swear to his born brother.
And up they started in their drunken rage
And made towards this village which the page
And publican had spoken of before.
Many and grisly were the oaths they swore,
Tearing Christ's blessed body to a shred;
"If we can only catch him, Death is dead!"
When they had gone not fully half a mile,
Just as they were about to cross a stile,
They came upon a very poor old man
Who humbly greeted them and thus began,
"God look to you, my lords, and give you quiet!"
To which the proudest of these men of riot
Gave back the answer, "What, old fool? Give place!
Why are you all wrapped up except your face?
Why live so long? Isn't it time to die?"
The old, old fellow looked him in the eye
And said, "Because I never yet have found,
Though I have walked to India, searching round
Village and city on my pilgrimage,
One who would change his youth to have my age.
And so my age is mine and must be still
Upon me, for such time as God may will.
"Not even Death, alas, will take my life;
So, like a wretched prisoner at strife
Within himself, I walk alone and wait
About the earth, which is my mother's gate,
Knock-knocking with my staff from night to noon
And crying, 'Mother, open to me soon!
Look at me, Mother, won't you let me in?
See how I wither, flesh and blood and skin!
Alas! When will these bones be laid to rest?
Mother, I would exchange—for that were best—
The wardrobe in my chamber, standing there
So long, for yours! Aye, for a shirt of hair
To wrap me in!' She has refused her grace,
Whence comes the pallor of my withered face.
"But it dishonored you when you began

10 What is the nature of the **group** that the three rioters form at this point? Do you think they will be able to keep their group intact long enough to fulfill their purpose?

11 ■ Why do you suppose the rioters treat the old man the way they do?

70 mother's gate, the grave, the entrance to "mother earth."

78 shirt of hair, rough shirt made of horsehair, worn to make the wearer suffer as a penance.

MINI-LESSON: GRAMMAR
Misplaced Modifiers

Teach Remind students that a word or phrase must be clearly attached to what it modifies. When such rules are compromised for reasons of rhyme, meter, and other elements, it is called *poetic license.* In line 24, page 48, note the line "Then, cased in metal, I've a shoulder-bone." Because of the placement, "cased in metal" modifies the subject, "I," instead of "shoulder-bone." While poets justify this kind of error, good writers of modern prose cannot.

Activity Idea Using Chaucer's text, students might find, write, and correct sentences with dangling modifiers. After they have found and corrected six to eight examples, suggest they attempt to correct Chaucer's modifiers while maintaining his meter and rhyme.

To speak so roughly, sir, to an old man,
Unless he had injured you in word or deed.
It says in holy writ, as you may read,
'Thou shalt rise up before the hoary head
And honor it.' And therefore be it said
'Do no more harm to an old man than you,
Being now young, would have another do
When you are old'—if you should live till then.
And so may God be with you, gentlemen,
For I must go whither I have to go."
"By God," the gambler said, "you shan't do so,
You don't get off so easy, by St. John!
I heard you mention, just a moment gone,
12 A certain traitor Death who singles out
And kills the fine young fellows hereabout.
And you're his spy, by God! You wait a bit.
Say where he is or you shall pay for it,
By God and by the Holy Sacrament!
I say you've joined together by consent
To kill us younger folk, you thieving swine!"
"Well, sirs," he said, "if it be your design
To find out Death, turn up this crooked way
Towards that grove, I left him there today
Under a tree, and there you'll find him waiting.
He isn't one to hide for all your prating.
You see that oak? He won't be far to find.
And God protect you that redeemed mankind,
Aye, and amend you!" Thus that ancient man.
At once the three young rioters began
To run, and reached the tree, and there they found
A pile of golden florins on the ground,
New-coined, eight bushels of them as they thought.
No longer was it Death those fellows sought,
For they were all so thrilled to see the sight,
The florins were so beautiful and bright,
That down they sat beside the precious pile.
The wickedest spoke first after a while.
"Brothers," he said, "you listen to what I say.
I'm pretty sharp although I joke away.
It's clear that Fortune has bestowed this treasure
To let us live in jollity and pleasure.
Light come, light go! We'll spend it as we ought.
God's precious dignity! Who would have thought
This morning was to be our lucky day?
"If one could only get that gold away,

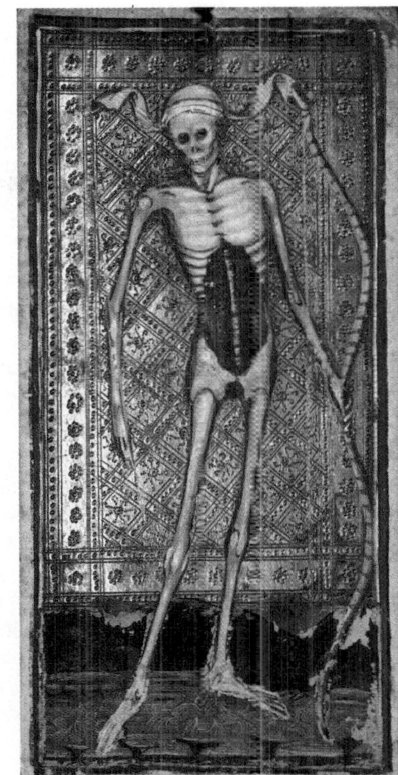

This tarot card, part of a deck of playing cards from the 1400s, shows Death as a skeleton grasping an archer's bow in one hand and an arrow in the other. How is this representation of Death similar to the way Death is portrayed in *The Pardoner's Tale*? How is it different?

104 grove (grōv), *n.* group of trees.
112 florin, coin originally issued in Florence, Italy; various coins of the same name were later used in other European countries.

Art Study

Response to Caption Question
Both representations personify the idea of death. They differ in that Chaucer's personification is an ancient figure who cannot himself die, while the tarot figure is a corpse who stalks the living.

Visual Literacy Over the centuries, death has been given many personae, who carry a variety of implements.

Question Can you think of other personifications of death? *(Possible responses: the shrouded grim reaper who carries a scythe; the skull-and-crossboned Jolly Roger; beautiful, seductive women [particularly in literature] and elegant gentlemen [in movies])*

12 Historical Note
The Black Death

The irony of three young men looking for the ravager, Death, may reflect the author's experience: when Chaucer was nine, one-third to one-half of England's population died of the Black Death, an epidemic of bubonic plague from which there was little escape.

BUILDING ENGLISH PROFICIENCY

Exploring Personification

Ask students to compare different views of Death in this tale. (To the boy, Death is a "privy thief"; to the rioters, Death is a "traitor" they seek to kill. The old man wrapped in a shroud also personifies Death.) Tell students that when writers talk about a quality or a nonhuman thing as if it were human, they are using personification. Extend discussion by using one or both of the following activities.

Activity Ideas
- Ask students to share different views of death that they may have heard about or seen in movies or TV, or that they know from folk tales and cultural traditions.
- Suggest that students imagine Death as a person. Have students draw a picture of the kind of person they visualize Death to be.

Art Study

Response to Caption Question
Images of death were widespread because death was widespread, due to near-constant warfare, poor nutrition and living conditions, and waves of plague, which regularly decimated the population.

Visual Literacy This ceremonial shield reflects the medieval ideal of chivalry. One aspect of this code was courtly love, in which a young, unmarried knight paid court to the wife of a superior nobleman. These "loves" almost never went beyond extravagant flirtation. Courtly love may have been an antidote to the nearly universal practice of marrying children off into loveless marriages of convenience.

Back to my house, or else to yours, perhaps—
For as you know, the gold is ours, chaps—
We'd all be at the top of fortune, hey?
But certainly it can't be done by day.
People would call us robbers—a strong gang,
So our own property would make us hang.
No, we must bring this treasure back by night
Some prudent way, and keep it out of sight.
And so as a solution I propose
We draw for lots and see the way it goes;
The one who draws the longest, lucky man,
Shall run to town as quickly as he can
To fetch us bread and wine—but keep things dark—
While two remain in hiding here to mark
Our heap of treasure. If there's no delay,
When night comes down we'll carry it away,
All three of us, wherever we have planned."
He gathered lots and hid them in his hand
Bidding them draw for where the luck should fall.
It fell upon the youngest of them all,
And off he ran at once towards the town.
As soon as he had gone the first sat down
And thus began a parley with the other:
"You know that you can trust me as a brother;
Now let me tell you where your profit lies;
You know our friend has gone to get supplies
And here's a lot of gold that is to be
Divided equally amongst us three.
Nevertheless, if I could shape things thus
So that we shared it out—the two of us—
Wouldn't you take it as a friendly act?"
"But how?" the other said. "He knows the fact
That all the gold was left with me and you;
What can we tell him? What are we to do?"
"Is it a bargain," said the first, "or no?
For I can tell you in a word or so
What's to be done to bring the thing about."
"Trust me," the other said, "you needn't doubt
My word. I won't betray you, I'll be true."
"Well," said his friend, "you see that we are two,
And two are twice as powerful as one.
Now look; when he comes back, get up in fun
To have a wrestle; then, as you attack,
I'll up and put my dagger through his back
While you and he are struggling, as in game;

134 prudent (prüd′nt), *adj.* sensible; discreet.

This shield from the late 1400s was not intended for combat but for display at a tournament. The image of Death reflects the knight's willingness to die in battle to honor his lady. Why might images of death have been so widespread in medieval art?

MINI-LESSON: READING/THINKING SKILLS

Synthesize

Teach Tell students that irony depends upon the perspective, or point of view, of an observer. For example, the plight of an employee who resigns just before he or she is to receive a promotion is ironic only when one steps back from the situation.

Activity Idea Ask students to consider the elements of the Pardoner's prologue and tale from the standpoint of two people, one who believes the Pardoner's pitch and one who does not.

Then draw your dagger too and do the same.
Then all this money will be ours to spend,
Divided equally of course, dear friend.
Then we can gratify our lusts and fill
The day with dicing at our own sweet will."
Thus these two miscreants agreed to slay
The third and youngest, as you heard me say.
The youngest, as he ran towards the town,
Kept turning over, rolling up and down
Within his heart the beauty of those bright
New florins, saying, "Lord, to think I might
Have all that treasure to myself alone!
Could there be anyone beneath the throne
Of God so happy as I then should be?"
And so the Fiend, our common enemy,
Was given power to put it in his thought
That there was always poison to be bought,
And that with poison he could kill his friends.
To men in such a state the Devil sends
Thoughts of this kind, and has a full permission
To lure them on to sorrow and perdition;
For this young man was utterly content
To kill them both and never to repent.
And on he ran, he had no thought to tarry,
Came to the town, found an apothecary
And said, "Sell me some poison if you will,
I have a lot of rats I want to kill
And there's a polecat too about my yard
That takes my chickens and it hits me hard;
But I'll get even, as is only right,
With vermin that destroy a man by night."
The chemist answered, "I've a preparation
Which you shall have, and by my soul's salvation
If any living creature eat or drink
A mouthful, ere he has the time to think,
Though he took less than makes a grain of wheat,
You'll see him fall down dying at your feet;
Yes, die he must, and in so short a while
You'd hardly have the time to walk a mile,
The poison is so strong, you understand."
This cursed fellow grabbed into his hand
The box of poison and away he ran
Into a neighbouring street, and found a man
Who lent him three large bottles. He withdrew
And deftly poured the poison into two.

177 miscreant (mis′krē ənt), *n.* wicked person; villain.

186 Fiend, Satan; the devil.

13 ■ Who do you think is going to come out on top of this situation?

192 perdition (pər dish′ ən), *n.* damnation.

196 apothecary (ə poth′ə-ker′ē), *n.* pharmacist

202 vermin (vėr′mən), *n. pl. or sing.* small animals, such as roaches and mice, that are troublesome or destructive.

13 Reading/Thinking Skills
Analyze

Before students answer this question, suggest that they analyze, or critically examine, what they know about the characters and the story so far.

Questions

- What is the narrator? *(a hypocrite)*
- Does the narrator's character have anything to do with the character of the story? *(possibly, but the slant may be ironic)*
- What does the young men taunting the old man suggest? *(that they are toying with death)*
- How do the young men respond to the pile of gold? *(Their greed makes them the prey of the devil.)*

Analyze The clues suggest that young men, drunk with greed and under the sway of Satan, are toying with death.

Response Now, who do you think is going to come out on top of this situation? *(In the end, Death will have his way.)*

The World of Work
Pharmacist

For the life experiences of a pharmacist, use the pages referenced below.

The World of Work
pp. 3–4

BUILDING ENGLISH PROFICIENCY

Relating Key Concepts

Exploring the effects of greed upon friendship will help students understand the Pardoner's moral: *Radix malorum est cupiditas.*

1. Have students copy this chart and work in pairs to complete it.

2. Ask one partner to jot down three notes about the friendship that the men shared.

3. Ask the other partner to jot down three notes about the greed that destroyed the friendship.

Friendship		Greed
1.	versus	1.
2.		2.
3.		3.

Art Study

Response to Caption Question Students may respond that the Pardoner in this illustration appears a little pastey or sickly, but not particularly evil.

Visual Literarcy While stories of Chaucer's time are populated with characters that personify goodness, evil, and death, Chaucer's original audience, unaffected by stock movie and TV characters, may have had fewer preconceptions than we do about how goodness and evil come wrapped.

14 Literary Focus
Irony

Question The climax of the Pardoner's tale supplies what kind of irony—verbal, dramatic, or situational? Why? *(situational; the irony results from an unexpected event—the murderers being murdered by their victim; another source of irony is Death's clever trap—taking them through the device of their own greed.)*

He kept the third one clean, as well he might,
For his own drink, meaning to work all night
Stacking the gold and carrying it away.
And when this rioter, this devil's clay,
Had filled his bottles up with wine, all three,
Back to rejoin his comrades sauntered he.
Why make a sermon of it? Why waste breath?
Exactly in the way they'd planned his death
They fell on him and slew him, two to one.
Then said the first of them when this was done,
"Now for a drink. Sit down and let's be merry,
For later on there'll be the corpse to bury."
And, as it happened, reaching for a sup,
He took a bottle full of poison up
And drank; and his companion, nothing loth,
Drank from it also, and they perished both.
There is in Avicenna's long relation
Concerning poison and its operation,
Trust me, no ghastlier section to transcend
What these two wretches suffered at their end.
Thus these two murderers received their due,
So did the treacherous young poisoner too.

"'O cursed sin! O blackguardly excess!
O treacherous homicide! O wickedness!
O gluttony that lusted on and diced!
O blasphemy that took the name of Christ
With habit-hardened oaths that pride began!
Alas, how comes it that a mortal man,
That thou, to thy Creator, Him that wrought thee,
That paid His precious blood for thee and bought thee,
Art so unnatural and false within?
"'Dearly beloved, God forgive your sin
And keep you from the vice of avarice!
My holy pardon frees you all of this,
Provided that you make the right approaches,
That is with sterling, rings, or silver brooches.
Bow down your heads under this holy bull!
Come on, you women, offer up your wool!
I'll write your name into my ledger; so!
Into the bliss of Heaven you shall go.
For I'll absolve you by my holy power,
You that make offering, clean as at the hour
When you were born. . . .' That, sirs, is how I preach.
And Jesu Christ, soul's healer, aye, the leech
Of every soul, grant pardon and relieve you

The Pardoner, from the Ellesmere Manuscript copy of *The Canterbury Tales,* about 1410. In this illuminated manuscript, the text was copied out by hand, and marginal drawings and highly ornate capital letters were used for decoration. How does this compare with the way you visualized the Pardoner?

233 Avicenna's long relation. Avicenna was an eleventh-century Arab physician who wrote a reference book (the "long relation") on poison.

242 blasphemy (blas′fə mē), *n.* abuse of or contempt for God.

257 absolve (ab solv′), *v.* free a person from guilt or punishment for sin.

260 leech, here, doctor. In earlier times physicians used leeches to draw blood from patients as a method of treating diseases.

MINI-LESSON: VOCABULARY

Recognize Slang

Teach Explain to students that money is very important to the Pardoner; things very important to people are usually given many names. The Japanese, for example, have many synonyms for rice.

Question What names for money does the Pardoner use on pages 49 and 53? *(pence, groat, mark, pelf, florin, gold)*

Activity Idea Have students look up the following words and their etymologies. Ask which terms are in the dictionary; which are slang; which are standard English; and which they have previous used, heard, or come across while reading. Ask in what context each term would most likely be used.

Word List	
brass	dollar
bread	dough
buck	gold
cabbage	lucre
cash	mammon
change	moolah
currency	silver
dead presidents	simoleons

Of sin, for that is best, I won't deceive you.
"One thing I should have mentioned in my tale,
Dear people. I've some relics in my bale
And pardons too, as full and fine, I hope,
As any in England, given me by the Pope.
If there be one among you that is willing
To have my absolution for a shilling
Devoutly given, come! and do not harden
Your hearts but kneel in humbleness for pardon;
Or else, receive my pardon as we go.
You can renew it every town or so
Always provided that you still renew
Each time, and in good money, what is due.
It is an honor to you to have found
A pardoner with his credentials sound
Who can absolve you as you ply the spur
In any accident that may occur.
For instance—we are all at Fortune's beck—
Your horse may throw you down and break your neck.
What a security it is to all
To have me here among you and at call
With pardon for the lowly and the great
When soul leaves body for the future state!
And I advise our Host here to begin,
The most enveloped of you all in sin.
Come forward, Host, you shall be the first to pay,
And kiss my holy relics right away.
Only a groat. Come on, unbuckle your purse!"
"No, no," said he, "not I, and may the curse
Of Christ descend upon me if I do!
You'll have me kissing your old breeches too
And swear they were the relic of a saint. . . ."
The Pardoner said nothing, not a word;
He was so angry that he couldn't speak.
"Well," said our Host, "if you're for showing pique,
I'll joke no more, not with an angry man."
The worthy Knight immediately began,
Seeing the fun was getting rather rough,
And said, "No more, we've all had quite enough.
Now, Master Pardoner, perk up, look cheerly!
And you, Sir Host, whom I esteem so dearly,
I beg of you to kiss the Pardoner.
"Come, Pardoner, draw nearer, my dear sir.
Let's laugh again and keep the ball in play."
They kissed, and we continued on our way.

264 bale, bundle.

268 absolution (ab′sə-lü′shən), *n.* a declaration that frees a person from guilt or punishment for sin.

285 Host, the keeper of the Tabard Inn where the pilgrims gather before setting out. The Host proposes the story-telling and accompanies the pilgrims to judge which tale is best.

296 pique (pēk), *n.* anger; wounded pride.

298 Knight, another one of the pilgrims.

EDITORIAL NOTE At line 294, the following—

"And swear they were the relic of a saint
Although your fundament supplied the paint!
Now by St. Helen and the Holy Land
I wish I had your ballocks in my hand
Instead of relics in a reliquarium;
Have them cut off and I will help to carry 'em.
We'll have them shrined for you in a hog's turd.' "

has been edited to—

"And swear they were the relic of a saint. . . .' "

Check Test

1. According to the narrator, who do people go to pay homage to at Canterbury? *(the martyred Saint Thomas à Becket)*
2. What is the Pardoner's hypocritical motto? *(Avarice is the root of all evil.)*
3. The Pardoner says his exclusive purpose is to win (money), not to do what? *(pardon people for their sins in order to reconcile them with God)*
4. In the Pardoner's tale, what made the three men so angry at Death? *(Death had just taken the life of a friend.)*
5. Who intervened in the unpleasant exchange between the Pardoner and the Host? *(the Knight, another pilgrim)*

Unit 1 Resource Book
Alternate Check Test, p. 29

BUILDING ENGLISH PROFICIENCY

Exploring Characterization

After telling a story about the tragic effects of greed, the Pardoner prays that his listeners would not fall into "the vice of avarice"—and then proceeds to make a sales pitch. Encourage students to see how this point illuminates his character.

1. Write the following statement on the chalkboard: You should buy "my holy pardon" because _____.
2. Ask students to look through lines 260–289 for answers and express those answers in their own words. *(Sample answers: You will be forgiven; you will go to heaven; my pardons can be renewed, for a price; you never know when Death may take you.)*
3. Ask: If you heard this sales pitch, would you buy a pardon? Why or why not?

After Reading

MAKING CONNECTIONS

1. Possible responses: hypocritical, avaricious, dishonest, vicious

2. Possible responses: Yes, everyone has inconsistencies in his or her character. No; while most people have inconsistencies in their characters, they are not so completely dishonest and hypocritical.

3. Students should recognize the old man as a personification of death or, possibly, Satan.

4. It is unlikely, because he has shown himself to be dishonest and a hypocrite, and he has been ridiculed by the host.

5. Yes, on at least two levels—the tale the Pardoner relates and the example the Pardoner offers.

6. Students might mention greedy stock and bond traders and bankers who have gone to prison for fraud; hoteliers who have gone to prison for tax evasion; or Congressmen who have been forced to resign because of illegal or highly suspect behavior.

After Reading

Making Connections

Shaping Your Response

1. In one word or phrase, describe the Pardoner.
2. The Pardoner admits to being a "wholly vicious man" (line 133) and yet he preaches moral tales designed to show that avarice is a vice. Do you think he represents typical human behavior? Explain.

Analyzing the Narrative Poem

3. The three rioters set out to find "this traitor Death." Instead, they find the old man, who directs them to the tree where they find the money. Who do you think the old man is?
4. After relating his tale, the Pardoner tries to sell the pilgrims his pardon and offers his relics for kissing. How likely is it that the pilgrims will buy his indulgences?
5. In your opinion, does *The Pardoner's Tale* illustrate the **theme** of his Latin text, "Radix malorum est cupiditas"? Explain.

Extending the Ideas

6. Chaucer wrote *The Pardoner's Tale* in the 1300s. Relate some examples you have heard from the 1990s of people like the three rioters who cause their own downfalls or deaths.

Literary Focus: Irony

Irony lies in the contrast between what appears to be and what really is. In situational irony, something occurs contrary to what the characters expect or intend. Explain the irony in these situations from *The Pardoner's Tale:*

1. The tavern keeper tells the rioters, "you'd best be wary" of Death, but they swear that when they catch him, "Death is dead!"
2. The "very poor old man" claims that Death won't take his life.
3. The three rioters look for Death under a tree in a nearby grove. When they find money instead, they forget about looking for Death.
4. After his tale, the Pardoner tells the other pilgrims that it is "an honor" for them to have found him.

Vocabulary Study

An analogy is a relationship. An analogy can be expressed this way:

TREE : GROVE :: house : village (Read: "Tree is to grove as house is to village.")

Word analogy tests require you to determine the relationship between a pair of words and then to choose another pair of words with the same relationship. In this example, you would first determine that a tree is found in a grove and then look for another pair of words in

LITERARY FOCUS: IRONY

1. Contrary to their threat, it is the rioters who are doomed.

2. Death can't take him, because he is death.

3. They forget about looking for Death, but it is at that moment that they have found death.

4. It is not an honor he offers them, but a genial holdup.

which something (house) is found in something else (village). Word analogies may reflect relationships such as antonyms (love : enmity); synonyms (abject : miserable); cause-effect (gunshot : injury); or person-place (teacher : classroom).

Study the relationship of each of the following pairs of words in capital letters; then choose another pair that has the same relationship.

1. AVARICE : GREED ::
   a. vice : wickedness **b.** church : tavern
   c. minister : sermon **d.** spring : fall
2. PUBLICAN : TAVERN ::
   a. rage : anger **b.** death : life
   c. preacher : pulpit **d.** writer : poet
3. ADVERSARY : FRIEND ::
   a. fish : water **b.** heat : cold
   c. wheat : grain **d.** wing : bird
4. SIN : ABSOLUTION ::
   a. rainstorm : flooding **b.** fever : medicine
   c. imagination : fancy **d.** sadness : tears
5. INSULT : PIQUE ::
   a. dislike : hate **b.** twilight : night
   c. velvet : cloth **d.** praise : pleasure

Expressing Your Ideas

Writing Choices

Writer's Notebook Update Choose some of the people you have listed who are representative of society today and who might go on a modern-day pilgrimage. Write character descriptions of two or three of them.

The Homeville Tales Use the notes you wrote in your notebook and plan a **television series** in which the travelers and their tales would be updated. Describe the cast of characters and the place where they meet to share their stories.

Other Options

In the Flesh? Create an **illustration** for *The Pardoner's Prologue* or *Tale* in any medium that you wish. Your work might be on paper, modeled in clay, or created from cloth or canvas. Or, you might choose to mime or to act out the story using simple costumes and props.

Heaven for Sale In order to increase business, the Pardoner has hired you as his publicity agent. Create a **poster** that will advertise what the Pardoner has to offer and that will increase sales of indulgences. Remember that an effective picture and a good, snappy headline may be more effective than a lot of words.

VOCABULARY STUDY

1. A—synonyms
2. C—person/place
3. B—antonyms
4. B—cause/effect
5. D—cause/effect

More Practice Suggest that students make up their own set of analogies using the five relationships exemplified in the Vocabulary Study.

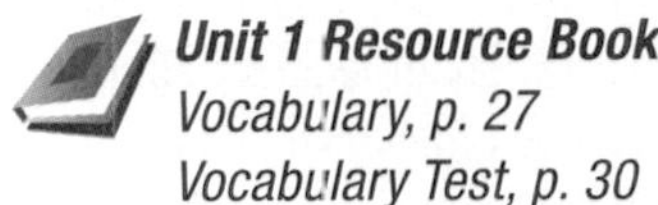

Unit 1 Resource Book
Vocabulary, p. 27
Vocabulary Test, p. 30

WRITING CHOICES

Writer's Notebook Update

Remind students to make their character descriptions as complete as possible, describing not only the appearance of the characters but also their mannerisms—unique and individual characteristics of speech and action.

The Homeville Tales

Support students in this activity by asking the following questions as prompts:

Are all pilgrimages religious?

What are some destinations to which people in our time are drawn?

- to honor someone
- to be in a place where a personally meaningful event occurred
- for recreation
- for thrill-seeking

OTHER OPTIONS

In the Flesh?

Suggest that students look at art in this selection if they need ideas. They could also illustrate what they think is the most dramatic scene.

Heaven for Sale

If students have a hard time getting started with this activity, suggest they look through magazines and at billboards for examples of popular advertising and public relations techniques.

Selection Test

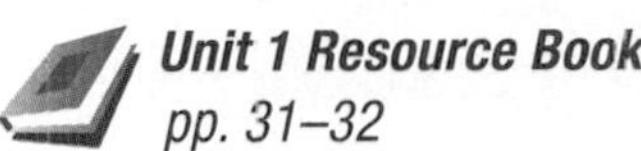

Unit 1 Resource Book
pp. 31–32

Before Reading

Building Background

Ask students to share with the class the kinds of missions various comic-book heroes impose upon themselves.

Literary Focus

Suggest to students that they are already familiar with the use of foreshadowing from watching movies and television. Both mediums use a variety of techniques—music, lighting, costumes, even weather—to hint at what is to come.

Writer's Notebook

Have students list examples of contemporary knights in shining armor. Remind them that, today, being a hero is an equal-opportunity occupation.

More About the Gawain Poet

The author, a contemporary of Chaucer, is considered an urbane and sophisticated poet whose known works include

- *Patience*
- *Purity*
- *Cleanness*
- *Pearl*

Before Reading

from Sir Gawain and the Green Knight

The Gawain–poet
late 1300s

Who is the author? We don't know. Although four of his works, including *Sir Gawain* (gä′wän) *and the Green Knight,* survive in a single manuscript, we don't even know the author's name. What was he like? There at least we can make some guesses. He wrote in a provincial dialect which suggests he lived in the West Midlands, northwest of London. He entertained his aristocratic audience with descriptions of the grandeur of English castles and the fierceness of the English countryside. He knew details of castle life and courtly behavior. He believed in the search for knightly perfection.

Building Background

The Medieval Romance In the medieval period the term *romance* had little to do with romantic love; it meant instead a long narrative in verse or prose telling of the adventures of a hero. These stories usually include knights, ladies in distress, kings, villains—and often a touch of the supernatural. Central to the medieval romance is the **code of chivalry,** the rules and customs connected with knighthood. Originally *chivalry* (from the French word *chevalier,* meaning "knight" or "horseman") referred to the training of knights for warfare. The concept broadened to include qualities of courtly behavior: bravery, honor, courtesy, generosity, respect for women, protection of the weak, and fairness to enemies. The materials for the medieval romance in English are mainly drawn from the stories of King Arthur and the knights of the Round Table at Camelot, where Arthur held his court (see also pages 88–93), as is *Sir Gawain and the Green Knight*.

Literary Focus

Foreshadowing Many authors make a point of dropping hints to their readers, suggestions about what's to come later in the action. This technique, called **foreshadowing,** creates suspense and encourages the reader to guess about future events and the outcome of the story. Sometimes a single word, sometimes a description, sometimes a character's action—or lack of action—will be just the hint that starts the reader guessing. As you read this romance, look for hints about what Gawain will face.

Writer's Notebook

Knight in Shining Armor When you hear the phrase "knight in shining armor," you might imagine a handsome, heroic figure charging into battle. Yet the medieval code of chivalry extended far beyond strength and bravery. Create a diagram in which you list in one circle qualities that you imagine a medieval knight would possess. In the other circle, list the traits you think a modern "knight" should possess. What traits do they share? List them where the circles overlap.

Medieval Knight | strength, bravery | Modern Knight

SUPPORT MATERIALS OVERVIEW

Unit 1 Resource Book
- Graphic Organizer, p. 33
- Study Guide, p. 34
- Vocabulary, p. 35
- Grammar, p. 36
- Alternate Check Test, p. 37
- Vocabulary Test, p. 38
- Selection Test, pp. 39–40

Building English Proficiency
- Selection Summaries
- Activities, p. 208

Reading, Writing, & Grammar SkillBook
- Reading, pp. 71–73
- Grammar, Usage, and Mechanics, pp. 149–152

Technology
- Audiotape
- Personal Journal Software.
- Custom Literature Database: For other selections dealing with Codes of Honor, see *The Second Shepherd's Play* and *Everyman* on the database.
- Test Generator Software

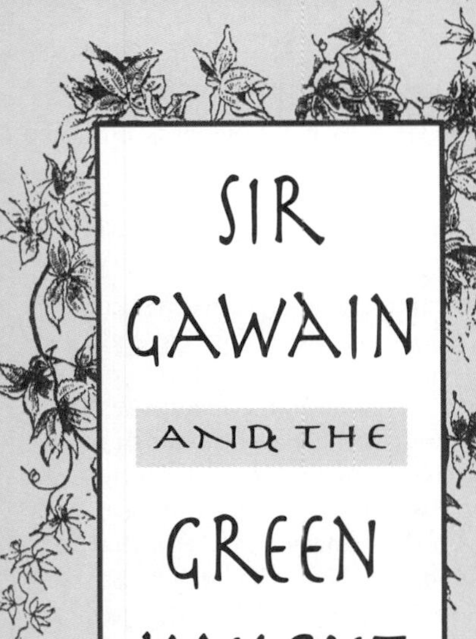

SIR GAWAIN AND THE GREEN KNIGHT

translated by
M.R. RIDLEY

Part 1

King Arthur lay at Camelot at Christmas, with many of his lords, great knights, all the noble brotherhood of the Round Table, and they kept high revel with carefree merrymaking. There were many tourneys, with gallant jousting of knights, and after the jousting they rode to the court for song

Legends of King Arthur and his Knights of the Round Table have inspired writers, poets, and artists for centuries. This painting entitled *Sir Galahad* by George Frederick Watts (1817–1904) shows an interpretation from the 1800s. What elements of knighthood are idealized here? ➤

During Reading

Selection Objectives

- to read an example of a Middle English romance
- to identify and understand foreshadowing as a literary device
- to explore the theme of accepting personal imperfection
- to recognize and correct run-on sentences

Unit 1 Resource Book
Graphic Organizer, p. 33
Study Guide, p. 34

Theme Link

In this excerpt from "Sir Gawain and the Green Knight," the Code of Honor theme is examined through Gawain's courageous but impulsive offer to do battle with the Green Knight.

Vocabulary Preview

hauberk, a flexible coat of armor made of chain mail
prodigious, huge
boon, favor
liege, honorable; having a right to respect and service
spate, a sudden flood
recreant, coward
dolorous, sorrowful
lissomely, limberly; supplely
doughty, brave
baldric, a belt hung from one shoulder to support a sword

Students can add the words and definitions to their Writer's Notebooks.

SELECTION SUMMARY

Sir Gawain and the Green Knight

A knight, green of skin and clothing, appears at Arthur's court and challenges anyone to an exchange of ax blows; he will receive the first stroke if he can deliver the second a year hence. Gawain beheads the knight. The headless knight then reminds Gawain of their bargain. A year later Gawain, en route to meet his fate, accepts from an amorous hostess a girdle that makes him invincible. When he faces the Green Knight, the ax blow barely cuts him. He confesses that he wears a magic girdle; the knight reveals that the challenge was Morgan la Fay's scheme to discredit Arthur. Gawain resolves to wear the girdle as a reminder of his own imperfection.

*For summaries in other languages, see the **Building English Proficiency** book.*

Art Study

Response to Caption Question
The idealized warrior appears noble and courageous, yet sensitive and poetic.

1 Literary Focus
Foreshadowing

Question What in this passage foreshadows that something is about to occur? *(Arthur's restlessness; discussion of strange tales, feats of arms)*

2 Literary Element
Personification

The Green Knight is introduced with an elaborate description. Begin by asking students why they think he might be green.

Question Why do you think the Green Knight is carrying holly? *(Possible responses: It's Christmas, with which holly is associated; the "green" knight carries what is "greenest of all when the leaves fall.")*

Point out various "green" associations: e.g., during the shortest days of the year, we bring in "evergreen"—holly and Christmas trees; political parties interested in ecology are called Green parties; people who are considered young and innocent are often called "green."

Question What do you think this "green" man might represent or personify? *(Possible responses: nature; its renewal; the promise of rebirth; life everlasting)*

EDITORIAL NOTE This excerpt has been shortened for length. For a more complete version of "Sir Gawain and the Green Knight," see the Custom Literature Database.

and dance; the festival went on full fifteen days, with all the banqueting and jollity that could be devised.

On New Year's Day there was a great banquet, with double portions, for the whole company. First, Mass was sung in the chapel, with loud chanting of the priests and the rest, and they celebrated the octave of Christmas.[1] When the service came to an end, the King came into the great hall with his knights, and some hurried forward with the New Year's gifts held high above their heads, and there was a busy contest for them; those that won a prize were glad, but even the ladies who won nothing laughed at their failure. So they made merry till it was time for dinner, and then they washed and went to their appointed seats, the noblest, as was right, at the high table. In the center of the dais[2] sat the Queen, Guenevere,[3] with her clear gray eyes, loveliest of ladies, splendidly gowned.

1 But Arthur would not sit down to eat till all the rest were served. He was so glad in his youth, and boyish in his eagerness, and his young blood ran high and his mind was restless, so that he never could be idle or sit still for long. But there was something else that kept him from his seat, a custom that his high heart had devised, that on a great festival such as this he would eat no meat till he had heard some strange tale of adventure, of the deeds of princes, or feats of arms, some great wonder which he might listen to and believe; or it might be that some strange knight would come, and ask him to name one of his own true knights to joust[4] with him, each staking his life on his skill, and granting the other such advantage as fortune should bring him.

So the tables were set with the choicest fare, and the trumpets sounded a fresh fanfare as a sign that the feast might begin. But the notes had hardly died away when there swung in at the hall door a fearsome warrior, the tallest of all on earth. From the neck to the waist he was so thick-set and squarely built, and he was so long in flank and limb, that one might have thought he was half a giant; but he was in fact a man, as mighty as any horse could bear in saddle, but yet shapely in his mightiness, burly in back and breast, but slender in the waist and with clean-run limbs. They were all amazed at his color, for they saw that he was bright green all over. His clothes were green, too. He wore a plain close-fitting coat of green, and over that a gay green mantle, lined with close-trimmed white fur. The hood of the mantle was the same, green outside and lined with white fur, and he had thrown it back off his hair so that it lay on his shoulders. His legs were clothed in long green hose, close-fitting, so that you could see the play of the muscles under them. He rode a huge green horse; his mane and his tail, green as the rest of him, were curled and combed and plaited with thread-of-gold and adorned with emeralds.

They all looked at him in wonder, as he sat there on his great horse, flashing and bright as the lightning; and they thought that if it came to fighting there could be no man in the world who could withstand him, so mighty a warrior he seemed. But he wore no armor, no helmet, nor hauberk, nor gorget;[5] he carried no shield, nor lance, nor sword. In one hand he held a bunch of 2
holly, the tree that stays greenest of all when the leaves fall from others in autumn. But in the other hand he grasped his one weapon, and a terrible enough weapon it was, a prodigious[6] battle-ax, with a spike sticking out beyond the head.

The Green Knight rode up the hall, right to the dais, fearless of danger. He greeted no one as he rode, but looked straight before him over

1. **the octave of Christmas.** The observance of major feasts like Christmas occupied a full week, concluding on the eighth day.
2. **dais** (dā′is), *n.* a raised platform at one end of a hall for a throne or seats of honor.
3. **Guenevere** (gwen′ə vir).
4. **joust** (joust), *v.* fight on horseback with spear-like lances.
5. **hauberk** (hô′bərk), *n.* . . . **gorget** (gôr′jit), *n.* A hauberk was a flexible coat of armor made of small loops of chain linked together. A gorget was a piece of armor for the throat.
6. **prodigious** (prə dij′əs), *adj.* huge.

MINI-LESSON: GRAMMAR
Recognizing Run-on Sentences

Teach Tell students that a *run-on sentence* combines two sentences but omits coordinating conjunctions or appropriate punctuation. Write the following on the board:

> On New Year's Day there was a great banquet, with double portions, for the whole company first, Mass was sung in the chapel, with loud chanting of the priests and the rest, they celebrated the octave of Christmas.

Point out that the text just runs on in a confusing manner. Then have students note the actual text at the top of column 1. One sentence ends with a period after *company.* Then, two independent clauses are combined with *and* after *rest.*

Good writers do not write run-on sentences. What may look like a run-on (e.g., column 1, paragraph 2, the third sentence) is just a compound-complex sentence with several dependent clauses.

Activity Idea Have students make run-on sentences out of several sentences in the story. A partner can correct the run-ons. Then, to see that there is more than one correct way to rewrite *if the meaning is not changed,* they can compare theirs with the actual text.

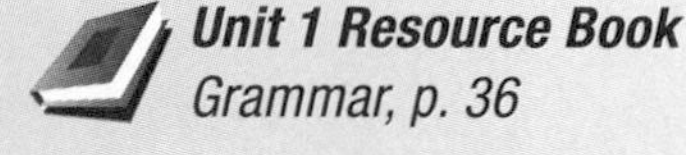

Unit 1 Resource Book
Grammar, p. 36

their heads, and the first words he spoke were: "Where is the ruler of this company? It is he that I want to see and to have plain speech with him." And with that he let his eyes rove over the company, and scanned each man to see who might seem to be a knight of renown.

> THEY HAD SEEN MANY MARVELS, BUT NEVER BEFORE SUCH A MARVEL AS THIS. . . .

Long they gazed at him, astonished what this marvel might mean, the Green Knight on the green horse, greener than grass, both gleaming more like a piece of jewelry, green enamel on gold, than like flesh and blood. They all scanned him, to see what it was that stood there, and walked round him, wondering what his purpose was. They had seen many marvels, but never before such a marvel as this, and they thought he must be some phantom from the land of Faërie.[7] And all were amazed at his words, and some were afraid to answer, and some waited in courtesy for the King to make reply. So they sat still as stones, and there was heavy silence through the great hall, as though they were all asleep.

There was Arthur's adventure for him, plain before his eyes. He stood before the dais, fearless, and gave the stranger a ready salutation. "You are welcome, sir, to this place. I am the master of this house, and my name is Arthur. Light down from your horse, I pray you, and stay and eat with us, and after that let us know what your will is."

But the Green Knight answered him: "Not so; so God help me, who sits throned above the skies, it was none of my errand to wait any while in this dwelling. But your renown, my lord, is spread wide about the world, and the warriors that live in your castle are held to be the best, the stoutest to ride out in their steel-gear, bravest and worthiest of all men on earth, valiant to contend with in all fair contests, and here, I have heard it told, all the true ways of courtesy are known. It is that which has drawn me hither today. You may be sure by this branch which I bear in my hand that I come in peace, seeking no danger. For if I had made my journey with battle in my thoughts, I have a hauberk at home, and a helmet, a shield and a sharp spear, bright-shining, and other weapons too, and I can wield them. But since I look for no war, I wear the softer clothes of a traveler. If you are bold as all men tell, you will grant me freely the sport that I ask for."

Arthur said, "Sir knight, even if it is just a combat that you crave, we can find a man to fight you."

"No," said he. "I am telling you the truth, it is no fight that I am seeking. All who are sitting around the hall are no more than beardless 3 children, and if I were buckled in my armor, and riding my war charger, there is no man here who could match his feeble might against mine in combat. All I ask in this court is just a Christmas game, seeing that it is the time of Noel and New Year, and here are many young warriors. If there is any man in this hall who counts himself bold enough, hot in blood and rash in brain, stoutly to change stroke for stroke with me, I will give him, as a free gift, this battle-ax. It is heavy enough, and he can wield it as he pleases. I shall abide the first blow, unarmed as I am now. If any man is bold enough to test what I say, let him come swiftly to me and grasp this weapon—I quit-claim[8] it forever, and he can keep it for his own—and I shall stand up to his stroke, steady on the floor of this hall. But you must proclaim my right to have a free blow at him in return, though I will grant him the respite

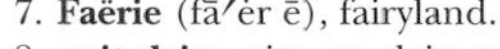

7. **Faërie** (fā′ər ē), fairyland.
8. **quit-claim,** give up claim to.

3 Reading/Thinking Skills
Compare and Contrast

Ask students to compare and contrast "All who are sitting around the hall are no more than beardless children . . ." with the Green Knight's previous statement: "The warriors that live in your castle are held to be the best, the stoutest to ride out in their steel-gear, bravest and worthiest of all men on earth."

Questions

- Does the second statement contradict the first? *(Possible responses: It would appear to; however, he might be saying the "best and stoutest warriors on earth" are "but beardless children" compared to himself.)*
- Do you think Arthur and his knights are being insulted? Why? *(Possible response: Yes, the Green Knight seems to want to provoke.)*

BUILDING ENGLISH PROFICIENCY

Considering a Key Concept

Exploring the meaning of *courage* will help students better understand the characters and themes in this story.

Activity Ideas

- Suggest that students think about times when they (or people they know personally) have shown courage. Have them write about one of these times in a private journal (which they may keep in their first language). Later, when students discuss personal reactions to the story, encourage them to draw upon these comments.
- Bring a set of newspapers to class. Ask students to find stories about times when others, people they do not know, have shown courage in the face of different kinds of danger. Ask them to summarize one of these stories for their journal and write a personal reaction to it.

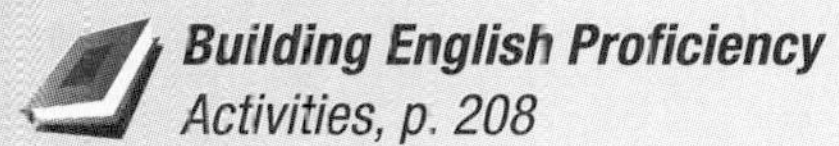

Building English Proficiency
Activities, p. 208

4 Active Reading
Summarize

Response To exchange blows with him, each taking a blow unarmed.

5 Historical Note
Origin of a Theme in the Selection

The author of "Sir Gawain and the Green Knight" did not invent the story of a challenger who proposes matching blows with an ax. A similar scene was originally presented in a ninth-century Irish narrative, "Bricriu's Feast."

6 Active Reading
Clarify

Possible Responses

- Why does he speak so humbly?
- What prompts him to ask Arthur to allow him to accept the challenge in Arthur's stead?
- How do his manner and speech relate to the code of chivalry?
- Is it unseemly for a knight to suggest to his king that the king's behavior is unseemly?

of a year and a day. Now let us see quickly, dares any man speak?"

4 **SUMMARIZE: What Christmas challenge does the Green Knight offer to the court?**

They had been astonished at first, when he rode into the hall, but they were stiller than ever now, both high and low. The Green Knight turned in his saddle, and his angry eyes roved savagely over the rows of sitting men, and he bent his bristling eyebrows, that flashed green as he moved, and he waved his beard as he sat and waited for someone to rise. And when no
5 one answered his challenge he coughed scornfully, and gave himself a great stretch with an air of insulting them, and started to speak.

"Well," said he, "is this Arthur's house, of which the renown runs through so many kingdoms? What has happened to your conceit and your boasted conquests, the fierceness of your wrath and your high words? All the revels and the renown of the famous Round Table are overturned with one word of one man, for you are all cowering for fear, and no one has lifted a finger." And he threw back his head, and laughed loud in their faces. The King felt the insult, and shame made the blood rush to his fair forehead and cheek, as the tempest of his anger rose, and he felt the anger also of his knights rising all round him. And he moved boldly forward, and stood by the Green Knight's stirrup, and spoke.

"Sir, by heaven, what you ask is foolishness. If it is folly that you seek, it is folly you shall rightly find. There is not a man in this hall that is afraid of your big words. Give me your battle-ax, for God's sake, and I will grant you myself the boon[9] you have asked for." He gave him his hand, and the knight got proudly down from the saddle to the floor. Arthur took the ax in his hand, and grasped the helve,[10] and swung it this way and that, trying the weight to see what the feel of it would be when he struck. The stout warrior stood there before him, towering head and shoulders above any man in the hall. He stood grimly stroking his beard, and not a muscle in his stern face moved as he drew down his coat, no more daunted or dismayed for the stroke that was coming than if someone on the seat beside him had offered him a goblet of wine.

Then Gawain, from where he sat by the Queen's side, leaned forward and spoke to the King. "I pray you, my lord, in plain words, let this combat be mine. Bid me rise from my seat and stand by you, so that without discourtesy to my liege[11] lady the Queen I can leave her side; and I will give you my counsel before all this noble company. In truth it is not seemly, when such a challenge is thrown out in your hall, that you yourself should be so eager to take it up, when there are sitting all round you so many of your knights. There are none in the world firmer of will, or stauncher fighters on a stricken field. I may be the weakest of all of them, and the feeblest of wit; there is nothing about me to praise except that you are my uncle, and all the virtue that is in me is the blood I share with you. But since this business is so foolish, and beneath your dignity as King, and since I have made my request first, grant it to me. Whether I have spoken fittingly or not, I leave to this company to decide. Let them speak their minds freely."

QUESTION: What questions do you have about the way Gawain describes himself and his behavior to this point? 6

So the knights whispered together, and they were all of one mind, that the crowned King should be relieved of the challenge, and Gawain given the game.

Then the King commanded Gawain to rise from his place; and he rose quickly, and came

9. **boon** (bŭn), *n.* favor.
10. **helv** (helv), *n.* handle.
11. **liege** (lēj), *adj.* honorable; having a right to respect and service.

MINI-LESSON: READING/THINKING SKILLS
Cause and Effect

Teach Suggest to students that a person's action may stem from a variety of causes.

- Personal background or beliefs may trigger certain actions.
- One event can trigger another, as a reflex action.
- A philosophical cause, or pursuit of individual goals, often dictates action, good and bad.

Activity Idea Ask groups of students to analyze Gawain's response to the Green Knight's challenge by deciding what may have motivated him. Suggest that they brainstorm among themselves, keeping lists of possibilities, which could include the three above, before deciding on one or two causes to be reported orally.

and knelt before the King, and grasped the great ax. And the king let him take it, and lifted up his hand and gave him the blessing of God, and cheerfully bade him be hardy both of heart and hand. "Take care, cousin,"[12] he
7 said, "over your blow; and if you direct it aright I am well sure that you will stand up to the blow that he will deal you later."

Gawain went to the Green Knight with the battle-ax in hand, and the Knight waited for him, calm and undismayed, and spoke to Gawain. "Before we go forward with this business, let us say over again our covenant.[13] First, I ask you, sir, tell me truly your name."

"I am called Gawain," he said, "I that am to deal you this buffet,[14] whatever happens later; and a year from today I will come, and no man else with me, and you shall deal me another blow in return, with what weapon you will."

> THE FAIR HEAD FELL FROM THE NECK AND ROLLED AMOUNG THE FEASTERS, WHO PUSHED IT AWAY WITH THEIR FEET.

And the Green Knight answered. "Sir Gawain, so may I thrive as I am wondrously eager that you shall let drive at me. By God, sir, I am glad that it is from your hand that I am to get what I asked for here; and you have rehearsed exactly, point by point, all the covenant that I sought of the King, except this—Promise me, on your honor, that at the year's end you yourself will come and seek me out wherever you think I may be found, and take from me the wages for whatever you deal me today before this noble company."

"Where am I to look for you?" said Gawain. "Where do you live? By God who made me, I know nothing of your dwelling, nor from what king's court you come, nor your name. Tell me truly your name, and where you live, and I will use all the skill I have to win my way thither; and that I swear on my troth[15] as a true knight."

"That is enough for New Year," said the Green Knight; "I need no more. If, when you have done me the courtesy of your blow, I tell you my house and my home and my own name, you will know all about me and be able to keep tryst.[16] And if I do not speak, you will be all the better off, for you can stay in your own land, and seek no further. But enough words! Take your grim tool in your hand, and let us see what kind of a man you are with the ax!"

"Gladly, sir knight," said Gawain, and ran his finger along the edge of the ax.

The Green Knight at once took up his stand, with his head a little bent, and his long hair thrown forward over the crown of his head, so that the naked flesh of his neck showed ready for the stroke. Gawain gripped his ax, and put his left foot forward to get his balance; then he hove up the ax above his head and brought it down swiftly and surely on the bare flesh, so that the sharp steel shore clean through the flesh and the bones and clove his neck in two, and the bright blade drove on and bit into the ground. The fair head fell from the neck and rolled among the feasters, who pushed it away with their feet. The blood spurted from the body and shone bright on the green mantle. The Green Knight did not fall nor even stagger, but 8

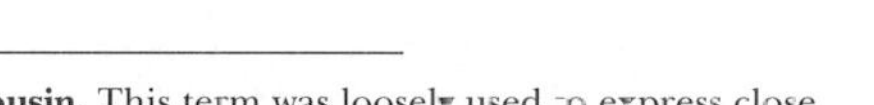

12. **cousin.** This term was loosely used to express close kinship.
13. **covenant** (kuv′ə nent), *n.* solemn agreement.
14. **buffet** (buf′it), *n.* blow; strike.
15. **troth** (trôth), *n.* faithfulness; loyalty.
16. **tryst** (trist), *n.* appointed meeting.

7 Literary Focus
Foreshadowing

Question What does King Arthur's advice to his nephew foreshadow? *(that Gawain will survive this challenge)*

8 Historical Note
Beheading

The idea of guests at a Christmas feast watching a man literally losing his head and then kicking it about is certainly a shocking image. But at the time "Sir Gawain and the Green Knight" was written (c. 1370), beheadings were not uncommon. This form of capital punishment was, however, reserved for offenders of high rank. The notion that beheading was "nicer" than hanging may have derived from ancient times; Greeks and Romans regarded it as an honorable form of death.

Lord Lovat, the last Englishman to be beheaded, was executed in April 1747. Subsequently, offenders of high birth were hanged, just like common folk, but with a silk rope. Bodies of previously hanged traitors continued to be beheaded until 1820; heads were displayed to serve as an example.

BUILDING ENGLISH PROFICIENCY

Expanding Vocabulary Notebooks

Students may be confused by words that have multiple meanings.

1. Encourage students to add such words to their vocabulary notebooks, perhaps using the chart shown. Some examples of multiple-meaning words from pages 64–65 are *fair, stout, drew, buffet, drive, shore,* and *clove.*

2. You may want to have students act out two meanings of the multiple-meaning words. See if the rest of the class can guess which words are being acted out.

Word	Meaning in Story	Sentence	Another Meaning
fair	good-looking	A fair lady waited beneath the tree.	just or honest

Reader's Response

Making Personal Connections

9

Questions

- Does this scene of the Green Knight on horseback, holding his head under his arm, remind you of anything? any other fictional character? *(Possible response: the headless horseman in Washington Irving's* The Legend of Sleepy Hollow, *which was based upon medieval folk tales)*
- Does this image suggest anything to you, other than a source of horror? *(Possible response: that humanity's attempts to control nature may be futile or will eventually backfire)*

strode firmly forward among the knights, and laid hold of his fair head and lifted it up. Then he turned to his horse, gathered the reins, put his foot in the stirrup-iron and swung himself into the saddle. He held his head by the hair, in his hand, and settled himself in his seat as 9 calmly as though nothing had happened to him, though he sat there headless; and he turned himself about, his gruesome bleeding trunk, and many were in dread of him before he had ended what he had to say.

For he held the head in his hand, and turned it so that it faced full at the guests on the high table. And the eyelids lifted, and the eyes gazed at them wide open; and the lips moved, and the head spoke.

"Sir Gawain, be prompt to come as you have promised and seek faithfully till you find me, as you have sworn now in this hall in the hearing of these knights. Make your way to the Green Chapel, I charge you, to receive such a blow as you have just dealt—well you deserve it—to be promptly paid on the morning of next New Year's Day. For men know me as the Knight of the Green Chapel. Seek therefore to find me and fail not, but come, or be called recreant[17] for ever."

With that he gave a roar, and wheeled his horse, and flung out at the hall door with his head in his hand; and the sparks flashed from the flints beneath his horse's hooves. To what land he went no man knew, any more than they had known whence he had come to them. The King and Gawain laughed together at the strangeness of the adventure, but all men there kept it in their hearts for a marvel.

Now take good heed, Sir Gawain, that you do not shrink, but go through to the end with this perilous venture that you have taken upon you.

A year later, after a feast in his honor, Sir Gawain sets off to keep his promise to the Green Knight. After journeying through grim landscapes and fighting dragons, ogres, and wild beasts, Gawain arrives, half dead with the cold and the sleet, at a shimmering castle. There he is warmly welcomed by the lord of the castle. Following days filled with Christmas feasting, games, and music, the lord of the castle plans three days of hunting in the forests and fields, but urges Gawain to rest in the castle in preparation for his upcoming challenge. The lord also offers a bargain to Gawain: "Whatever game I kill in the forest, it shall be yours, and whatever good fortune you come by here, give me that in exchange, whether it is of trifles or of something better." They agree to exchange their winnings at the end of each day.

On the first day the lord and his men hunt and kill many swift deer. In the meantime, Gawain, approached in his bed by the queen, reluctantly accepts a single kiss from her. At day's end the king gives Gawain his kill; in return Gawain kisses the king. At the end of the second day, the king returns with a huge boar for Gawain, who, having had a second visit from the queen, kisses the king twice.

Part 2

Gawain lay and slept quietly and sound all night, but the lord, who was full of his hunting, was up and about with the dawn. After they had heard Mass they ate a hasty breakfast, and the lord asked for his horse and went out to meet his knights, who were ready for him, dressed and mounted before the gates of the hall. It was a glorious morning; the hoarfrost sparkled bright on the ground, and the sun rose fiery red against the cloudrack, and his bright rays cut through the mists overhead. The huntsmen uncoupled by the side of a coppice,[18] and the rocks in the wood rang to the notes of the horns. Some of the hounds picked up the scent of the fox where he was lying, and they dashed this way and that across it as they were trained. One of them gave

17. recreant (rek′rē ənt), *n.* coward.
18. **coppice** (kop′is), *n.* a thicket of small trees.

MINI-LESSON: VOCABULARY

Word Choice

Teach Point out to students that the characters' choice of words creates the tone of a passage.

Activity Idea Invite students to look on pages 63–65 and note terms used by the characters for

- the Green Knight's challenge to Gawain
- the actions he and Gawain agree to take toward each other

Suggest that students brainstorm how use of these words cloak the horror of what the Green Knight and Gawain are about to do.

tongue on it, the huntsman called to him, and all the rest made after him, panting in full cry on a high scent. The fox ran before them, and soon they made him break covert, and as soon as they saw him they bayed furiously. He twisted and turned through many a rough patch of undergrowth, and doubled back, and often waited in the bottom of a hedge to listen. So the cunning fox led them, the lord and his men, all round and about, over hill and dale, till noon.

Meantime Gawain at home slept soundly through the cold morning within the fair curtains. But the lady could not sleep for she was still set in her heart on making love to him. She came in and closed the door behind her. Then she threw open a window, and called to Gawain and mocked him gaily.

"Gawain, Gawain, how can you sleep so sound on so bright a morning?"

Gawain was deep sunk in sleep, but at this he woke and heard her.

He had been deep in gloomy dreams, and muttering as he dreamed, like a man troubled with a throng of dreary thoughts, how that day he had to meet his destiny at the Green Chapel, when he encountered the Green Knight, and had to stand up to his stroke and make no resistance. But when that gracious lady came in he came to his waking senses, and swam up out of his dreams, and made haste to answer her greeting. The lady came to him, laughing sweetly, and bent over him and softly kissed him, and he welcomed her with good cheer. And when he saw her so lovely and so gaily arrayed, with her flawless beauty and her sweet color, joy welled up and warmed his heart. And they smiled gently at each other, and fell into gay talk, and all was joy and happiness and delight between them. It would have been a perilous[19] time for both of them, if Mary[20] had not taken thought for her knight. For that noble princess urged him so, and pressed him so hard to confess himself her lover, that at last he must needs either accept her love or bluntly refuse her. And he was troubled for his courtesy, for fear that he should behave like a churl, but more afraid of a wound to his honor, if he behaved badly to his host, the lord of the castle. And that at any rate, he said to himself, should not happen. So he laughed a little, though kindly, and put aside all the fond loving words that sprang to her lips. 10

And she said, "You are to blame, Gawain, if you have no love for the woman that holds you so near her heart, of all women on earth most sorely stricken, unless it is that you already have a lover that pleases you better, and you plighted your troth to her so surely that you will not break faith—and that is what I am coming to believe. Tell me the truth now, for God's sake, and do not hide it, nor make any pretense."

With a kindly smile, said Gawain, "By St. John I have no lover, nor will have one now."

"That," said she, "hurts more than anything else you could say. But I have my answer, and it wounds. Give me one kiss, and I will leave you. There is nothing left for me but sorrow, for I love you dearly." She stooped with a sigh and gave him a sweet kiss, and then she stood up, and said as she stood by him, "Now, my dear, as I go away, do at least this for me; give me some gift, if it is only your glove, that I can have something to remind me of you and lessen my grief."

"I wish I had here," said Gawain, "for your sake, the most precious thing I have in the world. You have deserved ten times over a richer gift of thanks than any I could offer. But to give you a love gift 
would avail but little, and it is not fitting for your honor to have a glove as a keepsake of Gawain."

"Well," said the lovely lady, "Gawain, noblest of knights, even if I can have nothing of yours, you shall have something of mine." And she held out to him a rich ring of the red gold, with a bright jewel blazing on it that flashed as bright as the sunrays. It was worth a king's ransom, but Gawain refused it.

---

19. **perilous** (per′ə ləs), *adj.* dangerous.
20. **Mary,** the mother of Jesus, here thought of as Gawain's guardian saint.

10 Critical Thinking
Evaluate

Question What do you think is most precious to Gawain? *(Possible responses: honor; respect of the king; courage)*

11 Historical Note
Courtly Love

Gawain's dilemma with respect to his hostess reflects the medieval rituals of "courtly love," which would not allow him to behave "churlishly" toward a lady, that is, to totally ignore her attentions. At the same time, they must not exchange tokens that would imply a dishonorable—that is, adulterous—alliance offensive to Gawain's host and to his own principles.

BUILDING ENGLISH PROFICIENCY

Making Inferences

Help students understand that readers make inferences, or guesses, about what will happen next in a story. Inferences are based not only upon clues that the writer provides but also upon the reader's own knowledge of life. Encourage students to share their inferences with others in a small group, using questions such as the following:

- What secret reason might lie behind the king's strange bargain with Gawain?
- What do you think of the queen's behavior? Whose side would you say she is on?
- What do you think of the kind of person Gawain is?
- Suppose that you like Gawain and don't want him to get hurt. Based on what you think might happen next, what kind of message might you send him?

12 Critical Thinking
Make Judgments

Questions

- Why do you think Gawain accepts the magic girdle? *(It would be "churlish" to refuse, and the girdle could prove useful.)*
- Do you think it is a form of cheating to use it? *(Yes, because Gawain accepted the challenge without the girdle; no, the Green Knight obviously has access to magic as well.)*

13 Active Reading
Clarify

Response He accepts a magic silk belt that protects the wearer from death "by any skill on earth."

14 Literary Focus
Foreshadowing

Question Why do you think the author has included this scene of a fox hunt? *(Possible response: It foreshadows "the peril that lay before.")*

She said, "If you refuse my ring, because it seems too rich, and you will not be so beholden to me, then I will give you my girdle, which is a cheaper gift." And she took hold of a belt that was fastened round her waist, clasped over her tunic under the bright mantle. It was fashioned of green silk, and trimmed with gold, embroidered only round the edges and adorned with pendants. That she offered to him, and besought him to take it, unworthy gift though it was. But he said that he would accept nothing, neither gold nor keepsake.

"Now are you refusing this silk," said she, "Because it seems so cheap a gift? It seems so, I know, a small thing and of little value. But if a man knew the powers that are knit into its fabric, he might hold it at a higher rate. Any man that is girt with this green girdle, when it is close clasped around him, there is no man under heaven that can cut him down, and he cannot be slain by any skill upon earth."

Then Gawain thought about it again, and it came into his head that this was the very thing for the peril that lay before him, when he came to the chapel to meet his doom, and that if he could escape death he would owe much to the
12 charmed girdle. So he was more patient with her as she pressed it on him, and let her speak on. She offered it to him again, and prayed him earnestly to take it, and in the end he consented, and she gave it him eagerly. But she besought him for her sake never to reveal it, but to keep it loyally hidden from her lord. And he promised her that no man should ever know of it, but themselves only. And he thanked her many times and deeply from the bottom of his heart. And she kissed him the third time. Then she took her leave and left him there.

13 **CLARIFY: What gift does Gawain accept from the queen? What special powers does she claim it possesses?**

Let us leave him there at his ease, with love all about him, and go back to the lord who was still out in the country at the head of his hunt. By now he had killed the fox that he had hunted all day. As he jumped a hedge to get a view of the rascal, and heard the pack that sped after him, he had seen the fox making his way through a tangled thicket, and all the pack in full cry at his heels. He watched him and waited carefully and drew his bright sword and aimed at him. The fox swerved from the steel, and would have drawn back, but a hound was on him before he could recover, and there right before the horse's hooves they all fell on him and worried[21] him.

The lord dismounted in haste and
grasped the fox, snatching him quickly 14
from the hounds' mouths, and held him high over his head and hollaed at the top of his voice, while the hounds bayed fiercely round him. The huntsmen hurried to his call, and then they skinned the fox, and then turned homeward, for it was near nightfall, blowing great blasts on the horns as they rode. At length the lord got down at his own castle, and found there a fire burning brightly on the hearth, and Gawain beside it.

He met his host in the middle of the hall, and greeted him merrily, and said to him courteously, "Tonight I will be the first to make good our covenant, that we made with so happy an outcome, and sealed it with the draught of wine." Then he embraced the lord and give him three kisses, as loving and eager as he could make them.

"By God!" said the lord, "you are doing well at your new trade, if you made a cheap bargain."

"No matter for the bargain," said Gawain at once, "so long as I have paid you in full what I owed you."

"Marry," said the other, "mine are poor winnings to set beside yours, for I have hunted all day and I have nothing to show for it but this miserable fox skin—the devil take it!—and that is a poor exchange for the precious things that

21. **worry** (wėr′ē), *v.* seize with the teeth.

MINI-LESSON: READING/THINKING SKILLS
Identify Alternatives

Teach In this tale, Sir Gawain engages in battle in order to fulfill his code of honor and ideal of courage. He seems not to consider any alternatives, once Arthur has agreed to let Gawain take his place.

Question Can you image a code of honor that would require Sir Gawain to respond differently to the Green Knight's provocation? *(Responses will probably focus on Gawain's responsibilities to family or fellow subjects—duties that make it undesirable for him to risk his life.)*

Activity Idea Invite students to consider alternative codes of honor and courage and to write a short monologue in which Gawain answers the Green Knight's challenge, but in noncombative terms.

A knight and a lady are shown in a garden in this painting from the 1400s. What **group** codes or rules for behavior do they seem to you to be obeying—or breaking?

you have pressed on me, three such warm and loving kisses."

"None the less," said Gawain, "I thank you."

And the lord told him all the tale of the hunt as they stood there. And he appointed one of his men to set Gawain on his way, and bring him over the hills, so that he should have no trouble with his road, and guide him through woodland and brake by the shortest track. Gawain thanked him for his kindness, and then he took his leave of the noble ladies. Then they brought him with lights to his room, and left him to go content to bed. Perhaps he slept less soundly than before, for he had much on his mind for the morrow to keep him awake.

Let him lie there peacefully, for now he is near the goal that he has been seeking. If you will listen, I will tell you how they fared.

Part 3

And New Year's Day drew near, and the night passed, and day drove hard on the heels of the dark. And all the wild weather in the world 15
seemed to be about the castle. There were clouds above that sent their cold breath down to the ground, and there was bitter cold from the north, torturing all ill-clad men. And the snow shivered down bitingly, and pinched all the wild creatures. And the whistling wind swooped down from the heavens and in the dales drove the snow into great drifts.

Art Study

Response to Caption Question
Courtly love—while knights might flirt and declare undying love to married ladies, such relationships were suppose to remain platonic.

Visual Literacy The couple meet in a garden. Typically combining flowers, herbs, and vegetables arranged in a geometric pattern, medieval gardens were walled or planted within a courtyard for protection.

Question Do the wall, hedge, trees, and fence surrounding the knight and lady suggest anything about their meeting? *(Possible response: While the details are historically accurate, they may be included to suggest that the couple has had to breach many barriers to meet in this fashion.)*

15 Literary Element: Foreshadowing

Question What do you think this description of the weather portends? *(Possible responses: danger, doom, otherworldly forces)*

BUILDING ENGLISH PROFICIENCY

Understanding Causes and Effects

Completing a cause-and-effect chart will help students check their comprehension as Part 2 of the story concludes.

1. Ask students to copy and complete a chart like the one shown. Point out that each effect, followed by the question "Why?" is listed on the left-hand side of the chart.
2. Have students work in pairs to find and record at least one cause for each effect on the right-hand side of the chart.

Effects	Causes
Gawain accepts the sash. Why?	
Gawain gives the king three kisses. Why?	
Gawain doesn't give the king the sash. Why?	

16 Reading/Thinking Skills
Making Judgments

Question Why do you think the narrator calls Gawain "the brave knight" when he has just equipped himself with magical protection? *(Possible response: It still takes great courage for Gawain to go forward—the belt may be useless.)*

17 Literary Element
Allusion

Remind students that an allusion is a brief reference to a person, event, place, work of art, and so on. This allusion to the Trojan War is particularly apt. Hector, like Gawain, is terrified, but faces his foe, Achilles, knowing he will surely die.

18 Literary Element
Characterization

The squire has just painted a terrifying picture of what is in store for Gawain and offers a way out.

Question How will Gawain respond? Why? *(He will reject the offer; it would be out of character for him to behave in any other way.)*

Sir Gawain listened as he lay in his bed, and for all that he kept his eyes shut it was little he slept. And as each cock crew he knew that his hour was coming nearer. Swiftly he got up, before the dawn, by the dim light of a lamp that gleamed in his room, and he called to his servant, who answered him straightaway, and bade him bring his mail shirt and saddle his horse. The servant rose and brought Gawain his clothes, and dressed him in his full armor. Gawain put this armor on, as gleaming a warrior as any between Britain and the far land of Greece, and he thanked his man, and told him to bring his horse.

And while he put on the glorious clothes—his coat, with the badge clearly worked on velvet, trimmed and set about with precious stones, with embroidered seams, and lined inside with fur—yet he did not leave off the love lace, the lady's gift. That, you may be sure, Gawain for his own sake did not forget. When he had belted on his sword round his hips, then he wound twice round his waist, swiftly and close, the green silken girdle, fit for a fair knight and shining out against the splendid scarlet of the cloth. But it was not for its richness that he wore it, or for pride in its pendants that glittered with the gleam of polished gold, but to save his life, when he had to stand in the face of danger, and, by his covenant, not stir a weapon in his
16 own defense. And now the brave knight was ready to go out to his fate.

There was Gringolet[22] ready waiting for him, his great war-charger. So Gawain rode his way with the one squire who was to guide him on his road to the dolorous[23] place where he was to abide the grim onslaught. They passed by banks where all the boughs were bare, and the icy cold seemed to cling to the cliffs under which they rode. The clouds rode high, but there was ill weather under them. The mist drizzled on the moor and was heavier on the tops of the hills, so that each had a cap and a cloak of mist about it. The streams swirled and broke about their banks, and foamed white as they came down in spate.[24] It was a hard wandering way they had to find when it lay through woods, till it came to the hour of dawn. Then they were high on a hill, and the white snow lay all round them. And his squire bade Gawain halt.

"Now I have brought you hither, my lord, and you are not far from the place which you have asked for and sought so earnestly. But now I shall tell you the truth, since each day that I have known you the more I have grown to love you; if you would do as I advise, you would fare the better. The place that you press forward to is held full perilous. In that waste land there dwells a man as evil as any on earth. He is stalwart, and grim, and a lover of blows, and mightier than any man on middle-earth, huger than Hector of
Troy[25] or any four knights of Arthur's house. 17
And this is what he does at the Green Chapel. There is never a man passes that way, however proud of his prowess in arms, but he smites him down and kills him. He is a violent man, and he knows no mercy in his heart, and I tell you the truth, if once you come there, no matter if you had twenty lives, you are a dead man, if the knight has his will with you. He has dwelt here a long time, and fought many combats, and there is no guard against his grim blows.

"Therefore, for God's sake, sir, leave the man well alone, and go some other way and ride to another country, where Christ may be your speed. And I will turn home again, and I promise you besides that I will keep our secret truly, and never let drop a word that you
flinched from meeting any man." 18

"All the thanks of my heart," said Gawain, slowly, "and good luck to you, who wish me well.

---

22. **Gringolet** (gring′gə let).
23. **dolorous** (dol′ər əs), *adj.* sorrowful.
24. **spate** (spāt), *n.* a sudden flood.
25. **middle-earth . . . Hector of Troy.** Middle-earth is an archaic term for the world. Hector was the greatest warrior in the ancient Trojan War.

MINI-LESSON: LITERARY FOCUS
Foreshadowing

Teach Remind students that foreshadowing is a hint given to the reader of what is to come. Explain that the hint may be given at any time in the narrative—even very early on.

Activity Idea Suggest that students, working in groups of three or four, write an additional scene to this tale that foreshadows one of the following existing episodes:

- the arrival of the Green Knight
- the Green Knight's imperviousness to being beheaded
- Gawain's courtly response to his hostess's attentions
- Gawain's acceptance of magical means of self-protection at the cost of honor

I am sure that you would truly keep my secret; but however close you kept it, if I now turned aside, and made haste to flee in the way you tell me to, then I should be a coward knight, and there could be no excuse."

Then he spurred Gringolet, and picked up the track, and made his way along the bank by the side of a shaw,[26] and rode along the rough bank right down to the dale. He reined in Gringolet and halted, and turned on this side and that, looking for the chapel.

> IN THAT WASTE LAND THERE DWELLS A MAN AS EVIL AS ANY ON EARTH.

He saw nothing like it anywhere, and he thought this strange. Then a little way away over the field he saw a small mound, a smooth swelling knoll, by the waterside where a cascade fell down, and the water of the brook bubbled in the basin as though it were boiling. Gawain gave Gringolet his head and came to the mound, and got down quietly and fastened the reins to the rough bough of a lime tree. Then he walked over to the mound, and strode all round it, wondering what it was. There was a hole in one end, and one on each side, and it was all overgrown with patches of grass; whether it was only an old cave or just a split in a rock, he could not make out.

"Well!" said he, "is this the Green Chapel? This is the kind of place where the devil might say matins[27] at midnight! It is a desolate place, and this chapel, if it is the chapel, is evil looking, all overgrown. It is the right place for the knight in green to perform his devotions after the devil's fashion. I am beginning to think in my heart that it is the fiend that has appointed me this tryst, to destroy me here. It is an unchancy chapel, bad luck to it, the least hallowed church that ever I came into!"

With helm on head and lance in hand he came up to the mound, and then he heard, from a rock high up on a hill beyond the brook, a wondrous loud noise. Hark! it re-echoed on the cliff with the sound of a 19 scythe being whetted on a grindstone. Hark! it whirred and rasped, like water at a mill; it rushed and rang, fearful to hear. Then said Gawain, "By God, this device, I think, is meant to greet me and to sound the challenge for me as I come. God's will be done. To say 'Woe is me!' does not help in the least. And though I may have to give up my life, no mere noise is going to scare me."

Then Gawain called aloud, "Who is master here, to keep tryst with me? For now am I, Sir Gawain, walking here and ready. If any man wants aught[28] of me, let him come hither quickly, now or never, to work his will."

"Stay," said a voice from the bank above his 20 head, "and swiftly you shall have all that I once promised you."

Yet the speaker went on for a while with the noise of his whetting before he would come down. Then he made his way down by the side of a crag, and came hurtling out of a crack in the rock with a grim weapon, a new Danish ax, with a massive blade on it, curving by the haft, whetted with a whetstone, and four foot long, measured by the thong that gleamed bright on the haft. There was the Green Knight, appareled as before, the same in his face and his limbs, his locks and his beard, except that this time he strode firmly on his feet, setting the haft to the ground beside him as he walked. And when he came to the water, not wanting to wade

26. **shaw,** a small wood or grove.
27. **matins** (mat′nz), morning prayers.
28. **aught** (ôt), *pron.* anything.

19 Literary Element
Simile

Question Is "It re-echoed on the cliff with the sound of a scythe being whetted on a grindstone" an example of simile? Why or why not? *(Although the narrator does not use "like" or "as," it is a simile; two unlike things are compared.)*

20 Literary Element
Imagery

Question What does the image of the disembodied voice emanating from above the hero's head evoke? *(Possible responses: fear, suspense; the hero's vulnerability; the supernatural; the talking, disembodied head of the Green Knight)*

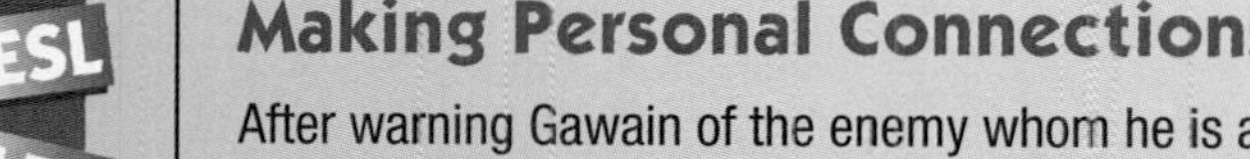

After warning Gawain of the enemy whom he is about to fight, Gawain's squire begs him to escape and promises to tell no one. Yet Gawain rides forward to meet the terrible Green Knight. Help students relate Gawain's actions to experiences that they know about both from fiction and real life.

1. Call on volunteers to describe how they think Gawain feels at this point in the story. Invite them to share a situation similar to Gawain's that they heard about, read about, or saw on TV or in the movies.

2. Ask: Why do you think that Gawain—or anyone else, including yourself—might choose to show courage, even when it's possible to get out of harm's way?

21 Reading/Thinking Skills
Find the Main Idea

Question Why do you think Gawain rejects the Green Knight's offer of combat, saying "keep yourself to the one stroke"? *(Possible responses: Gawain's only motive is to conclude the pact honorably, stroke for stroke; or perhaps he does not trust the knight's offer.)*

22 Reading/Thinking Skills
Recognize Values

Questions

- Do you think this title "better knight" is worth what it took to determine it? *(Possible responses: Yes, it was a test of discipline and faithfulness to a code of honor; no, this did not prove any inner qualities, only war-like attitudes.)*
- Are there contests like this in our time? *(Athletics and Outward Bound are similar challenges.)*

it, he used his ax as a jumping pole and leaped over, and came striding lissomely[29] forward, fierce and fell,[30] over the broad stretch of snow that lay all around.

Sir Gawain bent his head no farther than he must for courtesy, and greeted him. The other said, "Sir knight, now men may know that you are one who keeps tryst. Gawain, so God guard me, I tell you you are very welcome to my dwelling, and you have timed your travelings as a true man should. You know the covenants that we made between us. Twelve months ago today you took what chance gave you and I was to give you prompt quittance this New Year's Day. Here we are in this valley by our two selves, and there are no men to part us, however tight we lock swaying in combat. Take your helm off your head, and take your wages, making no more resistance than I made then, when you whipped my head off at one blow."

21 "Nay," said Gawain, "by the Lord God who gave me life, I shall have no grudge against you, not a grain, for any harm that may fall to me. But keep yourself to the one stroke, and I will stand still, and give you free leave to strike as you will." So he leaned his head down and bared his neck, showing the white skin, making as though he did not care, and giving no sign of fear.

Then the Green Knight got himself quickly ready, took firm hold of his grim tool to smite Gawain, and gathered every ounce of strength in his body together as he rose to the stroke, and drove at him as mightily as though he had a mind to destroy him. And if it had fallen as hard and as true as he seemed to intend, the doughtiest[31] warrior alive would have been dead of the blow. But Gawain glanced sideways at the blade as it came swooping down to strike him to the earth, and he could not help his shoulders shrinking a little from the keen steel. And the Green Knight with a turn of his wrist swerved the blade aside, and then he told Gawain what he thought of him.

"You cannot be Gawain, that is held so good a knight, who never, they say, quailed for any host of men on hill or on dale. And now you flinched like a coward before you felt even a scratch. That is not what I have ever heard of Gawain. I did not flinch nor flee when you aimed your blow at me, and I made no evasions in Arthur's hall. My head fell at my feet, but did I flinch? Not I. And now you quail before any harm comes to you. So I deserve to be called a better knight than you are." 22

Said Gawain, "I shrank once, but I will not again, even if my head falls on the stones, though I cannot, like you, put it back again on my shoulders if it does! Get ready again, and come to the point. Deal me my doom, and do it out of hand. I will stand up to your stroke, and start away no more till your ax has struck me, and I pledge my troth to that."

"Have at you then," said the other, and hove up the ax, and looked at him as fiercely as though he were mad with anger, and aimed a mighty blow at him; but just as the blade came down he held back before it could wound him. Gawain awaited the stroke steadfastly, and flinched this time not the least, but stood still as a stone or the stump of a tree that is anchored with a hundred roots round a rock in the ground.

Then merrily spoke the Green Knight: "Hm! Now that you have got your courage back, it is time to hit you in earnest. Throw back the hood that Arthur gave you, and see whether your neck can stand the blow that is coming."

To which Gawain, now full of wrath, replied in anger, "Drive on, fierce knight; you are too long over your threats. I wonder that you are not scared by your own fierceness."

"Faith," said the Green Knight, "if you are so furious, I will not delay, nor be slow in letting you have what you have come for. Ready!" Then he took his stance for the stroke, and set his lips and

29. lissomely (lis′əm lē), *adv.* limberly; supplely.
30. **fell** (fel), *adj.* fierce; savage.
31. doughtiest (dou′tē əst), *adj.* bravest.

knit his brows. It was no wonder that Gawain, with no hope of rescue, little liked the look of him.

He lifted the ax lightly and let it deftly down just by the bare neck. And though he swung at him hard he did him no more hurt than to graze him on one side, so that the very tip of the blade just broke the skin, and the bright blood spurted over his shoulders to the ground. And when Gawain saw the blood red on the snow, he leapt forward more than a spear length, and seized his helm and set it on his head, and gave a twitch with his shoulders to bring his shield round in front of him, and flashed out his bright sword, and spoke fiercely—Never since his mother bore him had he been so gay, now that his trial was over.

"Stop your blows, sir, and deal me no more. I have endured one stroke in this place without making any return; but if you deal me another, be very sure that I will pay it back forthwith, and give you blow for blow again. There is only the one blow due to fall to me here—those were the terms of the covenant made between us in Arthur's hall—so now, good sir, hold your hand."

The Green Knight held off and rested on his ax, the haft on the ground and his arms on the blade, and he watched Gawain standing there, bold and fearless, full armed again, and with never a thought of flinching. And he was glad to see it, and he spoke cheerfully to him in a great voice, so that his words rang clear like bells.

"Good knight, be not so wrathful. No man has here misused you unmannerly, or treated you otherwise than as the covenant allowed, which we made at the King's court. I promised you a stroke, and you have had it and you can count yourself well paid. That blow is full quittance[32] of all that you owe me. Had I wished, I could perhaps have dealt you a buffet more harshly, and done you injury. But, as it was, first I threatened you with a feint, and gave you no wound. That was for the agreement we made the first night at my castle, and for the next day, when you kept troth loyally, and gave me back, like a true man, your gains for the day. And the second feint was for the next day after, when again you had my dear lady's kisses and gave me them again. For those two days I aimed the two strokes at you that were no more than feints and did you no scathe. A true man pays his debts and then need fear no danger. But the third time you failed in your trust, and for that you had to take your third blow and the wound.

"For it is my own green girdle that you are wearing, and it was my own wife that gave it you. I know all about your kisses, and the love-making of my wife, and how you bore yourself, for it was I myself that brought it about. I sent her to make trial of you, and surely I think that you are the most faultless knight that ever trod upon earth. As a pearl for price by the side of a white pea, so, by God's truth, is Gawain beside other gay knights. But just over the girdle, sir, you failed a little, and came short in your loyalty; yet that was not for any intrigue nor for love-making, but just that you loved your life, and I do not blame you for it." 23 24

Gawain stood in thought a long while, so overcome with grief that he groaned in his heart, and all the blood in his body seemed to rush to his face as he winced for shame at what the Green Knight said. And the first words that he said were, "Curse upon cowardice and covetousness both; there is evil power in them to destroy a man's virtue." 25 Then he laid his hand to the knot of the girdle, and loosed it, and threw it savagely from him to the Green Knight, and said, "Lo, there is my broken faith, curse on it. I was afraid of your blow, so cowardice taught me to make terms with covetousness, and forget my true nature, the generosity and loyalty that belong to true knights. Now I have shown myself false, I that ever was afraid of any treachery or untruth, and hated them. I make my confession to you, sir knight, between the two of us. I have behaved very ill. Let me now do what I can to gain your good will; and afterwards I will show that I have learned my lesson."

32. **quittance** (kwit′ns) *n.* release from debt or obligation.

23 Reading/Thinking Skills
Making Analogies

Question What is implied in the Green Knight's analogy? *(Gawain's worth is to that of other knights' as a pearl's worth is to a white pea's.)*

24 Literary Element
Tone

Question Do you think the tone of the Green Knight's speech is in keeping with the tone of the beginning of the tale? *(Possible responses: Yes, it is lighthearted; no, his speech at the banquet is curt and sinister.)*

25 Reader's Response
Challenging the Text

The Green Knight explains the three blows by stating that Gawain has been put to three trials; he passed the first two, but failed the third.

Question In your opinion, is this failure serious? *(While recognizing that Gawain failed to live up to a code of honor, the Green Knight doesn't find the failing egregious; yet, Gawain is compromised and knows it.)*

The seriousness of Gawain's dishonor might make an interesting class discussion.

BUILDING ENGLISH PROFICIENCY

Responding to a Character

Gawain emerges from his test alive but distraught. Help students relate to and understand Gawain's feelings.

Activity Ideas

- Suggest that students write to Gawain in response to a letter from him requesting help in overcoming feelings of shame and guilt.
- Do students think that Gawain is too hard on himself? Have them copy this chart. In the first three sections, have them summarize different responses to Gawain's behavior. Later, ask them to add the response of Arthur's court.

What People Think of Gawain	
Gawain himself:	The Green Knight:
You:	Arthur's Court:

Art Study

Response to Caption Question Chain mail, shield, sword, and tunic are the garb of a warrior.

Visual Literacy While this figure wears partial battle dress, he does not appear at all warlike.

Question Why do you think he has been depicted in this way? *(Possible response: He may be depicted as an unwarlike warrior to suggest the "noble soldier" who only battles the force of evil.)*

26 Reading/Thinking Skills
Drawing Conclusions

Question Why doesn't Gawain want to return to the castle? *(Possible responses: It is where he dishonored himself by accepting the magic belt; and with their tricks and deceptions, the knight and his wife were hardly perfect hosts.)*

This illuminated (highly decorated) capital letter from the manuscript of a romance of the 1300s shows Sir Gawain. What does his costume suggest to you about the job of a knight?

The Green Knight laughed, and said to him friendlily, "Such harm as I took, I count it wholly cured. You have made such free confession that all your faults are cleansed, and besides you have done your penance at the edge of my blade. I hold you purged of all your offenses and as clean as if you had never failed in virtue since the day you were born. And I give you the gold-hemmed girdle that is green as my gown. Sir Gawain, you will be able to think back on this day's contest when you ride out among great princes. It will be a noble token of the meeting of two chivalrous knights at the Green Chapel. And now, this very New Year's Day, you shall come back with me to my castle, and we will finish off happily the rest of the revel[33] that we left." He pressed him to come, and said, "We must put you on good terms again with my wife, who behaved as your enemy."

"Nay," said Gawain, and took hold of his helm and lifted it from his head, and thanked the Green Knight. "I have stayed too long already. All happiness be yours, and may the great God grant it you, he that brings honor to men. Commend me to your fair and gracious lady, and to that other also, those two whom I honor, who with their devices so cunningly beguiled[34] me. But it is no marvel if a fool goes astray in his wits, and through the wiles of women comes to sorrow. 26

"But for your girdle—and may God reward you for your kindness—that I will wear with the best will in the world, not for the sake of the splendid gold, nor the silk, nor the pendants that hang from it, nor its costliness, nor the lovely work in it, nor for the honor that I shall get when I am seen wearing it, but as a memorial of my sin. I shall look at it often when I ride out proudly, and I shall feel remorse in my heart for the fault and frailty of the erring flesh, which is so ready to catch the infection and the stain of ill-doing. So when pride stirs in my heart for my prowess in arms, one glance at the love lace will humble me. But there is one thing I would ask you. Will you tell me your true name that you are called by? Then I will ask no more."

"I will tell you truly," said the other. "Bercilak de Haut-desert[35] I am called in my own land. And it is the might of Morgan la Fay[36] that has brought all this about. She dwells in my house, and she knows all the cunning of magical lore and the crafty ways of it, and has learned the mysteries of Merlin,[37] for once she had dealings in love with that great wizard, who knows all your knights at home. And so Morgan the goddess is her name, and there is never a man so high and proud but she can humble and tame him.

"It was she who sent me to your splendid halls, to make trial of your pride, and to see

---

33. **revel** (rev′əl) *v.* noisy good time.
34. **beguile** (bi gīl′) *v.* entertain; amuse.
35. **Bercilak de Haut-desert** (bėr′sə läk də ō′dā ser).
36. **Morgan la Fay,** "Morgan the Fairy," King Arthur's half-sister, a witch who continually plots against him.
37. **Merlin,** a wizard, Arthur's teacher and counselor.

whether there was truth in the report that runs through the world of the great renown of the Round Table. She sent this marvel to steal your wits away from you, and she hoped to have daunted Guenevere and brought her to death with dismay at that same strange figure that stood like a phantom before the high table, and spoke from the head that he held in his hand. She is that ancient lady whom you saw at my castle, and she is your own aunt, Arthur's half-sister, daughter of that Duchess of Tintagel on whom Uther[38] later begat Arthur, that now is King. So now I ask you, sir knight, come back to my halls and meet your aunt again, and by my faith I wish you as well as any man on earth for your true loyalty."

But Gawain still said no, and could not be persuaded. So they embraced and kissed and commended each other to the Prince of Paradise, and parted there in the snow. Gawain mounted and rode off, hasting to the King's castle, and the knight in the bright green went his own way.

And Gawain on Gringolet, with his life given back to him, rode through many wild ways, sometimes with a roof over his head at night, and sometimes sleeping under the stars. He had many adventures by the way, and won many victories. The wound in his neck was healed, and he wore the shining girdle about it, slantwise like a baldric[39] to his other side, and fastened under his left arm in a knot, the token of his fault, to remind him of the stain of it. So he came to the court, sound and whole. And great joy rose in the castle when the great King knew that the good Sir Gawain was come, and rejoiced over it. And the King kissed the knight, and the Queen too, and then many a true knight thronged round him to greet him and ask him how he had fared. He told them all the wonders, all the hardships he had, the adventure at the chapel, and the way the Green Knight dealt with him, the love of the lady, and at last the love lace. And he bared his neck and showed them the wound that he took at the knight's hand as punishment for his failure in troth. When he came to the telling of this part he was tormented, and groaned for grief and sorrow, and the blood rushed to his cheeks with the shame of what he had to confess.

"See, my lord," said Sir Gawain, and laid his hand on the girdle, "this is the band that is sign of my fault, my disgrace, the mark of the cowardice and the covetousness that I yielded to, the token of my broken troth. And I must needs wear it as long as I live. For no man can hide his scar, nor rid himself of it; when once it is fastened upon him it will never depart."

Predict: Why will Gawain always wear the green belt? How will the brotherhood of the Round Table demonstrate their group solidarity with Gawain? 27

The King comforted the knight, and all the court laughed kindly, and agreed, to cheer him, that all the lords and ladies of the Round Table, everyone of the brotherhood, should wear a slanting baldric of bright green, just like Gawain's. So that became a part of the glory of 28
the Round Table, and ever after a man that wore it was honored. So the ancient books of romance tell us.

And may He that wore the crown of thorns bring us to His bliss.

---

38. **Tintagel** (tin taj′əl) . . . **Uther.** Tintagel is an area in Cornwall, in southwest England, associated in legend with Arthur's birth. Uther Pendragon was Arthur's Father.

39. **baldric** (bôl′drik), *n.* a belt hung from one shoulder to the opposite side of the body, to support the wearer's sword.

27 Multicultural Note
Group

Response Gawain will wear the green belt to remind himself that he is human, thus imperfect. Other knights will follow his example.

28 Multicultural Note
Mythic Models

An Irish, mythical hero, Cuchulain, is thought to be the model for Sir Gawain. Descended from a Celtic sun god, Cuchulain is described as having a reddish complexion from sundown to sunrise; Gawain's strength was said to wax until noon and wane thereafter. The Irish hero arrived in England via Wales, where he was called Gwri Gwallt-evryn or "golden haired." Both he and Gawain were foundlings discovered swaddled in rich cloth, denoting a high, if ambiguous, birth. Both were fostered by noble families, exhibited precociousness, and joined King Arthur as knights.

Check Test

1. Why wouldn't King Arthur sit down to dinner until the others were served? *(His mind was naturally restless, and he traditionally heard an adventure tale before eating.)*
2. Why did Gawain persuade King Arthur not to take the Green Knight's challenge? *(It was beneath his dignity to take up the challenge himself when all his knights were present.)*
3. What was magical about what happened after Gawain beheaded the Green Knight? *(Beheading did not kill him.)*
4. What was the first gift the lady of the castle offered Sir Gawain? *(a jeweled, golden ring)*
5. What relation was Morgan la Fay to Sir Gawain? *(his aunt)*

Unit 1 Resource Book
Alternate Check Test, p. 37

BUILDING ENGLISH PROFICIENCY

ESL LEP ELD SAE LD

Exploring Symbols

"This day's context" occurs on New Year's Day. To help students explore the symbolism of New Year's Day:

1. Ask students to create a New Year's Day web, as shown. Encourage them to jot down phrases that tell what that day means to them. Have them circle each idea and draw lines to show how the ideas are connected.

2. As students share their webs, ask them to speculate about why the contest takes place on New Year's Day. *(Sample answer: A new year means a fresh start for Gawain, with new resolutions.)*

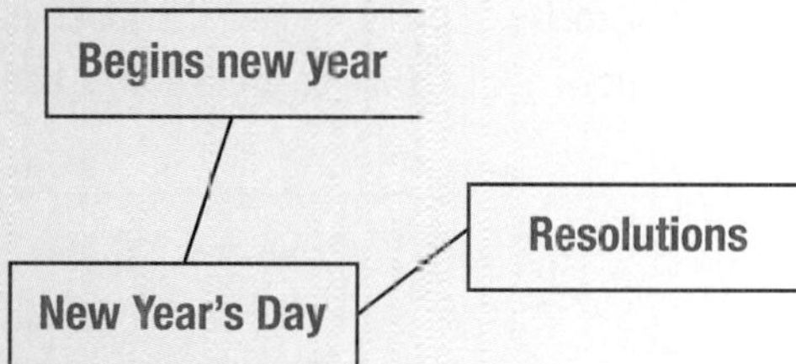

After Reading

MAKING CONNECTIONS

1. Possible responses: Magic makes the challenge unfair; Gawain cannot survive a beheading; facing such an opponent and fulfilling his promise makes Gawain a greater hero; or, Gawain is less a hero for accepting a magical instrument to save himself.

2. Possible responses: The king is above such challenges; Gawain's volunteering in his stead proves the virtues of the Round Table knights and their code.

3. Supernatural elements include the green man and horse; a talking, disembodied head; a magic girdle; a boiling brook; the transformations of the Green Knight; Morgan la Fay's magic. They suggest nature's challenge of humanity and reveal Gawain's bravery, goodness, and human frailties.

4. Gawain accepts the challenge in place of his king; fulfills his promise to the Green Knight; deals with the lady's attentions without dishonoring himself. The Green Knight honors virtue.

5. He is ashamed to have broken faith for fear of his life. He keeps it as a reminder of his imperfection and need for greater faith.

6. The reaction of Arthur and his knights shows that insults to honor must be rebuked at any cost. The same point of view is exhibited today by urban gangs.

7. Accept all reasonable responses. Students might respond that circumstances and relationships can change. Honor, keeping faith, or fear of losing face might steel one to fulfill a promise.

After Reading

Making Connections

Shaping Your Response

1. In your opinion, does the fact that the Green Knight uses magic make him more or less a challenge? Does it make Gawain more or less a hero?

Analyzing the Romance

2. Why is it appropriate that the Green Knight's challenge is taken up by Sir Gawain instead of by King Arthur himself?
3. Point out elements of magic or the supernatural that appear throughout this legend. Why do you suppose they are included?
4. How does the author illustrate examples of the code of chivalry and courtly love? Use examples from the text in your answer.
5. Why does Gawain throw away the green girdle? Why does he retrieve it?

Extending the Ideas

6. What does the behavior of the members of King Arthur's court reveal about how these people as a **group** regard insults to honor? Compare their reactions with the reactions of people today who are insulted or mocked.
7. It is important for Gawain to keep his part of the bargain with the Green Knight, yet he has very good reasons to want to break his promise. What circumstances would cause you to break—or keep—a promise you had made?

Literary Focus: Foreshadowing

The warning of the squire who guides Sir Gawain, the appearance of the Green Chapel, the strange sound Gawain hears: each is a different kind of **foreshadowing** of Gawain's second meeting with the Green Knight. What does each hint about what might happen at that meeting? What other examples of foreshadowing can you find?

Vocabulary Study

Many of the words in *Sir Gawain and the Green Knight* are archaic, or at least they are not used very much today. Match each numbered definition with its lettered word. You will not use all the words.

1. brave	a. hauberk	f. recreant
2. favor	b. prodigious	g. dolorous
3. sudden flood	c. boon	h. lissomely
4. sorrowful	d. liege	i. doughtiest
5. huge	e. spate	j. baldric

LITERARY FOCUS: FORESHADOWING

Hint	What Might Happen
Warning of squire	Overwhelming, danger, death
Green Chapel	Evil, danger, the supernatural
The sound	Danger, great power, fate

Other examples:	
Disembodied, talking head	Future supernatural events; Gawain's survival
King's advice	Gawain's survival
Green Knight's identity	His multiple identities

Expressing Your Ideas

Writing Choices

Writer's Notebook Update Look again at the qualities you listed for a modern "knight in shining armor." Select a characteristic that you consider to be important and write a paragraph explaining why that trait is desirable for a modern knight.

How Perfect Can You Get? Sir Gawain has often been called the perfect knight. The challenges he faces at the hands of the Green Knight test his character greatly, yet he comes through. Write a one-page **character sketch** of Sir Gawain in which you describe how he changes or matures as a result of his experiences.

Destroyers of Virtue "Curse upon cowardice and covetousness both; there is evil power in them to destroy a man's virtue," says Gawain after he learns from the Green Knight the truth about his ordeal. Write an **essay** in which you agree or disagree with Gawain's claim. Support your position with specific examples from other literary sources or with anecdotes from real life.

Well-Versed Choose one of the exploits of Sir Gawain and turn it into a **poem, song lyric,** or **rap.** Perform your work for the class.

Other Options

What's Important to Me The medieval knight, proud of his heritage, his skill, and his devotion to duty, displayed his personal heraldic shield, a colorful coat of arms. This carefully constructed design immediately indicated to any observer those elements of his life that were most important to him. Design a **coat of arms** for Sir Gawain or for yourself. Your coat of arms should reflect family background, personal character, interests, and accomplishments.

True Then, True Now You are a television journalist working on a magazine show. (Think of *Sixty Minutes*.) Create an **interview** with Sir Gawain (or any one of the other characters). Ask about what the character did and why he or she did it. You might want to confront one character with what another character says. (For example: "Morgan la Fay, Bercilak de Haut-desert claims that you can humble and tame any man, no matter how high and proud. Why would you want to do that?") If possible, videotape your segment to screen in class.

VOCABULARY STUDY

1. i
2. c
3. e
4. d
5. b

More Practice Suggest that students write sentences that include the unused words from the Vocabulary Study list.

Unit 1 Resource Book
Vocabulary, p. 35
Vocabulary Test, p. 38

WRITING CHOICES

Writer's Notebook Update

Remind students that the strongest arguments anticipate objections and counter additional argument. Suggest that any quality that characterizes a modern knight is probably one that all people possess to some degree.

How Perfect Can You Get?

Support students in this activity by asking the following questions:

- What events trigger Gawain's character growth?
- How does he react to these events?
- How does he change as a result?
- Why did Gawain profit by his experiences, when others might not?
- How is he different at the end?

Well-Versed

Encourage students to jot down images that come to mind and to use foreshadowing.

OTHER OPTIONS

What's Important to Me

Invite students to invent symbols for their coats of arms. Suggest to those who are having trouble that they try associative thinking to generate meaningful imagery. You may also wish to have students brainstorm associations.

True Then, True Now

You may wish to distribute roles among the class, then have them interview each other—or conduct a "round-table" discussion.

Selection Test

Unit 1 Resource Book
pp. 39–40

Before Reading

Building Background

Why do students think the tales of King Arthur and the Round Table have endured for so long?

Literary Focus

Suggest that one way to recognize the protagonist is to look for the character mentioned most often. Even today, writers often make it simple to distinguish between protagonist and antagonist in books, films, and television shows.

Writer's Notebook

Encourage students to consider qualities that remain valid regardless of place or period of history.

More about Sir Thomas Malory and Morte Darthur

- *Morte Darthur* is actually a skillful translation of a number of French Arthurian tales.
- William Caxton introduced movable type in England less than 10 years before publication of *Morte Darthur*—one of the first books printed in England.

Before Reading

The Day of Destiny from Morte Darthur

by Sir Thomas Malory

Sir Thomas Malory
1400?–1471

We are not sure of the exact identity of the author of the *Morte Darthur* ("The Death of Arthur"). The most likely candidate is Sir Thomas Malory of Newbold Revell, a knight from Warwickshire who led a very different life from the chivalrous and gallant knights of the story. Malory served in Parliament briefly and may have fought in France. In 1450 he seems to have become involved in a feud with another noble. Such feuds were common in England at the time. Malory and his men rustled cattle, kidnapped prisoners, and raided churches. He was arrested in 1451. Malory seems to have made powerful enemies, who kept him in jail off and on for years awaiting trial, though he was eventually released. Later in life Malory was again jailed, probably for siding against the Yorkist faction in the Wars of the Roses. While in Newgate Jail, Malory gathered the tales of Arthur and retold them in *Morte Darthur,* the most complete single version of the legends of King Arthur and his court. Malory may have died in jail.

Building Background

History or Legend? According to Gerald of Wales, a writer who was alive at the time, on a cool morn in 1190 four monks, carrying pickaxes and shovels, stole away to the burial ground at Glastonbury Abbey, a Christian monastery in the southwest of England. There, under the cover of mist, they began to dig. Several feet down, metal clinked on stone. The monks soon uncovered a grave marker and a cross with the words: "Here lies buried the renowned King Arthur in the Isle of Avalon." A few feet farther down, they unearthed a huge oak log, inside of which was a large skeleton with a smashed skull and a smaller skeleton with wisps of golden hair—the remains of the legendary King Arthur and Queen Guinevere! Fact or fiction? Truth or hoax? History or legend? That there was a historical figure behind the legend of Arthur is generally accepted. But through many centuries the imaginations of storytellers in many nations have transformed history into something very different from fact.

In *Morte Darthur,* when Arthur's illegitimate son Mordred discovers the secret love affair between Guinevere and Sir Lancelot, he brings about a crisis that leads to war between him and King Arthur. In this selection, the war is coming to its end.

Literary Focus

Protagonist / Antagonist The **protagonist,** the main or lead character, is always the character most central to the action of a story. Often the protagonist possesses heroic qualities. In contrast to the protagonist is the **antagonist,** the character who opposes or is in conflict with the main character. As you read, observe the techniques the author uses to signal the reader who is the protagonist here.

Writer's Notebook

Leading the Way King Arthur, the leader of his country, is renowned for establishing order in a lawless land and for defending what is right and just. Do these same principles hold true for leaders throughout history? Make a list of characteristics you expect any leader in any nation must have in order to be effective.

SUPPORT MATERIALS OVERVIEW

Unit 1 Resource Book
- Graphic Organizer, p. 41
- Study Guide, p. 42
- Vocabulary, p. 43
- Grammar, p. 44
- Alternate Check Test, p. 45
- Vocabulary Test, p. 46
- Selection Test, pp. 47–48

Building English Proficiency
- Selection Summaries
- Activities, p. 209

Reading, Writing & Grammar SkillBook
- Grammar, Usage, and Mechanics, pp. 233–234

Technology
- Audiotape
- Personal Journal Software.
- Custom Literature Database: Additional selections by Sir Thomas Malory can be found on the database.
- Test Generator Software

Sir Thomas Malory

1 And quickly King Arthur moved himself with his army along the coastline westward, toward Salisbury. And there was a day assigned betwixt King Arthur and Sir Mordred, that they should meet upon a field beside Salisbury and not far from the coast. And this day was assigned as Monday after Trinity Sunday,[1] whereof King Arthur was passing glad that he might be avenged[2] upon Sir Mordred.

Then Sir Mordred stirred up a crowd of people around London, for those from Kent, Sussex and Surrey, Essex, Suffolk, and Norfolk stayed for the most part with Sir Mordred. And many a full noble knight drew unto him and also to the King; but they that loved Sir Lancelot drew unto Sir Mordred.

So upon Trinity Sunday at night King Arthur dreamed a wonderful dream, and in his dream it seemed that he saw upon a platform a chair, and the chair was fixed to a wheel,[3] and there upon sat King Arthur in richest cloth of gold that might be made. And the King dreamed there was under him, far below him, a hideous deep black water, and therein were all kinds of serpents and dragons and wild beasts foul and horrible. And suddenly the King dreamed that the wheel turned up side down, and he fell among the serpents, and every beast took him by a limb. And the King cried out as he lay in his bed,

"Help! help!"

And then knights, squires, and yeomen[4] awaked the King, and then he was so amazed that he knew not where he was. And so he remained awake until it was nearly day, and then he fell into a slumber again, neither sleeping nor completely awake.

Then it seemed to the King that there came Sir Gawain unto him with a number of fair ladies with him. So when King Arthur saw him he said,

1. **Trinity Sunday,** the eighth Sunday after Easter.
2. avenge (ə venj′), *v.* revenge.
3. **wheel.** The wheel of fortune, symbolizing the rapid changes of human destiny, was a favorite medieval image.
4. **squires . . . yeomen.** A squire (skwīr) was a personal attendant to a knight; a yeoman (yō′mən) was a member of the king's bodyguard.

During Reading

Selection Objectives

- to read a Middle English legend
- to learn to identify protagonists and antagonists
- to explore various codes of honor
- to learn about English words sources

Unit 1 Resource Book
Graphic Organizer, p. 41
Study Guide, p. 42

Theme Link

While *Morte Darthur* depicts the end of Arthur and his dreams, the Arthurian code of honor triumphs in its survival through the centuries.

Vocabulary Preview

avenge, revenge
brandish, wave or shake threateningly
entreat, beg
grovel, crawl humbly on the ground
plunder, steal, especially during war
slay, kill with violence
smite, hit; give a hard blow to
swoon, faint
tarry, delay
wrought, past tense and past participle of *to work*

Students can add the words and definitions to their Writer's Notebooks.

1 Geographical Note
Salisbury

Salisbury is a Wiltshire town famous for its 13th-century cathedral.

SELECTION SUMMARY

The Day of Destiny

This excerpt from *Morte Darthur* begins with the massing of armies—the forces of King Arthur opposing those of Mordred, his miscreant son. Arthur has dreams that foretell his doom if he fights the next morning. While he is able to forestall the battle, one of his knights inadvertently triggers it. At battle's end, Arthur and Mordred deal each other fatal wounds. Bedivere, the one surviving knight loyal to Arthur, carries the mortally wounded King to the water, where Arthur is conveyed by barge to Avalon. Bedivere later stumbles upon the chapel where Arthur is buried and devotes the rest of his life to fasting and prayers in service there.

*For summaries in other languages, see the **Building English Proficiency** book.*

Art Study

Response to Caption Question The horses, lances, and armor suggest that they are nobles, who were entitled to and able to afford such trappings. The fact that Arthur personally fights his own battle suggests a nobility of spirit as well as birth.

Visual Literacy While the artist's scale, particularly of humans and horses, is naive, the sense of movement and tension that exists between Arthur and Mordred and their rearing horses is accomplished.

Questions How do you think the artist achieved this effect? Suggest that students consider the role played by the upright lances and waving flags. *(Possible responses: The tension is heightened by the contrast between upright and horizontal lances and the angles of the two warriors and their horses. Arthur and Mordred encircle the locked lances like parentheses. The jaunty flags reiterate the angles of the battle while making sport of its deadliness.)*

EDITORIAL NOTE This excerpt has been shortened for length. For a more complete version of *Morte Darthur,* see the Custom Literature Database.

MINI-LESSON: LITERARY FOCUS

Protagonist/Antagonist

Teach Review the meanings of the terms *protagonist* and *antagonist.*

Question Is it possible to have a protagonist without an antagonist? *(one usually defines the other)*

Activity Idea Have students look up the etymologies of *antagonist, protagonist,* and *agony.* (Students may need to check related words to find them.)

- *Antagonist* comes from *antagonize,* which combines two ancient Greek words meaning "against the contest."
- *Protagonist* comes from two ancient Greek words meaning "first actor or contestant," which suggests that even in ancient times the star got the best part.
- *Agony* comes from a Greek word meaning "contest," which suggests that athletes have always known the "agony of defeat."

Ask students to name the protagonists and antagonists of Beowulf (Beowulf/Grendel), "Gawain and the Green Knight" (Gawain/Green Knight), and Morte Darthur (Arthur/Mordred). If time allows, lead a discussion on who or what are the protagonist(s) and antagonist(s) of Chaucer's "The Pardoner's Tale."

"Welcome, my sister's son. I thought you had died! And now I see thee alive, great is my debt to Almighty Jesus. Ah, fair nephew, who be these ladies that come hither with you?"

"Sir," said Sir Gawain, "all these be fair ladies for whom I have fought for, when I was a living man. And all these are those that I did battle for in righteous quarrels, and God hath given them that aid for their earnest prayers; and because I did battle for them for their rights, they brought me hither unto you. Thus hath God given me leave for to warn you of your death: for if ye fight tomorrow with Sir Mordred, as ye both have agreed, doubt ye not ye shall be slain,[5] and the greatest part of your people on both sides. And for the great concern and good that Almighty Jesus has had for you, and for pity of you and many other good men that shall be slain, God
2 hath sent me to you of His special grace to give you warning that in no way ye do battle tomorrow, but instead that ye make a treaty for a month and a day. And request this urgently, so that tomorrow you can delay. For within a month shall come Sir Lancelot with all his noble knights, and rescue you loyally, and slay Sir Mordred and all that ever will stay with him."

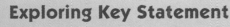

3 **PREDICT: What visions come to King Arthur in his dreams? What do they foreshadow might happen?**

Then Sir Gawain and all the ladies vanished, and at once the King called upon his knights, squires, and yeomen, and charged them quickly to fetch his noble lords and wise bishops unto him. And when they were come the King told them of his vision; that Sir Gawain had told him and warned him that if he fought on the morn, he should be slain. Then the King commanded Sir Lucan the Butler and his brother Sir Bedivere the Bold, with two bishops with them, and charged them in any way to make a treaty for a month and a day with Sir Mordred:

"And spare not, offer him lands and goods as much as ye think reasonable."

So then they departed and came to Sir Mordred where he had a grim host of a hundred thousand, and there they entreated[6] Sir Mordred a long time. And at the last Sir Mordred agreed for to take over Cornwall and Kent during King Arthur's lifetime; and after that all England, after the days of King Arthur.

Then were they agreed that King Arthur and Sir Mordred should meet betwixt both their hosts, and each of them should bring fourteen persons. And so they came with this word unto Arthur. Then he said,

"I am glad that this is done"; and so he went into the field.

And when King Arthur departed he warned all his host that if they saw any sword drawn, "look ye come on fiercely 4 and slay that traitor, Sir Mordred, for I in no way trust him." In like manner Sir Mordred warned his host that "and ye see any manner of sword drawn, look that ye come on fiercely and so slay all that before you stand, for in no way will I trust in this treaty." And in the same way said Sir Mordred unto his host: "for I know well my father will be avenged upon me."

And so they met as they had arranged, and were agreed and accorded thoroughly. And wine was fetched, and they drank together. Just then came an adder out of a little heath-bush, and it stung a knight in the foot. And so when the knight felt himself so stung, he looked down and saw the adder; and at once he drew his sword to slay the adder, and thought of no other harm. And when the host on both sides saw

This illustration from the 1400s shows King Arthur and his son Mordred battling each other at Camlan. What does their style of fighting suggest about what kind of people they were?

5. slay (slā), *v.* **slew, slain, slaying.** kill with violence.
6. entreat (en trēt′), *v.* beg.

2 Literary Focus
Protagonist/Antagonist

Question How does this passage suggest that Arthur is the protagonist? *(God is on his side; he is referred to as a good man.)*

3 Active Reading
Predict

Responses Arthur dreams of the turning of the wheel of fortune, then of Gawain, who warns against fighting a battle on the following day. They foreshadow Arthur's demise and his being taken to Avalon.

4 Literary Element
Foreshadowing

Question What do Arthur's warning about Mordred and Mordred's warning about his father foreshadow? *(that their fates are sealed; they will kill each other)*

BUILDING ENGLISH PROFICIENCY

Exploring Key Statement

On page 81, we read that "Sir Gawain had told him and warned him that if he fought on the morn, he should be slain." Ask students how this statement relates to the title of the story. (In the vision, Gawain has foretold Arthur's destiny—what indeed will happen to him if he battles Mordred on the next day.)

Activity Ideas

- Invite students to share their views about the importance of dreams. Discuss what might cause dreams and nightmares. Have volunteers tell (from personal experiences or from seeing TV shows or movies) about dreams that seemed to come true.
- To accommodate different learning styles, give students the option of (1) drawing or painting a dream, (2) creating a musical composition or song about a dream, or (3) writing a "dream poem."

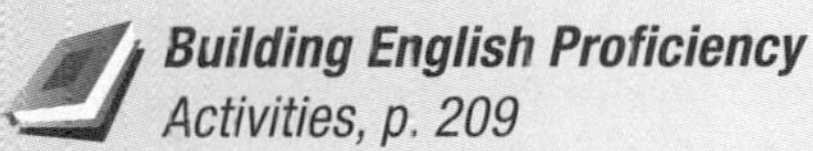
Building English Proficiency
Activities, p. 209

5 Literary Focus
Protagonist/Antagonist

Question Compare how the author characterizes King Arthur and Sir Mordred in this passage. *(The author glorifies Arthur's character and bravery, while the description of Mordred is restrained.)*

6 Reading/Thinking Skills
Recognize Values

Question What do you think King Arthur is expressing about his belief system with the line "Now come death, come life"? *(Possible response: Arthur may believe that his intention to rid the earth of Mordred is more important than his own life.)*

7 Reader's Response
Making Personal Connections

Malory uses extremely violent, bloody images in the struggle between antagonist/protagonist.

Question Is this violence, like the violence in many movies today, gratuitous? *(Possible response: perhaps, but it does display their hatred in a highly effective way)*

that sword drawn, then they blew trumpets and horns, and shouted grimly, and so both hosts attacked each other. And King Arthur mounted his horse and said, "Alas, this unhappy day!" and so rode to his men, and Sir Mordred in like wise.

And never since was there seen a more grievous battle in no Christian land, for there was only slashing and riding, thrusting and striking, and many a grim word was there spoken of one to the other, and many a deadly stroke. But ever King Arthur rode through the battle against Sir
5 Mordred many times and acted full nobly, as a noble king should do, and at all times he never hesitated. And Sir Mordred did his utmost that day and put himself in great peril.

And thus they fought all the day long, and never ceased 'till the noble knights were fallen on the cold earth. And yet they fought still 'till it was near night, and by then was there a hundred thousand lay dead upon the earth. Then was King Arthur wild with wrath beyond measure, when he saw his people so slain because of him.

And so he looked about himself and could see no more of all his host and of good knights left no more alive but two knights: Sir Lucan the Butler and his brother, Sir Bedivere; and yet they were very badly wounded.

"Jesus have mercy!" said the King, "where are all my noble knights gone? Alas, that ever I should see this grievous day! For now," said King Arthur, "I am come to mine end. But would to God," said he, "that I knew now where were that traitor Sir Mordred that hath caused all this mischief."

Then King Arthur looked about and was aware where stood Sir Mordred leaning upon his sword among a great heap of dead men.

"Now give me my spear," said King Arthur unto Sir Lucan, "for yonder I have seen the traitor that all this woe hath wrought."[7]

"Sir, let him be," said Sir Lucan, "for he brings misfortune. And if ye pass this unfortunate day ye shall be right well revenged. And, good lord, remember ye of your night's dream and what the spirit of Sir Gawain told you last night, and God of His great goodness hath preserved you hitherto. And for God's sake, my lord, leave this battle, for, blessed be God, ye have won the field; for yet be here three alive, and with Sir Mordred is not one alive. And therefore if ye leave now, this wicked day of destiny is past!"

"Now come death, come life," said the King, 6
"now I see him yonder alone, he shall never escape my hands! For at a better advantage shall I never have him."

"God speed you well!" said Sir Bedivere.

Then the King took his spear in both his hands, and ran towards Sir Mordred, crying out and saying,

"Traitor, now is thy death-day come!"

And when Sir Mordred saw King Arthur he ran towards him with his sword drawn in his hands, and there King Arthur struck Sir Mordred under the shield, with a thrust of his spear, through and beyond the body more than a foot. 7
And when Sir Mordred felt that he had his death's wound he thrust himself with the might that he had up to the hand guard of King Arthur's spear, and then he smote[8] his father, King Arthur, with his sword holding it in both his hands, upon the side of the head, so that the sword pierced the helmet and the outer membrane of the brain. And with that Sir Mordred dashed down stark dead to the earth.

And noble King Arthur fell in a swoon[9] to the earth, and there he swooned several times, and Sir Lucan and Sir Bedivere several times lifted him up. And so weakly betwixt them they led him to a little chapel not far from the sea, and when the King was there, he thought himself reasonably eased.

Then heard they people cry in the field.

"Now go thou, Sir Lucan," said the King,

7. wrought (rôt), *v.* ARCHAIC. a past tense and a past participle of **work.**
8. smite (smīt), *v.* **smote, smit ten** or **smote, smiting.** hit; give a hard blow to.
9. swoon (swün), *n., v.* faint.

MINI-LESSON: GRAMMAR
Beginning Sentences with Conjunctions

The sometimes-taught "rule" never to begin a sentence with a conjunction such as *and, but,* or *so* is not a valid one; in fact, skilled authors begin sentences with conjunctions.

Teach A conjunction such as *and* or *but* does not have to be in the same sentence to link it to the previous sentence. Have students find an example on this page where the author links a sentence to the previous one by beginning the second sentence with a conjunction. *(Many do so, including many paragraphs.)* Beginning a sentence with *and* or *but* can emphasize and strengthen the link or the contrast with the previous sentence. Point out that beginning a sentence with a conjunction was a more common practice in medieval and later times and is still done by skilled writers. However, for the sake of clarity, **most new writers should avoid** beginning sentences with conjunctions.

Activity Ideas

- Have students rewrite several paragraphs to avoid beginning sentences with *and* or *but.* What effect does this have on the writing?
- Have students check their own writing for sentences beginning with a conjunction and rewrite to avoid the conjunction.

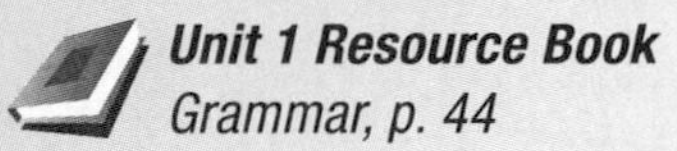

Unit 1 Resource Book
Grammar, p. 44

"and help me to learn what means that noise in the field."

So Sir Lucan departed, though he was grievously wounded in many places; and as he rode he saw and noticed by the moonlight how the plunderers and robbers were come into the field to plunder[10] and to rob many a full noble knight of brooches and bracelets and of many a good ring and many a rich jewel. And those that were not yet dead, there they slew them for their armor and their gold.

When Sir Lucan understood this he came to the King as soon as he might, and told him all which he had heard and seen.

"Therefore by my advice," said Sir Lucan, "it is best that we bring you to some town."

"I would that it were so," said the King, "but I may not stand, my head fails so. . . . Ah, Sir Lancelot!" said King Arthur, "this day have I missed thee! And alas, that ever I was against thee! For now I have my death, whereof Sir Gawain warned me in my dream."

Then Sir Lucan took up the King on one side and Sir Bedivere the other side, and in the lifting up the King swooned, and in the lifting Sir Lucan fell in a swoon, and
8 part of his guts fell out of his body, and with that the noble knight's heart burst. And when the King awoke he beheld Sir Lucan, how he lay foaming at the mouth and part of his guts lay at his feet.

"Alas," said the King, "this is to me a very sad sight, to see this noble duke die so for my sake, for he would have helped me that had more need of help than I! Alas, that he would not complain for himself, for his heart was so set to help me. Now Jesu have mercy upon his soul!"

Then Sir Bedivere wept for the death of his brother.

"Now leave this mourning and this weeping, gentle knight," said the King, "for all this will not help me. For know thou well, if I might live myself, the death of Sir Lucan would grieve me evermore. But my time passeth on fast," said the King. "Therefore," said King Arthur unto Sir Bedivere, "take thou here Excalibur,[11] my good sword, and go with it to the yonder water side; and when thou comest there, I charge thee throw my sword in that water, and come again and tell me what thou seest there."

"My lord," said Sir Bedivere, "your commandment shall be done, and lightly bring you word again."

So Sir Bedivere departed. And on the way he beheld that noble sword, and the pommel and the haft[12] was all precious stones. And then he said to himself, "If I throw this rich sword in the water, of this shall never come good, but harm and loss." And then Sir Bedivere hid Excalibur under a tree, and so as soon as he might he came again unto the King and said he had been at the water and had thrown the sword into the water.

"What saw thou there?" said the King.

"Sir," he said, "I saw nothing but waves and wind."

"That is untruly said by thee," said the King. "And therefore go thou lightly again, and do my commandment; as thou art to me beloved and dear, spare not, but throw it in."

Then Sir Bedivere returned again and took the sword in his hand; and yet he thought it a sin and shame to throw away that noble sword. And so again he hid the sword and returned again and told the King that he had been at the water and done his commandment.

"What sawest thou there?" said the King.

"Sir," he said, "I saw nothing but lapping waters and darkening waves."

"Ah, traitor unto me and untrue," said King Arthur, "now hast thou betrayed me twice! Who

10. **plunder** (plun′dər), *v.* steal by force, especially during war.
11. **Excalibur** (ek skal′ə bər), the sword that Arthur had received as a young man from the Lady of the Lake and that he must return at the time of his death. It served as his symbol of kingship.
12. **pommel . . . haft.** A pommel is a rounded knob on the haft, which is the handle of a sword.

8 Reader's Response
Challenging the Text

When Arthur is mortally wounded, the world seems to go haywire—the dead and dying are plundered; when Sir Lucan attempts to help Arthur, he swoons and turns inside out, so to speak.

Question Is this depiction necessary to the story? Can it be justified? *(Possible responses: Some students may think Malory is playing to the lowest common denominator; others may suggest that Malory depicts a world in which civilization is at risk.)* If time allows, this might make an interesting topic for class discussion.

BUILDING ENGLISH PROFICIENCY

Tracking Story Events

Completing the following chart will help small groups of students keep track of the important events in the story. Instruct groups to fill in the missing information wherever they see a question mark.

When	Where	What happened
1. Trinity Sunday night	Near Salisbury	?
2. Next morning	Battlefield	?
3. Nearly night	Battlefield	?
4. ?	Close to sea	?
5. After two false attempts	?	?
6. Later	Lake	?
7. ?	Chapel in woods	?

Art Study

Response to Caption Question
The mood, as dark and somber as the dirges the ladies sing, results from dark, rich colors, a highly stylized arrangement, and flattened perspective.

Visual Literacy Burne-Jones was a Pre-Raphaelite—an English artist of the middle 19th century who disliked neo-classical art, which was traced to Renaissance-artist Raphael. Disturbed by the upheavals of the Industrial Revolution, these artists saw a purer expression in "romantic dreams" of the Gothic. Pre-Raphaelite art, despised for much of the 20th century, has only recently been "rediscovered."

9 Literary Element
Symbolism

Arthur received the sword Excalibur from a misty, supernatural figure, the Lady of the Lake, who inhabited a castle in an underwater kingdom.

Question What do you think the sword Excalibur might symbolize? *(Students should recognize in some fashion that Excalibur was an instrument in the battle between good and evil, "right* vs. *might.")*

10 Multicultural Note
The Barge to Avalon

The belief that the dead travel over water to an afterlife led a number of cultures—the ancient Greeks, the Vikings, the Tongans and Samoans of the Pacific, among others—to bury or cremate the dead in a boat.

In *The Last Sleep of Arthur in Avalon,* painted by Sir Edward Burne-Jones between 1881 and 1898, the dying King is cared for by a queen and her ladies. What is the mood of the painting? How does the artist create that mood? ➤

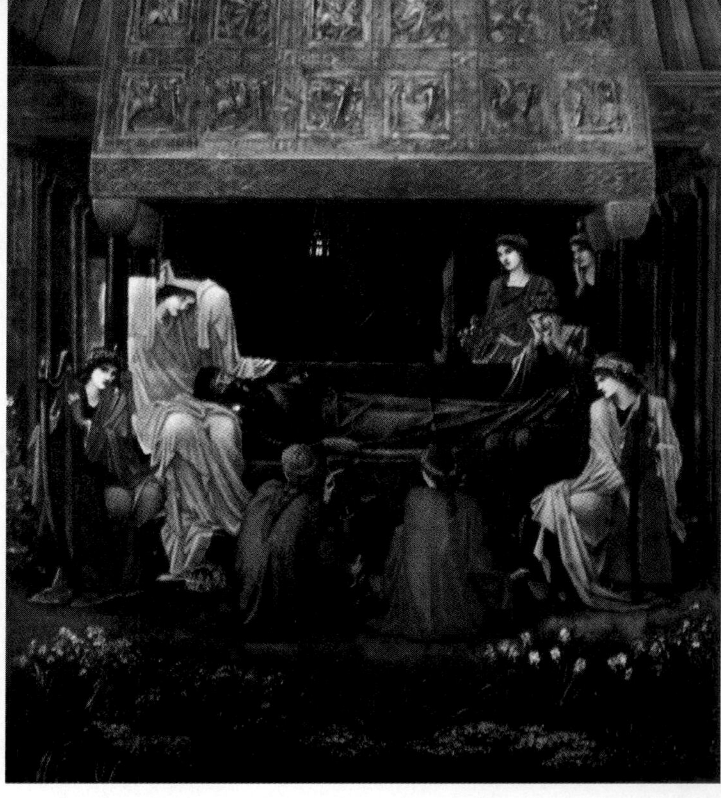

would believe that thou hast been to me so beloved and dear, and also named so noble a knight, that thou would betray me for the wealth of this sword? But now go again lightly; for thy long tarrying putteth me in great jeopardy of my life, for I am growing cold. And if thou do not now as I bid thee, if ever I may see thee, I shall slay thee by mine own hands, for thou wouldst for my rich sword see me dead."

Then Sir Bedivere departed and went to the sword and lightly took it up, and so he went unto the water side. And there he bound the belt about the hilt, and threw the sword as far into the water as he might. And there came an arm
9 and an hand above the water, and took it and seized it, and shook it thrice and brandished,[13] and then vanished with the sword into the water.

So Sir Bedivere came again to the King and told him what he saw.

"Alas," said the King, "help me hence, for I dread me I have tarried[14] over long."

Then Sir Bedivere took the King upon his back and so went with him to the water side. And when they were there, even close by the bank floated a little barge with many fair ladies on it, and among them all was a queen, and all of them had black hoods. And all of them wept and shrieked when they saw King Arthur.

"Now put me into that barge," said the King. 10

And so he did softly, and there received him three ladies with great mourning. And so they set him down, and in one of their laps King Arthur laid his head. And then the queen said,

13. brandish (bran′dish), *v.* wave or shake threateningly.
14. tarry (tar′ē), *v.* delay.

MINI-LESSON: USAGE

Origins and Development of the English Language

Teach Remind students that the English of Sir Thomas Malory's day had been shaped by Celtic, Latin, Anglo-Saxon, and French, as well as by Scandinavian languages. Today, when people wish to speak and write English in a formal manner, they use words derived in large part from Latin and French.

Activity Idea Have students recast the following passage from page 84 into contemporary English. Have them check the origins of the words they choose, using as few words derived from Latin as possible.

> "Alas," said the King, "help me hence, for I dread me I have tarried over long."

"Ah, my dear brother! Why have ye tarried so long from me? Alas, this wound on your head hath caught overmuch cold!"

And then they rowed away from the land, and Sir Bedivere beheld all those ladies go away from him. Then Sir Bedivere cried out and said,

"Ah, my lord Arthur, what shall become of me, now ye go from me and leave me here alone among mine enemies?"

"Comfort thyself," said the King, "and do as well as thou mayest, for in me is no trust for to trust in. For I must go into the vale of Avilion[15] to heal me of my grievous wound. And if thou hear never more of me, pray for my soul!"

But ever the queen and ladies wept and shrieked, that it was pitiful to hear. As soon as Sir Bedivere had lost sight of the barge he wept and wailed, and so entered the forest and traveled all night.

11 **CLARIFY: How is King Arthur transported to his resting place?**

And in the morning he was aware, betwixt two wan woods, of a chapel and a hermitage. Then was Sir Bedivere fearful, and thither he went, and when he came into the chapel he saw where lay a hermit groveling[16] on all fours, close there by a tomb was new dug. When the hermit saw Sir Bedivere he knew him well, for he was but little before Bishop of Canterbury that Sir Mordred put to flight.

"Sir," said Sir Bedivere, "what man is there here buried that ye pray so earnestly for?"

"Fair son," said the hermit, "I know not truly but only guess. But this same night, at midnight, there came a number of ladies and brought here a dead corpse and prayed me to bury him. And here they offered a hundred candles, and they gave me a thousand coins."

"Alas!" said Sir Bedivere, "that was my lord King Arthur, which lieth here buried in this chapel."

Then Sir Bedivere swooned, and when he awoke he prayed the hermit that he might stay with him still, there to live with fasting and prayers:

"For from hence will I never go," said Sir Bedivere, "by my will, but all days of my life stay here to pray for my lord Arthur."

"Sir, ye are welcome to me," said the hermit, "for I know you better than you think that I do: for ye are Sir Bedivere the Bold, and the full noble Duke Sir Lucan the Butler was your brother."

Then Sir Bedivere told the hermit all as ye have heard before, and so he remained with the hermit that was before the Bishop of Canterbury. And there Sir Bedivere put upon himself poor clothes, and served the hermit full lowly in fasting and in prayers.

Thus of Arthur I find no more written in books that have been written, nothing more of the very certainty of his brave death I never read . . .

Yet some men say in many parts of England 12
that King Arthur is not dead, but had by the will of Our Lord Jesu gone into another place; and men say that he shall come again, and he shall win the Holy Cross. Yet I will not say that it shall be so, but rather would I say: here in this world he changed his life. And many men say that there is written upon the tomb this:

HIC IACET ARTHURUS,
REX QUONDAM REXQUE FUTURUS.

Here Lies Arthur,
King Once and King That Will Be.

15. **Avilion** (ə vil′yən), often called **Avalon** (av′ə lon), a legendary island, an earthly paradise, the final resting place of King Arthur.

16. **grovel** (gruv′əl), *v.* crawl humbly on the ground.

11 Active Reading
Clarify

Response He is moved over water by barge.

12 Literary Criticism
Malory's Language

". . . if 'The Day of Destiny' has the quality that raises Malory to a high place among English authors, the reason is . . . its language. Malory used a plain, crisp, cadenced prose . . . was often vivid . . . and . . . often reproduced the directness and vigor of living speech."

Fredrick Whitehead
Professor of Old French Language and Literature, Victoria University of Manchester

Check Test

1. What day was assigned between King Arthur and Mordred for their battle to be held? *(Monday after Trinity Sunday)*
2. Why did King Arthur seek to postpone the battle? *(In dreams, he learned he would die if he fought on the assigned day.)*
3. Approximately how many people were killed in the battle? *(100,000)*
4. How many times did Bedivere lie to King Arthur about Excalibur? *(twice)*
5. What was the previous occupation of the hermit whom Bedivere found? *(Bishop of Canterbury)*

Unit 1 Resource Book
Alternate Check Test, p. 45

BUILDING ENGLISH PROFICIENCY

Analyzing a Conclusion

Help students understand how Malory offers readers a sense of closure.

1. Ask students who is speaking in the last two paragraphs. (Malory himself.)
2. Divide the class into groups. Have the groups discuss the information (not much, mostly rumors) and the mood (decidedly upbeat—Arthur may come back) in the final two paragraphs.
3. Ask each group to copy and complete the chart shown.

Malory . . .		
	Learned Through Research	Concluded on His Own
About Arthur's death:		
His greatest achievement:		

After Reading

MAKING CONNECTIONS

1. Possible responses: Students might say that they would have acted the same; Arthur would soon be dead. Or, they would have obeyed out of curiosity or to keep his principles alive.

2. Possible responses: Arthur's anger gets the best of him—this is his best chance to avenge himself; or Arthur knows this is his fate.

3. Arthur's principles and civilization will be abandoned.

4. Students may say that the description of the battle is sketchy, while the fight between Arthur and Mordred is graphic and realistic.

5. The first dream portends the turning of Arthur's fortunes; the second foretells his death and passage to Avalon.

6. After all Arthur's efforts to avert war, an "accident" causes the battle and its tragic aftermath.

7. Supernatural elements include the fulfillment of Arthur's dreams; the hand in the lake that catches Excalibur; the barge with the ladies who escort Arthur to Avalon.

8. Many people wish to believe in immortality, in superheroes who don't really die, e.g., Elvis; other people may believe that certain ideals can only be realized by those who espouse them.

9. Possible response: The legend combines the dream of a moral, just society with an exciting, exotic story containing elements of magic; at the same time, elements of the story—husband/wife and father/son conflict—are more realistic than most legends.

After Reading

Making Connections

Shaping Your Response

1. If you were Sir Bedivere, do you think you would react the same way he does about the sword Excalibur?
2. Why do you think Arthur insists on fighting Mordred man-to-man?
3. What do the plunderers Sir Lucan sees on the battlefield suggest to you about England's future after Arthur's death?

Analyzing the Tale

4. In your opinion, how realistic are Malory's descriptions of battle scenes?
5. On the night before he is scheduled to go into battle Arthur has two dreams. What do these dreams seem to **foreshadow?**
6. What is **ironic** about the episode with the adder?
7. What elements of magic or the supernatural do you find in this legend?

Extending the Ideas

8. According to Malory, people have continued to believe for centuries that King Arthur did not die, but that he is waiting to return to rule again. Why might people be attracted to such a belief?
9. The tales of Authur and his court have continued to intrigue writers and readers for centuries. Modern authors such as John Steinbeck, Mary Stewart, and Marion Zimmer Bradley have all penned their versions of the legend, and dozens of movies have dealt with characters and events of Arthur's court. Why do you think this story still holds such fascination?

Literary Focus: Protagonist/Antagonist

How is it made clear that King Arthur is the **protagonist** and that Mordred is the **antagonist?** Draw a chart like the following. Under each character's name list descriptive phrases from the text that help to establish the character's role. Then do the same thing for Gawain as the protagonist and the Green Knight as the antagonist.

Protagonist	Antagonist
King Arthur	Mordred
Sir Gawain	Green Knight

LITERARY FOCUS

Protagonist / Antagonist

Arthur	Mordred
noble	stirred up crowds
brave	agrees to take over . . . all England
"good that . . . Jesus has for you"	traitor
lord	grim
king	"slay all"

Protagonist / Antagonist

Sir Gawain	Green Knight
a true knight	a man as evil as any other on earth
noblest of knights	"fail not or be called a recreant"
if Mary had not . . . for her knight	lover of blows
the most faultless knight	violent
the good Sir Gawain	knows no mercy

avenge
brandish
entreat
grovel
plunder
slay
smite
swoon
tarry
wrought

Vocabulary Study

Malory uses strong verbs in his telling of the events surrounding the final battle between Arthur's and Mordred's forces. Among the most descriptive verbs Malory uses are forms of those in the list. Copy the words and write out their definitions (use the Glossary or the footnotes with the selection). Then use at least five of the words in a paragraph about a fight between a protagonist and antagonist such as King Arthur and Mordred.

Expressing Your Ideas

Writing Choices

Writer's Notebook Update Written on Arthur's tomb are these now famous words: "Here Lies Arthur, King Once and King That Will Be." Assume that King Arthur has indeed returned. List some of the challenges he would face.

A Different Angle You are Sir Bedivere, the only survivor of this fierce battle. Write a **narrative** of Arthur's last day from your own, first-person point of view; that is, use the pronoun "I." Include your account of Arthur's combat with Mordred, your reasons for hiding Excalibur, and your feelings and actions after Arthur departs in the barge. Be sure not to include information you couldn't know without someone's telling you.

A Tale of a Vale Arthur tells Bedivere that the queen and her ladies are taking him "into the vale of Avilion" where he will be healed. What do you think this miraculous land is? Is it an afterlife, or a special, magical spot here on earth? What else can it do, besides heal grievous wounds? Use your imagination to write a **description** of Avilion and its wonders.

Other Options

The Round Table Revisited Form a group with other classmates to create some new knights and new adventures. Work together to create a **skit** in which your knights return to King Arthur's court to share the stories of their conquests.

More Court News You have met only a few of the exciting characters of King Arthur's court; there are many more in the various legends, including Galahad, Guinevere, Lancelot, Merlin, Morgan la Fay, Percival, and Tristram. Research one of these characters and prepare a **picture essay** (a combination of pictures and captions) in the form of a bulletin board, a scrapbook, or a file in a multimedia computer program.

Hanging Around Lining the walls of medieval castles were tapestries, large woven panels picturing historic events, mythical characters, and other compositions. Create a design for a **wall hanging** that pictures one of the adventures you have read about. If possible, cover a wall with white paper or butcher paper and make your design full-sized.

VOCABULARY STUDY

Vocabulary words, as used in context, should reflect correct meanings and connotations.

More Practice Invite students to make up sentences about protagonists and antagonists from past selections. using the selection words.

Unit 1 Resource Book
Vocabulary, p. 43
Vocabulary Test, p. 46

WRITING CHOICES

Writer's Notebook Update

Remind students that Arthur would have to overcome not only the specific evils of any era to which he returned, but also unfamiliar social, cultural, and technological conditions.

A Different Angle

Point out to students that completing this assignment will require strong identification with Sir Bedivere. Tell them to imagine that they are an actor playing Sir Bedivere in a play or movie. "Becoming" the knight in their minds will help them write from the first-person point of view.

A Tale of a Vale

Encourage students to brainstorm ideas about Avalon before they begin writing.

Selection Test

Unit 1 Resource Book
pp. 47–48

Transparency Collection
Fine Art Writing Prompt 2

OTHER OPTIONS

The Round Table Revisited

Advise students to use the selections they have just read for hints as to characterization, language, and plot.

Hanging Around

You may wish to have students work on this project in small groups. Suggest that between planning, drawing, and adding color, there is a job for everyone and for every skill.

Interdisciplinary Study

Theme Link

Every human society has its own code of honor. Chivalry is here taken as the model for such codes. Oddly, one society's code of honor may seem fantastic or barbaric to another. The interdisciplinary study explores this perspective.

Curricular Connection: Humanities

Use the information presented here as the basis for a discussion of codes of honor in contemporary social groupings, from corporations to street gangs.

Terms to Know

vassal (vas′ əl), a person who held land from a lord or superior, to whom in return he gave homage and allegiance, usually in the form of military service.

courtly, having manners fit for a royal court; polite, elegant.

largesse (lär jes′), a generous giving.

lists, place where knights fought in tournaments.

liaison (lē ā′zon), intimacy between a man and a woman.

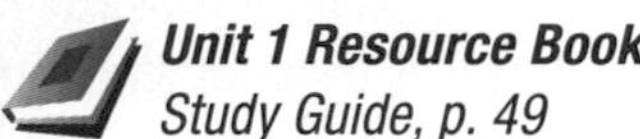

Unit 1 Resource Book
Study Guide, p. 49

INTERDISCIPLINARY STUDY

Codes of Honor

Legends of Arthur

Humanities Connection
The various tales and legends of King Arthur and his court became connected with a new concept of behavior called chivalry. Different versions developed different—and often conflicting—details of Arthur's life. Here are some of the highlights.

CHIVALRY

by Barbara Tuchman

Chivalry was a moral system governing the whole of noble life. It developed at the same time as the great crusades of the 12th century as a code intended to fuse the religious and martial spirits and somehow bring the fighting man into accord with Christian theory. A moral gloss was needed that would allow the Church to tolerate the warriors in good conscience and the warriors to pursue their own values in spiritual comfort. A code evolved that put the knight's sword arm in the service of justice, right, piety, the Church, the widow, the orphan, and the oppressed.

Chivalry developed its own principles. Prowess, that combination of courage, strength, and skill, was the prime essential. Honor and loyalty were the ideals, and so-called courtly love the presiding genius. Courtly love required its disciple to be in a chronically amorous condition, and largesse was the necessary accompaniment.

Prowess was not mere talk, for the function of physical violence required real stamina. To fight on horseback or foot wearing 55 pounds of plate armor, to give and receive blows with sword or battle-ax that could cleave a skull or slice off a limb at a stroke, to spend half of life in the saddle through all weathers and for days at a time, was not a weakling's work.

Loyalty, meaning the pledged word, was chivalry's fulcrum. The extreme emphasis given to it derived from the time when a pledge between lord and vassal was the only form of government. A knight who broke his oath was charged with "treason" for betraying the order of knighthood. The concept of loyalty did not preclude treachery or the most egregious trickery as long as no knightly oath was broken.

Chivalry was regarded as a universal order of all Christian knights, a trans-national class moved by a single ideal, much as Marxism later regarded all workers of the world. It was a military guild in which all knights were theoretically brothers.

Sir Lancelot hands down his shield to a lady as a mark of chivalry.

MINI-LESSON: STUDY SKILLS

Locate, Use, and Evaluate Reference Sources

Teach Tell students that encyclopedias are meant only to give an abstract or précis of knowledge on a subject. To do an in-depth study, you can use the computerized catalog of sources available at most modern libraries. These catalogs are extremely user-friendly, providing access to materials through author's name, source, title, and key subject words. Such searches yield lists of potentially useful materials which include bibliographic information and an abstract of the material's content.

Apply An essential for success using a computerized catalog is to be able to think of well-targeted key words for subject searches. Have students volunteer specific subjects, allowing you to demonstrate the above point by offering two to four good and bad key words for subject searches. Explain the stray paths a search can take because of ill-chosen key words.

Activity Take students to the nearest library with a computerized catalog. Allow them to take turns doing subject searches on the topic of chivalry.

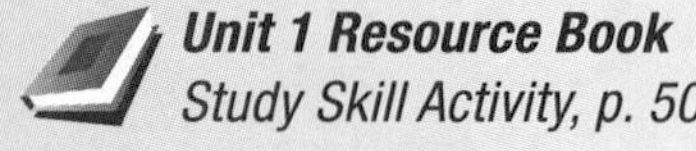

Unit 1 Resource Book
Study Skill Activity, p. 50

THE REGAL KING ARTHUR IS PORTRAYED IN THIS DETAIL FROM A FRENCH TAPESTRY, ABOUT 1385.

In the performance of his function, the knight must be prepared, as John of Salisbury wrote, "to shed your blood for your brethren— and, if needs must, to lay down your life."

Fighting filled the noble's need of something to do, a way to exert himself. It was his substitute for work. His leisure time was spent chiefly in hunting, otherwise in games of chess, backgammon, and dice, in songs, dances, pageants, and other entertainments. Long winter evenings were occupied listening to the recital of interminable verse epics. The sword offered the workless noble an activity with a purpose, one that could bring him honor, status, and, if he was lucky, gain. If no real conflict was at hand, he sought tournaments, the most exciting, expensive, ruinous, and delightful activity of the noble class.

Tournaments started without rules or lists as an agreed-upon clash of opposing units. Though justified as training exercises, the impulse was the love of fighting.

If tournaments were an acting-out of chivalry, courtly love was its dreamland. Courtly love was understood by its contemporaries to be love for its own sake, romantic love, true love, physical love, unassociated with property or family, and consequently focused on another man's wife, since only such an illicit liaison could have no other aim but love alone.

As its justification, courtly love was considered to ennoble a man, to improve him in every way. It would make him concerned to show an example of goodness, to do his utmost to preserve honor, never letting dishonor touch himself or the lady he loved.

If the fiction of chivalry molded outward behavior to some extent, it did not, any more than other models that man has made for himself, transform human nature. Yet, if the code was but a veneer over violence, greed, and sensuality, it was nevertheless an ideal, as Christianity was an ideal, toward which man's reach, as usual, exceeded his grasp.

Research Topics

- Walter of Henley (fl.1250), author of *Husbandry,* a work about estate management
- Causes of and principal leaders of the Peasants' Revolt in 1381
- Life of Joan of Arc (1412?–1431)
- Life of Richard III (1452–1485)

Art Study

The painting on page 88 is a detail from *Sir Lancelot Gives His Shield Into Elaine's Keeping* by Arthur A. Dixon. There are six people named Elaine in Arthurian legend; this is probably the daughter of Bernard of Astolat or the Lady of Shalott.

The Nine Heroes Tapestries were made in France and probably commissioned either by or for Jean, duc de Berry. The Nine Heroes (or Worthies) were Hector of Troy, Alexander the Great, Julius Caesar, Joshua, David, Judas Maccabaeus, Arthur, Charlemagne, and Godefroi de Bouillon. All are pictured in the tapestry in fourteenth-century dress. The tapestries are attributed to the workshop of Nicolas Bataille in Paris, and this one measures approximately 160 by 91 inches.

BUILDING ENGLISH PROFICIENCY

Analyzing Key Terms

This article offers an extended definition of the word *chivalry.* Help students check their understanding by creating a semantic web. They also can refer to the web as they continue on to pages 90–93.

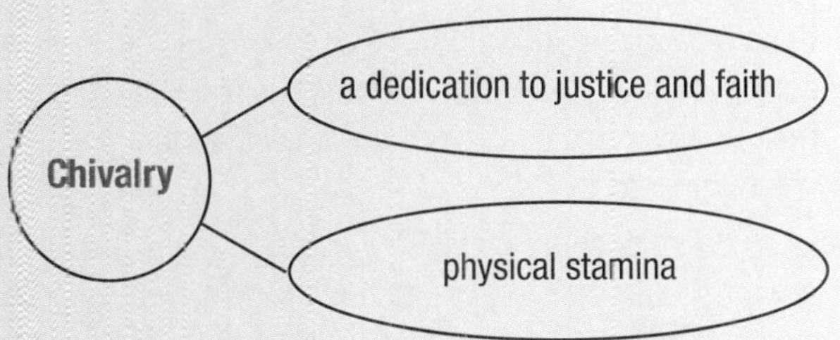

Art Study

Sir Launcelot in the Queen's Chamber (the background picture) was painted in 1867 by Dante Gabriel Rosetti (1828–1882). It was executed in pen and black and brown ink. Rosetti was one of the founders of the Pre-Raphaelite Brotherhood, which included Holman Hunt, Sir John Everett Millais, Edward Burne-Jones, and others. Rosetti was also a poet. The Pre-Raphaelite Brotherhood was a group of artists, poets, and critics who first met in 1848. D. G. Rosetti was a brother of writer Christina Rosetti.

The upper left picture is a detail from *Lancelot and Guinevere* by Herbert Draper (1864–1920).

The lower left picture is a detail from an engraving from an 1895 edition of Spenser's *The Faerie Queen.*

Beautiful Guinevere is surrounded by her ladies-in-waiting.

Merlin, the bearded magician, leads Arthur down the path to his kingship.

MINI-LESSON: STUDY SKILLS

Using a Thesaurus

Teach Remind students that a print thesaurus is a dictionary in which synonyms, antonyms, and other related words are classified under certain headings. Whether electronic or in a book, a thesaurus is a useful tool for finding just the right word.

Apply Have students become familiar with a print thesaurus by finding the following words in the alphabetical index: *absolve, benevolence,* and *cheerful.* Then have them turn to the sections designated after each word to see what synonyms or antonyms are shown.

Activity Have students use any thesaurus to find a suitable synonym for each italicized word in the following sentences.

- Sometime during the Middle Ages, Arthur became *connected* with the code of chivalry.
- "The Day of Destiny" describes the *dissolution* of the order he had established.
- According to *story,* Arthur will return.

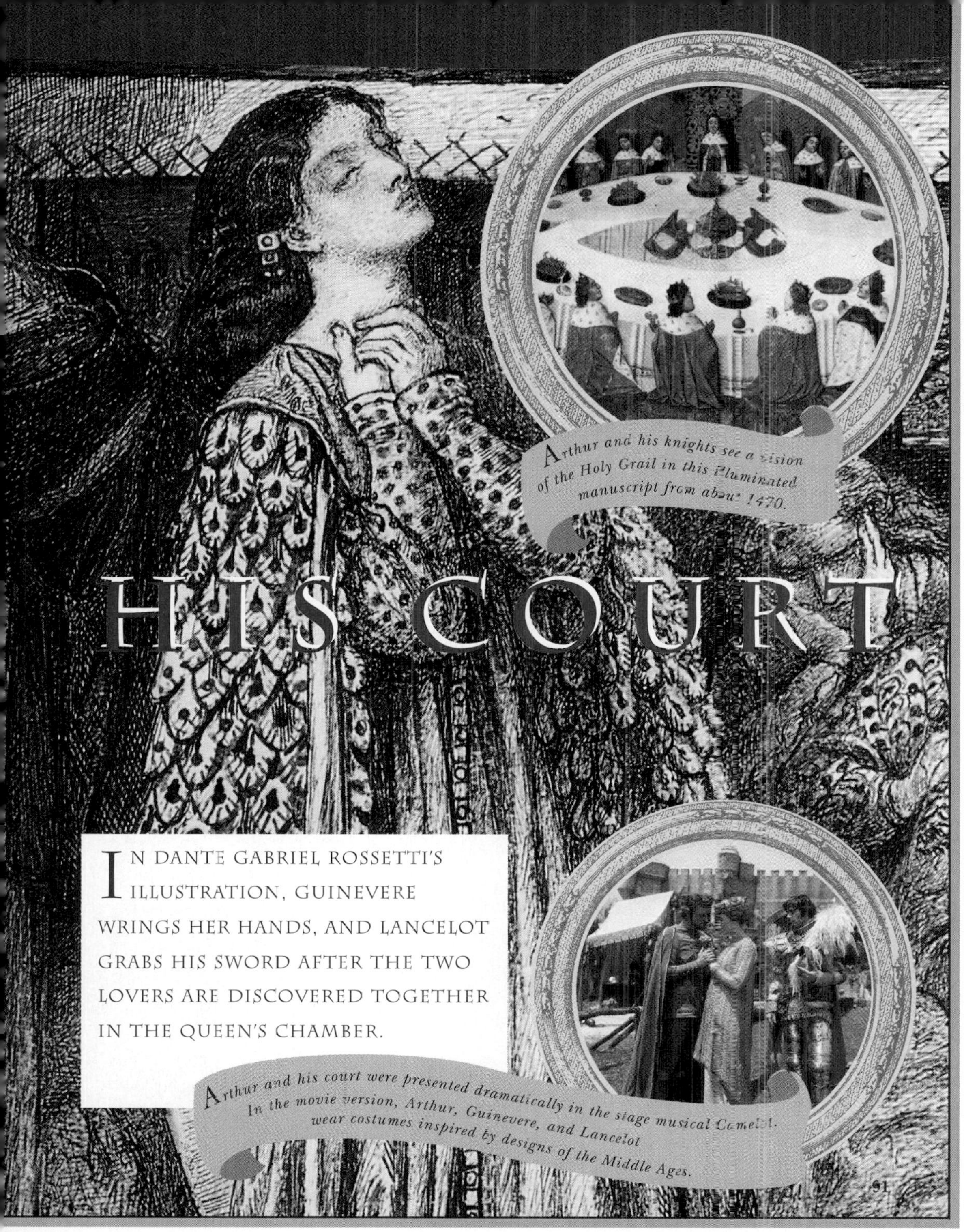

HIS COURT

Arthur and his knights see a vision of the Holy Grail in this illuminated manuscript from about 1470.

IN DANTE GABRIEL ROSSETTI'S ILLUSTRATION, GUINEVERE WRINGS HER HANDS, AND LANCELOT GRABS HIS SWORD AFTER THE TWO LOVERS ARE DISCOVERED TOGETHER IN THE QUEEN'S CHAMBER.

Arthur and his court were presented dramatically in the stage musical Camelot. In the movie version, Arthur, Guinevere, and Lancelot wear costumes inspired by designs of the Middle Ages.

91

Art Study

The upper right picture is from an early fourteenth-century French illuminated manuscript, *Le Roman de Lancelot du Lac.*

The words and music for *Camelot* (1967) were by Alan Jay Lerner and Frederick Lowe. The film starred Richard Harris and Vanessa Redgrave and won Academy Awards for art direction, music direction, and costumes.

BUILDING ENGLISH PROFICIENCY

Responding to Visual Cues

Students will become more familiar with interpreting art by studying this spread and doing the following activity.

1. Assemble students in five groups, one for each of the scenes on the spread.

2. Have each group interpret its scene—tell what is going on and how the characters may feel.

3. Have groups explain on what they based their interpretations (for example, through symbolism, color, and facial expressions).

4. Encourage group members to record in their dialogue journals their own interpretations of the other scenes on the spread.

Additional Background

Glastonbury, in southwest England, is often associated with Avalon. According to one legend, the abbey is supposed to have been founded by Joseph of Arimathea. Other legends suggest that it was founded by French monks. The discovery of two bodies there in the 1180s, supposedly Arthur and Guinevere, led to the connection of Avalon to Glastonbury.

Art Study

Daniel Maclise (1806–1870), the artist who created the engraving of Arthur being taken to Avalon, was an Irish history and portrait painter. He was a friend of Charles Dickens and his portrait of Dickens is in the National Portrait Gallery in London. He often painted subjects from Shakespeare.

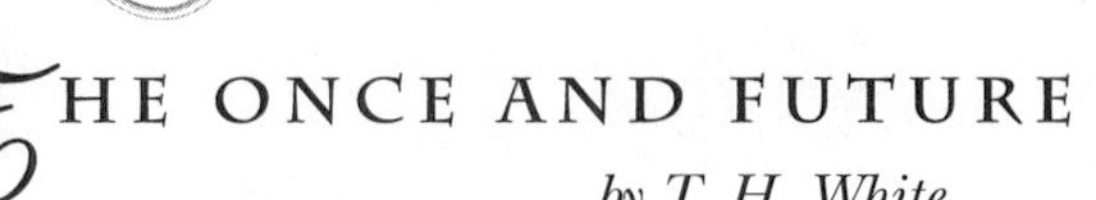

The Once and Future King

by T. H. White

In this novel excerpt, King Arthur talks to his page, a young servant, on the night before he meets Mordred for their final battle.

"Oh page?"

"My lord?"

"What is your name?"

"Tom, my lord," [the boy] said politely.

"Where do you live?"

"Near Warwick, my lord. At a place called Newbold Revell. It is a pretty one."

"How old are you?"

"I shall be thirteen in November, my lord."

"Tell me, Tom, what do you intend to do tomorrow?"

"I shall fight, sir. I have a good bow."

"And you will kill people with this bow?"

"Yes, my lord. A great many, I hope."

"Suppose they were to kill you?"

"Then I should be dead, my lord."

"I see."

"Shall I take the letter now?"

"No, Tom. Sit down and try to listen. Could you understand if I asked you not to fight tomorrow?"

"I should want to fight," [Tom] said stoutly.

"Everybody wants to fight, Tom, but nobody knows why. Suppose I were to ask you not to fight, as a special favor to the King? Would you do that?"

"I should do what I was told."

"Listen, then. I am a very old man, Tom, and you are young. When you are old, you will be able to tell what I have told tonight, and I want you to do that. Do you understand this want?"

"Yes, sir. I think so."

Arthur is taken to the island of Avalon to heal his wound.

"Put it like this. There was a king once, called King Arthur. That is me. When he came to the throne of England, he found that all the kings and barons were fighting against each other like madmen, and, as they could afford to fight in expensive suits of armor, there was practically nothing which could stop them from doing what they pleased. They did a lot of bad things, because they lived by force. Now this king had an idea, and the idea was that force ought to be used, if it were used at all, on behalf of justice, not on its own account. Follow this, young boy. He thought that if he could get his barons fighting for truth, and to help weak people, and to redress wrongs, then their fighting might not be such a bad thing as once it used to be. So he gathered together all the true and kindly people that he knew, and he dressed them in armor, and he made them knights, and taught them his idea, and set them down, at a Round Table. There were a hundred and fifty of them in the happy days, and King Arthur loved his Table with all his heart. He was prouder of it than he was of his own dear wife, and for many years his new knights went about killing ogres, and rescuing damsels, and saving poor prisoners, and trying to set the world to rights. That was the King's idea."

"I think it was a good idea, my lord."

"It was, and it was not. God knows."

"What happened to the King in the end?"

"For some reason, things went wrong. The Table split into factions, a bitter war began, and all were killed."

The boy interrupted confidently.

"No," he said, "not all. The King won. We shall win."

"Everybody was killed," he repeated, "except a certain page. I know what I am talking about."

"My lord?"

"This page was called young Tom of Newbold Revell near Warwick, and the old

King Arthur accuses his son Mordred of being a traitor and vows to kill him.

King sent him off before the battle, upon pain of dire disgrace. You see, the King wanted there to be somebody left, who would remember their famous idea. He wanted badly that Tom should go back to Newbold Revell, where he could grow into a man and live his life in Warwickshire peace—and he wanted him to tell everybody who would listen about this ancient idea, which both of them had once thought good. Do you think you could do that, Thomas, to please the King?"

The child said, with the pure eyes of absolute truth: "I would do anything for King Arthur."

Responding

1. How do you think King Arthur might have adapted the code of chivalry so that his people could live more at peace with each other?

2. What elements of the code seem to be most responsible for the downfall of the Round Table?

3. In your opinion, what elements of chivalry are still alive today? What elements should we try to revive?

Art Study

The upper right painting is by N(ewell) C(onvers) Wyeth (1882–1945) from *The Boy's King Arthur.*

Responding

1. Possible responses King Arthur could have greatly curtailed the number of instances when physical fighting was allowed to settle even legitimate disputes. He could have mandated discussion and compromise as the major and accepted methods of conflict resolution.

2. Possible responses an uncompromising philosophy, competition, emphasis on physical responses to problems

3. Possible responses Physical contests to bring honor and some traces of the idea of romantic love are two common phenomena. A sense of loyalty and honor should be revived, provided the loyalty is to a good cause and not an evil one.

Interdisciplinary Activity Ideas

- Students can form small groups to design a new code of conduct for their school. Tell them that some aspect of the new code must provide courtesies that demand real effort or care.
- Students can prepare a report on the United Nations Charter and the Declaration of Human Rights, analyzing and evaluating them as a code of conduct for the twenty-first century.

BUILDING ENGLISH PROFICIENCY

Analyzing Dialogue

This conversation expresses some key ideas relating to chivalry. Use one or more of the following activities to help students recognize those ideas as they read the dialogue.

Activity Ideas

- Have students explain what is meant by the title *The Once and Future King.*
- Encourage students to comment upon the concept of complete obedience implicit in the last line.
- Discuss why King Arthur believes that his dreams for England were both good and bad.

Language History

Teaching Objectives

- To understand reasons for changes in English from the eleventh to fourteenth centuries.
- To understand that the English language has always been in a state of flux.

Introduce

Ask students to volunteer some examples of words that have entered English from Spanish or Mexican Spanish. (Suggest that they think of names of foods.) They might mention taco, tortilla, guacamole, frijole, tostada, and chili. Ask them to speculate about why these words came into English and why English speakers often adopt names of foods from other languages. Then have students read the article.

Follow Up

Many words that entered English from French were originally based on Latin words. Encourage students to find the origins of the following words: chivalry, crown, robe, and noble.

Language History

The Language of Court and Chapel

There were many tourneys with gallant jousting of knights, and after the jousting they rode to the court for song and dance . . . .

When you read this passage at the beginning of *Sir Gawain and the Green Knight*, you encounter a number of words that entered the English language during the Middle Ages: *tourneys, gallant, jousting, dance*. What kind of social world do these words reflect?

In 1066, French-speaking Normans conquered England. The Norman Conquest had major long-term consequences for the English language. For the next three and a half centuries, English was substantially altered and expanded by contact with the French spoken by the invaders. For the first two centuries (1066–1250), the infusion of French words was relatively slight. Words adopted from the French during this period reflect the outlook of the ruling class (*noble, dame, chivalry, servant, messenger*) or religious concerns (*sermon, communion, confession, clergy, convent*).

By 1250, when ties between England and Normandy had loosened and English nationalism was making itself felt, many more French words began to be assimilated into English—particularly words associated with government, law, and business, such as *crown, state, reign, authority, tax, judge, pardon*. Also notable are the number of words from social and cultural life (*dance, recreation, poet, tragedy, story, music, art*) and food and clothing (*beef, bacon, olive, gown, boot, robe*).

During these same centuries, the dialect of Old English spoken by the people of the East Midlands, the area that included London, was becoming looked upon as the standard form of the language, as "the King's English." Around 1370 Geoffrey Chaucer wrote in this dialect, giving it literary status. Both modern English and American English are directly descended from this East Midlands dialect.

Writing Workshop

Is Chivalry Dead?

Assignment You have read about the code of honor known as chivalry, a value system that some people believed in and strove for during medieval times. Write an essay in which you discuss to what extent chivalry exists in today's society.

WRITER'S BLUEPRINT

Product	An essay of opinion
Purpose	To convince readers of your opinions on chivalry, past and present
Audience	People who have only a vague idea of what chivalry is about
Specs	As the writer of a successful essay, you should:

- ❑ Discuss chivalry as it was seen in medieval times. Focus on three of the following aspects: self-control, courtesy, loyalty, truthfulness, honor, keeping promises, courage, generosity.
- ❑ Discuss to what extent you think chivalry exists in today's society. Base your discussion on the three aspects you chose above. Support your opinions by citing events you have witnessed in your life and learned of through newspapers, radio, and TV.
- ❑ End by giving your conclusions about what has happened to the concept of chivalry since medieval times, based on your discussion. Define your terms clearly throughout.
- ❑ Follow the rules of grammar, usage, spelling, and mechanics. Pay special attention to subject-verb agreement.

STEP 1 PREWRITING

Brainstorm aspects of chivalry in medieval times. Working with a group, discuss the literature and interdisciplinary materials. Organize your notes in a chart like the one on the next page.

Writing Workshop

WRITER'S BLUEPRINT

Specs

The Specs in the Writer's Blueprint address these writing and thinking skills:

- taking a position
- supporting an opinion
- comparing and contrasting
- drawing conclusions
- defining abstract terms
- making generalizations
- avoiding errors in subject-verb agreement

These Specs serve as your lesson objectives, and they form the basis for the **Assessment Criteria Specs** for a superior paper, which appear on the final TE page for this lesson. You might want to review the *Assessment Criteria Specs* with students when you begin the lesson.

Linking Literature to Writing

Look for examples of chivalric behavior in the literature.

STEP 1 PREWRITING

Brainstorm aspects of chivalry

For additional support, see the worksheet referenced below.

Unit 1 Resource Book
Prewriting Worksheet, p. 51

WRITING WORKSHOP OVERVIEW

Product
Expository/Persuasive writing: An essay of opinion

Prewriting
Brainstorm aspects of chivalry—Discuss aspects of chivalry—Plan your essay
Unit 1 Resource Book
Prewriting Worksheets pp. 51–52

Drafting
Before you draft—As you draft
Transparency Collection
Student Models for Writing Workshop 3, 4

Revising
Ask a partner—Strategy: Clarifying Abstract Terms
Unit 1 Resource Book
Revising Worksheet p. 53

Editing
Ask a partner—Strategy: Making Subjects and Verbs Agree
Unit 1 Resource Book
Grammar Worksheet p. 54
Grammar Check Test p. 55

Presenting
Point-counterpoint
Poll
Cover Page

Looking Back
Self-evaluate—Reflect—For Your Working Portfolio
Unit 1 Resource Book
Assessment Worksheet p. 56
Transparency Collection
Fine Art Writing Prompt 2

Discuss aspects of chivalry

Remind students to use the group discussion to expand their own ideas of what each aspect means. For additional support, see the worksheet referenced below.

Unit 1 Resource Book
Prewriting Worksheet, p. 52

Plan your essay

Some students may find they can keep their ideas and writing focused if they first write a strong thesis statement.

Connections to
Writer's Notebook

For selection-related prompts, refer to Writer's Notebook.

Connections to
Writer's Resource

For additional writing prompts, refer to Writer's Resource.

STEP 2 DRAFTING

As you draft

If students seem overly concerned with correctness in their first drafts, try requiring a series of quick drafts that do not allow time for revisions but encourage fluency.

The Student Models

The **transparencies** referenced below are authentic student models. Review them with the students before they draft. These questions will help:

1. How did the writer of model 3 define terms for the reader? Cite examples.
2. What does the writer of model 4 think of chivalry in today's culture?.
3. Which model comes closer to fulfilling the Specs in the Writer's Blueprint? Why?

Transparency Collection
Student Models for Writing Workshop 3, 4

LITERARY SOURCE
"Thus the fair lady tested him, and tempted him to wrong, whatever else she wished of him. But he kept her at a distance so skillfully that he failed in neither courtesy nor honor, . . ."
from *Sir Gawain and the Green Knight*

Aspects of medieval chivalry	Notes
Self-Control	It's an ideal you strive for, especially knights. You keep the object of temptation at a distance at all times. (Gawain)
Courtesy	Especially with a man toward a woman. It's a skill, an art. (Gawain)

Discuss aspects of chivalry in modern times. Make notes on your discussion and organize them in a chart like the one above.

Plan your essay. The three-part plan that follows is closely based on the Writer's Blueprint. If you decide to use it, make notes about each bulleted point.

OR . . .
Do it your way. Create your own writing plan. Just be sure it deals with the points in the Writer's Blueprint.

Part One (chivalry in medieval times)
- A general statement about my three aspects
- Discussion of aspect #1

and so on . . .

Part Two (chivalry in modern times)
- A general statement about my three aspects
- Opinions about aspect #1
- Facts to support #1 opinions

and so on . . .

Part Three (conclusions about chivalry in modern times)
- My conclusions based on Part 2
- A closing statement

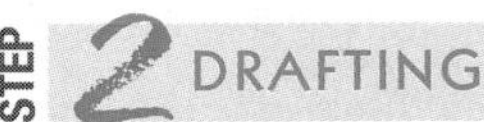

STEP 2 DRAFTING

Before you draft, review the Blueprint and your writing plan.

As you draft, think about your point of view. If you'd like to write from an unusual point of view, try one of these ideas:

- Write as if you were someone from medieval times who's been taken by a time machine into the present.
- Write as if you're someone from the present who's traveled back in time, and you're explaining things to people from medieval times.

But if you choose an unusual point of view, don't forget that you still need to write in the form of an essay.

MINI-LESSON: WRITING STYLE

Clarifying Abstract Terms

Teach Discuss ways in which an individual's perspective shapes her or his understanding of the world, and how a word can have different meanings to different people. Ask students to share their personal experiences of what courtesy means to them.

Activity Have students do several quickwrites about the state of courtesy in America today, each one from the perspective of a different person, (e.g. a student, a school cafeteria worker, a young woman, on older man, a visitor from Japan, a visitor from the Middle Ages).

Apply Students may want to assume or consider the perspective of one of these voices as they construct their essay.

STEP 3 REVISING

Ask a partner for comments on your draft before you revise it.

✔ Did I support my opinions with facts?

✔ Have I clearly defined my terms?

Revising Strategy

Clarifying Abstract Terms

Abstract terms like *self-control, courtesy,* and *loyalty* mean different things to different people. Be sure to give your readers an idea of what they mean to you. If you don't, they may be left with questions like these.

Unclear Maintaining self-control is beneficial. (*What do you mean by self-control?*)

Better Self-control, the ability to stay calm in times of stress, is beneficial. (*Beneficial? How?*)

Clear Self-control, the ability to stay calm in times of stress, helps you to make rational decisions.

Look through your draft and circle any abstract terms that still need clarifying. One way to clarify abstract terms is by adding concrete examples, as in the student model that follows. The last two sentences were added during revising.

A man who was chivalrous in medieval times was loyal to his king and his country. He would give up his life, if necessary, in order to protect the lives and honor of those around him. Such loyalty was apparent in "Day of Destiny." Sir Gawain's loyalty to the throne was apparent when he chose to combat the stranger who appeared in search of a duel.

to clarify "loyal"

STUDENT MODEL

STEP 3 REVISING

Ask a partner (Peer assessment)

Encourage students to reach beyond simple 'yes' or 'no' answers to the two peer assessment questions. For example, the reader should be able to point to specific facts that support an opinion; and if the reader believes the writer was successful in clearly defining important terms, the reader should be able to restate those definitions in his own words.

Revising Strategy: Clarifying Abstract Terms

Have students look over the student model and note the changes that were made. How did the addition of the last two sentences clarify the meaning of *loyal?*

For additional support, see the mini-lesson at the bottom of the previous page and the worksheet referenced below.

Unit 1 Resource Book
Revising Worksheet, p. 53

Connections to **Writer's Resource**

Refer to the Grammar, Usage, and Mechanics Handbook on Writer's Resource.

BUILDING ENGLISH PROFICIENCY

Working with Partners

Remind students that for a writer to benefit from a partner's feedback, both the writer and the partner must agree on ground rules such as these:

- The writer should listen with an open mind, ask questions about what isn't clear, and take notes if necessary.
- Writers should try not to argue with partners; instead, they simply should take in the feedback and decide later how much they agree with.
- The partner should point out strengths as well as weaknesses, should be clear and specific, and should avoid personal judgments.

STEP 4 EDITING

Ask a partner (Peer assessment)

Have students reading the drafts underline the subjects once and the verbs twice. Then, have students check that the singular subjects have a singular verb and the plural subjects have a plural verb.

Editing Strategy: Making Subjects and Verbs Agree

Model for students how to isolate the simple subject and verb in long, complicated sentences. After they isolate the subject and verb, students can check for agreement by saying this simplified sentence (the subject and the verb) out loud.

For additional support, see the mini-lesson at the bottom of this page and the worksheets referenced below.

Unit 1 Resource Book
Grammar Worksheet, p. 54
Grammar Check Test, p. 55

Connections to **Writer's Resource**

Refer to the Grammar, Usage, and Mechanics Handbook on Writer's Resource.

STEP 4 EDITING

Ask a partner to review your revised draft before you edit. As you edit, watch for errors in grammar, usage, spelling, and mechanics. Pay special attention to errors in subject-verb agreement.

Editing Strategy

Making Subjects and Verbs Agree

When you edit your sentences, keep these two simple rules in mind:

- A singular subject takes a singular verb. (A *knight* always *treats* a woman with courtesy.)
- A plural subject takes a plural verb. (*Knights* never *treat* women with disrespect.)

Be especially careful about sentences where several other words come between the subject and verb:

A list of important aspects appears in the final paragraph. (The verb, *appears,* must agree with the subject, *list,* not the nearer word *aspects.*)

The opinions expressed in this essay are entirely my own. (The subject is *opinions,* not *essay.*)

Notice how this writer edited to correct errors in subject-verb agreement.

FOR REFERENCE
You'll find more rules for subject-verb agreement in the Language and Grammar Handbook at the back of this book.

COMPUTER TIP
If you use a spell-checker, remember that it won't catch mistakes like writing *your* when you mean *you're*. Always proofread carefully for spelling.

> Honor to one's country, family, and friends ~~are~~ *is* lacking in modern American society. An example of how modern day society lacks honor among its members ~~are~~ *is* the actions of politicians. Politicians often express the view on socio-economic issues that will get them the most votes.

STUDENT MODEL

MINI-LESSON: GRAMMAR

Making Subjects and Verbs Agree

Alert students to mistakes in subject-verb agreement that often occur when a phrase or clause comes between the subject and verb. Write the following sentences on the board and have students choose the verb that agrees with the subject. Subjects are underlined and correct verbs are in italics.

1. The rings around Saturn (is, *are*) made up of billions of pieces of ice.
2. The linemen, as well as the quarterback, (is, *are*) working on a new series of plays.
3. The starling, along with other birds, (*does,* do) not migrate south in winter.
4. Constant use by heavy trucks (*causes,* cause) damage to bridges and highways.
5. Huge clams living in the world today (weighs, *weigh*) nearly 500 pounds.

Unit 1 Resource Book
Grammar Worksheet, p. 54
Grammar Check Test, p. 55

STEP 5 PRESENTING

Here are three ideas for presenting and enhancing your paper.

- Have a point-counterpoint reading/discussion. Work with a partner whose opinions are significantly different from yours. Read your papers to the class or a small group and discuss the opposing points of view.
- Conduct a poll of your classmates, asking if they agree or disagree that chivalry still exists in today's world. Add a statistical table to your paper reporting your findings, and discuss the results.
- Include a cover page with writing and drawings that have a medieval look.

STEP 6 LOOKING BACK

Self-evaluate. What grade would *you* give your essay? Look back at the Writer's Blueprint and evaluate yourself on each point, from 6 (superior) down to 1 (inadequate).

Reflect. Think about what you have learned from writing this essay as you write answers to these questions.

✔ What insights have you gained into your own code of honor by writing this paper?

✔ Compare your rough draft with your finished copy. Jot down comments about the kinds of changes you made. What do they tell you about your strengths and weaknesses as a writer?

For Your Working Portfolio Add your essay and reflection responses to your working portfolio.

STEP 5 PRESENTING

Point-counterpoint

Students might agree on a few rules of discussion beforehand, such as time limits and choice of an impartial moderator who will keep the discussion on topic and prevent one speaker from dominating the discussion.

Poll

Students might wish to expand their poll to include the entire twelfth grade. The school newspaper might be interested in publishing their findings.

Cover page

Encourage students to research the relationship between art and text during the Middle Ages and base their illustrations on real examples from the period.

STEP 6 LOOKING BACK

Self-evaluate

The *Assessment Criteria Specs* at the bottom of this page are for a superior paper. You might want to post these in the classroom. Students can then evaluate themselves based on these criteria. For a complete scoring rubric, use the *Assessment Worksheet* referenced below.

Unit 1 Resource Book
Assessment Worksheet, p. 56

Reflect

Students' own reflections on the differences between their rough drafts and final papers will be helpful evidence of their growth when you evaluate student performance.

To further explore the theme, use the Fine Art Transparency referenced below.

Transparency Collection
Fine Art Writing Prompt 2

ASSESSMENT CRITERIA SPECS

Here are the criteria for a superior paper. A full six-level rubric for this paper appears on the Assessment Worksheet referenced below.

6 Superior The writer of a 6 paper impressively meets these criteria:

- Focuses discussion on three clearly defined aspects of chivalry.
- Effectively illustrates abstract concepts with concrete examples from literature, life, and media.
- Makes generalizations that grow logically from examples.
- Follows a clearly apparent plan to compare and contrast medieval and modern chivalry.
- Provides supporting examples that persuasively lead to a concluding opinion.
- Avoids errors in subject-verb agreement.
- Correctly uses paragraphing, punctuation, grammar, and spelling to present a polished paper.

Unit 1 Resource Book
Assessment Worksheet, p. 56

Beyond Print

Teaching Objectives

- To explore the power of film to create the illusion of a past era
- To describe the formal production techniques that affect a period film's effectiveness
- To analyze the common pitfalls that detract from a film's historical authenticity

Curricular Connection: Media Literacy

Use the material in this article to help students sharpen their ability to view films with a critical eye.

Introduce

- Ask students to describe movies they have seen that depict life in the Middle Ages: for example, *Monty Python and the Holy Grail, The Hunchback of Notre Dame, Excalibur, First Knight, Robin Hood, Camelot,* and *Braveheart.*
- Discuss the thematic focus of each film and the visual techniques that were employed to explore it.
- The movies have a tendency to create and depict stereotypes and stock characters from distant historical eras. Suggest that students write down the visual images that they usually associate with the Middle Ages and to consider how many of these images were created or influenced by popular films.
- You might discuss the relationship between photographic technology and narrative filmmaking. Ask students to consider how several remakes of one film, for example, *Robin Hood,* can reflect the technological advances of cinematic media.

Beyond Print

The Middle Ages in the Movies

Knights, ladies, castles, wizards, tournaments—all these are standard elements in films that use the Middle Ages as a background. Some of these films are basically fantasies that employ medieval settings. Other films attempt to create the authentic look and feel of the historical Middle Ages. Many films mix history and romance. But whether a film primarily aims at fantasy or fact, it must feel right; that is, it must meet the audience's expectations about what the Middle Ages were like—and, of course, provide a satisfying spectacle. In trying to create a vivid impression of a remote time such as the Middle Ages, movie makers concentrate on the following areas.

Dialogue What the actors are given to say is critically important in establishing a period feeling. In a film about the Middle Ages, the dialogue has to avoid two dangers: (1) language so authentically "medieval" that it sounds stilted; or (2) language so modern that it sounds out-of-place. The first problem occurs when the characters use too many *thee's* and *thou's* and archaic words like *prithee* and *forsooth*. The second problem can result from overuse of highly contemporary speech, such as slang, or simply speech that makes romantic medieval characters sound too "everyday." If, as happens in one film, King Richard the Lionheart's queen complains to him, "War, war! That's all you think about, Dick Plantagenet!" the audience may think she sounds a bit too much like a bored housewife in a sitcom complaining about her husband's addiction to football.

Spectacle Whether a film presents medieval reality or fantasy, spectacle is a vital element. The quality of battle scenes—whether they emphasize the picturesque aspects of war or its butchery—is important. So are the special effects often used in medieval fantasies to produce images of fire-breathing dragons or Arthur's enchanted sword rising from the lake.

Set Design The basic set for most films about the Middle Ages is a castle. Some films try to glamorize these damp and drafty fortresses, while others make a more serious attempt to convey how uncomfortable living in them must have been.

ANOTHER APPROACH

A less common but equally challenging approach to making a movie of a medieval story is to set it in contemporary or modern times. For example, a recent production of *Richard III* set the late medieval drama in England in the 1940s, maintaining the Elizabethan dialogue, but providing authentic mid-twentieth century sets, costumes, and historical backdrop. It therefore presents an intriguing blend of several time periods. Have students work in groups to adapt a scene from this unit to fit a modern day setting, considering dialogue, costume, set design, spectacle, and music.

Costume In general, filmmakers probably do a better job with period costume than with other areas of historical research. Medieval clothing, from the richly embroidered gowns of courtiers to peasants' muddy rags, is convincingly recreated. The knight in armor is the most familiar image of the Middle Ages, and filmmakers have generally taken care to depict vividly these warriors clanking about in their steel suits.

Music Period music is frequently employed in films to help create historical atmosphere. However, when the period is the Middle Ages this is less likely to be true, since most modern audiences would probably find the sound of authentic medieval melodies and instruments very strange. What's most important with music is that it contribute to creating the proper mood, whether the mood is heroic or romantic or eerie.

Activity Options

1. Collect examples of dialogue from films dealing with the Middle Ages that you feel show either a successful or a disastrous attempt to give a contemporary feel to this historical period.
2. With other students, look at a videotape of a film dealing with some medieval subject—for example, King Arthur, Robin Hood, or the Crusades—and discuss how the filmmakers have dealt with the issues of dialogue, spectacle, set design, costume, and music. What impression of the Middle Ages does the film create—gritty or glamorous?
3. Create a collage that collects historical portraits of famous medieval figures, such as Richard the Lionheart and Eleanor of Aquitaine, with images of the actors that have played them.

This poster advertised Warner Brothers' 1938 classic *The Adventures of Robin Hood.* What version of the Middle Ages—history or romance—does this poster convey? ➤

Activity Options

Activity 1 Have students transcribe the lines and act out the scene in class. How do the tone and inflection of the delivery affect the authenticity or believability of the language?

Activity 2 You might suggest that students choose a fictional film and a historical documentary that treat the same subject. Compare and contrast the formal techniques of each.

Activity 3 You might suggest that students research film almanacs and encyclopedias, entertainment magazines, and biographies of film actors, actresses, and famous medieval figures to find these images.

Art Study

The Adventures of Robin Hood was made in 1938 and was praised for its fast action and swordplay. At a cost of two million dollars, it was the studio's most expensive film to that date. Errol Flynn was Sir Robin of Locksley, Olivia de Havilland was Maid Marian, Basil Rathbone was Guy of Gisbourne, and Claude Rains was Prince John. Erich Korngold won an Academy Award for his music, and though the picture was nominated for an Academy Award, it was edged out by *You Can't Take It With You.* Sherwood Forest was filmed at Chico, California.

The poster conveys a romantic view of the Middle Ages.

BUILDING ENGLISH PROFICIENCY

Linking Past and Present

You may want to introduce this feature by having students think about modern action films. Work, in reverse order, through the elements, asking questions such as the following:

Music: How do soundtracks let you know that a person is a hero (or a villain)? That a film is about to reach its climax?

Costume: What authentic costumes (such as police uniforms) and personal equipment do you expect to see in action films?

Set Design: What kinds of locations suggest "action" or "danger" to you? When we see characters alone, how might a hero's sets differ from a villain's?

Spectacle: What kinds of spectacles attract audiences to movies today? Why?

Dialogue: What kinds of things do action heroes say? Can you imagine any manner of speaking that would be completely out of character for an action hero?

Unit Wrap-Up

MULTICULTURAL CONNECTION

Remind students that during the Middle Ages the threat of invasion, civil war, and disease made adherence to a group necessary for survival. Lack of social mobility within the feudal system meant choices for most individuals were limited.

Choice

Remind students that in Anglo-Saxon times, rules were enforced by chieftains. Later, manorial lords were often responsible for making and enforcing rules, which varied greatly from manor to manor. Point out that in the absence of a national system of laws or of a universal system of justice, many people took the law into their own hands.

Possible Response Beowulf defends his tribal loyalty, Lord Randal is the victim of love gone awry, Edward is tortured by family ties, and the good man and wife test their marriage.

Groups

Possible Response The rioters all die as a result of their treachery. Bedivere almost denies Arthur the mystical journey to Avalon which the magical sword initiates. Gawain's concealment of the green girdle causes him shame and weakens his sense of honor.

Activities

Activity 1 Have students consider what groups people belong to by choice and which group identities are imposed by external circumstances.

Activity 2 You might discuss group interaction, and ask students to consider situations when identity with one group causes conflict with other groups or individuals.

Activity 3 This activity might be the basis for an essay on personal choice.

Multicultural Connections

Choice

Part One: Getting Even In *Beowulf,* the monster Grendel gets even with humans by killing and eating them, but the hero Beowulf takes the ultimate revenge on Grendel. In the folk ballads "Lord Randal" and "Edward," revenge seems implicit in the motives for the murders, but it is explicit in the curses that the speakers leave. "In Get Up and Bar the Door," the goodman and goodwife almost bring mischief on themselves through stubbornly trying to get even with each other.

■ How do the groups these characters belong to determine the choices they make in to deal how with their enemies?

Groups

Part Two: Codes of Honor In "The Pardoner's Tale" the three rioters swear to be brothers, but they violate their code when they kill each other off trying to keep all the gold. Sir Gawain is true to his code when he accepts the Green Knight's challenge, when he submits himself a year later, and when he gives the lord the lady's kisses, but he violates it by not reporting the green girdle. Because neither Arthur nor Mordred trusts the other to keep their agreement, a simple misunderstanding in killing a snake leads to the battle in which almost all are killed. Sir Bedivere almost violates his code when he lies to Arthur about disposing of Excalibur.

■ Discuss how the choices made by the rioters, Gawain, and Bedivere to stray from their group values bring negative results to all of them.

Activities

1. Create a graphic organizer to display different kinds of groups to be found in your community or in the country. Consider this question: How many groups might an average person belong to at the same time? during his or her lifetime?
2. Discuss when it may be desirable for teenagers to break out of various groups they belong to and when it is more desirable not to.
3. Share the most difficult choice you have had to make. What were the pressures on you to choose one way or the other? What determined your final choice?

Put Yourself in the Picture How would you have fit in medieval English society? To which of the classes of people shown on pages 42–43 would you have wanted to belong? Would you have had to work for a living? What would you have done when you weren't working? Describe your life as a medieval person and tell about yourself in a five-minute presentation—in costume if you wish.

Media

Not Easy Being Green We're never told how Gawain's foe became green—was he born that way, or did something colorful happen to him? For that matter, we know little enough about many of the characters in this unit. With a group, develop a talk show with one person playing a host or hostess and others representing various characters. Plan in advance what questions to ask and what answers to give. You might also want to plan some amusing chitchat among all the participants.

Art

Package Tours! Create a travel brochure designed to appeal to medieval travelers who wish to make the pilgrimage to Canterbury or any other places mentioned in this unit. You may want to include a map, a list of possible places to stay or stop for a meal along the way, and a description of sights to see. You might do some research about travel in the Middle Ages to find out what travelers' options were. (Hint: They were few.) Include advertising, illustrations, and a price list as well.

Research

Digging Up the Past There are many ancient—and mysterious—monuments in Britain, dating from medieval times and from long before. Research one of these sites, such as Tintagel Castle, Stonehenge, the stones at Avebury, the Cerne Giant at Cerne Abbas, or the White Horse of Uffington. (See your teacher for some other interesting research topics.) After you have done the appropriate research give a multimedia presentation on the historic place of your choice.

103

UNIT 1 OPTIONS

Oral Presentation

Chaucer provides detailed physical descriptions and characterizations of his pilgrims. Offer students the option of researching another of Chaucer's pilgrims and giving a talk from his or her point of view.

Media

Point out that a key element of a successful interview is background research. Encourage students to consult other versions of Arthurian legend, as well as mythology and symbolism reference resources, to deepen their understanding of each character.

Art

You might use this as an opportunity for students to expand their desk-top publishing skills.

- Encourage students with computer access to explore the design capabilities of simple graphics programs.
- Discuss strategies for layout, paste-up, typography, and reproduction. Students might request brochures from a travel agent to use as visual models.

Research

Suggest that students explore a wide range of media for their presentations. For example, they might create audio collages, video trailers culled from documentaries and dramatic films, overhead maps of England, slide shows and printed picture collections, including artistic interpretations of these monuments.

Unit Test

Unit 1 Resource Book,
New Selection, pp. 57–63
Test 1, pp. 64–65
Test 2, pp. 66–67

The Lure of Ambition

Planning Unit 2: The Elizabethan Era

Literature	Integrated Language Arts			
	Literary	**Writing/Grammar, Usage and Mechanics**	**Reading, Thinking, Listening, Speaking**	**Vocabulary/Spelling**
Shakespeare Sonnets 18, 29, 71, 116, 130 *by William Shakespeare* Poems *(average)* p. 111	Shakespearean sonnet	List Write a sonnet Personal letter Using *Like* and *As*	Recognize assumptions and implications	
Macbeth *by William Shakespeare* Play *(challenging)* **Act 1** p. 118	Plot structure, meter Theme, characterization Hyperbole, imagery, irony	Diagramming simple sentences Allusion and added stress Pronoun antecedent agreement Conveying state of mind through soliloquy	Compare and contrast Synthesize, infer Figurative language Find the main idea Visualize Understand persuasion Generalize/draw conclusions Recognize values Recognize propaganda	Archaic adverbs
Macbeth **Act 2** p. 135	Plot structure Connotation/denotation Symbolism Figurative language Irony, foreshadowing Theme	Relative pronouns *Which* and *That* Punctuation of quotations Diagramming sentences with direct and indirect objects	Find the main idea Understanding sequence Generalize/draw conclusions Compare and contrast Apply	Most similar meaning
Macbeth **Act 3** p. 148	Plot structure Irony Characterization Tone Figurative language Pun, simile	Diagramming reversed sentences Proper adjectives Using parts of speech effectively in sentences	Find the main idea Draw conclusions Understand sequence Analyze, generalize Compare and contrast Recognize values Essential and incidental information Recognize cause and effect	Opposite meaning Connotation/denotation Multiple-meaning words Puns
Macbeth **Act 4** p. 163	Plot structure Style, theme Dialogue Metaphor Characterization Symbolism, irony	Using *Shall* and *Will* Negative constructions Diagramming adjectives, adverbs and prepositional phrases Recognizing the function of the vocative part of speech	Compare and contrast Generalize, infer Recognize use of persuasion Find the main idea Recognize cause and effect Draw conclusions	Word analogies Etymology
Macbeth **Act 5** p. 178	Plot structure Theme, symbolism Foreshadowing Figurative language Irony, style Characterization Imagery, allusion	List of characters Analyze predictions Diary entry Diagramming verb forms Using descriptive language Subjunctive mood Allusion	Find the main idea Generalize Compare and contrast Recognize values Analyze Draw conclusions	Negative prefixes

Meeting Individual Needs

Multi-modal Activities	Mini-Lessons
Creating an artwork Converting a sonnet to rock lyrics Exploring sonnet structure	Using *Like* and *As*
Exploring character Analyzing characterization Analyzing stage directions Using gloss notes Exploring motivation Analyzing character Expanding vocabulary notebooks Sequencing plot events	Simple sentences Ellision and added stress Archaic adverbs Pronoun-antecedent agreement Dramatic irony Synthesize Conveying state of mind through soliloquy
Exploring relationships among characters Contrasting characters Analyzing metaphors Exploring rhyme	Relative pronouns Punctuation Direct and indirect objects Reading a play Map reading
Analyzing characters Making personal connections Exploring key statements Checking comprehension Analyzing key events Exploring key concepts Making real-life connections	Connotation /denotation Diagramming reversed sentences, puns Multiple-meaning words Proper adjectives Using parts of speech effectively in sentences
Relating parts of speech Mapping opposing character traits Analyzing characters Making cultural connections Expanding vocabulary notebooks Exploring motivation	Researching Using *Shall* and *Will* Negative constructions Diagramming adjectives, adverbs and prepositional phrases Etymology
Choreographing a scene Developing stage directions Paraphrasing Shakespeare Reviewing events Exploring a climax Evaluating a battle plan Looking to the future	Diagramming verb forms Negative prefixes Using descriptive language Subjunctive mood Allusion

Interdisciplinary Studies
The Burden of Guilt

Format	Content Area	Highlights	Skill
from The Book of the Dead	Humanities	This excerpt reveals ancient Egyptian beliefs on final judgment.	Prepared speech
from The Furies *by Aeschylus* **from Crime and Punishment** *by Fyodor Dostoevski*	Humanities	These selections describe forms of punishment and guilt.	Draw conclusions about art
from The Trial of Adolf Eichmann			Use both primary and secondary sources
Lady Macbeth in Therapy	Career	A mental health care professional designs a treatment plan for Lady Macbeth.	

Writing Workshop

Mode	Writing Format	Writing Focus	Proofreading Skills
Persuasive writing	A persuasive essay	Connecting cause to effect	Correcting comma splices

Program Support Materials

For Every Selection	For Every Writing Workshop
Unit Resource Book Graphic Organizer Study Guide Vocabulary Worksheet Grammar Worksheet Spelling, Speaking and Listening, or Literary Language Worksheet Alternate Check Test Vocabulary Test Selection Test	**Unit Resource Book** Prewriting Worksheet Revising Strategy Worksheet Editing Strategy Worksheet Presentation Worksheet Writing Rubric **Transparency Collection** Fine Art Transparency Student Writing Model Transparencies

For Every Interdisciplinary Study	Assessment
Unit Resource Book Study Guide Mini-Lesson Skill Worksheet	**Unit Resource Book** TE Check Tests Alternate Check Test (blackline master) Vocabulary Test (blackline master) Selection Test (blackline master) **Test Generator Software** **Assessment Handbook**

Unit 2 Supplemental Resources
Media and Technology

Sonnets 18, 29, 71, 116, and 130

Audiotape Sir John Gielgud performs 120 of Shakespeare's Sonnets in *Sonnets of William Shakespeare*, 2 hours, Harper, 1995.

Videotape The poetry of Shakespeare is explored in *Shakespeare's Sonnets*, 150 minutes, Films for the Humanities & Sciences, 1984.

Community Resources In 1983 Professor Donald Foster found a little-known elegy in the Bodleian Library at Oxford. It was bound as a pamphlet, signed W. S., and printed in 1612 by Shakespeare's publisher. Foster developed a computer program named Shaxicon to analyze the choice of words in the elegy. His database indexed all the words in Shakespeare's plays that appear twelve times or fewer. The result? Thirteen years later, Foster, and others, said the analysis proved the elegy was written by Shakespeare. Using local library resources students might like to investigate the story, the elegy, the subject of the elegy, and what the elegy seems to reveal about the author.

Macbeth

Audiotape Anthony Quayle and others perform in *Macbeth*, 2 hours 11 minutes, Harper, 1989. An audio program which is a helpful study of the play and includes social and political background is *Study Guide to William Shakespeare's Macbeth*, 1 hour, Time Warner Audio, 1994.

Connections to
Custom Literature Database

or "The Lure of Ambition" Selections with Lessons

- Sonnets 30 and 55 by William Shakespeare
- "All the world's a stage" from *As You Like It* by William Shakespeare

Additional theme-based selections can be accessed on the ScottForesman database.

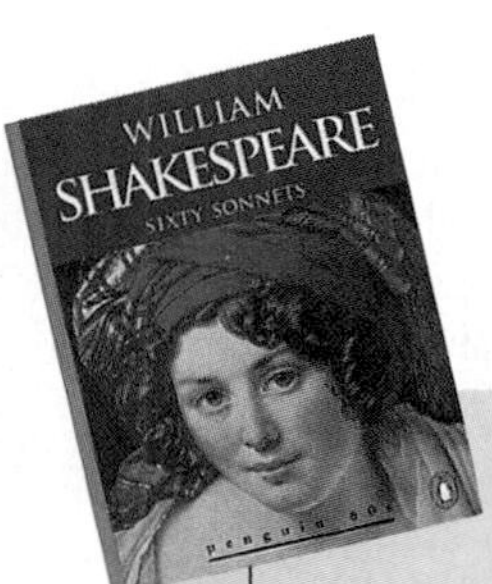

Listen to the Sonnets

An excellent audiotape collection of the sonnets is available in *Sonnets of William Shakespeare,* read by Sir John Gielgud.

Videotape Students will enjoy *Shakespeare: The Man and His Times*, 38 minutes, Educational Audio Visual, 1989. *Macbeth,* 1 hour 30 minutes, Goldhil Home Media, 1993, from the *Understanding Shakespeare Series*, contains reenactments and discussions of key scenes. Also consider the classic film version starring Orson Welles, *Macbeth*, 112 minutes, Library Video Company, 1948. *Macbeth,* 90 minutes, from the *Understanding Shakespeare Series,* Library Video Company, contains easy-to-follow dramatic interpretations of the play.

Computer Software The CD-ROM program, *Macbeth*, for Macintosh and Windows, is a multimedia program available from Voyager, 1994, featuring the Royal Shakespeare Company. *The Time, Life and Works of Shakespeare*, CD-ROM for IBM, Macintosh, and Windows, is available from Clearvue, 1995. Also consider *Much Ado About Shakespeare,* CD-ROM for Windows, from the Bureau of Electronic Publishing.

Community Resources If there is a member of a theater group in your area or someone who has studied or worked in the theater and could speak to the class, any of the follow topics will be of interest to students, depending on the speaker's area of expertise: makeup for the stage, staging fight scenes, designing costumes, special problems in producing Shakespeare, staging the Scottish play, and how the witches have been portrayed through the centuries.

Connections to
BBC Shakespeare on CD-ROM Series

The BBC Shakespeare on CD-ROM series: *Macbeth* offers a rich variety of unique materials for teaching the play. Also available on the BBC Shakespeare on CD-ROM series is *Hamlet* and *The Tempest.*

A Classic Macbeth

Orson Welles's classic firm portrayal of Macbeth is newly available for rental at commercial video stores.

Unit 2

The Elizabethan Era

Art Study

The Procession of Queen Elizabeth I, pp. 104–105 is thought to have been painted by Sir Robert Peake in about 1600. Sir Robert—known as "the Elder" because his son Sir Robert Peake was a printmaker—was the serjeant-painter to James I, and is thought to have painted many of the portraits of James I.

Question What does the men's clothing reveal about them? *(Possible responses: They must be very wealthy to afford such elaborate outfits; they are people of leisure because their clothing is not suited for much activity.)*

Question Do you think Queen Elizabeth I would have liked this painting? Why or why not? *(Possible responses: yes, because she is obviously portrayed as queenly and with loyal courtiers.)*

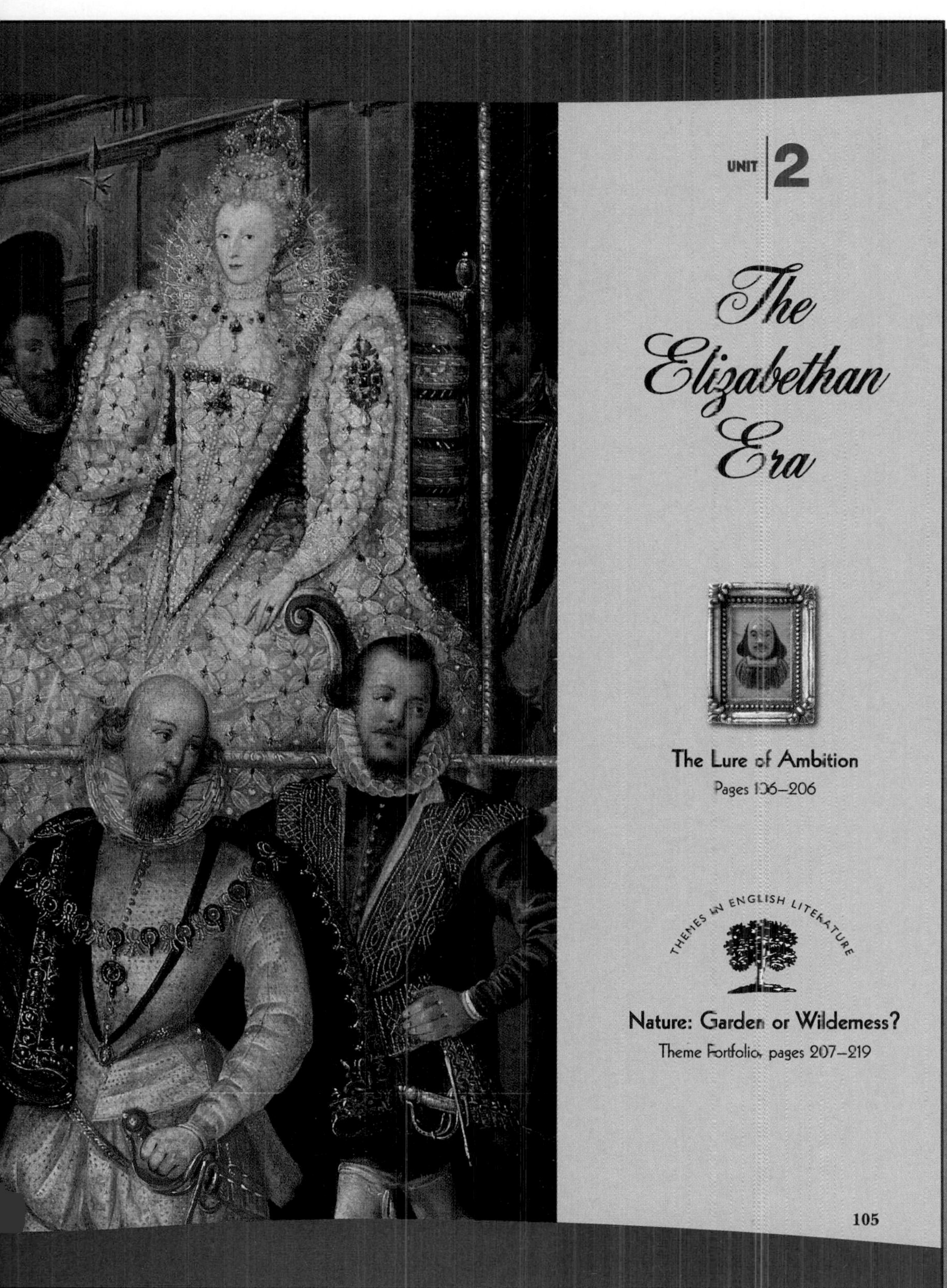

Thematic Connections

One of the most influential works of the Renaissance, *The Prince* by Machiavelli, instructs rulers on laying aside moral principles as they work to consolidate and strengthen their rule. Despite being banned by the Church, Machiavelli's book found its way to England, and the character of the ambitious and unprincipled villain-hero known as "the Machiavel," became widely used by English play-wrights, including Shakespeare, Marlowe, and Webster.

The Lure of Ambition

The literature in this unit considers how strong a hold ambition has on people and their differing responses to its call.

Ideas to Explore

- Can ambition ever be a good trait or used for a good end?
- What are the consequences of unbridled ambition?

Part One: The Lure of Ambition

Historical Overview

EXPLORING CONCEPTS

- The term "Renaissance," first appeared in French in the nineteenth century and was picked up in English in the 1840s.
- Roger Ascham (1515/16–1568) wrote of Queen Elizabeth I in *The Scholemaster* that "beside her perfect readiness in Latin, Italian, French, and Spanish, she readeth here now at Windsor [castle] more Greek every day than some prebendary [clergymen] of this Church doth read Latin in a whole week."

Art Study

The portrait of Queen Elzabeth I is by Marcus Gheeraerts the Younger (1562–1636) and was painted about 1592. A Flemish-born painter, he settled in England with his father Marcus the Elder. The queen is wearing a hoop skirt known as a farthingale.

Students who note her lavish attire may be interested to learn that at the time it was characterized as "beseeming her calling, but not sumptuous nor excessive" by contemporary standards. While her expenses for her yearly wardrobe for the final four years of her reign ran only £9,535 per year, James I, in the final five years of his reign, spent £36,377 per year on his wardrobe.

The other objects on these two pages include an armillary sphere, an old astronomical instrument ; a telescope; Leonardo da Vinci's model of a helicopter; his self portrait; sheet music from 1597 showing a motet; and a lute, a stringed musical instrument.

The Renaissance

The Lure of Ambition

Historical Overview

The Renaissance was marked by the rebirth of humanity's belief in its potential. "Men can do all things if they will," exulted the Italian architect LeonBattista Alberti, who made good his boast by mastering a dozen fields, from poetry to engineering. Two notable examples of this Renaissance ideal of multifaceted achieve- ment—Queen Elizabeth I of England (1553–1603) and the Italian artist Leonardo da Vinci (1452–1519)—appear on these pages, surrounded by objects reflecting the range of their interests. In addition to being a skillful ruler, Elizabeth was a poet, linguist, musician, and scholar. Leonardo was a painter, inventor, architect, engineer, and scientist. Both these individuals reflect the creative energy of the Renaissance and its delight in new discoveries.

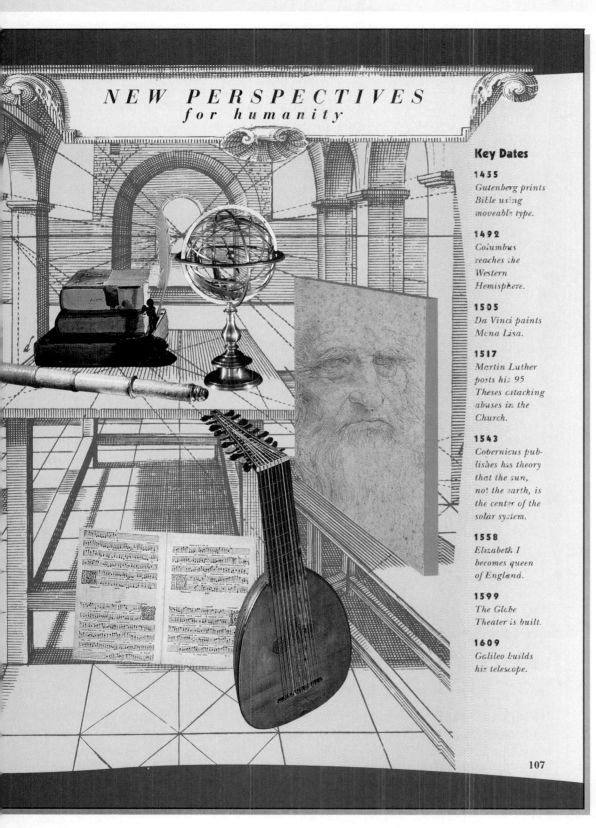

NEW PERSPECTIVES *for humanity*

Key Dates

1455 *Gutenberg prints Bible using moveable type.*

1492 *Columbus reaches the Western Hemisphere.*

1505 *Da Vinci paints Mona Lisa.*

1517 *Martin Luther posts his 95 Theses attacking abuses in the Church.*

1543 *Copernicus publishes his theory that the sun, not the earth, is the center of the solar system.*

1558 *Elizabeth I becomes queen of England.*

1599 *The Globe Theater is built.*

1609 *Galileo builds his telescope.*

107

Key Dates

1531 King Henry VIII of England breaks away from the Catholic Church and declares himself head of the Church of England.

1588 England's naval force defeats the Spanish Armada.

1592 The plague kills 15,000 inhabitants of London.

1603 Elizabeth I dies. James Stuart becomes James VI, King of Scotland and England.

1607 First permanent colony of England in the Americas (Jamestown) is settled.

MATERIALS OF INTEREST

Books

- *The Elizabethan World Picture* by E. M. W. Tillyard (Random House: Vintage Books, n.d.).
- *The Notebooks of Leonardo da Vinci* ed. by Edward MacCurdy (Reynal & Hitchcock, 1939).
- *Renaissance Profiles* edited by J. H. Plumb (American Heritage, 1961).

Multimedia

- *An Evening of Elizabethan Verse and Its Music* read by W. H. Auden with New York Pro Musica Antiqua directed by Noah Greenberg (Odyssey Mono 32 16 0171/CBS Library of Congress Card Catalog R67–3911).
- *Macbeth* (1948) [videotape]. 112 min., b/w, VHS. Republic Pictures Home Video 2514. Directed by Orson Welles.

Connections to **Custom Literature Database**

For further historical background, under **Background Articles,** see **Renaissance England 1500–1660.**

Preview

The Lure of Ambition

FOR ALL STUDENTS

Have students imagine ambition as a person who approaches them one day. Have them consider the following questions:

- Is ambition a man or a woman? What does ambition look like?
- What kind of clothes does ambition wear?
- Is ambition friendly or stern? What might ambition say?

To further explore the theme, use the transparency referenced below.

Transparency Collection
Fine Art Transparency 3

For At-Risk Students

Students might create a bulletin board entitled "The Lure of Ambition." They can include clippings from current newspapers and magazines, pictures of historical figures and events, and quotes from novels, plays, and movies. Students might divide the board to represent the positive and negative ramifications of ambition.

For Students Who Need Challenge

Ask students to research a figure from history that they feel exemplifies the power of strong ambition. They might try to answer the following questions: Is ambition an inborn quality? a result of social circumstances? a hard-won character trait? What were this person's greatest achievements?

MULTICULTURAL CONNECTION

Macbeth recklessly stumbles into death because he believes that he cannot be killed by another man. He makes foolish decisions based on the delusion that he is exempt from the laws that govern others.

The Lure of Ambition

Who doesn't desire to be best-loved, to be well-known, to be powerful? Ambition, the desire to distinguish oneself in some way, has led many people to great achievements in all areas of human endeavor. It has led others to ruthless, immoral, and sometimes deadly acts.

Multicultural Connection **Individuality** may arise either from accepting or rejecting different cultural norms or group standards. Yet selfish actions that lead to success and power today may still bring about loss or even destruction tomorrow. People in positions of leadership remain responsible to the groups to which they belong; in a sense they may be *more* responsible than others. To what degree does Macbeth's rejection of cultural norms contribute to his downfall?

IDEAS THAT WORK

Motivating with a Trial

"Shakespeare was more interested in character than plot. His plays aren't so much about the things human beings do as they are about why we do them. It's the job of the audience to put the characters on trial, decide who is motivated by good or bad intentions, who is just or unjust, and who is really the Fool. Kids are that audience in the classroom. And so we put the characters on trial (a tool of Shakespeare's, too) with students playing the roles of tragic heroes, their friends, their enemies, their accomplices. It's a great way to draw students into the workings of the play, after which you can hint ever so carefully about what a genius the man was with words. They just might listen—to you *and* to Shakespeare!"

Judith Edminster
Tampa, Florida

Before Reading

Sonnets 18, 29, 71, 116, and 130

by William Shakespeare

William Shakespeare
1564 –1616

Born to a prosperous glove maker at Stratford-on-Avon, William Shakespeare attended grammar school only until age 14. By age 18 he was married to 26-year-old Anne Hathaway, and by age 21 he was the father of three children: Susanna, and the twins Judith and Hamnet. While his family stayed behind in Stratford, Shakespeare journeyed to London. There he lived for much of the next 25 years, acting and writing over 200 poems and over 40 plays.

(For more about Shakespeare, see page 117.)

Building Backround

A Conventional Love Isolated from his family, Shakespeare wrote poems of praise, love, and despair. Many of these are addressed to a young man or to a "dark lady." Were they real people with whom he had real love affairs? Perhaps. But during the Elizabethan era writers often wrote to fulfill a **literary convention**—a device that becomes an accepted element through habitual use. One of the conventions of the day was for a poet to choose a fancy name (usually inspired by Greek or Roman mythology) for an imaginary woman and then complain to her—in elaborate verse—that she didn't love the poet enough.

Literary Focus

Shakespearean Sonnet The Shakespearean sonnet, adapted from an Italian form, follows tight literary conventions:

The sonnet is 14 lines long.

Each line follows the rhythmic meter of iambic pentameter. (See the Glossary of Literary Terms.)

The rhyme scheme is *a b a b c d c d e f e f g g*.

The ideas are divided into four sections: three parts of four lines each (quatrains) plus a final part of two lines (couplet). The quatrains may present three statements or examples, while the couplet usually comments on the preceding lines or provides a conclusion or application.

Some sonnets also reflect their Italian origins by having the ideas divided into eight lines of statement (octave) and six lines of conclusion (sestet).

As you read the sonnets, notice how Shakespeare divides his ideas.

Writer's Notebook

What Do Poets Write About? Two common **themes** you will see developed in this sampling of Shakespeare's sonnets are the immortalization of love and beauty and the inevitable decay that comes with time. List some other general themes, applicable to all men and women, that you think are appropriate for short poems.

Before Reading

Building Background

Students might discuss current literary conventions: placing fictional characters in historical situations (e.g., *Forrest Gump*); the theater's "fourth wall," through which one views characters "unaware" of being watched; dialogue balloons, which allow cartoon characters to speak.

Literary Focus

You might discuss the meter of the Shakespearean sonnet form. An iambic pentameter line of verse consists of five feet; each foot has an unstressed and a stressed syllable.

Writer's Notebook

Students might look through poetry anthologies for further ideas.

More About William Shakespeare

Shakespeare's sonnets were first published in 1609, under the title *Shakespeares Sonnets. Never before Imprinted.* Other poems include:

- *Venus and Adonis*
- *The Rape of Lucrece*
- "The Phoenix and the Turtle"

SUPPORT MATERIALS OVERVIEW

Unit 2 Resource Book
- Graphic Organizer, p. 1
- Study Guide, p. 2
- Vocabulary, p. 3
- Grammar, p. 4
- Alternate Check Test, p. 5
- Vocabulary Test, p. 6
- Selection Test, pp. 7–8

Building English Proficiency
- Selection Summaries
- Activities, p. 210

Reading, Writing & Grammar SkillBook
- Reading, pp. 58–60, 61–62

Technology
- Audiotape
- Personal Journal Software
- Custom Literature Database: Additional sonnets by Shakespeare can be found on the database.
- Test Generator Software

Art Study

Response to Caption Question The pose, clothing, and surroundings suggest that the young man is a wealthy man of leisure, one to whom the finer things in life are important. Students probably can imagine him having the time and desire to write or recite sonnets.

Visual Literacy The young man wears a doublet called a *peasecod* (meaning "pea sack" or "pod") that was padded to create a pointed bulge over his abdomen. His face and artificially curled hair are highlighted by a ruff, a large starched collar, then worn by both men and women. Such costumes were worn by courtiers, attendants, at the court of Elizabeth I, who also wore decidedly rich and elaborate costumes (see p. 106).

Questions How and why do people today reshape and decorate themselves? *(with clothing, hair styles, jewelry, body piercing, tattoos, body building; to present themselves in a certain light; to attract)* How will today's styles appear to people 400 years from now? *(Responses will vary, but exaggerated clothing and body styles always end up looking outlandish.)*

SELECTION SUMMARY

Shakespeare's Sonnets

Sonnet 18 In an extended metaphor, the poet compares his love to a summer's day.

Sonnet 29 The speaker bemoans his failures until the memory of his love provides recompense.

Sonnet 71 The poet, fearing that his memory would cause his love grief, asks to be forgotten after death.

Sonnet 116 The poet defines "true love" through metaphor.

Sonnet 130 The poet ridicules the literary convention of describing one's love as if she were a goddess.

For summaries in other languages, see the ***Building English Proficiency*** *book.*

Sonnet 18

Shall I compare thee to a summer's day?
Thou art more lovely and more temperate.
Rough winds do shake the darling buds of May,
And summer's lease hath all too short a date.
Sometimes too hot the eye of heaven shines,
And often is his gold complexion dimmed;
And every fair from fair sometimes declines,
By chance or nature's changing course untrimmed.
But thy eternal summer shall not fade
Nor lose possession of that fair thou owest;
1 Nor shall Death brag thou wanderest in his shade,
When in eternal lines to time thou growest.
So long as men can breathe or eyes can see,
So long lives this, and this gives life to thee.

2 **temperate** (tem′pər it), *adj.* moderate.

8 **untrimmed,** reduced; deprived of beauty
10 **fair thou owest,** beauty you possess.

Sonnet 29

When, in disgrace with Fortune and men's eyes,
I all alone beweep my outcast state,
And trouble deaf heaven with my bootless cries,
And look upon myself and curse my fate,
Wishing me like to one more rich in hope,
Featured like him, like him with friends possessed,
Desiring this man's art and that man's scope,
With what I most enjoy contented least;
2 Yet in these thoughts myself almost despising,
Haply I think on thee, and then my state,
Like to the lark at break of day arising
From sullen earth, sings hymns at heaven's gate;
For thy sweet love remembered such wealth brings
That then I scorn to change my state with kings.

3 **bootless** (büt′lis), *adj.*

9 **despise** (di spīz′), *v.* scorn.

Sonnet 71

No longer mourn for me when I am dead
Than you shall hear the surly sullen bell
Give warning to the world that I am fled
From this vile world, with vilest worms to dwell.
Nay, if you read this line, remember not
The hand that writ it; for I love you so
That I in your sweet thoughts would be forgot

2 **sullen** (sul′ən), *adj.* gloomy.
2 **bell.** The bell was rung after someone had died so that those who heard it might pray for the departed soul.

◄ Nicholas Hilliard painted this miniature portrait, known as *A Young Man Among Roses,* around 1588. What do the young man's pose and his surroundings seem to suggest about his outlook on life? Can you imagine the young man's writing or reciting a sonnet to his love? Why or why not?

During Reading

Selection Objectives

- to read a sample of Shakespeare's sonnets
- to explore The Lure of Ambition
- to examine the Shakespearean sonnet form and its conventions
- to explore the uses of imagery and figurative language

Unit 2 Resource Book
Graphic Organizer, p. 1
Study Guide, p. 2

Theme Link

Although each sonnet is uniquely linked to the theme, they all exhibit an awareness of the dichotomy between values inherent in love and those involved in ambition.

Vocabulary Preview

belie, misrepresent
bootless, useless
despise, scorn
impediment, obstruction
temperate, moderate
sullen, gloomy

Students can add the words and definitions to their Writer's Notebooks.

1 Literary Focus
Sonnet

Question How do lines 10–12 fit the 10-beat meter? *(On the last syllable of* owest, wanderest, growest , e *is "swallowed," cutting a syllable.)*

2 Literary Focus
Sonnet

Questions Would you say this sonnet has four or two sections? Why? *(The change at line 9 argues for two sections of eight and six lines each.)*

BUILDING ENGLISH PROFICIENCY

ESL LEP ELD SAE LD

Exploring Sonnet Structure

Help students understand that each of these sonnets may be divided into four related "chunks" of ideas.

1. Show students that the divisions fall after lines 4, 8, and 12.

2. Suggest that pairs of students work together at rephrasing or summarizing each set of lines into modern, conversational English.

3. Have them write their rephrased lines or summaries on the chart shown.

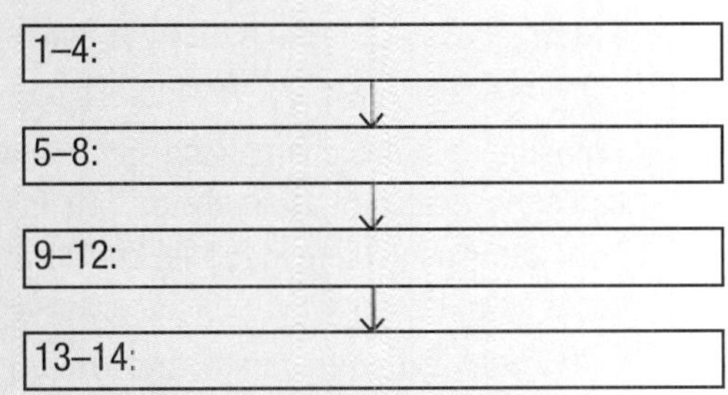

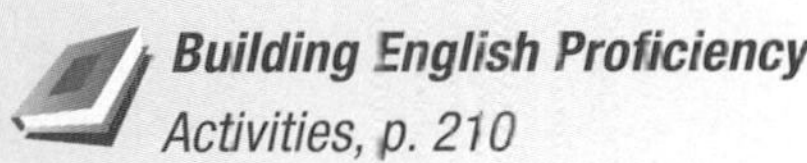

Building English Proficiency
Activities, p. 210

3 Literary Focus
Sonnet

Question Identify the rhyming words and scheme in Sonnet 71. *(a dead;* b *bell;* a *fled;* b *dwell;* c *not;* d *so;* c *forgot;* d *woe;* e *verse;* f *clay;* e *rehearse;* f *decay;* g *moan;* g *gone [a slant rhyme in modern English])*

4 Reading/Thinking Skills
Recognize Assumptions and Implications

Questions How does the speaker define "true love"? If he's right, what does it mean to us today? *(Possible response: True love is eternal and a changeless commitment; according to this definition, there may not be much true love in the world today.)*

5 Historical Note
Sonnet

Many poets of the period honored their loves with hyperbolic praise. Here, Shakespeare parodies that tradition.

Check Test

1. To what does the narrator of Sonnet 18 compare his love? *(a summer's day)*
2. Name three things that the Sonnet 29 narrator wishes for? *(Possible responses: hope, better looks, friends, greater talent)*
3. What does the Sonnet 71 speaker ask his love not to say after he dies? *(his name)*
4. What does the Sonnet 116 speaker define? *(love)*
5. Name three things to which the Sonnet 130 speaker compares his love? *(the sun, coral, snow, wires, roses, perfumes, music, a goddess)*

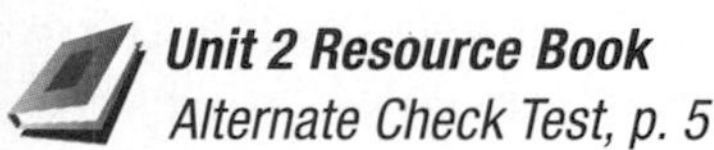

Unit 2 Resource Book
Alternate Check Test, p. 5

If thinking on me then should make you woe.
O, if, I say, you look upon this verse
When I perhaps compounded am with clay,
Do not so much as my poor name rehearse,
But let your love even with my life decay,
Lest the wise world should look into your moan
3 And mock you with me after I am gone.

Sonnet 116

Let me not to the marriage of true minds
Admit impediments. Love is not love
Which alters when it alteration finds,
Or bends with the remover to remove.
Oh no! It is an ever-fixèd mark,
That looks on tempests and is never shaken;
It is the star to every wandering bark,
Whose worth's unknown although his height be taken.
Love's not Time's fool, though rosy lips and cheeks
Within his bending sickle's compass come;
Love alters not with his brief hours and weeks,
But bears it out even to the edge of doom.
If this be error and upon me proved,
4 I never writ, nor no man ever loved.

2 **impediment** (im ped′ə mənt), *n.* obstruction.
4 **or bends . . . remove,** or changes when the loved one is unfaithful.
7 **bark,** ship.
10 **within . . . come,** Time is often represented as an old man carrying a sickle, a curved blade used for cutting down tall grasses or, metaphorically, human souls. Youth ("rosy lips and cheeks") also comes within his range ("compass").

Sonnet 130

5 My mistress' eyes are nothing like the sun;
Coral is far more red than her lips' red;
If snow be white, why then her breasts are dun;
If hairs be wires, black wires grow on her head.
I have seen roses damasked, red and white,
But no such roses see I in her cheeks;
And in some perfumes is there more delight
Than in the breath that from my mistress reeks.
I love to hear her speak, yet well I know
That music hath a far more pleasing sound.
I grant I never saw a goddess go;
My mistress, when she walks, treads on the ground.
And yet, by heaven, I think my love as rare
As any she belied with false compare.

3 **dun,** dull gray.
5 **damasked,** variegated; multicolored.
11 **go,** walk.
14 **any she,** any woman.
14 **belie** (bi lī′), *v.* misrepresent.

MINI-LESSON: GRAMMAR
Using Like and As

Teach Point out these lines from Sonnet 130:

My mistress' eyes are nothing *like* the sun;

Explain that in this comparison, *like* is a preposition and is followed by an object. *Like* is rarely used as a conjunction in formal English and is never to introduce a subordinate clause.

And yet, by heaven, I think my love *as* rare *As* any she belied with false compare.

Here *as* is being used as a conjunction to make a positive comparison. *As* should be used to introduce subordinate clauses.

CORRECT: You are *like* the gentle dove.

NOT: You sing sweetly *like* a chickadee does.

BUT: You sing sweetly *as* a chickadee does.

Activity Idea Invite students to write a sonnet that focuses on comparison between two things. Have students make sure they use *like* and *as* properly in their comparisons.

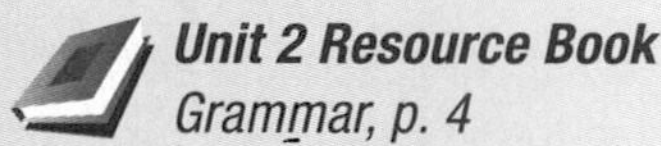

Unit 2 Resource Book
Grammar, p. 4

After Reading

Making Connections

Shaping Your Response

1. Like most Elizabethan sonneteers, Shakespeare uses **imagery** drawn from nature and common experience. Which image in these sonnets can you picture most clearly?
2. Some readers feel that Shakespeare, in Sonnet 18, is paying greater tribute to **poetic convention** than to his love. What do you think?

Analyzing the Sonnets

3. According to the speaker in Sonnet 18, his beloved's "eternal summer shall not fade." How is this possible?
4. Point out the contrast in Sonnet 29 that carries the meaning of the poem.
5. Sonnet 71 contains many words and phrases that suggest the unpleasantness of death. In your opinion, what, if anything, seems to lift it out of the grave?
6. How is **metaphor** used in Sonnet 116 to demonstrate how firm and steady love should be?
7. Sonnet 130 seems to celebrate **individuality**. How does the speaker first upset your expectations about the beauty of the beloved and then fulfill your expectations about the beloved?
8. Which sonnets contain elements of **hyperbole,** or exaggeration? Point them out and explain what effect they have on the poems.

Extending the Ideas

9. So popular have sonnets been that poets have continued writing them well into the 1900s. Why do you suppose poets choose an art form like the sonnet to express themselves?
10. How do the ideas expressed about fame and beauty in Shakespeare's sonnets compare with ideas about fame and beauty that people hold today?

Literary Focus: Shakespearean Sonnet

A Shakespearean **sonnet** is a fourteen-line poem in iambic pentameter. In each sonnet, statements or examples are presented, and then a conclusion is reached. For each of Shakespeare's sonnets, show where the conclusion begins. (What word or words does the poet use to signal that a new idea is coming?) Write a one-sentence summary of each sonnet to show how the statements and conclusions work together to present one main idea.

After Reading

MAKING CONNECTIONS

1. Possible responses: "darling buds of May" and "gold complexion dimmed" from Sonnet 18; "the lark . . . arising from sullen earth, sings hymns at heaven's gate" from Sonnet 29; "this vile world, with vilest worms to dwell" from Sonnet 71; "rosy lip and cheeks within his bending sickle's compass come" from Sonnet 116; and lines 1–11 from Sonnet 130

2. Students might mention the lack of specifics about his love.

3. Possible response: The love's "eternal summer" is captured in this poem and, thus, lives forever.

4. Possible response: Love and ambition are contrasted.

5. Students might respond that it is overdone and has nothing to redeem it; others might feel that redemption is found in the poem's expression of tender feelings.

6. a fixed mark, a star, from which one navigates one's way in a tempest

7. He negates standard comparisons of beauty; he fulfills expectation by affirming that in his eyes, she is the most wonderful of women.

8. Sonnet 18: The comparisons of his love to a summer day make the love seem exquisite. Sonnet 71: The speaker's pleas for his love to forget him in death makes him seem overly noble. Sonnet 130: The speaker exaggerates the ways in which the lover falls short to poke fun at other sonnets.

9. Possible responses: Some may like the challenge of working within the confines of the form; some may imitate poems that have moved them; others may parody the form.

10. Possible responses: While ideas of beauty change through time, the contrasting values of love versus ambition for fame and fortune remain as valid today as in Shakespeare's time.

LITERARY FOCUS: SONNET

Sonnet 18: signal—line 9/But; summary—While the speaker's love compares favorably to summer, the lover's youth will never fade; the sonnet preserves it for eternity. **Sonnet 29:** signal—line 9/Yet; summary—The speaker despairs at his failures to fulfill ambitions, but the thought of the one who loves him offers him solace. **Sonnet 71:** signal—line 13/Lest; summary—The speaker asks that his love forget him at his death; the lovers must not feel pain or be mocked for their love. **Sonnet 116:** signal—line 13/If; summary—True love is eternal, unchanging; if it isn't, there's no such thing as love or the poem. **Sonnet 130:** signal—line 13/And yet; summary—The speaker's mistress fails when compared to hyperbolic standards; to the speaker, she is beautiful; women who meet such standards are misrepresented.

VOCABULARY STUDY

1. belie
2. temperate
3. sullen
4. despise
5. impediment

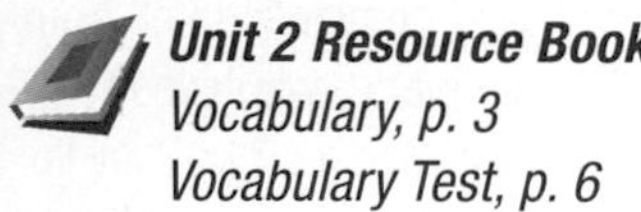

Unit 2 Resource Book
Vocabulary, p. 3
Vocabulary Test, p. 6

WRITING CHOICES

The Poet in You

Before students begin, discuss how approaches to writing poetry differ from those for prose; some poets, for example, decide meter and rhyme scheme and even choose some of their rhyme words before beginning. Poets often make major revisions during the drafting stage in order to make the parts work.

Dear Will

In a class discussion, review the literary conventions of the personal letter. Encourage the students to write in the real or an imaginary persona of a person of the Elizabethan era.

Selection Test

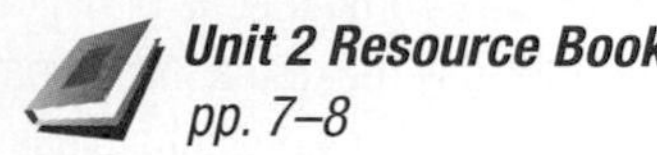

Unit 2 Resource Book
pp. 7–8

Vocabulary Study

Match each example with the appropriate vocabulary word. You will not use all the words.

belie
bootless
despise
impediment
temperate
sullen

1. "Why no—all those things you heard about me are lies. I swear I've never even looked at another woman!"
2. "Sure, I believe in getting involved in a relationship, but not *too* involved."
3. "Oh, I guess I'm just feeling miserable because I never seem to be able to talk to people without making a fool of myself."
4. "I hate him, that's all. I just can't stand to be in the same room with him."
5. "Yes, I'd like to go out with you, but you know my parents are very strict about my dating anyone."

Expressing Your Ideas

Writing Choices

Writer's Notebook Update Look back at the poetic themes you listed. Can you add to that list? Select a theme you like and jot down some ideas about statements and conclusions you could use to express it and about images that would help get the idea across.

The Poet in You Try your hand at writing a **sonnet.** Use this check list to make sure that you follow the conventions of the sonnet.

- ☐ 14 lines
- ☐ Rhythmic scheme
- ☐ Rhyme scheme
- ☐ Idea change after line 8 or line 12

Dear Will . . . Imagine that William Shakespeare has dedicated one of his sonnets to you. Write him a **personal letter** acknowledging receipt of the poem, expressing your opinion of the quality of the writing, and explaining your feelings at having this poem dedicated to you.

Other Options

Shakespeare in Art In his sonnets Shakespeare creates a word picture of his emotions. Select one of these poems and find a painting or a photograph that expresses similar emotions. If you prefer, create an **artwork** of your own. Be prepared to explain your choice of artwork to the class.

Shakespeare Rocks! Shakespeare's words have been set to music time and time again, from classical opera to modern jazz. Try your hand at adapting any of his sonnets into a contemporary **rock lyric.** You may use the entire poem or just a phrase or two to base your lyric on. If you can, set your lyric to music and perform your rock song for the class.

OTHER OPTIONS

Shakespeare in Art

Suggest the following research tips:

- Identify the emotions that you feel are expressed by the poem you have chosen.
- Ask a librarian to help you locate the oversized art books or slide collections. The school's art teacher might have some leads.

Shakespeare Rocks!

Mention to students that they are free to make the following changes: cut, reorganize, repeat, reword. You might suggest that students who do not wish to sing create a raplike song.

Reading a Shakespearean Play

The words may look old-fashioned. The sentences may seem awkward. Don't worry. There are a lot of things you can do to make reading Shakespearean drama easier. Here are some guidelines you can follow.

Read the scene summary. Because Shakespeare based many of his plays on old, familiar stories, his audiences often knew the plot lines of the play before they attended a performance. If you read the summary of each scene (in a colored box immediately after the scene heading) before you read the scene, you'll know what to expect.

Read the scene straight through. Try to get the sense of an entire passage by reading each scene straight through, without stopping to struggle with difficult words or sentences. Once you understand the action of the entire scene, you can go back and concentrate on the details.

Use the marginal notes. In the margins you will find definitions of unfamiliar words. When a passage is quite difficult, you will find an entire phrase or sentence rewritten in language you can understand.

Now reread the scene summary. Does it make sense? Through your own reading, do you see each event described in the summary? If so, you're ready to move on. If not, find a partner and reread the scene together.

Think about the characters. Concentrate on the major **characters.** Listen to what they say to others and to themselves. (That may mean that you'll need to reread a long speech.) Listen to what other characters say about them. Watch how other characters relate to them. Look for alliances between characters. Look for conflicts. Try to figure out what makes each character tick! What motivates him? What troubles her? It may even help to visualize each character's physical appearance.

Understand the stage conventions. Shakespearean theater had its own conventional way of doing things. Watch for a character to speak in an **aside,** which means that the audience can hear his or her thoughts, but that the other characters on stage cannot. At other times, a character alone on stage will deliver a **soliloquy,** a speech that gives voice to his or her inmost thoughts and feelings.

Rearrange inverted sentences. In common usage speakers most often place the subject of a sentence before the verb. Many of Shakespeare's sentences, however, are inverted; for example, Lady Macbeth's doctor says, "More needs she the divine than the physician." When you encounter such passages, simply rearrange the word order to place the subject first. Rearranged, this sentence would read: "She needs the divine [priest] more than the physician."

Interpret metaphors. Many important ideas in the play are developed through **metaphor.** Ask yourself what comparison is suggested and how this comparison affects the overall meaning of the passage. For example, when King Duncan greets Macbeth, whom he has just rewarded with a new title, he says, "I have begun to plant thee, and will labor / To make thee full of growing." Here he uses *plant* and *growing* metaphorically to tell Macbeth that other honors will be forthcoming.

Read passages aloud. You are, after all, reading a script meant to be performed by

READING A SHAKESPEAREAN PLAY

Teaching Objectives

- to become familiar with some features of Shakespearean plays
- to be ready to read a play by Shakespeare with understanding

Introduce

Tell students that the next selection they will read is a play by Shakespeare. Point out that reading Shakespeare's plays is not exactly like reading modern plays and other selections. Shakespeare used language that has since changed and techniques that are no longer necessary because of modern lighting, sound, and stages. The tips on these pages will help students understand the play they are about to read.

BUILDING ENGLISH PROFICIENCY

ESL LEP ELD SAE LD

Understanding the Reading Tips

While all students will benefit from understanding these pages on how to read a Shakespearean play, it is even more important that students who are not proficient in English understand these tips.

1. Assign one tip each to pairs or small groups. Students should work together to understand their assigned tip and, if appropriate, find examples in *Macbeth* of the feature being explained.

2. Have groups decide whether their tip would help them read any selection or whether that tip is specific only to reading Shakespeare's plays.

3. Then have a representative from each group explain its assigned tip to the class.

Follow Up

- Ask students to define these terms that apply to a play by Shakespeare: marginal note, aside, soliloquy, inverted sentence, plot, conflict, rising action, climax, falling action, resolution.
- Have students think of a simple story with which they are all familiar, such as "Goldilocks and the Three Bears." Have them plot the events on a plot chart similar to the one on this page.

actors. Try reading speeches aloud and visualizing the action as it unfolds. You'll soon discover that most of the play is in verse. Don't let this throw you. Read for the sense, using the punctuation as an aid to understanding the sentence structure.

Understand the plot structure. The structure of any narrative may be visualized as in this diagram. The introduction or **background** (also called *exposition*) is what the viewer or reader needs to know about the characters and their situation at the beginning. The **conflict** is what sets the events of the story in motion. What the main character does to battle the conflict and achieve the goal constitutes the **rising action** (also called the *complication*); in this part also the conflict may be renewed or new conflicts introduced. The **climax** is the turning point (also called the *crisis*), at which the main character takes the decisive action that will bring about the conclusion. The climax is often also the most exciting point of the story. The **falling action** is attended by a lessening of tension. The outcome or conclusion is the **resolution** (also called *denouement*) of the conflict and the events that occur thereafter. In a Shakespearean play, generally act 1 will contain the exposition and conflict; act 2 the rising action; act 3 the climax; act 4 the falling action; and act 5 the resolution.

Do the literary focus activities. These brief writing and plotting exercises after each act will help you understand the development of the **plot.** You will see that events do not happen in isolation. Rather, one event leads to the next, which leads to the next, and so on. Look for these chains of causes and effects. You'll then begin to understand what events happen and why they happen.

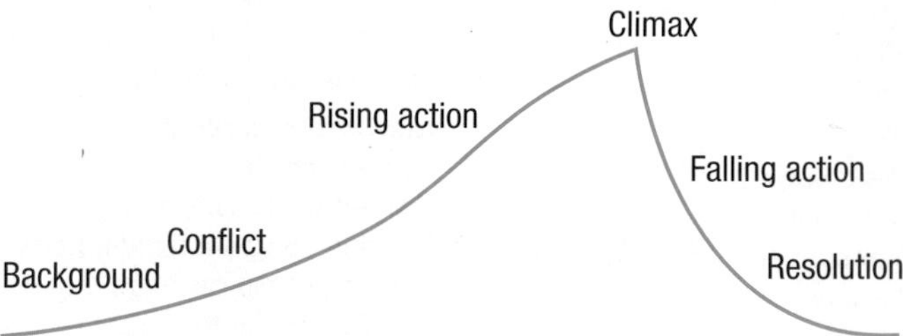

Before Reading

Macbeth

by William Shakespeare

During the time that Shakespeare lived in London, he wrote poetry and plays, acted, and helped to manage the theater. He became a full shareholder in his acting company (the Lord Chamberlain's Men, later the King's Men), and he was part owner of the Globe Theater (see pages 146–147) and later of Blackfriars Theater. Shakespeare made frequent visits back to Stratford, where he bought one of the finest houses in town. He returned home in 1610 to be with his wife until his death six years later. Although some of Shakespeare's plays were published during his lifetime, not until after his death was an effort made to collect them in a single volume. The *First Folio,* the first edition of Shakespeare's collected plays, appeared in 1623.

Building Background

That Scottish Play It's August 7, 1606, and the first production of Shakespeare's *Macbeth* has begun. King James of England, entertaining the visiting King Christian IV of Denmark, delights in the opening scene with the three weird sisters, for he believes that witches have cast spells on his own life. He hails the appearance of the noble Banquo, for he has traced his lineage back to this Scottish nobleman. He appreciates the dark, foreboding mood Shakespeare has created. Only after the play is over does King James learn that the black mood has extended to the play itself: Hal Berridge, the boy actor playing Lady Macbeth, has died backstage. From that first performance and from a series of other mishaps, disasters, and deaths associated with the play, *Macbeth* has come to be considered a tragedy so unlucky that some actors and directors never call it by name. They simply call it "that play" or "that Scottish play."

Literary Focus

Plot Structure The **plot,** a series of related events that make up a story, is the organizational pattern for a narrative work. The structure of a five-act Shakespearean play can be described as a rising and falling of the fortunes of the main character, as is shown in the diagram on page 116. In act 1, the background, sometimes called *exposition,* tells the viewers or readers what they need to know about the characters, setting, and so on—particularly what has happened previously to bring the characters to this situation. Watch for ways in which Shakespeare transmits such information through action and dialogue.

Writer's Notebook

What Makes a Tragedy? In 1598 John Florio, Shakespeare's contemporary, defined tragedy: "A tragedy or mournful play being a lofty kind of poetry and representing personages of great state and matter of much trouble, a great broil or stir; it beginneth prosperously and endeth unfortunately. . . ." Make a list of people you know or have read about whose lives began prosperously and ended unfortunately.

Before Reading

Building Background

Ask students if they have read or seen *Macbeth* or other Shakespeare plays and, if so, ask for their reactions.

Literary Focus

As an aid to tracking plot, students might keep a chart on which they record vivid images from each scene.

Writer's Notebook

Before students begin, reiterate Florio's requirements: great personages; much trouble; begin prosperously; end unfortunately.

More About William Shakespeare

Shakespeare died on April 23, 1616; his tombstone in Stratford reads:

"Good friend for Jesus' sake forbear,
To dig the dust enclosed here!
Blest be the man that spares these stones,
And curst be he that moves my bones."

Among his other great tragedies are

- *Hamlet* (first performed 1601)
- *Othello* (first performed 1604)
- *King Lear* (first performed 1605?)

SUPPORT MATERIALS OVERVIEW

Unit 2 Resource Book
- Graphic Organizer, pp. 9, 17, 25, 33, 41
- Study Guide, pp. 10, 18, 26, 34, 42
- Vocabulary, pp. 11, 19, 27, 35, 43
- Grammar, pp. 12, 20, 28, 36, 44
- Alternate Check Test, pp. 13, 21, 29, 37, 45
- Vocabulary Test, pp. 14, 22, 30, 38, 46
- Selection Test, pp. 15–16, 23–24, 31–32, 39–40, 47–48

Building English Proficiency
- Selection Summaries
- Activities, pp. 211–215

Reading, Writing & Grammar SkillBook
- Vocabulary, pp. 1–2
- Reading, pp. 74–76
- Writing, pp. 131–133
- Grammar, Usage, and Mechanics, pp. 143–144, 145–146, 147–148, 153–154, 155–156, 180–182, 187–188, 189–190, 191–192, 193–196, 236–238, 246–246

The World of Work
- Politician, p.5
- Activity, p. 6

Technology
- Audiotape
- Personal Journal Software
- Custom Literature Database: Additional plays by Shakespeare can be found on the database.
- Test Generator Software
- Writers Help Desk

During Reading

Selection Objectives

- to read a tragedy by Shakespeare
- to explore the theme of ambition
- to identify plot elements
- to analyze a tragedy

Unit 2 Resource Book
Graphic Organizer, p. 9
Study Guide, p. 10

Theme Link

When it is prophesied that he will be king, the lure of ambition drives Macbeth and Lady Macbeth into a series of acts—including regicide—that ultimately destroy them both.

Vocabulary Preview

disdain, scorn
minion, favorite; darling
flout, treat with scorn or contempt
disburse, pay out
content, fight; struggle
solicit, tempt
surmise, guesswork
recompense, reward
harbinger, forerunner
commendation, praise
mettle, courage

Students can add the words and definitions to their Writer's Notebooks.

1 Historical Note
Heir to the Throne

Macbeth and Duncan were cousins, representatives of two branches of the same royal family that ruled Scotland. At the time they lived, the law forbade that fathers pass the crown to sons; rather, the head of one branch succeeded the head of the other branch.

Macbeth

WILLIAM SHAKESPEARE

CHARACTERS
DUNCAN, *King of Scotland*
MALCOLM, DONALBAIN } *his sons*

1

MACBETH, *Thane of Glamis, later of Cawdor, later King of Scotland*
LADY MACBETH

BANQUO, *a thane of Scotland*
FLEANCE, *his son*
MACDUFF, *Thane of Fife*
LADY MACDUFF
SON *of Macduff and Lady Macduff*

LENNOX, ROSS, MENTEITH, ANGUS, CAITHNESS } *thanes and noblemen of Scotland*

SIWARD, *Earl of Northumberland*
YOUNG SIWARD, *his son*

SEYTON, *an officer attending Macbeth*
Another LORD
ENGLISH DOCTOR
SCOTTISH DOCTOR
GENTLEWOMAN *attending Lady Macbeth*
CAPTAIN *serving Duncan*
PORTER
OLD MAN
Three MURDERERS *of Banquo*
FIRST MURDERER *at Macduff's castle*
MESSENGER *to Lady Macbeth*
MESSENGER *to Lady Macduff*
SERVANT *to Macbeth*
SERVANT *to Lady Macbeth*
Three WITCHES *or* WEIRD SISTERS
HECATE, *leader of the Witches*
Three APPARITIONS

Lords, Gentlemen, Officers, Soldiers, Murderers, and Attendants

This poster, created by Edmund Dulac for a 1911 staging of *Macbeth,* shows Macbeth with the three Witches who foretell his future. What is the mood of this illustration? How does the artist create that mood? ➤

ACT ONE SUMMARY

Macbeth

Three witches agree to approach Macbeth. King Duncan learns that the rebellion has been put down and the traitorous thane of Cawdor overcome, principally by Macbeth. When Macbeth and Banquo meet the witches, Macbeth is hailed thane of Cawdor, king thereafter; Banquo will beget kings without being king. Duncan, after rewarding Macbeth with the thanehood of Cawdor, names his son Malcolm heir to the throne. Stirred by the partial fulfillment of the prophecy, Macbeth's plots the king's murder. Lady Macbeth, reading a letter telling of the king's imminent arrival, decides the time is right for his murder. She steels Macbeth for the deed. Duncan arrives, but Macbeth cannot bring himself to murder the king until his wife taunts him into action.

*For summaries in other languages, see the **Building English Proficiency** book.*

Art Study

Responses to Caption Questions The mood is malevolent: the witches' pupil-less eyes horrify; their gestures are ominous.

Question What do you think the structure and supporting details of this poster suggest? *(Possible response: The structure and details might suggest the inevitability of tragedy: the malevolence and power of the witches boils up like the steam from their cauldron to meet Macbeth's implacable stance head-on. Nothing good can result from this collision of forces.)*

Connections to BBC Shakespeare on CD-ROM

The BBC Shakespeare on CD-ROM series: *Macbeth* offers a rich variety of unique materials for teaching the play. Also available on the BBC Shakespeare on CD-ROM series are *Romeo and Juliet, Hamlet, The Tempest, Julius Caesar,* and *A Midsummer Night's Dream.*

BUILDING ENGLISH PROFICIENCY

Exploring Character

All that students know about *Macbeth* thus far is its list of characters. To spark interest, ask students to infer relationships and imagine how these people might look and act.

1. Have each student pick a character that he or she will "be" throughout the play (even though others may read that character's lines). Alternatively, write the characters' names on slips of paper and let students draw one from a hat.

2. Tell your student-characters that at any point during the play other students may ask them questions about their character's feelings and actions. They should try to give answers that are true to Shakespeare's characterization (and use their imagination for whatever Shakespeare does not reveal).

3. At the end of each act, have students write or dictate a journal-style entry from their character's perspective.

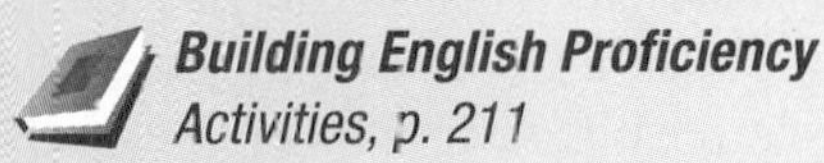

Building English Proficiency
Activities, p. 211

2 Literary Element
Meter

Instead of speaking in the usual iambic pentameter, the witches often speak in rhymed couplets set in trochaic tetrameter—that is, a line of verse with four metrical feet; each foot consists of a stressed syllable followed by an unstressed syllable.

Question Why do you think the witches speak differently than other characters? (Possible response: *to emphasize their weird or supernatural state)*

3 Literary Element
Theme

Question What major theme of *Macbeth* does this couplet introduce? *(the blurring of good and evil; a reversal of values)*

4 Literary Focus
Plot

Plot often turns on physical, social, or psychological conflict that involves a struggle with nature, society, another person, or oneself.

Question What kind of conflict opens this scene? *(The individual fighting is physical conflict; war and rebellion is social conflict.)*

Act One

SCENE 1

Summary *Three Witches agree to meet Macbeth on a lonely wasteland later that day.*

A wasteland somewhere in Scotland. Thunder and lightning. Enter three WITCHES.

FIRST WITCH. When shall we three meet again?
In thunder, lightning, or in rain?
[2] **SECOND WITCH.** When the hurlyburly's done,
When the battle's lost and won.
THIRD WITCH. That will be ere the set of sun.
FIRST WITCH. Where the place?
SECOND WITCH. Upon the heath.
THIRD WITCH. There to meet with Macbeth.
FIRST WITCH. I come, Grimalkin!
SECOND WITCH. Paddock calls.
THIRD WITCH. Anon.
ALL. Fair is foul, and foul is fair,
[3] Hover through the fog and filthy air.

9 **Graymalkin,** a gray cat.
10 **Paddock,** a toad.
11 **anon** (ə non′), *adv.* soon.

SCENE 2

Summary *King Duncan learns from the Captain of his army that his chief rival Macdonwald has been killed by the brave Macbeth. Ross, a nobleman, tells him that Macbeth has also defeated a traitor, the Thane of Cawdor. Duncan orders Cawdor executed and names Macbeth the new Thane of Cawdor.*

thane, a Scottish nobleman, just below an earl.

A camp near Forres, north of Edinburgh. Battle noises sound offstage. Enter DUNCAN, MALCOLM, DONALBAIN, LENOX, *with* ATTENDANTS, *meeting a bleeding* CAPTAIN.

DUNCAN. What bloody man is that? He can report,
[4] As seemeth by his plight, of the revolt
The newest state.
MALCOLM. This is the sergeant
Who like a good and hardy soldier fought
'Gainst my captivity. Hail, brave friend!
Say to the King the knowledge of the broil
As thou didst leave it.
CAPTAIN. Doubtful it stood,
As two spent swimmers that do cling together
And choke their art. The merciless Macdonwald—
Worthy to be a rebel, for to that
The multiplying villainies of nature

9 **choke their art,** hinder each other's ability to swim.

MINI-LESSON: GRAMMAR
Diagramming Simple Sentences

Teach Diagramming is a way of showing the structure of a sentence and how the parts are related. The simple subject and verb are placed on a horizontal line, with a vertical line separating them and crossing the horizontal line. The vertical line divides the complete subject and the complete predicate. Modifiers, such as adjectives and adverbs, are connected by slanted lines coming down from the horizontal line beneath the word they modify. The object of a verb (direct object) is separated from the verb by a vertical line that does not cross the horizontal line. If the verb is a linking verb, the adjective linked to the subject is separated from the verb by a slanted line. Show the examples for: The captain gave his report. He was wounded and tired. The old soldier could still swing his sword powerfully.

Activity Idea Have students diagram simple sentences based on sentences on this spread.

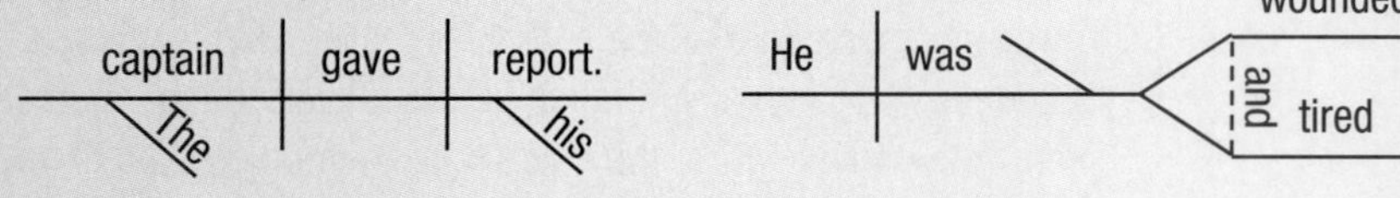

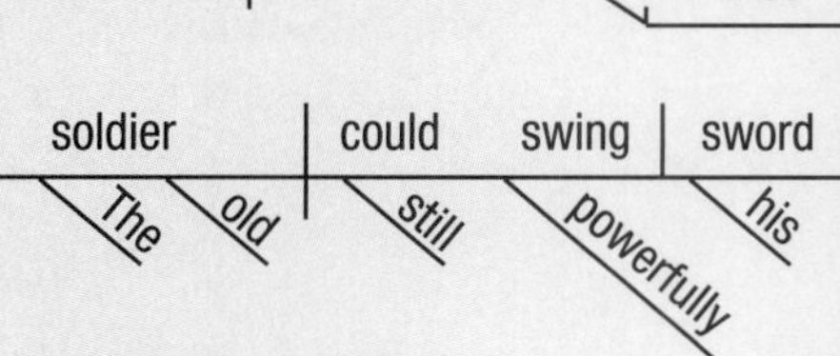

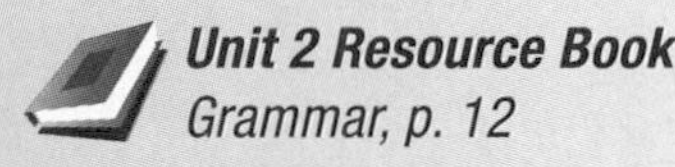

Unit 2 Resource Book
Grammar, p. 12

Do swarm upon him—from the Western Isles
Of kerns and gallowglasses is supplied;
And Fortune, on his damnèd quarrel smiling
Showed like a rebel's whore. But all's too weak;
For brave Macbeth—well he deserves that name—
Disdaining Fortune, with his brandished steel,
Which smoked with bloody execution,
Like valor's minion carved out his passage
Till he faced the slave,
Which ne'er shook hands nor bade farewell to him
Till he unseamed him from the nave to th' chops,
And fixed his head upon our battlements.

DUNCAN. O valiant cousin, worthy gentleman!

CAPTAIN. As whence the sun 'gins his reflection
Shipwrecking storms and direful thunders break,
So from that spring whence comfort seemed to come
Discomfort swells. Mark, King of Scotland, mark.
No sooner justice had, with valor armed,
Compelled these skipping kerns to trust their heels
But the Norweyan lord, surveying vantage,
With furbished arms and new supplies of men,
Began a fresh assault.

DUNCAN. Dismayed not this our captains, Macbeth and Banquo?

CAPTAIN. Yes, as sparrows eagles, or the hare the lion.
If I say sooth, I must report they were
As cannons overcharged with double cracks,
So they doubly redoubled strokes upon the foe.
Except they meant to bathe in reeking wounds
Or memorize another Golgotha,
I cannot tell.
But I am faint. My gashes cry for help.

DUNCAN. So well thy words become thee as thy wounds;
They smack of honor both. Go get him surgeons.

(*Exit* CAPTAIN, *attended. Enter* ROSS *and* ANGUS.)

Who comes here?

MALCOLM. The worthy Thane of Ross.

LENNOX. What a haste looks through his eyes!
So should he look that seems to speak things strange.

ROSS. God save the King!

DUNCAN. Whence cam'st thou, worthy thane?

ROSS. From Fife, great King,
Where the Norweyan banners flout the sky
And fan our people cold.
Norway himself, with terrible numbers,
Assisted by that most disloyal traitor,

12 the western isles, Ireland and the Hebrides.
13 kerns and gallowglasses, Irish foot soldiers.
14–15 Fortune . . . whore. Fortune at first smiled upon him then deserted him.

■ According to the captain, what kind of a soldier and leader is Macbeth?

17 disdain (dis dān′), *v.* scorn.
17 brandish (bran′dish), *v.* wave threateningly.
19 minion (min′yən), *n.* favorite; darling.
20 slave, Macdonwald.
22 unseamed him . . . chaps, split him from navel to jaws.
24 cousin, Duncan and Macbeth are first cousins, but the term is often used to describe other family relationships.
31 Norweyan, Norwegian.

36 sooth, (süth), *n.* truth.

40 memorize . . . Golgotha, make the area as memorable for bloodshed as the place where Jesus was crucified.

51 flout, (flout), *v.* treat with scorn or contempt.
53 Norway himself, the king of Norway.

5 Literary Element
Characterization

Response brave, persistent, inspiring, audacious

6 Literary Element
Hyperbole

When the king asks the captain if Macbeth and Banquo were dismayed by the fresh assault, he answers yes. Remind students that hyperbole is a figure of speech involving great exaggeration.

Question How is this an example of hyperbole? *(The captain's response—"yes, as eagles are dismayed by sparrows or lions are dismayed by hares"— is a highly exaggerated "no, they were not dismayed.")*

BUILDING ENGLISH PROFICIENCY

Analyzing Characterization

To help students understand Macbeth's character, introduce this graphic organizer.

1. Ask students to think of a military leader with whom they are familiar. Have them list three words that describe the leader on the left side of the chart.

2. Have students read the captain's description of Macbeth in Scene 2, lines 16–23. On the right side of the chart, ask students to list three words that describe Macbeth.

MILITARY LEADERS	
A Modern Leader	Macbeth

7 Reading/Thinking Skills
Compare and Contrast

Question How are Cawdor and Macbeth compared and contrasted? *(They are both trusted thanes, equally strong, and equally good warriors. But, Cawdor is a traitor while Macbeth is loyal to Duncan.)*

8 Reader's Response
Making Personal Connections

So far, the witches' appearances have been accompanied by a clap of thunder.

Question What feeling does this give you? *(Possible responses: Students may say that it makes them feel creepy or that it evokes a sense of horror or the supernatural.)*

9 Multicultural Note
Numbers

Various cultures have special associations with particular numbers. In our culture, seven is considered lucky and thirteen unlucky. Note that the number three is closely associated with the witches. Encourage students to look for various groups of threes when the witches make their appearances.

7 The Thane of Cawdor, began a dismal conflict,
Till that Bellona's bridegroom, lapped in proof,
Confronted him with self-comparisons,
Point against point, rebellious arm 'gainst arm,
Curbing his lavish spirit; and to conclude,
The victory fell on us.

DUNCAN. Great happiness!

ROSS. That now
Sweno, the Norways' king, craves composition;
Nor would we deign him burial of his men
Till he disbursèd at Saint Colme's Inch
Ten thousand dollars to our general use.

DUNCAN. No more that Thane of Cawdor shall deceive
Our bosom interest. Go pronounce his present death,
And with his former title greet Macbeth.

ROSS. I'll see it done.

DUNCAN. What he hath lost noble Macbeth hath won.

SCENE 3

Summary *Macbeth and Banquo meet the three Witches. They call Macbeth Thane of Glamis, Thane of Cawdor, and king hereafter. They tell Banquo that his descendants will be kings. After the Witches vanish, one of their prophecies is confirmed when two noblemen tell Macbeth he has been named Thane of Cawdor.*

8 *Thunder. Enter the three* WITCHES.

FIRST WITCH. Where hast thou been, sister?

SECOND WITCH. Killing swine.

THIRD WITCH. Sister, where thou?

9 **FIRST WITCH.** A sailor's wife had chestnuts in her lap,
And munched, and munched, and munched. "Give me," quoth I.
"Aroint thee, witch!" the rump-fed runnion cries.
Her husband's to Aleppo gone, master o' the *Tiger*,
But in a sieve I'll thither sail,
And like a rat without a tail
I'll do, I'll do, and I'll do.

SECOND WITCH. I'll give thee a wind.

FIRST WITCH. Thou'rt kind.

THIRD WITCH. And I another.

FIRST WITCH. I myself have all the other,
And the very ports they blow,
All the quarters that they know
I' the shipman's card.
I'll drain him dry as hay.
Sleep shall neither night nor day

56–57 Bellona's bridegroom . . . self-comparisons. Macbeth, dressed in armor, matched him with equal strength. Bellona (bə lō′nə) was the Roman goddess of war.
62 composition, a peace treaty.
64 disburse (dis pėrs′), *v.* pay out.
64 Saint Colme's Inch, an island off the coast of Scotland.
67 bosom interest, intimate trust.

6 aroint (ə roint′) **thee,** get out of here.
6 runnion (ron′yən), *n.* mangy creature.
7 Aleppo, city in NW Syria, famous as a trading center.
9 without a tail. It was believed that witches could change themselves into animals, but could be detected by some deformity.
17 shipman's card, compass card or chart.

MINI-LESSON: WRITING STYLE
Ellision and Added Stress

Teach Spelling and pronunciation in Shakespeare's writing do not always conform to modern usage. Point out these lines on page 122:

- "Point against point, rebellious arm 'gainst arm." (line 58)
- "Till he disbursèd at Saint Colme's Inch" (line 64)
- "Thou'rt kind." (Scene 3, line 12)

Note that the first and third examples, *'gainst* and *Thou'rt,* are referred to as ellision; the second, *disbursèd,* is called "added stress."

Question How and why did Shakespeare change the words in these three lines? *(To control meter and sound, he dropped the first syllable of* against; *added a stressed syllable to* disbursed; *and combined* thou art *into a single, one-syllable word.)*

Activity Idea Students might try their hands at writing short poems in which they employ ellision and added stress to control meter.

Hang upon his penthouse lid.
He shall live a man forbid.
Weary sev'nnights nine times nine
Shall he dwindle, peak, and pine.
Though his bark cannot be lost,
Yet it shall be tempest tossed.
Look what I have.

SECOND WITCH. Show me, show me.

FIRST WITCH. Here I have a pilot's thumb,
Wrecked as homeward he did come.
(A drum sounds offstage.)

THIRD WITCH. A drum, a drum!
Macbeth doth come.

ALL *(dancing).* The Weird Sisters, hand in hand,
Posters of the sea and land,
Thus do go about, about,
Thrice to thine, and thrice to mine,
And thrice again, to make up nine.
Peace! The charm's wound up.

(*Enter* MACBETH *and* BANQUO.)

11 **MACBETH.** So foul and fair a day I have not seen.

BANQUO. How far is 't called to Forres? What are these,
So withered and so wild in their attire,
That look not like th' inhabitants o' th' earth
And yet are on 't? Live you? Or are you aught
That man may question? You seem to understand me
By each at once her chappy finger laying
Upon her skinny lips. You should be women,
And yet your beards forbid me to interpret
That you are so.

MACBETH. Speak, if you can. What are you?

FIRST WITCH. All hail, Macbeth! Hail to thee, Thane of Glamis!

SECOND WITCH. All hail, Macbeth! Hail to thee, Thane of Cawdor!

THIRD WITCH. All hail, Macbeth, that shalt be king hereafter!

BANQUO. Good sir, why do you start and seem to fear
Things that do sound so fair? I' the name of truth,
Are ye fantastical or that indeed
Which outwardly ye show? My noble partner
You greet with present grace and great prediction
Of noble having and of royal hope,
That he seems rapt withal. To me you speak not.
If you can look into the seeds of time
And say which grain will grow and which will not,
Speak then to me, who neither beg nor fear
Your favors nor your hate.

20 **penthouse lid,** eyelid.
21 **forbid,** accursed.
22 **sev'nnights,** seven-nights; weeks.

10 ■ What kind of power do the witches seem to have?

▲ Illustration by Charles Ricketts from *The Tragedie of Macbeth,* reproduced in the players' Shakespeare, after the Folio of 1623 (Ernest Benn, 1923). How do you predict the presence of the witches will affect the development of the plot?

48 **Glamis** (glämz).

57 **rapt withal,** completely absorbed by it.

10 Reading/Thinking Skills
Clarify

Response They can change shape, fly, call up winds, and curse, predict, or decree the future.

Art Study

Response to Caption Question While responses will vary, students should note that the prophecies foreshadow plot, and the witches may embody that which has seduced Macbeth and his wife through their insatiable ambitions.

Visual Literacy The artist has given the stone, the sky, and even the witches similar colors and textures.

Question What do you think this might suggest? (*Possible response: In the world Shakespeare creates in* Macbeth, *everything below the heavens is hard, dark, rough, and tainted with evil.)*

11 Reading/Thinking Skills
Synthesize

Point out Macbeth's first statement and remind students of scene 1, line 12: "Fair is foul, and foul is fair."

Questions What connection can you draw between Macbeth's first line and the earlier line? What are the implications of this connection? *(Possible responses: It connects Macbeth with the evil witches; it suggests that Macbeth may not be what he seems, that nothing may be what it seems; it suggests a reversal of values, that everything will be turned upside down.)*

BUILDING ENGLISH PROFICIENCY

ESL LEP ELD SAE LD

Analyzing Stage Directions

Unlike modern playwrights, Shakespeare offers little guidance about *how* actors should say lines. Help students see why his stage directions still are important.

1. Have pairs of students speculate on the purpose for Shakespeare's italicized directions on pages 122–123 and record their ideas on a chart, as shown.

2. Invite partners to imagine that they are co-directing *Macbeth* and offer directions that would tell the actors playing witches how to say lines (*softly*, for instance).

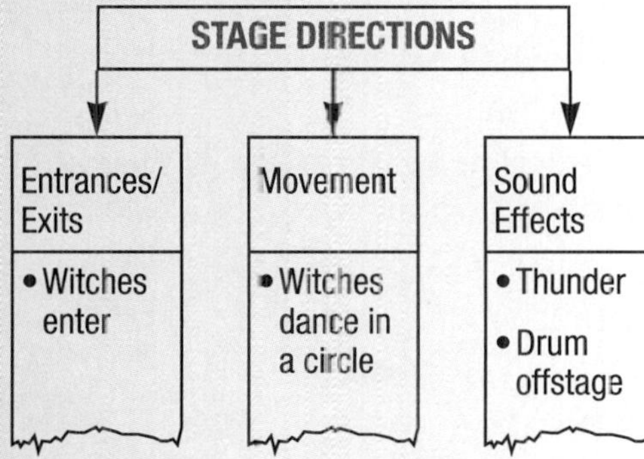

12 Reading/Thinking Skills

Literal and Figurative Language

Question These lines seem paradoxical. How would you make sense of them? *(Possible responses: that things are not always as they seem; that "the great" at times turn out not so great)*

Question Can you think of specific examples of "Less than [somebody], and greater"? *(Responses will vary: one example is Shakespeare, who in his day was not the "great man" compared to others now nearly forgotten.)*

13 Reader's Response

Challenging the Text

Remind students that foreshadowing is a hint of what is to come.

Questions Do you think Shakespeare's use of the witches as a device to foreshadow plot is effective? Why or why not? *(While the device is not exactly subtle, it is effective; no one forgets the weird sisters or their forecasts.)*

FIRST WITCH. Hail!
SECOND WITCH. Hail!
THIRD WITCH. Hail!
12 FIRST WITCH. Lesser than Macbeth, and greater.
SECOND WITCH. Not so happy, yet much happier.
13 THIRD WITCH. Thou shalt get kings, though thou be none.
So all hail, Macbeth and Banquo!
FIRST WITCH. Banquo and Macbeth, all hail!
MACBETH. Stay, you imperfect speakers, tell me more!
By Sinel's death I know I am Thane of Glamis,
But how of Cawdor? The Thane of Cawdor lives
A prosperous gentleman; and to be king
Stands not within the prospect of belief,
No more than to be Cawdor. Say from whence
You owe this strange intelligence, or why
Upon this blasted heath you stop our way
With such prophetic greeting? Speak, I charge you.
(The WITCHES *vanish.)*
BANQUO. The earth hath bubbles, as the water has,
And these are of them. Whither are they vanished?
MACBETH. Into the air; and what seemed corporal melted,
As breath into the wind. Would they had stayed!
BANQUO. Were such things here as we do speak about?
Or have we eaten on the insane root
That takes the reason prisoner?
MACBETH. Your children shall be kings.
BANQUO. You shall be king.
MACBETH. And Thane of Cawdor too. Went it not so?
BANQUO. To th' selfsame tune and words. Who's here?
(Enter ROSS *and* ANGUS.)
ROSS. The King hath happily received, Macbeth,
The news of thy success; and when he reads
Thy personal venture in the rebels' fight,
His wonder and his praises do contend
Which should be thine or his. Silenced with that,
In viewing o'er the rest o' the selfsame day
He finds thee in the stout Norweyan ranks,
Nothing afeard of what thyself didst make,
Strange images of death. As thick as tale
Came post with post, and every one did bear
Thy praises in his kingdom's great defense,
And poured them down before him.
ANGUS. We are sent
To give thee from our royal master thanks,
Only to herald thee into his sight,

67 get, beget; father.

71 Sinel, Macbeth's father. Macbeth had inherited the title.

84 insane root, a root that causes hallucinations or insanity.

92 contend, (kən tend′), *v.* fight; struggle.
93 silenced, speechless with admiration.

96–97 nothing . . . death. Macbeth killed, but did not fear death for himself.
98 post with post, one messenger after another.

MINI-LESSON: VOCABULARY

Archaic Adverbs

Teach Explain that Shakespeare used adverbs of place that are no longer commonly used. Point out the words in these lines from page 124: "*Whither* are they vanished?" and "Say from *whence* you owe this strange intelligence." Others from *Macbeth* in the chart.

Question Why might a poet find those words attractive when used as adverbs? *(They pack a lot of words into one or two syllables.)*

Activity Idea Students might

- find three or four examples of the use of these adverbs
- rephrase them in modern English
- compare their restatements with those of classmates

Word	Meaning
hence	this place *or* from this place
thence	that place *or* from that place
whence	where *or* from what place
hither	here *or* to this place *or* from this place
thither	that place *or* to that place
whither	where *or* to what place

Not pay thee.
ROSS. And, for an earnest of a greater honor,
He bade me, from him, call thee Thane of Cawdor;
In which addition, hail, most worthy thane.
For it is thine.
BANQUO. What, can the devil speak true?
MACBETH. The Thane of Cawdor lives. Why do you dress me
In borrowed robes?
ANGUS. Who was the thane lives yet,
But under heavy judgment bears that life
Which he deserves to lose. Whether he was combined
With those of Norway, or did line the rebel
With hidden help and vantage, or that with both
He labored in his country's wrack, I know not;
But treasons capital, confessed and proved,
Have overthrown him.
MACBETH *(aside).* Glamis, and Thane of Cawdor!
The greatest is behind. (*To* ROSS *and* ANGUS.) Thanks for your pains.
(*Aside to* BANQUO.) Do you not hope your children shall be kings
14 When those that gave the Thane of Cawdor to me
Promised no less to them?
BANQUO (*to* MACBETH). That, trusted home,
Might yet enkindle you unto the crown,
Besides the Thane of Cawdor. But 'tis strange;
And oftentimes to win us to our harm
The instruments of darkness tell us truths,
Win us with honest trifles, to betray 's
In deepest consequence.
Cousins, a word, I pray you.
(*He converses apart with* ROSS *and* ANGUS.)
MACBETH *(aside).* Two truths are told,
16 As happy prologues to the swelling act
Of the imperial theme. I thank you, gentlemen.
(*Aside.*) This supernatural soliciting
17 Cannot be ill, cannot be good. If ill,
Why hath it given me earnest of success
Commencing in a truth? I am Thane of Cawdor.
If good, why do I yield to that suggestion
Whose horrid image doth unfix my hair
And make my seated heart knock at my ribs,
Against the use of nature? Present fears
Are less than horrible imaginings.
My thought, whose murder yet is but fantastical,
Shakes so my single state of man

104 earnest, promise.

112 line, support.

117 behind, to come.

120–121 That . . . crown. Complete belief in the witches may arouse in you the ambition to become king.

15 ■ Compare Macbeth's reaction to the witches' prophecies with Banquo's reaction. What do you think Macbeth might be willing to do in order to see the witches' prophecy fulfilled?

131 soliciting (sə lis′it ing), *n.* temptation.

14 Reading/Thinking Skills
Infer

Question What can we infer from Macbeth's question to Banquo? *(that the question is disingenuous; that he is really asking if Banquo thinks Macbeth will be king)*

15 Reading/Thinking Skills
Find the Main Idea

Response The comparison suggests that Macbeth is willing to do anything. Banquo's warning contains the main idea: "The instruments of darkness tell us truths/Win us with honest trifles, to betray 's." The forces of darkness—Satan—tempt them both with truths, which they must resist.

16 Literary Focus
Plot

Question What is Macbeth's goal now? *(He wants to be king—the "swelling act of the imperial theme.")*

17 Literary Element
Theme

Question How does "Cannot be ill, cannot be good" fit the "Fair is foul, and foul is fair" theme? *(While a thing can be neither good nor bad, the dichotomy does suggest a reversal of values, of good and evil.)*

BUILDING ENGLISH PROFICIENCY

ESL LEP ELD SAE LD

Using Gloss Notes

Ask students to review the marginal notes on these pages. Explain that each such note is called a *gloss.*

1. Have students find one example of each kind of gloss:
- vocabulary help
- a difficult line paraphrased
- background
- a question directed to readers

2. Have pairs of students create three notes that they think might be helpful to others who are reading Scene 4.

18 Reading/Thinking Skills
Literal and Figurative Language

Question What might Macbeth's line "nothing is but what is not" mean, figuratively and literally? *(Possible responses: Figuratively, it echoes the "fair is foul" paradox; literally, it means "nothing is" as real as "what is not," that is, becoming king.)*

The World of Work
Politician

For real-life experiences of how political power works, use the pages referenced below.

The World of Work
pp. 5–6

19 Literary Element
Characterization

Question How does this response to the description of Cawdor's death characterize Duncan? *(While responses will vary, students should note that he rather cynically states that "one can't judge a book by its cover." He shows little humanity and makes no attempt to understand the whys behind Cawdor's betrayal.)*

That function is smothered in surmise,
18 And nothing is but what is not.
BANQUO. Look how our partner's rapt.
MACBETH *(aside)*. If chance will have me king, why, chance may
crown me
Without my stir.
BANQUO. New honors come upon him,
Like our strange garments, cleave not to their mold
But with the aid of use.
MACBETH *(aside)*. Come what come may,
Time and the hour runs through the roughest day.
BANQUO. Worthy Macbeth, we stay upon your leisure.
MACBETH. Give me your favor. My dull brain was wrought
With things forgotten. Kind gentlemen, your pains
Are registered where every day I turn
The leaf to read them. Let us toward the King.
(*Aside to* BANQUO.) Think upon what hath chanced,
and at more time,
The interim having weighed it, let us speak
Our free hearts each to other.
BANQUO (*to* MACBETH). Very gladly.
MACBETH (*to* BANQUO). Till then, enough. Come, friends.

SCENE 4

Summary *The king thanks Macbeth and Banquo for their brave fighting. He names his son Malcolm as his successor. Macbeth, his ambition growing, realizes that Malcolm is an obstacle to fulfilling the witches' prophecy that he will be king. He begins to plan to murder King Duncan.*

Trumpets sound offstage. Enter DUNCAN, LENNOX, MALCOLM, DONALBAIN, *and* ATTENDANTS.

DUNCAN. Is execution done on Cawdor? Are not
Those in commission yet returned?
MALCOLM. My liege,
They are not yet come back. But I have spoke
With one that saw him die, who did report
That very frankly he confessed his treasons,
Implored Your Highness' pardon, and set forth
A deep repentance. Nothing in his life
Became him like the leaving it. He died
As one that had been studied in his death
To throw away the dearest thing he owed
As 'twere a careless trifle.
DUNCAN. There's no art
19 To find the mind's construction in the face.

142 surmise (sər mīz′), *n.* guesswork.
140–143 My thought . . . is not. My thought, in which the murder is still only a fantasy, so disturbs me that all power of action is smothered by imagination, and only unreal imaginings seem real to me.
147 strange garments, new clothes.

150 we stay . . . leisure, we stand ready to serve when you call.

153–154 where . . . read them, in my mind and heart.

11–12 There's no art . . . face. There is no way of judging a person's thoughts from his or her appearance.

MINI-LESSON: GRAMMAR
Pronoun-Antecedent Agreement

Teach You might write the following lines from *Macbeth* on the board or pass out copies to students:

- "Noble Banquo,/*that* hast no less deserved . . ." (p. 127, lines 29–30)
- ". . . know/*We* will establish our estate . . ." (p. 127, lines 36–37)
- "*It* is a peerless kinsman." (p. 128, line 58)
- "Conduct me to *mine* host." (p. 131, line 29)

Remind students that the language, including grammatical usage, is continuously changing. Shakespeare's usage is not necessarily standard now.

Activity Idea Ask students to examine the pronouns and antecedents in the four lines above, correct any archaic usage, and explain why. *(Answers: **1st line:** no change—Duncan's usage is called "the royal we," which is still employed by royalty and the pope when making proclamations. **2nd line:** substitute* who *for* that*;* that *is used for an inanimate object,* who *for a person. **3rd line:** substitute he for it; kinsman, a person, calls for the third-person masculine pronoun* he*, not the neuter* it*. **4th line:** substitute* my *for* mine*, a pronoun no longer current [in Shakespeare's day,* mine *was a form of* my*, used to modify a noun beginning with a vowel or* h*].)*

He was a gentleman on whom I built
An absolute trust.
(*Enter* MACBETH, BANQUO, ROSS, *and* ANGUS.)
O worthiest cousin!
The sin of my ingratitude even now
Was heavy on me. Thou art so far before
That swiftest wing of recompense is slow
To overtake thee. Would thou hadst less deserved,
That the proportion both of thanks and payment
Might have been mine! Only I have left to say,
More is thy due than more than all can pay.
MACBETH. The service and the loyalty I owe,
In doing it, pays itself. Your Highness' part
Is to receive our duties; and our duties
Are to your throne and state children and servants,
Which do but what they should by doing everything
Safe toward your love and honor.
DUNCAN. Welcome hither!
I have begun to plant thee, and will labor
To make thee full of growing. Noble Banquo,
That hast no less deserved, nor must be known
No less to have done so, let me infold thee
And hold thee to my heart.
BANQUO. There if I grow,
The harvest is your own.
DUNCAN. My plenteous joys,
Wanton in fullness, seek to hide themselves
In drops of sorrow. Sons, kinsmen, thanes,
And you whose places are the nearest, know
We will establish our estate upon

Our eldest, Malcolm, and whom we name hereafter
The Prince of Cumberland; which honor must

Not unaccompanied invest him only,
But signs of nobleness, like stars, shall shine
On all deservers. From hence to Inverness,
And bind us further to you.
MACBETH. The rest is labor which is not used for you.
I'll be myself the harbinger and make joyful
The hearing of my wife with your approach;
So humbly take my leave.
DUNCAN. My worthy Cawdor!
MACBETH *(aside)*. The Prince of Cumberland! This is a step
On which I must fall down or else o'erleap,
For in my way it lies. Stars, hide your fires;
Let not light see my black and deep desires.

17 recompense (rek′əm pens), *n.* reward.

37 establish . . . upon, name as heir to the throne.

42 Inverness, the location of Macbeth's castle, Dunsinane.

44 the rest . . . you. Resting is work for me, when I am doing nothing to help you.

45 harbinger (här′bən jər), *n.* forerunner.

22 ■ What are Macbeth's "black and deep desires"? What stands in his way?

20 Literary Focus
Plot

Question How does Duncan's naming Malcolm heir to the throne move the plot? *(Possible response: According to the witches, "chance" will crown Macbeth without any action on his part; now, with Malcolm named heir, Macbeth is unwilling to leave the outcome to chance.)*

21 Historical Note
Royal Succession

As today's heir to the throne of Great Britain is named Prince of Wales, the heir to the throne of Scotland was given the title Prince of Cumberland.

22 Literary Element
Imagery

Responses His desire is to be king for which he will pay any price; Malcolm is now ahead of him in line for the throne.

Question Why doesn't Macbeth just say "I must not expose my desire to become king"? *(Possible response: The light and dark imagery of "hide your fires; /Let not light see my black desires" vividly exposes his burning ambition.)*

BUILDING ENGLISH PROFICIENCY

ESL LEP ELD SAE LD

Exploring Motivation

The following activities might help students understand Macbeth's ambition, which begins to become obvious on page 127.

Activity Ideas

- Bring newspapers to class. Ask students in small groups to look for examples of ambitious people. Have them identify what each hopes to gain. You also might have them speculate about what a highly ambitious person might end up losing.
- Have students create a web for the word *ambitions,* as shown in this sample.

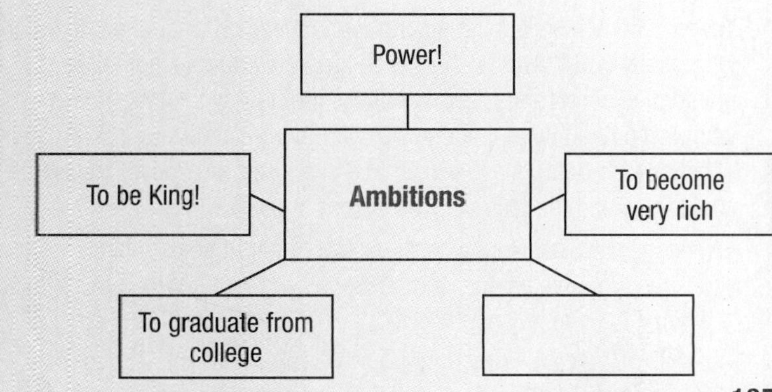

Response to Caption Question While responses will vary, students should note that an effective Lady Macbeth must have great presence and must radiate strength and ruthlessness; youth and beauty are unnecessary and might even detract from the characterization.

Visual Literacy This painting is a portrait of an actress, Ellen Terry, not a portrait of Lady Macbeth. John Singer Sargent has simply costumed and posed Miss Terry as a character she first played in 1888.

Question What do you think Sargent implies by posing his subject as Lady Macbeth crowning herself? *(Possible response: that Miss Terry was the queen of the English stage, a position she had earned through her interpretations of such characters as Lady Macbeth)*

The acclaimed actress Ellen Terry (1847–1928) is shown in her role as Lady Macbeth in this 1889 painting by John Singer Sargent. If you were casting a contemporary production of *Macbeth,* what actress would you choose to play the role of Lady Macbeth? Explain your choice.

The eye wink at the hand; yet let that be
Which the eye fears, when it is done, to see. *(Exit.)*
DUNCAN. True, worthy Banquo. He is full so valiant,
And in his commendations I am fed;
It is a banquet to me. Let's after him,
Whose care is gone before to bid us welcome.
It is a peerless kinsman. *(Trumpets sound.)*

55 commendation (kom′ən dā′shən), *n.* praise.

SCENE 5

Summary *When she reads Macbeth's letter about the witches' prophecies, Lady Macbeth begins to plot also—especially when she learns that Duncan will spend the night as their guest. When Macbeth returns, she encourages him to commit the murder soon.*

MINI-LESSON: LITERARY ELEMENT

Dramatic Irony

Teach Irony results from a contrast between what appears to be and what really is. *Situational irony* is triggered by an unexpected or unintended occurrence. *Verbal irony* is created by a contrast between what is said and what is meant. *Dramatic irony* refers to a situation in which events or facts not known to a character are known to the audience. Read the following lines from pages 127–128:

- MACBETH: "Stars, hide your fires;/Let not light see my black and deep desires./The eye wink at the hand; yet let that be/Which the eye fears, when it is done, to see."
- DUNCAN: "True, worthy Banquo. He is full so valiant,/And in his commendations I am fed . . . It is a peerless kinsman."

Questions What kind of irony is displayed here? Why? *(Dramatic irony: Duncan is praising a "peerless kinsman" who is in the process of planning Duncan's murder.)*

Activity Idea Suggest that students search scenes 1–4 for other examples of irony to discuss with the class.

Macbeth's castle at Inverness. Enter LADY MACBETH *reading a letter.*

LADY MACBETH *(reads).* "They met me in the day of success; and I have learned by the perfect'st report they have more in them than mortal knowledge. When I burnt in desire to question them further, they made themselves air, into which they vanished. Whiles I stood rapt in the wonder of it came missives from the King, who all-hailed me 'Thane of Cawdor,' by which title, before these Weird Sisters saluted me, and referred me to the coming on of time with 'Hail, king that shalt be!' This have I thought good to deliver thee, my dearest partner of greatness, that thou mightst not lose the dues of rejoicing by being ignorant of what greatness is promised thee. Lay it to thy heart, and farewell."

23
Glamis thou art, and Cawdor, and shalt be
What thou art promised. Yet do I fear thy nature;
It is too full o' the milk of human kindness
To catch the nearest way. Thou wouldst be great,
Art not without ambition, but without
The illness should attend it. What thou wouldst highly,
That wouldst thou holily; wouldst not play false,
And yet wouldst wrongly win. Thou'dst have, great Glamis,
That which cries "Thus thou must do," if thou have it,
And that which rather thou dost fear to do
Than wishest should be undone. Hie thee hither,
That I may pour my spirits in thine ear
And chastise with the valor of my tongue
All that impedes thee from the golden round
Which fate and metaphysical aid doth seem
24 To have thee crowned withal. *(Enter a* MESSENGER.*)*
What is your tidings?

MESSENGER. The King comes here tonight.

LADY MACBETH. Thou'rt mad to say it!
Is not thy master with him, who, were't so,
Would have informed for preparation?

MESSENGER. So please you, it is true. Our thane is coming.
One of my fellows had the speed of him,
Who, almost dead for breath, had scarcely more
Than would make up his message.

LADY MACBETH. Give him tending;
He brings great news. *(Exit* MESSENGER.*)*
The raven himself is hoarse
25 That croaks the fatal entrance of Duncan
Under my battlements. Come, you spirits
That tend on mortal thoughts, unsex me here
And fill me from the crown to the toe top-full
Of direst cruelty! Make thick my blood;

5 **missive** (mis′iv), *n.* message.

■ What does this letter reveal about the relationship between Macbeth and Lady Macbeth?

17 **illness . . . it,** the unscrupulousness you need to achieve that ambition.

25 **golden round,** the crown.
25 **metaphysical,** supernatural.

32 **had the speed of him,** outdistanced him.

35 **raven.** Long believed to be a bird of ill omen, the raven was said to foretell death by its croaking.
38 **mortal thoughts,** murderous thoughts.

23 Literary Element
Characterization

Response The two are soulmates—they fully understand each other and share a single ambition to gain great power.

Question What might this say about Lady Macbeth's character? *(Possible response: that her principles are as compromised by ambition as her husband's)*

24 Literary Element
Characterization

Question After reading Lady Macbeth's response to her husband's letter, how would you describe her character? *(Possible response: She is even more ambitious, more ruthless than her husband; she may push him into murder.)*

25 Literary Focus
Plot

Question What does the line "The raven himself is hoarse/That croaks the fatal entrance of Duncan/Under my battlements" suggest about what happens next? *(that Duncan rides to his death within the battlements of Glamis Castle)*

BUILDING ENGLISH PROFICIENCY

ESL LEP ELD SAE LD

Analyzing Character

The soliloquy on page 129 introduces Lady Macbeth. Help students focus on her character in greater detail.

1. Have students begin a character web about Lady Macbeth, beginning with traits that she displays in Scene 5.

2. Ask students to add a trait and an example, on a new line and circle, as they read the following scenes:

- Act One, Scenes 6 and 7
- Act Two, Scenes 2 and 3
- Act Two, Scenes 2 and 4
- Act Five, Scene 2

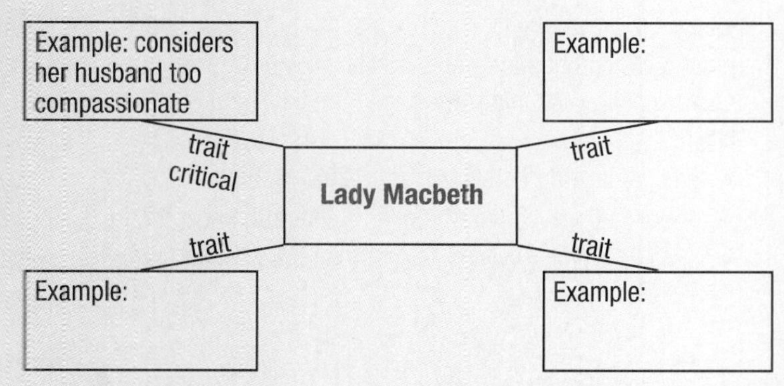

26 Literary Focus
Plot

Question How do Lady Macbeth and Macbeth resolve to deal with the prophecy now? *(Possible response: to murder Duncan in the night)*

27 Literary Element
Irony

Question What is ironic about Duncan's statement? *(Possible response: He praises the place of his own murder.)*

Literary Criticism

"It is true that Lady Macbeth is not naturally depraved or conscienceless. . . . But she deliberately chooses evil, her choice being more deliberate than her husband's. Macbeth speaks of ambition being his only spur; but he would never have overcome his reluctance to commit murder without the chastisement of his wife's tongue. She, not metaphorically or symbolically, but in deadly earnest, invokes the powers of darkness to take possession of her. . . ."

Kenneth Muir
The Arden Edition of the Works of William Shakespeare: Macbeth

---

Stop up th' access and passage to remorse,
That no compunctious visitings of nature
Shake my fell purpose, nor keep peace between
Th' effect and it! Come to my woman's breasts
And take my milk for gall, you murdering ministers,
Wherever in your sightless substances
You wait on nature's mischief! Come, thick night,
And pall thee in the dunnest smoke of hell,
That my keēn knife see not the wound it makes,
Nor heaven peep through the blanket of the dark
To cry "Hold, hold!" (*Enter* MACBETH.)
Great Glamis! Worthy Cawdor!
Greater than both by the all-hail hereafter!
Thy letters have transported me beyond
This ignorant present, and I feel now
The future in the instant.

MACBETH. My dearest love,
Duncan comes here tonight.

LADY MACBETH. And when goes hence?

MACBETH. Tomorrow, as he purposes.

LADY MACBETH. O, never
Shall sun that morrow see!
Your face, my thane, is as a book where men
May read strange matters. To beguile the time,
Look like the time; bear welcome in your eye,
Your hand, your tongue. Look like th' innocent flower,
But be the serpent under 't. He that's coming
Must be provided for; and you shall put
26 This night's great business into my dispatch,
Which shall to all our nights and days to come
Give solely sovereign sway and masterdom.

MACBETH. We will speak further.

LADY MACBETH. Only look up clear.
To alter favor ever is to fear.
Leave all the rest to me.

42 compunctious . . . nature, natural feelings of compassion.
43–44 keep peace . . . and it, come between my intention and my carrying out of it.

48 pall (pôl), *v.* wrap.
48 dunnest, darkest; murkiest.

60 beguile (bi gīl′), *v.* deceive.
60–61 To beguile . . . time, to deceive people, act as they expect you to act.

69 to alter . . . fear, to change facial expression shows fear.

SCENE 6

Summary *Duncan and his sons arrive at Macbeth's castle and are welcomed by Lady Macbeth.*

Outside Macbeth's castle. Music sounds offstage. Enter DUNCAN, MALCOLM, DONALBAIN, BANQUO, LENNOX, MACDUFF, ROSS, ANGUS, *and* ATTENDANTS *carrying torches.*

DUNCAN. This castle hath a pleasant seat. The air
27 Nimbly and sweetly recommends itself

MINI-LESSON: READING/THINKING SKILLS

Synthesize

Teach Explain that literary themes are not stated explicitly. Readers must put together statements and observations from throughout a work and synthesize meaning. Then read the following quotations from the play:

- "Fair is foul, and foul is fair." (p. 120)
- "There's no art /To find the mind's construction in the face." (p. 126)
- "Look like th' innocent flower,/But be the serpent under 't." (p. 130)

Question What thematic statement can you synthesize from these quotations? *(Possible responses: Appearances are deceiving; evil and good are not external qualities.)*

Activity Idea Suggest that students, working in groups, put together other sets of quotes and synthesize thematic statements from them. Ask groups to share their ideas with the class.

Unto our gentle senses.
BANQUO. This guest of summer,
The temple-haunting martlet, does approve
By his loved mansionry that the heaven's breath
Smells wooingly here. No jutty, frieze,
Buttress, nor coign of vantage but this bird
Hath made his pendent bed and procreant cradle.
Where they most breed and haunt, I have observed
The air is delicate. (*Enter* LADY MACBETH.)
DUNCAN. See, see, our honored hostess!
The love that follows us sometimes is our trouble,
Which still we thank as love. Herein I teach you
How you shall bid God 'ild us for your pains,
And thank us for your trouble.
LADY MACBETH. All our service
In every point twice done, and then done double,
Were poor and single business to contend
Against those honors deep and broad wherewith
Your Majesty loads our house. For those of old,
And the late dignities heaped up to them,
We rest your hermits.
DUNCAN. Where's the Thane of Cawdor?
We coursed him at the heels, and had a purpose
To be his purveyor; but he rides well,
And his great love, sharp as his spur, hath holp him
To his home before us. Fair and noble hostess,
We are your guest tonight.
LADY MACBETH. Your servants ever
Have theirs, themselves, and what is theirs in compt
To make their audit at Your Highness' pleasure,
Still to return your own.
DUNCAN. Give me your hand.
Conduct me to mine host. We love him highly,
And shall continue our graces towards him.
By your leave, hostess.

4 martlet . . . does approve, swallow demonstrates.

6–8 no jutty . . . procreant cradle. The swallow has built a nest in every architectural space available.

13 God 'ild, literally "God yield," used in returning thanks.

20 We rest your hermits. Like religious hermits, we will pray for you.

22 purveyor (pər vā′ ər), *n.* forerunner.

25–28 Your servants . . . own. Since we are your servants, all that we have is ready to be delivered to you.

SCENE 7

Summary *Macbeth decides he cannot murder Duncan, but Lady Macbeth convinces him once more. They plan to drug Duncan's servants and to murder him in his sleep.*

Outside a dining hall in MACBETH'S *castle. Music sounds offstage. Attendants with torches and servants with dishes of food cross the stage and exit.*

MACBETH. If it were done when 'tis done, then 'twere well
It were done quickly. If th' assassination

28 Reading/Thinking Skills
Visualize

Form a mental picture as you read Banquo's description of how the birds nest about the castle.

Question How does this increase the sense of irony? *(Possible response: It enlarges the disparity between the appearance of the castle and the character of its owners.)*

29 Reading/Thinking Skills
Recognizing the Use of Persuasion

Questions

- What is the purpose of Lady Macbeth's speech to Duncan? *(She plays the perfect hostess, throwing Duncan and everyone off the trail.)*
- How successful is she in achieving her purpose? *(Judging by Duncan's response, she is quite successful—he suspects nothing.)*
- How do her persuasive techniques for Duncan differ from those she uses on Macbeth? *(She uses deference and exaggerated good manners with Duncan; she goads and makes demands of her husband.)*

BUILDING ENGLISH PROFICIENCY

Expanding Vocabulary Notebooks

Help students develop the habit of looking up unfamiliar words in the dictionary and adding them to their vocabulary notebooks.

1. Point out the word *pall* on page 130, Scene 5, line 48. Explain that this verb is now almost always used only in its infinitive form, as in this sentence:

"All this gossip is beginning to *pall* on me."

2. Encourage students to write, define, and make up original sentences using these words from pages 130–131: *access, purpose, nimbly, purveyor, pall, sway, delicate, audit.*

Word	Meaning	Sentence
access	right to enter	Students were denied access to their lockers.

30 Reading/Thinking Skills

Generalize/Draw Conclusions

Question What does Macbeth fear? *(Possible responses: He fears having to live with himself after committing the murder; he fears that he will be damned in the next life.)*

31 Reading/Thinking Skills

Recognize Values

Questions

- What values does Macbeth hold that would argue against the murderous plan? *(Possible responses: family loyalty, patriotism, etiquette, esteem of Duncan's character, concern about the nation's mourning, pride in the honors he has received and the good opinions he has won)*
- What pushes him toward murder? *(Possible responses: ambition; his wife's disdain)*

32 Reading/Thinking Skills

Recognize Propaganda Techniques

Question What technique does Lady Macbeth use to goad husband? *(She calls him a coward.)*

Could trammel up the consequence, and catch
With his surcease success—that but this blow
Might be the be-all and the end-all!—here,
But here, upon this bank and shoal of time,
We'd jump the life to come. But in these cases
30 We still have judgment here, that we but teach
Bloody instructions, which, being taught, return
To plague th' inventor. This evenhanded justice
Commends th' ingredience of our poisoned chalice
To our own lips. He's here in double trust:
First, as I am his kinsman and his subject,
Strong both against the deed; then, as his host,
Who should against his murderer shut the door,
Not bear the knife myself. Besides, this Duncan
Hath borne his faculties so meek, hath been
So clear in his great office, that his virtues
Will plead like angels, trumpet-tongued, against
The deep damnation of his taking-off;
And Pity, like a naked newborn babe
Striding the blast, or heaven's cherubin, horsed
Upon the sightless couriers of the air,
Shall blow the horrid deed in every eye,
That tears shall drown the wind. I have no spur
To prick the sides of my intent, but only
31 Vaulting ambition, which o'erleaps itself
And falls on th' other— (*Enter* LADY MACBETH.)
How now, what news?

LADY MACBETH. He has almost supped. Why have you left the chamber?
MACBETH. Hath he asked for me?
LADY MACBETH. Know you not he has?
MACBETH. We will proceed no further in this business.
He hath honored me of late, and I have bought
Golden opinions from all sorts of people,
Which would be worn now in their newest gloss,
Not cast aside so soon.
LADY MACBETH. Was the hope drunk
Wherein you dressed yourself? Hath it slept since?
And wakes it now, to look so green and pale
At what it did so freely? From this time
Such I account thy love. Art thou afeard
To be the same in thine own act and valor
As thou art in desire? Wouldst thou have that
32 Which thou esteem'st the ornament of life,
And live a coward in thine own esteem,
Letting "I dare not" wait upon "I would,"

4 surcease (sər sēs′), *n.* death.

7 jump, risk.

17 faculties, royal powers.

20 taking-off, murder.

22 striding the blast, riding the wind.

23 couriers of the air, winds.

25–28 I have . . . th' other. I have nothing to stimulate me to accomplishing my purpose but ambition, which is apt to become too great.

43 ornament of life, the crown.

MINI-LESSON: WRITING STYLE

Conveying State of Mind Through Soliloquy

Teach You might read Macbeth's soliloquy (pp. 131–132) to the class and point out that Macbeth, in a highly disturbed state of mind, is thinking to himself, not speaking out loud.

Question What stylistic devices has Shakespeare introduced to show Macbeth's state of mind? *(Possible responses: interruptions [lines 4–5]; repetition [lines 5–6]; changes in logical structure* [first, *line 13, is not followed by* second]; *quick change from plain speech to high-flown imagery [lines13–25]; paradoxical statements* [ambition, which o'erleaps itself]*)*

Activity Idea Students might write a monologue or soliloquy that shows a character who is disturbed about something. Encourage them to use some of the same stylistic devices that Shakespeare employed. Students might perform their speeches for the class.

Like the poor cat i' the adage?
MACBETH. Prithee, peace!
I dare do all that may become a man;
Who dares do more is none.
LADY MACBETH. What beast was't, then,
That made you break this enterprise to me?
When you durst do it, then you were a man;
And, to be more than what you were, you would
Be so much more the man. Nor time nor place
Did then adhere, and yet you would make both.
33 They have made themselves, and that their fitness now
Does unmake you. I have given suck, and know
How tender 'tis to love the babe that milks me;
I would, while it was smiling in my face,
Have plucked my nipple from his boneless gums
And dashed the brains out, had I so sworn as you
Have done to this.
MACBETH. If we should fail?
LADY MACBETH. We fail?
But screw your courage to the sticking place
And we'll not fail. When Duncan is asleep—
Whereto the rather shall his day's hard journey
Soundly invite him—his two chamberlains
Will I with wine and wassail so convince
That memory, the warder of the brain,
Shall be a fume, and the receipt of reason
A limbeck only. When in swinish sleep
Their drenchèd natures lies as in a death,
What cannot you and I perform upon
Th' unguarded Duncan? What not put upon
His spongy officers, who shall bear the guilt
Of our great quell?
MACBETH. Bring forth men-children only!
For thy undaunted mettle should compose
Nothing but males. Will it not be received,
When we have marked with blood those sleepy two
Of his own chamber and used their very daggers,
That they have done 't?
LADY MACBETH. Who dares receive it other,
As we shall make our griefs and clamor roar
Upon his death?
MACBETH. I am settled, and bend up
Each corporal agent to this terrible feat.
Away, and mock the time with fairest show.
False face must hide what the false heart doth know.

46 cat . . . adage. The adage, or proverb, is "The cat would eat fish, but would not wet her feet."

52–53 nor time . . . adhere, there was no suitable time or place to commit the murder.

66–68 memory . . . only, memory and reason both will disappear, like the vapor of the alcohol they drink.

72 spongy, drunken.

73 quell, murder.

74 mettle (met'l), *n.* courage.

34 ■ What does Lady Macbeth reveal about herself in this scene?

80–81 bend up . . . feat, direct all my bodily powers to executing the murder.

33 Reader's Response
Challenging the Text

Critics have long argued about the occasion to which Lady Macbeth refers. Encourage students to enter into the debate by asking the following.

Question Can you make sense of Lady Macbeth's charge that Macbeth previously introduced the idea of murdering Duncan and promised to carry it out? *(Possible responses: The suggestion was in the beginning of Macbeth's letter; a scene has been lost from the play; Macbeth and Lady Macbeth had discussed the possibility before the action of the play.)*

34 Literary Element
Characterization

Response She is ambitious, clever, manipulative, devious, implacable, self-assured, and utterly ruthless.

Check Test

1. What do the witches predict? *(Macbeth will become thane of Cawdor and king; Banquo will father kings.)*
2. What leads Duncan to honor Macbeth? *(Macbeth defeats the King of Norway.)*
3. What honor does Duncan bestow on Malcolm? *(He names him successor to the throne.)*
4. What is the main conflict for Macbeth in Act One? *(whether to murder the king)*
5. How will Macbeth and Lady Macbeth act when Duncan's death is discovered? *(They will pretend to be grief-stricken.)*

Unit 2 Resource Book
Alternate Check Test, p. 13

BUILDING ENGLISH PROFICIENCY

ESL LEP ELD SAE LD

Sequencing Plot Events

This activity may help students keep track of the plot as they finish each Act.

1. Organize a small group to summarize, in two or three simple sentences, key events in each Scene. Ask them to write on large cards, one per Scene. Instruct them not to put scene numbers on the cards.

2. Shuffle the cards and ask another group to sort them in sequential order.

3. Choose a different group to write summaries for each Act. Number and post the cards in correct sequence.

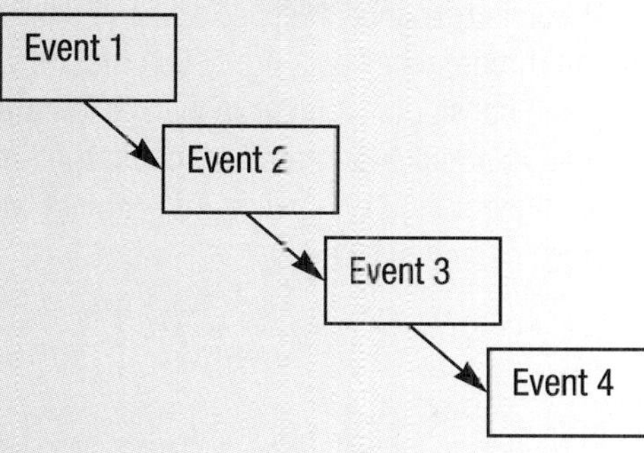

After Reading

MAKING CONNECTIONS

1. Possible response: Lady Macbeth seems stronger—she is able to bend Macbeth to her will and overcome his objections. She also seems less affected by conscience.

2. Possible response: Unbridled ambition is a serious defect in Macbeth's character, so the witches' suggestion plays on this flaw. Banquo has more integrity, so he finds it easier to make an objective judgment and not be drawn in.

3. the plot to murder Duncan

4. Possible response: He is not thinking clearly and is disturbed by the conflict between his conscience and his ambition.

5. Possible response: Ambition can lead to the destruction of others for selfish reasons; the Golden Rule is one idea of how far it is safe to assert oneself.

VOCABULARY STUDY

1. disdains
2. recompense
3. disburses
4. harbinger
5. mettle

Unit 2 Resource Book
Vocabulary, p. 11
Vocabulary Test, p. 14

Selection Test

Unit 2 Resource Book
pp. 15–16

Act 1

After Reading

Making Connections

Shaping Your Response

1. Which character do you believe is the stronger, Macbeth or Lady Macbeth? Why do you think so?

Analyzing the Play

2. Why do you think Macbeth and Banquo react in the ways they do to the prophecies of the witches and to their fulfillment?
3. An **aside** is a dramatic convention in which a character voices his or her thoughts so that the audience—but not the other characters—can hear. What is foreshadowed by Macbeth's aside in scene 3, lines 128–143?
4. A **soliloquy** is a dramatic convention in which a character voices his or her thoughts while alone on stage. What does Macbeth's soliloquy in scene 7, lines 1–28 reveal about his state of mind?

Extending the Ideas

5. Macbeth and Lady Macbeth seem to be very ambitious. How far can ambition lead a person into asserting his or her **individuality** over that of others? How far is too far?

Literary Focus: Plot Structure

In act 1, Shakespeare establishes the setting and the mood, introduces the characters and presents the conflicts that will drive the **plot.**

1. Write the names of the characters you feel will be key in the plot.
2. In one sentence describe the situation and identify the conflicts.
3. List the steps Macbeth and Lady Macbeth plan to follow in the assassination of King Duncan.

Vocabulary Study

Select the word that fits the meaning of each sentence.

1. King Duncan (disdains, contends) the Thane of Cawdor because he is a traitor.
2. Duncan gives Macbeth Cawdor's title as a (surmise, recompense) for his brave fighting.
3. The Scottish army will not allow the Norwegian king to bury his men until he (disburses, flouts) money to them.
4. Macbeth wants to be the (harbinger, minion) of the news of the witches' predictions.
5. Macbeth praises Lady Macbeth for her (commendation, mettle) in wanting to proceed with the murder of Duncan.

134 UNIT TWO: THE ELIZABETHAN ERA

LITERARY FOCUS: PLOT

1. Lady Macbeth, Macbeth, Duncan, Banquo, Malcolm

2. Possible response: Macbeth, who is next in line for the throne, receives a prediction that he will be king and considers whether to wait or to murder Duncan and make the prophecy come true immediately; this decision brings him into conflict with his conscience and his wife.

3. Once Duncan is asleep, Lady Macbeth will spike the wine of his chamberlains; Macbeth and Lady Macbeth will steal the chamberlains' daggers and use them to kill Duncan; they will smear the chamberlains with Duncan's blood to make them seem guilty; they will act grief-stricken as part of the cover-up.

Act Two

SCENE 1

Summary *Macbeth seeks to gain the loyalty of Banquo. As he waits for Lady Macbeth's signal that all is in order for the murder of Duncan, a vision of a dagger appears before him.*

Courtyard of MACBETH'S *castle. Enter* BANQUO *and* FLEANCE, *carrying a torch.*

BANQUO. How goes the night, boy?
FLEANCE. The moon is down, I have not heard the clock.
BANQUO. And she goes down at twelve.
FLEANCE. I take 't, 'tis later, sir.
BANQUO. Hold, take my sword. *(He gives him his sword.)*
There's husbandry in heaven;
Their candles are all out. Take thee that too.
(He gives him his belt and dagger.)
A heavy summons lies like lead upon me,
And yet I would not sleep. Merciful powers,
Restrain in me the cursèd thoughts that nature
Gives way to in repose. 1
(Enter MACBETH *and a* SERVANT *with a torch.)*
Give me my sword. Who's there? *(He takes the sword.)*
MACBETH. A friend.
BANQUO. What, sir, not yet at rest? The King's abed.
He hath been in unusual pleasure,
And sent forth great largess to your offices.
This diamond he greets your wife withal,
By the name of most kind hostess, and shut up
In measureless content. *(He gives a diamond.)*
MACBETH. Being unprepared,
Our will became the servant to defect,
Which else should free have wrought.
BANQUO. All's well.
2 I dreamt last night of the three Weird Sisters.
To you they have showed some truth.
MACBETH. I think not of them.
Yet, when we can entreat an hour to serve,
We would spend it in some words upon that business,
If you would grant the time.
BANQUO. At your kind'st leisure.
MACBETH. If you shall cleave to my consent when 'tis,
It shall make honor for you.
BANQUO. So I lose none
In seeking to augment it, but still keep
My bosom franchised and allegiance clear,

4 **husbandry,** economy.

■ At this point, what questions might you ask Banquo about his "cursèd thoughts"?

14 **great largess . . . offices,** many gifts of money to be distributed among your servants.
16–17 **shut up . . . content,** has ended his day greatly contented.
17–19 **being unprepared . . . wrought.** The unexpectedness of Duncan's visit has prevented us from entertaining him as we would have liked.

26 **if you . . . when 'tis,** if you ally yourself with me when the time comes.

28 augment (ôg ment′), *v.* increase.

During Reading

Vocabulary Preview

augment, increase
palpable, definite
requite, repay
scruple, doubt
suborn, hire or bribe

Students can add the words and definitions to their Writer's Notebooks.

1 Reading/Thinking Skills
Find the Main Idea

Response Are your thoughts about making sure your son becomes king or about your suspicions about Macbeth? Were these dreams or daydreams?

2 Literary Element
Connotation/Denotation

Questions What do you think Banquo's line "I dreamt last night of the three Weird Sisters" connotes? *(The witches' prophecies regarding Macbeth and Banquo's heirs have been on his mind.)* What do you think Macbeth's reply, "I think not of them" connotes? *(that Macbeth thinks of little else)*

Unit 2 Resource Book
Graphic Organizer, p. 17
Study Guide, p. 18

ACT TWO SUMMARY

Macbeth

While excited by the witches' prophecy, Banquo resolves to remain loyal to the king. Macbeth, by contrast, plans to murder Duncan. As Macbeth awaits a signal that all is ready, a vision of a dagger appears to him. After murdering Duncan, the unnerved Macbeth carries away the bloody daggers. His wife returns them and smears blood on the sleeping grooms. A knocking at the gate sends Macbeth and his wife to bed. The gate is finally opened to Macduff and Lennox by a drunken porter. Macduff, who has business with the king, discovers the murder. In simulated fury, Macbeth kills the grooms. Malcolm and Donalbain, fearing a fate like their father's, the king, flee. Macduff pointedly states that he will go to Fife, not to Scone where Macbeth has gone to be crowned.

*For summaries in other languages, see the **Building English Proficiency** book.*

3 Literary Element
Symbolism

Questions What do you think the dagger Macbeth sees before him symbolizes? *(the murder he is contemplating)* When Macbeth draws his own dagger, he sees blood on it; what does the blood symbolize? *(Possible response: the guilt he feels for even contemplating the act)*

4 Literary Element
Figurative Language

Questions Can you identify examples of personification, metaphor, and simile in lines 48 to 57? *(personification—nature, witchcraft, and murder; a metaphor compares Murder's steps to Tarquin's strides; a simile compares Murder's movement to that of a ghost)* What do you think this language tells us about Macbeth? *(Possible response: He has a vivid imagination and a highly developed conscience that makes him sensitive to the power of evil.)*

5 Reading/Thinking Skills
Understanding Sequence

Question What is this bell Macbeth hears? *(Lady Macbeth's signal that all has been made ready for murder)*

I shall be counseled.
MACBETH. Good repose the while!
BANQUO. Thanks, sir. The like to you.
(Exit BANQUO *with* FLEANCE.)
MACBETH (*to* SERVANT). Go bid thy mistress, when my drink is ready,
She strike upon the bell. Get thee to bed. (*Exit* SERVANT.)
Is this a dagger which I see before me,
The handle toward my hand? Come, let me clutch thee.
I have thee not, and yet I see thee still.
Art thou not, fatal vision, sensible
To feeling as to sight? Or art thou but
A dagger of the mind, a false creation,
Proceeding from the heat-oppressèd brain?
I see thee yet, in form as palpable
As this which now I draw. *(He draws a dagger.)*
Thou marshall'st me the way that I was going,
And such an instrument I was to use.
Mine eyes are made the fools o' th' other senses,
Or else worth all the rest. I see thee still,
3 And on thy blade and dudgeon gouts of blood,
Which was not so before. There's no such thing.
It is the bloody business which informs
Thus to mine eyes. Now o'er the one half world
Nature seems dead, and wicked dreams abuse
The curtained sleep. Witchcraft celebrates
Pale Hecate's offerings, and withered Murder,
Alarumed by his sentinel, the wolf,
Whose howl's his watch, thus with his stealthy pace,
With Tarquin's ravishing strides, towards his design
4 Moves like a ghost. Thou sure and firm-set earth,
Hear not my steps which way they walk, for fear
Thy very stones prate of my whereabouts
And take the present horror from the time
Which now suits with it. Whiles I threat, he lives;
5 Words to the heat of deeds too cold breath gives. *(A bell rings.)*
I go, and it is done. The bell invites me.
Hear it not, Duncan, for it is a knell
That summons thee to heaven or to hell.

27–30 So I . . . counseled. As long as I do not lose my honor in trying to increase it, and keep myself free and my loyalty to Duncan unstained, I will listen to you.

41 palpable (pal′pə bəl), *adj.* definite.
43 thou marshal'st me, you lead me.

47 dudgeon (duj′ən), *n.* handle.
49 inform, appear.

53 Hecate (hek′ə tē), goddess of witchcraft.

56 Tarquin (tär′kwən), one of the tyrannical kings of early Rome, who raped the chaste Lucrece.
59 prate, talk foolishly.

SCENE 2

Summary *Macbeth murders Duncan, but, in his confused state, fails to leave the daggers behind to incriminate Duncan's servants. Lady Macbeth returns the daggers to the bedchamber.*

A room in the castle. Enter LADY MACBETH.

MINI-LESSON: USAGE
Relative Pronouns Which and That

Teach Read the following lines from page 136:

"I see thee yet, in form as palpable/As this *which* now I draw./ Thou marshall'st me the way *that* I was going."

Point out that in modern usage, the word *that* is used for restrictive clauses; that is, clauses that provide information that defines the antecedent. *Which*, on the other hand, is used for nonrestrictive clauses; that is, clauses that provide parenthetical or incidental information. *Which* clauses are usually set off by commas.

Question How can you explain Shakespeare's use of the two relative pronouns? *(Possible response: The two relative pronouns seem to be interchangeable, and his decision to use one or the other seems to be based on sound; for example, "As this that now I draw" (line 42) would sound strange because of the juxtaposition of* this *and* that, *so Shakespeare used* which.*)*

Activity Ideas

- Have students rewrite Macbeth's soliloquy in modern English, using the appropriate relative pronouns.
- Have students work in small groups to make a list of props needed for Acts One and Two (so far)—diamond, dagger, and so on. Have them describe each prop, using a sentence with the relative pronoun *which* or *that*.

This illustration by Charles Ricketts is from *The Tragedie of Macbeth,* published in 1923. How does the dagger in Lady Macbeth's hand symbolize the guilt that she and her husband share? How do their differing poses illustrate their distinct reactions to the king's murder?

LADY MACBETH. That which hath made them drunk hath made me bold;
What hath quenched them hath given me fire. Hark! Peace!
It was the owl that shrieked, the fatal bellman,
Which gives the stern'st good-night. He is about it.
The doors are open; and the surfeited grooms
Do mock their charge with snores. I have drugged their possets,
That death and nature do contend about them
Whether they live or die.
MACBETH *(offstage).* Who's there? What, ho!
LADY MACBETH. Alack, I am afraid they have awaked,
And 'tis not done. Th' attempt and not the deed
Confounds us. Hark! I laid their daggers ready;
He could not miss 'em. Had he not resembled
My father as he slept, I had done 't.

3 owl . . . bellman. The screech of an owl was often interpreted as an omen of death.
6 posset, drink made of hot milk curdled with wine or ale.

Art Study

Responses to Caption Questions The dagger represents the murder plot—the means by which they procure their ends and incur guilt. Whispering seductively, Lady Macbeth leans into the act of murder, tempting him with the dagger. Macbeth recoils from it, blocking its way. Yet his eyes stray toward her face. He tries to resist, but will fail.

Visual Literacy Artists often use color to suggest character and mood.

Question What does the artist's use of color suggest? *(Possible response: Her red and orange scarves suggest blood flowing from her body; his orange and black scabbard and socks suggest that blood is rubbing off on him.)*

BUILDING ENGLISH PROFICIENCY

ESL LEP ELD SAE LD

Exploring Relationships Among Characters

Creating a character sociogram is one way to help students define and understand relationships among characters.

1. Ask students to make a diagram like the one shown. Have them write the names of the characters in the boxes.
2. Have students draw arrows between the boxes. Tell them to write on each arrow one word that describes the dominant feeling that characters have for one another at this point in the play (before Duncan's murder).

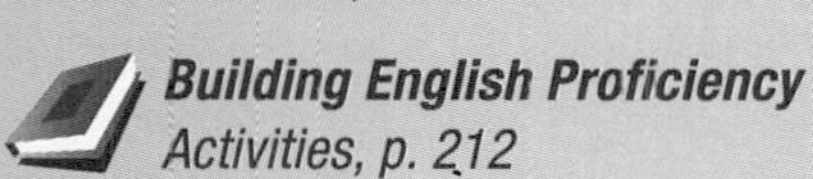

Building English Proficiency
Activities, p. 212

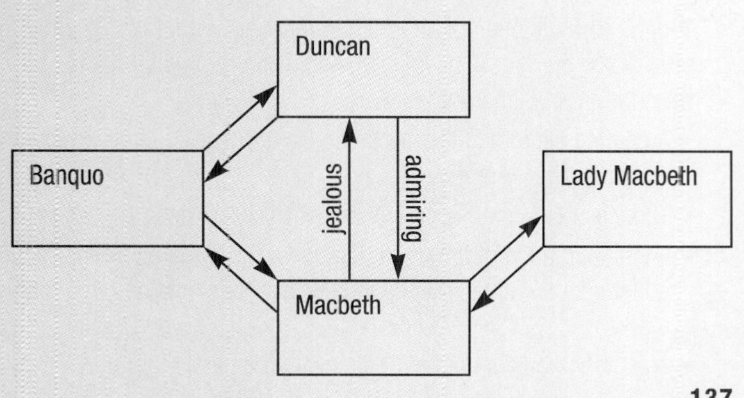

6 Literary Focus
Plot

Question What new conflict is introduced here? *(Possible response: As Macbeth predicted, the blow is not the be-all and end-all for him; he is in conflict with his sensitive conscience from the moment he commits the murder.)*

7 Literary Focus
Imagery

Question What attributes of sleep does this passage convey? *(Possible responses: Sleep is the province of the innocent with guilt-free consciences; it soothes worry, putting an end to each day's woes; it restores the body from the work of the day and eases the mind; it is essential to health.)*

8 Reading/Thinking Skills
Generalize/Draw Conclusions

Question What elements of Lady Macbeth's personality are revealed here? *(Possible responses: She is unimaginative, practical, sharp.)*

(Enter MACBETH *carrying bloody daggers.)*
My husband!
MACBETH. I have done the deed. Didst thou not hear a noise?
LADY MACBETH. I heard the owl scream and the crickets cry.
Did not you speak?
MACBETH. When?
LADY MACBETH. Now.
MACBETH. As I descended?
LADY MACBETH. Ay.
MACBETH. Hark! Who lies i' the second chamber?
LADY MACBETH. Donalbain.
MACBETH *(looking at his hands).* This is a sorry sight.
LADY MACBETH. A foolish thought, to say a sorry sight.
MACBETH. There's one did laugh in 's sleep, and one cried
"Murder!"
That they did wake each other. I stood and heard them.
But they did say their prayers, and addressed them
Again to sleep.
LADY MACBETH. There are two lodged together.
MACBETH. One cried "God bless us!" and "Amen!" the other,
As they had seen me with these hangman's hands.
List'ning their fear, I could not say "Amen"
When they did say "God bless us!"
LADY MACBETH. Consider it not so deeply.
MACBETH. But wherefore could not I pronounce "Amen"?
I had most need of blessing, and "Amen"
Stuck in my throat.
LADY MACBETH. These deeds must not be thought
After these ways; so, it will make us mad.
MACBETH. Methought I heard a voice cry "Sleep no more!
Macbeth does murder sleep," the innocent sleep,
Sleep that knits up the raveled sleave of care,
The death of each day's life, sore labor's bath,
Balm of hurt minds, great nature's second course,
Chief nourisher in life's feast—
LADY MACBETH. What do you mean?
MACBETH. Still it cried "Sleep no more!" to all the house;
"Glamis hath murdered sleep, and therefore Cawdor
Shall sleep no more; Macbeth shall sleep no more."
LADY MACBETH. Who was it that thus cried? Why, worthy thane,
You do unbend your noble strength to think
So brainsickly of things. Go get some water
And wash this filthy witness from your hand.
Why did you bring these daggers from the place?
They must lie there. Go, carry them and smear

29 two, Malcolm and Donalbain.
31 hangman's hands. In Elizabethan England, the hangman also had to "draw"—remove the entrails from—some of his victims.

41 raveled sleave, tangled thread.

MINI-LESSON: MECHANICS
Punctuation of Quotations

Teach Draw students' attention to Macbeth's quotation of other characters' words on page 138, lines 26–47. Then remind students of the basic rules for punctuating quotations:

- A comma separates the quotation from the attribution, whether it occurs before or after.
- The exact words of a speaker are enclosed in quotation marks.
- End punctuation of the quotation goes within the quotation marks, but punctuation of the sentence as a whole goes outside the quotation marks.
- A sentence that is quoted begins with a capital letter.

Question Which of these rules did Shakespeare (or his editor) follow on page 138? *(He used punctuation for the exact words of a speaker, used end punctuation properly, and began quoted sentences with capitals. He did not use commas to separate the attribution from the quotation.)*

Activity Idea For practice, students can pretend they are characters from Acts One and Two.

- Divide students into pairs and have students choose characters to be.
- Have each pair write a scene in which they express their views on the action and quote other characters (including each other) to make their points. Have each pair read their scene to the class.

The sleepy grooms with blood.

MACBETH. I'll go no more.
I am afraid to think what I have done;
Look on 't again I dare not.

LADY MACBETH. Infirm of purpose!
Give me the daggers. The sleeping and the dead
Are but as pictures. 'Tis the eye of childhood
That fears a painted devil. If he do bleed,
I'll gild the faces of the grooms withal,
For it must seem their guilt.

9

(She takes the daggers and exits. Knocking sounds offstage.)

MACBETH. Whence is that knocking?
How is 't with me, when every noise appalls me?
What hands are here? Ha! They pluck out mine eyes.
Will all great Neptune's ocean wash this blood
Clean from my hand? No, this my hand will rather
The multitudinous seas incarnadine,
Making the green one red.

(*Enter* LADY MACBETH.)

LADY MACBETH. My hands are of your color, but I shame
To wear a heart so white. *(Knock.)* I hear a knocking
At the south entry. Retire we to our chamber.
A little water clears us of this deed.
How easy is it, then! Your constancy
Hath left you unattended. *(Knock.)* Hark! More knocking.
Get on your nightgown, lest occasion call us
And show us to be watchers. Be not lost
So poorly in your thoughts.

10

MACBETH. To know my deed, 'twere best not know myself. *(Knock.)*
Wake Duncan with thy knocking! I would thou couldst.

56 infirm (in fėrm′), *adj.* weak.

60–61 I'll gild . . . guilt. I'll paint the servants' faces with Duncan's blood to indicate their guilt.

66 incarnadine, redden.
67 making . . . red, staining the green sea blood red.

72–73 Your constancy . . . unattended. You look disturbed and uneasy.
75 watchers, awake.
77 To know . . . myself. It is better to be lost in my thoughts than to be aware of what I have done.

SCENE 3

Summary *A drunken porter opens the castle gate for Macduff and Lennox. Macduff discovers Duncan's body and awakens the household. Macbeth kills Duncan's servants in a fury—he says—over their having murdered the king. Duncan's sons, Malcolm and Donalbain, now fearing for their own lives, flee the country.*

The courtyard. Knocking sounds offstage. Enter a PORTER.

PORTER. Here's a knocking indeed! If a man were porter of hell gate, he should have old turning the key. *(Knock.)* Knock, knock, knock! Who's there, i' the name of Beelzebub? Here's a farmer that hanged himself on th' expectation of plenty. Come in time! Have napkins enough about you; here you'll sweat for 't. *(Knock.)* Knock, knock! Who's there, in th' other devil's name? Faith, here's

■ Who is the porter pretending to be as he talks to the farmer, the equivocator, and the tailor? 11

2 old, plenty of.
3 Beelzebub (bē el′zə bub), a Devil.
4 on the expectation of plenty, because he tried illegally to earn an excess profit on his crops.
5 napkins enough, handkerchiefs to wipe off the sweat caused by the heat of Hell.

9 Reading/Thinking Skills
Compare and Contrast

Question How does Macbeth's reaction to the murder compare with Lady Macbeth's? *(Possible response: Macbeth is conscience-stricken and unable to act. Lady Macbeth is practical, objective, and does not understand his reaction at all; she knows what has to be done to avoid discovery.)*

10 Literary Element
Connotation/ Denotation

Questions What does Macbeth's speech (lines 65–67) regarding the washing of his hands connote? *(that nothing will ever "cleanse" him of this crime)* What does Lady Macbeth's comment (line 71) connote? *(Guilt washes away as easily as blood.)*

11 Literary Element
Irony

Response the porter or doorman at the gates of Hell

Question How is this pretense ironic? *(While unaware of the murder of the king, of the evil unleashed in the castle—which will become a kind of hell for Macbeth—the man jokes when he refers to himself as the porter of hell gate.)*

BUILDING ENGLISH PROFICIENCY

Contrasting Characters

Help students understand the role-reversal in this scene by having them contrast Macbeth's and Lady Macbeth's reactions to Duncan's murder.

1. Before students read Scene 2, ask them to write two sentences—one predicting Macbeth's reaction to the murders and another predicting Lady Macbeth's reaction.
2. After students have read Scene 2, work with them to complete this chart by drawing an arrow from each adjective to the person that the arrow describes.

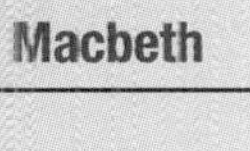

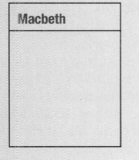

Macbeth		Lady Macbeth
	calm	
	confused	
	controlling	
	decisive	
	distracted	
	energetic	
	regretful	
	terrified	

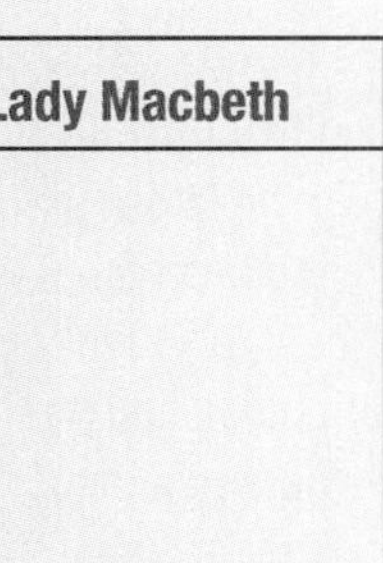

12 Reader's Response
Challenging the Text

Many critics have questioned the purpose of the porter's scene. Invite students to share views on this scene.

Question Do you think that this humorous scene is appropriate at this point? *(Possible responses: no—the porter's attempts at humor break the mood; or, yes—as Shakespeare has previously added irony by shifts of mood between scenes—e.g., Act One, Scenes 5 and 6—he increases the sense of horror by contrasting murder with very earthy humor.)*

an equivocator, that could swear in both the scales against either scale, who committed treason enough for God's sake, yet could not equivocate to heaven. O, come in, equivocator. *(Knock.)* Knock, knock, knock! Who's there? Faith, here's an English tailor come hither for stealing out of a French hose. Come in, tailor. Here you may roast your goose. *(Knock.)* Knock, knock! Never at quiet! What are you? But this place is too cold for hell. I'll devil-porter it no further. I had thought to have let in some of all professions that go the primrose way to th' everlasting bonfire. *(Knock.)* Anon, anon! *(He opens the gate.)* I pray you, remember the porter.

(*Enter* MACDUFF *and* LENNOX.)

MACDUFF. Was it so late, friend, ere you went to bed,
That you do lie so late?

PORTER. Faith, sir, we were carousing till the second cock; and drink, sir, is a great provoker of three things.

MACDUFF. What three things does drink especially provoke?

12

PORTER. Marry, sir, nose-painting, sleep, and urine. Lechery, sir, it provokes and unprovokes: it provokes the desire but it takes away the performance. Therefore much drink may be said to be an equivocator with lechery: it makes him and it mars him; it sets him on and it takes him off; it persuades him and disheartens him, makes him stand to and not stand to; in conclusion, equivocates him in a sleep and, giving him the lie, leaves him.

MACDUFF. I believe drink gave thee the lie last night.

PORTER. That it did, sir, i' the very throat on me. But I requited him for his lie, and, I think, being too strong for him, though he took up my legs sometimes, yet I made a shift to cast him.

MACDUFF. Is thy master stirring? (*Enter* MACBETH.)
Our knocking has awaked him. Here he comes. (*Exit* PORTER.)

LENNOX. Good morrow, noble sir.

MACBETH. Good morrow, both.

MACDUFF. Is the King stirring, worthy thane?

MACBETH. Not yet.

MACDUFF. He did command me to call timely on him.
I have almost slipped the hour.

MACBETH. I'll bring you to him.

MACDUFF. I know this is a joyful trouble to you,
But yet 'tis one.

MACBETH. The labor we delight in physics pain.
This is the door.

MACDUFF. I'll make so bold to call,
For 'tis my limited service. (*Exit* MACDUFF.)

LENNOX. Goes the King hence today?

MACBETH. He does; he did appoint so.

LENNOX. The night has been unruly. Where we lay,

7 equivocator (i kwiv′ ə - kāt′ər), *n.* person who uses expressions with double meaning in order to mislead.

11 stealing . . . hose. Tailors were often accused of stealing cloth. Since French hose (breeches) at this period were short and tight, it would take a clever tailor to cut them smaller so as to steal the excess cloth.

12 goose, a pressing iron used by a tailor.

15 primrose . . . bonfire, path of pleasure leading to everlasting damnation in Hell.

19 second cock, about 3:00 in the morning.

30 requite (ri kwīt′), *v.* repay.

37 timely, early.

41 physics pain, relieves that labor of its troublesome (painful) aspect.

43 limited, appointed.

MINI-LESSON: GRAMMAR

Diagramming Sentences with Direct and Indirect Objects

Teach Read this sentence portion from line 29 to students: . . . drink gave thee the lie. . . .

Point out that in this sentence *the lie* is the direct object, and *thee* is the indirect object. A direct object follows an action verb and tells *whom* or *what.* An indirect object is placed between the action verb and the direct object, and it tells *to what* or *to whom* or *for what* or *whom.* Remind students that in a sentence diagram a direct object is placed after a vertical line following the verb. An indirect object is placed on a line under the verb and connected by a slanted line extending below the horizontal line. Show the examples.

Activity Idea Have students find (or alter) and diagram four other examples of sentences with direct or direct and indirect objects.

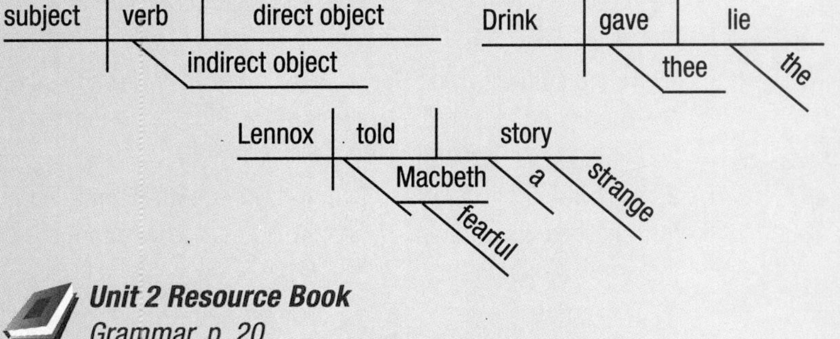

Unit 2 Resource Book
Grammar, p. 20

Our chimneys were blown down, and, as they say,
Lamentings heard i' th' air, strange screams of death,
And prophesying with accents terrible
Of dire combustion and confused events
New hatched to the woeful time. The obscure bird
Clamored the livelong night. Some say the earth
Was feverous and did shake.

14 **MACBETH.** 'Twas a rough night.
LENNOX. My young remembrance cannot parallel
A fellow to it. (*Enter* MACDUFF.)
MACDUFF. O, horror, horror, horror!
Tongue nor heart cannot conceive nor name thee!
MACBETH AND LENNOX. What's the matter?
MACDUFF. Confusion now hath made his masterpiece!
Most sacrilegious murder hath broke ope
The Lord's anointed temple and stole thence
The life o' the building!
MACBETH. What is 't you say? The life?
LENNOX. Mean you His Majesty?
MACDUFF. Approach the chamber and destroy your sight
With a new Gorgon. Do not bid me speak;
See, and then speak yourselves. (*Exit* MACBETH *and* LENNOX.)
Awake, awake!
Ring the alarum bell. Murder and treason!
Banquo and Donalbain, Malcolm, awake!
15 Shake off this downy sleep, death's counterfeit,
And look on death itself! Up, up, and see
The great doom's image! Malcolm, Banquo,
As from your graves rise up and walk like sprites
To countenance this horror! Ring the bell. (*Bell rings.*)
(*Enter* LADY MACBETH.)
LADY MACBETH. What's the business,
That such a hideous trumpet calls to parley
The sleepers of the house? Speak, speak!
MACDUFF. O gentle lady,
'Tis not for you to hear what I can speak.
The repetition in a woman's ear
Would murder as it fell. (*Enter* BANQUO.)
O Banquo, Banquo,
Our royal master's murdered!
LADY MACBETH. Woe, alas!
What, in our house?
BANQUO. Too cruel anywhere.
Dear Duff, I prithee, contradict thyself
And say it is not so.

13 ■ Visualize the unruly night Lennox describes. What state of the times is suggested by these events?

51 obscure bird, owl.

55 A fellow to it, an equal to it.

60 Lord's . . . temple, an allusion to the idea that a king is God's representative. The metaphorical temple is the king's body.

65 Gorgon, a horrible monster of Greek legend. Whoever looked at her was turned to stone. (See the picture of Medusa on page 33.)

71 great doom's image, sight as awful as Judgment Day.

13 Reading/Thinking Skills
Apply

Response This passage—a description of evil portents—suggests that bad times are in store.

14 Literary Element
Irony

Question What is the irony in Macbeth's statement "'Twas a rough night"? *(This understate-ment is an example of dramatic irony—Macbeth and the audience know just how rough a night it was; Lennox does not.)*

15 Reading/Thinking Skills
Generalize

Look at the comments about sleep that have appeared in Act One, Scene 3, lines 19–23; Act Two, Scene 2, lines 12–13 26–30, 39–47, 58, and Scene 3, lines 67–69.

Question What generalizations can you make about the meaning of these comments? *(Possible responses: The innocent, like Donalbain, sleep, while the guilty cannot; sleep marks time, one day to the next; Macbeth's reaction to the murder keeps that day ever present in his mind—as if time cannot pass beyond it; sleep is akin to death, perhaps even preparing the way for death.)*

BUILDING ENGLISH PROFICIENCY

Analyzing Metaphor

In lines 59–61, Macduff expresses his grief and honor for his king through a metaphor. Expand upon the gloss note as you help students grasp this figurative language.

1. Review that a metaphor compares two unlike things without using words such as *like, as,* or *resembles.* Offer these examples: *she's a whirlwind of activity; he's ice-cold.* Have students translate. *(She's very active. He shows no feelings.)*

2. As time permits, ask volunteers for examples of metaphors from their first language or from popular songs.

3. Ask students what Macduff is comparing in lines 59–61. *(He is comparing the king to a temple, anointed—that is, consecrated—by God.)* Explain that in Shakespeare's days people believed that a ruler was chosen by God. Ask: Why does this belief make Macbeth's crime more serious? *(Possible response: Murdering a king violates God's order and invites God's judgment upon the murderer.)*

16 Literary Element
Irony

Question How is this speech ironic? *(It is ironic in that the speech is both hypocritical and sincere; while displaying hypocritical grief, Macbeth expresses real grief, acknowledging too much space that life has lost all meaning.)*

17 Reading/Thinking Skills
Generalize

Response his love for Duncan and the evidence of guilt

18 Reading/Thinking Skills
Generalize

Questions Is the faint real? Why might Lady Macbeth choose to feint a faint? *(Possible responses: yes—she is overwhelmed by the murder of the grooms; no—appalled at Macbeth's feeble sounding excuses and overreaction [lines 102–112], she attempts to draw attention away from him)*

19 Literacy Focus
Plot

Questions What is Donalbain saying? How does this move the plot? *(He suspects Macbeth, fears for his own life, and intends to flee. Macbeth and Lady Macbeth are exposed.)*

(*Enter* MACBETH, LENNOX, *and* ROSS.)

MACBETH. Had I but died an hour before this chance
I had lived a blessèd time; for from this instant
There's nothing serious in mortality.
All is but toys. Renown and grace is dead;
The wine of life is drawn, and the mere lees
Is left this vault to brag of.

(*Enter* MALCOLM *and* DONALBAIN.)

DONALBAIN. What is amiss?

MACBETH. You are, and do not know 't.
The spring, the head, the fountain of your blood
Is stopped, the very source of it is stopped.

MACDUFF. Your royal father's murdered.

MALCOLM. O, by whom?

LENNOX. Those of his chamber, as it seemed, had done 't.
Their hands and faces were all badged with blood;
So were their daggers, which unwiped we found
Upon their pillows. They stared and were distracted;
No man's life was to be trusted with them.

MACBETH. O, yet I do repent me of my fury,
That I did kill them.

MACDUFF. Wherefore did you so?

MACBETH. Who can be wise, amazed, temp'rate and furious,
Loyal and neutral, in a moment? No man.
Th' expedition of my violent love
Outran the pauser, reason. Here lay Duncan,
His silver skin laced with his golden blood,
And his gashed stabs looked like a breach in nature
For ruin's wasteful entrance; there the murderers,
Steeped in the colors of their trade, their daggers
Unmannerly breeched with gore. Who could refrain
That had a heart to love, and in that heart
Courage to make 's love known?

LADY MACBETH (*fainting*). Help me hence, ho!

MACDUFF. Look to the lady.

MALCOLM (*aside to* DONALBAIN). Why do we hold our tongues,
That most may claim this argument for ours?

DONALBAIN (*aside to* MALCOLM). What should be spoken here, where our fate,
Hid in an auger hole, may rush and seize us?
Let's away. Our tears are not yet brewed.

MALCOLM (*aside to* DONALBAIN). Nor our strong sorrow upon the foot of motion.

BANQUO. Look to the lady. (LADY MACBETH *is helped out.*)
And when we have our naked frailties hid,

87 mortality, human life.

89–90 The wine of life . . . brag of. Duncan is dead, and those men who are left behind cannot compare to him.

■ What reasons does Macbeth give for murdering the servants?

104 expedition (ek′spə-dish′ən), *n.* haste.

115 that most . . . ours, we who are most concerned with this death.

117 augur (ô′gər) **hole,** obscure hiding place.

121 our . . . hid, gotten dressed.

MINI-LESSON: SPEAKING AND LISTENING
Reading a Play

Students who have never read a verse play aloud may be unsure how to approach it. You can provide them with the following tips for guidance:

- Speak as the character, not as yourself.
- Pay attention to the poetry, but do not force every line into iambic pentameter—Shakespeare varied the verse. Do not stop at the end of a line unless there is end punctuation.
- Use pitch and volume to reveal meaning.
- Check the pronunciation of difficult words before you read.
- Go over your part a few times to become familiar with it.

That suffer in exposure, let us meet
20 And question this most bloody piece of work
To know it further. Fears and scruples shake us.
In the great hand of God I stand, and thence
Against the undivulged pretense I fight
Of treasonous malice.

MACDUFF. And so do I.

ALL. So all.

MACBETH. Let's briefly put on manly readiness
And meet i' the hall together.

ALL. Well contented.

(Exit all but MALCOLM *and* DONALBAIN.*)*

MALCOLM. What will you do? Let's not consort with them.
To show an unfelt sorrow is an office
Which the false man does easy. I'll to England.

DONALBAIN. To Ireland, I. Our separated fortune
Shall keep us both the safer. Where we are,
There's daggers in men's smiles; the nea'er in blood,
The nearer bloody.

MALCOLM. This murderous shaft that's shot
Hath not yet lighted, and our safest way
Is to avoid the aim. Therefore to horse,
And let us not be dainty of leave-taking,
But shift away. There's warrant in that theft
Which steals itself when there's no mercy left.

124 scruple (skrü′pəl), *n.* doubt.

126–127 **against . . . malice,** I will fight against the unknown purpose which prompted this act of treason.

128 **put . . . readiness,** get dressed.

21 ■ Why do Malcolm and Donalbain decide to flee?

135–136 **the nea'er . . . bloody,** the closer in kinship to Duncan, the greater the chance of being murdered.

139 **dainty of,** ceremonious about.

140–141 **there's warrant . . . left,** we are justified in stealing away in these merciless times.

SCENE 4

Summary *Macduff tells Ross that Malcolm and Donalbain are suspected of murdering their father and that Macbeth has been named king.*

Outside MACBETH'S *castle. Enter* ROSS *with an* OLD MAN.

OLD MAN. Threescore and ten I can remember well,
Within the volume of which time I have seen
Hours dreadful and things strange, but this sore night
Hath trifled former knowings.

ROSS. Ha, good father,
Thou seest the heavens, as troubled with man's act,
Threatens his bloody stage. By th' clock 'tis day,
22 And yet dark night strangles the traveling lamp.
Is 't night's predominance or the day's shame
That darkness does the face of earth entomb
When living light should kiss it?

OLD MAN. 'Tis unnatural,
Even like the deed that's done. On Tuesday last
A falcon, towering in her pride of place,

7 **traveling lamp,** the sun.

20 Literary Focus
Plot

Question Why do you think Banquo and Macduff want to explore the murder further? *(Possible responses: They are suspicious of Macbeth and want to find out if he did it. They want to be sure that justice is done.)*

21 Reading/Thinking Skills
Draw Conclusions

Response They are afraid of being murdered.

22 Reading/Thinking Skills
Compare and Contrast

Questions What similarities do you see between "'tis day,/And yet dark night strangles" and "Fair is foul, and foul is fair" from Act One? *(Possible responses: Both reverse the norm, suggesting that things are turned upside-down; both portend disaster.)* How are they different? *(While day is night, there is no suggestion that night will be day; rather, night will likely be even darker than the norm.)*

BUILDING ENGLISH PROFICIENCY

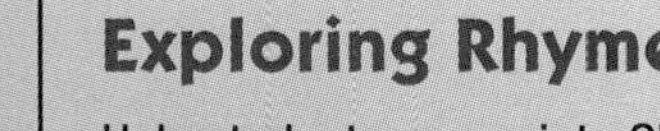

Exploring Rhyme

Help students appreciate Shakespeare's use of unrhymed iambic pentameter (blank verse).

1. Have students tap out the rhythm in several lines—for example, Scene 3, lines 95–99, on page 142. Help them discover the usual pattern: an unstressed syllable followed by a stressed one (iamb) with five beats in most lines (pentameter).
2. Challenge students to find lines that vary the pattern, usually for emphasis (lines 102–103). Point out, as well, that the witches speak mostly in rhymes, four beats to a line.
3. Help students find lines where Shakespeare "cheats" by using contractions (as in lines 91 and 112), and where he uses run-on lines, with speakers changing (as in lines 101 and 112), to avoid a singsongy regularity.

23 Literary Element
Foreshadowing

Response The hawk and owl foreshadow the predator, Macbeth, brought down by Malcolm; the flight of Duncan's horses foreshadows the flight of Duncan's sons out of Scotland to raise armies against the usurper.

24 Literary Element
Theme

Question How might Ross's statement apply to Macbeth, rather than to the sons? *(It is Macbeth, rather than Duncan's sons, who exhibits such ambition. "Thriftless ambition, that will ravin up/Thine own Life's means!"—the central theme of the play—foreshadows Macbeth's doom.)*

25 Literary Focus
Plot

Questions Why isn't Macduff going to Scone? What does this signal? *(Macduff suspects Macbeth of the murder; Macbeth is losing his allies and, thus, his base of power.)*

Check Test

1. Why doesn't Banquo want to sleep? *(He's afraid of evil dreams.)*
2. What vision does Macbeth have as he waits to kill Duncan? *(He sees an imaginary dagger before him.)*
3. Why does Lady Macbeth go to the king's chamber? *(to plant the daggers and smear the grooms with blood)*
4. Who discovers the murder? *(Macduff)*
5. What do Duncan's sons do when they discover Duncan is dead? *(They flee to Ireland and England.)*

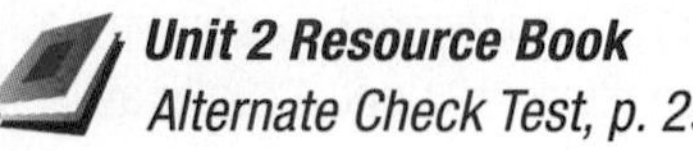

Unit 2 Resource Book
Alternate Check Test, p. 29

Was by a mousing owl hawked at and killed.
ROSS. And Duncan's horses—a thing most strange and certain—
Beauteous and swift, the minions of their race,
23 Turned wild in nature, broke their stalls, flung out,
Contending 'gainst obedience, as they would
Make war with mankind.
OLD MAN. 'Tis said they eat each other.
ROSS. They did so, to th' amazement of mine eyes
That looked upon 't. (*Enter* MACDUFF.)
Here comes the good Macduff.
How goes the world, sir, now?
MACDUFF. Why, see you not?
ROSS. Is 't known who did this more than bloody deed?
MACDUFF. Those that Macbeth hath slain.
ROSS. Alas the day,
What good could they pretend?
MACDUFF. They were suborned.
Malcolm and Donalbain, the King's two sons,
Are stol'n away and fled, which puts upon them
Suspicion of the deed.
ROSS. 'Gainst nature still!
24 Thriftless ambition, that will ravin up
Thine own life's means! Then 'tis most like
The sovereignty will fall upon Macbeth.
MACDUFF. He is already named and gone to Scone
To be invested.
ROSS. Where is Duncan's body?
MACDUFF. Carried to Colmekill,
The sacred storehouse of his predecessors
And guardian of their bones.
ROSS. Will you to Scone?
25 **MACDUFF.** No, cousin, I'll to Fife.
ROSS. Well, I will thither.
MACDUFF. Well, may you see things well done there. Adieu,
Lest our old robes sit easier than our new!
ROSS. Farewell, father.
OLD MAN. God's benison go with you, and with those
That would make good of bad, and friends of foes!

■ Visualize the unusual and unnatural events described by Ross and the old man. What might these events **foreshadow?**

24 what . . . pretend, what profit could they have been seeking?
24 suborn (sə bôrn′), *v.* hire or bribe.

28 ravin up, devour.
29 own life's means, parent.

31 Scone, the place where Scottish kings were crowned.
32 invest, (in vest′), *v.* install in office with a ceremony.
33 Colmekill, Iona Island, off the west coast of Scotland.

40 benison (ben′ə zən), *n.* blessing.

MINI-LESSON: STUDY SKILLS
Map Reading

Students who want to identify the locales mentioned in the play may wish to use a large map of Scotland. Remind them that an alphabetical listing of places with map grid plots often accompanies a map. They should begin by finding the place on the listing, and then note the letter and number assigned to it. Next, they should find that letter and number on the map grid marked at the map's edges and locate the corresponding square of area. Finally, they should search the square until they locate the place in question.

Activity Idea Students can practice locating places on a map and make a map of Scotland with all the places mentioned in the play. Have students

- make a list of places mentioned so far and find them on a map of Scotland
- record the places on a map of their own
- label their map with information about what happened at each place
- add to their maps as the play progresses

Act 2

After Reading

Making Connections

Shaping Your Response

1. Based on what you have seen of their characters and actions, do you think Macbeth and Lady Macbeth will make a good king and queen? Explain.

Analyzing the Play

2. Explain how Macbeth's and Lady Macbeth's states of mind after the murder are expressed through their speeches and actions.
3. The drunken porter's speeches are an example of **comic relief.** Why do you think Shakespeare might have placed this scene immediately after the murder scene?
4. Explain how Macduff, Banquo, Malcolm, and Donalbain each react to Duncan's murder in a way that reflects his personal position.

Extending the Ideas

5. How important an issue do you think gender is in physical strength? in mental strength? in moral strength? Have your opinions on the strengths of Macbeth and Lady Macbeth changed since act 1?

Literary Focus: Plot Structure

"What's done is done," says Lady Macbeth in act 3. In the second act of a Shakespearean play, the protagonist usually takes an action that cannot be reversed or undone. In this act Macbeth murders Duncan. Use a plot diagram like the one shown on page 116 to chart the rising action of the plot. Write the events that occur on the night of the murder and the characters who cause them to happen.

Vocabulary Study

Select the word that is most nearly similar in meaning to the numbered word.

1. augment — **a.** decrease **b.** motivate **c.** move **d.** increase
2. suborn — **a.** bribe **b.** cover **c.** obey **d.** raise
3. requite — **a.** repeat **b.** pay back **c.** honor **d.** set up
4. palpable — **a.** capable **b.** deadly **c.** honest **d.** definite
5. scruple — **a.** doubt **b.** sum of money **c.** vague thought **d.** escape

After Reading

MAKING CONNECTIONS

1. Possible response: Such selfish and ambitious (and disturbed) people are unlikely to make good rulers.

2. Lady Macbeth's calm acceptance of the deed is reflected in her attention to the practical details that will protect them from discovery; Macbeth's distress is reflected in the images he sees and his inability to return the daggers and bloody the grooms.

3. He may have done it to create dramatic irony and heighten tension.

4. Possible responses: Macduff and Banquo are suspicious; while they do not accuse Macbeth outright, they make their scepticism felt, e.g., Macduff's refusal to attend the coronation. Donalbain and Malcolm are highly suspicious of Macbeth's and Lady Macbeth's overreactions; fearing for their lives, they flee.

5. Possible response: Men are generally physically stronger than women; in every other way, gender is not a factor in strength. While responses will vary, we only see Macbeth's and Lady Macbeth's strengths/weaknesses increase in these first acts.

VOCABULARY STUDY

1. d
2. a
3. b
4. d
5. a

Unit 2 Resource Book
Vocabulary, p. 19
Vocabulary Test, p. 22

LITERARY FOCUS: PLOT

Encourage students to take note of the plot sequence by adding events in Act Two of *Macbeth* to the "rising action" part of the plot diagram they are making. These are the most significant events in Act Two:

Macbeth murders Duncan
Macbeth's conscience is bothered
Lady Macbeth tidies up details
Macbeth kills the servants
Duncan's sons flee

Macbeth is crowned; Macduff won't attend

Selection Test

Unit 2 Resource Book
pp. 23–24

1 Historical Note
Audience

Contemporary estimates suggest that an audience of between 2,000 and 3,000 people could fit into the theater.

2 Geographical Note
Location

The Globe stood in Southwarke across the Thames River from the City of London.

3 Reading/Thinking Skills
Identify Alternatives

Questions In what ways might a playwright deal with lack of artificial light in the theater? *(Possible response: have characters mention the time of day or perform activities that reveal time of day)* How did Shakespeare handle this problem in Act Two, Scene 1? *(The scene begins with characters casually discussing the time of day.)*

4 Historical Note
Appearance

Some sources state that there are no contemporary drawings of the Globe. Others insist that Hallar's topographic drawings of London show an accurate depiction of the theater.

The Globe Theater

The flag has just been raised high above the
roof of the Globe theater. The play is ready to
1 begin. London Bridge is crowded with men on
horseback riding to the theater. Others come
2 by boat along the Thames River. They come for
afternoon performances only, because there
3 are no artificial lights. As they stream into this
many-sided, three-story structure, which looks like a large Elizabethan town house, the men separate according to class. The groundlings (apprentices and the lower class) mingle about in the large open yard area. A rowdy bunch, they shove and push. The middle class folks wend their way to the galleries. The noblemen strut up to the special seats in boxes or on the stage. Vendors wander through the crowd hawking food and drink. The mood is festive, carnival-like. It is a man's afternoon out. There are no women in the audience, just as there are no women on stage.

The first Globe theater, completed in 1599, burned to the ground in 1613. The second Globe, which was built immediately afterward, stood until 1644. From a few surviving maps,
carpenters' contracts, and verbal descriptions,
4 we can put together the following picture of the
Globe. The main acting area, the Platform, extended well into the yard so that the spectators almost surrounded the actors. At the back was the Study, a curtained room used for interior scenes. In the floor of the Platform were several trap doors. Imagine smoke, fog, and apparitions, or ghosts, rising and falling! Macbeth's witches would appear and vanish via these trap doors. The main stage entrances, on either side of the Platform, were large permanent doors.

On the second level was another curtained room, the Chamber, typically used for domestic scenes. In front of this was a narrow balcony called the Tarras (ter′is). Often the Tarras and the Platform would be used together with the Tarras representing a hill, the wall of a town, or a gallery from which observers watched the action below. On the third level was a narrow musicians' gallery. Above it were the Huts which housed a pulley system for lowering objects supposed to appear from midair. Sound effects such as thunder or battle alarums (sounds of fighting) also came from the Huts.

There was very little scenery in a Shakespearean play. A desk, a bed, or a chair suggested the setting. Notice how often Shakespeare announces a change of scene with a trumpet or a few lines of dialogue. Costumes were usually not historically accurate. Instead, actors would be dressed in typical Elizabethan clothing. There were no actresses; all women's parts were played by boys.

Around the world Shakespearean-type theaters have been designed with permanent open stages meant to capture the style of the original. A full-size replica of the Globe, part of a Shakespearean complex, opened in 1996 close to the original site in London.

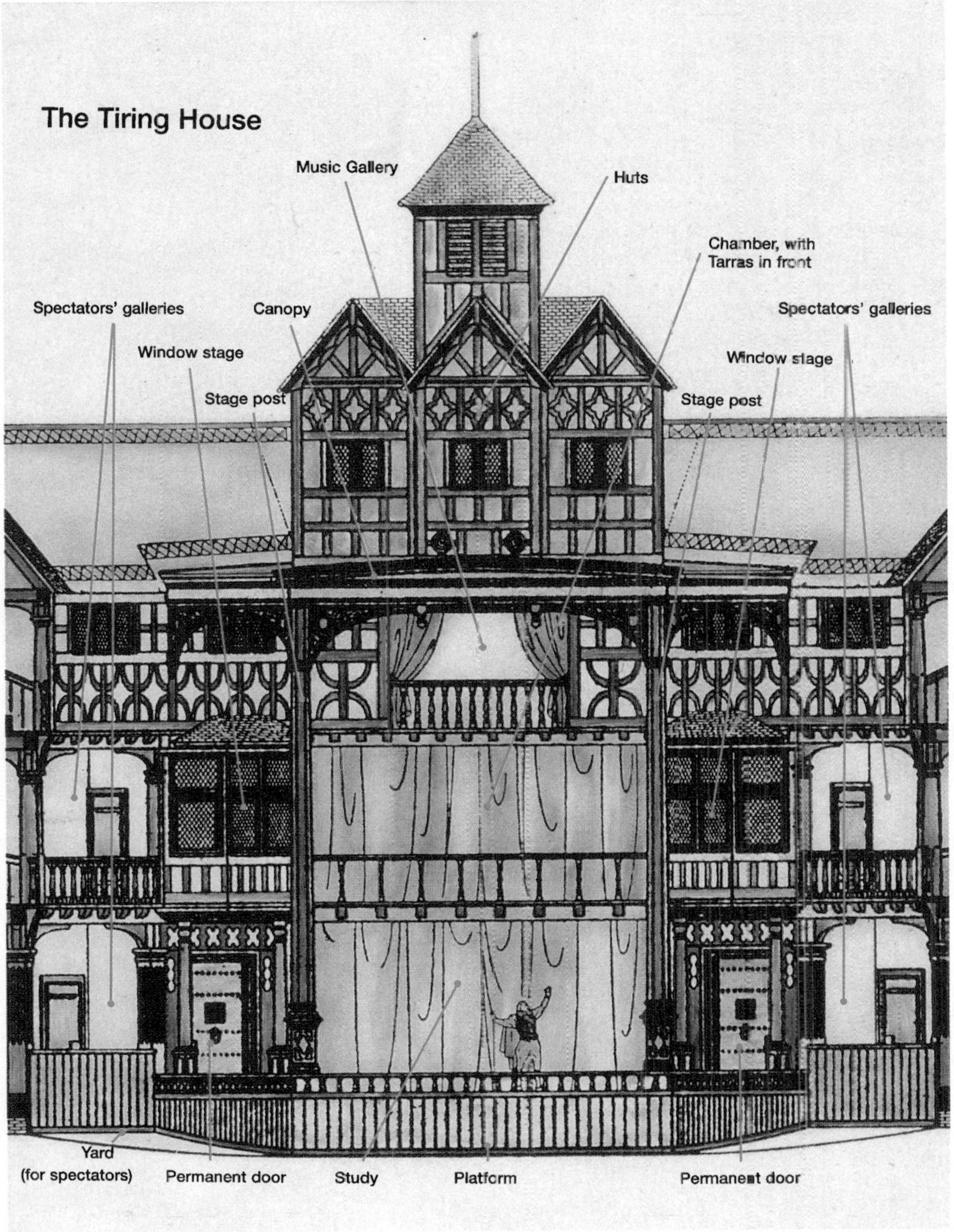

The Tiring House

Music Gallery
Huts
Chamber, with Tarras in front
Spectators' galleries
Canopy
Spectators' galleries
Window stage
Window stage
Stage post
Stage post
Yard (for spectators)
Permanent door
Study
Platform
Permanent door

Art Study

The diagram of the Tiring House, or "attiring house," at the Globe Theater shows the various levels upon which actors might perform. The Platform, Study, and Tarras may have provided playwrights and actors with more flexibility than is available in many modern playhouses. Because the Platform was nearly surrounded by audience, it may have functioned in a manner similar to modern theater-in-the-round; the multiple "stages" made movement possible in all directions instead of simply along the length of a narrow stage; it also allowed for a scene to follow quickly on the heels of the previous scene.

The multi-gabled structure of the Tiring House is typical of Tudor or Elizabethan architecture. It was constructed of wood, probably English oak, in a manner called "post and beam"—a building system that can be studied today in many old barns. In English buildings of the Tudor period, small timbers, called half-timbers, were inserted between the posts and beams. Usually cut from a curving limb or from the crotch of a tree, the half-timbers were often fitted together to form geometric shapes, such as the diamonds seen on this diagram. Spaces between the posts, beams, and half-timbers were filled with brick, stone, or more typically, plaster. The contrast between the dark timbers and light plaster provided the Elizabethan building with its characteristic lively facade.

BUILDING ENGLISH PROFICIENCY

Linking Past and Present

Briefly discuss the differences between watching a movie and seeing live actors perform a play. Encourage students to share any theatrical experiences.

Activity Idea Have groups create Venn diagrams to compare and contrast going to the theater in modern and Elizabethan times.

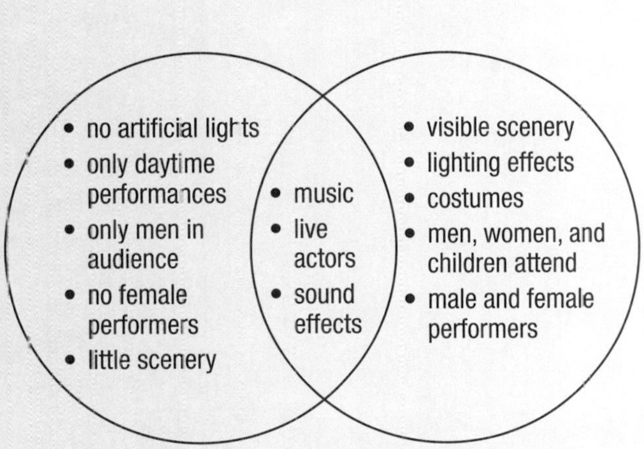

- no artificial lights
- only daytime performances
- only men in audience
- no female performers
- little scenery

- music
- live actors
- sound effects

- visible scenery
- lighting effects
- costumes
- men, women, and children attend
- male and female performers

During Reading

Vocabulary Preview

verity, truth
dauntless, brave
chide, scold
jovial, cheerful
malevolence, ill will

Students can add the words and definitions to their Writer's Notebooks.

1 Reading/Thinking Skills
Find the Main Idea

Question What is the main idea of Banquo's speech? *(Banquo informs the audience of his suspicions of Macbeth, and he reveals that he has ambitions and has become, like Macbeth, secretive in his plans.)*

2 Reading/Thinking Skills
Draw Conclusions

Response Macbeth determines that Banquo is going riding, how far he is going, when he expects to return, and that Fleance will accompany him (on p. 149). These "none-too-polite" questions of a guest suggest that Macbeth is becoming paranoid; that he might be attempting to determine if Banquo, in league with other thanes, is plotting against him; that he recalls the witches' prophecy to Banquo and might just "get rid of" Banquo and his sons and, thus, keep the throne in his own family.

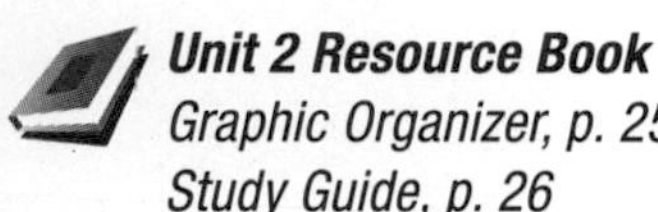
Unit 2 Resource Book
Graphic Organizer, p. 25
Study Guide, p. 26

Act Three

SCENE 1

Summary *Because the Witches have promised that the descendants of Banquo will be kings, Macbeth hires Murderers to kill Banquo and his son, Fleance.*

MACBETH'S *castle. Enter* BANQUO.

1
BANQUO. Thou hast it now—King, Cawdor, Glamis, all
As the weird women promised, and I fear
Thou played'st most foully for 't. Yet it was said
It should not stand in thy posterity,
But that myself should be the root and father
Of many kings. If there come truth from them—
As upon thee, Macbeth, their speeches shine—
Why, by the verities on thee made good,
May they not be my oracles as well
And set me up in hope? But hush, no more.
(*Music sounds offstage. Enter* MACBETH *as king,* LADY MACBETH, LENNOX, ROSS, LORDS, *and* ATTENDANTS.)
MACBETH. Here's our chief guest.
LADY MACBETH. If he had been forgotten,
It had been as a gap in our great feast
And all-thing unbecoming.
MACBETH. Tonight we hold a solemn supper, sir,
And I'll request your presence.
BANQUO. Let Your Highness
Command upon me, to the which my duties
Are with a most indissoluble tie
Forever knit.
2
MACBETH. Ride you this afternoon?
BANQUO. Ay, my good lord.
MACBETH. We should have else desired your good advice,
Which still hath been both grave and prosperous,
In this day's council; but we'll take tomorrow.
Is 't far you ride?
BANQUO. As far, my lord, as will fill up the time
Twixt this and supper. Go not my horse the better,
I must become a borrower of the night
For a dark hour or twain.
MACBETH. Fail not our feast.
BANQUO. My lord, I will not.
MACBETH. We hear our bloody cousins are bestowed
In England and in Ireland, not confessing
Their cruel parricide, filling their hearers

8 verity (ver′ə tē), *n.* truth.

13 **all-thing,** in every way.

■ Macbeth wants to know about Banquo's plans. What do you think he will do with this information?

22 **which . . . prosperous,** which always has been thoughtful and fruitful.

33 **parricide** (par′ə sīd), *n.* crime of killing a father.

ACT THREE SUMMARY

Macbeth

Macbeth decides Banquo must be killed because he suspects Macbeth of murder and because the witches have promised kingship to his descendants. Macbeth hires assassins. As Banquo and Fleance approach the palace, Banquo is killed; Fleance escapes. At a banquet in the palace, Macbeth, surrounded by his lords, sees the ghost of Banquo. In his terror, Macbeth's actions and words are such that the lords begin to suspect him. After Lady Macbeth dismisses the company, Macbeth voices his suspicions of Macduff and resolves to consult the witches again. Hecate rebukes the witches for trafficking with Macbeth and plots his downfall. After stating his opinion of Macbeth, Lennox is told that Macduff is in England raising an army against Macbeth.

For summaries in other languages, see the ***Building English Proficiency*** *book.*

In this Charles Ricketts illustration from *The Tragedie of Macbeth* (1923), a servant brings in the two Murderers whom Macbeth persuades to kill Banquo and his son, Fleance. The Second Murderer claims, "I am reckless what I do to spite the world!" What sort of events can bring people to the condition where they don't care what happens to them?

With strange invention. But of that tomorrow,
When therewithal we shall have cause of state
Craving us jointly. Hie you to horse. Adieu,
Till you return at night. Goes Fleance with you?
BANQUO. Ay, my good lord. Our time does call upon 's.
MACBETH. I wish your horses swift and sure of foot,
And so I do commend you to their backs.
Farewell. (*Exit* BANQUO.)
Let every man be master of his time
Till seven at night. To make society

35–36 cause . . . jointly, affairs of state demanding the attention of both of us.

Art Study

Response to Caption Question
Events that might bring people to the condition of not caring what happens to them can include crime, poverty, deaths of loved ones, injustice, discrimination, illness, physical and mental abuse, lack of self-esteem.

Visual Literacy You might suggest that students compare this illustration with the one by the same artist on page 137. Charles Ricketts, the artist, again suggests character through the use of color, pattern, and shape.

Questions What does the shape of Macbeth's crown suggest? *(Possible response: The deadly-looking points suggest cruelty.)* What does the color of his cloak suggest? *(that he is awash in blood [and clad in the same shades of red and orange that Lady Macbeth was when she incited him to murder])* Can you think of any predatory animals with skins similar to Macbeth's black and orange, striped sleeves and patterned socks? *(Possible response: tigers and leopards)* What does the color of the servant's garb suggest? *(that he is as bloodied as his master)*

BUILDING ENGLISH PROFICIENCY

ESL
LEP
ELD
SAE
LD

Analyzing Characters

Creating an "open-mind" drawing as shown will help students analyze Banquo's state of mind during his soliloquy on page 148, lines 1–10. You might suggest these topics:

- the witches
- suspicions about Macbeth
- his children

Encourage students to compare diagrams to check their comprehension.

Building English Proficiency
Activities, p. 213

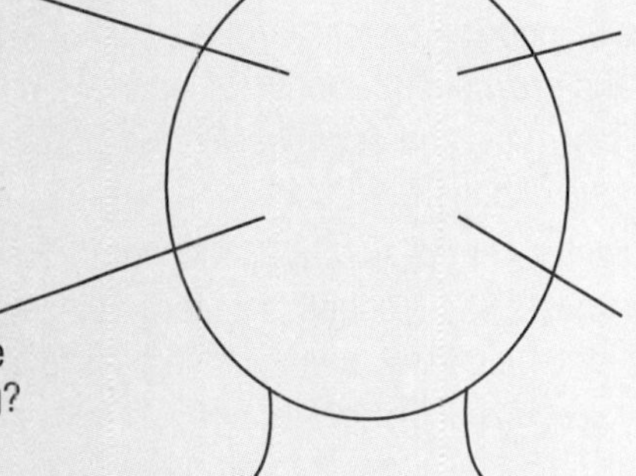
The witches' promises are coming true.
How can my children become kings?
How could Macbeth have killed my king?
I have hope, yet I worry.

3 Literary Focus
Plot

Question What new conflict is revealed here? *(Macbeth is turning against Banquo.)*

4 Multicultural Note
Individuality

Response Like many individuals who gain great power over a group, Macbeth's thirsts have become insatiable. No longer satisfied with simply being king, he wants "to be safely thus." He wants to be out from under the shadow of Banquo's talents so his "own genius" will shine. And he wants his descendants, not Banquo's, to sit on the throne. Macbeth is the classic tyrant—paranoid and insatiable.

5 Reading/Thinking Skills
Understand Sequence/ Order Events

Questions Who is "he" in line 78? How do you know? *("He" is Banquo; this is clear both from reading ahead to line 85 and from looking back to Macbeth's previous speech, which continues here with the murderers.)*

The sweeter welcome, we will keep ourself
Till suppertime alone. While then, God be with you!
(Exit all but MACBETH *and a* SERVANT.*)*
Sirrah, a word with you. Attend those men
Our pleasure?

SERVANT. They are, my lord, without the palace gate.

MACBETH. Bring them before us. *(Exit* SERVANT.*)*
To be thus is nothing,
3 But to be safely thus. Our fears in Banquo
Stick deep, and in his royalty of nature
Reigns that which would be feared. 'Tis much he dares;
And to that dauntless temper of his mind
He hath a wisdom that doth guide his valor
To act in safety. There is none but he
Whose being I do fear; and under him
My genius is rebuked, as it is said
Mark Antony's was by Caesar. He chid the sisters
When first they put the name of king upon me,
And bade them speak to him. Then, prophetlike,
They hailed him father to a line of kings.
Upon my head they placed a fruitless crown
And put a barren scepter in my grip,
Thence to be wrenched with an unlineal hand,
No son of mine succeeding. If 't be so,
For Banquo's issue have I filed my mind;
For them the gracious Duncan have I murdered,
Put rancors in the vessel of my peace
Only for them, and mine eternal jewel
Given to the common enemy of man
To make them kings, the seeds of Banquo kings.
Rather than so, come fate into the list,
And champion me to th' utterance! Who's there?
(Enter SERVANT *and two* MURDERERS.*)*
Now go to the door, and stay there till we call. *(Exit* SERVANT.*)*
Was it not yesterday we spoke together?

MURDERERS. It was, so please Your Highness.

MACBETH. Well then, now
Have you considered of my speeches? Know
5 That it was he in the times past which held you
So under fortune, which you thought had been
Our innocent self. This I made good to you
In our last conference, passed in probation with you
How you were borne in hand, how crossed, the instruments,
Who wrought with them, and all things else that might
To half a soul and to a notion crazed

46 Sirrah (sir′ə), ordinary form of address used in speaking to children and servants.

53 dauntless (dônt′lis), *adj.* brave.

55–58 There is none . . . Caesar. Macbeth's ambition is silently condemned by Banquo's loyalty. Mark Antony feared Octavius Caesar as a political, not personal, enemy, and this is how Macbeth regards Banquo.

58 chid (chid), past tense of *chide* (chīd), *v.* scold.

66 filed, defiled; made impure.

68 rancor, (rang′kər), *n.* ill will; hatred.

69–70 mine eternal . . . man, given my soul to the Devil.

72 list, battlefield.

73 champion . . . utterance, fight me to the death.

4 To become King would seem to be about the greatest achievement of **individuality** that anyone could hope for. Why is Macbeth still dissatisfied?

81 passed in probation, gave detailed proof.

82 borne in hand, deceived.

84 notion crazed, half-wit.

MINI-LESSON: VOCABULARY
Connotation/Denotation

Teach Read Macbeth's speech to the murderers (p. 151, lines 93–96):

"Ay, in the catalogue ye go for men,
As hounds and greyhounds, mongrels, spaniels, curs,
Shoughs, water-rugs, and demi-wolves are clept
All by the name of dogs."

Explain that simply knowing that all the words denote kinds of dogs is not enough to understand Macbeth's speech. It is important to know what they connote—the emotional meanings and associations connected to them—to interpret Macbeth's point.

Activity Idea Have students work toward understanding Macbeth's speech by looking up the following words in a dictionary (for example, the *ScottForesman Advanced Dictionary*) that discusses their usage, that is, their connotative meaning: *cur, mongrel, spaniel, hound.*

Tell students to pay special attention to what the words mean when they are applied to human beings. Then have them infer Macbeth's meaning by grouping these types of dogs together.

Say, "Thus did Banquo."
FIRST MURDERER. You made it known to us.
MACBETH. I did so, and went further, which is now
Our point of second meeting. Do you find
Your patience so predominant in your nature
That you can let this go? Are you so gospeled
To pray for this good man and for his issue,
Whose heavy hand hath bowed you to the grave
And beggared yours forever?
FIRST MURDERER. We are men, my liege.
6 **MACBETH.** Ay, in the catalogue ye go for men,
As hounds and greyhounds, mongrels, spaniels, curs,
Shoughs, water-rugs, and demi-wolves are clept
All by the name of dogs. The valued file
Distinguishes the swift, the slow, the subtle,
The housekeeper, the hunter, every one
According to the gift which bounteous nature
Hath in him closed, whereby he does receive
Particular addition from the bill
That writes them all alike; and so of men.
Now, if you have a station in the file,
Not i' the worst rank of manhood, say 't,
And I will put that business in your bosoms
Whose execution takes your enemy off,
Grapples you to the heart and love of us,
Who wear our health but sickly in his life,
Which in his death were perfect.
SECOND MURDERER. I am one, my liege,
Whom the vile blows and buffets of the world
Hath so incensed that I am reckless what
I do to spite the world!
FIRST MURDERER. And I another,
So weary with disasters, tugged with fortune,
That I would set my life on any chance
To mend it or be rid on 't.
MACBETH. Both of you
Know Banquo was your enemy.
MURDERERS. True, my lord.
MACBETH. So is he mine, and in such bloody distance
That every minute of his being thrusts
Against my near'st of life. And though I could
With barefaced power sweep him from my sight
And bid my will avouch it, yet I must not,
For certain friends that are both his and mine,
Whose loves I may not drop, but wail his fall

89 **gospeled,** religious.

95 **shoughs . . . clept,** shaggy dogs, water dogs, and half-wolves are called.

96 **valued file,** list according to worth.

101–102 **particular . . . alike,** specific qualifications along with the general characteristics.

7 ■ Why do you think Macbeth feels it necessary to convince the Murderers that Banquo is their enemy, instead of simply hiring them to kill him?

113 **tugged with,** pulled about by.

117 **in such bloody distance,** with such hostility.

118–119 **thrusts . . . life,** threatens my very existence.

121 **bid . . . avouch it,** take responsibility for it.

123 **but . . . fall,** I must pretend to weep for his death.

6 Literary Element
Irony

Question Do you see any irony in Macbeth's comparison of types of men with varieties of dogs? *(Possible response: Macbeth certainly suggests that these murderers are mongrels and curs, rather than greyhounds or spaniels. The irony is that we know that Macbeth, a king, is as much of a demi-wolf as they are.)*

7 Reading/Thinking Skills
Analyze

Response Macbeth attempts to remove himself from the crime by providing the assassins with a motive. Possibly, he is trying to protect himself from his own conscience and imagination, which caused him such suffering during the planning and carrying out of Duncan's murder. Lines 49–55 also suggests that Macbeth fears discovery and loss of the throne. If he sends men who have a legitimate motive for killing Banquo, others may accept that the paid assassins, not Macbeth, are the true instigators of the crime.

BUILDING ENGLISH PROFICIENCY

Making Personal Connections

In lines 96–102, Macbeth tells the murderers that there are all kinds of people, each with his or her own unique worth. Invite students to consider what "gift" (talent, unusual quality, strength, ability) has been "closed" in them. Allow for optional, voluntary sharing.

Activity Ideas

- Discuss some different "gifts" that make people unique. Ask students: How do people find their "gift"? What can you do if you know your "gift," but others (like your parents) think you have another "gift"?
- Have students write (for their eyes only, if they prefer) a brief paragraph in which they describe themselves, perhaps to a future employer or marriage partner. Suggest that they emphasize their outstanding qualities, especially the "gift" that distinguishes them from other people.

8 Reading/Thinking Skills
Draw Conclusions

Responses Macbeth's "weighty reason" is that he does not want "certain [powerful] friends" to suspect him of Banquo's murder because they already suspect him of regicide. It is also likely that Macbeth is afraid to interfere directly in the prophecy of the witches. Responses will vary on the wisdom of Macbeth's action; it is probably wise to distance himself from another murder; it might be wiser still to ignore Banquo and the witches' prophesy.

9 Literary Element
Characterization

Questions How does Lady Macbeth's state of mind change after her husband's arrival? *(She goes from being despondent to badgering her husband for his despondency.)* What does this suggest about a change in Lady Macbeth's character? *(Possible response: As she is now more concerned about their crimes, her conscience may be bothering her; she states that they "dwell in doubtful joy," but hides her thoughts from her husband and assumes the role of the strong, ruthless helpmate.)*

Who I myself struck down. And thence it is
That I to your assistance do make love,
Masking the business from the common eye
For sundry weighty reasons. [8]

SECOND MURDERER. We shall, my lord,
Perform what you command us.

FIRST MURDERER. Though our lives—

MACBETH. Your spirits shine through you. Within this hour at most
I will advise you where to plant yourselves,
Acquaint you with the perfect spy o' the time,
The moment on 't, for 't must be done tonight,
And something from the palace; always thought
That I require a clearness. And with him—
To leave no rubs nor botches in the work—
Fleance his son, that keeps him company,
Whose absence is no less material to me
Than is his father's, must embrace the fate
Of that dark hour. Resolve yourselves apart;
I'll come to you anon.

MURDERERS. We are resolved, my lord.

MACBETH. I'll call upon you straight. Abide within. (*Exit* MURDERERS.)
It is concluded. Banquo, thy soul's flight,
If it find heaven, must find it out tonight.

■ What reasons does Macbeth give for not killing Macduff himself? How wise do you think his action is?

133 something from, some distance from.
134 clearness, freedom from suspicion.

139 resolve yourselves, make up your minds.

SCENE 2

Summary *Lady Macbeth scolds Macbeth for brooding about Duncan's murder. Macbeth hints to Lady Macbeth about his plan to murder Banquo and Fleance.*

Another room in the castle. Enter LADY MACBETH *and a* SERVANT.

LADY MACBETH. Is Banquo gone from court?

SERVANT. Ay, madam, but returns again tonight.

LADY MACBETH. Say to the King I would attend his leisure
For a few words.

SERVANT. Madam, I will.

LADY MACBETH. Naught's had, all's spent, [9]
Where our desire is got without content.
'Tis safer to be that which we destroy
Than by destruction dwell in doubtful joy. (*Enter* MACBETH.)
How now, my lord? Why do you keep alone,
Of sorriest fancies your companions making,
Using those thoughts which should indeed have died
With them they think on? Things without all remedy
Should be without regard. What's done is done.

13–14 Things . . . regard. You shouldn't worry about things you can't change.

MINI-LESSON: GRAMMAR
Diagramming Reversed Sentences

Teach Read this part of line 39 on page 153 to students:

. . . full of scorpions is my mind . . .

Point out that here, the complement (in this case, a predicate adjective) is first, the verb follows, and the subject comes last. We would normally expect the order to be reversed. However, diagramming the sentence is relatively easy—the same sentence part is always in the same place, no matter where it was in the actual sentence. Also tell students that prepositional phrases are diagrammed in the same way as indirect objects except that the preposition is on the slanted line and the phrase goes under whatever part of speech it modifies. The sentence above is diagrammed as shown.

Activity Idea Have students make up four reversed sentences that they think Lady Macbeth and Macbeth might have said to each other as they left the banquet at which Banquo's ghost appeared. Then students should work in pairs to diagram the eight sentences.

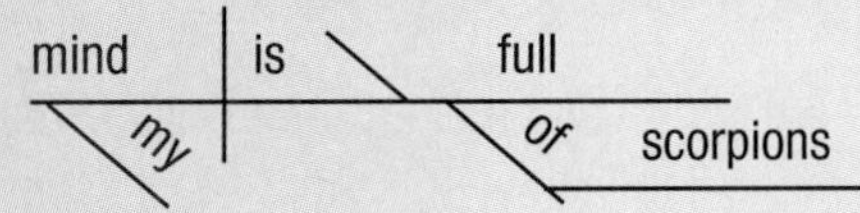

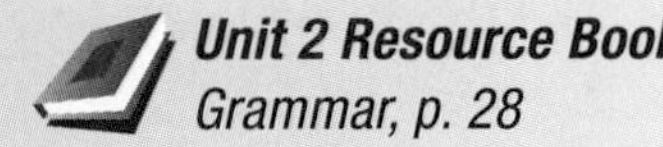
Unit 2 Resource Book
Grammar, p. 28

MACBETH. We have scorched the snake, not killed it.
She'll close and be herself, whilst our poor malice
Remains in danger of her former tooth.
But let the frame of things disjoint, both the worlds suffer,
Ere we will eat our meal in fear and sleep
In the affliction of these terrible dreams
That shake us nightly. Better be with the dead,
Whom we, to gain our peace, have sent to peace,
Than on the torture of the mind to lie
In restless ecstasy. Duncan is in his grave;
After life's fitful fever he sleeps well.
Treason has done his worst; nor steel, nor poison,
Malice domestic, foreign levy, nothing
Can touch him further.
LADY MACBETH. Come on,
Gentle my lord, sleek o'er your rugged looks.
Be bright and jovial among your guests tonight.
11 MACBETH. So shall I, love, and so, I pray, be you.
Let your remembrance apply to Banquo;
Present him eminence, both with eye and tongue—
Unsafe the while, that we
Must lave our honors in these flattering streams
And make our faces vizards to hearts,
Disguising what they are.
LADY MACBETH. You must leave this.
12 MACBETH. O, full of scorpions is my mind, dear wife!
Thou know'st that Banquo and his Fleance lives.
LADY MACBETH. But in them nature's copy's not eterne.
MACBETH. There's comfort yet; they are assailable.
Then be thou jocund. Ere the bat hath flown
His cloistered flight, ere to black Hecate's summons
The shard-borne beetle with his drowsy hums
Hath rung night's yawning peal, there shall be done
A deed of dreadful note.
LADY MACBETH. What's to be done?
MACBETH. Be innocent of the knowledge, dearest chuck,
Till thou applaud the deed. Come, seeling night,
Scarf up the tender eye of pitiful day,
And with thy bloody and invisible hand
Cancel and tear to pieces that great bond
Which keeps me pale! Light thickens,
And the crow makes wing to th' rooky wood;
Good things of day begin to droop and drowse,
Whiles night's black agents to their preys do rouse.
Thou marvel'st at my words, but hold thee still.

15 scorched, cut.

18 let the frame . . . suffer, if the universe breaks apart, earth and heaven will perish.

10 ■ What evidence is there that Macbeth's deeds are beginning to trouble his conscience?

24 restless ecstasy, suffering.

27 malice . . . levy, civil war, foreign invasion.

31 jovial (jō′vē əl), *adj.* cheerful.

34 present him eminence, show him special favor.
37 vizard (viz′ərd), *n.* mask.
35–38 unsafe the while . . . what they are. We are unsafe as long as we must flatter and appear to be what we are not.

41 But . . . eterne. They will not live forever.
43 jocund (jok′ənd) *adj.* cheerful; merry.

49 seeling, blinding. To *seel* is a technical term used in falconry for sewing up the eyelids of a young hawk to make him used to the hood.
50 scarf up, blindfold.

10 Literary Element
Tone

Response Macbeth states that it would be better to die, like Duncan, than continue being tortured by his thoughts.

Question What is the tone of this passage (lines 21–24)? *(His tone sounds anguished; but he just arranged a murder, which would appear to negate real anguish.)*

11 Reading/Thinking Skills
Compare and Contrast

Question How is the relationship of Macbeth and Lady Macbeth different here than it was in Act One, Scene 5? *(Possible response: Previously, Lady Macbeth had to tell Macbeth how to behave; now he gives her instruction. Then, she was the master plotter; now he is so much the master that she knows nothing of the plot.)*

12 Literary Element
Figurative Language

Question What does Macbeth's scorpion metaphor suggest? *(Possible response: that Macbeth's obsession with the prophecy regarding Banquo's lineage is like deadly scorpions poisoning his thoughts)*

BUILDING ENGLISH PROFICIENCY

Exploring Key Statements

Macbeth's advice that he and his wife should "make our faces vizards to hearts,/Disguising what they are" (Scene 2, lines 37–38) is quite telling. Invite students to explore this statement by having them work with you or an art teacher to create hand-held masks.

1. Suggest that students make masks that represent good qualities (for instance, a smiling angel or a dove).
2. When they are reading the play aloud in class, ask students to hold their masks in front of their faces whenever a character speaks falsely, tries to deceive someone, tells a lie, or hides true feelings.
3. Ask groups of students, using their masks, to role-play modern situations where people "speak falsely" to gain advantage at school, at work, in dating, or in politics.

13 Reading/Thinking Skills
Recognize Values

Question What change of values does the line "Things bad begun make strong themselves by ill" suggest? *(Possible response: He is entering more fully into evil in an attempt to strengthen himself and his position.)*

14 Literary Element
Pun

Response When the light goes out, Fleance escapes into the dark.

You might note that Shakespeare, near the end of this scene, sets up a pun based on the "light and dark" imagery that he uses throughout this scene and the play. Relate that a pun is a play on words, sometimes on different senses of the same word or on the sound of different words.

Question Can you find the pun? *(Response: line 27—". . . the son is fled." Both the son and the sun have fled into darkness, which suggests that Banquo's son [and descendants] will return, like the sun, to bring a new day to Scotland. The pun is set up when Macbeth, in the previous scene, asks for the sun to set; the murderer notes the "west glimmers with streaks of day"; and the murder scene is a confusion of light and darkness.)*

15 Reading/Thinking Skills
Compare and Contrast

Question How does Duncan's murder compare and contrast with Banquo's? *(Duncan is killed offstage; Banquo, on stage. Duncan is killed by Macbeth; Banquo, by Macbeth's minions. Duncan's murder comes off perfectly; Banquo's murder is fumbled when Fleance escapes.)*

13
Things bad begun make strong themselves by ill.
So, prithee, go with me.

59 prithee, I pray you.

SCENE 3

Summary *Banquo is killed by the Murderers, but Fleance escapes.*

A park near MACBETH'S *castle. Enter three* MURDERERS.

FIRST MURDERER. But who did bid thee join with us?
THIRD MURDERER. Macbeth.
SECOND MURDERER (*to the* FIRST MURDERER). He needs not our mistrust, since he delivers
Our offices and what we have to do
To the direction just.
FIRST MURDERER. Then stand with us.
The west yet glimmers with some streaks of day.
Now spurs the lated traveler pace
To gain the timely inn, and near approaches
The subject of our watch.
THIRD MURDERER. Hark, I hear horses.
BANQUO *(offstage)*. Give us a light there, ho!
SECOND MURDERER. Then 'tis he. The rest
That are within the note of expectation
Already are i' the court.
FIRST MURDERER. His horses go about.
THIRD MURDERER. Almost a mile; but he does usually—
So all men do—from hence to th' palace gate
Make it their walk.
(Enter BANQUO *and* FLEANCE, *with a torch.)*
SECOND MURDERER. A light, a light!
THIRD MURDERER. 'Tis he.
FIRST MURDERER. Stand to 't.
BANQUO. It will be rain tonight.
FIRST MURDERER. Let it come down! (*They attack* BANQUO.)
BANQUO. O, treachery! Fly, good Fleance, fly, fly, fly!
Thou mayst revenge. O slave! (*He dies.* FLEANCE *escapes.*)
14
THIRD MURDERER. Who did strike out the light?
FIRST MURDERER. Was 't not the way?
THIRD MURDERER. There's but one down; the son is fled.
SECOND MURDERER. We have lost best half of our affair.
15
FIRST MURDERER. Well, let's away and say how much is done.

2–4 He needs not . . . just. We need not distrust him, since he reports accurately what we are to do.

12 note of expectation, list of expected guests.

14 go about, take the long way to the castle.

■ How is Fleance able to escape being murdered?

MINI-LESSON: VOCABULARY
Multiple-meaning Words

Teach Read aloud the following lines from page 155: "Ourself will mingle with society/And play the humble host."

Point out that "play the humble host" can be understood in two ways because of the multiple meanings of the word *play.* First, Macbeth's straightforward meaning is that he will mingle with his nobles, fulfilling the duties of a host. A second meaning of *play* is evoked by the readers' knowledge that Macbeth is by no means humble. He is going to be "acting a part" for the evening, pretending to be something he isn't.

Activity Idea Students can create a piece of writing or an oral presentation in which multiple meanings of a word are important. It can center around a misunderstanding, create irony, or just be a play on words. Allow students to perform their work for the class when they're done.

▲ In *The Three Witches,* painted by Henry Fuseli in 1783, the heads of the three evil hags from *Macbeth* are shown in profile, overlapping each other. Compare this painting with the Dulac poster on page 119. How are the two artists' conceptions of the witches similar? How are they different?

Art Study

Responses to Caption Questions These witches, which seem far less malevolent than Dulac's witches (p. 119), look like men, normal except for their claw-like hands. They all lay one finger to their lips as they point out something with their other hands. The closest looks hesitant, even apologetic; the second looks serious; the third looks suspicious. While Dulac's witches seem to confront Macbeth, Fuseli's seem to direct his attention and impose silence on him.

Question Witches are usually thought of as female, and Shakespeare refers to his witches as sisters. Why do you think Fuseli gave these witches so masculine an appearance? *(Responses will vary; he may be suggesting that evil hardens femininity or that beauty and evil are incompatible.)*

SCENE 4

Summary *At a banquet Macbeth praises the absent Banquo, but then he is terrified by the appearance of the ghost of Banquo which only he can see. Because of Macbeth's odd behavior, Lady Macbeth dismisses the guests. Macbeth vows to return to the witches for more information.*

A hall in the castle. There is a banquet prepared. Enter MACBETH, LADY MACBETH, ROSS, LENNOX, LORDS *and* ATTENDANTS.

MACBETH. You know your own degrees; sit down. At first
And last, the hearty welcome. *(They sit.)*
LORDS. Thanks to Your Majesty.
MACBETH. Ourself will mingle with society
And play the humble host.
Our hostess keeps her state, but in best time,
We will require her welcome.

1 **degrees,** rank. Guests at state banquets were seated according to social or political rank.

5 **keeps her state,** remains seated on her throne.

BUILDING ENGLISH PROFICIENCY

Checking Comprehension

Use dramatics and class discussion to help students evaluate their own reading progress as Scene 3 concludes.

1. Encourage five volunteer actors and a director to act out Scene 3. Then follow up by discussing questions such as these:

- Who escapes, and why is that important? *(Fleance, Banquo's son; the witches had foretold he would be king)*
- Who do you think the third murderer might be? *(possibly a friend of the two murderers Macbeth spoke with, possibly Macbeth himself)*
- What is the double meaning of it in the murderer's shout, "Let it come down"? (It *refers to the fall of rain and of the attackers' knives.)* What is the double meaning of *light*: "Who did strike out the light?" (Light *refers to the torch and to Banquo's life.)*

2. Ask another group of volunteers to update both the situation and dialogue to modern times and act out the scene.

16 Literary Focus
Plot

Response He mingles with his guests to establish an alibi for the latest murders; because of earlier suspicions and his over-reaction to Duncan's murder, he wants the guests to remember that he was present and calm, even playful, at the time Banquo was killed.

17 Literary Element
Simile

Question What do Macbeth's similes suggest? *(Possible response: If he no longer had to worry about Fleance, life would be perfect—flawless, built on a strong foundation; the prophecy about Banquo would be null and void, and his rule would be as all-encompassing as the air.)*

18 Literary Focus
Plot

Question How is Fleance's escape important to the plot? *(Possible responses: The conflict Macbeth feels about the witches' prophecy remains unresolved; Fleance will likely return for revenge.)*

LADY MACBETH. Pronounce it for me, sir, to all our friends,
For my heart speaks they are welcome.
(FIRST MURDERER *appears at the door.*)
MACBETH. See, they encounter thee with their hearts' thanks.
Both sides are even. Here I'll sit i' the midst. *(He sits.)*
Be large in mirth; anon we'll drink a measure.
The table round. *(He goes to the* MURDERER.) 16
There's blood upon thy face.
FIRST MURDERER. 'Tis Banquo's, then.
MACBETH. 'Tis better thee without than he within.
Is he dispatched?
FIRST MURDERER. My lord, his throat is cut. That I did for him.
MACBETH. Thou art the best o' the cutthroats.
Yet he's good that did the like for Fleance;
If thou didst it, thou art the nonpareil.
FIRST MURDERER. Most royal sir, Fleance is scaped.
MACBETH. Then comes my fit again. I had else been perfect,
17 Whole as the marble, founded as the rock,
As broad and general as the casing air.
But now I am cabined, cribbed, confined, bound in
To saucy doubts and fears. But Banquo's safe?
FIRST MURDERER. Ay, my good lord. Safe in a ditch he bides,
With twenty trenchèd gashes on his head,
The least a death to nature.
MACBETH. Thanks for that.
There the grown serpent lies; the worm that's fled
18 Hath nature that in time will venom breed,
No teeth for th' present. Get thee gone. Tomorrow
We'll hear ourselves again. *(Exit* FIRST MURDERER.)
LADY MACBETH. My royal lord,
You do not give the cheer. The feast is sold
That is not often vouched, while 'tis a-making,
'Tis given with welcome. To feed were best at home;
From thence, the sauce to meat is ceremony;
Meeting were bare without it.
(The GHOST OF BANQUO *appears and sits in* MACBETH'S *place.)*
MACBETH. Sweet remembrancer!
Now, good digestion wait on appetite,
And health on both!
LENNOX. May 't please Your Highness sit?
MACBETH. Here had we now our country's honor roofed
Were the graced person of our Banquo present,
Who may I rather challenge for unkindness
Than pity for mischance.
ROSS. His absence, sir,

■ Why do you think Macbeth doesn't sit on his throne during the banquet?

14 'Tis better . . . within. The blood is better on you than in him.

19 nonpareil (non′pə rel′), *n.* one without equal.

23 casing, enveloping.

32 hear ourselves, talk it over.

33–37 The feast is . . . without it. Unless a host keeps his guests assured of their welcome, the meal is like one bought at an inn, and one might as well dine at home. When one is away from home, ceremony should accompany the meal.

40 here had . . . roofed, we would have all our country's most honored men here.

42–43 who may I . . . mischance, who is, I hope, absent because he has chosen not to attend rather than because he has been prevented from coming by some misfortune.

MINI-LESSON: VOCABULARY
Puns

Teach One reason it is important to read Shakespeare's plays aloud is to hear the use of puns that are not always caught by eye, especially when they involve homophones that are not homonyms. Read lines 36–37 on page 156:

> ". . . the sauce is meat to ceremony;
> Meeting were bare without it."

Explain the pun: "If meat didn't have sauce it would be bare; and to meet without ceremony is bare."

Activity Idea Point out these other puns in the play and have students work in small groups to explain them:

- Act One, Scene 7, line 69 (p. 133)
- Act Two, Scene 2, lines 60–61 (p. 139)
- Act Two, Scene 3, lines 11–12 (p. 140)

Allow students to share their interpretations with the class.

Lays blame upon his promise. Please 't Your Highness
To grace us with your royal company?
MACBETH *(seeing his place occupied).* The table's full.
LENNOX. Here is a place
reserved, sir.
MACBETH. Where?
LENNOX. Here, my good lord. What is 't that moves Your Highness?
MACBETH. Which of you have done this?
LORDS. What, my good lord?
19 **MACBETH.** Thou canst not say I did it. Never shake
Thy gory locks at me.
ROSS. Gentlemen, rise. His Highness is not well.
(They start to get up from the table.)
20 **LADY MACBETH.** Sit, worthy friends. My lord is often thus,
And hath been from his youth. Pray you, keep seat.
The fit is momentary; upon a thought
He will again be well. If much you note him
You shall offend him and extend his passion.
Feed, and regard him not. *(She confers apart with* MACBETH.*)*
Are you a man?
MACBETH. Ay, and a bold one, that dare look on that
Which might appall the devil.
LADY MACBETH. O, proper stuff!
This is the very painting of your fear.
This is the air-drawn dagger which, you said,
Led you to Duncan. O, these flaws and starts,
Impostors to true fear, would well become
A woman's story at a winter's fire,
Authorized by her grandam. Shame itself!
Why do you make such faces? When all's done,
You look but on a stool.
MACBETH. Prithee, see there!
Behold, look! Lo, how say you?
Why, what care I? If thou canst nod, speak too.
If charnel houses and our graves must send
Those that we bury back, our monuments
Shall be the maws of kites. *(The* GHOST *disappears.)*
LADY MACBETH. What, quite unmanned in folly?
MACBETH. If I stand here, I saw him.
LADY MACBETH. Fie, for shame!
MACBETH. Blood hath been shed ere now, i' th' olden time,
Ere humane statute purged the gentle weal;
Ay, and since, too, murders have been performed
Too terrible for the ear. The time has been
That, when the brains were out, the man would die,

55 **upon a thought,** in a moment.

57 **extend his passion,** prolong his fit.

61 **painting,** representation.

64 **imposters to,** imitations of.

21 ■ Who can see the ghost of Banquo and who cannot?

71–73 **If charnel . . . kites.** If morgues and graves cannot keep our bodies buried, our burial place should be the stomachs of birds of prey.

77 **ere . . . weal,** before laws allowed us to protect society from violent persons.

19 Reading/Thinking Skills
Draw Conclusions

Questions When Macbeth sees Banquo's ghost sitting in his place, he says, "Thou canst not say I did it. Never shake/Thy gory locks at me." To whom is he speaking? *(to the ghost)* To what does "gory locks" refer? *(bloody hair—the ghost bears the "twenty trenched gashes" described earlier)* Why do you think Macbeth bothers to deny his guilt to a ghost? *(Possible responses: He may be cracking under the strain and may somehow feel that his elaborate preparations to distance himself from Banquo's murder have absolved him of guilt; or it may be simply self-denial.)*

20 Reading/Thinking Skills
Compare and Contrast

Question How is Lady Macbeth's reaction similar to her response after Duncan's murder? *(Possible response: Once again, she is calm and practical in a crisis and irritated with her husband's irrational and dangerous behavior.)*

21 Reading/Thinking Skills
Infer

Response Only Macbeth sees the ghost.

BUILDING ENGLISH PROFICIENCY

Analyzing Key Events

Enrich students' understanding of this famous ghost scene.

1. Divide students into groups and have them share ghost stories they have read (such as Dickens's *A Christmas Carol*), seen in the media (for instance, Casper), or heard about as they were growing up.

2. Assign a group leader to keep the discussion moving and another group member to take notes on the discussion.

3. Later, the recorders can share their notes with the class.

Students may want to consider questions such as these:

- According to tradition, what is a ghost? Do all ghosts have "unfinished business" on Earth?
- Why do people "believe" in ghosts?
- Why might certain people see ghosts, while others don't? In particular, why is it Macbeth (not Lady Macbeth) who sees Banquo's ghost?

22 Reader's Response
Making Personal Connections

Questions

- If you were one of the guests, what would you think of Macbeth's behavior? *(Possible responses: that he might be drunk, hallucinating, ill, or bewitched; with rumors connecting him with Duncan's murder in circulation, one might be suspicious that he has a guilty conscience)*
- Do you believe that what Lady Macbeth says is true? If not, offer an explanation for her comments. *(Possible responses: It might be true, or she may be covering for him. If one remembers what has been said of Macbeth's overreaction to Duncan's murder, Lady Macbeth may be attempting to pass a mental state off as a medical condition.)*

23 Literary Focus
Plot

Question In what kind of danger does Macbeth place himself with his ravings? *(Possible response: He is in danger of revealing his complicity in the murder of Duncan.)*

And there an end; but now they rise again
With twenty mortal murders on their crowns,
And push us from our stools. This is more strange
Than such a murder is.
LADY MACBETH. My worthy lord,
Your noble friends do lack you.
MACBETH. I do forget.
Do not muse at me, my most worthy friends;
I have a strange infirmity, which is nothing
To those that know me. Come, love and health to all!
Then I'll sit down. Give me some wine. Fill full.
(He is given wine. The GHOST *reappears.)*
I drink to the general joy o' th' whole table,
And to our dear friend Banquo, whom we miss.
Would he were here! To all, and him, we thirst,
And all to all.
LORDS. Our duties and the pledge. *(They drink.)*
MACBETH (*seeing* GHOST). Avaunt, and quit my sight! Let the earth
hide thee!
Thy bones are marrowless, thy blood is cold;
Thou hast no speculation in those eyes
Which thou dost glare with!
LADY MACBETH. Think of this, good peers,
22 But as a thing of custom. 'Tis no other;
Only it spoils the pleasure of the time.
MACBETH. What man dare, I dare.
Approach thou like the rugged Russian bear,
The armed rhinoceros, or th' Hyrcan tiger;
Take any shape but that, and my firm nerves
Shall never tremble. Or be alive again
And dare me to the desert with thy sword.
If trembling I inhabit then, protest me
The baby of a girl. Hence, horrible shadow!
Unreal mockery, hence! (*Exit* GHOST.) Why, so; being gone,
I am a man again. Pray you, sit still.
LADY MACBETH. You have displaced the mirth, broke the good meeting
With most admired disorder.
MACBETH. Can such things be,
And overcome us like a summer's cloud,
Without our special wonder? You make me strange
Even to the disposition that I owe,
When now I think you can behold such sights
And keep the natural ruby of your cheeks
23 When mine is blanched with fear.
ROSS. What sights, my lord?

82 mortal . . . crowns, deadly wounds on their heads.

86 muse, wonder.

92 thirst, wish to drink.

94 avaunt (ə vônt′), *interj.* begone; go away.

96 speculation, power to see.

98 thing of custom, customary (usual) thing.

102 Hyrcan, of Hyrcania, in ancient times a region near the Caspian Sea.

106–107 If trembling . . . girl. If I still tremble, call me a girl's doll.

111 admired, wondered at.

113–114 You make . . . owe. You make me wonder at my own nature.

MINI-LESSON: USAGE
Proper Adjectives

Teach Remind students that proper adjectives do not follow a single rule of formation. So, the proper adjective formed from Russia is Russian, but Hyrcania forms Hyrcan (lines 101–102, p. 158).

Question What similarities are there in the two proper adjectives? *(Both begin with a capital letter and end with the letters* an*).*

Activity Idea For practice, each student can

- choose ten countries and/or states
- use a dictionary to locate the proper adjective for each
- make a list of rules that seem to govern the formation of proper adjectives
- discuss findings with the class

LADY MACBETH. I pray you, speak not. He grows worse and worse;
Question enrages him. At once, good night.
Stand not upon the order of your going,
But go at once.

LENNOX. Good night, and better health
Attend His Majesty!

LADY MACBETH. A kind good night to all!

(*Exit* LORDS *and* ATTENDANTS.)

MACBETH. It will have blood, they say; blood will have blood.
Stones have been known to move, and trees to speak:
24 Augurs and understood relations have
By maggotpies and choughs and rooks brought forth
The secret'st man of blood. What is the night?

LADY MACBETH. Almost at odds with morning, which is which.

MACBETH. How sayst thou, that Macduff denies his person
25 At our great bidding?

LADY MACBETH. Did you send to him, sir?

MACBETH. I hear it by the way; but I will send.
There's not a one of them but in his house
I keep a servant fee'd. I will tomorrow—
26 And betimes I will—to the Weird Sisters.
More shall they speak, for now I am bent to know
By the worst means the worst. For mine own good
All causes shall give way. I am in blood
Stepped in so far that, should I wade no more,
Returning were as tedious as go o'er.
Strange things I have in head, that will to hand,
Which must be acted ere they may be scanned.

LADY MACBETH. You lack the season of all natures, sleep.

MACBETH. Come, we'll to sleep. My strange and self-abuse
Is the initiate fear that wants hard use.
We are yet but young in deed.

SCENE 5

Summary *Hecate reprimands the Witches for dealing with Macbeth without her permission.*

A wilderness. Thunder. Enter the three WITCHES, *meeting* HECATE.

FIRST WITCH. Why, how now, Hecate? You look angerly.

HECATE. Have I not reason, beldams as you are?
Saucy and overbold, how did you dare
To trade and traffic with Macbeth
In riddles and affairs of death,
And I, the mistress of your charms,
The close contriver of all harms,

120 stand not . . . going, don't take the time to leave in order of rank.

125–127 Augurs . . . blood. Through talking birds (magpies, crows, and rooks), omens correctly interpreted have led to the discovery of the most secretive of murderers.

133 fee'd, paid (a fee) to spy.

133–134 I will . . . sisters. I will go very early to the witches.

141 which . . . scanned, which must be done before they can be discussed.

143–144 My strange . . . use. My peculiar actions arise from the fact that I am inexperienced at crime.

2 beldam (bel′dəm), *n.* old hag.

7 contriver, planner; schemer.

24 Reading/Thinking Skills
Find the Main Idea

Question What do you think is the main idea of this passage? (*Possible response: Blood will have blood, that is, violence begets violence; and even birds and inanimate objects, stones and trees, whisper of murder.)*

25 Literary Focus
Plot

Macbeth asks Lady Macbeth what she makes of Macduff's failure to appear at the banquet.

Question How is Macduff's absence important to the plot? *(Possible response: It is a grave social offense to not respond to the invitation of a head of state; Macduff's absence is, thus, a deliberate insult announcing his lack of confidence and withdrawal of support.)*

26 Reading/Thinking Skills
Essential and Incidental Information

Question What is the essential reason behind Macbeth's return to the witches? *("To know/By the worst means the worst"—it is better to know the worst than be tortured by one's fears.)*

BUILDING ENGLISH PROFICIENCY

Exploring Key Concepts

Macbeth says that he intends to visit the witches again so that he can "know . . . the worst" (Scene 4, lines 135–136). Invite students to consider in greater detail the concept of trying to know the future.

1. Ask students what Macbeth wants to know. *(He wants to know what Macduff will do next.)* Why does he expect that he won't like the answer? *(He worries that he has done such evil that things never will be right for him again.)*

2. Talk about whether it's better to know or not know the future. Have each student write a question about the future and drop it (anonymously) into a box. Ask a group to review and report on their classmates' questions.

3. Ask students to imagine they could send a telegram (or e-mail) of no more than thirty words to Macbeth. Have each student write such a message, making a prediction and advising Macbeth about what he should and shouldn't do at this point.

27 Reading/Thinking Skills

Generalize

Question How would you generalize Hecate's speech? Be sure to state the main idea and give important details. *(Possible response: Hecate announces that through the use of magic she will draw Macbeth to his doom by playing on his arrogance and overconfidence. She chastises her witches for trading and trafficking with Macbeth, who like all mortals is selfish, spiteful, and unworthy of her power.)*

27

Was never called to bear my part
Or show the glory of our art?
And, which is worse, all you have done
Hath been but for a wayward son,
Spiteful and wrathful, who, as others do,
Loves for his own ends, not for you.
But make amends now. Get you gone,
And at the pit of Acheron
Meet me i' the morning. Thither he
Will come to know his destiny.
Your vessels and your spells provide,
Your charms and everything beside.
I am for th' air. This night I'll spend
Unto a dismal and a fatal end.
Great business must be wrought ere noon.
Upon the corner of the moon
There hangs a vaporous drop profound;
I'll catch it ere it comes to ground,
And that, distilled by magic sleights,
Shall raise such artificial sprites
As by the strength of their illusion
Shall draw him on to his confusion.
He shall spurn fate, scorn death, and bear
His hopes 'bove wisdom, grace, and fear.
And you all know, security
Is mortals' chiefest enemy.
(Music offstage and a song: "Come away, come away," *etc.)*
Hark! I am called. My little spirit, see,
Sits in a foggy cloud and stays for me. *(Exit.)*

FIRST WITCH. Come, let's make haste. She'll soon be back again.

11 wayward (wā′wərd), *adj.* disobedient; willful.

14 amends (ə mendz′), *n.* compensation.

15 Acheron (ak′ə ron′), a river in Hell.

26 sleight (slīt), *n.* trick.

29 confusion, destruction.

32 security, overconfidence.

SCENE 6

Summary *Lennox says he is suspicious of Macbeth. He learns that Macduff has gone to England to meet Malcolm and to seek the help of the English king against Macbeth.*

MACBETH'S *castle. Enter* LENNOX *and another* LORD.

LENNOX. My former speeches have but hit your thoughts,
Which can interpret farther. Only I say
Things have been strangely borne. The gracious Duncan
Was pitied of Macbeth; marry, he was dead.
And the right valiant Banquo walked too late,
Whom you may say, if 't please you, Fleance killed,
For Fleance fled. Men must not walk too late.
Who cannot want the thought how monstrous

1–2 My former . . . farther. My earlier speeches have only given you ideas, from which you can draw your own conclusions.

3 borne, conducted; carried out.

MINI-LESSON: GRAMMAR

Using Parts of Speech Effectively in Sentences

Teach Read aloud lines 30–31 (p. 160): "He shall spurn fate, scorn death, and bear/His hopes 'bove wisdom, grace, and fear."
Point out the items in series used to create a compound predicate and a compound object of the preposition *'bove*. Show that each part of the compound predicate is parallel—it has a verb and an object. Point out that each object of the preposition *'bove* is a noun.

Question How does this technique benefit Shakespeare? *(Possible response: He is able to transmit a complex thought in a single sentence.)*

Activity Idea For practice, students can create sentences with multiple examples of parallel construction by writing a short piece about the ruler of a country (real or imaginary) and his or her agenda for a day.

It was for Malcolm and for Donalbain
To kill their gracious father? Damnèd fact!
How it did grieve Macbeth! Did he not straight
In pious rage the two delinquents tear
That were the slaves of drink and thralls of sleep?
Was not that nobly done? Ay, and wisely too;
For 'twould have angered any heart alive
To hear the men deny 't. So that I say
He has borne all things well; and I do think
That had he Duncan's sons under his key—
As, an 't please heaven, he shall not—they should find
What 'twere to kill a father. So should Fleance.
But peace! For from broad words, and 'cause he failed
His presence at the tyrant's feast, I hear
Macduff lives in disgrace. Sir, can you tell
Where he bestows himself?

LORD. The son of Duncan,
From whom this tyrant holds the due of birth,
Lives in the English court, and is received
Of the most pious Edward with such grace
That the malevolence of fortune nothing
Takes from his high respect. Thither Macduff
Is gone to pray the holy king, upon his aid,
To wake Northumberland and warlike Siward,
That by the help of these—with Him above
To ratify the work—we may again
Give to our tables meat, sleep to our nights,
Free from our feasts and banquets bloody knives,
Do faithful homage, and receive free honors—
All which we pine for now. And this report
Hath so exasperate the King that he
Prepares for some attempt of war.

LENNOX. Sent he to Macduff?

LORD. He did; and with an absolute "Sir, not I,"
The cloudy messenger turns me his back
And hums, as who should say, "You'll rue the time
That clogs me with this answer."

LENNOX. And that well might
Advise him to a caution, t' hold what distance
His wisdom can provide. Some holy angel
Fly to the court of England and unfold
His message ere he come, that a swift blessing
May soon return to this our suffering country
Under a hand accursed!

LORD: I'll send my prayers with him.

13. **thrall** (thrôl), *n.* slave.

28 ■ Do you think Lennox is speaking sincerely here, or with **irony?**

21 from broad words, because he spoke frankly.

27 Edward, Edward the Confessor, King of England 1042–1066.

28 malevolence (mə lev′ə ləns), *n.* ill will.

30 ■ What seems to be the general mood in Scotland? Do people have reason to feel this way?

42 cloudy, displeased.

43 rue, regret.

44 clogs, obstructs.

45 advise him . . . provide, warn him (Macduff) to keep what safe distance he can (from Macbeth).

28 Literary Element
Irony

Response Lennox's speech is a near perfect example of verbal irony. Nearly every statement is either an example of understatement—"Men must not walk too late"—or can be interpreted as defense or offense—"How it did grieve Macbeth."

29 Literary Focus
Plot

Question How is the plot affected by Macduff's absence from Scotland? *(Macduff has gone to England, presumably to urge Malcolm to raise an army against Macbeth.)*

30 Reading/Thinking Skills
Recognize Cause and Effect

Response The mood is negative. Food is scarce. People are afraid, unable to sleep, and feel coerced into loyalty to Macbeth.

Check Test

1. Why does Macbeth want to kill Banquo? *(to keep Banquo's progeny from the throne)*
2. What is the outcome of the murder attempt? *(Banquo is dead; Fleance has fled.)*
3. What disturbs Macbeth at the banquet? *(Banquo's ghost)*
4. What major characters, besides Banquo, suspect Macbeth? *(Macduff and Lennox)*
5. What does Hecate plan for Macbeth? *(his destruction)*

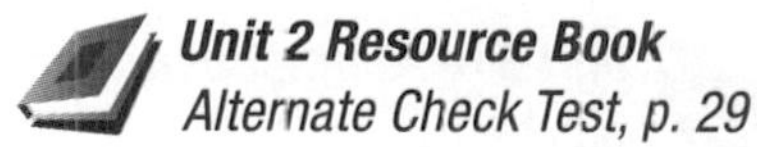
Unit 2 Resource Book
Alternate Check Test, p. 29

BUILDING ENGLISH PROFICIENCY

Making Real-Life Connections

Help students relate to Scene 5, lines 32–33 (p. 160)—the witches' claim that overconfidence is "mortals' chiefest enemy."

Activity Ideas

- Ask students what problems Macbeth has already had with overconfidence. *(He thought he could get away with murder.)*
- Have groups of students brainstorm some perils of overconfidence (for example, driving too fast, taking someone that you love for granted, not believing that health warnings on cigarette packs apply to you). Ask each group to find a way to present one situation to the class (for example, by dramatizing it or drawing a comic strip).

After Reading

MAKING CONNECTIONS

1. Possible response: Flee Scotland or prepare for all-out war.

2. Macbeth fears Banquo's suspicions and the witches' prophesy regarding Banquo's descendants.

3. He convinces them of the wrongs Banquo supposedly did them, and he attacks their legitimacy as men.

4. Possible responses: He may want to prove something to her, accomplish some plan independently, or avoid hearing her response to his plan.

5. not effectively; although as well as could be expected under the circumstances

6. It is dangerous to speak frankly, so Lennox screens his remarks toward Macbeth with irony. Up until line 19, everything he says can be interpreted in two ways. The passage shows that Lennox believes Macbeth guilty of the murders of Duncan and Banquo.

7. Possible responses: stupidity, desperation, arrogance, overconfidence, lust for power, indifference to outcome

VOCABULARY STUDY

1. c
2. d
3. a
4. c
5. b

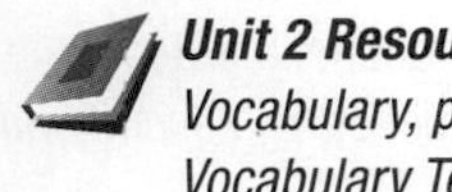

Unit 2 Resource Book
Vocabulary, p. 27
Vocabulary Test, p. 30

Selection Test

Unit 2 Resource Book
pp. 31–32

Act 3

After Reading

Making Connections

Shaping Your Response

1. At this point, what advice would you give to Macbeth and Lady Macbeth?

Analyzing the Play

2. Why do you think Macbeth fears Banquo as he does?

3. How does Macbeth manipulate the two murderers into agreeing to kill Banquo?

4. Why do you think Macbeth doesn't tell Lady Macbeth about the plans he has made to have Banquo and Fleance murdered?

5. How well do you think Lady Macbeth manages to cover up for Macbeth's odd behavior at the banquet?

6. Trace the **irony** in Lennox's speech to the Lord in scene 6. What special meaning does it give his speech?

Extending the Ideas

7. Macbeth talks about giving his soul to the common enemy of man, the Devil. He knows his actions so far are wrong, yet he persists. What causes people to take actions they know are clearly evil?

Literary Focus: Plot Structure

Act 3 is considered the **climax** of the play. Macbeth and Lady Macbeth have achieved their greatest desire—Macbeth is king. However, the escape of Fleance changes their fortune; it is the **turning point** or **dramatic reversal** of the plot. List other events in this act that that might reverse the fortunes of Macbeth and Lady Macbeth. Place them on a chart such as the one on page 116.

Vocabulary Study

Select the word that is most nearly *opposite* in meaning to the numbered word.

1. dauntless — **a.** brave **b.** bright **c.** fearful **d.** feeble

2. jovial — **a.** clever **b.** greedy **c.** sincere **d.** unhappy

3. malevolence — **a.** good will **b.** untruthfulness **c.** ill will **d.** mystery

4. verity — **a.** seriousness **b.** truth **c.** falsehood **d.** profit

5. chide — **a.** lower **b.** praise **c.** raise **d.** separate

---

LITERARY FOCUS: PLOT

Possible Responses

Part of Rising Action or Complication

- Macbeth hallucinates in front of his noblemen.
- Macduff fails to respond to Macbeth's invitation.
- Hecate plans Macbeth's fall.

Part of Climax

- Lennox realizes the truth about Macbeth and the murders.

Part of Falling Action

- It is reported that Macduff is in England raising an army against Macbeth.

Act Four

SCENE 1

Summary *Macbeth visits the witches again and asks them to prophesy his future. They show him three visions: an armed head, a bloody child, and a child wearing a crown and carrying a tree. They also show a line of eight kings followed by the ghost of Banquo, indicating that Banquo's descendants will rule. Later, learning that Macduff has gone to England, Macbeth plans the murders of Macduff's wife and children.*

A cave. In the middle, a large cooking pot. Thunder. Enter the three WITCHES.

1 **FIRST WITCH.** Thrice the brinded cat hath mewed.
SECOND WITCH. Thrice, and once the hedgepig whined.
THIRD WITCH. Harpier cries. 'Tis time, 'tis time!
FIRST WITCH. Round about the cauldron go;
In the poisoned entrails throw.
Toad, that under cold stone
Days and nights has thirty-one
Sweltered venom, sleeping got,
Boil thou first i' the charmèd pot.
ALL *(dancing round the cauldron).* Double, double, toil and trouble;
Fire burn, and cauldron bubble.
SECOND WITCH. Fillet of a fenny snake,
In the cauldron boil and bake;
Eye of newt and toe of frog,
Wool of bat and tongue of dog,
Adder's fork and blindworm's sting,
Lizard's leg and owlet's wing,
For a charm of powerful trouble,
Like a hell-broth boil and bubble.
ALL. Double, double, toil and trouble;
Fire burn, and cauldron bubble.
THIRD WITCH. Scale of dragon, tooth of wolf,
Witches' mummy, maw and gulf
Of the ravined salt-sea shark,
Root of hemlock digged i' the dark,
2 Liver of blaspheming Jew,
Gall of goat, and slips of yew
Slivered in the moon's eclipse,
Nose of Turk and Tartar's lips,
Finger of birth-strangled babe
Ditch-delivered by a drab,
Make the gruel thick and slab.
Add thereto a tiger's chaudron
For th' ingredients of our cauldron.

1 brinded, brindled; spotted or streaked.
2 hedge pig, hedge hog.
3 Harpier, the Third Witch's familiar spirit.
4 cauldron (kôl′drən), *n.* large kettle.
5 entrails (en′trālz), *n. pl.* intestines.
12 fillet . . . snake, slice of a snake from a fen, or swamp.
17 owlet, a small owl.
23 maw and gulf, stomach and throat.
24 ravined (rav′ənd), *adj.* ravenous; very hungry.
27 yew, evergreen tree, thought to be poisonous.
31 drab, whore.
32 slab, slimy.
33 chaudron (chô′drən), *n.* intestines.

During Reading

Vocabulary Preview

cauldron, large kettle
diminutive, very small
laudable, praiseworthy
cistern, reservoir for holding water
abjure, take back

Students can add the words and definitions to their Writer's Notebooks.

1 Historical Note
Witchcraft

Shakespeare, who wrote *Macbeth* for King James I of England, was aware that the monarch took a keen interest in witchcraft. Besides ordering the execution of all witches of the realm, James wrote a book on the subject entitled *Dæmonologie.* The King came to believe that his cousin, Francis Lord Bothwell, was a witch when the cousin attempted to murder him.

2 Historical Note
Racism

Students may find racial references in this passage offensive. Point out that in 17th-century England, racial bias was not viewed in the same light as it is today. Also, point out that it is the witches who use these terms. You might lead a discussion on how this trait fits their characterization.

Unit 2 Resource Book
Graphic Organizer, p. 33
Study Guide, p. 34

ACT FOUR SUMMARY

Macbeth

The witches show Macbeth three apparitions: an armed head warns Macbeth to beware Macduff; a bloody child assures that "none of woman born" shall harm Macbeth; a crowned child bearing a branch foretells that Macbeth will not be conquered until Birnam Wood comes to Dunsinane Hill. Macbeth is then shown the future: eight kings, followed by the smiling ghost of Banquo. When Macbeth learns that Macduff has fled to England, he orders the slaughter of Macduff's wife and children. In England, Malcolm tests the loyalty of Macduff. When finally assured of Macduff's loyalty, Malcolm invites Macduff to join in an invasion of Scotland, led by Siward. The news of the murder of Lady Macduff and her children steels them for the attack.

*For summaries in other languages, see the **Building English Proficiency** book.*

3 Literary Element
Theme

Questions What is the "wicked" thing that approaches? *(Response: Macbeth)* To what theme in the play does this title "wicked" refer? *(Possible response: As the witches predict at the outset, fair is foul, that is, fair Macbeth is now foul [wicked] Macbeth.)*

4 Reader's Response
Making Personal Connections

Question Why do you think the witches allow Macbeth to choose who will answer his questions? *(Possible responses: This is a device the author uses to heighten dramatic tension; the witches know Macbeth will choose the more powerful source of information; the witches toy with him, making him believe that he has power over them when he actually does not; the witches are luring Macbeth deeper into Hecate's destructive web.)*

ALL. Double, double, toil and trouble;
Fire burn, and cauldron bubble.
SECOND WITCH. Cool it with a baboon's blood,
Then the charm is firm and good. (*Enter* HECATE.)
HECATE. O, well done! I commend your pains,
And everyone shall share in' the gains.
And now about the cauldron sing
Like elves and fairies in a ring,
Enchanting all that you put in.
(*Music and a song: "Black spirits," etc. Exit* HECATE.)
SECOND WITCH. By the pricking of my thumbs,
3 Something wicked this way comes.
Open, locks,
Whoever knocks! (*Enter* MACBETH.)
MACBETH. How now, you secret, black, and midnight hags?
What is 't you do?
ALL. A deed without a name.
MACBETH. I conjure you, by that which you profess,
Howe'er you come to know it, answer me.
Though you untie the winds and let them fight
Against the churches, though the yeasty waves
Confound and swallow navigation up,
Though bladed corn be lodged and trees blown down,
Though castles topple on their warders' heads,
Though palaces and pyramids do slope
Their heads to their foundations, though the treasure
Of nature's germens tumble all together,
Even till destruction sicken, answer me
To what I ask you.
FIRST WITCH. Speak.
SECOND WITCH. Demand.
THIRD WITCH. We'll answer.
FIRST WITCH. Say if thou'dst rather hear it from our mouths
Or from our masters?
4 **MACBETH.** Call 'em. Let me see 'em.
FIRST WITCH. Pour in sow's blood, that hath eaten
Her nine farrow; grease that's sweaten
From the murderer's gibbet throw
Into the flame.
ALL. Come high or low.
Thyself and office deftly show!
(*Thunder. The* FIRST APPARITION, *a soldier's head, appears.*)
MACBETH. Tell me, thou unknown power—
FIRST WITCH. He knows thy thought.
Hear his speech, but say thou naught.

50 conjure (kən jůr′), *v.* request earnestly; entreat

53 yeasty, foamy.

55 though . . . lodged, though grain, still green, may be beaten down.
56 warder, guard or watchman.
59 nature's germens, the seeds by which nature's cycles operate.
60 sicken, is in excess.

65 farrow (far′ō), piglets; baby pigs.
66 gibbet (jib′it), gallows used for hanging.

apparition (ap ə rish′ən), *n.* ghost; phantom.

70 naught (nôt), *n.* nothing.

MINI-LESSON: STUDY SKILLS
Researching

Teach Students who want to explore *Macbeth* in greater depth will benefit from instruction in using electronic card catalogs. A topic of particular use may be key-word searches. Students can learn how to combine topics, as well as how to organize a search and what to do if their first approach fails to provide the information they need.

Activity Idea Students can
- suggest topics related to their reading so far and then write those topics on the board or an overhead projector.
- brainstorm how they would conduct a key-word search.

Macbeth, Banquo, and the Witches by George Cattermole is a watercolor of the 1800s. How does the style of this picture suggest the mystery and horror of the apparition scene?

Art Study

Response to Caption Question The mystery and horror of this scene from *Macbeth* is echoed in this painting by the artist's use of contrasts: the radiant light in which the apparitions appear compared to the brooding darkness surrounding the mortal characters; the calm in which the unearthly figures dwell compared to the violent winds that buffet Macbeth and the witches.

Visual Literacy This 19th-century watercolor by George Cattermole depicts the ghost of Banquo pointing out to Macbeth "the apparition of eight" from Act Four, Scene 1, lines 112–123. The "apparition of eight" is Banquo's line of descendants—eight future kings of Scotland, the last of whom holds a mirror to the future.

Question How does the subject of this painting relate to what has happened so far in the play? *(Banquo points out to Macbeth that his line, his descendants, will sit upon the throne; this prediction, in Act One, is what prompts Macbeth, in Act Three, to murder Banquo and attempt to murder his son, Fleance.)*

BUILDING ENGLISH PROFICIENCY

ESL
LEP
ELD
SAE
LD

Relating Parts of Speech

Help students explore one difficulty in learning English—namely, that some words are spelled the same in both noun and verb forms (for example, *trouble, lock*) whereas others are spelled differently *(enchant/enchantment, do/deed).*

Have students complete this chart (shown completed here), identifying whether the word, as used on page 164, is a noun or verb, then supplying the other part of speech. Discuss how the forms differ.

Word	Noun/Verb	Changes to . . .
charm	*noun*	*charm (verb)*
sing	*verb*	*song (noun)*
profess	*verb*	*profession (noun)*
swallow	*verb*	*swallow (noun)*
destruction	*noun*	*destroy (verb)*
thought	*noun*	*think (verb)*

Building English Proficiency
Activities, p. 214

5 Reader's Response
Challenging the Text

Questions What do you think the line "none of women born shall harm Macbeth" could mean? *(Possible response: that no living person can kill Macbeth; that he will die of natural causes or old age)* Can you think of any possible way a human being could be not "of women born"? *(Many students will not be able to think of anything; some may cite scientific advancements of the 20th century, e.g., "test-tube babies.")*

6 Literary Element
Style

Questions How does the style of this speech differ from the style of Macbeth's other speeches? *(Possible responses: This is the first time that Macbeth speaks entirely in rhymed couplets; it is also the first time that he refers to himself in the third person.)* What explanation can you offer for these stylistic changes? *(Possible responses: Macbeth's assumption of the rhymed couplet style of the witches suggests that he is either utterly enthralled with their revelations or completely under their spell; his use of the third person suggests how far he has grown away from his true self.)*

FIRST APPARITION. Macbeth! Macbeth! Macbeth! Beware Macduff,
Beware the Thane of Fife. Dismiss me. Enough. *(It disappears.)*
MACBETH. Whate'er thou art, for thy good caution, thanks;
Thou hast harped my fear aright. But one word more—
FIRST WITCH. He will not be commanded. Here's another,
More potent than the first.
(Thunder. The SECOND APPARITION, *a bloody child.)*
SECOND APPARITION. Macbeth! Macbeth! Macbeth!
MACBETH. Had I three ears, I'd hear thee.
SECOND APPARITION. Be bloody, bold, and resolute; laugh to scorn
5 The power of man, for none of woman born
Shall harm Macbeth. *(It disappears.)*
MACBETH. Then live, Macduff; what need I fear of thee?
But yet I'll make assurance double sure,
And take a bond of fate. Thou shalt not live,
That I may tell pale-hearted fear it lies,
And sleep in spite of thunder.
(Thunder. The THIRD APPARITION, *a child crowned, with a tree in his hand.)*
What is this
That rises like the issue of a king
And wears upon his baby brow the round
And top of sovereignty?
ALL. Listen, but speak not to 't.
THIRD APPARITION. Be lion-mettled, proud, and take no care
Who chafes, who frets, or where conspirers are.
Macbeth shall never vanquished be until
Great Birnam Wood to high Dunsinane Hill
Shall come against him. *(It disappears.)*
6 **MACBETH.** That will never be.
Who can impress the forest, bid the tree
Unfix his earthbound root? Sweet bodements, good!
Rebellious dead, rise never till the wood
Of Birnam rise, and our high-placed Macbeth
Shall live the lease of nature, pay his breath
To time and mortal custom. Yet my heart
Throbs to know one thing. Tell me, if your art
Can tell so much: shall Banquo's issue ever
Reign in this kingdom?
ALL. Seek to know no more.
MACBETH. I will be satisfied. Deny me this,
And an eternal curse fall on you! Let me know.
(The cauldron sinks out of sight. Music sounds offstage.)
Why sinks that cauldron? And what noise is this?
FIRST WITCH. Show!
SECOND WITCH. Show!

74 harped, guessed.

84 take . . . fate, make sure that fate's promise is fulfilled.

88–89 round and top, crown.

93 Dunsinane, (dun′sə nān′).

95 impress, force to serve as soldiers.
96 bodement (bōd′mənt), *n.* prophecy.

99–100 pay his breath . . . custom, die a natural death.

MINI-LESSON: GRAMMAR
Using Shall and Will

Teach Point out Macbeth's first sentence in line 104 on page 166. Explain that it used to be a hard and fast rule that futurity or expectation were expressed by *shall* in the first-person present indicative in a declarative sentence, whereas *will* expressed determination, threat, command, willingness, or promise. These rules are no longer strictly followed, so readers and listeners must rely on context to determine the meaning of the word *will.*

Activity Idea Debate Macbeth's use of the verb *will* in line 104 and connect it with the development of his character. Divide the class into two groups, having one argue that Shakespeare was indicating futurity and the other that he was indicating Macbeth's determination or a threat.

THIRD WITCH. Show!
ALL. Show his eyes, and grieve his heart;
Come like shadows, so depart!
(*A show of eight* KINGS, *the last carrying a magic mirror. They are followed by* BANQUO'S GHOST.)
7 **MACBETH.** Thou art too like the spirit of Banquo. Down!
Thy crown does sear mine eyeballs. And thy hair,
Thou other gold-bound brow, is like the first.
A third is like the former. Filthy hags,
Why do you show me this? A fourth? Start, eyes!
What, will the line stretch out to th' crack of doom?
Another yet? A seventh? I'll see no more.
And yet the eighth appears, who bears a glass
Which shows me many more; and some I see
That twofold balls and treble scepters carry.
Horrible sight! Now I see 'tis true,
For the blood-boltered Banquo smiles upon me
And points at them for his. (*The apparitions disappear.*)
What, is this so?
FIRST WITCH. Ay, sir, all this is so. But why
Stands Macbeth thus amazedly?
Come, sisters, cheer we up his sprites
And show the best of our delights.
I'll charm the air to give a sound,
While you perform your antic round,
That this great king may kindly say
Our duties did his welcome pay.
(*Music. The* WITCHES *dance; then they disappear.*)
MACBETH. Where are they? Gone? Let this pernicious hour
Stand aye accursèd in the calendar!
Come in, without there! (*Enter* LENNOX.)
8 **LENNOX.** What's Your Grace's will?
MACBETH. Saw you the Weird Sisters?
LENNOX. No, my lord.
MACBETH. Came they not by you?
LENNOX. No, indeed, my lord.
MACBETH. Infected be the air whereon they ride,
And damned all those that trust them! I did hear
The galloping of horse. Who was 't came by?
LENNOX. 'Tis two or three, my lord, that bring you word
Macduff is fled to England.
MACBETH. Fled to England!
LENNOX. Ay, my good lord.
MACBETH (*aside*). Time, thou anticipat'st my dread exploits.
The flighty purpose never is o'ertook

119 glass, a magic mirror showing the future.
121 twofold . . . scepters. The balls and scepters symbolize the sovereignty of England and Scotland, and the kingdoms of England, Scotland, and Ireland which were united for the first time under James I, eighth of the Stuart kings.
123, blood-boltered, having hair matted with blood.
127, sprites, spirits.
130 antic round, grotesque dance in a circle.
133 pernicious, (pər nish′əs), *adj.* fatal; deadly.
134 aye, (ā), *adv.* forever.

■ Summarize the prophecies that the apparitions have brought Macbeth.

7 Reading/Thinking Skills
Compare and Contrast

After students have read lines 112–124, suggest that they turn back to the illustration on page 165.

Question How would you compare or contrast Shakespeare's "word picture" of the "apparition of eight" with George Cattermole's painting of the same scene? *(While responses will vary, students might note that Cattermole's painting differs in many small details: Banquo wears no crown; his hair is not matted with blood. The painting also seems far more tame, static, and less colorful than the picture Shakespeare paints with words: "sear mine eyeballs," "filthy hags," "th' crack of doom," and "blood-boltered Banquo.")*

8 Reading/Thinking Skills
Generalize

Response Macbeth should beware of Macduff; he cannot be hurt by any man born of woman; he will not be conquered until Birnam Wood comes to the castle on Dunsinane Hill; and Banquo's line will sit on the throne of Scotland for at least eight generations.

BUILDING ENGLISH PROFICIENCY

Mapping Opposing Character Traits

Drawing a character wheel like the example shown will help students contrast and discuss characters. Have them put opposing characteristics at opposite ends of each line.

1. Ask students to think about which character in the play most demonstrates each quality at this time. Have them write his or her name on the rim of the wheel.

2. After students have completed their wheels, encourage them to compare and defend their opinions in small groups.

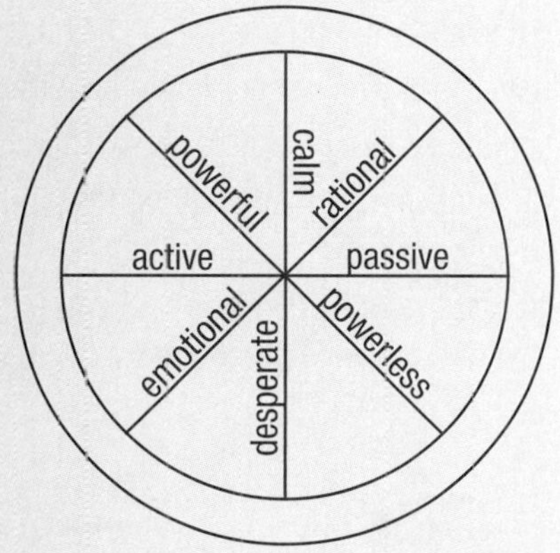

9 Literary Focus
Plot

Questions What simmering conflict does Macbeth plan to bring to a head? *(his conflict with Macduff)* What do you think the consequences might be? *(Possible response: The murder of Macduff's family could provoke open warfare with Macduff and rebellion among the other thanes.)*

10 Thinking/Reading Skills
Infer

Response The conversation suggests that Lady Macduff has received a message that her husband has fled to England.

11 Reader's Response
Making Personal Connections

If this speech can be taken at face value, Lady Macduff interprets her husband's flight as cowardice and states that he does not show proper concern for his family.

Questions What do you think of Macduff's actions? *(Possible responses: Macduff has placed the welfare of the nation ahead of the welfare of himself and his family; or Macduff has callously forsaken his family, possibly out of personal fear.)*

Unless the deed go with it. From this moment
The very firstlings of my heart shall be
The firstlings of my hand. And even now,
To crown my thoughts with acts, be it thought and done:
The castle of Macduff I will surprise,
9
Seize upon Fife, give to th' edge o' the sword
His wife, his babes, and all unfortunate souls
That trace him in his line. No boasting like a fool;
This deed I'll do before this purpose cool.
But no more sights! Where are these gentlemen?
Come, bring me where they are.

145–148 The flighty . . . hand. One must act at once if one is to accomplish one's purpose. From now on I shall put my thoughts into immediate action.

SCENE 2

Summary *Ross tells Lady Macduff that her husband has fled the country. Murderers hired by Macbeth kill Lady Macduff and her children.*

MACDUFF'S *castle at Fife. Enter* LADY MACDUFF, *her* SON, *and* ROSS.

LADY MACDUFF. What had he done to make him fly the land? 10

ROSS. You must have patience, madam.

LADY MACDUFF. He had none.
His flight was madness. When our actions do not,
Our fears do make us traitors.

ROSS. You know not
Whether it was his wisdom or his fear.

11

LADY MACDUFF. Wisdom? To leave his wife, to leave his babes,
His mansion, and his titles in a place
From whence himself does fly? He loves us not,
He wants the natural touch; for the poor wren,
The most diminutive of birds, will fight,
Her young ones in her nest, against the owl.
All is the fear and nothing is the love,
As little is the wisdom, where the flight
So runs against all reason.

ROSS. My dearest coz,
I pray you, school yourself. But, for your husband,
He is noble, wise, judicious, and best knows
The fits o' the season. I dare not speak much further,
But cruel are the times when we are traitors
And do not know ourselves, when we hold rumor
From what we fear, yet know not what we fear,
But float upon a wild and violent sea
Each way and none. I take my leave of you;
Shall not be long but I'll be here again.
Things at the worst will cease, or else climb upward
To what they were before. My pretty cousin,

■ What message has Ross apparently brought to Lady Macduff?

7 titles, possessions.

9 he wants. . . . touch, he lacks natural human affection.

10 diminutive (də min′yə-tiv), *adj.* very small.

14 coz, cousin.

15 school, control.

16 judicious (jü dish′ əs), *adj.* sensible; showing good judgment.

17 fits . . . season, violence of the times.

18–19 are traitors . . . ourselves, are accused of treason without thinking of ourselves as traitors.

19–20 hold rumor. . . . fear, believe rumors that grow out of fears.

MINI-LESSON: USAGE
Negative Constructions

Teach Read lines 35–36 on page 169:

"Thou'dst never fear/ The net nor lime, the pitfall nor the gin."

Explain that *nor* is a variant of *or.* It is used in the following situations:

- When one alternative is preceded by *neither,* the next alternative must be preceded by *nor.*
- When one alternative is made negative by *not* or another negative word, the next alternative is preceded by *nor* in order to continue the negation.

Activity Idea Have students look through newspapers, magazines, and other contemporary writing to find examples of the use of *nor* and bring them in for class discussion.

Blessing upon you!
12 **LADY MACDUFF.** Fathered he is, and yet he's fatherless.
ROSS. I am so much a fool, should I stay longer
It would be my disgrace and your discomfort.
I take my leave at once. (*Exit* ROSS.)
LADY MACDUFF. Sirrah, your father's dead;
And what will you do now? How will you live?
13 **SON.** As birds do, Mother.
LADY MACDUFF. What, with worms and flies?
SON. With what I get, I mean; and so do they.
LADY MACDUFF. Poor bird! Thou'dst never fear
The net nor lime, the pitfall nor the gin.
SON. Why should I, Mother? Poor birds they are not set for.
My father is not dead, for all your saying.
LADY MACDUFF. Yes, he is dead. How wilt thou do for a father?
SON. Nay, how will you do for a husband?
LADY MACDUFF. Why, I can buy me twenty at any market.
SON. Then you'll buy 'em to sell again.
LADY MACDUFF. Thou speak'st with all thy wit,
And yet, i' faith, with wit enough for thee.
SON. Was my father a traitor, Mother?
LADY MACDUFF. Ay, that he was.
SON. What is a traitor?
LADY MACDUFF. Why, one that swears and lies.
SON. And be all traitors that do so?
LADY MACDUFF. Every one that does so is a traitor,
And must be hanged.
SON. And must they all be hanged that swear and lie?
LADY MACDUFF. Every one.
SON. Who must hang them?
LADY MACDUFF. Why, the honest men.
SON. Then the liars and swearers, are fools, for there are liars and swearers enough to beat the honest men and hang them up.
LADY MACDUFF. Now, God help thee, poor monkey!
But how wilt thou do for a father?
SON. If he were dead, you'd weep for him; if you would not, it were a good sign that I should quickly have a new father.
14 **LADY MACDUFF.** Poor prattler, how thou talk'st!
(*Enter a* MESSENGER.)
MESSENGER. Bless you, fair dame! I am not to you known,
Though in your state of honor I am perfect.
I doubt some danger does approach you nearly.
If you will take a homely man's advice,
Be not found here. Hence with your little ones!
To fright you thus, methinks, I am too savage;

36 lime, birdlime, a sticky substance used to catch birds.
36 gin, trap.

48 swears and lies, swears allegiance and then breaks his oath.

62 prattler, (prat′lər) *n.* babbler; foolish talker.
64 in your . . . perfect, I know of your honorable rank.
65 doubt, suspect.

BUILDING ENGLISH PROFICIENCY

ESL LEP ELD SAE LD

Analyzing Characters

Creating an "open-mind" diagram for Lady Macduff, as shown, will help students grasp what is shaping her thoughts in what turns out to be her final moments. You might suggest these topics:

- her husband
- Ross
- her son
- her emotions

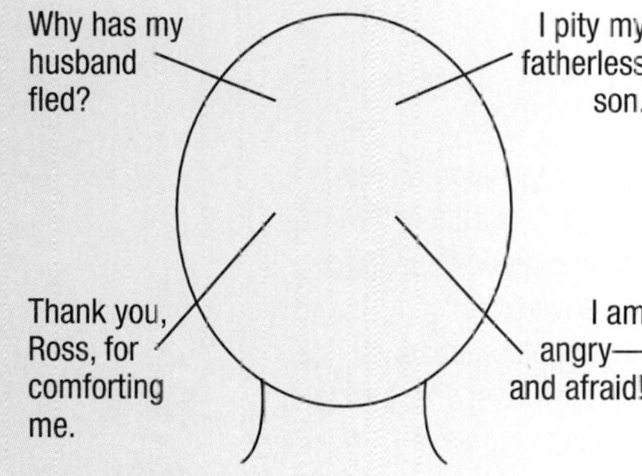
Why has my husband fled?
I pity my fatherless son.
Thank you, Ross, for comforting me.
I am angry—and afraid!

12 Literary Element
Theme

Question What theme of the play does "Fathered he is, and yet he's fatherless" suggest? *("Fair is foul, and foul is fair"—good and evil and all values are reversed. Lady Macduff states that while her son has a father, he is essentially fatherless because Macduff fails in his duty to his family.)*

13 Multicultural Note
The Bible

In line 34, Macduff's son alludes to Jesus' Sermon on the Mount (Matthew 6:26): "Behold the fowls of the air: for they sow not, neither do they reap, nor gather into barns; yet your heavenly Father feedeth them. Are ye not much better than they?"

14 Literary Element
Dialogue

Remind students that dialogue can serve many purposes, including characterization, mood, plot, and theme.

Question What purpose do you think this dialogue between mother and son serves? *(Possible responses: Both son and mother speak the truth; they are in great danger because Macduff has left them unprotected; yet, Lady Macduff may be too quick to judge her husband's motives, for which her son cleverly chides her; he also suggests that the accusers, including Lady Macduff, not the accused, Macduff, are the real traitors, which all serves a theme of the play. The dialogue also functions as a way to very quickly introduce and breathe life into new characters.)*

15 Literary Element
Theme

Question How does Lady Macduff's statement fit the theme of reversal of values? *(Possible response: She says that now it has become praiseworthy to do harm and dangerously foolish to do good—values have been reversed.)*

16 Literary Element
Dialogue

Question After reading this scene, can you think of other purposes that the dialogue between Lady Macduff and her son serves? *(Possible responses: The dialogue serves the plot by setting up this newest round of murder; and it intensifies the horror of the murders, serving the mood of the play, by allowing the audience to get to know the victims.)*

17 Reading/Thinking Skills
Recognize Use of Persuasion

Response He tries to convey Scotland's present desperation.

Question What is he trying to persuade Malcolm to do? *(to take up arms against Macbeth)*

To do worse to you were fell cruelty,
Which is too nigh your person. Heaven preserve you!
I dare abide no longer. (*Exit* MESSENGER.)

LADY MACDUFF. Whither should I fly?
I have done no harm. But I remember now
I am in this earthly world, where to do harm
15 Is often laudable, to do good sometimes
Accounted dangerous folly. Why then, alas,
Do I put up that womanly defense
To say I have done no harm? (*Enter* MURDERERS.)
What are these faces?

FIRST MURDERER. Where is your husband?

LADY MACDUFF. I hope in no place so unsanctified
Where such as thou mayst find him.

FIRST MURDERER. He's a traitor.

SON. Thou liest, thou shag-haired villain!

FIRST MURDERER. What, you egg?
(*He stabs him.*) Young fry of treachery!

SON. He has killed me, Mother.
16 Run away, I pray you! (*He dies.*)

(*Exit* LADY MACDUFF *crying* "Murder!" *followed by the* MURDERERS *with the* SON'S *body.*)

74 laudable (lô′də bəl), *adj.* praiseworthy.

SCENE 3

Summary *Malcolm tests Macduff's loyalty. Convinced that Macduff is not allied to Macbeth, Malcolm invites him to join with the forces that will attempt to overthrow Macbeth. They learn from Ross that Lady Macduff and the children have been murdered, and Macduff and Malcolm prepare to return to Scotland.*

The palace of the King of England. Enter MALCOLM *and* MACDUFF.

MALCOLM. Let us seek out some desolate shade, and there
Weep our sad bosoms empty.

MACDUFF. Let us rather
Hold fast the mortal sword, and like good men
Bestride our downfall'n birthdom. Each new morn
New widows howl, new orphans cry, new sorrows
Strike heaven on the face, that it resounds
As if it felt with Scotland and yelled out
Like syllable of dolor.

MALCOLM. What I believe, I'll wail;
What know, believe; and what I can redress,
As I shall find the time to friend, I will.
What you have spoke it may be so, perchance.
This tyrant, whose sole name blisters our tongues,

17 ■ In his meeting with Malcolm what attitude toward his country is Macduff trying to convey?

4 bestride. . . . birthdom, defend our fallen fatherland.

8 dolor, (dōlor), *n.* grief.
9 redress, (ri dres′) *v.* set right; remedy.
10 to friend, suitable.

MINI-LESSON: GRAMMAR

Diagramming Adjectives, Adverbs, and Prepositional Phrases

Teach Read these lines from pages 170 and 171:

I have done no harm.

I think our country sinks beneath the yoke;

Point out the noun *harm,* its adjective *no,* the preposition *beneath,* and its object *yoke.* In sentencediagramming, a modifier is attached to the word it modifies witha a slanted line. A similar technique is used for prepositional pharses that act as adjectives or adverbs, except that the preposition goes on the slanted line and its object on a horizontal line above the end of the slanted line. Diagram a noun clause like a regular sentence and attach it by a "tree" to the main clause in whatever position a noun would occupy. Show these examples.

Activity Idea Have partners create three sentence diagrams withmodifiers in the subject and three with modifiers in the predicate.

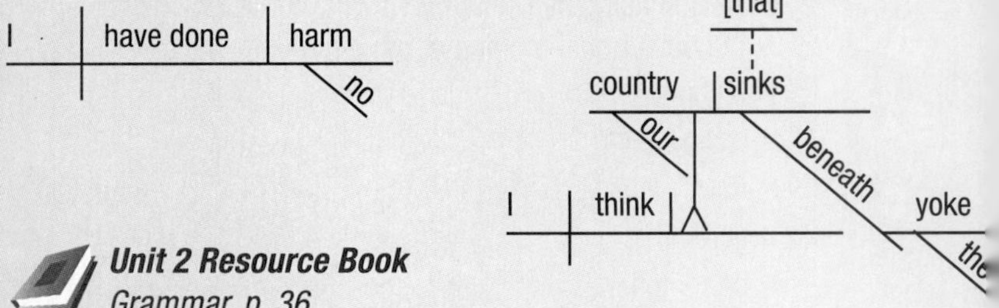

Unit 2 Resource Book
Grammar, p. 36

Was once thought honest. You have loved him well;
He hath not touched you yet. I am young; but something
You may deserve of him through me, and wisdom
To offer up a weak, poor, innocent lamb
18 T' appease an angry god.

MACDUFF. I am not treacherous.

MALCOLM. But Macbeth is.
A good and virtuous nature may recoil
In an imperial charge. But I shall crave your pardon.
That which you are my thoughts cannot transpose;
Angels are bright still, though the brightest fell.
Though all things foul would wear the brows of grace,
Yet grace must still look so.

MACDUFF. I have lost my hopes.

MALCOLM. Perchance even there where I did find my doubts.
Why in that rawness left you wife and child,
Those precious motives, those strong knots of love,
Without leave-taking? I pray you,
Let not my jealousies be your dishonors,
But mine own safeties. You may be rightly just,
Whatever I shall think.

MACDUFF. Bleed, bleed, poor country!
Great tyranny, lay thou thy basis sure,
For goodness dare not check thee; wear thou thy wrongs,
The title is affeered! Fare thee well, lord.
I would not be the villain that thou think'st
For the whole space that's in the tyrant's grasp,
And the rich East to boot.

MALCOLM. Be not offended.
I speak not as in absolute fear of you.
I think our country sinks beneath the yoke;
It weeps, it bleeds, and each new day a gash
Is added to her wounds. I think withal
There would be hands uplifted in my right;
And here from gracious England have I offer
Of goodly thousands. But, for all this,
When I shall tread upon the tyrant's head,
Or wear it on my sword, yet my poor country
Shall have more vices than it had before,
More suffer, and more sundry ways than ever,
By him that shall succeed.

MACDUFF. What should he be?

MALCOLM. It is myself I mean, in whom I know
All the particulars of vice so grafted
That, when they shall be opened, black Macbeth

14–15 but something . . . me, but you may win favor from Macbeth by betraying me.

20–21 recoil. . . . charge, reverse itself through loyalty to the king.
22 transpose, change.
23 brightest fell, Satan, once the "brightest" angel in Heaven, warred with God and was defeated by him.

27 rawness, haste.

30–31 let not . . . safeties, I am suspicious not to dishonor you but because I wish to assure my own safety.

35 The title . . . affeered. Your (tyranny's) title is confirmed.
44 England, the king of England.

Murderers creep up on Lady Macduff and her son in this illustration by Charles Ricketts (1923). How does this picture convey the mood of the scene?

18 Reading/Thinking Skills

Compare and Contrast

In this scene, Malcolm speaks sharply to Macduff, even suggesting that Macduff, working for Macbeth, is attempting to lure Malcolm back to Scotland to his doom.

Question Keeping in mind King Duncan's behavior and responses in Act One, how would you compare him to his son, Malcolm? Give specific examples. *(Possible response: Duncan trusted Cawdor and was betrayed; he then placed his trust in Macbeth, who murdered him. In contrast, Malcolm is far less trusting than his father and tries to pierce through appearances by questioning Macduff sharply.)*

Art Study

Response to Caption Question An ominous mood is conveyed by the posture of the man sneaking down the stairs and by the second man skulking in the doorway. The sallow yellows are colors often associated with cowardice and sickness. In contrast to the vertical angles that predominate in the picture, oblique angles—formed by the stairs, a curtain, the murderer's head, Lady Macduff's leg, and the child's arm—point, directly and ominously, at the victims' heads.

BUILDING ENGLISH PROFICIENCY

Making Cultural Connections

In Scene 3 Macduff and Malcolm describe the effects of war, especially internal strife. Use a chart to relate situations that students have heard or read about (and perhaps even experienced).

1. Have current newspapers and history texts available so that students can research examples if necessary.
2. Draw a chart on the chalkboard. Help students complete it, as shown, to reflect what characters in Scene 3 say about Scotland.
3. Divide students into small groups. Have each group find and suggest another example from history or current events.

Country	Sides	Effects
Scotland	Macbeth versus Malcolm	widows and orphans, sorrow, death

19 Literary Element
Metaphor

Question What do you think the metaphor "the cistern of my lust" suggests? *(Possible response: It may suggest "the great depths of my lust" or more aptly, "the great store of my lust," as cisterns are general large but shallow storage tanks.)*

20 Multicultural Note
Individuality

Response He accuses himself of voluptuousness and lust (lines 62, 64); willfulness (line 66); avarice (lines 79–85); he lacks all "king-becoming graces" (lines 92–96); he delights in crime and disorder (lines 96–98); and wishes to destroy the world (lines 98–101). Answers will vary: many may judge the two to be equal.

21 Reading/Thinking Skills
Find the Main Idea

Question What is the main idea that Macduff is conveying? *(Possible response: Although lust and avarice are not ideal traits for a ruler, they are bearable flaws.)*

Will seem as pure as snow, and the poor state
Esteem him as a lamb, being compared
With my confineless harms.

MACDUFF. Not in the legions
Of horrid hell can come a devil more damned
In evils to top Macbeth.

MALCOLM. I grant him bloody,
Luxurious, avaricious, false, deceitful,
Sudden, malicious, smacking of every sin
That has a name. But there's no bottom, none,
In my voluptuousness. Your wives, your daughters,
Your matrons, and your maids could not fill up
19 The cistern of my lust, and my desire
All continent impediments would o'erbear
That did oppose my will. Better Macbeth
Than such an one to reign.

MACDUFF. Boundless intemperance
In nature is a tyranny; it hath been
Th' untimely emptying of the happy throne
And fall of many kings. But fear not yet
To take upon you what is yours. You may
Convey your pleasures in a spacious plenty,
And yet seem cold; the time you may so hoodwink.
We have willing dames enough. There cannot be
That vulture in you to devour so many
As will to greatness dedicate themselves,
Finding it so inclined.

MALCOLM. With this there grows
In my most ill-composed affection such
A stanchless avarice that, were I king,
I should cut off the nobles for their lands,
Desire his jewels and this other's house,
And my more-having would be as a sauce
To make me hunger more, that I should forge
Quarrels unjust against the good and loyal,
Destroying them for wealth.

MACDUFF. This avarice
21 Sticks deeper, grows with more pernicious root
Than summer-seeming lust, and it hath been
The sword of our slain kings. Yet do not fear;
Scotland hath foisons to fill up your will
Of your mere own. All these are portable,
With other graces weighed.

MALCOLM. But I have none. The king-becoming graces,
As justice, verity, temperance, stableness,

56 confineless harms, unlimited evil.
59 luxurious (lug zhůr′ē əs), *adj.* lustful.
59 avaricious (av′ə rish′əs), *adj.* greedy for money.
60 sudden, violent.
61–62 but . . . voluptuousness (və lup′chü əs nis), but I need my senses pleased far more than Macbeth does.
64 cistern (sis′tərn), *n.* reservoir for holding water.

20 Summarize the charges that Malcolm levels against himself. Is the kind of **individuality** he is expressing here truly worse than Macbeth's?

72 convey (kən vā′), *v.* obtain secretly.
73 the time . . . hoodwink, the age you may thus deceive.

78 ill-composed affection, evil disposition.
79 stanchless avarice, excessive greed.

87 summer-seeming, short-lived.
89 foisons (foi′zənz), *n.* resources; plenty.
90–91 All these . . . weighed. These weaknesses are bearable, considering your other virtues.

MINI-LESSON: GRAMMAR
Recognizing the Function of the Vocative Part of Speech

Teach Read lines 101, 104–105, and 114–115 on page 173:

"O Scotland, Scotland!"

"O nation miserable,/With an untitled tyrant bloody-sceptered . . ."

"O my breast,/Thy hope ends here!"

Explain that when someone or something is called with a serious or earnest intent, the expression is in the vocative case. The *O* is part of the vocative address and the vocative is rarely used in modern English.

Question Although this is not the first time the vocative case is used in this play, it is used very often in this scene. Why do you think Shakespeare does this? *(Possible response: to express the strong feelings that Macduff is experiencing as he finds his hopes dashed for a restoration of the monarchy to the rightful heir and overthrow of the bloody tyrant who usurped the throne)*

Activity Idea For practice, students can

- write an ode that begins with a vocative
- search for examples of the vocative case in works of literature
- share their work with the class

Bounty, perseverance, mercy, lowliness,
Devotion, patience, courage, fortitude,
I have no relish of them, but abound
In the division of each several crime,
Acting it many ways. Nay, had I power, I should
22 Pour the sweet milk of concord into hell,
Uproar the universal peace, confound
All unity on earth.

MACDUFF. O Scotland, Scotland!

MALCOLM. If such a one be fit to govern, speak.
I am as I have spoken.

MACDUFF. Fit to govern?
No, not to live. O nation miserable,
With an untitled tyrant bloody-sceptered,
When shalt thou see thy wholesome days again,
Since that the truest issue of thy throne
By his own interdiction stands accurst
And does blaspheme his breed? Thy royal father
Was a most sainted king; the queen that bore thee,
Oft'ner upon her knees than on her feet,
Died every day she lived. Fare thee well.
These evils thou repeat'st upon thyself
Hath banished me from Scotland. O my breast,
Thy hope ends here!

MALCOLM. Macduff, this noble passion,
Child of integrity, hath from my soul
Wiped the black scruples, reconciled my thoughts
To thy good truth and honor. Devilish Macbeth
By many of these trains hath sought to win me
Into his power, and modest wisdom plucks me
From overcredulous haste. But God above
23 Deal between thee and me! For even now
I put myself to thy direction and
Unspeak mine own detraction, here abjure
The taints and blames I laid upon myself
For strangers to my nature. I am yet
Unknown to woman, never was forsworn,
Scarcely have coveted what was mine own,
At no time broke my faith, would not betray
24 The devil to his fellow, and delight
No less in truth than life. My first false speaking
Was this upon myself. What I am truly
Is thine and my poor country's to command—
Whither indeed, before thy here-approach,
Old Siward with ten thousand warlike men,

99 **concord** (kon′kôrd), *n.* agreement.

108 **interdiction** (in′tər-dik′shən), *n.* decree.
109 **blaspheme his breed,** slander his parentage.

112 **died . . . lived,** prepared for death by daily prayers and self-sacrifice.

117 **black scruples,** suspicions of Macduff's treachery.
119 **trains,** plots.

124 **abjure** (ab jůr′), *v.* take back.

22 Reading/Thinking Skills
Recognize Cause and Effect

Question What finally causes Macduff to decide that Malcolm is no more fit to rule Scotland than Macbeth? *(Possible response: when Malcolm states he has no "king-becoming graces" and would relish sowing war and disunity)*

23 Literary Element
Characterization

Question When does this game that Malcolm has played with Macduff suggest about his true character? *(Possible responses: that he is a very careful young man; that he can be tricky in his dealings with others and holds his own council when necessary)*

24 Reading/Thinking Skills
Draw Conclusions

Question What does Malcolm's statement about the devil mean? *(Possible response: Malcolm's sense of loyalty is so strong that he would not betray even the most wicked being.)*

BUILDING ENGLISH PROFICIENCY

Expanding Vocabulary Notebooks

In lines 93–95 Malcolm lists twelve "king-becoming graces," the characteristics of a good king. Help students add these words to their personal vocabulary.

1. Ask students to include each word, its definition, and a sentence using the word in their Vocabulary Notebooks.

2. Divide students into pairs. Invite each pair to choose the grace that they consider most important. (Alternatively, you might want to write the name of each grace on a slip of paper, put the slips in a basket, and have each pair select one.) Ask each pair to use pantomime or a brief enactment of a dramatic situation to show the class what its "king-becoming grace" means.

3. To extend the activity, have students think of a real person who demonstrates one or more of the graces. Allow them to write or dictate a description of the person.

25 Literary Element
Symbolism

Questions What might King Edward's ability to cure the disease called "the evil" symbolize? *(Possible response: a similar ability to "cure" evil or wickedness)* How would you compare Edward's "touch" as king to Macbeth's? *(Possible response: While Edward's touch "cures" evil, Macbeth's touch fosters evil.)*

26 Historical Note
The Healing Benediction

The monarch for whom Shakespeare wrote *Macbeth*, James I of England and James VI of Scotland, was believed to share "the healing benediction"—the capability of curing "the evil," or scrofula (a form of tuberculosis), with his touch.

Already at a point, was setting forth.
Now we'll together; and the chance of goodness
Be like our warranted quarrel! Why are you silent?
MACDUFF. Such welcome and unwelcome things at once
'Tis hard to reconcile. (*Enter a* DOCTOR.)
MALCOLM. Well, more anon. Comes the King forth, I pray you?
DOCTOR. Ay, sir. There are a crew of wretched souls
That stay his cure. Their malady convinces
The great essay of art; but at his touch—
Such sanctity hath heaven given his hand—
They presently amend.
MALCOLM. I thank you, Doctor. (*Exit* DOCTOR.)
MACDUFF. What's the disease he means?
25 MALCOLM. 'Tis called the evil.
A most miraculous work in this good king,
Which often, since my here-remain in England,
I have seen him do. How he solicits heaven
Himself best knows; but strangely-visited people,
All swoll'n and ulcerous, pitiful to the eye,
The mere despair of surgery, he cures,
Hanging a golden stamp about their necks
Put on with holy prayers; and 'tis spoken,
To the succeeding royalty he leaves
26 The healing benediction. With this strange virtue
He hath a heavenly gift of prophecy,
And sundry blessings hang about his throne
That speak him full of grace. (*Enter* ROSS.)
MACDUFF. See who comes here.
MALCOLM. My countryman, but yet I know him not.
MACDUFF. My ever-gentle cousin, welcome hither.
MALCOLM. I know him now. Good God betimes remove
The means that makes us strangers!
ROSS. Sir, amen.
MACDUFF. Stands Scotland where it did?
ROSS. Alas, poor country,
Almost afraid to know itself. It cannot
Be called our mother, but our grave; where nothing
But who knows nothing is once seen to smile;
Where sighs and groans and shrieks that rend the air
Are made, not marked; where violent sorrow seems
A modern ecstasy. The dead man's knell
Is there scarce asked for who, and good men's lives
Expire before the flowers in their caps,
Dying or ere they sicken.
MACDUFF. O, relation

136 at a point, prepared.
137–138 and the chance . . . quarrel, and may our chance of success be as strong as the justness of our cause.
143 stay his cure, wait for him to cure them.
143–144 convinces . . . art, defies cure by any medical skill.

147 the evil, scrofula, a disease characterized by swelling of the lymphatic glands. It was called "the king's evil" because of a belief that it could be healed by the touch of a king.
150 solicit (sə lis′it), *v.* appeal to.

167–168 nothing . . . smile, no one except a person who knows nothing ever smiles.
171 modern ecstasy, common feeling.
171 dead man's knell (nel), the sound of a bell rung for a person who has died.

MINI-LESSON: VOCABULARY
Etymology

Teach Read lines 186 and 189 on page 175:

" . . . I saw the tyrant's power afoot."

"To doff their dire distresses."

Tell students that there are some words formed by combining a preposition with another word. *Afoot* comes from the joining of *a* (a shortened form of *on*) and *foot* and means "in the process of being carried out." *Doff* comes from the joining of *do* and *off*. It means "to take off." Other words like these include: *astir, abed, ashore, afield,* and *aloft.*

Activity Idea For practice, students can

- work in groups to brainstorm more words that include a preposition
- look up the words to check their etymologies
- discuss their findings with the class

Too nice, and yet too true!
MALCOLM. What's the newest grief?
ROSS. That of an hour's age doth hiss the speaker;
Each minute teems a new one.
MACDUFF. How does my wife?
ROSS. Why, well.
MACDUFF. And all my children?
ROSS. Well too.
MACDUFF. The tyrant has not battered at their peace?
27 **ROSS.** No, they were well at peace when I did leave 'em.
MACDUFF. Be not a niggard of your speech. How goes 't?
ROSS. When I came hither to transport the tidings
Which I have heavily borne, there ran a rumor
Of many worthy fellows that were out,
Which was to my belief witnessed the rather
For that I saw the tyrant's power afoot.
Now is the time of help. (*To* MALCOLM.) Your eye in Scotland
29 Would create soldiers, make our women fight,
To doff their dire distresses.
MALCOLM. Be 't their comfort
We are coming thither. Gracious England hath
Lent us good Siward and ten thousand men;
An older and a better soldier none
That Christendom gives out.
ROSS. Would I could answer
This comfort with the like! But I have words
That would be howled out in the desert air,
Where hearing should not latch them.
MACDUFF. What concern they?
The general cause? Or is it a fee-grief
Due to some single breast?
ROSS. No mind that's honest
But in it shares some woe, though the main part
Pertains to you alone.
MACDUFF. If it be mine,
Keep it not from me; quickly let me have it.
ROSS. Let not your ears despise my tongue forever,
Which shall possess them with the heaviest sound
That ever yet they heard.
MACDUFF. Hum! I guess at it.
ROSS. Your castle is surprised, your wife and babes
Savagely slaughtered. To relate the manner
Were, on the quarry of these murdered deer,
To add the death of you.
MALCOLM. Merciful heaven!

174–175 **relation too nice,** report too exact.

176 **doth hiss the speaker,** causes the speaker to be hissed because his news is already out of date.

177 **teems,** brings forth.

28 ■ Why do you think Ross doesn't tell Macduff immediately what has happened to his family?

184 **out,** in arms; prepared for war.

196 **latch,** catch the sound of.

197 **fee-grief,** personal sorrow.

207 **quarry,** heap of dead bodies.

27 Literary Element
Irony

Question How is Ross's remark—"they were well at peace"—ironic? (Possible response: *The audience and Ross are aware that Macduff's family is dead, and the dead are often spoken of as being "at peace."*)

28 Reader's Response
Making Personal Connections

Response His own feelings about the death of his relatives make it hard for him to speak; he feels guilty, thinking he could have prevented it; he fears Macduff's reaction.

Question If you were put in the same position as Ross, would you blurt out the bad news or try to soften the blow? *(While responses will vary, most people behave in a fashion similar to Ross and try to soften the news.)*

29 Multicultural Note
Women Warriors

Holinshed—whose chronicles of Scotland are the source for many of the details in *Macbeth*—noted that Scottish women were accustomed to going to war along with the men.

BUILDING ENGLISH PROFICIENCY

Exploring Motivation

Help students understand why Ross at first lies to Macduff about his family.

1. Ask three students to present a Readers Theater dramatization from Ross's entrance until the end of Scene 3. Appoint a director who will be able to focus on building the emotional intensity with change of pace and volume.

2. Ask students why Shakespeare has Ross lie *(to build suspense)*, and why someone might lie if this were a real-life situation *(to delay bad news, to postpone hurting someone)*.

3. Have students take a class survey on this question: If you were in a stressful situation, would you want to know the truth, even if it might make you feel worse? Discuss the results.

30 Literary Criticism

Comment

"There are three explanations of this passage [line 217]. (i) *He* refers to Malcolm who, if he had children of his own, would not suggest revenge as a cure for grief. . . . (ii) *He* refers to Macbeth, on whom he cannot take an appropriate revenge. (iii) *He* refers to Macbeth, who would never have slaughtered Macduff's children if he had any of his own. . . . I adhere to (ii)."

Kenneth Muir
The Arden Edition of the Works of
William Shakespeare: Macbeth

Check Test

1. What three apparitions does Macbeth see? *(armed head, bloody child, child crowned with tree branch in hand)*
2. What characters are murdered in this act? *(Lady Macduff and her children)*
3. With which two vices does Malcolm begin his attack on himself? *(lust and avarice)*
4. Who does Macduff blame for the deaths that Ross reports? *(He blames himself.)*
5. What aid is Edward offering Malcolm? *(10,000 men led by Siward)*

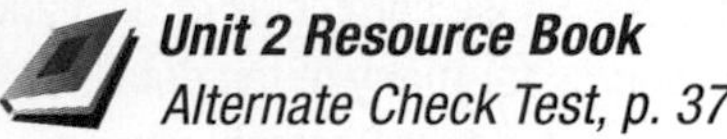
Unit 2 Resource Book
Alternate Check Test, p. 37

What, man, ne'er pull your hat upon your brows;
Give sorrow words. The grief that does not speak
Whispers the o'erfraught heart and bids it break.
MACDUFF. My children too?
ROSS. Wife, children, servants, all
That could be found.
MACDUFF. And I must be from thence!
My wife killed too?
ROSS. I have said.
MALCOLM. Be comforted.
Let's make us medicines of our great revenge
To cure this deadly grief.
30 **MACDUFF.** He has no children. All my pretty ones?
Did you say all? O hell-kite! All?
What, all my pretty chickens and their dam
At one fell swoop?
MALCOLM. Dispute it like a man.
MACDUFF. I shall do so;
But I must also feel it as a man.
I cannot but remember such things were,
That were most precious to me. Did heaven look on
And would not take their part? Sinful Macduff,
They were all struck for thee! Naught that I am,
Not for their own demerits, but for mine,
Fell slaughter on their souls. Heaven rest them now!
MALCOLM. Be this the whetstone of your sword. Let grief
Convert to anger; blunt not the heart, enrage it.
MACDUFF. O, I could play the woman with mine eyes
And braggart with my tongue! But, gentle heavens,
Cut short all intermission. Front to front
Bring thou this fiend of Scotland and myself;
Within my sword's length set him. If he scape,
Heaven forgive him too!
MALCOLM. This tune goes manly.
Come, go we to the King. Our power is ready;
Our lack is nothing but our leave. Macbeth
Is ripe for shaking, and the powers above
Put on their instruments. Receive what cheer you may.
The night is long that never finds the day.

228 demerit (dē mer′it), *n.* fault or defect.
230 whetstone (hwet′stōn′), *n.* stone for sharpening knives or tools.

239 Our lack . . . leave. We only need the King's permission to depart.

After Reading

Act 4

Making Connections

Shaping Your Response

1. How much influence do you think the witches have on Macbeth's decisions? Assign a number of stars—from ★ for *Little* to ★★★★★ for *A Great Deal*—to their influence. Explain your rating.

Analyzing the Play

2. Why does Macbeth decide to murder Macduff's family?
3. What is the cause and what is the effect of Malcolm's accusing himself of so many vices when Macduff comes to see him?
4. In your opinion, does Shakespeare's portrait of Macduff bearing his grief at the news of the murder of his wife and children seem realistic?

Extending the Ideas

5. What kinds of prophecies do some people in our time seek and follow?

Literary Focus: Plot Structure

By now Macbeth has murdered King Duncan and his servants, Banquo, and Macduff's wife and children. What is his motive—or justification—for each murder? Can you see a pattern emerging from these murders? What can you predict about Macbeth's future?

Vocabulary Study

An analogy is a relationship. Word analogies may reflect relationships such as antonyms, synonyms, object to action, quality to object, and so on. Study the relationship of each of the following pairs of words in capital letters; then choose another pair that has the same relationship.

1. LAUDABLE : COMMENDABLE ::
   a. sensible : lively **b.** intelligent : dumb
   c. careful : cautious **d.** impatient : angry
2. DIMINUTIVE : ATOM ::
   a. rainfall : rainbow **b.** fast: meteor
   c. overshoe : foot **d.** anxiety : worry
3. CAULDRON : BOIL ::
   a. oven : roast **b.** potato : slice
   c. pull : wagon **d.** toast : butter
4. ABJURE : EXPRESS ::
   a. calm : tranquil **b.** agile : clumsy
   c. greedy : cruel **d.** unpleasant : unkind
5. CISTERN : WATER ::
   a. hay : loft **b.** bucket : handle
   c. mountain : snow **d.** vase : flowers

After Reading

MAKING CONNECTIONS

1. While responses will vary, students should note that the murder of Banquo and attempted murder of Fleance suggest that Macbeth fully believes the witches' prophesy regarding Banquo's descendants; his visit to the witches in Act Four reinforces the idea that he is highly influenced by them.

2. Macbeth punishes Macduff for defiance and for fleeing to England; he may also be using this "punishment" as an example of how he deals with disloyalty.

3. Cause—to test Macduff to see if he is in league with Macbeth; effect—he determines that Macduff is trustworthy.

4. Possible responses: Yes, he is probably in shock. No, the grief seems forced; before leaving Scotland, Macduff chose to put the nation ahead of his family's safety.

5. astrologers, palm readers, horoscopes, religious cult leaders

VOCABULARY STUDY

1. c
2. b
3. a
4. b
5. d

Unit 2 Resource Book
Vocabulary, p. 35
Vocabulary Test, p. 38

Selection Test

Unit 2 Resource Book
pp. 39–40

LITERARY FOCUS: PLOT

Murder Victim	Macbeth's Motive
King Duncan	To become king
Duncan's grooms	To pin the blame for Duncan's murder on them without their being able to deny it
Banquo	To prevent Banquo's suspicions about the murder of Duncan from being shared with others and to prevent Banquo's progeny from ruling
Macduff's wife and children	To punish Macduff for openly defying him and for fleeing to England

Possible Response About Patterns:	Possible Prediction
All murders after the initial killing of Duncan are "damage control"; he kills to maintain his position. The fact that it is becoming easier and easier for Macbeth to kill provides a secondary pattern.	With Malcolm and Macduff leading an army, Macbeth may meet his match and his doom.

During Reading

Vocabulary Preview

valiant, courageous
upbraid, find fault with
epicure, lover of luxury
oblivious, unmindful; forgetful
pristine, original
bane, destruction
arbitrate, decide a dispute
avouch, affirm
clamorous, noisy
bruit, announce by a great noise

Students can add the words and definitions to their Writer's Notebooks.

1 Literary Element
Theme

When Macbeth is unable to sleep, he notes that "sleep knits up the ravell'd sleave of care."

Question What does Lady Macbeth's sleepwalking suggest about sleep's effects on "care's ravell'd sleave"? *(that one cannot escape guilt and the consequence of one's acts)*

2 Literary Element
Symbolism

Response Because Lady Macbeth now lives in the darkness of her deeds, she wants a light at all times.

3 Reading/Thinking Skills
Find the Main Idea

Question What is the main idea of Lady Macbeth's speech? *(Possible response: As Lady Macbeth attempts to cleanse herself of guilt by washing the "blood" from her hands, she relives the part she played in Duncan's murder.)*

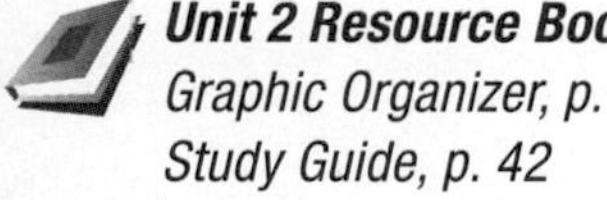

Unit 2 Resource Book
Graphic Organizer, p. 41
Study Guide, p. 42

Act Five

SCENE 1

Summary *Walking and talking in her sleep, Lady Macbeth reveals to a Doctor and a Gentlewoman the crimes she and Macbeth have committed.*

MACBETH'S *castle. Enter a* DOCTOR OF PHYSIC *and a* WAITING-GENTLEWOMAN.

DOCTOR. I have two nights watched with you, but can perceive no truth in your report. When was it she last walked?

GENTLEWOMAN. Since His Majesty went into the field, I have seen her rise from her bed, throw her nightgown upon her, unlock her closet, take forth paper, fold it, write upon 't, read it, afterwards seal it, and again return to bed; yet all this while in a most fast sleep. [1]

DOCTOR. A great perturbation in nature, to receive at once the benefit of sleep and do the effects of watching! In this slumbery agitation, besides her walking and other actual performances, what, at any time, have you heard her say?

GENTLEWOMAN. That, sir, which I will not report after her.

DOCTOR. You may to me, and 'tis most meet you should.

GENTLEWOMAN. Neither to you nor anyone, having no witness to confirm my speech. *(Enter* LADY MACBETH, *with a candle.)* Lo, you, here she comes! This is her very guise, and, upon my life, fast sleep. Observe her. Stand close. *(They stand aside.)*

DOCTOR. How came she by that light?

GENTLEWOMAN. Why, it stood by her. She has light by her continually. 'Tis her command.

DOCTOR. You see her eyes are open.

GENTLEWOMAN. Ay, but their sense are shut.

DOCTOR. What is it she does now? Look how she rubs her hands.

GENTLEWOMAN. It is an accustomed action with her to seem thus washing her hands. I have known her continue in this a quarter of an hour.

LADY MACBETH. Yet here's a spot.

DOCTOR. Hark, she speaks. I will set down what comes from her, to satisfy my remembrance the more strongly. *(He writes.)*

[3] **LADY MACBETH.** Out, damned spot! Out, I say! One—two—why then 'tis time to do 't. Hell is murky. Fie, my lord, fie, a soldier, and afeard? What need we fear who knows it, when none can call our power to account? Yet who would have thought the old man to have had so much blood in him?

DOCTOR. Do you mark that?

LADY MACBETH. The Thane of Fife had a wife. Where is she now? What, will these hands ne'er be clean? No more o' that, my lord, no more o' that; you mar all with this starting.

8 perterbation (pėr′tər bā′shən), *n.* disturbance.

13 meet, suitable.

16 guise (gīz), *n.* appearance.

■ The contrasts between darkness and light have been emphasized throughout the play. Why do you think Lady Macbeth must have light by her at all times? [2]

ACT FIVE SUMMARY

Macbeth

While talking in her sleep, Lady Macbeth reveals her involvement in the murders to witnesses. Scottish leaders decide to abandon Macbeth and join forces with Malcolm. When the combined forces have gathered at Birnam Wood, soldiers cut branches to carry before them in their march toward Dunsinane. Macbeth is informed that Lady Macbeth is dead. When told that Birnam Wood is moving toward Dunsinane, he curses the witches and abandons the castle for the field of battle. Young Siward is killed by Macbeth, who is then found by Macduff. When Macduff reveals that he was pulled from the womb, rather than delivered, Macbeth refuses to fight, but is finally goaded into it and killed. Malcolm is hailed king.

For summaries in other languages, see the ***Building English Proficiency*** *book.*

Mr MARSTON AS MACDUFF.
London Published by J. REDINGTON, 73 Hoxton Street, Formerly called 208 Hoxton Old Town.

◄ This hand-colored engraving from the early 1800s shows the actor M. Marston costumed for his role of Macduff in a contemporary revival of *Macbeth.* What does the pose the artist has chosen to capture suggest about the acting styles of the period?

DOCTOR. Go to, go to. You have known what you should not.

GENTLEWOMAN. She has spoke what she should not, I am sure of that. Heaven knows what she has known.

LADY MACBETH. Here's the smell of the blood still. All the perfumes of Arabia will not sweeten this little hand. O, o, o!

DOCTOR. What a sigh is there! The heart is sorely charged.

GENTLEWOMAN. I would not have such a heart in my bosom for the dignity of the whole body.

DOCTOR. Well, well, well.

GENTLEWOMAN. Pray God it be, sir.

Art Study

Response to Caption Question The pose suggests that acting in the early 1800s was probably histrionic, that is, excessively dramatic or emotional. It also suggests that theatrical producers and directors of the day sold tickets by "playing up" all possible action, including violence, in their advertisements.

Questions Does this type of advertisement remind you of contemporary movie ads? How? *(Possible response: Both attempt to attract audiences with the promise of violent action.)*

BUILDING ENGLISH PROFICIENCY

ESL LEP ELD SAE LD

Analyzing Characters

We have not seen Lady Macbeth since Act Three. Help students understand the changes that have come over her.

1. Have students in small groups discuss how a guilt-ridden conscience eventually might cause someone to become insane.

2. Ask visual learners to tell what images dominate this scene. *(blood, death, murder, candles)*

3. To help students compare Lady Macbeth's behavior here with her earlier behavior, have them complete the chart shown.

LADY MACBETH	
Earlier	**Now**
in control	distracted

Building English Proficiency
Activities, p. 215

4 Literary Element
Foreshadowing

Question What does the doctor's statement about sleepwalking foreshadow about Lady Macbeth? *(Possible response: that she will not die "holily" in her bed)*

5 Literary Criticism
Characterization

"The last act brings the tragedy to its close. It begins with the sleepwalking scene, which sums up and concentrates the full horror of the whole business. The resistance of this hard, practical woman has broken down. She was the real cause and the agent of the tragedy. In the words which she utters in her sleep, she gives her own answer to the casual remark that 'a little water clears us of this deed.' This is true dramatic irony, tragic and terrible, where the easiest remarks have the most ghastly significance and are echoed by a kind of devilish chuckle."

G. B. Harrison
Shakespeare: The Complete Works

6 Historical Note
Siward

According to Holinshed, Siward was the father of Duncan's wife; thus, Malcolm's grandfather, not uncle.

DOCTOR. This disease is beyond my practice. Yet I have known those
4 which have walked in their sleep who have died holily in their beds.

LADY MACBETH. Wash your hands, put on your nightgown; look not so pale! I tell you yet again, Banquo's buried. He cannot come out on 's grave.

DOCTOR. Even so?

5 **LADY MACBETH.** To bed, to bed! There's knocking at the gate. Come, come, come, come, give me your hand. What's done cannot be undone. To bed, to bed, to bed! (*Exit* LADY MACBETH.)

DOCTOR. Will she go now to bed?

GENTLEWOMAN. Directly.

DOCTOR. Foul whisperings are abroad. Unnatural deeds
Do breed unnatural troubles. Infected minds
To their deaf pillows will discharge their secrets.
More needs she the divine than the physician.
God, God forgive us all! Look after her;
Remove from her the means of all annoyance,
And still keep eyes upon her. So, good night.
My mind she has mated, and amazed my sight.
I think, but dare not speak

GENTLEWOMAN. Good night, good Doctor.

63 More needs . . . physician. She needs a priest more than a doctor.
65 annoyance, injury to herself.
67 mated, confused.

SCENE 2

Summary *The Scottish leaders agree to march toward Birnam Wood to join Malcolm and Macduff's forces.*

The countryside near Dunsinane. Drums sound and banners wave. Enter MENTEITH, CAITHNESS, ANGUS, LENNOX, *and* SOLDIERS.

MENTEITH. The English power is near, led on by Malcolm,
6 His uncle Siward, and the good Macduff.
Revenges burn in them, for their dear causes
Would to the bleeding and the grim alarm
Excite the mortified man.

ANGUS. Near Birnam Wood
Shall we well meet them; that way are they coming.

CAITHNESS. Who knows if Donalbain be with his brother?

LENNOX. For certain, sir, he is not. I have a file
Of all the gentry. There is Siward's son,
And many unrough youths that even now
Protest their first of manhood.

MENTEITH. What does the tyrant?

CAITHNESS. Great Dunsinane he strongly fortifies.
Some say he's mad, others that lesser hate him
Do call it valiant fury; but for certain
He cannot buckle his distempered cause

3–5 their dear causes . . . man, their deeply felt causes would arouse a dead man to bloody battle.
10 unrough, beardless.
11 protest . . . manhood, call themselves men for the first time.
14 valiant (val′yənt), *adj.* courageous.

MINI-LESSON: GRAMMAR
Diagramming Verb Forms

Teach Read this sentence about Scene 1:

Being plagued by guilt, Lady Macbeth alarms the doctor with her walking in her sleep to find relief.

Explain that the words *being plagued* are a participle—a verb form used as an adjective. A participle, whether one word or two, is diagrammed attached to the word it modifies partly on a slanting and partly on a horizontal line. The word *walking* is a gerund—a verb form ending in *-ing* that is used as a noun. Here it is the object of the preposition *with*. It is diagrammed similar to a prepositional phrase but with a stepped line. An infinitive—a verb form usually preceded by *to* that functions as a noun or as a modifier—is diagrammed similar to a prepositional phrase.

Activity Idea Have three groups find sources that give more details about diagramming gerunds, infinitives, and participles respectively. Have each group present its findings.

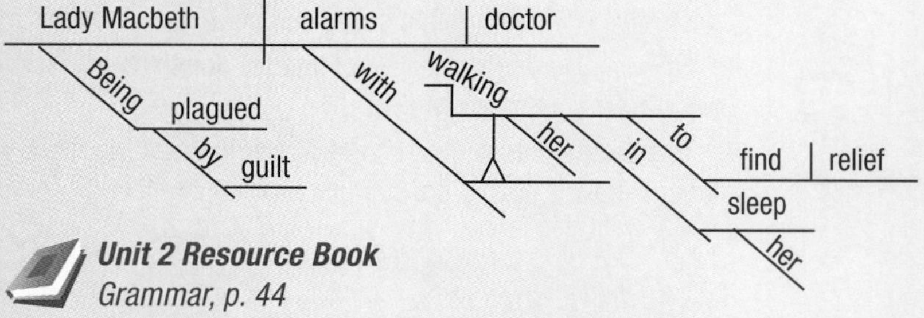

Unit 2 Resource Book
Grammar, p. 44

Within the belt of rule.
ANGUS. Now does he feel
His secret murders sticking on his hands;
Now minutely revolts upbraid his faith-breach.
Those he commands move only in command,
Nothing in love. Now does he feel his title
7 Hang loose about him, like a giant's robe
Upon a dwarfish thief.
MENTEITH. Who then shall blame
His pestered senses to recoil and start,
When all that is within him does condemn
Itself for being there?
CAITHNESS. Well, march we on
To give obedience where 'tis truly owed.
Meet we the med'cine of the sickly weal,
And with him pour we in our country's purge
Each drop of us.
LENNOX. Or so much as it needs
To dew the sovereign flower and drown the weeds.
8 Make we our march towards Birnam.

15–16 He cannot . . . rule. He cannot control the situation.
18 upbraid (up brād′), *v.* find fault with.
18 now . . . faith-breach, every minute, those who revolt against him blame his faithlessness.

27–29 Meet we . . . us. We go to meet Malcolm, who will heal the sickness of our country, and to offer our lives in the curing process.

SCENE 3

Summary *Macbeth hears reports from the Doctor about Lady Macbeth's illness and from a Servant about the advancing armies. Still he relies on the prophecies of the Witches.*

MACBETH'S *castle. Enter* MACBETH, DOCTOR, *and* ATTENDANTS.
MACBETH. Bring me no more reports. Let them fly all!
Till Birnam Wood remove to Dunsinane,
I cannot taint with fear. What's the boy Malcolm?
Was he not born of woman? The spirits that know
All mortal consequences have pronounced me thus:
"Fear not, Macbeth. No man that's born of woman
Shall e'er have power upon thee." Then fly, false thanes,
And mingle with the English epicures!
The mind I sway by and the heart I bear
Shall never sag with doubt nor shake with fear. (*Enter* SERVANT.)
The devil damn thee black, thou cream-faced loon!
Where gott'st thou that goose look?
SERVANT. There is ten thousand—
MACBETH. Geese, villain?
SERVANT. Soldiers, sir.
MACBETH. Go prick thy face and over-red thy fear,
Thou lily-livered boy. What soldiers, patch?
Death of thy soul! Those linen cheeks of thine

1 them, the thanes.

3 taint (tānt), *v.* become infected.

8 epicure (ep′ə kyůr), *n.* lover of luxury.
9 I sway by, I am directed by.

14 prick thy face . . . fear, go prick or pinch your pale cheeks to bring some color into them.
15 patch, fool.

7 Literary Element
Figurative Language

Caithness refers to Macbeth's rule as a belt that cannot be buckled. Angus states that Macbeth's title fits him like a giant's robe fits a dwarfish thief.

Questions What figures of speech are they using? *(Caithness uses a metaphor; Angus uses a simile.)* Earlier in the play Macbeth himself states that the title *thane of Cawdor* is "a borrowed robe." What do you think these figures of speech suggest? *(Possible response: As clothes do not make the man, assuming a title does not legitimize usurpation of power.)*

In lines 29–30, Lennox refers to dewing "the sovereign flower" and drowning "the weeds." **Question** What does this metaphor suggest? *(that the battle will water, or nurture, the flower [Malcolm] and wash away the weeds [Macbeth and Lady Macbeth])*

8 Literary Focus
Plot

Question What effect does this scene have on the plot? *(More and more of Macbeth's lords desert him and join forces with his enemies.)*

BUILDING ENGLISH PROFICIENCY

Paraphrasing Shakespeare

Give students practice in paraphrasing by having them focus on the doctor's final speech in Scene 1 (9 sentences, p. 180) and Macbeth's first speech in Scene 3 (11 sentences, p. 181).

1. Divide students into small groups; assign one speech to each group.

2. Suggest that the group first get a sense of the whole speech. Then, a group leader should assign an equal number of sentences to each group member. Students should paraphrase their assigned sentences on their own.

3. Ask all members of the group to collaborate on a final paraphrased version of the whole speech. Discuss and compare versions that different groups create.

9 Reading/Thinking Skills
Generalize

Response Rather than the blessings of old age, love, honor, obedience, friends, Macbeth will have only curses, unlike Duncan who was deeply mourned and honored by his countrymen.

10 Literary Element
Symbolism

Question Why do you think Macbeth wants to put on his armor? *(Possible responses: For Macbeth, armor may symbolize courage—his one undiminished virtue; or the armor, a hard outer covering, may represent an emotional hard outer covering that he needs to don in order to face his situation.)*

11 Literary Element
Irony

Question What is ironic about Macbeth's question? *(Macbeth, of all people, knows that there is no antidote for what ails his wife.)*

Are counselors to fear. What soldiers, whey-face?
SERVANT. The English force, so please you.
MACBETH. Take thy face hence. (*Exit* SERVANT.) Seyton! I am
sick at heart
When I behold—Seyton, I say!—This push
Will cheer me ever, or disseat me now.
9 I have lived long enough. My way of life
Is fall'n into the sere, the yellow leaf.
And that which should accompany old age,
As honor, love, obedience, troops of friends,
I must not look to have, but in their stead
Curses, not loud but deep, mouth-honor, breath
Which the poor heart would fain deny and dare not.
Seyton! (*Enter* SEYTON.)
SEYTON. What's your gracious pleasure?
MACBETH. What news more?
SEYTON. All is confirmed, my lord, which was reported.
MACBETH. I'll fight till from my bones my flesh be hacked.
Give me my armor.
SEYTON. 'Tis not needed yet.
10 **MACBETH.** I'll put it on.
Send out more horses. Skirr the country round.
Hang those that talk of fear. Give me mine armor.
How does your patient, Doctor?
DOCTOR. Not so sick, my lord,
As she is troubled with thick-coming fancies
That keep her from her rest.
MACBETH. Cure her of that.
11 Canst thou not minister to a mind diseased,
Pluck from the memory a rooted sorrow,
Raze out the written troubles of the brain,
And with some sweet oblivious antidote
Cleanse the stuffed bosom of that perilous stuff
Which weighs upon the heart?
DOCTOR. Therein the patient
Must minister to himself.
MACBETH. Throw physic to the dogs! I'll none of it.
Come put mine armor on. Give me my staff.
(ATTENDANTS *arm him.*)
Seyton, send out. Doctor, the thanes fly from me—
Come, sir, dispatch—If thou couldst, Doctor, cast
The water of my land, find her disease,
And purge it to a sound and pristine health,
I would applaud thee to the very echo,
That should applaud again—Pull 't off, I say—

20 push, attack.

9 ■ Summarize Macbeth's "I have lived long enough" speech. Compare Macbeth's life to that of Duncan, the first person Macbeth killed.

36 skirr (skėr), *v.* scour.

45 oblivious (ə bliv′ē əs), *adj.* unmindful; forgetful.

51 send out, send out more scouts.
52–53 cast . . . land, diagnose my country's illness.
54 pristine (pris′tēn′), *adj.* original.
56 pull 't off, referring to some part of his armor.

MINI-LESSON: VOCABULARY
Negative Prefixes

Teach Read these lines spoken by Macbeth (lines 20–21) from page 182, "This push/Will cheer me ever, or disseat me now." Point out that today there are two forms of the negative of the verb *seat* listed in many unabridged dictionaries: *unseat* and *disseat.* Remind students that there are a variety of negative prefixes available that have a similar effect on the base word they modify: *a-, dif-, dis-, im-, in-, mis-,* and *un-.*

Activity Idea For practice
- have the class predict which of the prefixes is the most common and rank the rest down to the least common
- divide students into seven small groups
- assign each group one of the prefixes listed
- have the group brainstorm and locate in the dictionary as many words as possible beginning with the prefix
- have the class revisit their rankings and see how they did

12 What rhubarb, senna, or what purgative drug
Would scour these English hence? Hear'st thou of them?
DOCTOR. Ay, my good lord. Your royal preparation
Makes us hear something.
MACBETH. Bring it after me.
I will not be afraid of death and bane,
Till Birnam Forest come to Dunsinane. (*Exit all but the* DOCTOR.)
DOCTOR. Were I from Dunsinane away and clear,
Profit again should hardly draw me here.

57 purgative (pėr′gə tiv), *adj.* causing the bowels to empty.
60 it, the armor.
61 bane (bān), *n.* destruction.

SCENE 4

Summary *The Scottish and English forces come together at Birnam Wood. In order to conceal their numbers, each man cuts a branch from a tree and carries it before him.*

Drums sound and banners wave. Enter MALCOLM, SIWARD, MACDUFF, SIWARD'S SON, MENTEITH, CAITHNESS, ANGUS, LENNOX, ROSS, *and* SOLDIERS, *marching.*

MALCOLM. Cousins, I hope the days are near at hand
That chambers will be safe.
MENTEITH. We doubt it nothing.
SIWARD. What wood is this before us?
MENTEITH. The wood of Birnam.
13 **MALCOLM.** Let every soldier hew him down a bough
And bear 't before him. Thereby shall we shadow
The numbers of our host and make discovery
Err in report of us.
SOLDIERS. It shall be done.
SIWARD. We learn no other but the confident tyrant
Keeps still in Dunsinane and will endure
Our setting down before 't.
MALCOLM. 'Tis his main hope;
For where there is advantage to be given,
Both more and less have given him the revolt,
And none serve with him but constrainèd things
Whose hearts are absent too.
MACDUFF. Let our just censures
Attend the true event, and put we on
Industrious soldiership.
SIWARD. The time approaches
That will with due decision make us know
What we shall say we have and what we owe.
Thoughts speculative their unsure hopes relate,
But certain issue strokes must arbitrate—
Towards which advance the war.

6 discovery, Macbeth's scouts.

10 setting down before 't, laying siege to it (the castle at Dunsinane).

12 both more and less, both nobles and common people.

14–15 let . . . event, let our judgment await the actual outcome of the battle.
19–21 Thoughts . . . war. We are now speculating on the basis of our hopes; only after the battle will we know the real outcome.
20 arbitrate (är′bə trāt), *v.* decide a dispute.

12 Reading/Thinking Skills
Compare and Contrast

Question How would you compare Macbeth's statements on the health of the land to comments made by Caithness and Lennox in Scene 2, lines 25–31? *(Possible responses: All three speak in medical terms and refer to Scotland as a diseased land that needs purging. While Macbeth asks the doctor to cast the water for a diagnosis, Lennox proposes drowning its weeds—its king and queen. While Macbeth asks for a drug to purge the English, Caithness proposes purging the "distempered cause"—Macbeth.)*

13 Literary Focus
Plot

Question Why is Malcolm's order important to the plot? *(Possible response: It fulfills a prophecy Macbeth received from the apparitions, and it shows the prophesy to be equivocal; Birnam Wood, in the form of cut branches carried by soldiers, is about to come to Dunsinane. This calls into question the other prophecies that led Macbeth to believe he would succeed in battle and escape unharmed.)*

BUILDING ENGLISH PROFICIENCY

Reviewing Events

Help students review the events that brought the anti-Macbeth forces to attempt the overthrow of his rule.

1. Have students collaborate to find four key events leading to the beginning of Act Five, Scene 4. *(Possible responses: Macbeth kills the king; Macbeth has Banquo killed; Macbeth has Macduff's wife and children killed; the Scottish leaders combine forces with Malcolm and Macduff.)*

2. Have students record their responses in the graphic organizer shown.

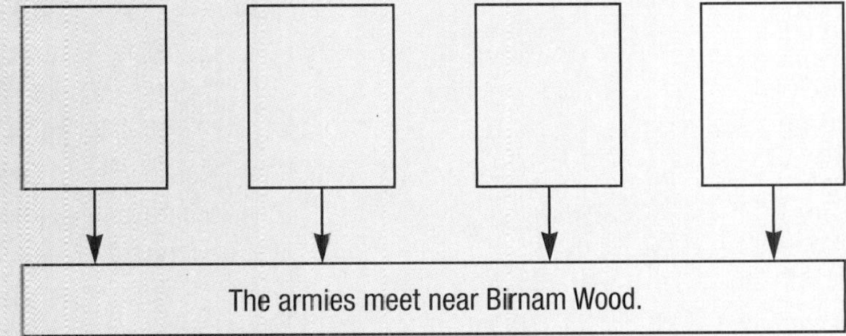

14 Reading/Thinking Skills
Recognize Values

Questions How have Macbeth's values changed? *(Possible response: The once sensitive and sympathetic man is now emotionally unresponsive and inured to sorrow, evil, and suffering.)* What do you think changed him? *(His humanity has been degraded by inhumanity.)*

15 Multicultural Note
Individuality

Response Individuality is worthless in a world without meaning—a dull, meaningless repetition of days.

16 Reader's Response
Challenging the Text

The most famous speech of the play (lines 19–28), and among the famous passages in the language, present the views of the character, Macbeth, not the author.

Question What do you think Shakespeare's view of life might be? *(Possible responses: From the fate suffered by Lady Macbeth, it would appear that Shakespeare believed that human beings had a strong sense of good and evil and that those who played with evil would be brought down by it. Students might also suggest that tragedy cannot be written by someone who believes that life has no moral meaning and value.)*

SCENE 5

Summary *Macbeth learns that Lady Macbeth has died. Hearing next that Birnam Wood is moving toward Dunsinane, Macbeth suspects the Witches have deceived him. He decides to fight actively.*

Outside MACBETH'S *castle. Enter* MACBETH, SEYTON, *and* SOLDIERS, *with drums and banners.*

MACBETH. Hang out our banners on the outward walls.
The cry is still, "They come!" Our castle's strength
Will laugh a siege to scorn. Here let them lie
Till famine and the ague eat them up.
Were they not forced with those that should be ours,
We might have met them dareful, beard to beard,
And beat them backward home. *(Crying is heard offstage.)*
What is that noise?

SEYTON. It is the cry of women, my good lord. *(He goes to the door.)*

MACBETH. I have almost forgot the taste of fears.
The time has been my senses would have cooled
To hear a night-shriek, and my fell of hair
Would at a dismal treatise rouse and stir
As life were in 't. I have supped full with horrors;
Direness, familiar to my slaughterous thoughts,
Cannot once start me. *(SEYTON returns.)*
Wherefore was that cry?

SEYTON. The Queen, my lord, is dead.

14

MACBETH. She should have died hereafter;
There would have been a time for such a word.
Tomorrow, and tomorrow, and tomorrow
Creeps in this petty pace from day to day
To the last syllable of recorded time,
And all our yesterdays have lighted fools
The way to dusty death. Out, out, brief candle!
Life's but a walking shadow, a poor player
That struts and frets his hour upon the stage
And then is heard no more. It is a tale
Told by an idiot, full of sound and fury,
Signifying nothing. *(Enter a MESSENGER.)*
Thou com'st to use thy tongue; thy story quickly.

15

16

MESSENGER. Gracious my lord,
I should report that which I say I saw,
But know not how to do 't.

MACBETH. Well, say, sir.

MESSENGER. As I did stand my watch upon the hill,
I looked toward Birnam, and anon, methought,
The wood began to move.

4 **ague** (ā′gyü), *n.* fever.
5 **forced,** reinforced.

12 **dismal treatise** (trē′tis), tragic account.

What implications does such a philosophy have for any person's feelings of **individuality?**

Macduff, holding Macbeth's head, kneels before the new King of Scotland in this Charles Ricketts illustration from *The Tragedie of Macbeth* (1923). Do you think Macbeth deserves his fate? Why or why not? ➤

MINI-LESSON: WRITING STYLE
Using Descriptive Language

To encourage students to describe carefully and precisely, have a discussion about ways to organize a description. Tell students that their descriptions will be better understood if they move in a logical way around the scene or illustration they are describing and designate the location of important objects. Have the class think of a list of possible approaches, such as moving from left to right, from front to back, or from the center outwards.

Activity Idea For practice, students can

- choose one of the illustrations that accompanies *Macbeth*
- write a detailed description of it
- compare and contrast their descriptions with students who described the same illustration
- have each group choose one description to share with the class

Art Study

You may wish to discuss these caption questions after students finish the play.

Responses to Caption Questions Responses will vary. Macbeth may have deserved his fate because he was an unrepentant murderer and traitor. Or, he did not deserve his fate because the throne should have gone to him, but Duncan unlawfully tried to give it to Malcolm; also Banquo was having "cursed thoughts" that may have led him to kill Macbeth to obtain the throne for his son; also Lady Macbeth tempted and bullied her husband into the first murder; and finally, the witches and Hecate seduced him with their evil games and played with his fate.

Visual Literacy The artist, Ricketts, again uses color in a suggestive manner.

Question What do you think the artist's use of red suggests about Macduff and Malcolm? *(Possible response: While Macduff and Malcolm have bloodied themselves in battle, their persons, as opposed to their swords and banners, are clean, suggesting that they will have far less trouble cleansing their souls than did Macbeth and Lady Macbeth.)*

BUILDING ENGLISH PROFICIENCY

Exploring a Climax

To help students relate to Macbeth's problems as the play approaches its ending, ask them to imagine that the telephone was invented before Macbeth's time.

1. Ask pairs of students to complete the chart shown. Under *Options,* have them list two to four different choices for Macbeth. Under *Consequences,* have them list what might happen if Macbeth took each course of action.

2. Have each pair of students improvise a telephone call between Macbeth and a friend. Let the friend advise Macbeth; have Macbeth respond to the advice.

Options	Consequences

17 Literary Element
Style

Macbeth, in lines 47–52, again speaks in rhyming couplets.

Question What do you think this might suggest? *(Possible response: When Macbeth speaks in the witches' rhyming couplet style, he is either recalling their words or somehow under their influence; at this point, Macbeth is not using sound military judgment, which suggests a fulfillment of Hecate's promise that he will be brought down through arrogance.)*

18 Reading/Thinking Skills
Analyze

Question Why is Macbeth's new battle strategy not a wise move? *(Possible responses: Macbeth has stated earlier that his forces are greatly outnumbered, but that the castle can withstand an attack and its inhabitants can outlast a siege. Also, Macbeth is failing to take into account the prophecy to beware Macduff.)*

MACBETH. Liar and slave!
MESSENGER. Let me endure your wrath if 't be not so.
Within this three mile may you see it coming;
I say, a moving grove.
MACBETH. If thou speak'st false,
Upon the next tree shall thou hang alive
Till famine cling thee. If thy speech be sooth,
I care not if thou dost for me as much.
I pull in resolution, and begin
To doubt th' equivocation of the fiend
That lies like truth. "Fear not, till Birnam Wood
Do come to Dunsinane," and now a wood
Comes toward Dunsinane. Arm, arm, and out!
[17] If this which he avouches does appear,
There is nor flying hence nor tarrying here.
I 'gin to be aweary of the sun,
And wish th' estate o' the world were now undone.
Ring the alarum bell! Blow wind, come wrack,
[18] At least we'll die with harness on our back.

40 cling, shrivel up.

42 I pull in resolution, I weaken in confidence.
43 doubt the equivocation (i kwiv′ə kā′shən), fear the deception.

47 avouch (ə vouch′), *v.* affirm.

SCENE 6

Summary *The army prepares for battle.*

Near the castle. Drums sound and banners wave. Enter MALCOLM, SIWARD, MACDUFF, *and their army, with tree branches.*

MALCOLM. Now near enough. Your leafy screens throw down,
And show like those you are. You, worthy uncle,
Shall with my cousin, your right noble son,
Lead our first battle. Worthy Macduff and we
Shall take upon 's what else remains to do,
According to our order.
SIWARD. Fare you well.
Do we but find the tyrant's power tonight,
Let us be beaten, if we cannot fight.
MACDUFF. Make all our trumpets speak! Give them all breath,
Those clamorous harbingers of blood and death.

2 uncle, Siward.

10 clamorous (klam′ər əs), *adj.* noisy.

SCENE 7

Summary *Young Siward attacks Macbeth, and Macbeth kills Young Siward.*

Another part of the field. Enter MACBETH.

MACBETH. They have tied me to a stake. I cannot fly,
But bearlike I must fight the course. What's he
That was not born of woman? Such a one
Am I to fear, or none. (*Enter* YOUNG SIWARD.)

1–2 They have . . . course. In bearbaiting, a popular sport in Shakespeare's time, a bear was tied to a stake and forced to fight rounds with dogs set upon it in relays.

MINI-LESSON: GRAMMAR

Understanding the Subjunctive Mood

Teach Read line 48 on page 189: "Why then, God's soldier be he." Point out that this sentence is in the subjunctive mood, which today is found almost exclusively in stock phrases like:

- far be it from me
- be that as it may
- come what may
- so be it
- if I were you

Point out that these statements express a wish, a command, a desire, or something improbable or contrary to fact.

Question How would you characterize what Siward's statement expresses? *(Possible response: a wish or a blessing)*

Activity Idea So that students better understand the subjunctive, have them

- find other examples of the subjunctive mood in *Macbeth* and explain the intent of those statements
- explain why a statement such as "If I was a bird, I'd fly away" is incorrect and what the correct statement should be
- look in newspapers and magazines for subjunctives used correctly and incorrectly

YOUNG SIWARD. What is thy name?

MACBETH. Thou'lt be afraid to hear it.

YOUNG SIWARD. No, though thou call'st thyself a hotter name
Than any is in hell.

MACBETH. My name's Macbeth.

YOUNG SIWARD. The devil himself could not pronounce a title
More hateful to mine ear.

MACBETH. No, nor more fearful.

YOUNG SIWARD. Thou liest, abhorrèd tyrant! With my sword
I'll prove the lie thou speak'st. (*They fight, and* MACBETH *kills* YOUNG SIWARD.)

MACBETH. Thou was born of woman.
But swords I smile at, weapons laugh to scorn,
Brandished by man that's of a woman born. (*Exit.*)

(*Sounds of battle offstage. Enter* MACDUFF.)

19 MACDUFF. That way the noise is. Tyrant, show thy face!
If thou be'st slain, and with no stroke of mine,
My wife and children's ghosts will haunt me still.
I cannot strike at wretched kerns, whose arms
Are hired to bear their staves. Either thou, Macbeth,
Or else my sword with an unbattered edge
I sheathe again undeeded. There thou shouldst be;
By this great clatter one of greatest note
Seems bruited. Let me find him, Fortune,
And more I beg not.

(MACDUFF *exits. Sounds of battle offstage. Enter* MALCOLM *and* SIWARD.)

SIWARD. This way, my lord. The castle's gently rendered:
The tyrant's people on both sides do fight,
The noble thanes do bravely in the war,
The day almost itself professes yours,
And little is to do.

MALCOLM. We have met with foes
That strike beside us.

SIWARD. Enter, sir, the castle.

23 bruit (brüt), *v.* announce by a great noise.

25 rendered, surrendered.

30 strike beside us, join us and fight on our side.

SCENE 8

Summary *Macbeth fights and is killed by Macduff. Malcolm is hailed as king of Scotland. He vows to right the wrongs created by Macbeth and Lady Macbeth.*

Another part of the field. Enter MACBETH.

MACBETH. Why should I play the Roman fool and die
On mine own sword? Whiles I see lives, the gashes
Do better upon them. (*Enter* MACDUFF.)

20 MACDUFF. Turn, hellhound, turn!

1–2 Why . . . sword? Why should I kill myself, as the Romans did? (The Romans considered suicide more honorable than capture.)
2 lives, living persons.

19 Literary Element
Characterization

Question What does this speech reveal about Macduff's character? *(He is courageous—willing to fight the country's best warrior in single combat; he is just—having no quarrel with the kerns, he will not fight them; he focuses his anger; he is humble—he asks, not demands, fortune's help.)*

20 Literary Element
Imagery

Questions Can you recall any other dog images in the play? *(Macbeth compares Banquo's assassins to the lowest order of dogs—mongrels, curs, demi-wolves [Act Three, Scene 1]; tongue of dog is mentioned as an ingredient in the witches' brew [Act Four, Scene 1]; Macbeth seems to unintentionally refer to himself when he responds to a doctor's advice with "Throw physic to the dogs!" [Act Five, Scene 3])* Keeping these images in mind, what do you think Macduff's hellhound epithet might suggest? *(Possible response: Macbeth has sunk lower, become more evil than the curs and mongrels he employed as assassins; he has become an animal.)*

BUILDING ENGLISH PROFICIENCY

Evaluating a Battle Plan

Have volunteers improvise a scene showing Malcolm creating a battle plan with other leaders named in the play.

1. Ask the student portraying Malcolm to describe one plan before the assembled leaders. This plan should have problems; let the others evaluate and suggest alternatives.
2. Suggest that students use a chart like the one shown to keep track of details of the plans.
3. Eventually, the leaders should agree on Malcolm's plan.

Questions	Plan A	Plan B	Plan C
Who What Where When Why How			

21 Literary Focus
Plot

Questions What do these lines suggest? Is Macbeth a coward who is afraid of Macduff? *(Possible response: He is neither a coward nor afraid; he avoids Macduff because of the apparition's "Beware Macduff" warning; and he avoids Macduff because his soul is already darkened with the blood of that family.)*

22 Literary Element
Allusion

The angel to which Macduff alludes is Satan, the fallen angel and chief devil in the Christian belief system.

23 Reading/Thinking Skill
Find the Main Idea

Question What excuse does Macbeth give for refusing to fight Macduff? *(He now understands that the prophecy of the second apparition was also an equivocation and that Macduff is the man who will kill him.)*

24 Reading/Thinking Skills
Draw Conclusions

Question What virtues does Macbeth still seem to possess? *(Possible responses: pride and courage)*

21 MACBETH. Of all men else I have avoided thee.
But get thee back! My soul is too much charged
With blood of thine already.
MACDUFF. I have no words;
My voice is in my sword, thou bloodier villain
Than terms can give thee out! *(They fight.)*
MACBETH. Thou losest labor.
As easy mayst thou the intrenchant air
With thy keen sword impress as make me bleed.
Let fall thy blade on vulnerable crests;
I bear a charmèd life, which must not yield
To one of woman born.
MACDUFF. Despair thy charm,
22 And let the angel whom thou still hast served
Tell thee, Macduff was from his mother's womb
Untimely ripped.
23 MACBETH. Accursèd be that tongue that tells me so,
For it hath cowed my better part of man!
And be these juggling fiends no more believed
That palter with us in a double sense,
That keep the word of promise to our ear
And break it to our hope. I'll not fight with thee.
MACDUFF. Then yield thee, coward,
And live to be the show and gaze o' the time!
We'll have thee, as our rarer monsters are,
Painted upon a pole, and underwrit,
"Here may you see the tyrant."
24 MACBETH. I will not yield
To kiss the ground before young Malcolm's feet
And to be baited with the rabble's curse.
Though Birnam Wood be come to Dunsinane,
And thou opposed, being of no woman born,
Yet I wll try the last. Before my body
I throw my warlike shield. Lay on, Macduff,
And damned be him that first cries, "Hold, enough!"
(They fight and exit. Enter, with drums sounding and banners waving, MALCOLM, SIWARD, ROSS, THANES, *and* SOLDIERS.*)*
MALCOLM. I would the friends we miss were safe arrived.
SIWARD. Some must go off; and yet, by these I see
So great a day as this is cheaply bought.
MALCOLM. Macduff is missing, and your noble son.
ROSS. Your son, my lord, has paid a soldier's debt.
He only lived but till he was a man,
The which no sooner had his prowess confirmed
In the unshrinking station where he fought,

6 blood of thine, that is, Macduff's wife and children.

9 intrenchant (in tren′-chənt), *adj.* invulnerable; incapable of being hurt.

15–16 from his mother's . . . ripped, born in a Caesarean operation.

18 cow (kou), *v.* frighten.

20 palter (pôl′tər), *v.* trifle deceitfully; play tricks.

26. painted . . . pole, your picture painted on a board which will be displayed from a pole.

36 go off, die.

MINI-LESSON: WRITING STYLE
Allusion

Teach An allusion is a brief reference to a person, event, place, work of art, or the words that someone has spoken or written.

In lines 65–68 on page 189 (in his first speech as the royal leader of Scotland), Malcolm uses allusion. He uses an image that Duncan had used in his final official speech. Duncan had said to Macbeth (Act One, Scene 4, lines 27–29): "Welcome hither!/I have begun to plant thee, and will labor/To make thee full of growing." Malcolm now says (Act Five, Scene 7, lines 65–74): "What's more to do/Which would be planted newly with the time . . . this, and what needful else/That calls upon us, by the grace of Grace/We will perform in measure, time, and place."

Activity Idea You can

- put up a piece of butcher paper, and have students bring in newspaper or magazine articles that contain allusions. Alert them to look particularly for quotations from Shakespeare and from the Bible—two of the most popular sources.
- display these examples on the butcher paper
- have students discuss their findings

But like a man he died.
SIWARD. Then he is dead?
ROSS. Ay, and brought off the field. Your cause of sorrow
Must not be measured by his worth, for then
It hath no end.
25 **SIWARD.** Had he his hurts before?
ROSS. Ay, on the front.
SIWARD. Why then, God's soldier be he!
Had I as many sons as I have hairs
I would not wish them to a fairer death.
And so, his knell is knolled.
MALCOLM. He's worth more sorrow,
And that I'll spend for him.
SIWARD. He's worth no more.
26 They say he parted well and paid his score,
And so, God be with him! Here comes newer comfort.
(Enter MACDUFF, *with* MACBETH'S *head.)*
MACDUFF. Hail, King! For so thou art. Behold where stands
Th' usurper's cursèd head. The time is free.
I see thee compassed with thy kingdom's pearl,
That speak my salutation in their minds,
Whose voices I desire aloud with mine.
27 Hail, King of Scotland!
ALL. Hail, King of Scotland! *(Music sounds offstage.)*
MALCOLM. We shall not spend a large expense of time
Before we reckon with your several loves
And make us even with you. My thanes and kinsmen,
Henceforth be earls, the first that ever Scotland
In such an honor named. What's more to do
Which would be planted newly with the time,
As calling home our exiled friends abroad
That fled the snares of watchful tyranny,
Producing forth the cruel ministers
Of this dead butcher and his fiendlike queen—
Who, as 'tis thought, by self and violent hands
Took off her life—this, and what needful else
That calls upon us, by the grace of Grace
We will perform in measure, time, and place.
So, thanks to all at once and to each one,
Whom we invite to see us crowned at Scone.

56 compassed . . . pearl, surrounded by the nobles of your kingdom.

62 reckon (rek′ən), *v.* settle accounts.

25 Reading/Thinking Skills
Infer

Questions Why does Siward ask "Had he his hurts before"? What does the answer mean to him? *(Possible responses: He wants to know if his son died engaged in battle or while running away; when he learns his son died in battle, he can accept his son's death.)*

26 Reading/Thinking Skills
Compare and Contrast

Question How would you compare this description of young Siward's death with Macbeth's final moments? *(Young Siward is hailed for dying bravely and well. In contrast, Macbeth refuses to fight when he learns that Macduff's birth was abnormal; he is finally goaded into defending himself when called a coward and told he will be exhibited as a monster; in death, he is accorded no honor.)*

27 Literary Focus
Plot

Question What is the resolution of the drama? *(Macbeth and Lady Macbeth are dead; Malcolm is to be king; order is restored to Scotland.)*

Check Test

1. How does Lady Macbeth reveal her involvement in the murder of Duncan? *(by talking in her sleep)*

2. What's Malcolm's idea for approaching Dunsinane without being seen? *(His soldiers carry tree branches from Birnam Wood.)*

3. Who is the last person Macbeth kills? *(Siward's son)*

4. Who kills Macbeth? *(Macduff)*

5. What honor does Malcolm bestow on his thanes? *(He makes them earls.)*

Unit 2 Resource Book
Alternate Check Test, p. 45

BUILDING ENGLISH PROFICIENCY

Looking to the Future

According to tradition, a tragedy should end on a note of hope. Help students relate to the signs of a hopeful future at the end of *Macbeth,* based upon Malcolm's final speech.

Activity Ideas

- Ask a group to produce a one-page special edition of a newspaper. Have the reporters and feature writers emphasize Malcolm's victory and the good that may come of it.
- Challenge a group to create a musical background for Malcolm's final speech. Have them find a martial or patriotic melody; capable students may also compose music that conveys strength.
- Ask students to write a letter from the point of view of Malcolm or one of the new earls, telling the parents of a slain soldier why their son did not die in vain.

After Reading

MAKING CONNECTIONS

1. depressed, paranoid, delusional, confused, distracted; responses will vary on Shakespeare's portrait.

2. While answers will vary, students should note that Macbeth and Lady Macbeth chose evil and share responsibility for their actions.

3. He believes the prophecies made by the apparitions.

4. The witches conjure apparitions that equivocate to mislead Macbeth.

5. He understands himself well enough to accept the consequences of his choice for evil. She misjudges her ability to deal with guilt.

6. Duncan, a good king, provides contrast to Macbeth's rule of ambition and ruthlessness. Young Siward's death in battle reminds one of Macbeth's defense of his king and shows how far he has fallen. While Malcolm appears "foul" when he is "fair," Macbeth appears "fair" while plotting evil. Lady Macduff's banter with her son contrasts with Lady Macbeth's desire to "unsex" herself and deny natural tenderness.

7. Possible response: He has suffered most during Macbeth's reign of terror.

8. Possible response: Execution is a punishment, not an equalizer; nothing makes up for the crime.

9. People who turn to an outside force can be genuinely religious, but it may often be the weak and frightened who turn to the supernatural. People often realize they do not have all the answers, that wiser, more experienced heads offer good council.

Maintaining individuality is a matter of direction and degree: the degree of power one person allows an outside force to exert, and the direction of the force—moral or otherwise.

Act 5

After Reading

Making Connections

Shaping Your Response

1. List five words to describe Lady Macbeth's behavior. Do you think Shakespeare gives a convincing portrayal of her mental illness?
2. On a scale of 1 to 10, how responsible do you think Macbeth is for his own downfall? On the same scale, how responsible is Lady Macbeth for Macbeth's downfall? Be prepared to explain your answers.

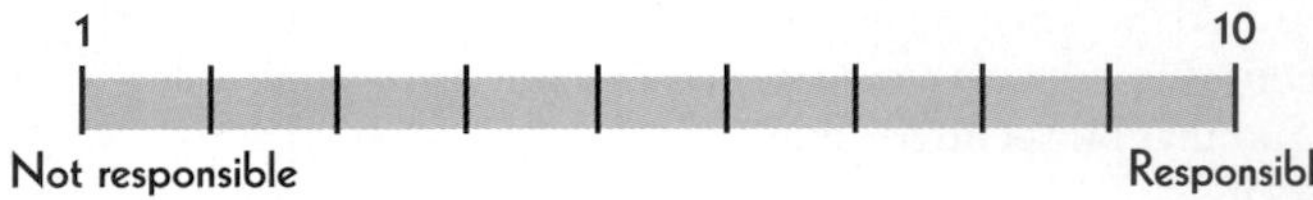

Analyzing the Play

3. Even though he hears about an advancing army, why does Macbeth still feel that he is safe?
4. To *equivocate* is to use expressions of double meaning in order to mislead. Explain whether or not the witches have equivocated.
5. How well do both Macbeth and Lady Macbeth seem to understand themselves, their strengths, and their limitations?
6. In literature, characters are frequently used as **foils;** that is, the traits of one point up by contrast the traits of another. What traits of Macbeth are pointed up by contrast with Duncan? with Young Siward? with Malcolm? How does Lady Macduff serve as a foil for Lady Macbeth?
7. Why is it particularly appropriate that Macduff is the one who finally kills Macbeth?

Extending the Ideas

8. Does the execution of a murderer make up for his or her crime? How? For whom?
9. Why do you think people turn to an outside or supernatural force for help in living their lives? Does depending on another force heighten or lessen one's own **individuality?**

Literary Focus: Plot Structure

Write down the three prophecies the Witches make in act 1. Each of these prophecies causes Macbeth to take some action that advances the plot. Trace the cause-effect actions that result from each prophecy. Do the same for act 4.

Vocabulary Study

In each of the following sentences, select the word in parentheses that best fits the meaning of the sentence.

1. Macbeth is often so absorbed in his thoughts of murder that he is

LITERARY FOCUS: PLOT

Act I Prophecies	Effects
Prophecy 1: Thane of Glamis	He is surprised to hear the witches call him by name.
Prophecy 2: Thane of Cawdor	When this prophecy is quickly realized he begins to seriously consider what his future may hold.
Prophecy 3: King hereafter	He soon determines that he will kill Duncan.
Prophecy 4: Banquo will father kings	Macbeth murders Banquo.
Act IV Prophecies	**Effects**
Prophecy 1: Beware Macduff	Macbeth tries to avoid fighting Macduff.
Prophecy 2: No harm from someone born of a woman	He believes himself invulnerable; prepares for battle.
Prophecy 3: No harm until Birnam Wood moves	He believes himself invulnerable; prepares for battle.

(oblivious, pristine) to the words and actions of those around him.

2. With a tyrant in charge, there is no one who can (upbraid, arbitrate) with him to help ease the awful conditions.
3. Macbeth believes he need not fear death and (bane, epicure) until Birnam Wood comes to Dunsinane.
4. When the messenger (avouches, bruits) that Birnam Wood is moving toward Dunsinane, Macbeth knows the end is near.
5. When Macbeth decides to leave his castle to fight, he once again becomes the (clamorous, valiant) warrior.

Expressing Your Ideas

Writing Choices

Writer's Notebook Update Review the definition of *tragedy* on page 117. Generally, the downfall of the main character in a tragedy is brought about through a tragic flaw in the character's personality or through a tragic error. Review the list of unfortunate people in your notebook. Were the forces that brought about their downfalls tragic flaws or tragic errors?

It's Fate After All The word *weird* comes from an Anglo-Saxon word meaning "fate." One interpretation of the three "weird sisters" is that they represent the beings who determine fate: the Past, the Present, and the Future. Write an **analysis** of the predictions of the witches, discussing to what extent you believe Macbeth is guided or controlled by them.

Dear Diary You are one of the invited guests at Macbeth's banquet. After you are dismissed by Lady Macbeth, you decide to record everything in your diary for future reference. Write a **diary entry** in which you describe your host and hostess and the events of the evening. You may wish to include your own theories about what was happening. Remember, *you* couldn't see Banquo's ghost.

Other Options

The Old Song and Dance The scenes with the three witches and Hecate offer the contrast of song and dance to the seriousness of the tragedy. Join with other classmates to choose appropriate music and to **choreograph** one or more of the witches' scenes. Add costumes and props, if you wish, and perform your dance for your class.

Block the Scene The banquet in act 3, scene 4 requires very careful positioning and moving of characters because of the many activities going on simultaneously. Work in a small group to block out this scene on paper, indicating where the various characters should be positioned and where they should move. Once you have developed your **stage directions,** assign parts and stage the scene.

Advertise *Macbeth* The illustration on page 119 is from a poster used to advertise a production of Macbeth in 1911. You have been selected to promote your school's production of *Macbeth.* Create a **poster** emphasizing an important theme, character, or event in the play. You might include an appropriate quote. Display your poster in the classroom.

VOCABULARY STUDY

1. oblivious
2. arbitrate
3. bane
4. avouches
5. valiant

Unit 2 Resource Book
Vocabulary, p. 43
Vocabulary Test, p. 46

WRITING CHOICES

Writer's Notebook Update

You might give students more background on tragic flaws by reading to them from Aristotle's *Poetics* before they begin the exercise.

Selection Test

Unit 2 Resource Book
pp. 47–48

Transparency Collection
Fine Art Writing Prompt 3

OTHER OPTIONS

The Old Song and Dance

Before students begin, ask them to brainstorm some words that describe what they want the dance to convey.

Block the Scene

Point out before students begin that the placement of the murderers is especially important because their conversation with Macbeth is understood not to be overheard by the company. Students should decide how the ghost will move and how he will appear and disappear.

Interdisciplinary Study

Theme Link

When the lure of ambition leads people to crime, how do they cope with the resulting burden of guilt? This is the topic explored in this interdisciplinary study.

Curricular Connection: Humanities

Use the information in this interdisciplinary study to explore with students the way that different cultures in different times view evil, guilt, and responsibility.

Terms to Know

blaspheme (bla sfēm′), speak about God or sacred things with abuse or contempt.

abhor (ab hôr′), regard with horror or disgust; detest; loathe.

malign (mə līn′), speak evil of.

plummet, a weight.

Additional Background

The *Egyptian Book of the Dead* was compiled between 1600 and 1500 B.C., though its individual texts date from much earlier.

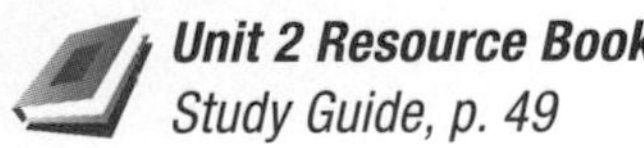

Unit 2 Resource Book
Study Guide, p. 49

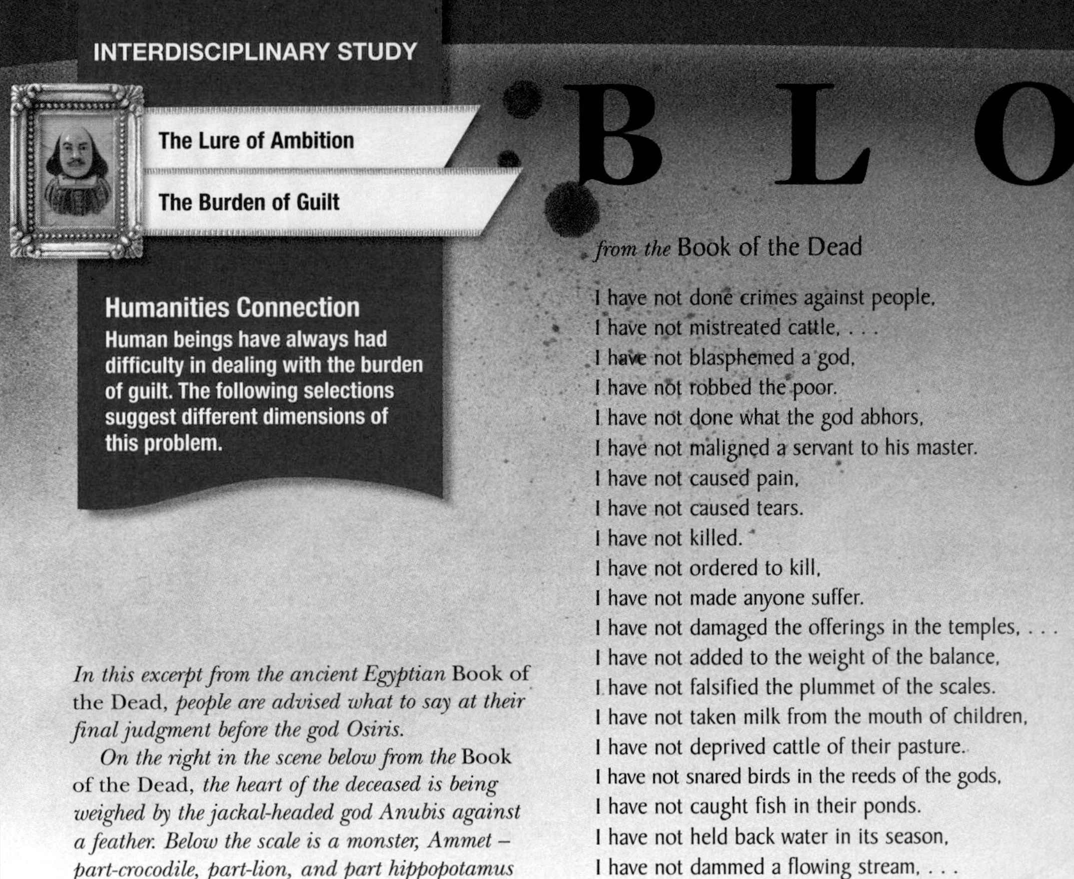

INTERDISCIPLINARY STUDY

The Lure of Ambition

The Burden of Guilt

Humanities Connection

Human beings have always had difficulty in dealing with the burden of guilt. The following selections suggest different dimensions of this problem.

B L O

from the Book of the Dead

I have not done crimes against people,
I have not mistreated cattle, . . .
I have not blasphemed a god,
I have not robbed the poor.
I have not done what the god abhors,
I have not maligned a servant to his master.
I have not caused pain,
I have not caused tears.
I have not killed.
I have not ordered to kill,
I have not made anyone suffer.
I have not damaged the offerings in the temples, . . .
I have not added to the weight of the balance,
I have not falsified the plummet of the scales.
I have not taken milk from the mouth of children,
I have not deprived cattle of their pasture.
I have not snared birds in the reeds of the gods,
I have not caught fish in their ponds.
I have not held back water in its season,
I have not dammed a flowing stream, . . .
I am pure, I am pure, I am pure, I am pure! . . .

In this excerpt from the ancient Egyptian Book of the Dead, *people are advised what to say at their final judgment before the god Osiris.*

On the right in the scene below from the Book of the Dead, *the heart of the deceased is being weighed by the jackal-headed god Anubis against a feather. Below the scale is a monster, Ammet – part-crocodile, part-lion, and part hippopotamus – that devours the hearts of the wicked.*

MINI-LESSON: SPEAKING

Prepared Speech

Teach The selection on this page is a model for a prepared speech. Point out the use of repetition, and the connection between some of the statements and those around them (e.g. "I have not killed, I have not ordered to kill"; following a statement that refers to a balance with one that refers to scales; a section on relations with nature). Point out the summation statement in this speech. Tell students that these techniques make a speech easier to memorize and deliver.

Activity Idea Provide students with an opportunity to practice their speech preparation skills in class. Emphasize that the purpose of this activity is not to analyze their ideas on the subject, but to provide them with practice in speech writing and confident presentation.

- Have students pretend that they are going to appear before Osiris.
- Give them time to prepare a short (1–2 minute) speech and practice it.
- Call on students at random to present their cases to Osiris.

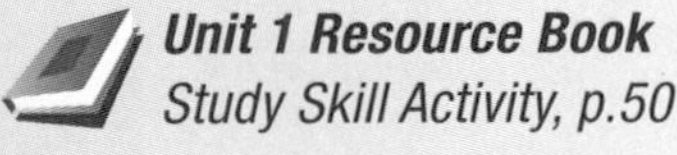

Unit 1 Resource Book
Study Skill Activity, p.50

O D Y

from The Furies *by Aeschylus*

Before the start of the Trojan War, the Greek King Agamemnon (ag′ə mem′non) *sacrifices his daughter Iphigenia* (if′ə jə nī′ə) *to the gods to obtain favorable winds for his warships, as shown in this ancient vase painting.*

After the war, Queen Clytemnestra (klī′tem nes′trə) *and her lover Aegisthus* (ē jis′thŭs) *murder Agamemnon on his return and take his throne. Her son Orestes* (ō res′tēs) *later murders Clytemnestra and Aegisthus in retribution for his father's death. In these speeches, the Furies, goddesses of vengeance, threaten what they will do to punish Orestes for his deed.*

So. Here the man has left a clear trail behind; keep on, keep on, as the unspeaking accuser tells us, by whose sense, like hounds after a bleeding fawn, we trail our quarry by the splash and drip of blood. And now my lungs are blown with abundant and with wearisome work, mankilling. My range has been the entire extent of land, and, flown unwinged across the open water, I am here, and give way to no ship in my pursuit. Our man has gone to cover somewhere in this place. The welcome smell of human blood has told me so.

Look again, look again,
search everywhere, let
not the matricide
steal away and escape...

You must give back for her blood from the living man
red blood of your body to suck, and from your own
I could feed, with bitter-swallowed drench,
turn your strength limp while yet you live and
drag you down
where you must pay for the pain of the murdered mother,
and watch the rest of the mortals stained with violence
against god or guest
or hurt parents who were close and dear,
each with the pain upon him that his crime deserves...
You are consecrate to me and fattened for my feast,
and you shall feed me while you live, not cut down first
at the altar. Hear the spell I sing to bind you in.

Come then, link we our choral. Ours
to show forth the power
and terror of our music, declare
our rights of office, how we conspire
to steer men's lives.
We hold we are straight and just. If a man
can spread his hands and show they are clean,
no wrath of ours shall lurk for him.
Unscathed he walks through his life time.
But one like this man before us, with stained
hidden hands, and the guilt upon him,
shall find us beside him, as witnesses
of the truth, and we show clear in the end
to avenge the blood of the murdered.

H A N D S

193

Terms to Know

The Furies, also known as the Eumenides (yü men′ə dēz′)—a euphemistic name meaning "the gracious goddesses"—are the avenging deities. They pursue those who have not atoned for their crimes.

quarry, prey of hunters.

matricide (mat′rə sīd), act of killing one's mother.

drench, medicine administered to an animal by pouring the liquid down its throat.

unscathed, unharmed.

Additional Background

The reason for the Trojan War arose when Paris, one of the princes of Troy, carried off Helen, the wife of King Menelaus of Sparta. Menelaus appealed to all the Greeks to help restore his wife, but relied chiefly on his brother, Agamemnon, King of Argos. They gathered a fleet in Aulis, but had no wind because Agamemnon had killed a stag of Artemis, who caused the unfavorable weather as a punishment. Told by a prophet that only the sacrifice of his daughter, Iphigenia, would satisfy Artemis and let the fleet sail, Agamemnon had Iphigenia brought to Aulis on the pretext of marrying her to the great hero Achilles who, when he discovered the plot, offered to rescue Iphigenia.

BUILDING ENGLISH PROFICIENCY

Linking Past and Present

The *Book of the Dead* (page 192) offers a self-defense of long ago. Invite students to create an update.

1. Discuss which statements from the *Book of the Dead* might seem to apply to any time and place (for example, *I have not done crimes against people; I have not caused pain).* Then have students locate statements that they think would not apply today (for example, *I have not mistreated cattle; I have not snared birds in the reeds of the gods).*
2. Have groups of students create new versions by listing 8–10 statements beginning with *I have not.* Urge students to keep some statements from the original and to include some that pertain to present-day life. Have them end with the original's conclusion: *I am pure, I am pure, I am pure, I am pure!*
3. Compare and discuss the groups' statements.

Terms to Know

delirium (di lir′ē əm), a temporary disorder of the mind; state of mental confusion.

faculty, power of the mind or body, such as thought, memory, hearing, and so on.

fray, make worn or ragged at the edge.

distraught (dis trôt′), in a state of mental conflict and anxiety.

Additional Background

The character being described, Raskolnikov, has just murdered two women: a cruel moneylender, by striking her repeatedly on the head with the blunt side of an axe, and her sister, whom he killed with a single blow to the head.

The photograph is of Peter Lorre in the 1935 film *Crime and Punishment.*

BLOODY HANDS

from *Crime and Punishment*
by Feodor Dostoevski

All at once, in one flash, he recollected everything. For the first moment he thought he was going mad. A dreadful chill came over him; but the chill was from the fever that had begun long before in his sleep. Now he was suddenly taken with violent shivering, so that his teeth chattered and all his limbs were shaking. He opened the door and began listening; everything in the house was asleep. With amazement he gazed at himself and everything in the room around him, wondering how he could have come in the night be fore without fastening the door, and have flung himself on the sofa without undressing, without even taking his hat off. It had fallen off and was lying on the floor near his pillow.

"If anyone had come in, what would he have thought? That I'm drunk but . . ."

He rushed to the window. There was light enough, and he began hurriedly looking himself all over from head to foot, all his clothes; were there not traces? But there was no doing it like that; shivering with cold, he began taking off everything and looking over again. He turned everything over to the last threads and rags, and mistrusting himself, went through his search three times. But there seemed to be nothing, no trace, except in one place, where some thick drops of congealed blood were clinging to the frayed edge of his trousers. He picked up a big claspknife and cut off the grayed threads. There seemed to be nothing more.

Suddenly he remembered that the purse and the things he had taken out of the old woman's box were still in his pockets! He had not thought till then of taking them out and hiding them! He had not even thought of them while he was examining his clothes! What next? Instantly he rushed to take them out, and fling them on the table. When he had pulled out everything, and turned the pocket inside out to be sure there was nothing left, he carried the whole heap to the corner. The paper had come off the bottom of the wall and hung there in tatters. He began stuffing all the things into the hole under the paper: "They're in! All out of sight, and the purse too!" he thought gleefully, getting up and gazing blankly at the hole which bulged out more than ever. Suddenly he shuddered all over with horror; "My God!" he whispered in despair: "what's the matter with me? Is that hidden? Is that the way to hide things?" He had not reckoned on having trinkets to hide. He had only thought of money, and so had not prepared a hiding-place. "But now, now, what am I glad of?" he thought. "Is that hiding things? My reason's deserting me—simply!" He sat down on the sofa in exhaustion and was at once shaken by another unbearable fit of shivering. Mechanically he drew from a chair beside him his old student's winter coat, which was still warm though almost in rags, covered himself up with it and once more sank into drowsiness and delirium. He lost consciousness.

MINI LESSON: VISUAL LITERACY

Draw Conclusions About Art

Teach Sometimes, as on this page, students will find illustrations with no caption or identifying information in a work of literature. Present students with the following questions to help them interpret illustrations under these conditions.

- Does the illustration show an actual moment in the story, or is it independent, intended to either resonate with or respond to the literature?
- What character(s) do(es) the illustration portray?
- What actions and/or emotions are depicted?
- How does the illustration relate to your ideas about the story? How is your interpretation different?
- What insights on the story does the illustration reveal?

Activity Idea Have students use these questions to interpret the illustration on page 194.

Not more than five minutes had passed when he jumped up a second time. . . . and with painful concentration he fell to gazing about him again, at the floor and everywhere, trying to make sure he had not forgotten anything. The conviction, that all his faculties, even memory, and the simplest power of reflection were failing him, began to be an insufferable torture.

"Surely it isn't beginning already! Surely it isn't my punishment coming upon me? It is!"

The frayed rags he had cut off his trousers were actually lying on the floor in the middle of the room, where any one coming in would see them!

"What is the matter with me!" he cried again, like one distraught.

Then a strange idea entered his head; that, perhaps, all his clothes were covered with blood, that, perhaps, there were a great many stains, but that he did not see them, did not notice them because his perceptions were failing, were going to pieces . . . his reason was clouded. . . .

Responding

1. How did these societies differ in values from ours today?
2. Which of the acts considered sinful by the ancient Egyptians would still be unacceptable behavior now?
3. Do you believe that a person is responsible for his or her own actions even if that person has been told or ordered by others to perform those actions?

During World War II over six million Jews and other people died or were murdered in Nazi concentration camps. After the war, Adolph Eichmann was captured in Argentina, where he had fled, and was brought to Israel to stand trial for his part in the killings. He was convicted in December, 1961, and was hanged the next year. Here is part of his statement.

from the trial of Adolph Eichmann

It is difficult to say what constitutes guilt, and I must make the distinction between guilt from the legal point of view and from the human aspect. . .

[The] guilt must be borne by those who were responsible for political decisions. when there is no responsibility there can be no guilt or blame. . .

The head of state ordered the deportations, and the part I played in them emanated from the master at the top. . . I had to obey. . .

Ethically I condemn myself and try to argue with myself. I wish to say, in conclusion, that I have regret and condemnation for the extermination of the Jewish people which was ordered by the German rulers, but I myself could not have done anything to prevent it. I was a tool in the hands of the strong and the powerful and in the hands of fate itself. . .

I do not consider myself guilty from the legal point of view. I was only receiving orders and carrying out orders. . . .

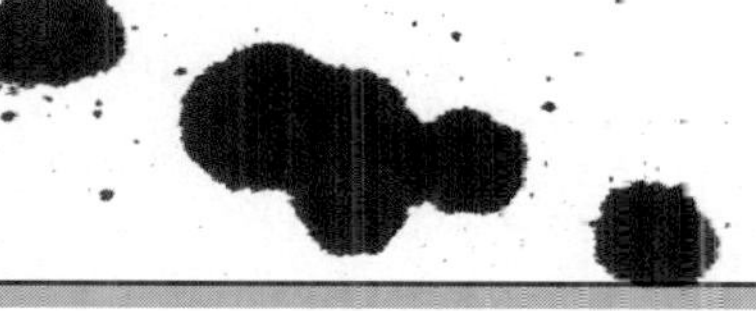

195

Terms to Know

deportation, usually meaning "banishment from a nation," here it refers to the collection and transportation of people to concentration camps.

emanate (em′ə nāt), originate from a person or thing as a source.

extermination (ek stėr′mə nā′shən), complete destruction.

Responding

1. Possible Responses The values are quite similar. In Egyptian society it was wrong to kill, cheat, and rob, for example. Greek society believed in divine punishment for offenses against a god or guest and for murder.

2. Possible Response Many students will say that most of these acts are still unacceptable.

3. Possible Responses Students should support their answers with reasons. Some will think that it is better to die for one's beliefs than to commit acts that are against one's conscience. Others may discuss the responsibility of those in power and the difficulty of choosing to disobey when a) it means certain death and b) those in power will just find someone else to perform the actions.

BUILDING ENGLISH PROFICIENCY

Exploring Key Concepts

Underlying both accounts on pages 194–195 is the concept of guilt—what it means (from both legal and personal standpoints) and how it affects the guilty. Help students focus on that concept by creating semantic webs arising from the word *guilt.*

1. After reading from *Crime and Punishment,* use a semantic web to explore with students how guilt might make a person feel and act. Use details from Dostoevski's account; add other details that students suggest from their own experience.
2. After reading from Eichmann's trial statement, have students respond to his idea that "It is difficult to say what constitutes guilt." Ask them to jot down words, phrases, or images that help define *guilt.*
3. To conclude, ask: What does it mean to be guilty? Invite students to offer responses from their semantic webs.

Terms to Know

trauma, an emotional shock which has a lasting effect on the mind.

psychiatric (sī′kē at′rik), having to do with the diagnosis and treatment of mental and emotional disorders.

clinical, of or having to do with the study of disease by observation of the patient rather than by experiment.

Responding

1. **Possible Response** She cannot live with the guilt she feels. Students may argue vehemently that Lady Macbeth was guilty, not insane; that her mental disturbance clearly arose after the murder that she planned and participated in; that a guilty conscience is not the equivalent of mental illness.

2. **Possible Response** Some students will feel very strongly that there is such a thing as choosing to be evil, that this is distinct from mental illness, and that this defense must only be used in certain very specific cases, for example, when a person has a documented case of schizophrenia or another psychosis. Students may struggle with the issue of temporary insanity and recall times when they became violently angry and felt out of control.

INTERDISCIPLINARY STUDY

Career Connection

Does Lady Macbeth go insane from feelings of guilt over her part in Duncan's murder? Here a mental-health care professional considers Lady Macbeth's case.

Lady Macbeth in Therapy

Interview with Diane Bray

Most of Diane Bray's clients are adults and older adolescents experiencing emotional distress. They are anxious or depressed, having relationship problems, addiction problems or difficulties as a result of emotional trauma or abuse. In private practice in Connecticut, Ms. Bray is a Certified Psychiatric Clinical Nurse Specialist and has been doing therapy for twenty-three years.

"Many factors influence our thoughts, feelings, behavior, and the choices we make in life. My goal as Lady Macbeth's therapist would be to help her become aware of these factors and how they've affected her behavior. I would want to know about her childhood and the kind of parenting she received. Sometimes in current relationships, we act out previous conflicts we've had with those closest to us, especially our parents. I would want to know about her relationship with her husband. How do they handle conflict and intimacy issues and how does she really feel about him? Is he really as soft-hearted as she thinks? He ends up killing Duncan, and later she has more trouble with the remorse than Macbeth.

"Culture and society also influence our roles and behavior. I wonder what it was like to be a female at the time of the play. Was a woman's only means of self-expression through her husband? How angry is Lady Macbeth about her limited opportunities?

"The development of Lady Macbeth's conscience is another important issue. I don't typically see people who have committed major crimes. Many people feel rage, but most find healthy ways to deal with their anger. Their conscience and control over their impulses keep them from acting out the rage. At first glance, Lady Macbeth looks cold-blooded as she and Macbeth plot the murder. But even in that scene in act 1, she wants to remove her remorse so she can carry out the deed. After the murder, she warns her husband not to think of it or it will make him mad. She is the voice of conscience and the predictor of what actually happens to her. Macbeth himself is responsible for the act, but doesn't seem to feel remorse and, in fact, goes into battle and orders additional murders.

"The goals of treatment are self knowledge, self acceptance, and being able to take responsibility for behavior and its consequences. Most treatment is done on an outpatient basis. However, Lady Macbeth, so out of touch with reality and unable to care for herself, would be put in a psychiatric hospital. She would get medication and therapy and would continue treatment after she left the hospital."

Responding

1. Why do you think Lady Macbeth commits suicide?

2. In your opinion, should a person be allowed to plead not guilty to a crime by reason of insanity? You might want to express your opinions in "Lady Macbeth on Trial," the Writing Workshop that begins on page 198.

MINI-LESSON: STUDY SKILLS

Use Both Primary and Secondary Sources

Teach Point out to students that while we, of course, do not have the opportunity to interview Lady Macbeth, there are ways in which we can discover more about her. Holinshed's *Chronicles,* the main source that Shakespeare used for the play, reveals a great deal about Scottish society. Other primary sources that can be useful include King James's writings on witchcraft.

Activity Idea Have each student choose either a primary or secondary source that touches on Lady Macbeth or Scottish society and culture in the time the Macbeths or Shakespeare lived, and report to the class on information they find that helps enlarge their understanding of Lady Macbeth's situation, actions, and choice to kill herself.

Language History

The Language of the Elizabethans

When we landed we founde fewe people, for the Lorde of that place was gone with divers Canoas above 400 miles of, upon a journey towardes the heade of Orenoque to trade for gold, and to buy women of the Canibals . . . .

Sir Walter Raleigh, *The Discoverie of Guiana* (1596)

By the time of Shakespeare, about half the population of London knew how to read, and that number continued to increase. Writers went on spelling words according to their own tastes or their dialectal backgrounds, however; the word *fellow,* for example, was spelled variously as *fallow, felowe, felow,* and *fallowe.*

The growth of the printing press increased the necessity for uniformity in language, and numerous "how-to" books on spelling and usage were printed during the late 1500s. On the one hand, preoccupation with a uniform language grew out of a strong sense of national identity. On the other hand, experimentation with new vocabulary and new means of expression grew out of the adventurous spirit of the Elizabethans.

The language grew to accommodate the new discoveries being made in scholarship and science. Experts estimate that more than ten thousand words were added to English during the last part of the 1500s. Words were borrowed or adapted from Latin and Greek *(antipathy, catastrophe, external, halo, anachronism, emphasis, strenuous);* French *(bigot, alloy, detail);* Italian *(balcony, cameo, stanza);* and Spanish and Portuguese *(alligator, negro, potato, tobacco, cannibal).*

Shakespeare himself was a notorious coiner and borrower of words. Many words originated by Shakespeare are still in common use today—for example, *monumental, lonely, hurry, castigate, assassination, majestic, excellent, fretful,* and *obscene.* As an originator of phrases, Shakespeare is preeminent. To him we are indebted for such phrases as *disgraceful conduct, flesh and blood, cold comfort, a foregone conclusion, the sound and the fury,* and *vanish into thin air.* Through his contributions not only to literature but also to English vocabulary and everyday speech, Shakespeare continues to speak to us across the centuries.

Language History

Teaching Objectives

- To understand the Elizabethan contribution to English vocabulary
- To understand how new words enter the language

Introduce

Mention at least one example of—or ask a volunteer to identify—a word that has more than one acceptable spelling (theater/theatre). Tell students that a number of words are spelled differently in Britain (honor/honour). Explain that until the Elizabethan era, there was no attempt to make spelling uniform.

Question What new words, meanings, or phrases can you think of that have entered the English language in the last five, ten, or fifteen years? *(Some examples are these: ethnic cleansing, drive-by, cocooning, infotainment)*

Then have them read the lesson.

Follow Up

Most libraries will have one or more sources for new words. *The Third Barnhart Dictionary of New English* by Robert K. Barnhart and Sol Steinmetz with Clarence Barnhart (H. W. Wilson, 1990) is a good source. Have students find this or a similar volume and bring to class five words that have entered the English language in recent years.

Writing Workshop

WRITER'S BLUEPRINT

Specs

The Specs in the Writer's Blueprint address these writing and thinking skills:

- summarizing
- taking and supporting a position
- evaluating evidence
- reasoning logically
- anticipating objections
- identifying cause and effect
- making judgments
- using commas correctly

These Specs serve as your lesson objectives, and they form the basis for the **Assessment Criteria Specs** for a superior paper, which appear on the final TE page for this lesson. You might want to read through the Assessment Criteria Specs with students when you begin the lesson.

Linking Literature to Writing

Ask students to think about how a lawyer would go about defending Lady Macbeth in today's court system. Briefly discuss high-profile court cases as examples of defenses that could be used.

Writing Workshop

Lady Macbeth on Trial

Assignment Do you think Lady Macbeth was as guilty of Duncan's murder as Macbeth? Write an essay in which you argue to what extent you think Lady Macbeth is guilty of the crime. See the Writer's Blueprint for details.

WRITER'S BLUEPRINT

Product	A persuasive essay
Purpose	To convince readers of your views on the degree to which Lady Macbeth is responsible for the murder of Duncan
Audience	People who have read or seen *Macbeth*
Specs	To write an effective essay, you should:

- ❑ Summarize the events leading to Duncan's murder in order to create a context for your argument.
- ❑ Give your opinion about the degree of Lady Macbeth's guilt and cite ample evidence from the text to support it, including direct quotations where appropriate.
- ❑ Address opposing points of view and refute them with logical reasons.
- ❑ Present clear cause-and-effect relationships throughout.
- ❑ Close by saying what you think should happen to Lady Macbeth as a result of her part in the murder, and why.
- ❑ Follow the rules of grammar, usage, spelling, and mechanics. Take special care to avoid comma splices.

WRITING WORKSHOP OVERVIEW

Product
Persuasive writing: A persuasive essay

Prewriting
Chart the events—Tally the evidence—Quickwrite your conclusions—Make your decision—Consider opposing points of view—Plan your essay—Ask a partner
Unit 2 Resource Book
Prewriting Worksheets pp. 51–52

Drafting
Before you draft—As you draft
Transparency Collection
Student Models for Writing Workshop 5, 6

Revising
Ask a partner—Strategy: Connecting Cause to Effect
Unit 2 Resource Book
Revising Worksheet p. 53

Editing
Ask a partner—Strategy: Correcting Comma Splices
Unit 2 Resource Book
Grammar Worksheet p. 54
Grammar Check Test p. 55

Presenting
Jury
Illustrate

Looking Back
Self-evaluate—Reflect—For Your Working Portfolio
Unit 2 Resource Book
Assessment Worksheet p. 56
Transparency Collection
Fine Art Transparency 3

STEP 1 PREWRITING

Chart the events that led to the murder. Review the play and make an evidence chart like the one below. List any evidence—actions, words—that relate to Lady Macbeth's involvement in the crime. For each piece of evidence, list a source: the act and scene where you found it. Include quotes where appropriate. Also, decide what this evidence shows about Lady Macbeth's part in the crime. (You might also want to reread "Lady Macbeth in Therapy" on page 196.)

Pieces of Evidence	Sources	What Evidence Shows
In his letter about the witches, Macbeth calls her "partner" and appeals to her ambition.	"My dearest partner of greatness . . . what greatness is promised thee." (act 1, scene 5)	

Tally the evidence. Put a plus sign next to the pieces of evidence that point to Lady Macbeth's guilt and a minus sign next to those that indicate she is either not guilty or is being persuaded to participate in the crime by Macbeth.

Quickwrite your conclusions. Look over your chart and spend a few minutes writing about what the evidence seems to show. Is Lady Macbeth:

- as guilty as Macbeth?
- less guilty but still responsible for the crime?
- not guilty by reason of insanity?
- an innocent victim of circumstances beyond her control?

Make your decision and circle the pieces of evidence from your chart that support it. Look back at the play if you feel you need more evidence.

Consider opposing points of view. Now look over the pieces of evidence from your chart that do not support your decision. What arguments could someone make to support a position different from yours? What logical reasons could you offer to refute them? Quickwrite for a few minutes about opposing points of view.

OR. . .
Get together with a partner who's taking an opposing point of view and discuss your positions. Take notes on your partner's position and ask questions.

STEP 1 PREWRITING

Chart the events

Students would probably benefit from working together in groups on this activity. Provide pieces of posterboard so students can make easy-to-read charts.

Tally the evidence

After students complete this activity individually, have them defend their positions in a class debate. If students create their charts in a group, this activity would provide another opportunity for group discussion and input from different points of view. For additional support see the worksheets referenced below.

Unit 2 Resource Book
Prewriting Worksheet, p. 51
Prewriting Worksheet, p. 52

Quickwrite your conclusions

Students may want to explore all of the possible charges against Lady Macbeth in their quickwrite before they settle on their position.

Make your decision

Remind students that supporting evidence will be crucial to building a persuasive essay.

Consider opposing points of view

During the quickwrite, students may want to write as if they are trying to prove the other position in order to get to know their opponents' arguments from the inside-out. Again, a group discussion prior to the quickwrite may help those students who have difficulty shifting from one position to another.

BUILDING ENGLISH PROFICIENCY

Exploring Key Concepts

The degree to which students consider Lady Macbeth guilty may depend upon their grasp of the concept of murder. Help students focus on the crime by creating a semantic web. Have students jot down thoughts that they associate (through Macbeth or through other experiences) with the murder of (1) any individual, (2) a husband and father, and (3) a king.

Plan your essay

Discuss with students the different structures a writer can use to frame an argument and discuss the strengths of each option.

Ask a partner

Have students highlight the strengths and probe the weaknesses of the writer's arguments.

Connections to
Writer's Notebook

For selection-related prompts, refer to Writer's Notebook.

Connections to
Writer's Resource

For additional writing prompts, refer to Writer's Resource.

STEP 2 DRAFTING

Before you draft

Students might work on their skills in persuasive rhetoric by taking on the tone of a trial lawyer during their early drafts.

Plan your essay. Reread the Writer's Blueprint. Then use your prewriting notes to help you create an outline like the one shown. As you plan, make sure you're presenting a sound argument based on solid evidence. See the Revising Strategy in Step 3 of this lesson.

- **Introduction**
  Events leading to the murder
- **Body–Part One**
  Your opinion on the degree of Lady Macbeth's guilt
  Piece of evidence + source
  Piece of evidence + source
  and so on . . .

OR . . .
Do Body–Part Two before Body–Part One. Refute opposing points of view before offering yours as the logical alternative.

(Note: present your pieces of evidence in time order, carrying the reader through the play from start to finish, or present them in order of strength, from weakest to strongest.)

- **Body–Part Two**
  An opposing point of view
  Reasons to support it
  Reasons to refute it
  Another opposing point of view
  and so on . . .
- **Conclusion**
  What should happen to Lady Macbeth
  Reasons why

Ask a partner to comment on your plan before you begin drafting. Use your partner's responses to help you revise your plan.

✔ Have I gathered strong evidence to support my opinion?

✔ Have I followed the Specs in the Writer's Blueprint?

STEP 2 DRAFTING

Before you draft, gather together your prewriting materials and review the Writer's Blueprint.

MINI-LESSON: WRITING STYLE

Connecting Cause to Effect

Activity Idea Have students arrange the following list of possible cause-and-effect statements regarding inflation into a flow chart using "if-then" statements. For example:

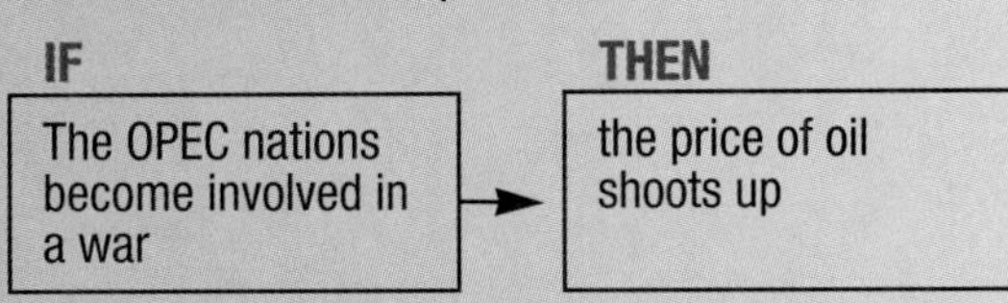

farmers spend more on fuel
truckers raise their fees
bread costs more at the store
OPEC nations become involved in war
salaries raised in response to higher food and heating prices
price of oil shoots up
prices are raised to compensate for higher wages

Apply Encourage students to "map" their own essays using a flow chart as a model.

As you draft, use your writing plan. These drafting tips may help:

- Begin with a quote from the play that strongly supports your opinion, and return to it later on when you state your opinion.
- Devote a paragraph to each of your three or four strongest pieces of evidence. Try to weave the other pieces of evidence into these paragraphs where they belong.

STEP 3 REVISING

Ask a partner for comments on your draft before you revise it.

✔ Have I clearly stated and supported my views on Lady Macbeth's guilt or innocence?

✔ Have I refuted opposing points of view?

✔ Have I presented strong cause-effect connections?

COMPUTER TIP
As you revise, save each version of your essay with a slightly different name, for example, MacbVer1, MacbVer2, and so on. This way you can always return to a previous version if you need to.

Revising Strategy

Connecting Cause to Effect

Test the strength of your arguments by asking yourself whether you have presented clear connections between causes and effects. The connection might be clear in your mind, but that's not enough. It's your responsibility to make it as clear to your readers as it is to you.

Weak Connection	After the witches spoke to Macbeth, he did the murder. *(Just because event #1 occurred a little while before event #2 doesn't mean that #1 caused #2.)*
Strong Connection	While speaking to Macbeth, the witches appealed to his latent ambition, and this appeal helped push him to commit the murder. *(Now we see how the witches helped cause the murder.)*

Notice how the writer has strengthened cause-effect connections in the student model on the next page.

As you draft

Remind students to use the proper format when quoting from the text. Remind students to read the drafting tips before they start writing.

The Student Models

The **transparencies** referenced below are authentic student models. Review them with the students before they draft. These questions will help:

1. The writer of model 5 says that Lady Macbeth "bullied Macbeth" into committing the murder. Does she support this conclusion? If so, how?

2. Compare the two writer's opinions about the degree of Lady Macbeth's guilt. Which writer do you think does a better job of proving his/her point?

3. Where and how does the writer of model 6 address opposing points of view?

Transparency Collection
Student Models for Writing Workshop 5, 6

STEP 3 REVISING
Ask a partner (Peer assessment)

Students may want to rank their peer's arguments in order of persuasiveness so that the writer will know which areas need strengthening.

Revising Strategy: Connecting Cause to Effect

Have students explain, through discussion, the importance of establishing relationships between causes and effects.

For additional support, see the mini-lesson at the bottom of page 200 and the worksheet referenced below.

BUILDING ENGLISH PROFICIENCY

Using Revising Helps

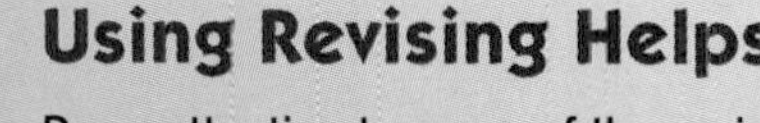

Draw attention to some of the revising helps provided on page 201.

- Expand upon the *Computer Tip* by pointing out that most word-processing software allows users to view more than one document at a time. Thus, if students save multiple versions of their drafts, they can view them on-screen, side by side.
- As students discuss the Revising Strategy, explain that even a clear connection will not help a weak cause. Urge students to consider each cause-and-effect argument in their draft to see if there might be other—and stronger—causes.

Unit 2 Resource Book
Revising Worksheet, p. 53

Connections to
Writer's Resource

Refer to the Grammar, Usage, and Mechanics Handbook on Writer's Resource.

STEP 4 EDITING

Ask a partner (Peer assessment)

You might have students divide into small editing groups, with each group member reading all the papers, but being responsible for one aspect of editing, such as spelling.

Editing Strategy: Correcting Comma Splices

Have students write several alternative revisions to the sentences in the example. Then list the strategies the class comes up with for rewriting sentence combinations containing comma splices.

For additional support, see the mini-lesson at the bottom of this page and the worksheets referenced below.

Unit 2 Resource Book
Grammar Worksheet, p. 54
Grammar Check Test, p. 55

Connections to **Writer's Resource**

Refer to the Grammar, Usage, and Mechanics Handbook on Writer's Resource.

Some people might think that Macbeth was innocent and it ~~was all Lady Macbeth's fault.~~ *But Macbeth knew what he was doing. While thinking about killing Duncan he said,* ~~Macbeth said:~~ "We still have judgement here, that we but teach bloody instructions, which, being taught, return to plague th' inventor" (act 1, scene 7).

Ask a partner to review your revised draft before you edit. When you edit, look for errors in grammar, usage, spelling, and mechanics. Be sure to look for comma splices.

Editing Strategy

Correcting Comma Splices

Thinking about complex topics may lead you to write separate sentences as if they were one long sentence, spliced together with commas. For example:

Comma Splice Macbeth knew what he was doing, he was aware of the terrible act he was about to commit well before he did it.

Corrected Macbeth knew what he was doing. He was aware of the terrible act he was about to commit well before he did it.

As you edit, be on the lookout for comma splices. Correct them by separating the individual sentences.

FOR REFERENCE. . .
More tips on correcting comma splices can be found in the Language and Grammar Handbook at the back of this book.

MINI-LESSON: GRAMMAR

Correcting Comma Splices

Have students correct the following comma splices by adding a coordinating conjunction (as in the example), by adding a semicolon, or forming two separate sentences. Example:

Williams was respected by many of the other players, the fans still did not vote her an All-Star.

Williams was respected by many of the other players, but the fans still did not vote her an All-Star.

Brad knows where the fish are, he's been fishing this river since he was seven.

Andre's mother worked during the day, she went to nursing school at night.

The turtles are now an endangered species, their eggs are a local delicacy.

Unit 2 Resource Book
Grammar Worksheet p. 54
Grammar Check Test p. 55

STEP 5 PRESENTING

To present your essay, consider these ideas.

- Find classmates whose points of view differ from yours. Read your essays to a jury of classmates, who will then confer and vote to select the most convincing argument.
- Illustrate your essay with drawings of Lady Macbeth that show her thinking thoughts or speaking words that exemplify your feelings about her.

STEP 6 LOOKING BACK

Self-evaluate. Evaluate your essay on each item in the Writer's Blueprint, giving yourself a score for each one from 6 (superior) down to 1 (inadequate).

Reflect. What did you learn from writing this essay? Write your thoughts in response to these questions:

✔ After arguing in favor of your point of view, what do you think of yourself as a persuasive thinker? Do you think you might someday be good at, say, writing ads or practicing law?

✔ What are your overall feelings about Lady Macbeth? Does she show strengths of character? If so, what do you think about how she uses those strengths?

For Your Working Portfolio Add your essay and your reflections to your working portfolio.

STEP 5 PRESENTING

Jury

Ask students to comment on whether their thinking was altered by any of their peers' arguments, and if so, how.

Illustrate

Students might look over comic strips for ideas bout how to combine drawings and text.

STEP 6 LOOKING BACK

Self-evaluate

The *Assessment Criteria Specs* at the bottom of this page are for a superior paper. You might want to post these in the classroom. Students can then evaluate themselves based on these criteria.
For a complete scoring rubric, use the *Assessment Worksheet* referenced below.

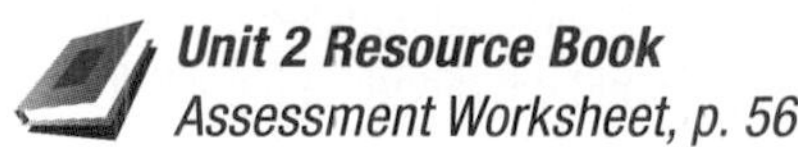
Unit 2 Resource Book
Assessment Worksheet, p. 56

Reflect

After students reflect on Lady Macbeth's character, ask them to consider ways in which their reactions to her can be applied to situations they face today.

To further explore the theme, use the Fine Art Transparency referenced below.

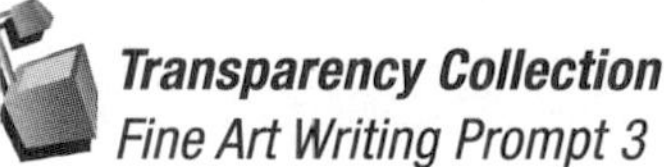
Transparency Collection
Fine Art Writing Prompt 3

ASSESSMENT CRITERIA SPECS

Here are the criteria for a superior paper. A full six-level rubric for this paper appears on the *Assessment Worksheet* referenced below.

6 Superior The writer of a 6 paper impressively meets these criteria:

- Provides a concise synopsis of events leading to the murder.
- Makes a convincing case for the degree of Lady Macbeth's guilt, supporting it with specific examples from the play, including direct quotations where appropriate.
- Addresses opposing points of view and refutes them with logical reasons.
- Presents clear cause-and-effect relationships in support of the case.
- Closes with a strong argument as to the punishment Lady Macbeth should receive.
- Has few, if any, errors in the conventions of standard written English. Avoids comma splices.

Unit 2 Resource Book
Assessment Worksheet, p. 56

Beyond Print

Teaching Objectives

- To perform key scenes from a Shakespearean play
- To understand Shakespeare's language
- To compare and contrast a class performance with a professional performance

Curricular Connection: Speaking/Listening Skills

Use the material in this article to give students practice in the speaking and listening skills necessary for dramatic performance of key scenes.

Introduce

Shakespeare's language can be daunting. Performing it can give students a good reason to search more deeply for meaning, and can also provide insights and understanding beyond what can be gained from independent, silent reading. As students go through the steps of preparing a performance, encourage them to take notes on strategies they find useful in interpreting and memorizing parts.

Activity Options

Activity 1 Areas that students may wish to focus on refining include

- delivery
- timing
- gesticulation

Activity 2 Students may begin by referring to the strategy notes they made during preparation. They might describe what aspects they found hardest to do and what the easiest part was.

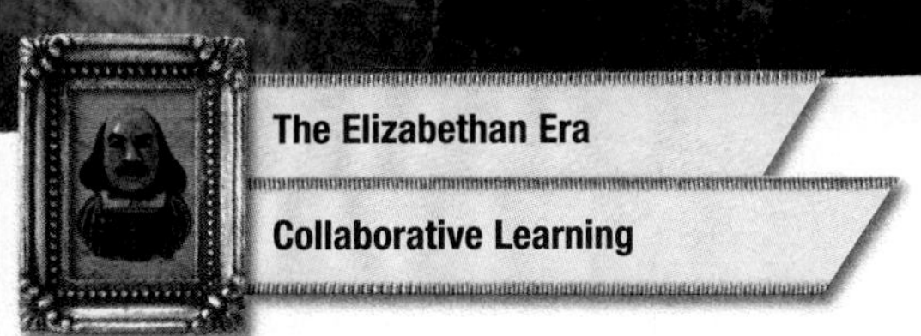

Beyond Print

Performing Shakespeare

One way to get familiar with any play is to act it out. This will help you get a better sense of what the words mean, who the people are, and what they're doing and feeling. Here are some tips on performing *Macbeth* in your classroom.

Select Scenes. Get familiar with the characters and the story. Then single out key scenes you might perform. In small groups, read and discuss these scenes. Take your time. Try to understand as much as possible. When passages are difficult, refer to the notes and talk them over.

Rehearse. Read through your scenes and learn the language. Then read through again and try to act the character. Next block out scenes, which means getting up and moving about. Decide where to make entrances and exits. Plan who will stand where and what actions are needed. Finally, have a dress rehearsal—at least one run-through with no stops.

Reading the Poetry. When you watch movies or listen to recordings of Shakespearean plays, you may notice the actors using a heightened style, a kind of delivery that emphasizes the poetry of the language. Don't worry about it. Read to get the meaning across and to express the emotions.

Perform the Scenes. Perform the various scenes in the order they come in the play. You might introduce scenes with brief descriptions of what took place before.

Afterwards. Discuss the play. What did you learn by performing it—about your character? about the themes? about the difficulties of putting on this play? Watch a movie version of *Macbeth* and compare your interpretations with those of the movie.

Activitiy Options

1. Polish your scenes and put them on for other classes.
2. Write a brief description of what you did to prepare the play for performance and what you learned from your experience.

ANOTHER APPROACH

Without a Stage: Readers Theater

Students who do not have access to a performance site can present a Readers Theater version of their chosen scenes. The actors can sit on chairs or stools arranged in a semicircle, or they may wish to group their seating in some other meaningful way. Students can still use gesture and posture for characterization, if they wish.

Multicultural Connections

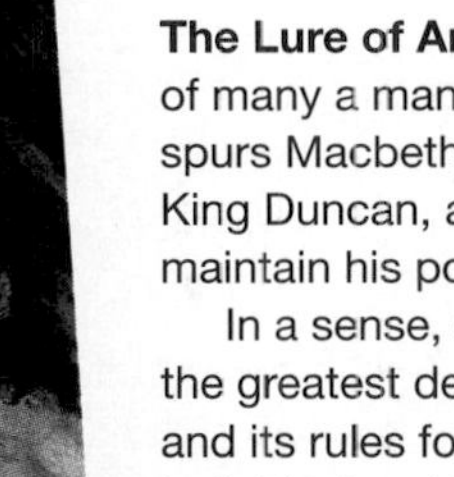

Individuality

The Lure of Ambition Uncontrolled ambition has been the downfall of many a man and woman throughout history. It is ambition that spurs Macbeth and Lady Macbeth to commit the first murder, that of King Duncan, and it is ambition that causes Macbeth to kill others to maintain his position.

In a sense, ambition is a desire to express one's individuality to the greatest degree possible. It is the desire to break out of the group and its rules for behavior. But it is the group that acknowledges an individual and keeps him or her special, and that means that the individual still has responsibilities to the group.

Macbeth wants the glory of kingship, but he shirks the responsibilities of leading his people in a sensible and dignified way and of assuring their personal safety—one of the bases for founding a society in the first place. His is, in a sense, individuality run amok.

■ How do you think Macbeth might have realized his ambition to express his individuality and yet not have crossed that line that alienates him from his society?

Activities

1. Watch a videotape of a production of *Macbeth*. Discuss how the actor playing the protagonist manages, through voice and body movements, to get across the motivations that cause him to commit so many murders.
2. Stage a number of scenes from *Macbeth*. You can work with your books or with scripts so that you don't have to memorize all the lines, but you should rehearse enough to be able to speak the lines with some facility. See Performing Shakespeare on page 204.
3. Although there was very little costuming in Shakespeare's day, modern productions of his plays often include elaborate costumes. Design costumes for Macbeth, Lady Macbeth, and their guests to wear in the banquet scene in act 3. Since all the guests are noblemen themselves, and since a tartan was a common pattern for Scotsmen to wear (see the illustration on page 179), how will you show Macbeth's individuality and his position as king?

Unit Wrap-Up

MULTICULTURAL CONNECTION

Shakespeare's *Macbeth* is based on real historical characters. Some critics believe that the play was intended to flatter James I, King of England, who claimed to be a descendant of the heroic Banquo. James had also written a treatise on witchcraft. You might discuss how ambition, in this case Shakespeare's desire to be patron-ized by his king, shapes the development of literature and even historical interpretations. This approach might help students understand that ambition is a driving force behind many human achievements.

Individuality

You might point out that although Macbeth is driven by his ambition, he is also greatly influenced by his wife's dark suggestions. Further, he is spurred on by the temptations of the witches' prophecies. Duncan, a more temperate advisor, becomes a victim of Macbeth's violence.

- Discuss how the system of checks and balances in democracy might have been a reaction to this kind of abuse of power under monarchy.
- Explore the loneliness that resulted from Macbeth's abandonment of responsibility for the group. Group support is often vital to individual achievement.

Possible Responses Macbeth could have chosen his political advisors more wisely. He could have depended on group loyalty rather than violence to secure his political power.

Activities

Activity 1 You might have students analyze the camera techniques employed to adapt a play to the screen. Point out that when the action is private and intimate, the camera moves in close. Ask: In what other ways does the movement of the camera supplement the methods of the actors and actresses?

Activity 2 Dramatic performance is an excellent example of how group interaction and solidarity nurture individual achievement. Ask students to consider the collaborative roles of performers, directors, and set technicians in theater arts.

Activity 3 Suggest that students research the costumes of the day through primary sources, such as textile encyclopedias, and through secondary sources, such as film adaptations of Shakespearean drama and films that depict life in early modern England.

UNIT 2 OPTIONS

Media

Students might consider including a video or audio interview, photographs of their subject in action, quotes from others who appreciate the subject's achievement, and a biographical timeline that lists the chronology of the subject's skills and achievements.

Oral Presentation

Students might bring "imaginary" witnesses to the stand to defend or condemn the organization. Artists and politicians they might choose to impersonate are writer William Shakespeare, writer Alice Walker, Senator Jesse Helms, actress Jane Alexander, President Clinton.

Panel Discussion

You might discuss the distinction between gratuitous violence, or violence for its own sake, and violence that seems to be an integral part of the dramatic narrative. You might also discuss the range of options for the cinematic depiction of violence: as large scale visual spectacle, as graphically shocking detail, and as an abstract tragic consequence of human interaction.

Research

Encourage students to carefully annotate their resources in a bibliographical format. Suggest that they write a brief description of each source, with a rating from 1–10 based on its helpfulness regarding their topic. Students can compile these bibliographies into an Elizabethan Reference Manual for use with future projects.

Unit Test

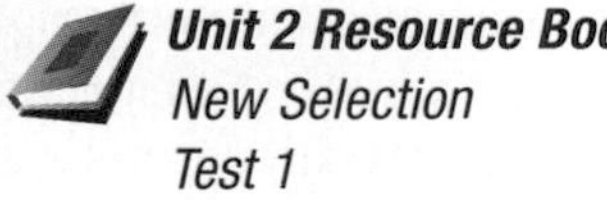

Unit 2 Resource Book,
New Selection
Test 1
Test 2

Independent and Group Projects

Media

A (Wo)man for All Seasons Someone who does a great variety of things is often described as a Renaissance man. Who in today's world might be described as a Renaissance man or woman? Make a list of the characteristics of your ideal Renaissance person. You might consider your grandmother, your social studies teacher, your science laboratory partner. Use a scrapbook or a multimedia computer program to assemble a personal profile of this person as a Renaissance man or woman.

Oral Presentation

Support for the Arts Throughout the history of England and many other nations as well, writers, musicians, and artists have been encouraged to pursue their talents through pensions or grants from their governments. Since 1965 in the United States, creativity has been encouraged by the National Endowment for the Arts. With a partner, research the National Endowment for the Arts and prepare a debate on whether grants from the organization should continue.

Panel Discussion

Violence Today Today's American society has been called the most violent in all of history, perhaps because of the violence presented in the movies and on television. Watch a television show known for its violence. Record the number of violent acts. Join classmates who have watched similar programs and have a panel discussion on the impact of violence in the media. Are your chosen programs more or less violent than *Macbeth?*

Research

Researching the Elizabethan Era Select one of the following topics or choose a topic of your own on which to do independent research. Then write a report of your findings.

- Elizabethan attitudes toward ghosts and witchcraft
- Adult and child acting companies
- Public and private theaters
- Critical theories on Macbeth's or Lady Macbeth's character
- The role of women in Shakespeare's day

206

Nature
Garden
or Wilderness?
THEMES in
ENGLISH
LITERATURE

THEMES IN ENGLISH LITERATURE

About Jean Jacques Rousseau

Rousseau (1712–1778) was the most important French philosopher of the Age of Reason. His work foreshadowed Romanticism by valuing feeling more than reason, impulse and spontaneity more than self-discipline. Rousseau's philosophy helped shape the political events that led to the French Revolution. The quotation is from *Emile; or, On Education* (1762), Book 3.

About Lord Byron

One of the most dashing and romantic of the Romantic poets, George Gordon, Lord Byron (1788–1824) published the first two cantos of *Childe Harold's Pilgrimage* upon returning from the traditional Grand Tour of Europe after his graduation from Cambridge. The poem was so popular that, as he put it, "I awoke one morning and found myself famous." This verse, number 178 in the fourth canto (1818), expresses a typically Romantic fascination with nature and the lessons one can learn from it (see also p. 462).

Nature

Garden or Wilderness?

We are all undeniably a part of nature, but how people feel about nature takes many forms. Some look upon nature as benevolent, a teacher, a parent, a healer, the source of all that is good in life. Some think that nature is neutral, in itself neither helpful nor harmful to humankind. And some look upon nature as an enemy, set to destroy individuals—who are, after all, comparatively helpless in its power. How you feel about nature may influence whether you prefer it wild and natural, as in wilderness, or tamed, as in a garden.

NATURE NEVER DECEIVES US; IT IS ALWAYS WE WHO DECEIVE OURSELVES.

Jean Jacques Rousseau (1762)

Love of Nature

There is a pleasure in the pathless woods,
There is a rapture[1] on the lonely shore,
There is society, where none intrudes,
By the deep Sea, and music in its roar:
I love not Man the less, but Nature more,
From these our interviews, in which I steal
From all I may be, or have been before,
To mingle with the universe, and feel
What I can ne'er express, yet cannot all conceal.

Lord Byron (1812)

1. **rapture** (rap′chər), *n.* strong feeling of delight or joy.

THEME LINK TO THE LITERATURE

Some other selections in the text that deal with the themes of the wilderness and the relationship between people and the land are listed below.

Thomas Gainsborough, Mr. and Mrs. Robert Andrews (1748)

Rural Leisure

Oh friendly to the best pursuits of man,
Friendly to thought, to virtue, and to peace,
Domestic life in rural leisure passed!
Few know thy value, and few taste thy sweets,
Though many boast thy favors, and affect
To understand and choose thee for their own.
But foolish man foregoes his proper bliss,
Even as his first progenitor,[1] and quits,
Though placed in paradise (for earth has still
Some traces of her youthful beauty left)
Substantial happiness for transient joy.
Scenes formed for contemplation and to nurse
The growing seeds of wisdom; that suggest,
By every pleasing image they present,
Reflections such as meliorate[2] the heart,
Compose the passions, and exalt the mind . . . .

William Cowper (1785)

1. **progenitor** (prō jen′ə tər), *n.* ancestor.
2. **meliorate** (mē′lyə rāt′), *v.* improve.

Art Study

Visual Literacy English painting before the Romantic era is largely portraiture. Landscapes were bought or commissioned, but they were usually portraits of a patron's house or estate. Thomas Gainsborough (1727–1788) wanted to paint landscapes, but he was forced to paint portraits for a living. Sometimes he compromised by posing his subjects in a landscape, combining English informality with the grace of French models of the genre.

Question What impression of themselves do you imagine Mr. and Mrs. Andrews wanted a viewer to get? *(Possible response: that they are important, sensible people, who have, nevertheless, a love for beauty)*

About William Cowper

For a decade or two after the publication of *The Task* in 1785, William Cowper (1731–1800) was the foremost poet in England. As the chief exponent in poetry of the moral and humanitarian values of the Evangelical Revival, Cowper enjoyed a wide readership well into the middle years of the Victorian era, a far wider readership than he had ever known in his lifetime. The quotation is from Book 2 of this long philosophical poem; this book is entitled "The Time-Piece" because it was "intended to strike the hour that gives notice of approaching judgment."

BUILDING ENGLISH PROFICIENCY

Exploring Key Concepts

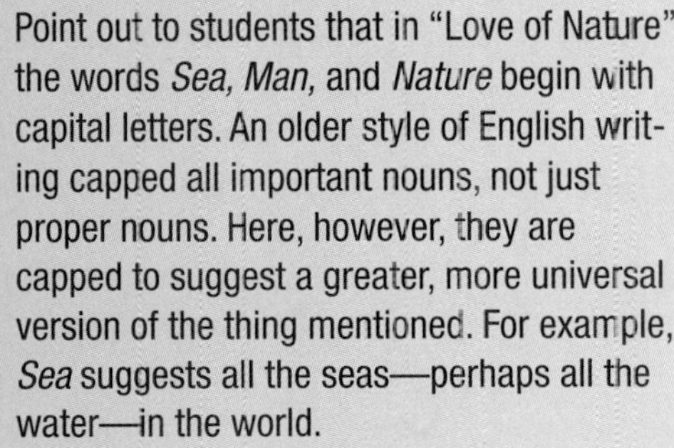

Point out to students that in "Love of Nature" the words *Sea, Man,* and *Nature* begin with capital letters. An older style of English writing capped all important nouns, not just proper nouns. Here, however, they are capped to suggest a greater, more universal version of the thing mentioned. For example, *Sea* suggests all the seas—perhaps all the water—in the world.

1. In line 5, how does *Man* differ from *man? (It suggests all of humanity.)*
2. How does *Nature* differ from *nature* in the same line? *(It suggests the entire natural world.)*

Art Study

Visual Literacy Lines 15–22 of Thomas Gray's "The Bard" describe the poet who inspired the painting:

On a rock whose haughty brow
Browns o'er old Conway's foaming flood,
Robed in the sable garb of woe,
With haggard eyes the poet stood
(Loose his beard and hoary hair
Streamed, like a meteor, to the troubled air),
And with a master's hand and prophet's fire
Struck the deep sorrows of his lyre. . . .

Question Why do you suppose the artist, John Martin, composed this picture so that the human characters are dwarfed by their natural setting? *(Possible response: to emphasize that human conquests—and even constructions, like the castle—are indeed small and transitory in comparison to nature)*

MINI-LESSON: LITERARY ELEMENT

Apostrophe

The figure of speech in which an absent person, an abstract concept, or an inanimate object is directly addressed is called apostrophe.

Teach Ask: To whom—or to what is the speaker in "Blow, winds . . ." talking? *(The winds, waterfalls, waterspouts, lightning, thunder, and all the other natural elements.)* Why is he doing this? What is the effect of his addressing inanimate elements. *(His address makes it seem as though the elements are personally out to get him; this makes his situation seem more pathetic or more tragic.)*

Activity Idea Have students do a quickwrite, addressing a particular element or all of nature with their praises, complaints, or comments.

Summer Is Gone

My tidings for you: the stag bells,
Winter snows, summer is gone.

Wind high and cold, low the sun,
Short his course, sea running high.

Deep-red the bracken, its shape all gone—
The wild-goose has raised his wonted cry.

Cold has caught the wings of birds;
Season of ice—these are my tidings.

Anonymous (800s)

NATURE, TO BE

COMMANDED,

MUST BE OBEYED.

Francis Bacon (1620)

"Blow, winds..."

Blow, winds, and crack your cheeks! Rage, blow!
You cataracts and hurricanoes,[1] spout
Till you have drenched our steeples, drowned the cocks![2]
You sulfurous and thought-executing fires,[3]
Vaunt-couriers[4] of oak-cleaving thunderbolts
Singe my white head! And thou, all-shaking thunder,
Strike flat the thick rotundity[5] o' the world!
Crack nature's molds, all germens[6] spill at once
That makes ingrateful man! . . .
I tax not you, you elements, with unkindness;
I never gave you kingdom, called you children.
You owe me no subscription.[7] Then let fall
Your horrible pleasure. Here I stand your slave,
A poor, infirm, weak, and despised old man.

William Shakespeare (1605)

John Martin's painting The Bard *(1817) illustrates Thomas Gray's poem in which a Welsh poet delivers a bitter prophesy to Edward I as the British king and his army invade Wales.*

1. **cataract** (kat′ə rakt′) . . . **hurricano** (hėr′ə kā′nō), waterfall and waterspout.
2. **cocks,** weathervanes.
3. **thought-executing fires,** lightning, acting with the quickness of thought.
4. **vaunt-courier,** forerunner.
5. **rotundity** (rō tun′də tē), *n.* roundness.
6. **germen** (jėr′mən), *n.* seed.
7. **subscription,** allegiance.

About "Summer is Gone"

After the retreat from England of the Roman legions, Celtic Britons struggled to defend their land against the next wave of invaders—the Anglo-Saxon tribes. Many Celts fled to what would become Ireland, Wales, and Scotland. Because of the early and rapid spread of Christianity in Ireland, Latin was already in use there by the fifth century, but poetry in the vernacular Irish language from the 500s to the 800s still survives—the oldest vernacular literature in Western Europe. In the 600s, a new sort of poetry—short lyrics with regular meter and end rhyme—started to develop. Probably derived from Latin models, it nevertheless spoke in an authentic Irish voice.

About Francis Bacon

Francis Bacon (1561–1626) was an English philosopher and statesman, one of the earliest and most influential supporters of experimental methods in solving scientific problems. This quotation is Aphorism 129 from his *Novum Organum,* part of a projected but unfinished major survey of the methods, theories, and achievements of experimental science. Bacon also wrote witty and original essays.

About "Blow, winds . . ."

In Shakespeare's *King Lear,* the old king foolishly divides his kingdom between two daughters who flatter him, disinheriting the daughter who speaks truth. In Act Three, Scene 2, Lear, driven mad by his false daughters' rejection, wanders the countryside in a terrifying rainstorm. In this speech he defies the malign—or at least indifferent—universe in which human life seems meaningless and brutal.

BUILDING ENGLISH PROFICIENCY

Exploring Key Concepts

Sometimes literature can be difficult to read because of the length and/or complexity of the sentences. This is especially true of Shakespeare, who uses frequent and lengthy interrupters (although it is not so true of this excerpt as it is of *Macbeth*).

1. What is the subject and verb of the sentence in lines 4–6? (You singe; fires *is an appositive to the subject pronoun.)*
2. What does line 5 describe? *(It is an appositive describing* fires.)

About William Wordsworth

In his childhood and youth, William Wordsworth (1770–1850) had a strong intuition that the soul, which is eternal, comes into a human body at birth from a glorious heavenly home. Gradually, as he grew older, he lost the vision of his childhood belief. In manhood, experiences with nature brought him comfort and renewed his earlier beliefs. His "Ode: Intimations of Immortality from Recollections of Early Childhood" is his strongest statement of his view of nature as a source of spiritual insight (see also p. 408).

About Thomas Gray

Best known for his "Elegy Written in a Country Churchyard," Thomas Gray (1716–1771) had a small poetic output. However, his letters—now considered among the best in an age when letter-writing was an art—show Gray's affectionate nature and gentle humor. This quotation is from a letter Gray wrote to schoolmate and friend Richard West about his journey up to the Grande Chartreuse (the motherhouse of the Carthusian monks) near Grenoble, France.

About "Fern Hill"

Derek Stanford comments, "If one sought to describe this poem within the compass of a single phrase, it might be called 'an elegy in praise of lost youth.' Lament and celebration sound throughout the work: the latter strongly at the beginning, the former gaining tone as the poem progresses. . . . Nostalgic recollection of a child's farm holiday is the leaping-off point for the poem; but—once launched—so intense and poignant a memory overtakes the poet, that his words convey more than a merely topographical homesickness. . . ."

from *Intimations of Immortality* . . .

There was a time when meadow, grove, and stream,
The earth, and every common sight,
To me did seem
Appareled[1] in celestial[2] light,
The glory and the freshness of a dream.
It is not now as it hath been of yore;
Turn wheresoe'er I may,
By night or day,
The things which I have seen I now can see no more.

The Rainbow comes and goes,
And lovely is the Rose,
The Moon doth with delight
Look round her when the heavens are bare;
Waters on a starry night
Are beautiful and fair;
The sunshine is a glorious birth;
But yet I know, where'er I go,
That there hath passed away a glory from the earth.

William Wordsworth (1807)

Religion and Poetry in Nature

. . . I do not remember to have gone ten paces without an exclamation that there was no restraining: not a precipice,[1] not a torrent, not a cliff, but is pregnant with religion and poetry. There are certain scenes that would awe an atheist into belief without the help of other argument.

Thomas Gray (1739)

from FERN HILL

Now as I was young and easy under the apple boughs
About the lilting house and happy as the grass was green,
The night above the dingle[1] starry,
Time let me hail and climb
Golden in the heydays of his eyes,
And honored among wagons I was prince of the apple towns
And once below a time I lordly had the trees and leaves
Trail with daisies and barley
Down the rivers of the windfall light.

And as I was green and carefree, famous among the barns
About the happy yard and singing as the farm was home,
In the sun that is young once only,
Time let me play and be
Golden in the mercy of his means,
And green and golden I was huntsman and herdsman, the
calves
Sang to my horn, the foxes on the hills barked clear and cold,
And the sabbath[2] rang slowly
In the pebbles of the holy streams. . . .

Dylan Thomas (1946)

1. **appareled** (ə par′əld), *adj.* dressed.
2. **celestial** (sə les′chəl), *adj.* heavenly.

1. **precipice** (pres′ə pis), *n.* cliff or steep mountainside.

1. **dingle** (ding′gəl), *n.* a small, deep, shady valley.
2. **sabbath** (sab′əth), *n.* day of worship.

212

MINI-LESSON: LITERARY ELEMENT

Inversion

When elements of a sentence are out of their regular noun-verb-object order, it is called inversion.

Teach Inversion may be used to help achieve a certain rhythm or rhyme or to emphasize certain words or ideas. Have students find and put into regular order the subjects and verbs in lines 7 *(I may turn)*, and 18 *(glory hath passed).*

Activity Idea Ask students to suggest other words or phrases that seem strangely out of order. *(Possible responses: The prepositional phrase* to me *[line 3] comes before the verb* did seem; *the prepositional phrase* with delight *[line 12] comes between the two parts of the verb* doth look)

O Glorious Nature!

[Theocles] turned away his eyes from me, musing awhile by himself; and soon afterwards, stretching out his hand, as pointing to the objects round him, he began:

"Ye fields and woods, my refuge from the toilsome world of business, receive me in your quiet sanctuaries[1] and favor my retreat and thoughtful solitude. Ye verdant[2] plains, how gladly I salute ye! Hail all ye blissful mansions! known seats! delightful prospects![3] majestic beauties of this earth, and all ye rural powers and graces! Blessed be ye chaste abodes[4] of happiest mortals, who here in peaceful innocence enjoy a life unenvied, though divine; whilst with its blessed tranquillity it affords a happy leisure and retreat for man, who, made for contemplation, and to search his own and other natures, may here best meditate the cause of things, and, placed amidst the various scenes of Nature, may nearer view her works.

"O glorious nature! supremely fair and sovereignly[5] good! all-loving and all-lovely, all-divine! whose looks are so becoming and of such infinite grace; whose study brings such wisdom, and whose contemplation such delight; whose every single work affords an ampler scene, and is a nobler spectacle than all which ever art presented! O mighty Nature! wise substitute of Providence![6] impowered creatress! Or thou impowering Deity, supreme creator! Thee I invoke and thee alone adore. To thee this solitude, this place, these rural meditations are sacred; whilst thus inspired with harmony of thought, though unconfined by words, and in loose numbers,[7] I sing of Nature's order in created beings, and celebrate the beauties which resolve in thee, the source and principle of all beauty and perfection . . . ."

This image of St. James Park in London is from a history of gardens published in 1887.

Here he stopped short, and starting as out of a dream: "Now, Philocles," said he, "inform me, how have I appeared to you in my fit? Seemed it a sensible kind of madness, like those transports which are permitted to our poets? or was it downright raving?"

Anthony Ashley Cooper, Third Earl of Shaftesbury (1709)

1. **sanctuary** (sangk′chü er′ē), *n.* place of refuge or protection.
2. **verdant** (vėrd′nt), *adj.* green.
3. **prospect** (pros′pekt), *n.* view; scene.
4. **chaste** (chāst) **abode** (ə bōd′), simple, plain home.
5. **sovereignly** (sov′rən lē), *adv.* powerfully.
6. **Providence** (prov′ə dəns), *n.* God.
7. **in loose numbers,** unconfined by strict poetic meter.

About Anthony Ashley Cooper

Anthony Ashley Cooper, Third Earl of Shaftesbury (1671–1713), was a Whig in sentiment, dedicated to the idea of liberty, and radically distrustful of church doctrines. His *The Moralists: A Philosophical Rhapsody* is one of six treatises that he collected in 1711 under the title *Characteristics of Man, Manners, Opinions, Times,* a book that had enormous European influence in the eighteenth century. In it Shaftesbury provides a philosophic ground for the love of wild nature and for the release of the divine in human nature.

Art Study

Visual Literacy In the 1700s there were two opposing schools of landscape design: the simple *vs.* the ornamental. The former interpreted a garden as a landscape park, a sculptural approach to nature. The latter preferred more than a hint of wildness, often creating caves or waterfalls where there had been none. This illustration suggests the ornamental approach, but the important thing to note is that the natural appearance is still artificial.

Question What characteristics does this scene share with the scene described by Shaftesbury on this page? What characteristics are different? *(Possible response: While both are beautiful and may be sources of restful solitude or religious insight, Shaftesbury's scene is of wild, untamed nature, and St. James Park is nature tamed and ordered for human convenience.)*

BUILDING ENGLISH PROFICIENCY

ESL LEP ELD SAE LD

Exploring Key Concepts

In the stanzas from "Fern Hill" students may not recognize some of Dylan Thomas's word usages, such as "lilting house" and "happy as the grass was green" and honored among wagons." That's because Thomas *coined,* or invented, many such usages.

1. Have students locate unfamiliar word combinations and phrases in these stanzas. *(Possible responses: heydays of his eyes, prince of the apple towns, once below a time, green and carefree, famous among the barns, mercy of his means, sabbath rang slowly.)*

2. Let students respond to each phrase in terms of how it makes them feel or what it makes them think. Encourage students to coin their own words and phrases when they want to achieve special effects in their writing.

About Jane Austen

Jane Austen (1775–1817), one of England's greatest novelists, wrote of the manners of the upper-middle class who lived in the villages and the adjoining country at a time when owning land was the most genteel of occupations. Character portrayal and analysis were Austen's chief concern, and her style was that of delicate satire. In recent years, Austen has enjoyed a revival of interest due to the success of several movies based on her novels.

Picturesque Principles

Edward returned to them with fresh admiration of the surrounding country; in his walk to the village, he had seen many parts of the valley to advantage; and the village itself, in a much higher situation[1] than the cottage, afforded a general view of the whole, which had exceedingly pleased him. This was a subject which ensured Marianne's attention, and she was beginning to describe her own admiration of these scenes, and to question him more minutely on the objects that had particularly struck him, when Edward interrupted her by saying, "You must not inquire too far, Marianne—remember I have no knowledge in the picturesque,[2] and I shall offend you by my ignorance and want of taste if we come to particulars. I shall call hills steep, which ought to be bold; surfaces strange and uncouth,[3] which ought to be irregular and rugged; and distant objects out of sight, which ought only to be indistinct through the soft medium of a hazy atmosphere. You must be satisfied with such admiration as I can honestly give. I call it a very fine country—the hills are steep, the woods seem full of fine timber, and the valley looks comfortable and snug—with rich meadows and several neat farm houses scattered here and there. It exactly answers my idea of a fine country, because it unites beauty with utility—and I dare say it is a picturesque one too, because you admire it; I can easily believe it to be full of rocks and promontories,[4] gray moss and brush wood, but these are all lost on me. I know nothing of the picturesque."

"I am afraid it is but too true," said Marianne; "but why should you boast of it?"

"I suspect," said Elinor, "that to avoid one kind of affectation,[5] Edward here falls into another. Because he believes many people pretend to more admiration of the beauties of nature than they really feel, and is disgusted with such pretensions,[6] he affects greater indifference and less discrimination in viewing them himself than he possesses. He is fastidious[7] and will have an affectation of his own."

"It is very true," said Marianne, "that admiration of landscape scenery is become a mere jargon.[8] Every body pretends to feel and tries to describe with the taste and elegance of him who first defined what picturesque beauty was. I detest jargon of every kind, and sometimes I have kept my feelings to myself, because I could find no language to describe them in but what was worn and hackneyed[9] out of all sense and meaning."

"I am convinced," said Edward, "that you really feel all the delight in a fine prospect which you profess[10] to feel. But, in return, your sister must allow me to feel no more than I profess. I like a fine prospect, but not on picturesque principles. I do not like crooked, twisted, blasted trees. I admire them much more if they are tall, straight and flourishing. I do not like ruined, tattered cottages. I am not fond of nettles, or thistles, or heath blossoms. I have more pleasure in a snug farm-house than a watch-tower—and a troop of tidy, happy villagers please me better than the finest banditti[11] in the world."

Jane Austen (1811)

1. **situation** (sich′ü ā′shən), *n.* location; place.
2. **picturesque** (pik′chə resk′), *adj.* quaint or interesting enough to be used as the subject of a picture.
3. **uncouth** (un küth′), *adj.* crude.
4. **promontory** (prom′ən tôr′ē), *n.* high point of land.
5. **affectation** (af′ek tā′shən), *n.* pretense; unnatural behavior to impress others.
6. **pretension** (pri ten′shən), *n.* showy display.
7. **fastidious** (fa stid′ē əs), *adj.* hard to please; dainty in taste.
8. **jargon** (jär′gən), *n.* language of a special group or profession.
9. **hackneyed** (hak′nēd), *adj.* used too often; commonplace.
10. **profess** (prə fes′), *v.* claim.
11. **banditti** (bän dē′tē), bandits. *[Italian]*

MINI-LESSON: READING/THINKING SKILLS

Detect Bias/Identify Assumptions

Identifying assumptions is finding the unstated beliefs that underlie an argument or piece of writing.

Teach The assumptions are not so much unstated here; rather the characters are trying to state their own and each other's assumptions in their attempts to communicate. Have students summarize Marianne's and Edward's assumptions about nature, as they express them.

Activity Idea Have students consider whether sharing one's own assumptions and discussing the differences in people's assumptions must lead to improved understanding and agreement between people. What if you think someone else's assumptions are foolish or wrong?

Thomas Tyndale, A Cottage Garden

Anthony Green, The Flower Arranger *(1932)*

This tapestry depicts a formal garden from the late 1600s.

215

Art Study

Visual Literacy The formal garden in the tapestry and Tyndale's *A Cottage Garden* demonstrate many of the opposites expressed by formality/informality; among them are straight lines/curved lines, balance/asymmetry, human scale/larger-than-human scale, planned complementary colors/accidental colors, coziness/distance.

Question Do you think that a small garden must be informal and friendly and that a large garden must be formal and proper, or may gardens of any size exhibit whatever characteristics their creators wish? *(Possible response: Formal or informal characteristics are possible on any scale.)*

Art Study

Visual Literacy Two of the features that make Green's *The Flower Arranger* unique are its octagonal shape and the fact that the painting is extended onto the frame.

Question What do these features contribute to the overall effect of the painting? *(Possible response: The octagonal frame adds to the cozy, informal mood, and the painted frame seems to put the flower arranger in the middle of his own garden.)*

BUILDING ENGLISH PROFICIENCY

Exploring Key Concepts

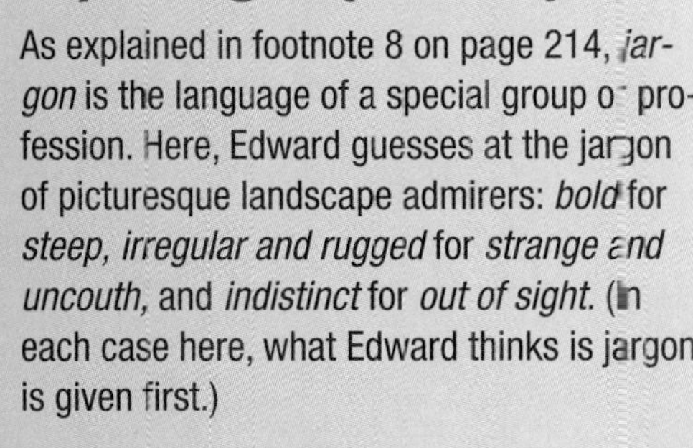

As explained in footnote 8 on page 214, *jargon* is the language of a special group or profession. Here, Edward guesses at the jargon of picturesque landscape admirers: *bold* for *steep, irregular and rugged* for *strange and uncouth,* and *indistinct* for *out of sight.* (In each case here, what Edward thinks is jargon is given first.)

1. Have students choose a topic and contribute some jargon they know while a volunteer lists words on the board. Some possible topics: computers, football or basketball, fashions.

2. When the speaker asks a question like "Where [has] the man [gone]?" what is he really saying? *(Possible response: Life is short, and we all—even I—must soon leave this world.)*

About Joseph Conrad

Romantic novels gave Conrad the desire to go to sea, and finally, when his uncle (who was his guardian) agreed, he joined the French merchant marine at age 17, feeling "like a man in a dream." He served as apprentice and then steward on ships in the West Indies and South America and even smuggled guns to guerrilla bands in Spain. Finally he joined the British merchant navy and, over the next 16 years, worked his way up to ship's captain—seeing the world in the process (see also p. 585).

About Mary Wollstonecraft

After being abandoned by American writer and adventurer Gilbert Imlay, with whom she had a daughter, Wollstonecraft attempted suicide. In 1796 she published a travel book, *Letters Written During a Short Residence in Sweden, Norway, and Denmark,* which, besides portraying the austere landscape, contains astute observations on the lot of women in northern countries. The quotation is from Letter 22 (see also p. 455).

Thames River at Twilight

. . . The day was ending in a serenity[1] of still and exquisite brilliance. The water shone pacifically;[2] the sky, without a speck, was a benign[3] immensity of unstained light; the very mist on the Essex marshes was like a gauzy and radiant fabric, hung from the wooded rises inland, and draping the low shores in diaphanous[4] folds. Only the gloom to the west, brooding over the upper reaches, became more somber[5] every minute, as if angered by the approach of the sun.

And at last, in its curved and imperceptible[6] fall, the sun sank low, and from glowing white changed to a dull red without rays and without heat, as if about to go out suddenly, stricken to death by the touch of that gloom brooding over a crowd of men.

Forthwith a change came over the waters, and the serenity became less brilliant but more profound.[7] The old river in its broad reach rested unruffled at the decline of day, after ages of good service done to the race that peopled its banks, spread out in the tranquil[8] dignity of a waterway leading to the uttermost ends of the earth. We looked at the venerable[9] stream not in the vivid flush of a short day that comes and departs forever, but in the august[10] light of abiding memories. And indeed nothing is easier for a man who has, as the phrase goes, "followed the sea" with reverance and affection, than to evoke the great spirit of the past upon the lower reaches of the Thames. The tidal current runs to and fro in its unceasing service, crowded with memories of men and ships it had borne to the rest of home or to the battles of the sea. It had known and served all the men of whom the nation is proud, from Sir Francis Drake to Sir John Franklin, knights all, titled and untitled—the great knights-errant of the sea . . . . Hunters for gold or pursuers of fame, they all had gone out on that stream, bearing the sword, and often the torch, messengers of the might within the land, bearers of a spark from the sacred fire. What greatness had not floated on the ebb of that river into the mystery of an unknown earth! . . . The dreams of men, the seed of commonwealths, the germs of empires . . .

Joseph Conrad (1902)

IT IS THE PRESERVATION OF THE SPECIES, NOT OF INDIVIDUALS, WHICH APPEARS TO BE THE DESIGN OF DEITY THROUGHOUT THE WHOLE OF NATURE.

Mary Wollstonecraft (1796)

1. **serenity** (sə ren′ə tē), *n.* peace and quiet; calmness.
2. **pacifically** (pə sif′ik lē), *adv.* peacefully.
3. **benign** (bi nīn′), *adj.* kindly in feeling.
4. **diaphanous** (dī af′ə nəs), *adj.* transparent.
5. **somber** (som′bər), *adj.* dark; gloomy.
6. **imperceptible** (im′pər sep′tə bəl), *adj.* gradual; very slight.
7. **profound** (prə found′), *adj.* very deep.
8. **tranquil** (trang′kwəl), *adj.* calm; peaceful.
9. **venerable** (ven′ər ə bəl), *adj.* deserving respect because of age or importance.
10. **august** (ô gust′), *adj.* majestic; inspiring admiration.

MINI-LESSON: LITERARY ELEMENT

Imagery

Imagery involves sensory details in writing that provide vividness and tend to arouse emotions in a reader.

Teach Have students locate effective sensory details in Conrad's description of the Thames. To which sense—sight, hearing, touch, taste, smell—does each detail appeal?

Activity Idea Suggest that students try to picture the scene that Conrad is painting; then have them list more details that might be consistent with this scene.

J. M. W. Turner, Fishermen upon a Lee Shore (about 1805)

from THE WANDERER

A wise man must fathom how frightening it will be
When all the riches of the world stand waste,
As now in diverse[1] places in this middle-earth
Old walls stand, tugged at by the winds
And hung with hoar-frost, buildings in decay.
The wine-halls crumble, heartbroken lords
Lie dead, all the proud followers
Have fallen by the wall . . . .
Thus the Creator laid this world waste
Until the ancient works of the giants were deserted,
Hushed without the hubbub of milling inhabitants.
Then he who contemplates these noble ruins,
And who deeply ponders this dark life,
Wise in his mind, will often remember
The countless slaughters of the past and speak these words:
Where has the horse gone? Where the man? Where the giver of gold?
Where is the feasting-place? And where the pleasures of the hall?
I mourn the gleaming cup, the warrior in his corselet,[2]
The glory of the prince. How time has passed away,
Darkened under the shadow of night even as if it had never been . . . .
Storms crash against these rocky slopes;
Falling sleet and snow fetter[3] the world;
Winter howls, then darkness draws on,
The night-shadow casts gloom and brings
Fierce hailstorms from the north to frighten men.
Nothing is ever easy in the kingdom of earth,
The world beneath the heavens is in the hands of fate.
Worldly possessions are ephemeral,[4] friends pass away,
Here man is transient[5] and kinsman transient,
The whole world becomes a wilderness.

Anonymous (900s?)

1. **diverse** (də vėrs′), *adj.* different; varied.
2. **corselet** (kôrs′lit), *n.* armor for the upper part of the body.
3. **fetter** (fet′ər), *v.* bind; restrain.
4. **ephemeral** (i fem′ər əl), *adj.* lasting for only a very short time.
5. **transient** (tran′shənt), *adj.* passing soon.

About "The Wanderer"

When the Anglo-Saxons came to England, they brought with them a relatively well-developed society organized around the family, the clan, the tribe, and finally the kingdom. "The Wanderer" consists of a monologue spoken by a character whose fate it is to roam the seas in search of a lord to replace his dead "gold-friend." Until the end of the sixth century, the Anglo-Saxons worshipped various pagan gods—gods associated today with Norse mythology. Perhaps the monk who finally wrote down the poem tried to make its essentially pagan spirit more acceptable to a Christian audience.

Visual Literacy Joseph M. W. Turner (1775–1851) is best known for his Romantic landscapes and seascapes. He developed a very individual style to depict the most extreme and fleeting effects of weather, time of day and night, light and atmosphere—a style that shocked the public and offended the critics of his time.

Question What artistic techniques does Turner use to suggest a storm at sea? *(Possible response: His colors are dark, including a dangerous-looking green; his brush strokes are vague, suggesting turbulent motion.)*

BUILDING ENGLISH PROFICIENCY

Exploring Key Concepts

A *rhetorical question* is a question asked for effect, not for an answer.

1. Have students locate the five questions in this passage from "The Wanderer." Ask: To whom is the speaker addressing these questions? *(Possible response: To himself, as he contemplates the ruins and ponders life.)* Ask: Does he expect an answer? *(Possible response: Not really; it is obvious that they are gone.)*

2. When the speaker asks a question like "Where [has] the man [gone]?" what is he really saying? *(Possible response: Life is short, and we all—even I—must soon leave this world.)*

About H. G. Wells

H. G. Wells voiced the divided mixture of anxiety and enthusiasm that characterized his age. Some of his work reflects the optimism of the new century; *The Time Machine,* however, is one of his darker works, reflecting a sense of catastrophe and doom. As the traveler explores the future, he finds that humans have evolved—or perhaps devolved—into groups of vicious, cannibalistic creatures and placid victims. Finally humans disappear from the earth altogether.

World's End

In H. G. Wells's classic science fiction novel, The Time Machine, *the Traveler has invented a machine that takes him back or forward in time. Here he decides to travel as far into the future as he can.*

"I cannot convey the sense of abominable[1] desolation that hung over the world. The red eastern sky, the northward blackness, the salt Dead Sea, the stony beach crawling with these foul, slow-stirring monsters, the uniform poisonous-looking green of the lichenous[2] plants, the thin air that hurt one's lungs; all contributed to an appalling effect. I moved on a hundred years, and there was the same red sun—a little larger, a little duller—the same dying sea, the same chill air, and the same crowd of earthly crustacea[3] creeping in and out among the green weed and the red rocks. And in the westward sky I saw a curved pale line like a vast new moon.

"So I traveled, stopping ever and again, in great strides of a thousand years or more, drawn on by the mystery of the earth's fate, watching with a strange fascination the sun grow larger and duller in the westward sky, and the life of the old earth ebb away. At last, more than thirty million years hence, the huge red-hot dome of the sun had come to obscure nearly a tenth part of the darkling[4] heavens. Then I stopped once more, for the crawling multitude of crabs had disappeared, and the red beach, save for its livid green liverworts[5] and lichens, seemed lifeless. And now it was flecked with white. A bitter cold assailed[6] me. Rare white flakes ever and again came eddying[7] down. To the north-eastward, the glare of snow lay under the starlight of the sable sky, and I could see an undulating[8] crest of hillocks pinkish-white. There were fringes of ice along the sea margin, with drifting masses further out; but the main expanse of that salt ocean, all bloody under the eternal sunset, was still unfrozen.

"I looked about me to see if any traces of animal-life remained. A certain indefinable apprehension still kept me in the saddle of the machine. But I saw nothing moving, in earth or sky or sea. The green slime on the rocks alone testified that life was not extinct. A shallow sandbank had appeared in the sea and the water had receded from the beach. I fancied I saw some black object flopping about on this bank, but it became motionless as I looked at it, and I judged that my eye had been deceived, and that the black object was merely a rock. The stars in the sky were intensely bright and seemed to me to twinkle very little.

"Suddenly I noticed that the circular westward outline of the sun had changed; that a concavity,[9] a bay, had appeared in the curve. I saw this grow larger. For a minute perhaps I stared aghast[10] at this blackness that was creeping over the day, and then I realised that an eclipse was beginning. Either the moon or the planet Mercury was passing across the sun's disk. Naturally, at first I took it to be the moon, but there is much to incline me to believe that what I really saw was the transit of an inner planet passing very near to the earth.

"The darkness grew apace; a cold wind began to blow in freshening gusts from the east, and the showering white flakes in the air increased in number. From the edge of the sea came a ripple and whisper. Beyond these lifeless sounds the world was silent. Silent? It would be hard to convey the stillness of it. All the sounds of man, the bleating of sheep, the cries of birds, the hum of insects, the stir that makes the background of our lives—all that was over. As the darkness thickened, the

1. **abominable** (ə bom′ə nə bəl), *adj.* disgusting; hateful.
2. **lichenous** (lī′kə nəs), *adj.* of lichens, combinations of fungus and alga.
3. **crustacea** (krus′tā′shə), *n.* class of shellfish including crabs, lobsters, and shrimp.
4. **darkling** (därk′ling), *adj.* dark; dim.
5. **liverwort** (liv′ər wėrt′), *n.* plant related to and resembling moss.
6. **assail** (ə sāl′), *v.* attack.
7. **eddy** (ed′ē), *v.* move in a whirling motion.
8. **undulating** (un′jə lā ting), *adj.* waving.
9. **concavity** (kon kav′ə tē), *n.* hollow; curving in.
10. **aghast** (ə gast′), *adj.* struck with surprise or horror.

MINI-LESSON: READING/THINKING SKILLS

Visualize

To visualize is to form mental pictures in order to help recall information, define new tasks, or respond to a piece of writing.

Teach Have students close their eyes as you or a volunteer reads aloud the excerpt from H. G. Wells. Tell them to try to see the scene in their imagination and to respond as well to the other sensory imagery.

Activity Idea Have students debate whether or not this scenario is a conceivable end to the world we know.

eddying flakes grew more abundant, dancing before my eyes; and the cold of the air more intense. At last, one by one, swiftly, one after the other, the white peaks of the distant hills vanished into blackness. The breeze rose to a moaning wind. I saw the black central shadow of the eclipse sweeping towards me. In another moment the pale stars alone were visible. All else was rayless obscurity. The sky was absolutely black.

"A horror of this great darkness came on me. The cold, that smote[11] to my marrow,[12] and the pain I felt in breathing overcame me. I shivered, and a deadly nausea seized me. Then like a red-hot bow in the sky appeared the edge of the sun. I got off the machine to recover myself. I felt giddy and incapable of facing the return journey. As I stood sick and confused I saw again the moving thing upon the shoal—there was no mistake now that it was a moving thing—against the red water of the sea. It was a round thing, the size of a football perhaps, or, it may be, bigger, and tentacles trailed down from it; it seemed black against the weltering[13] blood-red water, and it was hopping fitfully about. Then I felt I was fainting . . . ."

H. G. Wells (1895)

LINEAGE

In the beginning was Scream
Who begat Blood
Who begat Eye
Who begat Fear
Who begat Wing
Who begat Bone
Who begat Granite
Who begat Violet
Who begat Guitar
Who begat Sweat
Who begat Adam
Who begat Mary
Who begat God
Who begat Nothing
Who begat Never
Never, Never, Never

Who begat Crow

Screaming for Blood
Grubs, crusts
Anything
Trembling featherless elbows in the nest's filth.

Ted Hughes (1970)

RESPONDING

1. *Do you agree more with people who see nature as a healer, as neutral, or as a destroyer? Explain your reasons.*
2. *Have you ever learned anything from nature? Explain the lesson and the circumstances.*
3. *A large number of "doomsday" books and movies have depicted life in a much-changed society after civilization as we know it has been destroyed—often in a nuclear war. Do you think it is possible for people to destroy nature? Why or why not?*
4. *Do you prefer neat, tidy gardens or "irregular and rugged" wilderness? Describe your favorite outdoor view.*

11. **smite** (smīt), *v.* give a hard blow to.
12. **marrow** (mar′ō), *n.* inmost part.
13. **weltering** (wel′tər ing), *adj.* rolling or tumbling about.

About Ted Hughes

Much of Ted Hughes's poetry deals with the natural world. He writes unsentimentally of the savagery and cunning of animals and of similar qualities in human beings. *Crow* (1970) is a cycle of poems in which Hughes attempts to create a fragmentary mythology centered on a trickster figure drawn from primitive mythology. The book became something of a best-seller (at least for books of verse). Hughes was appointed poet laureate in 1984.

Responding

1. Students' responses. Life's experiences are varied enough to be used as reasons for either "healer" or "destroyer"; although today perhaps more people are coming to believe in a neutral nature that we use as a mirror for our own emotions.

2. Students' responses. Even a person who thinks that nature is neutral might yet learn a lesson from it.

3. Possible response: We can destroy civilization, but not nature; life could struggle on in caves, under ice, or at the bottom of the ocean if human beings were gone.

4. Possible response: Both the comfort and familiarity of a tidy garden and the challenge and exhilaration of wilderness might be desired at different times.

Part One: The Meaning of Life

Planning Unit 3: The Seventeenth Century

Literature	Integrated Language Arts			
	Literary	Writing/Grammar, Usage and Mechanics	Reading, Thinking, Listening, Speaking	Vocabulary/Spelling
Song *by John Donne* Poem *(average)* p. 226 **A Valediction: Forbidding Mourning** *by John Donne* Poem *(challenging)* p. 226 **Meditation 17** *by John Donne* Sermon *(average)* p. 227	Metaphor and conceit Simile Personification Hyperbole	Greeting card phrases Design a greeting card Guest editorial Understanding a parallel structure	Recognize values	Break the code
To the Virgins, to Make Much of Time *by Robert Herrick* Poem *(average)* p. 233 **Upon Julia's Clothes** *by Robert Herrick* Poem *(easy)* p. 233 **Delight in Disorder** *by Robert Herrick* Poem *(average)* p. 234 **To His Coy Mistress** *by Andrew Marvell* Poem *(average)* p. 235	Hyperbole Theme	Make a list Write a reply Brief essay Using *that* and *which*	Recognize values	

Meeting Individual Needs

Multi-modal Activities	Mini-Lessons
Monologue Musical setting Making personal connections Exploring main ideas	Understanding a parallel structure
Illustrated talk Design and present an illustrated time line Musical lecture Making personal connections	Using *that* and *which* Hyperbole

Interdisciplinary Studies
No Man is an Island

Format	Content Area	Highlights	Skill
from Six Degrees of Separation	Humanities	John Guare describes how people are bound together internationally.	Unabridged dictionaries
The Bubble Boy *by Carol Ann with Kent Demaret*	Science	This article relates the life of a young boy born without an immune system.	
One to One	Humanities	This article is about people helping others to overcome obstacles.	Use media as a means of expression
We Are the World	Humanities	This song, released in the early 1980's, is about helping people in need.	On-line communication

Writing Workshop

Mode	Writing Format	Writing Focus	Proofreading Skills
Expository/descriptive writing	A collage, summary, and speech	Making your intentions clear	Using adjectives and adverbs correctly

Program Support Materials

For Every Selection	For Every Writing Workshop
Unit Resource Book Graphic Organizer Study Guide Vocabulary Worksheet Grammar Worksheet Spelling, Speaking and Listening, or Literary Language Worksheet Alternate Check Test Vocabulary Test Selection Test	**Unit Resource Book** Prewriting Worksheet Revising Strategy Worksheet Editing Strategy Worksheet Presentation Worksheet Writing Rubric **Transparency Collection** Fine Art Transparency Student Writing Model Transparencies

For Every Interdisciplinary Study	Assessment
Unit Resource Book Study Guide Mini-Lesson Skill Worksheet	**Unit Resource Book** TE Check Tests Alternate Check Test (blackline master) Vocabulary Test (blackline master) Selection Test (blackline master) **Test Generator Software** **Assessment Handbook**

Part Two: The Fall from Grace

Planning Unit 3: The Seventeenth Century

Literature	Integrated Language Arts: Literary	Writing/Grammar, Usage and Mechanics	Reading, Thinking, Listening, Speaking	Vocabulary/Spelling
On His Having Arrived at the Age of Twenty-Three *by John Milton* Poem *(average)* p. 254 **On His Blindness** *by John Milton* Poem *(average)* p. 254 **from Paradise Lost** *by John Milton* Epic Poem *(challenging)* p. 255	Symbol Meter Allusion Style Characterization	Develop a symbol Short story One page description of Hell Understanding restrictive and unrestrictive modifiers	Find the main idea Draw conclusions Generalize Essential and incidental information Analyze Synthesize	
from Genesis *The King James Bible* Narrative *(average)* p. 268 **The Twenty-third Psalm** *The King James Bible* Poem *(average)* p. 272	Style Symbolism Theme	Describe the Garden of Eden Letter of advice Illuminated manuscript Verbs		Select the best definition Using dictionaries for word meaning

Meeting Individual Needs

Multi-modal Activities	Mini-Lessons
Collage Work of art Exploring key concepts Tracking plot events Exploring oxymorons Responding to key statements	Understanding restrictive and nonrestrictive modifiers Symbolism Expanding reading vocabulary Recognize cause and effect
Stage a children's play Analyzing and dramatizing a passage Understanding causes and effects	Verbs Using dictionaries for word meaning

Interdisciplinary Studies
Heaven, Hell, and Paradise

Format	Content Area	Highlights	Skill
The Peach-Blossom Fountain *by T'ao Ch'ien*	Humanities	This selection offers differing cultural glimpses of heaven, hell, and paradise.	Create and use diagrams
Hell from the Inferno *by Dante Alghieri*	Humanities	This selection shows various depictions of hell.	Evaluate nonprint media
Postcard from Paradise *by Chris Williamson*	Humanities	This song describes what might have happened if Columbus had abandoned ship.	

Writing Workshop

Mode	Writing Format	Writing Focus	Proofreading Skills
Expository writing	An interpretive essay	Using parallel structure Using adverbs and adjectives correctly	Editing strategy

Program Support Materials

For Every Selection	For Every Writing Workshop
Unit Resource Book Graphic Organizer Study Guide Vocabulary Worksheet Grammar Worksheet Spelling, Speaking and Listening, or Literary Language Worksheet Alternate Check Test Vocabulary Test Selection Test	**Unit Resource Book** Prewriting Worksheet Revising Strategy Worksheet Editing Strategy Worksheet Presentation Worksheet Writing Rubric **Transparency Collection** Fine Art Transparency Student Writing Model Transparencies

For Every Interdisciplinary Study	Assessment
Unit Resource Book Study Guide Mini-Lesson Skill Worksheet	**Unit Resource Book** TE Check Tests Alternate Check Test (blackline master) Vocabulary Test (blackline master) Selection Test (blackline master) **Test Generator Software** **Assessment Handbook**

Media and Technology

Part One Selections

Song/A Valediction: Forbidding Mourning/Meditation 17

Audiocassette The poems of Donne are presented in *The Treasury of John Donne,* Spoken Arts. Donne is included on *Sonnets of Shakespeare and Other Elizabethan Lyrics, Spoken Arts.*

Community Resources Some students might like to research the Gunpowder Plot, the failed attempt to blow up King James I and Parliament. Twelve conspirators, including Guy Fawkes, who resented the government's hostile attitude toward Catholics, planned the explosion for November 5, 1605. (Writer Garry Wills in his 1994 book *Witches and Jesuits: Shakespeare's Macbeth* argues convincingly that *Macbeth,* first performed in 1606, should be understood in the context of the Gunpowder Plot.)

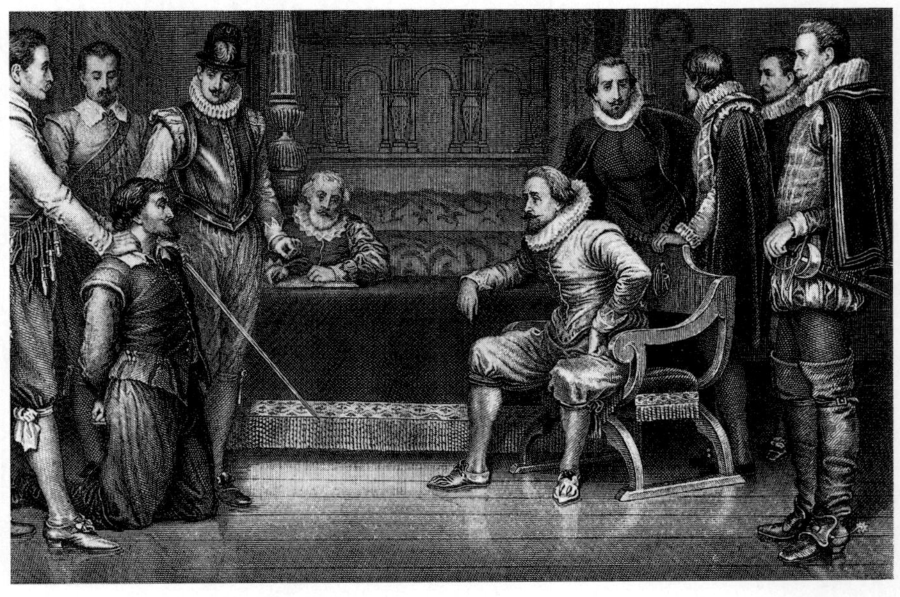

To the Virgins, to Make Much of Time/Upon Julia's Clothes/Delight in Disorder/To His Coy Mistress

Audiotape *Poetry of the Early 17th Century,* Spoken Arts, includes the work of Herrick, Marvell, Donne, and others.

Videotape *Metaphysical and Devotional Poetry,* 28 minutes, Films for the Humanities & Sciences, includes the work of Marvell and others.

Home Connection Some families might discuss what they know or believe about the question of life after death, mentioned on page 224 of the student text, and the relation of this question to the carpe diem theme. (Different faiths have different beliefs regarding life after death.) Students may have heard this expression or a similar one: Eat, drink, and be merry for tomor-

Connections to
Custom Literature Database

For Part One "The Meaning of Life" Selections with Lessons

- Sonnets 4 and 10 by John Donne
- "Easter Wings" and "Virtue" by George Herbert

Additional theme-based selections can be accessed on the ScottForesman database.

Are We Donne Yet?

The poems of John Donne can be played for your students using *The Treasury of John Donne,* Spoken Arts.

row we die. What does this philosophy imply? Do students subscribe to it? Do their parents or guardians? Why or why not?

Part Two Selections

On His Having Arrived at the Age of Twenty-three/On His Blindness,/from Paradise Lost

Audiotape *Treasury of John Milton*, Spoken Arts, includes excerpts from "Paradise Lost," and other works.

Videotape *Milton and 17th-Century Poetry,* 35 minutes, Films for the Humanities & Sciences, focuses on the Metaphysical poets.

Community Resources Some students might like to research seventeenth-century architecture. Two of the most famous architects were Inigo Jones (1573-1652) and Sir Christopher Wren (1632-1723). Jones introduced the Palladian style of architecture to England and greatly influenced theatrical design. Wren's most famous building is St. Paul's Cathedral, although he redesigned many smaller churches rebuilt after the 1666 fire.

from Genesis/The Twenty-third Psalm

Videotape Consider showing *The Bible as Literature*, 2 videos available from Britannica.

Home Connection Students might like to compare the King James version of the Genesis account in the pupil book with a different version they may have in a Bible at home. They might also find another psalm that speaks to them in a deep and personal way.

Connections to
Custom Literature Database

For Part Two "The Fall from Grace"

Selections with Lessons

- from *Paradise Lost,* Book IX, by John Milton
- *The French Revolution* by Thomas Carlyle

Additional theme-based selections can be accessed on the ScottForesman database.

The Bible as Literature

Britannica has produced a two-video collection called *The Bible as Literature.*

Unit 3

The Seventeenth Century

Art Study

The Suitor's Visit, a detail of which appears here, was painted about 1658 by Dutch artist Gerard Ter Borch (ter borH′) the Younger (1617–1681). It now hangs in the National Gallery in Washington. Ter Borch studied with his father, Gerard the Elder, in Zwolle and then in Haarlem.

Question What is a suitor, and what do you think the suitor in the painting is saying? *(A suitor is a man who courts a woman with the intention of marrying her. He is probably greeting her, asking after her health.)*

Question Where does the scene probably take place? *(in the lady's home, as evidenced by her little dog and her musical companion)*

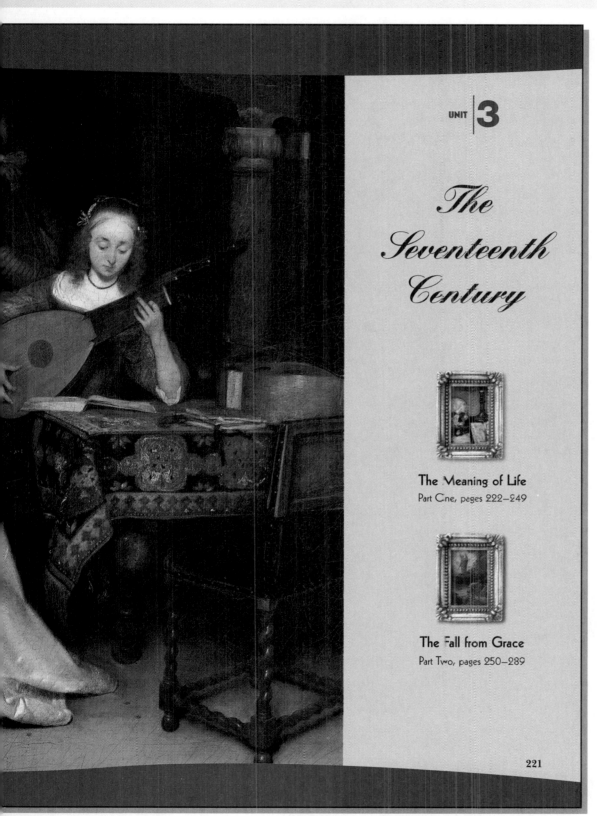

UNIT 3

The Seventeenth Century

THEMATIC CONNECTIONS

The seventeenth century was an era of major changes in Britain. Questions of religion and rule drove people to take up arms throughout the 1600s.

Part One

The Meaning of Life

Part One features writing that stresses finding meaning in life, no matter how brief that life is, as well as living in the moment.

Ideas to Explore

- Why was life relatively short in the seventeenth century?
- What are some likely human responses to the brevity or uncertainty of life?

Part Two

The Fall from Grace

This section focuses on ideas about people's relationship to God, as well as ideas of heaven and hell.

Ideas to Explore

- What was the relationship between church and state in England in the 1600s?
- What happens when religious factions within a country cannot get along?

Art Study

The skull symbolizes the transiency of life; the lower image is of Satan as depicted by Gustave Doré. Satan is often described as the chief fallen angel.

Part One: The Meaning of Life

Historical Overview

EXPLORING CONCEPTS

- Life in the 1600s was brief and difficult.
- Writers of the era struggled with the ideas of mortality and making life meaningful.
- The melding of physical and spiritual love was an ideal expressed in poetry.
- People are all connected to each other by the facts of life and death.

Art Study

Antonio de Pereda's paintings are in the Baroque style. The Baroque era of art was a combination of the Renaissance's use of classical themes and idealized human forms, and the Mannerists' artifice and decorativeness. Baroque paintings such as *The Knight's Dream* usually have a figure in the foreground, and contain many symbolic objects. There is also a typical sense of motion suggested by flowing folds of cloth. Pereda was active mainly in Madrid. The painting reproduced here is his most famous work and was painted around 1655.

Question How does Pereda's use of light and shadow emphasize his themes? *(Students may note that the faces of the dreamer and the angel are in light, as is one of the skulls. This highlighting emphasizes the fate of the dreamer and the presence of the spiritual world. The background is shadowed, giving dreamy, dark context.)*

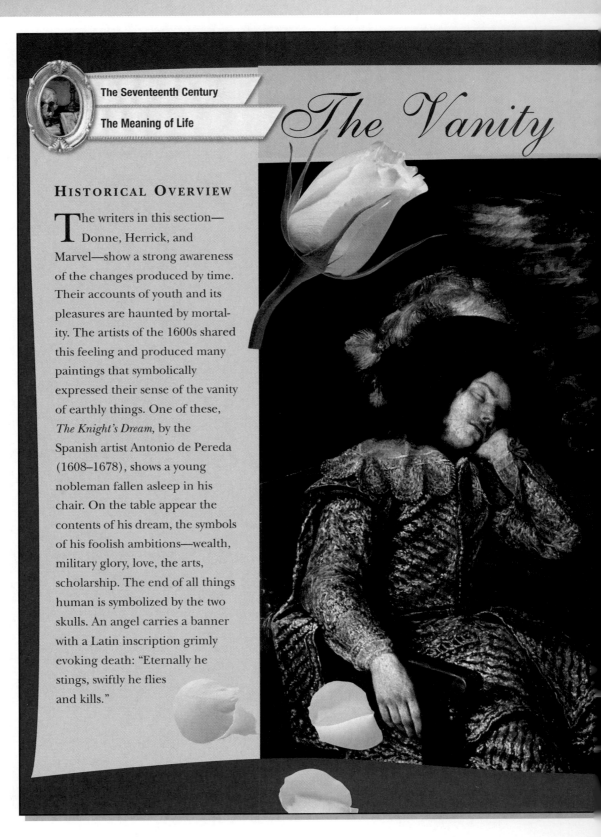

The Seventeenth Century

The Meaning of Life

The Vanity

HISTORICAL OVERVIEW

The writers in this section—Donne, Herrick, and Marvel—show a strong awareness of the changes produced by time. Their accounts of youth and its pleasures are haunted by mortality. The artists of the 1600s shared this feeling and produced many paintings that symbolically expressed their sense of the vanity of earthly things. One of these, *The Knight's Dream,* by the Spanish artist Antonio de Pereda (1608–1678), shows a young nobleman fallen asleep in his chair. On the table appear the contents of his dream, the symbols of his foolish ambitions—wealth, military glory, love, the arts, scholarship. The end of all things human is symbolized by the two skulls. An angel carries a banner with a Latin inscription grimly evoking death: "Eternally he stings, swiftly he flies and kills."

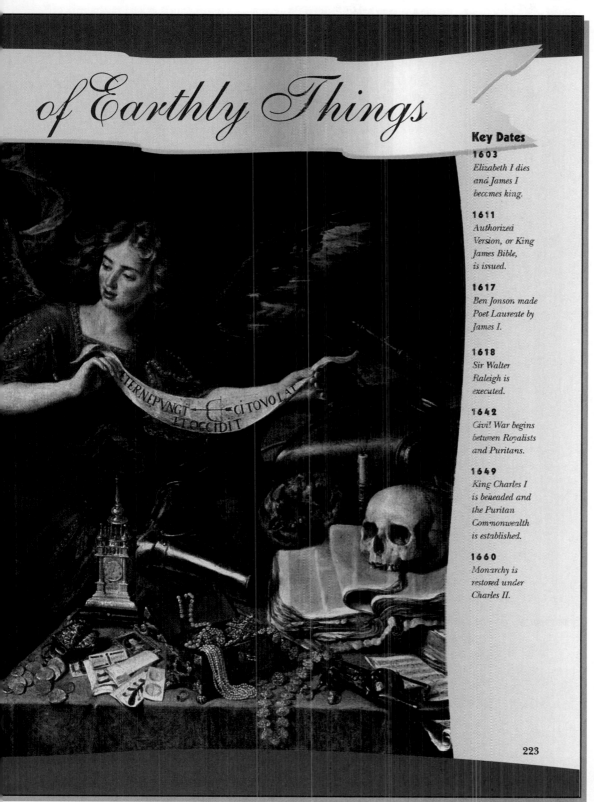

of Earthly Things

Key Dates

1603 *Elizabeth I dies and James I becomes king.*

1611 *Authorized Version, or King James Bible, is issued.*

1617 *Ben Jonson made Poet Laureate by James I.*

1618 *Sir Walter Raleigh is executed.*

1642 *Civil War begins between Royalists and Puritans.*

1649 *King Charles I is beheaded and the Puritan Commonwealth is established.*

1660 *Monarchy is restored under Charles II.*

Key Dates

1640–1641 "Bloodless Revolution": Charles I, in deep financial trouble, asks Parliament to help. It does, but on the condition that he give it much more decision-making power. Parliament abolishes the Star Chamber, a juryless trial court which arbitrarily sentenced people to torture and death.

1645 Anti-Royalist forces organize into the New Model Army, which combines Puritan and Parliamentarian causes and wins a victory against the Royalists at Naseby.

1647 Parliamentarians split into two factions. The more conservative one allies itself with Charles. Cromwell leads the radical group, the Independents, to victory.

1653–1658 Cromwell rules England as Lord Protector. A brilliant strategist and politician, he manages to keep domestic order, make peace with the Dutch, and successfully fight Spain. When he dies in 1658, his son Richard becomes Lord Protector but is ousted in 1659.

MATERIALS OF INTEREST

Books

- *The Century of Revolution: 1603–1714* by Christopher Hill (Second Edition, Norton, 1980).
- *The Oxford History of Britain* edited by Kenneth O. Morgan (Oxford, 1988).

Multimedia

European Monarchs CD-ROM, Charles I and Charles II articles (Quanta Press, 1995).

Connections to **Custom Literature Database**

For further historical background, under **Background Articles,** see **Renaissance England 1500-1660.**

Preview

The Meaning of Life

FOR ALL STUDENTS

- How do we learn about the meaning of life?
- How much does the meaning of one's life depend on others?

After students read the first paragraph on page 224, tell them that the selections in this part express several, not necessarily opposing, viewpoints about life.

To further explore the theme, use the transparency referenced below.

Transparency Collection
Fine Art Transparency 4

For At-Risk Students

- Ask students to think of someone they love or who is very dear to them. They can then write a letter to this person using ten adjectives.
- Ask students to design a simple greeting card using words or symbols.

For Students Who Need Challenge

Students could research works of other poets. For example, they can examine the works of Ben Jonson, Richard Lovelace, or George Herbert.

For Visual Learners

After students have studied the painting on pages 222–223, ask them to sketch things that mean the most to them.

MULTICULTURAL CONNECTION

In seventeenth-century England, dissenters from the dominant religion were usually not tolerated.

- What nations do you know of who have a national religion today?
- How are minorities in that nation treated?

Part One

The Meaning of Life

"Who am I? Why am I here? Where am I going?" Such questions have been asked since the beginnings of human consciousness. For answers, some people turn to religion, seeking meaning not in life now, but in life after death. Others deny that there is a life after death, seeking meaning in the here and now. Most of the British writers of the 1600s probably believed in a Christian God (worshipped according to either the Catholic or Protestant faiths). But most of them also followed the literary conventions of the day, protesting their spiritual love and physical desire in highly formalized verse forms.

Multicultural Focus As you read the literature in Part One, reflect on how this search for truth and the meaning of life is influenced by the different writers' differering viewpoints, or **perspectives.**

Literature

IDEAS THAT WORK

Motivating with Images

Time and distance, the limitations of life on earth, are the enemies of love. "Song" uses the images of "a falling star," "the devil's foot," and "envy's stinging" to build an image of a woman who cannot remain "true and fair" while her lover is away. In "A Valediction: Forbidding Mourning" the poet asserts that a "refined love" does not need constant physical contact to maintain its intensity. How do the two poems encompass the range of emotions that lovers feel toward one another? What kind of "love" is being described in "Song"? Which poem presents the most accurate view of the effect that separation has on a relationship? If one of these poems were addressed to you, would you be flattered, insulted, in agreement?

Lucia Podraza
Chicago, Illinois

Before Reading

Song
A Valediction: Forbidding Mourning
Meditation 17 by John Donne

John Donne
1572–1631

During a time when Catholics were often persecuted in England, John Donne's religion prevented him from receiving a university degree, and his brother was imprisoned for protecting a Catholic priest. Donne studied law and became secretary to the politically influential Sir Thomas Egerton. When Donne secretly married Egerton's niece, her father had him imprisoned, Egerton dismissed him, and he was unable to find suitable work for many years. Donne renounced the Catholic faith and, at the urging of King James, became an Anglican (Church of England) priest. In 1621 Donne was made Dean of St. Paul's Cathedral in London, where he became a celebrated preacher.

Building Background

His Life and Work John Donne's writing parallels his life. Before he married Anne More he had several love affairs, and his early poetry reflects a cynical view about women. Poet John Dryden wrote that Donne "perplexes the minds of the fair sex with nice speculations of philosophy, when he should engage their hearts, and entertain them with the softnesses of love." After he married Anne, Donne composed ardent love poems for her. When he became a priest he wrote religious poetry and prose. He even wrote attacks on Catholics, despite his early upbringing, perhaps to gain the favor of the king.

Literary Focus

Metaphor and Conceit A figure of speech that shows a comparison between two basically unlike things that have something in common is called a **metaphor.** The comparison may be stated or implied. For example, "Scarlet and yellow kites were bright patches on a quilt of dark clouds" compares kites to patches and clouds to a quilt. A **conceit** is an elaborate and surprising metaphor comparing two very dissimilar things. It has been described as stretching a metaphor to the breaking point. As you read these works by Donne, look for the metaphors and the conceits.

Writer's Notebook

Finding the Right Words In the 1600s and 1700s, it was customary to write elaborate poetry or letters to convey one's feelings. Today we might search for a greeting card to express our thoughts, satisfied to let an anonymous writer or artist convey our thanks or affections. In your notebook jot down several occasions for which a personal note or a greeting card might be appropriate. (You might glance at the greeting card racks in a local store to get ideas for unusual occasions.)

Before Reading

Building Background

You might begin by asking students if they are familiar with the Ernest Hemingway novel title *For Whom the Bell Tolls,* and then lead a discussion on what this phrase might mean.

Literary Focus

Question How is a conceit different than a normal metaphor? *(It is an elaborate, surprising metaphor that compares two very different things.)* Suggest that students list metaphors they find in Donne's work and then decide which are conceits.

Writer's Notebook

In preparation for writing greeting-card notes or verses, students might jot down images and ideas that Donne's work evokes.

More About John Donne

Donne wrote with wit and much humor. When imprisoned for marrying, he summarized his predicament as "John Donne, Anne Donne, Undone." During his final illness, he preached a sermon on dying and then posed for a portrait in a funeral shroud.

SUPPORT MATERIALS OVERVIEW

Unit 3 Resource Book
- Graphic Organizer, p. 1
- Study Guide, p. 2
- Vocabulary, p. 3
- Grammar, p. 4
- Alternate Check Test, p. 5
- Vocabulary Test, p. 6
- Selection Test, pp. 7–8

Building English Proficiency
- Selection Summaries
- Activities, p. 216
- "Song" and "A Valediction: Forbidding Mourning" in Spanish

Reading, Writing & Grammar SkillBook
- Reading, pp. 55–57
- Grammar, Usage, and Mechanics, pp. 167–170

Technology
- Audiotape
- Personal Journal Software.
- Custom Literature Database: Additional selections by John Donne can be found on the database.
- Test Generator Software

During Reading

Selection Objectives

- To contrast the poet's early and later views of romantic love
- To distinguish between metaphor and conceit
- To analyze Donne's argument for connections between all life

Unit 3 Resource Book
Graphic Organizer, p. 1
Study Guide, p. 2

Theme Link

Reflections of 17th-century writers still shed light on The Meaning of Life. Donne found meaning in marriage and religion.

Vocabulary Preview

breach, break or gap
toll, ring
piety, reverence for God
promontory, high point of a coastal land extending into the water
affliction, pain, misery
recourse, appeal for protection

Students can add the words and definitions to their Writer's Notebooks.

1 Reading/Thinking Skills
Recognize Values

Question Is faithfulness as large an issue today as it was for Donne? *(While responses will vary and might include references to divorce rates, parental absence, and portrayals of unfaithfulness on TV and in movies, students might note that the pain and anguish caused by unfaithfulness remains constant.)*

Art Study

Response to Caption Question
Possibilities include ginseng, alum, wolfsbane, garlic, and mistletoe.

Song

John Donne

Go and catch a falling star,
    Get with child a mandrake root,[1]
Tell me where all past years are,
    Or who cleft the devil's foot;
Teach me to hear mermaids singing,
Or to keep off envy's stinging,
    And find
    What wind
Serves to advance an honest mind.

If thou beest born to strange sights,
    Things invisible to see,
Ride ten thousand days and nights,
    Till age snow white hairs on thee;
Thou, when thou returnest, will tell me
All strange wonders that befell thee,
    And swear
    Nowhere
Lives a woman true, and fair.

If thou findest one, let me know;
    Such a pilgrimage were sweet.
Yet do not; I would not go,
    Though at next door we might meet.
Though she were true when you met her,
And last till you write your letter,
    Yet she
    Will be
1 False, ere I come, to two or three.

1. **get . . . mandrake root.** Mandrake (man′drāk) is an herb with a forked root that supposedly resembles a human figure. Recognizing this resemblance as well as the impossibility of a plant's reproducing as humans do, Donne includes this in his catalogue of fantastic achievements.

A mandrake *(Solanaceae mandragora)* is shown in this woodcut from *Commentaries on the Six Books of Dioscorides* by Dierandrea Mattiolo (Prague, 1563). Mandrakes were known to have medicinal properties and were thought by some to be magical as well. What other plants do you know of that are considered magical by some people?

SELECTION SUMMARY

Song; A Valediction: Forbidding Mourning; Meditation 17

Song A young and disappointed man expresses skepticism that a woman both beautiful and faithful might exist.

A Valediction An older Donne expresses the passionate and faithful love that he shares with his wife. Separation cannot diminish their relationship, as their souls are as interrelated as the two branches of a compass.

Meditation 17 Donne reflects on the individual's connection to humanity. The death of an individual diminishes us all; sharing in others' afflictions is sharing in a treasure, as it prepares one for meeting God.

For summaries in other languages, see the ***Building English Proficiency*** *book.*

A Valediction: Forbidding Mourning

John Donne

As virtuous men pass mildly away,
  And whisper to their souls to go,
Whilst some of their sad friends do say,
  The breath goes now, and some say, no;

So let us melt, and make no noise,
  No tear-floods, nor sigh-tempests move,
'Twere profanation of our joys
  To tell the laity our love.

Moving of the earth brings harms and fears,
  Men reckon what it did and meant,
But trepidation of the spheres,
  Though greater far, is innocent.[1]

Dull sublunary[2] lovers' love
  (Whose soul is sense)[3] cannot admit
Absence, because it doth remove
  Those things which elemented[4] it.

But we, by a love, so much refined
  That our selves know not what it is,
Inter-assurèd of the mind,
  Care less, eyes, lips, and hands to miss.

Our two souls therefore, which are one,
  Though I must go, endure not yet
A breach,[5] but an expansion,
  Like gold to airy thinness beat.

If they be two, they are two so
  As stiff twin compasses[6] are two;
Thy soul the fixed foot, makes no show
  To move, but doth, if the other do.

And though it in the center sit,
  Yet when the other far doth roam,
It leans, and hearkens after it,
  And grows erect, as that comes home.

Such wilt thou be to me, who must
  Like the other foot, obliquely run;
Thy firmness makes my circle just,
  And makes me end where I begun.

---

valediction (val′ə dik′shən), *n.* a bidding farewell. Donne wrote this poem to his wife before he left on an extended trip to France.

1. **trepidation . . . innocent.** Movements of the heavenly spheres, though greater than those of an earthquake, provoke no fears in nor danger to humans.
2. **sublunary** (sub lü′nər ē), *adj.* beneath the moon; that is, earthly and subject to change.
3. **whose soul is sense,** that is, loves that are confined to physical perceptions.
4. **element** (el′ə ment′), *v.* compose; make up.
5. breach (brēch), *n.* break or gap.
6. **compasses.** The image is of the instrument used for drawing a circle. One branch or leg of the compass is held steady, while the other leg is rotated to draw the circle. Anne is the "fixed foot."

2 Literary Element
Simile

Question Donne states that his soul and his wife's soul are one, which expands during periods of separation. What simile does he use to illustrate this expansion? *(The expansion is compared to gold beaten into leaf.)*

3 Literary Focus
Metaphor and Conceit

Questions What is this poem's primary metaphor? *(souls compared to the branches of a compass)* Do you think this metaphor is an example of conceit? *(Possible response: The metaphor satisfies the definition of conceit by being both highly elaborate and surprising in its comparison of very unlike things.)*

Literary Criticism

"The first impression of an unbiased reader . . . of Donne is unfavourable. He is repulsed by the . . . harsh and crabbed versification . . . by the oddity of the thought. In time, however, he perceives that behind the fantastic . . . language there is an earnest and vigorous mind, an imagination . . . and . . . insight into the mysteries of spiritual life . . . ."

Sir Edmund Gosse
Encyclopedia Brittanica, 14th Edition

BUILDING ENGLISH PROFICIENCY

ESL LEP ELD SAE LD

Making Personal Connections

Help students relate to what the poet is saying in "Song."

Activity Ideas

- Invite students to bring in (or sing) examples of modern songs (in English or another language) about lack of faithfulness in relationships. Ask: Why do you think this is a favorite subject for poets and singers through the ages?
- Ask students to write one sentence describing a present-day behavior type that they consider extremely rare.
- Have students create a web to record "strange" sights (line 10) from the modern world. Or, let visual learners draw "strange sights" if they prefer.

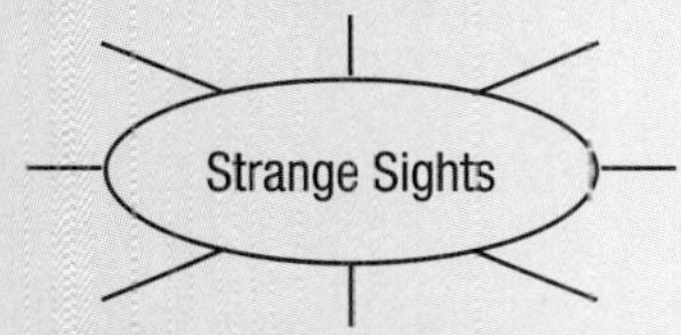

Building English Proficiency
Activities, p. 216
"Song" and "A Valediction: Forbidding Mourning" in Spanish

MULTICULTURAL NOTE

In Europe, in Donne's day, church bells called people to prayer and served as timekeepers, as most people had no clocks. They were also tolled to mark the death of an individual.

4 Literary Element
Personification

Remind students that personification is the representation of abstractions, ideas, animals, or inanimate objects as human beings by endowing them with human qualities.

Question What does Donne personify here? *(Possible response: the church as a woman. The church has traditionally been personified as the "bride of Christ"—a single body comprised of all its members.)*

5 Literary Focus
Metaphor and Conceit

Question What extended metaphor does Donne employ in the first paragraph? *(He compares humanity with a book written by a single author; the death of an individual is compared to a chapter of that book translated into a better language; heaven is compared to a library of all these chapters.)*

Art Study

Responses to Caption Questions
The mood, somber and contemplative, results from the dark colors, the elongated, vertical lines, and the contrast of scale between architecture and the human figures.

Meditation 17

John Donne

Now this bell, tolling softly for another, says to me, Thou must die.

Perchance he for whom this bell tolls[1] may be so ill as that he knows not it tolls for him; and perchance I may think myself so much better than I am, as that they who are about me and see my state, may have caused it to toll for me, and I know not that. The church is catholic, universal;
4 so are all her actions; all that she does belongs to all. When she baptizes a child, that action concerns me, for that child is thereby connected to that head which is my head too, and ingrafted into that body whereof I am a member.[2] And when she buries a man, that action concerns me. All mankind is of one author and is one vol-
5 ume; when one man dies, one chapter is not torn out of the book, but translated into a better language, and every chapter must be so translated. God employs several translators; some pieces are translated by age, some by sickness, some by war, some by justice; but God's hand is in every translation and his hand shall bind up all our scattered leaves again for that library where every book shall lie open to one another. As therefore the bell that rings to a sermon calls not upon the preacher only, but upon the congregation to come, so this bell calls us all; but how much more me, who am brought so near the door by this sickness.

1. toll (tōl), *v.* ring.
2. **When she baptizes . . . member.** The church, referred to as "she," is the head of all, as well as a body made up of its members.

MINI-LESSON: GRAMMAR
Understanding Parallel Structure

Teach Parallel structure is the repeating of phrases or sentences that are similar (parallel) in meaning and structure. Parallel structure helps make sentences more graceful and balanced. Examples: The first sentence uses parallel structure by beginning two clauses with *perchance.* "God employs several translators; *some* pieces are translated by age, *some* by sickness, *some* by war, *some* by justice . . . "—each phrase in the series begins with the same word.

Activity Idea Give students practice rewriting or restating unparallel sentences by using parallel construction. (An example to correct: In our school, the students pass time after school by studying, hanging out, or at a job.) What examples can students find or think of to challenge classmates?

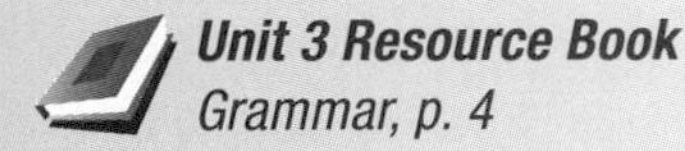

Unit 3 Resource Book
Grammar, p. 4

There was a contention as far as a suit[3] (in which both piety[4] and dignity, religion and estimation,[5] were mingled) which of the religious orders should ring to prayers first in the morning; and it was determined that they should ring first that rose earliest. If we understand aright the dignity of this bell that tolls for our evening prayer, we would be glad to make it ours by rising early, in that application, that it might be ours as well as his whose indeed it is. The bell doth toll for him that thinks it doth; and though it intermit[6] again, yet from that minute that that occasion wrought upon him, he is united to God. Who casts not up his eye to the sun when it rises? But who takes off his eye from a comet when that breaks out? Who bends not his ear to any bell which upon any occasion rings? But who can remove it from that bell which is passing a piece of himself out of this world? No man is an island, entire of itself; every man is a piece of the continent, a part of the main. If a clod be washed away by the sea, Europe is the less, as
6 well as if a promontory[7] were, as well as if a manor of thy friend's or of thine own were. Any man's death diminishes me, because I am involved in mankind; and therefore never send to know for whom the bell tolls; it tolls for thee.

Neither can we call this a begging of misery or a borrowing of misery, as though we were not miserable enough of ourselves, but must fetch in more from the next house, in taking upon us the misery of our neighbors. Truly it were an excusable covetousness[8] if we did; for affliction[9] is a treasure, and scarce any man hath enough of it. No man hath affliction enough that is not matured and ripened by it, and made fit for God by that affliction. If a man carry treasure in bullion, or in a wedge of gold, and have none coined into current monies, his treasure will not defray him as he travels. Tribulation[10] is treasure in the nature of it, but it is not current money in 7
the use of it, except we get nearer and nearer our home, heaven, by it. Another man may be sick too, and sick to death, and this affliction may lie in his bowels, as gold in a mine, and be of no use to him; but this bell, that tells me of his affliction, digs out and applies that gold to me, if by this consideration of another's danger, I take mine own into contemplation, and so secure myself by making my recourse[11] to my God, who is our only security.

3. **contention . . . suit,** a controversy that went as far as a lawsuit.
4. **piety** (pī′ə tē), *n.* reverence for God.
5. **estimation** (es′tə mā′shən), *n.* self-esteem.
6. **intermit** (in′tər mit′), *v.* break off.
7. **promontory** (prom′ən tôr′ē) *n.* a high point of land extending from the coast into the water.
8. **covetousness** (kuv′ə təs nis), *n.* desire for things that belong to others.
9. **affliction** (ə flik′shən), *n.* pain; misery.
10. **tribulation** (trib′yə lā′shən), *n.* great trouble.
11. **recourse** (rē′kôrs), *n.* appeal for help or protection.

◄ *Cathedral in Winter* was painted by Ernst Ferdinand Oehme in 1821. What mood does the artist create in this painting? How does he create that mood?

6 Literary Element
Hyperbole

Questions Remind students that hyperbole is a figure of speech that employs great exaggeration. Donne writes: "If a clod be washed away by the sea, Europe is less." Is a continent really diminished by the loss of a single clump of dirt? *(While it is not perceptibly diminished, it is diminished.)* What does this hyperbole suggest? *(Possible response: the connectedness of all life; the importance of each individual)*

7 Literary Focus
Metaphor and Conceit

Questions To what does Donne compare tribulation? *(a treasure)* At what point does this metaphor reach the level of conceit? Why? *(Possible response: It becomes conceit when he compares an affliction of the bowels with gold in a mine. It elaborates on an earlier metaphor, and it stretches the comparison of two very different things nearly to the breaking point.)*

Check Test

1. What is mandrake? *(a plant root with medicinal qualities)*
2. Why won't Donne visit a "true and fair" woman? *(By the time he sees her, she will become false.)*
3. In "Valediction," what will bring Donne back in a full circle? *(his wife, his true compass)*
4. Why does the bell toll? *(to announce someone's death)*
5. Why shouldn't one ask for whom the bell tolls? *(Everyone is connected, so whoever dies is a loss to all.)*

Unit 3 Resource Book
Alternate Check Test, p. 5

BUILDING ENGLISH PROFICIENCY

Exploring Main Ideas

Help students focus on the main idea in Donne's essay.

1. Have small groups talk about the important role that an individual plays in a family, a classroom, and a democracy. Encourage groups to share their ideas.
2. Most students have thrown a rock into water and watched ripples expand in circles from it. Relate this experience to Donne's ideas. Have students draw concentric circles for names of people to whom they are connected in ever-decreasing degrees, as shown.

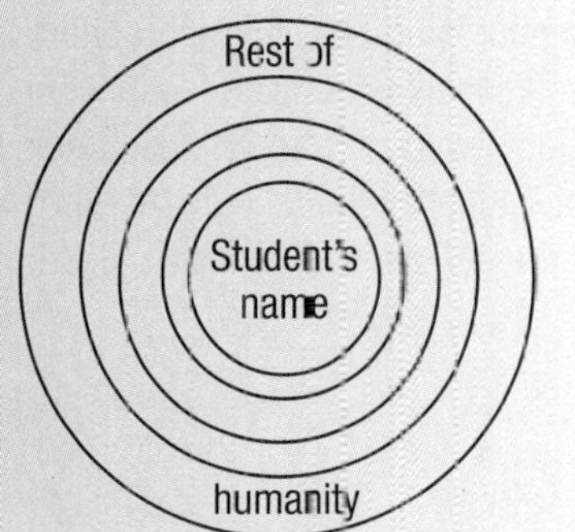

After Reading

MAKING CONNECTIONS

1. While student responses may break along gender lines, it should be noted that gender has nothing to do with faithfulness.

2. Responses will vary. Many students may find the comparison unromantic.

3. All command the impossible.

4. Students may describe the speaker as cynical, disappointed, bitter, or sarcastic because of disappointment in love.

5. The speaker and his love may be spiritual, ethereal, idealistic, or romantic in contrast to dull, earthly, pedestrian, sublunary lovers incapable of separation.

6. A bell may be tolled as an alarm; as a call to assemble or to pray; or to announce death. For Donne, death is most important because of our connection to it.

7. While responses will differ, students might note that Donne's vision of the connectedness of all humanity is a philosophy at odds with much of modern life.

After Reading

Making Connections

Shaping Your Response

1. Do you agree with Donne, in "Song," that all women are untrue? What about men?
2. If someone wrote a love poem to you, how would you react to being compared to a compass foot?

Analyzing the Selections

3. The speaker issues seven commands in the first stanza of "Song." What do they have in common?
4. What seems to be the speaker's state of mind in "Song," and what do you **infer** might account for it?
5. Compare the speaker and his love in "A Valediction: Forbidding Mourning" with the "dull sublunary lovers" of stanza 4 by listing descriptions that you imagine would apply to either couple.
6. For what general reasons might a bell be tolled? According to "Meditation 17," which reason is most important? Why?

Extending the Ideas

7. In "Meditation 17," Donne writes that "any man's death diminishes me because I am involved in mankind." Would most people today be likely to agree with this **perspective?** Explain.

Literary Focus: Metaphor and Conceit

A **metaphor** compares two basically unlike things that have something in common. A **conceit** is also a metaphor but a more elaborate one. In "A Valediction: Forbidding Mourning," Donne compares his and Anne's souls to twin compasses (really the two legs of one compass). Which soul is compared to the "fixed foot," and why does this comparison seem appropriate? Would you classify this as a conceit? Why or why not? In "Meditation 17," Donne compares man to a chapter in a book and to a piece of the continent. (He probably meant *man* to include all people, women as well.) Choose one of these metaphors and explain the similarity between a person and the thing to which he or she is compared.

Vocabulary Study

On your paper, write the listed word that fits each description (you will not use all the listed words). Then assign numbers to some of the letters, following the pattern in parentheses after the description. Finally put those letters in numerical order 1–12 to get the answer to the last description.

LITERARY FOCUS: METAPHOR AND CONCEIT

Possible Responses

- Donne compares his wife's soul to the "fixed foot." The metaphor is unusual but appropriate for such a close relationship: the fixed foot anchors the rotating foot, which in turn rotates around the fixed foot. Students should note that the metaphor satisfies the definition of conceit.
- Humanity is a book by a single author; the individual is a chapter; when the individual dies, his chapter, translated into a better language, is stored in the library of heaven.
- Humanity is the continent of Europe; Europe is as lessened by the washing away of a clod—by the death of a single person—as by the dropping away of a great promontory—by the death of a great man (or the death of huge numbers of people).

affliction
breach
piety
promontory
recourse
toll

1. A fee or a charge or the sound of a bell. (• 10 • •)
2. If you practice this, then you may escape hell. (9 • 7 • •)
3. A quarrel, a breakthrough, or often, a gap. (• • 11 4 • 6)
4. This prominent feature is found on a map. (1 • • • • • 12 • 8 •)
5. When you need protection, you ask for the same. (• 3 5 • • 2 • •)

To honor his monarch, what John Donne became.
(1 2 3 4 5 6 7 8 / 9 10 11 12)

Expressing Your Ideas

Writing Choices

Writer's Notebook Update Look again at your list of occasions for sending a greeting card. Jot down a few words or phrases for each occasion that seem appropriate for expressing the emotions that occasion brings out.

Pick a Card . . . Any Card Design a **greeting card** to someone you admire, love, or want to thank. Use some of the words and phrases you listed in your notebook to describe your feelings toward that person or your wishes upon a certain occasion. Write in rhymed verse if you wish. Illustrate your greeting card with an original drawing or with magazine art or photographs.

Taking a Toll Suppose you accept that "the bell tolls for thee." Does this change the way you behave (*ought* it to?), or do you put this thought aside and live life as usual? Write a response to Donne's statement in the form of a guest **editorial** for your school or community newspaper. To prove your point, include a personal anecdote or one that you have read about that illustrates how what happens to some people affects others.

Other Options

Up Close and Personal Choose a historic figure from the 1500s or the 1600s such as one of the following and portray that person in a one-man or one-woman show of no more than ten minutes: Mary Queen of Scots, Sir Walter Raleigh, the Earl of Essex, Christopher Marlowe, Queen Elizabeth I, King Charles I. After doing some research, write a **monologue** in the first person that helps to explain the person to a modern audience. Then, portray your chosen person as you read your sketch to your audience.

Words and Music Donne's poem is entitled "Song," and the word suggests music. Find and play a **musical setting** that these words can be sung to, or else write a melody or some chords that can be played on a guitar or a synthesizer while the poem is being recited. Make a recording of your best performance to share with other classes.

VOCABULARY STUDY

1. toll
2. piety
3. breach
4. promontory
5. recourse

John Donne became a preacher/poet.

More Practice Change the following verbs to adjectives by adding a suffix to each: *afflict, estimate, intermit, contend, covet*

Change the verbs to nouns by adding suffixes to verbs, as needed.

(Adjectives: afflicted, estimated, intermittent, contentious, covetous)

(Nouns: affliction, estimate, intermission, contention, covetousness)

Unit 3 Resource Book
Vocabulary, p. 3
Vocabulary Test, p. 6

WRITING CHOICES

Writer's Notebook

To help students get started, brainstorm examples of occasions or themes for greeting cards and list on newsprint or the chalkboard.

Taking a Toll

Furnish examples of editorials from school and local newspapers. Discuss the length and other characteristics of the sample editorials: Is it signed or unsigned? Is it written in the first person? Does it urge action or just express an opinion?

Selection Test

Unit 3 Resource Book
pp. 7–8

OTHER OPTIONS

Up Close and Personal

Enlist the speech or drama teacher to coach students on delivery of their monologues. Does the drama department have period costumes to borrow?

Words and Music

Ask students to write down and bring to class the words of a contemporary song that deals with the issue of fidelity.

Before Reading

Building Background

You might begin by asking students for current phrases that express the idea of *carpe diem* or "seize the day." *("Take time to smell the roses," "Go for the gusto," "Grab all the gusto you can," "Life is short, do it now," "So many men [women], so little time," "Live hard, die young, and leave a beautiful corpse")*

Literary Focus

Suggest that as students read, they look for the use of hyperbole by questioning whether phrases are exaggerated.

Writer's Notebook

Explain that after reading the poems, students will be asked to reply to the speakers' arguments to "seize the day." In their replies, they may want to employ contemporary words in unusual ways. Suggest that as they read, they record possible inspirations of how to use words in new, interesting ways.

More About Herrick and Marvel

- Herrick's poetry has alternately been applauded for its lyricism and condemned for its "obscenities."
- Author, tutor, and MP (Member of Parliament), Andrew Marvell may also have been a spy.

Before Reading

To the Virgins, to Make Much of Time
Upon Julia's Clothes by Robert Herrick
Delight in Disorder by Robert Herrick
To His Coy Mistress by Andrew Marvell

Robert Herrick
1591–1674

Herrick spent nearly thirty years of his life as a country parson. When the Puritans came to power in 1647, he was expelled from his ministry for his loyalty to the Royalist cause. Following the literary convention of the day, Herrick addressed many of his poems to imaginary mistresses.

Andrew Marvell
1621–1678

Born in Yorkshire, Andrew Marvell received a degree at Cambridge. In 1659, Marvell was elected a member of Parliament. He wrote both poetry and prose; the latter, often critical of royal power and therefore dangerous, was published anonymously.

Building Background

Revolution, Plague, and Fire These are turbulent times. The stubbornness of King Charles I leads to civil war between the Royalists and the Parliamentary party. In 1649, Charles is executed, his head chopped off. Puritan leader Oliver Cromwell assumes power. In 1660 Charles II reclaims the throne of his father, but England suffers further turmoil with an outbreak of the plague in 1665 and the Great Fire of London in 1666. Among the types of literature new to England during the Renaissance is **carpe diem** (kär′pe dē′em) poetry. *Carpe diem* is Latin for "seize (take advantage of) the day," and this poetry emphasizes that life is brief and that youth must pursue the pleasures of the present. The theme is popular, for disease or politics could quickly shorten one's life, if one lives past childhood to begin with. Obviously, it is necessary to "seize the day" at an early age.

Literary Focus

Hyperbole Writers sometimes use an extravagant statement or a figure of speech involving great exaggeration called **hyperbole** (hī pėr′ bə lē). "My love stretches to the farthest reaches of the universe," or "If I fail this test, I'll die" are both examples of hyperbole. Often used for emphasis or to demonstrate sincerity, hyperbole sometimes is used to create humor.

Writer's Notebook

Some experts estimate that during the later years of the 1500s, more than ten thousand words were added to the English language, partly through the importation of foreign terms. Shakespeare both borrowed and coined many words still in use today. Herrick didn't make up the word *liquefaction* (line 3 in "Upon Julia's Clothes"), but he used it in an unusual way. Find the word in an unabridged dictionary or in the *Oxford English Dictionary* and study the entry. As you read through these poems and others to come, keep a list of words in your notebook that you find particularly colorful or useful.

SUPPORT MATERIALS OVERVIEW

Unit 3 Resource Book
- Graphic Organizer, p. 9
- Study Guide, p. 10
- Vocabulary, p. 11
- Grammar, p. 12
- Alternate Check Test, p. 13
- Vocabulary Test, p. 14
- Selection Test, pp. 15–16

Building English Proficiency
- Selection Summaries
- Activities, p. 217

Reading, Writing & Grammar SkillBook
- Grammar, Usage, and Mechanics, pp. 157–158

The World of Work
- Fashion Designer, p. 7
- Activity, p. 8

Technology
- Audiotape
- Personal Journal Software.
- Custom Literature Database: Additional selections by Robert Herrick and Andrew Marvell can be found on the database.
- Test Generator Software

To the Virgins, to Make Much of Time

ROBERT HERRICK

Gather ye rosebuds while ye may,
Old time is still a-flying;
And this same flower that smiles today,
Tomorrow will be dying.

The glorious lamp of heaven, the sun,
The higher he's a-getting,
The sooner will his race be run,
And nearer he's to setting.

That age is best which is the first,
When youth and blood are warmer,
But being spent, the worse, and worst
Times still succeed the former.

Then be not coy, but use your time,
And while ye may, go marry;
For having lost but once your prime,
You may forever tarry.

16 tarry (tar′ē), *v.* remain; stay.

Upon Julia's Clothes

ROBERT HERRICK

Whenas in silks my Julia goes,
Then, then, methinks, how sweetly flows
That liquefaction of her clothes.

Next, when I cast mine eyes and see
1 That brave vibration each way free,
O, how that glittering taketh me!

5 brave, bright; splendid.

SELECTION SUMMARY

To the Virgins, to Make Much of Time; Upon Julia's Clothes; Delight in Disorder; To His Coy Mistress

To the Virgins, to Make Much of Time A young lady is urged to gather her rosebuds, or succumb to the narrator's ardor, while still young and in her prime.

Upon Julia's Clothes The narrator takes sensual pleasure in the sight and sound of silk and the movement of a woman's body beneath it.

Delight in Disorder The narrator finds the artful disarray of a young woman's costume fascinating and seductive.

To His Coy Mistress The narrator launches a campaign of seduction with hyperbolic descriptions of how he would woo the reluctant young lady if there were but time. But, time's flight toward the desert of eternity cannot be stopped. So, he urges her to outdistance time by joining him in devouring the life one has.

*For summaries in other languages, see the **Building English Proficiency** book.*

During Reading

Selection Objectives

- To understand the centrality of romance to the meaning of life for these poets
- To identify and analyze examples of hyperbole and its significance in *carpe diem* poetry
- To compare the 17th century and current times for reasons that make *carpe diem* a popular theme

Unit 3 Resource Book
Graphic Organizer, p. 9
Study Guide, p. 10

Theme Link

During times of great transformation, uncertainty often prompts people, especially young people and writers such as Herrick and Marvell, to question the Meaning of Life and to seize the day.

Vocabulary Preview

wantonness, lack of restraint
erring, wandering, straying
enthrall, hold captive
bewitch, to charm
transpire, breathe out
languish, become weak

Students can add the words and definitions to their Writer's Notebooks.

1 Literary Element
Theme

Questions How does this poem seem modern? What is the theme? *(Girl-watching is always modern, as is the theme—the mystery of sexual aesthetics. Herrick explores the relationship between appearance and attraction, why a person is more appealing in one type of clothing or material than another. The narrator finds sensual pleasure in the movement, rustle, and reflection of Julia's silk.)*

2 Reader's Response
Making Personal Connections

Question Do you agree with Herrick's contention that a little "disorder" in dress can bewitch? *(Responses will vary. If student responses don't touch on the subject, you might note that perfection is often rather intimidating.)*

Geographical Note

In 1641, Marvell's father drowned in the Humber estuary at Hull, England, made famous by his son's poem "To His Coy Mistress."

3 Literary Focus
Hyperbole

Question What are examples of hyperbole in this poem? Explain why. *(Possible responses: In "I would love ten years before the Flood," he exaggerates time by referring to ten years before the biblical flood of Noah; in "refuse till the conversion of the Jews," he exaggerates time to infinity by the unlikeliness of the outcome; in "my vegetable love should grow vaster than empires and more slow," he exaggerates time and place in his references to the size of his love and the centuries it took to assemble the Roman Empire; in "an hundred years should go to praise/two hundred to adore/thirty thousand to . . . " he exaggerates time beyond a life span.)*

Portrait of Lady Castelmaine by Sir Peter Lely. What does Lady Castlemaine's pose and the expression on her face suggest about her personality? ➤

Delight in Disorder

Robert Herrick

2 A sweet disorder in the dress
Kindles in clothes a wantonness.
A lawn about the shoulders thrown
Into a fine distraction;
An erring lace, which here and there
Enthralls the crimson stomacher;
A cuff neglectful, and thereby
Ribbons to flow confusèdly;
A winning wave, deserving note,
In the tempestuous petticoat;
A careless shoestring, in whose tie
I see a wild civility—
Do more bewitch me than when art
Is too precise in every part.

2 wantonness (won′tən nis), *n.* lack of restraint.
3 **lawn,** linen scarf.
5 erring (ėr′ing), *adj.* wandering; straying.
6 enthrall (en thrôl′), *v.* hold captive.
6 **stomacher,** an ornamental covering for the stomach and bodice.
13 bewitch (bi wich′), *v.* charm; fascinate.

To His Coy Mistress

Andrew Marvell

Had we but world enough, and time,
This coyness, Lady, were no crime.
We would sit down, and think which way
To walk, and pass our long love's day.
Thou by the Indian Ganges' side
Shouldst rubies find; I by the tide
Of Humber would complain. I would
3 Love you ten years before the Flood,
And you should, if you please, refuse
Till the Conversion of the Jews.
My vegetable love should grow
Vaster than empires and more slow;
An hundred years should go to praise
Thine eyes, and on thy forehead gaze;

7 **Humber,** the river that flows through Marvell's home town of Hull.
7 **complain,** that is, sing sad love songs.
8 **flood,** the biblical flood.
10 **conversion of the Jews.** It was a popular belief among Christians that Jews would convert to Christianity just before the end of the world.
11 **vegetable,** growing as slowly as vegetation.

MINI-LESSON: GRAMMAR
Using That and Which

Teach A relative pronoun is a pronoun that relates the subject before it to the action coming after it. Follow these rules:

- Use *that* to refer to animals or nonliving objects.
- Use *who,* not *which* or *that,* to refer to people unless it is a general reference to an impersonal group.
- Use *which* for nondefining or parenthetical clauses (clauses that can be put in parentheses or between commas or left out entirely without taking away from the full meaning of the rest of the sentence) and *that* for clauses that cannot be put between parentheses because they are necessary for defining the subject.
- Whenever *that* appears twice (one soon after the other), for ease of reading change the second *that* to *which.*

Activity Idea For practice, have students

- find an example from "To the Virgins . . . " illustrating the rule about changing a second *that* to *which* for ease of reading *(line 9: That age is best which is the first)*
- find an example from "Delight in Disorder" with *which* in a parenthetical phrase *(lines 5–6: . . . lace, which here and there . . .)*

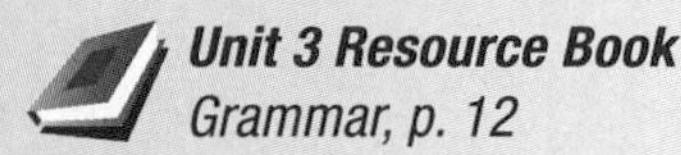

Unit 3 Resource Book
Grammar, p. 12

Art Study

Response to Caption Question The pose, head on hand, is informal. The expression might suggest boredom or even flirtation. The expression and pose together give the idea that Lady Castlemaine is quite human and approachable, rather than formidable as one might expect of a person of her social position. There is something about the pose and expression that also suggest indolence or even world-weariness. Has she seized too many days?

Visual Literacy The artist uses light and shadow most effectively. The shadows in the folds of the material give the painting depth and dimension; the play of light on the shimmering silk presents a sumptuous, yet playful, image.

Question Why do you think the artist posed this lady so that part of her face and shoulder are in shadow? *(Possible response: to impart a sense of mystery; to suggest that one can never truly know her; to suggest that her personality contains contradictory, "dark" and "light," elements)*

The World of Work

Fashion Designer

For real-life experiences of a fashion designer, use the pages referenced below.

The World of Work
pp. 7–8

BUILDING ENGLISH PROFICIENCY

ESL LEP ELD SAE LD

Making Personal Connections

Help students connect with an element shared by these poems—telling about characteristics that make a person "delightful."

Activity Ideas

- Ask students to find a picture of a famous person whom they'd like to date. Allow them to write or talk about the characteristics of that person that make him or her "delightful."
- Students might enjoy contrasting characteristics that they find "delightful" with those that they think their parents would so identify.

The Ideal Mate for Me	
What I Think	What My Parents Think
• clever	• dependable

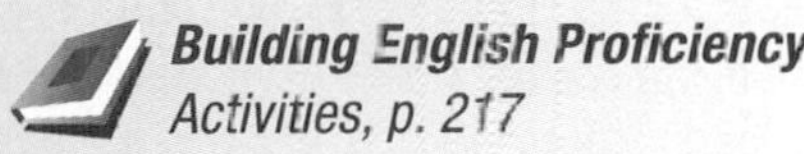

Building English Proficiency
Activities, p. 217

4 Reading/Thinking Skills
Recognize Values

Question What do you think the line "Deserts of vast eternity" and Marvell's images of death suggest about his values? *(Possible response: It seems to suggest that Marvell did not believe in an afterlife—eternity is a vast desert; honor, goodness, and of course beauty are feasted upon by worms.)*

5 Literary Element
Theme

Question How do lines 38 to 46 express the theme of *carpe diem? (Possible response: The image of devouring birds of prey tearing pleasure with rough strife and living with such energy as to make the sun run all the faster suggests the idea of seizing and devouring all that life has to offer because time moves relentlessly on.)*

Check Test

1. In "To the Virgins, to Make Much of Time," what is Herrick urging? *(that they not be coy, but gather their rosebuds, or take lovers, and marry while they are young)*
2. In "Upon Julia's Clothes," what unusual phrase does the poet use to describe his admiration of the movement of silks over her body? *(the liquefaction of her clothes)*
3. In "Delight in Disorder," what does he find so appealing about the young lady? *(her artfully disheveled clothing)*
4. What reason does the writer in "To His Coy Mistress" give for not wooing her in an elaborate, lengthy way? *(He doesn't have time.)*
5. According to Marvell, why shouldn't a lady be reluctant or coy? *(She'll lose her beauty, get old, and miss her chance for happiness and love.)*

Unit 3 Resource Book
Alternate Check Test, p. 13

Two hundred to adore each breast,
But thirty thousand to the rest;
An age at least to every part,
And the last age should show your heart.
For, Lady, you deserve this state;
Nor would I love at lower rate.

But at my back I always hear
Time's wingèd chariot hurrying near;
And yonder all before us lie
4 Deserts of vast eternity.
Thy beauty shall no more be found,
Nor, in thy marble vault, shall sound
My echoing song; then worms shall try
That long-preserved virginity,
And your quaint honor turn to dust,
And into ashes all my lust.
The grave's a fine and private place,
But none, I think, do there embrace.

Now therefore, while the youthful hue
Sits on thy skin like morning dew,
And while thy willing soul transpires
At every pore with instant fires,
Now let us sport us while we may,
And now, like amorous birds of prey,
5 Rather at once our time devour
Than languish in his slow-chapped power.
Let us roll all our strength and all
Our sweetness up into one ball,
And tear our pleasures with rough strife
Thorough the iron gates of life;
Thus, though we cannot make our sun
Stand still, yet we will make him run.

19 **state,** dignity.

27 **try,** test.

29 **quaint,** fastidious; out-of-fashion.

35 **transpire** (tran spīr′), *v.* breathe out.

40 **languish** (lang′guish), *v.* become weak or worn out.
40 **slow-chapped,** slow-jawed.

44 **thorough,** through.

MINI-LESSON: LITERARY FOCUS

Hyperbole

Help students to identify several examples of hyperbole in Marvell's "To His Coy Mistress."

Teach Hyperbole is a figure of speech or a statement using overstatement or exaggeration to make a point. To help identify hyperbole, ask yourself if it's a gross overstatement or such an exaggeration that it couldn't really be true.

Question Why might hyperbole be useful in a seduction poem? *(Possible responses: Exaggeration can convey sincerity, make a point and raise emotional response, delight, amuse, and enchant.)*

Activity Ideas Students can

- identify examples of Marvell's hyperbole and explain why it is hyperbole *(Possible responses: line 10—all Jews will never convert to Christianity; line 22—allusion to time as a chariot; lines 35 and 36—overstatement)*
- give examples of how they use exaggeration, or hyperbole, to be funny, be sincere, or make a point. Suggest they fill in the blanks: "If I fail this test, _____." "They were so stingy that _____."

After Reading

Making Connections

Shaping Your Response

1. Is the advice in "To the Virgins, to Make Much of Time" the kind of advice you would be likely to take, or not? Explain.
2. How would a person sympathetic to women's rights be likely to respond to "To His Coy Mistress"?

Analyzing the Poems

3. One reader has commented that the speaker in "Upon Julia's Clothes" seems to be "hooked" in line 6, much as a fish on a line. What justification can you find in the poem for this interpretation?
4. Which poems here are examples of **carpe diem** poems? What makes them so?
5. If stanza 1 of "To His Coy Mistress" speaks of an ideal world and stanza 2 brings us back to reality, what does stanza 3 do? Fill in a chart like the following as a help in answering.

To His Coy Mistress	
Stanza 1	In an ideal world, I would . . .
Stanza 2	But in the real world . . .
Stanza 3	Therefore . . .

Extending the Ideas

6. If you were writing the copy for a newspaper ad for clothing, how would you describe the kind of clothes and style the speaker in "Delight in Disorder" seems to prefer?
7. From what **perspective** do most *carpe diem* poems seem to be written? How would these poems be likely to differ if they were written from the perspective of a young woman? a much older man? a parent? a twentieth-century person?

Literary Focus: Hyperbole

A figure of speech or a statement involving great exaggeration is called **hyperbole.** Hyperbole is often used to heighten emotional effect. What is exaggerated in the first stanza of "To His Coy Mistress"? Why might the speaker use hyperbole here?

After Reading

MAKING CONNECTIONS

1. Possible responses: Yes, because life can pass you by before you know it; no, because someone has to be responsible and think of the future.

2. that it is terribly sexist

3. The glittering of a lure hooks a fish as the glittering of silk hooks the speaker.

4. Both "To the Virgins" and "To His Coy Mistress" urge the lady not to be coy, but to give in now, before looks, youth, and opportunities are lost.

5. Stanza 1: In an ideal world, I would take endless time for the elaborate seduction you deserve. Stanza 2: But in the real world, time is flying because death is always in the wings. Stanza 3: Therefore, let's seize our moment and push life to the edge; if we can't stop the sun, let's outrun it.

6. Possible descriptions: bared shoulder; peek-a-boo lace; tantalizingly transparent; a tangle of ribbons; undulating ruffles; carelessly casual cuffs; bright red bodice, and so on

7. Most *carpe diem* poems seem to be written from the male perspective. Written from a young woman's perspective, such a poem may include persuasions to respect whatever her wishes are, to linger or to wait, or to get equal gratification. From a much older man's perspective, such a poem might be less insistent, more romantic, less lustful. From a parent's perspective, such a poem might urge the reader to wait, to be responsible, to be safe, careful, celibate. From the perspective of a 20th-century person, such a poem might discuss mutual agreement, planning ahead, and taking precautions.

LITERARY FOCUS: HYPERBOLE

In such lines as "I would love ten years before the Flood" and "my vegetable love should grow vaster than empires and more slow," the narrator wildly exaggerates time and place to highlight the pleasures of seduction he could offer if only he had all the time in the world. This was employed to impress the lady with his sincerity, tantalize her with his prowess and imagination, "romance" her, and heighten her emotions.

VOCABULARY STUDY

1. enthralls
2. erring
3. bewitch
4. wantonness
5. transpire

More Practice Classify these words into three columns (noun, verb, adjective) according to which part of speech they are.

tarry	wantonness
bewitch	enthrall
erring	try
languish	complain
through	transpire
brave	quaint

(Nouns: wantonness)

(Verbs: tarry, bewitch, enthrall, try, languish, complain, transpire)

(Adjectives: erring, thorough, brave, quaint)

Unit 3 Resource Book
Vocabulary, p. 11
Vocabulary Test, p. 14

WRITING CHOICES
Writer's Notebook

Spark imaginations by sharing unusual or interesting words of your own choice and asking volunteers to do the same.

To Her Eager Lover

Students interested in writing replies in verse might find inspiration in Christopher Marlowe's "The Passionate Shepherd to His Love" and Sir Walter Raleigh's "The Nymph's Reply to the Shepherd." Both can be found in major anthologies.

Selection Test

Unit 3 Resource Book
pp. 15–16

Transparency Collection
Fine Art Writing Prompt 4

Vocabulary Study

Write the word from the list that best completes the meaning of each sentence (and maintains the rhythm). You will not use all the words.

bewitch
enthralls
erring
languish
transpire
wantonness

1. Though she ____ a crowd with wit,
2. Her ____ ways we must admit.
3. Her beauty does ____, it's true;
4. Her ____ is charming too;
5. But one could ____ ere she's through!

Expressing Your Ideas

Writing Choices

Writer's Notebook Update Try using the word *liquefaction* in a sentence of your own and continue to add unusual or interesting words to your notebook.

To Her Eager Lover Suppose you are the "coy mistress" that the speaker addresses in Marvell's poem. (Or, you might be a "coy mister.") Write a **reply** to the speaker. Do you buy his "seize the day" argument, or not? If you wish, write your reply in verse, using Marvell's poem as a model.

Seize the What? Is *carpe diem* a sensible motto for today's world? Write a brief **essay** exploring the advantages and disadvantages of living for the now. You might include examples of people who have lived both ways. Conclude by telling how you would prefer to live and why.

Other Options

Style Guide In England of the 1600s, dress varied according to one's social class or religious leanings. Research the styles of clothing worn by women, men, royalty, commoners, and Puritans and present your findings to the class in the form of an **illustrated talk.** You might display photocopies, colored drawings, or fashion dolls, or else you might use a multimedia computer program that allows you to include text, illustrations, and sound effects.

Time and Time Again Design and present an illustrated **timeline** that helps clarify the turbulent social and political events in England from the death of Elizabeth I in 1603 to the restoration of the monarchy in 1660. Do some additional research to find out what other people and events you might add. (See Up Close and Personal on page 231 for a partial list of people of the period.)

Musical Notes Work with a partner to prepare a series of short presentations on composers through the ages. Henry Purcell (1659–1695) wrote over 600 musical works, including anthems, works for royal occasions, and one opera, *Dido and Aeneas.* Find a short account of his life and recordings of some of his work and prepare and give a **musical lecture** on this famous English composer.

OTHER OPTIONS
Style Guide

Ask students to collect and display newspaper or magazine photos illustrating whether or how dress today varies according to one's social class or religious leanings.

Time and Time Again

Ask students to create time lines of social and political events during their own lifetimes by interviewing family members and reviewing information sources from their year of birth to the present. How is their motto for living or philosophy for living influenced by the times and events of their lifetime?

Musical Notes

Play background music recorded by various English composers during class for several days. Invite interested students to bring their suggestions and share what they know.

The Meaning of Life

No Man is an Island

Science Connection

No man...nor woman, nor child...is an island. David proved that physical isolation from the world does not have to mean a life of solitude and loneliness. Although he lived his short twelve years in a plastic bubble and never felt the direct touch of a hand, David was strongly connected to his family and friends.

THE BUBBLE BOY

by Carol Ann with Kent Demaret

In September 1971 a Texas baby, identified only as David, was born in Houston with a rare disorder: severe combined immunodeficiency (SCID). This left him with no defense against germs and bacteria. Because his older brother, also named David, had died of the same affliction a year before at seven months, doctors decided from the moment of the new boy's birth to isolate him in a sterile plastic bubble. Their hope was that, in time, David might develop his own immune system or that a cure would be found for SCID, a condition that affects 200 U.S. babies annually. In the following . . . David's mother, Carol Ann (the family withholds its surname), tells of raising her son in his sterile world. . . .

Love but don't touch. That was the rule for the dozen years of David Phillip's life. He spent 12 years in plastic bubbles, isolated from germs or bacteria. Isolated, too, from any human touch or kiss. But never isolated from love, and he knew that. . . . We wanted David to live as normally as possible, to marvel at whatever part of the world he could reach but never to consider himself a curiosity. . . .

David . . . was born at 7 A.M. on September 21, 1971, but not before extraordinary precautions had been taken for his birth . . . When the doctor lifted my tiny, just-born son in his double-gloved hands, . . . he was placed in a plastic isolator bubble. . . . It was three days before I got to see David. When I got to the door of his room I was overwhelmed by the apparatus. I guess I was expecting something smaller, like the bassinet-size isolators used for premature babies. Instead there was the isolator bubble for David, and another for his supplies. Large, floppy black gloves were attached to the sides of the bubbles. Hoses were pumping in filtered air and there was the hum of the motors. I never forgot that moment, and in later years it helped me in dealing with visitors to our home who were startled at the sight of David's equipment. The first two months of his life were spent in the hospital, and the fact that we got to take him home at all was a wonderful surprise. His life-support systems seemed so formidable and there were always so many people hovering over him that realistically we didn't think he would ever leave the hospital. . .

ALONE

Five-year-old David can only be an observer from his plastic bubble at Texas Children's Hospital. David's family and the medical staff hoped that David would either develop a normal immune system as he matured or that a cure would be discovered for his deadly disease.

Interdisciplinary Study

Theme Link

David's life was short, but a sense of his own limits may have made his appreciation for living greater.

Curricular Connection: Science

Discuss the role of science (or medicine) in society. Without extreme measures, David would have died as a baby. Ask students if they feel there are any instances in which medicine should intervene less, or if lives should always be saved.

Interdisciplinary Activity Ideas

- If possible arrange for students to visit a hospital pediatric wing. Back in the classroom, discuss whether these children were much different from ones who are well. What did the children enjoy? How did they talk about themselves? What did students learn from meeting them?
- Students might be interested in watching and discussing a videotape of the made-for-television movie *The Boy in the Plastic Bubble* (1977).The film stars John Travolta, Glynnis O'Connor, and Ralph Bellamy.

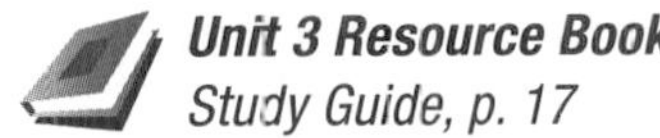

Unit 3 Resource Book
Study Guide, p. 17

BUILDING ENGLISH PROFICIENCY

Making Real-Life Connections

Perhaps students did not know about "David" before now, but they well may identify with feelings of being set apart or isolated. Invite students to explore these thoughts in greater detail.

1. Ask volunteers to improvise the following scenes:

- a neighbor comes home after having suffered a disabling accident
- a new student joins the cast of a school play late into the rehearsal process, after the star has quit

2. Afterward, discuss how being isolated or out of touch has guided characters' words and/or actions. Ask: Why might we isolate those who are "different"? How can we change that sort of behavior?

3. Encourage students to jot down their thoughts and to refer to them as they read "Case Studies from *One to One*."

Research Topics

- disorders of the immune system
- the use of bone marrow transplants in medicine
- the role of the lymph system in defense against illness
- findings on how mood affects healing

Responding

1. Possible Responses Students may point out that David's mother managed to hold and cuddle her baby with gloves even though she could not touch him directly. They allowed him to develop emotionally, and encouraged him to be as independent as possible.

2. Possible Responses Some students may feel they would be much more discouraged by the situation than David was. Others may feel they would try to be as normal and independent as possible. They might also feel angry and frustrated. Sharing feelings, keeping a sense of humor, and encouraging visits might keep one linked to one's loved ones.

REACHING OUT

In the first glorious days David spent at home . . . I really began to feel the excitement of caring for David by myself. He slept on ultrasoft sheepskin, and I could cradle him with the gloves at feeding time and sometimes I kissed him through the plastic. If I held him long enough I could feel the warmth of his skin, and I was certain that he could feel mine. I liked to position him so he could feel my heartbeat; I had read someplace that that was important to a newborn. Often he would nap in my arms as I held him with the gloves. . .

In spite of his isolation David seemed to go through all the normal stages other children did. There was a period when he got very sassy with me and . . . he . . . also went through a tantrum stage. Outbursts were understandable because it bothered him that he had so little control over his life. Someone would have to turn on the TV set for him, or change the channel or turn off the light. He was independent minded and later improvised ways to help himself. Reaching into the gloves on the side of the bubble, he would manipulate a stick about five feet long to turn lights on and off and open and shut doors. . .

There was no one dramatic moment when David learned that he had an immune deficiency. I'm sure it was more of an evolving understanding for him, with much of the awareness coming during his frequent stays in the hospital. He was told, however, that his older brother had died of the same disorder.

All his life he . . . tried to keep us from being gloomy. . . I remember thinking I couldn't live without him, that if he died, I would too. But I didn't feel that way at the end. I think he did something to me. I don't know what. In some ways I could never understand my little boy—his courage, and how he took it all so gracefully all those years. If he had the courage to die as he did, how could I not have the courage to go on living?

David was able to spend an occasional hour outside in his NASA– designed space suit. Because his time outdoors was so limited, David noticed and appreciated things that most people miss or take for granted. One day, after looking at leaves, David commented, "Mom, did you notice that they are one color on one side and another color on the other side?"

David spent most of his life in the hospital, encased in plastic bubbles to protect him from bacteria and viruses. David was one of about two hundred children who are born every year with severe combined immunodeficiency (SCID). Since doctors are now able to treat the disease successfully with bone marrow transplants, David's bubble is a thing of the past.

Responding

1. A baby can be warm, well–fed, and rested, but without sufficient touching cannot thrive. Since David could not be touched directly, what kind of nurturing did he receive from his parents and the hospital personnel that insured his normal psychological development?

2. You saw how David was able to cope with his disability and stay connected to family and friends. How would you manage in David's situation? What would you do to keep linked to loved ones?

MINI-LESSON: VOCABULARY

Unabridged Dictionaries

Teach Some words used in seventeenth- and eighteenth-century writing are no longer much in use but must be understood in order to interpret the literature. Tell students that most of these words are still in dictionaries but that they are likely to be in unabridged dictionaries. An unabridged dictionary is not a shortened or condensed dictionary such as a pocket or desk dictionary but a large work containing thousands of words.

Activity Idea Have students answer the following questions with the use of an unabridged dictionary:

- What is the meaning of *ere?*
- Does the word *didst* have a usage label? If so, what does that label mean?
- What is the present tense of *durst?*
- What is the Middle or Old English spelling of *thence?*

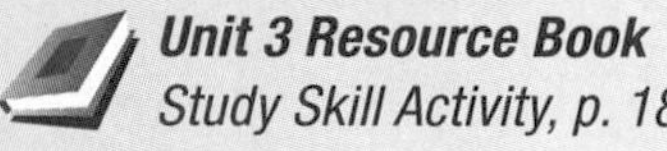

Unit 3 Resource Book
Study Skill Activity, p. 18

INTERDISCIPLINARY STUDY

Humanities Connection

John Donne's famous words in "Meditation 17" have resounded down through the years and, if possible, mean more today than ever before. In literature, in music, in art, in world events and in our daily lives, the message comes to us over and over—we are responsible for each other.

CASE STUDIES FROM *ONE TO ONE*
by George L. Beiswinger

The following case studies are from the files of the Big Brother/ Big Sister organization. This organization pairs children in need of guidance with adult volunteers from the community.

COMING TOGETHER

KATHY wanted to expose Anita (9 years old) to an environment that was quite different from the only one she had known. Kathy showed Anita how to wash and style her hair and care for her skin. Together, they worked on a new dress for Anita. Kathy chose the pattern, and Anita selected the material—possibly the first meaningful decision that she had ever made. After several months, and hours of practicing good table manners at Kathy's, the pair went to a nice restaurant. Anita wore her new dress.

Anita is beginning to understand that she need not accept what fate hands her. She has choices, and she is learning that desired goals can be attained through planning and self-discipline.

FRED never learned to assume responsibilities that he was quite capable of handling. Instead, he had developed a whining, complaining personality, often using his handicap as an excuse for lack of accomplishment.

His mother referred him to Big Brothers / Big Sisters. He was matched with Robert, who was disabled as a result of infantile paralysis and had to wear leg braces. Needless to say, Robert gave Fred little sympathy, and the latter quickly learned not to expect any. Instead, Robert focused attention on the many things that Fred could do. Fred learned responsibility and concern for others when he and Robert participated in fund-raising campaigns for the BB/BS agency, as well as for another social-service organization.

BOB attempted to build Mike's self-esteem by pointing out his good attributes. Mike lived in a neighborhood where there were many Hispanics, from whom he had picked up a fair knowledge of Spanish. Bob, too, spoke Spanish, and he sought to capitalize on this coincidence by helping Mike improve this skill through further study. They even visited a Spanish art exhibit. Mike was also encouraged to participate in organized sports. His pride knew no bounds when he won a bowling trophy. Mike learned to ice-skate at a local sports arena. These physical activities provided an excellent, socially acceptable outlet for his former, negatively-channeled aggression, and his new language skills gave a wondrous boost to his self-esteem. These gains were reflected in his relations with others. His grades improved. As he once helped, Bob now hopes to obtain scholarship aid for Mike.

Theme Link

Since we are all bound together on this planet, connecting with others often gives life more meaning.

Curricular Connection: Humanities

Use the examples in this interdisciplinary study to explore individuals' responsibility to society. Discuss with students things they may have done, or plan to do, to contribute to social causes or their communities.

MULTICULTURAL NOTE

Growing up can be tough. The children in these case studies were helped by having role models. Some cultures have rituals that move a person from childhood to adulthood. The aboriginal people of Australia have a rite for adolescents called a *walkabout*. It is a long walk on foot, all alone in the desert, with very few provisions. During a walkabout, a person has visions and becomes wiser, and returns to the community with a new, adult status.

BUILDING ENGLISH PROFICIENCY

Making Personal Connections

In all three accounts on page 241, young people are helped by focusing on their strengths. Invite students to do the same by creating a personal t-chart. In the left-hand column, have them list, realistically, some things at which they know that they do not excel. In the right-hand column, have them list abilities and strengths. Allow for optional, voluntary sharing.

I Cannot . . .	But I can . . .
do some kinds of math well	tell a story so that everyone wants to listen help my friends figure out their problems

Terms to Know

gondolier (gon dl ir′) person who rows or poles a gondola, a flat-bottomed boat.

Chinese water torture a torture method in which single drops of water land on the forehead of a person who is forcibly restrained.

Tierra del Fuegan person from Tierra del Fuego (tyer′ə del fwā′gō), "land of fire" in Spanish, islands at the southern tip of South America.

catechise (kat′ə kīz) to question closely.

Research Topics

- changes in German society since the opening of the Berlin Wall
- the history of the Make a Wish Foundation
- the history of the Big Brother/Big Sister organization
- the theme of human connection in the plays of John Guare

Geographical Note

Berlin, the capital of Germany, is in the northeastern part of Germany, about 50 miles from the border of Poland, and 120 miles from the Baltic Sea. After World War II, Germany was occupied by the allied powers for four years. During this time, East Germany was in the Russian zone.

FROM **SIX DEGREES OF SEPARATION**
by John Guare

I read somewhere that everybody on this planet is separated by only six other people. Six degrees of separation. Between us and everybody else on this planet. The president of the United States. A gondolier in Venice. Fill in the names. I find that A] tremendously comforting that we're so close and B] like Chinese water torture that we're so close. Because you have to find the right six people to make the connection. It's not just big names. It's anyone. A native in a rain forest. A Tierra del Fuegan. An Eskimo. I am bound to everyone on this planet by a trail of six people. It's a profound thought. . . . How every person is a new door, opening up into other worlds. Six degrees of separation between me and everyone else on this planet. But to find the right six people. . . .

In 1948, three years after the end of the second world war, East and West Berlin established separate governments. East Germany built a concrete and barbed wire wall in 1961 dividing the city and making it almost impossible for citizens to travel between the two sections. Many who tried were shot. The wall was finally opened in 1989 after massive protests by East Germans demanding more freedom.

S E P A R

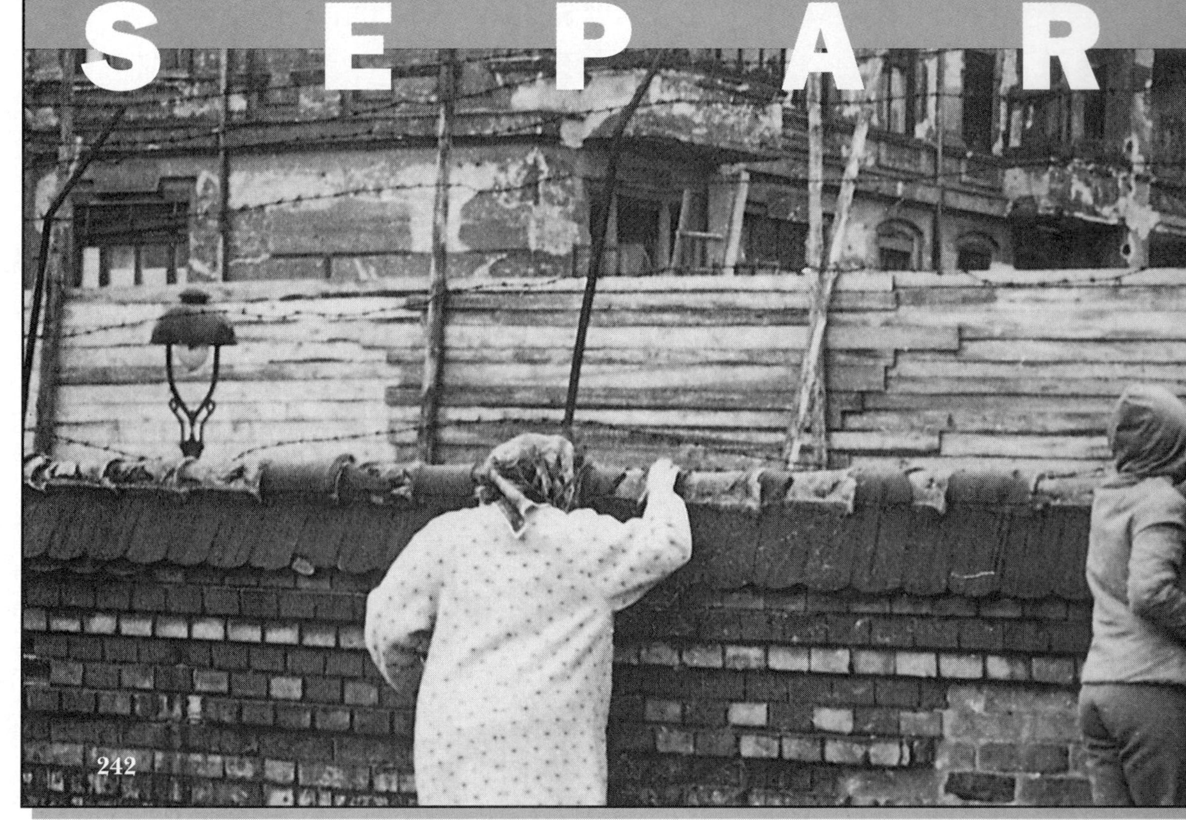

MINI-LESSON: VISUAL LITERACY

Use Media as a Means of Expression

The photo on pages 242–243 expresses the sense of separation created by the Berlin Wall. The people with their backs to the camera, the woman alone to the left of the others, and all the lines cutting horizontally accentuate the division.

Activity Idea Students can break up into groups and collaborate on expressing themes visually. They may use photography or video to express one of the following themes:

- separation between people
- science interacting with nature
- mortality and faith
- people helping people
- deception

Students may divide responsibilities on the project: some may perform in the videos or appear in photos, some may be camera operators, others will be in charge of lighting and scheduling.

FROM THE TASK
by William Cowper

'Twere well, says one sage erudite, profound,
Terribly arched and aquiline his nose,
And overbuilt with most impending brows,
'Twere well could you permit the world to live
As the world pleases. What's the world to you?
Much. I was born of woman, and drew milk
As sweet as charity from human breasts.
I think, articulate, I laugh and weep
And exercise all functions of a man.
How then should I and any man that lives
Be strangers to each other? Pierce my vein,
Take of the crimson stream meandering there,
And catechise it well. Apply your glass,
Search it, and prove now if it be not blood
Congenial with thine own. And if it be,
What edge of subtlety canst thou suppose
Keen enough, wise and skilful as thou art,
To cut the link of brotherhood, by which
One common Maker bound me to the kind. . . .

FROM MENDING WALL
by Robert Frost

Before I built a wall I'd ask to know
What I was walling in or walling out,
And to whom I was like to give offense.
Something there is that doesn't love a wall,
That wants it down. . . .

ATION

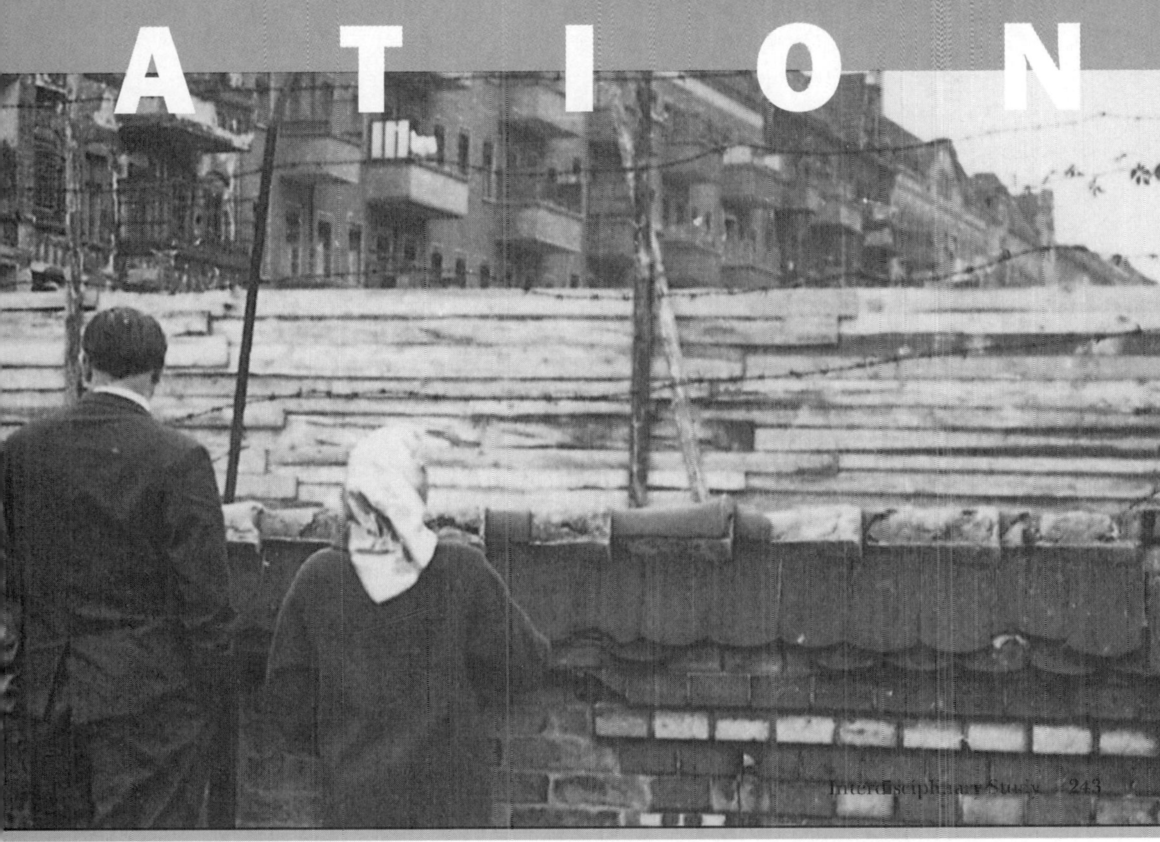

Interdisciplinary Activity Ideas

- Using magazines and newspapers as sources, students can divide into groups and make collages of pictures that say something about connection and separation. Suggest they also cut out words that relate to these themes, such as "alone," "love," "community."
- In small groups, students can look at the school community and decide where they see separations: for example, divisions between staff and faculty, male and female students, athletically and artistically inclined students. Students can spend a "coming together day" trying to address and bridge these separations.
- Students can view a video of the film *Six Degrees of Separation.* Afterwards, they can discuss how characters perpetuate or try to overcome separation.

BUILDING ENGLISH PROFICIENCY

Making Cultural Connections

Use one or more of the following activities to expand upon the international implications of this feature.

Activity Ideas

- Ask: What walls do we put up between nations, races, or cultures? Invite students to respond through small-group discussion or panel discussion, through sharing of personal experience, or through artwork.
- Review Guare's comment from *Six Degrees of Separation* that "you have to find the right six people to make the connection" and then review the people whom he names. Ask: If you could choose six people from anywhere on earth to be your "connection," whom would you choose? Why?
- Ask: What interests and dreams do you think unite people, no matter who they are or where they live? Invite discussion.

Additional Background

"We Are the World" was recorded by a group of popular musicians in 1984 and was produced by Quincy Jones as a fund raising effort for USA for Africa, a group formed to combat famine in Ethiopia.

Responding

1. Possible Responses Students might say they can share their knowledge with others, contribute time or money towards helping someone, or create art and music to make life more rewarding.

2. Possible Responses Students may start with their friends or families, move on to teachers and adults in the community, people in local government or in the arts, or a penpal far away.

3. Possible Responses Students may point out that since we are all parts of a whole, by saving the lives of others, we save our own. They may also point out that giving to others brings meaning to one's life.

WE ARE THE WORLD

WORDS AND MUSIC BY MICHAEL JACKSON AND LIONEL RICHIE

There comes a time when we heed a certain call
When the world must come together as one
There are people dying
And it's time to lend a hand to life
The greatest gift of all

We can't go on pretending day by day
That someone, somewhere will soon make a change
We are all a part of God's great big family
And the truth, you know,
Love is all we need

CHORUS:
We are the world, we are the children
We are the ones who make a brighter day
So let's start giving
There's a choice we're making
We're saving our own lives
It's true and we'll make a better day
Just you and me

Send them your heart so they'll know that someone cares
And their lives will be stronger and free
As God has shown us by turning stones to bread
So we all must lend a helping hand

(REPEAT CHORUS)

When you're down and out, there seems no hope at all
But if you just believe there's no way we can fall
Let us realize that a change can only come
When we stand together as one

Responding

1. What do you have to offer another person to help him or her cope with the world?
2. Think of a person–any person. What other people connect you?
3. "There's a choice we're making," go to the words of the song, "We're saving our own lives." In what sense is this true?

MINI LESSON: TECHNOLOGY

On-line Communication

There are more ways to communicate with other people now than ever before in history. One of the most recent developments is on-line communication with computers. Information can be passed in moments between computers via phone lines. Many different companies provide services that enable this communication.

Apply If on-line service is available at your school or local library, you or a librarian can demonstrate to students how people communicate on the Internet. You may want to explore the "rooms" in which people with special interests "talk" to each other.

Activity Idea Students can divide into small groups and work together to design the perfect on-line service. How would they structure it? What kinds of graphics would they include to make it easy to use? For which different special interests would they provide forums?

Writing Workshop

Making the Abstract Concrete

Assignment You've read writing in which the authors deal with big, abstract ideas, such as brotherhood and the nature of time, in remarkably specific, down-to-earth ways. Now see how well you can do the same thing.

WRITER'S BLUEPRINT

Product A collage, summary, and speech
Purpose To illustrate an abstract idea
Audience An assembly of your classmates
Specs As the creator of a successful collage and speech, you should:

- ❑ Choose an abstract idea drawn from the literature, such as brotherhood, living fully in the moment, true love, or time and change.
- ❑ Assemble a collage of fifteen or more images and quotations that illustrate your topic. For example, to illustrate brotherhood, you might use a photo of a family picnic and the John Donne quote "No man is an island." Look for images in magazines and newspapers, or sketch them yourself. For quotations, consider sources such as poems, song lyrics, bumper stickers, ads, and journal entries.
- ❑ Write a summary in which you list the five most significant elements in your collage and briefly give your thoughts on how each element illustrates your topic.
- ❑ Make note cards from your summary for a speech about your topic, using your collage as a graphic aid.
- ❑ Begin your speech by introducing your topic and collage. Then deal with each of the five most significant elements in turn. Conclude by summarizing your thoughts on the topic.
- ❑ Follow the rules of grammar, usage, mechanics, and spelling. Take special care not to confuse adjectives and adverbs.

Writing Workshop

WRITER'S BLUEPRINT

Specs

The Specs in the Writer's Blueprint address these writing and thinking skills:

- defining a concept
- using specific details
- integrating visuals and the written and spoken word
- summarizing
- keeping to the main idea
- clarifying your intentions
- using adjectives and adverbs correctly

These Specs serve as your lesson objectives, and they form the basis for the **Assessment Criteria Specs** for a superior paper, which appear on the final TE page for this lesson. You might want to read through the Assessment Criteria Specs with students when you begin the lesson.

Linking Literature to Writing

Look back at the literature in this part of the unit and have students pick out abstract concepts that they feel the writers are dealing with. Try to come up with a list of a dozen or so concepts, which students may use to help them get started in the "Review the literature" activity that follows.

WRITING WORKSHOP OVERVIEW

Product
Expository Writing: A collage, summary, and speech

Prewriting
Review the literature—Create your collage—Rate the elements—Plan your written summary
Unit 3 Resource Book
Prewriting Worksheets pp. 19–20

Drafting
Before you draft—As you draft
Transparency Collection
Student Models for Writing Workshop 7, 8

Revising
Ask a partner—Strategy: Making Your Intentions Clear
Unit 3 Resource Book
Revising Worksheet p. 21

Editing
Ask a partner—Strategy: Using Adjectives and Adverbs Correctly
Unit 3 Resource Book
Grammar Worksheet p. 22
Grammar Check Test p. 23

Presenting
Prepare a speech

Looking Back
Self-evaluate—Reflect—For Your Working Portfolio
Unit 3 Resource Book
Assessment Worksheet p. 24
Transparency Collection
Fine Art Transparency 4

STEP 1 PREWRITING

Review the literature

Remind students that the different members of their group may interpret the abstract ideas found in the selections differently and the listening to these differing interpretations may give them new insights.

Create your collage

Encourage students to be creative in choosing their materials. Have them look for unique objects to combine with images and text. For additional support, see the worksheet referenced below.

Unit 3 Resource Book
Prewriting Worksheet, p. 19

Rate the elements

Students may want to rank order all the elements they have chosen in order to choose the five. For additional support, see the worksheet referenced below.

Plan your written summary

Students might want to organize the elements into groups of visuals and text.

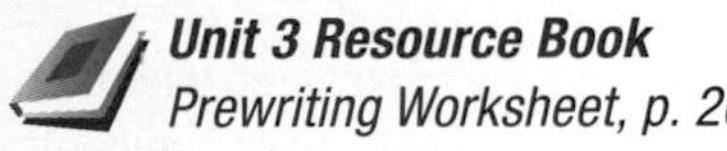

Unit 3 Resource Book
Prewriting Worksheet, p. 20

Connections to
Writer's Notebook

For selection-related prompts, refer to Writer's Notebook.

Connections to
Writer's Resource

For additional writing prompts, refer to Writer's Resource.

STEP 2 DRAFTING

Before you draft

Some students may want to tape these elements to a facing wall or bulletin board.

STEP 1 PREWRITING

LITERARY SOURCE
"If they be two, they are two so/As stiff twin compasses are two;/Thy soul the fixed foot, makes no show/To move, but doth, if the other do."
from "A Valediction: Forbidding Mourning" by John Donne

Review the literature. In a small group, look back at the selections for the abstract ideas the writers deal with and the images they use to bring those ideas to life. Use a chart like the one shown. When you finish, look your chart over and select the topic you'll be using.

Topics	Images/Words	My Reactions
True love	lovers compared to twin compasses ("A Valediction: Forbidding Mourning")	love so strong that you can overcome differences and see eye-to-eye

Create your collage. Follow these steps:

- Gather your materials. Make sketches of your own. Find pictures from magazines and newspapers. Look for song lyrics, bumper stickers, lines of poetry, single words—whatever works for you. Use your chart as a guide.
- Do a rough diagram of where you plan to place each element.
- Assemble the elements on paper, poster board, a cardboard box, or whatever medium seems to work best for you.

OR . . .
Get together with a partner or small group of classmates who've chosen the same topic and brainstorm ideas.

Rate the elements in your collage. Look back at what you've created and choose the five elements you think are most significant. Then rank those five in order of significance, from least (1) to most (5).

Plan your written summary by making a chart for your five chosen elements like the one you made in "Review the literature." This will serve as your writing plan.

STEP 2 DRAFTING

Before you draft your summary, be sure you have your writing plan and collage laid out in front of you.

As you draft, follow your writing plan, moving from the least significant element to the most significant. For your most significant element, be sure to tell why it's most significant. You might draft your summary as a numbered list or as a series of paragraphs, with one paragraph per element.

MINI-LESSON: WRITING STYLE

Making Your Intentions Clear

Teach Impress upon students that to make your intentions clear through your writing, you must guide your audience by making connections between ideas and examples, by building bridges between and among them.

Activity Idea Have students respond to the following paragraph, and discuss ways the author could fill in any gaps between the examples and the intended meanings they illustrate.

Each of these images speaks to the nature of time in its own way. A river flows through a canyon today as it did a thousand years ago. A newborn baby reaches for her father. A student looks anxiously at the clock on the school wall. These images all communicate to us, even though they are very different. They are all about time.

Apply As students revise, have them look for gaps in their own writing that need to be bridged for the reader.

STEP 3 REVISING

Ask a partner to comment on your draft before you revise it. Use this checklist as a guide.

✔ Have I chosen an abstract idea as my topic?

✔ Have I summarized the significance of five elements from my collage?

✔ Do all the elements relate clearly to the topic?

Revising Strategy

Making Your Intentions Clear

In writing, knowing what you want to say is only half the battle. The other half is putting your thoughts down so they're as clear to the reader as they are to you. For example, you may have a crystal-clear picture of exactly how the elements in your collage illustrate your topic, but you still have to communicate this vision. You have to make your intentions clear.

In the student model below, the writer hasn't quite made it clear, in her initial draft, exactly what an image of a starry night sky has to do with her topic: Time. Notice how she's revised to make her intentions clearer.

> 3. Image of a starry night sky: Time slips away. Stars are like memories.
>
> We forget far more of our past than we remember. So many moments are lost to us forever, like the stretches of empty space between the stars. Time is loss as well as opportunity. . . .

STUDENT MODEL

STEP 4 EDITING

Ask a partner to review your revised draft before you edit. When you edit, look for errors in grammar, usage, spelling, and mechanics. Look over each sentence to make sure you have not confused adjectives and adverbs.

BUILDING ENGLISH PROFICIENCY

Organizing Multimedia Presentations

Multimedia presentations can benefit from some of the same organizational strategies that students use in writing. Writing strategies such as the following can help students make their collages more effective.

- Emphasis: Have students place the most important images in their collages at a focal point, such as the center. They also may make these images larger.
- Unity: Ask students to consider whether all their collage items contribute to a central theme. (For example, would they put a picture of hearts and flowers with the lyrics "Love is a battlefield"?)

The Student Models

Review the **transparencies** referenced below with students before they draft. These questions will help:

1. Read model 7 and make note cards for a speech, as if you were the writer.

2. Which elements does the writer of model 8 deal with? How well do these elements illustrate the topic?

Transparency Collection
Student Models for Writing Workshop 7, 8

STEP 3 REVISING

Ask a partner (Peer assessment)

Have students write a list of the connections they see between the different elements in their peer's project. Through this activity the writer can see if he or she is pulling all of the disparate parts together to make a meaningful whole.

Revising Strategy: Making Your Intentions Clear

To help them focus, have students list the exact meanings they want to communicate.

For additional support, see the mini-lesson at the bottom of page 246 and the worksheet referenced below.

Unit 3 Resource Book
Revising Worksheet, p. 21

Connections to **Writer's Resource**

Refer to the Grammar, Usage, and Mechanics Handbook on Writer's Resource.

STEP 4 EDITING

Ask a partner (Peer assessment)

If students are unsure of any mechanics in their peer's paper, have them talk through their questions with other students.

Editing Strategy: Using Adjectives and Adverbs Correctly

Before students read the editing strategy, have them discuss the functions of adjectives and adverbs and how to determine which is appropriate to use when.

For additional support, see the worksheets referenced below.

Unit 3 Resource Book
Grammar Worksheet, p. 22
Grammar Check Test, p. 23

Connections to
Writer's Resource

Refer to the Grammar, Usage, and Mechanics Handbook on Writer's Resource.

STEP 5 PRESENTING

Prepare a speech

Have students discuss strategies they found effective as they prepared and presented their speeches.

STEP 6 LOOKING BACK

Self-evaluate

The *Assessment Criteria Specs* at the bottom of this page are for a superior paper. You might want to post these in the classroom. Students can then evaluate themselves based on these criteria. For a complete scoring rubric, use the *Assessment Worksheet* referenced below.

Unit 3 Resource Book
Assessment Worksheet, p. 24

Reflect

After students finish responding to the first question, you might want them to hold a discussion about learning styles based on their responses.

To further explore the theme, use the Fine Art Transparency referenced below.

Transparency Collection
Fine Art Writing Prompt 4

Editing Strategy

FOR REFERENCE
See the Language and Grammar Handbook for more information about adjectives and adverbs.

Using Adjectives and Adverbs Correctly

Good, real, and *strong* are adjectives that modify nouns or pronouns, not verbs. *Well*, *really*, and *strongly* are adverbs. Use them to modify verbs, adjectives, or other adverbs.

Don't write:	I think this image works *real good*.
Write:	I think this image works *really well*.
Don't write:	I feel *strong* about this image.
Write:	I feel *strongly* about this image.

Take care to avoid confusing adjectives and adverbs in your writing.

STEP 5 PRESENTING

Prepare a speech based on your collage and summary. Make note cards for each of your five elements, based on what you wrote in your summary. See the Beyond Print article that follows this lesson for information on delivering a speech.

STEP 6 LOOKING BACK

Self-evaluate. Look back at the Writer's Blueprint and give your paper a score for each item, from 6 (superior) to 1 (inadequate).

Reflect. Respond to these questions in writing.

✔ In this assignment you worked in three different modes: visual, written, and spoken. Which one did you like best? Why?

✔ Did finding concrete images to illustrate an abstract concept make that concept more meaningful to you? Why or why not?

For Your Working Portfolio Add your collage, note cards, and reflection responses to your working portfolio.

ASSESSMENT CRITERIA SPECS

Here are the criteria for a superior paper. A full six-level rubric for this paper appears on the Assessment Worksheet referenced below.

6 Superior The writer of a 6 paper impressively meets these criteria:

- Makes an abstract concept specific and concrete through a combination of visuals and the written and spoken word.
- Presents the concept visually through a collage of images and quotations.
- Presents the concept verbally through a written summary that highlights five key elements of the collage, and through a speech based on the summary.
- Makes the creator's intentions clear to the audience.
- Makes few, if any, mistakes in grammar, usage, mechanics, and spelling. Uses adjectives and adverbs correctly.

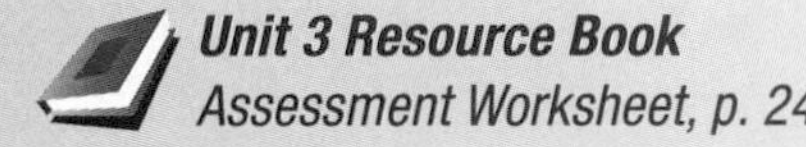

Unit 3 Resource Book
Assessment Worksheet, p. 24

Beyond Print

Talking to an Audience

Speaking before an audience worries many people, but it needn't; after all, you talk to other people every day. Here are some pointers on how to make your audience pay attention to what you have to say.

Rehearse. You're not making a fool of yourself. Successful speakers do rehearse—by themselves, out loud, and perhaps several times over. Not only do you become more familiar with your material, but you can also try out different gestures and vocal emphasis.

Get organized. If you spend the first minute or so in front of an audience shuffling your notes, they may suspect that you aren't quite ready to talk to them. Get everything in order before you walk to the front. This includes any visuals you may use.

Maintain good posture. Good posture actually helps you project your voice better. Stand on both feet so that you are in balance when you want to gesture or move. If there is a desk or podium for your notes, you may grasp it—lightly—but don't lean your weight on it.

Make eye contact. Talk *to* your audience. Pick one person and direct a sentence or two right at her or him; then pick another, and so on.

Speak loudly and clearly. You don't have to shout, but your speech is worthless if your audience can't hear you. Speak in a normal voice, but try to project your voice to the back wall of the room.

Avoid meaningless vocalisms. Some people fill every pause with "Ummm" or "Uhhh" or other noises. You may not be able to avoid these altogether, but try. Silence is better.

Make simple, meaningful gestures. You may have seen speakers waving their arms all over the place. While making some gestures is preferable to standing stock still, keep them simple and natural.

Activity Option

Use these pointers when you deliver the speech you wrote in the Writing Workshop, "Making the Abstract Concrete."

Beyond Print

Teaching Objectives

- To effectively communicate with an audience
- To recognize and understand the essentials of good oral presentation
- To connect with the audience while focusing on fundamentals and not straying from the topic

Curricular Connection: Speaking Skills

Highlight the essentials of an effective oral presentation. Maintaining audience interaction and attention while not straying away from the key fundamentals of the topic is important to a good oral presentation.

Introduce

Students have probably listened to speeches on television, radio, or even to live presentations. As they are exposed to different presentation techniques, students should be able to highlight the essentials that make a speaker good or a presentation interesting.

Activity Options

Activity 1 Encourage students to select a topic of interest and present a speech to the class. They can videotape their presentation and watch it later to identify their strong and weak points.

Activity 2 Divide students into small groups of five or six and have them give an impromptu autobiography to the small group. After the presentations, suggestions could be offered from group members with respect to style and clarity.

ANOTHER APPROACH

Technique Development

Students can practice speaking in front of a mirror or on an empty stage. Alternatively they can also video or audiotape themselves speaking. They can play back the recording to different individuals and to themselves in order to examine and refine presentation skills.

HISTORICAL OVERVIEW

EXPLORING CONCEPTS

- Seventeenth-century England became embroiled in a bitter three-sided struggle among religious groups.
- British literature in the seventeenth century was influenced by the passionate religious climate of this time.

Research Activity Small groups of students might use library or on-line resources to investigate Milton's involvement with the Puritans or his battle with blindness. Then, as they read *Paradise Lost,* students can consider how the poem was influenced by Milton's own "fall from grace" and by his personal struggles.

Gustave Doré (1832–1883), although a French illustrator, was known in England for his illustrations for the Bible and his engravings of life in London. *The Last Judgment* by Fra Angelico (1387–1455), two details of which appear here, depicts both heaven and hell. Fra Angelico, an Italian, was a member of the Dominican Order. *The Garden of Eden* (detail) was painted by Jacob Bouttats, who flourished in the Netherlands about 1700.

Questions What does the artist imagine heaven to be like? the Garden of Eden? hell? *(Possible responses: Heaven is depicted as a calm, contemplative place; the Garden of Eden is shown as a paradise of plentiful animals who seem to live peacefully with each other; hell is depicted as a place of burning torment.)*

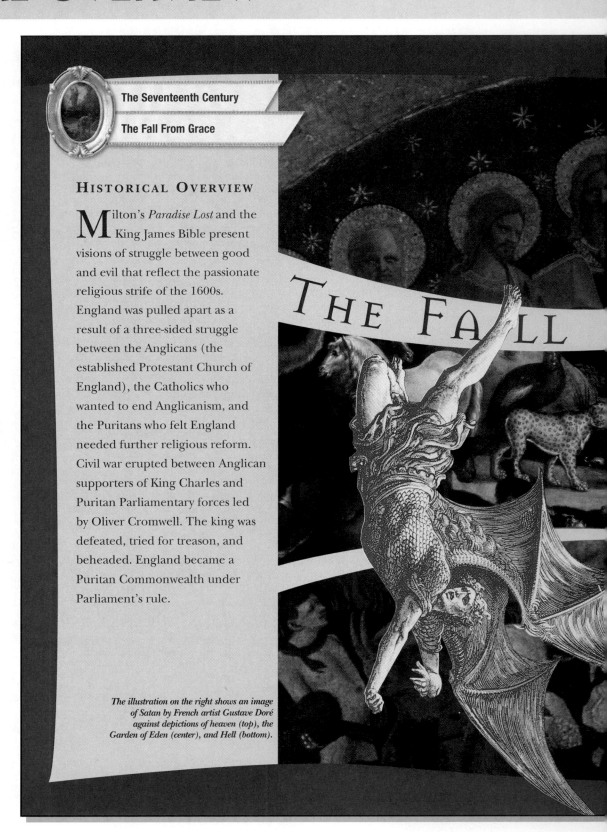

The Seventeenth Century

The Fall From Grace

HISTORICAL OVERVIEW

Milton's *Paradise Lost* and the King James Bible present visions of struggle between good and evil that reflect the passionate religious strife of the 1600s. England was pulled apart as a result of a three-sided struggle between the Anglicans (the established Protestant Church of England), the Catholics who wanted to end Anglicanism, and the Puritans who felt England needed further religious reform. Civil war erupted between Anglican supporters of King Charles and Puritan Parliamentary forces led by Oliver Cromwell. The king was defeated, tried for treason, and beheaded. England became a Puritan Commonwealth under Parliament's rule.

THE FALL

The illustration on the right shows an image of Satan by French artist Gustave Doré against depictions of heaven (top), the Garden of Eden (center), and Hell (bottom).

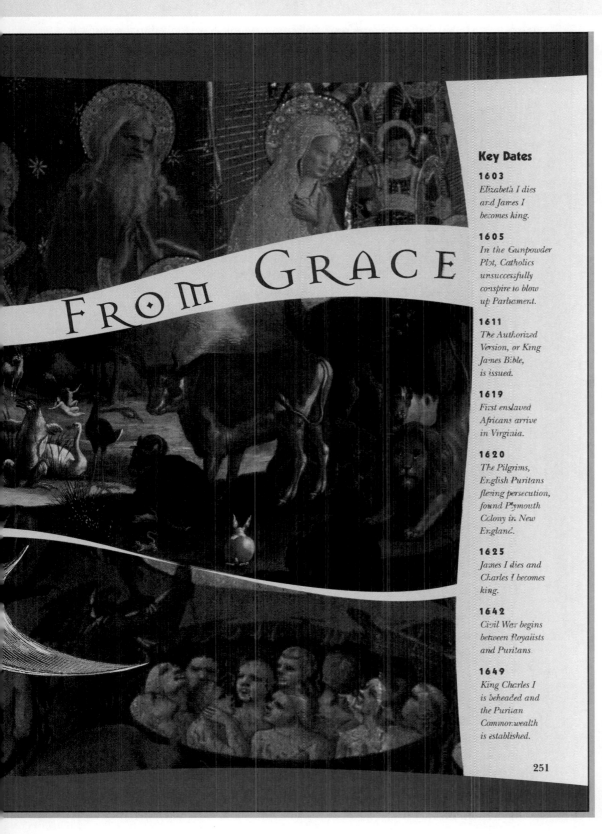

FROM GRACE

Key Dates

1603
Elizabeth I dies and James I becomes king.

1605
In the Gunpowder Plot, Catholics unsuccessfully conspire to blow up Parliament.

1611
The Authorized Version, or King James Bible, is issued.

1619
First enslaved Africans arrive in Virginia.

1620
The Pilgrims, English Puritans fleeing persecution, found Plymouth Colony in New England.

1625
James I dies and Charles I becomes king.

1642
Civil War begins between Royalists and Puritans.

1649
King Charles I is beheaded and the Puritan Commonwealth is established.

251

Key Dates

When Charles I (1600–1649) becomes king in 1625, he immediately offends his Protestant subjects by marrying the Catholic sister of Louis XIII of France, Henrietta Maria.

MATERIALS OF INTEREST

Books

- *The Bible As / In Literature* by James Ackerman and Thayer Warshaw, rev. ed. (Scott, Foresman, 1996).
- *British Writers*, Vol. II, article on John Milton by E. M. W. Tillyard (Scribner's, 1979).
- *The Great Rebellion, 1642–1660* by I. A. Roots (1968).

Multimedia

- *Paradise Lost* by John Milton [sound recording] 7 cassettes, unabridged (Blackstone Audio Books, 1994).
- Encarta [CD-ROM] reference work, John Milton article (Microsoft, 1996).
- America On-line Reference Desk—*Compton's Living Encyclopedia,* King James Bible article.
- On-line—*King James Bible.* **http://www.iadfw.net/webchap/kjvb/index.html**
- On-line—The English Server (a large and eclectic collection of humanities resources). **http://english-server.hss.cmu.edu** or **gopher://english-server.hss.cmu.edu**

Connections to **Custom Literature Database**

For further historical background, under **Background Articles,** see **Renaissance England 1500–1660**

Preview

The Fall from Grace

FOR ALL STUDENTS

Read the first paragraph on page 252 and discuss why so many stories arose around the theme of a fall from grace. Explain that in this context *grace* means the "love and favor of God."

To further explore the theme, use the transparency referenced below.

Transparency Collection
Fine Art Transparency 5

For At-Risk Students

Ask students to

- recall images of heaven and hell from movies, TV shows, or comic books
- recall characters and scenery from these depictions—St. Peter in heaven, for instance, or flames in hell

For Students Who Need Challenge

Suggest that students research William Tyndale and Miles Coverdale, whose work was used as a basis for the King James Bible.

For Social Learners

Suggest that a small group of students create a script based on this excerpt from *Paradise Lost.*

MULTICULTURAL CONNECTION

Students might compare the rather abstract images of the deity in these works with deities worshipped in other cultures with which they are familiar or that they have studied. For instance, how do they feel this God is different from Zeus or Apollo, early Egyptian deities, Norse gods and goddesses, and so on?

Part Two

The Fall from Grace

Since the beginnings of civilization, people have looked to the past with envy and regret for a "golden age" of simplicity and perfection, when everyone enjoyed God's grace, the favor and love of God. The stories of how people lost that favor and love—how they fell from grace—are many and varied.

Multicultural Connection **Communication** involves cultural uses of language that come down to us over time as well as new forms of language that are constantly evolving as cultures change over time. The language of Milton and the King James Bible has influenced for hundreds of years the way people communicate (and the way they think about religion). How do the styles of the following selections contribute to the meanings they communicate?

IDEAS THAT WORK

Motivating with Writing and Video Skits

Students write sonnets titled "On Having Reached the Age of Eighteen"; they reflect on their lives in high school and look into their future. For "On His Blindness," students write reflective essays on the parable of the talents (Matthew 25: 14-30); they speculate on whether they have invested their "talent," or "buried" abilities and potential.

For *Paradise Lost,* students write reflective essays that contemplate the function of evil in society, explain and rationalize the purposes of evil, and reflect on what the individual can learn from understanding how evil works. Students make video skits in groups, doing a part of *Paradise Lost,* reenacting 100 lines per group; they film the scenes and add music, transpose lines into modern English, and include modern references, allusions, and similes.

Diego Davalos
Jacumba, California

Before Reading

On His Having Arrived at the Age of Twenty-three
On His Blindness
from Paradise Lost by John Milton

John Milton
1608–1674

John Milton's father, a London notary, provided him with the best of educations: St. Paul's School, Christ College at Cambridge, six years of private study at his country house, and a year's tour of Europe. Returning home, Milton tutored and wrote poetry (he had mastered Greek, Latin, and Hebrew, as well as a number of modern European languages). A Puritan, he served as a secretary in the Commonwealth, the government declared after Charles I was executed for treason. He became totally blind in 1652. At the end of the Puritan regime, Milton was considered an enemy of the government; he was heavily fined and lost most of his property. At that time he began to write *Paradise Lost.*

Building Background

A Dream Come True For most of his lifetime, John Milton dreamed of writing an epic poem better than all others. His notebooks list the ninety-nine topics he considered; among them, Samson, King Arthur, and Macbeth. In 1660, ousted from government service, Milton finally began his grand poem, choosing as its setting the entire universe and as its theme mankind's fall from grace as told in the biblical story of the temptation of Adam and Eve. With his three teenage daughters serving as his secretaries, Milton dictated for hours each day. Finally in 1665, he completed the twelve books of what is still regarded as the finest epic poem in the English language.

Literary Focus

Symbol A **symbol** is something concrete, such as an object or an action, that signifies something abstract, such as an idea. The same object can symbolize different things to different people: a lily might symbolize beauty to one person but death to another. To determine whether an author is using a symbol, ask the following questions:

- Is a particular object or action stressed or repeated?
- Does a character think about something abstract whenever that object or action is mentioned? Do you, as a reader, do so?

Writer's Notebook

From Concrete to Abstract These objects are often used symbolically: sun, skull, lion, rose, flag, champagne bottle, diamond ring, black cat, light bulb, dark clouds. What abstract idea does each concrete **symbol** convey to you? Create a chart like the following and jot down a few words in response to each word or phrase. Compare your interpretations with those of your classmates. Continue the chart with symbols you find as you read the following selections.

Symbol	Abstract Idea	Symbol	Abstract Idea
sun	warmth, understanding	skull	death

Before Reading

Building Background

Ask students to imagine that their life's ambition, like Milton's, is to write an epic poem. What topics, either universal or contemporary, would they consider appropriate?

Literary Focus

Invite students to suggest possible symbols for the following ideas: youth, life, old age, justice, love, and time. *(Possible responses: youth—a flower; life—a river; old age—a gnarled tree; justice—a blindfolded woman holding a scale; love—a heart or a rose; time—a clock)*

Writer's Notebook

Invite students to compare the abstract ideas conveyed by these words. Which conveyed similar ideas to all students? Which conveyed a variety of ideas?

More About John Milton

Paradise Lost was Milton's only poem that sold well. With its publication, he was finally recognized as a poet, rather than the Puritan propagandist hated by many of his countrymen. Other works by the author include

- *Paradise Regained* (1671)
- *Samson Agonistes* (1671)

SUPPORT MATERIALS OVERVIEW

Unit 3 Resource Book
- Graphic Organizer, p. 25
- Study Guide, p. 26
- Vocabulary, p. 27
- Grammar, p. 28
- Alternate Check Test, p. 29
- Vocabulary Test, p. 30
- Selection Test, pp. 31–32

Building English Proficiency
- Selection Summaries
- Activities, p. 218

Reading, Writing & Grammar SkillBook
- Reading, pp. 65–66
- Writing, pp. 111–112

The World of Work
- Theologian, p. 9
- Activity, p. 10

Technology
- Audiotape
- Personal Journal Software
- Custom Literature Database: Additional selections by John Milton can be found on the database.
- Test Generator Software

During Reading

Selection Objectives

- to analyze John Milton's poetry
- to identify forms of poetry
- to recognize and analyze symbols

Unit 3 Resource Book
Graphic Organizer, p. 25
Study Guide, p. 26

Theme Link

Milton examines The Fall from Grace through Satan's expulsion from heaven.

Vocabulary Preview

transgress, sin against
restraint, limit; restriction
guile, deceit
vanquish, defeat
baleful, destructive
deluge, a heavy fall, as of rain
tempestuous, stormy; violent
desolation, sad loneliness
dire, dreadful
abject, miserable

Students can add the words and definitions to their Writer's Notebook.

1 Literary Focus
Symbolism

Question What symbols might Milton be using in these poems? *(In the first poem, spring symbolizes youth; in the second, light and dark refer to sight and Milton's blindness, but symbolize his talent, to which the "wide world" turns a blind eye.)*

2 Literary Element
Meter

Questions What is the meter of the poems? *(iambic pentameter)* Considering the meter and 14-line structure, what is the form? *(sonnet)* How do the first eight lines of "On His Having Arrived . . ." relate to the final six? *(The first eight present a problem, which the final six resolve.)*

On His Having Arrived at the Age of Twenty-Three

John Milton

1 How soon hath Time, the subtle thief of youth,
Stolen on his wing my three and twentieth year!
My hasting days fly on with full career,
But my late spring no bud or blossom showeth.
Perhaps my semblance might deceive the truth,
That I to manhood am arrived so near,
And inward ripeness doth much less appear,
That some more timely-happy spirits endueth.
Yet be it less more, or soon or slow,
It shall be still in strictest measure even
To that same lot, however mean or high,
Toward which Time leads me, and the will of Heaven;
All is, if I have grace to use it so,
As ever in my great Task-Master's eye.

3 with full career, at full speed.
5 semblance (sem′bləns), *n.* youthful appearance.
8 endue (en dü′), *v.* provide.
10 even, adequate; that is, his "inward ripeness," or inner readiness, will be up to whatever destiny Time and Heaven are leading him to.

On His Blindness

John Milton

When I consider how my light is spent,
Ere half my days, in this dark world and wide,
And that one talent which is death to hide
Lodged with me useless, though my soul more bent
To serve therewith my Maker, and present
My true account, lest He, returning, chide;
"Doth God exact day-labor, light denied!"
I fondly ask. But Patience, to prevent
That murmur, soon replies: "God doth not need
Either man's work or His own gifts; who best
Bear His mild yoke, they serve Him best. His state
Is kingly—thousands at His bidding speed
And post o'er land and ocean without rest;
2 They also serve who only stand and wait."

3 talent, the gift of writing. This is an allusion to Jesus's parable of the "unprofitable servant," condemned for burying his one talent, or coin, instead of investing it. (Matthew 25:15–30)
8 fondly, foolishly.

SELECTION SUMMARY

On His Having Arrived at the Age of Twenty-Three; On His Blindness; Paradise Lost

On His Having Arrived at the Age of Twenty-Three The narrator relates his concerns that time is passing, and he is wasting his talents.

On His Blindness The sonnet begins with the narrator's declaration of dismay and expression of sorrow at the loss of his sight; it resolves with acceptance of his state as God's will.

Paradise Lost In this excerpt from Book I of the epic poem, Satan falls from grace and prepares to do future battle with the forces of heaven.

*For summaries in other languages, see the **Building English Proficiency** book.*

Paradise Lost

John Milton

Opening with the ***invocation,*** *or call for poetic inspiration, and the posing of the question he will answer in the poem, Milton begins his epic* ***in medias res,*** *or "in the middle of things." The archangel Satan and "his horrid crew," having waged war against God in Heaven, have been plunged down into Hell where they roll in the "fiery gulf."*

Of man's first disobedience, and the fruit
Of that forbidden tree, whose mortal taste
Brought death into the world, and all our woe,
With loss of Eden, till one greater Man
Restore us, and regain the blissful seat,
3 Sing, heavenly Muse—that on the secret top
Of Oreb, or of Sinai, didst inspire

4 That shepherd who first taught the chosen seed
In the beginning how the heavens and earth
Rose out of Chaos; or if Sion hill
Delight thee more, and Siloa's brook that flowed
Fast by the oracle of God, I thence
Invoke thy aid to my adventurous song,
That with no middle flight intends to soar

6 Muse, In Greek myth nine Muses each watched over a different field of art or science and inspired its artists. Urania (yů rā′nē ə) was the muse of astronomy.
7–8 Oreb (ôr′eb) . . . **Sinai** (sī′nī) . . . **chosen seed.** Oreb and Sinai are two names for the peak in the Sinai peninsula of Egypt where Moses received the word of God to bring to the the Jewish people (the "chosen seed").
10 Chaos (kā′os), the infinite space in which formless matter was thought to have existed before God created the heavens and earth.
10–11 Sion (sī′ən) **hill** . . . **Siloa's** (sī lō′əz) **brook,** places near the temple in Jerusalem.

3 Reading/Thinking Skills
Find the Main Idea

Question In his invocation of the muse, of what subject does Milton ask the Muse to sing? *(Milton asks the Muse to tell of Adam and Eve's temptation by Satan in the Garden of Eden, where they ate the forbidden fruit and from which they were subsequently expelled.)*

4 Literary Element
Allusion

Question To whom does Milton allude when he writes of the shepherd inspired on Oreb and Sinai? *(He directly alludes to Moses, who spoke to God on Oreb and Sinai; he may indirectly allude to Jesus, to whom the title "shepherd" is more commonly applied.)*

EDITORIAL NOTE This excerpt has been shortened for length. For a more complete version of *Paradise Lost,* see the Custom Literature Database.

BUILDING ENGLISH PROFICIENCY

ESL LEP ELD SAE LD

Exploring Key Concepts

In "On His Having Arrived at the Age of Twenty-Three," young Milton—like many young people—wrestles with mixed emotions. Encourage students to consider those emotions.

1. Have small groups of students complete these sentences, based on the sonnet, and share their responses with the class:

- I feel angry because _____.
- I feel confused because _____.
- I feel hopeful because _____.

2. Invite students, working on their own, to complete these same statements so that they reflect students' thoughts about themselves.

3. Allow for optional, voluntary sharing. Encourage students to save their responses for use with the first of the Other Options on page 266.

Building English Proficiency
Activities, p. 218

5 Multicultural Note
Perspective on the Classics

This is one of many references in *Paradise Lost* to classical (ancient Greek and Roman) literature. The poem's form and style—that of an epic poem—is based on Homer's *Iliad* and Virgil's *Aeneid.* Milton's ambition, however, was to create a Christian epic; although the poem takes the form of a Greco-Roman epic, it is dominated by Christian ideals.

6 Reading/Thinking Skills
Find the Main Idea

Response Why did "our grand parents" (Adam and Eve) fall from grace? Why were they expelled from Eden?

7 Literary Focus
Symbolism

Questions What does the serpent symbolize? *(Satan, evil)* Why is the snake a standard symbol for Satan? *(In biblical Eden, Satan takes the form of a serpent; also, snakes may have been feared by homo sapiens from time immemorial.)*

8 Reading/Thinking Skills
Draw Conclusions

Responses The proud and hateful cannot bear for others to succeed; the envious and vengeful try to destroy the accomplishments of others.

---

5 Above the Aonian mount, while it pursues
Things unattempted yet in prose or rhyme.
And chiefly Thou, O Spirit, that dost prefer
Before all temples the upright heart and pure,
Instruct me, for Thou knowest; Thou from the first
Wast present, and, with mighty wings outspread,
Dove-like satest brooding on the vast abyss
And madest it pregnant: what in me is dark,
Illumine; what is low, raise and support—
That to the height of this great argument
I may assert eternal providence,
And justify the way of God to men.
    Say first, for Heaven hides nothing from thy view,
Nor the deep tract of Hell, say first what cause
Moved our grand parents in that happy state,
Favored of Heaven so highly, to fall off
From their Creator, and transgress His will
For one restraint, lords of the world besides?
Who first seduced them to that foul revolt?
7 The infernal serpent—he it was whose guile,
Stirred up with envy and revenge, deceived
The mother of mankind, what time his pride
Had cast him out from Heaven, with all his host
Of rebel angels, by whose aid aspiring
To set himself in glory above his peers,
He trusted to have equalled the Most High,
If he opposed; and with ambitious aim
Against the throne and monarchy of God
Raised impious war in Heaven and battle proud
With vain attempt. Him the Almighty Power
Hurled headlong flaming from the ethereal sky
With hideous ruin and combustion down
To bottomless perdition, there to dwell
In adamantine chains and penal fire,
Who durst defy the Omnipotent to arms.
    Nine times the space that measures day and night
To mortal men, he with his horrid crew
Lay vanquished, rolling in the fiery gulf
Confounded though immortal. But his doom
Reserved him to more wrath; for now the thought
Both of lost happiness and lasting pain
Torments him; round he throws his baleful eyes,
That witnessed huge affliction and dismay
Mixed with obdúrate pride and steadfast hate.
At once as far as Angels' ken he views

15 Aonian (ā ō′nē ən) **mount,** a Greek mountain, the home of the Muses. Milton intends to write a Christian epic greater than earlier non-Christian Greek and Latin poetry.

6 ■ What is the **epic question** that Milton poses?

29 grand parents, Adam and Eve.
31 transgress (trans gres′), *v.* sin against.
32 restraint (ri strānt′), *n.* limit; restriction.
34 guile (gīl), *n.* deceit.

8 ■ What kind of behavior do you expect from someone motivated by envy and revenge? by pride and hate?

48 adamantine (ad′ə-man′tēn), *adj.* immovable.
52 vanquish (vang′kwish), *v.* defeat.
53 confounded (kən-found′id), *adj.* overthrown.
56 baleful (bāl′fəl), *adj.* destructive.
58 obdurate (ob′dər it), *adj.* unrepentant.
59 ken (ken), *n.* range of vision.

Angel Michael Binding the Dragon by William Blake shows one interpretation of the war in Heaven that resulted in the expulsion of Satan and his rebel angels from Heaven. How does this interpretation compare with Milton's version? ➤

MINI-LESSON: GRAMMAR
Restrictive and Nonrestrictive Modifiers

Teach A restrictive modifier (either a phrase or a clause) tells which particular person or thing is meant. It is necessary for understanding and is NOT set off by commas from the word it modifies.

- The angel who stirred up rebellion was Satan. (Of several angels, only one stirred up rebellion; the modifier is required, or restrictive.)
- The angels rebelling against God were punished. (Of several angels, only certain ones were punished; the modifier is restrictive.)

A nonrestrictive phrase or clause that modifies merely adds descriptive or explanatory information, could be deleted and have the sentence still make sense, and is therefore set off by commas.

- The angel, who stirred up rebellion, was Satan. (The reader knows which angel is being referred to, so the clause gives information, is nonrestrictive, and could be omitted.)
- The angels, rebelling against God, were punished. (All the angels were punished, so the phrase just adds information.)

Activity Idea Have students find examples of restrictive and nonrestrictive modifiers in a story, remove them from the sentences, and tell how this helps distinguish between the two types of modifiers.

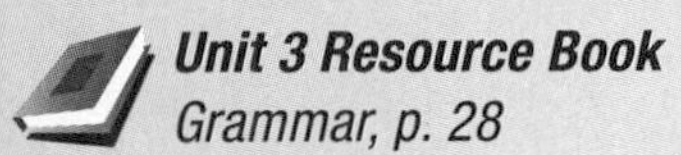

Unit 3 Resource Book
Grammar, p. 28

Response to Caption Question The interpretations differ in the manner the story is presented: Milton informs us (as does Isaiah 14:12–15) that God cast Satan out of heaven into bottomless perdition; we don't witness the battle. Blake vividly illustrates the titanic battle between the dragon, Satan, and St. Michael (Revelation, 12:7–9).

Visual Literacy William Blake (1757–1827), visionary and recluse, began having visions of angels at age nine. A gifted poet as well as an artist, he produced his own books of poems with engraved, hand-colored illustrations. An admirer of the arts and crafts of the Middle Ages, Blake attempted to recreate in his books the artistry and craftsmanship of medieval illuminated manuscripts.

Question Keeping in mind that Satan is often referred to as the Prince of Darkness, why do you think Blake pictured the dragon in dark colors and St. Michael in light colors? *(Possible response: to highlight the struggle between the forces of darkness, i.e., evil, with the forces of light, or goodness)*

BUILDING ENGLISH PROFICIENCY

Tracking Plot Events

After wondering how Adam and Eve could have fallen, the speaker jumps further back in time to tell his story. Encourage students to use a time line to sequence the plot events.

1. Have students record Milton's question (lines 27–32) as a statement at the far right-hand side of the time line.
2. Have them note Satan's rebellion at the far left-hand side.
3. As students read on, have them add other events.

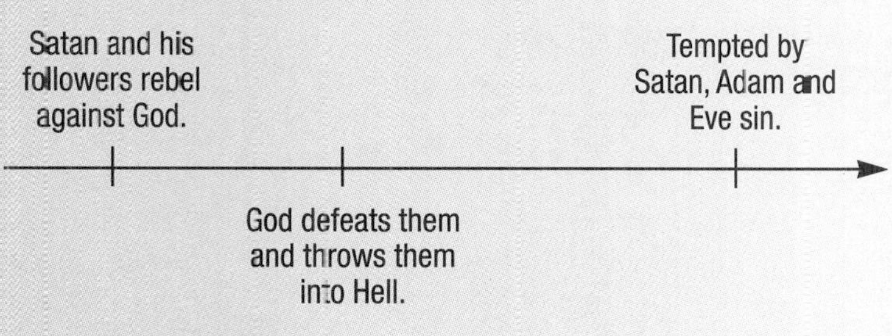

Satan and his followers rebel against God.

God defeats them and throws them into Hell.

Tempted by Satan, Adam and Eve sin.

9 Literary Focus
Symbolism

Question What do you think this image—flames that cast no light, darkness that illuminates only sights of woe—might symbolize? *(Possible response: that when one dwells in evil, one is incapable of seeing anything but evil; or that without the light of God, of goodness, one is blind to anything but evil)*

10 Reading/Thinking Skills
Generalize

Response Milton pictures a dungeon surrounded by walls of fire that cast no light; all is dark, except for visible scenes of despair; it is a place without hope of salvation, a place of endless torture.

11 Literary Criticism
Imagery

"Falling and separation are the major images of evil . . . Satan's 'progress' from the brightest angel . . . closest to God's high throne, to a serpent groveling on the deep throne of Hell sets the limits of evil. His physical separation and his fall . . . correspond precisely to his moral fall."

David M. Miller
John Milton: Poetry

12 Reading/Thinking Skills
Essential and Incidental Information

Question What does Satan mean when he states that "All is not lost"? *(Possible response: While he has lost freedom, hope of salvation, and the delights of heaven, his will, hatred, and courage remain.)*

The dismal situation waste and wild:
A dungeon horrible, on all sides round
As one great furnace flamed, yet from those flames
9 No light, but rather darkness visible
Served only to discover sights of woe,
Regions of sorrow, doleful shades, where peace
And rest can never dwell, hope never comes
That comes to all; but torture without end
Still urges, and a fiery deluge, fed
With ever-burning sulphur unconsumed:
Such place eternal justice had prepared
For those rebellious, here their prison ordained
In utter darkness, and their portion set
As far removed from God and light of Heaven
As from the center thrice to the utmost pole.
11 O how unlike the place from whence they fell!
There the companions of his fall, overwhelmed
With floods and whirlwinds of tempestuous fire,
He soon discerns, and weltering by his side
One next himself in power, and next in crime,
Long after know in Palestine, and named
Beelzebub. To whom the arch-enemy,
And thence in Heaven called Satan, with bold words
Breaking the horrid silence thus began. . . .

Addressing Beelzebub, Satan boldly declares that, although he has been thrown into Hell, he will continue to fight God with all his might.

12 "All is not lost; the unconquerable will,
And study of revenge, immortal hate,
And courage never to submit or yield—
And what is else not to be overcome?
That glory never shall His wrath or might
Extort from me. To bow and sue for grace
With suppliant knee, and deify His power—
Who from the terror of this arm so late
Doubted His empire—that were low indeed,
That were an ignominy and shame beneath
This downfall; since by fate the strength of gods
And this empyreal substance cannot fail,
Since through experience of this great event,
In arms not worse, in foresight much advanced,
We may with more successful hope resolve
To wage by force or guile eternal war. . . ."

67 to all. The greatest torment of Hell was the absence of hope of salvation.
68 deluge (del′yüj), *n.* downpour; a heavy fall, as of rain.

10 ■ Summarize Milton's idea of Hell.

77 tempestuous (tem pes′chü əs), *adj.* stormy; violent.
78 weltering (wel′tər ing), *adj.* tossing.
80 Palestine (pal′ə stīn), the Holy Land, now divided chiefly between Israel and the Palestinians.
81 Beelzebub (bē el′zə bub), Satan's chief associate.

85 study of, search for.

91 who, I (Satan) who.
92 doubted, feared.
93 ignominy (ig′nə min′ē), *n.* disgrace.
95 this empyreal (em pir′ē əl) **substance cannot fail.** The fallen angels are still heavenly, and therefore immortal; they cannot die ("fail").

MINI-LESSON: LITERARY FOCUS
Symbolism

Teach Help students develop a list of questions, like the following, for determining and analyzing symbols in literary works: Does the author directly equate an event or object with an abstract meaning? Does characterization suggest that the author intends a character, human or animal, to represent an idea? Do images or patterns of imagery suggest symbols? Are connotative words emphasized in a way that suggests they should be read symbolically? Are there allusions that suggest symbolism? Does context alter the original idea of an allusion?

Activity Ideas

- Students might choose a symbol from the charts they began on page 253 and explain how it might be used in a literary work.
- Have students work in pairs, choose a symbol from *Paradise Lost,* and analyze its meaning.

Beelzebub is afraid that God is too strong to be overcome, but Satan, scolding him for his fears, begins to make plans.

13 "Fallen cherub, to be weak is miserable,
Doing or suffering: but of this be sure,
To do aught good never will be our task,
But ever to do ill our sole delight,
As being the contrary to His high will
Whom we resist. If then His providence
Out of our evil seek to bring forth good,
Our labor must be to pervert that end,
And out of good still to find means of evil. . . .
Seest thou yon dreary plain, forlorn and wild,
The seat of desolation, void of light,
Save what the glimmering of these livid flames
Casts pale and dreadful? Thither let us tend
From off the tossing of these fiery waves,
There rest, if any rest can harbor there,
And reassembling our afflicted powers,
Consult how we may hence forth most offend
Our enemy, our own loss how repair,
How overcome this dire calamity,
What reinforcement we may gain from hope;
If not, what resolution from despair. . . ."
Forthwith upright he rears from off the pool
His mighty stature; on each hand the flames
Driven backward slope their pointing spires, and rolled
In billows, leave in the midst a horrid vale.
Then with expanded wings he steers his flight
Aloft, incumbent on the dusky air
That felt unusual weight, till on dry land
He lights, if it were land that ever burned
With solid, as the lake with liquid fire;
And such appeared in hue; as when the force
Of subterranean wind transports a hill
Torn from Pelorus, or the shattered side
15 Of thundering Etna, whose combustible
And fuelled entrails thence conceiving fire,
Sublimed with mineral fury, aid the winds,
And leave a singéd bottom all involved
With stench and smoke: such resting found the sole
Of unblest feet. Him followed his next mate,
Both glorying to have scaped the Stygian flood
As gods, and by their own recovered strength,
Not by the sufferance of supernal power.

100 cherub (cher′əb), *n.* one of the second highest order of angels.
102 aught (ôt), *pron.* anything.

110 desolation (des′ə-lā′shən), *n.* sad loneliness.

115 afflicted (ə flikt′id), *adj.* cast out.

118 dire (dīr), *adj.* dreadful.

14 ■ What does Satan tell Beelzebub about the work the fallen angels must do?

126 incumbent (in-kum′bənt), *adj.* pressing down.

132 Pelorus (pə lôr′əs), northeastern Sicily.
133 Etna (et′nə), the volcano of Mount Etna in Sicily.

139 Stygian (stij′ē ən) **flood,** waters of the river Styx (stiks) in Hell.

13 Literary Element
Meter

You might remind students that blank verse is unrhymed iambic pentameter and is frequently used in poetic drama, perhaps because it is closer to speech than most metrical lines. Within the regularity of the meter, poets vary blank verse by shifting pauses within lines, by using run-on lines, or by making slight alterations of the iambic pattern.

Questions Do you agree with the poet's decision to compose his epic in blank verse? Or do you think rhymed lines would be more effective? *(While responses will vary, students might note that blank verse is a highly effective way to tell the story; while it has an "epic" quality, it sounds more natural than rhyming poetry.)*

14 Reading/Thinking Skills
Find the Main Idea

Response They must prevent the bringing forth of good; reassemble their powers; offend their enemy, i.e., God; and overcome their calamity.

15 Literary Element
Setting

Question To what does Milton compare Hell in this section? *(to a volcano)*

BUILDING ENGLISH PROFICIENCY

ESL
LEP
ELD
SAE
LD

Exploring Oxymorons

Milton's *darkness visible* (line 63) is a classic example of an oxymoron. A brief study of oxymorons can extend students' vocabularies—and their imaginations.

1. Explain that an oxymoron is a phrase that matches opposing ideas to create a new meaning. Discuss how *darkness visible* helps describe the horror that is Hell.

2. Offer these additional examples: *sad happiness, deafening silence,* and *pleasant pain.* Call on volunteers to suggest situations in which the terms might apply.

3. Invite pairs of students to complete these further examples: _____ *sweetness,* _____ *tears,* and _____ *beauty.* (Alternatively, allow students to create their own.) Have students, as a class, choose the five oxymorons that they find most interesting.

The World of Work

Theologian

For a real-life discussion of good and evil, use the pages referenced below.

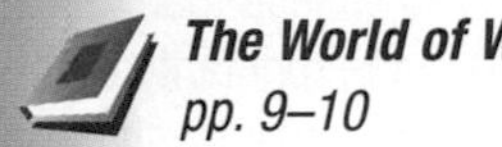

The World of Work
pp. 9–10

16 Reading/Thinking Skills
Analyze

Questions What do you think this phrase, "The mind is its own place . . .," might mean? *(Possible response: The mind is capable of erecting a reality more real than the outer world. With imagination and attitude, one can turn a negative into a positive or vice versa.)* Have you ever known anyone who saw hell in heaven or heaven in hell? *(Responses will vary.)*

17 Literary Focus
Symbolism

Response He wears a massive, round shield that is strapped across his shoulders onto his back.

Question What might this shield symbolize? *(Possible response: The shield is compared to the moon at which astronomers stare in the night sky [p. 261]. If the shield across Satan's back is the moon, then he is the night sky; the image of a shield that glows like the moon is another "darkness visible," capable only of illuminating evil and despair.)*

"Is this the region, this the soil, the clime,"
Said then the lost archangel, "this the seat
That we must change for Heaven, this mournful gloom
For that celestial light? Be it so, since He
Who now is sovereign can dispose and bid
What shall be right. Farthest from Him is best,
Whom reason hath equalled, force hath made supreme
Above His equals. Farewell, happy fields,
Where joy for ever dwells: hail, horrors! hail,
Infernal world! and thou, profoundest Hell,
Receive thy new possessor: one who brings
A mind not to be changed by place or time.
The mind is its own place, and in itself
16 Can make a heaven of Hell, a hell of Heaven.
What matter where, if I be still the same,
And what I should be, all but less than He
Whom thunder hath made greater? Here at least
We shall be free; the Almighty hath not built
Here for His envy, will not drive us hence:
Here we may reign secure, and in my choice
To reign is worth ambition, though in Hell.
Better to reign in Hell than serve in Heaven.
But wherefore let we then our faithful friends,
The associates and co-partners of our loss,
Lie thus astonished on the oblivious pool,
And call them not to share with us their part
In this unhappy mansion, or once more
With rallied arms to try what may be yet
Regained in Heaven, or what more lost in Hell?"
So Satan spake, and him Beelzebub
Thus answered: "Leader of those armies bright,
Which but the Omnipotent none could have foiled,
If once they hear that voice, their liveliest pledge
Of hope in fears and dangers, heard so oft
In worst extremes, and on the perilous edge
Of battle when it raged, in all assaults
Their surest signal, they will soon resume
New courage and revive, though now they lie
Grovelling and prostrate on yon lake of fire,
As we erewhile, astounded and amazed—
No wonder, fallen such a pernicious height!"
He scarce had ceased when the superior fiend
Was moving toward the shore; his ponderous shield,
Ethereal temper, massy, large, and round,
Behind him cast; the broad circumference 17

145 celestial (sə les′chəl), *adj.* heavenly.

159 Almighty (ôl mī′tē), God, also called Creator.

166 oblivious (ə bliv′ē əs) **pool,** lake of forgetfulness.

173 Omnipotent (om nip′ə tənt), *n.* all-powerful one; God.

176 perilous (per′ə ləs), *adj.* dangerous.

182 pernicious (pər nish′əs), *adj.* causing great harm or damage.

■ Describe Satan's armor.

MINI-LESSON: VOCABULARY

Expand Reading Vocabulary

Teach Poets delight in language, often using words that have fallen into disuse. Reading poetry and then using unfamiliar words in another context is a way to expand students' reading vocabulary.

Activity Idea Divide the class into groups and assign these words from the selection to each group: infernal (lines 34, 151), obdurate (line 58), oblivious (line 166), ponderous (line 184), perfidious (line 208), myriads (line 253). Ask each group to

- define each word, using a dictionary if necessary
- write a poem, a paragraph, a short-short story, or a dialogue using all the words
- read the results to the class

Hung on his shoulders like the moon, whose orb
18 Through optic glass the Tuscan artist views
At evening from the top of Fesole,
Or in Valdarno, to descry new lands,
Rivers or mountains in her spotty globe.
His spear, to equal which the tallest pine
Hewn on Norwegian hills, to be the mast
Of some great ammiral, were but a wand,
He walked with to support uneasy steps
Over the burning marl, not like those steps
On heaven's azure; and the torrid clime
Smote on him sore besides, vaulted with fire.
Nathless he so endured, till on the beach
Of that inflamèd sea, he stood and called
His legions, angel forms, who lay entranced,
Thick as autumnal leaves that strew the brooks
In Vallombrosa, where the Etrurian shades
High over-arched embower; or scattered sedge
Afloat, when with fierce winds Orion armed
Hath vexed the Red Sea coast, whose waves overthrew
19 Busiris and his Memphian chivalry,
While with a perfidious hatred they pursued
The sojourners of Goshen, who beheld
From the safe shore their floating carcasses
And broken chariot wheels—so thick bestrewn,
Abject and lost, lay these, covering the flood,
Under amazement of their hideous change.
He called so loud that all the hollow deeps
Of Hell resounded: "Princes, Potentates,
Warriors, the flower of Heaven, once yours, now lost,
If such astonishment as this can seize
Eternal Spirits; or have ye chosen this place
After the toil of battle to repose
Your wearied virtue, for the case you find
To slumber here, as in the vales of Heaven?
Or in this abject posture have ye sworn
To adore the Conqueror, who now beholds
Cherub and seraph rolling in the flood
With scattered arms and ensigns, till anon
His swift pursuers from Heaven gates discern
The advantage, and descending tread us down
Thus drooping, or with linkèd thunderbolts
Transfix us to the bottom of this gulf?
21 Awake, arise, or be for ever fallen!". . .

188–190 through optic glass . . . Fesole (fē′sōl) **. . . Valdarno** (val där′nō). Through the telescope the astronomer Galileo uses on the hills and in the valleys near Florence, Italy.
194 ammiral, admiral's flagship.
196 marl (märl) *n.* earth.
199 nathless (nāth′ les), *adv.* nevertheless.

203 Vallombrosa (val′əm brō′sə) **. . . Etrurian** (ē trůr′ē ən) **shades,** a valley near Florence in the Etruscan area of Italy.
205 Orion (ô rī′ən), the constellation of the hunter, visible in autumn, the time of harsh storms.
206 Red Sea, an arm of the Indian Ocean between Africa and the Arabian peninsula.
207–209 Busiris (bü sī′rəs) **. . . Gosen** (gō′shən). Busiris is the name Milton gives to the pharaoh of Egypt who enslaved the Israelites. At the time, the Israelites lived in Goshen, a part of Egypt. When Moses led them out of slavery, the pharaoh pursued them with his army (the "Memphian chivalry"). The Egyptians were drowned when the Red Sea closed over them after God had parted it for the Israelites.

20 ■ While Satan and Beelzebub are making plans, where are the other fallen angels?

212 abject (ab′jekt), adj. miserable.
224 seraph (ser′əf), *n.* one of the highest order of angels.

18 Literary Element
Style

Question Why do you think Milton employs such a grand, ornate style? *(Possible responses: The style matches the poem's grand themes, is similar to the style of the heroic, classical epic, and highlights the breadth of Satan's arrogance and evil.)*

19 Literary Element
Allusion

Question Why does Milton couple the image of the fallen angels with an allusion to the drowned army of the pharaoh? *(Possible response: Like the fallen angels, the army of the pharaoh, by pursuing the Israelites, attempted to thwart the will of God.)*

20 Reading/Thinking Skills
Find the Main Idea

Response in the "inflamed sea," a burning lake

21 Historical Note
The Restoration

Milton experienced his own fall with the death of Cromwell and the restoration of Charles II. Milton had publicly defended Parliament's execution of Charles I (father of Charles II) and had held a post in the Commonwealth. With the Restoration, many of his colleagues were put to death. He escaped this fate, in part, because of his blindness and through a deal arranged by his brother (a Royalist lawyer). For Milton, the Restoration was a major disappointment, professionally and philosophically, but the resulting disillusionment forged insights into humanity and a depth of character that illuminate *Paradise Lost.*

BUILDING ENGLISH PROFICIENCY

Responding to Key Statements

Use one or more of the following activities to help students focus on Satan's declaration in lines 154–155.

Activity Ideas

- Invite students to create artwork that reflects the idea that one's mind has the power to "make a heaven of Hell, a hell of Heaven."
- Ask students to recall (from history, movies, and so on) or to create a character whose attitude brought the best out of a bad situation or ruined a good situation.
- Discuss whether one's attitude—one's "mind"—is, by itself, able to effect such a drastic change. Ask: Do you think that Satan really believes what he says here, or do you think he's just acting brave to keep his followers' loyalty?

22 Reading/Writing Skills
Synthesize

Response We were told earlier that Satan looks upon the fallen angels with "signs of remorse and passion"; that he appreciates their faithfulness; and that his first three attempts at addressing the fallen angels were choked in tears. Thus, we can assume that he addresses them with a certain remorse, with appreciation for what they have sacrificed, and with sorrow and regret at their mutual loss. However, we also know that it would be in character for him to enflame them into bold, new attacks.

23 Literary Element
Style

Questions You might begin by noting that Satan's oration (from line 253) is in the oratorical style common to epic poetry. How does Satan begin his address? *("Oh myriads of immortal spirits! O powers/ Matchless, but with the Almighty!")* How are many of his comments framed? *(as rhetorical questions)* What is the purpose of the oration? *(to stir his forces of darkness into war with the forces of good)*

The fallen angels rise from the burning lake and fly to the plain, where they assemble in military formation before their "dread commander," Satan.

. . . Above them all the archangel: but his face
Deep scars of thunder had intrenched, and care
Sat on his faded cheek, but under brows
Of dauntless courage, and considerate pride
Waiting revenge. Cruel his eye, but cast
Signs of remorse and passion, to behold
The fellows of his crime, the followers rather
(Far other once beheld in bliss), condemned
For ever now to have their lot in pain—
Millions of spirits for his fault amerced
Of Heaven, and from eternal splendors flung
For his revolt—yet faithful how they stood,
Their glory withered; as, when heaven's fire
Hath scathed the forest oaks or mountain pines,
With singed top their stately growth, though bare,
Stands on the blasted heath. He now prepared
To speak; whereat their doubled ranks they bend
From wing to wing, and half enclose him round
With all his peers: attention held them mute.
Thrice he assayed, and thrice, in spite of scorn,
Tears, such as angels weep, burst forth: at last
Words interwove with sighs found out their way:
"O myriads of immortal spirits! O powers
23 Matchless, but with the Almighty!—and that strife
Was not inglorious, though the event was dire,
As this place testifies, and this dire change,
Hateful to utter. But what power of mind,
Foreseeing or presaging, from the depth
Of knowledge past or present, could have feared
How such united force of gods, how such
As stood like these, could ever know repulse?
For who can yet believe, though after loss,
That all these puissant legions, whose exile
Hath emptied Heaven, shall fail to re-ascend,
Self-raised, and re-possess their native seat?
For me, be witness all the host of Heaven,
If counsels different, or danger shunned
By me have lost our hopes. But He who reigns
Monarch in Heaven till then as one secure
Sat on His throne, upheld by old repute,
Consent or custom, and His regal state

240–241 amerced (ə mėrst′) . . . **Heaven,** exiled from Heaven.

250 assay (ə sā′), *v.* attempt.

22 ■ With what emotions do you think Satan delivers his speech to his angel comrades?

258 presage (pri sāj′), *v.* predict.

263 puissant (pwis′nt), *adj.* powerful.

This picture of the fallen angels appeared in the first illustrated edition of *Paradise Lost,* published in London in 1688. What qualities of Satan seem to be emphasized here? of hell? ➤

MINI-LESSON: CRITICAL THINKING
Recognizing Cause and Effect

Teach *Paradise Lost* is difficult to read. Students may find it easier to follow the plot if they track causes and effects. Review with students that every action, event, or effect has a cause. Each event in a story can affect another, or cause a new event to take place.

Activity Idea Have students start a cause-and-effect chart of major events in the poem. The events up until now might look something like the following.

Cause-and-Effect Chart

Satan wages war against God in Heaven.
Satan and his confederates are thrown into Hell.
Satan plots his revenge, resolving to wage an "eternal war."
Satan calls the other fallen angels together to battle the forces of Heaven.

Art Study

Responses to Caption Questions Satan's repellent features, animal-like ears, and snake-like hair emphasize his loathsomeness and evil; the contrast of light and shadows on his body creates a sense of "darkness visible" as described by Milton; the edges of his wings are ragged and give the appearance of flames fanned by wind. Hell also is "darkness visible" and arranged much as Milton describes.

Visual Literacy One surprising note is Hell's classical Roman architecture and the Roman soldiers' uniforms worn by Satan and the fallen angels.

Question Keeping in mind that Milton wrote for a Christian audience, why do you think the illustrator depicts Hell as a Roman city and Satan and the fallen angels in the garb of a Roman soldier? *(Possible response: Ancient Rome is often depicted as a place of extreme decadence; Pontius Pilate, who ordered the execution of Christ, and the soldiers who carried it out would have been dressed in this manner. The artist, thus, connects Rome and the Crucifixion to Satan.)*

BUILDING ENGLISH PROFICIENCY

Analyzing Character

Milton's Satan is a complex character. As Satan prepares to address the other fallen angels, have students begin a character web. Students should record at least one trait that they feel Satan has exhibited thus far. They also might record their suspicions about other characteristics and then look for more evidence as they continue to read.

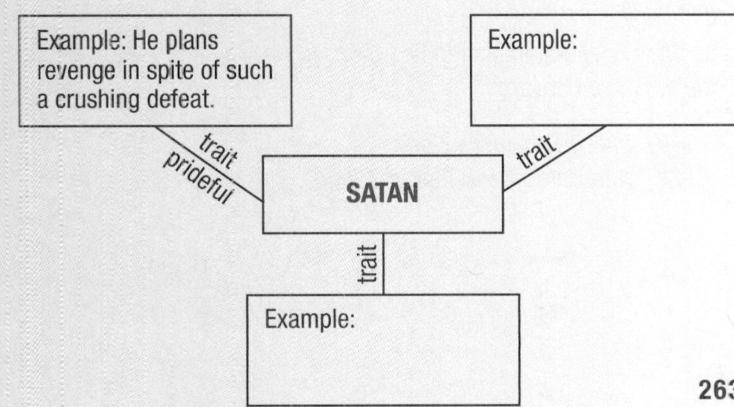

24 Reading/Thinking Skills
Find the Main Idea

Response "a generation . . . equal to the sons of Heaven," i.e., Adam and Eve and their offspring

25 Multicultural Note
Communication

Response The chances are nil. Satan is intent upon making a Heaven of Hell and a Hell of Heaven.

26 Literary Element
Characterization

Questions How has Milton characterized Satan? *(as courageous, proud, arrogant, vengeful, regretful, resolved, intelligent, stupid, and as an eloquent leader)* How would you characterize these traits? *(Responses will vary. Some students might note that Satan's contradictory nature is typically human.)* If time allows, this human-like portrayal of Satan and what it suggests might provide an interesting topic for class discussion.

Check Test

1. What worries the poet in "On His Having Arrived at the Age of Twenty-three"? *(Time is passing, and he may never achieve his ambitions.)*

2. What does the poet conclude in "On His Blindness"? *(that God is best served by those who bear whatever troubles He sends them)*

3. Who does Milton invoke in the first lines of *Paradise Lost*? *(a Muse to inspire his story)*

4. Where has Satan been cast by God? *(into Hell)*

5. What does Satan plan to do? *(fight the forces of Heaven)*

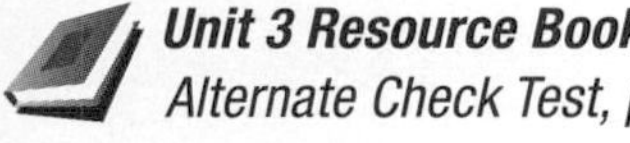

Unit 3 Resource Book
Alternate Check Test, p. 29

Put forth at full, but still His strength concealed—
Which tempted our attempt, and wrought our fall.
Henceforth His might we know, and know our own,
So as not either to provoke, or dread
New war provoked. Our better part remains,
To work in close design, by fraud or guile,
What force effected not; that He no less
At length from us may find, who overcomes
By force hath overcome but half his foe.
Space may produce new worlds; whereof so rife
There went a fame in Heaven that He ere long
Intended to create, and therein plant
A generation whom his choice regard
Should favor equal to the sons of Heaven.
Thither, if but to pry, shall be perhaps
Our first eruption—thither, or elsewhere;
For this infernal pit shall never hold
Celestial spirits in bondage, nor the abyss
Long under darkness cover. But these thoughts
Full counsel must mature. Peace is despaired;
For who can think submission? War, then, war
Open or understood, must be resolved."

Book 1 ends with the building of the palace of Pandemonium (that is, "All Demons") and with preparations for a council of war. The story of Satan's meeting with Adam and Eve in the Garden of Eden follows. Satan tempts Eve, who in turn persuades Adam to eat the forbidden fruit of the Tree of Knowledge. For this disobedience, Adam and Eve are driven from Paradise out into the world. The twelfth and last book of the poem closes with the pair standing hand in hand upon the threshold of the world. Paradise, "so late their happy home," lies behind them. Sadly and penitently they face the future, their punishment softened only by the promise of the ultimate redemption of man by Christ.

281 rife (rīf), *adj.* widespread.
282 fame, rumor.

■ Against what rumored creation of God does Satan intend to wage his war? (24)

Given the character of Satan as Milton has presented him, what are the chances of meaningful **communication** ever occurring between the forces of evil and the forces of good? (25)

After Reading

Making Connections

Shaping Your Response

1. Jot down two words that describe Milton as a young man and two words that describe him as an older man. Do you think he has changed? In what way?
2. Explain how "On His Having Arrived . . ." makes use of the **sonnet** structure. How do the last six lines relate to the first eight lines?

Analyzing the Poems

3. In "On His Blindness" what do you think the speaker means by asking, "Doth God exact day-labor, light denied?"
4. How would you interpret Patience's answer, "They also serve who only stand and wait"? How does that thought console the speaker?
5. Describe Satan, pointing out the methods of **characterization** Milton uses to create this picture.
6. Explain how you think pride has brought Satan to his current position and how it influences the plans he is making.
7. In light of his recent defeat by God, evaluate Satan's intent to wage a different kind of war from now on.
8. How might Milton's blindness and political exile have influenced his **communication** of ideas and attitudes in *Paradise Lost?*

Extending the Ideas

9. Compare Milton's vision of Satan and Hell with other images you are familiar with from literature or movies.

Literary Focus: Symbol

Beginning with lines 22–23 (". . . what in me is dark, / Illumine . . .") and throughout *Paradise Lost,* Milton emphasizes the **symbols** of darkness and light. Find at least three other examples of the darkness / light symbolism. In each example, what do you think darkness and light stand for?

Vocabulary Study

Select the word that is most nearly similar in meaning to the numbered word.

1. guile — **a.** association **b.** deceit **c.** guilt **d.** leadership
2. dire — **a.** dreadful **b.** made visible **c.** spoken **d.** without end
3. vanquish — **a.** change **b.** disappear **c.** diminish **d.** defeat

After Reading

MAKING CONNECTIONS

1. Possible responses: The younger man is ambitious and impatient; the older man, ambitious, but resigned; while still hungry for success, he accepts God's plans.

2. The first eight present a problem, which the final six lines resolve.

3. Possible responses: Does God expect a blind man to do the work of people who can see? Does He expect a man to forever waste his true talents in trivial, day-to-day work?

4. Possible response: Even those who do not do useful work serve God. It consoles the speaker to remember that God does not need man's work, but rather man's forbearance.

5. Using description, imagery, and dialogue, Milton characterizes Satan as courageous, resolved, proud, angry, vengeful, regretful, eloquent, and both clever and stupid, i.e., as human.

6. Pride led Satan to believe that he could best God. This led to war against God, who then flung Satan into Hell. Pride does not allow him to admit defeat, so he begins again to plan God's overthrow.

7. Satan believes the experience he has gained will help him wage the next war successfully. If force doesn't work, guile might.

8. Milton may have thought of himself as fallen, like Satan: the government he worked so hard to establish had been overthrown; blind, poor, and imprisoned, he may have felt as if he were in Hell.

9. Milton's portrayal of Satan is more thought-provoking and complicated. Satan is typically depicted as one-dimensional, totally evil. Most images of Hell coincide with Milton's vision.

LITERARY FOCUS: SYMBOLISM

Question When students are done, ask: In general, what do the darkness and light symbolize in the poem? *(Possible responses: good and evil; Heaven and Hell)*

Example	What It Means
line 63: "No light, but rather darkness visible"	The fires of Hell do not cast light but rather illuminate the darkness, that is, they illuminate evil.
line 110: "The seat of desolation, void of light"	Hell is a desolate, sad place, void of light, whose source is God.
lines 143-145: Satan asks if he must exchange "this mournful gloom/For that celestial light"	Hell is a dark, gloomy place; Heaven is a light-filled place.

VOCABULARY STUDY

1. b. deceit
2. a. dreadful
3. d. defeat
4. d. sin against
5. a. destructive
6. c. sad loneliness
7. d. stormy
8. b. limit; restriction
9. c. miserable
10. a. downpour

More Practice Students might write antonyms for each vocabulary word.

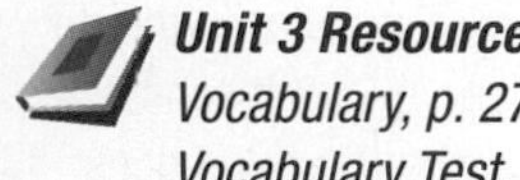

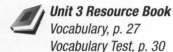

Unit 3 Resource Book
Vocabulary, p. 27
Vocabulary Test, p. 30

WRITING CHOICES

Writer's Notebook Update

Students can refer to the entries they made while reading Milton's poems. Students should consider whether the symbol has several meanings. Could it mean one thing to one person and something else to another?

Sin at Work

Review with students that a short-short story is often less than 1,000 words and usually centers around a single, pivotal incident.

So This Is Hell

As a prewriting activity, students might create a word web describing Hell.

Selection Test

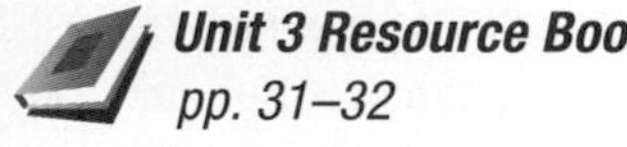

Unit 3 Resource Book
pp. 31–32

4. transgress	**a.** ask about	**b.** give up	
	c. give back	**d.** sin against	
5. baleful	**a.** destructive	**b.** fortunate	
	c. mysterious	**d.** stubborn	
6. desolation	**a.** comfort	**b.** meanness	
	c. sad loneliness	**d.** place to live	
7. tempestuous	**a.** cold	**b.** mischievous	
	c. soft	**d.** stormy	
8. restraint	**a.** new attempt	**b.** limit; restriction	
	c. question	**d.** freedom	
9. abject	**a.** descriptive	**b.** incomplete	
	c. miserable	**d.** sufficient	
10. deluge	**a.** downpour	**b.** misunderstanding	
	c. great hope	**d.** specialty	

Expressing Your Ideas

Writing Choices

Writer's Notebook Update Select one of the symbols you identified earlier and write a few lines in which you develop that symbol by describing a concept or idea that you want your reader to understand better. If you wish, write the lines in poetic form.

Sin at Work Satan's sin of pride is one of the traditional "seven deadly sins"; the others are envy, anger, lust, avarice, gluttony, and sloth. Do a little research on the seven deadly sins. Then select one of the other sins and write a **short story** showing that sin at work.

So This Is Hell What's your idea of what Hell might be like? Write a one-page **description** of that infamous place where people are said to go after death and of the people that go there. (You might want to study the visions of Hell in the Interdisciplinary Study on pages 276–280 before you begin writing.)

Other Options

On My Having Arrived . . . Inspired by Milton's poem "On His Having Arrived at the Age of Twenty-three," create a **collage** that illustrates your current state in life and your attitude toward life as you arrive at the age of—whatever you are. You can use drawings, pictures cut from magazines or newspapers, and even words and phrases in your collage.

Worth a Thousand Words? Select one of the scenes from *Paradise Lost* and create a **work of art** that depicts the emotions and tensions of the scene. You might choose to do a painting or a sculpture, for example, or an abstract piece that makes use of line and color. Add an appropriate quote from Milton as a caption.

OTHER OPTIONS

On My Having Arrived

Students might consider the use of color in their collages. A color might be chosen to represent a particular mood or feeling, as well as to provide background unity to the many images in the collage.

Worth a Thousand Words?

Students might consider the effect of color in this activity as well. What color represents anger? pride? cruelty? the torments of Hell? Discuss why people generally use warm oranges and reds to represent these passionate emotions.

Before Reading

from Genesis
The Twenty-third Psalm

The King James Bible

As the Hampton Court Conference of 1604 draws to a close, those assembled propose that they honor King James for his peacemaking work among the hostile religious factions of Great Britain. They authorize a new translation of the Bible. And so fifty-four scholars and students of divinity, divided into six teams, begin their research. Working at Westminster, at Cambridge, and at Oxford, the teams read earlier English translations, and they read in the original languages, Hebrew, Aramaic, and Greek. They write with an eye to simplifying the language. Each team then submits its work to a review team who hear each verse read aloud. The final judgment is on the sound and the flow of the words. In 1611, eight years after it was began, the Authorized Version of the Bible, known as the King James Bible, is published. In the introduction to this work, the translators explain that from many good Bibles they have created "one principal good one."

Building Background

The Bible is not one book but a collection of many books including many different types of literature. Christians divide the Bible into two sections—the Old Testament, containing the laws, history, and literature of the Jews, and the New Testament. Jews do not include the New Testament in their Bibles. The first book in the Bible is called *Genesis* (jen′ə sis), from Greek, "be born," and most of it is devoted to the history of the tribal ancestors of the Jews, the patriarchs Abraham, Isaac, and Jacob. In order to set this history in the widest possible context, the first chapters of Genesis give an account of the creation of the world and of the parents of the human race, Adam and Eve. Other books in what Christians call the Old Testament include sermons and visions of Jewish prophets and miscellaneous psalms, proverbs, moral tales, and love songs. Despite the many types of literature included in the Bible, the subject of all these works is basically the same—the divine order of human events, the ways in which God operates in the lives of people on Earth.

Literary Focus

Style The way a writer uses language to convey his or her ideas is called **style.** Style involves an author's choice of words and the arrangement of those words into sentences and paragraphs. An author's style may be simple or elaborate, elegant or folksy, conversational or formal. As you read, look especially for these elements of style:

- concrete terms and images
- straightforward phrases and sentences
- repetition and parallel structure

Writer's Notebook

The Garden of Eden Most cultures of the world have some counterpart of the Garden of Eden, the perfect land in which God originally placed the first human beings, Adam and Eve. Jot down a few descriptive words and phrases that come to your mind when you think of the Garden of Eden.

Before Reading

Building Background

Ask students to relate what they know about the Bible, especially Genesis.

Literary Focus

While the writing of the Bible is generally prose, many of the same stylistic elements as poetry are employed: symbolism, figurative and concrete language, repetition, and parallel structure. Much of the prose of the King James Bible is highly rhythmic, although not as metrically exact as blank verse.

Writer's Notebook

Inform students that when they finish reading the selection they will use their lists of descriptive words as the basis for writing a paragraph describing the Garden of Eden.

More About the Bible

The King James Bible was translated for the Protestant Anglican Church. (English-speaking Roman Catholics used the earlier Douay-Rheims translation.) The King James Version, a standard in Protestant churches for more than 200 years, is still treasured for the grace and beauty of its prose.

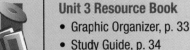

SUPPORT MATERIALS OVERVIEW

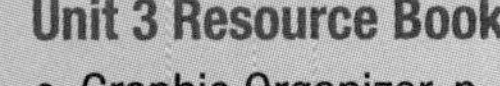

Unit 3 Resource Book
- Graphic Organizer, p. 33
- Study Guide, p. 34
- Vocabulary, p. 35
- Grammar, p. 36
- Alternate Check Test, p. 37
- Vocabulary Test, p. 38
- Selection Test, pp. 39–40

Building English Proficiency
- Selection Summaries
- Activities, p. 219

Reading, Writing & Grammar SkillBook
- Grammar, Usage, and Mechanics, pp. 189–190, 191–192, 193–196

Technology
- Audiotape
- Personal Journal Software
- Custom Literature Database: Additional selections from the Bible can be found on the database.
- Test Generator Software

Art Study

Response to Caption Questions They are leaving a place of peace, warmth, and plenty where it was not necessary to work in order to survive. They go to a cold, harsh place of conflict, where they will wear clothes to keep warm and struggle for their daily bread.

Visual Literacy Tapestries were woven of linen or wool on a loom. Working from the back, the weaver created the pattern by following a cartoon, which was drawn, full scale, by an artist. The completed design, most often illustrating a myth or Bible story, was a mirror opposite of the cartoon. Workshops in Paris and Brussels, which flourished in the 14th, 15th, and 16th centuries, wove tapestries in sets designed with related subject and color schemes by famous artists. These were commissioned as decoration for churches and castles, but also served the practical function of insulating very cold spaces.

Question Why do you think designs based on Bible stories were so popular in this period? *(Possible response: It was an intensely religious period, and Bible stories were well known to the people. The stories were, however, generally known through an artistic medium, such as carvings or stained glass, rather than through reading; the vast majority of people, including the nobles, were illiterate.)*

Genesis

The King James Bible

This large (21 feet by 15 feet, 3 inches) tapestry showing Adam and Eve being driven from the Garden of Eden was woven in Brussels, Belgium, in the 1500s. What do details in the tapestry—including the border—suggest about what they are leaving behind? about what they have to look foward to?

Chapter 1

In the beginning God created the heaven and the earth. And the earth was without form and void; and darkness was upon the face of the deep. And the Spirit of God moved upon the face of the waters. And God said, "Let there be light": and there was light. And God saw the light, that it was good: and God divided the light from the darkness. And God called the light Day, and the darkness he called Night. And the evening and the morning were the first day.

And God said, "Let there be a firmament[1] in the midst of the waters, and let it divide the waters from the waters." And God made the firmament, and divided the waters which were under the firmament from the waters which were above the firmament: and it was so. And God called the firmament Heaven. And the evening and the morning were the second day.

And God said, "Let the waters under the heaven be gathered together unto one place, and let the dry land appear": and it was so. And God called the dry land Earth; and the gathering together of the waters called he Seas: and God saw that it was good.

And God said, "Let the earth bring forth grass, the herb yielding seed, and the fruit tree yielding fruit after his kind, whose seed is in itself, upon the earth": and it was so. And the earth brought forth grass, and herb yielding seed after his kind, and the tree yielding fruit, whose seed was in itself, after his kind: and God saw that it was good. And the evening and the morning were the third day.

And God said, "Let there be lights in the firmament of the heaven to divide the day from the night; and let them be for signs, and for seasons, and for days, and years: And let them be for lights in the firmament of the heaven to give light upon the earth": and it was so. And God made two great lights; the greater light to rule the day, and the lesser light to rule the night: he made the stars also. And God set them in the firmament of the heaven to give light upon the earth, and to rule over the day and over the night, and to divide the light from the darkness: and God saw that it was good. And the evening and the morning were the fourth day.

And God said, "Let the waters bring forth abundantly the moving creature that hath life, and fowl that may fly above the earth in the open firmament of heaven." And God created great whales, and every living creature that moveth, which the waters brought forth abundantly, after their kind, and every winged fowl after his kind: and God saw that it was good. And God blessed them, saying, "Be fruitful, and multiply, and fill the waters in the seas, and let fowl multiply in the earth." And the evening and the morning were the fifth day.

And God said, "Let the earth bring forth the living creature after his kind, cattle, and creeping thing, and beast of the earth after his kind": and it was so. And God made the beast of the earth after his kind, and cattle after their kind, and every thing that creepeth upon the earth after his kind: and God saw that it was good.

And God said, "Let us make man in our image, after our likeness: and let them have dominion[2] over the fish of the sea, and over the fowl of the air, and over the cattle, and over all the earth, and over every creeping thing that creepeth upon the earth." So God created man in his own image, in the image of God created he him; male and female created he them. And God blessed them, and God said unto them, "Be fruitful, and multiply, and replenish[3] the earth, and subdue[4] it: and have dominion over the fish of the sea, and over the fowl of the air, and over every living thing that moveth upon the earth."

And God said, "Behold, I have given you every herb bearing seed, which is upon the face of all **1**

1. **firmament** (fėr′mə mənt), *n.* sky.
2. **dominion** (də min′yən), *n.* control.
3. **replenish** (ri plen′ish), *v.* refill.
4. **subdue** (səb dü′), *v.* conquer.

During Reading

Selection Objectives

- to explore the themes of creation and the fall from grace
- to analyze style
- to compare and contrast different translations of the same passages

Unit 3 Resource Book
Graphic Organizer, p. 33
Study Guide, p.34

Theme Link

Genesis describes the creation of the world and relates the story of Adam and Eve and their Fall from Grace and expulsion from Eden.

Vocabulary Preview

replenish, refill
subdue, conquer
sanctify, make holy
beguile, trick
enmity, hatred

Students can add the words and definitions to their Writer's Notebook.

1 Literary Focus
Style

Question What elements of style do you notice on this page?

Possible responses:

- repetition of phrases—
  "And God said, let . . ."
  "And God saw that . . . "
- repetition of "And" to begin sentences
- repetition in responses (e.g., in paragraph 4)—"And God said, 'Let . . .'" and what is wrought is described in closely related words
- use of parallel structure—"And God called the light Day, and the darkness he called Night"
- "unto" to mean "in" or "to"
- archaic verb forms, such as *creepeth* and *moveth*

SELECTION SUMMARY

The King James Bible

Genesis The excerpt from Genesis tells the story of creation. After God creates light, heaven, and dry land and populates the earth with living things, He places the first man and woman in the garden of Eden. They live as innocents until a serpent tempts Eve to eat the fruit of a forbidden tree; after eating, she offers the fruit to Adam, who also eats. For the first time, they realize they are naked, and they are ashamed when God comes to the garden. Realizing Adam and Eve have eaten of the forbidden fruit, God drives them from Eden.

The Twenty-third Psalm The last selection contains four versions of the Twenty-third Psalm, a sacred poem that describes God's promise to the faithful.

*For summaries in other languages, see the **Building English Proficiency** book.*

2 Multicultural Note
The Sabbath

The seventh day, the day on which God rested, is Saturday in our week. Jews and some Christians observe the Sabbath, a word that comes from a Hebrew word meaning "to rest," on Saturday. Most Christians, however, observe the Sabbath on the first day of the week. Sunday was adopted as the Sabbath because Christians believe that Jesus rose from the dead on Sunday.

3 Historical Note
The Creation

Genesis includes two accounts of the creation. There is evidence that the Adam and Eve account was the first. The second version may have been added to clarify God's awesomeness and perfection. The inclusion of the two versions suggests that the Bible that has come down to us is the result of multiple points of view.

4 Literary Element
Symbolism

Questions What might Adam and Eve's nakedness symbolize? *(Possible responses: the natural state of a newborn baby; their lack of material possessions; their purity and innocence)* Who or what might the serpent symbolize? *(Possible responses: Satan; evil in the world; the disobedient side of people)*

5 Multicultural Note
Communication

Response Yes, he informs her that she will not die from eating the forbidden fruit, but will be like a god by knowing good and evil.

the earth, and every tree, in which is the fruit of a tree yielding seed; to you it shall be for meat. And to every beast of the earth, and to every fowl of the air, and to every thing that creepeth upon the earth, wherein there is life, I have given every green herb for meat": and it was so.

And God saw every thing that he had made, and behold, it was very good. And the evening and the morning were the sixth day.

Chapter 2

Thus the heavens and the earth were finished,
and all the host of them. And on the seventh day
God ended his work which he had made; and he
2 rested on the seventh day from all his work which
he had made. And God blessed the seventh day,
and sanctified[5] it: because that in it he had rested
from all his work which God created and made.

These are the generations of the heavens and of the earth when they were created, in the day that the Lord God made the earth, and the Heavens, and every plant of the field before it was in the earth, and every herb of the field before it grew: for the Lord God had not caused it to rain upon the earth, and there was not a man to till the ground. But there went up a mist from the earth, and watered the whole face of the ground. And the Lord God formed man of the dust of the ground, and breathed into his nostrils the breath of life; and man became a living soul.

3 And the Lord God planted a garden east-
ward in Eden; and there he put the man whom
he had formed. And out of the ground made
the Lord God to grow every tree that is pleasant
to the sight, and good for food; the tree of life
also in the midst of the garden, and the tree of
knowledge of good and evil. . . .

And the Lord God took the man, and put him into the garden of Eden to dress it and to keep it. And the Lord God commanded the man, saying, "Of every tree of the garden thou mayest freely eat: But of the tree of knowledge of good and evil, thou shalt not eat of it: for in the day that thou eatest thereof thou shalt surely die."

And the Lord God said, "It is not good that the man should be alone; I will make him a help meet for him." And out of the ground the Lord God formed every beast of the field, and every fowl of the air, and to every beast of the field; but for Adam there was not found a help meet for him.

And the Lord God caused a deep sleep to fall upon Adam, and he slept: and he took one of his ribs, and closed up the flesh instead thereof; and the rib, which the Lord God had taken from man, made he a woman, and brought her unto the man.

And Adam said, "This is now bone of my bones, and flesh of my flesh; and she shall be called Woman, because she was taken out of Man."

Therefore shall a man leave his father and his
mother, and shall cleave unto his wife: and they
shall be one flesh. And they were both naked, the
man and his wife, and were not ashamed. 4

Chapter 3

Now the serpent was more subtle than any beast of the field which the Lord God had made. And he said unto the woman, "Yea, hath God said, 'Ye shall not eat of every tree of the garden'?"

And the woman said unto the serpent, "We may eat of the fruit of the trees of the garden: but of the fruit of the tree which is in the midst of the garden, God hath said, 'Ye shall not eat of it, neither shall ye touch it, lest ye die.' "

And the serpent said unto the woman, "Ye shall not surely die: for God doth know that in the day ye eat thereof, then your eyes shall be opened, and ye shall be as gods, knowing good and evil."

EVALUATE: Is the serpent using his ability to communicate in order to trick Adam and Eve? 5

5. sanctify (sangk′tə fī), *v.* make holy.

MINI-LESSON: GRAMMAR
Verb Forms

Teach Verbs on these pages such as *multiply, said, will make,* and *have given* illustrate various forms of verbs, respectively the present, past, future, and past participle forms. Many verbs are called *regular* because the past and participle are formed by adding *-d* or *-ed* to the present tense: *create, created, (have) created.* Many other verbs are *irregular* because they don't merely add *-d* or *-ed* to the present tense—the whole form changes: *see, saw, (have) seen; take, took, (have) taken; bring, brought, (have) brought; is, was, (have) been.*

Activity Idea Have students give the main verb forms (present, past, and participle) for ten other verbs in this excerpt from Genesis and state whether the verb is regular or irregular.

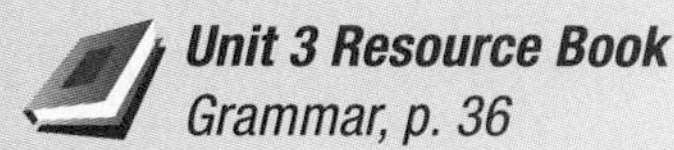

Unit 3 Resource Book
Grammar, p. 36

6 And when the woman saw that the tree was good for food, and that it was pleasant to the eyes, and a tree to be desired to make one wise, she took of the fruit thereof, and did eat, and gave also unto her husband with her; and he did eat. And the eyes of them both were opened, and they knew that they were naked; and they sewed fig leaves together, and made themselves aprons.

And they heard the voice of the Lord God walking in the garden in the cool of the day: and Adam and his wife hid themselves from the presence of the Lord God amongst the trees of the garden.

And the Lord God called unto Adam, and said unto him, "Where art thou?"

And he said, "I heard thy voice in the garden, and I was afraid, because I was naked; and I hid myself."

And he said, "Who told thee that thou wast naked? Hast thou eaten of the tree, whereof I commanded thee that thou shouldest not eat?"

And the man said, "The woman whom thou gavest to be with me, she gave me of the tree, and I did eat."

And the Lord God said unto the woman, "What is this that thou hast done?" And the woman said, "The serpent beguiled[6] me, and I did eat."

And the Lord God said unto the serpent, "Because thou hast done this, thou art cursed above all cattle, and above every beast of the field, upon thy belly shalt thou go, and dust shalt thou eat all the days of thy life: and I will put enmity[7] between thee and the woman, and between thy seed and her seed; it shall bruise thy head, and thou shalt bruise his heel."

Unto the woman he said, "I will greatly multiply thy sorrow and thy conception; in sorrow thou shalt bring forth children; and thy desire shall be to thy husband, and he shall rule over thee."

And to Adam he said, "Because thou hast hearkened unto the voice of thy wife, and hast eaten of the tree, of which I commanded thee, saying, 'Thou shalt not eat of it': cursed is the ground for thy sake; in sorrow shalt thou eat of it all the days of thy life; thorns also and thistles shall it bring forth to thee; and thou shalt eat the herb of the field, in the sweat of thy face shalt thou eat bread, till thou return unto the ground; for out of it wast thou taken; for dust thou art, and unto dust shalt thou return."

And Adam called his wife's name Eve; because she was the mother of all living. Unto Adam also and to his wife did the Lord God make coats of skins, and clothed them.

And the Lord God said, "Behold, the man is become as one of us, to know good and evil: and now, lest he put forth his hand, and take also of the tree of life, and eat, and live for ever": therefore the Lord God sent him forth from the garden of Eden, to till the ground from whence he was taken. So he drove out the man; and he placed at the east of the garden of Eden Cherubim,[8] and a flaming sword which turned every way, to keep the way of the tree of life. 7

6. **beguile** (bi gīl′), *v.* trick.
7. **enmity** (en′mə tē), *n.* hatred.
8. **cherubim** (cher′ə bim), *n.* angels.

6 Literary Element
Symbolism

Questions What do you think the forbidden tree symbolizes? *(forbidden knowledge)* What might Eve and Adam's eating of the tree's fruit and the opening of their eyes symbolize? *(Possible responses: loss of innocence; knowledge of good and evil; self-awareness)* Can you think of anything in life that is akin to what happens when Adam and Eve eat the fruit? *(Possible response: As babies, we are unaware of ourselves, of the difference between good and evil; in the process of growing up, our eyes are slowly opened as we absorb knowledge, and we become very aware of ourselves.)*

7 Literary Element
Theme

Question Bible stories often contain an underlying message, or theme. What do you think is the theme of this story of Adam and Eve? *(Possible response: that humanity must obey God's orders or face expulsion from His presence; that there are some things that human beings are not meant to know)*

BUILDING ENGLISH PROFICIENCY

Analyzing and Dramatizing a Passage

Use one or more of these activities to help students grasp the Genesis passages from the King James Bible.

Activity Ideas

- Divide students into six groups; have each group report on one of the six days of creation. Encourage groups to use visuals that give examples of the things created.
- Discuss questions such as these: Each day's work was "good"; what might that mean? Male and female were created in the image of God; what qualities do you think we share with God? Do God's closing commands give people the right to use up natural resources and drive animal species into extinction? Why or why not?
- Have volunteers enact any of these events: the creation and instruction of Adam; the creation of Eve; the serpent's temptation of Eve; or Adam and Eve's excuse-making and expulsion from Eden. Then ask students to explain how dramatization helped them understand the story better.

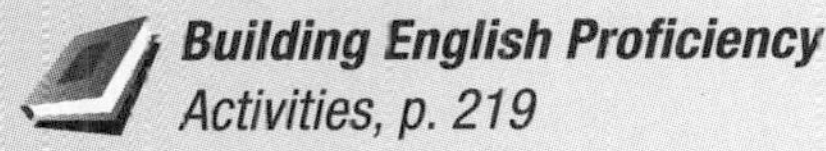
Building English Proficiency
Activities, p. 219

8 **Literary Focus**
Style

While style is not what is said but how it is said, it does have an effect on how we interpret what is said.

Question How do the differing styles of the phrase "valley of the shadow of death" affect how we interpret it?

Possible responses:

- *(In the Great Bible and King James Bible, the phrase is figurative and suggests that the knowledge of death throws its shadow over all of life.)*
- *(In the Bay Psalm Book, the phrase is the same figurative suggestion that life is lived with the knowledge of death, but here "in valley of" seems to suggest "deep in," which darkens the phrase to "deep in death's shadow I live.")*
- *(In the New English Bible, the phrase seems to have become either a literal walk in a valley or a figurative bout of hard times; changing "shadow of death" to "valley dark as death" removes the specter of death from life, which changes the meaning of the phrase and how one views life.)*

The Twenty-third Psalm

There have been many translations of the Bible. Judge the achievement of the King James version by comparing it with some other translations. Here are four versions of the Twenty-third Psalm (säm)*, a sacred song or poem—the King James translation, one published before it, and two versions published later.*

The Great Bible (1539)

The Lord is my shepherd; therefore can I lack nothing. He shall feed me in a green pasture, and lead me forth beside the waters of comfort. He shall convert my soul, and bring me forth in the paths of righteousness for his name's sake. Yea, though I walk through the valley of the shadow of death, I will fear no evil, for thou art with me. Thy rod and thy staff comfort me. Thou shalt prepare a table before me against them that trouble me; thou has anointed my head with oil, and my cup shall be full. But thy loving-kindness and mercy shall follow me all the days of my life and I will dwell in the house of the Lord forever.

The King James Bible (1611)

The Lord is my shepherd; I shall not want.
He maketh me to lie down in green pastures:
he leadeth me beside the still waters.
He restoreth my soul: he leadeth me in the
paths of righteousness for his name's sake.
8 Yea, though I walk through the valley of the
shadow of death, I will fear no evil: for thou
art with me; thy rod and thy staff they
comfort me.
Thou preparest a table before me in the
presence of mine enemies: thou anointest
my head with oil; my cup runneth over.
Surely goodness and mercy shall follow me all
the days of my life: and I will dwell in the
house of the Lord forever.

MINI-LESSON: VOCABULARY

Use Dictionaries for Word Meaning

Teach Review that a dictionary entry includes the word, its pronunciation, the part of speech, its definition(s), and often its etymology (origins).

Activity Idea Divide the class into groups, and assign two of these words to each group: firmament, dominion, replenish, subdue, sanctify, beguile, enmity, cherubim. Point out that each word is defined in footnotes in the Genesis passages, but that the dictionary may contain more information or a fuller definition. Ask each group to

- look up its words in a dictionary
- compare and contrast the dictionary definition(s) with the selection's definition
- consider the word's etymology to see if that adds to the group's understanding of the word's meaning
- write up its findings in a clear, easily-read way so that you can post each result on a bulletin board for the class to consider

The Bay Psalm Book (1640)

The Lord to me a shepherd is,
    want therefore shall not I.
He in the folds of tender grass,
    doth cause me down to lie:
To waters calm me gently leads,
    restore my soul doth he:
He doth in paths of righteousness
    for his name's sake lead me.
Yea though in valley of death's shade
    I walk, none ill I'll fear:
Because thou art with me, thy rod
    and staff my comfort are.
For me a table thou hast spread,
    in presence of my foes:
Thou dost anoint my head with oil,
    my cup it overflows.
Goodness and mercy surely shall
    all my days follow me:
And in the Lord's house I shall dwell
    so long as days shall be.

These two paintings of Shepherds with their flocks are from medieval illuminated manuscripts. Why do you think such a common image was used by the writer of the Twenty-third Psalm as a metaphor for God?

The New English Bible (1970)

The Lord is my shepherd; I shall want nothing.
    He makes me lie down in green pastures,
and leads me beside the waters of peace;
    he renews life within me,
and for his name's sake guides me in the right path.
Even though I walk through a valley dark as death
I fear no evil, for thou art with me,
thy staff and thy crook are my comfort.

Thou spreadest a table for me in the sight of
my enemies;
thou hast richly bathed my head with oil,
    and my cup runs over.
Goodness and love unfailing, these will
follow me
    all the days of my life,
    and I shall dwell in the house of the Lord
    my whole life long.

Art Study

Response to Caption Question God leads and cares for His people much as a shepherd cares for his flock. Also, it was to shepherds that the angel announced that "unto you is born this day in the city of David a Saviour, which is Christ the Lord" (Luke 2:11).

Visual Literacy Before the invention of the printing press, manuscripts were hand-copied by monks. They often added illustrations done in clear, jewel-like tones, showing the influence that stained glass windows had on medieval art.

Check Test

1. What was the first thing God created? *(light)*

2. Why does God create man? woman? *(Man was created to have dominion over the earth and its creatures; woman was created to help man.)*

3. Why did Adam and Eve hide from God? *(They had eaten from the tree of knowledge of good and evil and were afraid to show themselves naked.)*

4. How did God punish Eve and Adam? *(For Eve, childbirth will be difficult and her husband will rule over her; Adam will have to work hard to obtain food.)*

5. Based on the Twenty-third Psalm, what will the Lord provide the believer? *(peace and restoration of one's soul; direction in life; comfort in the face of death; goodness and love in life; and a place in the house of the Lord through eternity)*

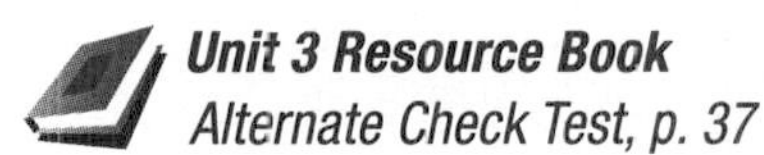

Unit 3 Resource Book
Alternate Check Test, p. 37

BUILDING ENGLISH PROFICIENCY

Understanding Causes and Effects

All four versions of Psalm 23 emphasize what is true for the psalmist because the Lord is his shepherd. Help students relate these causes and effects.

1. Have students read the most recent version, the one from the New English Bible.

2. Encourage students to use a t-chart as they work in small groups. In the left column, they should note the things that the Lord does (e.g., He guides me in the right path); in the right column, they should record either what the psalmist says about his response or what they think their own response would be (e.g., I don't have to worry about the future, because the path is right).

3. Suggest that they use their t-charts as a guide to the other versions and refine the charts as they read.

After Reading

MAKING CONNECTIONS

1. Students should explain why they do or do not feel sympathy for Adam and Eve.

2. Some students may choose the King James translation or another older translation because they sound more biblical or more familiar, or perhaps because they prefer the poetry. Those who choose the New English Bible translation may find it easier to comprehend, since it is written in the English of today.

3. The sun, stars, planets, and moon were used by astronomers to predict and interpret important events and were used by ordinary people to tell the season, day, and year.

4. Possible response: Human beings have the best-developed brains and so can make decisions regarding animals.

5. They realize that they are naked, so they try to clothe themselves, then hide from God. This behavior is due to the knowledge that the fruit conferred upon them and the knowledge that they had disobeyed God.

6. Responses will vary. Students concerned with women's rights may find the punishments particularly hard on women and a rationale to deny equality in the work place.

7. Students might research creation myths in books of mythology and then retell them to the class.

After Reading

Making Connections

Shaping Your Response

1. Do you feel sympathy for Adam and Eve in the story? Why or why not?
2. Which version of the Twenty-third Psalm do you prefer? Why?

Analyzing the Selections

3. What do you think God means by saying that the lights in the firmament can be "for signs, and for seasons, and for days, and years."?
4. Why do you suppose God gives man dominion over all of the animals on earth?
5. How and why does the behavior of Adam and Eve change after they have eaten the forbidden fruit?
6. Do the particular punishments God inflicts upon Eve, Adam, and the serpent seem appropriate? Explain.

Extending the Ideas

7. All cultures of the world **communicate** from generation to generation their versions of how the world—along with its people and animals—was created. Share with the class some stories you have heard.

Literary Focus: Style

Style is not what is said, but *how* it is said. The authors of the King James Bible use a style that is simple and straightforward, yet elegant and dignified. Review the first three chapters of Genesis, noting the following elements of style. Find and write down other examples of these style elements.

Style Element	Example	Further Examples
Use of *and* to begin sentences	"And God said . . . ."	
Use of repetition	". . . and God saw that it was good."	
Use of parallel structure	". . . the greater light to rule the day, and the lesser light to rule the night."	

LITERARY FOCUS: STYLE

The *Further Examples* column may include:

- Row 1: "And God saw every thing that he had made . . . "; "And the Lord God took the man . . . "
- Row 2: "And God said . . . "; "And the evening and the morning were the . . . day."
- Row 3: "And God called the light Day, and the darkness he called Night"; "This is now bone of my bones, and flesh of my flesh . . . "

Encourage students to also look for examples of the King James Bible's simple and straightforward style. For example, the first creation story is told in short, simple paragraphs. There are few adjectives or adverbs. For the most part, the words used are common English words that are still in use today; there is a lack of "flowery" language.

Vocabulary Study

Select the letter of the situation that best demonstrates the meaning of the numbered word.

1. enmity
   a. a teenager getting ready for her first date
   b. a politician addressing the voters
   c. a soldier confronting the opposition on the battlefield
2. replenish
   a. a stock boy putting merchandise on empty shelves
   b. a farmer harvesting his fields
   c. a zookeeper cleaning animal cages
3. beguile
   a. a beggar with his hand out
   b. a guide leading a tour group
   c. a salesman selling worthless land
4. sanctify
   a. a scholar studying in a quiet place
   b. a minister blessing a marriage
   c. a teacher approving a theme topic
5. subdue
   a. a debtor paying a bill
   b. an army gaining control over new territory
   c. an employee giving a suggestion to the boss

Expressing Your Ideas

Writing Choices

Writer's Notebook Update How does your list of descriptive words about the Garden of Eden compare with the picture created in Genesis? What words can you add to your list? Using some of the words on your list, write your own paragraph describing the Garden of Eden.

Advise Adam and Eve At the end of Genesis, Chapter 3, Adam and Eve have been banished by God from the Garden of Eden. They are ready to enter the world. Write a **letter of advice** to Adam and Eve, telling them what they should expect and how they can best survive in this new, unfamiliar world.

Illuminate the Text During the Middle Ages monks copied out texts by hand, often adding fanciful capital letters (see pages 46 and 79) and illustrations of daily life or of their notions of biblical times (see pages 56, 74, and 272–273). Create your own **illuminated manuscript** by copying out your favorite version of the Twenty-third Psalm—perhaps on poster-sized cardboard. Add whatever capital letters and illustrations you please, and perhaps some fancy borders or curlicues.

Other Option

Stage a Children's Play Choose another story from the Bible. (Your teacher may be able to suggest some possibilities.) Working with a small group, write a dramatic version of this story suitable for presentation to young children. If possible, stage your **play** for a grade school class.

VOCABULARY STUDY

1. c
2. a
3. c
4. b
5. b

More Practice Students might research each word's etymology.

Unit 3 Resource Book
Vocabulary, p. 35
Vocabulary Test, p. 38

WRITING CHOICES

Writer's Notebook Update

Students can refer to the list they made describing Eden. Encourage them to use words that engage all five senses as they write their paragraphs.

Advise Adam and Eve

As a prewriting activity, students might make a chart comparing the couple's life in Eden to life in the outside world.

Eden	Outside World
All food provided	Must grow own food
No need for shelter or clothing	Must build own shelter and make own clothing
No other people	Must deal with other people, both good and bad

Selection Test

Unit 3 Resource Book
pp. 39–40

Transparency Collection
Fine Art Writing Prompt 5

OTHER OPTIONS

Stage a Children's Play

Review with students the conventions of writing a play:

- All characters are listed and described at the beginning of the play.
- The story is told mostly through dialogue, although a narrator can provide a bridge for some parts.
- The action is divided into acts, and the acts into scenes. A one-act play is possible.
- Directions to the characters are written in italics or set off in some way from the dialogue.

Interdisciplinary Study

Theme Link

Ideas of perfect worlds untouched by time have given people hope throughout the ages. Places of eternal suffering and punishment have made people think twice about actions for which they may be judged later.

Curricular Connection: Humanities

You can use the writings and visuals in this interdisciplinary study to explore the role that these "other worlds" have played in human consciousness.

Art Study

U.S. painter Edward Hicks (1780–1849) is considered a primitive painter, meaning he was self-taught, not formally trained.

Question How is this painting different from paintings done by artists schooled in technique? *(Possible responses: The perspective is unusual; the people and animals in the foreground are all looking straight ahead; the animals have human expressions; proportions are not realistic.)*

Question What images in this work are symbolic of peace? *(Possible responses: The animals are all sitting calmly with each other; a person is standing in the midst of the animals; the men in the background are not fighting; the light is very calm.)*

Unit 3 Resource Book
Study Guide, p.17

INTERDISCIPLINARY STUDY

The Fall From Grace

Heaven, Hell, and Paradise

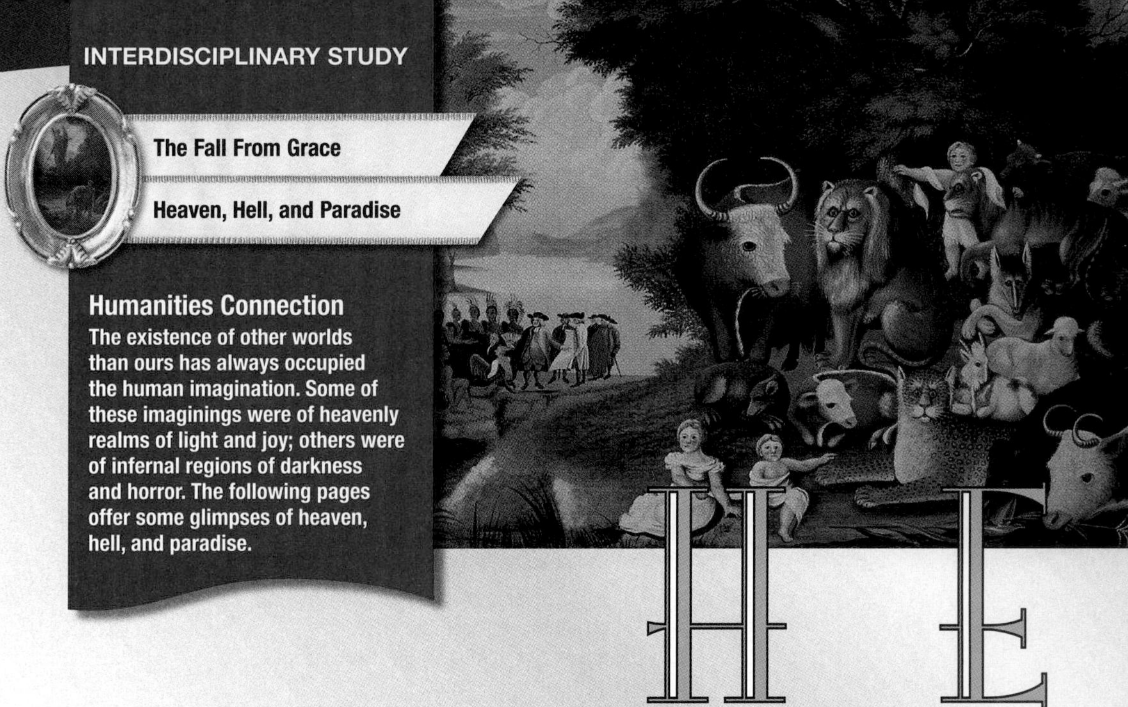

Humanities Connection
The existence of other worlds than ours has always occupied the human imagination. Some of these imaginings were of heavenly realms of light and joy; others were of infernal regions of darkness and horror. The following pages offer some glimpses of heaven, hell, and paradise.

HE

The Peach-Blossom Fountain

T'ao Ch'ien, translated by Herbert Giles

Towards the close of the fourth century A.D., a certain fisherman of Wu-ling, who had followed up one of the river branches without taking note whither he was going, came suddenly upon a grove of peach trees[1] in full bloom, extending some distance on each bank, with not a tree of any other kind in sight. The beauty of the scene and the exquisite perfume of the flowers filled the heart of the fisherman with surprise, as he proceeded onwards, anxious to reach the limit of this lovely grove. He found that the peach trees ended where the water began, at the foot of a hill; and there he espied what seemed to be a cave with light issuing from it. So he made fast his boat, and crept in through a narrow entrance, which shortly ushered him into a new world of level country, of fine houses, of rich fields, of fine pools, and of luxuriance of mulberry and bamboo. Highways of traffic ran north and south; sounds of crowing cocks and barking dogs were heard around; the dress of the people who passed along or were at work in the fields was of a strange cut; while young and old alike appeared to be contented and happy.

One of the inhabitants, catching sight of the fisherman, was greatly astonished; but, after learning whence he came, insisted on carrying him home, and killed a chicken and placed some wine before him. Before long, all the people of the place had turned out to see the visitor, and they informed him that their ancestors had sought refuge here, with their wives and families, from the troublous times of the house of Ch'in[2] adding that they had thus become finally cut off from the rest of the human race. They then enquired about the politics of the day, ignorant of the establishment of the Han dynasty[3] and of course of the

1. **peach trees**, symbols of immortality in Chinese tradition.
2. **Ch'in**, or **Qin** (chin), short-lived dynasty that ruled China at the end of the third century B.C.
3. **Han dynasty**, one of the greatest Chinese dynasties, ruling from 202 B.C. to A.D. 220; successors of the Qin.

MINI-LESSON: STUDY SKILLS

Create and Use Diagrams

Teach Putting information into an easily interpreted diagram is a skill that extends across disciplines. Explain to students that a diagram is a visual guide that explains and/or accompanies written information.

Apply Show students some examples of diagrams from directions for an appliance, from a science book, or from an atlas.

Activity Idea Working in small groups, students can use an encyclopedia and an atlas, or do research in the library, to make one of the following diagrams:

- changing territories of the Chinese Dynasties, starting with the Chou
- the growth in Chinese trade from 100 B.C. to the Middle Ages
- family tree of the Han emperors of China

Unit 3 Resource Book
Study Skills Activity, p. 41

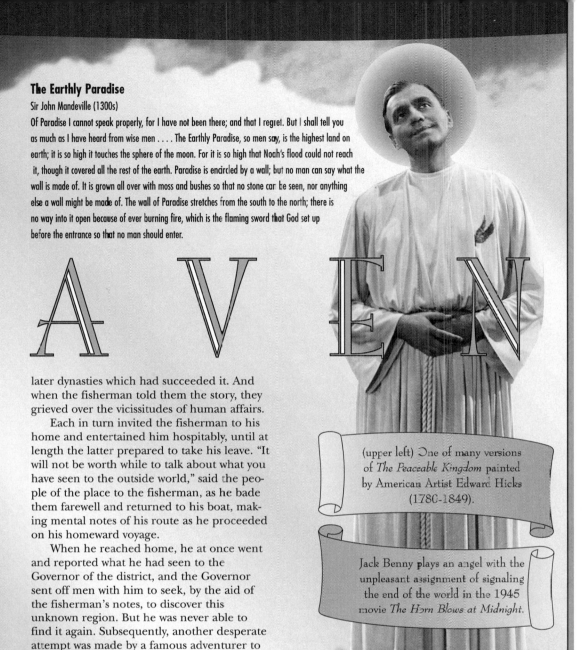

The Earthly Paradise

Sir John Mandeville (1300s)

Of Paradise I cannot speak properly, for I have not been there; and that I regret. But I shall tell you as much as I have heard from wise men . . . . The Earthly Paradise, so men say, is the highest land on earth; it is so high it touches the sphere of the moon. For it is so high that Noah's flood could not reach it, though it covered all the rest of the earth. Paradise is encircled by a wall; but no man can say what the wall is made of. It is grown all over with moss and bushes so that no stone can be seen, nor anything else a wall might be made of. The wall of Paradise stretches from the south to the north; there is no way into it open because of ever burning fire, which is the flaming sword that God set up before the entrance so that no man should enter.

A V E N

later dynasties which had succeeded it. And when the fisherman told them the story, they grieved over the vicissitudes of human affairs.

Each in turn invited the fisherman to his home and entertained him hospitably, until at length the latter prepared to take his leave. "It will not be worth while to talk about what you have seen to the outside world," said the people of the place to the fisherman, as he bade them farewell and returned to his boat, making mental notes of his route as he proceeded on his homeward voyage.

When he reached home, he at once went and reported what he had seen to the Governor of the district, and the Governor sent off men with him to seek, by the aid of the fisherman's notes, to discover this unknown region. But he was never able to find it again. Subsequently, another desperate attempt was made by a famous adventurer to pierce the mystery; but he also failed, and died soon afterwards of chagrin, from which time forth no further attempts were made.

(upper left) One of many versions of *The Peaceable Kingdom* painted by American Artist Edward Hicks (1780-1849).

Jack Benny plays an angel with the unpleasant assignment of signaling the end of the world in the 1945 movie *The Horn Blows at Midnight.*

MULTICULTURAL NOTE

The story of Noah, mentioned by Mandeville, is told in Genesis. He is chosen by God to be the sole survivor of a flood, along with his family and a male and female of all kinds of animals. Flood accounts are common in many of the world's literatures. For example, in Hindu mythology, Manu is warned by a fish of the deluge. He survives but is all alone in the world. When he prays to the gods for a wife, they create one for him.

Additional Background

Comedian Jack Benny died in 1975 at the age of 81. Born Benjamin Kubelsky in Waukegan, Illinois, he started out as a vaudeville performer when he was 17. He hosted *The Jack Benny Show,* first on radio, then on TV. An accomplished musician, he used his violin as a comic prop.

Historical Note

Though the Ch'in Dynasty only lasted for the reign of one emperor, Shih Huang Ti, many changes occurred in those forty-nine years (259–210 B.C.): the country was divided into thirty-six provinces, and the written language was standardized across the land, as were weights, measures, and coins.

BUILDING ENGLISH PROFICIENCY

Comparing Descriptions

Both T'ao Ch'ien and Sir John Mandeville describe a paradise on earth, but do they see it the same way? Encourage pairs or groups of students to create a Venn diagram, listing similarities and differences between the descriptions. Afterward, invite them to discuss which description better matches their own view of paradise or seems more appealing.

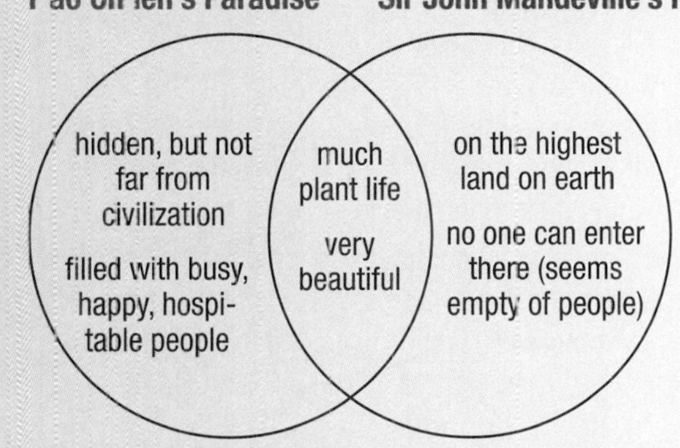

Art Study

Baroque sculpture, such as these wax figures, was characterized by many surface details. Folds of cloth and swirling patterns of wavy hair were decoratively rendered.

Visual Literacy Have students contrast the Blessed figure with the Damned.

Activity Options

Activity 1 Students can divide into groups and research various cultural and religious ideas about one's journey after death. For instance, Hades and the Elysian Fields may be studied by one group, Avalon by another, and so on. Each group can report to the class.

Activity 2 The class may divide into small groups and create collages with modern images of and allusions to heaven, hell, or paradise. They may cut out pictures and words from magazines and newspapers. Hint: advertisements for vacation spots often refer to paradise, ads for foods may refer to heaven, or heavenly aromas, and images of devils and angels sometimes appear as aspects of people's consciences.

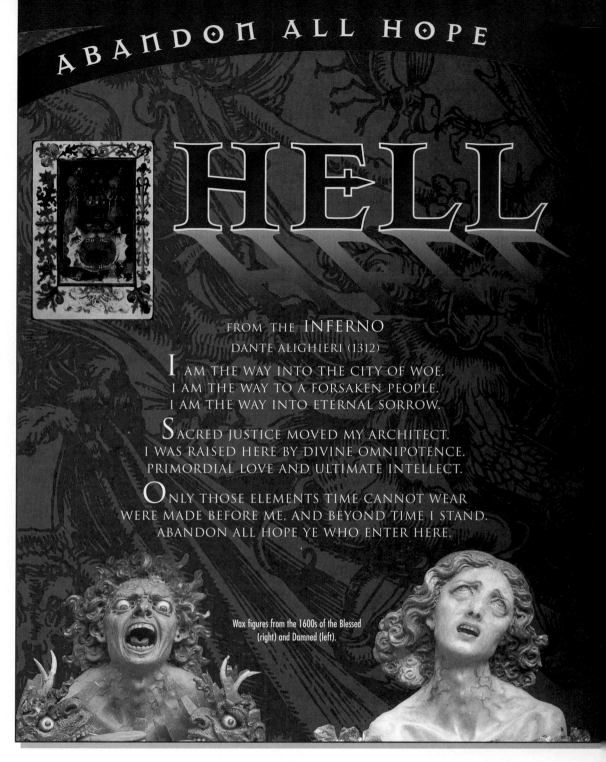

ABANDON ALL HOPE

HELL

FROM THE INFERNO

DANTE ALIGHIERI (1312)

I AM THE WAY INTO THE CITY OF WOE.
I AM THE WAY TO A FORSAKEN PEOPLE.
I AM THE WAY INTO ETERNAL SORROW.

SACRED JUSTICE MOVED MY ARCHITECT.
I WAS RAISED HERE BY DIVINE OMNIPOTENCE.
PRIMORDIAL LOVE AND ULTIMATE INTELLECT.

ONLY THOSE ELEMENTS TIME CANNOT WEAR
WERE MADE BEFORE ME, AND BEYOND TIME I STAND.
ABANDON ALL HOPE YE WHO ENTER HERE.

Wax figures from the 1600s of the Blessed (right) and Damned (left).

MINI-LESSON: SPEAKING AND LISTENING

Asking Questions

Being able to ask a question may seem simple, but when you are listening to someone lecture or read, keeping track of questions you want to ask can be difficult. Students may be helped by the following pointers:

- Jot down the speaker's thesis, or main idea. Then if there are points you don't understand, jot *them* down. When you have a chance to ask a question, try to relate it to the thesis.
- If you have a factual question that does not affect your overall understanding of the lecture, write it down. You can look up a fact later, whereas more complex questions will need to be asked now.
- Before you ask your question, have the wording clear in your head.

Activity Idea Have the class divide into groups. In each group, one person will be the "lecturer," giving a short report on any topic with which he or she feels comfortable: a hobby, an anecdote, a book. While the lecturer speaks, the other group members, the "audience," will jot down notes for questions, keeping in mind the above pointers. After the report, each person will ask the lecturer a clear, concise question.

YE WHO ENTER HERE

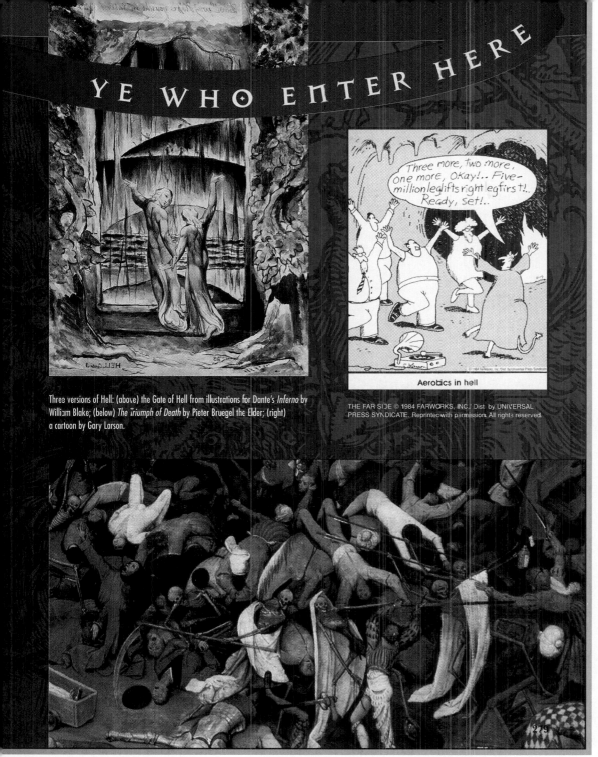

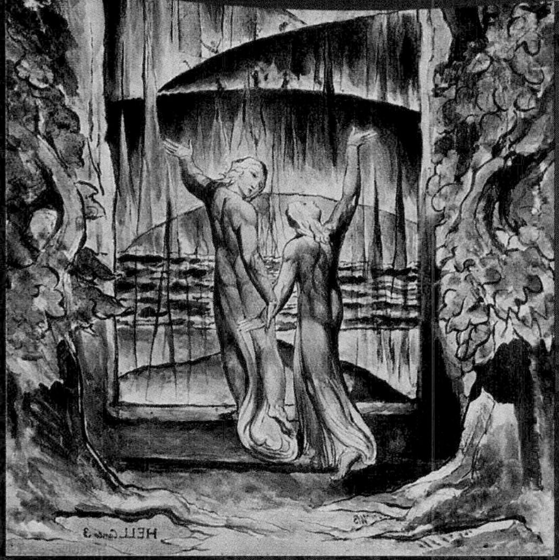

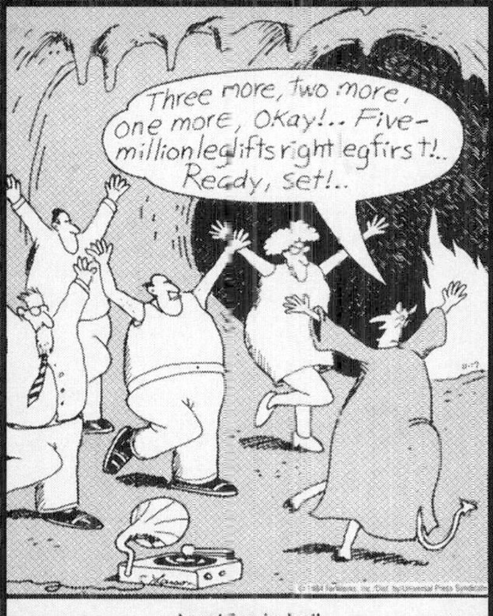

Aerobics in hell

Three versions of Hell: (above) the Gate of Hell from illustrations for Dante's *Inferno* by William Blake; (below) *The Triumph of Death* by Pieter Bruegel the Elder; (right) a cartoon by Gary Larson.

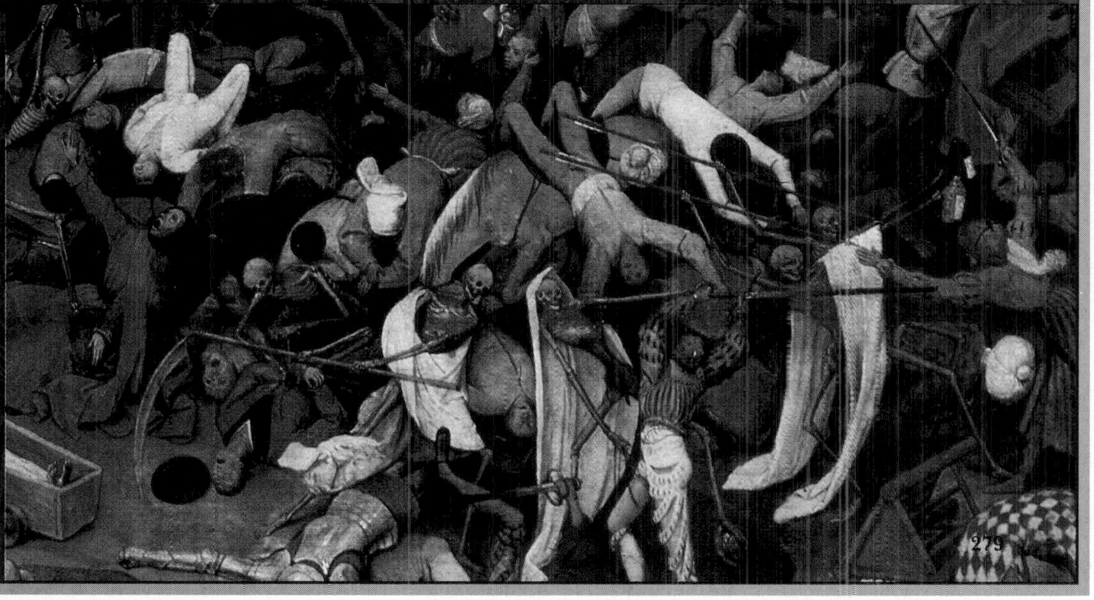

BUILDING ENGLISH PROFICIENCY

ESL LEP ELD SAE LD

Responding to Visual Cues

Use one or more of the following activities to expand upon the images and explanatory text in this feature.

Activity Ideas

- Direct students' attention to the wax figures on page 278. Have two groups of students create paired free-verse poems, one expressing the thoughts of the Blessed and the other expressing the thoughts of the Damned.
- Ask students to imagine that this spread is to be expanded. Challenge students to find or describe pictures from modern life that would indicate what hell would mean to them.
- Ask students to find or create pictures that could add to the illustrations on pages 276–277.

Additional Background

Dante Alighieri (1265–1321), usually referred to simply as Dante, spent the first part of his life in the city-state of Florence, where he was one of the rulers. He wrote *The Divine Comedy,* of which the *Inferno* is one section, after he had been exiled. *The Divine Comedy* is Dante's visionary tour of the afterlife; the other two sections are *Heaven* and *Purgatory*. While in exile, he depended on the patronage of wealthy nobles for survival, and he died penniless in Ravenna.

Research Topics

- Dante Alighieri, his life and works
- Pieter Bruegel (broi′gəl) the Elder, Pieter Bruegel the Younger, and Jan Bruegel the Elder: their place in Flemish art

Art Study

William Blake (see Unit 5) lived during the late eighteenth and early nineteenth centuries and as an artist and writer relied on his inner vision to express his beliefs. Pieter Brueghel the Elder was a Flemish artist in the 1600s. He painted mostly landscape scenes with several, sometimes many, figures in them. His horrific view of hell contains his trademark elements. Larson's *Far Side* comic, which ran from the early 1980s to the mid-1990s, satirized the human condition irreverently.

Geographical Note

Flemish artists, such as Brueghel, were from Flanders, now part of Belgium. It borders France in the southwest, touches the Netherlands in the northeast, and is on the coast of the North Sea. During Brueghel's time, Flanders flourished on its cloth manufacturing; to this day, flax is one of the major products of the region.

Terms to Know

Arawak (ä′rä wäk), member of a South American Indian tribe, now living mostly in Brazil.

The Little Girl The *Niña,* which means "little girl" in Spanish, was one of Columbus's three ships.

Colón (kō lōn′), the Spanish name for Columbus.

Responding

1. Possible responses Students may describe versions they have seen in movies or on TV, perhaps in music videos. Some students may have heard descriptions of heaven and hell in a place of worship.

2. Possible reponses Students may list delicious foods, listening to music, sunbathing, watching TV, or being with loved ones among pleasures they would choose to have in heaven.

3. Possible responses Students might mention everyday hassles such as tests or traffic jams. They also might mention earthly horrors such as starvation, war, or nuclear weapons.

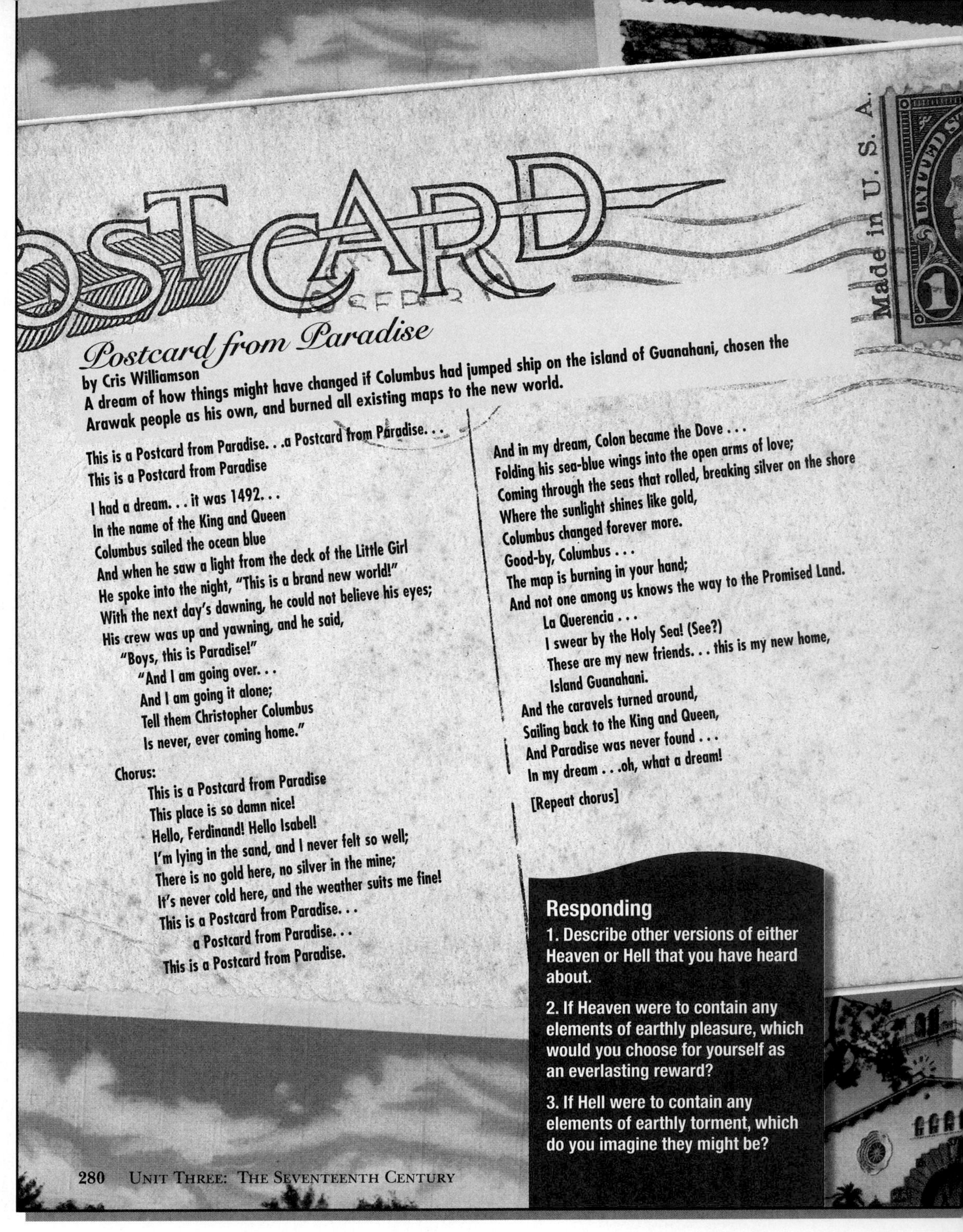

Postcard from Paradise

by Cris Williamson

A dream of how things might have changed if Columbus had jumped ship on the island of Guanahani, chosen the Arawak people as his own, and burned all existing maps to the new world.

This is a Postcard from Paradise. . .a Postcard from Paradise. . .
This is a Postcard from Paradise

I had a dream. . . it was 1492. . .
In the name of the King and Queen
Columbus sailed the ocean blue
And when he saw a light from the deck of the Little Girl
He spoke into the night, "This is a brand new world!"
With the next day's dawning, he could not believe his eyes;
His crew was up and yawning, and he said,
"Boys, this is Paradise!"
"And I am going over. . .
And I am going it alone;
Tell them Christopher Columbus
Is never, ever coming home."

Chorus:
This is a Postcard from Paradise
This place is so damn nice!
Hello, Ferdinand! Hello Isabel!
I'm lying in the sand, and I never felt so well;
There is no gold here, no silver in the mine;
It's never cold here, and the weather suits me fine!
This is a Postcard from Paradise. . .
a Postcard from Paradise. . .
This is a Postcard from Paradise.

And in my dream, Colon became the Dove . . .
Folding his sea-blue wings into the open arms of love;
Coming through the seas that rolled, breaking silver on the shore
Where the sunlight shines like gold,
Columbus changed forever more.
Good-by, Columbus . . .
The map is burning in your hand;
And not one among us knows the way to the Promised Land.
La Querencia . . .
I swear by the Holy Sea! (See?)
These are my new friends. . . this is my new home,
Island Guanahani.
And the caravels turned around,
Sailing back to the King and Queen,
And Paradise was never found . . .
In my dream . . .oh, what a dream!

[Repeat chorus]

Responding

1. Describe other versions of either Heaven or Hell that you have heard about.
2. If Heaven were to contain any elements of earthly pleasure, which would you choose for yourself as an everlasting reward?
3. If Hell were to contain any elements of earthly torment, which do you imagine they might be?

MINI-LESSON: VISUAL LITERACY

Evaluate Nonprint Media

Teach Tell students that although television is part of almost everyone's daily life, usually we view it passively. For instance, we often watch the news on TV with the assumption that it presents an objective truth. However, just as a movie or situation comedy is scripted and edited, so is the TV news.

Apply Show the class a videotape of a TV news show that contains anchor people reading the news and an "on the street" segment. Ask students to pay careful attention to what is shown in the frame of each shot, what kind of language is used for the news items, and when each shot ends and begins.

Activity Idea Have students choose an "on the street" segment of the news and answer the following questions about it. They may want to watch the segment several times.

- What happens in this segment?
- What do you think happened just before that?
- What might be going on outside the edges of the frame?
- What do you think might happen after the cameras are turned off?
- What are some descriptive phrases used by the news anchor person?
- Did you learn anything about the TV news by doing this exercise?

After students write their answers, discuss what they learned.

Language History

The Language of the King James Bible

And the Lord God formed man of the dust of the ground, and breathed into his nostrils the breath of life; and man became a living soul.

Genesis 2:7

This eloquent passage, taken from the book of Genesis in the King James Bible, illustrates why that work has been called "the noblest monument of English prose." The sheer brilliance of its language makes the King James version deserving of that epithet. In contrast to the ornamental style characteristic of some prose in the early 1600s, the King James version preserves the old language and plain style of the earlier English versions of the Bible. Its extensive use of concrete terms and images, its straightforward phrases and sentences, its balance and parallelism in many passages—all make for a dignified simplicity most compatible with religious feeling and ritual.

The profound impact of the King James Bible can be seen in the work of a multitude of writers and speakers, who—generation after generation—have been deeply influenced by the plain, yet poetic, language and style of the King James version. Abraham Lincoln, for example, used the language of the King James Bible in this sentence from a famous speech about slavery: "A house divided against itself cannot stand." Many phrases and expressions commonly used in everyday speech also have their origins in the King James Bible—for example, *the salt of the earth; a sign of the times; the apple of my eye; a thorn in the flesh; all is vanity;* and *to everything there is a season*. Still widely read and quoted nearly four hundred years after its first printing, the King James Bible has had a unique influence not only on religious thought but on English language and literature as well.

Language History

Teaching Objectives

- to appreciate the language of the King James Bible
- to understand the unique influence of the King James Bible on English language and literature

Introduce

Students can work in small groups to find other translations or versions of Genesis 2:7 and compare the wording. For example, some versions substitute the words *being* or *creature* for the word *soul.* Students might discuss which words and which versions they prefer, and why.

Follow Up

After students have read page 281, discuss the meaning of the biblical phrases in the second paragraph. Then have them scan a book of quotations, such as *Bartlett's*, looking for Bible quotations, that they have encountered in the past. Did they realize how many common expressions and quotations come from the Bible?

CONTENT AREA READING

Use Reference Sources

From time to time, students may need to locate quotations such as those in the lesson on this page. Show them a book of quotations, such as *Bartlett's*. Discuss that such books may be divided into sections, usually by author, but also by topics such as the Koran or the Bible, or by historical periods such as ancient Egypt.

If only part of a quotation is known, but its source is not, students should look in the index, which lists quotations by first lines and key words.

If one is looking for a quotation to illustrate a particular subject in a speech or a paper, a book of quotations organized entirely by topic is useful. Such books will include quotations under topics such as aviation, food, gardening, money, movies, working, or writing, for example.

Writing Workshop

WRITER'S BLUEPRINT

Specs

The Specs in the Writer's Blueprint address these writing and thinking skills:

- analyzing symbols in literature
- drawing conclusions
- using supporting details
- synthesizing
- incorporating visuals with text
- using parallel structure
- using adjectives and adverbs correctly

These Specs serve as your lesson objectives, and they form the basis for the **Assessment Criteria Specs** for a superior paper, which appear on the final TE page for this lesson. You might want to read through the *Assessment Criteria Specs* with students when you begin the lesson.

Linking Literature to Writing

Ask students to point out several features of the landscape of Hell. You might make a list on the board. Then have students speculate on the relationships of two or three of these landmarks to Satan's character.

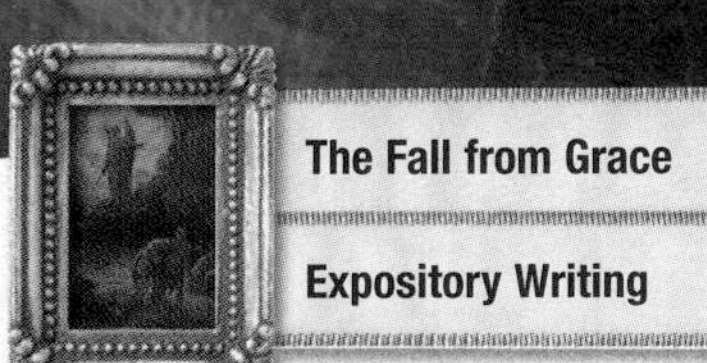

Writing Workshop

A Landscape of Symbols

Assignment In *Paradise Lost*, Milton uses vivid imagery to describe the landscape to which Satan has been banished, a landscape meant to symbolize Satan's character. Write an essay in which you interpret the landscape of Hell as symbolic of Satan's character.

WRITER'S BLUEPRINT

Product	An interpretive essay
Purpose	To analyze symbols in literature
Audience	People who have read *Paradise Lost*
Specs	As the writer of a successful essay, you should:

- ❑ Begin in a dramatic way to engage the reader.
- ❑ Present your conclusions about the symbolic relationships between landscape and character. Back up these conclusions with evidence from the poem, including direct quotations.
- ❑ End by drawing your separate conclusions together into a paragraph that restates them with a fresh emphasis.
- ❑ Include any visuals—sketches, diagrams, maps—that will liven up or clarify your conclusions.
- ❑ Use parallel structure for emphasis and clarity.
- ❑ Follow the rules of grammar, usage, spelling, and mechanics. Pay special attention to forms of adjectives and adverbs.

WRITING WORKSHOP OVERVIEW

Product
Expository writing: An interpretive essay

Prewriting
Interpret a familiar landscape—Create a sketch—Chart the symbolic relationships—Plan your essay—Ask a partner
Unit 3 Resource Book
Prewriting Worksheets pp. 43–44

Drafting
Before you write—As you draft
Transparency Collection
Student Models for Writing Workshop 9, 10

Revising
Ask a partner—Strategy: Using Parallel Structure
Unit 3 Resource Book
Revising Worksheet p. 45

Editing
Ask a partner—Strategy: Using Adjectives and Adverbs Correctly
Unit 3 Resource Book
Grammar Worksheet p. 46
Grammar Check Test p. 47

Presenting
Read Around
Another Class

Looking Back
Self-evaluate—Reflect—For Your Working Portfolio
Unit 3 Resource Book
Assessment Worksheet p. 48
Transparency Collection
Fine Art Transparency 5

STEP 1 PREWRITING

Interpret a familiar landscape. Practice interpreting a familiar landscape before you work with Milton's. Visualize a room that's familiar to you, your own or someone's close to you. Make a list of objects in the room that say something important about the person who lives there.

Create a sketch. To help you visualize Milton's landscape, use colored pencils or markers to sketch the landscape described in the poem. On the back of your landscape, explain at least two ways you have represented the symbolic relationship between Satan and his landscape.

Chart the symbolic relationships in *Paradise Lost.* With a partner, search Milton's poem for quotations that show relationships between aspects of Satan's character and the landscape of Hell.

Character Elements (Satan)	Landscape Elements (Hell)
inability to see truth and goodness	"As one great furnace flamed, yet from those flames/No light, but rather darkness visible. . . ." (lines 62–63)

Plan your essay. Organize your ideas in a plan similar to the one that follows.

Introduction
- Dramatic quote or strong statement (to engage the reader)

Body
- First conclusion (an element from the landscape and how it symbolizes an aspect of Satan's character)
  Evidence from poem
- Second conclusion
  Evidence from poem

  and so on . . .

Conclusion
- Summary of conclusions from body
- Fresh emphasis on Satan and landscape of Hell

Visuals
- Sketches or other graphics to include

OR . . .
Before you make your sketch, do research to see how various artists have illustrated *Paradise Lost* since Milton's time. See the interdisciplinary study on Heaven and Hell beginning on page 278.

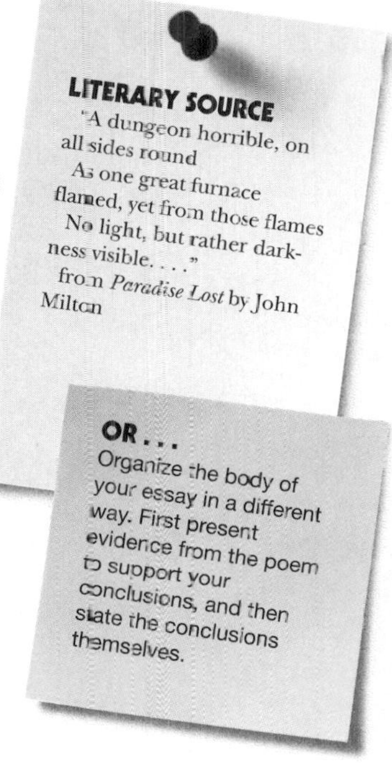

LITERARY SOURCE
"A dungeon horrible, on all sides round
As one great furnace flamed, yet from those flames
No light, but rather darkness visible. . . ."
from *Paradise Lost* by John Milton

OR . . .
Organize the body of your essay in a different way. First present evidence from the poem to support your conclusions, and then state the conclusions themselves.

STEP 1 PREWRITING

Interpret a familiar landscape

Have students discuss their interpretations in groups or as a class. Some students may want to sketch a familiar landscape. For additional support, see the worksheet referenced below.

Unit 3 Resource Book
Prewriting Worksheet, p. 43

Create a sketch

You may want to treat this as you might a quickwrite. As you read a passage aloud, have students visually represent the feelings or emotions that first strike them.

Chart the symbolic relationships

Students may find it helpful to break down this problem into parts. Have them first list all the descriptions of Hell and all the elements characteristic of Satan. Then they can go back and match any elements from the two lists that seem to share commonalties. For additional support, see the worksheet referenced below.

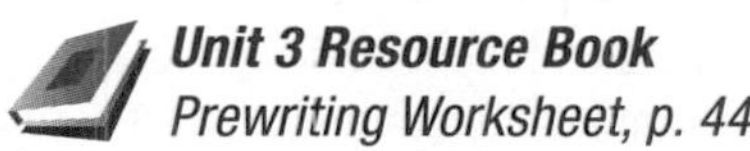

Unit 3 Resource Book
Prewriting Worksheet, p. 44

Plan your essay

Have students choose a strong quote from the text around which to build their essay. Make sure students are aware of the "Or . . ." option.

BUILDING ENGLISH PROFICIENCY

Planning Use of Artwork

Offer to students who wish to use sketches or other graphics in their essays recommendations such as the following:

- Always refer to your artwork within the text (as in "see the drawing below "or "the sketch on the following page").
- If the piece of artwork is small enough to share a page with text, place it after the section of text that mentions it. If it is full page, try to place it on the page immediately following the one on which it was mentioned.
- Use captions to identify your graphics.

Ask a partner (Peer assessment)

After students respond to their peer's essay in general, have them read the opening and closing again in order to focus on these important areas of the essay.

Connections to **Writer's Notebook**

For selection-related prompts, refer to Writer's Notebook.

Connections to **Writer's Resource**

For additional writing prompts, refer to Writer's Resource.

STEP 2 DRAFTING

As you draft

Have students take a moment to write one sentence that sums up their main argument to use as a reminder of their focus.

The Student Models

The **transparencies** referenced below are authentic student models. Review them with the students before they draft. These suggestions may help:

1. Focus on the conclusion of model 9. How well does it fulfill the third spec in the Writer's Blueprint?

2. How could the writer of model 10 improve the conclusion with a fresh emphasis?

Transparency Collection
Student Models for Writing Workshop 9, 10

STEP 3 REVISING

Ask a partner (Peer assessment)

Remind students to point out the effective parts of their peer's essays as well as the areas that need improvement.

Ask a partner to review your plan.

- ✔ Have I come up with strong conclusions, supported by evidence from the poem, to show the relationship between landscape and character?
- ✔ Are my conclusions restated at the end of my paper in a fresh and emphatic way?
- ✔ Am I following the Specs in the Writer's Blueprint?

Use your partner's comments to help you revise your plan.

STEP 2 DRAFTING

Before you write, review the Writer's Blueprint, your character and landscape chart, visual representations, and writing plan.

As you draft, don't spend time correcting mistakes in spelling and punctuation. Concentrate on getting your ideas on the page. Consider these suggestions.

- Instead of writing your essay in your own voice, consider writing it from the point of view of an eyewitness visiting Milton's version of Hell, or as Satan himself. If you write as Satan, be sure to have him interpret the landscape from a point of view that is favorable to himself.
- Use parallel structure to emphasize and clarify the points you make. (See the Revising Strategy in Step 3 of this lesson.)

COMPUTER TIP
Save the revised version of your essay in a new file with a new name. This allows you to compare the two versions, or even incorporate something from the first draft back into the revised version.

STEP 3 REVISING

Ask a partner for comments on your draft before you revise it.

- ✔ Have I concentrated on the relationship between Satan and the landscape of Hell?
- ✔ Have I supported my conclusions with examples from the poem?
- ✔ Have I used parallel structure for emphasis and clarity?

MINI-LESSON: WRITING STYLE

Using Parallel Structure

Teach When a reader has to reread a sentence to make sense of it, the writer is often to blame. Sentences with problems in parallelism often force readers to stumble over the shift in structure and to retrace their paths.

Activity Idea Have students identify the errors in parallel structure in the examples below before revising.

1. The Meals on Wheels volunteers spend a few hours each week either cooking meals, loading and dispatching, or they deliver the lunches to the clients.

2. Min Lu is a college student, married, and cares for her daughter.

3. I have dedicated myself to making the soccer team and to practice every day this semester.

Apply Have students read aloud any of their sentences that might contain errors in parallel structure. Ask them to notice the parts that cause them to pause because they don't *sound* quite right, and to revise them so they sound right.

Revising Strategy

Using Parallel Structure

Sentences with parallel structure use the same grammatical form to express similar ideas of equal importance. Parallel structure creates balance and rhythm within paragraphs and within individual sentences. It is essential when you list items in a series. Read these two sentences aloud to hear how much smoother the revised, parallel version is.

Not Parallel: Milton believed that the Christian religion was a matter involving God, the Bible, and to include the individual human being. (two nouns and a phrase)

Parallel: Milton believed that the Christian religion was a matter involving God, the Bible, and the individual human being. (three nouns)

When you revise, read your draft aloud to yourself. When a sentence sounds awkward, check it with the idea of parallel structure in mind. See the student model that follows.

Satan must be in control at all times. His thirst for power can only be quenched in a setting where his power is able to grow without challenge, complication, or contradiction ~~is ever contradicted in any way~~. He must realize his goal "To set himself in glory among his peers" (line 39). In order to succeed at this he must be in control of a place "as far removed from God and light of Heaven / As from the center thrice to the utmost pole." (lines 73–74)

STUDENT MODEL

STEP 4 EDITING

Ask a partner to review your revised draft before you edit. As you edit, look for errors in grammar, usage, spelling, and mechanics. Look especially for problems with forms of adjectives and adverbs.

Revising Strategy: Using Parallel Structure

Before discussing the revising strategy, have students discuss possible meanings of the term *parallel structure,* drawing from what they know of *parallel* from mathematics and geography.

For additional support, see the mini-lesson at the bottom of page 284 and the worksheet referenced below.

Unit 3 Resource Book
Revising Worksheet, p. 45

Connections to **Writer's Resource**

Refer to the Grammar, Usage, and Mechanics Handbook on Writer's Resource.

STEP 4 EDITING

Ask a partner (Peer assessment)

Remind students to use proofreading symbols rather than just circling errors. See the symbols on the inside back cover of the text.

MINI-LESSON: GRAMMAR

Using Adjectives and Adverbs Correctly

Have students change the following adjectives and adverbs to the comparative and superlative degrees. Then have them compile some guidelines to use as they write. For example:

deep—deeper—deepest

One-syllable modifiers usually add *-er* or *-est.*

gentle	innocent
lovely	rapidly
fearful	warm

Unit 3 Resource Book
Grammar Worksheet p. 46
Grammar Check Test p. 47

Editing Strategy: Using Adjectives and Adverbs Correctly

For additional support, see the mini-lesson at the bottom of page 285 and the worksheets referenced below.

Unit 3 Resource Book
Grammar Worksheet, p. 46
Grammar Check Test, p. 47

Connections to **Writer's Resource**

Refer to the Grammar, Usage, and Mechanics Handbook on Writer's Resource.

STEP 5 PRESENTING

Read Around

Have students extend their discussion of symbols to any previous class readings that used the technique effectively.

STEP 6 LOOKING BACK

Self-evaluate

The *Assessment Criteria Specs* at the bottom of this page are for a superior paper. You might want to post these in the classroom. Students can then evaluate themselves based on these criteria. For a complete scoring rubric, use the *Assessment Worksheet* referenced below.

Unit 3 Resource Book
Assessment Worksheet, p. 48

Reflect

After gathering all of the students' reflections regarding effective writing strategies, discuss with the class any activities that a majority of students feel are helpful. Begin to compile a list of the strategies that could be carried over to other assignments.

To further explore the theme, use the Fine Art Transparency referenced below.

Transparency Collection
Fine Art Writing Prompt 5

Editing Strategy

Using Adjectives and Adverbs Correctly

FOR REFERENCE
Look for more information about forms of adjectives and adverbs in the Language and Grammar Handbook at the back of this text.

When you edit, take care to see that you've formed the comparative and superlative forms of adjectives and adverbs correctly. Most of the time, use *-er* or *-est*: holier, quicker, yellowest, soonest.

For some longer words, use *more* or *most* instead: more corrupt, most carelessly.

Never use *more* and *-er* or *most* and *-est* together. Write *more dangerous,* not *more dangerouser.* Write *latest,* not *most latest.*

STEP 5 PRESENTING

- Have a read around. In a small group, pass your essays around until everyone has read each one. Use your essays as the basis for a round-table discussion on the subject of symbols in literature.
- If another class has read and written about *Paradise Lost*, exchange papers with them. Get together and compare ideas.

STEP 6 LOOKING BACK

Self-evaluate. What grade would *you* give your essay? Look back at the Writer's Blueprint and give yourself a score for each item, from 6 (superior) to 1 (inadequate).

Reflect. Think about what you've learned while writing this essay.

✔ Write a note to your teacher describing how you developed your essay. What prewriting and planning activities helped you most? Attach this note to your essay when you hand it in.

✔ Look at the various drafts of your paper. What are three major improvements you made in the final version?

For Your Working Portfolio Add your essay and your reflection responses to your working portfolio.

ASSESSMENT CRITERIA SPECS

6 Superior The writer of a 6 paper impressively meets these criteria:

- Insightfully analyzes the relationships between the landscape of Hell and Satan's character as reflected in Milton's poem.
- Offers an engaging introduction that hooks the reader.
- Refers to specific images and symbols from the text that reveal Satan's personality, psyche, beliefs, and temperament and clearly interprets their significance.
- Backs up conclusions with compelling evidence from the poem, including quotations where appropriate.
- Includes visuals that help clarify conclusions.
- Ends by restating the writer's premise with a fresh emphasis that offers new insights.
- Uses parallel structure for emphasis and clarity.
- Makes few, if any, mistakes in grammar, usage, mechanics, and spelling. Uses adjectives and adverbs correctly throughout.

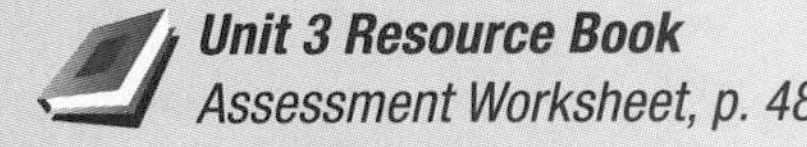

Unit 3 Resource Book
Assessment Worksheet, p. 48

Beyond Print

Basic Word Processing

Some people don't take full advantage of word processing, possibly because they're not yet familiar enough with it. Here are some pointers on using this powerful tool to create your documents.

Compose at the keyboard. Many people still use pen and paper to write and then retype it. However, as your keyboarding skills improve you should be able to eliminate using a pen and compose your entire document using only the word processor.

Don't worry about mistakes. Since editing text is so simple on the computer, let yourself go and *just write!* You can always go back and fix your mistakes later.

Learn the capabilities. Every time you use your word processor, try a different tool or function. Learn to perform a spelling check or grammar check, center headings, insert page numbers, create footnotes or endnotes, create charts or graphs.

Use the available tools. But don't use them blindly. The spelling checker is a marvelous help; however, don't forget that it only checks spelling, not usage. Always proofread your documents.

Save your documents. Power outages and system errors can cause the computer to lose hours worth of writing, so get into the habit of saving often. A good rule of thumb is to save after every paragraph.

Limit the number of fonts. Generally, more than three fonts in the same document become confusing to read. Serif fonts like Times, Bookman, or Palatino are easier to read in the body of a document, while sans-serif fonts like Helvetica make nice headings and titles. Use special font styles like outline, shadow, bold, and italic sparingly.

Fonts
Times
Bookman
Palatino
Helvetica

Styles
outline
shadow
bold
italic

Activity Options

1. Start by brainstorming essay ideas on the screen. Print out this list.
2. Open a new document and create an outline. Print it out.
3. Compose your essay on screen, using the outline as a guide.

Beyond Print

Teaching Objectives

- to learn the potential uses of a word processor
- to recognize the limits of a word processor
- to make stylistic choices when using a word processor

Curricular Connection: Technology

You can use these pointers to aid students in using a word processor to its full potential.

Introduce

Formatting, editing, changing fonts—these are just a few of the many things a basic word processor can do. Suggest to students that they make a list comparing and contrasting the uses of a typewriter with those of a word processor.

Activity Options

Activity 1 Since they are writing these essays as practice material, they can pick whimsical or humorous ideas.

Activity 2 When outlining, students can practice setting tabs, changing spacing, and making the type bold or italic. Or students can experiment with an outline template.

Activity 3 While composing their essays, students can practice moving sentences or whole paragraphs to different parts of the essay by using a cut-and-paste function.

BUILDING ENGLISH PROFICIENCY

Expanding upon Factual Information

Use one or both of the following activities to help students grasp this feature's information about basic word processing.

- Invite a teacher or student who is familiar with word-processing software (or an adult who uses it in his or her daily work) to demonstrate the software's capabilities. For example, have him or her cut and paste, save a document, change fonts, and use a spelling checker.
- Arrange time in the school's computer lab for students to try some basic word processing. Invite them to write and save a paragraph; then allow them to experiment on "pasted" copies of that paragraph—changing details, moving sentences, and so on—and print a final copy. Afterward, encourage students to share their thoughts about composing at the keyboard.

Unit Wrap-Up

MULTICULTURAL CONNECTION

Ethnicity is one aspect of culture that students may be aware of; they may be less conscious of how historical time, geographical location, and class contribute to the formation of culture. It may be helpful to take these aspects into account when discussing the culture from which the literature of Unit 3 came.

Perspectives

The awareness of life's shortness and difficulty can cause people to reach out to each other and feel connected.

Possible Response Students may choose the Donne works for the way he mixes the personal with the philosophical; they may choose Herrick for the intimate specificity of his *carpe diem* subjects; they may choose Marvell for the vivid sensuality expressed in his work.

Communication

The King James Bible and *Paradise Lost* are products of a specific time and place and the minds of their authors.

Possible Response Students may say it depends on whether a writer is trying to represent the opinion of a group, or his or her own. Many will say that since no one knows what heaven or hell, for example, are actually like, writers are free to interpret these places as they wish.

Activity Options

Activity 1 Suggest students listen to rock musicians of the 1950s, such as Buddy Holly and Elvis Presley, to find some good examples.

Activity 2 Suggest students look into some non-monotheistic religions for creation stories.

Activity 3 It has been said that a scene needs to contain a change to be complete. Suggest to students that at least one character in each scene experiences some sort of change.

Multicultural Connections

Perspectives

Part One: The Meaning of Life The relative shortness and difficulty of life in the 1600s undoubtedly contributed toward the unique perspective of *carpe diem* ("seize the day") literature, a perspective that John Donne, Robert Herrick, Andrew Marvell, and hundreds of other writers have communicated over the centuries. The same shortness and difficulty may lead to other perspectives as well, such as Donne's declaration that "no man is an island," that we are all a part of each other and responsible for each other.

■ Which of the selections in this part do you feel does the best job of communicating a particular perspective?

Communication

Part Two: The Fall from Grace The religious faith of Christianity is in itself a unique perspective, but it is one that has been susceptible to various interpretations at various times, depending on how its tenets have been communicated, by whom and to whom. Although both *Paradise Lost* and the King James Bible are landmarks in Christian literature, both were the products of a particular time and place, and both reflect the perspectives of their creators.

■ When a writer undertakes to communicate a particular perspective, or to create a narrative that dramatizes that perspective, how much individuality do you think that writer can—or should be allowed to—put into his or her work?

Activities

1. Find examples of *carpe diem* writings from other periods of history, for example in song lyrics of the 1900s (such as "You'd Better Stop and Smell the Roses" or "It's Today" from the musical *Mame*).
2. Research creation stories from some other religions. Each group member can research a different religion and then give a brief oral summary to the group or to the whole class.
3. Develop a skit that illustrates the concept that no man is an island. Your skit should run about 10 minutes. You can use any place and any time in history as a setting. Rehearse and present it in reader's theater format—with scripts in hand—to the class.

Independent and Group Projects

Music

Perform a Poem Hundreds of seventeenth-century poems have been set to music by composers of their day or by later composers. Find and listen to a recording of a musical setting for one or two poems, or compose music for one of the poems in this unit and perform the song for the class. Your composition can be in a modern or traditional idiom.

Media

Defining the Age What is your general impression of the seventeenth century, its people, and its literature? Do some further research on the political or social history of the era or on a seventeenth century author and his writing. Use a multimedia computer program or a video camera to prepare a documentary that explains your subject to a new audience of your classmates. Use any kinds of graphics, music, and sound effects you think appropriate.

Panel Discussion

What Is Sin? Milton and other writers of the period often pondered the nature of sin and evil. Topics such as the widespread presence of evil in the world, possible reasons for sin, and the notion that humans are becoming more and more evil are troubling ones. Although there may be no definitive explanations, you might at least come close to demonstrating what evil is or what it does. Organize a panel discussion in your class. If possible, include people from a variety of cultures. Make certain that there are guidelines to assure that everyone's beliefs will be heard respectfully.

Art

Rebus Verse Seventeenth century writers loved word play and elaborate conceits. A rebus is a game in which pictures substitute for syllables, words, or phrases. For example, a rebus for the first line of Donne's "Song" might be: Go and [picture of a catcher's mitt] a falling [picture of a star]. Devise a rebus for the rest of "Song" or for another poem of your choosing and display it on a bulletin board.

UNIT 3 OPTIONS

Music

Some composers of the seventeenth century are Claudio Monteverdi, Jean Baptiste Lully, Antonio Vivaldi, and Arcangelo Corelli. The foremost English composer of the time was Henry Purcell.

Media

Suggest to students that they narrate the documentaries themselves, include their opinions, and ask questions.

Panel Discussion

A discussion of good and evil may quickly become heated. To keep the panel from becoming hurtful, suggest that students

- start by defining what will be broadly meant by the terms "good" and "evil"
- call "time out" when they need to take a break from the discussion

Rebus Verse

Students may look at some of the art work from this unit, or other examples of baroque art, and try drawing the pictorial elements of their rebuses in the style of the day.

Unit Test

Unit 3 Resource Book
New Selection, pp. 49–50
Test 1, pp. 51–52
Test 2, pp. 53–58

Part One: A Focus on Society

Planning Unit 4: The Age of Reason

Literature	Integrated Language Arts			
	Literary	Writing/Grammar, Usage and Mechanics	Reading, Thinking, Listening, Speaking	Vocabulary/Spelling
A Modest Proposal *by Jonathan Swift* Essay *(challenging)* p. 296	Satire Connotation/denotation Metaphor Irony	Modern targets for satire Essay on irony Satirical column Sentence structure Use commas in a series	Compare and contrast Detect bias Find the main idea	Word origins
The Education of Women *by Daniel Defoe* Essay *(average)* p. 306	Theme Figure of speech	Take a position Letter to the editor Essay Understand subordinate and coordinate clauses The rhetorical question	Find the main idea Recognize propaganda techniques	
from The Rape of the Lock *by Alexander Pope* Epic Poem *(challenging)* p. 314 **from An Essay on Criticism** *by Alexander Pope* Poem *(average)* p. 325	Heroic couplet/epigram Foreshadowing Alliteration Mood Onomatopoeia Simile	Write a heroic couplet Profile a satirist Letter to the editor Dialogue Use consistent verb tense Epics and mock epics	Find the main idea Essential and incidental information Recognize values Draw conclusions Infer Generalize	Connotation/denotation

Meeting Individual Needs

Multi-modal Activities	Mini-Lessons
Stage a radio talk show Satirical drawing Linking past and present Exploring key concepts Exploring different points of view	Sentence structure Word origins Using commas in a series
Oral report Debate Picture/diagram of best learning environment Planning a reading strategy Expanding vocabulary notebook	Understanding subordinate and coordinate clauses The rhetorical question
Editorial cartoon Illustrated report on Handel Choreograph a fight Improving comprehension Understanding elevated language Making personal connections Making cultural connections Responding artistically to poetry	Connotation/denotation Using consistent verb tense Heroic couplets /epigrams Epics and mock epics

Interdisciplinary Studies
Satirical Thrusts

Format	Content Area	Highlights	Skill
Article: **Our Glorious Leaders**	Popular Culture	A collection of political cartoons and puppet caricatures.	Distinguish between fact and opinion
Interview: **Hoping for a Visceral Reaction**	Career	A political cartoonist talks about his job.	Distinguish between fact and opinion

Writing Workshop

Mode	Writing Format	Writing Focus	Proofreading Skills
Persuasive writing	A satirical essay	Making smooth transitions	Avoiding careless spelling mistakes

Program Support Materials

For Every Selection	For Every Writing Workshop
Unit Resource Book Graphic Organizer Study Guide Vocabulary Worksheet Grammar Worksheet Spelling, Speaking and Listening, or Literary Language Worksheet Alternate Check Test Vocabulary Test Selection Test	**Unit Resource Book** Prewriting Worksheet Revising Strategy Worksheet Editing Strategy Worksheet Presentation Worksheet Writing Rubric **Transparency Collection** Fine Art Transparency Student Writing Model Transparencies

For Every Interdisciplinary Study	Assessment
Unit Resource Book Study Guide Mini-Lesson Skill Worksheet	**Unit Resource Book** TE Check Tests Alternate Check Test (blackline master) Vocabulary Test (blackline master) Selection Test (blackline master) **Test Generator Software** **Assessment Handbook**

Part Two: Other People's Lives

Planning Unit 4: The Age of Reason

Literature	Integrated Language Arts			
	Literary	Writing/Grammar, Usage and Mechanics	Reading, Thinking, Listening, Speaking	Vocabulary/Spelling
from The Diary *by Samuel Pepys* Diary *(average)* p. 340	Imagery Characterization Tone	Keep a personal diary Descriptive narrative Brief news story Proper nouns, titles and adjectives	Compare and contrast Draw conclusions Infer	Match synonyms and use in a sentence Word meanings
Dignity and Uses of Biography *by Samuel Johnson* Essay *(average)* p. 351 **from the Dictionary of the English Language** *by Samuel Johnson* Dictionary *(easy)* p. 355 **Letter to Chesterfield** *by Samuel Johnson* Letter *(easy)* p. 357	Denotation/connotation Characterization Sound devices Satire	Describe an unfair act Compile a dictionary of teenage expressions Brief essay Run-on sentences	Find the main idea Detect bias/identify assumptions Compare and contrast Fact and opinion Recognize cause and effect	Using dictionaries for word meanings
from The Life of Samuel Johnson, LL.D. *by James Boswell* Biography *(average)* p. 361	Characterization Simile Apply	Make a list Write a biographical sketch Write a biographical anecdote Personal pronouns	Find the main idea Draw conclusions Recognize values Compare and contrast	Describe a verbal argument Using adjectives

Meeting Individual Needs

Multi-modal Activities	Mini-Lessons
Tell a human interest story Design a personal book plate Planning a reading strategy Linking past and present Using context clues Making real-life connections	Proper nouns, titles and adjectives Word meanings Using a time line
Bulletin board display Chart the famous Improving comprehension Exploring key ideas	Run-on sentences Using dictionaries for word meaning Exploring connotation
Creating an advertisement Constructing a time line Conducting an interview Considering an interviewing strategy Exploring biography	Personal pronouns Characterization Using adjectives

Interdisciplinary Studies
Celebrity

Format	Content Area	Highlights	Skill
Article: **A Short History of Fame** *by Clive James*	History	A brief account of how the celebrity system began.	Use an anthology
Article: **Seeing Stars**	Fine Art	Various artists paintings of famous people.	Interpretive reading/speech

Writing Workshop

Mode	Writing Format	Writing Focus	Proofreading Skills
Narrative writing	A biographical sketch	Avoiding choppy writing Interview your subject	Punctuating quotations correctly

Program Support Materials

For Every Selection	For Every Writing Workshop
Unit Resource Book Graphic Organizer Study Guide Vocabulary Worksheet Grammar Worksheet Spelling, Speaking and Listening, or Literary Language Worksheet Alternate Check Test Vocabulary Test Selection Test	**Unit Resource Book** Prewriting Worksheet Revising Strategy Worksheet Editing Strategy Worksheet Presentation Worksheet Writing Rubric **Transparency Collection** Fine Art Transparency Student Writing Model Transparencies

For Every Interdisciplinary Study	Assessment
Unit Resource Book Study Guide Mini-Lesson Skill Worksheet	**Unit Resource Book** TE Check Tests Alternate Check Test (blackline master) Vocabulary Test (blackline master) Selection Test (blackline master) **Test Generator Software** **Assessment Handbook**

Media and Technology

Part One Selections

A Modest Proposal

Videotape Students may enjoy another work of Swift's in *BBC: Gulliver in Lilliput*, 107 minutes, Library Video Company.

Community Resources The problems of poor people still concern society. Invite a local public official to class to discuss current state or national proposals that are designed to help poor people. Students might submit questions to the speaker beforehand.

The Education of Women

Videotape *Daniel Defoe*, 30 minutes, International Historic Films, 1991, profiles the life and work of Daniel Defoe.

Home Connection Students might query their parents or other older adults in the family who attended school with members of the opposite sex about whether teachers treated boys and girls differently in the classroom, and if so, how.

The Rape of the Lock/from An Essay on Criticism

Audiotape Selections from the works of Pope are presented in *Treasury of Alexander Pope,* and *Alexander Pope: The Rape of the Lock*, both from Spoken Arts.

Community Resources If a local, daily paper employs an editorial cartoonist, invite that per

Connections to
Custom Literature Database

For Part One "A Focus on Society" Selections with Lessons

- "Will Wimble" from *The Spectator* by Joseph Addison
- "A Description of a City Shower" by Jonathan Swift

Additional theme-based selections can be accessed on the ScottForesman database.

A New Gulliver

Ted Danson stars in a new Hallmark Hall of Fame production of *Gulliver's Travels,* available on video.

son to speak to the class. Students might ask questions such as these: Where do cartoon ideas come from? Are people ever angered enough by a satirical cartoon to write a letter? How does one become an editorial cartoonist?

Part Two Selections

from The Diary

Audiotape *The Diary of Samuel Pepys,* Spoken Arts, contains extracts from the famous diary.

Community Resources Some communities have had devastating fires, which someone in the community usually remembers or knows about. If your community has had a memorable fire, ask someone with knowledge of it to talk to the class.

Dignity and Uses of Biography/from the Dictionary of the English Language/Letter to Chesterfield

Videotape *The Age of Reason,* 2 sound filmstrips, Films for the Humanities & Sciences, includes Johnson, Pope, and Boswell.

Home Connection Biographies are often shown on public television, and a variety of types of people are portrayed: actors, politicians, inventors, royalty, explorers, writers, and musicians are all featured from time to time. Students might watch a biography, perhaps on video if none is scheduled on

television, and analyze the point of view as evidenced in both words and pictures. Is it admiring? critical? slanted?

from The Life of Samuel Johnson, LL. D.

Videotape *Boswell for the Defence,* 90 minutes, and *Boswell in London,* 1 hour 52 minutes, Films for the Humanities & Sciences, are both insightful portraits of the man and his times.

Community Resources When the Stuarts were returned to power in 1660, the literary name of the period came to be known as the Restoration Age. Some students might like to find and read a Restoration comedy by Congreve or Wycherly.

Connections to
Custom Literature Database

For Part Two "Other People's Lives" Selections with Lessons

- from *The Life of Milton* by Samuel Johnson
- "Elegy Written in a Country Churchyard" by Thomas Gray

Additional theme-based selections can be accessed on the ScottForesman database.

Diary on Tape

Students can listen to excerpts from *The Diary of Samuel Pepys,* from Spoken Arts.

Unit 4

The Age of Reason

Art Study

This anonymous work, *View of Broad Quay, Bristol,* was painted about 1735. Bristol is a seaport in southwest England on the Avon, near the confluence of the Severn estuary, which flows into the Bristol Channel.

Question What can you tell about life in this locale from the picture? *(Possible responses: The economy of the town may depend on fishing and shipping. There is an active civic life with children playing and people talking, gossiping, and transacting business on the street.)*

Visual Literacy Introduce the term "vanishing point," the point toward which receding parallel lines seem to converge, and ask students to find the vanishing point in this picture.

Question What was the artist's vantage point? (*Possible response: The artist seems to have been at the end of and a little above the street, perhaps in a second- or third-story window.)*

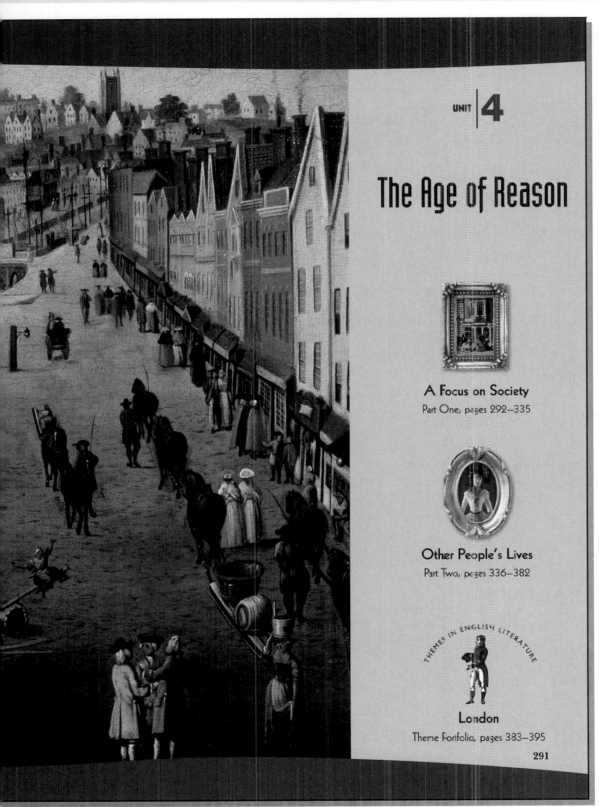

UNIT 4

The Age of Reason

A Focus on Society
Part One, pages 292–335

Other People's Lives
Part Two, pages 336–382

THEMES IN ENGLISH LITERATURE

London
Theme Portfolio, pages 383–395

291

THEMATIC CONNECTIONS

During the Age of Reason, there was an emphasis on self-knowledge, rationalism, discipline, and decorum. Literature was realistic and satiric.

Part One
A Focus on Society

Part One features literature that explores some important social issues of the Age of *Reason.*

Ideas to Explore

- What are some dictionary definitions of reason?
- What are the alternatives to living a life according to reason?
- What issues did people try to address using reasoned persuasion?

Part Two
Other People's Lives

The literature in Part Two focuses on how the men who considered themselves primarily rational beings chose to live their lives.

Ideas to Explore

- Why do some people keep diaries?
- What makes people want to write autobiographies and biographies?
- How is nonfiction an appropriate category of writings for this age?

The top icon is a picture of Arthur's Club, a once-popular gaming center on St. James's Street in London.

Historical Overview

EXPLORING CONCEPTS

- There were great inequalities between rich and poor and male and female in seventeenth- and eighteenth-century Britain.
- Satire was a powerful weapon against social injustice and an amusing one when directed at the leisured class.

Research Activity Small groups of students might use library or on-line resources to find out and report on the Royal Society, St. Paul's Cathedral, the Duke of Monmouth, Queen Anne, William III and Mary, Angelica Kauffmann, Sarah Siddons, and Sir Joshua Reynolds.

The art on these two pages is a composite, with details from several sources. An Unhappy Seaman at lower left and A Troubled Pedestrian, extreme lower right, are from a cartoon (1797) by George Cruikshank. Other types of people are (page 292) The Lady of Fashion, An Elegant Trio, The Brooding Curate; (page 293) A Hobbling Crone, Family, A Merry Milkmaid, and A Chimney Sweep and his Helper.

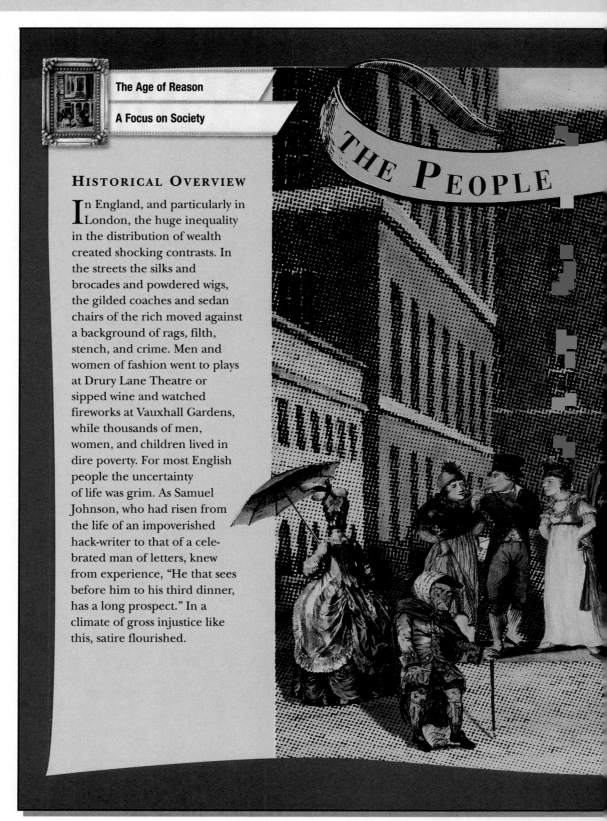

THE PEOPLE

HISTORICAL OVERVIEW

In England, and particularly in London, the huge inequality in the distribution of wealth created shocking contrasts. In the streets the silks and brocades and powdered wigs, the gilded coaches and sedan chairs of the rich moved against a background of rags, filth, stench, and crime. Men and women of fashion went to plays at Drury Lane Theatre or sipped wine and watched fireworks at Vauxhall Gardens, while thousands of men, women, and children lived in dire poverty. For most English people the uncertainty of life was grim. As Samuel Johnson, who had risen from the life of an impoverished hack-writer to that of a celebrated man of letters, knew from experience, "He that sees before him to his third dinner, has a long prospect." In a climate of gross injustice like this, satire flourished.

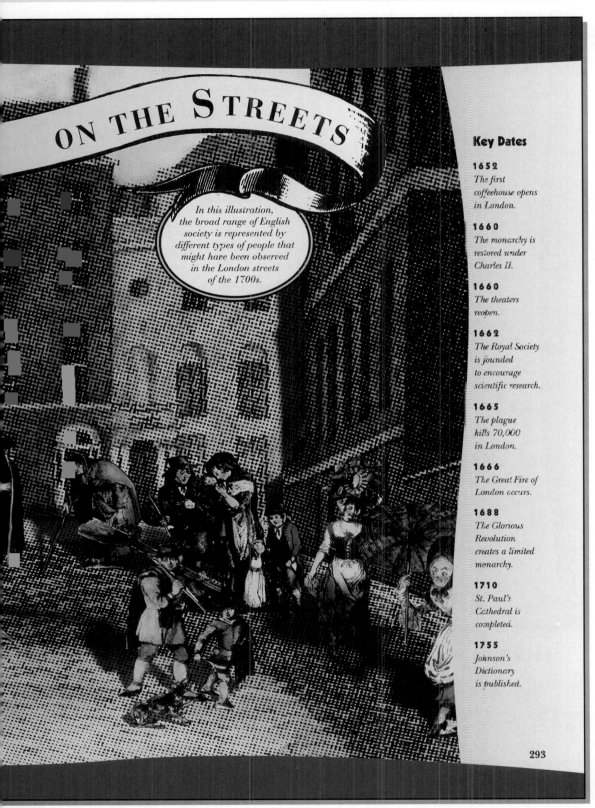

ON THE STREETS

In this illustration, the broad range of English society is represented by different types of people that might have been observed in the London streets of the 1700s.

Key Dates

1652
The first coffeehouse opens in London.

1660
The monarchy is restored under Charles II.

1660
The theaters reopen.

1662
The Royal Society is founded to encourage scientific research.

1665
The plague kills 70,000 in London.

1666
The Great Fire of London occurs.

1688
The Glorious Revolution creates a limited monarchy.

1710
St. Paul's Cathedral is completed.

1755
Johnson's Dictionary is published.

Key Dates

London coffeehouses were gathering places for literary, theatrical, political, and business people. Garraway's was a meeting place for dealers in stocks and shares. Will's Coffee House was patronized by Addison, Pope, and Congreve; Dryden had his own chair there. Bedford Coffee House was at the northeast corner of Covent Garden and was frequented by actors and artists, including David Garrick and William Hogarth. White's was a chocolate house started in 1697. It was converted into a club by Arthur, founder of Arthur's Club, and became a gaming center.

MATERIALS OF INTEREST

Books

- *Gulliver's Travels and Other Writings* by Jonathan Swift. (Bantam Classics, 1984).
- *Restoration Literature 1660–1700,* edited by James R. Sutherland. Includes Dryden, Bunyan, and Pepys. (Oxford History of English Literature Series, Vol. VIII, 1990. Out of print.)

Multimedia

- *The British Achievement, 1720–1850* [videotape], 28 min., color, VHS. The National Gallery, A Private View Series. Order #345.
- *The Puritan Revolution: Cromwell and the Rise of Parliamentary Democracy* [videotape] 33 min., color, VHS. Learning Corp. of America. Order #DF-LEN421.

Connections to **Custom Literature Database**

For further historical background, under **Background Articles,** see **Neoclassical England 1660–1780.**

Preview

A Focus on Society

FOR ALL STUDENTS

The three selections highlight three different issues: treatment of the poor, rights of women, and relationships between men and women. Identify ways in which these issues are alive today. Note that satire may be, but is not necessarily, political. Any human shortcoming or weakness can be satirized.

To further explore the theme, use the transparency referenced below.

Transparency Collection
Fine Art Transparency 6

For At-Risk Students

Ask students to identify examples of satire in movies and television programs. Late twentieth-century television examples include *The Simpsons*, *Saturday Night Live*, and *Roseanne*.

For Students Who Need Challenge

You might ask students to collect examples of satirical essays.

For Visual Learners

The New Yorker magazine is an excellent source of satiric cartoons. Comic strips ranging from *Sylvia* to *Doonesbury* also represent political satire. Ask students to collect cartoons, bring them to class, and identify political attitudes in each.

MULTICULTURAL CONNECTION

Two plays that poke fun at traditional Roman Catholic schooling of the 1950s and 1960s *(Nunsense* and *Do Patent Leather Shoes Really Reflect Up?)* were very popular with some Catholics and denounced by others. Is satire better written from a point of view that is "inside" the group being satirized or from the point of view of an "outsider"? *(Student answers will vary.)*

Part One

A Focus on Society

In an age when scientists, astronomers, and navigators were using their newly developed instruments to focus on the microscopic world or on the heavens, writers were using their intelligence and their wit to focus on the society in which they lived. What they saw sometimes moved them to anger or righteous indignation. Sometimes it moved them to laughter.

Multicultural Connection **Interactions** refer to encounters between people of diverse cultural backgrounds. The results may be varied: confusion, conflict, attempts to shut out or welcome in. Sometimes when people see things they don't like in other people they try to change those things; sometimes they simply scorn them. What different cultural notions do people in the following selections bring to their various encounters?

IDEAS THAT WORK

Motivating with Cartoons

"When recounting Swift's line, 'Satire is a sort of glass, wherein beholders do generally discover everybody's face but their own,' I'm reminded of *Milwaukee Journal* satirist Joel McNally who, in his column concerning Mother Theresa's visit to Milwaukee, referred to her as the "Calcutta Clipper" because during her short stay, large donations expeditiously left area pockets for Indian relief. Careful reading showed that McNally neither begrudged the money nor criticized the cause, but did satirically observe that it would be nice if these philanthropists would act equally generously aiding area poor.

Nonetheless, hundreds of outraged calls swamped the *Journal*'s complaint desk. All this is mentioned to demonstrate that the point of satire is often misunderstood; difficult to write well; and generally confounding to inexperienced readers. Ease into the subject of satire with a display and discussion of political cartoons. Students love it when they 'get' it!"

Jim Liska, Mequon, Wisconsin

Before Reading

A Modest Proposal

by Jonathan Swift

Jonathan Swift
1667–1745

Swift summed up his own life: "Perhaps I may allow, the Dean / Had too much satire in his veins / And seemed determined not to starve it, / Because no age could more deserve it." He was born in Dublin, Ireland. After receiving a degree at Trinity College, he served for some years as secretary to Sir William Temple, a writer and diplomat. Ordained an Anglican priest, in 1713 he was made Dean of St. Patrick's Cathedral in Dublin, a great disappointment to him, for he had been hoping to receive a church in England. He was known as England's greatest prose satirist, although much of his work was published anonymously. His most famous work, *Gulliver's Travels,* was published in 1726 and became a best seller.

Building Background

The Evils of Tyranny In Swift's time, Ireland was ruled by England, and absentee English landlords collected all the revenues while making few improvements to the land. According to Swift, Ireland was "a bare face of nature, without houses or plantations; filthy cabins, miserable, tattered, half-starved creatures, scarce in human shape; one insolent, ignorant, oppressive squire [chief landowner in a district] to be found in twenty miles riding; a parish church to be found only in a summer day's journey; a bog of fifteen miles round; every meadow a slough [swamp], and every hill a mixture of rock, heath, and marsh. . . . There is not an acre of land in Ireland turned to half its advantage, yet it is better improved than the people; and all these evils are effects of English tyranny." In "A Modest Proposal," Swift pretends to be a "projector," an expert planner, who has a scheme to solve Ireland's problems.

Literary Focus

Satire Gentle or bitter, **satire** is the use of irony, sarcasm, or wit to expose a human weakness or social evil, usually with the purpose of inspiring reform. The title of Swift's essay is an example of *irony* since, as you will see, his proposal is not modest at all. *Sarcasm* is the use of language to hurt or ridicule; for example, Swift says he doesn't want to hear of any other solutions until there is "at least some glimpse of hope that there will ever be some hearty and sincere attempt to put them in practice." *Wit* is the power to express cleverly ideas that are unusual, striking, or amusing. As you read "A Modest Proposal," look for unusual ideas and examples of irony and sarcasm, and then decide whether Swift's satire is effective.

Writer's Notebook

Skewering with the Pen Swift was kind to people in trouble or in need, but he scorned those who were boring, stupid, lazy, or corrupt. Although he felt that no times deserved satire more than the age in which he lived, would he alter that view if he could observe today's society? What types of people or political situations today are ripe for satire? Jot down some ideas in your notebook.

Before Reading

Building Background

Ask students whether they know of contemporary examples of absentee landlords who make substantial profits from tenants who living in poor conditions. *(Examples might include urban slumlords; owners of share-cropped farmland; tiny minorities that own nearly all the arable land in underdeveloped countries.)*

Literary Focus

Cartoonists are among the most visible satirists in today's media. Ask students to look through newspapers for examples of political satire.

Writer's Notebook

You might ask students to brainstorm ideas for satire before making notes in their Writer's Notebooks.

More About Jonathan Swift

Swift lived in England, writing political satire, during the first decade of the 18th century. When his political fortunes changed in 1713, Swift reluctantly returned to Ireland. Other works by the author include

- *A Tale of a Tub* (1704)
- *Journal to Stella* (1710–1713)
- *Gulliver's Travels* (1726)

SUPPORT MATERIALS OVERVIEW

Unit 4 Resource Book
- Graphic Organizer, p. 1
- Study Guide, p. 2
- Vocabulary, p. 3
- Grammar, p. 4
- Alternate Check Test, p. 5
- Vocabulary Test, p. 6
- Selection Test, pp. 7–8

Building English Proficiency
- Selection Summaries
- Activities, p. 220

Reading, Writing & Grammar SkillBook
- Reading, pp. 71–73, 77–78
- Writing, pp. 115–116
- Grammar, Usage, and Mechanics, pp. 163–164, 165–166, 239–242

Technology
- Audiotape
- Personal Journal Software
- Custom Literature Database: Additional selections by Swift can be found on the database.
- Test Generator Software

During Reading

Selection Objectives

- to identify satire and its purpose
- to apply satire to contemporary situations
- to master rudiments of complex sentence structure

Unit 4 Resource Book
Graphic Organizer, p. 1
Study Guide, p. 2

Theme Link

Swift turns his Focus on Society in this essay that outlines a modest proposal for solving the problems of poverty.

Vocabulary Preview

raiment, clothing
ragout, a highly seasoned meat stew
gibbet, gallows for hanging criminals
vintner, wine merchant
parsimony, stinginess

Students can add the words and definitions to their Writer's Notebooks.

1 Literary Focus
Satire

Question What is illogical in this reference to the Pretender? *(Beggars would lack funds and probably the inclination to join the Pretender; the reference probably satirizes paranoid politicians who see plots everywhere.)*

A Modest PROPOSAL

FOR PREVENTING THE CHILDREN OF POOR PEOPLE IN IRELAND FROM BEING A BURDEN TO THEIR PARENTS OR COUNTRY, AND FOR MAKING THEM BENEFICIAL TO THE PUBLIC

Jonathan Swift

It is a melancholy object to those who walk through this great town,[1] or travel in the country, when they see the streets, the roads, and cabin doors crowded with beggars of the female sex, followed by three, four, or six children, all in rags, and importuning[2] every passenger for an alms. These mothers, instead of being able to work for their honest livelihood, are forced to employ all their time in strolling to beg sustenance[3] for their helpless infants—who, as they grow up, either turn thieves for want of work, or leave their dear
1 native country in flight for the Pretender[4] in Spain, or sell themselves to the Barbados.[5]

I think it is agreed by all parties that this prodigious number of children in the arms, or on the backs, or at the heels of their mothers, and frequently of their fathers, is, in the present deplorable state of the kingdom, a very great additional grievance; and therefore whoever could find out a fair, cheap, and easy method of making these children sound and useful members of the commonwealth would deserve so well of the public as to have his statue set up for a preserver of the nation.

But my intention is very far from being confined to provide only for the children of professed beggars: it is of a much greater extent and shall take in the whole number of infants at a certain age who are born of parents in effect as little able to support them as those who demand our charity in the streets.

As to my own part, having turned my thoughts for many years upon this important subject and maturely weighed the several schemes of other projectors, I have always found them grossly mistaken in their computation. It is true, a child just dropped from its dam may be supported by her milk for a solar year

1. **this great town,** Dublin, Ireland.
2. **importune** (im′pôr tün′), *v.* ask urgently; beg.
3. **sustenance** (sus′tə nəns), *n.* support; means of living.
4. **the Pretender,** James Stuart (1688–1766), son of King James II and "pretender," or claimant, to the throne. He was Catholic, and Ireland was loyal to him.
5. **sell . . . Barbados.** Many poverty-stricken Irish "sold" themselves to work for a specified number of years in the West Indies or other British possessions in exchange for boat fare across the Atlantic.

SELECTION SUMMARY

A Modest Proposal

Swift presents the problem of poverty in Ireland with a statistical analysis of numbers of infants born annually to the poor. He announces that the problem could be solved by converting Irish one-year-olds into food stuffs and, thereafter, raising Irish children for the table—thus, turning a vexing burden into a cash crop. He calculates numbers of meals that might be realized from the weight of a typical one-year-old; discusses utilizing adolescents as a venison substitute; and debates the relative merits of male versus female flesh. He offers logical arguments in support of his proposal. While he will listen to no proposals for moral, social, or political reform, he outlines several, but with the caveat that "visionary thoughts" are never implemented. His modest proposal is altogether more traditional, practical, and convenient.

For summaries in other languages, see the ***Building English Proficiency*** *book.*

with little other nourishment: at most, not above the value of two shillings, which the mother may certainly get, or the value in scraps, by her lawful occupation of begging; and it is exactly at one year old that I propose to provide for them in such a manner, as, instead of being a charge upon their parents or the parish, or wanting food and raiment[6] for the rest of their lives, they shall, on the contrary, contribute to the feeding, and partly to the clothing, of many thousands.

There is likewise another great advantage in my scheme: that it will prevent those voluntary abortions and that horrid practice of women murdering their bastard children, alas!, too frequent among us, sacrificing the poor innocent babes, I doubt more to avoid the expense than the shame, which would move tears and pity in the most savage and inhuman breast. 2

The number of souls in this kingdom being usually reckoned one million and a half, of these I calculate there may be about two hundred thousand couple whose wives are breeders; 3 from which number I subtract thirty thousand couple who are able to maintain their own children (although I apprehend there cannot be so many, under the present distresses of the kingdom); but this being granted, there will remain

6. raiment (rā′mənt), *n.* clothing.

In *The Vagrants* (1868), Frederick Walker depicts the harsh reality of poverty, as experienced by a family of wanderers. How does Swift use his satiric skills to express his own concern about poverty and injustice? Give at least one example.

2 Reader's Response
Making Personal Connections

Question Do the social conditions Swift describes remind you of anything in contemporary society? *(Possible responses: discussions of Welfare reform and getting people off Welfare rolls; debate over fatherless families, street people, abortion, violence)*

3 Literary Element
Connotation/Denotation

Question What does Swift's use of the words *breeders* and *dams* denote and connote? *(Possible response: Usually associated with animal husbandry, the words denote a female parent of livestock. In this context, their use connotes equating human beings with animals.)*

Art Study

Response to Caption Question One example is Swift's use of words that point out how the poor are regarded as less than human. By referring to a human being as a dam or a breeder, he shocks the reader into wondering if he or she may also dehumanize the poor by accepting platitudes and political strategies as truth.

BUILDING ENGLISH PROFICIENCY

Linking Past and Present

Help students grasp what Swift was trying to accomplish in this essay by asking them to think about problems in nations today.

1. Divide students into groups. Try to include in each group at least one student who may know about conditions in another country.
2. Ask groups to list two or more countries, including the United States. Have them list problems that they have seen in U.S. cities and in one other country.
3. Have group members discuss what they have seen done to try to solve these problems. Ask: Which problems can be solved by new laws? Which require a change in people's attitudes? Which may require countries to work together?
4. As students read "A Modest Proposal," have them think about how Swift might really be trying to solve problems that he sees in Ireland.

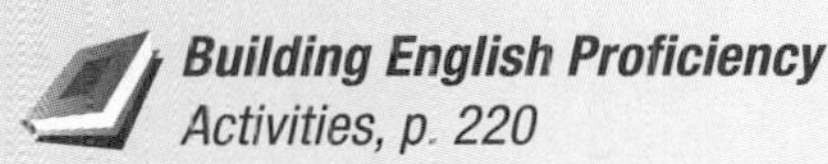

Building English Proficiency
Activities, p. 220

4 Reading/Thinking Skills
Compare and Contrast

Questions How would you compare this comment with what led up to it? *(Possible response: Until we reach this comment, the intent of the essay seems serious; the outrageousness of the comment informs the reader that this must be satire.)* What is the effect of the contrast? *(Contrasting dry statistical copy with a matter-of-fact discussion of the nominal age for becoming a thief exaggerates comic effect while taking deadly aim at a very real problem.)*

5 Reading/Thinking Skills
Detect Bias

Question Why do you think Swift cites an American as an authority on cannibalism? *(Possible response: This may be an 18th-century "ethnic joke"; it suggests that the English have long been poking fun at their "primitive" American cousins.)*

6 Active Reading
Question

Response While answers may vary, most students will begin to raise questions when Swift describes the age at which children may qualify for a life of crime. The main question that comes to mind is what is the point of Swift's modest proposal.

. . . A YOUNG HEALTHY CHILD, WELL NURSED, IS, AT A YEAR OLD, A MOST DELICIOUS, NOURISHING, AND WHOLESOME FOOD . . . .

an hundred and seventy thousand breeders. I again subtract fifty thousand for those women who miscarry, or whose children die by accident or disease within the year. There only remain a hundred and twenty thousand children of poor parents annually born. The question therefore is: How this number shall be reared and provided for? which, as I have already said, under the present situation of affairs, is utterly impossible by all the methods hitherto proposed. For we can neither employ them in handicraft or agriculture; we neither build houses (I mean in the country) nor cultivate land: they can very seldom pick up a
4 livelihood by stealing until they arrive at six years old, except where they are of towardly[7] parts; although I confess they learn the rudiments[8] much earlier; during which time they can, however, be properly looked upon only as probationers; as I have been informed by a principal gentleman in the county of Cavan, who protested to me that he never knew above one or two instances under the age of six, even in a part of the kingdom so renowned for the quickest proficiency in that art.

I am assured by our merchants that a boy or a girl before twelve years old is no saleable commodity; and even when they come to this age they will not yield above three pounds or three pounds and half-a-crown at most, on the exchange; which cannot turn to account either to the parents or kingdom, the charge of nutriment and rags having been at least four times that value.

I shall now, therefore, humbly propose my own thoughts, which I hope will not be liable to the least objection.

I have been assured by a very knowing
5 American of my acquaintance in London that a young healthy child, well nursed, is, at a year old, a most delicious, nourishing, and wholesome food, whether stewed, roasted, baked, or boiled; and I make no doubt that it will equally serve in a fricassee or a ragout.[9]

I do therefore humbly offer it to public consideration, that of the hundred and twenty thousand children already computed, twenty thousand may be reserved for breed, whereof only one-fourth part to be males; which is more than we allow to sheep, black cattle, or swine; and my reason is that these children are seldom the fruits of marriage, a circumstance not much regarded by our savages; therefore one male will be sufficient to serve four females. That the remaining hundred thousand may, at a year old, be offered in sale to the persons of quality and fortune through the kingdom—always advising the mother to let them suck plentifully in the last month, so as to render them plump and fat for a good table. A child will make two dishes at an entertainment for friends; and when the family dines alone, the fore or hind quarter will make a reasonable dish, and, seasoned with a little pepper or salt, will be very good boiled on the fourth day, especially in winter.

I have reckoned upon a medium that a child just born will weigh twelve pounds, and in a solar year, if tolerably nursed, increases to twenty-eight pounds.

QUESTION: At what point during this essay did you, the reader, begin to question just what Swift was getting at? What questions come to mind? 

I grant this food will be somewhat dear, and therefore very proper for landlords, who, as

7. **towardly** (tôrd′lē), *adj.* promising; ready to learn.
8. **rudiment** (rü′də mənt), *n.* basic understanding.
9. ragout (ra gü′), *n.* a highly seasoned meat stew.

MINI-LESSON: GRAMMAR
Sentence Structure

Complex sentences can be broken down into parts to facilitate student understanding.

Teach Swift frequently uses long, involved sentences. While these sentences can look intimidating, they can be broken down into simpler sentences that are easier to understand. The complex sentences may be more elegant and interesting.

Activity Idea Choose a long sentence or a paragraph containing several complicated sentences. (For example, you might choose the last sentence of the paragraph at the beginning of page 298, which begins: "For we can neither employ them in handicraft or agriculture . . . ") Ask students to rewrite the sentence or paragraph, using only simple, declarative sentences. Which version is easier to understand? Which version is more interesting to read?

7 they have already devoured most of the parents, seem to have the best title to the children.

Infants' flesh will be in season throughout the year, but more plentifully in March, and a little before and after: for we are told by a grave author, an eminent French physician,[10] that fish being a prolific diet, there are more children born in Roman Catholic countries about nine months after Lent than at any other season; therefore, reckoning a year after Lent, the markets will be more glutted than usual, because
8 the number of popish infants is at least three to one in this kingdom; and therefore it will have one other collateral[11] advantage, by lessening the number of papists among us.

I have already computed the charge of nursing a beggar's child (in which list I reckon all cottagers, laborers, and four-fifths of the farmers) to be about two shillings per annum, rags included; and I believe no gentleman would repine[12] to give ten shillings for the carcass of a good fat child, which, as I have said, will make four dishes of excellent nutritive meat when he has only some particular friends or his own family to dine with him. Thus the squire will learn to be a good landlord and grow popular among his tenants; the mother will have eight shillings net profit and be fit for work till she produces another child.

Those who are more thrifty (as I must confess the times require) may flay the carcass—the
9 skin of which, artificially[13] dressed, will make admirable gloves for ladies and summer-boots for fine gentlemen.

As to our city of Dublin, shambles[14] may be appointed for this purpose in the most convenient parts of it, and butchers we may be assured will not be wanting; although I rather recommend buying the children alive and dressing them hot from the knife, as we do roasting pigs.

A very worthy person, a true lover of his country, and whose virtues I highly esteem, was lately pleased, in discoursing on this matter, to offer a refinement upon my scheme. He said that many gentlemen of this kingdom, having of late destroyed their deer, he conceived that the want of venison might be well supplied by the bodies of young lads and maidens, not exceeding fourteen years of age, nor under twelve; so great a number of both sexes in every country being now ready to starve for want of work and service; and these to be disposed of by their parents, if alive, or otherwise by their nearest relations. But with due deference to so excellent a friend and so deserving a patriot, I cannot be altogether in his sentiments; for as to the males, my American acquaintance assured me from frequent experience, that their flesh was generally tough and lean, like that of our schoolboys, by continual exercise, and their taste disagreeable; and to fatten them would not answer the charge. Then as to the females, it would, I think, with humble submission, be a loss to the public, because they soon would become breeders themselves; and besides, it is not improbable that some scrupulous people might be apt to censure such a practice (although indeed very unjustly) as a little bordering upon cruelty; which, I confess, has always been with me the strongest objection against any project, how well soever intended.

But in order to justify my friend, he confessed that this expedient was put into his head by the famous Psalmanazar,[15] a native of the island Formosa, who came from thence to London above twenty years ago, and in conversation told my friend that in his country, when any young

10. **grave author . . . physician,** Francois Rabelais (1495?–1553), who was not a "grave" (serious) author but a satirical one.
11. **collateral** (kə lat′ər əl), *adj.* secondary; indirect.
12. **repine** (ri pīn′), *v.* fret; complain.
13. **artificially** (är′tə fish′əl ē), *adv.* artfully; skillfully.
14. **shambles,** slaughterhouses.
15. **Psalmanazar,** a Frenchman who passed himself off in England as a Formosan and wrote a fictitious "true" account of Formosa in which he described cannibalism.

7 Literary Element
Metaphor

Question What does Swift mean when he states that landlords have already devoured the parents? *(Possible response: Swift uses eating as a metaphor. Landlords have "devoured most of the parents" by exploiting the weak for profit. The essay essentially asks, "As long as one is devouring parents, why not eat children as well?")*

8 Multicultural Note
Popish Infants

Roman Catholics were in the majority in Ireland, which at this time was ruled by Great Britain. *Papist* and *popish* are derogatory terms for Roman Catholics, referring to their allegiance to the pope as head of their church. Swift notes the prejudice of the English against the poor Irish and their religion by elaborating how his scheme will reduce the number of Roman Catholics in Ireland.

9 Reader's Response
Challenging the Text

Question Do you think Swift goes "over the top" at his point? *(While responses will vary, it might be noted that this passage was probably more amusing before various horrors of the twentieth century outdistanced his satire.)*

BUILDING ENGLISH PROFICIENCY

Exploring Key Concepts

To help students relate better to the essay, have them work on any of these group activities.

Activity Ideas

- Ask each group to come up with phrases that describe the kind of person Swift *pretends* to be. Have them decide on a word they would substitute for "Modest" in the title. Invite groups to compare their responses.
- Have each group estimate the cost of raising a child to age 16 today: Add the weekly expenses for housing, food, and so on divide by the number of people in a family they consider "average," multiply by 52 (weeks), and finally multiply by 16 (years).
- Challenge each group to brainstorm the causes of poverty. Ask: In your opinion, which solutions work? Which don't work? Have group representatives meet for a panel discussion on the topic.

10 Reading/Writing Skills
Find the Main Idea

Question What is the main idea of this passage? *(On one level, Swift suggests that since Irish tenants have no crops, livestock, or money with which to pay rent, children would provide a much needed cash crop. On a deeper level, he points out the desperate plight of tenants and rapaciousness of landlords.)*

11 Multicultural Note
Interactions

Response The poor are despised by the rest of society and are exploited for profits. The nonpoor think of the poor as a burden and of value only as a source of cheap labor.

person happened to be put to death, the executioner sold the carcass to persons of quality as a prime dainty; and that in his time the body of a plump girl of fifteen, who was crucified for an attempt to poison the emperor, was sold to his Imperial Majesty's prime minister of state and other great mandarins[16] of the court, in joints from the gibbet,[17] at four hundred crowns. Neither indeed can I deny that if the same use were made of several plump young girls in this town who, without one single groat to their fortunes, cannot stir abroad without a chair, and appear at playhouse and assemblies in foreign fineries which they will never pay for, the kingdom would not be the worse.

Some persons of a desponding spirit are in great concern about that vast number of poor people who are aged, diseased, or maimed; and I have been desired to employ my thoughts what course may be taken to ease the nation of so grievous an encumbrance. But I am not in the least pain upon that matter, because it is very well known that they are every day dying and rotting, by cold and famine, and filth and vermin, as fast as can be reasonably expected. And as to the younger laborers, they are now in almost as hopeful a condition: they cannot get work, and consequently pine away for want of nourishment to a degree that if at any time they are accidentally hired to common labor, they have not strength to perform it; and thus the country and themselves are happily delivered from the evils to come.

I have too long digressed and therefore shall return to my subject. I think the advantages by the proposal which I have made are obvious and many, as well as of the highest importance.

For first, as I have already observed, it would greatly lessen the number of papists with whom we are yearly overrun, being the principal breeders of the nation, as well as our most dangerous enemies; and who stay at home on purpose with a design to deliver the kingdom to the Pretender, hoping to take their advantage by the absence of so many good Protestants, who have chosen rather to leave their country than stay at home and pay tithes against their conscience to an idolatrous Episcopal curate.[18]

Secondly, the poorer tenants will have something valuable of their own, which by law may be made liable to distress,[19] and help to pay their landlord's rent; their corn and cattle being already seized, and money a thing unknown. **10**

CLARIFY: What seem to be the interactions between the poor people and the rest of society, especially the landlords? **11**

Thirdly, whereas the maintenance of an hundred thousand children, from two years old and upwards, cannot be computed at less than ten shillings a piece per annum, the nation's stock will be thereby increased fifty thousand pounds per annum—besides the profit of a new dish introduced to the tables of all gentlemen of fortune in the kingdom who have any refinement in taste. And the money will circulate among ourselves, the goods being entirely of our own growth and manufacture.

Fourthly, the constant breeders, besides the gain of eight shillings sterling per annum by the sale of their children, will be rid of the charge of maintaining them after the first year.

Fifthly, this food would likewise bring great custom to taverns, where the vintners[20] will certainly be so prudent as to procure the best

16. **mandarin** (man′dər ən), *n.* a powerful or influential person.
17. gibbet (jib′it), *n.* gallows, a structure for hanging criminals.
18. **Protestants . . . curate.** Swift is here attacking dissenting Protestants who have left Ireland and avoided paying tithes on the grounds that Anglican Church practices were "idolatrous."
19. **distress,** distraint, the legal seizure of property for payment of debts.
20. vintner (vint′nər), *n.* wine merchant.

MINI-LESSON: VOCABULARY
Word Origins

What makes a word an English word?

Teach English is a constantly changing language, with new words coming into use all the time. English words are derived from many different languages. Part of the function of dictionaries is to identify the origins of words. Another function of dictionaries is to say which words are part of the English language.

Activity Ideas

- Have students consult a dictionary to find the origin of the following words: ragout, shambles, mandarins, animosity, distress.
- As a class, begin a dictionary of contemporary slang. Include both words and definitions. Students can compare their list with the entries in a published dictionary of American slang.

receipts[21] for dressing it to perfection and, consequently, have their houses frequented by all the fine gentlemen, who justly value themselves upon their knowledge in good eating: and a skilful cook, who understands how to oblige his guests, will contrive to make it as expensive as they please.

I CAN THINK OF NO ONE OBJECTION THAT WILL POSSIBLY BE RAISED AGAINST THIS PROPOSAL. . . .

12 Sixthly, this would be great inducement to marriage, which all wise nations have either encouraged by rewards or enforced by laws and penalties. It would increase the care and tenderness of mothers towards their children, when they were sure of a settlement for life to the poor babes, provided in some sort by the public, to their annual profit instead of expense. We should soon see an honest emulation[22] among the married women, which of them could bring the fattest child to the market. Men would become as fond of their wives during the time of their pregnancy as they are now of their mares in foal, their cows in calf, or sows when they are ready to farrow; nor offer to beat or kick them (as is too frequent a practice) for fear of a miscarriage.

13 Many other advantages might be enumerated. For instance, the addition of some thousand carcasses in our exportation of barrelled beef; the propagation[23] of swine's flesh, and improvement in the art of making good bacon, so much wanted among us by the great destruction of pigs, too frequent at our tables—which are no way comparable in taste or magnificence to a well-grown, fat yearling child, which, roasted whole, will make a considerable figure at a Lord Mayor's feast, or any other public entertainment. But this and many others I omit, being studious of brevity.

Supposing that one thousand families in this city would be constant customers for infants' flesh, besides others who might have it at merry meetings, particularly weddings and christenings, I compute that Dublin would take off annually about twenty thousand carcasses; and the rest of the kingdom (where probably they will be sold somewhat cheaper) the remaining eighty thousand.

I can think of no one objection that will possibly be raised against this proposal, unless it should be urged, that the number of people will be thereby much lessened in the kingdom. This I freely own, and it was indeed one principal design in offering it to the world. I desire the reader will observe that I calculate my remedy for this one individual kingdom of Ireland, and for no other that ever was, is, or, I think, ever can be upon earth. Therefore let no man talk to me of other expedients:[24] of taxing our absentees at five shillings a pound; of using neither clothes nor household furniture except what is of our own growth and manufacture; of utterly rejecting the materials and instruments that promote foreign luxury; of curing the expensiveness of pride, vanity, idleness, and gaming in our women; of introducing a vein of parsimony,[25] prudence, and temperance; of learning to love our country, wherein we differ even from Laplanders, and the inhabitants of Topinamboo;[26] of quitting our animosities[27] and factions, nor act any longer like the Jews, who were murdering one another at the very moment their city was taken;[28] of

21. **vintners . . . receipts,** that is, wine merchants will be sure to find the best recipes
22. **emulation** (em′yə lā′shən), *n.* rivalry.
23. **propagation** (prop′ə gā′shən), *n.* breeding and raising.
24. **expedient** (ek spē′dē ənt), *n.* means of bringing about a desired result.
25. **parsimony** (pär′sə mō′nē), *n.* stinginess.
26. **Topinamboo,** an area of Brazil.
27. **animosity** (an′ə mos′ə tē), *n.* dislike; ill will.
28. **city was taken.** While the Roman Emperor Titus was besieging Jerusalem, which he destroyed in A.D. 70, groups of fanatics within the city were fighting each other.

12 Literary Element
Irony

Questions What effect would Swift's proposal have on marriage? *(Possible response: It would turn husband and wife into business partners and marriage into a business proposition.)* What is the irony in this suggestion? *(Possible response: Swift suggests that poverty in Ireland would be "fixed" if parents were to exploit their marriage and children exactly as landlords exploit them.)*

13 Literary Focus
Satire

Irony and sarcasm are key elements of satire. Ask students to carefully read Swift's comparisons between raising livestock and raising children.

Question What elements of sarcasm can you identify? *(Possible responses: He maintains that women will take better care of their children if they know the children can be sold for a profit; that men will care for their wives as effectively as they do for pregnant livestock and will not beat or kick pregnant women; that eating domestic children and selling pork and beef abroad will have a positive effect on the balance of trade.)*

BUILDING ENGLISH PROFICIENCY

Exploring Different Points of View

To help students understand Swift's satire, have them explore how he might have defended his essay.

1. Divide students into five groups. Assign each group to assume the persona of one of these people: an unemployed Irish father; a poor Irish mother; a landlord; an elderly person; and a poor, young teenager.

2. Ask the groups to imagine that these people hear about the essay shortly after it was written. They think that Swift is sincere in his cruel proposal. Have each group brainstorm three questions for their person to ask Swift.

3. Invite a volunteer to play the role of Swift in the "hot seat." Each group, speaking from the viewpoint of its assigned character, should fire its questions at "Swift." Have Swift, in character, explain and defend his ideas.

14 Reading/Thinking Skills
Find the Main Idea

Question What economic expedients does Swift outline? *(taxing landlords' profits; buying English-made goods; rejecting foreign luxury goods; reducing wasteful consumption; fostering prudence and temperance; reducing class and political factions; instilling pride for oneself and one's country; fostering civilized treatment of tenants by landlords; fostering honesty and integrity among merchants)*

15 Active Reading
Evaluate

Response The "other expedients" would foster a society and an economy in which devouring other people would be unnecessary and morally repugnant. The expedients seem quite sensible.

Check Test

1. How many people live in Ireland, according to Swift? *(1.5 million)*
2. What does Swift say that a newborn child weighs? *(12 pounds)*
3. What does Swift suggest making from the skins of children? *(gloves and boots)*
4. Who are papists? *(Roman Catholics)*
5. What argument does Swift offer to prove that he is not planning to profit personally from his scheme? *(His youngest child is nine years old, and his wife is past child-bearing age.)*

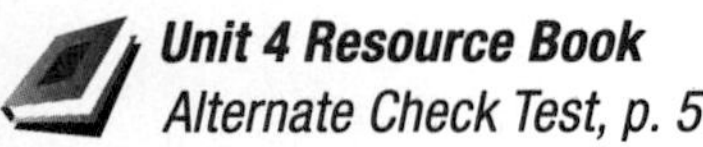
Unit 4 Resource Book
Alternate Check Test, p. 5

being a little cautious not to sell our country and consciences for nothing; of teaching landlords to have at least one degree of mercy towards their tenants; lastly, of putting a spirit of honesty, industry, and skill into our shopkeepers, who, if a resolution could now be taken to buy only our native goods, would immediately unite to cheat and exact upon us in the price,
14 the measure, and the goodness, nor could ever yet be brought to make one fair proposal of just dealing, though often and earnestly invited to it.

15 **EVALUATE: What can you conclude about these "other expedients"? Are they sensible or not?**

Therefore, I repeat, let no man talk to me of these and the like expedients till he has at least some glimpse of hope that there will ever be some hearty and sincere attempt to put them in practice.

But as to myself, having been wearied out for many years with offering vain, idle, visionary thoughts, and at length utterly despairing of success, I fortunately fell upon this proposal, which, as it is wholly new, so it hath something solid and real, of no expense and little trouble, full in our own power, and whereby we can incur no danger in disobliging England. For this kind of commodity will not bear exportation, the flesh being of too tender a consistence to admit a long continuance in salt, although perhaps I could name a country which would be glad to eat up our whole nation without it.[29]

After all, I am not so violently bent upon my own opinion as to reject any offer proposed by wise men which shall be found equally innocent, cheap, easy, and effectual. But before something of that kind shall be advanced in contradiction to my scheme, and offering a better, I desire the author or authors will be pleased maturely to consider two points. First, as things now stand, how they will be able to find food and raiment for a hundred thousand useless mouths and backs? And, secondly, there being a round million of creatures in human figure throughout this kingdom whose whole subsistence, put into a common stock, would leave them in debt two millions of pounds sterling—adding those who are beggars by profession to the bulk of farmers, cottagers, and laborers, with the wives and children who are beggars in effect—I desire those politicians who dislike my overture,[30] and may perhaps be so bold as to attempt an answer, that they will first ask the parents of these mortals whether they would not at this day think it a great happiness to have been sold for food at a year old, in the manner I prescribe, and thereby have avoided such a perpetual scene of misfortunes as they have since gone through by the oppression of landlords, the impossibility of paying rent without money or trade, the want of common sustenance, with neither house nor clothes to cover them from the inclemencies of weather, and the most inevitable prospect of entailing the like, or greater miseries, upon their breed for ever.

I profess, in the sincerity of my heart, that I have not the least personal interest in endeavouring to promote this necessary work, having no other motive than the public good of my country, by advancing our trade, providing for infants, relieving the poor, and giving some pleasure to the rich. I have no children by which I can propose to get a single penny; the youngest being nine years old, and my wife past child-bearing.

29. **a country . . . without it.** Another way of saying that the English are devouring or swallowing the Irish.
30. **overture** (ō′vər chər), *n.* proposal or offer.

MINI-LESSON: GRAMMAR
Using Commas in a Series

Teach To review commas in a series, write this passage from this page on the board.

> . . . having no other motive than the public good of my country, by advancing our trade, providing for infants, relieving the poor, and giving some pleasure to the rich.

Point out the commas between the items in a series, and ask which parts of speech are joined. *(four gerunds as objects of the preposition* by*)* Review the rule: When three or more words or groups of words appear in a series, place a comma after each item except the last. Do not use commas when items in a series are joined by conjunctions.

Activity Idea Have partners each write three sentences about babies or satire that each contain an unpunctuated series of items and then punctuate each other's sentences.

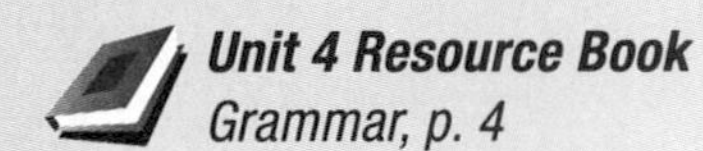
Unit 4 Resource Book
Grammar, p. 4

After Reading

Making Connections

Shaping Your Response

1. If you had not been told that this essay is a **satire,** at what point would you have realized it for yourself?
2. Do you find this essay shocking? Assign it a 1–12 rating on the shock meter.

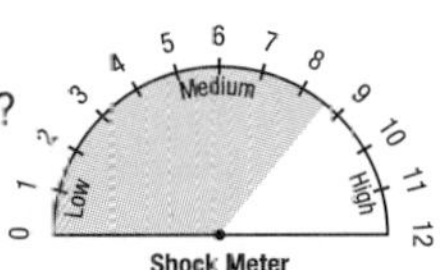

Analyzing the Essay

3. Paragraph 4 refers to "a child just dropped from its dam," and the essay contains other examples of terms usually applied only to animals. Why do you suppose the narrator uses such language?
4. In what ways, according to the narrator, are the Irish responsible for their own circumstances?
5. If the narrator truly believes that his other expedients aren't worth talking about, why do you think he includes them?
6. If Swift's intention is to inspire reform, what kind of reform is he suggesting?
7. Of the people living during Swift's time, who do you think would have been most annoyed by this essay? most approving?

Extending the Ideas

8. Many of the problems Swift mentions still exist in the world today. Are the reasons for these problems the same kinds of **interactions** as described here? Are there additional reasons? Discuss.

Literary Focus: Satire

Satirical writing, whether for television, films, or print, is usually aimed at reforming some human weakness or some evil of society. Irony, sarcasm, and wit are all part of the technique of **satire.**

1. Swift says that he is "wearied out . . . with offering vain, idle, visionary thoughts" and so "fell upon this proposal." What is ironic about this?
2. "Landlords," Swift says, "who, as they have already devoured most of the parents, seem to have the best title to the children." What makes this an example of sarcasm?
3. Find a passage that you think best illustrates Swift's wit.

Vocabulary Study

On your paper, write the letter of the word or phrase that best completes each of the following sentences.

1. *Raiment* is most likely to be kept in a ____.
   a. kitchen **b.** living room **c.** closet **d.** dining room

After Reading

MAKING CONNECTIONS

1. Students' responses will vary, but most are likely to mention p. 298: "they can very seldom pick up a livelihood by stealing until they arrive at six years old."

2. Student responses should be supported with examples.

3. to emphasize that the poor are treated like and viewed as animals by the landlords

4. They have too many children; they are lazy, and they depend on begging as a way of life.

5. He does not really believe that they are not worth talking about; they are the backbone of his proposal to address the problems of poverty.

6. He wants better treatment of the poor and less extravagance on the part of the wealthy.

7. Conservative members of Parliament and English landlords would probably have been most annoyed; English and Irish reformers, some clergymen, and of course, the poor would have been least annoyed.

8. Student responses will vary, but might note that the strong continue to exploit the weak; that the nonpoor continue to blame the poor for their plight; that pulling oneself out of poverty is not easy; and that the structure of society is as "market driven" today as it was in Swift's time. "Interactions" have changed only in detail, for example, the urban poor have replaced the rural poor.

LITERARY FOCUS: SATIRE

1. The irony lies in Swift's rationale for the essay: "since acceptable solutions to these problems are never adopted, are never thought acceptable, I will pose a completely unacceptable solution, a metaphor that mirrors the truth."

2. Swift uses "devour" as a metaphor; landlords "eat" their tenants by reducing them to penury and then exploiting their weak state. Eating, i.e., exploiting, the children of the poor is a logical step. The landlords have "best title" because "to the victors belong the spoils."

3. Examples could include Swift's suggestion that his proposal would be an inducement to marriage because such a marriage offers business opportunities beneficial to all parties; or his argument that the proposal would allow more domestic meat to be exported and, thus, benefit Britain's balance of trade.

VOCABULARY STUDY

1. c. closet
2. a. kitchen
3. a. refuse to give to the poor
4. d. been convicted of a crime
5. b. wine

Unit 4 Resource Book
Vocabulary, p. 3
Vocabulary Test, p. 6

WRITING CHOICES

Writer's Notebook Update

You might remind students that Swift knew a great deal about the situation of Ireland and of the poor of Ireland. They will be best able to write satire about topics on which they are well informed.

Not So Modest?

You might suggest that students begin by looking up the word *modest* and deciding which definition applies to Swift's title. *(The irony lies in the fact that Swift's title suggests a somewhat less excessive proposition than the remedy he actually proposes.)*

Music, Manners, and Malls

Students might brainstorm possible fads to serve as subjects for their satires.

Selection Test

Unit 4 Resource Book
pp. 7–8

2. *Ragout* would probably be found in a ____.
   a. kitchen **b.** porch **c.** field **d.** church
3. People who practice *parsimony* would probably ____.
   a. refuse to give to the poor **b.** exercise daily
   c. eat only vegetables **d.** refuse to wear leather or fur
4. Someone headed for a *gibbet* has probably ____.
   a. had too much to eat **b.** been visiting a zoo
   c. been suffering from overwork **d.** been convicted of a crime
5. *Vintners* are in the business of selling ____.
   a. cheese **b.** wine **c.** cloth **d.** medicine

Expressing Your Ideas

Writing Choices

Writer's Notebook Update Now that you've read "A Modest Proposal," think about some of the possible modern targets for satire that you jotted down in your notebook. Write a paragraph or so about one of the topics.

Not So Modest? Reread the full title on page 296. Then write an **essay** in which you explain why this title is meant to be taken ironically. Suggest some reasons why Swift might have used irony instead of making straightforward statements.

Music, Manners, and Malls Newspaper columnists often satirize some aspect of popular culture, and the fads and tastes of young people are frequently ripe areas for satire. Write a **satirical column** dealing with a current interest among your friends or acquaintances that could be published in a school paper or magazine.

Other Options

"In My Opinion . . ." Some people have objected to including Swift's essay in a textbook on the grounds that it is about "eating babies" and is generally unsuitable for high school readers. Do you agree that some topics are "unsuitable" for reading in school? If so, what might they be? Work with a partner to stage a call-in **radio talk show,** in which one person (either caller or talk-show host) objects to the essay and the other defends it.

Art as Social Commentary William Hogarth (1697–1764) was an English painter and engraver whose works often satirized English life. What does he seem to be satirizing in this caricature of British judges titled "The Bench"? Think of an issue that you feel strongly about and create a **satirical drawing** to represent your point of view.

OTHER OPTIONS

"In My Opinion . . ."

Students might chose various radio or TV talk show hosts and/or guests and assume their personae to argue for or against the suitability of the essay. Suggest that "hosts" and "guests" should stay in character during the debate.

Satirical Drawing

Hogarth is satirizing the judiciary.

Students might develop unused ideas from their Writer's Notebooks or elaborate on the subjects used for their essays.

Before Reading

The Education of Women

by Daniel Defoe

Daniel Defoe
1661?–1731

A candle merchant's son, born in London, Daniel Defoe attended Morton's Academy for Dissenters (Protestants who were not members of the Anglican Church). Never one to live a retiring life, he took part in an armed rebellion against King James II led by the Duke of Monmouth. He engaged in various commercial ventures that were mostly unsuccessful. He was imprisoned once for bankruptcy and a second time for writing a pamphlet attacking the government's religious policies. Later he was employed as a secret agent. He wrote hundreds of pamphlets and books, many anonymously or under a pseudonym. Defoe is considered one of the pioneers of the English novel and is best known for *Robinson Crusoe* (1719), *Moll Flanders* (1722), and *A Journal of the Plague Year* (1722).

Building Background

Should Women Be Educated? In 1698 when Defoe published this essay (which was included in a miscellany of schemes to improve social conditions) the number of educated women in England had changed little since medieval times, when only a few girls were taught in nunneries. Since most of the powerful people in society thought women were inferior to men and should not be educated beyond their expected roles as wife and mother, even upper-class women received little formal learning. Many middle- and lower-class parents were fearful that too much learning made girls dissatisfied with their lives and less attractive to men; their daughters usually received no education at all until the establishment by Parliament of charity schools. When girls of any social class were taught to read, they were discouraged from reading fiction. Clergymen in particular warned that novels were not instructive and were likely to corrupt the morals of young women.

Literary Focus

Theme An underlying meaning of a literary work is a **theme.** A theme may be implied, or it may be directly stated. One of Swift's themes in "A Modest Proposal," for example, is that English tyranny over Ireland has caused great misery. Themes in nonfiction are clarified by supporting examples, the author's stated point of view, and word choice. When Swift writes that there is no need to worry about "aged, diseased, or maimed" poor because they are dying every day of famine and filth, he is supporting his theme with a powerful satirical example, but he never states his point of view directly. To discover how Defoe supports his theme, consider the examples he uses to develop his topic, which is stated in the title of the essay.

Writer's Notebook

Reform Schools? In your notebook, jot down some current problems in American education. Consider school financing, student achievement, books, supplies and equipment, curriculum, or health and safety issues.

Before Reading

Building Background

Ask students to contemplate how their lives would be different if all females were denied education. What effect would such a "brain drain" have on the nation?

Literary Focus: Theme

Remind students that *theme* is the underlying meaning of a literary work. In an essay, such as "The Education of Women," the theme will be stated and supported through logical argument.

Writer's Notebook

Students might compare educational problems today with educational problems of a previous generation by interviewing their parents.

More About Daniel Defoe

Although Defoe was imprisoned for his defense of religious freedom, religion and politics remained favorite topics for public discourse and conversation. Defoe, who did not take up the writing of fiction until he was well into his fifties, is considered one of the early creators of the novel form.

SUPPORT MATERIALS OVERVIEW

Unit 4 Resource Book
- Graphic Organizer, p. 9
- Study Guide, p. 10
- Vocabulary, p. 11
- Grammar, p. 12
- Alternate Check Test, p. 13
- Vocabulary Test, p. 14
- Selection Test, pp. 15–16

Building English Proficiency
- Selection Summaries
- Activities, p. 221

Reading, Writing & Grammar SkillBook
- Reading, pp. 79–80
- Writing, pp. 125–126

Technology
- Audiotape
- Personal Journal Software
- Custom Literature Database: Additional selections by Daniel Defoe can be found on the database.
- Test Generator Software

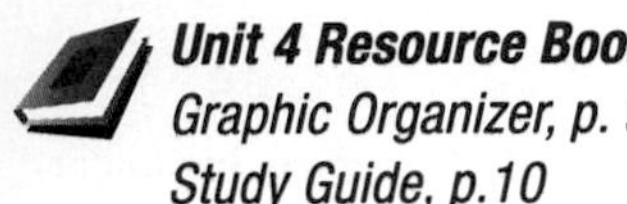

Selection Objectives

- to identify the theme of Defoe's essay
- to compare the status of women in 1698 and today
- to identify uses of satire

Unit 4 Resource Book
Graphic Organizer, p. 9
Study Guide, p.10

Theme Link

Daniel Defoe brings his Focus on Society by raising and answering the question: In an "age of reason," do women possess the ability to reason?

Vocabulary Preview

folly, being foolish, lack of sense
manifest, plain; clear
vie, compete
essay, trial
impertinent, rudely bold
prerogative, right or privilege than nobody else has

Students can add the words and definitions to their Writer's Notebook.

1 Reading/Thinking Skills
Find the Main Idea

Question What is the main idea of this passage? *(that a gentleman without education, regardless of wealth, background, and appearance, makes a sorry figure in society)*

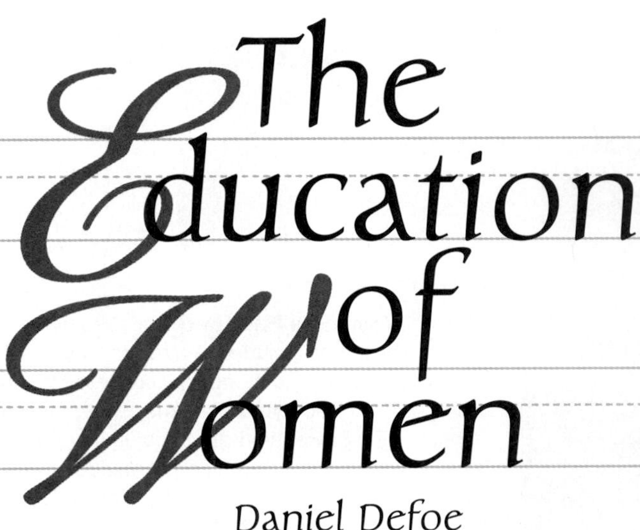

The Education of Women

Daniel Defoe

I have often thought of it as one of the most barbarous customs in the world, considering us as a civilized and a Christian country, that we deny the advantages of learning to women. We reproach the sex every day with folly[1] and impertinence, while I am confident, had they the advantages of education equal to us, they would be guilty of less than ourselves.

One would wonder, indeed, how it should happen that women are conversible[2] at all, since they are only beholding to natural parts[3] for all their knowledge. Their youth is spent to teach them to stitch and sew or make baubles. They are taught to read, indeed, and perhaps to write their names or so, and that is the height of a woman's education. And I would but ask any who slight the sex for their understanding, what is a man (a gentleman, I mean) good for that is taught no more?

1 I need not give instances or examine the character of a gentleman with a good estate and of a good family and with tolerable parts, and examine what figure he makes for want of education.

1. folly (fol′ē), *n.* a being foolish; lack of sense.
2. **that women are conversable,** that women can hold a conversation.
3. **beholding . . . parts,** dependent upon natural abilities.

SELECTION SUMMARY
The Education of Women

Defoe argues that women have the capacity to be educated and that, since they are able to learn, it is unfair to deprive them of the opportunity. He supports his argument by appealing to the self-interest of men: If a man owns a fine horse, he will train that horse well; in a similar manner, a fine women should be well-trained, so as to be most useful to men. He notes that women's virtues are fostered by education, and that lack of education fosters silliness and vice. He argues that as God has made the souls of both men and women equally capable of redemption, He has made their mental capacities and talents equally capable of training.

For summaries in other languages, see the ***Building English Proficiency*** *book.*

When Winslow Homer painted this watercolor, *Blackboard,* in 1877, educational opportunities for women had expanded from the time of Defoe, but women still did not have equal access to education. Do you think that women and men today have equal educational opportunities? Why or why not?

Art Study

Responses to Caption Questions
In theory, men and women in this country have equal access to educational opportunities. In reality, they do not. Traditionally, families—particularly those that equated education with earning power—have provided greater opportunities to sons than to daughters. Women also continue to encounter subtle discrimination, particularly in gaining admittance to certain fields of graduate study.

Visual Literacy The painting's title, *Blackboard,* and composition suggest that the young woman finds the geometry lesson "dark," i.e., unfathomable. Homer has covered her with an apron, suggesting that the elaborate dress (and the girl herself?) must be protected; her body is posed "with one hand tied behind her back," which may suggest she approaches her lessons at a disadvantage.

Question Can you think of ways in which female students of this period were at a disadvantage? *(Possible responses: Middle-class girls were typically "protected"; this often left them ill prepared to lead independent lives. Many were taught to be passive, to accept, rather than to question. Their restrictive clothes reflected the restricted lives that custom and class forced on them.)*

BUILDING ENGLISH PROFICIENCY

Planning a Reading Strategy

Filling in a K-W-L chart will help students focus on this essay.

1. Allow time for students to share prior knowledge about views of women and education in former eras. Encourage them to draw upon their knowledge of how their own ancestors were educated, as well as on what they know from movies and books.
2. Students should state questions they have about the topic.
3. After reading, students can share responses and complete the chart in small groups.

What We Know	What We Want to Know	What We Learned
Most women did not receive an education.	Why was educating women not considered important?	

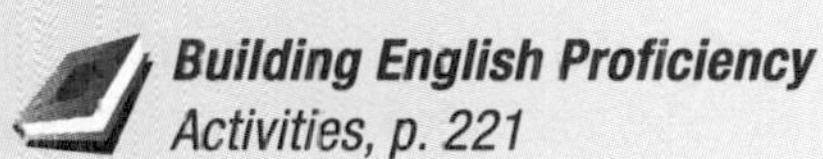

Building English Proficiency *Activities, p. 221*

2 Literary Element
Figure of Speech

Question What figure of speech does Defoe use when he compares a soul to a rough diamond? *(simile)* Continuing the simile, how might the diamond of the soul be polished? *(Possible responses: baptism; receiving religious training; accepting the tenets of Christianity)*

3 Active Reading
Clarify

It would need a moat to defend the women from anyone who might try to attack them, and to keep them isolated from the evil influences of the world.

4 Literary Element
Figure of Speech

Question Defoe refers to "giving a woman more tongues than one." What does this mean? *(A language is often called a "tongue"; French and Italian are additional tongues.)*

2 The soul is placed in the body like a rough diamond and must be polished, or the luster of it will never appear; and 'tis manifest[4] that as the rational soul distinguishes us from brutes, so education carries on the distinction and makes some less brutish than others. This is too evident to need any demonstration. But why then should women be denied the benefit of instruction? If knowledge and understanding had been useless additions to the sex, God Almighty would never have given them capacities, for He made nothing needless. Besides, I would ask such what they can see in ignorance that they should think it a necessary ornament to a woman? or how much worse is a wise woman than a fool? or what has the woman done to forfeit the privilege of being taught? Does she plague us with her pride and impertinence? Why did we not let her learn, that she might have had more wit? Shall we upbraid[5] women with folly, when 'tis only the error of this inhuman custom that hindered them being made wiser?

The capacities of women are supposed to be greater and their senses quicker than those of the men; and what they might be capable of being bred to is plain from some instances of female wit, which this age is not without; which upbraids us with injustice, and looks as if we denied women the advantages of education for fear they should vie[6] with the men in their improvements.

To remove this objection, and that women might have at least a needful opportunity of education in all sorts of useful learning, I propose the draft of an academy for that purpose. . . .

Wherefore the academy I propose should differ but little from public schools,[7] wherein such ladies as were willing to study should have all the advantages of learning suitable to their genius.[8] But since some severities of discipline more than ordinary would be absolutely necessary to preserve the reputation of the house, that persons of quality and fortune might not be afraid to venture their children thither, I shall venture to make a small scheme by way of essay.[9]

The house I would have built in a form by itself, as well as in a place by itself. The building should be of three plain fronts, without any jettings or bearing-work,[10] that the eye might at a glance see from one coign[11] to the other; the gardens walled in the same triangular figure, with a large moat, and but one entrance. When thus every part of the situation was contrived as well as might be for discovery, and to render intriguing dangerous, I would have no guards, no eyes, no spies set over the ladies, but shall expect them to be tried by the principles of honor and strict virtue. . . .

CLARIFY: Why does Defoe think the academy would need a moat? 3

In this house, the persons who enter should be taught all sorts of breeding suitable both to their genius and quality, and in particular, music and dancing, which it would be cruelty to bar the sex of, because they are their darlings; but besides this, they should be taught languages, as particularly French and Italian; and I would venture the injury of giving a woman more tongues 4
than one. They should, as a particular study, be taught all the graces of speech and all the necessary air of conversation, which our common education is so defective in that I need not expose it. They should be brought to read books, and especially history; and so to read as to make them

4. manifest (man′ə fest), *adj.* plain; clear.
5. **upbraid** (up brād′), *v.* find fault with; blame.
6. vie (vī), *v.* compete.
7. **public schools,** schools that prepared boys for the universities.
8. **their genius,** their special abilities.
9. essay (es′ā), *n.* trial.
10. **without any jettings or bearing-work.** Jettings are parts jutting out from a perpendicular wall; bearing-works are supports for these parts.
11. **coign** (koin), *n.* a stone-reinforced corner.

MINI-LESSON: GRAMMAR
Understanding Subordinate and Coordinate Clauses

Teach Read or write on the board this sentence from the middle of column 2 on page 309.

If her temper be bad, want of breeding makes her worse, and she grows haughty, insolent, and loud.

Point out the coordinate conjunction *and* connecting the two independent clauses, clauses that are really sentences that could stand on their own. Also point out the subordinate conjunction *if* introducing the subordinate clause *her temper be bad* (the verb would be *is* except that this is in the subjunctive mood). Remind students that independent clauses can stand alone and are connected with coordinate conjunctions, while subordinate clauses cannot stand alone and are introduced by subordinate conjunctions.

Activity Idea While many of Defoe's sentences are very complex, have students find other examples of sentences having subordinate clauses or sentences as short as they can find that have both a coordinate and a subordinate clause.

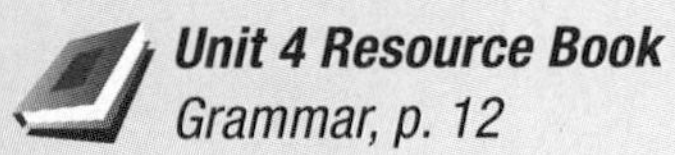

Unit 4 Resource Book
Grammar, p. 12

understand the world and be able to know and judge of things when they hear of them.

To such whose genius would lead them to it, I would deny no sort of learning; but the chief thing, in general, is to cultivate the understandings of the sex, that they may be capable of all sorts of conversation; that, their parts and judgments being improved, they may be as profitable in their conversation as they are pleasant.

. . . *You rarely see them lumpish and heavy when they are children, as boys will often be.*

Women, in my observation, have little or no difference in them, but as they are or are not distinguished by education. Tempers, indeed, may in some degree influence them, but the main distinguishing part is their breeding.

The whole sex are generally quick and sharp. I believe I may be allowed to say generally so, for you rarely see them lumpish and heavy when they are children, as boys will often be. If a woman be well bred, and taught the proper management of her natural wit, she proves generally very sensible and retentive;[12] and without partiality, a woman of sense and manners is the finest and most delicate part of God's creation, the glory of her Maker, and the great instance of His singular regard to man, His darling creature, to whom He gave the best gift either God could bestow or man receive. And 'tis the sordidest piece of folly and ingratitude in the world to withhold from the sex the due luster which the advantage of education gives to the natural beauty of their minds.

A woman well bred and well taught, furnished with the additional accomplishments of knowledge and behavior, is a creature without comparison; her society is the emblem of sublimer enjoyments; her person is angelic and her conversation heavenly; she is all softness and sweetness, peace, love, wit, and delight. She is every way suitable to the sublimest wish, and the man that has such a one to his portion has nothing to do but rejoice in her and be thankful. 6

On the other hand, suppose her to be the very same woman, and rob her of the benefit of education, and it follows thus:

If her temper be good, want of education makes her soft and easy. Her wit, for want of teaching, makes her impertinent[13] and talkative. Her knowledge, for want of judgment and experience, makes her fanciful and whimsical.[14] If her temper be bad, want of breeding makes her worse, and she grows haughty, insolent,[15] and loud. If she be passionate, want of manners makes her termagant[16] and a scold, which is much at one with lunatic. If she be proud, want of discretion (which still is breeding) makes her conceited, fantastic, and ridiculous. And from these she degenerates to be turbulent, clangorous,[17] noisy nasty, and the devil.

Methinks mankind for their own sakes—since, say what we will of the women, we all think fit at one time or other to be concerned with them—should take some care to breed them up to be suitable and serviceable, if they expected no such thing as delight from them. Bless us! what care do we take to breed up a good horse

12. **retentive** (ri ten′tiv), *adj.* able to remember easily.
13. **impertinent** (im pėrt′n ənt), *adj.* rudely bold.
14. **whimsical** (hwim′zə kəl), *adj.* having many odd notions or fancies.
15. **insolent** (in′sə lənt), *adj.* insulting.
16. **termagant** (tėr′mə gənt), *adj.* violent and quarrelsome.
17. **clangorous** (klang′ər əs), *adj.* with a loud, harsh, ringing sound.

5 Literary Focus
Theme

Questions According to Defoe, what virtues do women acquire through education? *(They become wonderful companions: they behave perfectly and converse intelligently; their tempers are sweet and their wit delightful.)* How do these virtues relate to the theme? *(They support Defoe's argument that women are equal to men in intelligence and should be educated.)*

6 Reading/Thinking Skills
Recognize Propaganda Techniques

Questions What do you think of Defoe's list of virtues? *(While responses may vary, many students will find the list condescending. They all benefit men, rather than women.)* Why do you think Defoe offers such a male-oriented list of virtues? *(Possible response: He appeals to the vanity of his male readers in an effort to convince them to support extending education to women.)*

BUILDING ENGLISH PROFICIENCY

Expanding Vocabulary Notebooks

Students may find much of Defoe's vocabulary a challenge. You might help them by narrowing their focus to words that relate to Defoe's key ideas.

1. Write the following words from pages 308–309 on the chalkboard: rational, fortune, tongues, wit, venture, breeding, upbraid, contrived, degenerates.

2. Model the use of a dictionary in defining these words—look up one of them and draw attention to ways in which meanings may have changed since Defoe's time.

3. Invite pairs or groups of students to create sentences for these or other words from the essay. If students are working with words whose meanings have changed, work with them to come up with sentences that illustrate both the "past" and "present" meanings.

7 **Literary Focus**
Theme

Question What is Defoe's main argument in favor of education for women? *(As God has given men and women souls equally capable of redemption, He has given them intelligence and talents equally capable of training through education.)*

8 **Active Reading**
Summarize

Response Women have the capacity to be educated; they will be better people and better companions for men for being educated; the entire society will be improved because they will be less ignorant and foolish.

Check Test

1. According to Defoe, what are women taught in their youths? *(to stitch and sew or make baubles, perhaps to read and to write their own names)*
2. Defoe compares the soul in the body to what? *(a rough diamond)*
3. Does Defoe advocate public education for men and women? *(No, he proposes educating women in a separate house behind a moat.)*
4. What are some of the vices of an uneducated woman? *(She is soft and easy, impertinent and talkative, fanciful and whimsical, haughty, insolent, and loud, termagant and scolding, conceited and ridiculous, noisy and nasty.)*
5. Does Defoe propose equal political rights for women? *(No, he thinks they should be educated to be companions for men, who will maintain their own prerogatives.)*

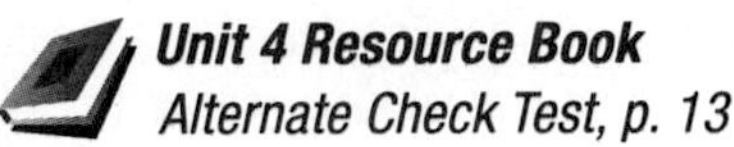
Unit 4 Resource Book
Alternate Check Test, p. 13

and to break him well! and what a value do we put upon him when it is done, and all because he should be fit for our use! and why not a woman? Since all her ornaments and beauty without suitable behavior is a cheat in nature, like the false tradesman who puts the best of his goods uppermost, that the buyer may think the rest are of the same goodness.

That Almighty First Cause which made us all is certainly the fountain of excellence, as it is of being, and by an invisible influence could have diffused equal qualities and perfections to all the creatures it has made, as the sun does its light, without the least ebb or diminution to Himself, and has given indeed to every individual sufficient to the figure His providence had designed him in the world.

7 I believe it might be defended if I should say that I do suppose God has given to all mankind equal gifts and capacities in that He has given them all souls equally capable, and that the whole difference in mankind proceeds either from accidental difference in the make of their bodies or from the foolish difference of education. . . . and this is manifested by comparing it with the difference between one man or woman and another.

And herein it is that I take upon me to make such a bold assertion that all the world are mistaken in their practice about women; for I cannot think that God Almighty ever made them so delicate, so glorious creatures, and furnished them with such charms, so agreeable and so delightful to mankind, with souls capable of the same accomplishments with men, and all to be only stewards of our houses, cooks, and slaves.

Not that I am for exalting the female government in the least; but, in short, I would have men take women for companions, and educate them to be fit for it. A woman of sense and breeding will scorn as much to encroach[18] upon the prerogative[19] of the man as a man of sense will scorn to oppress the weakness of the woman. But if the women's souls were refined and improved by teaching, that word would be lost; to say the *weakness of the sex* as to judgment would be nonsense, for ignorance and folly would be no more found among women than men. I remember a passage which I heard from a very fine woman. She had wit and capacity enough, an extraordinary shape and face, and a great fortune, but had been cloistered up all her time, and, for fear of being stolen, had not had the liberty of being taught the common necessary knowledge of women's affairs; and when she came to converse in the world, her natural wit made her so sensible of the want of education that she gave this short reflection on herself: "I am ashamed to talk with my very maids," says she, "for I don't know when they do right or wrong. I had more need go to school than be married."

SUMMARIZE: Summarize Defoe's reasons for proposing that women be educated. 8

I need not enlarge on the loss the defect of education is to the sex, nor argue the benefit of the contrary practice; 'tis a thing will be more easily granted than remedied. This chapter is but an essay at the thing, and I refer the practice to those happy days, if ever they shall be, when men shall be wise enough to mend it.

18. **encroach** (en krōch′), *v.* tresspass; intrude.
19. **prerogative** (pri rog′ə tiv), *n.* right or privilege that nobody else has.

MINI-LESSON: GRAMMAR

The Rhetorical Question

The first paragraph on page 308 contains several examples of rhetorical questions.

Teach A rhetorical question is a question that is asked for effect, rather than with the expectation of an answer. It is a device often used in argument, from great literary essays to commercial jingles. An example of the latter is a fast food ad campaign in the 1980s that asked, rhetorically, "Where's the beef?" Parents often furnish good examples: "Is this a bedroom or a pig sty?" and "What have you been up to until one A.M.?" are two classic examples.

Activity Idea Ask students to write a paragraph describing a contemporary social issue. After they have described the problem, they should compose three rhetorical questions that might be part of a speech or essay on that issue.

After Reading

Making Connections

Shaping Your Response

1. In your opinion, is this essay persuasive? Do you think it would have changed anyone's mind at the time it was written?

Analyzing the Essay

2. Defoe says that "the soul is placed in the body like a rough diamond and must be polished, or the luster of it will never appear." What does this **simile** have to do with education?
3. Why does Defoe seem to think it necessary to provide directions for building an academy for women?
4. Educating women would certainly change the **interactions** between men and women. Summarize the advantages to both men and women that Defoe claims would follow from providing an education for women.
5. Defoe says he is not "for exalting the female government" and that "A woman of sense and breeding will scorn . . . to encroach upon the prerogative of the man . . . ." What does he mean, and why do you think he includes such remarks?

Extending the Ideas

6. Have all the problems with women's education that Defoe criticizes been eliminated in the United States today? in the world? Explain.

Literary Focus: Theme

Theme, either directly stated or implied, is an underlying meaning of a work. Where does Defoe state his theme? What techniques does he use to support this theme? What do you think is his most effective argument? his least effective argument?

Vocabulary Study

On your paper, write the word from the list that best completes the meaning of each sentence. You will not use all the words.

essay
folly
impertinent
manifest
prerogative
vie

1. In the past, men often claimed the ____ of education.
2. Some individuals, however, thought it was ____ to deny education to women.
3. Defoe and others believed that lack of learning made women ____.
4. According to Defoe, it was ____ that denying education to women was an inhuman custom.
5. He wondered whether men feared that an educated woman would ____ with men.

After Reading

MAKING CONNECTIONS

1. While responses will vary, opinions should be supported by reasons.

2. Defoe states that as the souls of women are capable of polishing, i.e., redemption, their minds are capable of training.

3. He includes these directions as a way to demonstrate that such establishments could be proper and safe environments for daughters.

4. Defoe believes that women would be better companions for men and that they would no longer be subject to ignorance and folly. Women would enjoy having a wider view of the world and developing their abilities.

5. He is assuring readers that he does not intend women to have equal rights or to participate in political life, because most of his readers would vehemently oppose any such plan.

6. Student answers will vary, but should be supported by examples.

VOCABULARY STUDY

1. prerogative
2. folly
3. impertinent
4. manifest
5. vie

Unit 4 Resource Book
Vocabulary, p. 11
Vocabulary Test, p. 14

LITERARY FOCUS: THEME

Defoe's theme is stated in the title: the education of women. He supports his theme by appeals to religion and to the self-interest of men. He uses rhetorical questions to appeal to readers' generosity. His most effective argument is that men and women are equally intelligent and, thus, can benefit equally from education. His least effective argument is that educated women will make better companions for men.

WRITING CHOICES

Writer's Notebook Update

Remind students that if they are writing about current problems in education, then they should use arguments that appeal to current beliefs. If they are writing about Defoe's essay, they should use arguments that would have made sense in his time.

"In My Opinion . . ."

You might remind students that Defoe's ideas were, in his day, radical, even groundbreaking. This may help students to deal with his condescension toward women.

Selection Test

Unit 4 Resource Book
pp. 15–16

Expressing Your Ideas

Writing Choices

Writer's Notebook Update Look back at the list of current problems in education that you wrote in your notebook. Choose one of these and in a sentence or two state your position on this problem.

"In My Opinion . . ." Put yourself in the place of a man or woman of 1698 reading Defoe's essay. With which parts of it would you agree? With which would you disagree? Organize your thoughts and express them in a **letter to the editor** of a newspaper. (*The Review, The Tatler,* and *The Spectator* were weekly or bimonthly newspapers popular in the early 1700s.) Support your points with examples and write to convince other newspaper readers to share your opinions.

Be Reasonable! Both Swift and Defoe, as well as Alexander Pope, the author who comes next, were writing in a period (late 1600s to mid-1700s) that has come to be known as the Age of Reason. This period was characterized by a belief in reason rather than sensory experience or religious faith as the answer to life's problems. Pope wrote two lines that help to clarify this belief:

> Know then thyself, presume not God to scan;
> The proper study of mankind is Man.

Can you find any flaws in this belief? Examine this idea in an **essay.**

Other Options

Pressing the Issue Women's education is not a high priority in many parts of the world, and in fact, it is actively opposed in some countries. With a partner, research some of the reasons for lack of women's education and the efforts by international organizations such as UNESCO to raise literacy rates, and give an **oral report** to the class. Include visuals if possible.

A Better Job? Some people feel that men and women should be educated primarily for the work force; others feel that such an emphasis goes against the basic purpose of education: to develop the individual for any situation in life—moral, spiritual, and economic. With a partner, consider these ideas, develop an argument for each side, and present your **debate** to the class.

The Look of Learning Defoe has some rather particular ideas about how a school for women should be constructed. What does your ideal learning place look like? Draw a **picture** or **diagram** of a place that you feel would provide the best learning environment possible. Label or write captions for parts of your diagram that are not immediately apparent. (For example, would you put computers in every room, all together in a technology center—or not include them at all? For that matter, are there even rooms?) Display your picture in the classroom.

OTHER OPTIONS

Pressing the Issue

Students might wish to read reports of the conference on the status of women that took place near Beijing, China, in the summer of 1995.

A Better Job?

Students can gather facts and ideas for each side before choosing which partner will argue which side in the debate.

The Look of Learning

Students who need ideas might begin by considering how their own school could be modified to provide a more ideal learning environment.

Before Reading

from The Rape of the Lock
from An Essay on Criticism by Alexander Pope

Alexander Pope
1688–1744

Stricken with tuberculosis of the spine at an early age, Alexander Pope was crippled and in almost constant pain for most of his life. A Catholic in an age of violent anti-Catholicism, his religion prevented him from receiving a university education, holding public office, or voting, and he was educated chiefly at home. His *Essay on Criticism*, written when he was twenty-three, first made him famous. He earned a large income from his poetry, translations of the *Iliad* and the *Odyssey* (two ancient Greek epic poems), and other writings. In 1718 he moved with his mother to Twickenham, now a suburb of London. Here he devoted much time to landscape gardening and to entertaining friends. He later became known as the "wasp of Twickenham" because of his stinging satire.

Building Background

The Social Whirl "The Rape of the Lock" (here the word *rape* means simply "theft") is a poem written in the style of a serious epic poem but it is called a **mock-epic** because of its subject matter. On the surface, Pope's poem is about a quarrel between two families. Yet it contains much social criticism, as noted by biographer Maynard Mack: "Pope represents the absurdities of the fashionable world with affection, and with an eye to the delicate beauties that its best graces unfold. We recognize too the shrewdness of his perception that the contemporary counterpart of the epic hero in his own society—in prestige, influence, authority, and tribute exacted—is the beautiful, marriageable, well-dowered young woman: the profitable 'match.'"

In this society, where the death of a husband or a lap dog is equally serious and where the theft of a lock of hair is sufficient cause for war, values must be out of order.

Literary Focus

Heroic Couplet/Epigram A **heroic couplet** is a pair of rhymed lines that contain a complete thought. The lines are written in iambic pentameter (see the Glossary of Literary Terms), a meter that is often used for serious epics having to do with heroes, and thus the couplet is called "heroic." Heroic verse is now used more for satire or mock-epics, since few people write serious epic poems today.

An **epigram** is a short, witty verse, usually of two or four lines, that often ends with a twist. This heroic couplet by Pope is also an epigram:

Hope springs eternal in the human breast;
Man never is, but always to be blessed.

Writer's Notebook

Rhyming Pairs How would you go about writing rhymed verse? Would you start by making a list of rhyming words or think of the rhymes as you wrote? Choose a general topic (friendship, school, work) and jot down some rhyming words of one or two syllables that you could use to write about that topic.

Before Reading

Building Background

Ask students if they can recall trivial incidents blown wildly out of proportion by vanity or ego. You might begin by mentioning how people often "overreact" to a bad haircut.

Literary Focus

Question What is the difference between a heroic couplet and an epigram? *(A heroic couplet is two rhymed lines that contain a complete thought. An epigram is a witty verse, usually two or four lines, that often ends with a twist.)*

Writer's Notebook

Ask students to suggest key words on the topics of school, friends, or jobs and then brainstorm pairs of rhyming words for each of the key words.

More About Alexander Pope

Pope, embittered by his spinal deformity and experiences as a Roman Catholic in a Protestant country, was fond of saying, "Blessed are those who expect nothing, for they will never be disappointed." His other works include:

- *An Essay on Man* (1733)
- *The Dunciad* (1743)

SUPPORT MATERIALS OVERVIEW

Unit 4 Resource Book
- Graphic Organizer, p. 17
- Study Guide, p. 18
- Vocabulary, p. 19
- Grammar, p. 20
- Alternate Check Test, p. 21
- Vocabulary Test, p. 22
- Selection Test, pp. 23–24

Building English Proficiency
- Selection Summaries
- Activities, p. 222

Reading, Writing & Grammar SkillBook
- Grammar, Usage, and Mechanics, pp. 205–206, 207–208

The World of Work
- Cosmetologist, p. 11
- Activity, p. 12

Technology
- Audiotape
- Personal Journal Software
- Custom Literature Database: Additional selections by Alexander Pope can be found on the database.
- Test Generator Software

During Reading

Selection Objectives

- to identify examples of heroic couplet and epigram
- to identify how the formal devices of classical epic are used for comic effect in the mock epic
- to identify and write examples of consistent verb tense

Unit 4 Resource Book
Graphic Organizer, p. 17
Study Guide, p. 18

Theme Link

Pope, like other writers of the Age of Reason, brings to his Focus on Society the sharp edge of irony, sarcasm, and great wit.

1 Literary Focus
Heroic Couplet/Epigram

Questions Is this an example of heroic couplet? epigram? Why? *(It is heroic couplet; the pair of rhymed lines of iambic pentameter contain a complete thought; it is not an epigram; it is not an expression of wit, ending with a twist.)* Why is this a "mock" heroic couplet? *(Pope uses a heroic couplet to report the unheroic, in fact, inconsequential, news that Belinda sleeps. Rather than enriching, the form mocks the subject matter.)*

EDITORIAL NOTE This excerpt has been shortened for length. For a more complete version of *The Rape of the Lock,* see the Custom Literature Database.

THE RAPE OF THE Lock

An Heroic-Comical Poem

Alexander Pope

Pope wrote this poem at the request of a friend who asked him to make peace between both sides in a quarrel that had arisen when Lord Petre (the Baron in the poem) snipped off a lock of hair from the head of Arabella Fermor (Belinda in the poem). To show how trivial was the basis of the quarrel, Pope exaggerated it still further, puffing it up to epic importance in this "heroic-comical" form. Pope apparently succeeded in healing the breach between the families involved, but the real-life hero and heroine never married. Lord Petre married a younger and richer heiress and died of smallpox within a year. Arabella Fermor married another gentleman, and they had six children.

Canto 1

What dire offence from amorous causes springs,
What mighty contests rise from trivial things,
I sing—this verse to Caryll, Muse! is due;
This, even Belinda may vouchsafe to view.
Slight is the subject, but not so the praise,
If she inspire, and he approve my lays.
Say what strange motive, Goddess! could compel
A well-bred Lord to assault a gentle Belle?
O say what stranger cause, yet unexplored,
Could make a gentle Belle reject a Lord?
In tasks so bold, can little men engage,
And in soft bosoms dwells such mighty rage?
Sol through white curtains shot a timorous ray,
And oped those eyes that must eclipse the day.
Now lapdogs give themselves the rousing shake,
And sleepless lovers, just at twelve, awake.
Thrice rung the bell, the slipper knocked the ground,
And the pressed watch returned a silver sound.
Belinda still her downy pillow pressed,
1 Her guardian Sylph prolonged the balmy rest.
'Twas he had summoned to her silent bed

3 Caryll, John Caryll, who suggested that Pope write the poem to heal the breach between the two families.
18 pressed watch. When the stem is pressed on this type of watch, it chimes the nearest hour or quarter hour.
20 sylph (silf), *n.* one of the spirits which, according to an old belief, inhabit the air. This one is named Ariel.

The three illustrations with this poem were created by Aubrey Beardsley for an edition of *The Rape of the Lock* published in 1896. In this illustration, entitled "The Toilet," what does Belinda's elaborate grooming ritual suggest about the value she places on her appearance? ➤

SELECTION SUMMARY

The Rape of the Lock; An Essay on Criticism

The Rape of the Lock Beautiful Belinda is warned in a dream of a dread event. After completing an elaborate toilette, she sets off for Hampton Court by barge. During the voyage she is greatly admired by a baron, who covets the twin locks of hair that grace her neck. At the palace, he seizes his chance and severs a lock. Outraged, Belinda attacks him with snuff and a hairpin and demands restoration. Alas, the lock cannot be restored; the heavenly curl has been transformed into a heavenly body, which will attest to Belinda's beauty through eternity.

An Essay on Criticism With wit and wry humor, the speaker expounds on the intellectual qualities—including knowledge of personal limitations and defects—that characterize a thoughtful and enlightened human being.

For summaries in other languages, see the ***Building English Proficiency*** *book.*

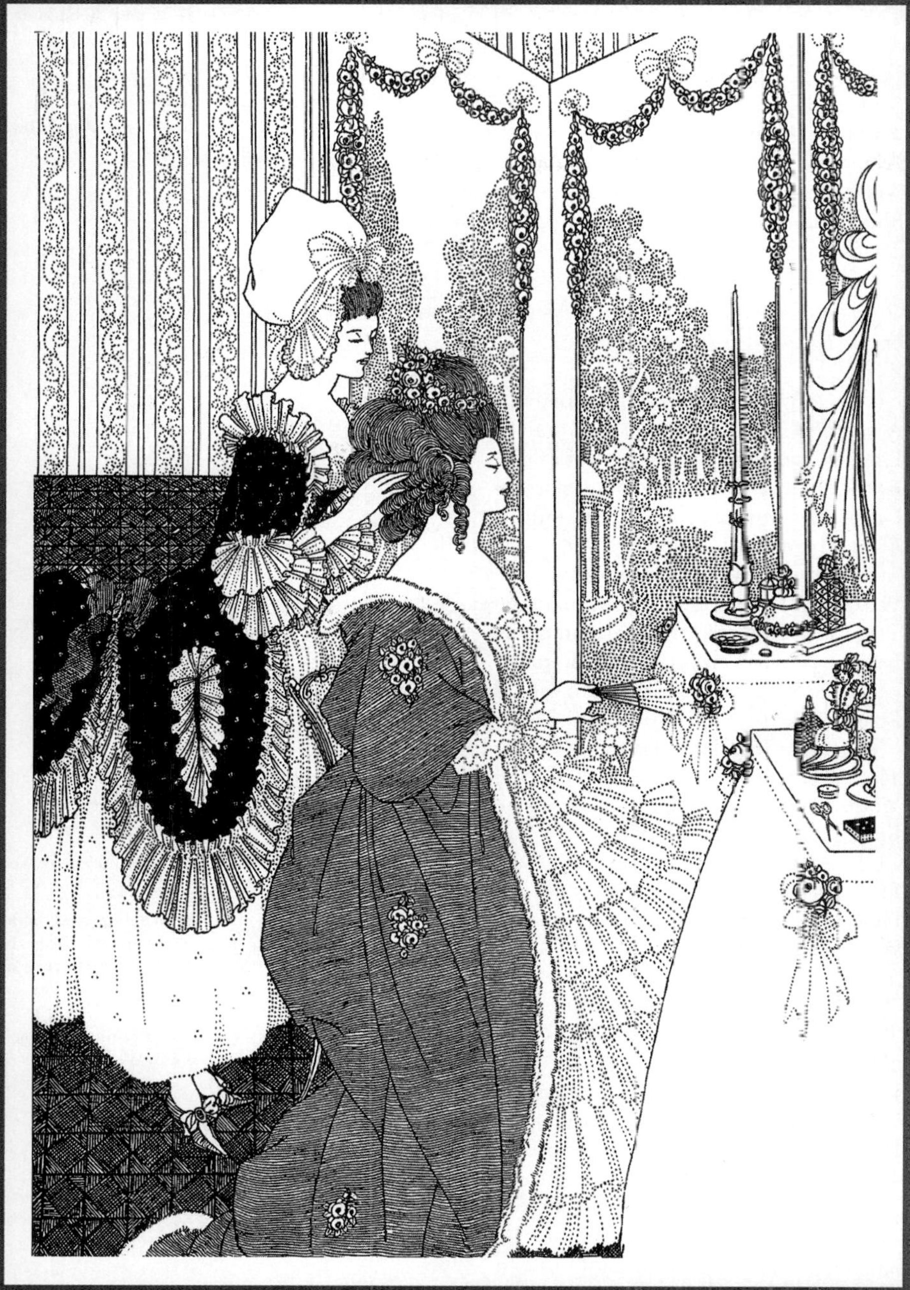

Response to Caption Question It suggests that her appearance is of the utmost importance to her.

Visual Literacy The artist, Aubrey Beardsley, was associated with an artistic movement called Aestheticism; the followers of the movement, sometimes referred to as decedents, believed that art should exist for its own sake, independent of moral or social concerns; beauty, however morbid or "unhealthy" in subject, is its own justification.

Question Do you think this illustration by Beardsley pokes fun at vanity or, in fact, celebrates it? *(Responses will vary. It might be noted that Beardsley does "dress" his illustration with the same exquisite care with which the Belindas of the world dress their hair. The details seem to exist for no other purpose than to amuse the artist and amaze his audience.)*

BUILDING ENGLISH PROFICIENCY

ESL LEP ELD SAE LD

Improving Comprehension

To help students grasp this poem, combine different ability levels in six groups. Assign each group to one canto, but let two groups handle Canto 5, dividing it at line 292.

1. Ask each group to become an expert on its assigned canto, ready to answer questions that the rest of the class may have about that part of the poem. Have group members work together, researching allusions and looking up difficult words.
2. Have each group summarize what happens in its canto.
3. Have the groups collaborate on creating a chain of canto summaries in correct sequence.

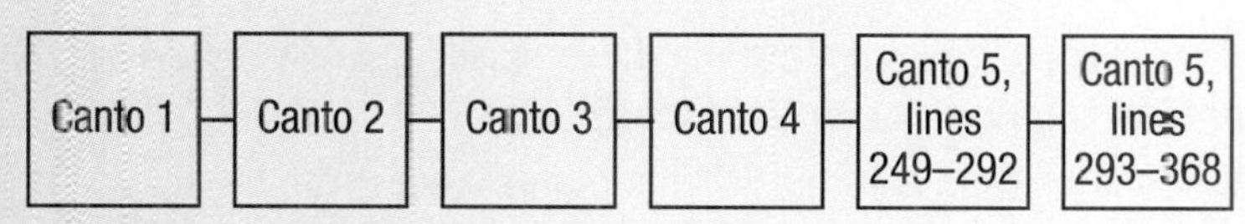

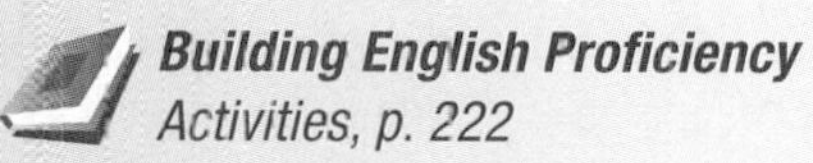

Building English Proficiency
Activities, p. 222

2 Reading/Thinking Skills
Find the Main Idea

Response a glittering youth who whispers of her importance

3 Historical Note
"Machinery"

The original two-canto, 334-line *The Rape of the Lock* was a great success when published in 1712. Not satisfied, Pope revised and expanded it in 1713, adding the delightful "machinery" (i.e., the supernatural agents in epic action) of the Sylphs, Belinda's toilette, the card game, and the visit to the Cave of Spleen in Canto 4. With the addition of Clarissa's speech on good humor, the poem assumed its final form in 1717.

4 Literary Element
Foreshadowing

Response that she may be "attacked" by a man

5 Reading/Thinking Skills
Infer

Response that she cares very much about her appearance; that she is vain

The morning dream that hovered over her head.
A youth more glittering than a birth-night beau
(That even in slumber caused her cheek to glow)
Seemed to her ear his winning lips to lay,
And thus in whispers said, or seemed to say . . . .
"Hear and believe! thy own importance know,
Nor bound thy narrow views to things below.
Some secret truths, from learnèd pride concealed,
To maids alone and children are revealed. . . ."

2 ■ What is Belinda dreaming about?

23 birth-night beau, a gentleman dressed in fine clothes for the sovereign's birthday.

Ariel explains that "unnumbered spirits" fly around Belinda and that sylphs can take whatever shape and sex they wish.

3

"A Sylph am I, who thy protection claim,
A watchful sprite, and Ariel is my name.
Late, as I ranged the crystal wilds of air,
In the clear mirror of thy ruling star
I saw, alas! some dread event impend,
Ere to the main this morning sun descend.
But heaven reveals not what, or how, or where:
Warned by the Sylph, oh pious maid, beware!
This to disclose is all thy guardian can:
Beware of all, but most beware of man!"
He said; when Shock, who thought she slept too long,
Leaped up, and waked his mistress with his tongue.
'Twas then, Belinda, if report say true,
Thy eyes first opened on a billet-doux;
Wounds, charms and ardors were no sooner read,
But all the vision vanished from thy head.
And now, unveiled, the toilet stands displayed,
Each silver vase in mystic order laid.
First, robed in white, the nymph intent adores,
With head uncovered, the cosmetic powers.
A heavenly image in the glass appears,
To that she bends, to that her eyes she rears;
The inferior priestess, at her altar's side,
Trembling, begins the sacred rites of pride.
Unnumbered treasures ope at once, and here
The various offerings of the world appear;
From each she nicely culls with curious toil,
And decks the goddess with the glittering spoil.
This casket India's glowing gems unlocks,
And all Arabia breathes from yonder box.
The tortoise here and elephant unite,
Transformed to combs, the speckled and the white.

4 ■ Prophetic dreams are part of the epic tradition. What might Ariel's warning foreshadow?

41 Shock, Belinda's dog.

44 billet-doux (bil′ē dü′), *n.* love letter. *[French]*

47 toilet, dressing table.

5 ■ What impression do you get of Belinda from the contents of her dressing table?

53 inferior priestess, Belinda's maid Betty.

57 cull (kul), *v.* pick out; select.
59 casket, here, a small box.
60 Arabia, source of perfumes.

MINI-LESSON: VOCABULARY
Connotation/Denotation

The Rape of the Lock contains a word used playfully—the word *rape*—that is seldom, if ever, used lightly today.

Teach Word meanings change with time: they are historical. A familiar example is the word "nice," which in earlier times meant "unruly," "lewd," or "silly." A word has both denotative meanings (dictionary definitions) and connotative meanings (suggested meanings with emotional impact). The context in which a word is used often determines its connotation. Thus in "This is a nice mess," the connotation of the word *nice* is "bad."

Activity Idea Discuss with students the use of the word *rape* in three circumstances that place the meanings historically.

- What does *rape* mean in *The Rape of the Lock*? *(attack on, seizure, capture)*
- What does *rape* mean in "the Rape of Poland" at the beginning of World War II? *(conquest, devastation)*
- What does *rape* mean in the criminal sense today? *(violation, sexual assault, sexual violence)*

Have students use a thesaurus to find synonyms for the word *rape* that would be usable and are used in each context. Ask whether the use of *rape* as a comedic device, as in *The Rape of the Lock,* would be possible today.

Here files of pins extend their shining rows,
6 Puffs, powder, patches, bibles, billet-doux.
Now awful beauty puts on all its arms;
The fair each moment rises in her charms,
Repairs her smiles, awakens every grace,
And calls forth all the wonders of her face;
Sees by degrees a purer blush arise,
And keener lightnings quicken in her eyes.
The busy Sylphs surround their darling care;
These set the head, and those divide the hair,
Some fold the sleeve, whilst others plait the gown;
And Betty's praised for labors not her own.

Canto 2

7 Not with more glories, in the ethereal plain,
The sun first rises over the purpled main,
Than issuing forth, the rival of his beams
Launched on the bosom of the silver Thames.
Fair nymphs and well-dressed youths around her shone,
But every eye was fixed on her alone. . . .
This nymph, to the destruction of mankind,
Nourished two locks, which graceful hung behind
In equal curls, and well conspired to deck
With shining ringlets the smooth ivory neck.
Love in these labyrinths his slaves detains,
And mighty hearts are held in slender chains.
With hairy springes we the birds betray,
Slight lines of hair surprise the finny prey,
Fair tresses man's imperial race ensnare,
And beauty draws us with a single hair.
The adventurous Baron the bright locks admired,
He saw, he wished, and to the prize aspired.
Resolved to win, he meditates the way,
By force to ravish, or by fraud betray;
For when success a lover's toil attends,
Few ask, if fraud or force attained his ends. . . .

64 patches, tiny pieces of black silk pasted on the face to show off fine skin.
65 awful, awe-inspiring.

75 ethereal plain, the sky.

78 launched . . . Thames. Belinda now sets forth on a Thames River boat on her way to Hampton Court, one of the royal palaces.

85 labyrinth (lab′ə rinth′), *n.* maze.
87 springe (sprinj), *n.* snare to catch birds.

The World of Work

Cosmetologist

For a real-life discussion of the perils of vanity, use the pages referenced below.

The World of Work
pp. 11–12

6 Literary Element
Alliteration

Remind students that alliteration is the repetition of consonant sounds at the beginning of words or within words.

Question What are examples of alliteration in lines 63–64? *(pins, puffs, powder, patches and bibles, billet-doux)*

7 Reading/Thinking Skills
Essential and Incidental Information

Question What is the essential information in lines 75–96? *(Possible response: Belinda sets forth on a boat on the Thames River. She is the center of attention. A Baron greatly admires two locks of hair that hang down her neck. He resolves, somehow, to have one of those locks.)*

BUILDING ENGLISH PROFICIENCY

Understanding Elevated Language

Students may find Pope's elevated language a challenge. Emphasize that Pope uses elegant language for comic effect, to mock events that he considers silly and unimportant.

Activity Ideas

- Have pairs of students paraphrase each couplet in lines 49–70.
- Ask pairs of students to make up two sentences—one using plain language and the other using elevated language—to tell about a simple activity, such as riding a bike. Encourage students to add these examples to their vocabulary notebooks.

PLAIN	ELEVATED
I got on my bike and took off.	Mounting my mechanical, bipedalled steed, I advanced on my journey.

8 Reading/Thinking Skills

Recognize Values

Response No, the dire disasters are not of equal importance. They alternate between the important and the trivial.

Question What does this coupling of the important and the trivial suggest about the values of these characters. *(Possible response: By equating a stain on honor with a stain on a dress, Pope suggests that these characters have false values.)*

The Author Speaks

"As to the following cantos, all the passages of them are as fabulous as the vision at the beginning, or the transformation at the end; (except the loss of your hair, which I always mention with reverence). The human persons are as fictitious as the airy ones; and the character of Belinda, as it is now managed, resembles you in nothing but in beauty."

Alexander Pope
"Letter to Mrs. Arabella Fermor"
The Norton Anthology of English Literature

The Baron has collected various items such as a glove and love letters from former lovers, but he now seeks to possess something of Belinda's. Ariel, aware of the threat to Belinda, summons his fellow sylphs and sends them to their various stations about Belinda to guard her every precious possession.

"This day, black omens threat the brightest fair
That ever deserved a watchful spirit's care;
Some dire disaster, or by force, or sleight,
But what, or where, the fates have wrapped in night— 8
Whether the nymph shall break Diana's law,
Or some frail China jar receive a flaw,
Or stain her honor, or her new brocade,
Forget her prayers, or miss a masquerade,
Or lose her heart, or necklace, at a ball;
Or whether Heaven has doomed that Shock must fall.
Haste then, ye spirits! to your charge repair:
The fluttering fan be Zephyretta's care;
The drops to thee, Brillante, we consign;
And, Momentilla, let the watch be thine;
Do thou, Crispissa, tend her favourite lock;
Ariel himself shall be the guard of Shock.
"To fifty chosen Sylphs, of special note,
We trust the important charge, the petticoat:
Oft have we known that sevenfold fence to fail,
Though stiff with hoops, and armed with ribs of whale.
Form a strong line about the silver bound,
And guard the wide circumference around.
"Whatever spirit, careless of his charge,
His post neglects, or leaves the fair at large,
Shall feel sharp vengeance soon overtake his sins,
Be stopped in vials, or transfixed with pins;
Or plunged in lakes of bitter washes lie,
Or wedged whole ages in a bodkin's eye:
Gums and pomatums shall his flight restrain,
While clogged he beats his silken wings in vain;
Or alum styptics with contracting power
Shrink his thin essence like a rivelled flower.
Or, as Ixion fixed, the wretch shall feel
The giddy motion of the whirling mill,
In fumes of burning chocolate shall glow,
And tremble at the sea that froths below!"
He spoke; the spirits from the sails descend;
Some, orb in orb, around the nymph extend,
Some thrid the mazy ringlets of her hair,

■ Are the "dire" disasters that might happen of equal importance?

101 Diana's law, chastity. Diana was the Roman goddess of the moon and protector of women.

109 drops, dangling earrings.

122 vial (vī′əl), *n.* small bottle for holding medicines or the like.
124 bodkin, a large needle.
125 pomatums, perfumed ointments for the hair.
128 rivelled (riv′ld) *adj.* wrinkled or shrivelled.
129 Ixion. In Greek myth, he was fastened to an endlessly revolving wheel in Hades as punishment for making love to Juno, queen of the gods.

135 thrid (thrid), *v.* past-tense of *thread,* pass through.

MINI-LESSON: GRAMMAR

Using Consistent Verb Tense

Couplets in this poem display consistent verb tense even though the tense may change from couplet to couplet, as in lines 13–16.

Sol through white curtains *shot* a timorous ray
And *oped* [opened] those eyes that must eclipse the day.
Now lap dogs *give* themselves the rousing shake,
And sleepless lovers, just at twelve, *awake.*

In the first couplet, main verbs are consistent in the past tense; in the second couplet, they are in the present tense.

Teach The verb tense is: **present** when it expresses action (or existence) that is happening now or that happens continually, regularly; **past** when it expresses action (or existence) that is completed at a particular time in the past; and **future** when it expresses action that will take place at some time after the present. Verb tenses should not be mixed unless there is a good expressive purpose for doing so.

Activity Idea Students can: find the main verbs in six consecutive couplets; write the tense of these verbs after each couplet; change the verb tense in each couplet, keeping tenses within each couplet consistent; and evaluate the alteration of meaning that results.

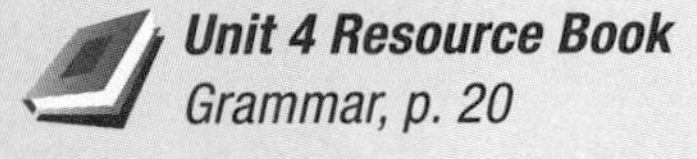
Unit 4 Resource Book
Grammar, p. 20

Some hang upon the pendants of her ear;
With beating hearts the dire event they wait,
Anxious and trembling for the birth of fate.

Canto 3
Close by those meads, for ever crowned with flowers,
Where Thames with pride surveys his rising towers,
There stands a structure of majestic frame,
Which from the neighboring Hampton takes its name.
Here Britain's statesmen oft the fall foredoom
Of foreign tyrants, and of nymphs at home;
Here thou, great Anna! whom three realms obey,
9 Dost sometimes counsel take—and sometimes tea.
Hither the heroes and the nymphs resort,
To taste awhile the pleasures of a court;
In various talk the instructive hours they passed,
Who gave the ball, or paid the visit last.
One speaks the glory of the British queen;
And one describes a charming Indian screen;
A third interprets motions, looks, and eyes;
At every word a reputation dies.
Snuff, or the fan, supply each pause of chat,
With singing, laughing, ogling, and all that. . . .

Belinda joins the pleasure-seekers at Hampton Court and wins at a card game called ombre over the Baron, who covets her locks of hair. As the game ends and they all have refreshments (including coffee, a new rage in London), the Baron seizes his opportunity.

Coffee (which makes the politician wise,
And see through all things with his half-shut eyes)
Sent up in vapors to the Baron's brain
New stratagems, the radiant lock to gain.
Ah cease, rash youth! desist ere 'tis too late,
Fear the just gods, and think of Scylla's fate!
Changed to a bird, and sent to flit in air,
She dearly pays for Nisus' injured hair!
But when to mischief mortals bend their will,
How soon they find fit instruments of ill!
Just then, Clarissa drew with tempting grace
A two-edged weapon from her shining case;
So ladies in romance assist their knight,
Present the spear, and arm him for the fight.
He takes the gift with reverence, and extends
10 The little engine on his fingers' ends;

"The Barge," an Aubrey Beardsley illustration dating from 1896, shows Belinda on the vessel that transports her to Hampton Court. Notice that the barge is as richly ornamented as its passengers. How might you react if you were to encounter the scene depicted in this illustration? What makes these people seem somewhat ridiculous to the modern observer?

145 Anna, Queen Anne, who reigned 1702–1714.
162 Scylla's fate. In Greek legend, Scylla (sil′ə), daughter of Nisus, was changed into a bird because she cut off a golden hair (and the source of his power) from her father's head and offered it to her lover.
168 two-edged weapon, scissors.

9 Historical Note
Queen Anne

Pope's note that "great Anna" sometimes takes "counsel" may satirize this queen's obstinate refusal to follow the advise of her ministers as well as her intellectual limitations; the reference to tea may poke fun at Anne's decided preference for more spirited liquids; in England, she is still sometimes referred to as "Brandy Anne."

Responses to Caption Questions
Most modern observers would be amazed at the sight of such a barge filled with such people. The extremes of their costumes, wigs, and hair styles make them ridiculous.

10 Reading/Thinking Skills
Draw Conclusions

Question What is "the two-edged weapon," the "little engine"?
(a pair of scissors)

BUILDING ENGLISH PROFICIENCY

Making Personal Connections

Relating the interests of today's young people to the ones Pope describes will help students understand the poem better.

Activity Ideas

- Ask students to listen to people their age talking in the cafeteria. Have them meet in groups to list four or five general topics that they heard discussed. Have them compare their list with the topics mentioned in lines 149–156.
- Ask students to work together to create a rap song (rhyming in couplets) about a topic that updates any event on these pages. Offer these examples:
  Young lovers have some kind of romantic conflict.
  Everyone has fun at a party.
  The crowd meets at its favorite place.

11 Reading/Thinking Skills
Find the Main Idea

Response Ariel's power expires when he reads Belinda's thoughts, which dwell on an earthly lover.

12 Literary Element
Mood

Question Pope, in lines 173–193, establishes a mood of suspense. How is this achieved? *(Possible response: Suspense is created by slowing the pace of the narrative and minutely describing each step as the baron, scissors in hand, approaches the lock.)*

13 Reading/Thinking Skills
Recognizing Values

Question What does the couplet "Not louder shrieks . . . are cast/ When husbands or when lapdogs breathe their last" suggest about the values of the people Pope satirizes? *(Possible response: Pope equates the loss of a lock of hair with the death or a husband and then compounds the comparison by equating the death of a husband with the death of a lapdog. It is all the same to these people, whose values are insubstantial.)*

This just behind Belinda's neck he spread,
As over the fragrant steams she bends her head.
Swift to the lock a thousand sprites repair,
A thousand wings, by turns, block back the hair,
And thrice they twitched the diamond in her ear;
Thrice she looked back, and thrice the foe drew near.
Just in that instant, anxious Ariel sought
The close recesses of the virgin's thought;
As, on the nosegay in her breast reclined,
He watched the ideas rising in her mind,
Sudden he viewed, in spite of all her art,
An earthly lover lurking at her heart.
Amazed, confused, he found his power expired,
Resigned to fate, and with a sigh retired.
The peer now spreads the glittering forfex wide,
To enclose the lock; now joins it, to divide.
Even then, before the fatal engine closed,
A wretched Sylph too fondly interposed;
Fate urged the shears, and cut the Sylph in twain
(But airy substance soon unites again),
12 The meeting points the sacred hair dissever
From the fair head, for ever and for ever!
Then flashed the living lightning from her eyes,
And screams of horror rend the affrighted skies.
13 Not louder shrieks to pitying heaven are cast,
When husbands or when lapdogs breathe their last;
Or when rich China vessels, fallen from high,
In glittering dust and painted fragments lie!
"Let wreaths of triumph now my temples twine,"
(The victor cried) "the glorious prize is mine!
While fish in streams, or birds delight in air,
Or in a coach and six the British fair,
As long as Atalantis shall be read,
Or the small pillow grace a lady's bed,
While visits shall be paid on solemn days,
When numerous wax-lights in bright order blaze,
While nymphs take treats, or assignations give,
So long my honor, name, and praise shall live!"
What time would spare, from steel receives its date,
And monuments, like men, submit to fate!
Steel could labor of the gods destroy,
And strike to dust the imperial towers of Troy;
Steel could the works of mortal pride confound,
And hew triumphal arches to the ground.

181 nosegay (nōz′gā′), *n.* bunch of flowers.

11 ■ Why can't Ariel protect Belinda?

187 forfex, scissors.

193 dissever (di sev′ər), *v.* separate.

205 Atalantis, a popular book of court scandal and gossip.

209 assignation (as′ig nā′shən), *n.* a secret meeting of lovers.

214 Troy, city in the northwest part of ancient Asia Minor (now Turkey), site of the legendary Trojan War.

MINI-LESSON: LITERARY FOCUS
Heroic Couplets/Epigrams

Pope was the undisputed master of the couplet, a pair of lines in poetry, usually rhymed.

Teach The word *heroic* has to do with the length of the couplet—the ten syllables in iambic pentameter. In the iambic pentameter couplet, each line has ten syllables, alternating unaccented and accented. Couplets can be either closed or open. Basically, by having two equal parts, the couplet is a simple structure that reflects so many other basic structures in and around us, such as the two arms, two ears, or two hands of the human body, or our thought patterns of yes/no, up/down, and good/bad. It can be used consciously with great effect. Students will be familiar with the effectiveness of this example: "Ask not what your country can do for you; ask what you can do for your country."—from John F. Kennedy's inaugural address on January 20, 1961

Activity Idea Ask students to think of something they would like to say with great effect. They should try to state it by writing a couplet, either rhymed or unrhymed.

What wonder then, fair nymph! thy hairs should feel
The conquering force of unresisted steel?

Canto 4

Belinda, furious, delivers an indignant speech.

. . ."For ever cursed be this detested day,
Which snatched my best, my favourite curl away!
Happy! ah ten times happy had I been,
If Hampton Court these eyes had never seen!
14 Yet am not I the first mistaken maid,
By love of courts, to numerous ills betrayed.
Oh had I rather unadmired remained
In some lone isle, or distant northern land;
Where the gilt chariot never marks the way,
Where none learn ombre; none ever taste bohea!
There kept my charms concealed from mortal eye,
Like roses that in deserts bloom and die.
What moved my mind with youthful lords to roam?
O had I stayed, and said my prayers at home!
'Twas this, the morning omens seemed to tell;
15 Thrice from my trembling hand the patch box fell;
The tottering china shook without a wind;
Nay, Poll sat mute, and Shock was most unkind!
A Sylph too warned me of the threats of fate,
In mystic visions, now believed too late!
See the poor remnants of these slighted hairs!
My hands shall rend what even thy rapine spares:
These, in two sable ringlets taught to break,
Once gave new beauties to the snowy neck;
The sister lock now sits uncouth, alone,
And in its fellow's fate foresees its own;
Uncurled it hangs, the fatal shears demands;
And tempts once more thy sacrilegious hands.
Oh hadst thou, cruel! been content to seize
Hairs less in sight, or any hairs but these!"

Canto 5

She said: the pitying audience melt in tears,
But fate and Jove had stopped the Baron's ears
In vain Thalestris with reproach assails,
For who can move when fair Belinda fails?
Not half so fixed the Trojan could remain,
While Anna begged and Dido raged in vain.

228 bohea (bō hā′), *n.* an expensive tea.

■ What does Belinda wish she had done to prevent her favorite curl from being snatched?

240 rend (rend), *v.* tear apart.

240 rapine (rap′ən), *n.* robbery by force; plunder.

251 Thalestris (thal es′trəs), Belinda's friend, named for a queen of the Amazons and thus fiercely militant.

254 Anna . . . vain. In the *Aeneid,* Anna was unable to persuade Aeneas to remain faithful to her sister Dido. The comparison is to Thalestris, friend of Belinda, whose reproaches to the Baron are also in vain.

14 Reading/Thinking Skills
Infer

Question What is inferred by Belinda's remark that she is not the first maid at court to fall victim to "numerous ills"? *(Possible response: The line infers that the loss of a lock is as ruinous as the loss of virtue—an equation similar to equating a stained honor with a stained dress.)*

15 Reading/Thinking Skills
Generalize

Response She wishes she had stayed on a lone isle or in some northern land or at home, saying her prayers.

BUILDING ENGLISH PROFICIENCY

Making Cultural Connections

Help students cope with Pope's many allusions to myths.

1. Explain that Pope is making fun of (while imitating for comic effect) the grand style of heroic epics such as the *Iliad,* by Homer.
2. Ask students to share stories about cultural heroes, such as Krishna and Sundiata, that they know about. Have them describe the qualities that each hero represents.
3. Have students contrast the *trivial* qualities that the Baron and Belinda represent with the qualities of a "true hero." Explain that Pope uses this difference to poke fun at his characters—but his tone is teasing, not mean.
4. Discuss elements in the poem that students may remember in other hero tales: omens, a battle with everyone taking sides, gods taking a part in human affairs, and supernatural beings protecting humans that they like.

16 Multicultural Note
Interactions

Response The poem presents a world of style over substance, in which all interactions are artificial.

17 Literary Element
Onomatopoeia

You might read aloud the following couplet: "All side in parties, and begin the attack;/Fans clap, silks rustle, and tough whalebones crack."

Question What uses of sound make the couplet unusual and effective? *(Possible response: The use of onomatopoeia creates the effect of hearing fans snapped shut, skirts in motion, and corset stays cracking under strain. The couplet is unusual because, in contrast to the meter and melodious tone of the rest of the poem, Pope uses odd, halting rhythm and juxtaposes words difficult to pronounce, e.g., "fans clap." The effect is the cacophony of combat.)*

18 Reading/Thinking Skills
Infer

Response At this point, the reader can infer that her weapons are words because "no weapons in their hands are found" while shouts "strike the skies."

Then grave Clarissa graceful waved her fan;
Silence ensued, and thus the nymph began.
"Say, why are beauties praised and honored most,
The wise man's passion, and the vain man's toast?
Why decked with all that land and sea afford,
Why angels called, and angel-like adored?
Why round our coaches crowd the white-gloved beaux,
Why bows the side-box from its inmost rows?
How vain are all these glories, all our pains,
Unless good sense preserve what beauty gains:
That men may say, when we the front-box grace,
'Behold the first in virtue, as in face!'
Oh! if to dance all night, and dress all day,
Charmed the smallpox, or chased old age away,
Who would not scorn what housewife's cares produce,
Or who would learn one earthly thing of use?
To patch, nay ogle, might become a saint,
Nor could it sure be such a sin to paint.
But since, alas! frail beauty must decay,
Curled or uncurled, since locks will turn to grey;
Since painted or not painted, all shall fade,
And she who scorns a man, must die a maid;
What then remains, but well our power to use,
And keep good humor still whatever we lose?
And trust me, dear! good humor can prevail,
When airs, and flights, and screams, and scolding fail.
Beauties in vain their pretty eyes may roll;
Charms strike the sight, but merit wins the soul."
So spoke the dame, but no applause ensued;
Belinda frowned, Thalestris called her prude.
"To arms, to arms!" the fierce virago cries,
And swift as lightning to the combat flies.
All side in parties, and begin the attack;
17 Fans clap, silks rustle, and tough whalebones crack;
Heroes' and heroines' shouts confusedly rise,
And bass and treble voices strike the skies.
No common weapons in their hands are found;
Like gods they fight, nor dread a mortal wound. . . .

271 ogle (ō′gəl), *v.* look at with desire.

16 ■ What generalization can you make about the **interactions** between the men and women of high society featured in this poem?

285 virago (və rā′gō), *n.* strong vigorous woman; here, Thalestris.

18 ■ What are Belinda's weapons?

MINI-LESSON: WRITING STYLE
Epics and Mock Epics

Pope could see similarities of motive, character, and conduct between eighteenth-century society and those he saw in the heroic epics of classical literature. To describe the theft of a lock of the heroine's hair, Pope used the devices and diction of epic poetry, offering a commentary on the values of upper-class English society that is both mocking and admiring.

Teach Writing style depends on subject matter, diction (word choice), and rhythm. In *The Rape of the Lock* there is a contrast between the warlike frame of reference of the subject matter and the delicate, whimsical choice of describing words. The stylistic effect of the poem depends on this contrast.

Activity Idea Have students

- choose two subjects for a one-paragraph story—for example, a murder mystery in a suburb of London
- write the one-paragraph story using diction appropriate to the subject matter
- revise the story, changing word choices to reflect a witty, light-hearted tone in which, for example, "blood-soaked shirt" might become "blushing chemise"

Belinda attacks the Baron, but they are both deprived of the precious lock as it rises into the skies, there to become changed into a heavenly body and thus immortalized.

See, fierce Belinda on the Baron flies,
With more than usual lightning in her eyes;
Nor feared the chief the unequal fight to try,
Who sought no more than on his foe to die.
But this bold lord, with manly strength endued,
She with one finger and a thumb subdued:
Just where the breath of life his nostrils drew,
A charge of snuff the wily virgin threw;
The Gnomes direct, in every atom just,
The pungent grains of titillating dust.
Sudden, with starting tears each eye overflows,
And the high dome re-echoes to his nose.
"Now meet thy fate," incensed Belinda cried,
And drew a deadly bodkin from her side.
(The same, his ancient personage to deck,
Her great great grandsire wore about his neck
In three seal rings; which after, melted down,
Formed a vast buckle for his widow's gown:
Her infant grandame's whistle next it grew,
The bells she jingled, and the whistle blew;
Then in a bodkin graced her mother's hairs,
Which long she wore, and now Belinda wears.)
"Boast not my fall" (he cried) "insulting foe!
Thou by some other shalt be laid as low.
Nor think, to die dejects my lofty mind;
All that I dread is leaving you behind!
Rather than so, ah let me still survive,
And burn in Cupid's flames—but burn alive."
19 "Restore the lock!" she cries; and all around
"Restore the lock!" the vaulted roofs rebound.
Not fierce Othello in so loud a strain
Roared for the handkerchief that caused his pain.
But see how oft ambitious aims are crossed,
And chiefs contend till all the prize is lost!
The lock, obtained with guilt, and kept with pain,
In every place is sought, but sought in vain:
With such a prize no mortal must be blest,
So Heaven decrees! with Heaven who can contest?
Some thought it mounted to the lunar sphere,
Since all things lost on earth are treasured there.
There heroes' wits are kept in ponderous vases,

297 endue (en dü′), *v.* furnish; supply.
301 gnome (nōm), *n.* spirit inhabiting the earth.
306 bodkin, here, an ornamental hairpin.
323–324 Othello . . . handkerchief. In Shakespeare's play *Othello*, the title character becomes enraged at his wife Desdemona when she cannot show him a prized handkerchief which he thinks she has given to a lover.

In "The Rape of the Lock" (Aubrey Beardsley, 1896), the Baron, scissors in hand, is poised to commit the dastardly deed. What kind of social world does this illustration reflect?

19 Reading/Thinking Skills
Generalize

Questions With what does Belinda first attack the Baron? What is the result? *(She blows snuff in his face; his eyes water, and he sneezes.)* What tack does she take next? *(She pulls a gold hairpin from her hair and threatens him with it.)* What does she demand? *(that her lock be restored)* What is absurd about this demand? *(The lock can be returned, but not restored.)*

Art Study

Response to Caption Question The illustration reflects a social world in which people do not work or devote their time to serious pursuits; a world of appearances and, probably, of boredom masked by gaiety.

BUILDING ENGLISH PROFICIENCY

Responding Artistically to Poetry

Give students a chance to share their knowledge of pages 322–323 in a way that they choose.

Activity Ideas

- Have a group present these two pages as Reader's Theater or act out the scene. In dramatizing the scene, let Clarissa and the Baron give short speeches, summarizing what Pope has them say in his poem.
- Have students create a cartoon sequence, using five panels to show the action. Let them use speech balloons to record brief dialogue that they create for the characters.

20 Reading/Thinking Skills
Find the Main Idea

Question What happens to the lock? *(It ascends into the sky and is transformed into a dazzling heavenly body.)*

21 Reading/Thinking Skills
Draw Conclusions

Response Students responses may vary. While Belinda lost her lock, she is compensated by the ultimate glory of its fate. The Baron lost out completely.

And beaus' in snuffboxes and tweezer cases.
There broken vows, and deathbed alms are found,
And lovers' hearts with ends of ribbon bound;
The courtier's promises, and sick man's prayers,
The smiles of harlots, and the tears of heirs,
Cages for gnats, and chains to yoke a flea,
Dried butterflies, and tomes of casuistry.
    But trust the Muse—she saw it upward rise,
Though marked by none but quick, poetic eyes:
(So Rome's great founder to the heavens withdrew,
To Proculus alone confessed in view.)
A sudden star, it shot through liquid air,
And drew behind a radiant trail of hair.
Not Berenice's locks first rose so bright,
The heavens bespangling with dishevelled light.
The Sylphs behold it kindling as it flies,
And pleased pursue its progress through the skies.
    This the beau monde shall from the Mall survey,
And hail with music its propitious ray.
This, the blessed lover shall for Venus take,
And send up vows from Rosamonda's lake.
This Partridge soon shall view in cloudless skies,
When next he looks through Galileo's eyes;
And hence the egregious wizard shall foredoom
20 The fate of Louis, and the fall of Rome.
    Then cease, bright nymph! to mourn thy ravished hair
Which adds new glory to the shining sphere!
Not all the tresses that fair head can boast
Shall draw such envy as the lock you lost.
For, after all the murders of your eye,
When, after millions slain, yourself shall die;
When those fair suns shall set, as set they must,
And all those tresses shall be laid in dust;
This lock, the Muse shall consecrate to fame,
And 'midst the stars inscribe Belinda's name! 21

340 tomes of casuistry, books containing overly subtle reasoning about ethical issues.

343–344 Rome's great founder . . . view, Romulus, who supposedly ascended to heaven, witnessed only by a Roman senator named Proculus.

347 Berenice's locks. According to legend, Berenice offered her hair to Venus for the safe return of her husband from war. The hair was transformed into a heavenly constellation.

351 beau monde . . . Mall, fashionable society will see the transformed lock of hair from the promenade in St. James's Park.

354 Rosamonda's lake, in St. James's Park.

355–358 Partridge . . . Rome. John Partridge (1644–1715) was an astrologer who annually predicted the downfall of the King of France and the Pope. "Galileo's eyes" is a reference to the telescope.

357 egregious (i grē′jəs), *adj.* extraordinarily bad.

359 ravished (rav′isht), *adj.* stolen.

■ Does this poem have a happy ending? Why or why not?

An Essay on Criticism

Alexander Pope

Pope's couplets and epigrams are often quoted. Here is a sample.

1. 'Tis with our judgments as our watches; none
   Go just alike, yet each believes his own.
2. Let such teach others who themselves excel,
   And censure freely who have written well.
3. Music resembles poetry; in each
   Are nameless graces which no methods teach.
4. Of all the causes which conspire to blind
   Man's erring judgment, and misguide the mind,
   What the weak head with strongest bias rules,
   Is pride, the never-failing vice of fools.
5. Trust not yourself: but your defects to know,
   Make use of every friend—and every foe.
6. A little learning is a dangerous thing;
   Drink deep, or taste not the Pierian spring.[1]
   There shallow draughts intoxicate the brain,
   And drinking largely sobers us again.
7. 'Tis not a lip, or eye, we beauty call,
   But the joint force and full result of all.
8. True wit is Nature to advantage dressed,
   What oft was thought, but ne'er so well expressed.
9. As shades more sweetly recommend the light,
   So modest plainness sets off sprightly wit.
10. Words are like leaves; and where they most abound,
    Much fruit of sense beneath is rarely found.
11. True ease in writing comes from art, not chance,
    As those move easiest who have learned to dance.
12. Be not the first by whom the new are tried,
    Nor yet the last to lay the old aside.
13. Some praise at morning what they blame at night,
    But always think the last opinion right.
14. We think our fathers fools, so wise we grow;
    Our wiser sons, no doubt, will think us so.
15. Good nature and good sense must ever join;
    To err is human, to forgive divine.

1. **Pierian** (pī ir′ē ən) **spring,** that is, inspiration; from Pieria, where the Greek Muses were born.

22 Literary Element
Simile

Questions What is the simile in the first couplet, and what does it suggest about human judgment? *(Pope compares an individual's judgment to his or her watch. As we blindly trust in the reliability of our watches, we blindly trust in the value and wisdom of our judgment. Neither may be particularly accurate.)*

23 Literary Focus
Heroic Couplet/Epigram

Questions Are all of these 15 verses from *An Essay on Criticism* heroic couplets? epigrams? Explain why. *(Numbers 4 and 6 are not couplets; a complete thought is not expressed in a pair of rhymed lines. All could be considered epigrams; each is a witty verse, is of two to four lines, and most end with a twist.)*

Check Test

1. What was Ariel's warning to Belinda in the beginning of the poem? *(that she beware of all, but especially of man)*
2. Why did the Baron want a lock of Belinda's hair? *(He is besotted by the lock and wants to possess something of Belinda's.)*
3. What were the omens that warned Belinda she would have a bad day? *(The patch box fell three times, the china shook, her dog rudely awakened her, and a Sylph warned her.)*
4. What ultimately happens to the lock of hair? *(It rises into the skies and turns into a heavenly body.)*
5. In *An Essay on Criticism*, what does the speaker say is the vice of fools? *(pride)*

Unit 4 Resource Book
Alternate Check Test, p. 21

BUILDING ENGLISH PROFICIENCY

Improving Comprehension

To help students remember the ideas in Pope's epigrams, write the numbers 1 to 15 on pieces of paper. Let each student pick one piece of paper from a basket and then find a way to "teach" his or her epigram to the class. Offer options such as the following.

- Translate it into another language.
- Present an original skit or song related to the epigram's meaning.
- Mime the words and let the class guess at the epigram.
- Hand-letter the words on nice paper; create a border suited to the subject.

After Reading

MAKING CONNECTIONS

1. Student responses will vary and may include such words as amusing, hard, long, or clever.
2. Students may say they would feel ridiculed and angry; or they may laugh it off, deciding it isn't worth being upset about.
3. The lines appropriately satirize Belinda's attitude toward her toilette as a sacred ritual.
4. Epics refer to large themes and great heroics. The classical references mock the trivialness of the incident around which the poem is written, thus mocking the trivial nature of fashionable society.
5. Pope is speaking through Clarissa to minimize the event and to urge Belinda to keep things in perspective. Clarissa reasons that "Charms strike the sight, but merit wins the soul."
6. *The Rape of the Lock* fits the definition of satire. It exposes human or societal weaknesses in a witty and ironic way. Students may feel it works because it inspires reform, or that it doesn't work because it is difficult to follow.
7. Some students may feel that, while equality has improved, the "warfare" and interactions between the sexes have not changed. Both sides might site society's greater awareness of rape and domestic violence to illustrate either how the situation is getting better or worse.
8. Students should back up their reasoning. For example, some may feel the final couplet still has much to say because everyone make mistakes and should, therefore, understand the need for forgiveness.

After Reading

Making Connections

Shaping Your Response

1. Write three words that you think describe "The Rape of the Lock." List all the words you and your classmates come up with and tally their frequency. Finally, create one or more word webs to show how your class feels about the poem.
2. Arabella Fermor and Lord Petre were apparently amused and flattered at being the subjects of this poem. How would you have reacted at reading such a treatment of your own experiences? Explain.

Analyzing the Poems

3. Line 53 refers to a priestess and an altar and line 54 refers to sacred rites. Are these references appropriate? Explain.
4. Epics often contain references to classical mythology. Explain how such references contribute to the **mock-epic** nature of this poem.
5. What do you think is the purpose of Clarissa's speech in canto 5 (lines 257-282)?
6. How does "The Rape of the Lock" fit the definition of **satire** (see page 295)? In your opinion, is it a successful satire?

Extending the Ideas

7. Has the "warfare" between the sexes changed since Pope's time, or are the **interactions** about the same today as they were then? Discuss.
8. Which of the quotations from "An Essay on Criticism" do you think has the most to communicate to today's world? Why?

Literary Focus: Heroic Couplet/Epigram

In a **heroic couplet,** a pair of rhymed lines written in iambic pentameter, the second line may complete the thought of the first, restate it, expand it, or contrast it. What does the second line do in this example?

> Beauties in vain their pretty eyes may roll;
> Charms strike the sight, but merit wins the soul.

An **epigram,** a short witty verse, usually ends with a wry twist. What clever turn of thought is contained in this epigram?

> Trust not yourself; but your defects to know,
> Make use of every friend—and every foe.

LITERARY FOCUS: HEROIC COUPLET/EPIGRAM

Heroic couplet The second line completes the thought by reversing the image created in the first and revealing Pope's view of reality.

Epigram The clever turn suggests that self-knowledge—through understanding of one's defects—is best studied through relationships, particularly with foes; that enmity is often the result of one's own defects reflected in others.

Expressing Your Ideas

Writing Choices

Writer's Notebook Update Try your hand at writing a heroic couplet (or an epigram). Use some of the ideas and rhyming words you jotted down.

Know Any Good Satirists? Who are some modern satirists? Research three or four columnists, radio commentators, or comedians on television. What are their topics? Write a **profile,** such as might appear in a popular magazine, of one or more of them. Describe their usual subject matter and their satirical techniques. End by telling which satirist you prefer and why.

How Far Is Too Far? How far should a comedian or talk-show host go in satirizing public figures or ethnic, religious, or social groups? Some people feel that satirists go too far and should respect some limits, while others feel that our freedom of speech means "anything goes." In a **letter to the editor** of your local newspaper, examine the difference, if any, between satire and spite, remembering the purpose of satire.

"Dah-h-h-ling—!" Imagine a meeting between Belinda and a young society woman of today. (If you don't know any society women, think of a character from a TV show.) What might they have to say to each other? Would they be friends or would they end up having a "cat fight"? Write the **dialogue** of their meeting. You might work with some classmates to read it aloud.

Other Options

Picture This Editorial cartoons are almost always satirical. Look through at least five issues of a daily paper, including a Sunday paper, to see what topics are currently the focus of the cartoons on the editorial page. ("Our Glorious Leaders" in the Interdisciplinary Study on pages 328–329 shows some examples of editorial cartoons.) Then try your hand at creating an **editorial cartoon.**

On a More Serious Note It's possible that Belinda might have settled down enough to attend a performance of one of George Frederick Handel's works. Handel (1685–1759) was born in Germany but settled permanently in England, where he wrote oratorios (including the well-known *Messiah),* operas, choral works, and works for orchestra. With one or more partners, prepare an **illustrated report** on Handel. Take turns describing his life and work, and supply some brief examples of his music.

"Begin the Attack" Physical conflict is a subject that is endlessly explored in various media from ballet to movie fight sequences. Plan the **choreography** of the fight between Belinda and the Baron. You could stage it as an elaborate dance of the 1700s or as a modern brawl. Include some of the other characters if you wish. Use sensible precautions; you know that even the most violent movie fight is carefully planned and thoroughly rehearsed so that no one gets injured.

WRITING CHOICES

Writer's Notebook Update

Ask students to share examples of wry observations that might be used in an epigram.

Know Any Good Satirists?

Help students to broaden their thinking by suggesting that satirists can be writers of printed materials, writers for television shows, such as *Roseanne,* or stand-up comics.

How Far Is Too Far?

Suggest that students might choose to write letters concerning the performances of contemporary stand-up comedians on cable comedy shows versus the tamer routines of comedians on late-night talk shows.

Selection Test

Unit 4 Resource Book
pp. 23–24

Transparency Collection
Fine Art Writing Prompt 6

OTHER OPTIONS

Picture This

Remind students that political cartoonists often make their points through the use of symbols, e.g., drawing crowns on politicians or giving rat-like or devil-like features to public figures of questionable character.

On a More Serious Note

Remind students that there will likely be many biographies of Handel and descriptions of his music in the public library. They should not rely solely on encyclopedias.

"Begin the Attack"

Students may want to work in groups to plan the choreography.

Interdisciplinary Study

Theme Link

One of the standard modern ways of critiquing society is through the political (or editorial) cartoon, which employs the same techniques of irony, sarcasm, satire, wit, and exaggeration used by writers in the Age of Reason.

Curricular Connection: Popular Connections

Use the information in this interdisciplinary study to explore with students the techniques employed by twentieth-century political cartoonists and the types of people who are popular targets.

Additional Background

In four of the cartoons, the presidents are portrayed using widely recognized cultural allusions. Use the Multicultural Notes to provide students with more information about these figures.

MULTICULTURAL NOTE

Boy Scouts

The Boy Scouts of America was founded in 1910.The cartoon of President Carter shows him wearing a Boy Scout uniform and repeating the Boy Scout Oath, substituting "Politician" for "Boy Scout."

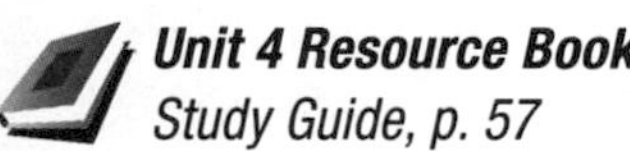

Unit 4 Resource Book
Study Guide, p. 57

Popular Culture Connection

No one in the public eye seems to be immune from being the subject of someone's satirical view. U.S. Presidents and the British Royal Family have been particulary vulnerable, as shown by these political cartoons and puppet caricatures.

Satirical Thrusts

Reprinted Courtesy of The Boston Globe

Lyndon Johnson

"We are not going to send American boys 9,000 or 10,000 miles away to do what Asian boys ought to be doing for themselves."
–Lyndon Johnson (1964 campaign)

THIS WAY! ...BUT I'M OPEN TO SUGGESTIONS...

Bill Clinton

MINI-LESSON: VISUAL LITERACY

Distinguish Between Fact and Opinion

Teach Explain that distinguishing fact from opinion in a political cartoon can be difficult. For example, it is a fact that Lyndon Johnson did not carry out his promise to keep Americans out of the war. He actually increased the number of American troops enormously, and by the end of the war, 58,000 Americans had died.

The cartoonist is not expressing a fact, however, in choosing to show Johnson as Pinocchio, the wooden boy whose nose grew longer every time he told a lie. Whether Johnson lied or changed his mind may be a matter of debate. The cartoonist is using the caricature to call attention to the difference between what Johnson said and what he subsequently did and to express his own opinion of Johnson's culpability. Emphasize to students how important it is to have the relevant facts when analyzing a political cartoon.

Activity Idea Have students focus on a cartoon on the spread or on one in a recent daily paper. Have them research the relevant facts and write a brief commentary telling which elements of the cartoon are factual and which express the cartoonist's opinion.

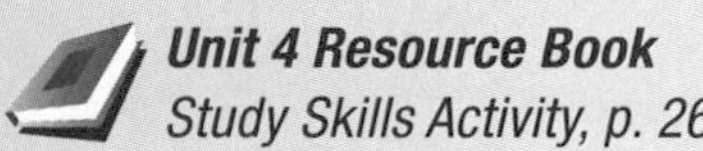

Unit 4 Resource Book
Study Skills Activity, p. 26

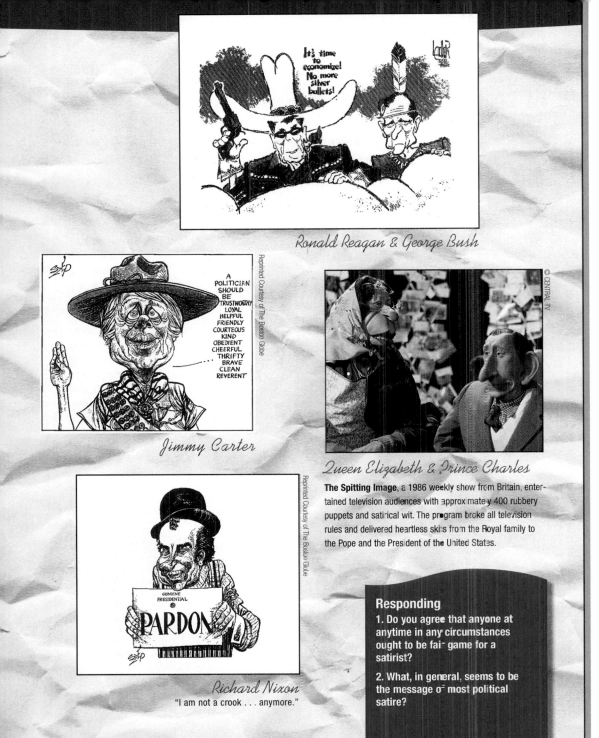

Ronald Reagan & George Bush

Reprinted Courtesy of The Boston Globe

Jimmy Carter

© CENTRAL TV

Queen Elizabeth & Prince Charles

The Spitting Image, a 1986 weekly show from Britain, entertained television audiences with approximately 400 rubbery puppets and satirical wit. The program broke all television rules and delivered heartless skits from the Royal family to the Pope and the President of the United States.

Reprinted Courtesy of The Boston Globe

Richard Nixon
"I am not a crook . . . anymore."

Responding

1. Do you agree that anyone at anytime in any circumstances ought to be fair game for a satirist?

2. What, in general, seems to be the message of most political satire?

MULTICULTURAL NOTES

Pinocchio

Pinocchio is a wooden puppet whose nose grows longer every time he tells a lie. *The Adventures of Pinocchio* is a nineteenth-century children's story written by Italian writer Carlos Collodi. President Johnson is portrayed as Pinocchio in the cartoon.

Three Musketeers

President Clinton is shown as one of the Three Musketeers, members of an elite guard who served King Louis XIII of France and who were fictionalized by Alexandre Dumas (Dumas père) in 1844.

The Lone Ranger and Tonto

President Reagan is depicted as The Lone Ranger, while Vice-President Bush appears as his sidekick, Tonto. The Lone Ranger was created in 1929 by George Trendle to bring life to his floundering Detroit radio station. The silver bullets reminded the hero of the value of human life and encouraged him to use his weapon only as a last resort.

Responding

1. Possible Response Students may feel that good taste or good manners would reject the idea that sick, grieving, or disaster-stricken people are targets for satire.

2. Possible Response Political satire, which can be directed at any public official, focuses on incompetence, aspects of domestic or foreign policy, dishonesty, and any other scandalous behavior. Students may mention other topics.

BUILDING ENGLISH PROFICIENCY

Making Historical Connections

If they are to understand the point of the satire on pages 328–329, students need to be aware of the historical background. You might want to team-teach this feature with a social studies teacher, covering material such as the following:

- The oldest historical reference in this spread dates to 1964, during the Johnson administration. Provide an overview of Johnson and the Vietnam War; then review the presidents from Johnson to the present.
- Discuss the Watergate scandal to provide a context for the Nixon cartoon. Contrast it with the Boy Scout image of Carter.
- Contrast the Lone Ranger image of Reagan with the Musketeer image of Clinton.
- Ask students whether they can identify the people pictured in the photo from *Spitting Image.*

Historical Note

Caricature

The term *caricature* was first used in Italy in the mid-1600s. It comes from the Italian word *caricate,* meaning "overloaded." A true caricature is a picture that conveys its message without words. The earliest recognized caricature of a political figure was done by Michelangelo in his painting "The Last Judgment" in the Sistine Chapel. His figure of King Minos, Prince of Hell, is recognizable as Biagio da Cesena, the papal master of ceremonies. Other famous caricaturists include Lucas Cranach, William Hogarth, and Honoré Daumier. Today, David Levine and Al Hirschfeld are two of the few true caricaturists, as opposed to political cartoonists.

Political Cartoonists

Political cartoons were popular in eighteenth- and nineteenth-century Europe. They first appeared in America in the late 1800s, usually in magazines. Thomas Nast (1840–1902) was the first outstanding American editorial cartoonist. Today there are about 125 full-time political cartoonists, of whom two are women.

INTERDISCIPLINARY STUDY

Career Connection

Satire is alive and well and living in many places, one of them being your daily newspaper. Here a political cartoonist talks about his job.

HOPING FOR A VISCERAL REACTION

Interview with Jack Higgins

One of only a few political cartoonists for major newspapers who prefer to use local rather than national or international politics as inspiration, Jack Higgins works for the *Chicago Sun-Times.* Two early interests of his—drawing and politics—merged in his college years to become his career.

"I've been drawing since about two-and-a-half. Through high school, I was largely self-taught from how-to books. In college, my major was economics, but I took anatomy and other art courses, and these took me to a higher skill level. With a teacher critiquing me, I could immediately see my mistakes.

"My interest in politics also came at a young age. On election day when I was a boy, the politicians gave us kids palm cards to pass out to voters. These were cards that could be hidden in the palm of the hand and listed who to vote for. No one was supposed to campaign within a hundred feet of the polling place, but kids passing out these little cards weren't noticed. Afterwards, the politicians took us out for ice cream. To me, politics was a sport.

"I started thinking about political cartooning in college when I saw Paul Szep's work for the *Boston Globe.* I liked his methods and meatiness, his directness, his wit and vinegar. He was doing cartoons on local politics in Boston. I thought, 'Chicago is a lot like Boston!' I realized that art came in handy for cartooning. I liked being able to study the personality of someone and put it into caricature, to capture the essence of the person. I did political cartooning for a couple of college newspapers.

"My creative method is to get up at 4:00 A.M. My mind is clear then. I start reading newspapers and taking notes. If I get angry about something, I write it down. Then I write down everything I can think of about what makes me angriest that day. From that, I develop a pencil sketch—usually with a humorous twist, get honest reactions from the folks at the *Sun-Times*, rework the picture in pencil, and then go over it with India ink and a brush.

"Although political cartoons are called satire, I don't like to use that term. Putting labels on takes the fun out. My art comes from deeply within me. I don't over analyze it. And I hope for a visceral reaction to my work from readers. The language of the cartoonist is very different from that of the writer, who analyzes an issue and fashions a logical argument. We cartoonists give you about ten seconds to let the picture sink in, and then we hope it will stay in the back of your mind to shape your thoughts."

HIGGINS

1. Discuss the ways in which your reaction as a viewer to a cartoon is different from your reaction as a reader to an essay or article.

2. Do you agree that labeling cartoons as satire takes the fun out of it? Why or why not?

3. Which of the issues in today's news gives you a visceral (gut) reaction?

MINI-LESSON: VISUAL LITERACY

Distinguishing Between Fact and Opinion

Teach Remind students that a factual statement is one that can be proved to be true or untrue. An opinion statement, no matter how valid or how widely held, is one that cannot be proved.

Activity Idea Have students identify each of the following statements as a factual statement or an opinion statement.

- Jack Higgins has been drawing since he was about two-and-a-half.
- All children draw at age two-and-a-half.
- Jack Higgins is a clever cartoonist.
- Paul Szep worked for the *Boston Globe.*
- Jack Higgins thought politics was a sport.
- Politicians in Chicago have always been dishonest.

Writing Workshop

My Modest Proposal

Assignment Using Jonathan Swift's "A Modest Proposal" as a model, offer your own satirical solution to one of society's problems.

WRITER'S BLUEPRINT

Product	A satirical essay
Purpose	To provoke change through ridicule
Audience	Readers of a magazine of current events
Specs	As the writer of an effective essay, you should:

- ❑ Imagine that you're writing for a magazine that publishes articles about current events. Focus on a controversial issue, a problem that people are divided on, such as what to do about homelessness, government inefficiency, smoking, litter, teen pregnancy, or illiteracy.
- ❑ Introduce the problem and your concerns in a serious, reasonable tone. Then propose your unrealistic, exaggerated solution, which will be the opposite of your true position on the issue. Present this solution step by step in this same reasonable tone, using some of the satirical techniques that Swift employs in "A Modest Proposal."
- ❑ Mention realistic alternatives to your solution and dismiss them in this same reasonable tone.
- ❑ Conclude by summing up how the world will be a better place after your solution is adopted.
- ❑ Make smooth transitions between ideas.
- ❑ Follow the rules of grammar, usage, spelling, and mechanics. Avoid careless spelling mistakes.

STEP 1 PREWRITING

Analyze the literature. Look back at Swift's "A Modest Proposal" and list quotes from the text that show Swift's use of each of these satirical techniques: sarcasm, exaggeration, flattering the reader, appealing to

Writing Workshop

WRITER'S BLUEPRINT

Specs

The Specs in the Writer's Blueprint address these writing and thinking skills:

- making judgments
- solving problems
- anticipating objections
- identifying alternatives
- establishing tone
- summarizing
- making transitions
- spelling

These Specs serve as your lesson objectives, and they form the basis for the **Assessment Criteria Specs** for a superior paper, which appear on the final TE page for this lesson. You might want to read through the Assessment Criteria Specs with students when you begin the lesson.

Linking Literature to Writing

While discussing Swift's use of satire, ask students about elements of satire that spice their everyday speech, jokes, or letters.

STEP 1 PREWRITING

Analyze the literature

Share a current example of satire with the class, such as a Dave Barry column or *Saturday Night Live* clip. For additional support, see the worksheet referenced below.

Unit 4 Resource Book
Prewriting Worksheet, p.27

WRITING WORKSHOP OVERVIEW

Product
Persuasive writing: A satirical essay

Prewriting
Analyze the literature—Choose an issue—Make a writing plan
Unit 4 Resource Book
Prewriting Worksheets pp. 27–28

Drafting
As you draft
Transparency Collection
Student Models for Writing Workshop 11, 12

Revising
Ask a partner—Strategy: Making Smooth Transitions
Unit 4 Resource Book
Revising Worksheet p. 29

Editing
Ask a partner—Strategy: Avoiding Careless Spelling Mistakes
Unit 4 Resource Book
Grammar Worksheet p. 30
Grammar Check Test p. 31

Presenting
Publish
Perform

Looking Back
Self-evaluate—Reflect—For Your Working Portfolio
Unit 4 Resource Book
Assessment Worksheet p. 32
Transparency Collection
Fine Art Transparency 6

Choose an issue

Ask students if they believe any issues are too sensitive or controversial to be effectively satirized. In a class discussion, students may find there are aspects of these sensitive issues that could be used. For additional support, see the worksheet referenced below.

Unit 4 Resource Book
Prewriting Worksheet, p. 28

Make a writing plan

Remind students that a writing plan is only a guide and revisions can always be considered. The plan in the lesson is a good model. Encourage students to begin with the plan given and then make changes as their essays take form.

Connections to
Writer's Notebook

For selection-related prompts, refer to Writer's Notebook.

Connections to
Writer's Resource

For additional writing prompts, refer to Writer's Resource.

STEP 2 DRAFTING

As you draft

Encourage students not to self-censor or revise too much during this part of the process. Let the ideas flow, no matter how outrageous, and worry about revisions later.

OR . . .
Working in a group, take turns reading "A Modest Proposal" aloud. Let group members identify satirical techniques as they hear them.

LITERARY SOURCE
"A child will make two dishes at an entertainment for friends; and when the family dines alone, the fore or hind quarter will make a reasonable dish. . . ."
from "A Modest Proposal"
by Jonathan Swift

OR . . .
Plan a series of visuals to go along with your writing. Make rough sketches of situations that illustrate your modest proposal in action.

logic and reason, creating an aura of objectivity, appealing to emotions, dehumanizing the subject. Then look for these techniques in other sources, such as the TV show *Saturday Night Live,* the writings of Woody Allen and Dave Barry, or articles in *Mad Magazine.*

Choose an issue to satirize. Select a controversial issue that will be familiar to your readers and about which you know enough to write convincingly.

Make a writing plan. Look over the examples that follow. Then complete a plan like this one for your own modest proposal.

Problem: the divisive controversy over smoking

My true position: that smoking should be banned

The unrealistic solution I will propose: (See the Literary Source.)

—Everyone will be forced to take up smoking.

—All laws regulating smoking will be struck down . . .

How this solution will be brought about:

—The U.S. Congress will pass a law stating that . . .

—Cigarettes will be made available to kids in candy machines and . . .

My reasons:

—Since this is a democratic society, we should all be equally at risk.

—People will smoke anyway, so why not . . .

Opposing positions—my responses:

—Smoking is hazardous to your health—true, but people smoke anyway, so why not . . .

How the world will be a better place:

—Since everyone will be smoking, there will be less conflict . . .
and so on . . .

STEP 2 DRAFTING

As you draft, keep these suggestions in mind:

- Keep your notes on satirical techniques at hand and look for places to use them.

MINI-LESSON: WRITING STYLE

Making Smooth Transitions

Teach The root *trans-* means "across" or "over." In writing, a transition guides the reader by connecting one idea to another. A transition word or phrase not only connects concepts, it can also show *how* they are related.

Activity Idea Have students generate a list of transitions and categorize them according to the most likely function: comparing ideas, contrasting ideas, showing cause and effect.

Apply Have students locate weak transition points in their essays and bolster them with transitions from the class-generated list.

- Don't make the mistake of telling your audience that you're not serious. The fun of reading satire is joining with the author in momentarily imagining that these outrageous ideas are reasonable.
- Connect one idea to the next, using smooth transitions. For more information, see the Revising Strategy in Step 3 of this lesson.

STEP 3 REVISING

Ask a partner for comments on your draft before you revise it. Pay special attention to making smooth transitions.

Revising Strategy

Making Smooth Transitions

Your satire will be full of different ideas. When you connect these ideas with smooth transitions, your readers will feel comfortable because they'll know where you're taking them. Notice how the writer of the student model added transitions to connect ideas.

There is only one option left at this point, ~~to~~ That is, we should enforce smoking everywhere and in everyone's lives. Of course nonsmokers are not used to the horrid smell and bitter taste that smokers have grown to love. On the other hand, it is not that difficult to get used to. If nonsmokers just gave in and tried it there would be no more controversy. Society would be in perfect harmony.

STEP 4 EDITING

Ask a partner to review your revised draft before you edit. When you edit, look for errors in grammar, usage, spelling, and mechanics. Pay special attention to catching careless spelling mistakes.

BUILDING ENGLISH PROFICIENCY

ESL LEP ELD SAE LD

Exploring Opposing Positions

Help students use a graphic organizer as they consider convincing ideas that support views that oppose their own.

1. Ask students to list solutions, methods, and reasons that support their position they are proposing

2. Next to each item in the list, have students write an opposing solution, method, or reason.

Your Views	Opposing Views
Ban all cigarette machines.	
Sell cigarettes in candy machines.	

The Student Models

The **transparencies** referenced below are authentic student models. Review them with students before they draft. These questions will help:

1. How does the writer of model 11 adopt a serious, reasonable tone?

2. Does the writer of model 12 address the third point in the blueprint? If not, what are some alternatives the writer could advance and counter?

3. Notice how the writer of model 12 begins the second-last paragraph with a transition. Look for other examples of transitions in the models.

Transparency Collection
Student Models for Writing Workshop 11, 12

STEP 3 REVISING

Ask a partner (Peer assessment)

Have students read their drafts aloud while their partner makes note of the most striking or humorous elements of the proposal. As the essays are read a second time, have partners listen for the transitions that tie paragraphs and ideas together.

Revising Strategy: Making Smooth Transitions

For additional support, see the mini-lesson at the bottom of page 332 and the worksheet referenced below.

Unit 4 Resource Book
Revising Worksheet, p. 29

Connections to **Writer's Resource**

Refer to the Grammar, Usage, and Mechanics Handbook on Writer's Resource.

STEP 4 EDITING

Ask a partner (Peer assessment)

Have students read their partners' essays and use proofreading and editing marks to indicate changes.

Editing Strategy: Avoiding Careless Spelling Mistakes

Remind students that not all mistakes are caught by a computer spell checker. Reading each line of an essay from right to left is one way to focus on each word and look for spelling errors.

For additional support, see the worksheets referenced below.

Unit 4 Resource Book
Grammar Worksheet, p. 30
Grammar Check Test, p. 31

STEP 5 PRESENTING

Publish

If students choose to create a satirical magazine, use magazines such as *Mad* and *Spy* as models.

Perform

Skits could be performed and videotaped, and shown to another class.

STEP 6 LOOKING BACK

Self-evaluate

The *Assessment Criteria Specs* at the bottom of this page are for a superior paper. You might want to post these in the classroom. Students can then evaluate themselves based on these criteria. For a complete scoring rubric, use the *Assessment Worksheet* referenced below.

Unit 4 Resource Book
Assessment Worksheet, p. 32

Reflect

As students struggle with the first question they may decide that neither satire nor straightforward criticism is appropriate, according to the context. This notion might spark an interesting class discussion about whether subject matter determines form.

To further explore the theme, use the Fine Art Transparency referenced below.

Transparency Collection
Fine Art Writing Prompt 6

Editing Strategy

COMPUTER TIP
If your word processing program has a spell check feature, use it to help you locate careless spelling mistakes that might otherwise go unnoticed.

Avoiding Careless Spelling Mistakes

Many simple words are misspelled because they're so familiar that we tend to overlook them. To catch careless misspellings, proofread your draft several times for different kinds of errors. Set aside one time just for spelling. Here are some commonly misspelled words to watch for:

friend	finally	something	usually
probably	really	themselves	because
favorite	especially	different	except

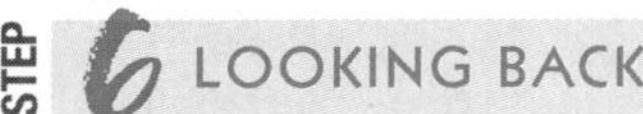

STEP 5 PRESENTING

Here are some ideas for presenting your modest proposal.

- With other members of your class, publish a satirical magazine complete with essays, cartoons, and an appealing cover.
- Collaborate with a small group to adapt your satirical essay into a sketch to be performed as part of a comedy revue.

STEP 6 LOOKING BACK

Self-evaluate. Look back at the Writer's Blueprint and give yourself a score on each point, from 6 (superior) to 1 (inadequate).

Reflect. Write your responses to these questions.

✔ In general, which do you think is the more effective way to make a controversial point: satire or straightforward criticism? Why?

✔ Compare your rough draft with your finished copy. Did you follow the Revising Strategy (using transitional phrases to connect ideas) and Editing Strategy (avoiding careless spelling mistakes)?

For Your Working Portfolio Add your satirical essay and your reflection responses to your working portfolio.

ASSESSMENT CRITERIA SPECS

6 Superior The writer of a 6 paper impressively meets these criteria:

- Proposes a deliberately unreasonable solution to a serious problem in a reasonable tone—a solution that is startling at first glance and humorous at second glance.
- Maintains this serious, reasonable tone throughout.
- Clearly and methodically presents this unreasonable solution, effectively using satirical techniques similar to those used by Swift.
- Considers opposing views and effectively dismisses them.
- Concludes with a clear presentation of the benefits of the proposed solution.
- Makes smooth transitions between ideas and paragraphs.
- Makes few, if any, mistakes in grammar, usage, mechanics, and spelling.

Unit 4 Resource Book
Assessment Worksheet, p. 32

Beyond Print

Analyzing Political Cartoons

All cartoons may use the same tools—including satire—to make a point, but political cartoons (also called editorial cartoons) may have more of a point, or a sharper one. Review the cartoons in Satirical Thrusts on pages 328–329. Consider these questions.

What is the central issue? What is it about in general? Poverty? Gun control? War in a foreign country? Look for labels on people or places, or look for familiar (if exaggerated) faces to help identify the issue.

How does the art comment on the issue? Political cartoon art is often exaggerated. Faces are distorted to look sly or stupid or evil. Look at what is included besides people. Unusual clothing may be symbolic; other symbols may be evident as well. The characters' physical relationships to each other and the actions they are performing are usually important.

What does a caption contribute? Political cartoons often include simple but punchy captions. These are not always straightforward but may be heavily ironic or sarcastic. Study how the caption works together with the art.

What is the cartoonist's viewpoint? Whatever the central issue is, does the cartoonist seem finally to be in favor of it or against it? Does the cartoonist seem to wish that the subjects of the cartoon were behaving differently? that you, the viewer, would do something in response?

Is it convincing? Finally, you be the judge. Is the cartoon funny and right on target? Does it work for you? Remember, you don't have to agree with all the political beliefs of a satirist in order to appreciate a satire; likewise, you can enjoy a cartoon and appreciate its effectiveness even if it doesn't make you want to change the world accordingly.

Activity Option

Work in a small group to collect and study a number of cartoons from around the country on the same theme or central issue. How many different viewpoints can you identify? How do the different cartoonists use their art to express their different viewpoints?

Beyond Print

Teaching Objectives

- to analyze political cartoons
- to apply given criteria to form a judgment
- to identify the point of view of a political cartoon

Curricular Connection: Critical Thinking

Use the material in this article to give students practice in thinking critically as they read editorial material.

Introduce

Have students recall questions and categories they have used to analyze art and literature. Discuss how these criteria might relate to analyzing a political cartoon, which includes both art and words. Then have them read the article.

Activity Option

Encourage students to use a variety of sources to collect cartoons: books, the Internet, foreign periodicals and newspapers, and so on.

ANOTHER APPROACH

Analyzing a Political Comedian

Have students choose a political commentator and satirist, such as Mark Russell, or a group, such as the Capitol Steps, and find a video of a performance. Then have them adapt the questions they used to analyze political cartoons to analyze this other form of political satire.

Historical Overview

EXPLORING CONCEPTS

- The audience for literature was growing in the 1700s, and many people wanted to read about their peers.
- The Age of Reason saw a proliferation of diaries, letters, autobiographies, and biographies, as well as other prose.
- The quotations beside each portrait are taken from each person's writing.

Question What do the quotes reveal about each person? *(Students might note that Goldsmith, Burney, Montagu, and Austen display a tart wit. Austen, Gibbon, and Montagu display a good deal of self-knowledge, and all of them are capable of shrewd insights.)*

Art Study

Fanny Burney (1752–1840) published her first novel, *Evelina,* in 1778. Her *Early Diary 1768–1778* includes lively descriptions of Johnson and others. Sir Joshua Reynolds painted this portrait of Samuel Johnson about 1756. Reynolds painted most of the famous people of his day, and he painted Johnson five times.

Cassandra Austen, Jane Austen's sister, completed this portrait about 1810. Lady Mary Wortley Montagu (1689–1762) was famous for her wit. In 1739 she left her husband and lived in France and Italy for over twenty years. She wrote many letters to her daughter, Lady Bute.

The portrait of Oliver Goldsmith (1730?–1774) was executed in the studio of Sir Joshua Reynolds. The portrait of historian Edward Gibbon (1737–1794) was completed about 1773 by Henry Walton. Gibbon was engaged to Suzanne Curchod (later Mme. Necker) before his father persuaded him to end it.

The Age of Reason

Other People's Lives

A Kaleidoscope

Historical Overview

The Age of Reason delighted in examining human character—in general and in particular individuals. Many of the writers of the period, including Samuel Pepys, Samuel Johnson, and James Boswell, produced a great variety of vivid and insightful descriptions of themselves and others in diaries, journals, letters, autobiographies, biographies, and other writings. One reason for this was the belief that literature, by presenting examples of human behavior—both good and bad—should serve the function of improving people's morals. Another reason was the growing influence of a middle-class audience for literature, who wanted to read about people like themselves. But the main reason, most likely, was simply the perennial fascination exerted by human personality.

EDWARD GIBBON

I sighed as a lover; I obeyed as a son.

1725 ~ Edward Gibbon, on his father's refusal to let him marry. *Memoirs of My Own Life*

OLIVER GOLDSMITH

He had some wit, . . . but it was of that sort which is rather happy than permanent. Once a week he might say a good thing.

1762 ~ Oliver Goldsmith, *The Life of Richard Nash*

MARY WORTLEY

I give my self sometimes admirable advice, but I am incapable of taking it.

1725 ~ Lady Mary Wortley Montagu, letter

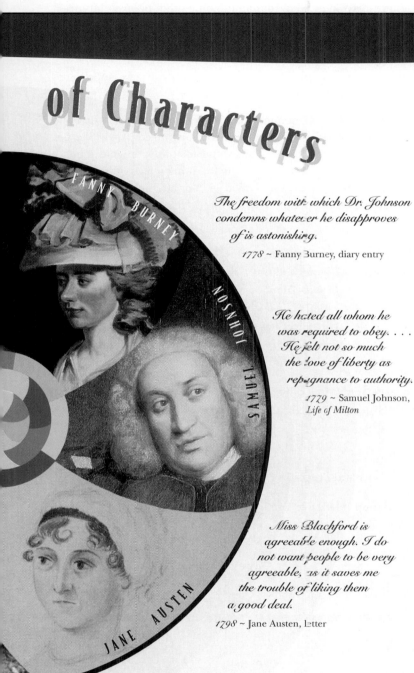

# of Characters

The freedom with which Dr. Johnson condemns whatever he disapproves of is astonishing.

1778 ~ Fanny Burney, diary entry

He hated all whom he was required to obey. . . . He felt not so much the love of liberty as repugnance to authority.

1779 ~ Samuel Johnson, *Life of Milton*

Miss Blachford is agreeable enough. I do not want people to be very agreeable, as it saves me the trouble of liking them a good deal.

1798 ~ Jane Austen, Letter

Key Dates

1652
First coffeehouse opens in London.

1660
The monarchy is restored under Charles II.

1660
The theaters reopen.

1662
The Royal Society is founded to encourage scientific research.

1665
The plague kills 70,000 in London.

1666
The Great Fire of London occurs.

1688
The Glorious Revolution creates a limited monarchy.

1710
St. Paul's Cathedral is completed.

1730
Hogarth completes his satirical graphic series The Rake's Progress.

1755
Johnson's Dictionary *is published.*

337

Key Dates

1687 Newton's *Principia Mathematica* is published.

1688 William III (of Orange) and Mary accede to the throne.

1694 Bank of England is founded.

1702 William III dies, and Anne is crowned.

1726 *Gulliver's Travels* is published.

1752 The Gregorian Calendar is adopted.

MATERIALS OF INTEREST

Books

- *Daily Life in Johnson's London* by Richard B. Schwartz (Wisconsin, 1983).
- *Letters* by Mary Montagu (Knopf, 1992).

Multimedia

- *Boswell in London* [videotape]. 112 min., color, VHS. Films for the Humanities. Order #AD-1315.
- *The Worldbook Multimedia Encyclopedia* [CD-ROM]. "Restoration Literature," "The Augustan Age," and "The Age of Johnson" under "English Literature" entry. World Book, 1994.

Connections to
Custom Literature Database

For further historical background, under **Background Articles,** see **Neoclassical England 1660-1780.**

Preview

Other People's Lives

FOR ALL STUDENTS

What makes us so interested in other people's lives? Read together the first paragraph on page 338 and tell students that the selections they will be reading illustrate the diverse ways that we find out about people's lives. To further explore the theme, use the transparency referenced below.

Transparency Collection
Fine Art Transparency 7

For At-Risk Students

Have students

- brainstorm ways in which they learn about people whom they know
- brainstorm ways in which they learn about people whom they do not know
- talk about what is gained by learning more about people

For Students Who Need Challenge

Have students research one of the six people shown on pages 336–337 to find out what kinds of resources can give them more insight into these people's lives.

MULTICULTURAL CONNECTION

To help students expand their understanding of different genres, ask them to

- compare a book they've read with a movie made from the book
- compare a movie they've seen with a book made from the movie
- compare an excerpted audio version of a book with their reading of the original book

Part 2

Other People's Lives

Is any pastime more widely enjoyed than minding other people's business? From watching our next-door neighbors through a window to reading a magazine article about a movie actor's divorce to watching television dramatizations of the sexy or tragic events in some celebrity's life story, we are fascinated by other people. Perhaps it is in part because we hope sometime, somehow to be able to tell about ourselves.

Multicultural Connection **Communication** plays an integral role when groups and persons of different backgrounds come into contact with each other, observe each other, attempt to talk with each other, or write about their perceptions of each other. Each of the following selections is in a different genre, or form. How are they similar in their attempts to communicate understandings about people's lives? How do they differ?

IDEAS THAT WORK

Motivating with Quirky Types

"Some powerful personal statement here! I encourage students to work past the distractions of seventeenth- and eighteenth-century British formality—the conventions of this idiom seen by many students as 'foreign'—to meet quirky celebs who would be at home on *Firing Line* or Letterman.

Play to students' awareness of the cult of personality. Lead them to see the relative nature of point of view in Johnson's broadside to the detached Chesterfield; look to Boswell's biography, Pepys's diary, and Johnson's 'Dignity and Uses. . . .' for pictures of those foibles and vulnerabilities we must recognize in ourselves and others. Read Pepys for insight into the media's fascination with circumstances, which might make any of us a victor or victim: war, natural disaster, selfish indiscretion. We all crave sight of our own possibilities, and in seeing the plights, triumphs, and vision of others, we see ourselves."

Rob Slater
Greensboro, North Carolina

Before Reading

from The Diary

by Samuel Pepys

Samuel Pepys
1633–1703

Educated at St. Paul's School, London, and Magdalene College, Cambridge, Samuel Pepys (pēps) spent much of his lifetime as a civil servant, working for many years as an official in the Admiralty, the government agency that runs the British navy. In 1673 he was promoted to Secretary to the Admiralty and that same year became a member of Parliament. He left public service in 1689. The remaining years of his life Pepys devoted to amassing and cataloguing a 3,000-volume library, which he donated to his college. In literary circles Pepys is remembered for his fresh and spontaneous diaries in which he recorded his life from age 26 to age 36.

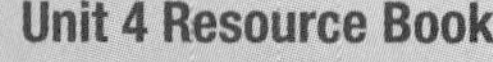

Building Background

Through Great Events—and Small Each evening Samuel Pepys took out his leather notebook and his pen and dashed down his impressions of the day. His mind worked quickly, and, because he used a special shorthand, his thoughts often tumbled together. He re-created the burned dinner his wife prepared, the headache he had because he drank too much wine, his wife's flirting with the dance instructor. He described his new silk suit with the gold buttons, his attempts to learn the multiplication tables, the crowd at a cock fight. He presented the silly sermon he heard at church, the first time he saw a woman acting on stage, the contracts he wrote as a member of the Navy Board. He depicted the Lord Chancellor snoring during Privy Council meetings, the King in his elegant velvet robes on coronation day, the Great Plague of 1665 striking at the houses of friends. Through great events—and small—for ten years (1660–1669) Pepys recorded the details of his life in London. A century and a half later, in 1819, a young scholar at Magdalene College labored over the six leather-bound diaries of Pepys, deciphering the chicken-scratch shorthand. Early editions of the diaries suppressed material considered unsuitable or scandalous. Not until the 1970s were Pepys's complete diaries published.

Literary Focus

Imagery The use of details that appeal to the senses (that is, call for a sensory response) is called **imagery**. Sensory images often help a reader experience an action or a scene by creating mental pictures. Which of your senses would you expect to be stimulated by reading an account of a great fire devastating a city?

Writer's Notebook

"Dear Diary . . ." Everyone enjoys talking about his or her life, but few are able to maintain the discipline necessary to record the events of their lives day after day for an extended period. Have you ever tried to keep a diary? Did you succeed? Why or why not? Write a brief account of your diary-keeping experience, or else write a diary entry for your most memorable day of this week.

Before Reading

Building Background

Ask students who have kept diaries to share their experiences. What are the difficulties of keeping a diary? What are the rewards?

Literary Focus

Remind students that vivid writing sparks the reader's imagination. One could expect the writer to describe the sights, sounds, and smells of a city on fire, as well as the feel of the heat against one's skin and the taste of the ash on one's lips and tongue. Then, invite students to brainstorm a list of sensory images.

Writer's Notebook

You might note to students that they will later expand on these notes by keeping a personal diary for a week.

More About Samuel Pepys

Pepys's diary was written in a combination of shorthand, foreign language, and a code of his own invention. The writing was not deciphered until 1822, more than a century after his death.

SUPPORT MATERIALS OVERVIEW

Unit 4 Resource Book
- Graphic Organizer, p. 33
- Study Guide, p. 34
- Vocabulary, p. 35
- Grammar, p. 36
- Alternate Check Test, p. 37
- Vocabulary Test, p. 38
- Selection Test, pp. 39–40

Building English Proficiency
- Selection Summaries
- Activities, p. 223

Reading, Writing & Grammar SkillBook
- Vocabulary, pp. 13–14
- Reading, pp. 42–44
- Writing, pp. 123–124
- Grammar, Usage, and Mechanics, pp. 236–238

The World of Work
- Firefighter, p. 13
- Activity, p. 14

Technology
- Audiotape
- Personal Journal Software
- Test Generator Software

During Reading

Selection Objectives

- to recognize features and conventions of the personal diary
- to recognize sensory images in description
- to explore historical events through the eyes of a participant

Unit 4 Resource Book
Graphic Organizer, p. 33
Study Guide, p. 34

Theme Link

Pepys's diary offers a rare glimpse into Other People's Lives as well as a vivid picture of an extraordinary event as witnessed by a humane and highly observant man.

Vocabulary Preview

infinite, endless
lamentable, sorrowful
loath, reluctant
combustible, easily burned
malicious, evil

Students can add the words and definitions to their Writer's Notebooks.

1 Geographical Note
London

In Pepys's day, London already consisted of many communities. The City, the site of the fire, is the oldest section; Westminster, where the king's palace was located, is west of the City; Southwark, where the Globe Theater stood, lies across the River Thames, south of the City.

2 Historical Note
Street Names

Many London street names derive from medieval commerce. Fish Street and Pudding Lane were where people bought and sold fish and puddings.

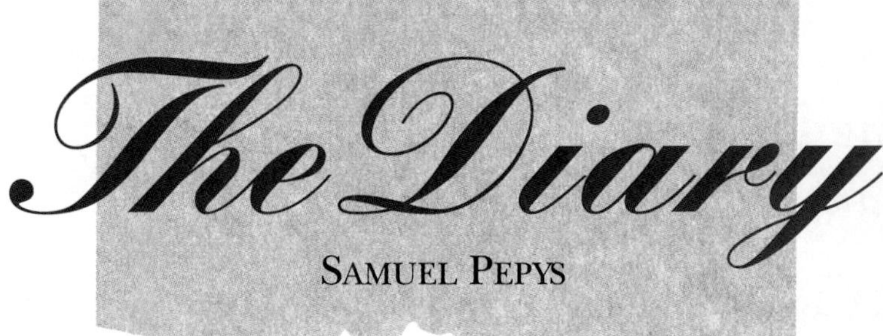

The Diary

SAMUEL PEPYS

The portion of Pepys's diary included here deals largely with the Great Fire of London, which started on September 2, 1666, and raged out of control for almost a week. Before it was extinguished, it had destroyed two-thirds of London. More than 13,000 houses were burned, plus other buildings, including 87 churches and St. Paul's Cathedral. Miraculously, fewer than ten people seem to have died in the fire, but tens of thousands were homeless, camping out in makeshift tents in the fields adjacent to London. It is difficult to comprehend what the burning of London meant in its day. Pepys helps us to realize some of this through his vivid eyewitness descriptions. One thing, however, he does not tell us, for he did not know it: never again was London paralyzed by the plague, perhaps because the fire destroyed the rats that carried the plague as well as the old buildings that harbored them.

SEPTEMBER 2, 1666 (Lord's day). Some of our maids sitting up late last night to get things ready against our feast today, Jane [Pepys's maid] called us up about three in the morning,
1 to tell us of a great fire they saw in the City.[1] So I rose and slipped on my nightgown, and went to her window; and thought it to be on the backside of Mark Lane at the farthest; but, being unused to such fires as followed, I thought it far enough off; and so went to bed again, and to sleep. About seven rose again to dress myself, and there looked out at the window, and saw the fire not so much as it was, and further off. So to my closet[2] to set things to rights, after yesterday's cleaning. By and by Jane comes and tells me that she hears that above 300 houses have been burned down tonight by the fire we saw, and that it is now burning down all Fish Street, by London Bridge. So I made myself ready presently, and walked to the Tower;[3] and there got up upon one of the high places, Sir J. Robinson's little son going up with me; and there I did see the houses at that end of the bridge all on fire, and an infinite[4] great fire on this and the other side the end of the bridge; which, among other people, did trouble me for poor little Michell and our Sarah on the bridge.[5] So down with my heart full of trouble, to the Lieutenant of the Tower, who tells me that it begun this morning in the King's baker's house in Pudding Lane, and that it hath burned St. Magnus's Church and most part of Fish Street 2
already. So I down to the waterside, and there

1. **the City,** the area within the medieval walls of London; the business district.
2. **closet,** study.
3. **Tower,** the Tower of London, a medieval fort on the Thames River.
4. infinite (in′fə nit), *adj.* endless.
5. **on the bridge.** In Pepys's time, London Bridge was covered with houses and shops.

SELECTION SUMMARY

The Diary

Samuel Pepys describes the Great Fire that leveled much of London in 1666. He details his role in communicating the perils of the fire to King Charles II; in helping to bring it under control; and in seeing to the protection of the goods and houses of his friends and family. In daily entries, Pepys analyzes the progress of the fire through the city, viewing it from various vantage points, including hilltops, steeples, and boats on the River Thames.

*For summaries in other languages, see the **Building English Proficiency** book.*

This painting, *The Great Fire of London, Showing Ludgate and Old St. Paul's,* was done by an unknown British artist in the late 1600s. Do you think the artist succeeds in depicting what Pepys refers to as the "extraordinary vehemence" of the fire? Explain your answer.

Art Study

Response to Caption Question The artist captures the frightening force and violence of the fire and its updraft, as well as recording what people would be doing during such a catastrophe.

Question Why do you think the artist may have painted such a scene? *(Possible responses: The artist, like Pepys, may have felt compelled to record his or her own memory of the event; or the artist may have been commissioned to record the memory of a patron.)*

The World of Work

Firefighter

For a real-life discussion of the adventures of battling fires, use the pages referenced below.

The World of Work
pp. 13–14

BUILDING ENGLISH PROFICIENCY

Planning a Reading Strategy

The text for Pepys's diary is likely to challenge students, so have them begin by considering the painting on page 341 and the topic of fires in particular.

1. Have students begin a K-W-L chart, listing any facts they know about fires (especially in densely populated city neighborhoods) and some questions that they hope to see answered in this selection. You might encourage students to think about how some fires spread very quickly and how they are fought.

2. Ask students to add answers and more questions to the charts as they read.

3. When students have finished reading, have them meet in small groups and compare charts. Ask: What is the most interesting or surprising thing you learned while reading Pepys's diary?

Building English Proficiency
Activities, p. 223

3 Literary Focus
Imagery

Questions What images does Pepys record in the early stages of the fire? *(Possible responses: houses burning; people throwing goods in the river or bringing them to boats; pigeons being singed or burned as they try to roost)* To what senses do these images appeal? *(Possible responses: smell—houses burning, smoke; sound—pigeons cooing, goods splashing into the water, people shouting; sight—all of these; taste—smoke; touch—the heat)*

4 Literary Element
Characterization

You might note that Pepys's diary not only records events, but offers a portrait of the writer.

Question What does this section reveal about Pepys's character? *(Possible response: He is a logical, levelheaded man of action. He notes that no one seems to be doing anything to stop the fire. Therefore, he goes to Whitehall to report conditions and to suggest ways of bringing the fire under control. These actions show that he takes his government position seriously; that he is willing to take a position of leadership and responsibility; that he cares about others.)*

got a boat,[6] and through bridge and there saw a lamentable[7] fire. Poor Michell's house, as far as the Old Swan, already burned that way, and the fire running further, that, in a very little time, it got as far as the Steelyard, while I was there. Everybody endeavoring to remove their goods, and flinging into the river, or bringing them into lighters[8] that lay off; poor people staying in their houses as long as till the very fire touched them, and then running into boats, or clambering[9] from one pair of stairs, by the waterside, to another. And, among other things, the poor pigeons, I perceive, were loath[10] to leave their houses, but hovered about the windows and balconies, till some of them burned their wings,
3 and fell down.

Having stayed, and in an hour's time seen the fire rage every way; and nobody, to my sight,
4 endeavoring to quench[11] it, but to remove their goods, and leave all to the fire, and having seen it get as far as the Steelyard, and the wind mighty high, and driving it into the city: and everything, after so long a drought,[12] proving combustible,[13] even the very stones of churches; and, among other things, the poor steeple by which pretty Mrs.—— lives, and whereof my old schoolfellow Elborough is parson, taken fire in the very top, and there burned till it fell down; I to Whitehall,[14] with a gentleman with me who desired to go off from the Tower, to see the fire, in my boat; to Whitehall, and there up to the King's closet in the Chapel, where people come about me, and I did give them an account dismayed them all, and word was carried into the King. So I was called for, and did tell the King and Duke of York what I saw; and, that unless his Majesty did command houses to be pulled down, nothing could stop the fire. They seemed much troubled, and the King commanded me to go to my Lord Mayor[15] from him, and command him to spare no houses, but to pull down before the fire every way. The Duke of York bid me tell him, that if he would have any more soldiers, he shall; and so did my Lord Arlington afterwards, as a great secret. Here meeting with Captain Cocke, I in his coach, which he lent me, and Creed with me to Paul's;[16] and there walked along Watling Street, as well as I could, every creature coming away loaden with goods to save, and here and there, sick people carried away in beds. Extraordinary good goods carried in carts and on backs. At last met my Lord Mayor in Canning Street, like a man spent, with a handkerchief about his neck. To the King's message, he cried like a fainting woman, "Lord! what can I do? I am spent; people will not obey me. I have been pulling down houses; but the fire overtakes us faster than we can do it." That he needed no more soldiers; and that, for himself, he must go and refresh himself, having been up all night. So he left me, and I him, and walked home, seeing people all almost distracted, and no manner of means used to quench the fire. The houses, too, so very thick thereabouts, and full of matter for burning, as pitch and tar, in Thames Street; and warehouses of oil, and wines, and brandy, and other things. Here I saw Mr. Isaake Houblon, that handsome man, prettily dressed and dirty at his door at Dowgate, receiving some of his brothers' things, whose houses were on fire; and, as he says, have been removed twice already; and he doubts (as it soon proved) that they must be, in a little time, removed from his house also, which was a sad consideration. And to see the churches all filling with goods by people who themselves should have been quietly there at this time.

6. **boat.** Small boats rowed by "watermen" were a common form of transportation in the city.
7. **lamentable** (lam′ən tə bəl), *adj.* sorrowful.
8. **lighter,** small, flat-bottomed boat.
9. **clamber** (klam′bər), *v.* climb awkwardly or with difficulty.
10. **loath** (lōth), *adj.* reluctant.
11. **quench** (kwench), *v.* drown out; put out.
12. **drought** (drout), *n.* period of dry weather.
13. **combustible** (kəm bus′tə bəl), *adj.* easily burned.
14. **Whitehall,** the king's residence and offices in London.
15. **Lord Mayor,** of London.
16. **Paul's,** St. Paul's Cathedral. Pepys travels back toward the fire, to one of the largest churches in London, which the fire is soon to destroy.

MINI-LESSON: GRAMMAR
Proper Nouns, Titles, and Adjectives

Teach Copy this "sentence" from page 343 on the board.

Met with the King and Duke of York in their barge, and with them to Queenhithe, and there called Sir Richard Browne to them.

Explain that proper nouns name a particular person, place, or thing and are capitalized. Point out the examples of proper nouns in the sentence—names of people (Richard Browne), places (Queenhithe), and titles (Duke of York, Sir, and King—as we capitalize *President* for the chief executive of the U.S.). Elsewhere, names of specific companies (Three Cranes) and buildings (St. Magnus's Church) are capitalized. Discuss other examples of proper nouns, such as names of countries, geographical features, and political organizations.

Explain that proper adjectives are adjectives usually derived from proper nouns, giving these noun/adjective pairs as examples: England/English, Shakespeare/Shakespearean, America/American.

Activity Idea Give students categories (for example, *titles, geographical features, organizations,* and *historical events and eras*) and ask them to name proper nouns within each category.

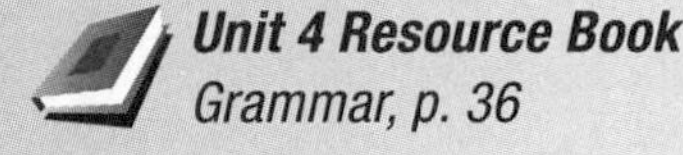
Unit 4 Resource Book
Grammar, p. 36

John Keeling's fire engine is shown in this illustration. Fire-fighting equipment such as this lacked efficient pumps and flexible hose. Do you think that a fire on the scale of the Great Fire of London could occur today in a city equipped with modern fire-fighting equipment? Why or why not?

By this time, it was about twelve o'clock; and so home, and there find my guests, which was Mr. Wood and his wife Barbary Shelden, and also Mr. Moone; she mighty fine, and her husband, for aught I see, a likely man. But Mr. Moone's design and mine, which was to look over my closet, and please him with the sight thereof, which he hath long desired, was wholly disappointed; for we were in great trouble and disturbance at this fire, not knowing what to think of it. However, we had an extraordinary dinner, and as merry as at this time we could be.

While at dinner, Mrs. Batelier come to enquire after Mr. Woolfe and Stanes (who, it seems, are related to them) whose houses in Fish Street are all burned, and they in a sad condition. She would not stay in the fright.

5 As soon as dined, I and Moone away, and walked through the City, the streets full of nothing but people and horses and carts loaden with goods, ready to run over one another, and removing goods from one burned house to another. They now removing out of Canning Street, which received goods in the morning, into Lombard Street, and further; and among others, I now saw my little goldsmith Stokes receiving some friend's goods, whose house itself was burned the day after. We parted at Paul's; he home, and I to Paul's Wharf, where I had appointed a boat to attend me, and took in Mr. Carcasse and his brother, whom I met in the street, and carried them below and above bridge too and again to see the fire, which was now got further, both below and above, and no likelihood of stopping it. Met with the King and Duke of York in their barge, and with them to Queenhithe, and there called Sir Richard Browne to them. Their order was only to pull down houses apace,[17] and so below bridge at the waterside; but little was or could be done, the fire coming upon them so fast. Good hopes there was of stopping it at the Three Cranes above, and at Buttulph's Wharf below bridge, if care be used; but the wind carries it into the city, so as we know not, by the waterside, what it do there. River full of lighters and boats taking in goods, and good goods swimming in the water; and only I observed that hardly one lighter or boat in three that had the goods of a house in, but there was a pair of virginals[18] in it. Having seen as much as I could now, I away to Whitehall by appointment, and there walked to St. James's Park; and there met my wife, and Creed, and Wood, and his wife, and walked to my boat; and there upon the water again, and to the fire up and down, it still increasing, and the wind great. So near the fire as we could for smoke; and all over the Thames, with one's face in the wind, you were almost burned with a shower of fire-drops. This is very true; so as houses were burned by these drops and flakes of fire, three or four, nay, five or six houses, one from
another. When we could endure no more upon 6
the water, we to a little ale house on the Bankside,

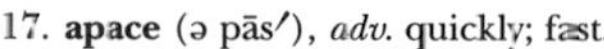

17. **apace** (ə pās′), *adv.* quickly; fast.
18. **virginal,** small legless piano.

Art Study

Responses to Caption Questions
Responses will vary. The combination of modern equipment and fire-fighting techniques, sprinkler systems, and building codes create a situation in which large fires are kept under control. However, the many small fires that result from an earthquake or from enemy bombing could overwhelm fire departments and spread across much of a city. This happened in San Francisco in 1906 and in Coventry, England, and Dresden, Germany, during World War II.

5 Reading/Thinking Skills
Compare and Contrast

Questions How would you compare Mr. Moone's response to the fire with the narrator's? *(Mr. Moone, who wants to see Pepys's study, seems oblivious to what is going on; Pepys is too preoccupied with the fire to oblige Mr. Moone. While Pepys acts the part of host, he soon goes back to the fire.)*

6 Literary Focus
Imagery

Question How does the imagery here heighten the sense of danger? *(Pepys describes how the smoke, wind, and shower of firedrops become more than he can endure.)*

BUILDING ENGLISH PROFICIENCY

ESL LEP ELD SAE LD

Linking Past and Present

Help students relate the 1666 fire of London to a 1990s disaster.

1. Remind students that in many years southern California experiences serious fires. Ask students to share their knowledge of these or other disasters they know about or have witnessed.

2. Have students imagine that a fire (or another disaster) is threatening their town. Have groups of students create Venn diagrams comparing what Pepys experienced in 1666 with what they might see, hear, and smell in a disaster today.

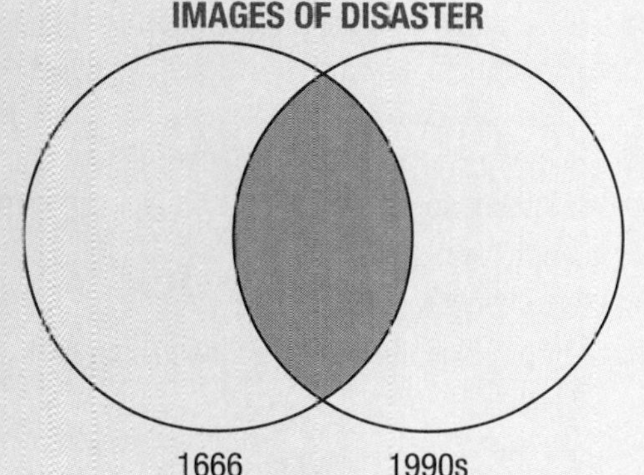

7 Multicultural Note
Communication

Response Communication is vital. Pepys receives news from friends and neighbors, and he keeps returning to the fire for reliable information, which he relays to the king.

8 Literary Element
Tone

Question Do you think the tone of Pepys's writing in this passage reflects the events he describes? *(While responses will vary, students might note that his calm and measured tone seems at odds with the picture he paints of himself, a gentleman of considerable position, riding through the streets in his nightgown. Pepys may have written this some time after the event.)*

over against the Three Cranes, and there stayed till it was dark almost and saw the fire grow; and, as it grew darker, appeared more and more; and in corners and upon steeples, and between churches and houses, as far as we could see up the hill of the city, in a most horrid, malicious,[19] bloody flame, not like the fine flame of an ordinary fire. Barbary and her husband away before us. We stayed till, it being darkish, we saw the fire as only one entire arch of fire from this to the other side the bridge, and in a bow up the hill for an arch of above a mile long; it made me weep to see it. The churches, houses, and all on fire, and flaming at once; and a horrid noise the flames made, and the cracking of houses at their ruin. So home with a sad heart, and there find everybody discoursing[20] and lamenting the fire; and poor Tom Hater come with some few of his goods saved out of his house, which was burned upon Fish Street Hill. I invited him to lie at my house, and did receive his goods; but was deceived in his lying there, the news coming every moment of the growth of the fire; so as we were forced to begin to pack up our own goods, and prepare for their removal; and did by moonshine, it being brave, dry, and moonshine and warm weather, carry much of my goods into the garden; and Mr. Hater and I did remove my money and iron chests into my cellar, as thinking that the safest place. And got my bags of gold into my office, ready to carry away, and my chief papers of accounts also there, and my tallies into a box by themselves. So great was our fear, as Sir W. Batten hath carts come out of the country to fetch away his goods this night. We did put Mr. Hater, poor man! to bed a little; but he got but very little rest, so much noise being in my house, taking down of goods.

7 **EVALUATE: How important a role does communication play in fighting the fire and in evacuating the city?**

SEPTEMBER 3. About four o'clock in the morning, my Lady Batten sent me a cart to carry away all my money and plate and best things to Sir W. Rider's at Bednall Green; which I did, riding myself in my nightgown in 8
the cart; and, Lord! to see how the streets and the highways are crowded with people, running and riding and getting of carts at any rate to fetch away things. I find Sir W. Rider tired with being called up all night and receiving things from several friends. His house full of goods, and much of Sir W. Batten and Sir W. Penn's. I am eased at my heart to have my treasure so well secured. Then home with much ado to find a way. Nor any sleep all this night to me nor my poor wife. But then, and all this day, she and I and all my people[21] laboring to get away the rest of our things, and did get Mr. Tooker to get me a lighter to take them in, and we did carry them (myself some) over Tower Hill, which was by this time full of people's goods, bringing their goods thither. And down to the lighter, which lay at the next quay[22] above the Towerdock. And here was my neighbor's wife, Mrs.——, with her pretty child and some few of her things, which I did willingly give way to be saved with mine. But there was no passing with anything through the postern,[23] the crowd was so great. At night, lay down a little upon a quilt of W. Hewer in the office (all my own things being packed up or gone); and after me, my poor wife did the like—we having fed upon the remains of yesterday's dinner, having no fire nor dishes, nor any opportunity of dressing anything.

SEPTEMBER 4. Up by break of day to get away the remainder of my things, which I did by a lighter at the Iron Gate; and my hands so few,

19. **malicious** (mə lish′əs), *adj.* evil.
20. **discourse** (dis kôrs′), *v.* talk.
21. **my people,** Pepys's servants.
22. **quay** (kē), *n.* landing place for ships.
23. **postern** (pō′stərn), *n.* a small door or gate.

MINI-LESSON: VOCABULARY
Word Meanings

Teach Samuel Pepys uses many words and phrases whose meanings may be obscure to today's students. Encourage students to use the context of confusing words or phrases as well as what they know about Pepys's place and time to make educated guesses about the meanings of the words. Also guide students to use footnotes and glossaries to assess meaning. You might ask:

- How much has language changed since Pepys's time?
- What are some words from today that might be indecipherable to Pepys?

Activity Idea Suggest to students that, as they read, they create lists of words or phrases they don't know. So that they create a personal understanding of the word meanings, encourage students to make semantic maps of the meaning of a word or several words using clues that come from context (What part of speech is it?), background knowledge (Where is the thing named? What does Pepys say about it?), and footnote information (What is the formal definition?).

that it was the afternoon before we could get them all away.

Sir W. Penn and I to Tower Street, and there met the fire burning three or four doors beyond Mr. Howells; whose goods, poor man (his trays and dishes, shovels etc., were flung all along Tower Street in the kennels,[24] and people working therewith from one end to the other), the fire coming on in that narrow street, on both sides, with infinite fury. Sir W. Batten, not knowing how to remove his wine, did dig a pit in the garden and laid it in there; and I took the opportunity of laying all the papers of my office that I could not otherwise dispose of. And in the evening Sir W. Penn and I did dig another and put our wine in it, and I my Parmesan cheese as well as my wine and some other things.

. . . the whole heaven on fire

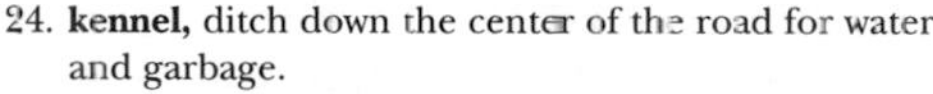

This night Mrs. Turner, who poor woman, was removing her goods all this day—good goods, into the garden, and knew not how to dispose of them—and her husband supped with my wife and I at night in the office, upon a shoulder of mutton from the cook's, without any napkin or anything, in a sad manner but were merry. Only, now and then walking into the garden and saw how horridly the sky looks, all on a fire in the night, was enough to put us out of our wits; and indeed it was extremely dreadful, for it looks just as if it was at us, and the whole heaven on fire. I after supper walked in the dark down to Tower Street, and there saw it all on fire at the Trinity house on that side and the Dolphin Tavern on this side, which was very near us—and the fire with extraordinary vehemence.[25] Now begins the practice of blowing up of houses in Tower Street, those next the Tower, which at first did frighten people more than anything; but it stopped the fire where it was done—it bringing down the houses to the ground in the same places they stood, and then it was easy to quench what little fire was in it, though it kindled nothing almost. W. Hewer this day went to see how his mother did, and comes late home, but telling us how he hath been forced to remove her to Islington, her house in Pye Corner being burned. So that it is got so far that way and all the Old Bailey, and was running down to Fleet Street. And Paul's is burned, and all Cheapside. I wrote to my father this night; but the posthouse being burned, the letter could not go.

SEPTEMBER 5. I lay down in the office again upon W. Hewer's quilt, being mighty weary, and sore in my feet with going till I was hardly able to stand. About two in the morning my wife calls me up, and tells me of new cries of "Fire!"—it being come to Barking Church, which is the bottom of our land. I up; and finding it so, resolved presently to take her away, and did, and took my gold (which was about £2350). W. Hewer, and Jane down by Proundy's boat to Woolwich; but, Lord! what a sad sight it was by moonlight, to see the whole city almost on fire, that you might see it plain at Woolwich, as if you were by it. There, when I come, I find the gates[26] shut, but no guard kept at all; which troubled me, because of discourse now begun, that there is plot in it,[27] and that the French had done it. I got the gates open, and to Mr. Shelden's, where I locked up my gold, and charged my wife and W. Hewer never to leave the room without one of them in it, night or day. So back again, by the way seeing my goods well in the lighters at Deptford, and watched well by people. Home,

24. **kennel,** ditch down the center of the road for water and garbage.
25. **vehemence** (vē′ə məns), *n.* forcefulness; violence.
26. **gates,** to the dockyard.
27. **that there is plot in it,** that is, that the fire has been deliberately set.

9 Reading/Thinking Skills
Drawing Conclusions

Ask students to use details on this page to draw conclusions about the state of affairs by September 5.

Questions

- Is it still worthwhile to try to move goods out of the fire's path? *(Possible response: Things have seemingly gone beyond worrying about household goods; Pepys is only moving gold, wine, and imported cheese.)*
- How effective has the destruction of houses been in stopping the spread of the fire? *(Possible response: This method has worked where it has been used, but the fire continues to flourish.)*
- What would you conclude at this point about the fate of London? Why? *(The entire city may well burn; the fire seems unstoppable.)*

10 Multicultural Note
Scapegoats

Londoners seem to be nominating France as a scapegoat for their troubles. For centuries, France was England's traditional enemy and was often blamed when things went wrong, e.g., during the Great Plague. The French, in turn, blamed their disasters on the English.

BUILDING ENGLISH PROFICIENCY

ESL LEP ELD SAE LD

Using Context Clues

Pepys used some words that are rarely used today. Help students find the meaning of such words from their context, that is, the surrounding words in the sentence or in nearby sentences.

1. Point out the word *moonshine* at about the middle of column 1 on page 344. Ask students for a modern synonym. *(moonlight)*

2. Ask groups of students to find the following words in the selection: ado (page 344, just above the middle of column 2), thither (page 344, middle of column 2), supped (page 345, beginning of paragraph 2 in column 1), discourse (page 345, near the bottom of column 2). For each word, have them read the entire sentence for the context and then tell what they think the word means.

3. Have students check a dictionary to make sure that their definitions are correct. Then have them write an original sentence for each.

11 Literary Focus
Imagery

Questions

- As Pepys walks through London, what does he see? hear? taste? smell? feel? *(Possible responses: He sees the results of the fire on the city and its inhabitants, human and animal; he hears explosions as buildings are blown up; he touches a buckled piece of glass from Mercer's Chapel; he tastes food and drink; he smells brimstone and burning oil; he feels the heat of burning coals.)*
- How do these scenes make him feel? *(sad, almost despairing)*
- Which of his images most affects you? *(While responses will vary, many students will remember Pepys's description of the scorched cat.)*

12 Reading/Thinking Skills
Infer

Question From Pepys's previous comments on the French and this description of the dangers faced by strangers, what can you infer about the mood of the people? *(Possible response: Discouraged and angry at their lot, the people are looking for someone to blame and punish.)*

and whereas I expected to have seen our house on fire, it being now about seven o'clock, it was not. But to the fire, and there find greater hopes than I expected; for my confidence of finding our office on fire was such, that I durst not ask anybody how it was with us, till I come and saw it not burned. But, going to the fire, I find, by the blowing up of houses, and the great help given by the workmen out of the King's yards, sent up by Sir W. Penn, there is a good stop given to it, as well as at Mark Lane end as ours; it having only burned the dial of Barking Church, and part of the porch, and was there quenched. I up to the top of Barking steeple, and there saw the saddest sight of desolation[28] that I ever saw; everywhere great fires, oil-cellars, and brimstone, and other things burning. I became afeard to stay there long, and therefore down again as fast as I could, the fire being spread as far as I could see it; and to Sir W. Penn's, and there eat a piece of cold meat, having eaten nothing since Sunday, but the remains of Sunday's dinner. Here I met with Mr. Young and Whistler; and having removed all my things, and received good hopes that the fire at our end is stopped, they and I walked into the town, and find Fenchurch Street, Gracious Street, and Lombard Street all in dust. The Exchange[29] a sad sight, nothing standing there, of all the statues or pillars, but Sir Thomas Gresham's picture in the corner. Walked into Moorfields, our feet ready to burn, walking through the town among the hot coals, and find that full of people, and poor wretches carrying their goods there, and everybody keeping his goods together by themselves; and a great blessing it is to them that it is fair weather for them to keep abroad night and day; drank there, and paid twopence for a plain penny loaf. Thence homeward, having passed through Cheapside, and Newgate Market, all burned; and seen Anthony Joyce's house in fire; and took up, which I keep by me, a piece of glass of Mercer's Chapel in the street, where much more was, so melted and buckled with the heat of the fire like parchment. I also did see a poor cat taken out of a hole in a chimney, joining to the wall of the Exchange, with the hair all burned off the body, and yet alive. So home at night, and find there good hopes of saving our office; but great endeavors of watching all night, and having men ready; and so we lodged them in the office, and had drink and bread and cheese for them. And I lay down and slept a good night about midnight; though, when I rose, I heard that there had been a great alarm of French and Dutch[30] being risen, which proved nothing. But it is a strange thing to see how long this time did look since Sunday, having been always full of variety of actions, and little sleep, that it looked like a week or more, and I had forgot almost the day of the week. 11

SEPTEMBER 6. Up about five o'clock, and there met Mr. Gawden at the gate of the office (I intending to go out, as I used every now and then to do, to see how the fire is) to call our men to Bishopsgate, where no fire had yet been near, and there is now one broke out—which did give great grounds to people, and to me too, to think that there is some kind of plot in this (on which many by this time have been taken, and it hath been dangerous for any stranger to walk in the streets); but I went 12
with the men and we did put it out in a little time, so that that was well again. It was pretty to see how hard the women did work in the kennels sweeping of water; but then they would scold for drink and be as drunk as devils. I saw good butts of sugar broke open in the street, and people go and take handfuls out and put into beer and drink it. And now all being pretty well, I took boat and over to Southwark, and took boat on the other side the bridge and so to Westminster, thinking to

28. **desolation** (des′ə lā′shən), *n.* ruin; destruction.
29. **the Exchange,** a large building in which merchants met to discuss business.
30. **French and Dutch,** England's enemies at the time.

MINI-LESSON: STUDY SKILLS
Using a Time Line

Teach Given that this selection is presented in chronological order, model the use of a time line to keep track of key events, images, or other aspects of Pepys's close-up account of the Great Fire. Ask questions such as the following, and summarize on a time line:

- How does Pepys's view of the fire's danger change over the week?
- At what point does Pepys become nervous about the fire's impact on London? When does he begin to fear for his own home?
- How long does it take for the fire to come under control?

Activity Idea Have students create a time line to track a week of

- events in their own lives
- a news event covered in the newspaper or by other media
- a historical or imaginary natural disaster

shift myself,[31] being all in dirt from top to bottom. But could not there find any place to buy a shirt or pair of gloves, Westminster Hall being full of people's goods—those in Westminster having removed all their goods, and the Exchequer money put into vessels to carry to Nonsuch.[32] But to the Swan, and there was trimmed. And then to Whitehall, but saw nobody, and so home. A sad sight to see how the River looks—no houses nor church near it to the Temple—where it stopped. At home did go with Sir W. Batten and our neighbor Knightly (who, with one more, was the only man of any fashion left in all the neighborhood hereabouts, they all removing their goods and leaving their houses to the mercy of the fire) to Sir R. Ford's, and there dined, in an earthen platter a fried breast of mutton, a great many of us. But very merry; and indeed as good a meal, though as ugly a one, as ever I had in my life. Thence down to Deptford, and there with great satisfaction landed all my goods at Sir G. Carteret's, safe, and nothing missed I could see, or hurt. This being done to my great content, I home; and to Sir W. Batten's, and there with Sir R. Ford, Mr. Knightly, and one Withers, a professed lying rogue, supped well; and mighty merry and our fears over. From them to the office and there slept, with the office full of laborers, who talked and slept and walked all night long there. But strange it was to see Clothworkers Hall on fire these three days and nights in one body of Flame—it being the cellar, full of Oil.

SEPTEMBER 7. Up by five o'clock and, blessed be God, find all well, and by water to Paul's Wharf. Walked thence and saw all the town burned, and a miserable sight of Paul's church, with all the roofs fallen and the body of the choir fallen into St. Faith's[33]—Paul's school also—Ludgate—Fleet Street—my father's house, and the church, and a good part of the Temple the like. So to Creeds lodging near the New Exchange, and there find him laid down upon a bed—the house all unfurnished, there being fears of the fire's coming to them. There borrowed a shirt of him—and washed. To Sir W. Coventry at St. James's, who lay without Curtains, having removed all his goods—as the King at Whitehall and everybody had done and was doing. He hopes we shall have no public distractions upon this fire, which is what everybody fears—because of the talk of the French having a hand in it. And it is a proper time for discontents—but all men's minds are full of care to protect themselves and save their goods. The militia is in arms everywhere.

SUMMARIZE: What are the possible theories about the origin of the fire? 13

This day our merchants first met at Gresham College, which by proclamation is to be their Exchange. Strange to hear what is bid for houses all up and down here—a friend of Sir W. Riders having £150 for what he used to let for £40/per annum. Much dispute where the Custom House shall be; thereby the growth of the City again to be foreseen. My Lord Treasurer, they say, and others, would have it at the other end of the town. I home late to Sir W. Penn, who did give me a bed—but without curtains or hangings, all being down. So here I went the first time into a naked bed, only my drawers on—and did sleep pretty well; but still, both sleeping and waking, had a fear of fire in my heart, that I took little rest.

31. **shift myself,** change clothes.
32. **Nonsuch,** a royal palace in Surrey, a district south of London.
33. **St. Faith's,** a chapel under St. Paul's Cathedral.

13 Active Reading
Summarize

Response Pepys first traces the fire's origin to a draught; he then mentions the French; later the French and Dutch; and finally, he discusses "discontents," i.e., political or religious dissenters.

Check Test

1. What is the effect of the fire on London? *(devastation and loss of property as well as suspension of all normal business)*
2. When the fire draws near, what does Pepys save besides gold and wine? *(a Parmesan cheese)*
3. How is Pepys's personal life affected by the fire? *(He does not lose his house or any of his property, but he has effectively lost his city, i.e., his world is forever changed.)*
4. To whom does Pepys offer information and advice during the fire? *(the king and Duke of York)*
5. Why is the militia patrolling streets at the end of the fire? (*to protect people and property from looters and those who want to take their troubles out on somebody; there was also fear of French invasion and of political discontents.)*

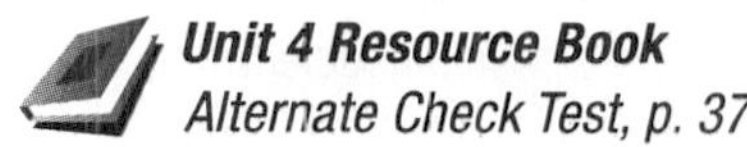
Unit 4 Resource Book
Alternate Check Test, p. 37

BUILDING ENGLISH PROFICIENCY

Making Real-Life Connections

The following activities may help your students come to closure on this selection.

Activity Ideas

- Ask a qualified speaker to address students about disaster preparedness.
- Have groups of students discuss how to help make a disaster plan for their families. Suggest such topics as food and water shortage, escape routes, first-aid kits, and meeting places.
- Ask students to imagine they have five minutes to throw things into a pillowcase before evacuating their house. (What is left will be destroyed.) Have them list and discuss what they would take.

After Reading

MAKING CONNECTIONS

1. Responses will vary. Sample: people throwing their goods into the river; a scorched cat rescued from a chimney

2. Pepys's normal home life seems to be happy and busy. The Pepys family seems to have many friends. There are maids to help with the housework, and Pepys is used to very good meals.

3. Pepys conducts himself well, giving good advice to the king on how to deal with the fire, making sure that his family is safe and his goods safely stored, and helping his friends to save their goods.

4. Pepys, who has the ear of the king, is greatly respected.

5. Pepys saves his bags of gold, his plate, his papers and accounts, and his wine and cheese. These specific items show that he is wealthy and thrifty, that he is organized, and that he values fine food and drink.

6. Possible response: He might have written things out in more complete form and—considering his public character—written in a more formal style. He might have been more reticent about revealing his feelings and intimate details of his home life.

7. Possible response: In the face of change and disaster, people often cling to what is familiar and comforting.

8. Possible response: to maintain law and order and to help those in need

After Reading

Making Connections

Shaping Your Response

1. Which episodes about the fire stand out most clearly in your mind? Why?

Analyzing the Diary

2. From this excerpt, what can you tell about Pepys's everyday home life in normal times?
3. During the fire how does Pepys conduct himself as a public official? as a husband? as a friend?
4. What can you tell about Pepys's reputation in the community by the way he is treated by the nobility and by his friends?
5. Make a list of the items Pepys chooses to save from his home. What does each item contribute toward a **characterization** of the man?
6. Pepys used a private shorthand to write his diaries for himself and was not concerned with **communication** to a reading public. How might he have written differently if he had known that you would be reading his intimate thoughts hundreds of years later?

Extending the Ideas

7. Pepys describes the people waiting too long to leave their homes that eventually burn down around them. You may have seen or read examples of similar behavior in media accounts of floods and hurricanes. What is it about human nature that causes people to react in this way?
8. Pepys says that "the militia is in arms everywhere." In times of disaster why are armed forces often involved?

Literary Focus: Imagery

Imagery may appeal to the sense of sight, hearing, taste, smell, or touch. Effective imagery often appeals to more than one sense at a time. Which of your senses were most aroused by Pepys's descriptive language? Chart some of the words or phrases that helped to stimulate those senses.

Sense	Examples
sight	
hearing	
taste	
smell	
touch	

LITERARY FOCUS: IMAGERY

Possible Responses

Sense	Example
sight	goods dumped in the river; pigeons with burnt wings; a scorched cat
hearing	the sound of the fire; the crack of timbers giving way; explosions
taste	various meals
smell	smoke; brimstone; oil burning
touch	buckled glass from a burnt chapel

Vocabulary Study

For each numbered word write the letter of its synonym. You will not use all the synonyms. Then use each of the numbered words in a sentence that shows you understand the meaning of the word.

1. combustible	**a.** sorrowful
2. infinite	**b.** easily burned
3. lamentable	**c.** full of joy
4. loath	**d.** endless
5. malicious	**e.** reluctant
	f. evil

Expressing Your Ideas

Writing Choices

Writer's Notebook Update Keep a personal diary for at least one week. Try to follow Pepys's example of recording not only your personal thoughts but also observations of the people and events around you. Don't worry about grammar and sentence structure. You might even want to use your own form of shorthand.

Tell It as It Was Write a **descriptive narrative** of an exciting or dangerous event in your life. (If your life hasn't been especially exciting or dangerous, write about a fictional event.) Write in the first person and look for ways to characterize yourself as one who's part of the action. Look for fresh, crisp verbs and adjectives to convey the spirit and emotion of the event.

London Burns! You are a newspaper reporter for an early version of *The Times* of London presenting the essential facts of the fire to the public. Write a brief **news story** for one of the six days, concentrating on *who, what, when, where,* and, if you wish, *why* and *how.*

Other Options

A Human Story In Pepys's account, the fire becomes a backdrop for a tale of human interest. Often human-interest tales can be captured in the looks exchanged between mother and child or in the wrinkles of an old face. Find a magazine photograph—or snap a picture yourself—that portrays human interest. Display the photograph and **tell the human story** it suggests with a small group or the class as your audience.

My Book This calligraphic sketch is one of many Samuel Pepys had created to decorate the title pages of his magnificent collection of books. Design a **personal bookplate** for your private book collection. Include designs that are meaningful—perhaps symbolic—in your own life.

From Pepys's calligraphical collection.

VOCABULARY STUDY

1. b. easily burned
2. d. endless
3. a. sorrowful
4. e. reluctant
5. f. evil

Vocabulary words, as used in context, should reflect correct meanings and connotations.

Unit 4 Resource Book
Vocabulary, p. 35
Vocabulary Test, p. 38

WRITING CHOICES

Writer's Notebook Update

Remind students that, since diaries are not (usually) for public consumption, they may write freely, without concern that their privacy will be intruded upon.

London Burns!

As students prepare their news stories, ask them to consider an imaginary interview with Pepys or with the king or the Duke of York.

Selection Test

Unit 4 Resource Book
pp. 39–40

OTHER OPTIONS

My Book

Ask the class to brainstorm interpretations for the symbols and design of Pepys's bookplate before designing their own. Interested students might also investigate the career of twentieth-century artist Rockwell Kent, who designed a number of bookplates and colophons.

Before Reading

Building Background

Ask students to recall the last time they used a dictionary and identify why they did so. Lead a discussion on what it would be like if there were no dictionaries or if dictionaries were never updated.

Literary Focus

Ask students to identify the following terms as synonyms for either *denote* or *connote:* stand for, imply, intimate, define, designate, suggest. *(synonyms for denote—stand for, define, designate; synonyms for connote—imply, intimate, suggest)*

Writer's Notebook

Suggest that students may want to give some thought to their examples of "unfairness" as they will later be writing about them more fully.

More About Samuel Johnson

The son of a bookseller, Samuel Johnson wrote the novel Rasselas, *Prince of Abyssinia* in seven days to raise money for his mother's funeral.

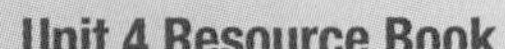

Before Reading

Dignity and Uses of Biography
from the Dictionary of the English Language
Letter to Chesterfield by Samuel Johnson

Samuel Johnson
1709–1784

Samuel Johnson was an unattractive figure: blind in one eye, half-deaf, misshapen by disease, and sloppy in dress and personal habits. He spent only one year at Pembroke College, Oxford, before leaving for lack of funds. After an unsuccessful attempt at teaching, Johnson went to London, where he began a long period of writing for magazines, eventually founding two periodicals, *The Rambler* and *The Idler.* The three major projects of his life, any one of which could be considered a life's work, were the *Dictionary of the English Language* (1755), a complete edition of Shakespeare (1765), and the ten-volume *Lives of the English Poets* (1781), a combination of biography and literary criticism.

Building Background

"Done by an Oxford Hand" Discouraged by the lack of a university degree and by the kinds of writing he was forced to do to earn his meager existence, Samuel Johnson seized upon the offer by bookseller Robert Dodsley to create a new dictionary of the English language. Guaranteed a fee of £1,575 Johnson rented a house, hired six clerks, and organized a dictionary workshop on the top floor. Using his own books and those borrowed from friends, Johnson read biography, drama, essays, history, poetry, and science. As he read, he underlined the words to be defined (40,000 in all) and marked passages to be quoted (116,000 quotations). The clerks copied the material on slips of paper which were pasted into 80 large notebooks. Johnson then wrote the definitions and the word origins. The process continued for nine years, being completed shortly after Johnson was awarded an honorary Master of Arts degree from Oxford. That he could include that degree on the title page was so important to Johnson! An Oxford man, however, was heard to say, "It is in truth doing ourselves more honor than him to have such a work done by an Oxford hand."

Literary Focus

Denotation / Connotation The dictionary meaning of a word is its **denotation.** The emotional associations that surround a word are the word's **connotation.** Denotations are constant; they are the same for everyone. Connotations vary from person to person based on individual attitudes and experiences. Copy the following words and write a denotation and a connotation for each of them: *school, winter, job, family, gun.* As you read Johnson's dictionary entries, look for examples of connotation in his definitions.

Writer's Notebook

That's Not Fair! Have you ever felt that you were the victim of unfairness—at home, at school, or among your friends? Write down two or three examples. If you can't think of personal examples, jot down examples of unfair acts you have observed being done to others.

SUPPORT MATERIALS OVERVIEW

Unit 4 Resource Book
- Graphic Organizer, p. 41
- Study Guide, p. 42
- Vocabulary, p. 43
- Grammar, p. 44
- Alternate Check Test, p. 45
- Vocabulary Test, p. 46
- Selection Test, pp. 47–48

Building English Proficiency
- Selection Summaries
- Activities, p. 224

Reading, Writing & Grammar SkillBook
- Grammar, Usage, and Mechanics, pp. 163–164, 165–166

Technology
- Audiotape
- Personal Journal Software
- Custom Literature Database: Additional selections by Samuel Johnson can be found on the database.
- Test Generator Software

Dignity and Uses of BIOGRAPHY

SAMUEL JOHNSON

All joy or sorrow for the happiness or calamities of others is produced by an act of the imagination that realizes the event, however fictitious, or approximates it, however remote, by placing us for a time in the condition of him whose fortune we contemplate. So that we feel, while the deception lasts, whatever motions would be excited by the same good or evil happening to ourselves.

Our passions are therefore more strongly moved in proportion as we can more readily adopt the pains or pleasure proposed to our minds by recognizing them at once our own or considering them as naturally incident to[1] our state of life. It is not easy for the most artful writer to give us an interest in happiness or misery which we think ourselves never likely to feel and with which we have never yet been made acquainted. Histories of the downfall of kingdoms and revolutions of empires are read with great tranquillity.[2] The imperial tragedy pleases common auditors only by its pomp of ornament and grandeur of ideas; and the man whose faculties have been engrossed by business, and whose heart never fluttered but at the rise or fall of stocks, wonders how the attention can be seized or the affection agitated by a tale of love.

Those parallel circumstances and kindred[3] images to which we readily conform our minds are, above all other writings, to be found in narratives of the lives of particular persons; and therefore no species of writing seems more worthy of cultivation than biography, since none can be more delightful or more useful, none can more certainly enchain the heart by irresistible interest, or more widely diffuse[4] instruction to every diversity of condition.

1 **CLARIFY: How does Johnson suggest that we can experience another's joy or sorrow?**

The general and rapid narratives of history, which involve a thousand fortunes in the business of a day and complicate innumerable incidents in one great transaction, afford few lessons applicable to private life, which derives its comforts and its wretchedness from the right or wrong management of things which nothing but their frequency makes considerable—"Parva si non fiunt quotidie,"[5] says Pliny—and which can have no place in those relations which never descend below the consultation of senates, the motions of armies, and the schemes of conspirators.

I have often thought that there has rarely passed a life of which a judicious[6] and faithful narrative would not be useful. For not only every man has, in the mighty mass of the world, great numbers in the same condition with himself, to whom his mistakes and miscarriages, escapes and expedients,[7] would be of immedi-

1. **incident to,** belonging to.
2. **tranquillity** (trang kwil′ə tē), *n.* peacefulness.
3. **kindred** (kin′drid), *adj.* similar.
4. **diffuse** (di fyüz′), *v.* spread.
5. **Parva . . . quotidie,** small things are important because they happen daily. *[Latin]*
6. **judicious** (jü dish′əs), *adj.* wise.
7. **expedient** (ek spē′dē ənt), *n.* method of bringing about desired results.

During Reading

Selection Objectives

- to understand Johnson's place and importance in English literature
- to identify and analyze denotation and connotation in Johnson's work
- to identify and correct run-on sentences

Unit 4 Resource Book
Graphic Organizer, p. 41
Study Guide, p. 42

Theme Link

Samuel Johnson, a keen observer of Other People's Lives, examines the art of biography in his essay "Dignity and Uses of Biography."

Vocabulary Preview

tranquillity, peacefulness
judicious, wise
expedient, method of bringing about desired results
fallacy, false idea
propriety, proper behavior
negligent, careless
impartiality, fairness
extrinsic, external
insolence, bold rudeness
censure, criticize
calumnious, slanderous
asperity, harshness

Students can add the words and definitions to their Writer's Notebooks.

1 Active Reading
Clarify

Response We experience the joys and sorrows of others by an act of imagination, which puts us, for a time, in another person's situation.

SELECTION SUMMARY

Dignity and Uses of Biography; Dictionary of the English Language; Letter to Chesterfield

Dignity and Uses of Biography Samuel Johnson explains why, in his opinion, biographies are superior to other forms of writing. The form expresses events and emotions that all human beings share and from which most can learn.

Dictionary of the English Language Selected entries from *Dictionary of the English Language* illustrate Johnson's attempt at comprehensiveness and tendency toward eccentric, connotative definitions.

Letter to Chesterfield Johnson rebuffs, with wit and irony, Lord Chesterfield's attempts to receive credit for the dictionary after its completion.

*For summaries in other languages, see the **Building English Proficiency** book.*

2 Reader's Response

Making Personal Connections

Question Do you agree with Johnson's statement that "We are all prompted by the same motives"? *(Possible responses: Students who agree with Johnson may identify motives that many humans share—love, need for security, or power; other students may argue that "all" is an overgeneralization.)*

3 Active Reading

Clarify

Response He seems to believe that we are more alike.

4 Reader's Response

Making Personal Connections

Question Since Johnson values "thoughts into domestic privacies" and "minute details of daily life," how do you think he would feel about how today's media intrude into people's private lives? *(Possible responses: Some will feel that Johnson would embrace the idea; others may say he would be shocked by the media's intrusiveness and lack of prudence and taste.)*

ate and apparent use, but there is such an uniformity in the state of man, considered apart from adventitious[8] and separable decorations and disguises, that there is scarce any possibility of good or ill but is common to human kind. A great part of the time of those who are placed at the greatest distance by fortune or by temper must unavoidably pass in the same manner, and though, when the claims of nature are satisfied, caprice[9] and vanity and accident begin to produce discriminations[10] and peculiarities, yet the eye is not very heedful or quick which cannot discover the same causes still terminating their influence in the same effects, though sometimes accelerated, sometimes retarded, or perplexed by multiplied combinations. We are all
2 prompted by the same motives, all deceived by the same fallacies,[11] all animated by hope, obstructed by danger, entangled by desire, and seduced by pleasure.

3 **CLARIFY: Does Johnson believe people are more alike or more different?**

It is frequently objected to relations of particular lives that they are not distinguished by any striking or wonderful vicissitudes.[12] The scholar who passed his life among his books, the merchant who conducted only his own affairs, the priest whose sphere of action was not extended beyond that of his duty, are considered as no proper objects of public regard, however they might have excelled in their several stations, whatever might have been their learning, integrity, and piety. But this notion arises from false measures of excellence and dignity, and must be eradicated[13] by considering that in the esteem of uncorrupted reason what is of most use is of most value.

It is, indeed, not improper to take honest advantages of prejudice and to gain attention by a celebrated name; but the business of the biographer is often to pass slightly over those performances and incidents which produce vulgar greatness, to lead the thoughts into domestic privacies, and display the minute details of 4
daily life where exterior appendages[14] are cast aside and men excel each other only by prudence[15] and by virtue. The account of Thuanus[16] is, with great propriety,[17] said by its author to have been written that it might lay open to pos-

8. **adventitious** (ad′ven tish′əs), *adj.* accidental.
9. **caprice** (ke prēs′), *n.* whim.
10. **discrimination** (dis krim′ə nā′shən), *n.* distinction.
11. fallacy (fal′ə sē), *n.* false idea.
12. **vicissitude** (və sis′ə tüd), *n.* change in fortune.
13. **eradicate** (i rad′ə kāt), *v.* erase.
14. **appendage** (ə pen′dij), *n.* addition.
15. **prudence** (prüd′ns), *n.* wisdom.
16. **Thuanus.** Each of the proper names found in the remainder of this essay refers to a biographer or to the subject of a biography.
17. propriety (prə prī′ə tē), *n.* proper behavior.

MINI-LESSON: GRAMMAR

Run-on Sentences

Some authors, like Samuel Johnson, express themselves with long, complicated sentences.

Teach A *run-on sentence* combines two sentences but omits coordinating conjunctions or appropriate punctuation; the reader becomes confused, not knowing where one sentence ends and the other begins. Good writers do not publish run-on sentences; they catch and correct them while proofreading their work.

Question Is the first sentence of Johnson's "Dignity and Uses of Biography" a run-on sentence? Why or why not? *(It is not a run-on sentence because it is not a case where two sentences were combined without punctuation or a conjunction; instead, it is an example of a long, complicated sentence.)*

Activity Ideas

- Have students rewrite the first sentence of "Dignity and Uses of Biography" as two separate sentences. Ask them whether the message is easier to understand as one sentence or as two sentences.
- Have students write five examples of run-on sentences. Then ask students to exchange papers and correctly punctuate each other's work.

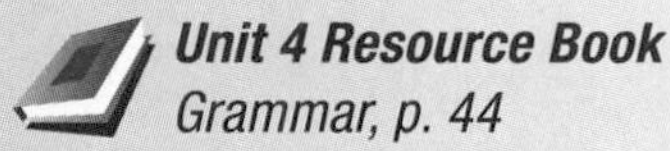

Unit 4 Resource Book
Grammar, p. 44

This biographical painting, by an unknown artist, showing scenes from the life and death of Sir Henry Unton (1557?–1596). According to Johnson, what is the purpose of biography? How is that purpose similar to what the artist tries to accomplish in this painting?

terity the private and familiar character of that man, *cujus ingenium et candorum ex ipsius scriptis sunt olim semper miraturi* ("whose candor and genius will to the end of time be by his writings preserved in admiration").

There are many invisible circumstances which, whether we read as inquirers after natural or moral knowledge, whether we intend to enlarge our science or increase our virtue, are more important than public occurrences. Thus Sallust, the great master of nature, has not forgot in his account of Cataline to remark that his walk was now quick and again slow, as an indication of a mind revolving something with violent com-
5 motion. Thus the story of Melanchthon affords a striking lecture on the value of time by informing us that when he made an appointment he expected not only the hour but the minute to be fixed, that the day might not run out in the idleness of suspense. And all the plans and enterprises of De Wit are now of less importance to the world than that part of his personal character which represents him as careful of his health and negligent[18] of his life.

But biography has often been allotted to writers who seem very little acquainted with the nature of their task or very negligent about the performance. They rarely afford any other

18. **negligent** (neg′lə jənt), *adj.* careless.

Responses to Caption Questions to examine not only the great events of life, but also the telling details of daily existence; the artist illustrates the great events, as well as the telling details.

Visual Literacy The painting details the life of a public figure who died on a diplomatic mission in France. On his death bed (top center), he asks to be buried in England; the funeral is shown bottom center and left. He is portrayed as a baby in his mother's arms (bottom right); he studies at Oxford (far right center); he tours the continent (upper right); and he distinguishes himself in battle (upper right). The large interior scene (right center) demonstrates his hospitality at a masque, a popular and elaborate diversion of the era.

Question Is there a modern equivalent of this visual biography? *(the TV biographical documentary)*

5 **Literary Element**
Characterization

Questions What does this detail reveal about Melanchthon? *(Possible response: He was either obsessed with time or with waste.)* How does the use of this detail support Johnson's views? *(Possible response: It demonstrates how a biographer can reveal character through detail.)*

Improving Comprehension

Help students attack the unfamiliar, abstract words and long, complicated sentences in Johnson's essay.

1. Beginning with "A great part of the time" in the first column on page 352, there are twelve complete sentences to the end of page 353. Assign two students to most sentences, and three to long sentences that are the most challenging.

2. Give students five minutes to figure out what their assigned sentence means and to translate it into informal English for the class. The reworded sentence should summarize Johnson's meaning in language that is as clear and specific as possible.

3. Ask students to choose one phrase in their sentence that they find especially interesting or challenging. Have them tell the class which phrase they have chosen, what it means, and why they chose it.

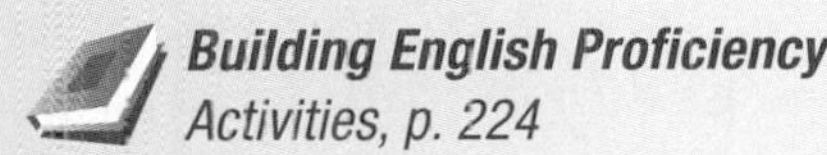
Building English Proficiency
Activities, p. 224

6 Reading/Thinking Skills
Find the Main Idea

Question What is the source of Johnson's irritation with the writers he cites in this passage? *(Possible response: the inclusion of details, e.g., Addison's irregular pulse, that offer no insight into the character of the subject of the biography)*

7 Active Reading
Predict

Response He probably would include the details of the subject's habits, quirks, and foibles, as well as details of physical description.

8 Literary Focus
Denotation/Connotation

Pity denotes sorrow for the suffering of another; compassion; sympathy.

Question What difference in connotation is there between the pity felt toward a criminal and the pity felt toward a country? *(While student responses may vary, it should be noted that pity toward a criminal suggests "feeling sorry for" while pity for a country suggests "deference to the needs of.")*

account than might be collected from public papers, but imagine themselves writing a life when they exhibit a chronological series of actions or preferments,[19] and so little regard the manners or behavior of their heroes, that more knowledge may be gained of a man's real character by a short conversation with one of his servants than from a formal and studied narrative begun with his pedigree and ended with his funeral.

If now and then they condescend[20] to inform the world of particular facts, they are not always so happy as to select the most important. I know not well what advantage posterity[21] can receive from the only circumstance by which Tickell has distinguished Addison from the rest of mankind, the irregularity of his pulse. Nor can I think myself overpaid for the time spent in reading the life of Malherbe by being enabled to relate, after the learned biographer, that Malherbe had two predominant opinions; one that the looseness of a single woman might destroy all her boast of ancient descent, the other that the French beggars made use very improperly and barbarously of the phrase *noble gentleman*, because either
6 word included the sense of both.

There are, indeed, some natural reasons why these narratives are often written by such as were not likely to give much instruction or delight, and why most accounts of particular persons are barren and useless. If a life be delayed till interest and envy are at an end, we may hope for impartiality[22] but must expect little intelligence. For the incidents which give excellence to biography are of a volatile[23] and evanescent[24] kind, such as soon escape the memory and are rarely transmitted by tradition. We know how few can portray a living

PREDICT: If Johnson were writing a biography, what kinds of details would he be likely to include about his subject? 7

acquaintance except by his most prominent and observable particularities and the grosser features of his mind; and it may be easily imagined how much of this little knowledge may be lost in imparting it, and how soon a succession of copies will lose all resemblance of the original.

If the biographer writes from personal knowledge and makes haste to gratify the public curiosity, there is danger lest his interest, his fear, his gratitude, or his tenderness overpower his fidelity and tempt him to conceal if not to invent. There are many who think it an act of piety to hide the faults or failings of their friends, even when they can no longer suffer by their detection. We therefore see whole ranks of characters adorned with uniform panegyric,[25] and not to be known from one another but by extrinsic[26] and casual circumstances. "Let me remember," says Hale, "when I find myself inclined to pity a criminal, that there is likewise a
pity due to the country." If we owe regard to the 8
memory of the dead, there is yet more respect to be paid to knowledge, to virtue, and to truth.

19. **preferment** (pri fėr′mənt), *n.* promotion.
20. **condescend** (kon′di send′), *v.* lower oneself.
21. **posterity** (po ster′ə tē), *n.* generations of the future.
22. **impartiality** (im′pär shē al′ə tē), *n.* fairness.
23. **volatile** (vol′ə təl), *adj.* changing rapidly.
24. **evanescent** (ev′ə nes′nt), *adj.* soon passing away.
25. **panegyric** (pan′ə jir′ik), *n.* extravagant praise.
26. **extrinsic** (ek strin′sik), *adj.* external.

MINI-LESSON: VOCABULARY
Using Dictionaries for Word Meanings

Vocabulary in Samuel Johnson's works presents many challenges to a contemporary reader.

Teach Open any dictionary and you will find that few words are limited to just one definition. Instead, one word can have several meanings. For example, the term *volatile* is defined as "fickle, changeable." Yet *volatile* also can be defined as "violent, explosive."

Question How would a different definition for the word *volatile,* such as "violent, explosive," change the meaning of the last sentence in column 1, in which it appears? *(It now would imply that excellence in biography would depend on fleeting incidents of violence.)*

Activity Idea Have students choose five of the vocabulary words in this selection and write out the sentences in which they appear. In each sentence, students should substitute the meaning given at the bottom of the page for the vocabulary word itself. Direct students to use a dictionary to find alternative meanings for each of their words. Students then should rewrite each sentence, substituting another meaning for each vocabulary word. Have different definitions changed the sentences' meanings?

Dictionary of the English Language

SAMUEL JOHNSON

Johnson's reputation as a scholar and writer was established in 1755 with the publication of his Dictionary. Selling for ninety shillings and filling two large volumes, the Dictionary was the most comprehensive English lexicon ever published. In Italy and France similar dictionaries, prepared under the direction of national academies, represented the work of forty or more men. Johnson prepared his single-handedly, with the help of six clerks. The following entries are selected either for their comprehensiveness or for the personal touches they show.

alliga′tor. The crocodile. This name is chiefly used for the crocodile of America, between which, and that of Africa, naturalists have laid down this difference, that one moves the upper, and the other the lower jaw; but this is now known to be chimerical,[1] the lower jaw being equally moved by both.

bu′lly. (Skinner derives this word from *burly,* as a corruption in the pronunciation; which is very probably right; or from *bulky,* or *bulleyed;* which are less probable. May it not come from *bull,* the pope's letter, implying the insolence[2] of those who came invested with authority from
9 the papal court?) A noisy, blustering, quarrelling fellow: it is generally taken for a man that has only the appearance of courage.

bu′tterfly. A beautiful insect, so named because it first appears at the beginning of the season for butter.

chi′cken. (3) A term for a young girl.

chiru′rgeon. One that cures ailments, not by internal medicines, but outward applications. It is now generally pronounced, and by many written, *surgeon.*

10 **cough.** A convulsion[3] of the lungs, vellicated by some sharp seriosity.[4] It is pronounced *coff.*

to cu′rtail. (*curto,* Latin It was anciently written *curtal,* which perhaps is more proper; but dogs that had their tails cut, being called *curtal* dogs, the word was vulgarly conceived to mean originally *to cut the tail,* and was in time written according to that notion.) (1) To cut off; to cut short; to shorten.

dedica′tion. (2) A servile address to a patron.

den. (1) A cavern or hollow running horizontally, or with a small obliquity,[5] under ground; distinct from a hole, which runs down perpendicularly.

dull. (8) Not exhilarating; not delightful; as, *to make dictionaries is* dull *work.*

e′ssay. (2) A loose sally[6] of the mind; an irregular indigested piece; not a regular and orderly composition.

exci′se. A hateful tax levied upon commodities,[7] and adjudged not by the common judges of property, but wretches hired by those to whom excise is paid.

fa′vorite. (2) One chosen as a companion by his superior; a mean wretch whose whole business is by any means to please.

fun. (A low cant[8] word) Sport; high merriment; frolicksome delight.

ga′mbler. (A cant word I suppose, for *game,*

1. **chimerical** (kə mer′ə kəl), *adj.* imaginary.
2. **insolence** (in′sə ləns), *n.* bold rudeness.
3. **convulsion** (kən vul′shən), *n.* spasm.
4. **vellicated . . . serosity,** with many fluids moving around.
5. **obliquity** (ə blik′wə tē), *n.* inclination.
6. **sally,** outburst.
7. **commodity** (kə mod′ə tē), *n.* anything bought and sold.
8. **cant** (kant), *adj.* slang; jargon.

9 Reading/Thinking Skills
Detect Bias/Identify Assumptions

Question What bias might Johnson's musings on the etymology of *bully* suggest? *(Possible response: His notion that* bully *comes from the arrogant attitude of those invested with authority by a Papal bull seems to suggest an anti-Roman Catholic bias, which was typical of Protestant Englishmen of his day.)*

10 Reading/Thinking Skills
Compare and Contrast

Question How does the information presented for *cough* compare and contrast with that presented in a modern dictionary? *(Possible responses: Both dictionaries offer pronunciations; while the definitions are similar, Johnson employs playful and pompous words, such as "vellicated" and "seriosity"; new dictionaries also tell part of speech and word origin, and usually offer more than one meaning for a term.)*

BUILDING ENGLISH PROFICIENCY

Exploring Key Ideas

Help students understand the process of creating the kind of dictionary that fills a special need, such as a picture dictionary for young children, a dictionary for adults who speak little English, or a dictionary for adults interested in the technical words of a special field, such as music, computers, or cars.

1. Let students find others willing to work on the same kind of dictionary.
2. Have each group choose ten words to define, draw (if appropriate), alphabetize, and present in a neatly finished form.
3. As students share their dictionaries, invite students to add interesting words to their vocabulary notebooks.

11 Literary Element
Sound Devices

Question What sound device is Johnson describing under *hiss? (onomatopoeia)*

12 Literary Focus
Denotation/Connotation

Question Are Johnson's definitions of *parasite* and *patron* denotative or connotative? *(Possible response: As they are not literal meanings, they are connotative, but in a personal, satirical way.)*

13 Literary Element
Satire

Question Does Johnson's definition of *pension* qualify as satire as he defines satire? *(Possible response: The definition is not satire as he defines it, as it is not a poem. The definition* is *satirical in the modern sense; it uses sarcasm and wit to attack an institution.)*

14 Reading/Thinking Skills
Distinguish Between Fact and Opinion

Question What part of the *sonnet* definition is fact and what is opinion? *(The first sentence is fact; the second is opinion.)*

or *gamester.*) A knave[9] whose practice it is to invite the unwary[10] to game and cheat them.

to gi′ggle. To laugh idly; to titter; to grin with merry levity. It is retained in Scotland.

goat. A ruminant[11] animal that seems a middle species between deer and sheep.

gra′vy. The serous juice that runs from flesh not much dried by the fire.

11 **to hiss.** To utter a noise like that of a serpent and some other animals. It is remarkable, that this word cannot be pronounced without making the noise which it signifies.

itch. (1) A cutaneous disease[12] extremely contagious, which overspreads the body with small pustules filled with a thin serum, and raised as microscopes have discovered by a small animal. It is cured by sulphur.

lexico′grapher. A writer of dictionaries; a harmless drudge, that busies himself in tracing the original, and detailing the signification of words.

lunch, lu′ncheon. As much food as one's hand can hold.

ne′twork. Any thing reticulated or decussated,[13] at equal distances, with interstices[14] between the intersections.

oats. A grain, which in England is generally given to horses, but in Scotland supports the people.

pa′rasite. One that frequents rich tables, and earns his welcome by flattery.

pa′stern. (1) The knee of a horse.

12 **pa′tron.** (1) One who countenances,[15] supports, or protects. Commonly a wretch who supports with insolence, and is paid with flattery.

13 **pe′nsion.** An allowance made to any one without an equivalent. In England it is generally understood to mean pay given to a state hireling for treason to his country.

pe′nsioner. (2) A slave of state hired by a stipend to obey his master.

sa′tire. A poem in which wickedness or folly is censured.[16] Proper *satire* is distinguished, by the generality of the reflections, from a *lampoon* which is aimed against a particular person; but they are too frequently confounded.[17]

shre′wmouse. A mouse of which the bite is generally supposed venomous, and to which vulgar tradition assigns such malignity,[18] that she is said to lame the foot over which she runs. I am informed that all these reports are calumnious,[19] and that her feet and teeth are equally harmless with those of any other little mouse. Our ancestors however looked on her with such terror, that they are supposed to have given her name to a scolding woman, whom for her venom they call a *shrew.*

so′nnet. (1) A short poem consisting of four- 14
teen lines, of which the rhymes are adjusted by a particular rule. It is not very suitable to the English language, and has not been used by any man of eminence since Milton.

To′ry. (A cant term, derived, I suppose, from an Irish word signifying a savage.) One who adheres to the ancient constitution of the state, and the apostolical hierarchy[20] of the Church of England, opposed to a Whig.[21]

Whig. (2) The name of a faction.

wi′tticism. A mean attempt at wit.

to worm. (2) To deprive a dog of something, nobody knows what, under his tongue, which is said to prevent him, nobody knows why, from running mad.

---

9. **knave** (nāv), *n.* rogue.
10. **unwary,** careless.
11. **ruminant** (rü′mə nənt), *adj.* cud chewing.
12. **cutaneous disease,** disease of the skin.
13. **reticulated** (ri tik′yə lā tid) **or decussated** (di kus′ā tid), *adjs.* intricately woven or crossed.
14. **interstice** (in tėr′stis), *n., pl.* **-stices** (-stə sēz), a narrow opening.
15. **countenance** (koun′tə nəns), *v.* encourage.
16. **censure** (sen′shər), *v.* criticize.
17. **confound** (kon found′), *v.* confuse.
18. **malignity** (mə lig′nə tē), *n.* ill will.
19. **calumnious** (kə lum′nē əs), *adj.* slanderous.
20. **apostolical** (ap′ə stol′ə kəl) **hierarchy** (hī′ə rär′kē), organization by rank within the church.
21. **opposed to a Whig.** Whigs were the political party supporting Parliamentary control of government. Tories, like Johnson, were royalists favoring the monarchy.

MINI-LESSON: LITERARY FOCUS
Connotation/Denotation

Some of the entries in Johnson's *Dictionary of the English Language* provide good examples of denotation, for a dictionary's purpose is to provide precise, reliable definitions.

Teach Today, dictionary publishers are careful to make sure the definitions they use are denotations, devoid of emotional colorings. Samuel Johnson, however, did not adhere as strictly to this rule. Many of his definitions reflect his own attitudes and experiences.

Question Which aspects of a word's definition would likely change from person to person, denotation or connotation? *(connotation)*

Activity Ideas

- Have students read the dictionary entry for the word *favorite,* which appears on page 355. Ask them to identify the part of the definition that is a connotation. *("a mean wretch whose whole business is by any means to please")*
- Have students choose ten of the vocabulary terms in this passage and write down what each word connotes to them. Then read aloud several of the terms, asking students to offer and compare their connotations for each word.

Letter to Chesterfield

SAMUEL JOHNSON

In 1746, when Johnson first proposed the idea of compiling a dictionary, he discussed the project with Lord Chesterfield, who expressed interest, and, in the custom of literary patronage, gave Johnson a gift of 10 pounds. Later Chesterfield apparently approved the plan for the dictionary and promised Johnson continued financial support. That support never materialized. When the Dictionary *finally appeared in 1755, Chesterfield expressed the desire to be regarded as its patron. Johnson wrote him this letter in response.*

To the Right Honorable
the Earl of Chesterfield
February 7, 1755.
My Lord,

I have lately been informed by the proprietor of *The World*,[1] that two papers, in which my *Dictionary* is recommended to the public, were written by your Lordship. To be so distinguished is an honor which, being very little accustomed to favors from the great, I know not well how to receive, or in what terms to acknowledge.

When, upon some slight encouragement, I first visited your Lordship, I was overpowered, like the rest of mankind, by the enchantment of your address; and could not forbear to wish that I might boast myself *"Le vainqueur du vainqueur de la terre,"*[2] that I might obtain that regard for which I saw the world contending; but I found my attendance so little encouraged, that neither pride nor modesty would suffer me to continue it. When I had once addressed your Lordship in public, I had exhausted all the art of pleasing which a retired and uncourtly scholar can possess. I had done all that I could; and no man is well pleased to have his all neglected, be it ever so little.

Seven years, my Lord, have now passed, since I waited in your outward rooms, or was repulsed[3] from your door; during which time I have been pushing on my work through difficulties, of which it is useless to complain, and have brought it, at last, to the verge of publication, without one act of assistance, one word of encouragement, or one smile of favor. Such treatment I did not expect, for I never had a patron before.

The shepherd in Virgil grew at last acquainted with Love, and found him a native of the rocks.[4]

Is not a patron, my Lord, one who looks with unconcern on a man struggling for life in the water, and, when he has reached ground, encumbers[5] him with help? The notice which you have been pleased to take of my labors, had it been early, had been kind; but it has been delayed till I am indifferent,[6] and cannot enjoy it; till I am solitary, and cannot impart it; till I am known, and do not want it. I hope it is no very cynical asperity[7] not to confess obligations where no benefit has been received, or to be unwilling that the public should consider me as owing that to a patron, which Providence has enabled me to do for myself.

Having carried on my work thus far with so little obligation to any favorer of learning, I shall not be disappointed though I should conclude it, if less be possible, with less; for I have been long wakened from that dream of hope, in which I once boasted myself with so much exultation. 15

My Lord,
Your Lordship's most humble,
Most obedient servant,

Sam. Johnson

1. ***The World,*** a newspaper run by a friend of Johnson's.
2. ***"Le vainqueur . . . de la terre,"*** "The conqueror of the conqueror of the world." *[French]*
3. **repulse** (ri puls′), *v.* drive away.
4. **The shepherd . . . rocks.** Johnson is referring to a passage in the *Eclogues,* a collection of pastoral poems by the Latin poet Virgil (70–19 B.C.), that speaks of the cruelty of love.
5. **encumber** (en kum′bər), *v.* burden.
6. **indifferent** (in dif′ər ənt), *adj.* not interested.
7. asperity (a sper′ə tē), *n.* harshness.

Reading/Thinking Skills
Recognize Cause and Effect

Question Can you recognize cause and effect between Lord Chesterfield's "patronage" and Johnson's definition of patron? *(Possible response: The definition was probably triggered by this experience; we know, from the letter, that the relationship predated the dictionary, and we know that Chesterfield's patronage was rude and neglectful. Thus, we can assume it is Chesterfield that Johnson describes as "a wretch who supports with insolence and is repaid with flattery.")*

Check Test

1. What kind of writing does Johnson find most worth supporting? *(biography)*
2. According to "Dignity and Uses of Biography," why does Johnson feel narratives of history rarely contain lessons that apply to private life? *(Johnson feels that history deals with great events, while people's private lives are made up of small but humanly significant events.)*
3. What established Johnson's reputation as a scholar and a writer? *(the 1755 publication of his* Dictionary of the English Language*)*
4. According to Johnson's dictionary, what is remarkable about the word *hiss? (It is an example of onomatopoeia.)*
5. According to Johnson's "Letter to Chesterfield," how was Johnson received when he first visited Lord Chesterfield? *(He was enchanted by Chesterfield's pleasant reception, but received no encouragement.)*

Unit 4 Resource Book
Alternate Check Test, p. 45

BUILDING ENGLISH PROFICIENCY

Exploring Connotations

Help students understand that certain words suggest a variety of images.

1. Point out the use of *pride* (second paragraph of the letter) and *obligation* (last paragraph of the letter).
2. Have groups of students work together to construct two webs: one for either *pride* or *obligation* and one for a listed synonym (such as *conceit* for *pride* or *duty* for *obligation*) that brings a different set of images to mind. Invite students to use a thesaurus for help.

After Reading

MAKING CONNECTIONS

1. Students may point out that the difficulty level of the terms varies; they also may say that some of the terms seem quaint and archaic.

2. Students may point out that since Lord Chesterfield has no effective defense, he might choose silence.

3. Words that have remained the same: *bully, to curtail, to hiss.* Words that have changed: *lunch, essay, favorite.* Words change when they are used in different ways by different groups of people; predominant usage often wins out; sometimes word connotation overtakes denotation through extensive usage.

4. Students may identify Johnson's feelings in the definitions of words like *excise, lexicographer, patron,* and *pensioner;* students might suggest that rules of objectivity for dictionary entries had not yet been established.

5. Possible responses: Such expressions were standard at this time; Johnson may also have been making a show of respect; his usage of certain words, e.g., *distinguished* and *honor,* suggests irony.

6. Student answers should indicate if they agree with Johnson's assessment of biography and, if they agree, give reasons why.

7. Student responses will vary, but opinions should be supported through comparison with Johnson's views.

After Reading

Making Connections

Shaping Your Response

1. What do you think of Johnson's choices of vocabulary in his dictionary definitions?
2. If you were Lord Chesterfield, how would you respond to Johnson's letter?

Analyzing the Selections

3. Some of the words in Johnson's *Dictionary* have the same meanings today as they did in Johnson's time; the meanings of other words have changed considerably. Find examples of each. What reasons can you give for changes in a word's meaning over time?
4. Find examples of Johnson's revealing his own personality through his definitions and discuss what each example shows. Why do you suppose Johnson writes so personally in a reference work?
5. A **communication** between members of different social classes often reflects the writer's sense of status. Why do you suppose Johnson uses polite expressions like "My lord" and "Most obedient servant" in a letter written basically to convey his anger?
6. Do you agree with the values that Johnson finds in the literary form of biography in his essay "Dignity and Uses of Biography"? Explain.

Extending the Ideas

7. In your opinion, should a biographer tell all the truth—good and bad—about his or her subject?

Literary Focus: Connotation / Denotation

Copy these words from Johnson's *Dictionary* and write his denotation and connotation for each of them: *favorite, lexicographer, oats, patron, pension.* Then write a denotation and a connotation that you know for each of these words: *beauty, taxes, home, yellow, car.* Compare your responses with those of your classmates.

Vocabulary Study

Answer the following questions, giving reasons for your answers.

1. If the biographer treated his subject with *impartiality,* would he be critical, fair, full of praise, or telling only half the story?
2. If a biography were *calumnious,* what advice might you give to the biographer?
3. Are the leather binding and elaborate lettering on Johnson's *Dictionary* better examples of *judicious* or *extrinsic* features?
4. If a clerk copying quotations displayed *negligent* work habits, would Johnson praise him, scold him, or send him to a doctor?

LITERARY FOCUS: CONNOTATION/ DENOTATION

	Denotation	Connotation
favorite	a chosen companion	wretch who pleases
lexicographer	a writer of dictionaries	a harmless drudge
oats	a grain for horse	food in Scotland
patron	one who supports	a wretch
pension	an allowance . . .	pay for treason
beauty	good looks	a trap
taxes	money to support government	money squandered by government
home	where a family lives	warmth, comfort; *or* pain and disunity
yellow	a primary color	cowardly
car	a vehicle on wheels	symbol of status and sexual image

5. If Johnson found a *fallacy* in a dictionary manuscript, would he correct it, pronounce it, or answer it?
6. If the clerks experienced a period of *tranquillity,* were they fighting, eating, relaxing, or copying?
7. In addressing Lord Chesterfield with respect, was Johnson behaving with *insolence* or *propriety?*
8. Would Johnson have been justified in treating Chesterfield with greater *asperity?* Explain.
9. Which is the better example of an *expedient*—borrowing books from friends or his not getting money from Chesterfield?
10. In which does Johnson *censure* the most—his essay, letter, or dictionary entries?

Expressing Your Ideas

Writing Choices

Writer's Notebook Update Look back at the instances of unfairness listed in your notebook. Select one of those unfair acts and write a few sentences describing the situation.

Defining Slang Select ten slang or colloquial expressions you and your friends use and prepare personalized definitions for them. Work with other members of your class to compile a **dictionary of teenage expressions.**

Johnson Right or Wrong Select one of the following quotations from Johnson and write a brief **essay,** with supporting examples, in which you agree or disagree with his viewpoint.

- "Every man wishes to be wise, and they who cannot be wise are almost always cunning."
- "No man ever yet became great by imitation."
- "It is better to suffer wrong than to do it, and happier to be sometimes cheated than not to trust."

Other Options

Find Celebrity Details Select a celebrity currently being featured in magazines and tabloids. Collect pictures and clippings to make a **bulletin board display** of the biographical information revealed about this personality. Categorize your display into important and non-important details, pointing out those items which might be made up or exaggerated.

Chart the Famous Work with a group of classmates to survey a general biographical reference source. Before you begin, make a list of professions, such as Theater, Business, Art, Music, and Science. Tally the number of famous people that belong to each profession. Then construct a graph or chart that graphically compares the number of famous people in the professions you have chosen. In your display or presentation to the class, what generalizations can you make about why the numbers compare as they do?

VOCABULARY STUDY

1. fair
2. to either rewrite or hire a lawyer
3. extrinsic
4. scold him
5. correct it
6. relaxing
7. propriety
8. Harshness was justified by Chesterfield's groundless claims.
9. borrowing books
10. the letter

Unit 4 Resource Book
Vocabulary, p. 43
Vocabulary Test, p. 46

WRITING CHOICES

Writer's Notebook Update

You might suggest that students use Johnson's letter as an example of fully describing an unfair situation.

Defining Slang

Begin this activity by relating some of the words that were "cool" when you were a teenager.

Johnson Write or Wrong

The class might discuss Johnson's quotations before individuals begin writing.

Selection Test

Unit 4 Resource Book
pp. 47–48

OTHER OPTIONS

Find Celebrity Details

You may wish to begin by asking students to bring in magazines and tabloids dealing with celebrities for students to use for their bulletin board display. If bulletin board space is limited, you might assign students into three or four groups.

Chart the Famous

To supplement the chart, some students might check if any biographies are on newspaper bestseller lists. Other students might visit a bookstore and list the subjects of 20 biographies currently on the market. List all the people on the board and ask students to create a chart similar to the chart they have already made. Are professions represented in the same proportion as on the original chart?

Before Reading

Building Background

Ask if any students have read biographies or watched biographical films that seemed to bring the subject to life. Ask them to relate details.

Literary Focus

As you review characterization, you might draw students into a discussion of what is unique to each technique and what overlaps; for example, how are interactions affected by speech and behavior.

Writer's Notebook

Before students begin, they might note questions they would ask a new student with whom they would like to become acquainted. Suggest that the answers to such questions might be the basis for their lists.

More About James Boswell

Boswell and Johnson met in a London bookstore in 1763; the biography was published 28 years later, to the day. For the next 150 years, Boswell was remembered chiefly for the biography. Then, in the 1940s, his private papers and journals were discovered and eventually published, revealing a lively and penetrating commentator and diarist. His other works include

- *Boswell's London Journal* (1950)
- *Boswell on the Grand Tour* (1955)

Before Reading

from The Life of Samuel Johnson, LL.D.

by James Boswell

James Boswell
1740–1795

Son of a distinguished Scottish judge and educated at the universities of Glasgow, Edinburgh, and Utrecht (in Holland), Boswell practiced law in Scotland and later in England. He spent most of his literary career chronicling the life of Samuel Johnson, first in *Journal of a Tour to the Hebrides* (1785), an account of a trip he and Johnson took to the western isles of Scotland, and later in his masterpiece of biography, *The Life of Samuel Johnson, LL.D.* (1791). Boswell, a member of the Literary Club, which met weekly for conversation at The Turk's Head Tavern, recorded Johnson's conversations and activities. Although Boswell himself was witty and charming, he is most remembered for his accurate reports of the brilliant witticisms of Johnson.

Building Background

The Perfect Biography "I am absolutely certain," wrote Boswell, "that my mode of biography, which gives not only a history of Johnson's visible progress through the world, and of his publications, but a view of his mind, in his letters and conversations, is the most perfect that can be conceived, and will be more of a Life than any work that has ever yet appeared." How had Boswell collected the material for this perfect biography? In the twenty-one years of his friendship with Samuel Johnson, Boswell kept a very detailed journal, often recording Johnson's conversations word for word as he spoke. Following Johnson's death, Boswell conducted extensive interviews with many of Johnson's contemporaries. He prepared questionnaires for Johnson's closest friends. He acquired letters written by Johnson and to Johnson. He ran "half over London" to verify a date or confirm a piece of information. Then Boswell selected those anecdotes which were most characteristic of the Johnson he knew and admired and transformed them into vivid, lifelike scenes.

Literary Focus

Characterization The techniques an author uses to develop the personality of a character, fictional or real, are called **characterization.** An author can describe any or all of the following in presenting each character:

- physical appearance
- personality traits
- thoughts and feelings
- speech and behavior
- interactions with other characters

As you read his characterization of Johnson, notice which techniques Boswell uses most often.

Writer's Notebook

Just the Facts? You are about to read portions of the biography of a famous literary figure. Make a list of the kinds of information you would expect to learn about the subject of any biography.

SUPPORT MATERIALS OVERVIEW

Unit 4 Resource Book
- Graphic Organizer, p. 49
- Study Guide, p. 50
- Vocabulary, p. 51
- Grammar, p. 52
- Alternate Check Test, p. 53
- Vocabulary Test, p. 54
- Selection Test, pp. 55–56

Building English Proficiency
- Selection Summaries
- Activities, p. 225

Reading, Writing & Grammar SkillBook
- Writing, pp. 119–120
- Grammar, Usage, and Mechanics, pp. 175–176, 180–181, 210–212

Technology
- Audiotape
- Personal Journal Software
- Custom Literature Database: Additional selections by James Boswell can be found on the database.
- Test Generator Software

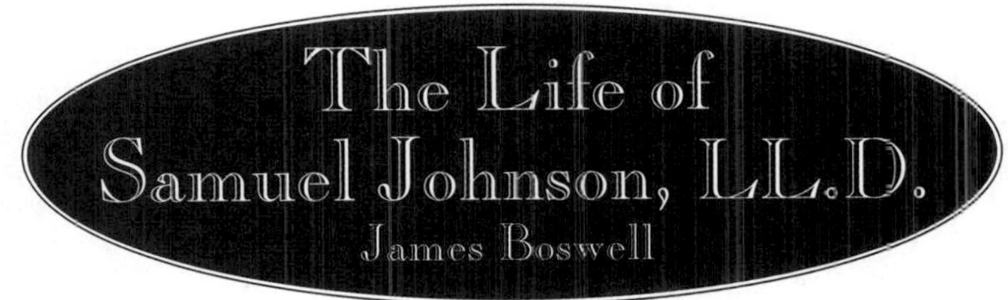

The Life of Samuel Johnson, LL.D.

James Boswell

On London

Talking of a London life, he said, "The happiness of London is not to be conceived but by those who have been in it. I will venture to say, there is more learning and science within the circumference of ten miles from where we now sit, than in all the rest of the kingdom."

BOSWELL. "The only disadvantage is the great distance at which people live from one another."

JOHNSON. "Yes, Sir; but that is occasioned by the largeness of it, which is the cause of all the other advantages."

BOSWELL. "Sometimes I have been in the humor of wishing to retire to a desert."

JOHNSON. "Sir, you have desert enough in
1 Scotland."

I suggested a doubt, that if I were to reside in London, the exquisite zest with which I relished it in occasional visits might go off, and I might grow tired of it.

JOHNSON. "Why, Sir, you find no man, at all intellectual, who is willing to leave London. No, Sir, when a man is tired of London, he is tired of life; for there is in London all that life can afford."

On Eating

At supper, this night he talked of good eating with uncommon satisfaction. "Some people (said he) have a foolish way of not minding, or pretending not to mind, what they eat. For my part, I mind my belly very studiously, and very carefully; for I look upon it that he who does not mind his belly will hardly mind anything else."

He now appeared to me *Jean Bull philosophe,*[1] and he was, for the moment, not only serious but vehement.[2] Yet I have heard him, upon other occasions, talk with great contempt of people who were anxious to gratify their palates; and the 206th number of his *Rambler* is a masterly essay against gulosity.[3] His practice, indeed, I must acknowledge, may be considered as casting the balance of his different opinions upon this subject, for I never knew any man who relished good eating more than he did. When at table, he was totally absorbed in the business of the moment; his looks seemed riveted to his plate; nor would he, unless when in very high company, say one word, or even pay the least attention to what was said by others, till he had satisfied his appetite, which was so fierce, and indulged with such intenseness, that while in the act of eating, the veins of his forehead swelled, and generally a strong perspiration was visible. To those whose sensations were delicate, this could not but be disgusting; and it was doubtless not very suitable to the character of a philosopher, who should be distinguished by self-command. But it must be owned that Johnson, though he could be rigidly *abstemious,*[4]
was not a *temperate* man either in eating or drink- 2
ing. He could refrain, but he could not use moderately. He told me that he had fasted two

1. ***Jean Bull philosophe,*** John Bull the philosopher. *[French]* John Bull is the personification of the British nation, the typical Englishman.
2. vehement (vē′ə mənt), *adj.* forceful.
3. **gulosity** (gyü los′i tē), *n.* excessive appetite.
4. abstemious (ab stē′mē əs), *adj.* moderate.

During Reading

Selection Objectives

- to identify and analyze characterization techniques
- to examine the role of adjectives in characterization
- to create a mental picture of Samuel Johnson, based on Boswell's writings

Unit 4 Resource Book
Graphic Organizer, p. 49
Study Guide, p. 50

Theme Link

The theme, Other People's Lives, is explored through Boswell's record of Johnson's life, particularly Boswell's exploration of the subject's motives, thought processes, and prejudices.

Vocabulary Preview

vehement, forceful
abstemious, moderate
arduous, difficult
salutary, beneficial
pernicious, harmful

Students can add the words and definitions to their Writer's Notebooks.

1 Literary Focus Characterization

In the dictionary, under *oats*, Johnson insults the Scots; here, he suggests that Scotland is an intellectual desert.

Question What do these feelings reveal about Johnson? *(that he has prejudices; that he enjoys trading "barbs" with his friend Boswell)*

2 Literary Focus Characterization

Question What does Boswell mean when he writes that Johnson was not temperate, but could be abstemious? *(Possible response: that Johnson's personality, like most people's, is a blend of contradictory elements)*

SELECTION SUMMARY

The Life of Samuel Johnson, LL.D.

In this excerpt from Boswell's biography of Johnson, the writer employs varied techniques to create character. In a series of conversations with the author, Johnson offers his views on a variety of subjects—from city life and eating to social structure and the human capacity for pity. In the final section, Boswell pictures the great man as he knew him, describing Johnson's appearance and how he moved; his personality, thoughts, feelings, and speech; and how Johnson interacted with colleagues and friends.

*For summaries in other languages, see the **Building English Proficiency** book.*

Art Study

Response to Caption Questions Johnson is "riveted to his plate." Boswell appears to be too busy observing Johnson to eat.

Visual Literacy Cartoons, such as "A Chop House," were published in newspapers and periodicals, more to amuse the reader than to satirize the subject.

Question From what you have learned about Johnson, would he have been insulted by this caricature? *(Possible response: It is unlikely that he would have minded the cartoon. In his essay on biography, he claimed that ordinary details, like eating, were important and that the truth should be told.)*

3 Literary Focus

Characterization

Question How would you characterize Johnson's interactions with others? *(Possible response: Johnson was opinionated and could be tart, irascible, and insulting; he could also be generous and charming and was, obviously, a great wit and a master conversationalist.)*

EDITORIAL NOTE This excerpt has been shortened for length. For different selections from *The Life of Samuel Johnson, LL.D.*, see the Custom Literature Database.

James Boswell (left) and Samuel Johnson (right) are shown dining in London in this cartoon entitled "A Chop House." In what ways does the cartoonist's depiction of Johnson's eating habits agree with Boswell's description of those habits? Why do you think Boswell is shown in this pose?

days without inconvenience, and that he had never been hungry but once. They who beheld with wonder how much he ate upon all occasions when his dinner was to his taste could not easily conceive what he must have meant by hunger, and not only was he remarkable for the extraordinary quantity which he ate, but he was, or affected to be, a man of very nice discernment[5] in the science of cookery. He used to descant[6] critically on the dishes which had been at table where he had dined or supped, and to recollect minutely what he had liked.

He about the same time was so much displeased with the performances of a nobleman's French cook, that he exclaimed with vehemence, "I'd throw such a rascal into the river"; and he then proceeded to alarm a lady at whose house he was to sup, by the following manifesto[7] of his skill: "I, Madam, who live at a variety of good tables, am a much better judge of cookery, than any person who has a very tolerable cook, but lives much at home; for his palate is gradually adapted to the taste of his cook; whereas, Madam, in trying by a wider range, I can more exquisitely judge."

When invited to dine, even with an intimate friend, he was not pleased if something better than a plain dinner was not prepared for him. I have heard him say on such an occasion, "This was a good dinner enough, to be sure: but it was not a dinner to *ask* a man to."

On the other hand, he was wont to express, with great glee, his satisfaction when he had been entertained quite to his mind. One day when he had dined with his neighbor and landlord, in Boltcourt, Mr. Allen, the printer, whose old housekeeper had studied his taste in everything, he pronounced this eulogy:[8] "Sir, we could not have had a better dinner, had there been a *Synod*[9] *of Cooks.*" **3**

5. **discernment** (də zėrn′mənt), *n.* judgment.
6. **descant** (des kant′), *v.* talk at great length.
7. **manifesto** (man′ə fes′tō), *n.* public declaration.
8. **eulogy** (yü′lə jē), *n.* speech of praise.
9. **synod** (sin′əd), *n.* convention.

MINI-LESSON: GRAMMAR

Personal Pronouns

On page 362, Boswell never refers to Johnson by name. He uses only personal pronouns to refer to his friend.

Teach Tell students that personal pronouns are either in the nominative case (I, we, he, she, they, it, you), the objective case (me, us, him, her, them, it, you), or the possessive case with no apostrophe (my, mine, our, ours, his, her, hers, their, theirs, its, your, yours). Ask students what pronouns they would expect to see most often in a biography. *(pronouns that refer to the biography's subject)*

Activity Ideas

- Have students test the answer to the above question. In the chart below, they should write in the appropriate column each personal pronoun on page 362 and tally the number of times it is used.
- For each pronoun on page 362, ask students to determine to whom the pronoun refers.

Frequency of Personal Pronouns Used on Page 362

Nominative	Objective	Possessive

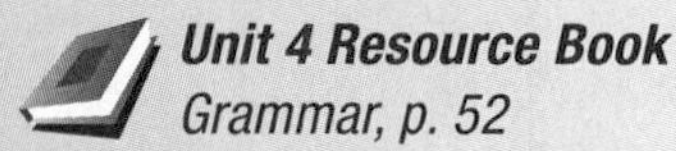

Unit 4 Resource Book
Grammar, p. 52

On the Dictionary

That he was fully aware of the arduous[10] nature of the undertaking, he acknowledges; and shows himself perfectly sensible of it in the conclusion of this "Plan"; but he had a noble consciousness of his own abilities, which enabled him to go on with undaunted spirit.

Dr. Adams found him one day busy at his Dictionary, when the following dialogue ensued.

ADAMS. "This is a great work, Sir. How are you to get all the etymologies?"[11]

JOHNSON. "Why, Sir, here is a shelf with Junius, and Skinner,[12] and others; and there is a Welsh gentleman who has published a collection of Welsh proverbs, who will help me with the Welsh."

ADAMS. "But, Sir, how can you do this in three years?"

JOHNSON. "Sir, I have no doubt that I can do it in three years."

ADAMS. "But the French Academy,[13] which consists of forty members, took forty years to compile their Dictionary."

JOHNSON. "Sir, thus it is. This is the proportion. Let me see; forty times forty is sixteen hundred. As three to sixteen hundred, so is the proportion of an Englishman to a Frenchman."

With so much ease and pleasantry could he talk of that prodigious[14] labor which he had undertaken to execute.

On Books and Reading

JOHNSON. "Sir, I love the acquaintance of young people; because, in the first place, I don't like to think myself growing old. In the next place, young acquaintances must last longest, if they do last; and then, Sir, young men have more virtue than old men; they have more generous sentiments in every respect. I love the young dogs of this age: they have more wit and humor and knowledge of life than we had; but then the dogs are not so good scholars. Sir, in my early years I read very hard. It is a sad reflection, but a true one, that I knew almost as much at eighteen as I do now. My judgment, to be sure, was not so good; but I had all the facts. I remember very well, when I was at Oxford, an old gentleman said to me, 'Young man, ply your book diligently now, and acquire a stock of knowledge; for when years come upon you, you will find that poring upon books will be but an irksome task.'"

JOHNSON. "Idleness is a disease which must be combated; but I would not advise a rigid adherence to a particular plan of study. I myself have never persisted in any plan for two days together. A man ought to read just as inclination leads him: for what he reads as a task will do him little good. A young man should read five hours in a day, and so may acquire a great deal of knowledge." 4

On Pity

JOHNSON. "Pity is not natural to man. Children are always cruel. Savages are cruel. Pity is acquired and improved by the cultivation of reason. We may have uneasy sensations for seeing a creature in distress, without pity; for we have not pity unless we wish to relieve them. 5
When I am on my way to dine with a friend, and finding it late, have bid the coachman make haste, if I happen to attend when he whips his horses, I may feel unpleasantly that the animals are put to pain, but I do not wish him to desist. No, sir, I wish him to drive on."

10. **arduous** (är′jü əs), *adj.* difficult.
11. **etymology** (et′ə mol′ə jē), *n.* word origin.
12. **Junius . . . Skinner.** Their books were sources for many of Johnson's etymologies for the Germanic languages.
13. **French Academy,** a society of men and women of letters whose purpose is to uphold correct usage of the French language.
14. **prodigious** (prə dij′əs), *adj.* vast.

4 Reading/Thinking Skills
Find the Main Idea

Question What do you think is the main idea of Johnson's comments on books and reading? *(One's teens and early twenties provide a great opportunity for reading and storing up knowledge; wisdom, however, comes through experience, over time; true learning comes only through pursuing what one is interested in.)*

5 Reading/Thinking Skills
Draw Conclusions

Questions Do you think that Johnson's views on pity reflect his character or the truth about humanity? *(Possible responses: Some will be convinced by Johnson's contention that pity exists only when one is willing to relieve it. Others may argue that Johnson's views reflected his own "hard shell.")* What does his reasoning on this subject suggest about his character? *(He is a man of reason; he is not sentimental.)*

Literary Criticism

"*The Life of Johnson* is assuredly . . . a very great work. Homer is not more decidedly the first of heroic poets, Shakespeare is not more decidedly the first of dramatists . . . than Boswell is the first of biographers. He has no second."

Thomas Babington Macaulay
Samuel Johnson

Considering an Interviewing Strategy

Help students focus on the way in which Boswell may have gathered information on Samuel Johnson.

1. Divide students into groups to invent a questionnaire to be filled out by *friends* of one of these subjects: a teacher or family member who just did something heroic, a famous author, a political figure, or an entertainment personality.

2. Have each group list ten questions that might produce original, interesting information for a TV interview.

3. Invite groups to exchange questionnaires and brainstorm answers for the questions they receive. Then ask groups to choose representatives to play the roles of interviewer and subject. Have students videotape their interviews and present them to the class.

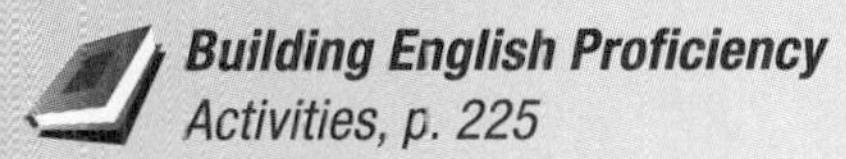
Building English Proficiency
Activities, p. 225

6 Reading/Thinking Skills
Recognizing Values

Question What values do you recognize in Johnson's positive reply to Boswell's question about dining after a hanging? *(Possible responses: Johnson places little value on pity or friendship; or Johnson values reason and controls his emotions.)*

7 Literary Focus
Characterization

You might review with students that an anecdote is a short account of an interesting incident or single event, especially one in the life of a person.

Questions How does Boswell use anecdote in his characterization of Johnson? *(Boswell includes anecdotes that illustrate various aspects of Johnson's personality.)* What does the anecdote about Mrs. Macaulay reveal about Johnson's beliefs? *(Possible responses: He upholds the social order of his day; he believes that human beings always create social orders.)*

8 Reading/Thinking Skills
Compare and Contrast

Questions How would you compare Johnson's thoughts on the existing social order with his beliefs on the subject of slavery? *(He upholds the social order while opposing slavery.)* Do you think there is a flaw in this reasoning? *(Some students may think his stance is illogical; others might note that the Macaulay anecdote suggests he believes less in the existing social order than in the human propensity for ordering society; while there may always be a lowest rung on the ladder, it need not be populated with the enslaved.)*

Talking of our feeling for the distresses of others:

JOHNSON. "Why, Sir, there is much noise made about it, but it is greatly exaggerated. No, Sir, we have a certain degree of feeling to prompt us to do good; more than that, Providence does not intend. It would be misery to no purpose."

BOSWELL. "But suppose now, Sir, that one of your intimate friends were apprehended for an offense for which he might be hanged."

JOHNSON. "I should do what I could to bail him, and give him any other assistance; but if he were once fairly hanged, I should not suffer."

BOSWELL. "Would you eat your dinner that day, Sir?"

JOHNSON. "Yes, Sir; and eat it as if he were eating it with me. Why, there's Baretti[15] who is to be tried for his life tomorrow, friends have risen up for him on every side; yet if he should be hanged, none of them will eat a slice of plum pudding the less. Sir, that sympathetic feeling
6 goes a very little way in depressing the mind."

The Social Order

I described to him an impudent[16] fellow from Scotland, who affected to be a savage, and railed at all established systems.

JOHNSON. "There is nothing surprising in this, Sir. He wants to make himself conspicuous. He would tumble in a hogsty, as long as you looked at him and called to him to come out. But let him alone, never mind him, and he'll soon give it over."

I added that the same person maintained that there was no distinction between virtue and vice.

JOHNSON. "Why, Sir, if the fellow does not think as he speaks, he is lying; and I see not what honor he can propose to himself from having the character of a liar. But if he does really think that there is no distinction between virtue and vice, why, Sir, when he leaves our houses let us count our spoons."

He again insisted on the duty of maintaining subordination of rank.

JOHNSON. "Sir, I would no more deprive a nobleman of his respect, than of his money. I consider myself as acting a part in the great system of society, and I do to others as I would have them to do to me. I would behave to a nobleman as I should expect he would behave to me, were I a nobleman and he Sam Johnson. Sir, there is one Mrs. Macaulay in this town, a great republican. One day when I was at her house, I put on a very grave countenance,[17] and said to her, 'Madam, I am now become a convert to your way of thinking. I am convinced that all mankind are upon an equal footing; and to give you an unquestionable proof, Madam, that I am in earnest, here is a very sensible, civil, well-behaved fellow-citizen, your footman; I desire that he may be allowed to sit down and dine
with us.' I thus, Sir, showed her the absurdity of 7
the leveling doctrine. She has never liked me since. Sir, your levelers wish to level *down* as far as themselves; but they cannot bear leveling *up* to themselves. They would all have some people under them; why not then have some people above them?"

On Slavery

After supper I accompanied him to his apartment, and at my request he dictated to me an argument in favor of the negro who was then claiming his liberty, in an action in the Court of Session in Scotland. He had always been very
zealous[18] against slavery in every form, in which 8
I with all deference[19] thought that he discovered "a zeal without knowledge." Upon one occasion, when in company with some very grave

15. **Baretti,** Johnson's friend who was tried and acquitted for murder.
16. **impudent** (im′pyə dənt), *adj.* very rude.
17. **countenance** (koun′tə nəns), *n.* expression.
18. **zealous** (zel′əs), *adj.* enthusiastic.
19. **deference** (def′ər əns), *n.* respect.

MINI-LESSON: LITERARY FOCUS
Characterization

Teach Have students use what they have learned in this selection to draw a picture of Samuel Johnson. For each element illustrated in the picture, the student should write how the author conveyed that piece of information. An arrow should connect each part of the picture to its corresponding explanation. Have students compare their pictures to determine similarities and differences. Students can use their explanations to defend their portraits.

Activity Ideas

- Have students write a paragraph that characterizes a friend or family member.
- Have students summarize the characterization of Samuel Johnson presented by Boswell. Ask students to discuss whether they would rather have dinner or a debate with Mr. Johnson, based on Boswell's observations.

men at Oxford, his toast was, "Here's to the next insurrection of the negroes in the West Indies."

His violent prejudice against our West Indian and American settlers appeared whenever there was an opportunity. Towards the conclusion of his "Taxation no Tyranny," he says "how is it that we hear the loudest yelps for liberty among the drivers of negroes?"

On Johnson's Character

9 His figure was large and well-formed, and his countenance of the cast of an ancient statue; yet his appearance was rendered strange and somewhat uncouth, by convulsive cramps, by the scars of that distemper which it was once imagined the royal touch could cure,[20] and by a slovenly[21] mode of dress. He had the use only of one eye; yet so much does mind govern, and even supply the deficiency of organs, that his visual perceptions, as far as they extended, were uncommonly quick and accurate. So morbid was his temperament, that he never knew the natural joy of a free and vigorous use of his limbs; when he walked, it was like the struggling gait of one in fetters;[22] when he rode, he had no command or direction of his horse, but was carried as if in a balloon. 10 That with his constitution and habits of life he should have lived seventy-five years, is a proof that an inherent *vivida vis*,[23] is a powerful preservative of the human frame.

He was prone to superstition, but not to credulity.[24] Though his imagination might incline him to a belief of the marvelous and the mysterious, his vigorous reason examined the evidence with jealousy. He was a sincere and zealous Christian, of high Church-of-England and monarchical principles, which he would not tamely suffer to be questioned; and had, perhaps, at an early period, narrowed his mind somewhat too much, both as to religion and politics. His being impressed with the danger of extreme latitude[25] in either, though he was of a very independent spirit, occasioned his appearing somewhat unfavorable to the prevalence of that noble freedom of sentiment which is the best possession of man. Nor can it be denied, that he had many prejudices; which, however, frequently suggested many of his pointed sayings, that rather show a playfulness of fancy than 11 any settled malignity. He was steady and inflexible in maintaining the obligations of religion and morality; both from a regard for the order of society, and from a veneration[26] for the Great Source of all order: correct, nay stern in his taste; hard to please, and easily offended; impetuous[27] and irritable in his temper, but of a most humane and benevolent heart, which showed itself not only in a most liberal charity, as far as his circumstances would allow, but in a thousand instances of active benevolence.

He was afflicted with a bodily disease, which made him often restless and fretful; and with a constitutional melancholy, the clouds of which darkened the brightness of his fancy, and gave a gloomy cast to his whole course of thinking: we, therefore, ought not to wonder at his sallies of impatience and passion at any time; especially when provoked by obtrusive ignorance, or presuming petulance;[28] and allowance must be made for his uttering hasty and satirical sallies even against his best friends. And, surely, when it is considered, that "amidst sickness and sorrow," he exerted his faculties in so many works for the benefit of mankind and particularly that he achieved the great and admirable Dictionary of our language, we must be astonished at his resolution.

20. **distemper . . . cure.** Johnson had scrofula which, it was believed, could be cured by the touch of a monarch. Although he was taken to Queen Anne as a young child, he was not cured.
21. **slovenly** (sluv′ən lē), *adj.* untidy.
22. **fetter** (fet′ər), *n.* chain or shackle for the feet.
23. ***vivida vis,*** life force. *[Latin]*
24. **credulity** (krə dü′lə tē), *n.* a too great readiness to believe.
25. **latitude** (lat′ə tüd), *n.* freedom.
26. **veneration** (ven′ə rā′shən), *n.* respect.
27. **impetuous** (im pech′ü əs), *adj.* impulsive.
28. **petulance** (pech′ə ləns), *n.* bad temper.

9 Literary Focus: Characterization

Question How does Boswell's characterization of Johnson differ in this passage from previous sections of the biography? *(Possible response: For the first time, Boswell describes Johnson's physical appearance.)*

10 Literary Element: Simile

Question How is this description of Johnson on horseback an example of simile? *(Boswell states that Johnson on horseback is "as if in a balloon.")*

11 Reading/Thinking Skills: Apply

Question Apply Boswell's comment on prejudices and humor to Johnson's remarks on Roman Catholics and Scots. Do you think such remarks were intended to amuse or to slight? *(Responses will vary. Boswell, himself a Scot, states that they "show a playfulness of fancy." It is probable that while they were delivered to amuse, they were reflections of his true feelings.)*

BUILDING ENGLISH PROFICIENCY

Exploring Biography

Boswell describes Johnson's good and bad qualities. He also tells anecdotes (little stories) about what Johnson said and did. Either of the following activities will give students some experience in creating biography.

Activity Ideas

- Have students write a biography of themselves as a middle-aged success. Encourage them to invent the kind of life they hope to have. Have them include details about achievements, health, family life, good and bad qualities or experiences, and an anecdote that readers might find "instructive."
- Ask groups of students to work together to invent life stories of a pet, wild animal, zoo animal, or barnyard animal. Like the biographydescribed above, this one should include positive and negative qualities and experiences.

12 Literary Focus
Characterization

Question What characterization techniques does Boswell use in his section "On Johnson's Character"? Give examples for each technique.

Possible responses

- *physical appearance*—"His figure was large and well-formed"
- *personality traits*—"He loved praise, when it was brought to him; but was too proud to seek for it."
- *thoughts and feelings*—"But his superiority over other learned men consisted chiefly . . . in the art of using his mind" *and* "He suffered from the gloom that perpetually haunted him"
- *speech and behavior*—"He had accustomed himself to such accuracy in his . . . conversation, that he at all times expressed his thoughts with great force, and an elegant choice of language"
- *interactions with others*—"the heartiest merriment was often enjoyed in his company"

Check Test

1. According to Johnson, what gives London its advantage over other places? *(its size)*

2. Why did Boswell think Johnson's eating habits might be found disgusting by some? *(His appetite was so fierce and intense that the veins of his forehead swelled, and he broke out in a sweat.)*

3. According to Johnson, how many hours a day should a young man spend reading? *(five hours a day)*

4. How did Johnson's illnesses affect his thinking? *(It gave his thinking a gloomy cast.)*

5. Why, according to Boswell, did Johnson not seek praise? *(He was too proud.)*

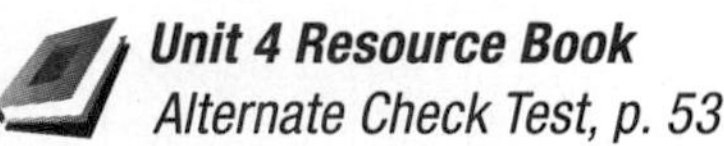

Unit 4 Resource Book
Alternate Check Test, p. 53

12 The solemn text, "of him to whom much is given, much will be required," seems to have been ever present to his mind, in a rigorous sense, and to have made him dissatisfied with his labors and acts of goodness, however comparatively great; so that the unavoidable consciousness of his superiority was, in that respect, a cause of disquiet. He suffered so much from this, and from the gloom which perpetually haunted him, and made solitude frightful, that it may be said of him, "If in this life only he had hope, he was of all men most miserable."

He loved praise, when it was brought to him; but was too proud to seek for it. He was somewhat susceptible of flattery. As he was general and unconfined in his studies, he cannot be considered as master of any one particular science; but he had accumulated a vast and various collection of learning and knowledge, which was so arranged in his mind, as to be ever in readiness to be brought forth. But his superiority over other learned men consisted chiefly in what may be called the art of thinking, the art of using his mind; a certain continual power of seizing the useful substance of all that he knew, and exhibiting it in a clear and forcible manner; so that knowledge, which we often see to be no better than lumber in men of dull understanding, was, in him true, evident, and actual wisdom.

His moral precepts[29] are practical; for they are drawn from an intimate acquaintance with human nature. His maxims carry conviction; for they are founded on the basis of common sense, and a very attentive and minute survey of real life. His mind was so full of imagery, that he might have been perpetually a poet; yet it is remarkable, that, however rich his prose is in this respect, his poetical pieces, in general, have not much of that splendor, but are rather distinguished by strong sentiment, and acute observation, conveyed in harmonious and energetic verse, particularly in heroic couplets. Though usually grave, and even awful in his deportment, he possessed uncommon and peculiar powers of wit and humor; he frequently indulged himself in colloquial pleasantry; and the heartiest merriment was often enjoyed in his company; with this great advantage, that, as it was entirely free from any poisonous tincture[30] of vice or impiety, it was salutary[31] to those who shared in it.

He had accustomed himself to such accuracy in his common conversation, that he at all times expressed his thoughts with great force, and an elegant choice of language, the effect of which was aided by his having a loud voice, and a slow deliberate utterance. In him were united a most logical head with a most fertile imagination, which gave him an extraordinary advantage in arguing: for he could reason close or wide, as he saw best for the moment. Exulting in his intellectual strength and dexterity, he could, when he pleased, be the greatest sophist[32] that ever contended in the lists of declamation; and, from a spirit of contradiction, and a delight in showing his powers, he would often maintain the wrong side with equal warmth and ingenuity: so that, when there was an audience, his real opinions could seldom be gathered from his talk; though, when he was in company with a single friend, he would discuss a subject with genuine fairness; but he was too conscientious to make error permanent and pernicious,[33] by deliberately writing it; and, in all his numerous works, he earnestly inculcated[34] what appeared to him to be the truth; his piety being constant, and the ruling principle of all his conduct.

Such was Samuel Johnson, a man whose talents, acquirements, and virtues were so extraordinary, that the more his character is considered the more he will be regarded by the present age, and by posterity, with admiration and reverence.

29. **precept** (prē′sept), *n.* principle.
30. **tincture** (tingk′chər), *n.* trace; tinge.
31. **salutary** (sal′yə ter′ē), *adj.* beneficial.
32. **sophist** (sof′ist), *n.* clever but misleading speaker.
33. **pernicious** (pər nish′əs), *adj.* harmful.
34. **inculcate** (in kul′kāt), *v.* teach by repetition.

MINI-LESSON: VOCABULARY
Using Adjectives

Teach Boswell's use of colorful adjectives helps to create details for his portrait of Johnson. Review with the class the vocabulary words in this selection. Then direct each student to list four adjectives that describe Johnson. For each word, students should write a sentence supporting its inclusion in the list. Have students share their choices and sentences with the class.

Activity Ideas

- Have students determine which part of speech they think told them the most vivid information about Johnson—adjectives, adverbs, verbs, or nouns.
- Have students use the lists they created above to identify other people those vocabulary words describe.
- Ask students to choose four of the adjectives to describe a modern celebrity.

After Reading

Making Connections

Shaping Your Response

1. List the personal qualities you think a biographer should have.
2. If ★ is *Okay* and ★★★★★ is *Excellent,* how many stars do you think Johnson would have given Boswell's biography?
3. Would you enjoy meeting and talking with Samuel Johnson? Why or why not?

Analyzing the Biography

4. What role does Boswell play in his biography of Johnson? Why might he act this way?
5. Why do you think Boswell sometimes reports Johnson's conversations as if they were part of a play?
6. List some of the negative characteristics of Boswell's Johnson. In your opinion, why might Boswell choose to reveal so many negative characteristics?
7. What do you think is the overall impression Boswell wants to give about Johnson?

Extending the Ideas

8. In your opinion, what is a proper balance between the public's "right to know" and an individual's right to privacy; that is, how much of a person's private life should be revealed by a biographer?
9. How might the **communication** of the facts of a person's life be affected by differences in group identities between a biographer and a subject?

Literary Focus: Characterization

Jot down ten characteristics of Samuel Johnson that stand out in Boswell's characterization. Then place each of the characteristics on a chart like the one below, under as many heads as you think are appropriate. Are the characteristics evenly divided among the techniques, or does your list suggest that Boswell favors one particular kind of characterization?

Techniques of Characterization	Characteristics Recalled
Physical appearance	
Personality traits	
Thoughts and feelings	
Speech and behavior	
Interactions with other characters	

After Reading

MAKING CONNECTIONS

1. Possible responses: integrity, objectivity, curiosity, keen interest, observational and analytical skills

2. Answers will vary. Sample: 4 stars—good use of details; masterful recreation of conversations; highly entertaining

3. Students may say no, that he seems slovenly and ill-mannered; others may say yes, that his wit and his views are interesting.

4. Students may respond that Boswell acts as a foil to Johnson's wit and wisdom, asking questions and providing transitions; students might say that Boswell saw this as a technique for presenting Johnson's views in the first person.

5. Students might respond that these dramatic scenes effectively characterize Johnson.

6. Students may say Johnson was prejudiced, stern, hard to please, easily offended, impetuous, irritable, and slovenly; Boswell felt his job was to present both strong and weak characteristics of his subject to present a true portrait.

7. Possible response: that Johnson was a brilliant, fascinating, complex, and eccentric man

8. Some students may say everyone has a basic right to privacy; others may say that public figures are aware that one of the prices of fame is the loss of privacy.

9. Possible response: A biographer born to privilege may find it difficult to comprehend the personal and professional struggles of a person from more modest circumstances. A biographer of modest background might resent the privileges enjoyed by his or her subject and inject that resentment onto the biography.

LITERARY FOCUS: CHARACTERIZATION

Techniques of Characterization	Characteristics Recalled
Physical appearance	1. large; well-formed 2. awkward; slovenly
Personality traits	1. sense of humor 2. highly prejudiced
Thoughts and feelings	1. upheld social order and state church 2. hated slavery
Speech and behavior	1. spoke with force 2. ate voraciously
Interactions with other characters	1. wonderful conversationalist 2. capable of great merriment

VOCABULARY STUDY

Vocabulary words, as used in context, should reflect correct meanings and connotations.

More Practice Write an antonym for each of the adjectives listed.

Possible responses

- abstemious/gluttonous
- arduous/easy
- impetuous/reasoned
- impudent/polite
- pernicious/beneficial
- salutary/harmful
- slovenly/neat
- vehement/calm
- zealous/noncommittal

Unit 4 Resource Book
Vocabulary, p. 51
Vocabulary Test, p. 54

WRITING CHOICES

Writer's Notebook Update

You might lead a discussion in which students discuss whether the expected or unexpected information added more color to Boswell's biography.

A Modern Boswell

You might suggest that students ask their subjects to give their thoughts on the topic of pity. Compare their responses to Johnson's response.

Selection Test

Unit 4 Resource Book
pp. 55–56

Transparency Collection
Fine Art Writing Prompt 7

Vocabulary Study

abstemeous
arduous
impetuous
impudent
pernicious
salutary
slovenly
vehement
zealous

Select five of the adjectives listed and write a description of a verbal argument between two rivals. Be sure that each sentence demonstrates your understanding of the word's meaning. Use your Glossary, if necessary.

Expressing Your Ideas

Writing Choices

Writer's Notebook Update Go back to your list of biographical information and place a check mark by each kind of information that you learned about Johnson. Did Boswell provide you with the information you expected to get? Make a list of the topics Boswell covered that you hadn't anticipated.

A Modern Boswell You have observed your friends and family members for many years. Who better, then, to write a **biographical sketch** of one of them than you? Recall a special incident that reveals an important aspect of your family member's personality. Following Boswell's example, you might retell the incident in dialogue, with characters' names added.

About Me Write—not the entire history of your life thus far—but one **autobiographical anecdote** that will reveal an important quality of your character. Review the techniques of characterization listed in the Literary Focus and try to use at least three of those techniques in your characterization of yourself.

Other Options

Advertise Boswell's Book Boswell's *The Life of Samuel Johnson, LL.D.* had to compete with several other biographies issued soon after Johnson's death. Create a **poster** for a bookseller's window to advertise Boswell's book. What about Boswell's portrait of Johnson can you emphasize to create interest in this particular biography?

The Time of Your Life Construct a **time line** of your life, including not only milestone events (maybe moving to a new town or getting your driver's license) but also small but memorable incidents (maybe the first holiday you can remember or your first bicycle). Illustrate your time line with your own drawings, family snapshots, and found objects such as ticket stubs, postcards, and letters.

"Let Me Ask You . . ." In the Writing Workshop that follows, you will have a chance to write a biography of someone you know. With your teacher's help, plan and conduct an **interview** of the subject of your biography. Be sure to have a list of questions before you talk to your subject. Listen carefully (see page 380) and be sure to record your subject's words accurately.

OTHER OPTIONS

Advertise Boswell's Book

Students might work in groups to decide which techniques of characterization or "scenes" from the book could be emphasized graphically in a poster.

"Let Me Ask You . . ."

Students should prepare a list of 10 questions to ask during their interview. They can share their proposed questions with a partner and then revise the questions in response to feedback.

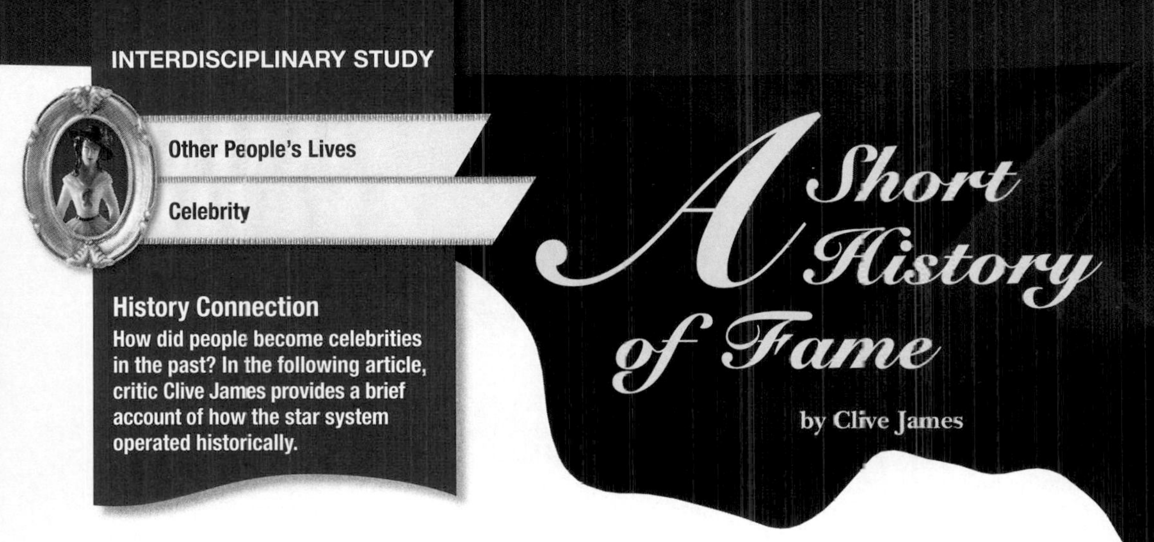

A Short History of Fame

by Clive James

History Connection
How did people become celebrities in the past? In the following article, critic Clive James provides a brief account of how the star system operated historically.

There was always fame. As long as there have been human beings, there has always been fame. It's a human weakness.

No other kind of living creature knows anything about fame, not even the peacock, who certainly craves attention but lacks the brain to know why. In every human group of any size, someone becomes famous, and it's a fair bet this has always been true. . . . When people lived in caves, every cave had someone famous in it. But that was as far as his, or her, fame went. There was no way of transmitting it except to write on the cave wall. By the time the cave dwellers found out how to do that, they were already on their way out of the cave, living in bigger and bigger groups that needed kings and queens whose importance had to be drummed into their own people and any other people they might conquer. It could be done by unsophisticated means, such as shouting the monarch's name in unison over and over so that it echoed in the surrounding hills. Or it could be done by sophisticated means: by song, by story, by some form of elementary graven image.

These elementary graven images grew less elementary as time went by. Showcases for them grew more elaborate. The famous person could order a showcase in advance of his own death and so transmit his fame through time. Pit, tumulus, mastaba: there was a steady line of progress in such devices which reached a peak—if the word is not too appropriate—in the pyramid. But as a means of transmitting the Pharaoh's fame the pyramid had one conspicuous drawback. People had to come and see it. They could see it from some distance because it was tall and—for the brief time between the occupant's interment and the arrival of the first thieves—clad in high-quality brick veneer. But it could not be sent to them. Out of sight, out of mind. Yet the pyramid also had a conspicuous virtue: relative permanence. Thus we still remember the name of Cheops, although only the Egyptologists among us know precisely what Cheops did that, say, Rameses II didn't. To the rest of us, Cheops is the man who built the big pointed building. We might guess, correctly, that he got to do that only because he ruled the known world, which at that time extended about a month's chariot ride each side of the Nile. We have only the vaguest idea of what he looked like because portraits at the time were so stylized that one Pharaoh looked pretty much like another: big hat, little beard, things to hold, one foot in front of the other.

A certain amount of time having gone by, Alexander the Great achieved fame for conquering as much of the world as he could reach. His fame was transmitted by several

Interdisciplinary Study

Theme Link

Other people's lives are even more fascinating if the people are famous. But are celebrities always admirable?

Curricular Connection: History

Use the information in this interdisciplinary study to explore with students the means by which fame is achieved and the results of fame.

Terms to Know

tumulus (tü′myə ləs), an ancient grave mound.

mastaba (mas′tə bə), an ancient Egyptian tomb with a flat roof and sloping sides.

Additional Background

Cheops, Ramses II, Alexander the Great

Cheops (c. 2680 B.C.) is remembered for directing the construction of the largest pyramid built to house a tomb. His funeral ship was uncovered in 1954.

Ramses II (r. 1304–1237 B.C.) built extensively and is noted for the temple of Abu Simbel.

The image of Alexander the Great (356–323 B.C.) is on a Greek coin in the British Museum. He was King of Macedonia from 336–323 B.C., and he conquered the Greek city-states and the whole Persian empire.

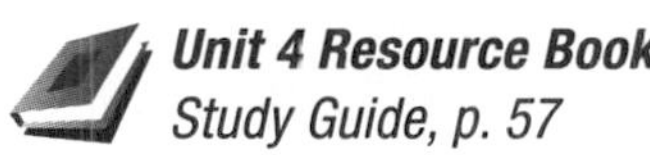
Unit 4 Resource Book
Study Guide, p. 57

BUILDING ENGLISH PROFICIENCY

Exploring a Theme

You may wish to preface students' reading of "A Short History of Fame" by having them consider their own ideas about fame. Ask: How are famous people treated? What can they do that other people cannot? What can they not do that other people can? Encourage students to create a details web similar to the one shown; then, as they read, have them look for ways in which the famous people discussed in the article match the responses.

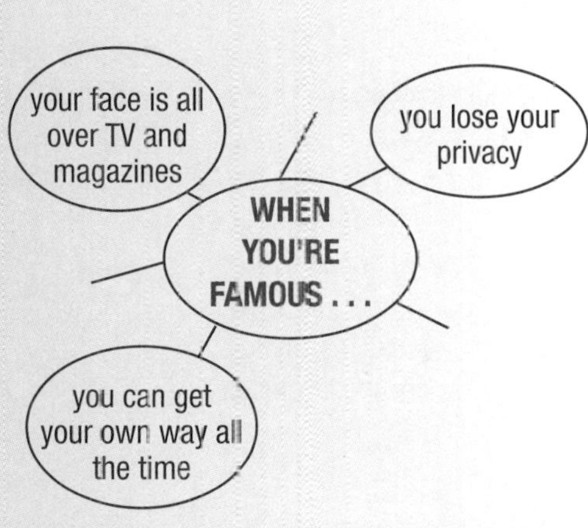

MULTICULTURAL CONNECTION

Lenin, Mao Tse-tung, Attila the Hun, Genghis Khan, Michelangelo, Vasari, Earl of Essex

Vladimir Ilich Lenin (1870–1924) led the Bolshevik Revolution of 1917. He was the founder of the Soviet government and its first premier.

Mao Tse-tung (1893–1976) [also Mao Zedong] helped found the Chinese Communist Party in 1921 and founded the Peoples Republic of China in 1949, unifying the country.

Attila the Hun (d. 453), known as the "Scourge of God," was the ruler of a nomadic tribe that caused so much damage to the Roman Empire that they were able to exact tribute from the emperor Theodosius II.

Genghis Khan (c. 1162–1227) led the Mongols in conquering much of the Asian mainland. His image is taken from a Persian miniature.

Michelangelo Buonarroti (1475–1564) was an Italian artist, chiefly remembered for his statues *Pietà, David*, and *Moses*, and his painting in the Sistine Chapel.

Giorgio Vasari (1511–1574) wrote *Lives of the Most Eminent Painters, Sculptors, and Architects,* a work containing a history of the Italian Renaissance and many biographies.

Robert Devereux, second Earl of Essex, (1567–1601) was Queen Elizabeth's favorite courtier after the death of Leicester. He led a rebellion and was convicted of treason and beheaded.

means. His body was embalmed and kept on show in Alexandria, a practice repeated recently with the corpses of Lenin in Moscow and Mao Tse-tung in Peking, and with the same limitations, largely to do with air conditioning. . . . After Alexander the pace picked up, although it remained a requirement for world fame that it was hard to get without conquering the world first. Julius Caesar was even better at that than Alexander. Caesar also had the advantage that he built roads, got home more often and was therefore easier to sculpt . . . . Coins, busts, bas-reliefs and cameos of Julius Caesar all looked at least roughly like the man himself. He also added a promising new device to the range of means by which fame could be transmitted. He wrote his memoirs. . . . Unfortunately they were mainly about battles . . . The commentaries would have served him better for containing some of the self-justification that modern politicians go in for. Caesar had a lot to justify: he owned gladiators, for example, until he was forced to sell them. . . .

Alexander the Great

The Dark Ages were a dark age for fame, too. Attila the Hun was another world conqueror in the old sense, but all he did was tear things down. He never put anything up, not even a statue to himself. Few eyewitnesses survived to say what he looked like. Outside his group of low-life associates, he had no ambitions to be remembered for anything except the usual Hunnish activities—pillage, raping and pyromania. He burned records rather than kept them, so the picture of his personality was never filled out even to the extent that later ages might speculate about it. Consequently he is just a name, without really being famous at all. Genghis Khan is almost in the same case. He was an Eastern Attila with the same attitude problem. Once again the globetrotting psychopath's chief monument was a long trail of smoking ruins. . . .

Conquering the world with a paintbrush and a chisel instead of the sword and the cross, Michelangelo was the man who spelled the Italian Renaissance to the civilized world, which had grown to be almost as big as the old classical world had been before the barbarians got loose. Michelangelo was keenly interested in his own glory. He thought big: king-sized sculptures, frescoes with a Cinerama spread, a whole ceiling laid out like a curved split screen.

He regarded himself as a cut above all those other hacks. Unfortunately he left us no reliable self-portrait beyond a flayed skin in the Last Judgment. Though a distinguished poet, he also neglected to write his memoirs, leaving the job principally to Vasari, who was a better writer than painter, though not by much. The consequence once again was lasting fame but little image control, allowing later generations complete latitude to concoct their own version of the greatest graphic artist of all time. . . . The emphasis on the judicious husbandry of national resources [by Queen Elizabeth I of England] extended to the control of her own publicity. Prominent playwrights of the period were not encouraged to include any character too closely resembling her in their five-act blank-verse outpourings. The portrait as a means of transmitting fame had always been hampered by how long it took to paint one. With Queen Elizabeth it took even longer because so many finely detailed jewels had to be included. She could write—if she had never been Queen she would still count among the accomplished minor poets of the period—but what she wrote was not for publication. Though word-of-mouth had it that she could be quite merry at court when the Earl of Essex was in town, the impression of the Great Queen that went down to the ages was of a woman hampered by a

Genghis Khan

MINI-LESSON: STUDY SKILLS

Use an Anthology

Teach Point out to students the reference on page 370 to Queen Elizabeth as a poet. Explain that a good place to begin looking for examples of a fairly well-known poet's work is in literary anthologies, particularly, those published by W. W. Norton. There are several Norton anthologies. *The Norton Anthology of English Literature, The Norton Anthology of American Literature,* and *The Norton Anthology of Literature by Women: The Tradition in English* are three examples. Writers, as well as the titles of their works and first lines, are listed in the index. The books provide historical background on periods, as well as on particular pieces of literature.

Activity Idea Have students look up Queen Elizabeth I in an appropriate Norton anthology, remembering to search under "Elizabeth," rather than under "Queen." Have them vote on their favorite of the two poems that appear in the anthology.

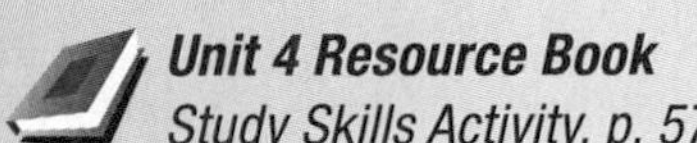

Unit 4 Resource Book
Study Skills Activity, p. 57

severe nature. . . . The great ruler thought fame unruly, and kept it on a short leash.

But it was bursting to get loose as more books and periodicals were published. In the next couple of centuries, rulers of various degrees of absoluteness acquired the habit of glorifying themselves by building whole cities—Peter the Great's Petersburg was merely the most conspicuous example—but what really spread their fame was movable type, moving by the million pieces every hour of the day. It could make you famous whether your blood was blue or not. By the early, romantic, unruly nineteenth century, the young poet John Keats wasn't just dreaming of being a great poet, he was dreaming of fame itself. The young poet Byron got what Keats dreamed of. He published a long poem, *Childe Harold's Pilgrimage,* that all the young ladies loved. He woke up to find that he had become famous overnight. From then on, all the young ladies loved him, and not just in Britain but on a European scale. He was written up week by week. The periodicals were making a difference.

Catherine the Great

Napoleon conquered Europe with the sword instead of the pen. But he realized that fame was a weapon too. He was written about constantly. His portraits took almost as long to turn out as Queen Elizabeth's, because the dedication to simple dress that he started off with gave way to a taste for the sumptuosity that impressed the populace. The huge painting of his coronation as Emperor took so long to complete that he had started rewriting European history all over again before it was finished. But engravings could be quickly turned out for the periodicals and they fixed the essentials of his appearance for all time. . . Images were growing more complex as time went on—still simple, but more like life. Napoleon would have approved. He wanted to be famous, and he wanted his fame to last after death. He was still giving interviews in his final exile.

Only forty years after Napoleon died, Abraham Lincoln was President of the United States. Lincoln didn't especially want to be famous, but by now there was no choice. America's political importance was growing and no politically powerful figure could any longer get out of being famous. If Lincoln was impatient about posing for his portrait, and too busy to meet all but the quickest sketch artists, there was a new device that could capture his image in a matter of minutes. With the advent of photography, fame started to accelerate. Here was a way for a face to be everywhere in almost no time. And it didn't have to hang on the wall, it could just appear in the periodical that came out every week—or, another new idea, in the newspaper that came out every day. When Lincoln spoke at Gettysburg, hardly anybody was there to hear it. Perhaps it was a good thing. He had a high, not very satisfactory voice, its timbre nothing like as sonorous as his syntax. With no means of transmitting the sound, the speech drifted away on the wind. But when the words appeared in the paper, it was almost like being there, and probably better. It had happened only yesterday. When Lincoln was assassinated, publications all over the country had the news by telegraph, and all over the world not long after. The press was speeding things up. It needed the news.

Responding

1. How do the types of people who became famous in the past differ from today's celebrities?

2. Are the rewards of fame worth its drawbacks? Why or why not?

Terms to Know

pyromania (pī rō mā′nē ə), an uncontrollable impulse to set fires

psychopath (sī′kə path), a person having a disorder of personality characterized by antisocial behavior, such as indifference to morality and aggressive criminal behavior

sumptuous (sump′chü əs), lavish indulgence

MULTICULTURAL CONNECTION

Peter the Great, John Keats, Byron, Napoleon, Abraham Lincoln

Peter I,(1672–1725) was the first Russian czar.

John Keats (1795–1821) and George Gordon, Lord Byron (1788–1824) were English poets. (See Unit 5.)

Napoleon I (1769–1821), emperor of France, conquered European coalitions to extend French rule to most of Europe. He was defeated by the Duke of Wellington at the Battle of Waterloo in 1815.

Abraham Lincoln (1809–1865) was the sixteenth president of the United States.

Responding

1. Possible Response Famous people of the past tended to be rulers, great military heroes, or adventurers, while today's famous people also include athletes and entertainers.

2. Possible Response Students may not be convinced that the drawbacks of fame are very serious compared to the wealth and prestige that it can bring.

BUILDING ENGLISH PROFICIENCY

Improving Comprehension

Students may better grasp this text-dense article by focusing on only a part of it. A jigsaw activity can increase understanding.

1. Divide students into eight groups and assign one of the following people to each group:

Cheops	Queen Elizabeth I
Alexander the Great	Lord Byron
Attila the Hun	Napoleon Bonaparte
Michelangelo	Abraham Lincoln

2. Have each group read and discuss its relevant part of the article. Ask group members to decide what made their person famous and to comment on whether the person suggests a positive or negative view of fame.

3. Call on a representative from each group to report the responses. Have the class work together to discuss the Responding questions.

Interdisciplinary Study

Theme Link

How do other people's lives appear to us when viewed through the medium of the portrait?

Curricular Connection: Fine Art

You can use the information in this interdisciplinary study to explore with students ways in which the visual arts capture and add to the fame of celebrities.

Additional Background

Marie Antoinette

The frivolous and irresponsible behavior of Marie Antoinette (1755–1793), wife of King Louis XVI and Queen of France, was partly responsible for laying the groundwork for the French Revolution. She was guillotined for treason after aiding Austria's invasion of France.

INTERDISCIPLINARY STUDY
Fine Art Connection
As Clive James observes, artists have long served to fix the the way the world pictures famous people. On these pages are four such celebrity portraits.
Seeing

LOUISE ELISABETH VIGÉE-LEBRUN
Marie Antoinette (1780s)
One of the few women who made a successful career as an artist before modern times, Vigée-Lebrun was both court painter and confidante of the Queen of France, Marie Antoinette.

ANTOINE JEAN GROS
Napoleon at Arcole (1796)
Gros made his reputation by contributing historical paintings that helped to embody vividly the legend of Napoleon Bonaparte.

MINI-LESSON: SPEAKING AND LISTENING

Interpretive Reading/Speech

Teach Give students copies of "The Gettysburg Address," by Abraham Lincoln, or another brief speech. Tell students that when they prepare to read a speech written by someone else, they need to practice, and may even wish to mark the speech to indicate how they will use the following:

- phrasing
- rate
- pitch
- modulation
- volume
- inflection

Work with the class to devise ways to record their decisions about these aspects of speech.

Activity Idea Have each student prepare the speech for presentation. Have them turn in their marked copy so you can see how they planned their approach to the speech.

MATHEW BRADY

Abraham Lincoln (1862)

Employing the new medium of photography, Brady recorded the terrible burden of leadership during the Civil War in a series of portraits of President Abraham Lincoln.

©1995 The Andy Warhol foundation, Inc./ARS

ANDY WARHOL

Elvis (1963)

One of the best known figures in the pop art style of painting, Warhol frequently created works that were multiple images of familar American icons, such as Marilyn Monroe and Elvis Presley.

Stars

"In the future, everyone will be world-famous for fifteen minutes."
—Andy Warhol

Responding

1. What one word would you use to sum up the impression created by each of these portraits?

2. If you were famous, which of these four artists would you choose to paint your portrait? Explain your answer.

Additional Background

Matthew Brady, Andy Warhol, Elvis Presley Photographer Matthew Brady (1823?–1896) was a portrait photographer who published a series of portraits of famous Americans as "The Gallery of Illustrious Americans." He took more than one-third of the 100 photographs of Lincoln and covered the Civil War with a crew of up to twenty photographers assisting him, changing the perception of war for those not at the battlefield.

Andy Warhol (1928?–1987) began as a commercial artist and later founded the Pop Art movement.

Elvis Aron Presley (1935–1977) popularized rock 'n' roll and appeared in thirty-three movies. Some of his most famous songs are "Heartbreak Hotel" and "Love Me Tender."

Responding

1. Possible Responses Napoleon—brooding; Marie Antoinette—elegant, frivolous; Lincoln—thoughtful, sad; Elvis—striking, forceful.

2. Possible Responses Students may prefer the romantic style of Gros or Vigée-Lebrun or they may opt for the more realistic style of Brady or Warhol.

BUILDING ENGLISH PROFICIENCY

Responding to Visual Cues

Use one or more of the following activities to expand upon the images and explanatory text in this feature.

Activity Ideas

- Allow time for students to use their dialogue journals to respond to the portraits and captions.
- Ask pairs of students to choose one of the portaits. Have them improvise a skit in which one student speaks as the artist and the other as the subject but both express comments about the nature of fame.
- Ask students to imagine that a portrait of themselves could be included in this spread. Ask: What would the portrait look like? What would the caption say about you?
- Invite an art teacher or speaker from an art museum to show the class portraits of other famous people. Apply the Responding questions to this expanded presentation.

Language History

Teaching Objectives

- To understand the impetus behind language changes in the seventeenth century
- To understand the limits on the ability to impose changes on language
- To understand the complex state of the English language in the mid-seventeenth century

Introduce

Ask students to volunteer some words or constructions that are not obscene but are considered unacceptable or nonstandard English. (For example, *ain't, scairt, he don't, this here, bestest, boughten, drownded*) Ask them to try to devise strategies for eliminating such words or grammatical constructions from the language. Do they think their strategies would achieve any measure of success? Then have students read the article.

Follow Up

Encourage students to look up the words to which Johnson and Swift objected. Have them try to come up with a rationale that Johnson and Swift might have had for eliminating those words. Discuss whether there are any words the students think should be eliminated, and if so, why.

Language History

Greater Simplicity and Precision

They have exacted from all their members a close, naked, natural way of speaking . . . .

Thomas Sprat,
The History of the Royal Society of London (1667)

During the late 1600s, the English people reacted against ornamental prose and unregulated spontaneity of expression, calling instead for an ordered, rational language. The Royal Society, founded by a group of learned men and scientists, demanded of its members "a close, naked, natural way of speaking, positive expressions, clear senses, a native easiness, bringing all things as near the Mathematical plainness as they can, and preferring the language of Artizans, Countrymen, and Merchants, before that of Wits or Scholars."

Those caught in the surge toward a simpler and more precise language—among them Swift, Johnson, and Lord Chesterfield—tended to disparage what they called "cant" or "low speech." These arbiters of language realized that the English language was in a muddle: words still had widely variant meanings, spellings, and pronunciations, and the general instability of the language was a barrier to clear communication.

The urge to introduce order into the language is evident in hundreds of projects undertaken during the course of the eighteenth century. Johnson's ponderous two-volume *Dictionary,* great achievement though it was, offered only a partial solution to the problems of standardizing the language, and before the century ended there were many other attempts.

While the neoclassicism of the 1700s did much to tone down the bizarre and freakish aspects of speech of the 1600s, it did not, in spite of its insistence on rules and rigidity, stamp out the rich variety of the English language. Although both Johnson and Swift objected to the use of such words as *humbug, prig, doodle, bamboozle, fib, bully, fop, banter, stingy, fun,* and *prude,* those words continued in use then as they do today, evidence of the fact that people—not grammar books or dictionaries—make and perpetuate language.

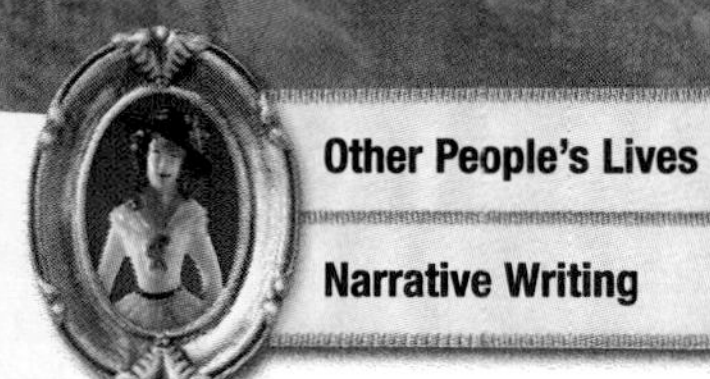

Writing Workshop

Someone You Should Know

Assignment In this part of the unit you read biographical writings. Now write a biographical sketch about someone you know.

WRITER'S BLUEPRINT

Product	A biographical sketch
Purpose	To bring a person to life on paper
Audience	Newspaper readers in your community
Specs	To write a successful paper, you should:

- ❑ Imagine that you are writing a biographical sketch for a feature in a local newspaper entitled "Someone You Should Know." Focus on someone in your community who interests you and whom you can observe and interview in person.
- ❑ Begin by showing your subject in action, doing something characteristic and interesting (to hook the reader), then by giving a few basic facts about him or her (to orient the reader).
- ❑ Go on to discuss three of the following elements of your subject's life: personality, likes and dislikes, occupation, interests, background. Include quotations from an interview.
- ❑ Conclude with your personal reactions to your subject.
- ❑ Write smoothly. Take care to avoid a succession of choppy sentences.
- ❑ Follow the rules of grammar, usage, spelling, and mechanics. Take care to punctuate quotations correctly.

STEP 1 PREWRITING

Brainstorm a list of possible subjects for a biographical sketch. You might consider family members or neighbors. Also, think about all the people you know through various activities, including school, sports, part-time jobs—even your doctor or hairstylist. Then choose one person

Writing Workshop

WRITER'S BLUEPRINT

Specs

The Specs in the Writer's Blueprint address these writing and thinking skills:

- hooking the reader
- orienting the reader
- interviewing
- organizing information
- drawing conclusions
- making judgments
- avoiding choppy sentences
- punctuating quotations

Linking Literature to Writing

After reviewing the literature, have students generate a list of techniques or qualities the writers incorporated to develop good biographies.

STEP 1 PREWRITING

Brainstorm a list of possible subjects

Urge students to begin by writing down every name that comes to mind. Then cut names from the list to eliminate the least likely candidates. Finally, choose the subject from this pared-down list. But urge students to keep a copy of the pared-down list in case their first choice doesn't work out. For additional support, see the worksheet referenced below.

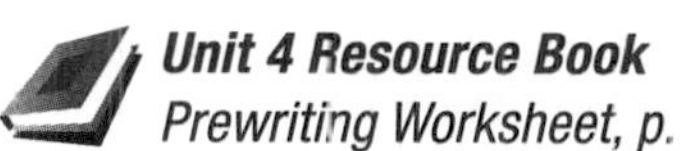

Unit 4 Resource Book
Prewriting Worksheet, p. 59

WRITING WORKSHOP OVERVIEW

Product
Narrative writing: A biographical sketch

Prewriting
Brainstorm a list of possible subjects—Gather background information—Make a web of interesting elements—Interview your subject—Try a quickdraw—Plan your biographical sketch
Unit 4 Resource Book
Prewriting Worksheets pp. 59–60

Drafting
Before you draft—As you draft
Transparency Collection
Student Models for Writing Workshop 13, 14

Revising
Ask a partner—Strategy: Avoiding Choppy Writing
Unit 4 Resource Book
Revising Worksheet p. 61

Editing
Ask a partner—Strategy: Punctuating Quotations Correctly
Unit 4 Resource Book
Grammar Worksheet p. 62
Grammar Check Test p. 63

Presenting
Wall of Fame
Copies for Subjects

Looking Back
Self-evaluate—Reflect—For Your Working Portfolio
Unit 4 Resource Book
Assessment Worksheet p. 64
Transparency Collection
Fine Art Transparency 7

Gather background information about your subject

Remind students to be sure they've contacted their subject and gotten his or her approval before beginning this step.

Make a web of interesting elements

Encourage students to experiment with a variety of categories before settling on an angle to pursue in their research.

Interview your subject

Go over with students the information in the Beyond Print article so they will have guidelines for conducting an interview. Students may want to bring a camera as well as an audio recorder to the interview. For additional support, see the mini-lessons at the bottom of this page and the page following. See also the worksheet referenced below.

Unit 4 Resource Book
Prewriting Worksheet, p. 60

from your list to be your subject. Remember that this should be someone you can observe and interview in person and who is willing to participate.

Gather background information about your subject. Make a list of people who know your subject—friends, co-workers, family members, former teachers, etc. Talk with two or three of these people about your subject, and take careful notes. Consider questions like: *What do you most admire about ____? What is the most interesting fact you know about ____? Can you think of an anecdote that would give an insight into ____'s personality?*

Make a web of interesting elements. Now that you know a little more about your subject, select three of these elements to focus on: personality, likes and dislikes, occupation, interests, background. Create a web similar to the one shown in which you list details you already know about each element.

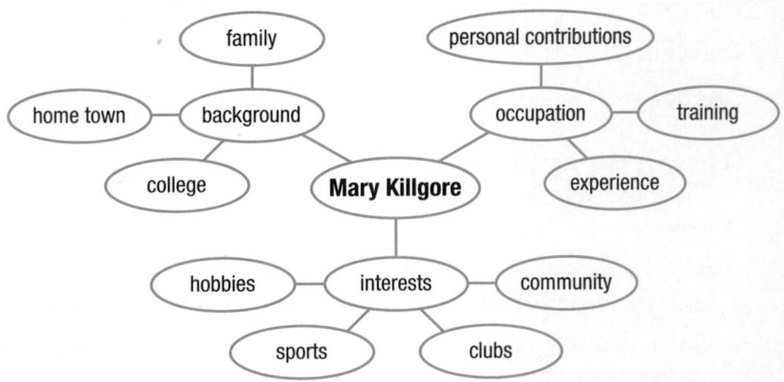

Interview your subject. Contact your subject and arrange a time and place to conduct an interview. Come prepared with questions that focus on the three elements you've selected. Think of asking these three kinds of questions:

- **General** questions: *What sorts of things do you do in your spare time?*
- **Specific** questions about details connected with the general questions: *Why did you take up skydiving?*
- **Follow-up** questions to expand on the information in the specific questions: *You say skydiving has made you a more careful person. What do you mean by "careful"?*

During the interview, listen carefully. For ideas on effective listening, see the Beyond Print article on page 380.

OR . . .
If you have access to a tape recorder and your subject feels comfortable about it, tape the interview. Later on, listen to it and take your notes then.

MINI-LESSON: PREWRITING

Interview Your Subject

Teach Advise students that a good interviewer develops strategies to encourage subjects to talk freely. For example, one can draw more information out of the person being interviewed by asking extending questions, as in, "That's fascinating; tell me more about your first days on the job." Allowing plenty of "wait time" after a speaker seems to have finished his or her thoughts often results in further dialogue as well.

Activity Idea Provide copies of interviews from newspapers or magazines so students can get an idea of the kinds of questions asked and the extent of the answers given to certain questions. Encourage students to use these published interviews for ideas for their questions.

Apply Have a few students role-play an interview for the class to critique their interviewing techniques.

Try a quickdraw. Sketch your subject in action, doing something characteristic. Insert dialogue bubbles with appropriate quotes. At the bottom, write a few of your personal reactions to your subject.

Plan your biographical sketch. Look back at the information you've gathered on your subject and organize your notes into a plan like the one shown here.

Introduction
My subject doing something characteristic
Basic facts about him or her

Body
First element of my subject's life
  Quotations from interview
Second element
  Quotations from interview
Third element
  Quotations from interview

Conclusion
My personal reactions to my subject

STEP 2 DRAFTING

Before you draft, look over your prewriting materials and reread the Writer's Blueprint.

As you draft, concentrate on putting your ideas on paper. Worry about spelling and punctuation mistakes in the revising and editing stages. Here are some drafting tips.

- For the body, begin each section with a topic sentence that clearly identifies the element you are describing. (See the Literary Source for an example.)
- For the conclusion, review your interview notes to find a quote that you feel characterizes your subject better than any other, and use it as a basis for your closing comments.

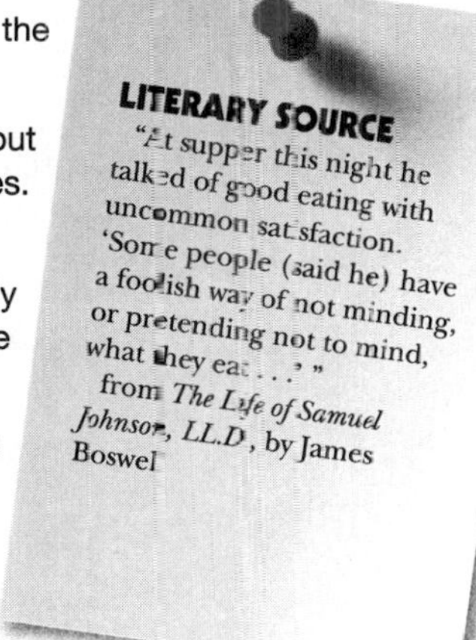

LITERARY SOURCE
"At supper this night he talked of good eating with uncommon satisfaction. 'Some people (said he) have a foolish way of not minding, or pretending not to mind, what they eat. . . .' "
from The Life of Samuel Johnson, LL.D., by James Boswell

STEP 3 REVISING

Ask a partner to comment on your draft before you revise it. Use the checklist on the next page as a guide.

BUILDING ENGLISH PROFICIENCY

ESL LEP ELD SAE LD

Planning for Interviews

Students who have never taken part in an interview may need some special preparation before approaching their subjects. Offer one or both of the following activities to help.

- Ask students to interview each other to help get a feel for drawing information out of their subject and making the most of questions.
- Ask an instructor or official from your school (such as the principal, a coach, or a social worker) to visit your class as a practice interview subject.

Try a quickdraw

Some students may just want to sketch a few items that represent some facet of the subject's character, such as the tools of her or his trade.

Plan your biographical sketch

Provide magazines that include biographical feature articles for the students to use as models for structure and content.

Connections to **Writer's Notebook**

For selection-related prompts, refer to Writer's Notebook.

Connections to **Writer's Resource**

For additional writing prompts, refer to Writer's Resource.

STEP 2 DRAFTING
The Student Models

The **transparencies** referenced below are authentic student models. Review them with students before they draft. These questions will help:

1. Which three elements of the subject's life does the writer of model 13 discuss?

2. Have students look over both models for smoothness. Are there any places where the sentences are too choppy?

Transparency Collection
Student Models for Writing Workshop 13, 14

STEP 3 REVISING
Ask a partner (Peer assessment)

Have students identify the most descriptive or telling details from their peer's essay.

Revising Strategy: Avoiding Choppy Writing

Have students examine the model closely to see how the choppy sentences were revised, taking note of how the sentences are now more closely related.

For additional support, see the worksheet referenced below.

Unit 4 Resource Book
Revising Worksheet, p. 61

Connections to
Writer's Resource

Refer to the Grammar, Usage, and Mechanics Handbook on Writer's Resource.

✔ Did I focus on three elements of the subject's life?

✔ Did I include details from an interview with the person?

✔ Does my writing flow smoothly?

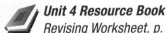

Revising Strategy

Avoiding Choppy Writing

Sometimes writers deliberately string together choppy sentences for dramatic effect:

> Lightning struck. Trees fell. The windows broke. The roof caved in.

More often, though, short, choppy sentences strung together call attention to themselves without the writer wanting them to:

> Mary Killgore went to college during the Sixties. She attended the University of Oregon. Mary majored in economics. She had a minor in Asian history. Mary went twelve months out of the year. She got her bachelor's degree in three years.

Effective writing moves along so smoothly that the reader often doesn't notice when one sentence ends and another begins:

> Mary Killgore attended the University of Oregon during the Sixties. She majored in economics with a minor in Asian history. By going twelve months out of the year, she got her bachelor's degree in three years.

When you revise, keep an eye out for successions of short sentences strung together, especially if they have the same structure. You might find that by combining some of them, you clarify meaning as well as make the writing flow, as in the student model below.

C. J. definitely has a full calendar. School is his top priority, but his job is also a high priority. Sports ~~are important~~ and leisure ~~is~~ are also important to a well-balanced life ~~is necessary~~. "I guess if I had to choose, the job would be the first thing to go," he noted. "I need the income to go toward future college expenses, though," he said.

STUDENT MODEL

MINI-LESSON: GRAMMAR

Punctuating Quotations Correctly

Have students edit the following paragraph, giving special attention to correct punctuation of the quotation.

At that point Miss Alvarez peeked over her eyeglasses and whispered you mean he didn't tell you about his expulsion from high school? she laughed and said sit back because this is going to take a while.

Unit 4 Resource Book
Grammar Worksheet p. 62
Grammar Check Test p. 63

STEP 4 EDITING

Ask a partner to review your revised draft before you edit. Look over each paragraph to make sure you are punctuating quotations correctly.

Editing Strategy

Punctuating Quotations Correctly

Enclose words taken directly from a printed source or speech in quotation marks: Mary said, "I had a happy childhood."

More than one quote can appear in the same paragraph as long as the speaker hasn't changed:

> Mary said, "My mother thinks I was a naughty child." She thought a moment and then smiled slyly. "But I wouldn't call it naughty. I'd call it mischievous," she winked.

FOR REFERENCE
More information on punctuating quotations appears in the Language and Grammar Handbook at the back of this text.

STEP 5 PRESENTING

- Create a "wall of fame" at your local library, using the biographical sketches from your class along with photographs of your subjects.
- Make a copy of your biographical sketch for the person featured in it.

STEP 6 LOOKING BACK

Self-evaluate. Look back at the Writer's Blueprint and give yourself a score for each item, from 6 (superior) to 1 (inadequate).

Reflect. Write answers to these questions.

✔ How closely did the interview with your subject follow your planned questions? What unexpected turns did it take?

✔ If you were to interview and write a biographical sketch of a famous person, who would you choose and why?

For Your Working Portfolio Add your biographical sketch and reflection responses to your working portfolio.

STEP 4 EDITING

Ask a partner (Peer assessment)

Advise students to pay particular attention to quotations.

Editing Strategy: Punctuating Quotations Correctly

For additional support, see the mini-lesson at the bottom of page 378 and the worksheets referenced below.

Unit 4 Resource Book
Grammar Worksheet, p. 62
Grammar Check Test, p. 63

Connections to **Writer's Resource**

Refer to the Grammar, Usage, and Mechanics Handbook on Writer's Resource.

STEP 5 PRESENTING

Wall of Fame

You may want to invite the students' interview subjects to school to see the "wall of fame."

STEP 6 LOOKING BACK

Self-evaluate

The *Assessment Criteria Specs* at the bottom of this page are for a superior paper. You might want to post these in the classroom. Students can then evaluate themselves based on these criteria. For a complete scoring rubric, use the *Assessment Worksheet* referenced below.

Unit Four Resource Book
Assessment Worksheet, p. 64

Reflect

You might have students discuss their choices for famous-person interviews and some of the questions they might ask.

To further explore the theme, use the Fine Art Transparency referenced below.

Transparency Collection
Fine Art Writing Prompt 7

ASSESSMENT CRITERIA SPECS

6 Superior The writer of a 6 paper impressively meets these criteria:

- Hooks the reader from the start by showing the subject in action performing some characteristic bit of behavior that serves as a key to the subject's personality.
- Firmly orients the reader by filing in basic details about the subject early on in the paper.
- Develops a detailed, intriguing, and insightful portrait of the subject.
- Includes quotations from a skillfully-conducted interview.
- Concludes with personal reactions to the subject, which reveal that the writer has learned something important about the subject from this experience.
- Writes smoothly.
- Punctuates quotations correctly.

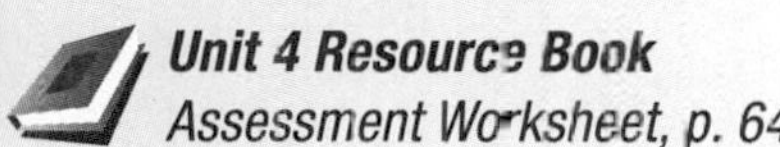

Unit 4 Resource Book
Assessment Worksheet, p. 64

Beyond Print

Teaching Objectives

- to develop an interview
- to listen and respond effectively during an interview.

Curricular Connection: Critical Thinking

You can use the material in this article to give students practice in becoming more at ease with interviewing techniques and strategies.

Introduce

Interviews can provide access to the most up-to-date research and previously unavailable discoveries, insights, and observations. They can connect the interviewer with authorities who are the experts in their field. Share these thoughts with students before asking them to read the article.

Activity Option

Encourage students to decide whether to conduct an interview

- in person
- by mail
- over the phone
- on-line

Beyond Print

Interviewing

Effective listening requires practice and discipline. When interviewing one or more subjects, you want to be sure that you are listening effectively so that you don't waste their time or yours. Here are some pointers.

Pay attention. Make as much eye contact as is comfortable for you both. Watch your subject's facial expressions and body language also.

Think as you listen. You should be working with a list of questions you prepared in advance, but that doesn't mean you should follow your list slavishly. Listen to be sure that your subject is actually answering the question you asked, but be prepared to follow your subject off on little bypaths if they seem interesting and possibly relevant to your project.

Give the speaker feedback. Look and sound interested in what the speaker is saying. It's good to give verbal responses such as "Oh, that's interesting," or "I didn't know that" as long as they are natural to you. Ask your subject for more details when you think they might be useful.

Take notes. Some interviewers like to use a tape recorder—with permission, of course—to be sure they have an accurate record of their subject's words. You can conduct an effective interview with a pen and notebook, however. Don't try to record the interview word for word. Just write down key words or particularly useful phrases as you hear them; then try to summarize the answer to each question. It may help to give your subject an oral summary so that you can both check your accuracy. After the interview, write up your notes as soon as possible. That way, it will be easier to remember what your notes mean.

Follow up. It should go without saying that you have been friendly and courteous throughout the interview and have thanked your subject sincerely for his or her time. It is a nice idea to send your subject a copy of the interview after have written it up.

Activity Option

Interview one or more subjects in the preparation of your biography, Someone You Should Know, pages 373–377.

ANOTHER APPROACH

Interviewing On-Line

When students conduct on-line interviews, they need to use different strategies to get the results they want. Here are some guidelines:

- Students should phone or write to arrange the interview—people don't always read their e-mail consistently.
- Students must plan most of their questions in advance, but can try to arrange a follow-up session for more questions after they have read the initial answers.
- Questions must be especially clear, since the interviewer will not be present to explain what he or she meant.
- Students should both save the file and print a hard copy to protect their data.
- Students should thank the interviewee after the conclusion of the interview.

Multicultural Connections

Interactions

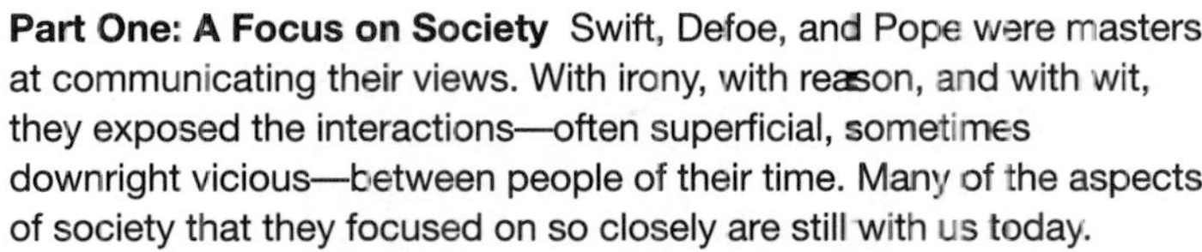

Part One: A Focus on Society Swift, Defoe, and Pope were masters at communicating their views. With irony, with reason, and with wit, they exposed the interactions—often superficial, sometimes downright vicious—between people of their time. Many of the aspects of society that they focused on so closely are still with us today.

■ People have written satire for years, yet little, apparently, has changed. If it seems certain that writing is not going to change society, why bother? Why should writers continue to expose social ills even when the people responsible for them don't pay attention?

Communication

Part Two: Other People's Lives Communication plays an integral role when groups and persons of different backgrounds come into contact and interact with each other. Pepys, Johnson, and Boswell all devoted their considerable energies to communicating their understandings about people's lives and interactions.

■ What do you think is the single most important piece of information you can get from learning about another person's life?

Activities

1. Collect several weeks' worth of tabloid newspapers and magazines that feature celebrities. Survey who's in the news and for what reasons. Devise some sort of graphic organizer to summarize your findings. What conclusions can you come to about who becomes a celebrity and why?
2. What's funny? Browse library shelves for jokebooks or ask adults of your acquaintance to tell you their favorite jokes. Collect jokes (in good taste) from at least two different cultures—more, if possible. Compare them in terms of subject matter, type of humor, and so on. You may come away with more questions than conclusions. Ask the questions.
3. Prepare a dialogue between at least two people demonstrating how communication—or the lack of it—affects their interaction.

381

Unit Wrap-Up

MULTICULTURAL CONNECTION

Communication about the ills they saw in society formed a fundamental part of the lives of the men whose works are showcased in Parts One and Two of Unit 4.

Interactions

- One way to approach social interactions that one finds faulty is to publicly critique them.
- An alternative approach is to ridicule them through irony or satire.

Possible Response Even if the people responsible for social ills do not respond, other people may step in and help to alleviate the effects of those ills.

Communication

Good communication is important when different types of people interact.

Possible Responses One may gain insight into how to live (or not live) one's own life, an understanding of the relationship between beliefs and actions, and clues as to how to attain rapport with that person

Activities

Activity 1 Suggest to students that they try to determine whether the celebrities are featured because of a recent accomplishment, because of the vicarious thrill their lives might provide to the general public, because of their looks, and so on.

Activity 2 You may want to encourage students to collect a specific type of joke—for example, fish stories, sports stories, and so on.

Activity 3 Students may wish to base their dialogue on a real conversation, either to portray it or to satirize or caricature it.

UNIT 4 OPTIONS

Drama

Students may wish to use costumes and make-up for their roles. After students present their "autobiographies," you might want to allow the "authors" a few minutes to interact with each other.

Research

Fielding aimed to use laughter rather than satire to turn people from folly and vice, and as such, his works do not provide a mirror of life in his times, but a fun-house reflection. Encourage students to use historical information, not the novel *Tom Jones*, to decide if the movie portrays life in the eighteenth century well or not.

Art

Encourage students to find out the names of the items of clothing popular in the 1700s and label their depiction.

Media

For ideas on presentation and columns, encourage students to read copies of *The Spectator* and *The Tatler, The Guardian*, and *The Englishman*— periodicals that contained essays by eighteenth-century authors Joseph Addison and Richard Steele. These publications were precursors of modern newspapers.

Unit Test

Unit 4 Resource Book
New Selection
Test 1
Test 2

Independent and Group Projects

Drama

"They Call Me the Wasp of Twickenham" Prepare an "autobiographical" sketch of one of the authors in this unit. Include his comments on a piece of his writing (or someone else's writing), details from a period of his life, and perhaps some of his personal idiosyncrasies. Present your sketch to the class in the form of a dramatic monologue in which you play the role of the author.

Research

Read the Book, See the Movie The first novels were written during the 1700s. Notable were *Pamela* by Samuel Richardson (1740), *Joseph Andrews* by Henry Fielding (1742), and *Tristram Shandy* by Laurence Sterne (1760), but perhaps the most popular was Fielding's *Tom Jones* (1749). Read enough of the book to get a feel for the style and the period details. Then view the modern movie version, noting especially the picture of eighteenth-century life it presents. Write a review in which you concentrate on how well the movie portrays life in an earlier time.

Art

Costume Models Costume in the 1700s was elaborate, colorful, and decorative, and the men's outfits were sometimes as fancy as the women's. Find some books on costume history and dress at least two dolls with period costumes. If you're better with paints or colored pencils than you are with needle and thread, prepare costume plates instead. If the information is available, label your models with the year and the name of the person depicted.

Media

The Eighteenth-century Scene Create a magazine that reflects the daily life of England in the 1700s. After doing a little research, you might include news stories, feature stories, fashions, sports, music commentary, illustrations, and advertisements. If you are working with a group, give each member a separate assignment, such as research, writing, cover design, or layout. If possible, use your school's desktop publishing facilities to print an issue of your magazine for circulation to your classmates.

LONDON
THEMES in
ENGLISH
LITERATURE

About William Dunbar

William Dunbar (1460?–1520?) was a Scottish poet attached to the court of James IV of Scotland, who granted him a life pension and employed him on diplomatic missions. Dunbar was noted for his versatility with occasional poems and for his earthy humor and satirical imagination. This quote is the refrain to "London."

About John Bancks

John Bancks (1709–1751) was a miscellaneous writer who published poetry; biography, including lives of Jesus and Oliver Cromwell; history; and newspaper articles.

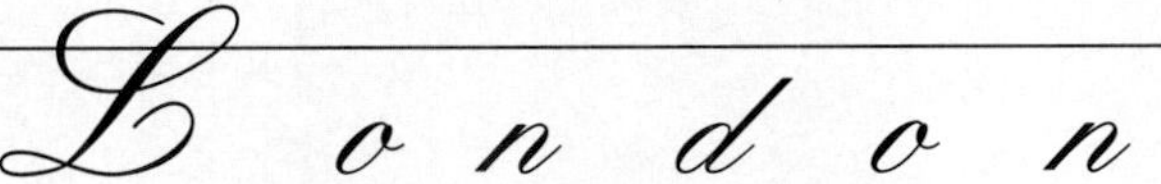

~ capital city of England and hub of the British Empire ~ is both loved and hated, enthusiastically embraced and viciously denounced. In this section you will experience what various writers and artists have expressed about their experiences in what was once the largest city in the world.

LONDON, THOU ART THE FLOWER OF CITIES ALL.

William Dunbar (1500s)

A Description of London

Houses, churches, mixed together,
Streets unpleasant in all weather;
Prisons, palaces contiguous,[1]
Gates, a bridge, the Thames irriguous.[2]

Gaudy things enough to tempt ye,
Showy outsides, insides empty;
Bubbles, trades, mechanic arts,
Coaches, wheelbarrows and carts.

Warrants, bailiffs,[3] bills unpaid,
Lords of laundresses afraid;
Rogues that nightly rob and shoot men,
Hangmen, aldermen and footmen.

Lawyers, poets, priests, physicians,
Noble, simple, all conditions:
Worth beneath a threadbare cover,
Villainy bedaubed all over.

Women black, red, fair and gray,
Prudes and such as never pray,
Handsome, ugly, noisy, still,
Some that will not, some that will.

Many a beau[4] without a shilling,[5]
Many a widow not unwilling;
Many a bargain, if you strike it:
This is London! How d'ye like it?

John Bancks (1738)

1. **contiguous** (kən tig′yü əs), *adj.* adjoining; near.
2. **irriguous** (i rig′yü əs), *adj.* watery.
3. **bailiff** (bā′lif), officer of the court.
4. **beau** (bō), *n.* young man courting a woman. *[French]*
5. **shilling,** coin equal to twelve pennies.

THEME LINK TO THE LITERATURE

Some other selections in the text that deal with the themes of London, Londoners, and how the English feel about their capital city are listed here.

- from *The Rape of the Lock* (p. 314)
- from *The Diary* (p. 340)
- from *The Life of Samuel Johnson, LL. D.* (p. 361)
- *Pygmalion* (p. 662)
- "A Cup of Tea" (p. 797)
- from *In the Ditch* (p. 881)
- *The Courtship of Mr. Lyon* (p. 933)

About Charles Dickens

Charles Dickens (1812–1870) is probably England's most popular novelist. All of his novels were written for serial publication; that is, they appeared chapter by chapter in periodicals. His plots are rich with incident, complex, and full of suspense, and his gallery of heroic, villainous, and eccentric characters is among the most memorable in all of literature. This quotation is from the opening of *Bleak House.*

Fog Everywhere

Implacable[1] November weather. As much mud in the streets, as if the waters had but newly retired from the face of the earth, and it would not be wonderful to meet a Megalosaurus,[2] forty feet long or so, waddling like an elephantine[3] lizard up Holborn Hill. Smoke lowering down from chimney-pots, making a soft black drizzle, with flakes of soot in it as big as full-grown snowflakes—gone into mourning, one might imagine, for the death of the sun. Dogs, undistinguishable in mire. Horses, scarcely better; splashed to their very blinkers.[4] Foot passengers, jostling one another's umbrellas, in a general infection of ill-temper, and losing their foot-hold at street-corners, where tens of thousands of other foot passengers have been slipping and sliding since the day broke (if this day ever broke), adding new deposits to the crust upon crust of mud, sticking at those points tenaciously[5] to the pavement, and accumulating at compound interest.

Fog everywhere. Fog up the river, where it flows among green aits and meadows; fog down the river, where it rolls defiled among the tiers of shipping, and the waterside pollutions of a great (and dirty) city. Fog on the Essex marshes, fog on the Kentish heights. Fog creeping into the cabooses of collier-brigs;[6] fog lying out on the yards, and hovering in the rigging of great ships; fog drooping on the gunwales[7] of barges and small boats. Fog in the eyes and throats of ancient Greenwich pensioners,[8] wheezing by the firesides of their wards; fog in the stem and bowl of the afternoon pipe of the wrathful skipper, down in his close cabin; fog cruelly pinching the toes and fingers of his shivering little 'prentice[9] boy on deck. Chance people on the bridges peeping over the parapets[10] into a nether sky of fog, with fog all round them, as if they were up in a balloon, and hanging in the misty clouds.

Charles Dickens (1853)

1. **implacable** (im plā′kə bəl), *adj.* unyielding.
2. **Megalosaurus** (meg′ə lō sôr′əs), *n.* a large dinosaur.
3. **elephantine** (el′ə fan′tēn), *adj.* elephant-like.
4. **blinkers,** leather flaps to keep a horse from seeing sideways.
5. **tenaciously** (ti nā′shəs lē), *adv.* stubbornly.
6. **collier-brigs,** coal barges.
7. **gunwale** (gun′l), *n.* the upper edge of the side of a ship.
8. **pensioners,** retired people.
9. **'prentice,** apprentice, a young person learning a trade.
10. **parapet** (par′ə pet), *n.* a low wall or barrier

BUILDING ENGLISH PROFICIENCY

Exploring Key Concepts

Help students analyze the Dickens selection for sentence structure. They should come to realize that none of the sentences is complete. Essentially this selection is a list of impressions of things seen, and it is made up of minor-type sentences that—out of context—would be called fragments. Here, however, the use of minor-type sentences contributes a sense of vagueness, perhaps of fragmentation, of seeing things through a fog.

1. **Question** Is "Implacable November weather" a complete sentence? *(No; it lacks a verb.)*
2. **Question** Is the last sentence, beginning "Chance people on the bridges . . . ." a complete sentence? *(No; it also lacks a verb.)*

About William Wordsworth

Wordsworth, when young, had a strong political bent. He returned from a trip to France radicalized in his political thinking and fired with enthusiasm for the French Revolution but later became disillusioned by the Reign of Terror and the advent of Napoleon. His poetry could be critical as well as complimentary; in "London, 1802" he calls England a "fen of stagnant waters" (see also p. 408).

About London Coffeehouses

In 1652 the opening of the first coffeehouse in London provided a place where men could meet their friends, drink coffee, smoke, and talk. Here the rising middle class rubbed shoulders with writers and members of the upper classes—and sometimes transacted business. In fact, the great insurance firm of Lloyd's of London drew its name, as well as its origin, from Lloyd's Coffeehouse. By the end of the century the coffeehouse had become an institution, with several thousand in existence.

WESTMINSTER BRIDGE

Earth has not anything to show more fair:
Dull would he be of soul who could pass by
A sight so touching in its majesty:
This City now doth, like a garment, wear
The beauty of the morning; silent, bare,
Ships, towers, domes, theaters, and temples lie
Open unto the fields, and to the sky;
All bright and glittering in the smokeless air.
Never did sun more beautifully steep
In his first splendor, valley, rock, or hill;
Ne'er saw I, never felt, a calm so deep!
The river glideth at his own sweet will:
Dear God! the very houses seem asleep;
And all that mighty heart is lying still!

William Wordsworth (1807)

Coffee Houses

In London there are a great number of coffee-houses, most of which, to tell the truth, are not over clean or well furnished, owing to the quantity of people who resort to these places and because of the smoke, which would quickly destroy good furniture. Englishmen are great drinkers. In these coffee-houses you can partake of chocolate, tea, or coffee, and of all sorts of liquors, served hot; also in many places you can have wine, punch, or ale. . . . What attracts enormously in these coffee-houses are the gazettes[1] and other public papers. All Englishmen are great newsmongers.[2] Workmen habitually begin the day by going to coffee-rooms in order to read the latest news. I have often seen shoeblacks and other persons of that class club together to purchase a farthing[3] paper. . . . Some coffee-houses are a resort for learned scholars and for wits; others are the resort of dandies or of politicians, or again of professional newsmongers.

Ferdinand de Saussure (1700s)

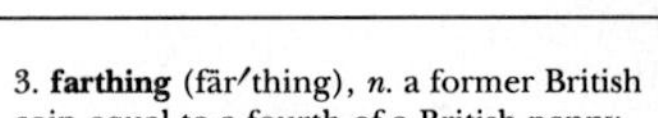

1. **gazette** (gə zet′), *n.* newspaper.
2. **newsmonger** (nüz′mung′gər), *n.* person who spreads news or gossip.
3. **farthing** (fär′thing), *n.* a former British coin equal to a fourth of a British penny.

MINI-LESSON: READING/THINKING SKILLS

Compare and Contrast

To compare is to show how things are alike; to contrast is to show how they are different.

Teach Ask students to list elements about these three pictures that are the same. *(Possible responses: They are all set in London; they all focus on people; they all show a number of people gathered in a public place.)* Then have them list elements that are different. *(Possible response: the clothes, the activities, the social classes.)*

Activity Idea Have students work in small groups. Each student should choose one subject from one of the pictures and make up a character and a brief personal history for that subject. Each responses should take the form of an interior monologue—what that character is thinking at this moment—of no more than one minute. After the groups have shared within, they can choose a variety of monologues to share with the rest of the class.

John Henry Henshall, Behind the Bar *(1882)*

Gustave Doré, Wentworth Street, Whitechapel *(1872)*

William Powell Frith, The Railway Station *(1862)*

LONDON,

that great cesspool[1] into which all the loungers of the Empire are irresistibly drained.

Sir Arthur Conan Doyle (1887)

1. **cesspool** (sis′pül′), *n.* sewer.

Art Study

Visual Literacy Victorian artists delighted in narrative painting, pictures that told stories.

Question What seems to be the narrative expressed in each work? *(Possible responses: Henshall—neighbors and acquaintances gather to spend the evening in a neighborhood pub; Doré—the impoverished residents have no gainful occupation, so they hang about the streets; Frith—the railway station is full of the bustle of hundreds of people intent on their separate journeys.)*

About Sir Arthur Conan Doyle

Sir Arthur Conan Doyle (1859–1930) was the author of the immensely popular Sherlock Holmes detective stories. These words are Dr. Watson's, the narrator of *A Study in Scarlet.*

BUILDING ENGLISH PROFICIENCY

Exploring Key Concepts

Literal language is words used in their usual meaning, without exaggeration or imagination. Figurative language is words used out of their usual meaning to add beauty or force.

1. Question Of the selections by Wordsworth and Saussure, which one uses figurative language? *(Wordsworth)*

2. Question Which lines in "Westminster Bridge" contain simile? *(4–5, 13)* metaphor? *(14)* personification? *(4, 12, 13, 14)* hyperbole? *(1, 9–10, 11)* apostrophe? *(13)* synecdoche? *(10)* If necessary, have students use the definitions in the Glossary of Literary Terms on page 968 to determine answers.

About William Blake

William Blake (1757–1827) wrote *Songs of Innocence and Experience* to dramatize the two contrary states of the human soul. Many of the songs of experience are harsh cries against the terrible living conditions that were coming with the Industrial Revolution and the moral conditions that would allow them (see also p. 401).

About Feodor Dostoevski

Feodor Dostoevski (1821–1881) is perhaps the most expressive writer of the troubled soul of Russia. His novels, such as *Crime and Punishment* (see p. 194), *The Brothers Karamazov,* and *The Possessed,* all show the conflict between the world of thought, aspiration, and reason, and the world of pure experience that opposes all rational definition. This quotation is from a travelogue entitled *Winter Notes on Summer Impressions.*

London

I wander through each chartered[1] street,
Near where the chartered Thames does flow.
And mark in every face I meet
Marks of weakness, marks of woe.

In every cry of every Man,
In every Infant's cry of fear,
In every voice: in every ban,[2]
The mind-forged manacles[3] I hear
How the Chimney-sweepers cry
Every blackening Church appalls,[4]
And the hapless Soldier's sigh,
Runs in blood down Palace walls.

But most through midnight streets I hear
How the youthful Harlots curse
Blasts the new-born Infant's tear
And blights with plagues the Marriage hearse.

William Blake (1794)

Saturday Night in London

In London the masses can be seen on a scale and in conditions not to be seen anywhere else in the world.

I have been told, for example, that on Saturday nights half a million working men and women and their children spread like the ocean all over town, clustering particularly in certain districts, and celebrate their sabbath[1] all night long until five o'clock in the morning, in other words guzzle and drink like beasts to make up for a whole week. They bring with them their weekly savings, all that was earned by hard work and with many a curse. Great jets of gas burn in meat and food shops, brightly lighting up the streets. It is as if a grand reception were being held for those white negroes. Crowds throng the open taverns and the streets. There they eat and drink. The beer houses are decorated like palaces. Everyone is drunk, but drunk joylessly, gloomily and heavily, and everyone is somehow strangely silent. Only curses and bloody brawls occasionally break that suspicious and oppressively sad silence. . . . Everyone is in a hurry to drink himself into insensibility. . . .wives in no way lag behind their husbands and all get drunk together, while children crawl and run about among them.

One such night—it was getting on for two o'clock in the morning—I lost my

1. **chartered,** given by written authority. Blake is making a bitter pun on freedom and limitations.
2. **ban,** prohibition.
3. **manacle** (man′ə kəl), *n.* handcuff.
4. **appall** (ə pôl′), *v.* fill with dismay; terrify.

1. **sabbath** (sab′əth), *n.* day of worship.

MINI-LESSON: READING/THINKING SKILLS

Recognize Values

Values are deeply held beliefs or philosophies. Sometimes it is a relatively simple matter to recognize people's values from what they say and do; at other times these values must be inferred.

Teach Ask students to infer the values that underlie Blake's "London" and Dostoevski's "Saturday Night in London."

Questions Are these writers happy with the scenes they witness? *(no)* Are their descriptions harsh or mild? (*harsh)* Do they seem sympathetic to the poor people they see? *(yes)* What, then, are they critical of? *(Possible response: The poverty and the social conditions that keep these people downtrodden.)*

Activity Idea Have students assume the identity of either Blake or Dostoevski and comment on a typical scene in their own neighborhoods in that identity, applying whatever values they have found in the literature.

way and for a long time trudged the streets in the midst of a vast crowd of gloomy people, asking my way almost by gestures, because I do not know a word of English. I found my way, but the impression of what I had seen tormented me for three days afterwards. The populace[2] is much the same anywhere, but there all was so vast, so vivid that you almost physically felt things which up till then you had only imagined. In London you no longer see the populace. Instead, you see a loss of sensibility, systematic, resigned and encouraged. . . . what we have here is a repudiation[3] of our social formula, an obstinate[4] and unconscious repudiation; an instinctive repudiation at any cost, in order to achieve salvation, a horrified and disgusted repudiation of the rest of us. Those millions of people, abandoned and driven away from the feast of humanity, push and crush each other in the underground darkness into which they have been cast by their elder brethren, they grope around seeking a door at which to knock and look for an exit lest they be smothered to death in that dark cellar. This is the last desperate attempt to huddle together and form one's own heap, one's own mass and to repudiate everything, the very image of man if need be, only to be oneself, only not to be with us. . . .

Feodor Dostoevski (1863)

In people's eyes, in the swing, tramp, and trudge; in the bellow and uproar; the carriages, motor cars, omnibuses,[1] vans, sandwich men[2] shuffling and swinging; brass bands; barrel organs; in the triumph and the jingle and the strange high singing of some airplane overhead was what she loved; life; London; this moment in June.

Virginia Woolf (1925)

Walking in London

London life was very favorable for such a break. There is no town in the world which is more adapted for training one away from people and training one into solitude than London. The manner of life, the distances, the climate, the very multitude of the population in which personality vanishes, all this together with the absence of Continental diversions[1] conduces[2] to the same effect. One who knows how to live alone has nothing to fear from the tedium of London. The life here, like the air here, is bad for

2. **populace** (pop′yə lis), *n.* the common people.
3. **repudiation** (ri pyü′dē ā′shən), *n.* rejection.
4. **obstinate** (ob′stə nit), *adj.* stubborn.

1. **omnibuses,** public busses.
2. **sandwich men,** men wearing advertising boards front and back.

1. **diversion** (də vėr′zhən), *n.* entertainment.
2. **conduce** (kən düs′), *v.* contribute.

About Virginia Woolf

In her fiction, considered experimental, Virginia Woolf (1882–1941) placed her emphasis on detailed descriptions of character and setting, expressing the timeless inner consciousness of her characters by means of interior monologues. This quotation is from her novel *Mrs. Dalloway* (see also p. 813).

About Alexander Herzen

Born in Moscow, Alexander Herzen (1812–1870) emigrated with his family to Paris in 1847. Because of his revolutionary activities, the Russian government ordered him home; when he refused, they confiscated his fortune and possessions. Disenchanted with the failed revolution, Herzen became a Swiss citizen. Personal tragedies and deaths in his family caused him finally to go to London in 1851, where he published a periodical in Russian called *The Pole Star* and began to write what would become his four-volume memoir, *My Past and Thoughts.* This excerpt is from Part VI, section 1, "The Fogs of London."

BUILDING ENGLISH PROFICIENCY

Exploring Key Concepts

Point out to students that the sentence structure of the Woolf quote is very unusual.

1. Question What is the main verb? *(was)*

2. Question What function does the dependent clause *what she loved* serve? *(It is a predicate adjective following the linking verb* be. *It describes what is on the other side of the linking verb.)*

3. Question What is the subject of the sentence? What is "what she loved"? *(Everything preceding the very, from "In peoples eyes . . ." to ". . . some airplane overhead." Probably "life; London; this moment in June" can be considered part of the subject as well.)*

About T. S. Eliot

T. S. Eliot (1888–1965) was a pivotal figure in modern English literature; his work reveals disillusionment with commercial values and hunger for spiritual revitalization that touched a responsive chord in many readers. This poem was published the same year he became a naturalized British citizen (see also p. 768).

the weak, for the frail, for one who seeks a prop outside himself, for one who seeks welcome, sympathy, attention; the moral lungs here must be as strong as the physical lungs, whose task it is to separate oxygen from the smoky fog. The masses are saved by battling for their daily bread, the commercial classes by their absorption in heaping up wealth, and all by the bustle of business; but nervous and romantic temperaments, fond of living among people, fond of intellectual sloth and of idly luxuriating in emotion, are bored to death here and fall into despair.

Wandering lonely about London, through its stony lanes and stifling passages, sometimes not seeing a step before me for the thick, opaline[3] fog, and colliding with shadows running—I lived through a great deal.

Alexander Herzen (1968)

C. R. W. Nevinson's Amongst the Nerves of the World *(about 1930) depicts London's newspaper district, Fleet Street, with St. Paul's Cathedral in the distance.*

PRELUDE 1

The winter evening settles down
With smell of steaks in passageways.
Six o'clock.
The burnt-out ends of smoky days.
And now a gusty shower wraps
The grimy scraps
Of withered leaves about your feet
And newspapers from vacant lots;
The showers beat
On broken blinds and chimney-pots,
And at the corner of the street
A lonely cab-horse steams and stamps.
And then the lighting of the lamps.

T. S. Eliot (1917)

3. **opaline** (ō′pə līn), *adj.* like an opal, with a peculiar play of colors.

MINI-LESSON: READING/THINKING SKILLS

Inference

An inference is a reasonable conclusion drawn from hints or from limited information.

Teach Have students explore the kinds of inferences they can make about the narrator in "Walking in London" and the speaker in "Prelude 1."

Questions Does the narrator or speaker seem to be a stranger, freshly arrived in London? How long has he been here? Is he a tourist? Does he have family or friends here? business? How old is he? How wealthy is he? Remind students that inferences are *reasonable* conclusions.

Activity Idea Have students do a quickwrite of the character they imagine for the narrator or the speaker, based on the inferences they and their classmates have made.

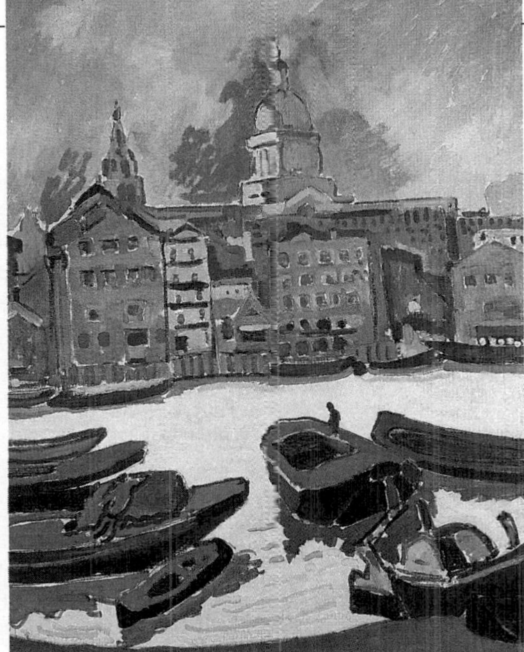

André Derain, St. Paul's from the Thames *(1906)*

St. Paul's stands amid the smoke after a German bombing raid in 1940.

391

Art Study

Visual Literacy In painting, style involves an artist's choices of color, lighting, composition, and line, as well as his or her degree of adherence to, or departure from, realism.

Question How realistic are these three pictures? *(Possible response: The subject matter is recognizable in all three, but Nevinson uses a style with cubistic influences, while Derain uses a style that verges on the primitive. Style choices also affect the photograph, as smoke obscures a clear image of St. Paul's.)*

BUILDING ENGLISH PROFICIENCY

Exploring Key Concepts

In extended sentences and in paragraphs, parallel structure helps comprehension. Point out that in sentence 3 of "Walking in London," the repetition of the word helps the reader identify the parts of the compound subject of the verb *conduces.*

1. Question What is the repeated parallel element in sentence 5? (for; *it introduces a series of prepositional phrases that modify* bad.)

2. Question What is the repeated parallel element in sentence 6? (by; *it introduces a series of prepositional phrases that modify* are saved, *the verb of the subject masses. That same verb is understood as the verb of the subjects* classes *and* all.)

About D. H. Lawrence

D. H. Lawrence (1885–1930) was a writer constantly in revolt against the Puritanism, mediocrity, and dehumanization he found in an industrial English society; he lived the last two decades of his life mostly outside of England. This quotation is from *Assorted Articles,* published after his death.

DULL LONDON

It begins the moment you set foot ashore, the moment you step off the boat's gangway. The heart suddenly, yet vaguely, sinks. It is no lurch of fear. Quite the contrary. It is as if the life-urge failed, and the heart dimly sank. You trail past the benevolent policeman and the inoffensive passport officials, through the fussy and somehow foolish customs—we don't *really* think it matters if somebody smuggles in two pairs of false-silk stockings—and we get into the poky but inoffensive train, with poky but utterly inoffensive people, and we have a cup of inoffensive tea from a nice inoffensive boy, and we run through small, poky but nice and inoffensive country, till we are landed in the big but unexciting station of Victoria, when an inoffensive porter puts us into an inoffensive taxi and we are driven through the crowded yet strangely dull streets of London to the cosy yet strangely poky and dull place where we are going to stay. And the first half-hour in London, after some years abroad, is really a plunge of misery. The strange, the gray and uncanny,[1] almost deathly sense of *dullness* is overwhelming. Of course, you get over it after a while, and admit that you exaggerated. You get into the rhythm of London again, and you tell yourself that it is *not* dull. And yet you are haunted, all the time, sleeping or waking, with the uncanny feeling: It is dull! It is all dull! This life here is one vast complex of dullness! I am dull! I am being dull! My spirit is being dulled! My life is dulling down to London dullness. . . .

Now to feel like this about one's native land is terrible. I am sure I am an exceptional, or at least an exaggerated case. Yet it seems to me most of my fellow-countrymen have the pinched, slightly pathetic look in their faces, the vague, wondering realization: It is dull! It is always essentially dull! My life is dull!

Of course, England is the easiest country in the world, easy, easy and nice. Everybody is nice, and everybody is easy. The English people on the whole are surely the *nicest* people in the world, and everybody makes everything so easy for everybody else, that there is almost nothing to resist at all. But this very easiness and this very niceness become at last a nightmare. It is as if the whole air were impregnated with chloroform or some other pervasive[2] anaesthetic, that makes everything easy and nice, and takes the edge off everything, whether nice or nasty. As you inhale the drug of easiness and niceness, your vitality begins to sink. Perhaps not your physical vitality, but something else: the vivid flame of your individual life. England can afford to be so free and individual because no individual flame of life is sharp and vivid. It is just mildly warm and safe. You couldn't burn your fingers at it. Nice, safe, easy: the whole ideal. And yet under all the easiness is a gnawing uneasiness, as in a drug-taker.

D. H. Lawrence (1932)

1. **uncanny** (un kan′ē), *adj.* strange and mysterious.

2. **pervasive** (pər vā′siv), *adj.* spreading throughout.

MINI-LESSON: LITERARY ELEMENT

Repetition

Teach Have students scan "Dull London" and write down words and phrases that are repeated. Have them consider why Lawrence may have used repetition as he did, instead of simply stating his idea and letting it go at that.

Questions By the time Lawrence has used the word *inoffensive* eight times, what do you think about his emotional reaction to the things he is describing in this way? *(He seems to be offended by the things he calls* inoffensive.) What about the word *nice? (It has the same effect: he seems to think the people are anything but nice.)*

Activity Idea Have students work in small groups to analyze the lyrics of rock songs they have chosen that have lots of repetition. Does the repetition in the rock songs create the same kind of ironic, negative impression that it does in Lawrence? Why do students think this might be true?

Entertainments

I will now try to describe what a ball was like in Victorian and Edwardian days. Your hostess and her daughter stood at the head of the staircase, each of these ladies holding a fan and a bouquet. The guests struggled up the stairs, as there was invariably a crush. No ball or entertainment was considered a success unless there were far more guests present than the ball-and-supper-rooms could accommodate with comfort. Your name, or names as the case might be, were announced, and after shaking hands with your hostess you drifted away to the ballroom, the young ladies in search of their partners and the mamas, dowagers, and chaperons proceeding to seat themselves on small gilt chairs along the wall. The daughters, unless they were dancing, stood by their side. The young girls who were not fortunate in finding partners were rather cruelly termed "wallflowers." I do not think that there are any "wallflowers" nowadays!

If you were seen dancing more than once with the same young man, the latter ran the risk of being questioned as to what were "his intentions," and I wonder how many budding romances came to nought owing to these very searching and rather tactless questions.

The following day, visiting-cards had to be left on one's hostess of the party, ball, or dinner of the preceding evening. I believe the leaving of visiting-cards has gone out of fashion, and a little note of "thank you," often accompanied by a few carefully chosen flowers, has taken their place.

Princess Marie Louise (1946)

All That Life Can Afford

I suggested a doubt, that if I were to reside in London, the exquisite zest with which I relished it in occasional visits might go off, and I might grow tired of it. JOHNSON. "Why, Sir, you find no man, at all intellectual, who is willing to leave London. No, Sir, when a man is tired of London, he is tired of life; for there is in London all that life can afford."

James Boswell (1791)

About Princess Marie Louise

Princess Marie Louise (1872–1956) was the daughter of Helena of Saxe-Coburg and Christian of Schleswig-Holstein. Marie Louise's grandmother was Queen Victoria (Helena was Victoria's third daughter). Related by blood or marriage to most of the ruling houses of Europe, Marie Louise herself was destined to marry royalty; in 1891 she married prince Aribert of the small Duchy of Anhalt, now a part of Germany. Their marriage was a distant one and was later annulled. Marie Louise lived the rest of her life in England. This quotation is from *My Memories of Six Reigns.*

About James Boswell

James Boswell (1740–1795) is best known as the biographer of the brilliant, idiosyncratic Samuel Johnson. This quotation is from Boswell's biography of Johnson (see p. 361).

BUILDING ENGLISH PROFICIENCY

Exploring Key Concepts

The second-person pronoun is *you.* The second person is rarely used in narrative writing, but Princess Marie Louise uses it here simply and effectively.

1. Question What is the effect of use of the second person in Princess Marie Louise's description? *(It adds a sense of immediacy and perhaps universality.)*

2. Question What other persons are used in this description? *(The first-person is used at the beginning and later in the sentences beginning "I do not think . . ."; "I wonder . . ."; and "I believe . . . " The third person is used in the remaining sentences.)*

About the London Blitzes

Blitz is short for the German word *blitz-krieg* meaning "lightning war." Aviation had had little effect in World War I because it was still in its infancy. Hitler considered bombing by air to be an important strategy in World War II, however. The plan was to soften British coastal defenses, transportation facilities, and population centers in preparation for a combined sea and air invasion. Ironically, the British fighter force, aided by newly developed radar, proved superior to German bombers, which were inadequately armed and unable to carry heavy loads of bombs.

"This is London . . ."

After the Fall of France in June 1940, Germany prepared to invade England. In an attempt to destroy British defenses, the Germans began an intensive air assault against England in August 1940. Early in September the focus of the German air raids shifted to the British capital, London. A 32-year-old American newsman, Edward R. Murrow (1908-1965), became famous for his radio broadcasts from London during the Battle of Britain. The following is an excerpt from his broadcast for October 10, 1940.

This is London, ten minutes before five in the morning. Tonight's raid has been widespread. London is again the main target. Bombs have been reported from more than fifty districts. Raiders have been over Wales in the west, the Midlands, Liverpool, the southwest, and northeast. So far as London is concerned, the outskirts appear to have suffered the heaviest pounding. The attack has decreased in intensity since the moon faded from the sky.

All the fires were quickly brought under control. That's a common phrase in the morning communiqués.[1] I've seen how it's done; spent a night with the London fire brigade. For three hours after the night attack got going, I shivered in a sandbag crow's-nest atop a tall building near the Thames. It was one of the many fire-observation posts. There was an old gun barrel mounted above a round table marked off like a compass. A stick of incendiaries[2] bounced off rooftops about three miles away. The observer took a sight on a point where the first one fell, swung his gun sight along the line of bombs, and took another reading at the end of the line of fire. Then he picked up his telephone and shouted above the half gale that was blowing up there, "Stick of incendiaries—between 190 and 220—about three miles away." Five minutes later a German bomber came boring down the river. We could see his exhaust trail like a pale ribbon stretched straight across the sky. Half a mile downstream there were two eruptions and then a third, close together. The first two looked like some giant had thrown a huge basket of flaming golden oranges high in the air. The third was just a balloon of fire enclosed in black smoke above the housetops. The observer didn't bother with his gun sight and indicator for that one. Just reached for his night glasses, took one quick look, picked up his telephone, and said, "Two high explosives and one oil bomb," and named the street where they had fallen. . . .

There was peace and quiet inside for twenty minutes. Then a shower of incendiaries came down far in the distance. They didn't fall in a line. It looked like flashes from an electric train on a wet night, only the engineer was drunk and driving his train in circles through the streets. One sight at the middle of the flashes and our observer reported laconically, "Breadbasket at 90—covers a couple of miles." Half an hour later a string of fire bombs fell right beside the Thames. Their white glare was reflected in the black, lazy water near the banks and faded out in midstream where the moon cut a golden swathe broken only by the arches of famous bridges.

We could see little men shoveling those fire bombs into the river. One burned for a few minutes like a beacon right in the middle of a bridge. Finally those white flames all went out. No one bothers about the white light, it's only when it turns yellow that a real fire has started.

I must have seen well over a hundred fire bombs come down and only three small fires were started. The incendiaries aren't so bad if there is someone there to deal with them, but those oil bombs present more difficulties.

As I watched those white fires flame up and die down, watched the yellow blazes grow dull and disappear, I thought, what a puny effort is this to burn a great city.

Edward R. Murrow (1940)

1. **communiqué** (kə myü′nə kā), *n.* official bulletin or statement. *[French]*

2. **incendiary** (in sen′dē er′ē), *n.* shell or bomb containing chemical agents that cause fire.

MINI-LESSON: READING/THINKING SKILLS

Visualize

Forming mental pictures as they read will help students respond to this description of an air raid.

Teach Have students close their eyes and listen while you or a volunteer reads "This is London . . ." Ask which of the sights Murrow describes was easiest to imagine. *(Possible response: The incendiary shower, because of the description of an electric train on a wet night.)* Point out that Murrow actually describes several different kinds of bombs, and that the reader or listener can tell the difference between them because of Murrow's exact descriptions and use of similes.

Activity Idea Have students write their own descriptions of some sort of light seen at night—fireworks, car headlights, lighted city windows, lightning bugs, and so on. They can then work in small groups to share their descriptions and, perhaps, to guess what is being described from the description alone.

THE LAST CIVILIZED METROPOLIS IN THE WORLD.

John Canaday (1972)

London Pride

There's a little city flower—every spring unfailing
Growing in the crevices by some London railing
Though it has a Latin name, in town and country-side
We in England call it London Pride.

London Pride has been handed down to us.
London Pride is a flower that's free.
London Pride means our own dear town to us,
And our pride it forever will be.

Woa Liza see the coster[1] barrows,
Vegetable marrows and the fruit piled high.
Woa Liza little London sparrows,
Covent Garden Market[2] where the costers cry.
Cockney[3] feet mark the beat of history.
Every street pins a memory down.
Nothing ever can quite replace
The grace of London Town.

In our city darkened now—street and squares and crescent
We can feel our living past in our shadowed present
Ghosts beside our starlit Thames who lived and loved and died
Keep throughout the ages London Pride.

London Pride has been handed down to us.
London Pride is a flower that's free.
London Pride means our own dear town to us,
And our pride it forever will be.

Gray city stubbornly implanted,
Taken so for granted for a thousand years.
Stay city smokily enchanted,
Cradle of our memories and hopes and fears.
Every Blitz[4] your resistance toughening
From the Ritz to the Anchor and Crown,[5]
Nothing ever could override
The Pride of London Town.

Noel Coward (1941)

RESPONDING

1. Summarize the sorts of reasons people have for loving London or for hating it. Do these reasons seem persuasive to you? Explain.
2. Do the details that make people respond positively or negatively seem to change over the years; that is, if you loved London then are you likely to hate it now (or vice versa)?
3. Which detail or description of London appeals to you the most? the least? Why?
4. Make a generalization about what happens when different artists look at the same monument or building (such as St. Paul's Cathedral on page 391) at different times over the years.
5. From the differing treatments of Londoners on page 387, what can you infer about the attitude of the artist in each case toward the particular group of people he portrays?

1. **coster,** street vendor.
2. **Covent Garden Market,** a large street market in the middle of London.
3. **cockney** (cok′nē), *n.* nickname for an inhabitant of the eastern section of London who speaks a particular dialect of English.
4. **blitz** (blits), *n.* Nazi bombing attack during World War II.
5. **Ritz . . . Crown,** that is, from the fine hotels to the corner taverns.

About Noel Coward

Sir Noel Coward (1899–1973) was a playwright, composer, and actor. Although best known for his light comedies and his lilting love songs, Coward showed high patriotism in such works as *Cavalcade* (1931) and the film *In Which We Serve* (1942). He was knighted in 1970.

About John Canaday

John Canaday (1907–1985) was an American mystery novelist and controversial art historian. For years he served as art critic with the *New York Times*. This quotation is from one of his *New York Times* columns.

Responding

1. Love: variety, beauty, humanity, bustle and excitement, high society, resistance, stubbornness and pride, grace, civilization; Hate: ostentation, crime and vice, foul weather, dirt, inhumanity, drunkenness and rowdy behavior, solitude, dullness.

2. No; poverty, for example, remains a problem no matter what efforts are made to eliminate it.

3. Every artist sees a building or monument differently, in terms of experiences and of what he or she wants to emphasize.

4. Henshall feels a shared humanity with the patrons of a neighborhood tavern. Doré finds compassion for the poor in Wentworth Street. Frith is impressed by the comings and goings of people in society.

Part One: Visions and Dreams

Planning Unit 5: The Romantic Era

Literature	Integrated Language Arts			
	Literary	Writing/Grammar, Usage and Mechanics	Reading, Thinking, Listening, Speaking	Vocabulary/Spelling
The Tyger *by William Blake* Poem *(average)* p. 402 **The Lamb** *by William Blake* Poem *(easy)* p. 404 **A New Jerusalem** *by William Blake* Poem *(challenging)* p. 404 **from Auguries of Innocence** *by William Blake* Poem *(average)* p. 405	Analogy Allusion Repetition Metaphor Symbol	Descriptive paragraph Essay Letter to Blake Standard capitalization	Find the main idea	
Titern Abbey *by William Wordsworth* Poem *(average)* p. 409 **My Heart Leaps Up** *by William Wordsworth* Poem *(easy)* p. 413 **The World Is Too Much with Us** *by William Wordsworth* Poem *(average)* p. 413	Blank verse Figurative language Imagery Paradox Theme	Journal Lyric poem Travel brochure Using dashes	Generalize	
Kubla Khan *by Samuel Taylor Coleridge* Poem *(average)* p. 417	Rhythm/meter Alliteration	Dream image poetry Travelogue Humorous summary Using nouns and pronouns	Visualize	
La Belle Dame Sans Merci *by John Keats* Poem *(average)* p. 423 **Ode to a Nightingale** *by John Keats* Poem *(average)* p. 426	Onomatopoeia Metaphor Point of view Personification Imagery	Phrases using onomatopoeia Essay—analyze imagery Rap poem Using adjectives	Find the main idea	Understand denotations

Meeting Individual Needs

Multi-modal Activities	Mini-Lessons
Illustrated time line Creating a visual Making cultural connections Making personal connections	Standard capitalization
Dialogue—Blake and Wordsworth Art talk Improving comprehension Responding to key statements	Using dashes
Illustrated map Video Oral description Responding to poetic ideas	Using nouns and pronouns
Performance Oral report—biographical Stream-of-consciousness monologue Making real-life connections Expanding vocabulary notebooks	Understand denotations Using adjectives

Interdisciplinary Studies
Visionary Experiences

Format	Content Area	Highlights	Skill
Article: **A World of Dreamers**	Multicultural	Accounts of how several cultures sought strength and wisdom in visionary experiences.	Using appropriate speaking behavior
Article: **The Power of Dreams**	Science	Explore research on what happens physically when people dream.	Encyclopedia
Art: **The Dark Side**	Fine Art	The dark side of visionary experience as represented by this painting.	Analyzing a painting

Writing Workshop

Mode	Writing Format	Writing Focus	Proofreading Skills
Descriptive writing	A travel article	Using spatial order terms	Getting letters in the right order

Program Support Materials

For Every Selection

Unit Resource Book
Graphic Organizer
Study Guide
Vocabulary Worksheet
Grammar Worksheet
Spelling, Speaking and Listening, or Literary Language Worksheet
Alternate Check Test
Vocabulary Test
Selection Test

For Every Writing Workshop

Unit Resource Book
Prewriting Worksheet
Revising Strategy Worksheet
Editing Strategy Worksheet
Presentation Worksheet
Writing Rubric
Transparency Collection
Fine Art Transparency
Student Writing Model Transparencies

For Every Interdisciplinary Study

Unit Resource Book
Study Guide
Mini-Lesson Skill Worksheet

Assessment

Unit Resource Book
TE Check Tests
Alternate Check Test (blackline master)
Vocabulary Test (blackline master)
Selection Test (blackline master)
Test Generator Software
Assessment Handbook

Part Two: The Outsider

Planning Unit 5: The Romantic Era

Literature	Integrated Language Arts			
	Literary	Writing/Grammar, Usage and Mechanics	Reading, Thinking, Listening, Speaking	Vocabulary/Spelling
A Man's a Man for A' That *by Robert Burns* Poem *(challenging)* p. 450 **A Red, Red Rose** *by Robert Burns* Poem *(easy)* p. 452 **Auld Lang Syne** *by Robert Burns* Poem *(average)* p. 452	Dialect	Complete similes Descriptive paragraph Letter to Burns Recognize colloquialism	Generalize	Translate poetry
from A Vindication of the Rights of Woman *by Mary Wollenstonecraft* Essay *(average)* p. 456	Allusions Tone	Essay Editorial Policy statement Recognizing propositions	Recognize use of persuasion	
She Walks in Beauty *by George Gordon, Lord Byron* Poem *(average)* p. 463 **When We Two Parted** *by George Gordon, Lord Byron* Poem *(average)* p. 464	Diction Rhyme Alliteration	Diction—characterization tool Description Poem Subject-verb agreement	Recognize values	Bulletin board display
Ode to the West Wind *by Percy Bysshe Shelley* Poem *(average)* p. 469 **Ozymandias** *by Percy Bysshe Shelley* Poem *(average)* p. 472	Apostrophe Figurative language Rhyme Mood Irony Theme	Description Write a poem Inscription Singular and plural nouns	Literal and figurative language Find the main idea	Synonym or antonym Denotation and connotation

Meeting Individual Needs

Multi-modal Activities	Mini-Lessons
Collections of photographs and drawings Exploring dialect	Recognize colloquialism
Prepare a speech Prepare a lesson Making cultural connections Expanding vocabulary notebooks	Recognizing propositions
Oral report Debate Making real-life connection	Subject-verb agreement
Happiest moments Oral report Design a monument Improving comprehension	Singular and plural nouns Denotation and connotation

Interdisciplinary Studies
Rebels with Causes

Format	Content Area	Highlights	Skill
Article: **Rebels with Causes**	Multicultural	Biographical sketches of historical rebels with important causes.	Photographs Specialized information sources
Article: **A Passion for Justice**	Career	An interview with a union organizer on what the job entails.	Analyzing a speech

Writing Workshop

Mode	Writing Format	Writing Focus	Proofreading Skills
Narrative/expository writing	A saturation research report	Using subordination Making note cards	Citing works in correct form

Program Support Materials

For Every Selection

Unit Resource Book
Graphic Organizer
Study Guide
Vocabulary Worksheet
Grammar Worksheet
Spelling, Speaking and Listening, or Literary Language Worksheet
Alternate Check Test
Vocabulary Test
Selection Test

For Every Writing Workshop

Unit Resource Book
Prewriting Worksheet
Revising Strategy Worksheet
Editing Strategy Worksheet
Presentation Worksheet
Writing Rubric
Transparency Collection
Fine Art Transparency
Student Writing Model Transparencies

For Every Interdisciplinary Study

Unit Resource Book
Study Guide
Mini-Lesson Skill Worksheet

Assessment

Unit Resource Book
TE Check Tests
Alternate Check Test (blackline master)
Vocabulary Test (blackline master)
Selection Test (blackline master)
Test Generator Software
Assessment Handbook

Part Three: Exceeding Human Limits

Planning Unit 5: The Romantic Era

Literature	Integrated Language Arts			
	Literary	Writing/Grammar, Usage and Mechanics	Reading, Thinking, Listening, Speaking	Vocabulary/Spelling
from Frankenstein *by Mary Shelley* Novel Excerpt *(average)* p. 492	Mood Genre Novel Metaphor Theme Foreshadowing Characterization Allegory Allusion Narrator Plot	Impressions Brief essay Descriptive paragraph Paragraph indentations	Visualize Make judgments	Expanding reading vocabulary

Meeting Individual Needs

Multi-modal Activities	Mini-Lessons
Debate Oral report Exploring key ideas Using figurative language to evoke horror Tracking characters Exploring predicate adjectives Making personal connections Evaluate arguments	Paragraph indentations Recognize cause and effect Mood Expanding reading vocabulary

Interdisciplinary Studies
Creating Life

Format	Content Area	Highlights	Skill
Article: **The Monster's Human Nature** *by Stephen Jay Gould*	Science	A scientists' argument that Hollywood consistently misinterprets the theme of Mary Shelley's novel.	Taking notes
Article: **Creators and Creatures**	Multicultural	Various artistic and literary cultural versions of creators.	Analyzing and responding to art
Article: **Mad Scientists?**	Popular Culture	Frankenstein has been the basis of many movies about mad scientists.	Recognize different purposes of art

Writing Workshop

Mode	Writing Format	Writing Focus	Proofreading Skills
Narrative writing	A scene for a horror story	Strengthening mood Getting started	Maintaining consistent verb tense

Program Support Materials

For Every Selection	For Every Writing Workshop
Unit Resource Book Graphic Organizer Study Guide Vocabulary Worksheet Grammar Worksheet Spelling, Speaking and Listening, or Literary Language Worksheet Alternate Check Test Vocabulary Test Selection Test	**Unit Resource Book** Prewriting Worksheet Revising Strategy Worksheet Editing Strategy Worksheet Presentation Worksheet Writing Rubric **Transparency Collection** Fine Art Transparency Student Writing Model Transparencies

For Every Interdisciplinary Study	Assessment
Unit Resource Book Study Guide Mini-Lesson Skill Worksheet	**Unit Resource Book** TE Check Tests Alternate Check Test (blackline master) Vocabulary Test (blackline master) Selection Test (blackline master) **Test Generator Software** **Assessment Handbook**

Unit 5 Supplemental Resources

Media and Technology

Part One Selections

The Tyger/The Lamb/A New Jerusalem/from Auguries of Innocence

Audiotape Students can hear a selection of Blake's poetry in *Essential Blake,* 58 minutes, Listening Library, 1987, and in *Poetry of William Blake*, Spoken Arts.

Community Resources Students might recall that King George III reigned from 1760-1820, most of Blake's life, and was on the throne during the American Revolution. Using library sources, some students might like to read about him, contrasting his views with those of Blake.

Lines Composed a Few Miles Above Tintern Abbey/My Heart Leaps Up/The World Is Too Much with Us

Audiotape *Treasury of William Wordsworth* is available from Spoken Arts.

Videotape *William Wordsworth*, 30 minutes, Britannica, is a program which traces the author's life. *William Wordsworth: William and Dorothy*, 52 minutes, Films for the Humanities & Sciences, is an award-winning film dramatization of the poet and his sister.

Home Connection What do family members do when the world closes in? Students might compile a list of favorite leisure-time activities and share them in the classroom, perhaps without revealing the name or the relationship of the family member.

Kubla Khan

Audiotape Students can hear "Kubla Khan" and poems of Blake, Wordsworth, and Keats on *Rime of the Ancient Mariner and Other Great Poems*, 1 hour 43 minutes, Listening Library, 1990.

Videotape Orson Welles delivers a reading of *Rime of the Ancient Mariner*, 42 minutes, Library Video Company, 1977. *Samuel Taylor Coleridge*, 52 minutes, Films for the Humanities & Sciences, focuses on the poet's tortured life.

Community Resources Visions are, or have been, important to many religions and cultures, including Celtic, Native American, medieval Christian, and Islamic. Some students might like to use local library sources to investigate the significance of visions over the centuries.

La Belle Dame Sans Merci/Ode to a Nightingale

Audiotape "Ode to a Nightingale" is included in the poems of *Essential Keats*, 59 minutes, Listening Library, 1987, and in *Treasury of John Keats*, Spoken Arts.

Videotape *John Keats: Poet,* 31 minutes, Britannica, portrays the poet and his life.

Community Resources Some students might like to research the life and work of English painters John Constable (1776-1837) and J. M. W. Turner (1775-1851).

Part Two Selections

A Man's a Man for A' That/A Red, Red Rose/Auld Lang Syne

Audiotape *Love Songs of Robert Burns,* containing several songs of love and loneliness, is available from Spoken Arts.

Videotape *Robert Burns: Love and Liberty*, 38 minutes, Films for the Humanities & Sciences, contains several poems sung or read.

Connections to
Custom Literature Database

For Part One "Visions and Dreams"

Selections with Lessons

- "Ode: Intimations of Immortality from Recollections of Early Childhood" by William Wordsworth
- "Ode on a Grecian Urn" by John Keats

Additional theme-based selections can be accessed on the ScottForesman database.

Connections to
Custom Literature Database

For Part Two "The Outsider"

Selections with Lessons

- "My Heart's in the Highlands" and "To a Louse" by Robert Burns
- "On This Day I Complete My Thirty-Sixth Year" by Lord Byron (George Gordon)

Additional theme-based selections can be accessed on the ScottForesman database.

Community Resources Burns led a colorful life, and some students might like to research more information about him than is given in the pupil edition. They may be interested in the Burns Night celebrations, often held in various places on January 25, his birthday, by Burns enthusiasts.

from A Vindication of the Rights of Woman

Videotape *Women in American Life: 1861-1955,* 60 minutes, National Women's History Project, combines fact-filled narrative with compelling images on women's roles.

Community Resources Mary Wollstonecraft was able to earn a living, though meager, by writing. Some students might like to investigate the occupations available to women in the l700s.

She Walks in Beauty/When We Two Parted

Audiotape *Treasury of George Gordon, Lord Byron,* Spoken Arts, includes "When We Two Parted," and others.

Home Connection Byron is said to have dressed as he thought a poet should look. At home students might like to discuss not only how a poet should look but how one's appearance affects others' perceptions. For example what would be the effect of a police force dressed in jeans instead of in uniform? supreme court justices dressed in yellow robes instead of black? dentists wearing black instead of white?

Ode to the West Wind/Ozymandias

Videotape *Percy Bysshe Shelley*, 30 minutes, Britannica, looks at the author's life. An impressive ensemble of actors bring the words of Byron, Keats, and Shelly to life in *The Glorious Romantics*, 1 hour 30 minutes, Monterey Home Video, 1994.

Community Resources Although Ozymandias's monument crumbled, students might like to investigate those still standing in their neighborhood or community, prepare a map showing the locations, and compile a list of who or what is commemorated by the monuments.

Part Three Selections

from Frankenstein

Audiotape An abridged reading of the novel is presented in *Frankenstein*, 3 hours, Simon & Schuster.

Videotape A wealth of material about the author and her work is presented in *Frankenstein, The Making of the Monster* and *The World of Mary Shelley*, Library Video Company. Also consider showing the classic version of the film starring Boris Karloff, *Frankenstein*, 1 hour 11 minutes, MCA Home Video, 1931. *True Story of Frankenstein*, 100 minutes, A&E/Library Video Company, 1996, explores Shelley's creation.

Computer Software *The Interactive History of Frankenstein*, available on CD-ROM for MPC and Macintosh, Library Video Company, contains a content-rich biography of Shelley. *The Essential Frankenstein*, CD-ROM for Windows, Byron Preiss Multimedia Company, 1994, is a multimedia exploration.

Community Resources Using local library resources, some students might like to research advances in animal or plant genetics and report to the class.

Connections to
Custom Literature Database

For Part Three "Exceeding Human Limits" Selections with Lessons

- "To a Skylark" by Percy Bysshe Shelley
- "The Lifted Veil" by George Eliot

Additional theme-based selections can be accessed on the ScottForesman database.

Connections to
AuthorWorks

Information about the life and times of William Blake, William Wordsworth, and Mary Shelley is available on ScottForesman's AuthorWorks CD-ROM.

Unit 5

The Romantic Era

Art Study

John Constable's *The Hay Wain* is a quiet nature scene of a family at work, painted in 1821. Ask students to describe the kind of painting they would choose to portray a unit called "The Romantic Era." Then compare their descriptions with the painting on this page. Is it effective in portraying romance?

Questions

- What are some dictionary definitions of *romantic? (Answers will depend on what dictionary students use.)*
- What about this scene is romantic? *(Possible responses: Feelings of romance are inspired by the pastoral, still scene; the cottage on a stream; the wholesome, outdoor work being performed; the beautiful trees and sky.)*

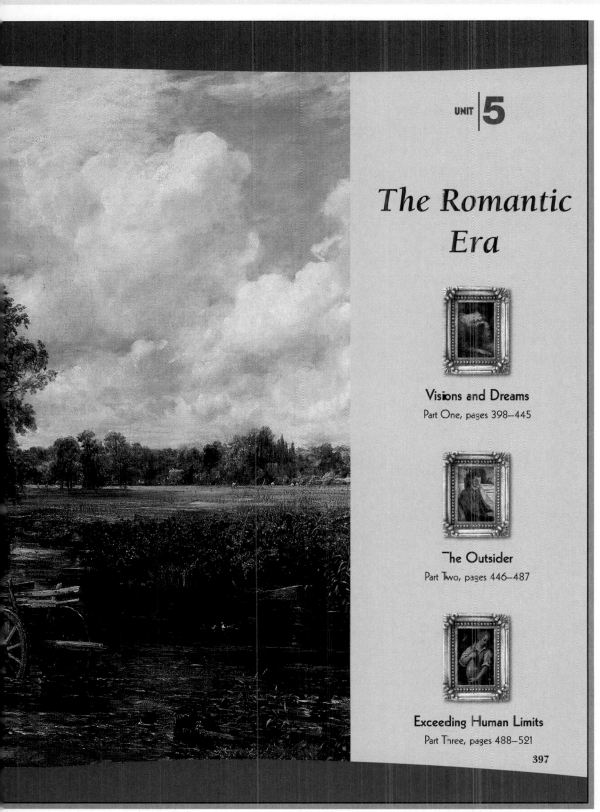

UNIT 5

The Romantic Era

Visions and Dreams
Part One, pages 398–445

The Outsider
Part Two, pages 446–487

Exceeding Human Limits
Part Three, pages 488–521

397

THEMATIC CONNECTIONS

The Romantic Age writers demonstrated a daring, individual, and imaginative approach to literature.

Part One

Visions and Dreams

The poetry in Part One illustrates the concept of the romantic as a dreamer.

Ideas to Explore

What ideas from the Age of Reason might be rejected by the Romantics?

Part Two

The Outsider

The role of the romantic writer as rebel and reformer is evident in the works of Burns, Shelley, Wollstonecraft, and Byron.

Ideas to Explore

- What is the definition of *outsider?*
- How do writers and artists outside the mainstream get their ideas recognized?

Part Three

Exceeding Human Limits

Frankenstein shows people's reactions to astonishing scientific and technological developments.

Ideas to Explore

What are the deep mysteries of creation that interest Dr. Frankenstein?

The "Visions and Dreams" icon is *Reverie* by Dante Gabriel Rossetti. "The Outsider" icon is *Self-Portrait in Weimar* by Edvard Munch. The "Exceeding Human Limits" icon is *Alchemist Laboratory* by Giovanni Stradano.

Part One: Visions and Dreams

Historical Overview

EXPLORING CONCEPTS

A reaction against the Age of Reason was partly responsible for the Age of Romanticism. The Romantic Era was characterized by

- a reverence for nature and childhood
- an interest in folklore, dreams, and visions
- an interest in the Middles Ages
- a focus on subjective experience, especially that of the artist

Art Study

Thomas Rowlandson (1756–1827) was an English caricaturist, best known for his wash-colored pen-and-ink sketches.

Henry Fuseli (1741–1825) was a professor of painting at the Royal Academy in London from 1799–1805 and from 1810–1825. He created illustrations for several Shakespeare plays, as well as for the works of Milton, Dante, and other poets. He was fascinated by the supernatural, and many of his works depict frenzied expressions on stylized figures.

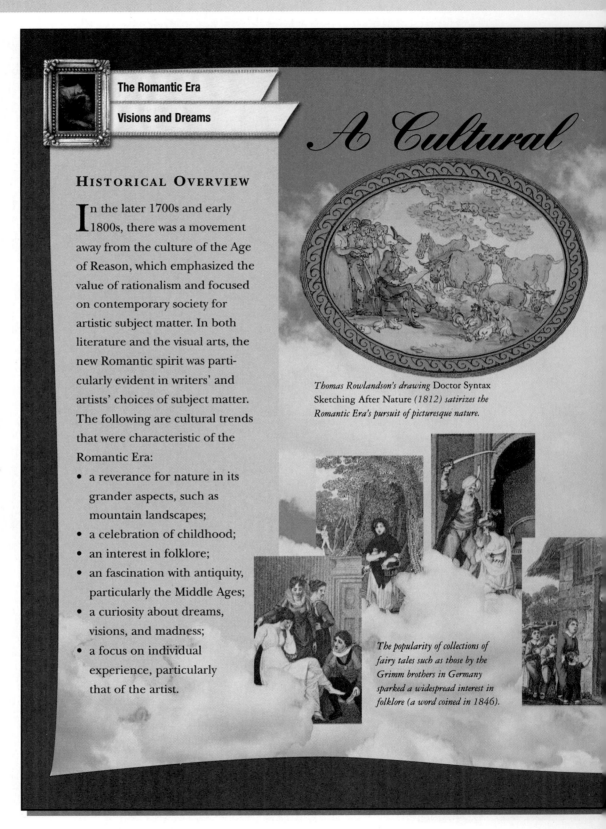

The Romantic Era

Visions and Dreams

A Cultural

HISTORICAL OVERVIEW

In the later 1700s and early 1800s, there was a movement away from the culture of the Age of Reason, which emphasized the value of rationalism and focused on contemporary society for artistic subject matter. In both literature and the visual arts, the new Romantic spirit was particularly evident in writers' and artists' choices of subject matter. The following are cultural trends that were characteristic of the Romantic Era:

- a reverance for nature in its grander aspects, such as mountain landscapes;
- a celebration of childhood;
- an interest in folklore;
- an fascination with antiquity, particularly the Middle Ages;
- a curiosity about dreams, visions, and madness;
- a focus on individual experience, particularly that of the artist.

Thomas Rowlandson's drawing Doctor Syntax Sketching After Nature *(1812) satirizes the Romantic Era's pursuit of picturesque nature.*

The popularity of collections of fairy tales such as those by the Grimm brothers in Germany sparked a widespread interest in folklore (a word coined in 1846).

Revolution

In the poems and pictures of his book Songs of Innocence *(1789), William Blake created images of childhood as paradise.*

The Romantic Era's fascination with the Middle Ages was reflected in the popularity of Gothic novels such as Horace Walpole's The Castle of Otranto. *Set in a medieval castle complete with underground passages, trap doors, dark stairways, and mysterious rooms, Walpole's novel began the fashion for strange tales full of weird landscapes, haunted ruins, sinister noblemen, and innocent heroines.*

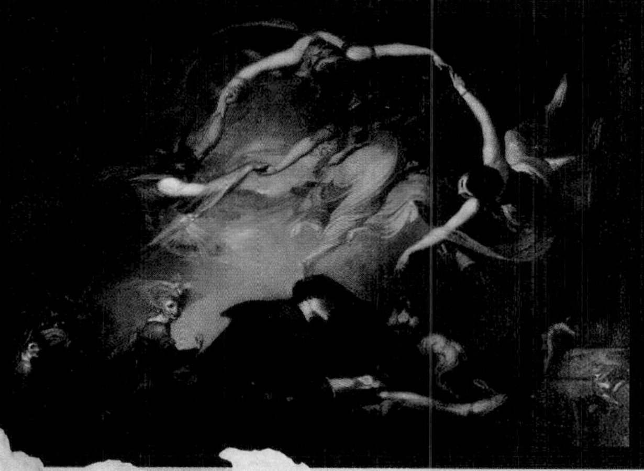

Henry Fuseli's painting The Shepherd's Dream *(1793), with its vision of fairies circling above the sleeping shepherd, suggests the Romantic interest in visionary experiences.*

Key Dates

1755
A massive earthquake in Lisbon undercuts belief in rational world order.

1764
The Castle of Otranto *starts fashion for Gothic novels.*

1785
Percy's collection of English and Scottish ballads published.

1798
Wordsworth and Coleridge's Lyrical Ballads *published.*

1799
Rosetta stone found in Egypt.

1812
Publication begins of Grimms' collection of German folktales.

1816
Elgin marbles removed from the Parthenon are purchased by the British Museum.

399

Key Dates

1760 Reign of George III begins.

1775 British war with colonies begins (The American Revolution); ends with American independence in 1783.

1789 French Revolution begins.

1812 The War of 1812 begins between America and Britain.

1812–13 George III is declared insane and the Regency (which lasts until 1820) begins, with the future George IV acting as Prince Regent.

1814 The Treaty of Ghent ends the War of 1812.

1815 Napoleon is defeated at Waterloo.

1818 Mary Shelley's *Frankenstein,* the first work of science fiction, is published.

MATERIALS OF INTEREST

Books

- *The Life and Death of Mary Wollstonecraft* by Claire Tomalin (Viking Penguin, 1992).
- *Lord Byron: Selected Letters and Journals* edited by Leslie A. Marchand (1984).
- *English Romantic Poets: Modern Essays in Criticism* edited by M. H. Abrams (Oxford UP, 1975).
- *The Romantic Age in Britain* by Boris Ford (Cambridge, 1992).

Multimedia

- *Frankenstein* [videotape] directed by James Whale; starring Boris Karloff (1931). 71 min., b&w, VHS. MCA Home Video. Order #23002
- *Frankenstein* directed by David Wickes; starring Patrick Bergan, Randy Quaid, John Mills, and Fiona Gillies (1992).
- *Romanticism: The Revolt of the Spirit* [videotape]. 24 min., color, VHS. (Learning Corporation of America, 1971).

Preview

Visions and Dreams

FOR ALL STUDENTS

What do the words *vision* and *dreams* mean? Discuss how they relate to the concept of romanticism.

To further explore the theme, use the Fine Art Transparency referenced below.

Transparency Collection
Fine Art Transparency 8

For At-Risk Students

After students have read over the poem titles and speculated on their content, ask them which poem they would choose to read first.

For Students Who Need Challenge

Have students choose a person mentioned in one of the poems. In a written report, students should answer these questions:

- What is the historical (or mythological) significance of this person?
- What is the significance of the person to the poem in which he or she appears?

For Visual and Social Learners

Students can plan and draw a comic strip that illustrates the poem of their choice.

MULTICULTURAL CONNECTION

Have students discuss what emotions the authors might have been experiencing as they wrote these works.

Part One

Visions and Dreams

Not all of life can be measured scientifically and considered logically. There are people who place greater trust in dreams, visions, and other heightened states of emotion.

Multicultural Connection One focus of the Romantic Era was on the **individuality** of the "common" men and women who made up most of the work force, and who, the poets felt, achieved dignity through their work. Some Romantic poets achieved their own individuality, however, above or beyond the cultural norms of the rest of society.

IDEAS THAT WORK

Motivating with Journals

"For my students, Romantic poetry means journaling—and lots of it! I want them to examine their own feelings, to think about their impressions of the world, and to use their imaginations. Many of the topics come directly from the titles or from lines in the poems.

The unit is perfect for a review of figurative language. Students can find examples of almost every poetic device—from alliteration to synecdoche—and note them in their journals. We don't just find and explain examples, however. We also write our own and then vote for the funniest, the most melancholy, and so on.

Culminating activities involve students in not only sharing their own writing, but also giving creative oral presentations of their favorite Romantic poems and designing their own visual aids to illustrate the poems."

Ruth Parkhurst
Hammond, Indiana

Before Reading

The Tyger
A New Jerusalem
The Lamb
from Auguries of Innocence

by William Blake

William Blake
1757–1827

William Blake was born in London and lived most of his life in a working class section of the city. Trained as an engraver, Blake supported himself as an illustrator throughout his life (See page 407.) As a child of four, Blake had his first mystical experience when he reported that he saw God's face. By the time he was eight, he related that he had seen angels in a field, the prophet Ezekiel, and a tree filled with angels. By the time of his marriage, Blake had become so consumed in mystical belief that his wife is said to have remarked: "I have very little of Mr. Blake's company. He is always in Paradise."

Building Background

A New Vision In his best-known works William Blake avoided the classical allusions and formal language that characterized the work of earlier poets. Instead he developed a childlike simplicity, lyricism, and visual immediacy that place him firmly with the group of Romantic poets, although his poetry is more visionary than that of most later Romantics. Largely unappreciated during his lifetime, he lived in poverty, his life driven by mystical experiences and a search for truth. Between 1783 and 1794 Blake wrote, illustrated, and printed his most famous lyric poems in *Songs of Innocence* and *Songs of Innocence and Experience: Shewing* [showing] *the Two Contrary States of the Human Soul.* He prepared his own illustrative engravings for these poems, and either he or his wife Catherine tinted each illustration by hand.

Literary Focus

Analogy An **analogy** is a comparison made between two situations, people, or ideas that are somewhat alike but unlike in most respects. Sometimes the comparison simply places two like things side by side and the reader must make the connection, as is often true of Blake. Sometimes a new, unfamiliar, or complex object or idea is explained through comparison to a familiar or simpler one. Look for the analogy or comparison as you read Blake's poetry, particularly "The Lamb."

Writer's Notebook

Look Around You Blake's poetry is characterized by strong **imagery,** which he achieves through careful choice of words. Look up from your reading at the scene around you—at the room you're in or outdoors through a window—and jot down some words and phrases that describe the scene. Try to choose words that call up specific and strong images. For example, not *door* but *golden oak door;* not *sound of an airplane* but *distant rumble of a 747.*

Before Reading

Building Background

Ask students to describe their images of the poet as genius. Note that Blake's life was largely as one might imagine the life of a poet: given to visions, he was driven to express himself; in an age of reason, he glorified intuition and imagination; unappreciated and poor, he personally manufactured each book he published. But contrary to the cliché, Blake, by all accounts, was a happy man, who relished life.

Literary Focus

You might note to students that the word *analogy* derives from an ancient Greek term used to express similarity in proportional relationships: "As *A* is to *B,* so *C* is to *D.*"

Writer's Notebook

Suggest that students use descriptive words and phrases that are connotative, as well as denotative.

More About William Blake

Blake, who had struggled with poverty all his life, was buried in a pauper's unmarked grave.

Connections to **AuthorWorks**

William Blake is a featured author in the AuthorWorks CD-ROM series.

SUPPORT MATERIALS OVERVIEW

Unit 5 Resource Book
- Graphic Organizer, p. 1
- Study Guide, p. 2
- Vocabulary, p. 3
- Grammar, p. 4
- Alternate Check Test, p. 5
- Vocabulary Test, p. 6
- Selection Test, pp. 7–8

Building English Proficiency
- Selection Summaries
- Activities, p. 226

Reading, Writing & Grammar SkillBook
- Grammar, Usage, and Mechanics, pp. 236–238

Technology
- Audiotape
- Personal Journal Software
- Custom Literature Database: Additional works by William Blake can be found on the database.
- Test Generator Software

During Reading

Selection Objectives

- to examine Blake's use of analogy
- to examine Blake's themes and "the contrary states of the human soul"
- to review conventions of standard capitalization

Unit 5 Resource Book
Graphic Organizer, p. 1
Study Guide, p. 2

Theme Link

Blake's lyrical visions and dreams reveal a world in which human beings, beset by evil, strive toward the divine within themselves.

Vocabulary Preview

immortal, living forever
symmetry, pleasing proportions; harmony
aspire, rise high
mead, meadow
bower, shelter

Students can add the words and definitions to their Writer's Notebooks.

1 Literary Element
Allusion

In lines 7 and 8, Blake alludes to characters in Greek mythology: Daedalus, who fashioned wings and flew; and Prometheus, who took fire from the gods and gave it to humanity.

2 Literary Focus
Analogy

Question What analogies can students find in the poem? *(Possible responses: The lamb is analogous to the tiger through their common creator; also, the blacksmith/industrial imagery, i.e., fire and anvil, suggests an analogy between God, the creator, and man, who dares seize the fire and create his own "fearful symmetry.")*

The Tyger

WILLIAM BLAKE

Tyger! Tyger! burning bright
In the forests of the night,
What immortal[1] hand or eye
Could frame thy fearful symmetry?[2]

In what distant deeps or skies
Burned the fire of thine eyes?
On what wings dare he aspire?[3]
1 What the hand dare seize the fire?

And what shoulder, & what art,
Could twist the sinews[4] of thy heart?
And when thy heart began to beat,
What dread Hand? & what dread feet?

What the hammer? what the chain?
In what furnace was thy brain?
What the anvil? what dread grasp
Dare its deadly terrors clasp?

When the stars threw down their spears
And watered heaven with their tears,
Did he smile his work to see?
Did he who made the Lamb make thee? 2

Tyger! Tyger! burning bright
In the forests of the night,
What immortal hand or eye
Dare frame thy fearful symmetry?

1. immortal (i môr′tl), *adj.* living forever.
2. symmetry (sim′ə trē), *n.* pleasing proportions between the parts of a whole; harmony.
3. aspire (ə spīr′), *v.* rise high.
4. **sinew** (sin′yü), *n.* tendon; also, strength; energy.

This hand-colored engraving, entitled *Tiger,* was created by the British artist Edward J. Detmold (1883–1957). In what ways does the artist's depiction of the tiger agree with the image Blake creates in "The Tyger"? ➤

SELECTION SUMMARY

The Tyger; The Lamb; The New Jerusalem; Auguries of Innocence

The Tyger Blake celebrates the tiger, an analogy for human experience. In this poem, the narrator glorifies God, recognizing that only an immortal could have created a creature as magnificent and terrible as the tiger.

The Lamb Blake looks at a lamb as the innocent side of the human character, symbolized by Jesus.

A New Jerusalem Blake expresses a determination to re-create a new Jerusalem, and all that implies, in England.

Auguries of Innocence The poem outlines the interconnection of all life on earth, as well as the interconnection of innocence and experience.

For summaries in other languages, see the ***Building English Proficiency*** *book.*

Art Study

Response to Caption Question Like Blake, the artist depicts a fearsome creature with fire in its eyes.

Visual Literacy The artist, Edward J. Detmold, juxtaposes two seemingly unlike things—a tiger head and a peacock feather—and compares their lines, patterns, and textures through meticulous technique.

Question Do students see an analogy between the tiger and the peacock feather? *(Possible response: While one is as soft and harmless as Blake's lamb and the other hard and fearsome, both have unique and immediately recognizable patterns much admired for their beauty. Detmold's highly detailed rendering seems to suggest that they are somehow more alike than different, as if they both spring from a common source.)*

BUILDING ENGLISH PROFICIENCY

Making Cultural Connections

Much of the power in "The Tyger" arises from a common understanding about symbols. Help students share their reactions to those symbols.

1. Have students read "The Tyger" a few times (or use the Audiotape).

2. On the chalkboard, list words from the poem that may have a larger meaning than the literal one. Among the possibilities are *tyger* (tiger), *forests, night, skies, fire, eyes, wings, hammer, furnace, anvil, stars, tears,* and *the Lamb.*

3. Call on volunteers to describe what each one means. Draw special attention to differences in interpretation. (For example, the Tyger may seem to be more a symbol of cunning than of dangerous power, and the Lamb loses some of its meaning for students unfamiliar with the Christian tradition.)

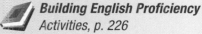

Building English Proficiency
Activities, p. 226

3 Literary Element
Repetition

Question In "The Lamb," how does Blake use repetition to enforce the mood of the poem? *(Possible response: The repetition suggests that a child is speaking and imparts the tone and rhythm of a nursery rhyme, reinforcing the innocent mood.)*

4 Literary Focus
Analogy

Question What analogy does Blake make in "The Lamb"? *(He draws an analogy between Jesus Christ as Redeemer and the innocence of the lamb.)*

5 Literary Element
Metaphor

Question In the poem, "A New Jerusalem," Blake compares human minds to mills, specifically Satanic mills. Completing this metaphor, what would such minds "mill" or grind out? *(Possible response: Satanic minds would mill greedy, dark, evil thoughts.)*

6 Literary Element
Symbol

Question What might Jerusalem symbolize? *(a righteous, Godly place)*

The Lamb

WILLIAM BLAKE

Little Lamb, who made thee?
Dost thou know who made thee?
Gave thee life & bid thee feed
By the stream & o'er the mead;[1]
Gave thee clothing of delight,
Softest clothing wooly bright;
Gave thee such a tender voice,
Making all the vales[2] rejoice!
3 Little Lamb who made thee?
Dost thou know who made thee?

Little Lamb, I'll tell thee,
Little Lamb, I'll tell thee!
He is callèd by thy name,
For he calls himself a Lamb:[3] 4
He is meek & he is mild;
He became a little child.
I a child & thou a lamb,
We are callèd by his name.
Little Lamb, God bless thee!
Little Lamb, God bless thee!

1. **mead** (mēd), *n.* meadow.
2. **vale** (vāl), *n.* valley.
3. **Lamb,** symbol of Jesus Christ as Redeemer: "Behold the Lamb of God, which taketh away the sin of the world." (John 1:29)

A New Jerusalem

WILLIAM BLAKE

And did those feet in ancient time[1]
Walk upon England's mountains green?
And was the holy Lamb of God
On England's pleasant pastures seen?

And did the Countenance Divine
Shine forth upon our clouded hills?
And was Jerusalem builded here,
5 Among these dark Satanic Mills?[2]

Bring me my Bow of burning gold!
Bring me my Arrows of desire!
Bring me my Spear! O clouds, unfold!
Bring me my Chariot of fire!

I will not cease from Mental Fight,
Nor shall My Sword sleep in my hand,
Till we have built Jerusalem 6
In England's green & pleasant Land.

1. **feet . . . time,** an allusion to legends that during the part of Jesus' life not described in the Bible, he traveled to many lands, including the British Isles.
2. **Satanic Mills,** mills of the mind, not industrial mills.

MINI-LESSON: GRAMMAR

Standard Capitalization

Many poets feel themselves exempt from the normal mechanics of the English language.

Teach Have students state rules they remember about capitalization. List their suggestions on the board. They will probably include these:

- Every sentence should begin with a capital letter.
- The first word of a direct quotation should begin with a capital letter.
- Every proper noun should be capitalized.
- Common nouns being personified may be capitalized.
- Capitalize a common noun when it is part of a specific name.
- In most poetry, every line begins with a capital letter.

Activity Idea Have students look at the first four lines of "Auguries of Innocence" and determine whether each capitalized word follows the guidelines listed on the board. Ask students why they think Blake broke so many capitalization rules in this poem. *(Possible responses: Blake used capitalization for emphasis; perhaps rules for capitalization were looser in his day; perhaps Blake's visionary style called for much personification.)*

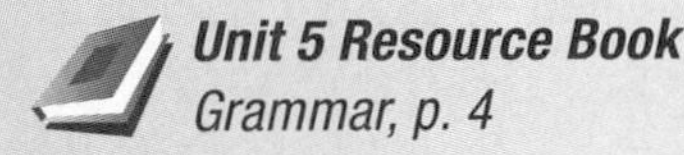

Unit 5 Resource Book
Grammar, p. 4

Auguries of Innocence

WILLIAM BLAKE

7 To see a World in a Grain of Sand
And a Heaven in a Wild Flower,
Hold Infinity in the palm of your hand
And Eternity in an hour.

A Robin Red breast in a Cage
Puts all Heaven in a Rage.
A dove house filled with doves & Pigeons
Shudders Hell through all its regions.
A dog starved at his Master's Gate
Predicts the ruin of the State.
A Horse misused upon the Road
Calls to Heaven for Human blood.
Each outcry of the hunted Hare
A fiber from the Brain does tear.
A Skylark wounded in the wing,
A Cherubim[1] does cease to sing.
The Game Cock clipped & armed for fight[2]
Does the Rising Sun affright.
Every Wolf's & Lion's howl
Raises from Hell a Human Soul.
The wild deer, wandering here & there,
Keeps the Human Soul from Care.
The Lamb misused breeds Public strife
And yet forgives the Butcher's Knife.
The Bat that flits at close of Eve
Has left the Brain that won't Believe.
The Owl that calls upon the Night
Speaks the Unbeliever's fright.
He who shall hurt the little Wren
Shall never be beloved by Men.
He who the Ox to wrath[3] has moved
Shall never be by Woman loved.
The wanton Boy that kills the Fly
Shall feel the Spider's enmity.[4]
He who torments the Chafer's[5] sprite
Weaves a Bower[6] in endless Night.
The Caterpillar on the Leaf
Repeats to thee thy Mother's grief.
Kill not the Moth nor Butterfly,
For the Last Judgment draweth nigh.
He who shall train the Horse to War
Shall never pass the Polar Bar.
The Beggar's Dog & Widow's Cat,
Feed them & thou wilt grow fat.
The Gnat that sings his Summer's song
Poison gets from Slander's tongue.
The poison of the Snake & Newt[7]
Is the sweat of Envy's Foot.
The Poison of the Honey Bee
Is the Artist's Jealousy.
The Prince's Robes & Beggar's Rags
Are Toadstools on the Miser's Bags.
A truth that's told with bad intent
Beats all the Lies you can invent.
It is right it should be so;
Man was made for Joy & Woe;
And when this we rightly know
Through the World we safely go. . . . 8

augury (ô′gyər ē), *n.* sign; omen.
1. **cherubim** (cher′ə bim), *n.* plural of *cherub,* one of the second highest order of angels.
2. **game cock . . . for fight,** in the sport of cockfighting, the natural spurs on the legs of specially bred roosters are often trimmed so that metal spurs can be fastened on.
3. **wrath** (rath), *n.* great anger.
4. **enmity** (en′mə tē), *n.* hostility; hatred.
5. **chafer** (chā′fər), *n.* beetle.
6. **bower** (bou′ər), *n.* shelter.
7. **newt** (nüt), *n.* salamander.

7 Literary Focus
Analogy

Question What are the analogies in the first quatrain? *(A grain of sand is to the world as a wildflower is to heaven; the human palm is to infinity as an hour is to eternity.)*

8 Reading/Thinking Skills
Find the Main Idea

Questions What is the main idea of "Auguries of Innocence"? *(While responses will vary, students should note that Blake describes the interconnections of all things; a grain of sand is a microcosm of the world; a starved dog testifies to the state of humanity.)* Does the poem remind you of an earlier text selection? *(Possible response: In Meditation 17, John Donne wrote about interconnections between all humanity: "when a clod be washed away . . ., Europe is the less . . . never send to know for whom the bell tolls; it tolls for thee . . .")*

Check Test

1. What is the first question the narrator poses to the tiger? *("What immortal hand or eye could frame thy fearful symmetry?")*

2. In "The Tyger," which imagery does Blake employ to describe its creation? *(blacksmithing or industrial imagery—fire, furnace, hammer, anvil, chain)*

3. In "The Lamb," how is the lamb's coat described? *(as delightful, soft, bright)*

4. In ancient times, who might have walked England's mountains? *(the Lamb of God—Jesus)*

5. According to the narrator of "Auguries of Innocence," what is the reward for feeding animals of the poor? *(The person will grow fat.)*

Unit 5 Resource Book
Alternate Check Test, p. 5

BUILDING ENGLISH PROFICIENCY

Making Personal Connections

Help students understand and apply "Auguries of Innocence" by creating two lists.

1. Have students work in groups to locate and list details that Blake offers as signs of an "innocent" person (for example, an innocent person does not mistreat animals; is not jealous, and so on).

2. Then have the same groups list details that they think would be "auguries of innocence" today.

3. As groups share responses, ask: Which "auguries" seem to be timeless? Which seem unique to today's world? Can you raise the level of your personal "innocence"?

After Reading

MAKING CONNECTIONS

1. Answers will vary, but should address the *visionary* quality of Blake's poetry or the *innocence* inherent in his beliefs.

2. Possible response: that the burning eye of the tiger, like the roar of the lion and the howl of the wolf, is of the mind of God, something too deep, awesome, and mysterious for humanity to comprehend

3. Possible responses: the tiger—fearsome, hard, fiery; the lamb—soft, wooly, tender-voiced

4. To Blake, the word *Jerusalem* seemed to connote a goal toward which people should strive; to the reader, the word indicates what England is not, but could become—a home to the righteous.

5. Possible responses: All life is interrelated; all life, particularly the lives of innocents, is sacred.

6. Students may respond that Blake's mystical visions, innocence in the face of contrary experiences, and idealism set him apart then, as they would now.

7. Possible responses: Blake might choose computer graphics; as his engraving techniques were new to his time, computer graphics are new to the present day; the medium would also allow him to work alone, which would probably suit him best.

After Reading

Making Connections

Shaping Your Response

1. Judging from his poetry only, what one word or phrase would you use to describe William Blake?

Analyzing the Poems

2. Blake also wrote (in "The Marriage of Heaven and Hell"), "The roaring of lions, the howling of wolves . . . are portions of eternity, too great for the eye of man." How does this help explain Blake's attitude toward the creature in "The Tyger"?
3. "The Lamb" is from *Songs of Innocence,* in which the poems recapture the happiness of childhood. "The Tyger" is from *Songs of Experience,* in which the poems are in part about social evils and reveal Blake's attempt to reconcile evil and good. He believed that the innocence of childhood must be balanced by the wisdom gained through experience, however painful and disenchanting. What qualities of the lamb and the tiger are emphasized in these matched poems?
4. The **connotation** of a word is what is suggested in addition to the literal meaning. What connotation does the word *Jerusalem* seem to have to Blake? to his readers?
5. Summarize one **theme** of "Auguries of Innocence."
6. Comment on the **individuality** of Blake—the person and the poet—based on what you have read of his poetry and what you have read about his life.

Extending the Ideas

7. What art form do you think Blake would choose to express his visions if he were living today—movies, multimedia, computer graphics, or what?

Literary Focus: Analogy

An **analogy** is a comparison made between two people, situations, or ideas that are somewhat alike but unlike in most respects. The analogy in "The Lamb" is between the innocent lamb with a "tender voice" and Jesus as the Lamb of God, also "meek and mild," who according to Christian belief came to earth as the son of God. The analogy deals in part with the mystery of creation. What does it mean for Jesus to be called by the names of the child and the lamb? What does it mean for the child and the lamb to be called by the same names as Jesus? What analogy can you find in "The New Jerusalem"?

406 UNIT FIVE: THE ROMANTIC ERA

LITERARY FOCUS: ANALOGY

Jesus is called a child because He was God transfigured or God reborn as the baby Jesus. Blake's line "For he calls himself a lamb" refers to biblical references to Jesus as the Lamb of God. In the line "We are called by his name," Blake may be saying "We are called Christians" or "We are called by or to Jesus, i.e., God."

Blake draws an analogy between England in the period when Christianity and its lessons first spread across the land—a holy place—and his England of dark Satanic mills. Using supernatural weapons and force of will, the narrator will again make a righteous, holy place—a Jerusalem—of his green and pleasant land.

Vocabulary Study

Write the letter of the word that is not related in meaning to the other words in the set.

aspire
bower
immortal
mead
symmetry

1. **a.** mead **b.** field **c.** hillside **d.** pasture
2. **a.** shelter **b.** bower **c.** refuge **d.** tombstone
3. **a.** wicked **b.** sinful **c.** immortal **d.** evil
4. **a.** concert **b.** symmetry **c.** opera **d.** play
5. **a.** aspire **b.** rise **c.** ascend **d.** hunt

Expressing Your Ideas

Writing Choices

Writer's Notebook Update Look over the words or phrases you jotted down to describe a scene, and write a descriptive paragraph of that scene using some of those words. You might use spatial order in your paragraph.

Digging Deep Choose one of Blake's poems, and in an **essay** describe how he has used one or more of the following literary techniques and discuss their effect on the poem: alliteration, repetition, metaphor, symbol, imagery, connotation.

Dear Mr. Blake Blake once wrote in a letter: "What is Grand is necessarily obscure to Weak men. That which can be made Explicit [clear] to the Idiot is not worthy my care." Suppose he had written this in a letter to you. Write a **letter** to Blake agreeing or disagreeing with his views.

Other Options

What Happened When Create an illustrated **time line** showing major events of the industrial revolution in England and America during Blake's lifetime (1757–1827). Include inventions and technical advances.

I Want! This is a metal engraving that William Blake created as an illustration for *The Gates of Paradise* (1793). Create a **visual expressing aspiration,** or ambition, and your views toward it. Your visual could be a piece of sculpture in paper, clay, or metal; it could be a collage; it could be computer art or animation. Even if you think that Blake's image of a stepladder to the moon is a bit of an exaggeration, you need not be limited by anything except your imagination.

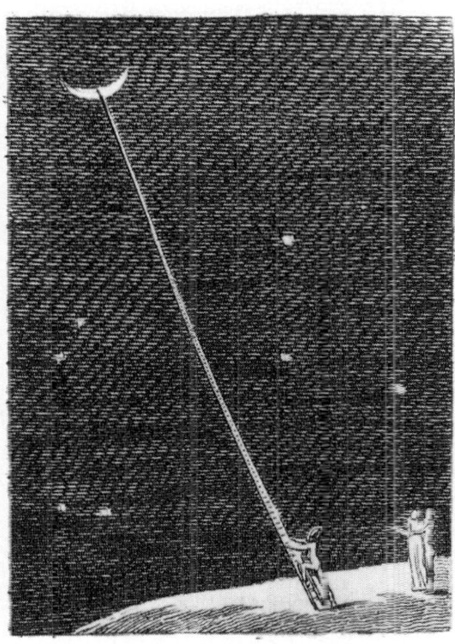

VOCABULARY STUDY

1. c.
2. d.
3. c.
4. b.
5. d.

More Practice Have students use other vocabulary terms from this selection to construct three more word sets similar to those shown in this activity. Ask students to exchange papers and answer each other's test questions.

Unit 5 Resource Book
Vocabulary, p. 3
Vocabulary Test, p. 6

WRITING CHOICES

Writer's Notebook Update

You may wish to explain that if a student decides to work in spatial order, he or she will choose a starting point, such as the classroom door or a tree seen through the window; from the starting point, he or she will describe the scene, moving left to right [or right to left] or up, over, and down.

Digging Deep

When students have finished this assignment, ask volunteers to identify examples of each of the literary techniques listed.

Dear Mr. Blake

Tell students that this is an opportunity to correspond with one of the great visionaries of history and that they should fully express their feelings.

OTHER OPTIONS

What Happened When

If student history texts do not give a complete summary of major events of the industrial revolution, suggest that students refer to encyclopedias.

I Want!

When students have completed their artwork, invite them to share their creations with the class; invite the class to guess what ambition is being illustrated in each.

Selection Test

Unit 5 Resource Book
Selection Test, pp. 7–8

Before Reading

Building Background

You might ask students if they have ever been *emotionally moved* by nature; if in the midst of natural surroundings, they have ever experienced a moment of perfection. Invite students to share such moments.

Literary Focus

You might note that of the three Wordsworth poems, only "Tintern Abbey" is written in blank verse.

Writer's Notebook

For journal entries, students might also visit a park, lake, public garden, or some other site of natural beauty.

More About William Wordsworth

Although Wordsworth's reputation remained high with the public and he was made poet laureate in 1843, he lost the admiration of the younger Romantic poets, who felt the power of his poetry had waned and his growing conservatism betrayed his own ideals.

Connections to **AuthorWorks**

William Wordsworth is a featured author in the AuthorWorks CD-ROM series.

Before Reading

Tintern Abbey
My Heart Leaps Up
The World Is Too Much with Us by William Wordsworth

William Wordsworth
1770–1850

During the summer of 1790 Wordsworth went on a walking tour of Switzerland and France and returned to England fired with enthusiasm for the French Revolution. After his graduation from Cambridge, he returned to France, where he fell in love with Annette Vallon. They had a daughter, but lack of funds forced his return to England, and declaration of war between Britain and France in 1793 prevented his return to France. He later saw Vallon and helped support their daughter, however. In 1802 he married a childhood friend, Mary Hutchinson, and they had five children, two of whom died at an early age. Wordsworth was not universally liked (poet John Keats thought him an egotist). However, Wordsworth achieved national recognition and great public respect before his death.

Building Background

Devising the Plan The beginning of Wordsworth's friendship with poet Samuel Taylor Coleridge in 1795 led to two revolutionary ideas about poetry. In 1798 they published *Lyrical Ballads.* The book was at first not well received by critics or other poets. In a preface to an expanded edition in 1800 Wordsworth stated that "all good poetry is the spontaneous overflow of powerful feelings" and that poetry must be in the language "really used by men"; that is, in simple, direct language. Both ideas were revolutionary in that they helped to free poetry from earlier rigid ideas about suitable subject matter and language.

Literary Focus

Blank Verse **Blank verse** is unrhymed and written in iambic pentameter—which, of all the various rhythms, is closest to the natural rhythms of English speech. (See the Glossary of Literary Terms.) The heroic couplets of Alexander Pope (see page 313) are also in iambic pentameter; the difference is that they rhyme and blank verse does not. As you read "Tintern Abbey," consider whether Wordsworth's poetic lines actually do sound like natural English speech.

Writer's Notebook

Dorothy's Journals The journals of Wordsworth's sister Dorothy contain vivid descriptions of landscape, walking, and weather:

"1st March [1798] . . . . The shapes of the mist, slowly moving along, exquisitely beautiful; passing over the sheep they almost seemed to have more of life than those quiet creatures. The unseen birds singing in the mist."

Try keeping a journal for several days of your walking and the weather and the landscape you travel through daily.

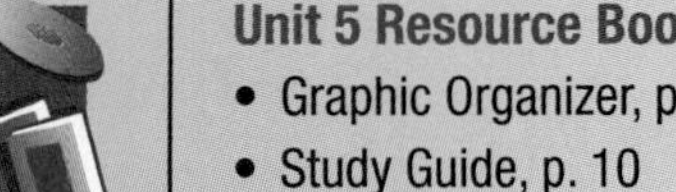

SUPPORT MATERIALS OVERVIEW

Unit 5 Resource Book
- Graphic Organizer, p. 9
- Study Guide, p. 10
- Vocabulary, p. 11
- Grammar, p. 12
- Alternate Check Test, p. 13
- Vocabulary Test, p. 14
- Selection Test, pp. 15–16

Building English Proficiency
- Selection Summaries
- Activities, p. 227

Reading, Writing & Grammar SkillBook
- Grammar, Usage, and Mechanics, pp. 247–248

The World of Work
- Conservationist, p. 15
- Activity, p. 16

Technology
- Audiotape
- Personal Journal Software
- Custom Literature Database: Additional selections by Wordsworth can be found on the database.
- Test Generator Software

Lines Composed a Few Miles Above Tintern Abbey

On Revisiting the Banks of the Wye During a Tour. July 13, 1798

William Wordsworth

Wordsworth wrote this poem during a walking tour with his sister Dorothy along the River Wye. The beautiful ruin of Tintern Abbey, once a monastery, is located in a deep valley at the river's edge. Wordsworth later wrote that "no poem of mine was composed under circumstances more pleasant for me to remember than this."

1

Five years have passed; five summers, with the length
Of five long winters! and again I hear
These waters, rolling from their mountain-springs
With a soft inland murmur. Once again
Do I behold these steep and lofty cliffs,
That on a wild secluded scene impress
Thoughts of more deep seclusion; and connect
The landscape with the quiet of the sky.
The day is come when I again repose
Here, under this dark sycamore, and view
These plots of cottage-ground, these orchard-tufts,
Which at this season, with their unripe fruits,
Are clad[1] in one green hue, and lose themselves
'Mid groves and copses.[2] Once again I see
These hedge-rows, hardly hedge-rows, little lines
Of sportive wood run wild: these pastoral farms,
Green to the very door; and wreaths of smoke
Sent up, in silence, from among the trees!
With some uncertain notice, as might seem
Of vagrant[3] dwellers in the houseless woods,
Or of some Hermit's cave, where by his fire
The Hermit sits alone.
These beauteous forms,
Through a long absence, have not been to me
As is a landscape to a blind man's eye:
But oft, in lonely rooms, and 'mid the din
Of towns and cities, I have owed to them
In hours of weariness, sensations sweet,
Felt in the blood, and felt along the heart;
And passing even into my purer mind,
With tranquil restoration:—feelings too
Of unremembered pleasure: such, perhaps,
As have no slight or trivial influence
On that best portion of a good man's life,
His little, nameless, unremembered acts
Of kindness and of love. Nor less, I trust,
To them I may have owed another gift,
Of aspect more sublime;[4] that blessed mood
In which the burthen[5] of the mystery,
In which the heavy and the weary weight

1. clad (klad), *adj.* clothed.
2. copse (kops), *n.* thicket of small bushes or shrubs.
3. vagrant (vā′grənt), *adj.* wandering.
4. **sublime** (sə blīm′), *adj.* noble; grand; exalted.
5. **burthen** (bėr′ᴛʜən), *n.* burden.

SELECTION SUMMARY

Lines Composed a Few Miles Above Tintern Abbey; My Heart Leaps Up; The World Is Too Much with Us

Tintern Abbey After five years, the poet returns to the Wye River valley. He again admires its beauty, recalling that his memories of it have inspired acts of love, serenity, and spiritual understanding. He foresees that memories of this moment will provide future understanding and solace for him and his sister.

My Heart Leaps Up The poet expresses hope that his response to nature will never diminish, that the child's love of nature, which fathered the same in the man, will continue unbroken, always providing meaning to life.

The World Is Too Much with Us The poet contends that humanity, in its getting and spending, is cut off from the natural world; he would prefer being a pagan, who at least retains the capacity to wonder at the glories of the earth.

*For summaries in other languages, see the **Building English Proficiency** book.*

During Reading

Selection Objectives

- to identify blank verse and compare it to rhymed iambic pentameter
- to analyze nature and individuality as themes of Romantic poetry
- to apply conventions of standard punctuation to dashes

Unit 5 Resource Book
Graphic Organizer, p. 9
Study Guide, p.10

Theme Link

Wordsworth, writing in an age of political and industrial revolution, found inspiration in nature for visions and dreams of a better and freer life.

Vocabulary Preview

clad, clothed
copse, thicket of small bushes
vagrant, wandering
corporeal, of or for the body
sylvan, of or flowing through woods
perplexity, confusion
cataract, waterfall
chasten, discipline
interfuse, blend; mix
exhortation, strong urging

Students can add the words and definitions to their Writer's Notebook.

1 Literary Focus
Blank Verse

You might ask a student to read the first eight lines aloud. Remind the reader to ignore line breaks and follow punctuation as he or she would follow traffic signals.

Questions What is the meter? *(iambic pentameter)* Compared to Shakespeare's rhymed iambic pentameter, how does blank verse sound? *(While responses will vary, students should note that it sounds much more like natural speaking.)*

2 Reading/Thinking Skills
Generalize

Question What general idea is expressed between lines 1 and 57? *(The narrator revisits this place after five years. He describes its beauty and how memories of this beauty have often restored his spirit; inspired him to treat others with love; and provided solace and spiritual understanding.)*

3 Literary Element
Figurative Language

Questions To what is the narrator referring in the "life and food" metaphor? *(renewed memories that will sustain him in the future)* To what does he compare his youthful self in the line 67 simile? *(a roe)*

4 Literary Element
Imagery

Questions To what senses do these images appeal? *(hearing [waterfall]; sight [waterfall, rock, mountain])* By bringing your memories of nature to a second reading of these images, are any additional senses appealed to? *(Possible responses: smell [the woods]; touch [rock, bark]; sound [birds, wind in trees, walking through leaves and over pine needles])*

Of all this unintelligible world,
Is lightened—that serene and blessed
mood,
In which the affections gently lead us on,
Until, the breath of this corporeal[6] frame
And even the motion of our human blood
Almost suspended, we are laid asleep
In body, and become a living soul:
While with an eye made quiet by the power
Of harmony, and the deep power of joy,
We see into the life of things.
If this
Be but a vain belief, yet, oh! how oft—
In darkness and amid the many shapes
Of joyless daylight; when the fretful stir
Unprofitable, and the fever of the world,
Have hung upon the beatings of my heart—
How oft, in spirit, have I turned to thee,
O sylvan[7] Wye! thou wanderer through
the woods,
2 How often has my spirit turned to thee!

And now, with gleams of half-
extinguished thought,
With many recognitions dim and faint,
And somewhat of a sad perplexity,[8]
The picture of the mind revives again:
While here I stand, not only with the sense
Of present pleasure, but with pleasing
thoughts
3 That in this moment there is life and food
For future years. And so I dare to hope,
Though changed, no doubt, from what I
was when first
I came among these hills; when like a roe[9]
I bounded o'er the mountains, by the sides
Of the deep rivers, and the lonely streams,
Wherever nature led: more like a man
Flying from something that he dreads
than one
Who sought the thing he loved. For
nature then
(The coarser pleasures of my boyish days,
And their glad animal movements all
gone by)
To me was all in all. I cannot paint
What then I was. The sounding cataract[10]
Haunted me like a passion: the tall rock, **4**
The mountain, and the deep and
gloomy wood,
Their colors and their forms, were
then to me
An appetite; a feeling and a love,
That had no need of a remoter charm,
By thought supplied, nor any interest
Unborrowed from the eye. That time
is past,
And all its aching joys are now no more,
And all its dizzy raptures. Not for this
Faint I, nor mourn nor murmur; other gifts
Have followed; for such loss, I would believe,
Abundant recompense.[11] For I have learned
To look on nature, not as in the hour
Of thoughtless youth; but hearing
oftentimes
The still, sad music of humanity,
Nor harsh nor grating, though of ample
power
To chasten[12] and subdue. And I have felt
A presence that disturbs me with the joy
Of elevated thoughts; a sense sublime
Of something far more deeply interfused,[13]
Whose dwelling is the light of setting suns,
And the round ocean and the living air,
And the blue sky, and in the mind of man:
A motion and a spirit, that impels
All thinking things, all objects of all thought,

6. corporeal (kôr pôr′ē əl), *adj.* of or for the body.
7. sylvan (sil′vən), *adj.* of or flowing through woods.
8. perplexity (pər plek′sə tē), *n.* confusion.
9. **roe** (rō), *n.* a small deer.
10. cataract (kat′ə rakt′), *n.* waterfall.
11. **recompense** (rek′əm pens), *n.* payment; reward.
12. chasten (chā′sn), *v.* discipline.
13. interfuse (in′tər fyüz′), *v.* blend; mix.

Tintern Abby, a 1931 poster created by Freda Lingstrom, advertised a package tour of the Wye Valley. Does the scene depicted in this poster make you want to visit the Wye Valley? Why or why not? ➤

MINI-LESSON: GRAMMAR

Using Dashes

The dash was a punctuation mark much favored by Romantic poets.

Teach A dash—a straight line—indicates pauses and marks off thoughts known as asides. A dash can be used singly or in parenthetical pairs when the main sentence is resumed after the pause. Its main uses are: (1) to indicate an additional statement or fact that calls for more emphasis than is given by commas; (2) to indicate a pause, especially for effect at the end of a sentence; (3) to add an afterthought.

Have students determine the reason for the dash in these lines of the poem: lines 50–54 (additional statement; commas would have been confusing because of the extra punctuation); lines 106–107 at the semicolon (additional explanation); lines 153 (after colon)–155 (add an afterthought).

Activity Ideas

- Ask students to write three sentences using dashes; each sentence should demonstrate a different use of the dash.
- Have students find a sentence from another selection that uses a dash or dashes and state the intended use.

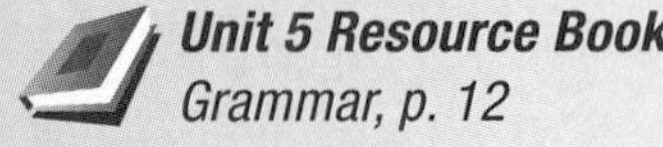

Unit 5 Resource Book
Grammar, p. 12

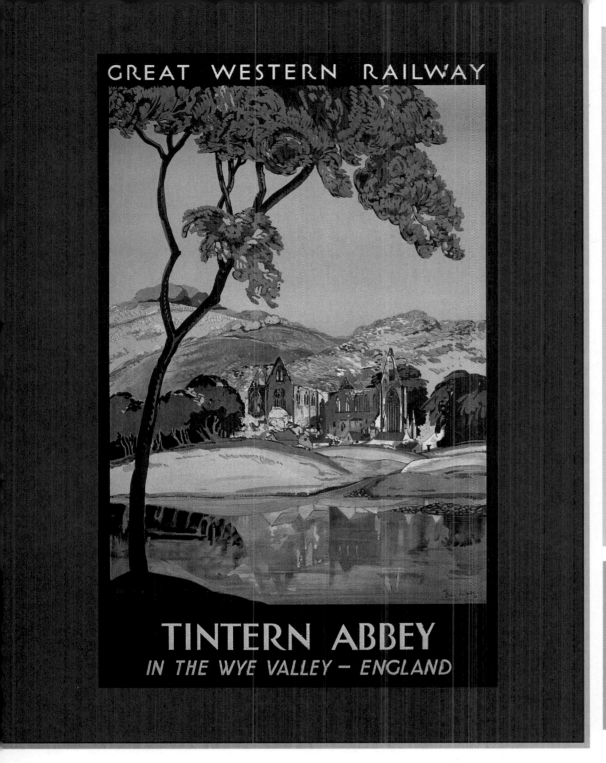

GREAT WESTERN RAILWAY

TINTERN ABBEY

IN THE WYE VALLEY – ENGLAND

Responses to Caption Questions
Most students will want to visit the Wye Valley as it is depicted—idyllic.

Visual Literacy The poster is typical of commercial art of this period, which generally was executed with a high degree of skill and style. The scene is intended to lure its viewer into a vacation; highlighting the abbey, the setting of a very famous poem, is not a coincidence; the artist plugs into the viewer's memory of Wordsworth's rhapsodic descriptions, exploiting that memory as part of the ad campaign. This idealized depiction also owes a debt to the composition, stylized delicacy, and flattened dimensions of the Japanese wood-block print.

Questions While the intent of this poster was commercial, the artist created a thing of beauty. Do students think commercial artists still blend commerce with beauty? *(Responses will vary. Students might mention the creativity of some television commercials.)*

The World of Work

Conservationist

For a discussion of conservation of natural beauty, use the pages referenced below.

The World of Work
pp. 15–16

BUILDING ENGLISH PROFICIENCY

Improving Comprehension

Students may better grasp Wordsworth's somewhat aesthetic contemplation if they try to mirror his thinking process.

1. Invite students to think back five years. Ask questions such as the following:

- At that time, what were your goals? your hopes?
- Are you now where you thought that you would be?
- Which goals or hopes have come true? Which have not?

Encourage students to respond in first languages other than English and to record some responses in their journals. Allow for optional, voluntary sharing.

2. Have students keep a response journal as they read. In addition to other kinds of notes, ask them to comment upon ways in which they see Wordsworth to be like themselves in this matter of reflecting upon the past.

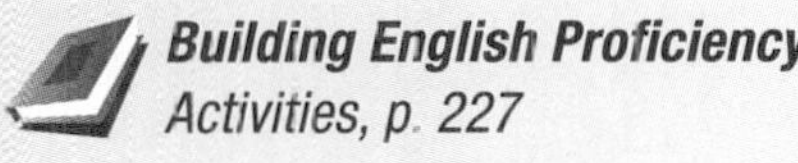
Building English Proficiency
Activities, p. 227

5 Reading/Thinking Skills
Generalize

Question What general ideas are expressed between lines 58 and 111? *(The poet relates that his memories were those of a different person—a coarse youth who bounded through the valley like an unthinking animal. His response is now tempered by intellect and a sense of the sublime that impels all thinking beings. He is still moved, but acknowledges that for him the beauties of nature have become the "guide and guardian" of his soul and moral being.)*

6 Literary Element
Imagery

Question To what "wild" simile earlier in the poem might the "shooting lights of wild eyes" image correspond? *(to the comparison between the youthful self and the bounding roe)*

7 Reading/Thinking Skills
Understand Sequence

Question What time sequence does the narrator follow? *(He begins in the present; recalls the past; and ends by projecting into the future.)*

8 Reading/Thinking Skills
Generalize

Question What is the general idea expressed between lines 112 and 159? *(In his sister's response, the narrator perceives the untamed pleasure of his youth. He prays that she finds in nature a joy and solace that will arm her against the coarseness and banality of life; that the memory of this time, and of his words, will heal the pain of solitude.)*

And rolls through all things. Therefore am I still
A lover of the meadows and the woods,
And mountains; and of all that we behold
From this green earth; of all the mighty world
Of eye, and ear—both what they half create,
And what perceive; well pleased to recognize
In nature and the language of the sense
The anchor of my purest thoughts, the nurse,
The guide, the guardian of my heart, and soul
5 Of all my moral being.
                    Nor perchance,
If I were not thus taught, should I the more
Suffer my genial spirits[14] to decay:
For thou art with me here upon the banks
Of this fair river; thou my dearest Friend,[15]
My dear, dear Friend; and in thy voice I catch
The language of my former heart, and read
My former pleasures in the shooting lights
6 Of thy wild eyes. Oh! yet a little while
May I behold in thee what I was once,
My dear, dear Sister! and this prayer I make,
Knowing that Nature never did betray
The heart that loved her; 'tis her privilege,
Through all the years of this our life, to lead
From joy to joy: for she can so inform[16]
The mind that is within us, so impress
With quietness and beauty, and so feed
With lofty thoughts, that neither evil tongues,
Rash judgments, nor the sneers of selfish men,
Nor greetings where no kindness is, nor all
The dreary intercourse of daily life,
Shall e'er prevail against us, or disturb
Our cheerful faith, that all which we behold
Is full of blessings. Therefore let the moon
Shine on thee in thy solitary walk;
And let the misty mountain-winds be free
To blow against thee: and, in after years, **7**
When these wild ecstasies shall be matured
Into a sober pleasure; when thy mind
Shall be a mansion for all lovely forms,
Thy memory be as a dwelling-place
For all sweet sounds and harmonies; oh! then,
If solitude, or fear, or pain, or grief,
Should be thy portion, with what healing thoughts
Of tender joy wilt thou remember me,
And these my exhortations![17] Nor, perchance—
If I should be where I no more can hear
Thy voice, nor catch from thy wild eyes these gleams
Of past existence—wilt thou then forget
That on the banks of this delightful stream
We stood together; and that I, so long
A worshipper of Nature, hither[18] came
Unwearied in that service: rather say
With warmer love—oh! with far deeper zeal[19]
Of holier love. Nor wilt thou then forget,
That after many wanderings, many years
Of absence, these steep woods and lofty cliffs,
And this green pastoral landscape, were to me
More dear, both for themselves and for thy sake! **8**

---

14. **genial spirits,** powers native to the poet.
15. **my dearest Friend,** Dorothy, Wordsworth's sister.
16. **inform,** inspire.
17. exhortation (eg′zôr tā′shən), *n.* strong urging to do something.
18. **hither** (hiтн′ər), *adv.* here.
19. **zeal** (zēl), *n.* eager desire.

My Heart Leaps Up

William Wordsworth

My heart leaps up when I behold
A rainbow in the sky:
So was it when my life began;
So is it now I am a man;
So be it when I shall grow old,
Or let me die!
9 The Child is father of the Man;
And I could wish my days to be
Bound each to each by natural piety.[1]

1. **piety** (pī′ə tē), *n.* godliness; devotion to God.

The World Is Too Much with Us

William Wordsworth

The world is too much with us; late and soon,
Getting and spending, we lay waste our powers:
Little we see in Nature that is ours;
We have given our hearts away, a sordid boon![1]
This Sea that bares her bosom to the moon,
The winds that will be howling at all hours,
And are up-gathered now like sleeping flowers;
For this, for everything, we are out of tune;
10 It moves us not. Great God! I'd rather be
A Pagan suckled in a creed outworn;
So might I, standing on this pleasant lea,
Have glimpses that would make me less forlorn;
Have sight of Proteus rising from the sea;
Or hear old Triton[2] blow his wreathèd horn.

1. **boon** (bün), *n.* benefit.
2. **Proteus** (prō′tē əs) . . . **Triton** (trīt′n), sea gods in classical Greek mythology.

BUILDING ENGLISH PROFICIENCY

Responding to Key Statements

Use one or more of the following activities to explore Wordsworth's belief that " . . . late and soon,/Getting and spending, we lay waste our powers."

Activity Ideas

- Moderate an informal debate over this statement. Ask: Is it our true nature to "get and spend"—or is our true nature something else? Would Wordsworth agree with you?
- Have students list things that they (or teens in general) are under pressure to do that "lay waste [their] powers."
- Ask students to create artwork that shows how people today "get and spend." (The artwork may help students respond to "Making Connections" number 5 on page 414.)

9 Literary Element
Paradox

Questions Remind students that a paradox is a statement that seems contradictory, but has valid meaning. What do they think the paradox in line 7 implies? *(that much of an adult's character is formed when he or she is a child)* How does the paradox connect with the poem's theme? *(The narrator prays that the child's love of nature, which fathered the same love in the man, continues unbroken into old age, giving life meaning.)*

10 Literary Element
Theme

Questions What does the narrator contend in the sonnet's first nine lines? *(He argues that materialism has deadened humanity's capacity to appreciate the great things of the earth—the beauty and majesty of nature.)* How is the contention resolved in the final six lines? *(Rather than be a man who gets and spends but sees nothing, the narrator would prefer being a pagan, who at least retains the capacity to wonder at the glory of the world.)*

Check Test

1. In "Tintern Abbey," what have memories of an earlier visit given the narrator? *(peace, solace)*
2. How has the narrator changed? *(No longer a wild, unthinking creature, he notes his response to nature is now tempered by intellect and moral vision.)*
3. To whom does the "Tintern Abbey" narrator speak? *(his sister)*
4. In "My Heart Leaps Up," during what periods of life has the poet been delighted by a rainbow? *(childhood and manhood)*
5. What does "The World" narrator claim is wrong with humanity? *(materialism; removal from nature)*

Unit 5 Resource Book
Alternate Check Test, p. 13

After Reading

MAKING CONNECTIONS

1. Possible responses: People visit places of beauty, of historic interest, of cultural and literary interest.

2. Possible responses: The poet has gained a sense of peace and joy and spiritual sustenance that he is a part of nature and vice versa.

3. Possible responses: the innocent pleasures of nature; the contrast between humanity and nature; the effects of experience on innocence; the compensations of experience over innocence—e.g., intellectual stimulation and spiritual sustenance offered by nature; and the shared pleasures of friendship and family

4. "The Child is father of the Man" states Wordsworth's philosophy that people's early childhood experiences can and should influence their later lives. What is wonderful and natural in childhood should remain a part of one's adulthood.

5. Most students will agree that the ideas in "The World Is Too Much with Us" apply to modern life. Explanations will vary, but should note how contemporary materialism affects how we view ourselves and the world.

6. Possible advantages: The reader may identify with the artist and learn that he or she shares experiences and is, therefore, not alone. The reader may be inspired to write of his or her own experiences or emotions. Possible disadvantages: The reader may not share the artist's emotions or experiences and find the work perplexing or self-indulgent. The reader may find art that focuses too narrowly on the individual, but ignores society as a whole.

After Reading

Making Connections

Shaping Your Response

1. The poster that accompanies "Tintern Abbey" dates from 1931. Why do you think people might still be interested in this place 130 years or more after Wordsworth published his poem?

Analyzing the Poems

2. What does Wordsworth seem to have gained from nature?
3. Discuss some of the **themes** you find in "Tintern Abbey."
4. "My Heart Leaps Up" is generally considered a summary of Wordsworth's philosophy. In your opinion, how does line 7 fit in with this philosophy?

Extending the Ideas

5. Do the ideas in "The World Is Too Much with Us" apply to modern life? Explain.
6. Most of Wordsworth's poetry is about himself—a common enough idea today but an idea unheard of in its time. What are the advantages and disadvantages of art focusing on the **individual** in this way?

Literary Focus: Blank Verse

Blank verse is unrhymed iambic pentameter. Of all the regular English verse forms it is the most fluid and comes closest to the natural rhythms of English speech, yet it is readily altered for passages of passion and grandeur. Look again at the beginning of "Tintern Abbey." Note that Wordsworth has varied the basic blank verse pattern. The end of line 2, for example, should be read as one unit with line 3 and the beginning of line 4. This avoids a sing-song effect.

1. Read aloud lines 9–14, paying attention to the punctuation and not stopping at the ends of lines.
2. A pause—called a **caesura** (si zhůr′ə)—can also affect the blank verse pattern. What line contains such a pause?
3. Read lines 22–24. How is the blank verse pattern altered here?

Vocabulary Study

Decide whether or not the statement made about each italicized word is correct. Write *Correct* or *Incorrect* on your paper.

1. A *copse* could be found in the ocean.
2. A *sylvan* retreat will probably have mosquitoes.
3. A *vagrant* teenager is likely to be on the honor roll.
4. "May I have a drink of water?" is an *exhortation*.

LITERARY FOCUS: BLANK VERSE

1. Call on one or two students to read aloud lines 9–14 to the class.

2. Line 14 contains the caesura: "Mid groves and copses. [caesura at period] Once again I see."

3. While there is a caesura after "alone" and "These beauteous forms" is placed on a separate line, the meter continues from "The hermit sits alone." Lines 22, 23, and 24 should be read as one continuous unit.

5. A *cataract* is sure to be damp.
6. A book with long, involved sentences and many hard words may add to a person's feeling of *perplexity.*
7. Green is the result of yellow and blue being *interfused.*
8. If joy is mixed with sorrow, it is *corporeal.*
9. A woman buying a heavy coat will find herself *clad* for cold weather.
10. A policeman is likely to stop and *chasten* a speeding driver.

Expressing Your Ideas

Writing Choices

Writer's Notebook Update If you are keeping a journal of your wanderings and weather, take a few minutes to review what you have written. Then beside each entry, tell how you felt or what you thought at those times. Read part of your journal to the class.

Keep it Brief A lyric poem such as "My Heart Leaps Up" is usually short, expresses some emotion, and is highly personal. Try writing a **lyric poem** based on an entry from your journal or on some other topic you have been thinking about.

Don't Miss It! The illustration of Tintern Abbey on page 411 is a travel poster issued by the Great Western Railway, and William and Dorothy Wordsworth were in effect playing tourists when they visited Tintern Abbey in 1798. What sort of publicity would draw tourists to such a place? Write a **travel brochure** for Tintern Abbey. It may help first to locate the River Wye on a map of England. (It winds back and forth across the border between England and Wales on its way to the Bristol Channel.) The beautiful ruin of Tintern Abbey is located in a deep valley at the river's edge. Review the poem for other details you might use. If you wish, add some graphics such as a map and a picture of the abbey.

Other Options

William and William What do you think Wordsworth and Blake might say to each other if they had a chance to meet? Each one expressed strong opinions about art and society; from what you've read of their work, do you think they would agree or disagree? Work with a partner to plan a **dialogue** in which William Blake and William Wordsworth meet and discuss their own—and each other's—work. Present your dialogue for the class.

Beauteous Forms The "beauteous forms" of the landscape around Tintern Abbey inspired Wordsworth to "see into the life of things" and to write his poem. Find a painting, photograph, or other graphic that expresses how you feel about nature. Find out some background about the work, if possible, and about the artist. Give a five-minute **art talk** in which you show and tell about your chosen work and explain your reaction to it.

VOCABULARY STUDY

1. False
2. True
3. False
4. False
5. True
6. True
7. True
8. False
9. True
10. True

Unit 5 Resource Book
Vocabulary, p. 11
Vocabulary Test, p. 14

WRITING CHOICE

Writer's Notebook Update

If students have difficulty describing what they thought or how they felt, suggest they review portions of "Tintern Abbey" for examples of how Wordsworth extended description into personal reflection.

Lyric Poem

Post students' lyric poems in the classroom; ask volunteers to illustrate some of these poems, and post the illustrations with the poems they illustrate.

Don't Miss It!

You might bring travel brochures to class to give students an idea of format.

Selection Test

Unit 5 Resource Book
pp. 15–16

OTHER OPTIONS

William and William

Students may need to do additional research on Blake and Wordsworth to discover their views on various issues. Partners should practice their dialogues once they have written them. Then call on volunteers to perform their William-and-William dialogues before the class.

Beauteous Forms

You may want to display a few art books with landscapes or photographs by noted artists. Suggest that students can find similar books in their school library or public library.

Before Reading

Building Background

You might suggest that Coleridge's dream was not unlike those vivid dreams that one has just before waking in the morning, the kind of dream one tries so hard to hold on to and later, recall. Ask students to share examples of particularly vivid dreams.

Literary Focus

You might point out the difference between rhythm and meter. Rhythm is the arrangement of stressed and unstressed sounds in writing; meter is the pattern of stressed and unstressed syllables in a line of poetry.

Writer's Notebook

Students might record recurring or particularly vivid dreams from the past. Inform students that they will use their notes later for an assignment.

More About Samuel Coleridge

Under the sway of the French Revolution, Coleridge and a friend planned a "pantisocracy" (equal rule by all), a Utopian community in the United States. The vision was never realized. In 1795, Coleridge met Wordsworth, with whom he collaborated on the highly influential *Lyrical Ballads* (1798), which included Coleridge's most famous work, "The Rime of the Ancient Mariner."

Before Reading

Kubla Khan

by Samuel Taylor Coleridge

Samuel Taylor Coleridge
1772–1834

Samuel Taylor Coleridge was a poet, critic, philosopher, theologian, lecturer, and journalist. He was also a great talker. "Charles, did you ever hear me preach?" he once asked essayist Charles Lamb. "I never heard you do anything else," his friend replied. Born in Devonshire, Coleridge was a precocious child. He attended school in London and college at Cambridge. His stimulating association with Wordsworth led to his writing "Kubla Khan." Coleridge struggled most of his life against an opium addiction. This, an unhappy marriage, and a quarrel with Wordsworth in 1810, which was never completely resolved, contributed to his physical and mental decline, and he died at 61 in London.

Building Background

Images on a Stream Coleridge himself described how "Kubla Khan" came to be written: In the summer of 1797 he was staying in a farmhouse in Exmoor, between Porlock and Linton. After taking a prescription drug (opium) for an illness, he fell asleep while reading about the Chinese emperor Kublai Khan (1216?–1294). "The author continued for about three hours in a profound sleep, at least of the external senses, during which time he has the most vivid confidence that he could not have composed less than from two to three hundred lines; if that indeed can be called composition in which all the images rose up before him as *things* . . . . On awaking he appeared to himself to have a distinct recollection of the whole, and taking his pen, ink, and paper, instantly and eagerly wrote down the lines that are here preserved. At this moment he was unfortunately called out by a person on business from Porlock, and detained by him above an hour, and on his return to his room, found, to his no small surprise and mortification, that though he still retained some vague and dim recollection of the general purport of the vision, yet, with the exception of some eight or ten scattered lines and images, all the rest had passed away like the images on the surface of a stream . . . ."

Literary Focus

Rhythm / Meter In speech or writing in general, the arrangement of stressed and unstressed syllables is called **rhythm;** in poetry the pattern is called **meter.** A **foot** is a group of syllables, usually consisting of one accented syllable and one or more unaccented syllables. Lines of poetry can be **scanned,** or divided into feet, by indicating the stressed and unstressed syllables. The result is called **scansion.** (See the Glossary of Literary Terms.) As you read "Kubla Khan," notice the varying meters Coleridge uses and the overall effect of their combination.

Writer's Notebook

How vividly do you dream? For two or three nights, try writing down what you remember of your dreams. Do this as soon as possible after you awake; dreams have a way of fading quickly from memory.

SUPPORT MATERIALS OVERVIEW

Unit 5 Resource Book
- Graphic Organizer, p. 17
- Study Guide, p. 18
- Vocabulary, p. 19
- Grammar, p. 20
- Alternate Check Test, p. 21
- Vocabulary Test, p. 22
- Selection Test, pp. 23–24

Building English Proficiency
- Selection Summaries
- Activities, p. 228

Reading, Writing & Grammar SkillBook
- Grammar, Usage, and Mechanics, pp. 173–174, 183–184

Technology
- Audiotape
- Personal Journal Software
- Custom Literature Database: Additional selections by Coleridge can be found on the database.
- Test Generator Software

SAMUEL TAYLOR COLERIDGE

1 In Xanadu[1] did Kubla Khan
A stately pleasure-dome decree:
Where Alph, the sacred river, ran
Through caverns measureless to man
Down to a sunless sea.
So twice five miles of fertile ground
With walls and towers were girdled round:
And there were gardens bright with sinuous rills,[2]
Where blossomed many an incense-bearing tree;
And here were forests ancient as the hills,
Enfolding sunny spots of greenery.

But oh! that deep romantic chasm[3] which slanted
Down the green hill athwart[4] a cedarn cover!
A savage place! as holy and enchanted
As e'er beneath a waning moon was haunted
By woman wailing for her demon-lover!
And from this chasm, with ceaseless turmoil seething,
2 As if this earth in fast thick pants were breathing,

1. **Xanadu** (zan′ə dü), an altered form of Xamdu, mentioned by Samuel Purchas as a residence of Kubla Khan. *Purchas's Pilgrimage* is the book Coleridge was reading when he fell asleep.
2. **sinuous** (sin′yü əs) **rills,** winding streams.
3. **chasm** (kaz′əm), *n.* deep opening; gap.
4. **athwart** (ə thwôrt′), *adv.* crosswise.

During Reading

Selection Objectives

- to understand the individuality and visionary nature of Coleridge's work
- to identify Coleridge's use of meter
- to apply standard usage to noun and pronoun forms in writing

Unit 5 Resource Book
Graphic Organizer, p. 17
Study Guide, p. 18

Theme Link

Coleridge's visions and dreams, transformed into poetry of startling originality, exemplify this period's reaction against the rationality of the Age of Reason.

1 Historical Note
Who Was Kubla Khan?

Kubla Khan (*Khan* means king) founded the Mongol dynasty in China in the thirteenth century. It was to this court that Marco Polo traveled in 1275.

2 Literary Focus
Rhythm/Meter

After students have read the first 18 lines, ask them to scan these lines. You might write on the board that a meter of three feet to the line is called *trimeter;* four feet to the line is called *tetrameter;* and five feet to the line is *pentameter.*

Questions What meters are used in lines 1–18? *(Lines 1–4 and 6–7 are tetrameter; 5 is trimeter; 8–18 are pentameter.)* What effect does the change in meter have on line 5? *(The abruptness reinforces the end of a thought.)* What effect does the change in meter have after line 7? *(Possible response: The change to a chant-like pentameter enhances the sensuous description.)*

SELECTION SUMMARY

Kubla Khan

In "Kubla Khan," the narrator describes Xanadu with its "stately pleasure-dome" and gardens. Outside the walls of the Khan's domain lies a asavage but holy place of exploding geysers and voices prophesying war. The narrator interrupts his descriptions to relate the memory of a vision, in which an Abyssinian maiden plays a dulcimer and sings. If he could but re-create her music, then he could build pleasure-domes in the air, holy visions that would strike fear in the hearts of his listeners.

*For summaries in other languages, see the **Building English Proficiency** book.*

3 Reading/Thinking Skills
Visualize

Question The narrator piles image on image and simile on simile. Can students visualize what is described here? *(Possible response: In an explosion of rock, a great geyser cleaves the earth and shoots into the air.)*

4 Literary Element
Alliteration

Question Coleridge makes frequent use of the repetition of consonant sounds at the beginnings of words or within words. What are the alliterative words in line 25? *(The words* miles, meandering, mazy, *and* motion *all begin with the consonant* m.)

5 Literary Focus
Rhythm/Meter

Question Note to students that the meter of lines 31–44 seems to change almost randomly. What do they think is the effect of this changing meter? *(Possible response: The poet's metric variation emphasizes the exoticism of his images and tone.)*

6 Multicultural Note
An Abyssinian Maid

In a sense, the Abyssinian maid with her dulcimer is the narrator's muse; if he could reproduce her music, he could scale the heights of human imagination and drink "the milk of Paradise." In western culture, the muse of lyric poetry is Euterpe, of Greek mythology. In creating his own muse of remote origin, the narrator displaces the classical for the exotic, a characteristic of Romanticism.

A mighty fountain momently was forced:
Amid whose swift half-intermitted burst
Huge fragments vaulted like rebounding[5] hail,
3 Or chaffy grain beneath the thresher's flail:[6]
And 'mid these dancing rocks at once and ever
It flung up momently the sacred river.
4 Five miles meandering with a mazy[7] motion
Through wood and dale the sacred river ran,
Then reached the caverns measureless to man,
And sank in tumult to a lifeless ocean:
And 'mid this tumult Kubla heard from far
Ancestral voices prophesying war!
5 The shadow of the dome of pleasure
Floated midway on the waves;
Where was heard the mingled measure
From the fountain and the caves.
It was a miracle of rare device,
A sunny pleasure-dome with caves of ice!
A damsel with a dulcimer[8]
In a vision once I saw:
It was an Abyssinian[9] maid,
6 And on her dulcimer she played,
Singing of Mount Abora.
Could I revive within me
Her symphony and song,
To such a deep delight 'twould win me,
That with music loud and long,
I would build that dome in air,
That sunny dome! those caves of ice!
And all who heard should see them there,
And all should cry, Beware! Beware!
His[10] flashing eyes, his floating hair!
Weave a circle round him thrice,
And close your eyes with holy dread,
For he on honey-dew hath fed,
And drunk the milk of Paradise.

Royal Lovers on a Terrace is a miniature portrait that was painted by Bal Chand in about 1633. What elements of the painting help to create its mood of tenderness and tranquillity? ➤

---

5. **rebounding** (ri bound′ing), *adj.* bouncing back.
6. **flail** (flāl), *n.* instrument for threshing—separating—grain by hand.
7. **mazy** (mā′zē), *adj.* like a maze, a network of paths.
8. **damsel** (dam′zəl) . . . **dulcimer** (dul′sə mər), a young girl with a stringed musical instrument.
9. **Abyssinian** (ab′ə sin′ē ən), from what is now Ethiopia, a country in East Africa.
10. **his,** the speaker's.

MINI-LESSON: GRAMMAR
Using Nouns and Pronouns

Teach Ask students to define a noun. *(a word that names a person, a place, a thing, or an abstraction such as an emotion or an idea)* Then ask them to define a pronoun. *(words that take the place of a noun, such as* he, she, you, them, *and so on)*

Point out that Coleridge has filled his poem with nouns and pronouns. Ask students to identify and list all the nouns in lines 19–28. Then ask them to state all the pronouns in lines 38–44 of "Kubla Khan." *(I, It, her, she, I, me, Her, me)*

Activity Ideas

- Have students copy a paragraph from another selection and identify the nouns and pronouns by circling them in two different colors of ink.
- Challenge students to compose a sentence that contains one verb, six nouns, and three pronouns. Ask authors of the most amusing or creative sentences to write them on the board.

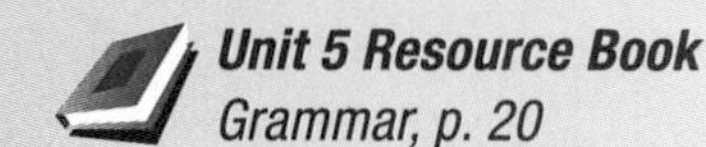

Unit 5 Resource Book
Grammar, p. 20

419

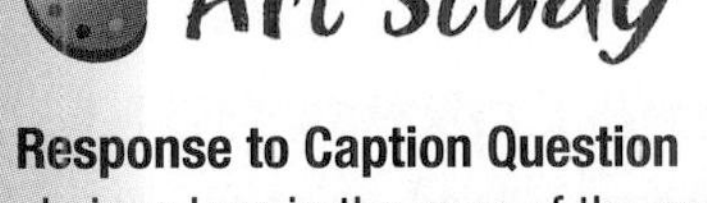

Art Study

Response to Caption Question The obvious love in the eyes of the couple—which is communicated with extraordinary artistry—is the primary source of tenderness. Her hand on his knee and his hand on her thigh contribute to the mood. A feeling of tranquillity is created by the painting's symmetry and perfect balance of "hot" and "cool" colors.

Literary Criticism

Coleridge's . . . "persons and characters supernatural" are no vulgar ghosts and phantoms, but archetypal figures from the depths of the mind itself, given a semblance of truth sufficient to procure for those shadows of imagination that willing suspension of disbelief for the moment, which constitutes poetic faith.

Kathleen Raine
Samuel Taylor Coleridge:
A Selection of His Poems and Prose

Check Test

1. What does the speaker describe in the first stanza? *(the kingdom of Xanadu and its pleasure-dome)*
2. How is the world outside the walls of Xanadu described? *(savage, holy, enchanted)*
3. What cleaves rock, momentarily throwing down a river? *(a mighty fountain or geyser)*
4. Who is the poet's muse or ideal inspiration? *(an Abyssinian maid)*
5. How would people react if the narrator could recreate the song of the Abyssinian maid? *(His holy visions would strike fear in them.)*

Unit 5 Resource Book
Alternate Check Test, p. 21

BUILDING ENGLISH PROFICIENCY

Responding to Poetic Ideas

This poem hints at interesting action and is filled with vivid imagery. To help students picture both, suggest that, for every 4 to 5 lines of the poem, they draw a small picture of what is happening. Then have students in groups share their pictures with each other and compare their interpretations. Together they can arrive at a common interpretation of what Coleridge is describing. This activity will also help students with the first of the "Other Options" on page 421.

Building English Proficiency
Activities, p. 228

After Reading

MAKING CONNECTIONS

1. Responses will vary; most will rate Coleridge above average because of his exotic images, names, and setting, as well as his irregular meter, word choice, and figurative language.

2. Possible responses: Visual images—pleasure-dome, caverns, sunless sea, gardens, waning moon, demon-lover, chasm, great fountain, shower of rocks, lifeless ocean, dome's shadow, ice caves, Abyssinian maiden, flashing eyes and floating hair. Auditory images—rills and rivers, wailing woman, seething fountain, explosion of rocks, ancestral voices, damsel's song, narrator's music. Students should conclude that most images are visual or auditory.

3. The damsel's music causes the narrator to wish, in turn, to build images in air, holy visions that would strike fear in his listeners.

4. Responses will vary, but should note some of the following: Coleridge claimed the images came to him in an opium dream. Initially, the narrator describes a place of beauty and peace, which blends nature and the fruits of human imagination; he then describes a savage, but holy place beyond the walls, where war, the dark side of human imagination, is foretold; finally, recalling a vision of an Abyssinian maiden at song, he longs to reproduce its sound and scale the heights of individual imagination. Responses will vary on whether or not an individual caught up in a personal vision can retain a measure of group identity.

5. One possible response: Because music is the most abstract of art forms, human beings respond to it with emotion, not intellect.

After Reading

Making Connections

Shaping Your Response

1. In their poems for *Lyrical Ballads,* Wordsworth set out to give "the charm of novelty to things of every day," while Coleridge set out to give "the interest of novelty by the modifying colors of imagination" by writing about more unusual and supernatural subjects. How well do you think he did? Give "Kubla Khan" a rating on the Novelty Meter. Be prepared to explain your rating.

Novel
10
9
8
7
6
5
4
3
2
1
0
Common

Analyzing the Poem

2. Find examples of Coleridge's use of **imagery** in this poem. To what senses do these images appeal, for the most part?

3. Trace the chain of causes and effects that the maid has upon the speaker and that the speaker expects to have upon others.

4. Summarize the elements in the poem—including the story of its creation (see page 416)—that express the poet's **individuality.** Discuss how possible it may be for anyone to be totally caught up in his or her personal vision and yet retain a measure of group identity.

Extending the Ideas

5. The speaker plans to create "music loud and long" such that hearers will not only be able to see the pleasure dome but will think that the speaker is having a holy vision. Why do you think people ascribe such great power to music? Can you relate some personal experiences that illustrate this power?

Literary Focus: Rhythm / Meter

Rhythm is the arrangement of stressed and unstressed syllables in speech or writing—called **meter** in poetry. A **foot** is a group of accented and unaccented syllables. An **iambic foot** has one unaccented syllable followed by an accented syllable (—´), as in the word *until*. Another kind of foot is the **trochaic,** with one accented syllable followed by an unaccented syllable (´—), as in the word *happen.* A three-foot line is called **trimeter;** a four-foot line is called **tetrameter;** a five-foot line is called **pentameter.** Choose five running lines of "Kubla Khan" and analyze the meter, demonstrating how Coleridge has combined different kinds of feet and different line lengths.

LITERARY FOCUS: RHYTHM/METER

Possible Responses:

Lines

42—iambic trimeter

43—iambic trimeter

44—iambic tetrameter

45 and 46—trimeter made up of one anapest (metrical foot of two unaccented and one accented syllables) and two iambs

Expressing Your Ideas

Writing Choices

Writer's Notebook Update If you have managed to record a few dream images, recast some of them into lines of poetry. You can use rhyme and meter, as Coleridge did, or let them flow in free verse.

Xanadu to You Coleridge modified the name *Xanadu* from one he had found in a travel book, probably intending it to sound exotic and foreign. Invent a name for a faraway land that might be used in a fantasy game or a television show. Then write a brief **travelogue,** mentioning some of the sights to be found there (perhaps some of the sounds, smells, and tastes as well). Are there supernatural elements in your land? Describe them.

In Short Here is a whimsical attempt to reduce "Kubla Khan" to just a few lines.

> Sleepy Samuel has a dream:
> Gardens, ice, and river mazy.
> There he spies a singing maid,
> And she really drives him crazy—
> Makes his eyes flash and his hair float.
> Some maid.
> Some poet.

Choose another selection from this book and write a brief **humorous summary** of it, using rhythm and rhyme.

Other Options

Decree a Pleasure Dome Create an illustration, an **illustrated map,** or a scene in miniature depicting the various images mentioned in "Kubla Khan." For example, you would probably include the pleasure dome, the River Alph, the caves of ice, and the "damsel with a dulcimer."

Mime a Rime Working with a small group, locate and read Coleridge's "The Rime of the Ancient Mariner." Choose a scene and draw up plans for a **video.** Consider whether to include music or sound effects; whether to use actual people, puppets, or animation; and whether you want a realistic or a fantastic depiction of the poem. If time and equipment allow, complete your plans and film the scene.

Exotic Means "Foreign" If you could choose to dream about any unusual place in the world, where would it be? Choose a country that interests you and do a little research on it. Then give a brief **oral description** of your chosen place, emphasizing its beauty or other interesting features. If possible, display some pictures to illustrate your talk.

WRITING CHOICES

Writer's Notebook Update

Call on volunteers to read aloud their poetic dream images. After each volunteer reads, ask the class whether the poetry was written in free verse or whether it used rhyme and meter.

Xanadu to You

From among the student travelogues, choose the most creative and read parts aloud to the class.

In Short

Because students may want to share their summaries with the class, suggest that they choose selections that have already been studied, which will allow everyone to understand the humor.

Selection Test

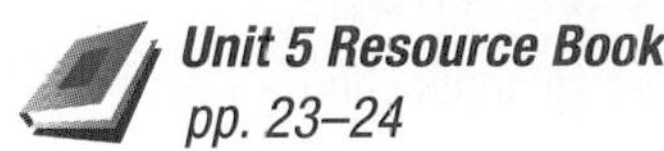

Unit 5 Resource Book
pp. 23–24

OTHER OPTIONS

Decree a Pleasure Dome

Students may want to divide the poem into groups of lines to analyze the images. They can then draw these images into a map or put them into a large picture of Xanadu.

Mime a Rime

Coleridge's "The Rime of the Ancient Mariner" is available on the Custom Literature Database.

Exotic Means "Foreign"

Besides researching in the library for unusual and interesting places to visit, students might contact travel agents for brochures.

Before Reading

Building Background

You might explain that the title "La Belle Dame Sans Merci" means "the beautiful lady without pity." The beautiful, pitiless woman is an archetypal figure in western culture. Ask students if they can think of examples of this character type. To get a discussion started, you could mention Salome or Delilah from the Bible, "dark" ladies of 1940s "noir" movies, or Erika of "All My Children."

Literary Focus

You might note to the class that onomatopoeia, like repetition, alliteration, assonance, and consonance, is a "sound device," which is defined in the Glossary of Literary Terms, page 968.

Writer's Notebook

Suggest that students choose their onomatopoetic words carefully, as they will be used later in a writing assignment.

More About John Keats

Lamia, Isabella, The Eve of St. Agnes, and Other Poems, published when Keats was 24, contains much of his best work, including selections in this text and

- "To Autumn"
- "Ode on a Grecian Urn"
- "Ode on Melancholy"

Before Reading

La Belle Dame Sans Merci

Ode to a Nightingale by John Keats

John Keats
1795–1821

John Keats wrote of himself and fellow poet Lord Byron: "There is this great difference between us: he describes what he sees—I describe what I imagine. Mine is the hardest task. . . ." His parents died when he was still young, and despite Keats's care, his brother Tom died of tuberculosis, a disease that would claim Keats as well. An intense and hopeless love affair with Fanny Brawne was anguish for the passionate young man who desired marriage but found himself thwarted by financial difficulties and worsening health. After a desperate flight to Italy to find a healthy climate, he died at age twenty-five and was buried in Rome under the epitaph he wrote for himself: "Here lies one whose name was writ in water."

Building Background

A Friend's Remembrance After the death of his brother Tom, Keats spent nearly a year with a friend, Charles Armitage Brown, who described the circumstances surrounding the writing of one of his poems as follows: "In the spring a nightingale had built her nest near my house. Keats felt a tranquil and continual joy in her song; one morning he took his chair from the breakfast table to the grass plot under a plum tree, where he sat for two or three hours. When he came into the house, I perceived he had some scraps of paper in his hand, and these he was quietly thrusting behind the books. On inquiry, I found those scraps, four or five in number; the writing was not well legible, and it was difficult to arrange the stanzas. With his assistance I succeeded, and this was his 'Ode to a Nightingale.'" The first and last stanzas constitute a frame for the succession of dreamlike thoughts.

Literary Focus

Onomatopoeia The use of words whose sound imitates the sound of the thing spoken of is called **onomatopoeia** (on′ə mat′ə pē′ə). The words *hiss, purr, boom,* and *gurgle* are all onomatopoetic words. Onomatopoeia creates images of sound and adds to the feeling or mood of a work. In line 50 of "Ode to a Nightingale," Keats writes of "The murmurous haunt of flies on summer eves." His use of *murmurous* and the repetition of the *m* sound in *summer* effectively create the drowsy sound and feeling of a warm evening out-of-doors, and the repeated *z* sound in *flies* and *eves* suggest the buzzing sound that insects make. Look for other instances of onomatopoeia in Keats's poems.

Writer's Notebook

What's that Sound? Stop reading for a few minutes and listen to the sounds around you. Then jot down some onomatopoetic words that seem to imitate those sounds. Some words such as *purr* are also called **echoic,** because they seem to echo or imitate a sound and are derived from that sound. For example, find the word *boom* in a dictionary and read the derivation.

SUPPORT MATERIALS OVERVIEW

Unit 5 Resource Book
- Graphic Organizer, p. 25
- Study Guide, p. 26
- Vocabulary, p. 27
- Grammar, p. 28
- Alternate Check Test, p. 29
- Vocabulary Test, p. 30
- Selection Test, pp. 31–32

Building English Proficiency
- Selection Summaries
- Activities, p. 229
- "La Belle Dame Sans Merci" and "Ode to a Nightingale" in Spanish

Reading, Writing & Grammar SkillBook
- Vocabulary, pp. 1–2, 3–4
- Grammar, Usage, and Mechanics, pp. 211–213

Technology
- Audiotape
- Personal Journal Software
- Custom Literature Database: Additional selections by Keats can be found on the database.
- Test Generator Software

La Belle Dame Sans Merci

JOHN KEATS

Translated from the French, the title means "the beautiful lady without pity." The poem is probably based on the centuries-old ballad "True Thomas," which tells how a man was enchanted by the Queen of Elfland and lured to her home, where he had to serve her for seven years. Keats takes up that story after the seven years are over, the spell has been broken, and the knight, now journeying home, meets a curious passerby.

O, what can ail thee, knight-at-arms,
Alone and palely loitering?
The sedge has withered from the lake,
And no birds sing.

O, what can ail thee, knight-at-arms,
So haggard and so woe-begone?
The squirrel's granary is full,
And the harvest's done.

1 I see a lily on thy brow,
With anguish moist and fever dew;
And on thy cheeks a fading rose
Fast withereth too.

2 I met a lady in the meads,
Full beautiful—a faery's child,
Her hair was long, her foot was light,
And her eyes were wild.

I made a garland for her head,
And bracelets too, and fragrant zone;[1]
She looked at me as she did love,
And made sweet moan.

1. **zone,** belt.

During Reading

Selection Objectives

- to recognize the joy and sorrow Keats found in nature
- to examine imagery in Keats's work
- to identify and understand onomatopoeia in Keats's poetry

Unit 5 Resource Book
Graphic Organizer, p. 25
Study Guide, p. 26

Theme Link

In his work, Keats expressed the passion of his visions and dreams; joy in the physical world; and sorrow that each of us must pass out of it.

Vocabulary Preview

steed, horse
grot, grotto; a cave or cavern
thrall, bondage; condition of being under some power or influence
gloam, gloaming; twilight
hemlock, a poison
verdurous, green and fresh
darkling, in the dark
requiem, musical service or hymn for the dead
casement, window
forlorn, abandoned; desolate

Students can add the words and definitions to their Writer's Notebooks.

1 Literary Element
Metaphor

Question What metaphors are developed in lines 9–12? *(The knight's pallor is compared to the whiteness of a lily; his lack of color to a faded, withered rose.)*

2 Literary Element
Point of View

You might point out that while the point of view remains first person, the knight begins speaking at line 13.

SELECTION SUMMARY

La Belle Dame Sans Merci; Ode to a Nightingale

La Belle Dame Sans Merci A narrator asks a knight why he is so haggard, so pale. The knight answers that he met a lady who took him to a grotto where he kissed her. She lulled him to dream of pale warriors, who warn of "La Belle Dame sans Merci." He awoke alone on a cold hillside, where now he "palely" loiters.

Ode to a Nightingale The song of a nightingale pulls the narrator from a stupor. He longs for a rare wine that might lift him from this world with its cares, sickness, and death. He muses that he might join the nightingale, not with drink, but on the wings of poetry. But it has grown dark, and the night brings thoughts of death, of his own mortality compared to the immortality of beauty. When the bird flies away, the narrator wonders if the song was but a dream, if he shall "wake or sleep."

For summaries in other languages, see the ***Building English Proficiency*** *book.*

Art Study

Response to Caption Question While the lady's attitude can be interpreted in a variety of ways, from indifference to bemusement, it should be noted that she is pitiless.

Visual Literacy There is something very modern about Cowper's "La Belle Dame"; no Victorian child/woman, she is emancipated and quite capable of taking care of herself. Cowper's knight, on the other hand, is an anachronism; incapacitated by his suit of armor, he is incapable of walking, let alone functioning in the modern world. He is no match for "La Belle Dame."

Question The pitiless lady sits amid poppies, and her costume is woven in a pattern of poppy blooms and pods. What do you think the artist (not the poet) might be suggesting about "La Belle Dame"? *(Possible responses: that she is like an opiate, addictive and dangerous; or that the beautiful, but pitiless woman may personify opium, a drug that was then misunderstood and over-prescribed for a variety of ailments—from "nerves" to tuberculosis)*

The inspiration for La Belle Dame Sans Merci, painted in 1926 by Frank Cadogan Cowper, was Keats's poem of the same title. What attitude does the beautiful lady seem to have toward the knight who lies at her feet?

I set her on my pacing steed,[2]
And nothing else saw all day long;
For sidelong would she bend, and sing
A faery's song.

She found me roots of relish sweet,
And honey wild, and manna dew,
And sure in language strange she said—
"I love thee true."

She took me to her elfin grot,[3]
3 And there she wept and sighed full sore.
And there I shut her wild wild eyes
4 With kisses four.

And there she lullèd me asleep
And there I dreamed—Ah! woe betide![4]
The latest dream I ever dreamed
On the cold hill side.

I saw pale kings and princes too,
Pale warriors, death-pale were they all;
They cried—"La Belle Dame sans Merci
Hath thee in thrall!"[5]

I saw their starved lips in the gloam,[6]
With horrid warning gapèd wide,
And I awoke and found me here,
On the cold hill's side.

And this is why I sojourn[7] here
5 Alone and palely loitering,
Though the sedge has withered from the lake,
And no birds sing.

2. steed, horse.
3. grot (grot), *n.* grotto; a cave or cavern. *[Archaic]*
4. **betide** (bi tīd′), *v.* happen [to me].
5. thrall (thrôl), *n.* bondage; condition of being under some power or influence.
6. gloam (glōm), *n.* gloaming; twilight.
7. **sojourn** (sō′jėrn′), *v.* stay for a time.

3 Literary Focus
Onomatopoeia

The original manuscript indicates that Keats considered changing line 30 to read, "sighed deep," instead of "sighed full sore." Which is a more effective example of onomatopoeia? *("Sighed full sore" uses the* s *sounds to draw the line out into a sigh.)*

4 The Author Speaks
Keats Counts Kisses

Keats wrote, "Why four Kisses—you will say—why four because I wish to restrain the headlong impetuosity of my Muse—she would have fain said 'score' without hurting the rhyme—but we must temper the Imagination, as the Critics say, with Judgment. I was obliged to choose an even number that both eyes might have fair play: and to speak truly I think two a piece quite sufficient."

5 Literary Element
Personification

The poem ends with the knight "palely loitering." Earlier, his cheeks are compared to the color of a faded rose. He dreams of pale warriors warning of "La Belle Dame."

Question What might Keats's "La Belle Dame" personify? *(a disease—most probably tuberculosis, from which Keats and his brother died; in its last stages, victims are left "palely loitering," waiting to die.)*

BUILDING ENGLISH PROFICIENCY

Making Real-Life Connections

Help students to see that although Keats uses a setting of fantasy, the feelings that he presents are very true to life. Encourage students to respond to the following questions by drawing upon their knowledge of popular American culture and on personal experience and/or cultural views.

1. Point out that the woman uses her beauty as a trap—even a form of destruction. Ask: How have you seen this "type" portrayed today? Who sees women in this way—all men? some men? some people of both genders? people in some cultures more than in others?

2. Explain that even without its supernatural elements, this poem can be read as an example of how devastating a romantic breakup can be. Ask: How do you know when a relationship is over? How does it feel to be the one who walks out? How does it feel to be the one who is left behind?

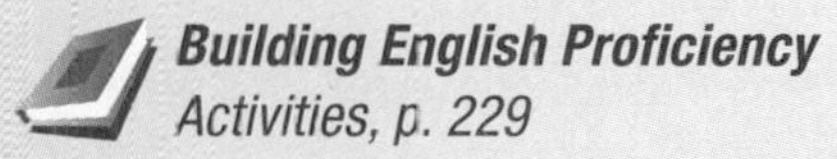
Building English Proficiency
Activities, p. 229

6 Historical Note
Keats's Odes

Between April and May of 1819, Keats wrote five odes. Four of these—"Ode to Psyche," "Ode to a Nightingale," "Ode on a Grecian Urn," and "Ode on Melancholy"—are considered by many critics to be among the greatest poems in the English language.

7 Literary Element
Imagery

In "Ode to a Nightingale," Keats uses imagery to relate several facts about this bird. For each of the facts below, have students locate the line or lines in which Keats relays the same information.

- The nightingale is a shy, rarely seen bird. *(lines 8 and 9: "In some melodious plot/Of beechen green, and shadows numberless"; line 20: "And with thee fade away into the forest dim")*
- The nightingale is famous for its beautiful song. *(line 10: "Singest of summer in full-throated ease"; lines 57–58: "While thou art pouring forth thy soul abroad/In such an ecstasy")*
- The nightingale is known for singing on moonlit nights. *(lines 35–36: "tender is the night,/And haply the Queen-Moon is on her throne")*

6

JOHN KEATS

My heart aches, and a drowsy numbness pains
  My sense, as though of hemlock[1] I had drunk,
Or emptied some dull opiate to the drains
  One minute past, and Lethe-wards[2] had sunk:
'Tis not through envy of thy happy lot,
  But being too happy in thine happiness—
    That thou, light-wingèd Dryad[3] of the trees,
7   In some melodious plot
  Of beechen green, and shadows numberless,
    Singest of summer in full-throated ease.

O, for a draught[4] of vintage![5] that hath been
  Cooled a long age in the deep-delved earth,
Tasting of Flora[6] and the country green,
  Dance, and Provençal[7] song, and sunburnt mirth!
O for a beaker full of the warm South,

---

1. **hemlock** (hem′lok), *n.* a poison.
2. **Lethe-wards,** towards Lethe (lē′thē), river of forgetfulness in Hades, the underworld home of the dead.
3. **dryad** (drī′əd), *n.* a tree nymph; in classical mythology, a nymph is one of the lesser goddesses of nature.
4. **draught** (draft), *n.* drink.
5. **vintage** (vin′tij), *n.* wine of fine quality.
6. **Flora** (flôr′ə), in Roman myths, the goddess of flowers and vegetation.
7. **Provençal** (prō′vən säl′) **song.** Provence, in southern France, was famous during the Middle Ages for its songs about love and chivalry.

MINI-LESSON: VOCABULARY
Understand Denotations

Often, context provides the clues to the definitions of unfamiliar terms.

Teach Remind students that a word's *denotation* is its dictionary definition. Explain that it is not always necessary to sit with an open dictionary when reading—that often students can figure out a word's denotation by the context of the sentence in which the word appears.

Activity Idea Have students first read this poem, "Ode to a Nightingale," without referring to the footnoted definitions. Instead, have them number a paper from 1 to 20. Then, each time they come to a footnote number in the poem, have them write down what they think that term means based on the meaning of the rest of the sentence. When they finish reading, have them compare their denotations to the definitions in the footnotes. Ask students to identify the terms they found most difficult to define and to explain why they think these were harder than the other terms. (Students will likely find terms that deal with Greek mythology the least possible to define from context since those require additional, outside knowledge in order to be completely understood.)

Full of the true, the blushful Hippocrene,[8]
With beaded bubbles winking at the brim,
And purple-stainèd mouth;
That I might drink, and leave the world unseen,
8 And with thee fade away into the forest dim:

Fade far away, dissolve, and quite forget
What thou among the leaves hast never known,
The weariness, the fever, and the fret
Here, where men sit and hear each other groan;
Where palsy shakes a few, sad, last grey hairs,
Where youth grows pale, and spectre-thin, and dies;
Where but to think is to be full of sorrow
And leaden-eyed despairs,
Where Beauty cannot keep her lustrous eyes,
Or new Love pine at them beyond tomorrow.

Away! away! for I will fly to thee,
Not charioted by Bacchus[9] and his pards,
But on the viewless[10] wings of Poesy,[11]
Though the dull brain perplexes and retards:
Already with thee! tender is the night,
And haply the Queen-Moon is on her throne,
Clustered around by all her starry Fays;[12]
But here there is no light,
Save what from heaven is with the breezes blown
Through verdurous[13] glooms and winding mossy ways.

9 I cannot see what flowers are at my feet,
Nor what soft incense hangs upon the boughs,
But, in embalmèd darkness, guess each sweet
Wherewith the seasonable month endows
The grass, the thicket, and the fruit-tree wild;
White hawthorn, and the pastoral eglantine;
Fast fading violets covered up in leaves;
And mid-May's eldest child,

---

8. **Hippocrene** (hip′ə krēn′), a fountain in Greece, regarded as a source of poetic inspiration.
9. **Bacchus** (bak′əs), god of wine, often represented in a carriage drawn by leopards (pards).
10. **viewless**, invisible.
11. **poesy** (pō′ə sē), *n.* poetry. *[Archaic]*
12. **fay** (fā), *n.* fairy.
13. verdurous (vėr′jər əs), *adj.* green and fresh.

8 Literary Element
Imagery

Question What senses does Keats's imagery appeal to in this stanza?

Possible responses:

- *touch*—"cooled," "deep-delved earth," "sunburnt," "warm South," "beaded bubbles winking," "purple-stainèd mouth"
- *taste*—"tasting of Flora and the country green," "beaded bubbles winking,'" "purple-stainèd mouth"
- *hearing*—"Provençal song," "sunburnt mirth"
- *sight*—"Flora," "country green," "Dance," "sunburnt mirth," "blushful," "beaded bubbles winking," "purple-stainèd mouth," "forest dim"
- *smell*—possibly "deep-delved earth"

9 Reading/Thinking Skills
Find the Main Idea

Question What is the main idea of this stanza? *(Possible response: The narrator speaks as if in the grave. Unable to see or smell, he recalls sensual images of meadows, trees, flowers, and insects.)*

BUILDING ENGLISH PROFICIENCY

Expanding Vocabulary Notebooks

The diction in "Ode to a Nightingale" is very "poetic" and rather challenging. Help students grasp Keats's vocabulary.

1. After discussing the poem in class, ask students to list any words that they still don't understand.

2. Collect the lists and see which words come up most often, or have students suggest words for discussion.

3. Explain the words for the class; then, work with students to create original sentences using the words.

4. Urge students to jot down words, definitions, and sample sentences in their vocabulary notebooks.

10 Literary Focus
Onomatopoeia

Question Can you find examples from this stanza and the following stanza of alliteration that echoes the onomatopoetic sounds of "murmurous haunt of flies on summer eves"?

Possible responses:

- The sound of "murmurous summer" is recalled in line 53, "Called him soft names in many a musèd rhyme"; and in lines 68–69, "The same that off-times hath/Charmed magic casements, opening on the foam."
- The sibilant sounds of "flies" and "eves" is echoed in line 52, "easeful death"; in line 56, "To cease upon the midnight"; in line 58, "In such an ecstasy!"; in line 59, "Still wouldst thou sing"; and in lines 65–68, "Perhaps the self-same song that wound a path/Through the sad heart of Ruth, when, sick for home,/She stood in tears amid the alien corn."

Check Test

1. In "La Belle Dame Sans Merci," where is the speaker when he awakens from his dream? *("on the cold hill's side")*

2. Who did the knight see in his dream? *(He saw "pale kings and princes too, pale warriors.")*

3. In "Ode to a Nightingale," what has the nightingale never known? *(weariness, fever, fret, sickness, death)*

4. What did Ruth hear as she stood in the cornfield? *(the nightingale's song)*

5. Why did the nightingale's music end? *(It flew away.)*

Unit 5 Resource Book
Alternate Check Test, p. 29

The coming musk-rose, fully of dewy wine,
The murmurous haunt of flies on summer eves.

10
Darkling[14] I listen; and, for many a time
I have been half in love with easeful Death,
Called him soft names in many a musèd rhyme,
To take into the air my quiet breath;
Now more than ever seems it rich to die,
To cease upon the midnight with no pain,
While thou art pouring forth thy soul abroad
In such an ecstasy!
Still wouldst thou sing, and I have ears in vain—
To thy high requiem[15] become a sod.

Thou wast not born for death, immortal Bird!
No hungry generations tread thee down;
The voice I hear this passing night was heard
In ancient days by emperor and clown:
Perhaps the self-same song that found a path
Through the sad heart of Ruth, when, sick for home,
She stood in tears amid the alien corn;[16]
The same that oft-times hath
Charmed magic casements,[17] opening on the foam
Of perilous seas, in faery lands forlorn.[18]

Forlorn! the very word is like a bell
To toll me back from thee to my sole self!
Adieu! the fancy[19] cannot cheat so well
As she is famed to do, deceiving elf.
Adieu! adieu! thy plaintive[20] anthem fades
Past the near meadows, over the still stream,
Up the hill-side; and now 'tis buried deep
In the next valley-glades:
Was it a vision, or a waking dream?
Fled is that music—Do I wake or sleep?

14. **darkling** (därk′ling), *adv.* in the dark.
15. **requiem** (rek′wē əm), *n.* musical service or hymn for the dead.
16. **Ruth . . . corn.** According to the Bible story, Ruth left her homeland to go with Naomi, her mother-in-law, to Judah, a country foreign to her, where she worked in the corn (wheat) fields. (Ruth 2:1–23).
17. **casement** (kās′mənt), *n.* window.
18. **forlorn** (fôr lôrn′), *adj.* abandoned; desolate.
19. **fancy**, imagination.
20. **plaintive** (plān′tiv), *adj.* mournful.

MINI-LESSON: GRAMMAR
Using Adjectives

Keats's superb use of adjectives is one criterion by which his writing is considered great.

Teach Remind students that adjectives are used to modify nouns or pronouns. Ask them to identify the adjectives Keats used in lines 7–10 in the first stanza of "Ode to a Nightingale." *(light-wingèd, melodious, beechen, numberless, full-throated)*

Activity Idea Have students copy lines 7–10 of "Ode to a Nightingale," inserting blank spaces for the adjectives. Lead a discussion in which students talk about the contribution adjectives make to Keats's poetry. Then have students substitute their own adjectives for the adjectives Keats chose. Invite students to share their revised lines.

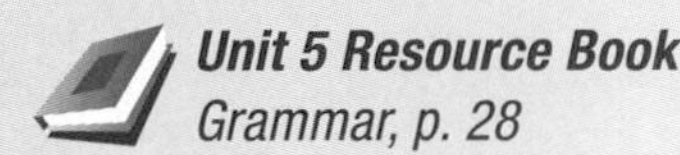

Unit 5 Resource Book
Grammar, p. 28

After Reading

Making Connections

Shaping Your Response

1. If Keats were living today, how do you think he would be making a living?

Analyzing the Poems

2. What emotions does the nightingale's song arouse in the speaker? What is it about the song that seems to cause these emotions?
3. What is the **mood** of "La Belle Dame Sans Merci," and how does the setting contribute to that mood?
4. To what senses does the **imagery** in "La Belle Dame Sans Merci" mainly appeal?
5. One of Keats's basic ideas was that beauty is permanent and changeless. Where is this idea made clear in "To a Nightingale"?
6. Compare the speakers in these two poems in terms of the degree of **individuality** each has gained or lost.

Extending the Ideas

7. American author F. Scott Fitzgerald titled one of his novels *Tender Is the Night* (from line 35 of "Ode to a Nightingale") What other phrases from the poem would make good book titles?
8. What kind of writing is being done about nature today?

Literary Focus: Onomatopoeia

Onomatopoeia refers to the use of words, like *murmur,* whose sound imitates the sound of the thing spoken of. In what way is the word *forlorn* "like a bell" tolling in lines 71–72 of "Ode to a Nightingale"? Find other examples in this poem of words or phrases you consider onomatopoetic.

Vocabulary Study

Some words are used frequently in discussing certain subjects. For example, *garlic* is a word you would expect to find in a cookbook. Match each lettered vocabulary word with the title of the book in which you would be most likely to find the word.

1. *The Abandoned Cottage*	a. verdurous
2. *The Fortunate Gardener*	b. casement
3. *The Case of the Poisoned Peach*	c. grot
4. *The Carpenter's Guide*	d. requiem
5. *Making Money at the Racetrack*	e. hemlock
6. *Exploring Caverns and Caves*	f. thrall

After Reading

MAKING CONNECTIONS

1. Possible responses: song lyricist, poet, humanities teacher, landscape architect, conservationist

2. The nightingale's music makes the writer think of death, for he contrasts his mortal life with the bird's immortal song.

3. The mystical and melancholy mood is supported by the desolate place where "the sedge has withered" and "no birds sing."

4. sight, hearing, taste, touch

5. The nightingale is described as never having known weariness, fever, or fret; as "not born for death"; and its song has been heard for centuries.

6. Students may say the knight lost his own identity, pining after the woman who lulled him to sleep and left him palely loitering; the speaker in "Ode to a Nightingale" wishes to join the song of the nightingale, but is reminded of his own mortality compared to its immortality and, in the end, returns to his "sole self."

7. Possible responses: And Shadows Numberless; The Deep-delved Earth; Where Youth Grows Pale; Beyond Tomorrow; Here There Is No Light; To Cease Upon the Midnight; Generations Tread; This Passing Night; Amid the Alien Corn; Magic Casements; Of Perilous Seas; Fancy Cannot Cheat So Well; Fled Is That Music.

8. Students may say current writing about nature is primarily scientific and ecological.

LITERARY FOCUS: ONOMATOPOEIA

By coupling "forlorn" with a bell simile, Keats suggests its onomatopoetic quality; the sound of its two syllables, stressed and unstressed, is comparable to the high/low, ding-dong pitch of a bell. Students may cite words like "dull" (line 3) or "melodious" (line 8). Students may also cite phrases like "blushful Hippocrene,/With beaded bubbles winking at the brim" (lines 16 and 17); "fade far away" (line 21); "winding mossy ways" (line 40); "fast fading violets" (line 47). Some of these words may create evocative images that are substantially visual or may appeal to physical feeling. These may be distinguished from those that evoke sound images, such as "melodious" or possibly "beaded bubbles winking at the brim."

VOCABULARY STUDY

1. h.
2. a.
3. e.
4. b.
5. i.
6. c.
7. d
8. f.
9. g.
10. j.

More Practice Have students create book titles in which two or more vocabulary words can be found. For example, a book title like *Galloping into the Twilight* could include both the words "steed" and "gloam."

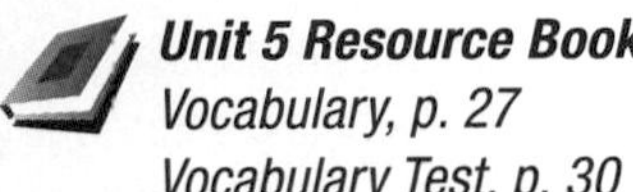

Unit 5 Resource Book
Vocabulary, p. 27
Vocabulary Test, p. 30

WRITING CHOICES

Writer's Notebook Update

Writing should demonstrate an understanding of onomatopoeia and echoic words.

Analyzing Imagery

Before students begin their essays, you might review what constitutes imagery: those sensory details that provide vividness and that tend to arouse emotions or feelings that abstract language does not.

Rap

You might ask for volunteers to perform their rap songs for the class.

Selection Test

Unit 5 Resource Book
pp. 31–32

Transparency Collection
Fine Art Writing Prompt 8

7. *Church Music Through the Ages* — **g.** darkling
8. *Slavery in Egypt During the Pharaohs* — **h.** forlorn
9. *Stories to Tell After Midnight* — **i.** steed
10. *A Song at Twilight* — **j.** gloam

Expressing Your Ideas

Writing Choices

Writer's Notebook Update Write some phrases using the onomatopoetic or echoic words you wrote in your notebook. Use as many of those words as you can.

Analyzing Imagery In an **essay** analyze Keats's use of imagery in "Ode to a Nightingale." Start by stating the purpose of the paper. Then analyze the images stanza by stanza. How does Keats achieve his visual and auditory effects? In your conclusion, tell to what degree an understanding of the imagery is essential to comprehending the meaning of the whole poem.

Rap What aspects of nature might be appropriate for a rap poem? Tornadoes? Earthquakes? Sunsets? Spring growth? Summer heat? Write a **rap poem** about some aspect of nature.

Other Options

Perform "Romantically" In a small group, prepare a **performance** by reading several short poems by any of the authors in this part, accompanied by suitable background music by a composer of the Romantic period. Research recordings of Franz Liszt or Frederic Chopin to find suitable pieces. Practice reading aloud before your presentation.

What Else Happened? Not just their work, but their lives as well place these poets within the Romantic tradition. Find biographical material on more aspects of any writer's life than are given in this part. Then present an **oral report** to the class.

The Romantic Poet in You Much of the writing of the Romantic poets consisted of describing their emotional reactions to scenes of nature. Take a portable tape recorder with you into a park or some other natural area. As you walk about, let your thoughts fly free, and describe what you see and your reactions to it in a kind of **stream-of-consciousness monologue.** As you listen to your tape later, you may or may not decide to edit out certain sections before sharing your monologue with a small group of classmates.

OTHER OPTIONS

Perform "Romantically"

You may want to suggest that students ask the music teacher for assistance in finding appropriate compositions from the Romantic period.

What Else Happened?

Suggest to students interested in this option that as they do their research, they pay particular attention to financial and health problems faced by the poets featured in this section of the text.

The Romantic Poet in You

You might note to the class that "stream-of-consciousness" is the re-creation of a character's flow of thought. Raw images, perceptions, and memories come and go in seemingly random, but actually controlled, fashion, much as they do in people's minds.

INTERDISCIPLINARY STUDY

Visions and Dreams

Visionary Experiences

Multicultural Connection

From the beginning, human beings have sought to understand dreams and visions. What did these experiences mean? Could they be a guide for life? On the following pages are accounts of how several cultures sought strength and wisdom in visionary experiences.

A World of Dreamers

The following fable about the Chinese philosopher Chuang Tzu suggests that our dreams may be as real—or unreal—as our waking expereiences.

Chuang Tzu and the Butterfly

translated by **Burton Watson**

Once Chuang Tzu dreamt he was a butterfly, a butterfly flitting and fluttering around, happy with himself and doing as he pleased. He didn't know he was Chuang Tzu. Suddenly he woke up and there he was, solid and unmistakable Chuang Tzu. But he didn't know if he was Chuang Tzu who had dreamt he was a butterly, or a butterfly dreaming he was Chuang Tzu. Between Chuang Tzu and a butterfly there must be *some* distinction! This is called the Transformation of Things . . . .

A delicate butterfly appears in this detail of a painting by Ch'en Hung-shou (1598–1652).

Interdisciplinary Study

Theme Link

The Romantic poets were not the first people to be influenced by visions and dreams. People throughout history have let their visions and dreams, as well as their reason influence their art, their philosophy, and their choices in life.

Curricular Connection: Multicultural

You can use the information in this interdisciplinary study to explore with students the ways that some different cultures have shown their respect for visions and dreams.

Historical Note

Chuang Tzu was a minor court official in China in the fourth century B.C. He taught Taoist thought through stories. The book that bears his name was compiled by others, and Chuang Tzu figures as a character in the stories.

Interdisciplinary Activity Ideas

- Have students read other anecdotes by Chuang Tzu and begin to flesh out their ideas of his philosophy.
- Students can then write their own anecdotes in the style of Chuang Tzu.

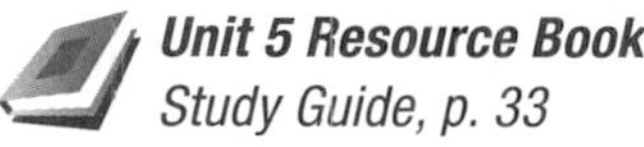

Unit 5 Resource Book
Study Guide, p. 33

BUILDING ENGLISH PROFICIENCY

Making Personal Connections

This fable passes by quickly and contains little action, so students may not consider it important. Use questions that build upon students' experiences—questions such as the following—to focus on the tale and what it says about the power of dreams.

- Why is being a butterfly a good dream for Chuang Tzu? If you could dream about yourself as an animal, what animal would it be, and why?
- Why is Chuang Tzu confused when he wakes up? Have you ever awakened from a dream confused? What were you thinking and feeling?
- What do you think Chuang Tzu means by describing the experience as *the Transformation of Things?* How often do you think such experiences happen to people? Has such an experience ever happened to you or someone you know?

Additional Background

Delphi is in Phocis, Greece, near the Gulf of Corinth. The oracle there was the one consulted by Oedipus in Sophocles' Greek dramas, and was also consulted by the fifth century philosopher Socrates. Besides being sacred to Apollo, Delphi was also sacred to the god Dionysus (the god of wine), and the nine Muses (the goddesses of the arts, music, literature, philosophy, and history). Delphi was excavated in the early part of the twentieth century, and the sanctuary of Apollo was found.

Historical Note

Theodosius I (347–395) was the last ruler of the eastern Roman empire. He is remembered for making peace with the Visigoths, and for convening the First Ecumenical Council of Constantinople, which brought many Arian Christians (followers of Arius) into the Catholic Church.

The Delphic Oracle

The Greeks sought wisdom by consulting oracles, visionaries who were associated with various sanctuaries throughout the Greek world. The most celebrated of these sites was Delphi, which was located on the lower slopes of Mount Parnassus in central Greece. The Greeks believed the spot to be the navel of the world, saying that their supreme god Zeus had released two eagles, one from the east and one from the west, and flying toward each other they had met there. The site was originally sacred to the earth-goddess Gaea (jeʹə).

The Greeks told the story of a monstrous serpent, Python, who guarded the spot. The god Apollo came to Delphi, slew Python, and established his oracle there. Apollo was called *Pythian* in memory of this deed. The priestess of Apollo at Delphi was called the *Pythia* or the *Pythoness.* The Delphic oracle was consulted on a variety of questions, both private and public.

Those who wished to consult the oracle first performed the rite of purification and sacrificed to Apollo. Precedence among pilgrims was generally determined by lot, although occasionally granted as a privilege. A male priest, the sole attendant of the Pythia, related the questions and interpreted the answer. The priestess, seated on the sacred tripod, delivered the god's word while in a frenzied state. How this condition was induced is not completely clear. Excavation at Delphi has shown as improbable the theory that the priestess inhaled vapors issuing from a hole in the earth. Such practices as chewing laurel leaves and drinking the water from the Castalian spring which flowed near the sanctuary may have assisted, but the major cause was probably the priestess's own complete faith in the power of the god to speak through her. The influence of Delphi, felt throughout the entire Mediterranean world for several centuries, began to decline from the fourth century B.C. onward. The sanctuary was finally closed by the Christian emperor Theodosius in A.D. 390.

This vase painting shows a petitioner standing before the priestess of Delphi, who is seated on her tripod and holding a branch of laurel sacred to her patron, the god Apollo.

MINI-LESSON: SPEAKING AND LISTENING

Use Appropriate Speaking Behavior

Teach Tell students that each language or dialect has customs about behavior between speakers. These tell us things like the following:

- how loudly to speak
- how close to stand to others
- how much to gesticulate
- what level of formality would be appropriate
- how turn-taking should work in a conversation

Activity Idea Have students reread the section of text on page 432 that deals with consulting the oracle. Divide the class into three groups. The groups will write customs they imagine governed the speaking behavior of the people involved in an oracular consultation as if they were publishing an ancient etiquette book. One group will write the proper behavior for the priestess; the second for the priest attendant; the third for the pilgrims. After students are done, they should share their work with the class.

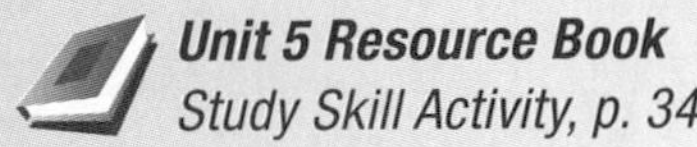

Unit 5 Resource Book
Study Skill Activity, p. 34

A shaman, or "medicine man," among the Crow, a Plains Indian people, is shown performing a healing ritual in this painting by George Catlin (1796–1872). Dreams and other visionary experiences were an important part of such shamanistic practices.

The Plains Indian Power Vision

The experience of the universe as mysterious and powerful is basic to the psychology of all human religion. The human awareness that in this mystery and power is the source of birth and sterility, strength and blight, food and want, life and death, has led all peoples to try to engage the more-than-human, the supernatural, to their benefit through religious practice. In American Indian cultures the supernatural was the object of a great deal of activity. The effort was not to organize a consistent body of beliefs, but rather through liturgy and ordeal to come to some direct experience of the supernatural, and from this experience to obtain guidance for life and protection from danger.

Among the small, semi-nomadic groups which formed the nations of the Great Plains, the emphasis was on ordeal and vision. The individual males sought visions which would enable them to be successful hunters and warriors. The ordeal involved isolation from the tribe, prolonged fasting, and sometimes self-inflicted injury to encourage visions when they did not come. The visions took a variety of forms but had a standard outline. The supernatural would manifest itself as a being combining animal and human natures. The hunter would accompany this being and when they arrived at its dwelling, which might be deep in the forest or above the clouds or under the sea, he would receive the "spirit power" which he sought, usually consisting of a song to be used when power was needed and some sort of fetish or talisman, the hunter's "medicine," which the being would give him or which he must find or make, and which involved a special ritual for its proper use. However, the procedure involved in gaining the power vision need not be so strenuous. A vision might even arrive unsought, coming as a dream in sleep, or accompanying a fever.

Responding

1. In the three cultures represented here—ancient China, ancient Greece, and Plains Indians—do dreams and visions seem to have been considered more or less significant than waking experience?

2. Do you think dreams are a useful guide to life decisions? Why or why not?

MULTICULTURAL NOTE

The role of the shaman originated in Siberia, before the early peoples crossed the Bering Strait into North America. The role and practice of shamanism was not identical in all tribes, but at least in some tribes, the role of the shaman was closely connected to the dream world. In the tribes of the Northeastern woodlands and the Southwestern tribes, for example, the shaman's power was believed to come from dreams.

Responding

1. Possible response Students may feel that in all three cultures, visions and dreams were used to inform waking decisions and thoughts, but that one was not more important than the other.

2. Possible response Students' answers will vary depending on their personal experiences and their understanding of dreams and the unconscious. You may wish to have students return to this question after they have read pages 434–435.

BUILDING ENGLISH PROFICIENCY

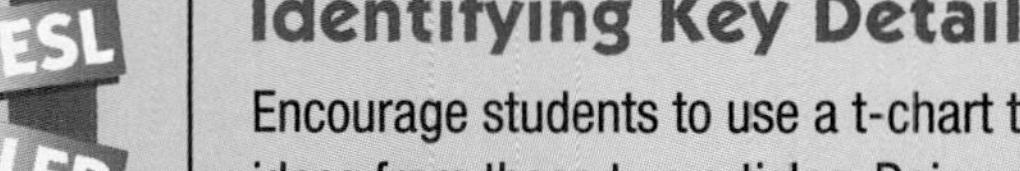

Identifying Key Details

Encourage students to use a t-chart to record important facts and ideas from these two articles. Doing so will help them not only to recall the ancient Greek and Plains Indian view of dreams but to compare those two cultural views.

ANCIENT GREEKS	PLAINS INDIANS
The Delphic Oracle was a kind of dream, sent by the gods.	The men needed supernatural dream visions to become warriors.
Only the pure could consult the oracle.	They purified themselves through fasting and self-injury.
The oracle influenced that whole part of the world.	Some dreams came "unsought."

Interdisciplinary Study

Theme Link

New understandings of dreams gained in the last two centuries have influenced the current views of people on the role of visions and dreams in the life experience.

Curricular Connection: Science

You can use the information in this interdisciplinary study to explore with students the new scientific understandings of the role of dreams in life.

Additional Background

Friedrich August Kekulé (1829–1896), who later became Kekulé von Stradonitz when he was made a noble, trained in architecture before switching to chemistry. In 1865, he conceptualized the benzene molecule in a dream as a snake biting its own tail, and this vision helped him clarify the concept of the six-carbon benzene ring.

INTERDISCIPLINARY STUDY

Science Connection

In recent years scientists have attempted to understand what happens to us physically when we dream. The following article explores some of this research. The illustrations are by people who were asked to draw their dreams right after waking up.

The Power of Dreams

by George Howe Colt

Dreams have tantalized humans since our earliest ancestors first curled up for a nap. Four thousand years before the birth of Freud, Egyptian priests were trying to interpret dreams. Aristotle believed that dreams are an early warning system for illness, and recent studies suggest he may have been right. Dreams have been credited with the creation of Mont St. Michel, the discovery of the structure of the benzene molecule, fixing Jack Nicklaus's golf swing, Lyndon Johnson's decision not to run for reelection in 1968, many of the routes mapped out by Harriet Tubman for the Underground Railroad, and enough novels, poems and paintings to fill the libraries and museums of a small civilization. There is something about the ephemeral nature of dreams that makes us insist they must have meaning—if we could just decipher what it is.

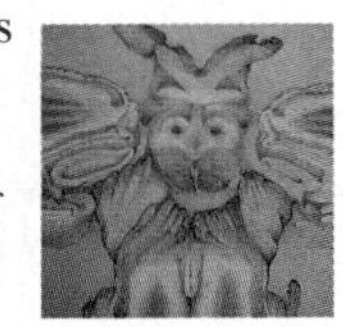

Each night, of course, hundreds of people dream what seems to be the Great American Novel but, on waking, find it to be gibberish. And studies of prophetic dreams are inconclusive. When it came out in court that O. J. Simpson had dreamed of killing his wife shortly before she was murdered, dream psychologist Gayle Delaney was asked if Simpson's dream was an indication of guilt. "We really don't have anything research-wise about whether dreams can predict future behavior," she says. "And lots of people dream of killing people when they have absolutely no intention of doing it." Which doesn't mean such dreams shouldn't be strip-mined for meaning. "Doing therapy without dream interpretation," Delaney says, "is like doing orthopedics without X-rays."

Dreams are so intimate, so fantastic, that many dreamers are not surprised—and perhaps are even secretly pleased—that dreams have proved so elusive to science. Over the years, people have believed dreams were caused by the weather, stars, God, the devil, indigestion, slamming doors, pickles and abusive parents. The physiological study of dreams didn't really take off until 1952, when a graduate student at the University of Chicago attached electrodes to his son and discovered REM sleep, the period characterized by rapid eye movement under eyelids. By waking sleepers up, the

MINI-LESSON: STUDY SKILLS

Encyclopedia

Teach Remind students that an encyclopedia is a good place to look for a quick introduction to a subject. The cross-references and works cited at the end of encyclopedia articles can help them begin to explore an area in more depth. Explain that this is true whether students consult a print encyclopedia, a CD-ROM encyclopedia, or one that is available online.

Activity Idea Have students choose one of the discoveries or inspirations listed in the second half of the first paragraph on page 434 and use an encyclopedia to make an initial exploration. They can then cite three other places they would look, were they to continue their research.

researcher was able to pinpoint, for the first time, exactly when a sleeping person was dreaming.

Here is some of what we have learned since then: We all dream, even if we don't remember our dreams. Our most fertile dreaming occurs in REM sleep. We enter REM about 90 minutes after nodding off, and it occurs more frequently and for longer periods as sleep progresses. We also dream sporadically during non-REM sleep, although in a less elaborate form. We spend two of every 24 hours dreaming, adding up to more than five years of our lives.

Here is something we don't know: Why dreaming is so much more bizarre and magical than waking. In 1988, Harvard neurophysiologist J. Allan Hobson shocked the dream world by announcing that he might have the answer. The chemistry of sleep, he said, is very different from the chemistry of the awake brain. "There are three neuromodulators in the brain stem," he explains. "They determine mood and memory, cognition and emotion. But they change during sleep. In REM sleep, your brain is being bathed in a totally different chemical bath." Dreams were not the "royal road to the unconscious," as Freud had it, but neurological misfirings, as random as the ramblings of an Alzheimer's patient. Says Hobson, "Under the adverse working conditions of REM sleep, the brain is making the best of a bad job."

If Hobson is right, Freud's psychoanalytic theory of dreams is as dated as the flat-earth theory—which explains why distressed analysands have been storming into therapists' offices wanting to know whether the dreams they'd spent years and fortunes recounting were meaningless chemical detritus; outraged dream workers called Hobson a spoilsport. But Hobson, who keeps a dream journal and loves discussing dreams with patients, has clarified his position: "We're not saying dreams have no meaning. We're saying dreams have meaning and they have nonsense. The problem is deciding which is which. In many instances the meaning of dreams is so clear they hardly need interpretation. The real question arises over the idea that images in dreams are symbols. When people interpret that stuff as if it were meaningful, and then sell those interpretations, it's quackery."

To many dreamers, such studies merely confirm what they have known all along—dreams are critical to good mental health. Even if we don't interpret them, even if we don't remember them, many experts agree that the unexamined dream is worth having. Dreaming is therapeutic. Precisely because of their bizarre and unfettered visual vocabulary, dreams make connections more broadly than we're able to when awake and may be able to solve problems our self-conscious conscious minds can't.

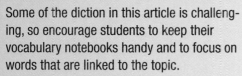

Responding
Try keeping a dream journal for a week, briefly recording your dreams in words or pictures on first awakening.

Terms to Know

strip mined, a type of mining that is particularly crude in its treatment of the earth; it is used figuratively to suggest an activity carried on with unnecessary destructive force.

orthopedics (ôr′ thə pē′diks), the branch of medicine which treats disorders of the skeletal system (the bones) and relies heavily on X-rays for exact diagnoses.

REM sleep, discovered by Nathaniel Kleitman and a group of sleep researchers. They were exploring the well-known fact that eyeballs of sleeping humans and animals move during sleep. Human beings have about 5 dreams a night; 136,000 in a lifetime.

neurophysiologist (nůr′ ō fiz′ ē ol′ə jist), a person who studies the function and activities of the nervous system.

Alzheimer's (älts′hī mərz), a disease that causes brain deterioration, and eventually death.

analysand (ə nal′ə sand′), person who undergoes psychological or psychiatric analysis with a therapist.

detritus (di trī′təs), debris.

quackery (kwak′ər ē) the practice of dispensing medical advice and treatment without training.

therapeutic (ther′ ə pyü′tik), having healing powers.

Responding

Students' journals will vary widely. Since some people cannot remember their dreams, some students may not be able to complete this assignment.

BUILDING ENGLISH PROFICIENCY

Exploring Topical Vocabulary

Some of the diction in this article is challenging, so encourage students to keep their vocabulary notebooks handy and to focus on words that are linked to the topic.

1. Offer examples of possibly difficult descriptive words that relate to the nature of dreams—for example, *ephemeral, gibberish, inconclusive, elusive, sporadically, elaborate, random,* and *unfettered.*

2. Work with students to identify challenging words that relate to the attempt to study dreams—for example, *decipher, strip-mined, physiological, sporadically, cognition, neurological, adverse, psychoanalytic, detritus, quackery,* and *therapeutic.*

3. Have students note these or other words, define each word, and then use it in an original sentence. Encourage students to share their sentences to reinforce understanding.

Interdisciplinary Study

Theme Link

Visions and dreams are not always experienced as a good and beneficial thing, as this work of art shows.

Curricular Connection: Fine Art

Use the information in this interdisciplinary study to explore with students another side of visions and dreams.

Responding

1. **Possible responses** overwhelming, frightening, unpleasant
2. **Possible responses** *The Nightmare* is more oppressive, darker, and more frightening. *The Shepherd's Dream,* while strange, and fantastical, is lighter and less threatening. Students may use the words *dream* and *nightmare* to help explain the differences.

INTERDISCIPLINARY STUDY

Fine Art Connection

The dark side of visionary experience is well represented by Henry Fuseli's famous painting, *The Nightmare* (1790–91).

THE DARK SIDE

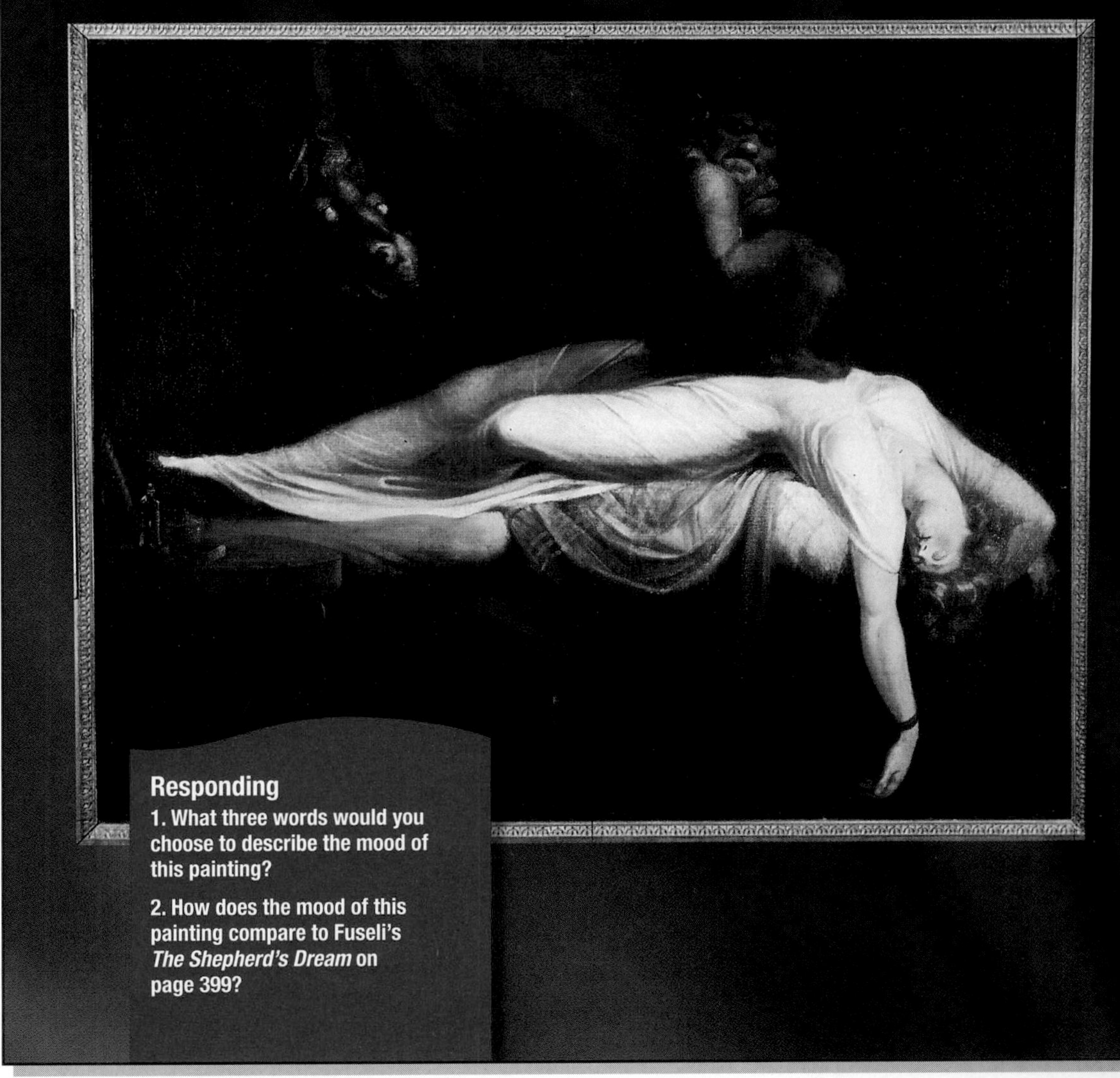

Responding

1. What three words would you choose to describe the mood of this painting?

2. How does the mood of this painting compare to Fuseli's *The Shepherd's Dream* on page 399?

MINI-LESSON: VISUAL LITERACY

Analyzing a Painting

Teach Introduce the terms *foreground* and *background. Foreground* is the portion of a scene nearest to the viewer; in the painting *The Nightmare,* the unconscious woman. *Background* is the portion of the scene in the rear, in this case, the demons.

Activity Idea Have students describe what they notice about the figure in the foreground of the painting. What do they notice about her posture, about the colors used to paint her, about the lighting of the picture? How do the figures in the background compare and contrast with her? What other images can students suggest as examples of nightmares?

Language History

The Language of the Romantic Era

It is an ancient Mariner,
And he stoppeth one of three.
"By thy long gray beard and glittering eye,
Now wherefore stopp'st thou me? . . ."

He holds him with his skinny hand;
"There was a ship," quoth he.
"Hold off! unhand me, graybeard loon!"
Eftsoons his hand dropt he.

During the Romantic Era, many archaic words and obsolete verb forms were reintroduced into the language, partly as a result of the Romanticists' interest in the Middle Ages. In "The Rime of the Ancient Mariner" (1798), Samuel Taylor Coleridge uses *thy* and *thou* for *your* and *you*, *quoth* for *said* and *eftsoons* for *immediately*; he uses the old verb forms *stoppeth*, *stopp'st*, and *dropt*; and he uses inverted sentence structure (in lines 4 and 8). These words, not only old but odd, were scarcely likely to be adopted in conversation, but they served to acquaint readers with the language of England's past. In their search for color the Romanticists also included slang and dialect terms, and although these forms were sparsely used in comparison with their use in literature today, they began to find acceptance in writing.

The years of the Romantic Movement are notable for the beginnings of really serious attempts to set up a standard of pronunciation. In 1773 William Kendrick published the first dictionary that indicated vowel sounds, and he was quickly copied by both English and American lexicographers. Because many lexicographers felt that words should be pronounced as they are spelled, there was a tendency to reestablish older pronunciations.

The Romantic writers were largely concerned with bringing naturalness and simplicity back into the language. Some of them felt that borrowed or foreign words should be eliminated because they corrupted the mother tongue. This discrimination against foreign words was not widespread, for English had become quite stabilized by this time.

Language History

Teaching Objectives

- to identify characteristics of the language of the Romantic Era
- to understand some of the influences that shape the history of language

Introduce

Have students read only the quotation from Coleridge's poem. Ask them to identify elements of language that are not used today, and list them on the board. Ask them to speculate on the factors that might cause language to develop and change. Then have them read the rest of the article.

Follow Up

After students have read the article, have them look back at the other poems in the cluster and identify other examples of the phenomena described here.

CONTENT-AREA READING

Using the Dictionary

Teach Ask students to look up the word *archaic* in the dictionary. The word is most commonly defined as being from an earlier time but rare in present day usage. When the Romantics incorporated words from the Middle Ages, they were using archaic language for their own time. Today those words, and others in use before 1900 are likely to be labeled *archaic* in the dictionary.

Activity Idea Assign students to look in the dictionary for *thy, thou quoth, eftsoons,* and *dropt.* What are the counterpart words in current usage? Ask students to browse through a few pages looking for other examples of words labeled *archaic.* List the words they find on the board.

Writing Workshop

WRITER'S BLUEPRINT

Specs

The Specs in the Writer's Blueprint address these writing and thinking skills:

- visualizing
- orienting the reader
- using sensory details
- using first-person point of view
- using spatial organization
- spelling

These Specs serve as your lesson objectives, and they form the basis for the **Assessment Criteria Specs** for a superior paper, which appear on the final TE page for this lesson. You might want to read through the Assessment Criteria Specs with students when you begin the lesson.

Linking Literature to Writing

Invite students to make a list of the writers' attitudes toward nature as reflected in the literature. Have students keep this list handy as they plan and write. It will help remind them that one of the purposes of their writing is to show the reader how they feel about their place.

Writing Workshop

A Place of One's Own

Assignment Romantic poets are enchanted by the beauty and power of nature. Write an article in which you describe a place in nature and its effect on you.

WRITER'S BLUEPRINT

Product	A travel article
Purpose	To re-create a scene from nature that is special to you
Audience	Readers of a travel magazine
Specs	As the writer of a successful article, you should:

- ❑ Imagine that you have been commissioned by a travel magazine to write an article for a regular feature entitled "Our Favorite Places." Choose a place in nature that you know well and that appeals to you: a well-known place of great beauty, such as the Grand Canyon, or a more ordinary location that nevertheless appeals greatly to you.
- ❑ Begin by introducing your place. Where is it? How can it be reached?
- ❑ Go on to describe this place so clearly and so vividly that readers can imagine themselves in it. Use at least three of the senses (sight, sound, smell, taste, touch) in your description. Use the first-person ("I") point of view to describe how this place makes you feel and why.
- ❑ Use a clear spatial organization to guide your readers through the scene, from one element to another. Since you're guiding your readers along, you may want to address them directly, as "you," from time to time.
- ❑ Follow the rules of grammar, usage, spelling, and mechanics.

WRITING WORKSHOP OVERVIEW

Product
Descriptive writing: A travel article

Prewriting
Revisit the literature—Brainstorm a list of places—Make a web of vivid imagery—Try a quickwrite—Talk a partner through your scene—Formulate a plan
Unit 5 Resource Book
Prewriting Worksheets pp. 35–36

Drafting
Before you write—As you draft
Transparency Collection
Student Models for Writing Workshop 15, 16

Revising
Ask a partner—Strategy: Using Spatial Order Terms
Unit 5 Resource Book
Revising Worksheet p. 37

Editing
Ask a partner—Strategy: Getting Letters in the Right Order
Unit 5 Resource Book
Grammar Worksheet p. 38
Grammar Check Test p. 39

Presenting
Column
Map

Looking Back
Self-evaluate—Reflect—For Your Working Portfolio
Unit 5 Resource Book
Assessment Worksheet p. 40
Transparency Collection
Fine Art Transparency 8

STEP 1 PREWRITING

Revisit the literature. Jot down a list of places described in the poems. For each place on your list, jot down key descriptive words and phrases from the poem—words and phrases that you feel helped bring the place to life. Think of this as making a collection of vivid imagery, which may give you ideas for your own writing later on in this lesson.

Brainstorm a list of places in nature that give you strong feelings, such as peace, sadness, happiness, fear. Then brainstorm descriptive words and phrases about the places on your list. Choose the place that brought forth the most vivid images.

OR . . . If you can, pay a visit to your place and gather firsthand observations.

Make a web of vivid imagery to describe your natural scene. Include words that appeal to as many of the senses as you can, and any comparisons that occur to you, as in this example:

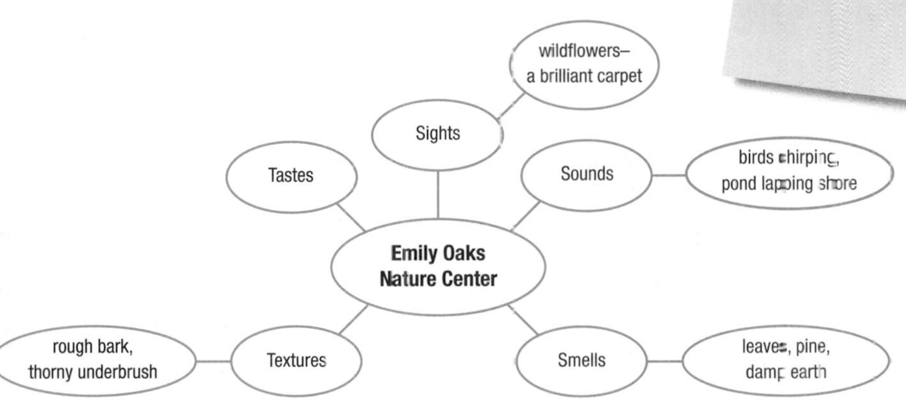

Try a quickwrite. Write for five minutes about the details in your web and about how the place makes you feel. Write quickly. The point of a quickwrite is to record your thoughts as they come to mind. Look back at the results and decide whether you need to do some more thinking and add more details to your web. You may even decide to choose another place instead.

OR . . . Draw a picture of the scene and label it with sensory details.

STEP 1 PREWRITING

Revisit the literature

Discuss with students some of the techniques the writers used to create such vivid images. Ask students to identify specific words that appeal to them and ask them to tell the images these words evoke. Have them make notes and use these notes when they plan and write.

Brainstorm a list of places

Remind students that their special place does not have to be a wilderness area. People can enjoy the stars from an apartment rooftop or gain a sense of peace by watching fish floating around in an aquarium.

Make a web of vivid imagery

If students are able to visit their special place again, encourage them to sit quietly for a while and write about everything their senses take in and the thoughts that run through their mind.

Try a quickwrite

Students may want to model their quickwrite on the poetic style of the readings and simply write down a series of images and metaphors. For additional support, see the worksheet referenced below.

Unit 5 Resource Book
Prewriting Worksheet, p. 35

BUILDING ENGLISH PROFICIENCY

Using Specific Details

Help students to achieve a high level of specific detail by evaluating and improving upon the images that they discovered in their prewriting imagery webs.

1. Ask students to mark any images in their webs that they would like to make more specific.

2. Have students add detail to those images or replace general words with specific words until they find a level of detail that pleases them—for example:

- leaves: oak leaves: brown, crunchy oak leaves of late fal
- old building: graying barn

Talk a partner through your scene

Have listeners make diagrams and put labels where they think each scenic element belongs. Then have listeners describe the place as they visualize it. This should give the writer a good idea of changes that need to be made in order to properly orient and guide the reader.

For additional support, see the mini-lesson at the bottom of this page and the worksheet referenced below.

Unit 5 Resource Book
Prewriting Worksheet, p. 36

Formulate a plan

Strongly urge students to choose a definite plan of spatial organization and stick to it as they plan the order of elements they'll present. If time allows, have them show their plan to a partner and ask for comments.

Connections to
Writer's Notebook

For selection-related prompts, refer to Writer's Notebook.

Connections to
Writer's Resource

For additional writing prompts, refer to Writer's Resource.

Talk a partner through your scene, using spatial organization, describing each element in order as you look around or move through the space, element by element. Here are some methods of spatial organization you might use.

- Near to far: "You enter the canyon through a narrow path between two tall pines. Immediately in front of you is a. . . ."
- Far to near: "In the distance is the roaring falls itself, which empties into a turbulent pool, which in turn empties into a narrow steam flowing toward you. . . ."
- Left to right: "At your left is a canyon wall, which winds right towards the falls. . . ."
- Right to left: "Immediately on your right hand is a pine forest whose needles crunch underfoot as you make your way out of it, to the left, where a twisting path leads into the canyon. . . ."
- Low to high: "A cushiony bed of pine needles crunches underfoot. Looking up, you discover. . . ."
- High to low: "The sky itself seems to flow into the canyon, as if sucked in by the sky-blue falls, which at its apex trembles as if in fear of falling over the edge, then tumbles dizzily downwards. . . ."

Choose one of these methods, or some other method of your choice, to lay out the elements of your scene. Think of it as taking your readers by the hand and leading them along. Remember, this is a guided tour, and the guide is you.

Formulate a plan. Look back at your prewriting materials as you make your writing plan. Here is one way to organize your notes.

- Introduction: where place is and how we can reach it
- First element of the scene (based on the method of spatial organization you've chosen)
  Sensory details
  Feelings
- Second element of the scene
  Sensory details
  Feelings

and so on . . .

MINI-LESSON: WRITING STYLE

Using Spatial Order Terms

Teach Explain to students that in a sense they are creating a verbal map for their readers. Note that maps indicate directions, distances, landmarks, and other physical features, and that by consulting it you can get an idea of what the territory is like and how to get around within it.

Activity Idea Invite students to revise the following paragraph in order to better guide the reader through the physical space. Encourage them to use the spatial order terms listed in the Revising Strategy.

The climb is difficult and I usually end up with several scratches or bruises, but from on top of the great oak I can see the entire flood plain. The river meanders like a rust-colored ribbon through the trees. In the hay field I usually spot a few deer if the rising sun isn't too hot. Over there I can see the old riverbed, left behind by shifting sands but still full of fat catfish.

Apply Have students draw an actual map of their scene before revising their essay further.

STEP 2 DRAFTING

Before you write, look back at your prewriting notes and writing plan. Then reread the Writer's Blueprint.

As you draft, concentrate on getting the ideas in your plan down on paper. Here are some tips to get you started.

- Start your article by explaining how you discovered this special place.
- Begin with a vivid sensory description that instantly transports the reader to your place.
- Begin by approaching the place, on foot or by some other mode of transportation, and describing what you see and hear as you approach. Similarly, you might end your article by describing how things look as you depart.
- Write a lead sentence that opens your introduction in an intriguing way: "A thick curtain of leaves blocked my view. As I lifted my hands to part it, something low to the ground made rustling noises on the other side, and I hesitated. Did I really want to intrude on this hidden, private world?"

STEP 3 REVISING

Ask a partner to comment on your draft before you revise it. Use this checklist as a guide.

✔ Have I explained how this place makes me feel?

✔ Have I appealed to at least three senses in the description?

✔ Did I use vivid imagery?

✔ Did I guide the reader through my place using spatial organization?

STEP 2 DRAFTING

Before you draft

Students may also want to read some of the literature again for inspiration.

As you draft

Have students work for a few minutes on their openings. Then have them share these beginnings with the class in order to gauge whether they are grabbing their readers from the start.

The Student Models

The **transparencies** referenced below are authentic student models. Review them with the students before they draft. These questions will help:

1. Look closely at the last paragraph of model 15. How could it be rewritten to be more clear and less awkward?

2. Which Specs in the blueprint has the writer of model 16 followed? Which ones has he not followed?

3. Find the spatial order terms the writers use to guide their readers through their scenes. Can you think of other terms that might improve clarity or add meaning?

Transparency Collection
Student Models for Writing Workshop 15, 16

STEP 3 REVISING

Ask a partner (Peer assessment)

Have students read their descriptions aloud and have partners try to visualize the scene as they listen.

BUILDING ENGLISH PROFICIENCY

Showing, Not Telling

Help students use description that reveals their feelings so that they do not have to rely on feeling words (*happy, comfortable, frightened, saddened*) to let readers know how they respond to the scene. This activity can help students practice.

1. Display a large photo of a landscape. Have students work in groups to write a positive or negative description of the scene.

2. Tell students to check their work to make sure that they have not used feeling words. Offer advice as requested.

3. Discuss differences in the groups' descriptions.

Revising Strategy: Using Spatial Order Terms

Suggest that students read their drafts over to themselves one more time and make a sketch of what they visualize, then compare it with their original plan and use the results to help them revise.

For additional support, see the mini-lesson at the bottom of page 440 and the worksheet referenced below.

Unit 5 Resource Book
Revising Worksheet, p. 37

Connections to
Writer's Resource

Refer to the Grammar, Usage, and Mechanics Handbook on Writer's Resource.

STEP 4 EDITING

Ask a partner (Peer Assessment)

If any students are unfamiliar with spell-checking applications, try to demonstrate this software feature.

Revising Strategy

Using Spatial Order Terms

Once you've chosen a method of spatial organization, it's important to use words and phrases that will help readers follow your organization. Spatial order words, like those listed below, provide information about spatial relationships that will guide readers along.

Distance	Direction	Position
beyond	to the right	in front of
in the distance	to the left	in back of
close by	ahead	above
near	up	below
far	down	behind

In the student model, notice how the writer has added spatial order words to guide the reader from near to far.

> My favorite trail is the pond trail. It starts out by meandering along a small stream. ^*Beyond the stream* ~~It~~ it travels through a forest of maple and oak. You can hear the wind blowing softly through the leaves and smell the damp spring earth. ^*Once through the forest,* ~~The~~ the stream empties into a large pond covered with waterlilies.

STUDENT MODEL

STEP 4 EDITING

Ask a partner to review your revised draft before you edit. When you edit, look for errors in grammar, usage, spelling, and mechanics. Watch for spelling errors caused by getting letters in the wrong order.

MINI-LESSON: GRAMMAR

Getting Letters in the Right Order

Have students edit the following paragraph, paying special attention to misspelled words.

I counted thriteen beuatiful hummingbirds around the roses: a sure sing that autunm was near. At times they fouhgt like minaiture fighter pilots, diving in and around the nieghbors' fence. These swift cretaures couldn't wiegh more than a few ounces each.

Unit 5 Resource Book
Grammar Worksheet, p. 38
Grammar Check Test, p. 39

COMPUTER TIP . . .
The spellchecking feature in your software can help you catch typing and spelling errors before submitting your article for publication.

Editing Strategy

Getting Letters in the Right Order

Some words are misspelled because they have combinations of letters that are easy to write in the wrong order, like these:

license	remodel	grateful	poetry	building	enemy
judged	beautiful	thirteen	tongue	thousand	neighbor
perform	soldier	pieces	through	unusual	prefer

When you edit your writing, pay special attention to words like these.

STUDENT MODEL

My cares are simply forgotten as soon as I enter the ~~perserve~~ *preserve*. I also feel excitement when I catch a glimpse of a deer or rabbit darting across the trail. Mostly, I feel ~~greatful~~ *grateful* for the serene ~~baeuty~~ *beauty* of this place.

STEP 5 PRESENTING

- Suggest to the editors of your school paper that they run a column called "Our Favorite Places," and include several of these articles.
- Include a picture or a map of your favorite place with your article.

STEP 6 LOOKING BACK

Self-evaluate. Look back at the Writer's Blueprint and give yourself a score for each item, from 6 (superior) to 1 (inadequate).

Reflect. Write answers to these questions.

✔ How was writing a descriptive article different from other forms of writing, such as research reports or analytical essays? How was it similar?

✔ How has this article changed your view of your special place?

For Your Working Portfolio Add your travel article and reflection responses to your working portfolio.

ASSESSMENT CRITERIA SPECS

Here are the criteria for a superior paper. A full six-level rubric for this paper appears on the *Assessment Worksheet* referenced below.

6 Superior The writer of a 6 paper impressively meets these criteria:

- Describes a particular place with fine sensory detail, re-creating it in such vivid detail that readers can easily imagine themselves in this place.
- Uses first-person point of view.
- Orients the reader by making it clear where the place is and how it can be reached.
- Shows how this place makes the writer feel and why.
- Successfully integrates details from at least three senses into the description.
- Skillfully uses spatial organization to guide the reader through the scene.
- Has few, if any, errors in grammar, usage, mechanics, or spelling.

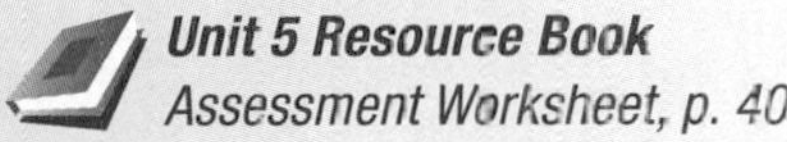
Unit 5 Resource Book
Assessment Worksheet, p. 40

Editing Strategy: Getting Letters in the Right Order

For additional support, see the mini-lesson at the bottom of page 442 and the worksheets referenced below.

Unit 5 Resource Book
Grammar Worksheet, p. 38
Grammar Check Test, p. 39

Connections to **Writer's Resource**

Refer to the Grammar, Usage, and Mechanics Handbook on Writer's Resource.

STEP 5 PRESENTING

Column

These articles could be published as a class travel magazine if it is difficult to get articles published in the school newspaper.

Map

Some students may want to include a photo essay with their text.

STEP 6 LOOKING BACK

Self-evaluate

The *Assessment Criteria Specs* at the bottom of this page are for a superior paper. You might want to post these in the classroom. Students can then evaluate themselves based on these criteria.
For a complete scoring rubric, use the *Assessment Worksheet* referenced below.

Unit 5 Resource Book
Assessment Worksheet, p. 40

Reflect

You might use students' responses to the first question as the basis for a discussion on different modes of writing, which could lead to a helpful list of characteristics.

To further explore the theme, use the Fine Art Transparency referenced below.

Transparency Collection
Fine Art Writing Prompt 8

Beyond Print

Teaching Objectives

- to understand the criteria used to analyze a painting
- to analyze a painting
- to evaluate a painting

Curricular Connection: Visual Literacy

Use the material in this article to give students practice in critical analysis of illustrations.

Introduce

Have students begin by simply looking at the painting for a few moments. Invite volunteers to mention what they find most striking about the painting. Encourage them to use the critical vocabulary they have been learning in the earlier visual literacy lessons. Then have them read the article. You may wish to have them work in pairs or small groups as they answer the questions.

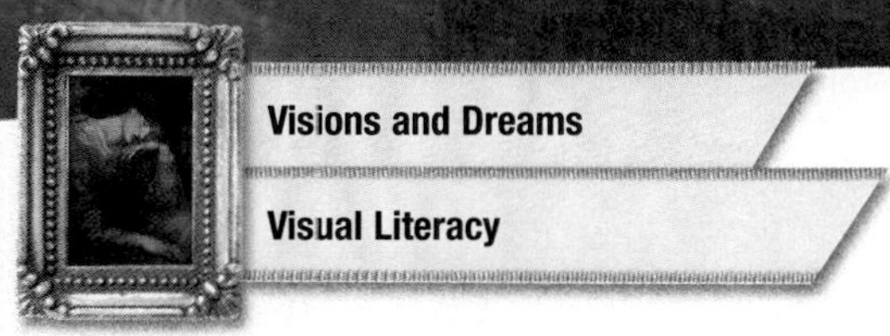

Beyond Print

Reading a Painting

Many Romantic poems are paintings with words. Think of the lines in Wordsworth's "Tintern Abbey" or Keats's "Ode to a Nightingale" that are devoted to description. The Romantics thought of nature as so much more than just trees and flowers: it was a metaphor for the unlimited spirit of mankind; it was a way to experience the perfection of God. This painting, *Hadleigh Castle* by John Constable (1776–1837), is typical of the Romantic era. As you look at it more closely, here are some questions to ask yourself by way of "reading" what the artist is trying to say.

Subject Matter What is shown in the picture? Where is the castle mentioned by the title? Are there humans or animals? What other aspects of nature are depicted? Of all these—architecture, humans, animals, and aspects of nature—which receives the most emphasis?

Composition Look closely at the shapes and at their arrangement in space. Which are stronger, vertical or horizontal elements? What major shape draws your eye? What balances that shape? Are there lines or other arrangements of shapes that cause your eye to follow a particular path through the painting?

Colors What colors are used, and how do they influence the mood of the painting? What do you think you are intended to feel? Where is the darkest part? Why there? Where does the painting lighten up? Why there?

Context Interpret the general meaning. How does a ruined castle fit in with the Romantics' fascination with things of the past? (Would you know these are castle ruins if you weren't told?) From what you know about the Romantics, why do you suppose Constable includes the thick, ominous clouds; the rough sea; the shore with its windswept shrubs? Why does he include the cows and men and dog at all? How about the boats? How do all these elements—and the overall mood—fit into Romantic ideas?

A Critical View What do you think the painter was trying to accomplish? How well did he accomplish it? Do you like or dislike the painting? Why?

ANOTHER APPROACH

Relating Literary Analysis to Art Criticism

Have students work in small groups to review the questions asked about the illustration. For each bold-faced heading and general analytical question, have them think of a corresponding question that they would ask about a poem.

When groups have completed their work, share with them another poem by one of the authors in this cluster, such as the following:

- "I Wandered Lonely as a Cloud" by William Wordsworth
- "When I Have Fears" by John Keats
- "This Lime-Tree Bower My Prison" by Samuel Taylor Coleridge

Activity Options

1. Using the criteria suggested and your own answers to the questions, explain to someone unfamiliar with this painting how it works and how it achieves its effects.
2. Write a Romantic poem based on this painting, using the poems in this part as models. You might call your poem "Ode to Hadleigh Castle." How can you make use of the various elements, including the men and animals? How can you transmit the mood? As an alternative, make up a story about this painting, giving the characters names and explaining what they are doing and why.

Activity Options

Activity 1 Encourage students to begin their explanation with a brief description of the painting. Have them choose an organizational strategy to help them convey the information in an orderly fashion. For example, they could move from the bottom to the top of the painting, or they could begin with the dominant shape and work around it.

Activity 2 As students work to try to capture the mood of the painting in the poem, encourage them to name the mood of the picture to make it more concrete for themselves. Then have them consider how mood is captured in poetry and plan the devices they will use to create the mood they want.

BUILDING ENGLISH PROFICIENCY

Making Personal Connections

Students may not think of themselves as qualified to interpret art. Assure them that they can offer valid interpretations.

1. Ask them either (a) to find a piece of artwork or a photograph that they like in a source of their own choosing (including magazine advertisements or covers of CDs) or (b) to create a piece of artwork that pleases them.

2. In small groups, have them display their visuals and explain what they think the choices say or what the artist's or photographer's purpose was. Invite other members of each group to ask questions and add other comments to clarify meaning.

3. Bring groups together for a sharing of responses.

4. Have the class choose from among the visuals submitted five pieces—one piece that they think best exemplifies each of the areas of questioning discussed on page 444.

Part Two: The Outsider

Historical Overview

EXPLORING CONCEPTS

- During the Romantic Era, people considered humans innately good.
- Romantics believed people are corrupted by economics, religion, education, and government.
- The Industrial Revolution brought great wealth to some, poverty and hardship to most.
- The French Revolution expressed the political and social idealism of the Romantics.
- The Reign of Terror and Napoleon's rule disillusioned many Romantics.
- The French Revolution sparked revolutions around the world.

Question What do the events depicted in the images on pages 446–447 tell you about the Romantic Period? *(Possible responses: It was a period of civil violence, nationalism, and social awareness.)*

Research Activity Ask students to work in pairs or small groups and to choose one of the events illustrated in the images or listed under Key Dates to research. Have them provide a brief summary of the events and their causes and effects for the class.

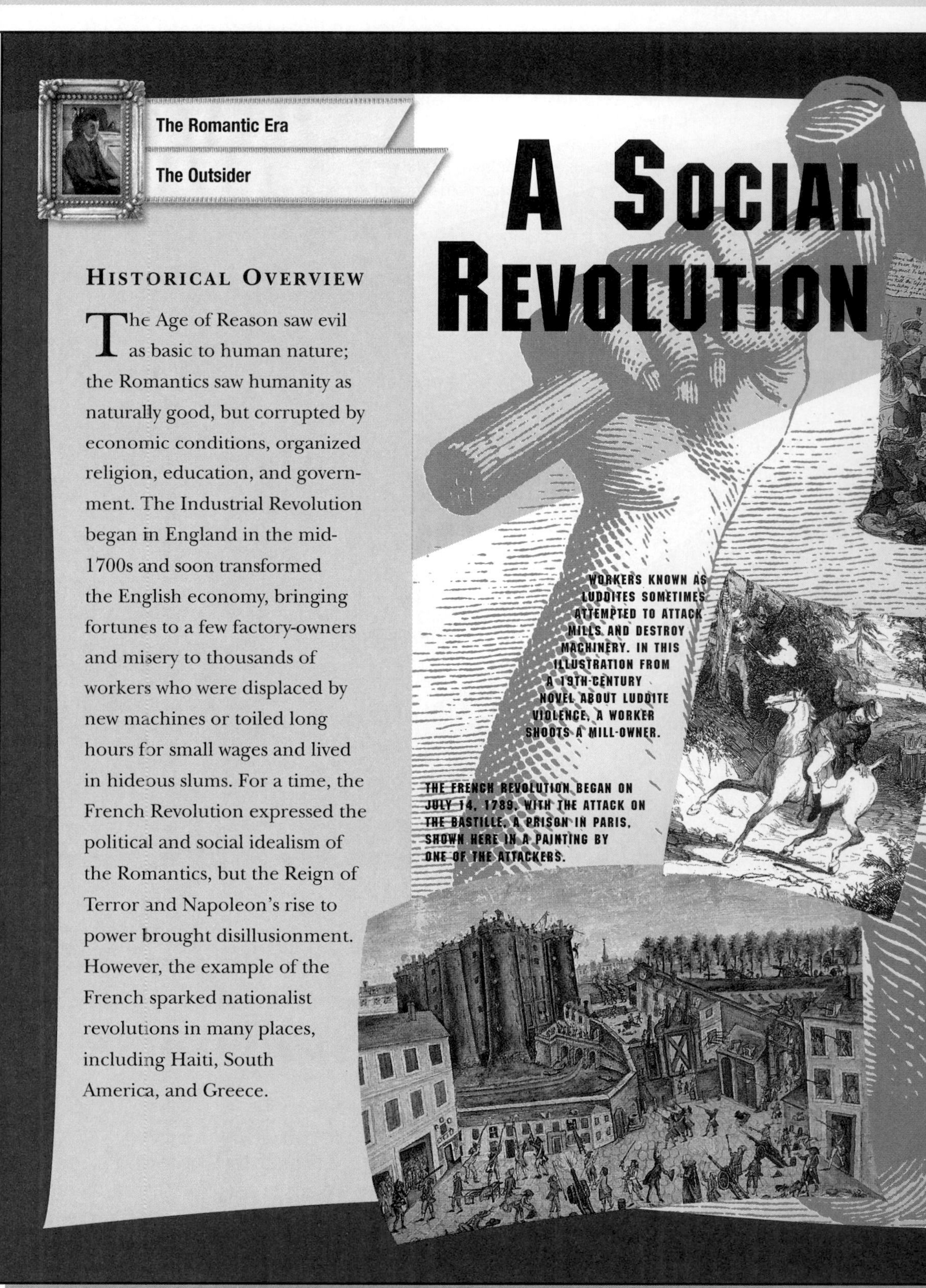

HISTORICAL OVERVIEW

The Age of Reason saw evil as basic to human nature; the Romantics saw humanity as naturally good, but corrupted by economic conditions, organized religion, education, and government. The Industrial Revolution began in England in the mid-1700s and soon transformed the English economy, bringing fortunes to a few factory-owners and misery to thousands of workers who were displaced by new machines or toiled long hours for small wages and lived in hideous slums. For a time, the French Revolution expressed the political and social idealism of the Romantics, but the Reign of Terror and Napoleon's rise to power brought disillusionment. However, the example of the French sparked nationalist revolutions in many places, including Haiti, South America, and Greece.

WORKERS KNOWN AS LUDDITES SOMETIMES ATTEMPTED TO ATTACK MILLS AND DESTROY MACHINERY. IN THIS ILLUSTRATION FROM A 19TH-CENTURY NOVEL ABOUT LUDDITE VIOLENCE, A WORKER SHOOTS A MILL-OWNER.

THE FRENCH REVOLUTION BEGAN ON JULY 14, 1789, WITH THE ATTACK ON THE BASTILLE, A PRISON IN PARIS, SHOWN HERE IN A PAINTING BY ONE OF THE ATTACKERS.

THE REFORM MILL
Key Dates
1789
The French Revolution begins.
1791
Slaves on Haiti rebel against the French.
1793
The Reign of Terror begins in France.
1807
England abolishes the slave trade.
1811
Luddites begin destroying machinery.
1804
Napoleon becomes emperor.
1819
The Peterloo Massacre occurs.
1821
Greeks begin their struggle for independence.
IN THE ENGLISH MANUFACTURING CITY OF MANCHESTER ON AUGUST 16, 1819, MOUNTED TROOPS CHARGED A CROWD OF 60,000 WORKING-CLASS MEN, WOMEN, AND CHILDREN PETITIONING FOR ECONOMIC AND POLITICAL REFORMS. THE SO-CALLED "PETERLOO MASSACRE" RESULTED IN 11 DEAD AND HUNDREDS INJURED.
IN 1832 THE BRITISH PARLIAMENT PASSED A REFORM BILL THAT INCREASED THE ELECTORATE BY FIFTY PERCENT. THIS CARTOON, IN SUPPORT OF THE MEASURE, SHOWS POLITICAL CORRUPTION BEING GROUND UP AND A TRIUMPHANT BRITANNIA EMERGING.
AFTER DECADES OF AGITATION, BRITISH ABOLITIONISTS (WHOSE MEDALLION BY JOSIAH WEDGEWOOD APPEARS HERE) WERE SUCCESSFUL IN OUTLAWING THE SLAVE TRADE IN 1807.
AM I NOT A MAN AND A BROTHER?
INSPIRED BY THE EXAMPLE OF THE FRENCH REVOLUTION, SLAVES ON HAITI REBELLED IN 1791. IN 1804 HAITI BECAME THE FIRST INDEPENDENT BLACK NATION IN THE WESTERN HEMISPHERE.
447

Key Dates

1791 Toussaint L'Ouverture participates in the slave rebellion on Haiti. Later he becomes governor for life and leader of an independent government.

1793 The Reign of Terror is led by Maximilian Robespierre. France's King Louis XVI is guillotined.

1802 France invades Haiti to restore it as a colony and captures L'Ouverture. French invasion ultimately fails.

1804 Napoleon initially continues reforms begun with French Revolution but soon disregards reform as he attempts to expand French empire.

1808 U. S. prohibits the importation of slaves from Africa.

1814 Napoleon abdicates; the French monarchy is restored under King Louis XVIII.

1815 Napoleon briefly regains throne but is defeated at Waterloo, ending his rule; Louis XVIII regains throne.

1837 Victoria becomes queen of Great Britain.

MATERIALS OF INTEREST

Books

- *The Age of Illusion: Manners and Morals 1750–1848* by James Laver (David McKay, 1972)
- *Blood Sisters: The French Revolution in Women's Memory* by Marilyn Yalom (Basic Books, 1993)
- *The Greek Adventure: Lord Byron and Other Eccentrics in the War of Independence* by David Armine Howarth (Atheneum, 1976)

Multimedia

The New Grolier Multimedia Encyclopedia, "French Revolution" article on CD-ROM (Grolier, 1993)

Preview

The Outsider

FOR ALL STUDENTS

Read the first paragraph on page 448 and answer these questions.

- Who are some well-known outsiders in our society? (Encourage students to think of examples from literature, popular culture, politics, and history).
- Who are the outsiders in our community?
- How and why do people become outsiders?

To further explore the theme, use the transparency noted below.

Transparency Collection
Fine Art Transparency 9

For At-Risk Students

- Discuss classic outsider figures in movies, such as outlaws in westerns and social outcasts in films about high school.
- Discuss the ways that outsiders are both admired (their rejection of society) and disdained (for their rejection of society).

For Students Who Need Challenge

Students may research and present an oral or written report about an outsider political figure, artist, writer, or musician who does not conform to society's expectations and norms.

For Kinesthetic Students

Students may creat a short skit featuring outsiders.

MULTICULTURAL CONNECTION

Discuss the ways in which our culture and society have changed as a result of influence from different groups of people.

Part Two

The Outsider

People find themselves in the position of an outsider for a variety of reasons, but it may be their own choice to stand apart, to assert their individuality. When people who rebel find important social causes to fight for, they can sometimes make a considerable difference in the lives of those around them.

Multicultural Focus **Change** creates challenges by introducing new dimensions to cultural situations. People respond both by clinging to existing cultural patterns and by changing those traditions to fit new situations. In this way, new cultures are created or old ones are modified, both by deliberate acts of people and by the simple fact that change is bound to occur. In the following selections, who are the rebels, what cultural situations do they face, and what changes do they hope to bring about?

Literature

Interdisciplinary Study Rebels with Causes

Writing Workshop Narrative / Expository Writing

Beyond Print Technology

IDEAS THAT WORK

Emphasizing the Lives of the Authors

"This is biography heaven! There's nothing dry in the facts of these authors' lives; teenagers find them fascinating and are eager to read their works. Indulge them; it's not every literary period that will afford you such ready-made motivation.

Burns, Byron, and Shelley are an English teacher's dream. I love to tell my students the juicy tales of the romantic entanglements, the battles with critics, the authors' dedication to the ideal of freedom, and even their early deaths. I cull books for photographs of people and places associated with their lives and make a large bulletin board display. Students produce a variety of written works including love letters, tabloid stories, and obituaries using the biographical details they have learned. Teenagers seem impressed with the knowledge that art is created by people who live lives as crazy—perhaps even crazier—than their own. I've seen that knowledge lead to a deeper appreciation of the literature.

Margaret Anne Doria
Brooklyn, New York

Before Reading

A Man's a Man for A' That
A Red, Red Rose
Auld Lang Syne by Robert Burns

Robert Burns
1759–1796

Robert Burns was born into poverty on a small farm in Scotland. His early years were spent as a plowboy. Although his formal schooling lasted no longer than two years, he read widely. Burns was considered a wild fellow: he drank heavily and he fathered several children by at least four different women. In 1786 the publication of *Poems, Chiefly in the Scottish Dialect* made him an overnight success, but polite society regarded him only as a rustic novelty. In 1787 he joined with James Johnson to begin the task of preserving the songs of his nation in *The Scots Musical Museum.* Before his early death at age 37, he had compiled and composed over 300 songs for this collection and for George Thomson's *Select Collection of Scottish Airs.*

Building Background

The "Untutored Ploughman" Although they were very poor, Robert Burns's father gave him books so that he could read the great English writers. His mother taught him Scottish songs and legends. But Burns claimed that his inspiration to be a poet came at age fifteen from a pretty girl who worked and sang alongside him in the fields. When she told him that one of the songs she was singing had been written by a nobleman's son, the "untutored ploughman" (as he later called himself) determined to compose a better song. Always fascinated with the sounds and the rhythms of the Scots language, Burns recreated the lilt of the language in this first poem, "Handsome Nell." As he continued to write, the poems he composed became intermingled with the songs his mother had sung. Thus, Burns became the poet of the Scottish people, the spokesman for the Scottish community, writing in their earthy, folksy language about everyday country life. In his collection of songs some are wholly Burns's own; some are traditional folk airs; most are his improvisations from fragments of songs from many nameless Scottish singers.

Literary Focus

Dialect A variety of language used in a particular region or by a particular social class is a **dialect.** Dialect is distinguished from standard language by vocabulary, pronunciation, and grammatical form. In the poetry of Robert Burns you will read the dialect of Scottish English. His poems are generally left as original instead of translated like Chaucer because Burns achieved fame as a dialect poet.

Writer's Notebook

My Love Is Like . . . Probably the most popular subject of poets is love: true love, unrequited love, lost love. Often a poet uses the technique of **simile,** a comparison using *like* or *as,* to relate his or her lover or situation to an object. Burns compares his love to a red, red rose and to a sweet melody. Jot down five or six other ways a lover might complete the sentence: "My love is like . . . ."

Before Reading

Building Background

You might discuss why people enjoy the poems and songs of their particular cultural heritage. Ask students to share poems or songs of their families' cultural heritage.

Literary Focus

You might note to the class that while twentieth-century media—particularly radio, and TV—have contributed to the standardization of English, dialects persist, and an "outsider" rarely goes unnoticed. Burns wrote in dialect to emphasize his "insider" status within the Scottish culture.

Writer's Notebook

Point out that Burns's comparison of love to a red, red rose was fresh and evocative in the eighteenth century, but has become a cliché. Challenge students to write fresh similes.

More About Robert Burns

Fifty years after Burns's death, he was elevated to the highest literary rank by Thomas Carlyle, who described Burns as the "most gifted British soul in all that century." Burns's greatest fame, however lies in his undisputed position as national poet of Scotland. As Scottish emigrants traveled the world, they carried two books—the Bible and Robert Burns's poetry.

SUPPORT MATERIALS OVERVIEW

Unit 5 Resource Book
- Graphic Organizer, p. 41
- Study Guide, p. 42
- Vocabulary, p. 43
- Grammar, p. 44
- Alternate Check Test, p. 45
- Vocabulary Test, p. 46
- Selection Test, pp. 47–48

Building English Proficiency
- Selection Summaries
- Activities, p. 230

Reading, Writing & Grammar SkillBook
- Writing, pp. 123–124

Technology
- Audiotape
- Personal Journal Software
- Custom Literature Database: Additional selections by Robert Burns can be found on the database.
- Test Generator Software

During Reading

Selection Objectives

- to identify and appreciate dialect
- to explore the theme of the outsider
- to identify and create similes
- to recognize colloquialisms

Unit 5 Resource Book
Graphic Organizer, p. 41
Study Guide, p. 42

Theme Link

Each poem celebrates the outsider. "A Man's a Man for A' That" applauds people who set themselves apart by common sense. "A Red, Red Rose" and "Auld Lang Syne" describe the faithful lover and long-time friends who will not allow time or distance to isolate them.

1 Literary Focus
Dialect

Question What are examples of dialect in the first stanza? *(Possible responses: "That hings," "a' that," "the gowd for a' that")*

2 Reading/Thinking Skills
Generalize

Question What is the main idea of the poem? *(Possible response: At the present time, a man's worth is measured by his wealth or by a title he has been given. A man should be measured by his common sense, honesty, and self-worth.)*

A Man's a Man for A' That

Robert Burns

1

Is there, for honest poverty,
That[1] hings[2] his head, and a' that;
The coward-slave, we pass him by,
We dare be poor for a' that!
For a' that, and a' that,
Our toils obscure, and a' that,
The rank is but the guinea's stamp,[3]
The man's the gowd[4] for a' that.

What though on hamely[5] fare we dine,
Wear hoddin-grey,[6] and a' that;
Gie[7] fools their silks, and knaves their
wine,
A man's a man for a' that.
For a' that, and a' that,
Their tinsel[8] show, and a' that;
The honest man, tho' e'er sae poor,
Is king o' men for a' that.

Ye see yon birkie, ca'd[9] a lord,
Wha struts, and stares, and a' that;
Tho' hundreds worship at his word,
He's but a coof[10] for a' that.
For a' that, and a' that,
His ribband, star,[11] and a' that,
The man of independent mind,
He looks and laughs at a' that.

A prince can mak a belted[12] knight,
A marquis, duke, and a' that;
But an honest man's aboon[13] his might,
Guid faith, he mauna fa'[14] that!
For a' that, and a' that,
Their dignities, and a' that,
The pith[15] o' sense, and pride o' worth,
Are higher rank than a' that.

Then let us pray that come it may,
As come it will for a' that,
That sense and worth, o'er a' the earth,
Shall bear the gree,[16] and a' that.
For a' that, and a' that,
It's coming yet, for a' that,
That man to man, the warld o'er,
Shall brothers be for a' that.

2

a', all.
1. **that,** one that; a person who.
2. **hings,** hangs.
3. **guinea's stamp,** stamped, bas-relief impression on a gold coin.
4. **gowd,** gold.
5. **hamely,** homely; simple.
6. **hoddin-grey,** coarse grey wool.
7. **gie,** give.
8. **tinsel** (tin′səl), *adj.* showy but not worth much.
9. **birkie . . . ca'd,** fellow . . . called.
10. **coof,** fool.
11. **ribband . . . star,** decorations of the order of knighthood.
12. **belted,** decorated; distinguished.
13. **aboon,** above.
14. **mauna fa',** must not claim.
15. **pith** (pith), *n.* essential part.
16. **bear the gree,** claim the first place.

SELECTION SUMMARY

A Man's a Man for A' That; A Red, Red Rose; Auld Lang Syne

A Man's a Man for A' That An honest man, no matter how poor, is above both the poor and the rich. Some day, sense and human worth will be the measure of a man, and men will be brothers.

A Red, Red Rose The speaker compares his love to a red rose in its first bloom. He will love his lass even until the seas go dry and rocks melt. The speaker says farewell, but promises to return, even if he must travel 10,000 miles.

Auld Lang Syne The speaker says old friends and old times should not be forgotten. In the years since their youth, he and a friend have wandered far apart, but now they should have a toast and keep the memories alive.

*For summaries in other languages, see the **Building English Proficiency** book.*

This 1908 oil painting by British artist Sir George Clausen (1852–1944) is entitled *The Boy and the Man.* Like so many of Clausen's works, this one depicts farm workers in the English countryside—strong, heroic figures doing the backbreaking work that was essential to an agricultural way of life. Do you think the artist might agree with the ideas Burns expresses in his poem "A Man's a Man for A' That"? Why or why not?

Art Study

Responses to Caption Questions It is likely that Clausen would have agreed with the ideas that Burns expresses in the poem. Clausen seems to depict his rural figures with a strength and nobility that Burns describes as "pith o' sense, and pride o' worth."

Visual Literacy Clausen gave his painting the title *The Boy and the Man.* The man is bent over his work. The boy, standing straight, has stopped work and stares off into the distance.

Question What do you think the title and the contrast between the boy and the man might suggest? *(Responses will vary. One possible interpretation is the age-old contrast between the idealism of youth and the lowered expectations and practicality that result from experience. The boy, unbent by time and life, dreams of the future, of the wide world; the man, having lost his dreams to the realities of day-to-day existence, concentrates on survival and the compensations of his work.)*

BUILDING ENGLISH PROFICIENCY

Exploring Dialect

Use one or more of the following activities to help students grasp the Scottish dialect and to expand upon the Literary Focus for the Burns selections.

Activity Ideas

- Call on volunteers to read aloud parts of "A Man's a Man for A' That." (You might want to play the Audiotape first.) Encourage them to start slowly, especially from lines 15 on, and to increase their pace in subsequent readings. Ask: Does the sense of the words improve as their sound becomes more familiar?
- Display words from the poem that might have modern slang counterparts—for example, *knaves, birkie, coof,* and *belted.* Invite students to suggest how Burns might express the same ideas using modern slang (in English or other languages).
- Have students focus on the final four lines. Have them use art, music, or drama to respond to Burns's vision of equality.

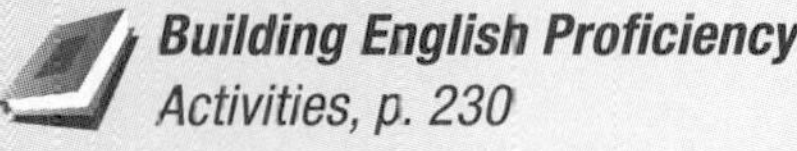

Building English Proficiency
Activities, p. 230

3 Literary Focus
Dialect

Question Remind students that Burns primarily wrote for the working people of Scotland. How does Burns's use of dialect make his poetry appealing to this audience? *(Possible reponse: The dialect implies that Burns, like his audience, is a working Scot, and that he speaks directly to them.)*

4 Reader's Response
Making Personal Connections

Question Why do you think "Auld Lang Syne" is sung on New Year's Eve? *(Students might note that the poem's nostalgia for one's youth and "the good old days" fits the mood of older people on New Year's Eve, when the passing of time is formally marked; the narrator's offers of "cups of kindness" also fit the spirited nature of New Year celebrations.)*

Check Test

1. In "A Man's a Man for A' That," what does the narrator mean by "rank is but the guinea's stamp"? *(Social standing is based on money.)*

2. What does the narrator pray will one day be the measure of a man? *(sense and self-worth)*

3. In "A Red, Red Rose," what promises does the speaker make to his love? *(to love her always and to return to her, even if it means traveling 10,000 miles)*

4. What is the meaning of the words "Auld Lang Syne"? *(old long ago* or *the good old days)*

5. How does the speaker want to celebrate memories of the old days with his friend? *(with a handshake and a goodwill toast)*

Unit 5 Resource Book
Alternate Check Test, p. 45

A Red, Red Rose

Robert Burns

O my luve's[1] like a red, red rose,
That's newly sprung in June;
O my luve's like the melodie
That's sweetly played in tune.

As fair art thou, my bonie[2] lass,
So deep in luve am I;
And I will luve thee still, my dear,
Till a' the seas gang[3] dry.

Till a' the seas gang dry, my dear,
And the rocks melt wi' the sun;
And I will luve thee still, my dear,
While the sands o' life shall run.

And fare thee weel,[4] my only luve!
And fare thee weel a while!
And I will come again, my luve,
3 Tho' it were ten thousand mile!

1. **luve,** love
2. **bonie,** bonnie; pretty.
3. **gang,** go.
4. **weel,** well.

Auld Lang Syne

Robert Burns

Should auld acquaintance be forgot,
And never brought to min'?
Should auld acquaintance be forgot,
And auld lang syne?
CHORUS:
For auld lang syne, my dear,
For auld lang syne,
We'll tak a cup o' kindness yet
For auld lang syne.

And surely ye'll be your pint-stowp,[1]
And surely I'll be mine!
And we'll tak a cup o' kindness yet
For auld lang syne.

We twa[2] hae run about the braes,[3]
And pu'd the gowans[4] fine;
But we've wandered monie a weary fit[5]
Sin'[6] auld lang syne.

We twa hae paidled i' burn[7]
From mornin' sun till dine;[8]
But seas between us braid[9] hae roared
Sin' auld lang syne.

And there's a hand, my trusty fiere,[10]
And gie's a hand o' thine;
And we'll tak a right guid-willie waught[11]
For auld lang syne. 4

auld lang syne, old long ago; the good old days.
1. **ye'll . . . pint-stowp,** you'll pay for your pint of drink.
2. **twa,** two.
3. **braes,** hillsides.
4. **pu'd the gowans,** pulled the daisies.
5. **monie . . . fit,** many a weary footstep.
6. **sin',** since.
7. **paidled i' burn,** paddled in the brook.
8. **dine,** noon.
9. **braid,** broad.
10. **fiere,** friend.
11. **right . . . waught,** hearty goodwill toast.

MINI-LESSON: GRAMMAR
Recognizing Colloquialisms

Teach A *colloquialism* (from the Latin word *colloquium* meaning "talk together" or "conversation") is a word or expression used in everyday, informal speech that is generally not acceptable in formal English. It is different from a dialect. When people say an experience is "colossal" or "weird," they are using colloquialisms. Burns's use of "for a' that," "cup o' kindness," and "guid-willie waught" are examples from his poetry. Burns knew formal English but used colloquialisms for the same reason that he used dialect—to make his poems sound like the everyday speech of working-class Scottish people.

Activity Idea Have students list colloquialisms they use every day and state what the expressions would be in formal English.

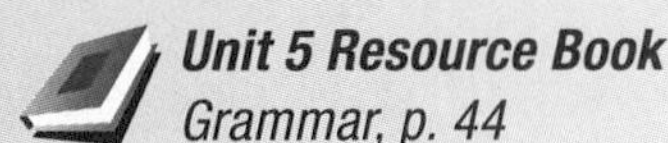
Unit 5 Resource Book
Grammar, p. 44

After Reading

Making Connections

Shaping Your Response

1. Imagine Robert Burns doing an oral reading of his poetry. With what emotions do you imagine Burns might have read each of these three poems?

Analyzing the Poems

2. In "A Man's a Man for A' That" why do you think Burns calls poverty "honest"?
3. What distinctions does Burns draw between the working man and the nobleman?
4. In this poem, inspired by the French Revolution, what **change** does Burns pray will be in the future for humankind?
5. Do you imagine the "bonie lass" in "A Red, Red Rose" is a new love or someone the speaker has loved for a while? What lines from the poem justify your response?
6. In "Auld Lang Syne" what might the speaker be suggesting about the longevity of friendships established when people are young?
7. What do the **images** Burns uses in his poetry suggest about his life?

Extending the Ideas

8. Do Burns's ideas about poverty, rank, dignity, and so on, have any application today? Do people still make these distinctions?
9. Why might an author choose to write in a dialect instead of a standard language, no matter what the language is?

Literary Focus: Dialect

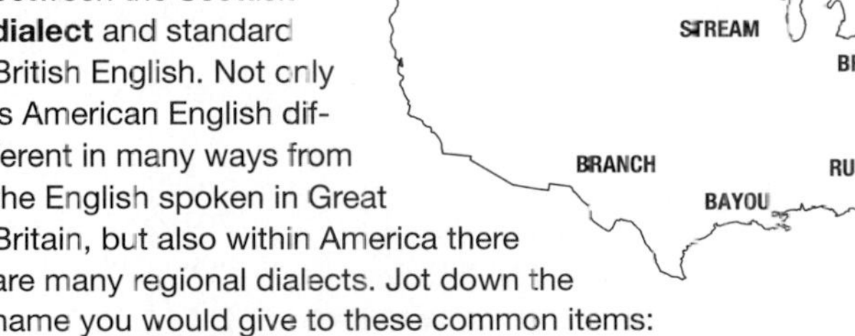

Burns's poetry demonstrates differences between the Scottish **dialect** and standard British English. Not only is American English different in many ways from the English spoken in Great Britain, but also within America there are many regional dialects. Jot down the name you would give to these common items: a carbonated soft drink, a sweet pastry, a long seat for more than one person, a person who acts in a stupid manner, a place to live. Compare your responses with those of your classmates. (Perhaps you can come up with other things that have different dialectal names.) If your responses are different, can you explain those differences based on region of the country?

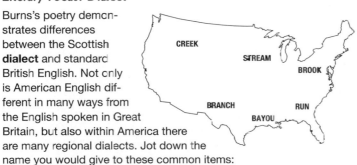

After Reading

MAKING CONNECTIONS

1. Possible responses: "A Man's a Man . . ."—fierce pride; "A Red, Red Rose"—sadness and longing; "Auld Lang Syne"—nostalgia

2. Possible response: He states that there is nothing wrong with being poor if a person is honest.

3. A working man eats homely food and wears coarse clothes, while a nobleman wears silk, drinks wine, struts and stares, and is honored.

4. Burns predicts that one day people will be ranked by honesty, sense, and personal values, not by wealth or title.

5. Possible response: that the bonnie lass is a new love is suggested by the statement that his love is like a rose "newly sprung"

6. People may wander far away, but the memories of times spent with friends will last through the years, and the friendship will endure.

7. The images suggest that the poet was poor, worked hard, loved deeply, valued and remembered his friends, and enjoyed good times and the countryside.

8. Possible response: Yes; people continue to make these distinctions. The nonpoor still consider themselves better than the poor, who are often regarded with contempt, as if poverty were a choice.

9. Possible responses: An author might feel more competent and expressive when writing in his or her native dialect. An author might wish to be identified with a specific regional culture. An author might be attempting to preserve the traditions and values of the culture.

LITERARY FOCUS: DIALECT

Possible Responses

A carbonated drink might be a *soda, pop,* or *soda pop.* A sweet pastry might be a *danish, doughnut,* or *sinker.* The long seat might be a *couch, sofa, davenport,* or *settee.* A person who acts in a stupid manner might be a *half-wit, dummy, fool, idiot, dunce,* or *dimwit.* A place to live might be a *house, home, quarters, digs, lodging, residence, flat,* or *pad.*

Emphasize to students that a dialect is not inferior or bad English. It is simply a variation that has evolved naturally as people speak to the people immediately around them. Point out that standard English is simply the most widely used dialect.

VOCABULARY STUDY

When in my arms, with all thy charms,
I clasp my countless treasure, O,
I seek no more of Heaven to share
Than such a moment's pleasure, O!
And by thy eyes so bonnie blue
I swear I'm thine for ever, O!
And on thy lips I seal my vow,
And break it shall I never, O!

Unit 5 Resource Book
Vocabulary, p. 43
Vocabulary Test, p. 46

WRITING CHOICES

Writer's Notebook Update

To get students started, invite them to share and discuss the similes for "My love is like . . . " that they wrote at the beginning of the lesson.

Capture a Holiday Spirit

Students might begin by brainstorming words and expressions that capture the essence of the holiday about which they are writing.

Brothers Be?

Point out that Burns was speaking literally about brothers and men, not women. Suggest that students consider the changes in sexual equality in composing their letters.

Selection Test

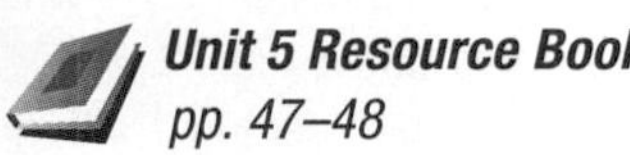

Unit 5 Resource Book
pp. 47–48

Vocabulary Study

The notes have helped you to translate Robert Burns's Scottish English. Now try your hand at translating the following lines taken from Burns's poem "And I'll Kiss Thee Yet." You'll need to concentrate on the underlined words. (See also the notes to the folk ballads on pages 25–29.)

When in my arms, wi' a' thy charms,
I clasp my countless treasure, O,
I seek nae mair o' Heav'n to share
Than sic a moment's pleasure, O!

And by thy een sae bonie blue
I swear I'm thine for ever, O!
And on thy lips I seal my vow,
And break it shall I never, O!

Expressing Your Ideas

Writing Choices

Writer's Notebook Update Complete the following **similes,** comparisons introduced by *like* or *as.* Share your favorite similes with your classmates.

Happiness is like. . . .
Trust is like. . . .
Peace is like. . . .
Friendship is like. . . .
School spirit is like. . . .

Capture a Holiday Spirit Burns's "Auld Lang Syne" is traditionally sung on New Year's Eve because people feel it captures the spirit of friendship and remembering the good old days. Select a favorite holiday and try to capture the spirit of that day in a short **descriptive paragraph.** Put your description together with paragraphs by your classmates to compile a Book of Holidays.

Brothers Be? Write a **letter** to Robert Burns in which you discuss for him the status of his 200-year-old prediction in "A Man's a Man for A' That":

"It's coming yet, for a' that,
That man to man, the warld o'er,
Shall brothers be for a' that."

Other Option

That Was Then; This Is Now Think about a good friend from your childhood who has moved to another town. You haven't seen your friend for several years now, but you still remember the good times you used to share. Assemble a **collection of photographs and drawings** that will bring your friend up to date and let him or her know how you've changed and how you've stayed the same. Entitle your collection "That Was Then; This Is Now." After comparing your collection with your classmates, send it to your friend.

OTHER OPTIONS

That Was Then; This Is Now

Suggest that students begin their collection with photographs and drawings of "Then"—the last time they saw their friends. Encourage them to think about events that have happened and people who have come into their lives and changed them in some way.

Before Reading

from A Vindication of the Rights of Woman

by Mary Wollstonecraft

Mary Wollstonecraft
1759–1797

Daughter of an abusive, alcoholic father and a submissive mother, from her early years on Mary Wollstonecraft was very conscious of the oppression of women. After working as a companion to an old woman and running a small school, she went to London to begin writing, an occupation traditionally reserved for men. Neglected and abandoned by an American writer whose child she bore, Mary Wollstonecraft attempted suicide twice. Later she found brief happiness when she married the social philosopher William Godwin. At age 38 Mary Wollstonecraft died of blood poisoning, just ten days after the birth of their daughter, Mary Godwin, the future author of *Frankenstein.*

Building Background

"I wish them to be taught to think" Mary Wollstonecraft arrived at her deep convictions about women's rights from the circumstances of her own life. She observed the women around her being abused and belittled by men. She saw women lacking self-respect and self-confidence. As a teenager Mary Wollstonecraft frequently intervened when her father assaulted her mother, often taking the blows herself. She watched the mother of her best friend sewing into the early morning hours in an endless struggle to earn a living for her family. As a young, single mother Mary faced criticism and prejudice. She helped her sister escape from the husband she was sure had driven her insane. She saw her best friend, already ill when she married, die shortly after childbirth. Mary believed that without an adequate education, which was denied to all but the wealthy, women would continue to be disadvantaged and oppressed. She knew women needed to be "taught to think."

Literary Focus

Allusion An **allusion** is a brief reference to a person, event, place, or work of art. An allusion, which may refer to myth, literature, history, religion, or any aspect of ancient or modern culture, can be a simple mention of a name or a brief quotation from a work. If you recognize an allusion, it should remind you of an idea that the author only wants to hint at in his or her work. Look for the allusions Wollstonecraft makes.

Writer's Notebook

Women's Rights? In 1792 Mary Wollstonecraft was one of the first spokeswomen for the rights of women. What do you imagine was the position of women during her time, not only in England but also in the United States? What rights did they have? What rights given to men did they not have? List some descriptions of life for women before—and even into—the twentieth century.

Before Reading

Building Background

Ask students what they know about the rights and education of women before this century and why they think it took so long for women to achieve equal rights.

Literary Focus

Explain that some allusions are direct; a writer clearly states the source of the allusion. Other allusions are indirect; the reader must recognize the source of a name, word, or phrase. Urge students to be alert for obvious and buried allusions.

Writer's Notebook

Invite partners to respond to the questions. Tell students that their answers will be helpful for a later writing project.

More About Mary Wollstonecraft

Wollstonecraft also wrote *A Vindication of the Rights of Man.*

Connections to **AuthorWorks**

Charlotte Brontë, also concerned with the outsider, is a featured author in the AuthorWorks CD-ROM series.

Connections to **NovelWorks**

NovelWorks: *Jane Eyre* offers a variety of unique materials for teaching the novel.

SUPPORT MATERIALS OVERVIEW

Unit 5 Resource Book
- Graphic Organizer, p. 49
- Study Guide, p. 50
- Vocabulary, p. 51
- Grammar, p. 52
- Alternate Check Test, p. 53
- Vocabulary Test, p. 54
- Selection Test, pp. 55–56

Building English Proficiency
- Selection Summaries
- Activities, p. 231

Reading, Writing & Grammar SkillBook
- Writing, pp. 125–126
- Grammar, Usage, and Mechanics, pp. 231–232

The World of Work
- EEOC Supervisory Investigator, p. 17
- Activity, p. 18

Technology
- Audiotape
- Personal Journal Software
- Test Generator Software

Art Study

Responses to Caption Questions Student responses may vary. As members of a privileged class, the men would be unlikely to favor social reform. While some of the women might favor reform for their sex, they would, most probably, keep such opinions to themselves.

Visual Literacy The world Sperling depicts in *Dynes Hall* is, essentially, the same world Jane Austen depicts in such novels as *Pride and Prejudice* (1813) and *Emma* (1816). Young men and women are shown interacting over cards and tea tables. While such people's dress, language, manners, and mores differ markedly from today's, their strengths, weaknesses, ambitions, and basic humanity are essentially like our own.

Question Do you find similarities between the scene Sperling depicts and how you might spend an evening with friends? *(Possible response: Friends continue to gather for parties, for games, and to attempt to get to know each other. While clothes and manners change, how people interact changes little.)*

A Vindication of the Rights of Woman

Mary Wollstonecraft

SELECTION SUMMARY

A Vindication of the Rights of Woman

In Chapter 2, the author argues that if women are often foolish and capricious, it is because they are uneducated. They are taught to be weak, obedient, and pretty so they will be taken care of by men. They get a disorderly education and, consequently, they think in a disorderly manner. This situation will not change until men change society. Women should have the right to an education.

In Chapter 9, the author says women have nothing to do but loiter about and look pretty. They should earn their living by some duty, rather than by cultivating their weakness and wasting life away. She appeals to men to emancipate women and to value them as rational companions.

*For summaries in other languages, see the **Building English Proficiency** book.*

◄ The people pictured in *Dynes Hall,* from a series created by Diana Sperling between 1812 and 1823, seem to lead lives of leisure and privilege. Do you think they might be in favor of the social reforms Wollstonecraft advocates in "A Vindication of the Rights of Woman"? Would the women be likely to have different opinions from the men?

Chapter 2

To account for, and excuse the tyranny of man, many ingenious[1] arguments have been brought forward to prove, that the two sexes, in the acquirement of virtue, ought to aim at attaining a very different character: or, to speak explicitly, women are not allowed to have sufficient strength of mind to acquire what really deserves the name of virtue. Yet it should seem, allowing them to have souls, that there is but one way appointed by providence[2] to lead *mankind* to either virtue or happiness.

If then women are not a swarm of ephemeron[3] triflers, why should they be kept in ignorance under the specious[4] name of innocence? Men complain, and with reason, of the follies and caprices of our sex, when they do not keenly satirize our headstrong passions and grovelling vices. Behold, I should answer, the natural effect of ignorance! The mind will ever be unstable that has only prejudices to rest on, and the current will run with destructive fury when there are no barriers to break its force. Women are told from their infancy, and taught by the example of their mothers, that a little knowledge of human weakness, justly termed cunning, softness of temper, *outward* obedience, and a scrupulous attention to a puerile kind of propriety,[5] will obtain for them the protection of man; and should they be beautiful, every thing else is needless, for at least twenty years of their lives. . .

SUMMARIZE: What are the lessons that Wollstonecraft sees young girls being taught?

1

The most perfect education, in my opinion is, such an exercise of the understanding as is best calculated to strengthen the body and form the heart. Or, in other words, to enable the individual to attain such habits of virtue as will render it independent. In fact, it is a farce to call any being virtuous whose virtues do not result from the exercise of its own reason. This was Rousseau's opinion respecting men.[6] I extend it to women, and confidently assert, that they have 2

vindication (vin′də kā′shən), *n.* defense; justification.
1. **ingenious** (in jē′nyəs), *adj.* cleverly planned.
2. **providence** (prov′ə dəns), *n.* God's care and help.
3. **ephemeron** (i fem′ər ən), *adj.* short-lived.
4. **specious** (spē′shəs), *adj.* apparently good, but not really so.
5. **propriety** (prə prī′ə tē), *n.* proper behavior.
6. **Rousseau's opinion . . . men.** Jean Jacques Rousseau (1712–1778) argued that an individual's natural goodness is distorted by the false values of civilization.

During Reading

Selection Objectives

- to identify and understand allusions
- to recognize the functions of prepositions in language
- to analyze reasons why women should have the right to an education

Unit 5 Resource Book
Graphic Organizer, p. 49
Study Guide, p. 50

Theme Link

Wollstonecraft argues that women should no longer be outsiders, but be admitted as full members of society.

Vocabulary Preview

ingenious, cleverly planned
specious, apparently good, but not really so
epithet, descriptive expression
indolent, lazy
factitious, artificial

Students can add the words and definitions to their Writer's Notebooks.

1 Active Reading
Summarize

Response cunning, soft temper, outward obedience, and attention to proper behavior

2 Literary Focus
Allusion

The allusion is a kind of shorthand; the author calls on the reader's knowledge of Rousseau's arguments to reinforce hers.

The World of Work
EEOC Investigator

For a contemporary look at equal opportunity, use the pages referenced below.

The World of Work
pp. 17–18

BUILDING ENGLISH PROFICIENCY

ESL LEP ELD SAE LD

Making Cultural Connections

Help students understand the system of cultural thinking Wollstonecraft wants to change.

1. Offer these paraphrases of statements from page 457, which Wollstonecraft will argue against.

- Men and women should be very different in character.
- The way to get a husband is to pretend to be obedient.
- A woman who is beautiful has all she needs.
- Women who want to be independent are too masculine.

2. Invite students to respond to the paraphrases, drawing upon their knowledge of history, their own cultural backgrounds and values, and their personal experiences.

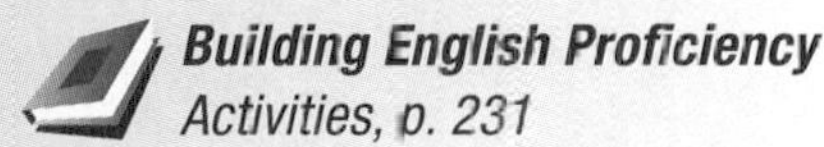

Building English Proficiency
Activities, p. 231

3 Literary Element
Tone

Question What is the author's tone, or attitude, toward her subject and her audience? *(Possible responses: reasonable, persuasive, respectful, serious)*

4 Active Reading
Clarify

Response She means that women are not taught to think carefully and logically.

5 Reading/Thinking Skills
Recognize Use of Persuasion

Question Are Wollstonecraft's techniques for persuading her readers confrontational or not? *(Possible responses: They are nonconfrontational. After calling Rousseau's view "nonsense," she appeals to men to be "great" and "to puff away the fumes" of pride. Then, rather than claiming women are by nature equal to men (which might antagonize readers who have never doubted the superiority of men), she asks only that her readers acknowledge that women's "virtues must be the same in quality, if not in degree." She does not demand that her readers give up all their beliefs, just a few critical ones.)*

been drawn out of their sphere by false refinement, and not by an endeavour to acquire masculine qualities. Still the regal homage which they receive is so intoxicating, that till the manners of the times are changed, and formed on more reasonable principles, it may be impossible to convince them, that the illegitimate power, which they obtain by degrading themselves, is a curse, and that they must return to nature and equality, if they wish to secure the placid satisfaction that unsophisticated affections impart. But for this epoch we must wait—wait, perhaps, till kings and nobles, enlightened by reason, and, preferring the real dignity of man to childish state, throw off their gaudy hereditary trappings; and if then women do not resign the arbitrary power of beauty, they will
3 prove that they have *less* mind than man. . . .

Many are the causes that, in the present corrupt state of society, contribute to enslave women by cramping their understandings and sharpening their senses. One, perhaps, that silently does more mischief than all the rest, is their disregard of order.

To do every thing in an orderly manner, is a most important precept,[7] which women, who, generally speaking, receive only a disorderly kind of education, seldom attend to with that degree of exactness that men, who from their infancy are broken into method, observe. This negligent kind of guesswork, for what other epithet[8] can be used to point out the random exertions of a sort of instinctive common sense, never brought to the test of reason? prevents their generalizing matters of fact, so they do today what they did yesterday, merely because they did it yesterday. . . .

4 **CLARIFY: Explain what Wollstonecraft means by a "disorderly kind of education."**

Women are, therefore, to be considered either as moral beings, or so weak that they must be entirely subjected to the superior faculties of men.

Let us examine this question. Rousseau declares, that a woman should never, for a moment feel herself independent, that she should be governed by fear to exercise her *natural* cunning, and made a coquettish[9] slave in order to render her a more alluring object of desire, a *sweeter* companion to man, whenever he chooses to relax himself. He carries the arguments, which he pretends to draw from the indications of nature, still further, and insinuates[10] that truth and fortitude, the corner stones of all human virtue, shall be cultivated with certain restrictions, because with respect to the female character, obedience is the grand lesson which ought to be impressed with unrelenting rigor.

What nonsense! when will a great man arise with sufficient strength of mind to puff away the fumes which pride and sensuality have thus spread over the subject! If women are by nature inferior to men, their virtues must be the same in quality, if not in degree, or virtue is a relative idea; consequently, their conduct should be founded on the same principles and have the same aim.

Connected with man as daughters, wives, 5
and mothers, their moral character may be estimated by their manner of fulfilling those simple duties; but the end, the grand end of their exertions should be to unfold their own faculties, and acquire the dignity of conscious virtue. They may try to render their road pleasant; but ought never to forget, in common with man, that life yields not the felicity[11] which can satisfy an immortal soul. I do not mean to insinuate, that either sex should be so lost, in abstract reflections or distant views, as to forget the affections and duties that lie before them, and

7. **precept** (prē′sept), *n.* rule of action or behavior.
8. epithet (ep′ə thet), *n.* descriptive expression.
9. **coquettish** (kō ket′ish), *adj.* like a flirt.
10. **insinuate** (in sin′yü āt), *v.* hint.
11. **felicity** (fə lis′ə tē), *n.* happiness.

MINI-LESSON: GRAMMAR
Recognizing Prepositions

Teach Explain that a *preposition* is a word that shows a relationship between a noun or pronoun, called the object of the preposition, and some other word in a sentence. If the object of the preposition is a pronoun, it MUST be in the objective case—*me, you, him, her, it, us,* or *them.* A preposition always introduces a phrase. Among many examples are *among, at, for, of, off, on, through, to,* and *with.*

Write this sentence from column 2 on the board. Have students identify each preposition. *(by, to, in, in, on)* Then point out how each preposition links the noun that follows it to the rest of the sentence.

If women are by nature inferior to men, their virtues must be the same in quality, if not in degree, or virtue is a relative idea; consequently, their conduct should be founded on the same principles and have the same aim.

Activity Ideas

- Have pairs of students find the prepositions in a paragraph.
- Have students find prepositions in a piece of their writing and check that pronoun objects of prepositions are in the objective case.

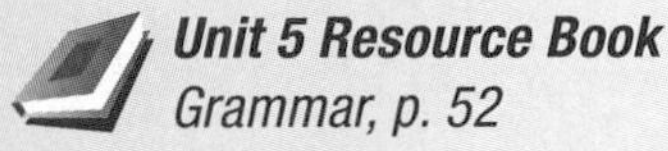

Unit 5 Resource Book
Grammar, p. 52

are in truth, the means appointed to produce the fruit of life; on the contrary, I would warmly recommend them, even while I assert, that they afford most satisfaction when they are considered in their true subordinate light.

CHAPTER 9

. . . But what have women to do in society? I may be asked, but to loiter with easy grace; surely you would not condemn them to suckle
6 fools and chronicle small beer![12] No. Women might certainly study the art of healing, and be physicians as well as nurses.

How much more respectable is the woman who earns her bread by fulfilling any duty, than the most accomplished beauty!—beauty did I say?—so sensible am I of the beauty of moral loveliness, or the harmonious propriety that attunes the passions of a well-regulated mind, that I blush at making the comparison; yet I sigh to think how few women aim at attaining this respectability by withdrawing from the giddy whirl of pleasure, or the indolent[13] calm that stupefies the good sort of women it sucks in.

Proud of their weakness, however, they must always be protected, guarded from care, and all the rough toils that dignify the mind. If this be the fiat[14] of fate, if they will make themselves insignificant and contemptible,[15] sweetly to waste "life away," let them not expect to be valued when their beauty fades, for it is the fate of the fairest flowers to be admired and pulled to pieces by the careless hand that plucked them. In how many ways do I wish, from the purest benevolence, to impress this truth on my sex; yet I fear that they will not listen to a truth that dear bought experience has brought home to many an agitated bosom, nor willingly resign the privileges of rank and sex for the privileges of humanity, to which those have no claim who do not discharge its duties.

CLARIFY: What does Wollstonecraft believe will happen to women who rely solely on their beauty? 7

Those writers are particularly useful, in my opinion, who make man feel for man, independent of the station he fills, or the drapery of factitous[16] sentiments. I then would fain convince reasonable men of the importance of some of my remarks, and prevail on them to weigh dispassionately the whole tenor of my observations. I appeal to their understandings; and, as a fellow-creature, claim, in the name of my sex, some interest in their hearts. I entreat them to assist to emancipate their companion, to make her a *help meet*[17] for them!

Would men but generously snap our chains, and be content with rational fellowship instead of slavish obedience, they would find us more observant daughters, more affectionate sisters, more faithful wives, more reasonable mothers—in a word, better citizens. We should then love them with true affection, because we should learn to respect ourselves; and the peace of mind of a worthy man would not be interrupted by the idle vanity of his wife, nor the babes sent to nestle in a strange bosom, having never found a home in their mother's.[18]

---

12. **to suckle . . . beer,** to breastfeed babies and keep track of trivial matters. In Shakespeare's *Othello* (act two, scene 1, line 160) Iago gives Desdemona this description of how a woman should spend her life.
13. **indolent** (in′dl ənt), *adj.* lazy.
14. **fiat** (fī′ət), *n.* command.
15. **contemptible** (kən temp′tə bəl), *adj.* worthless; deserving scorn.
16. **factitious** (fak tish′əs), *adj.* artificial.
17. ***help meet,*** companion or helper. In the Bible (Genesis, chapter 2), God creates Eve to be a help meet (suitable) for Adam.
18. **sent to nestle . . . mother's,** given to a nurse to be cared for.

6 Literary Focus
Allusion

You might point out that "to suckle fools and chronicle small beer" alludes to Shakespeare. Wollstonecraft's audience was familiar with Shakespeare's works and would have recognized the allusion.

7 Active Reading
Clarify

Response They will lose their value to men—their protectors and providers—when they grow older and are no longer beautiful.

Check Test

1. What is the "tyranny of man" that the author refers to in the opening sentence? *(the power men have exercised to deny women equal rights and equal access to education)*
2. What does the author say is the goal of the perfect education? *(to provide the individual with the capacity to live independently)*
3. What objection does the author have to women's role in society? *(She objects to keeping them "innocent"; to not allowing them to develop their minds and achieve their human potential.)*
4. According to the author, what does Rousseau consider the greatest virtue among women? *(obedience)*
5. How will men benefit from freeing women from "slavish obedience"? *(through rational fellowship, true love, more affectionate sisters, more observant daughters, better mothers, and freedom from the demands of idle and vain wives)*

Unit 5 Resource Book
Alternate Check Test, p. 53

BUILDING ENGLISH PROFICIENCY

Expanding Vocabulary Notebooks

Wollstonecraft's vocabulary is challenging, so encourage students to build their own word resources in addition to studying the selection vocabulary and footnotes.

1. Offer examples of words that may seem new—for example, *negligent, exertions, fortitude, rigor,* and *propriety.*
2. Then offer examples of words whose meaning here is not what students might expect—for example, *faculties, reflections, dear,* and *drapery.*
3. Have students note these or other words in their vocabulary notebooks, define each word, and then use it in an original sentence.

After Reading

MAKING CONNECTIONS

1. Answers will vary, but students should give reasons for their choices.

2. Wollstonecraft thinks young girls are not taught to think in an orderly, logical manner. Most students will agree with her.

3. Possible responses: Wollstonecraft's attitude toward men is sometimes one of irritation and impatience because of what they subject women to. Sometimes she also exhibits understanding because men, too, are victims of society. Her attitude toward women is usually one of sympathy for their situation, but sometimes she is impatient because they accept things as they are.

4. Answers will vary but should include the idea that people who can reason and think critically have stronger motives and make better companions than people who act out of obedience or from social pressure.

5. She means the writers who help people understand the nature and needs of others. Students should give reasons for naming the authors they do.

6. Defoe and Wollstonecraft make a similar point, that education would make women better companions of men, not worse. Some students may find the tone of Defoe's piece condescending. They may comment that Wollstonecraft seems more modern.

7. Answers will vary. Many students may say that education today should strengthen the mind and prepare people to succeed in a competitive job market.

After Reading

Making Connections

Shaping Your Response

1. What color would you use to describe the emotions of Mary Wollstonecraft as revealed through her essay? Explain your choice.

Analyzing the Essay

2. Why do you think Wollstonecraft feels the education of young girls is inadequate? Do you agree with her?
3. What attitudes does Wollstonecraft display towards men? towards other women? Why do you think she feels this way?
4. Wollstonecraft believes that educated women will be "more observant daughters, more affectionate sisters, more faithful wives, more reasonable mothers, . . . better citizens." Discuss how education could bring about the **change** Wollstonecraft describes.

Extending the Ideas

5. Wollstonecraft praises writers who "make man feel for man." What do you think she means? What authors have you read who have created such a feeling in you?
6. Compare the **theme** of Wollstonecraft's essay with that of Daniel Defoe's "The Education of Women" (see page 306). How are Defoe and Wollstonecraft alike and how are they different in the literary tools they use to get their themes across?
7. Is Wollstonecraft's prescription for a perfect education—"to strengthen the body and form the heart"—still valid today? Would you add any other goals for today's students and teachers?

Literary Focus: Allusion

In this selection Mary Wollstonecraft uses **allusion,** references to historical or literary writings, persons, events, or places. Locate the three allusions in the text. What do you think was Wollstonecraft's purpose in selecting each allusion?

Vocabulary Study

epithet
factitious
indolent
ingenious
specious

Many vocabulary words are misunderstood because they look like or sound like other words. Confusing one word for another can often lead to misinterpretation. In each of the following sentences, select the correct word. Use your Glossary or a dictionary, if necessary.

1. Mary Wollstonecraft believes that her plea for equality for women is not (indolent, insolent), but sensible for both men and women.
2. Wollstonecraft admits that some of the arguments used to prove the inferiority of women are (ingenious, ingenuous).

LITERARY FOCUS: ALLUSION

- *Allusion:* pages 457 and 458—"Rousseau's opinion . . . " and "Rousseau declares . . . " refer to French philosopher Jean Jacques Rousseau
  Purpose: to give weight to her argument; to introduce a rationale that she will later attack; and to show that Rousseau's logic is wrong
- *Allusion:* page 459—"to suckle fools . . . " Shakespeare
  Purpose: to emphasize the traditional view of women's role in society
- *Allusion:* page 459—"help meet . . . " from the Bible
  Purpose: to show that the Bible offers precedent for her view of the role of women

3. In arguing for the education of women, Wollstonecraft challenges what she considers to be the (spacious, specious) arguments of men.
4. Wollstonecraft wants to help women understand the difference between the (factitious, fictitious) and the real feelings of men.
5. An (epitaph, epithet) on Mary Wollstonecraft's tombstone might well include mention of her most famous work, *A Vindication of the Rights of Woman.*

Expressing Your Ideas

Writing Choices

Writer's Notebook Update Which of the conditions you listed in your notebook do you think has improved the most for women? Write a paragraph or so in which you discuss what the improvements have been, why you believe they occurred, and whether more improvements are necessary.

Schools Today The artist who created this cartoon seems to feel that education today is male-centered. Do you agree? Are girls today short-changed by American schools? From your personal experience in an American high school write an **editorial** for your school newspaper responding to the cartoon shown here.

Darkow. Reprinted with special permission of North America Syndicate.

Playing It Fair You are an employer who believes in equal-opportunity employment. Write a one-page equal opportunity **policy statement** to be given to all prospective employees. You may wish to consider such issues as gender, race, religion, age, appearance, marital status.

Other Options

Speak Your Mind! There is an international conference on the status of women in the world. You can be any woman from any country, or you can be yourself. Prepare a **speech** which you will present to the conference addressing what you feel is the single most critical issue in women's rights today. After your class has listened to all of the speeches, discuss which issue is most important.

Train Up a Child "Train up a child in the way he should go," says the Bible, "and when he is old, he will not depart from it." (Proverbs 22:6). Prepare a **lesson** on an aspect of women's rights that would be suitable for a class of fourth graders. Remember that you will be teaching both girls and boys. Include teaching aids such as dolls, toys, and photographs.

VOCABULARY STUDY

1. insolent
2. ingenious
3. specious
4. factitious
5. epitaph

Unit 5 Resource Book
Vocabulary, p. 51
Vocabulary Test, p. 54

WRITING CHOICES

Writer's Notebook Update

Before students begin writing you might bring up the "glass ceiling" (the invisible barrier beyond which women seldom rise in corporate hierarchy) and lead a discussion on its meaning and implications.

Schools Today

Ask the class to recall memories of grade and middle schools; and then discuss who led the class, who achieved more scholastically, and who performed better athletically in grade and middle school *vs.* high school—girls or boys. Have things changed and, if so, why?

Playing It Fair

Discuss the usual rationale and contents of such a policy statement.

Selection Test

Unit 5 Resource Book
pp. 55–56

OTHER OPTIONS

Speak Your Mind!

Remind students that their audience already supports women's rights. Their goal is to explain why one issue is more important than others.

Train Up a Child

Suggest that students observe some fourth graders or look at some fourth-grade, nonfiction books to develop an idea of the sophistication of fourth graders. The lesson they prepare should be appropriate for children of about nine to ten years of age.

Before Reading

Building Background

You might discuss the "Byronic hero" and how this term describes both the poet and his characters. The Byronic hero is brooding, romantic, rebellious, and capable of great evil, for which he feels great guilt. Above all, he values freedom.

Literary Focus

Suggest that students look for words that are used repeatedly or that catch their attention and try substituting synonyms. Do the substitutions change meaning, tone, mood, or rhythm of line?

Writer's Notebook

Suggest that students visualize themselves parting from the person closest to them. How do they feel?

More About Lord Byron

Byron was a man of paradoxes. He was born with a deformed foot, but became a great athlete. He was passionate for many things, but never satisfied. The public was as enthralled by the man, and the scandals that clung to him, as by his poetry. Other poems by Byron include

- "English Bards and Scotch Reviewers" (1809)
- *Don Juan* (1818–1821)

Before Reading

She Walks in Beauty
When We Two Parted

by George Gordon, Lord Byron

George Gordon, Lord Byron
1788–1824

At the age of ten, George Gordon inherited a fortune and became Lord Byron, the title which gave him a seat in the House of Lords. He lived an eccentric life. While on a tour of Europe, he swam the Hellespont (a strait in Turkey), lived with bandits, visited a sultan's harem, and wrote *Childe Harold's Pilgrimage.* After only one year of marriage, his wife took their young daughter and returned to her father. Rumors of madness, abandonment, and scandalous sexuality forced him to leave England, never to return. For a time he lived with Percy and Mary Shelley in Italy. Always a champion of liberty, Byron raised an army and contributed large sums of money to the Greek fight for independence from Turkey. He died of a fever in Greece, at the age of thirty-six.

Building Background

"Let us have wine and women, mirth and laughter,
Sermons and soda-water the day after."

This rhyming couplet, from his famous mock epic poem *Don Juan,* might well have served as a motto for the life—and the poetry—of the intense young poet, Lord Byron. His earliest love affair with Mary Duff, a cousin, when both were only seven, is celebrated in one of his first love poems, "When I Roved a Young Highlander." Enchanted by the beauty of his many lovely cousins, intrigued by the mystery of young ladies of aristocratic birth, Byron recorded his passions, his obsessions, his loves, and his regrets in lyric after lyric. Among the many subjects of his poetry were the "Maid of Athens," whom he met on his European tour; Caroline Lamb, who frequently dressed as a footman in order to get closer to Byron; his half sister Augusta, with whom he had more than one steamy affair; the young Claire Clairmont, stepdaughter of philosopher William Godwin; and Teresa Guioccioli, perhaps his last and greatest love. Indeed, it is difficult to separate the life and the poetry of the Byron once described by Caroline Lamb as "mad, bad, and dangerous to know."

Literary Focus

Diction The writer's choice of words and phrases is called **diction.** This choice may involve a range of words from formal to informal or from old-fashioned—even archaic—to modern and slangy. Sometimes a poet will make use of what are known as poetic contractions; for example, Byron uses *o'er* for *over*. This choice of words, involving both denotation and connotation, is meant to have a certain effect on a reader. As you read Byron's poems, think about what effect Byron's diction actually has on you.

Writer's Notebook

Taking Leave What sort of thoughts might you have and what sort of emotions might you feel if you had to go away from someone to whom you felt very close? Jot some impressions of your possible thoughts and emotions. Would you share them with the other person?

SUPPORT MATERIALS OVERVIEW

Unit 5 Resource Book
- Graphic Organizer, p. 57
- Study Guide, p. 58
- Vocabulary, p. 59
- Grammar, p. 60
- Alternate Check Test, p. 61
- Vocabulary Test, p. 62
- Selection Test, pp. 63–64

Building English Proficiency
- Selection Summaries
- Activities, p. 232

Reading, Writing & Grammar SkillBook
- Grammar, Usage, and Mechanics, pp. 205–206, 207–208

Technology
- Audiotape
- Personal Journal Software
- Custom Literature Database: Additional selections by Byron can be found on the database.
- Test Generator Software

She Walks in Beauty

GEORGE GORDON, LORD BYRON

She[1] walks in beauty, like the night
1 Of cloudless climes[2] and starry skies;
And all that's best of dark and bright
Meet in her aspect[3] and her eyes:
Thus mellowed to that tender light
Which heaven to gaudy day denies.

One shade the more, one ray the less,
Had half impaired the nameless[4] grace
Which waves in every raven tress,
Or softly lightens o'er her face;
Where thoughts serenely[5] sweet express
How pure, how dear their dwelling-place.

2 And on that cheek, and o'er that brow,
So soft, so calm, yet eloquent,
The smiles that win, the tints that glow,
But tell of days in goodness spent,
A mind at peace with all below,
A heart whose love is innocent!

---

1. **she,** Lady Wilmot Horton, Byron's beautiful young cousin by marriage, who had appeared in an evening dress of black mourning brightened with spangles.
2. **clime** (klīm), *n.* region.
3. **aspect** (as′pekt), *n.* facial expression.
4. **nameless,** indescribable.
5. **serenely** (sə rēn′lē), *adv.* peacefully.

SELECTION SUMMARY

She Walks in Beauty; When We Two Parted

She Walks in Beauty The narrator compares a woman to a star-filled night sky. She is so perfect that any change would detract. Even her thoughts seem serene and pure. Her smile is so winning and her color so glows that her mind must be at peace, her heart innocent.

When We Two Parted The narrator remembers parting, with silence and tears, from a woman he loved. When he hears her name, he silently shares the guilt of her lost reputation; his guilt remains silent because their association remains a secret. If they should meet again, how should he greet her? With silence and tears, he decides.

*For summaries in other languages, see the **Building English Proficiency** book.*

During Reading

Selection Objectives

- to recognize the themes of the Byronic hero in Romantic poetry
- to understand and appreciate diction in Byron's poetry
- to explore the theme of the outsider
- to apply subject-verb agreement

Unit 5 Resource Book
Graphic Organizer, p. 57
Study Guide, p. 58

Theme Link

In "She Walks in Beauty," the narrator is the outsider who stands apart to observe and marvel at the woman who walks in beauty. In "When We Two Parted," he grieves alone and in silence for the woman from whom he is parted, but still loves.

1 Literary Focus
Diction

Questions What other words might Byron have used instead of "climes"? *(Possible responses: regions, areas, locales, places)* What makes "clime" the best word choice? *(Possible response: The word "clime" suggests a region or locale by denoting its climate.)* You might discuss how the other word choices would have similar denotations, but would alter the sound, connotation, and tone.

2 Literary Element
Rhyme

Question You might call attention to the rhyme scheme. What word rhymes with brow? *(This is no rhyme.)* Explain that poets occasionally experiment with *sight* (or false) rhyme, and the effect, as here, can be playful and surprising.

3 Reading/Thinking Skills
Recognize Values

Questions What does the author mean that he shares in the shame? *(The woman's reputation has been ruined by her association with men. The speaker, though never connected with her publicly, feels guilty.)* Do you agree that the speaker should feel guilt? *(While answers will vary, students should understand that he shares in her shame because he shared in the kind of behavior that led to her shame; he may be unknown, but he is not innocent.)*

4 Literary Focus
Diction

You might point out the word *wert.* Explain that it is an archaic past tense of "to be," meaning *were.* Note that *wert*, along with other word choices, such as *knell, thou,* and *rue,* lend a poetic, antique sound because they are archaic. Invite students to discuss why Byron might have used such words.

5 Literary Element
Alliteration

Question Remind students that alliteration is the repetition of consonant sounds, which may occur at the beginning, the end, or within words. Can you find examples of alliteration in the final stanza? *(The* s *sound is repeated in the words* secret, silence, spirit, *and* deceive, *and in the last line,* silence *and* tears.*)*

When We Two Parted

George Gordon, Lord Byron

When we two parted
In silence and tears,
Half broken-hearted
To sever for years,
Pale grew thy cheek and cold,
Colder thy kiss;
Truly that hour foretold
Sorrow to this.

The dew of the morning
Sunk chill on my brow—
It felt like the warning
Of what I feel now.
Thy vows are all broken,
And light is thy fame;
I hear thy name spoken,
And share in its shame. **3**

They name thee before me,
A knell to mine ear;
A shudder comes o'er me—
4 Why wert thou so dear?
They know not I knew thee,
Who knew thee too well—
Long, long shall I rue thee,
Too deeply to tell.

5 In secret we met—
In silence I grieve,
That thy heart could forget,
Thy spirit deceive.
If I should meet thee
After long years,
How should I greet thee?—
With silence and tears.

In *Broken Vows,* an 1856 painting by Philip Hermogenes Calderon, a betrayed woman suffers in silence, while those who are the cause of her sorrow commune happily on the other side of the wall. Have you ever been betrayed by someone you loved and trusted? What feelings did you experience when you learned of the betrayal? Explain how the artist's choice of details and composition help to tell the story. ➤

18 **knell** (nel), *n.* mournful sound.

20 **wert,** were.

23 **rue** (rü), *v.* regret.

MINI-LESSON: GRAMMAR
Subject-Verb Agreement

Teach Write these lines on the board. Have students identify the subjects and verbs.

Thy vows are all broken,
And light is thy fame;

Remind students that verbs have singular and plural forms and the form used must agree in number with the subject. Point out that *vows* is the plural subject of the first line and *are* is the plural form of the verb *be.* In the second line, the subject, *fame,* is singular and so it takes *is,* the singular form of the verb *be.*

Activity Ideas

- Ask students to restate lines from the poem, changing plural subjects and verbs to singular, and vice versa.
- Have students check a current writing assignment for subject-verb agreement.

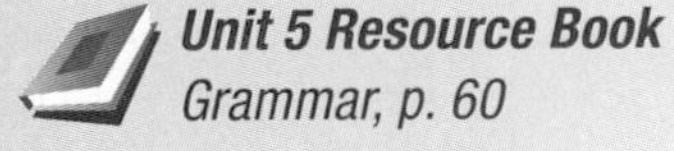

Unit 5 Resource Book
Grammar, p. 60

Art Study

Responses to Caption Questions Responses to the first two questions will vary. The story of *Broken Vows* is essentially told through the hands and mouths. A masculine hand drops a posy into the hand of a woman, who smiles at the gesture. On the other side of the wall, the position of the woman's hand suggests the pain of a broken heart; the ring on her finger tells us that the man is her husband; and the position of her mouth suggests that she is heartsick. An oblique angle of light connects the two scenes, showing cause and effect.

Visual Literacy The Victorians loved paintings that told stories, and various details suggest a conclusion to this one. The somber clothing and scarf of the "lady wronged" suggest mourning. The ivy gives the wall against which she leans the typical flat-surfaced, rounded-top look of a tombstone of the era. The ivy itself evokes an English churchyard.

Question What do these details suggest about the lady's fate? *(She may succumb to her "broken heart.")*

Check Test

1. To what does Byron compare the woman in "She Walks in Beauty"? *(a cloudless night)*

2. What does the woman's winning smile indicate? *(She spends her days in goodness, her mind is at peace, and her heart is innocent.)*

3. In "When We Two Parted," what does the pale cheek and cold kiss foretell? *(the sorrow he still feels)*

4. Why isn't anyone aware that the speaker knew the woman? *(They met and parted in secret.)*

5. If the speaker should ever meet this woman again, how will he greet her? *(with silence and tears)*

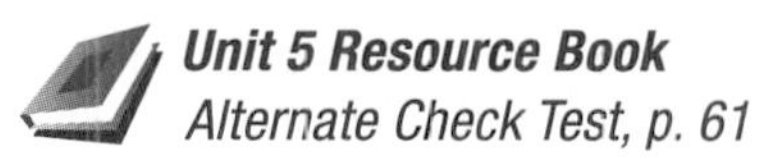

Unit 5 Resource Book
Alternate Check Test, p. 61

BUILDING ENGLISH PROFICIENCY

Making Real-Life Connections

Invite students to think of the world around them as they consider how Byron captures the feelings of a romantic break-up.

Activity Ideas

- Ask volunteers to name movies, TV shows, or songs that focus on a break-up. Ask: How did the break-up happen? Were both people at fault? How did each person feel afterward?
- The ending of the poem suggests a possible future meeting of the ex-lovers. Invite volunteers to role-play the ex-lovers and improvise a scene in which they actually do meet several years after they have broken up.

Building English Proficiency
Activities, p 232

After Reading

MAKING CONNECTIONS

1. Based on what students know about Byron, most will respond that the speaker is describing real emotions.

2. Answers will vary. Students may respond that starlight, which lends the lady a shimmering quality, is more romantic than the bright light of the day.

3. a graceful woman with black hair, a softly glowing cheek, a gentle smile, and innocence

4. She is a good person who is at peace in her mind and innocent in her heart.

5. Answers will vary. The poet devotes more lines to describing her physical beauty, but he seems to place more emphasis on the spiritual beauty by putting it at the end of the poem and ending the last line with an exclamation point.

6. The speaker says that at their separation, her cold kiss foretold sorrow to come. In the second stanza, he says the dew was cold on his brow and warned of the sorrow and guilt he feels now.

7. Answers will vary. Could the lady have been married and broken off the relationship to preserve her home? Could she have taken up with a new lover? Did she break off the relationship in order to protect the narrator's reputation at the expense of her own?

8. The emotions expressed in both poems are excessive in comparison to typical English reserve.

9. While answers will vary, students should note that Byron's combination of physical and spiritual ideals is lacking in modern definitions of ideal beauty, which dwell only on the physical.

After Reading

Making Connections

Shaping Your Response

1. Do you think the speaker in these two poems is describing real emotions or just being "poetic"? Explain your answer.

Analyzing the Poems

2. In "She Walks in Beauty" what do you think the speaker gains by describing his beauty in starlight rather than in daylight?
3. What seems to be the speaker's physical ideal?
4. What spiritual ideals are apparently present in the woman?
5. Which aspects of beauty—the physical or the spiritual—do you think the speaker emphasizes more?
6. In "When We Two Parted" what **foreshadowings** and warnings does the speaker seem to have about the future of the relationship?
7. Imagine some circumstances that might have brought about the **change** in their relationship that the speaker is so unhappy about.

Extending the Ideas

8. In what ways might one or both of these poems suggest that the author was in opposition to the traditional reserve of English society?
9. In your opinion, to what extent does Byron's picture of ideal physical and spiritual beauty correspond with modern definitions of ideal beauty?

Literary Focus: Diction

The writer's **diction,** or choice of words and phrases, influences a reader's reaction to the writer's work. List words and phrases from these two poems that are different from the words and phrases you use normally. After each word or phrase write the way you would say it. Finally, write a sentence or two describing Byron's overall diction and your reaction to it.

LITERARY FOCUS: DICTION

Possible Responses:

climes—regions
aspect—appearance or face
nameless—indescribable
raven—black
tress—braid of hair
o'er—over,
foretold—predicted
vows—promises
knell—sorrowful ringing
wert—were
rue—regret

Students' responses to Byron's diction will vary.

Expressing Your Ideas

Writing Choices

Writer's Notebook Update Writers of fiction and drama know that diction can be a powerful tool of **characterization.** First write a description of a distinctive diction that you're familiar with; for example: "teenager raised in Texas" or "immigrant from Vietnam, to whom English is a second language." Then rewrite your thoughts about leaving in this character's voice, controlling his or her diction through your choice of words and sentence structures.

Inside and Out Write a **description**—in either poetry or prose—of a person who has made a strong impression on you. Include not only a physical description but also a description of the person's inner character or spiritual qualities. Do the person's physical qualities reveal anything about his or her character and personality?

Meeting / Parting The lovers in "When We Two Parted" separate in "silence and tears." Think about a close relationship you have had with someone or imagine fictional characters in a relationship. Write a **poem** in which you describe your meeting and/or your parting. Begin and end your poem with strong words (like *silence* and *tears*) so that you capture your mood for the reader.

Other Options

That's My Ideal Select pictures from a variety of popular magazines and catalogues to put together a **bulletin board display** of what you believe to be the ideals of beauty in America today. You might add quotations about beauty or paragraphs from articles about cosmetics, health, and so on.

Westminster Abbey Although Lord Byron is regarded as one of the greatest English poets, he was denied burial in Poets' Corner of Westminster Abbey in London. Research this famous resting place of England's renowned writers and present your findings in an **oral report.** If possible, illustrate your report with pictures of Westminster Abbey and of the people who are buried there.

Mixing Art and Politics Although Byron lived a notorious life, he died a hero to the Greeks in whose cause he fought (see the Interdisciplinary Study beginning on page 475). Do you believe writers and other artists ought to involve themselves with politics or other causes, such as poverty or the environment—or should they be content to be good artists? Work with a partner to plan and present a **debate** on this question. You might want to use as examples artists (such as movie stars) from our time who have been particularly vocal on behalf of one cause or another.

WRITING CHOICES

Writer's Notebook Update

You might suggest that students first list characteristics of the diction they will use as a way of formulating their writing goals.

Inside and Out

Students may begin by brainstorming pairs of rhyming words or by freewriting, or both.

Meeting/Parting

Students might try freewriting about the relationship for two minutes before beginning their poem in order to develop ideas and identify key points.

Selection Test

Unit 5 Resource Book
pp. 63–64

OTHER OPTIONS

That's My Ideal

You may want to provide magazines and catalogs for students to cut apart. When students have completed their displays, you might have them present an informal discussion comparing their various ideals of beauty.

Westminster Abbey

In their reports, students may wish to include their reflections on the contradiction between the poet's greatness and fame on the one hand and, on the other, public attitudes toward his personal life.

Mixing Art and Politics

Ask students to follow formal debate procedures. They should begin by agreeing on and writing a clear proposition.

Before Reading

Building Background

Much of the power of the imagery of "Ode to the West Wind" lies in the contrast of a violent, summer-like thunderstorm in an autumnal landscape. Ask students to visualize a blustery, autumn day and brainstorm words or phrases to describe how it feels to be out on such a day.

Literary Focus

Discuss with the class why a writer might employ an apostrophe, and then, ask students to create apostrophes of their own.

Writer's Notebook

Urge students to think of fresh, interesting adjectives that evoke the special qualities of the place.

More About Shelley

A classmate described the young Shelley: "His imagination was always roving upon something romantic and extraordinary, such as spirits, fairies, fighting, volcanoes, etc., and he not unfrequently astonished his schoolfellows by blowing up the boundary palings [fence] of the playground with gunpowder." Shelley's major works include

- *Queen Mab* (1813)
- *The Cenci* (1819)
- *Prometheus Unbound* (1820)

Before Reading

Ode to the West Wind
Ozymandias

by Percy Bysshe Shelley

Percy Bysshe Shelley
1792–1822

Son of a conservative country squire, Percy Shelley was expelled after only a year at Oxford for collaborating on a pamphlet called *The Necessity of Atheism.* At nineteen he married sixteen-year-old Harriet Westbrook. Two years later he left England with a new love, Mary Godwin, daughter of philosopher William Godwin and writer Mary Wollstonecraft. Harriet was left behind with one child and another on the way. Following Harriet's suicide, Percy and Mary married and settled in Italy. Here the eccentric and passionate Shelley wrote many lyric poems and his masterpiece, *Prometheus Unbound.* In 1822, when he was nearing his thirtieth birthday, Shelley drowned when his boat was caught in a violent storm.

Building Background

"Be thou me, impetuous one" A true Romantic, Percy Bysshe Shelley often drew his inspirations from nature just as his poetic idol, William Wordsworth, did. Of the motivation for his "Ode to the West Wind," Shelley wrote: "This poem was conceived and chiefly written in a wood that skirts the Arno, near Florence [Italy], and on a day when that tempestuous wind, whose temperature is at once mild and animating, was collecting the vapors which pour down the autumnal rains. They began, as I foresaw, at sunset with a violent tempest of hail and rain, attended by the magnificent thunder and lightning peculiar to the Cisalpine regions." In calling upon the "impetuous" wind to be his guide, Shelley asks that his poetry may strike a spark of hope among mankind.

Literary Focus

Apostrophe A figure of speech in which an absent person, an inanimate object, or an abstract concept is directly addressed is called **apostrophe.** Following are examples of each kind. What apostrophe can you find in Shelley's poetry?

Kind	Example	Source
absent person	"Here thou, great Anna!. . ."	Pope's "The Rape of the Lock" (page 319, line 145)
inanimate object	"O sylvan Wye! thou wanderer through the woods. . ."	Wordsworth's "Tintern Abbey" (page 410, line 56)
abstract concept	"Time, thou anticipat'st my dread exploits. . ."	Shakespeare's *Macbeth,* act four, scene 1 (page 167, line 144)

Writer's Notebook

My Private Place When you want to be alone—to think, to dream, to talk to yourself—where do you go? Jot down five or more adjectives that describe a place where you go to be alone with your thoughts.

SUPPORT MATERIALS OVERVIEW

Unit 5 Resource Book
- Graphic Organizer, p. 65
- Study Guide, p. 66
- Vocabulary, p. 67
- Grammar, p. 68
- Alternate Check Test, p. 69
- Vocabulary Test, p. 70
- Selection Test, pp. 71–72

Building English Proficiency
- Selection Summaries
- Activities, p. 233
- "Ode to the West Wind" in Spanish

Reading, Writing & Grammar SkillBook
- Grammar, Usage, and Mechanics, pp. 175–177

Technology
- Audiotape
- Personal Journal Software
- Custom Literature Database: Additional selections by Shelley can be found on the database.
- Test Generator Software

ODE TO THE WEST WIND

PERCY BYSSHE SHELLEY

1

1

O wild West Wind, thou breath of Autumn's being,
Thou, from whose unseen presence the leaves dead
Are driven, like ghosts from an enchanter fleeing,

Yellow, and black, and pale, and hectic red,
Pestilence[1]-stricken multitudes: O thou,
Who chariotest to their dark wintry bed

The wingèd seeds, where they lie cold and low,
Each like a corpse within its grave, until
Thine azure sister of the Spring shall blow

Her clarion[2] o'er the dreaming earth, and fill
(Driving sweet buds like flocks to feed in air)
With living hues and odors plain and hill;

Wild Spirit, which art moving everywhere;
Destroyer and preserver; hear, oh, hear!

2

2

Thou on whose stream, mid the steep sky's commotion,
Loose clouds like earth's decaying leaves are shed,
Shook from the tangled boughs of Heaven and Ocean,

Angels of rain and lightning: there are spread
On the blue surface of thine airy surge,
Like the bright hair uplifted from the head

Of some fierce Maenad,[3] even from the dim verge
Of the horizon to the zenith's height,
The locks of the approaching storm. Thou dirge[4]

1. pestilence (pes′tl əns), *n.* epidemic disease.
2. **clarion** (klar′ē ən), *n.* trumpet call.
3. **maenad** (mē′nad), a priestess of Dionysus, Greek god of wine, who was worshipped with savage rites.
4. dirge (dėrj), *n.* funeral song.

During Reading

Selection Objectives

- to identify apostrophes as a literary device
- to explore the theme of the outsider
- to identify mood and irony

Unit 5 Resource Book
Graphic Organizer, p. 65
Study Guide, p. 66

Theme Link

In "Ode to the West Wind," the narrator sees himself as the outsider who has fallen on the thorns of life. In "Ozymandias," time has reduced the ultimate "insider" into the ruler of a kingdom of sand.

Vocabulary Preview

pestilence, epidemic disease
dirge, funeral song
sepulcher, tomb
tumult, commotion
impetuous, rash; hasty

Students can add the words and definitions to their Writer's Notebooks.

1 Literary Focus
Apostrophe

Questions What is the apostrophe in this poem? *(the narrator's address to the wind)* What effect is achieved by the apostrophe? *(The device lends immediacy and gives the wind the quality of being a living, responsive thing.)*

2 The Author Speaks
Romantic Style

"When my brain gets heated with thought, it soon boils and throws off images and words faster than I can skim them off. In the morning, when cooled down, out of the rude sketch, as you justly call it, I shall attempt a drawing."

Percy Bysshe Shelley
to Edward Trelawney

SELECTION SUMMARY

Ode to the West Wind; Ozymandias

Ode to the West Wind The narrator calls to the West Wind, destroyer and preserver, which drives autumn's leaves as well as seeds that, in spring, will burst into new life. The narrator asks to be the wind's lyre, to have his words scattered like seeds. His words may seem dead now, but like trees in spring, they will come back to life to spark humanity.

Ozymandias The narrator tells of a traveler to an ancient land, who has seen a colossal statue. The pedestal declares the image to be Ozymandias, king of kings, whose works leave the mighty in despair. Wrecked and decayed, the statue stares across an endless sea of sand.

For summaries in other languages, see the ***Building English Proficiency*** *book.*

3 Literary Element
Figurative Language

Questions What "death" simile does the narrator use in section 1? *(Seeds are compared to corpses in their graves.)* What "death" metaphors does he use in section 2? *(Possible responses: The wind is compared to a dirge; the autumn sky is compared to the dome of a sepulcher; dark clouds are compared to the vaults of the sepulcher.)*

4 Literary Element
Rhyme

You might point out that the rhyme scheme of "Ode to the West Wind" is called *terza rima,* a form invented by Dante for his *Divine Comedy.* In *terza rima,* the first and third lines of each three-line stanza, or triplet, rhyme, and the second line rhymes with the first and third lines of the next triplet. In "West Wind," the stanzas, four triplets and one couplet, form a sonnet. The final line rhymes with the preceding line of the couplet.

Of the dying year, to which this closing night
Will be the dome of a vast sepulcher,[5]
Vaulted with all thy congregated might

Of vapors, from whose solid atmosphere
3 Black rain, and fire, and hail will burst: oh hear!

3

Thou who didst waken from his summer dreams
The blue Mediterranean, where he lay,
Lulled by the coil of his crystàlline streams,

Beside a pumice isle in Baiae's bay,[6]
And saw in sleep old palaces and towers
Quivering within the wave's intenser day,

All overgrown with azure moss and flowers
So sweet, the sense faints picturing them! Thou
For whose path the Atlantic's level powers

Cleave themselves into chasms,[7] while far below
The sea-blooms and the oozy woods which wear
The sapless foliage of the ocean, know

Thy voice, and suddenly grow gray with fear,
4 And tremble and despoil[8] themselves: oh, hear!

4

If I were a dead leaf thou mightest bear;
If I were a swift cloud to fly with thee;
A wave to pant beneath thy power, and share

The impulse of thy strength, only less free
Than thou, O uncontrollable! If even
I were as in my boyhood, and could be

The comrade of thy wanderings over Heaven,
As then, when to outstrip the skyey speed
Scarce seemed a vision—I would ne'er have striven

MINI-LESSON: GRAMMAR
Singular and Plural Nouns

Teach Have students identify nouns in the stanzas above as singular or plural. Then review the rules for forming plurals.

- Most singular nouns are made plural by adding an *-s.*
- Some nouns are made plural by adding *-es.*
- Nouns ending in *y* that are preceded by a consonant are made plural by changing the *y* to an *i* and adding *-es.*
- Nouns ending in *y* that are preceded by a vowel are made plural by adding an *s.*
- Most nouns ending in *f* or *fe,* such as *life,* are made plural by changing the *f* to a *v* and adding *-s* or *-es.* Some are formed by simply adding *-s.*
- The plural of some nouns, such as *deer,* is the same as the singular form.
- Some nouns, such as *beau* and *child,* have special plural forms *(beaux* and *children).*

Activity Idea Have students change the singular nouns in the stanzas on this page to plural and the plural nouns to singular.

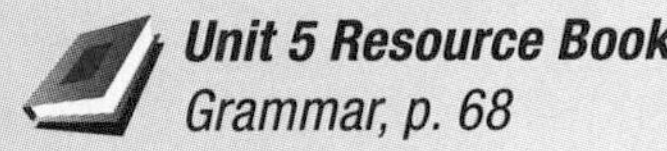
Unit 5 Resource Book
Grammar, p. 68

As thus with thee in prayer in my sore need.
Oh, lift me as a wave, a leaf, a cloud!
I fall upon the thorns of life! I bleed! 5

A heavy weight of hours has chained and bowed
One too like thee—tameless, and swift, and proud.

5

Make me thy lyre, even as the forest is:
What if my leaves are falling like its own!
The tumult[9] of thy mighty harmonies

Will take from both a deep, autumnal tone,
Sweet though in sadness. Be thou, Spirit fierce,
My spirit! Be thou me, impetuous[10] one!

Drive my dead thoughts over the universe 6
Like withered leaves to quicken a new birth;
And, by the incantation[11] of this verse,

Scatter, as from an unextinguished hearth
Ashes and sparks, my words among mankind!
Be through my lips to unawakened earth

The trumpet of a prophecy! O Wind,
If Winter comes, can Spring be far behind? 7

5. sepulcher (sep′əl kər), *n.* tomb.
6. **Baiae's** (bä′yäz) **bay.** Baiae, on the Bay of Naples in Italy, was a famous Roman seaside resort.
7. **the Atlantic's . . . into chasms,** the calm waters of the Atlantic Ocean stirred up into huge waves, with deep valleys between them.
8. **despoil** (di spoil′), *v.* undress.
9. tumult (tü′mult), *n.* commotion.
10. impetuous (im pech′ü əs), *adj.* rash; hasty.
11. **incantation** (in′kan tā′shən), *n.* magic spell.

5 Reading/Thinking Skills
Literal and Figurative Language

Questions What words or phrases in line 54 are figurative? *(fall, thorns of life, bleed)* How would you rephrase line 54 in literal language? *(Possible response: "I am having problems in life and am suffering from them.")* Why is the figurative language a more effective way of expressing the idea? *(Possible response: The reader is forced to confront the narrator's emotions and respond in kind, that is, emotionally, rather than intellectually.)*

6 Literary Element
Mood

Questions Remind students that mood is the feeling of atmosphere or overall emotional aura of a work of literature. What is the mood of "West Wind"? *(Possible response: agitated, brooding, funereal)* How is the mood created? *(Possible responses: through the description of the setting—dark, threatening, autumnal; through words referring to death—"ghosts," "corpse within its grave," "dirge," "dead leaf," "dying year," "dead thoughts"; and through the speaker's wish to join the wind and find redemption.)*

7 Reading/Thinking Skills
Find the Main Idea

Question What is the main idea of section 5? *(Possible response: The narrator asks the wind to make him its instrument; to drive his thoughts across the earth, as it drives autumn leaves. And as trees come back to life in the spring, his ideas, by the magic of poetry, will awaken to inspire humanity.)*

BUILDING ENGLISH PROFICIENCY

Improving Comprehension

A jigsaw activity may help students grasp the abstract ideas and poetic language in Shelley's ode.

1. Divide students into five groups; assign each group one section of the poem.

2. Have each group read and discuss its section. Ask them to

- express each sentence in modern English (Point out that Shelley uses run-on lines; thus, some sentences extend not only across lines but across stanzas.)
- summarize the thought of the section in a sentence or two (e. g., Section 4 might become "*I wish I were a leaf, a cloud, or a child so that I could feel your power again! However, age has taken away what I once shared with you, and life is painful.*")

3. Bring students together and have group representatives share discussion results.

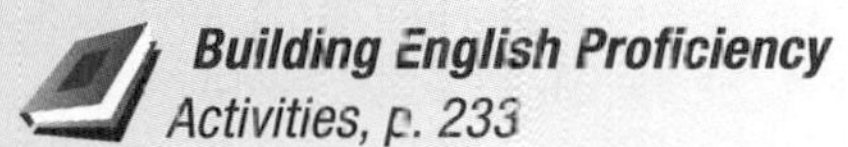
Building English Proficiency *Activities, p. 233*

8 Literary Element
Irony

Question What is the irony of the inscription on the pedestal? *(Possible response: If Ozymandias were to return and look upon his works, he, not the other "mighties" of the earth, would despair, for his works, and pride, lie in ruin.)*

9 Literary Element
Theme

Question Remind students that theme is the underlying meaning of a literary work. What do you think is the theme of "Ozymandias"? *(Possible response: Human aspirations, pride, and tyranny, even of a king of kings, is presumptuous and even pathetic against the tides of nature and time.)*

Art Study

Response to Caption Question
Students questions will vary. One might ask, "What have you seen over the last 5,000 years?"

Check Test

1. How does the West Wind show itself to be a preserver of life? *(It carries seeds to their beds where they will wait for spring.)*
2. Why does the poet want the West Wind to lift him as a wave, a leaf, or a cloud? *(He feels chained and bowed down and wants to be free.)*
3. What does the poet want the West Wind to do to his words? *(He wants the wind to scatter his words among humankind.)*
4. Where is the statue of Ozymandias? *(in a desert in an ancient land, specifically Egypt)*
5. What remains of Ozymandias's kingdom? *(nothing)*

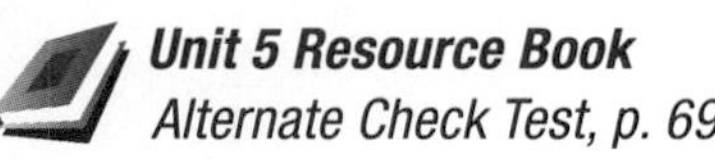

Unit 5 Resource Book
Alternate Check Test, p. 69

·OZYMANDIAS·

PERCY BYSSHE SHELLEY

I met a traveler from an antique land
Who said: Two vast and trunkless legs of stone
Stand in the desert . . . Near them, on the sand,
Half sunk, a shattered visage lies, whose frown,
And wrinkled lip, and sneer of cold command,
Tell that its sculptor well those passions read
Which yet survive, stamped on these lifeless things,
The hand that mocked them, and the heart that fed;
And on the pedestal these words appear:
"My name is Ozymandias, king of kings:
8 Look on my works, ye Mighty, and despair!"
Nothing beside remains. Round the decay
Of that colossal wreck, boundless and bare
9 The lone and level sands stretch far away.

Ozymandias (oz′i man′dē əs), more commonly known as Ramses II, was an Egyptian pharaoh who ruled about 1200 B.C. He had an evil reputation for persecuting the Israelites, making him a likely subject for Shelley, an opponent of tyranny.

8 **The hand . . . fed,** that is, the passions carved in the stone have outlived the hand that sculpted ("mocked") them and the pharaoh's heart that created them.

The Questioner of the Sphinx was painted in 1863 by American artist Elihu Vedder (1836–1923). Perhaps the "questioner" thinks that over the ages, the sphinx has accumulated extraordinary wisdom. Imagine that an ancient Egyptian sphinx were able to answer a question you posed to it. What would the question be? ➤

472

MINI-LESSON: VOCABULARY
Denotation and Connotation

Write these lines on the chalkboard:

I met a traveler from an antique land.
I met a tourist from a historic region.

Discuss the meanings of the lines. Point out that the denotative, or literal, meanings are almost the same. The connotative, or associated emotional, meanings are different. Discuss the shades of meaning the words have and how the emotions and other associations suggested by a word subtly change the meaning of writing.

Activity Ideas

- Have students substitute synonyms for some of the words in the poem and then discuss how the connotative meaning changes.
- Ask students to review a piece of their writing and replace some words with words having different connotations that will make their meaning clearer.

After Reading

Making Connections

Shaping Your Response

1. Which image of the wind stands out most in your mind?

Analyzing the Poems

2. Why do you think the speaker calls the wind both "destroyer and preserver" and also "thou dirge of the dying year"?
3. In what sense might the West Wind be a spirit "moving everywhere"?
4. In the fourth stanza the speaker draws a comparison between himself and the West Wind. How are they alike? In what ways are they different?
5. Why does the speaker call on the West Wind for assistance?
6. In the final stanza the speaker moves from wanting to be a sweet "lyre" to wanting to be a strong "trumpet." What do you think this change might indicate about the speaker's attitude toward himself? What shift in **tone** do you sense?
7. What do you think the "frown, / And wrinkled lip" and the "sneer of cold command" might indicate about either the sculptor's or the speaker's attitude toward Ozymandias? toward tyranny in general?
8. Given the description of the present condition of the statue and landscape, what **irony** is there in the inscription on the pedestal?

Extending the Ideas

9. How do lines 47–52 of "Ode to the West Wind" echo Wordsworth's pictures of childhood, as expressed in "Tintern Abbey" (see page 409)?
10. In "Ozymandias" what commentary, if any, might Shelley be making on **change** that comes with time?

Literary Focus: Apostrophe

Shelley uses **apostrophe,** or direct address, in several different phrases as he speaks to the West Wind. List as many phrases as you can find.

1. Why do you think Shelley uses apostrophe?
2. What does he gain in thought or feeling by addressing the Wind as a powerful being?

After Reading

MAKING CONNECTIONS

1. Answers will vary, but students should be able to explain what aspect of a particular image stands out, e.g., the wind as destroyer and preserver.

2. The wind is both a destroyer and a preserver because it ushers in the end of the year, but also buries the seeds that will grow when spring comes. The howling of the wind and the thunder of its storms are a dirge mourning the year's end.

3. The wind, representing the cycle of life and earth, is everywhere, moving leaves and seeds, clouds and seas.

4. The wind is swift, powerful, free. The speaker is also swift and untamed. However, the speaker has been bowed by the weight of hours, while the wind remains free.

5. The speaker needs inspiration. He asks the wind to guide him, to make him its lyre or instrument.

6. The poet moves from a position of passive melancholy (the lyre) to confident action (the trumpet). The tone changes from melodious to forceful and confident (like the wind).

7. The expression suggests that both the sculptor and speaker believe Ozymandias was an arrogant, contemptuous tyrant. The narrator despises tyranny in general.

8. The words challenge the viewer to look about at the greatness of Ozymandias, but there is nothing to see but boundless sand.

9. The lines suggest that Shelley shared Wordsworth's belief that children have a special affinity with nature and a visionary power.

10. Shelley suggests that nothing, including the tyranny of the most powerful empire on earth, will last forever. In time, everything changes.

LITERARY FOCUS: APOSTROPHE

Phrases of apostrophe include the following: "O wild West Wind," "Thou, from whose unseen presence," "O thou, Who chariotest," "hear, oh, hear!" "Thou on whose stream," "Thou who didst," "thou mightest bear," "Than thou, O uncontrollable," "Make me thy lyre," "Be thou me, impetuous one!" "Be through my lips," "O Wind."

Possible Responses

(1) Shelley makes the poem more personal by using apostrophe because he is speaking to someone rather than talking abstractly about a feeling or idea. (2) He creates the feeling that the wind is something that can respond to his call for help.

VOCABULARY STUDY

1. A
2. S
3. A
4. S
5. A

Unit 5 Resource Book
Vocabulary, p. 67
Vocabulary Test, p. 70

WRITING CHOICES

Writer's Notebook Update

Emphasize that students can add additional adjectives when writing. Invite them to share their descriptions.

I Am a . . .

You might encourage students to use apostrophe in their poems.

Immortal Architecture

Challenge students to consider what effect time will have on the structure. Will their inscription eventually have ironic overtones? Or will their structures, like the medieval cathedrals of Europe, be cared for and renewed by succeeding generations?

Selection Test

Unit 5 Resource Book
pp. 71–72

Transparency Collection
Fine Art Writing Prompt 9

Vocabulary Study

Decide whether the second word in each pair is a synonym or antonym of the italicized vocabulary word. On your paper, write *S* for synonym or *A* for antonym.

1. *dirge*—ditty
2. *pestilence*—disease
3. *sepulcher*—cradle
4. *tumult*—commotion
5. *impetuous*—cautious

Expressing Your Ideas

Writing Choices

Writer's Notebook Update Using the adjectives you listed to describe your quiet place, write a brief description of that place, telling why it is a source of comfort for you.

I Am a . . . Shelley compares himself to the West Wind, "tameless, and swift, and proud." In what element of nature can you find a similarity to yourself? Write a **poem** in which you compare yourself to the stars or the rain or the dawn or a river or some other element of nature. You can use Shelley's "Ode" as a model, or you might write instead in a freer verse form of your own

Immortal Architecture Shelley quotes the inscription on the pedestal of Ozymandias's statue. Select a physical structure—a statue, a monument, a prominent building, a bridge, a church—and write an **inscription** for it in which you express the statement this structure seems to be making to the world. Ozymandias was a person, but you might write as if the bridge or other structure you choose has a personality and can speak. Would it be conscious of or concerned about immortality?

Other Options

The Best and Happiest Shelley defined poetry as "the record of the best and happiest moments of the happiest and best minds." What form of personal expression would you choose to record a "best and happiest moment"? Music? Dance? Ceramics? Photography? Poetry? Select your favorite medium of artistic expression and record one of your **happiest moments.**

Shelley's Mysterious Death The death of Shelley is surrounded by mystery. Although the standard explanation is that he drowned in a violent storm, many believe he was the victim of a brutal murder. Research the various theories of Shelley's death and with a classmate present an **oral report** for your class.

R. I. P. Percy Bysshe Of all of the famous Romantic poets, Percy Bysshe Shelley had the shortest life: he died before his thirtieth birthday. Research the important facts of his life and death and **design a monument** for him. Monuments from the 1800s were often elaborate, and might include a short epitaph, a portrait bust, tools of a person's occupation, and/or symbols of fame, importance, or everlasting life.

OTHER OPTIONS

The Best and Happiest

Point out to students that "best and happiest" acquires deeper meaning when applied to a somber poem such as "Ode to the West Wind." In recording a "happiest moment," they might reflect on the deeper meaning of happiness.

Shelley's Mysterious Death

Suggest that students create a graphic organizer, listing the evidence that supports each theory of Shelley's death.

R.I.P Percy Bysshe

For inspiration, students might investigate various memorials constructed in the Poets' Corner of Westminster Abbey.

The Outsider

Rebels with Causes

Multicultural Connection
Some years ago a popular movie was entitled "Rebel Without a Cause." All the people you will read about here were rebels, in that their actions were often unpopular or put them in jeopardy. But they all had causes that they considered important enough to work for, to fight for, to dedicate their lives to.

"I hold it, that a little rebellion, now and then is a good thing, and as necessary in the political world as storms in the physical."

Thomas Jefferson, letter to James Madison January 30, 1787

Simón Bolívar

Simón Bolívar

Revolutionary Leader

Simón Bolívar (1783–1830) enjoyed a life of wealth and privilege as a member of one of Venezuela's oldest and most prosperous families. He married young and was settling into the life of a wealthy land-owner, when his beloved wife died suddenly and tragically. The young Bolívar left Venezuela and traveled to Europe where he pursued the life of a playboy, but true happiness eluded him. The emptiness of his personal life, along with the tumultuous political events then occurring in Europe, inspired Bolívar to work to liberate his homeland from Spanish rule. Back in Venezuela, Bolívar joined the struggle for independence and became one of South America's most important revolutionary leaders. Bolívar and his forces eventually liberated Venezuela, Colombia, Bolivia, Ecuador, and Peru. Although the struggle to oust the Spaniards lasted nearly fifteen years, Bolívar never wavered in his dedication to his cause. He is remembered and revered as "El Libertador" (The Liberator) of South America.

Bolivar traveled to Europe where he pursued a life of a playboy but true happiness eluded him

Interdisciplinary Study

Theme Link

Rebels are always outsiders. They fight for causes that are often not universally popular and that are always contrary to rules of their society. Despite their outsider status and the tremendous forces opposed to them, the rebels spotlighted in this interdisciplinary study labored for their causes throughout their lives.

MULTICULTURAL CONNECTION

This interdisciplinary study provides an opportunity to examine with students the contributions of people from many countries in forwarding the causes of freedom and equality.

Term to Know

diet (di Et) the general legislative assembly of certain countries, including Japan

Unit 5 Resource Book
Interdisciplinary Study Guide, p. 73

BUILDING ENGLISH PROFICIENCY

Exploring a Theme

The nine people profiled on pages 475–479 differed in many ways, but a common desire united them. Help students understand that the theme of "a rebel with a cause" can have various interpretations.

1. Begin a semantic web arising from the word *rebel.*
2. Have groups of students use the web to record qualities of a "rebel," based upon the various accounts.
3. Compare groups' responses, giving special attention to qualities that seem to be shared in two or more accounts.

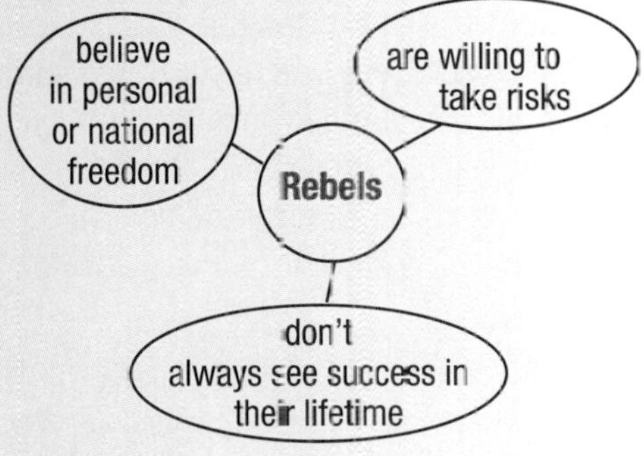

Historical Note

On various occasions, Emmeline Pankhurst led her followers in brick-throwing demonstrations. In 1912, she was arrested for vandalism, which included breaking the windows of the Prime Minister's residence. At her trial she explained her actions:

> "There comes a time in the life of a people suffering from an intolerable injustice when the only way to maintain one's self-respect is to revolt against that injustice. That time came for us. . . . Year after year, month after month, the fate of women is decided. How they are to live, their relationship with their children, the marriage laws under which they are joined in union and pledge their affections . . . and women have no voice. We will fight until we are given that voice."

When she died in 1928, just a few weeks after the passage of the law granting women the full right to vote, she was running for a seat in the British Parliament.

Historical Note

During the first half of the nineteenth century, much of the debate over women's rights involved their rights in marriage and in the home. One of Mott's early successes, achieved in conjunction with Elizabeth Cady Stanton, was the passage of the Married Women's Property Act of 1848 in New York. This law gave women certain limited rights to control their own property.

WOMEN PIONEERS

Emmeline Pankhurst

Equal Voting Rights Pioneer

Emmeline Pankhurst (1858 – 1928) dedicated her life to the cause of winning equal voting rights for British women. Her career as an activist began after her marriage to the radical Dr. Richard Pankhurst; together, the Pankhursts worked for a variety of social and political causes. In 1889, they established the Women's Franchise League to advance the cause of women's suffrage. After her husband's death, Pankhurst and her daughters Christabel and Sylvia continued to work, forming the Women's Social and Political Union in 1903. Pankhurst and her followers were activists: they staged rallies, demonstrations, and parades; lobbied Parliament; heckled the opposition; and finally resorted to acts of vandalism in order to make their voices heard. Many women, including Pankhurst and her daughter Christabel, were imprisoned because of their activities in support of full voting rights for women. The hunger strikes that Pankhurst waged in prison severely damaged her health, and she died in 1928, the same year that British women finally won equal voting rights.

Lucretia Mott

Women's Rights Convention

During her long and productive life, Lucretia Mott (1793 – 1880) dedicated herself to the abolition of slavery as well as the advancement of women's rights. Mott became a Quaker minister at the age of twenty-eight, following a series of family misfortunes, including the death of her young son. She helped to establish two antislavery organizations and gave impassioned speeches about the cause, despite the physical dangers abolitionists faced from hostile proslavery forces. At the World Anti-Slavery Convention in London in 1840, Mott was outraged when the male delegates would not allow her and the other female delegates to be seated. Along with Elizabeth Cady Stanton, whom she had met at the London gathering, Mott and Stanton organized the Women's Rights Convention that met in Seneca Falls, New York, in 1848. At this convention, the women's rights movement in the United States was formally launched. Until the end of her life, Mott continued to labor in the service of her causes. When slavery was finally abolished, she began to work on behalf of black voting rights.

MINI-LESSON: VISUAL LITERACY

Photographs

Point out that most photographs fall into one of two categories: posed and not posed. Posed photographs give the viewer a clear picture of what the person looks like. Unposed photographs may not aid identification quite as much, but they may provide insights into the person's personality or character. Compare, for example, the photographs of Emmeline Pankhurst and Lucretia Mott.

Questions

- Based on the photograph, what words might be used to describe Mott? *(Possible responses: elderly, neat)*
- What words might be used to describe Pankhurst? *(Possible responses: small, composed, courageous, rebellious)*

Activity Idea Have students examine other photographs of people in this unit and list words and phrases that tell what the photographs reveal about their subjects.

Fusaye Ichikawa

Women's Rights Activist

She founded the New Women's Association to fight for women's right to make political speeches– this in a time when women were not even allowed to listen to political speeches

Fusaye Ichikawa (1893 – 1981) began her adult life as a village schoolteacher. She went on to become the first female reporter for the newspaper *Nagoya Shimbun*, then a stockbroker's clerk, and finally a trade union worker. Between 1918 and 1920 she founded the New Women's Association to fight for women's right to make political speeches— this in a time when women were not even allowed to listen to political speeches or to attend political meetings. During the 1920s she directed the Women's Committee for the International Labour Organization. In 1924 Ichikawa was co-founder of the women's Suffrage League, and in 1945 she founded the League of Women Voters. Elected to the Upper House of Councillors in the Diet of 1952, the first woman member of the legislative branch of the Japanese government, she served there until 1970. All her life she remained in the forefront of the struggle for women's political rights, leading campaigns against licensed prostitution and corruption in elections, opposing pay raises for politicians, and donating part of her salary to women's causes.

Margaret Sanger

Planned Parenthood Pioneer

Many of these women, unable to adequately care for the children they already had, begged Sanger to tell them how to avoid becoming pregnant again

As a student nurse in the early 1900s, Margaret Sanger (1883 – 1966) often helped to deliver the babies of poor women. Many of these women, unable to adequately care for the children they already had, begged Sanger to tell them how to avoid becoming pregnant again. When Sanger tried to share this information in a newspaper column, she was stopped from doing so by "obscenity laws" then in effect. Wanting to help these women "whose miseries were as vast as the sky," Sanger went to Europe—where attitudes about birth control were more enlightened—to find more information. Sanger's attempts to publish this information in the United States resulted in her being arrested for violating obscenity laws. The charges were dropped, but the laws remained on the books. In her struggle to legalize the distribution of birth control information, she opened this country's first birth control clinic in New York City in 1916. In 1953, Sanger was named the first president of the International Planned Parenthood Federation.

Historical Note

As a nurse in New York City slums, Margaret Sanger not only observed women living in poverty as they struggled to raise children, she also witnessed the effects of self-induced abortions. The experience fed her desire to help women find safer methods of birth control. In 1914, Sanger gathered a group of friends in her cheap flat to plan the campaign for making birth control information available. During that meeting, a young friend, Otto Bobsein, coined the phrase "birth control" to replace the awkward, euphemistic terms such as "voluntary motherhood" and "family limitation," that were then in use.

Research Topics

- The Pankhurst sisters: Christabel, Sylvia, and Adela—their rivalries, careers, and public images
- Suffrage movements in countries other than the U. S. and Britain
- What contemporaries thought about the words and actions of the rebels portrayed on these pages.

Interdisciplinary Activity Ideas

As a class, ask students to brainstorm a list of causes that interest them. Have them organize into pairs or small groups that are interested in a specific cause. Ask groups to do research to learn about the cause, the people who are working for the cause, and the challenges and opportunities facing them. Then ask them to brainstorm present and future careers or roles for rebels in the cause. Have students share their information by organizing a career day for rebels with causes.

BUILDING ENGLISH PROFICIENCY

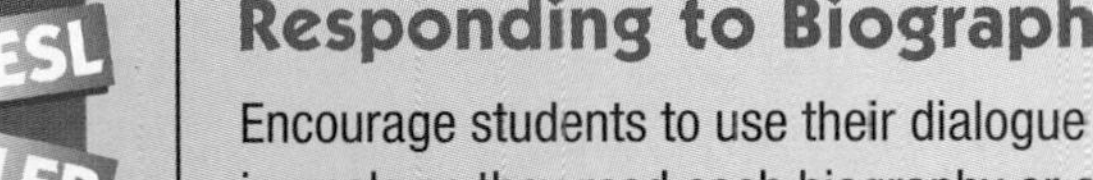

Responding to Biography

Encourage students to use their dialogue journals as they read each biography or compare biographies. For example, in the left-hand column of a T-chart, they could note specific information that catches their attention; in the right-hand column, they could express an opinion, jot down a question, and so on. Afterward, invite volunteers to share their comments.

Fact/Detail	My Response
Pankhurst and Mott both campaigned for voting rights.	How controversial they must have been!
Hideko published a women's magazine.	Which magazines today deal with the same subjects?

Historical Note

The Crimean War (1853–1856) took its name from the setting of a major battle of the war at Sevastopol, on the Crimean peninsula. The battle of Balaklava, which was also fought on the Crimean peninsula, was the subject of Alfred Lord Tennyson's poem "The Charge of the Light Brigade."

Additional Background

Toussaint L'Ouverture attained widespread fame during his lifetime. In fact William Wordsworth wrote a sonnet titled "To Toussaint L'Ouverture" in which he urged him to "live, and take comfort."

REBELS WITH CAUSES

Florence Nightingale

Founder of Modern Nursing

Nightingale wasted no time getting the filthy hospital cleaned up

As a young woman, Florence Nightingale (1820 – 1910) deeply resented the restrictions placed on her by her parents and the upper-class British society into which she was born. At the age of twenty-four, she began to study nursing on her own. Nightingale enrolled in a nursing school and later became the superintendent of a London hospital. In 1854, Nightingale was asked to sail to the Crimea to oversee the care of British soldiers who had been wounded in the Crimean War. Appalled by the conditions she found at the military hospital, Nightingale wasted no time in getting the filthy hospital cleaned up and demanding from British Army officials the supplies that were so sorely needed. A later visit to the front lines of the war nearly killed Nightingale, who contracted Crimean fever there. She never fully regained her health, but she continued to work tirelessly on behalf of her causes. When she died at the age of ninety, she had already secured her place in history as the founder of modern nursing.

Toussaint L'Ouverture

"The Black Napoleon"

Toussaint remained steadfast in his devotion to the cause of freedom

Toussaint L'Ouverture (1743 – 1803) was born into slavery in the French colony of Saint Domingue, now known as Haiti. After spending nearly fifty years as a slave, L'Ouverture became a leader of the slave rebellion that broke out in 1791. A brilliant military strategist, L'Ouverture commanded the black army that not only forced France to proclaim the freedom of the slaves, but also ousted the British and Spanish soldiers who had invaded the colony. The military leaders whom L'Ouverture defeated, as well as L'Ouverture himself, attributed much of his success to the extraordinary discipline he instilled in his soldiers. Saint Domingue remained under French control, however, and Napoleon Bonaparte sent a huge fleet to restore slavery. L'Ouverture —who came to be known as "The Black Napoleon"— then led a revolution whose goal it was to liberate Saint Domingue. Despite his failing health, L'Ouverture remained steadfast in his devotion to the cause of freedom. He died in a French prison less than a year before Saint Domingue became the independent nation of Haiti.

MINI-LESSON: STUDY SKILLS

Specialized Information Sources

Ask students to list types of information sources they might use when researching a topic. Guide them to identifying specialized information sources.

- Experts
- University professors, departments, organizations
- Museums, science centers, specialized libraries
- Organizations, clubs, associations
- Government agencies

Explain that many of these resources can be identified by using the *Yellow Pages, Encyclopedia of Associations, Organizations Master Index,* and *Selected List of U.S. Government Publications.* Other resources may be identified using periodicals, pamphlet files, and books.

Activity Idea Have students work in small groups to identify sources of information on nursing education.

Unit 5 Resource Book
Interdisciplinary Study Skills, p. 74

Lord Byron

Rebel Poet

Although best known as one of the most popular and influential of the English Romantic poets, George Gordon, Lord Byron (1788 – 1824), also involved himself in controversial social and political issues. The rebellious tone and spirit that often characterized his poetry were also reflected in Byron's own adventurous and unconventional life. Byron decided in 1823 to join the Greek struggle for liberation from Turkish rule. He set sail in July 1823, in a ship he had loaded with arms, ammunition, medical supplies, and cash, ending up at Missolonghi, capital of the Greek provisional government that represented the main group of rebels, where he advised the Greek military leaders on strategic planning, formed an artillery unit, commanded six hundred infantrymen—and helped to finance the whole operation. Despite the tremendous energy Byron devoted to the cause, his health was failing, and he died in Missolonghi on April 19, 1824.

Chavez, right, and supporters

Cesar Chavez

Labor Rights Organizer

Cesar Chavez (1927–1993) grew up on a farm in Yuma, Arizona. When he was ten, his family lost their land and took to the road as migrant farm workers. Wages were low and the conditions were harsh, but the Chavezes were determined to survive. As a teenager, Chavez quit school and began following the crops in California. After serving in World War II, he rejoined the ranks of migrant farm workers. As Chavez became involved with a group called the Community Service Organization (CSO), he developed strong political and organizational skills. He also became convinced that farm workers needed a union. In 1962 he founded the National Farm Workers Association which merged with another farm workers union and became the United Farm Workers of America (UFW) in 1973. During the 1960s and '70s, Chavez organized strikes and nationwide boycotts to force growers to bargain with the union. In his long career as a labor union organizer and leader, Chavez never wavered from his policy of nonviolence.

Responding

1. In your opinion, what do all these people have in common? What are their differences?

2. Who are the rebels working and fighting today? What are their causes?

3. What cause do you consider important enough to dedicate yourself to?

Responding

1. Possible Responses: All of these people were courageous and tireless in working toward their goals. They were willing to be different and to speak out for their beliefs. They were different in their approaches: Bolívar, Toussaint, and Byron engaged in warfare to reach their objectives; the others used more peaceful means to achieve their purposes, although Pankhurst did use vandalism to draw attention to her cause.

2. Answers will vary. Students should list contemporary persons engaged in social causes that set them apart as rebels or outsiders.

3. Answers will vary. Students should explain why the cause is so important to them.

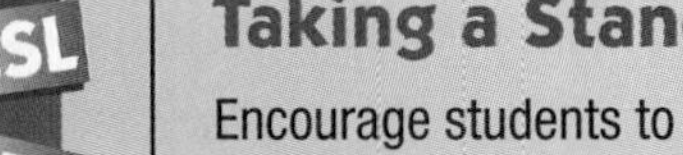

BUILDING ENGLISH PROFICIENCY

Taking a Stand

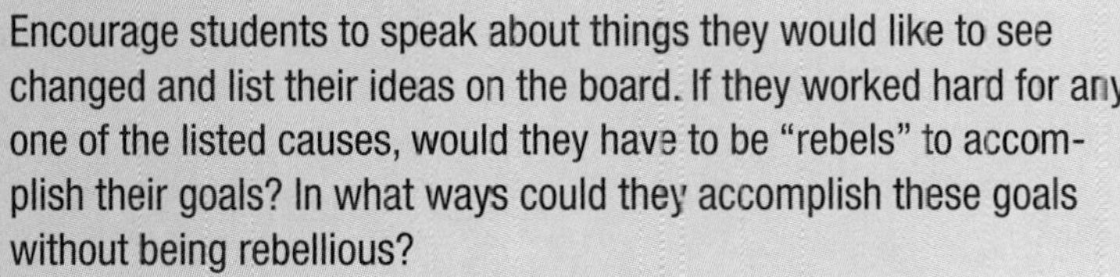

Encourage students to speak about things they would like to see changed and list their ideas on the board. If they worked hard for any one of the listed causes, would they have to be "rebels" to accomplish their goals? In what ways could they accomplish these goals without being rebellious?

Activity Idea Have two groups of students perform skits—one showing a peaceful confrontation between two people who disagree and the other demonstrating more conflict. Which approach do students think is more effective?

Interdisciplinary Study

Theme Link

In the interests of serving fellow workers, union organizers frequently are rebels in our society, fighting management for the rights of labor.

Curricular Connection: Careers

Use the information in this interdisciplinary study to explore career opportunities with students.

MULTICULTURAL CONNECTION

Labor unions exist in many countries, but their structure, affiliations, and roles in society differ. In the U. S., about 17 percent of all workers belong to unions. In some countries, such as Sweden and Norway, almost all workers are union members. All unions are politically active. In the U. S., they lobby government and endorse and financially support sympathetic candidates, but they are not affiliated with a particular party. In many Western European countries, unions are affiliated directly with political parties.

Responding

1. Possible Responses: Finding work that fulfills personal interests and goals, creates a sense of well-being and accomplishment, and provides a satisfactory income.

2. Possible Response: Wallace believes that unions give people dignity, respect, and a chance to share in the American dream. She's willing to confront those persons who don't share her views to help workers form unions.

INTERDISCIPLINARY STUDY

Career Connection

In most careers the employees work efficiently, serving the business interests of the employer. A union organizer, however, does not work smoothly or quietly to serve companies. Tanya Wallace brings strong opinions and energy to her work on behalf of other workers.

A PASSION FOR JUSTICE

Interview with

Tanya Wallace

In college, Ms. Wallace wanted a career in which she could help and empower people

Growing up in Chicago, Tanya Wallace knew about the benefits unions brought to workers: both of her parents were active in their unions. In college, Ms. Wallace wanted a career in which she could help and empower people. She "really had a passion about injustices in our society." But majoring in criminal justice, she had no thought of working for a union. In her senior year, a representative from the AFL-CIO Organizing Institute in California visited her campus to recruit organizers. After talking with the institute's recruiter, she realized that in a career as a union organizer, she could turn her passion for justice into action.

After completing four months of training with the Organizing Institute, Ms. Wallace became a union organizer for the Union of Needle Trades Industrial and Textile Employees (UNITE!), a member union of the AFL-CIO. Ms. Wallace now lives in the Atlanta area. Most of her work is in the South. She discusses her job as an organizer:

"Usually I get called in by dissatisfied workers. They don't like what's going on at their company. If a company doesn't have a union, it operates according to rules in an employee handbook, and in fine print, the handbook says the company reserves the right to change the rules as it sees fit. Such open-endedness can lead to uneven and unfair application of the regulations. When a union is established, management and labor discuss and agree upon the rules, which are put in a contract that's signed by and binding for both parties.

"The first thing I do when I get a call to organize a union is to go and meet the workers who asked for help. I talk with them and find out about the company and their problems. I start to identify the leaders and to enhance their skills. Then we make up a list of names and addresses of everyone in the work force and have what is called a blitz. This is a weekend to kick off the campaign, and we try to see every single person and talk to them before the company tries to scare them. Even though it's illegal, sometimes management will threaten employees, in both subtle and blatant ways, who show an interest in a union.

"Some workers have been fired for helping to organize, but they have all said to me, 'I knew what I was getting into, and I'd do it again.' My union has gotten all of those employees their jobs back with full back pay! People, including some in white-collar jobs, are getting tired of being stepped on, and they are thinking of the kind of work environment they want to leave their children. Too much money is being funneled into the pockets of a greedy few in big business, at the expense of the workers. Unions give people a chance for their slice of the American pie and to be treated with dignity and respect."

Responding

1. What do you think is important when choosing a career?

2. The title of this Interdisciplinary Study is "Rebels with Causes." How do you think Tanya Wallace fits that description?

MINI-LESSON: SPEAKING AND LISTENING

Analyzing a Speech

Explain that good listeners are not passive, but participate in a speech by active listening. Discuss the following elements of good listening. Suggest that students copy the chart and use it as a guide while listening to speeches.

Content of Speech

- Subject (appropriateness, interest-level)
- Knowledge of subject
- Organization (introduction, development, conclusion)

Delivery

- Use of standard English
- Nonverbal communication (posture, eye contact, gestures)
- Voice (loudness, enunciation, pronunciation)

Activity Idea Have students use the chart to analyze a speech by a classmate, a politician, a newscaster, or other.

Unit 5 Resource Book
Interdisciplinary Study Guide, p. 74

Writing Workshop

Changing the World

Assignment A saturation research paper is a unique kind of research report that uses both fictional and nonfictional techniques to report factual information in a vivid, dramatic manner. Write a saturation research paper about a special kind of outsider: a social reformer. Focus on an event from this person's life as seen through this person's eyes.

WRITER'S BLUEPRINT

Product — A saturation research paper

Purpose — To dramatize a significant event in the life of a social reformer

Audience — People interested in social reform

Specs — As the writer of a successful paper, you should:

- ❑ Saturate yourself in your topic. Use every reliable source you can find, including museum exhibits, interviews with experts, videos, diaries, history books, biographies and autobiographies, magazine and newspaper articles, and online sources.
- ❑ Use first-person ("I") point of view to narrate your event, as if you actually were this person living these moments in time. (You might include a third-person introduction to set the stage for your first-person account.)
- ❑ Begin by setting the scene, using vivid imagery, including sights, sounds, and smells, to give your reader a "you are there" feeling right from the start.
- ❑ Go on to narrate your event in present tense, as if it were happening now, using first-person narration and dialogue. Along the way, be sure you make it clear who your character is, what his or her goals are, and why this event is significant.
- ❑ Use subordination to help signal how ideas are related.
- ❑ Follow the rules of punctuation, spelling, grammar, and mechanics. Make sure the facts you present are drawn from reliable sources that you have documented in a Works Cited list.

Writing Workshop

WRITER'S BLUEPRINT

Specs

The Specs in the Writer's Blueprint address these writing and thinking skills:

- researching primary and secondary sources
- organizing information
- using first-person point of view
- using imagery
- recognizing values
- using subordination
- citing research materials

These Specs serve as your lesson objectives, and they form the basis for the **Assessment Criteria Specs** for a superior paper, which appear on the final TE page for this lesson. You might want to read through the *Assessment Criteria Specs* with students when you begin the lesson.

Linking Literature to Writing

As you review the literature, discuss with students the ways in which a social reformer can fit into the archetype of the "outsider." Do any students envision themselves in this role?

WRITING WORKSHOP OVERVIEW

Product
Narrative/expository writing: A saturation research paper

Prewriting
Choose a topic—Put your event into perspective—Organize your research questions—Brainstorm research sources—Carry out your research—Try a quickwrite—Plan the report
Unit 5 Resource Book
Prewriting Worksheets pp. 75–76

Drafting
Start drafting
Transparency Collection
Student Models for Writing Workshop 17, 18

Revising
Ask a partner—Strategy: Using Subordination
Unit 5 Resource Book
Revising Worksheet p. 77

Editing
Ask a partner—Strategy: Citing Works in Correct Form
Unit 5 Resource Book
Grammar Worksheet p. 78
Grammar Check Test p. 79

Presenting
Dramatic Monologue
Headlines

Looking Back
Self-evaluate—Reflect—For Your Working Portfolio
Unit 5 Resource Book
Assessment Worksheet p. 80
Transparency Collection
Fine Art Transparency 9

STEP 1 PREWRITING

Choose a topic

A guest speaker from a local civil rights organization or labor union might inspire students as they choose topics. For additional support, see the worksheet referenced below.

Unit 5 Resource Book
Prewriting Worksheet, P. 75

Put your event into perspective

Provide models of well-designed time lines for students, perhaps from history texts and encyclopedias.

Organize your research questions

Brainstorm possible types of questions with students, using a journalistic interview as a model. For additional support, see the worksheet referenced below.

Unit 5 Resource Book
Prewriting Worksheet, P. 76

Brainstorm research sources

After the class creates a list of sources, have students complete a "scavenger hunt" in which they locate a piece of information from each source.

Carry out your research

Remind students that careful documentation will save them much time during the writing phase of the process.

STEP 1 PREWRITING

Choose a topic. In a group, brainstorm potential topics. Use anything you've read or seen about social reformers, including the literature in this part. Each topic should consist of (1) a reformer and (2) an event in that person's life. On your own, review the list and choose the topic that you find most interesting. Here are sample topic ideas from the literature and from the Interdisciplinary Study on pages 475–480.

—Toussaint L'Ouverture fighting against French control of Haiti
—Lucretia Mott at the Seneca Falls Women's Rights Convention in 1848
—César Chávez leading a farm workers' strike
—Mary Wollstonecraft publishing her book on women's rights

Put your event into perspective. Make a time line that notes historical events that influenced your topic event or were influenced by it. Use your time line to help guide your research.

Organize your research questions. Begin by writing down everything you already know about your topic. Then make a list of questions you want to answer. Number the questions and use them to guide your research. The sample questions below are based on the publication of Mary Wollstonecraft's book advocating equal rights for women.

1. Who finally published her book?
2. What problems did she run into trying to find a publisher?
3. What inspired her to write the book?

LITERARY SOURCE

"Would men but generously snap our chains, and be content with rational fellowship instead of slavish obedience, they would find us more observant daughters, more affectionate sisters, more faithful wives, more reasonable mothers—in a word, better citizens."
from *A Vindication of the Rights of Woman* by Mary Wollstonecraft

Brainstorm research sources for gathering information in your school and community. Consider sources such as libraries, historical societies, museums, and the Internet.

Carry out your research, using your questions as a guide. Be prepared to add new questions as you learn more.

Consult **primary sources,** such as news accounts, letters, photos, and eyewitness accounts, as well as **secondary sources,** such as biographies, historical fiction, and history books.

Record each source you consult on a numbered **source card** in the order you find it. Then, as you take notes from various sources, mark each **note card** with the numbers of both the source of the information and the question it addresses.

MINI-LESSON: PREWRITING

Making Note Cards

Have students create a source card and note cards—summary, paraphrase, quote—from the following information about Langston Hughes.

Hughes used the sounds of jazz in Harlem after dark to create a vibrant new poetry. His first collection of poetry, *The Weary Blues*, established him as a major American writer. Hughes often said his poems were indelicate because he was honest about racial injustice. He felt that life was indelicate and wrote about the tragedies of the lower classes. The lower classes were the people he knew best and he wanted to catch the hurt in their lives. Hughes gave voice to African-American pride and hope. He wrote poetry, novels, stories, plays, essays, and newspaper columns from the 1920s to the 1960s.—from *The United States and its People* by David C. King, Norman McRae, Jaye Zola; published by Addison Wesley Publishing Company in New York, 1995, page 548

Source Card

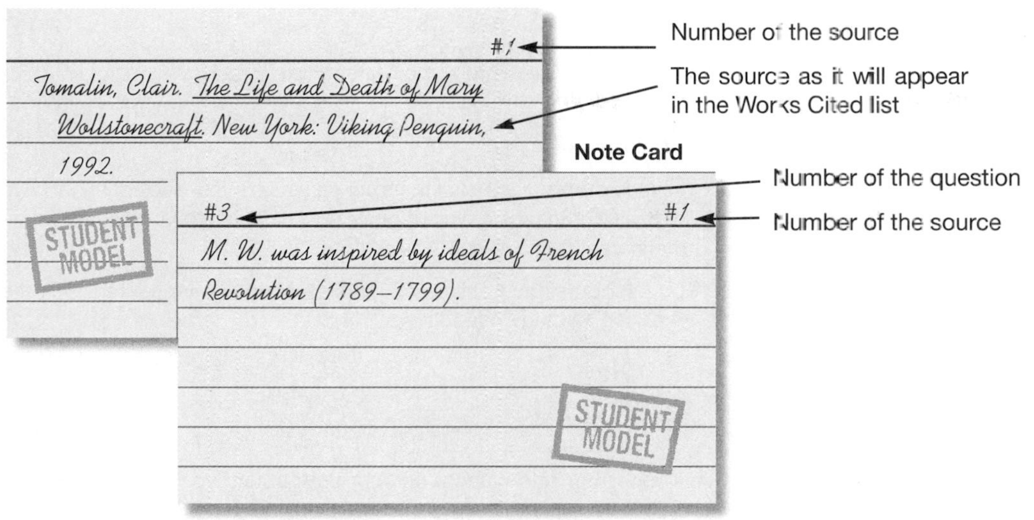

#1
Tomalin, Clair. The Life and Death of Mary Wollstonecraft. New York: Viking Penguin, 1992.
Number of the source
The source as it will appear in the Works Cited list
STUDENT MODEL
Note Card
#3
#1
M. W. was inspired by ideals of French Revolution (1789–1799).
Number of the question
Number of the source
STUDENT MODEL

As you research, look for answers to your questions.

Try a quickwrite. Write for five minutes in the voice of the person you chose. Describe the event as if you were actually living through it. If you find you can't describe the event because you don't have enough information, go back and gather more facts.

OR . . .
Conduct an interview in which the reformer (you) tells a reporter (a partner) what is happening, your feelings about the event, and why the event is significant. Make notes on the results and use them as you plan.

Plan the report. Organize your notes into a plan like the one shown here.

Setting the scene

Vivid images
—sights
—sounds
—smells
—movements

My reactions
—thoughts
—feelings

Narrating the event

What happened first
—vivid images
—my thoughts and feelings
—possible lines of dialogue

What happened next
—vivid images
—my thoughts and feelings
—possible lines of dialogue

and so on . . .

Try a quickwrite

If students choose the Or... activity, have the "reporters" use the writer's list of research questions as a basis for the interviews.

Plan the report

Encourage writers to enliven their essays by including dialogue to reveal character and move the story along.

Connections to **Writer's Notebook**

For selection-related prompts, refer to Writer's Notebook.

Connections to **Writer's Resource**

For additional writing prompts, refer to Writer's Resource.

BUILDING ENGLISH PROFICIENCY

Exploring Historical Detail

Encourage students to look for historical details that will help make their setting more authentic. You can guide their research with questions such as the following:

1. What kinds of clothing did people wear?
2. What kinds of transportation did they use?
3. What other technology was in use?
4. What kind of weather was common in that place at that time of year?
5. What commonplace personal belongings of that era might the social reformer have owned or used that were common to that place and time? (Mary Wollstonecraft, for example, would not have written *Frankenstein* with a ball-point pen.)

STEP 2 DRAFTING

Start drafting

Encourage students to set goals for the drafting stage to help them get started. For example, a student may set as a goal to write at least two pages during class time and two at home over the next week. The drafting tips include ideas to help them begin writing.

The Student Models

The **transparencies** referenced below are authentic student models. Review them with the students before they draft. These questions will help:

1. Look at the Works Cited lists for both models to make sure each writer used the correct format for all sources. If necessary, make corrections.

2. How could you improve the sentence structure of the opening paragraph of model 17?

3. What verb tense did the writer of model 18 use? If needed, make suggestions to improve the use of the verb tense.

Transparency Collection
Student Models for Writing Workshop, p 17, 18

STEP 3 REVISING

Ask a partner (Peer assessment)

Responders may review the writer's research questions to determine whether all have been answered.

Revising Strategy: Using Subordination

For additional support, see the mini-lesson at the bottom of this page and the worksheet referenced below.

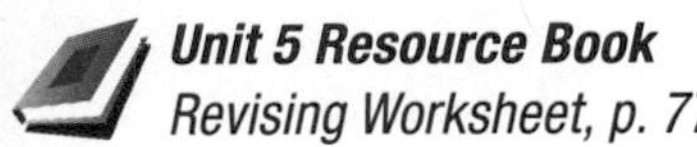

Unit 5 Resource Book
Revising Worksheet, p. 77

Connections to **Writer's Resource**

For additional writing prompts, refer to Writer's Resource.

STEP 2 DRAFTING

Start drafting. Here are some drafting tips.

- Close your eyes and visualize yourself taking part in the event as it unfolds around you.
- Include excerpts from fictitious conversations your subject might have had with others as a way of giving dramatic life to your factual information about the event.
- Use subordinating clauses to show how ideas are related. See the Revising Strategy that follows.

STEP 3 REVISING

Ask a partner to comment on your draft before you revise it. Use this checklist as a guide.

✔ Is it clear to you whom I'm writing as and what event I'm portraying?

✔ Have I made this person's goals clear to you?

✔ Have I included a Works Cited list?

✔ Could I use subordination to help emphasize relationships between ideas?

Revising Strategy

Using Subordination

Many of the statements you make in your writing will be related to each other in special ways. You can emphasize these relationships through subordination—that is, by linking these statements with conjunctions such as *although, because, if, when,* and *while,* or relative pronouns such as *who, which,* and *that*. Notice how the writer of the student model on the next page revised this passage in order to emphasize relationships.

MINI-LESSON: WRITING STYLE

Using Subordination

Teach Subordination helps a writer emphasize relationships among ideas. Read the student model aloud so students can hear the difference between the original version and the revised version.

Activity Idea Have students combine the following short, choppy sentences using subordination.

Sometimes the crop dusters would spray where we were working. We would run for any cover we could find.

I attended many different schools as a child. I was always behind in any schoolwork.

The rain went on for the rest of the afternoon. We continued picking beets until dusk.

Apply Have students look through their own papers looking for places where subordination could help connect ideas.

My book will finally be published this year. Although it may be considered controversial by many, I hope people will read it with an open mind. If society is to move forward, it must change its views toward women. People who cling to old prejudices must become enlightened.

~~Society must~~ ~~To do so~~ ~~These people~~

STEP 4 EDITING

Ask a partner to review your revised draft before you edit. When you edit, look for errors in grammar, usage, spelling, and mechanics. Be careful to use the correct form for a Works Cited list.

Editing Strategy

Citing Works in Correct Form

A research paper includes a list called *Works Cited* to tell the reader what sources you used in your research.

- List all the sources you actually consulted, in alphabetical order.
- Give page numbers for magazine articles, but not for books.
- Indent the second and subsequent lines of each entry.

The correct form changes slightly for different types of sources, as shown in the following student model.

Behrman, Cynthia. "Mary Wollstonecraft." World Book Encyclopedia, 1988 ed.

Janes, R. M. "On the Reception of Mary Wollstonecraft's 'A Vindication of the Rights of Women.'" Journal of Historical Ideas, Volume 39, pp. 293–302.

Tomalin, Claire. The Life and Death of Mary Wollstonecraft. New York: Viking Penguin, 1992.

STUDENT MODEL

STEP 4 EDITING

Ask a partner (Peer assessment)

Caution students to look carefully at Works Cited entries.

Editing Strategy: Citing Works in Correct Form

Discuss with students the importance of following an established format for entering sources on a Works Cited List. Remind students to record all of the bibliographic information they will need in order to cite their sources.

For additional support, see the mini-lesson at the bottom of this page and the worksheets referenced below.

Unit Five Resource Book
Grammar Worksheet, p. 78
Grammar Check Test, p. 79

Connections to **Writer's Resource**

Refer to the Grammar, Usage, and Mechanics Handbook on Writer's Resource.

MINI-LESSON: GRAMMAR

Citing Works in Correct Form

Students may be unfamiliar with the format for citing information gathered on the Internet. To cite an online source, give the author's name (if known), the full title of the work in quotation marks, the full http address, and the date the information was accessed.

Example: Ruiz, Albert. "Who Are America's Farmworkers?" http://www.nmrpoorg/pg3.htm (2 Jan. 96).

Ask students to share sources other than books or periodicals and make sure they have the correct form for putting these sources in a Works Cited list.

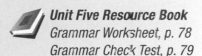

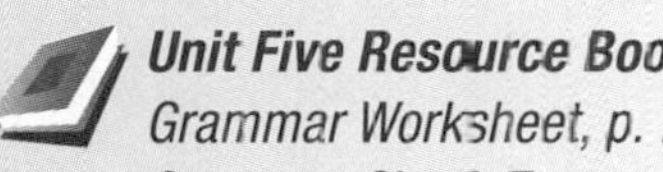

Unit Five Resource Book
Grammar Worksheet, p. 78
Grammar Check Test, p. 79

STEP 5 PRESENTING

Dramatic Monologue

A collage of pictures and headlines would create the appropriate background for a dramatic monologue or presentation.

Headlines

You might enlist students' help in gathering together a store of old magazines and newspapers from which to draw materials.

STEP 6 LOOKING BACK

Self-evaluate

The *Assessment Criteria Specs* at the bottom of this page are for a superior paper. You might want to post these in the classroom. Students can then evaluate themselves based on these criteria. For a complete scoring rubric, use the *Assessment Worksheet* referenced below.

Unit Five Resource Book
Assessment Worksheet, p. 80

Reflect

After students write about the sources that were most helpful, have them share their discoveries with each other.

To further explore the theme, use the Fine Art Transparency referenced below.

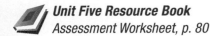

Transparency Collection
Fine Art Writing Prompt 9

STEP 5 PRESENTING

Consider these ideas for presenting your paper:

- Turn it into a dramatic monologue delivered by the subject himself or herself.
- Illustrate it with headlines and pictures from current periodicals that relate to the social issue your subject addressed.

STEP 6 LOOKING BACK

Self-evaluate. What grade would *you* give your paper? Look back at the Writer's Blueprint and evaluate yourself on each point, from 6 (superior) to 1 (inadequate).

Reflect. Think about what you've learned from writing this paper as you write answers to these questions.

✔ How do you, personally, feel about your subject's cause and his or her methods?

✔ What was the most helpful source you consulted? Why?

✔ What sorts of things did you have to think about in order to *become* your character and write in his or her voice?

For Your Working Portfolio Add your paper and reflection responses to your working portfolio.

ASSESSMENT CRITERIA SPECS

Here are the criteria for a superior paper. A full six-level rubric for this paper appears on the *Assessment Worksheet* referenced below.

6 Superior The writer of a 6 paper impressively meets these criteria:

- Chooses a significant event that demonstrates the reformer's cause.
- Brings that moment vivdly to life through telling details of setting, characterization, and action.
- Convincingly reveals character's thoughts and feelings through dialogue, interior monologue, imagery, and other fictional techniques.
- Clearly indicates why the event was significant.
- Maintains consistent point of view.
- Includes Works Cited list in correct format.
- Effectively uses subordination to show the relationship between ideas.
- Makes few, if any, mistakes in grammar, usage, mechanics, and spelling.

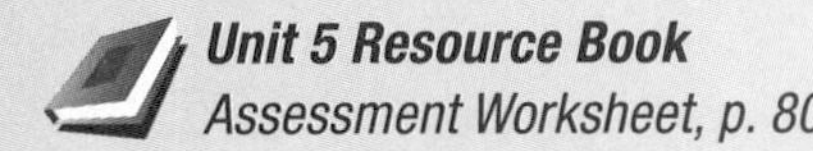

Unit 5 Resource Book
Assessment Worksheet, p. 80

Beyond Print

Electronic Research

Using today's technology can make researching quick and enjoyable. A **database** is any collection of information or data. A **self-contained database** is accessed through a computer terminal. The information is stored electronically, often on a CD-ROM.

- **Electronic Card Catalogs** Many libraries have transferred their traditional card catalog systems to computer systems. Printers connected to the system allow you to print out the information.
- **Electronic Reference Materials** An entire encyclopedia may be contained on an individual CD-ROM. There are also dictionaries, thesauruses, atlases, almanacs, and other references.
- **Periodical Databases** Some databases list magazine and newspaper articles, and may provide abstracts or entire articles.

An **on-line database** is located outside your immediate area; it is accessed through a telephone line and modem.

- **Library Memberships and Networks** Libraries often purchase on-line memberships to a variety of research services. You can search on-line for resources at other libraries. Often, these resources can be sent to you as an inter-library loan.
- **Individual Memberships** For a fee, members can access on-line encyclopedias, magazines, reviews, interviews and subject-specific databases. They can also post questions and receive answers.
- **The Internet** The Internet is a world-wide series of computers hooked together through telephone lines. It is accessed via modem through institutions or consumer on-line services.

Activity Options

1. Ask your school or local librarian for a tour of the library's electronic research resources. Keep lists of resources in your notebook.
2. Generate a list of keywords on a topic. Then try using these keywords on several different databases to search your topic.

Beyond Print

Teaching Objectives

- to learn about the kinds of electronic information resources
- to search for information using an electronic database

Curricular Connection: Technology Skills

Use the information in this article to help students understand the scope of electronic information resources that exist and develop familiarity with those available.

Introduce

Guide students in a review of techniques they would use for doing research using traditional library print resources, such as the card catalog and *Readers' Guide to Periodical Literature.* Explain that computers and online services have made research faster, more comprehensive, and easier than ever, but that many of the basic skills used in traditional research are equally important to electronic research. Then ask students to read the text.

Activity Options

Activity 1 As students list available resources, suggest that they include details and examples of information available on specific databases. They might also want to note helpful clues to accessing this information.

Activity 2 Invite students to compare the kinds and quality of information they access on different databases.

Activity 3 Prepare an index card file of the information compiled by students for use by the whole class.

ANOTHER APPROACH

Limited Electronic Resources

If your school or local library lacks or has limited electronic research resources, encourage students to visit larger city or university libraries in the area that have more extensive computer resources. As an additional alternative, challenge students to work in pairs or small groups and to interview computer users who have online, CD-ROM, and other electronic resources. Students should be able to find both individuals and business people with various computer capabilities. Have students share their infor-mation in class discussion.

Part Three: Exceeding Human Limits

Historical Overview

EXPLORING CONCEPTS

- During the Romantic Era, technology and science advanced rapidly.
- Technological inventions in weaving and steam power moved England to the forefront among industrial nations.
- Hot-air balloons developed in France.
- Faraday pioneered work on electricity.
- Darwin began work on natural history.
- Romantic writers were fascinated and fearful of scientific and technological changes.

Questions What scientific or technological development in your lifetime do you think will have the greatest impact on the future? *(Answers will vary. Use student responses to help them appreciate the scope of the changes that occurred during the Romantic Era.)*

Research Activity Ask students to work in pairs or small groups and to investigate one of the scientific and technological developments illustrated. Have them report back to the class on how people of the Romantic Era reacted to the development, and why they responded in that way.

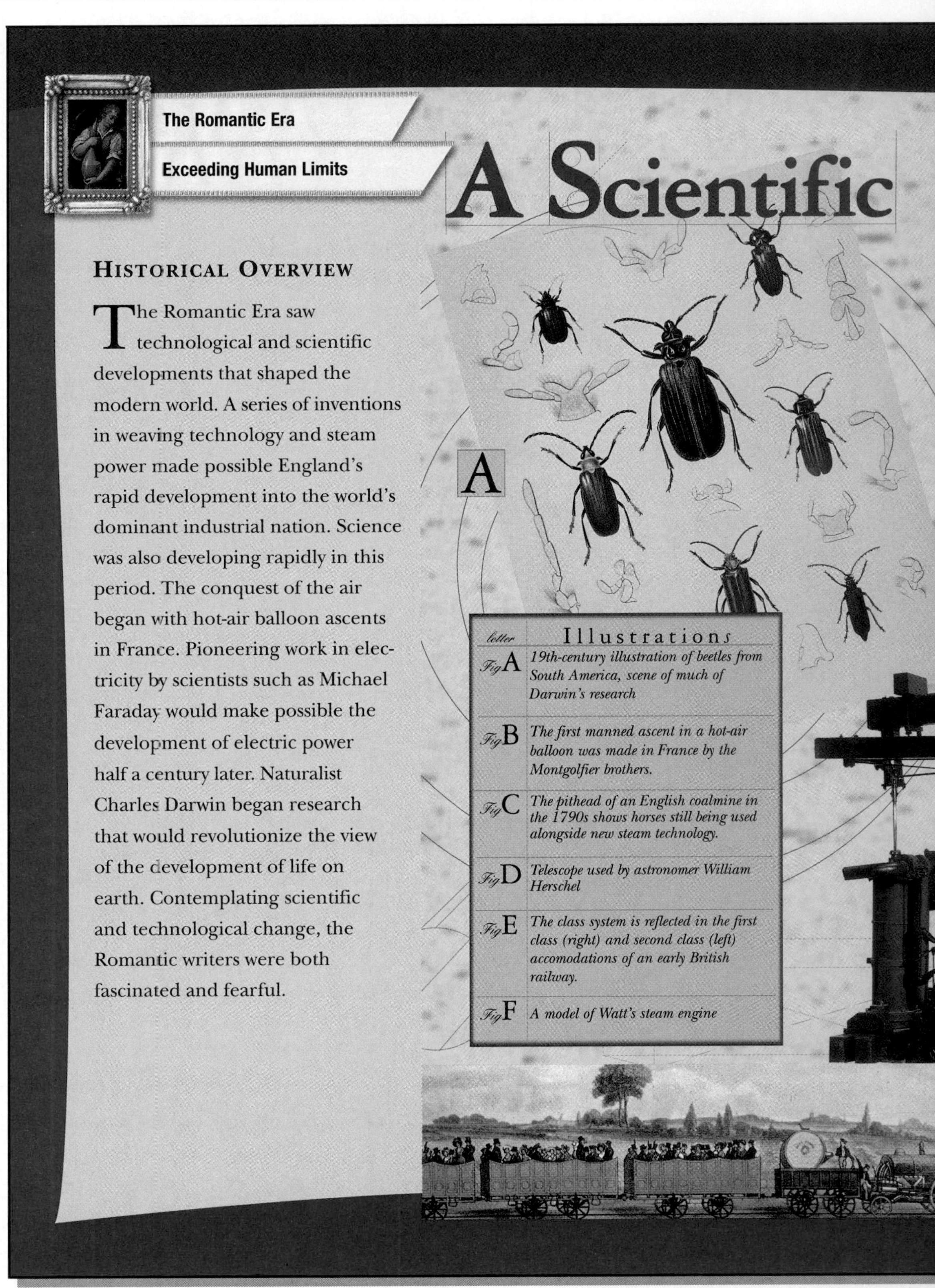

HISTORICAL OVERVIEW

The Romantic Era saw technological and scientific developments that shaped the modern world. A series of inventions in weaving technology and steam power made possible England's rapid development into the world's dominant industrial nation. Science was also developing rapidly in this period. The conquest of the air began with hot-air balloon ascents in France. Pioneering work in electricity by scientists such as Michael Faraday would make possible the development of electric power half a century later. Naturalist Charles Darwin began research that would revolutionize the view of the development of life on earth. Contemplating scientific and technological change, the Romantic writers were both fascinated and fearful.

letter	Illustrations
Fig A	*19th-century illustration of beetles from South America, scene of much of Darwin's research*
Fig B	*The first manned ascent in a hot-air balloon was made in France by the Montgolfier brothers.*
Fig C	*The pithead of an English coalmine in the 1790s shows horses still being used alongside new steam technology.*
Fig D	*Telescope used by astronomer William Herschel*
Fig E	*The class system is reflected in the first class (right) and second class (left) accomodations of an early British railway.*
Fig F	*A model of Watt's steam engine*

Revolution

B

C

D

E

F

Key Dates

1769 *Arkwright builds first textile factories.*

1776 *Watt invents a new type of steam engine.*

1781 *Herschel discovers the planet Uranus.*

1783 *First balloon ascension by Montgolfier brothers.*

1796 *Jenner begins vaccinating against smallpox.*

1800 *Volta builds forerunner of electric battery.*

1821 *Faraday demonstrates principle of electric generator.*

1829 *Stephenson wins prize with his locomotive.*

1831 *Darwin starts voyage of the* Beagle.

1833 *Babbage conceives forerunner of computer.*

489

Key Dates

1779 The first velocipedes (early bicycles) appeared on the streets of Paris.

1781 Sir William Herschel's discovery of Uranus was the first sighting of a new planet since ancient times.

1790 Antoine Lavoisier publishes *The Elements of Chemistry* and the "Table of Thirty-One Chemical Elements" and establishes the basis for modern chemistry.

1792 Gas first used for lighting in London.

1801 Robert Fulton constructs the world's first submarine.

1818 The *Savannah* becomes the first steamship to cross the Atlantic.

1827 John Walker invents the sulfur friction match.

1828 Charles Carroll begins construction of the first railroad in U.S., the Baltimore and Ohio.

1829 James Smithson bequeaths 100,000 pounds for the founding of the Smithsonian Institution in Washington, D.C.

MATERIALS OF INTEREST

Books

- *Frankenstein: Mary Shelley's Wedding Guest* by Mary Lowe-Evans (Twayne, 1993)
- *Mary Shelley: Her Life, Her Fiction, Her Monsters* by Anne K. Mellor (Methuen, 1988)

MultiMedia

- *Mary Shelley's Frankenstein,* an audio adaptation read by Kenneth Branagh (Simon & Schuster, 1994)
- *Gothic,* a film directed by Kenneth Russell, 87 min. (Distributed by Image Entertainment, 1987)

Preview

Exceeding Human Limits

FOR ALL STUDENTS

Ask students to define the following common phrases:

- "You've gone too far?"
- "You're out of bounds."
- "You've crossed the line."

How do students decide whether or not they have exceeded limits?

To further explore the theme, use the transparency noted below.

Transparency Collection
Fine Art Transparency 10

For At-Risk Students

Retelling a story can help students get a better understanding of plot, characters, and themes. Ask students to recount the Frankenstein story to someone who is unfamiliar with it.

For Students Who Need Challenge

Groups of students may want to make a short video of some part of the novel, using costumes, scenery, make-up, and other creative flourishes.

For Social Learners

Students may work with partners to prepare story boards of the events in the selection.

MULTICULTURAL CONNECTION

Ask students to consider the choices Frankenstein makes. When he chooses to ignore society's norms, is he freer or more limited than before?

Part Three

Exceeding Human Limits

A theme that was central to Romanticism was the desire to test and break through human limits—and the fear of the possible consequences of such an attempt. One of those limits is the borderline between life and death. People's fascination with creating life and conquering death was age-old during the Romantic era and remains very much with us today.

Multicultural Connection The cultural values of the society in which a person lives influence to a very large degree any **choice** that person makes. What is important to the society at large becomes important to individuals in society. When a person chooses to break out of those social boundaries, however, that person may find a greater degree of freedom—or may find that choice has become more limited than before.

IDEAS THAT WORK

Motivating with Relevancy

"Integration of curriculum bombarded me when I reread the novel. An integrated project with English, art, biology, and history began to format itself in my mind. The issues of right to life, quality of life, creationism, duty, the natural order, and genetic engineering suggested countless projects to me—from a mock trial with numerous sidebars to a creative writing project on traveling in cyberspace with the creature. The issues, combined with the fluid language of the novel, make studying *Frankenstein* appealing to both teachers and students. Mary Shelley offers a literary piece that defines *classic,* a work with relevancy, style, substantive content, and appeal."

Rosetta Tetteh
Chicago, Illinois

Before Reading

from Frankenstein

by Mary Shelley

Mary Shelley
1797–1851

Mary Shelley was only eighteen when she began writing *Frankenstein.* As the daugher of feminist Mary Wollstonecraft and the radical writer William Godwin, and as the wife of poet Percy Bysshe Shelley, she lived at the center of the Romantic Revolution. Mary Godwin first met Percy Shelley in 1812. They ran away to the Continent, leaving behind Shelley's wife Harriet and two children. Two years later, following Harriet's suicide, they married. By age twenty-four, Mary Shelley was a widow who had lost three of her four children and who struggled to support herself.

Building Background

Imagine the Scene Percy and Mary Shelley and the moody, brilliant young poet Lord Byron are on holiday together in Switzerland. Rainy weather forces them to remain indoors for days on end, and along with John William Polidori, Byron's physician, the group passes the time reading ghost stories. One night, Lord Byron proposes that they each try to write a ghost story. All four initially welcome the task, but only Mary Shelley perseveres, searching in vain for a story idea until one night when, after a long discussion of Erasmus Darwin's experiments to animate lifeless matter, she has a vivid dream. In her own words: "When I placed my head on my pillow I did not sleep, nor could I be said to think. My imagination, unbidden, possessed and guided me . . . I saw—with shut eyes but acute mental vision—I saw the pale student of unhallowed arts kneeling beside the thing he had put together." The next day she begins to write down what eventually becomes the novel *Frankenstein*.

Literary Focus

Mood The atmosphere or overall emotional content is the **mood** of a work. *Frankenstein* is considered a *gothic novel,* or novel of terror. Gothic novels became extremely popular in the 1700s, and the form has survived to this day in the novels of authors such as Stephen King and Thomas Tryon. As you read *Frankenstein,* consider how the author creates a mood of suspense and dread. What role does language play in establishing this mood?

Writer's Notebook

Frankly, Who's Frankenstein? Many people who have never read Mary Shelley's novel know a lot about Frankenstein's monster—through movies, comic books, cartoons, or even music videos. Write down your impressions of the creature based on how you've seen him portrayed in popular culture. Later you may want to compare your description with that of Mary Shelley's.

Before Reading

Building Background

You might introduce this selection by viewing *Frankenstein: The Making of the Monster,* which contains clips from the Karloff film and an interview with Ann Rice. (50 mins, color: Films for the Humanities & Sciences, 800-257-5126)

Literary Focus

Point out that the mood of a literary work may be created by

- description of setting(s)
- actions and words of characters
- tone of the author or narrator

Writer's Notebook

Tell students that they will eventually compare their impressions of Frankenstein's monster with Shelley's description. Encourage them as they read to jot notes about the creature's appearance and personality.

Connections to **AuthorWorks**

Mary Shelley is a featured author in the AuthorWorks CD-ROM series.

SUPPORT MATERIALS OVERVIEW

Unit 5 Resource Book
- Graphic Organizer, p. 81
- Study Guide, p. 82
- Vocabulary, p. 83
- Grammar, p. 84
- Alternate Check Test, p. 85
- Vocabulary Test, p. 86
- Selection Test, pp. 87–88

Building English Proficiency
- Literature Summaries
- Activities, p. 234

Reading, Writing & Grammar SkillBook
- Writing, pp. 123–124

The World of Work
- Chemical Engineer, p. 19
- Activity, p. 20

Technology
- Audiotape
- Personal Journal Software
- Custom Literature Database: For an opportunity to compare creation myths, see "Prometheus and Pandora" and "Pygmalion," by Thomas Bulfinch, on the database.
- Test Generator Software

During Reading

Selection Objectives

- to explore the theme of human limits—and whether it is wise to exceed them
- to recognize mood and its effect on a literary work
- to observe paragraph indentations

Unit 5 Resource Book
Graphic Organizer, p. 81
Study Guide, p. 82

Theme Link

Victor Frankenstein, who has unlocked the key to life, discovers the consequences of exceeding human limits.

Vocabulary Preview

procrastinate, put things off until later; delay
transitory, passing soon or quickly
incipient, just beginning; in an early stage
delineate, describe in words; portray
lassitude, lack of energy; weariness
dissipate, spread in different directions; scatter
clemency, mercy or leniency
commiserate, pity; sympathize with
odious, hateful; offensive
superfluous, needless; unnecessary

Students can add the words and definitions to their Writer's Notebooks.

1 Literary Element
Genre: The Novel

Frankenstein is in the eighteenth-century tradition of the epistolary novel. Robert Walton, an Arctic explorer, writes to his sister in England about a man, Victor Frankenstein, that his crew finds on an ice floe and takes on board. Walton's letters serve as a frame for both his own account and the doctor's story.

Caspar David Friedrich painted *Traveller Looking over a Sea of Fog* in about 1815. What is the mood of this work? What elements of the painting help to create that mood? ➤

Frankenstein

Mary Shelley

Part 1

Victor Frankenstein has left his home in Geneva, Switzerland, to study natural science at the University of Ingolstadt, Germany. There, Frankenstein astounds his professors by his mastery of chemistry and research procedures and his passion to probe "the deepest mysteries of creation." Eventually Frankenstein plans to return home to his family and fiancée, Elizabeth, but now his experiments take over his life. In this part, Frankenstein tells his story to Robert Walton, an explorer who has helped him. Victor Frankenstein is speaking.

One of the phenomena which had peculiarly attracted my attention was the structure of the human frame, and, indeed, any animal endued[1] with life. Whence, I often asked myself, did the principle of life proceed? It was a bold question, and one which has ever been considered as a mystery; yet with how many things are we upon the brink of becoming acquainted, if cowardice or carelessness did not restrain our inquiries. I revolved these circumstances in my mind, and determined thenceforth to apply myself more particularly to those branches of natural philosophy which relate to physiology. Unless I had been animated by an almost supernatural enthusiasm, my application to this study would have been irksome, and almost intoler-

1. **endued** (en düd′), *adj.* provided with a quality or power.

SELECTION SUMMARY

Frankenstein

In Part 1, Victor Frankenstein describes the labor that led to the monster's life and his horror upon first viewing his creation. Frankenstein flees, and when he finally returns, the monster is gone.

In Part 2, six years later, the creature has murdered Frankenstein's brother. When Frankenstein comes upon his creation in the Alps, the monster begs him to listen to his story. Frankenstein reluctantly consents.

In Part 3, the monster asks that Frankenstein create him a mate to relieve his loneliness. Frankenstein begins, but then destroys the female creature. In revenge, the monster murders Frankenstein's wife, Elizabeth. Frankenstein pursues the monster to the Arctic, where the scientist dies. The monster appears by his creator's corpse and vows to kill himself as well in order to put an end to his miserable, desolate existence.

For summaries in other languages, see the ***Building English Proficiency*** *book.*

Response to Caption Question
Students may find the mood to be lonely, pensive, or contemplative. The traveler is surrounded by rock outcroppings, a fog-covered landscape, and the sky. These features create a sense of humanity overwhelmed by nature's forces. The man's thoughtful posture makes the viewer wonder at his inner state.

Visual Literacy Caspar David Friedrich (1774–1840) is considered one of the most important German Romantic artists. His paintings often convey a feeling of lonely melancholy, a sense that human beings are overshadowed by the vastness of nature and an unseen Creator. One critic has said that Friedrich paints "religious art without an explicit religion." His paintings often depict features of landscape in meticulous detail, with a high degree of "realism." It is the selection and treatment of these details that creates Romantic mood.

Questions Where is the man placed in the picture and why is this significant? *(at the center; the individual is central to the Romantic vision.)* What is the effect of having the man face away from the viewer? *(isolation; dramatic impact)*

EDITORIAL NOTE This excerpt has been shortened for length. For a more complete version of *Frankenstein,* see the *Custom Literature Database.*

BUILDING ENGLISH PROFICIENCY

Exploring Key Ideas

Before they read, help students focus on Frankenstein's desire to master "the deepest mysteries of creation."

1. Have students create a semantic web arising from the phrase *the deepest mysteries of creation.* Ask them to jot down phenomena that they consider great mysteries. Responses may be serious (for example, when the universe began) or humorous (such as how to attract a boyfriend or girlfriend). Allow for voluntary sharing and discussion.

2. Have students choose one response. Ask: If you could solve that mystery, what would it mean to you? to the world? Students can create another web to explore the possibilities.

3. As students read about Victor Frankenstein, encourage them to draw parallels between his wish and their own.

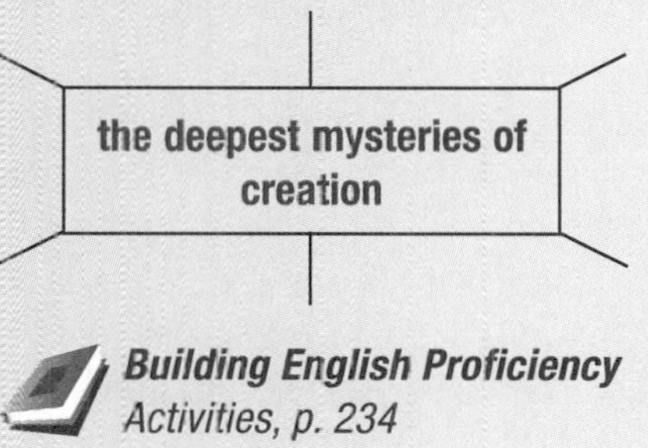

Building English Proficiency
Activities, p. 234

2 Literary Element
Metaphor

Frankenstein may be read as an extended metaphor for a woman's ability to "create" life by giving birth. Help students find phrases in the preceding paragraph that might also apply to women's labor and delivery. *(Possible responses: "stages of the discovery were distinct and probable," "days and nights of incredible labor and fatigue," "cause of generation and life")*

3 Active Reading
Clarify

Response Frankenstein may have several reasons.

- He knows now that humans are not meant to be creators of life.
- He is afraid Walton will misuse the secret.
- He knows the secret has resulted in Frankenstein's destruction and misery, and he does not wish for that to happen to Walton.

The World of Work
Chemical Engineer

For the real-life experiences of a chemical engineer, use the pages referenced below.

The World of Work
pp. 19–20

able. To examine the causes of life, we must first have recourse to death. I became acquainted with the science of anatomy: but this was not sufficient; I must also observe the natural decay and corruption of the human body. In my education my father had taken the greatest precautions that my mind should be impressed with no supernatural horrors. I do not ever remember to have trembled at a tale of superstition, or to have feared the apparition of a spirit. Darkness had no effect upon my fancy; and a churchyard was to me merely the receptacle of bodies deprived of life, which, from being the seat of beauty and strength, had become food for the worm. Now I was led to examine the cause and progress of this decay, and forced to spend days and nights in vaults and charnel houses.[2] My attention was fixed upon every object the most insupportable to the delicacy of the human feelings. I saw how the fine form of man was degraded and wasted; I beheld the corruption of death succeed to the blooming cheek of life; I saw how the worm inherited the wonders of the eye and brain. I paused, examining and analyzing all the minutiae[3] of causation, as exemplified in the change from life to death, and death to life, until from the midst of this darkness a sudden light broke in upon me—a light so brilliant and wondrous, yet so simple, that while I became dizzy with the immensity of the prospect which it illustrated, I was surprised that among so many men of genius who had directed their inquiries towards the same science, that I alone should be reserved to discover so astonishing a secret.

Remember, I am not recording the vision of a madman. The sun does not more certainly shine in the heavens, than that which I now affirm is true. Some miracle might have produced it, yet the stages of the discovery were distinct and probable. After days and nights of incredible labor and fatigue, I succeeded in discovering the cause of generation and life; nay, more, I became myself capable of bestowing animation upon lifeless matter.

The astonishment which I had at first experienced on this discovery soon gave place to delight and rapture. After so much time spent in painful labor, to arrive at once at the summit 2
of my desires was the most gratifying consummation of my toils. But this discovery was so great and overwhelming that all the steps by which I had been progressively led to it were obliterated, and I beheld only the result. What had been the study and desire of the wisest men since the creation of the world was now within my grasp. Not that, like a magic scene, it all opened upon me at once: the information I had obtained was of a nature rather to direct my endeavors so soon as I should point them towards the object already accomplished. . . .

I see by your eagerness, and the wonder and hope which your eyes express, my friend, that you expect to be informed of the secret with which I am acquainted; that cannot be: listen patiently until the end of my story, and you will easily perceive why I am reserved upon that subject. I will not lead you on, unguarded and ardent[4] as I then was, to your destruction and infallible misery. Learn from me, if not by my precepts, at least by my example, how dangerous is the acquirement of knowledge, and how much happier that man is who believes his native town to be the world, than he who aspires to become greater than his nature will allow.

CLARIFY: Why do you think Victor Frankenstein doesn't tell his listener, Robert Walton, the secret of life? 3

When I found so astonishing a power placed within my hands, I hesitated a long time con-

2. **charnel house,** place where dead bodies or bones are laid.
3. **minutiae** (mi nü′shē ē), *n. pl.* very small matters; trifling details.
4. **ardent** (ärd′nt), *adj.* very enthusiastic; eager.

MINI-LESSON: GRAMMAR
Paragraph Indentations

Teach Review the idea that paragraphs are indented so that readers may follow the writing more easily. (Alternatively, the writer may leave a space before new paragraphs.) A new paragraph signals a change in ideas or in speakers.

Point out the excerpt's long first paragraph pp. (492–493). Note that although this paragraph is long by today's standards and may be easier to read if broken down into several paragraphs, it nonetheless deals with one main idea (Frankenstein's search for the secret of life). Then have students note the two paragraph indentations on page 499. Discuss that the new paragraphs set off dialogue and show a change in speakers.

Activity Idea Have students write a short essay about *Frankenstein.* The essay should include dialogue between the creature and his creator. Students can exchange essays with a partner for proofreading, paying particular attention to the construction of paragraphs.

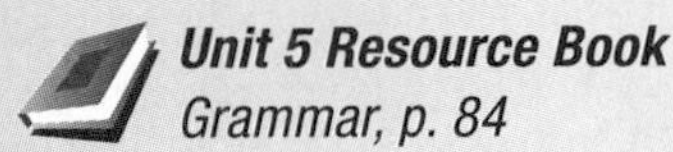

Unit 5 Resource Book
Grammar, p. 84

cerning the manner in which I should employ it. Although I possessed the capacity of bestowing animation, yet to prepare a frame for the reception of it, with all its intricacies of fibers, muscles, and veins, still remained a work of inconceivable difficulty and labor. I doubted at first whether I should attempt the creation of a being like myself, or one of simpler organization; but my imagination was too much exalted by my first success to permit me to doubt of my ability to give life to an animal as complex and wonderful as man. The materials at present within my command hardly appeared adequate to so arduous[5] an undertaking; but I doubted not that I should ultimately succeed. I prepared myself for a multitude of reverses; my operations might be incessantly baffled, and at last my work be imperfect: yet, when I considered the improvement which every day takes place in science and mechanics, I was encouraged to hope my present attempts would at least lay the foundations of future success. Nor could I consider the magnitude and complexity of my plan as any argument of its impracticability. It was with these feelings that I began the creation of a human being. As the minuteness of the parts formed a great hindrance to my speed, I resolved, contrary to my first intention, to make the being of a gigantic stature; that is to say, about eight feet in height, and proportionably large. After having formed this determination, and having spent some months in successfully collecting and arranging my materials, I began.

4 No one can conceive the variety of feelings which bore me onwards, like a hurricane, in the first enthusiasm of success. Life and death appeared to me ideal bounds, which I should first break through, and pour a torrent of light into our dark world. A new species would bless me as its creator and source; many happy and excellent natures would owe their being to me. No father could claim the gratitude of his child so completely as I should deserve theirs. Pursuing these reflections, I thought that if I could bestow animation upon lifeless matter, I might in process of time (although I now found it impossible) renew life where death had apparently devoted the body to corruption.

These thoughts supported my spirits, while I pursued my undertaking with unremitting ardor. My cheek had grown pale with study, and my person had become emaciated[6] with confinement. Sometimes, on the very brink of certainty, I failed; yet still I clung to the hope which the next day or the next hour might realize. One secret which I alone possessed was the hope to which I had dedicated myself; and the moon gazed on my midnight labors, while, with unrelaxed and breathless eagerness, I pursued nature to her hidden places. Who shall conceive the horrors of my secret toil, as I dabbled among the unhallowed damps of the grave, or tortured the living animal to animate the lifeless clay? My limbs now tremble and my eyes swim with the remembrance; but then a 5 resistless, and almost frantic, impulse urged me forward; I seemed to have lost all soul or sensation but for this one pursuit. It was indeed but a passing trance that only made me feel with renewed acuteness so soon as, the unnatural stimulus ceasing to operate, I had returned to my old habits. I collected bones from charnel houses; and disturbed, with profane fingers, the tremendous secrets of the human frame. In a solitary chamber, or rather cell, at the top of the house, and separated from all the other apartments by a gallery and staircase, I kept my workshop of filthy creation: my eyeballs were starting from their sockets in attending to the details of my employment. The dissecting room and the slaughter-house furnished many of my materials; and often did my human nature turn with loathing from my occupation, whilst, still urged on by an eagerness which perpetually increased, I brought my work near to a conclusion.

5. **arduous** (är′jü əs), *adj.* hard to do; requiring much effort.
6. **emaciated** (i mā′shē āt əd), *adj.* unnaturally thin.

4 Literary Element
Theme

Frankenstein exemplifies the Greek term *hubris*, the arrogant pride that led to the downfall of heroes in classical tragedies.

Questions

- How would you describe Frankenstein's feelings as he imagines a world filled with his creations? *(Possible responses: proud, self-satisfied, enthusiastic)*
- How could someone "exceeding human limits" achieve a beneficial outcome? *(Students might point to positive outcomes, such as the discovery of antibiotics or the technological applications that have resulted from the space program.)*

5 Multicultural Note
Creation Stories

Mary Shelley subtitled her work "The Modern Prometheus." The Greeks believed that Prometheus shaped the first humans out of clay, and this mention of "lifeless clay" may be an allusion to the myth. The Bible also refers to people being fashioned from earth.

Question Why do you think so many creation stories imply that the first humans were fashioned from earth? *(Possible response: Earth is a life source and nurturer.)*

BUILDING ENGLISH PROFICIENCY

ESL LEP ELD SAE LD

Using Figurative Language to Evoke Horror

Help students focus on Shelley's ability to evoke horror through figurative language.

Activity Ideas

1. Read aloud (or have a volunteer read) the paragraph in column 2 of page 495, while students close their eyes and imagine the scene. Ask them to share what they imagine.

2. Have a volunteer paraphrase this passage, using literal language: "I grew pale and obsessed trying to create life. I collected bones from graveyards and brought them to my lab. I worked until I was almost done."

3. Have small groups work together to explain how figurative language evokes more horror than literal language (for example, *unhallowed damps* rather than *graveyard; workshop of filthy creation* rather than *lab; my eyeballs were starting from their sockets* rather than *I stared)*.

4. Have students suggest how the horror in this passage would be communicated on a movie screen today.

6 **Reader's Response**

Making Personal Connections

Questions What do you think Frankenstein is implying in this paragraph? Do you agree? *(He seems to be blaming wars, enslavement, and other evils on passionate feelings—including the pursuit of a goal to the exclusion of all else. Student responses might acknowledge the difference between pursuing legitimate goals and becoming obsessed with them.)*

7 **Literary Element**

Foreshadowing

You might point out that creating the creature has come at great cost to Frankenstein. This foreshadows the pain and grief the monster will cause. Encourage students to note other foreshadowing as they read.

Literary Criticism

Frankenstein does not touch us because Victor Frankenstein is a scientist but because his creature was born ugly, because Victor abandoned him, because the creature's life is spent in a long, long pilgrimage toward his father/mother's love. The issue is not the scientist's laboratory; rather it is the "workshop of filthy creation" in which love and birth, and their consequence—death—take place.

Leonard Wolf
The Annotated Frankenstein

. . . I saw the dull yellow eye of the creature open . . . .

The summer months passed while I was thus engaged, heart and soul, in one pursuit. It was a most beautiful season; never did the fields bestow a more plentiful harvest, or the vines yield a more luxuriant vintage: but my eyes were insensible to the charms of nature. And the same feelings which made me neglect the scenes around me caused me also to forget those friends who were so many miles absent, and whom I had not seen for so long a time. I knew my silence disquieted them; and I well remembered the words of my father: "I know that while you are pleased with yourself, you will think of us with affection, and we shall hear regularly from you. You must pardon me if I regard any interruption in your correspondence as a proof that your other duties are equally neglected."

I knew well, therefore, what would be my father's feelings; but I could not tear my thoughts from my employment, loathsome in itself, but which had taken an irresistible hold of my imagination. I wished, as it were, to procrastinate[7] all that related to my feelings of affection until the great object, which swallowed up every habit of my nature, should be completed.

6 I then thought that my father would be unjust if he ascribed my neglect to vice, or faultiness on my part; but I am now convinced that he was justified in conceiving that I should not be altogether free from blame. A human being in perfection ought always to preserve a calm and peaceful mind, and never to allow passion or a transitory[8] desire to disturb his tranquillity. I do not think that the pursuit of knowledge is an exception to this rule. If the study to which you apply yourself has a tendency to weaken your affections, and to destroy your taste for those simple pleasures in which no alloy can possibly mix, then that study is certainly unlawful, that is to say, not befitting the human mind. If this rule were always observed; if no man allowed any pursuit whatsoever to interfere with the tranquillity of his domestic affections, Greece had not been enslaved; Caesar would have spared his country; America would have been discovered more gradually; and the empires of Mexico and Peru had not been destroyed.

But I forget that I am moralizing in the most interesting part of my tale; and your looks remind me to proceed.

My father made no reproach in his letters, and only took notice of my silence by inquiring into my occupations more particularly than before. Winter, spring, and summer passed away during my labors; but I did not watch the blossom or the expanding leaves—sights which before always yielded me supreme delight—so deeply was I engrossed in my occupation. The leaves of that year had withered before my work drew near to a close; and now every day showed me more plainly how well I had succeeded. But my enthusiasm was checked by my anxiety, and I appeared rather like one doomed by slavery to toil in the mines, or any other unwholesome trade, than an artist occupied by his favorite employment. Every night I was oppressed by a slow fever, and I became nervous 7
to a most painful degree; the fall of a leaf startled me, and I shunned my fellow creatures as if I had been guilty of a crime. Sometimes I grew alarmed at the wreck I perceived that I had become; the energy of my purpose alone sustained me: my labors would soon end, and I believed that exercise and amusement would then drive away incipient[9] disease; and I promised myself both of these when my creation should be complete.

It was on a dreary night of November that I beheld the accomplishment of my toils. With an

7. procrastinate (prō kras′tə nāt), *v.* put things off until later; delay.
8. transitory (tran′sə tôr′ē), *adj.* passing soon or quickly.
9. incipient (in sip′ē ənt), *adj.* just beginning; in an early stage.

MINI-LESSON: CRITICAL THINKING

Recognizing Cause and Effect

Teach A *cause* is a person, thing, or event that produces an *effect*, or result. A single cause may produce a chain of effects, as it does in *Frankenstein*. For example, it can be argued that the doctor's creation of life ultimately causes his own death.

Activity Idea Have students diagram the events in Part 1, in a cause-and-effect chain such as that pictured here. Students can diagram Parts 2 and 3 in the same way.

Cause-and-Effect Chain

Frankenstein discovers the principle of life.
Frankenstein gives his own creature life.
Frankenstein rejects his creature.

anxiety that almost amounted to agony, I collected the instruments of life around me, that I might infuse a spark of being into the lifeless thing that lay at my feet. It was already one in the morning; the rain pattered dismally against the panes, and my candle was nearly burnt out, when, by the glimmer of the half-extinguished light, I saw the dull yellow eye of the creature
8 open; it breathed hard, and a convulsive motion agitated its limbs.

How can I describe my emotions at this catastrophe, or how delineate[10] the wretch whom with such infinite pains and care I had endeavored to form? His limbs were in proportion, and I had selected his features as beautiful. Beautiful!—Great God! His yellow skin scarcely covered the work of muscles and arteries beneath; his hair was of a lustrous black, and flowing; his teeth of a pearly whiteness; but these luxuriances only formed a more horrid contrast with his watery eyes, that seemed almost of the same color as the dun white sockets in which they were set, his shriveled complexion and straight black lips.

9 **CONNECT: How does the description of the creature compare with the description you wrote in your Writer's Notebook?**

The different accidents of life are not so changeable as the feelings of human nature. I had worked hard for nearly two years, for the sole purpose of infusing life into an inanimate body. For this I had deprived myself of rest and health. I had desired it with an ardor that far exceeded moderation; but now that I had finished, the beauty of the dream vanished, and breathless horror and disgust filled my heart. Unable to endure the aspect of the being I had created, I rushed out of the room, and continued a long time traversing my bedchamber, unable to compose my mind to sleep. At length lassitude[11] succeeded to the tumult I had before endured; and I threw myself on the bed in my clothes, endeavoring to seek a few moments of forgetfulness. But it was in vain: I slept, indeed, but I was disturbed by the wildest dreams. I thought I saw Elizabeth, in the bloom of health, walking in the streets of Ingolstadt. Delighted and surprised, I embraced her; but as I imprinted the first kiss on her lips, they became livid with the hue of death; her features appeared to change, and I thought that I held the corpse of my dead mother in my arms; a shroud enveloped her
form, and I saw the grave-worms crawling in the 10
folds of the flannel. I started from my sleep with horror; a cold dew covered my forehead, my teeth chattered, and every limb became convulsed: when, by the dim and yellow light of the moon, as it forced its way through the window shutters, I beheld the wretch—the miserable monster whom I had created. He held up the curtain of the bed; and his eyes, if eyes they may be called, were fixed on me. His jaws opened, and he muttered some inarticulate sounds, while a grin wrinkled his cheeks. He might have spoken, but I did not hear; one hand was stretched out, seemingly to detain me, but I escaped, and rushed down stairs. I took refuge in the courtyard belonging to the house which I inhabited; where I remained during the rest of the night, walking up and down in the greatest agitation, listening attentively, catching and fearing each sound as if it were to announce the approach of the demoniacal corpse to which I had so miserably given life.

Oh! no mortal could support the horror of that countenance.[12] A mummy again endued with animation could not be so hideous as that wretch. I had gazed on him while unfinished; he was ugly then; but when those muscles and joints were rendered capable of motion, it became a thing such as even Dante[13] could not have conceived.

---

10. **delineate** (di lin′ē āt), *v.* describe in words; portray.
11. **lassitude** (las′ə tüd), *n.* lack of energy; weariness.
12. **countenance** (koun′tə nəns), *n.* face; features.
13. **Dante** (1265–1321), Italian poet, author of the *Inferno,* about a journey into Hell.

8 Reading/Thinking Skills
Visualize

Invite students to visualize the scene. Encourage them to use this as a model for creating mood and dramatic details to enliven their own writing.

9 Active Reading
Connect

Possible response Students might not have given the monster any "beautiful" characteristics, such as the flowing black hair and pearly white teeth described by Shelley.

10 Literary Focus
Mood

Review that mood is the overall atmosphere or prevailing emotional aura of a literary work.

Questions

- What mood does this description of the dream evoke? *(Possible response: stark terror)*
- How might this dream also serve to foreshadow events? *(Students might speculate on what could cause the death of the doctor's beloved Elizabeth.)*

Connections to **AuthorWorks**

Emily Brontë, another writer who explores the theme Exceeding Human Limits, is a featured author in the AuthorWorks CD-ROM series.

Connections to **NovelWorks**

NovelWorks: Wuthering Heights offers a rich variety of unique materials for teaching the novel.

BUILDING ENGLISH PROFICIENCY

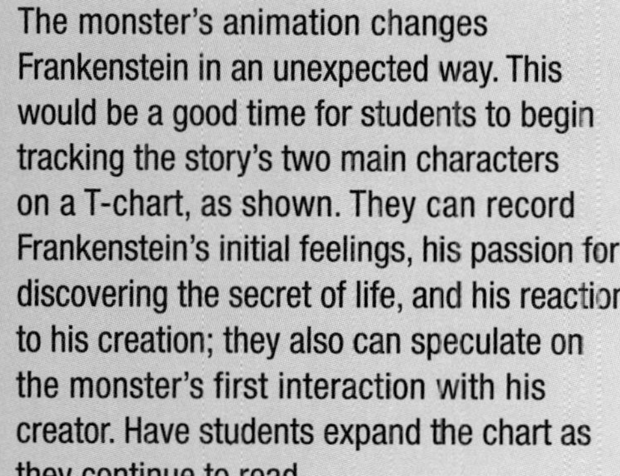

Tracking Characters

The monster's animation changes Frankenstein in an unexpected way. This would be a good time for students to begin tracking the story's two main characters on a T-chart, as shown. They can record Frankenstein's initial feelings, his passion for discovering the secret of life, and his reaction to his creation; they also can speculate on the monster's first interaction with his creator. Have students expand the chart as they continue to read.

Frankenstein	The Monster
optimistic, enthusiastic	happy to be alive?
obsessed	eager for acceptance?
disgusted, fearful	frightened?
________	________
________	________

11 Literary Focus

Mood

Draw students' attention to how setting is used to evoke various moods in the novel.

Questions

- What is the scene Frankenstein sees? *(a majestic, ice-covered mountain range)*
- What feelings do the mountains evoke in Frankenstein? *(awe, joy)*
- Is there anything foreboding in this setting? *(Possible response: Amid the impression of great beauty and majesty there is also a coldness; Frankenstein speaks of "icy and glittering peaks.")*

12 Literary Element

Genre: The Novel

In *Frankenstein*, Shelley overturns the conventions of the Gothic novel in an almost satirical way. In the Gothic fiction that emerged as a distinct literary genre in the mid-1700s, the central figure is usually a virginal young woman who faints at signs of trouble. She is usually pursued by a dark male figure with evil on his mind. The setting may be a cavern, a castle, or a ruin.

I passed the night wretchedly. Sometimes my pulse beat so quickly and hardly that I felt the palpitation[14] of every artery; at others, I nearly sank to the ground through languor and extreme weakness. Mingled with this horror, I felt the bitterness of disappointment; dreams that had been my food and pleasant rest for so long a space were now become a hell to me; and the change was so rapid, the overthrow so complete!

Morning, dismal and wet, at length dawned, and discovered to my sleepless and aching eyes the church of Ingolstadt, its white steeple and clock, which indicated the sixth hour. The porter opened the gates of the court, which had that night been my asylum, and I issued into the streets, pacing them with quick steps, as if I sought to avoid the wretch whom I feared every turning of the street would present to my view. I did not dare return to the apartment which I inhabited, but felt impelled to hurry on, although drenched by the rain which poured from a black and comfortless sky. . . .

PART 2

When Frankenstein finally returns to his rooms the creature has disappeared. He is greatly relieved and makes no attempt to search for him. After being away six years, Frankenstein receives news of the murder of his youngest brother, William, by an unknown strangler. Frankenstein intuitively realizes that the murderer is his own creation. In a terrible injustice, a former servant is executed for the crime. Crushed by feelings of guilt and despair, Frankenstein suffers a nervous collapse and impulsively wanders alone in the Alps. Finally he climbs Montanvert Mountain. Victor Frankenstein is speaking.

It was nearly noon when I arrived at the top of the ascent. For some time I sat upon the rock that overlooks the sea of ice. A mist covered both that and the surrounding mountains.
11 Presently a breeze dissipated[15] the cloud, and I descended upon the glacier. The surface is very uneven, rising like the waves of a troubled sea, descending low, and interspersed by rifts that sink deep. The field of ice is almost a league in width, but I spent nearly two hours in crossing it. The opposite mountain is a bare perpendicular rock. From the side where I now stood Montanvert was exactly opposite, at the distance of a league; and above it rose Mont Blanc, in awful majesty. I remained in a recess of the rock, gazing on this wonderful and stupendous scene. The sea, or rather the vast river of ice, wound among its dependent mountains, whose aerial summits hung over its recesses. Their icy and glittering peaks shone in the sunlight over the clouds. My heart, which was before sorrowful, now swelled with something like joy; I exclaimed—"Wandering spirits, if indeed ye wander, and do not rest in your narrow beds, allow me this faint happiness, or take me, as your companion, away from the joys of life."

As I said this, I suddenly beheld the figure 12
of a man, at some distance, advancing towards me with superhuman speed. He bounded over the crevices in the ice, among which I had walked with caution; his stature, also, as he approached, seemed to exceed that of man. I was troubled: a mist came over my eyes, and I felt a faintness seize me; but I was quickly restored by the cold gale of the mountains. I perceived, as the shape came nearer (sight tremendous and abhorred!) that it was the wretch whom I had created. I trembled with rage and horror, resolving to wait his approach, and then close with him in mortal combat. He approached; his countenance bespoke bitter anguish, combined with disdain and malignity, while its unearthly ugliness rendered it almost too horrible for human eyes. But I scarcely observed this; rage and hatred had at first deprived me of utterance, and I recovered only

14. **palpitation** (pal′pə tā′shən), *n.* rapid beating; throb.
15. dissipate (dis′ə pāt), *v.* spread in different directions; scatter.

MINI-LESSON: LITERARY FOCUS

Mood

Teach Remind students that mood is the atmosphere, or feeling, of a written work. Mood is created by factors such as the description of settings, the actions or feelings of characters, and the characters' words. Mood may create suspense or serve to unify a work.

Question What is the overall mood created in Frankenstein? *(Possible responses: dark, horror-filled, suspenseful)*

Activity Idea Small groups can look for elements that establish mood. An appointed recorder might chart answers under the three major heads shown in this sample:

Setting reflects characters' feelings

"black and comfortless sky" (p. 498)

Descriptions of characters' feelings or actions

"I trembled with rage and horror" (p. 498)

Dialogue

"Devil," "vile insect" (p. 499)

This still from the famous 1931 movie verson of *Frankenstein* shows one film maker's conception of Frankenstein's monster, played here by Boris Karloff. Compare this portrayal of the monster with the description Shelley gives in *Frankenstein*. How are the two similar? How are they different?

to overwhelm him with words expressive of furious detestation and contempt.

"Devil," I exclaimed, "do you dare approach me? and do not you fear the fierce vengeance of my arm wreaked on your miserable head? Begone, vile insect! or rather, stay, that I may trample you to dust! and, oh! that I could, with the extinction of your miserable existence, restore those victims whom you have so diabolically murdered!"

"I expected this reception," said the demon.
"All men hate the wretched; how, then, must I 13
be hated, who am miserable beyond all living

13 Literary Element
Characterization

Shelley has created a believable, complex monster who is horrible, yet sympathetic.

Questions In what ways is the creature repulsive? In what ways is he an object of sympathy? *(Possible responses: He is physically repulsive and has murdered an innocent man; on the other hand, he has been rejected by society and by the very man who created him.)*

Art Study

Response to Caption Question
Students may feel that Karloff evokes the spirit of the monster without resembling Shelley's description exactly—for example the square head and neck pegs.

Boris Karloff (1887–1969) was a British-born actor whose real name was William Henry Pratt. He refused to follow his family's profession, the diplomatic service, and moved to Hollywood, where he was cast for the part of the creature in *Frankenstein*. Karloff's horrifying yet sympathetic portrayal of the monster made him an instant star and led to a long film career. Since the 1931 production of *Frankenstein*, there have been scores of sequels, film adaptations, cartoons, and parodies.

BUILDING ENGLISH PROFICIENCY

Exploring Predicate Adjectives

You can use this excerpt from *Frankenstein* to offer a grammar refresher about predicate adjectives. Remind students that a predicate adjective follows a linking verb and gives more information about the subject.

1. Write the following sentences, based on sentences on page 498, on the board, indicating the subject and the predicate adjective. (Here, the subject is underlined, and the predicate adjective is in boldfaced type.)

- The <u>surface</u> is very **uneven**.
- <u>Montanvert</u> was exactly **opposite**.
- <u>I</u> was **troubled**.
- <u>I</u> felt **impelled** to hurry on.

2. Have students create sentences by using combinations of the following linking verbs and predicate adjectives.

Linking verbs: *am, has been, tastes, appears*

Predicate adjectives: *sour, nervous, busy, considerate*

14 Literary Element
Allegory

Invite students to consider *Frankenstein* as an allegory to be read on several levels: the relationship between a mother and child; the relationship of God and His creations; the consequences of overreaching human limits.

15 Literary Element
Allusion

With the reference to a "fallen angel," Shelley alludes to Lucifer or Satan, who was thrown out of heaven for plotting against God. This is a biblical allusion, but also one of the many allusions to Milton's *Paradise Lost* contained in the novel.

Question What does the creature mean when he says, "I ought to be thy Adam; but I am rather the fallen angel"? *(Possible response: Frankenstein should have loved and nurtured him as a son; instead the doctor was repulsed by the creature and rejected him. The creature is now more akin to Lucifer, the fallen angel, who sought to overthrow God.)*

16 Historical Note
Diction

You might note to the class that the cultivated speech of the monster is unrealistic, yet necessary to convey the dichotomy of good versus evil.

Wretched devil! you reproach me with your creation . . . .

14 things! Yet you, my creator, detest and spurn me, thy creature, to whom thou art bound by ties only dissoluble[16] by the annihilation of one of us. You purpose to kill me. How dare you sport thus with life? Do your duty towards me, and I will do mine towards you and the rest of mankind. If you will comply with my conditions, I will leave them and you at peace; but if you refuse, I will glut the maw of death, until it be satiated[17] with the blood of your remaining friends."

"Abhorred monster! fiend that thou art! the tortures of hell are too mild a vengeance for thy crimes. Wretched devil! you reproach me with your creation; come on, then, that I may extinguish the spark which I so negligently bestowed."

My rage was without bounds; I sprang on him, impelled by all the feelings which can arm one being against the existence of another.

He easily eluded me, and said—

"Be calm! I entreat you to hear me, before you give vent to your hatred on my devoted head. Have I not suffered enough that you seek to increase my misery? Life, although it may only be an accumulation of anguish, is dear to me, and I will defend it. Remember, thou hast made me more powerful than thyself; my height is superior to thine; my joints more supple. But I will not be tempted to set myself in opposition to thee. I am thy creature, and I will be even mild and docile to my natural lord and king, if thou wilt also perform thy part, the which thou owest me. Oh, Frankenstein, be not equitable to every other, and trample upon me alone, to whom thy justice, and even thy clemency[18] and affection, is most due. Remember, that I am thy creature; I ought to be thy Adam; but I am
15 rather the fallen angel, whom thou drivest from joy for no misdeed. Everywhere I see bliss, from which I alone am irrevocably excluded. I was benevolent and good; misery made me a fiend. Make me happy, and I shall again be virtuous."

"Begone! I will not hear you. There can be no community between you and me; we are enemies. Begone, or let us try our strength in a fight, in which one must fall."

"How can I move thee? Will no entreaties cause thee to turn a favorable eye upon thy creature, who implores thy goodness and compassion? Believe me, Frankenstein: I was benevolent; my soul glowed with love and humanity: but am I not alone, miserably alone? You, my creator, abhor me; what hope can I gather from your fellow creatures, who owe me nothing? they spurn and hate me. The desert mountains and dreary glaciers are my refuge. I have wandered here many days; the caves of ice, which I only do not fear, are a dwelling to me, and the only one which man does not grudge. These bleak skies I hail, for they are kinder to me than your fellow-beings. If the multitude of mankind knew of my existence, they would do as you do, and arm themselves for my destruction. Shall I not then hate them who abhor me? I will keep no terms with my enemies. I am miserable, and they shall share my wretchedness. Yet it is in your power to
recompense me, and deliver them from an evil 16
which it only remains for you to make so great that not only you and your family, but thousands of others, shall be swallowed up in the whirlwinds of its rage. Let your compassion be moved, and do not disdain me. Listen to my tale: when you have heard that, abandon or commiserate[19] me, as you shall judge that I deserve. But hear me. The guilty are allowed, by human laws, bloody as they are, to speak in their own defense before

16. **dissoluble** (di sol′yə bəl), *adj.* capable of being dissolved.
17. **satiate** (sā′shē āt), *v.* satisfy fully.
18. clemency (klem′ən sē), *n.* mercy or leniency.
19. commiserate (kə miz′ə rāt), *v.* pity; sympathize with.

they are condemned. Listen to me, Frankenstein. You accuse me of murder; and yet you would, with a satisfied conscience, destroy your own creature. Oh, praise the eternal justice of man! Yet I ask you not to spare me: listen to me; and then, if you can, and if you will, destroy the work of your hands."

17 **SUMMARIZE: What does the creature seem to think Victor Frankenstein owes him, as his creator?**

"Why do you call to my remembrance," I rejoined, "circumstances, of which I shudder to reflect, that I have been the miserable origin and author? Cursed be the day, abhorred devil, in which you first saw light! Cursed (although I curse myself) be the hands that formed you! You have made me wretched beyond expression. You have left me no power to consider whether I am just to you or not. Begone! relieve me from the sight of your detested form."

18 "Thus I relieve thee, my creator," he said, and placed his hated hands before my eyes, which I flung from me with violence; "thus I take from thee a sight which you abhor. Still thou canst listen to me, and grant me thy compassion. By the virtues that I once possessed, I demand this from you. Hear my tale; it is long and strange, and the temperature of this place is not fitting to your fine sensations; come to the hut upon the mountain. The sun is yet high in the heavens; before it descends to hide itself behind yon snowy precipices, and illuminate another world, you will have heard my story, and can decide. On you it rests whether I quit for ever the neighborhood of man, and lead a harmless life, or become the scourge of your fellow-creatures, and the author of your own speedy ruin."

As he said this, he led the way across the ice: I followed. My heart was full, and I did not answer him; but, as I proceeded, I weighed the various arguments that he had used, and determined at least to listen to his tale. I was partly urged by curiosity, and compassion confirmed my resolution. I had hitherto supposed him to be the murderer of my brother, and I eagerly sought a confirmation or denial of this opinion.

For the first time, also, I felt what the duties of a creator towards his creature were, and that I ought to render him happy before I complained of his wickedness. These motives urged me to comply with his demand. We crossed the ice, therefore, and ascended the opposite rock. The air was cold, and the rain again began to descend: we entered the hut, the fiend with an air of exultation, I with a heavy heart and depressed spirits. But I consented to listen; and, seating myself by the fire which my odious[20] companion had lighted, he thus began his tale. 19

Part 3

The creature describes his attempts to become part of the human family, studying in secret the ways of family life and reading books to develop his feelings and intellect. As a result, the creature comes to realize his similarity to humanity and yet his complete alienation and loneliness, which awakens in him stirrings of envy, resentment, and rebellion. The creature demands that Frankenstein create a female for him as a companion.

Frankenstein finds a lonely cottage on one of the Orkney Islands, off Scotland, to fulfill his promise. But he can scarcely bring himself to enter his laboratory for days at a time. Fearful that a female creation may be even more "malignant" than her mate, he destroys his work. The creature sees the act and tells Frankenstein angrily, ". . . I go; but remember, I shall be with you on your wedding-night."

The monster keeps his deadly promise and murders Elizabeth. Frankenstein's father perishes in grief. Frankenstein himself sets out in pursuit of his creation—a quest that takes him, finally, to the

20. odious (ō′dē əs), *adj.* hateful; offensive.

17 Active Reading
Summarize

Possible response He expects a chance at happiness or a chance to tell his story.

18 Reader's Response
Challenging the Text

Some critics argue that the creature has educated himself remarkably well in six years, as witnessed by his manner of speaking and his ability to read and to function in the world.

Questions

- Is the monster merely a mouthpiece for Shelley or a character in his own right? *(Possible response: Although the monster speaks on philosophical issues, he is a character in his own right, not just a vehicle for Shelley's ideas.)*
- Do you think Shelley's ideas would have been conveyed more effectively in a nonfiction work than a novel? *(It is unlikely that people would be reading this work today if it had been an essay. Elements of fiction, such as characterization, plot, and setting, help humanize and distinguish the work.)*

19 Reading/Thinking Skills
Make Judgments

Question What are the duties of a creator (or someone giving life) to the creature? *(Answers should reflect serious consideration of the issue.)*

BUILDING ENGLISH PROFICIENCY

Making Personal Connections

Help students focus on the monster's poignant plea on these pages by drawing upon their own experiences.

1. Ask students to think of times when they felt that they were outsiders—not like the people around them, even shunned by the people around them. If students want to share such information, allow them to do so.

2. Have students use their experiences to help them interpret these statements made by the monster (p. 500):

- "Have I not suffered enough that you seek to increase my misery?"
- "Everywhere I see bliss, from which I alone am irrevocably excluded."
- "Shall I not then hate them who abhor me?"

20 Literary Element
Narrator

Draw attention to the shift in point of view now that Walton is the narrator.

Questions

- Compare Walton's reactions to the monster with Frankenstein's. *(He initially is repulsed, but eventually he feels sympathy for him.)*
- Explain how Walton provides an opportunity for the monster to show his deep regret for his actions. *(He provides a certain distance, allowing the monster to meditate on his horrible acts and to acknowledge his creator as a "generous and self-devoted being"—admissions he couldn't have made to Frankenstein.)*

21 Literary Element
Plot

Motivation—why a character acts as she or he does—is important to an understanding of the plot. Discuss with students the creature's motivation for destroying Frankenstein's wife and relations.

Question What caused the creature's thirst for vengeance? (*Possible responses: Frankenstein's initial rejection of the creature and his destruction of the creature's mate; the creature's utter aloneness and unhappiness)*

Arctic wastes and into the protection of Robert Walton, an explorer who befriends Frankenstein and hears his story. Weakened by his exhausting and perilous journey, Frankenstein dies on Walton's ship. Later that night, Walton goes to investigate unearthly sounds in the cabin where Frankenstein's corpse lies. Robert Walton is speaking.

I entered the cabin where lay the remains of my ill-fated and admirable friend. Over him hung a form which I cannot find words to describe; gigantic in stature, yet uncouth and distorted in its proportions. As he hung over the coffin his face was concealed by long locks of ragged hair; but one vast hand was extended, in color and apparent texture like that of a mummy. When he heard the sound of my approach he ceased to utter exclamations of grief and horror and sprung towards the window. Never did I behold a vision so horrible as his face, of such loathsome yet appalling hideousness. I shut my eyes involuntarily and endeavored to recollect what were my duties with regard to this destroyer. I called on him to stay.

He paused, looking on me with wonder; and, again turning towards the lifeless form of his creator, he seemed to forget my presence, and every feature and gesture seemed instigated by the wildest rage of some uncontrollable passion.

"That is also my victim!" he exclaimed: "in his murder my crimes are consummated; the miserable series of my being is wound to its close! Oh, Frankenstein! generous and self-devoted being! what does it avail that I now ask thee to pardon me? I, who irretrievably destroyed thee by destroying all thou lovedst. Alas! he is cold, he cannot answer me."

His voice seemed suffocated; and my first impulses, which had suggested to me the duty of obeying the dying request of my friend, in destroying his enemy, were now suspended by a
20 mixture of curiosity and compassion. I approached this tremendous being; I dared not again raise my eyes to his face, there was something so scaring and unearthly in his ugliness. I attempted to speak, but the words died away on my lips. The monster continued to utter wild and incoherent[21] self-reproaches. At length I gathered resolution to address him in a pause of the tempest of his passion: "Your repentance," I said, "is now superfluous.[22] If you had listened to the voice of conscience, and heeded the stings of remorse, before you had urged your diabolical vengeance to this extremity, Frankenstein would yet have lived."

"And do you dream?" said the demon; "do you think that I was then dead to agony and remorse? . . . But when I discovered that he, the author at once of my existence and of its unspeakable torments, dared to hope for happiness; that while he accumulated wretchedness and despair upon me he sought his own enjoyment in feelings and passions from the indulgence of which I was for ever barred, then impotent envy and bitter indignation filled me with an insatiable[23] thirst for vengeance. I recollected my threat and resolved that it should be accomplished. . . . And now it is ended; there is my last victim!"

I was at first touched by the expressions of his 21
misery; yet, when I called to mind what Frankenstein had said of his powers of eloquence and persuasion, and when I again cast my eyes on the lifeless form of my friend, indignation was rekindled within me. "Wretch!" I said, "it is well that you come here to whine over the desolation that you have made. You throw a torch into a pile of buildings; and when they are consumed you sit among the ruins and lament the fall. Hypocritical fiend! if he whom you mourn still lived, still would he be the object, again would he become the prey, of your accursed vengeance. It is not pity that you feel; you lament only because the victim of your malignity is withdrawn from your power."

---

21. **incoherent** (in′kō hir′ənt), *adj.* having no logical connection of ideas; confused.
22. superfluous (sü pėr′flü əs), *adj.* needless; unnecessary.
23. **insatiable** (in sā′shə bəl), *adj.* extremely greedy; not able to be satisfied.

MINI-LESSON: VOCABULARY

Expanding Reading Vocabulary

Teach *Frankenstein* contains a vivid and varied vocabulary, with many words that may be unfamiliar to students. Students can expand their reading vocabularies by defining the unfamiliar words and suggesting synonyms for them.

Activity Ideas

Divide the class into groups, and assign some of these words from the selection to each group: *phenomena* (p. 492), *apparition* (p. 494, column 1), *consummation* (p. 494, column 2), *multitude* (p. 495, column 1), *corruption* (p. 495, column 2), *correspondence* (p. 496, column 1), *dun* (p. 497, column 1), *impelled* (p. 498, column 1), *abhorred* (p. 501, column 1)

Ask groups to

- find each word in the selection and then define it, using a dictionary if necessary
- rewrite the sentence in which the word appears, replacing the word with a synonym

22 **CLARIFY: What is Robert Walton's initial response to the creature? Why do you suppose he changes his mind?**

"Oh, it is not thus—not thus," interrupted the being; "yet such must be the impression conveyed to you by what appears to be the purport[24] of my actions. Yet I seek not a fellow-feeling in my misery. No sympathy may I ever find. When I first sought it, it was the love of virtue, the feelings of happiness and affection with which my whole being overflowed, that I wished to be participated. . . . But now crime has degraded me beneath the meanest animal. No guilt, no mischief, no malignity, no misery, can be found comparable to mine. When I run over the frightful catalogue of my sins, I cannot believe that I am the same creature whose thoughts were once filled with sublime and transcendent[25] visions of the beauty and the majesty of goodness. But it is even so; the fallen angel becomes a malignant devil. Yet even that enemy of God and man had friends and associates in his desolation; I am alone.

"You, who call Frankenstein your friend, seem to have a knowledge of my crimes and his misfortunes. But in the detail which he gave you of them he could not sum up the hours and months of misery which I endured, wasting in impotent passions. For while I destroyed his hopes, I did not satisfy my own desires. They

24. **purport** (pėr′pôrt), *n.* meaning; main idea.
25. **transcendent** (tran sen′dənt), *adj.* going beyond ordinary limits; superior; extraordinary.

In *Arctic Shipwreck,* an 1824 painting by Caspar David Friedrich, elements of nature unleash their fury, a ship sinks, and people become the victims of powerful natural forces. Victor Frankenstein himself perishes on a ship in the Arctic, in the midst of a barren, forbidding landscape. In *Frankenstein,* who are the victims? Who are the victimizers? Do some characters fill both roles?

22 Active Reading
Clarify

Possible response At first Walton describes the creature as horrible, loath-some, and hideous. He intends to kill the creature, in keeping with Frankenstein's dying request. However, after Walton hears the monster's self-reproaches and remorse, he feels a mixture of curiosity and compassion.

Art Study

Response to Caption Question The clear victims are Frankenstein's relations who die at the creature's hands. The doctor and the creature are both victims and victimizers: the doctor rejects the creature he has made, which then turns on him; the creature is rejected by his maker, and then attempts to destroy him.

Visual Literacy Caspar David Friedrich often based paintings on real events. The painting reproduced on page 503 was inspired by a dangerous incident in William Parry's Arctic expedition of 1819–1820. Friedrich has visualized the boat as it was caught and crushed by huge slabs of ice. The ice slabs dwarf the crushed ship, emphasizing human defeat in the face of nature's overwhelming power, a common theme in the artist's works.

BUILDING ENGLISH PROFICIENCY

ESL
LEP
ELD
SAE
LD

Evaluating Arguments

In the dialogue that concludes this excerpt, Walton and the monster argue over the extent to which the monster can be held accountable for Frankenstein's death. Have students use the "scales of justice" graphic shown at right to record the key points of each argument. Then have students determine who would win this case in a court of law—Walton (the prosecuting attorney) or the monster (the defendant, who is representing himself).

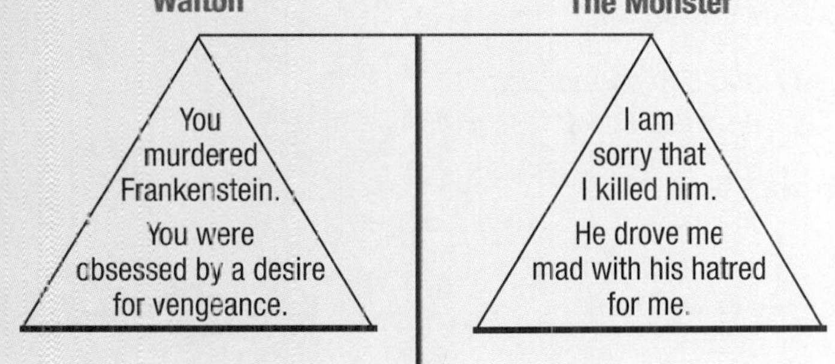
Walton
The Monster
You murdered Frankenstein.
You were obsessed by a desire for vengeance.
I am sorry that I killed him.
He drove me mad with his hatred for me.

23 Literary Element
Theme

Shelley opened her novel with a quote from Milton's *Paradise Lost:*

—Did I request thee, Maker, from my clay To mould me man? Did I solicit thee From darkness to promote me?—

Question How does this quote reflect a theme in *Frankenstein? (Possible response: It points out the abandonment of a creature by its creator and the obligations of a creator to the creation.)*

24 Reader's Response
Making Personal Connections

Questions

- Speculate on why Shelley chose not to destroy the monster. *(Possible response: Perhaps Shelley intended a sequel; perhaps living with his guilt is the monster's biggest punishment.)*
- Do you think this story merits a sequel? Explain. *(Those voting for a sequel should suggest a plot.)*

Check Test

1. What is Dr. Frankenstein's goal at the beginning of the novel? the end? *(to find the secret of life; to destroy what he has created)*

2. What does Frankenstein feel when he first beholds the living creature? *(shock, horror, revulsion)*

3. In Part 3, what does the creature ask Frankenstein to do for him? *(create a mate)*

4. How does Frankenstein end up in the Arctic? *(He is following the creature with the intent of destroying it.)*

5. Who narrates the final events of the story? *(Robert Walton)*

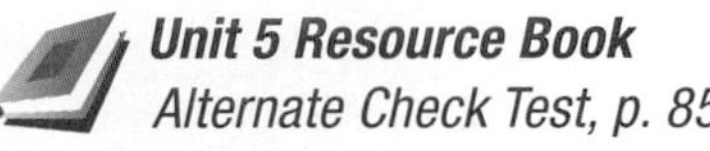

Unit 5 Resource Book
Alternate Check Test, p. 85

were for ever ardent and craving; still I desired love and fellowship, and I was still spurned. Was there no injustice in this? Am I to be thought the only criminal when all human kind sinned against me? . . . I, the miserable and the abandoned, am an abortion, to be spurned at, and kicked, and trampled on. Even now my blood boils at the recollection of this injustice.

"But it is true I am a wretch. I have murdered the lovely and the helpless; I have strangled the innocent as they slept, and grasped to death his throat who never injured me or any other living thing. I have devoted my creator, the select specimen of all that is worthy of love and admiration among men, to misery; I have pursued him even to that irremediable[26] ruin. There he lies, white and cold in death. You hate me; but your abhorrence cannot equal that with which I regard myself. I look on the hands which executed the deed; I think on the heart in which the imagination of it was conceived, and long for the moment when these hands will meet my eyes, when that imagination will haunt my thoughts no more.

"Fear not that I shall be the instrument of future mischief. My work is nearly complete. . . . I shall quit your vessel on the ice-raft which brought me thither, and shall seek the most northern extremity of the globe; I shall collect my funeral pile and consume to ashes this miserable frame, that its remains may afford no light to any curious and unhallowed wretch who would create such another as I have been. I shall die. I shall no longer feel the agonies which now consume me, or be the prey of feelings unsatisfied, yet unquenched. He is dead who called me into being; and when I shall be no more the very remembrance of us both will speedily vanish. I shall no longer see the sun or stars, or feel the winds play on my cheeks. Light, feeling, and sense will pass away; and in this condition must I find my happiness. Some years ago, when the images which this world affords first opened upon me, when I felt the cheering warmth of summer, and heard the rustling of the leaves and the warbling of the birds, and these were all to me, I should have wept to die; now it is my only consolation. Polluted by crimes, and torn by the bitterest remorse, where can I find rest but in death?

"Farewell! I leave you, and in you the last of human kind whom these eyes will ever behold. Farewell, Frankenstein! If thou wert yet alive, and yet cherished a desire of revenge against me, it would be better satiated in my life than in my destruction. . . .

"But soon," he cried, with sad and solemn enthusiasm, "I shall die, and what I now feel be no longer felt. Soon these burning miseries will be extinct. I shall ascend my funeral pile triumphantly, and exult in the agony of the torturing flames. The light of that conflagration[27] will fade away; my ashes will be swept into the sea by the winds. My spirit will sleep in peace; or if it 23
thinks, it will not surely think thus. Farewell."

He sprung from the cabin-window, as he said this, upon the ice-raft which lay close to the vessel. He was soon borne away by the waves and lost in darkness and distance. 24

26. **irremediable** (ir′i mē′dē ə bəl), *adj.* that cannot be corrected or remedied; incurable.

27. **conflagration** (kon′flə grā′shən), *n.* a great and destructive fire.

After Reading

Making Connections

Shaping Your Response

1. In your opinion, does this story still have the power to frighten readers? Explain.
2. For which character do you have more sympathy—Victor Frankenstein or his creature? Why?

Analyzing the Novel Excerpt

3. Compare Frankenstein's reaction to his creation as he is working on it to his reaction after it has come to life.
4. Do you believe the creature's explanation that he was once "benevolent and good" but is now changed? Explain.
5. Frankenstein declares that "there can be no community between you and me; we are enemies." What, in your opinion, makes them enemies? Why can't they make the **choice** to be otherwise?
6. The monster challenges Frankenstein, "Do your duty towards me, and I will do mine towards you . . . ." What do you think should be the duties of a creator toward a creation? of a creation toward a creator?
7. What do you think is the major **theme** of the story?

Extending the Ideas

8. Does *Frankenstein* remind you of any popular movies or stories of today? What do they have in common? How are horror stories and movies today different from Mary Shelley's tale?
9. Why do you think this story is still popular after so many years?

Literary Focus: Mood

The atmosphere or feeling of a written work is its **mood.** The mood of a selection may be romantic, sad, eerie, lighthearted, dreamlike—the possibilities cover the range of emotions. Authors create mood through the setting, characters, actions, and descriptive details. Gothic novels, like *Frankenstein,* try to create a mood of horror.

1. What details, descriptions, and events help create a mood of horror in this selection?
2. Jot down a list of at least a dozen words or phrases Mary Shelley uses that enhance the mood of this story.

Vocabulary Study

Which word does not belong? Write the letter of the word that is not related in meaning to the other words in the set.

1. **a.** beginning **b.** early **c.** incipient **d.** ridiculous
2. **a.** sympathize **b.** pity **c.** scorn **d.** commiserate

After Reading

MAKING CONNECTIONS

1. Responses will vary with students' perceptions and prior experiences. Students should keep in mind that only a few excerpts of the novel are included here; reading the novel in its entirety might evoke a different response.

2. Students may alternate between sympathy for the two characters. Frankenstein loses everything in his quest for the secret of life, and the creature is a lonely, rejected, and physically repulsive being.

3. While working on the creature, Frankenstein is excited and proud of his abilities. After the creature comes to life, he is shocked and repulsed by its ugliness.

4. Students might compare the newly created monster to an innocent, newborn baby or a young child, who is prepared to love and be good if treated kindly.

5. Perhaps the two are enemies because Frankenstein feels he has no choice but to destroy that which he created; both are fated to play out their lives to the inevitable end.

6. Possible response: The creator should love, care for, and accept responsibility for the creation; the creation should love and respect its creator in return.

7. Possible response: the tragic consequences of exceeding human limits

8. Students should provide examples to support their comparisons.

9. Perhaps the story is still popular because it can be read on so many levels—as a horror story, as science fiction, as a metaphor for the parent/child relationship, as a creation story, and so on.

LITERARY FOCUS: MOOD

Invite students to discuss the atmosphere established in *Frankenstein.* Which parts evoked excitement? horror? sadness? suspense? How did all these contribute to the overall mood? Then discuss the two numbered items on page 505.

Possible Responses

1. Students might mention the frequently rainy, dark setting, the "birth" of the creature, the creature's horrifying ugliness, the unnecessary deaths of innocent people, and so on.

2. Students should include words and phrases describing Frankenstein's workshop, the creature's appearance, the setting, and the dialogue between Frankenstein and the creature. These "mood" words should be listed in their notebooks for future use in their writing.

VOCABULARY STUDY

1. d
2. c
3. b
4. c
5. a
6. b
7. c
8. c
9. a
10. b

More Practice Students can create a crossword puzzle using the vocabulary words.

Unit 5 Resource Book
Vocabulary, p. 83
Vocabulary Test, p. 86

WRITING CHOICES

Writer's Notebook Update

Responses will vary. Students will probably find that their impressions were formed from films and television shows. Point out that a movie rarely captures a book completely and accurately; each should be considered its own genre.

Invent a Monster Character

As a prewriting exercise, you might have students think of a social evil and a "monster" that could reflect this evil. (For example, toxic waste could be reflected by a monster breathing noxious fumes.)

Selection Test

Unit 5 Resource Book
pp. 87–88

Transparency Collection
Fine Art Writing Prompt 10

clemency	3. **a.** leniency	**b.** disturbance	**c.** mercy	**d.** clemency
commiserate	4. **a.** needless	**b.** superfluous	**c.** unnatural	**d.** unnecessary
delineate	5. **a.** transitory	**b.** eternal	**c.** long lived	**d.** constant
dissipate	6. **a.** vitality	**b.** lassitude	**c.** enthusiasm	**d.** energy
incipient	7. **a.** delineate	**b.** portray	**c.** betray	**d.** describe
lassitude	8. **a.** odious	**b.** offensive	**c.** peculiar	**d.** hateful
odious	9. **a.** approve	**b.** procrastinate	**c.** delay	**d.** put off
procrastinate	10. **a.** spread	**b.** concentrate	**c.** dissipate	**d.** scatter
superfluous				
transitory				

Expressing Your Ideas

Writing Choices

Writer's Notebook Update Put your impressions of Frankenstein's creature into a double-column format. In the second column write words and phrases from Mary Shelley that either confirm your impressions or contradict them.

Modern Terrors Have monsters lost their power to scare, or have real modern terrors such as nuclear weaponry or AIDS diverted most of the public's fears toward themselves and away from fictional creatures? Write a brief **essay** in which you explore this question, citing specific public events or fictional creations.

Invent a Monster Character Mary Shelley invented the story of Frankenstein's monster to entertain friends during a rainy summer. If you were going to invent a character for a tale of terror, what would it be like? Write a **descriptive paragraph** that establishes your character and tells what special powers he or she has. (You might want to use this character in writing My Own Monster; see the Writer's Workshop on page 513.)

Other Options

For or Against? A **debate** is a formal way to argue for and against a particular statement, called a *proposition*. With a partner, consider one of the moral questions that arise in *Frankenstein,* and develop an argument for each side. Then present your debate to the class. Here are some possible propositions:

- Victor Frankenstein has no right to act as a creator.
- A creator has certain responsiblities toward his or her creation.
- Modern scientific experimentation is like a Frankenstein's monster.

Creating Life, Conquering Death The news media today present countless stories about people who are pushing, if not exceeding, the human limits of life and death—for example, keeping alive prematurely born babies or freezing people after death in hopes of reviving them at a later date. Locate one or more of these stories and share it with the class. (See also the Interdisciplinary Study on page 507.) If you find several stories on similar topics, you might combine them in an **oral report.**

506 UNIT FIVE: THE ROMANTIC ERA

OTHER OPTIONS

For or Against?

Encourage students to consider all the possible arguments for and against their chosen position so that they are prepared for any points their debating partner may bring up.

Creating Life, Conquering Death

Students might research topics, such as revivification, the care of premature infants, infertility clinics, "test-tube" babies, and euthanasia. They can locate articles by using the *Readers' Guide to Periodical Literature* or the Internet.

Exceeding Human Limits

Creating Life

Science Connection

In the following article, scientist Stephen Jay Gould argues that Hollywood has consistently misinterpreted the theme of Mary Shelley's novel.

The Monster's Human Nature

Stephen Jay Gould

Hollywood knows only one theme in making monster movies, from the archetypal *Frankenstein* of 1931 to [the recent] megahit, *Jurassic Park*. Human technology must not go beyond an intended order decreed by God or set by nature's laws. No matter how benevolent the purposes of the transgressor, such cosmic arrogance can only lead to killer tomatoes, very large rabbits with sharp teeth, giant ants in the Los Angeles sewers, or even larger blobs that swallow entire cities. Yet these films often use far more subtle books as their sources and, in so doing, distort the originals beyond all thematic recognition.

The trend began in 1931 with *Frankenstein*, Hollywood's first great monster "talkie" (although Boris Karloff only grunted, while Colin Clive, as Henry Frankenstein, emoted). Hollywood decreed its chosen theme by the most "up-front" of all conceivable strategies. The film begins with a prologue (even before the titles roll), featuring a well-dressed man standing on stage before a curtain, to issue both a warning about potential fright and to announce the film's deeper theme as the story of "a man of science who sought to create a man after his own image without reckoning upon God."

This 1831 illustration shows a terror-struck Victor Frankenstein fleeing from his creation.

In the movie, Dr. Waldman, Henry's old medical school professor, speaks of his pupil's "insane ambition to create life," a diagnosis supported by Frankenstein's own feverish words of enthusiasm: "I created it. I made it with my own hands from the bodies I took from graves, from the gallows, from anywhere."

The best of a carload of sequels, *The Bride of Frankenstein* (1935) makes the favored theme even more explicit in a prologue featuring Mary Wollstonecraft Shelley (who wrote *Frankenstein* when she was only nineteen years old and published the story two years later in 1818). In conversation with her husband, Percy, and their buddy Lord Byron, she states: "My purpose was to write a moral lesson of the punishment that befell a mortal man who dared to emulate God."

Shelley's *Frankenstein* is a rich book of many themes, but I can find little therein to support the Hollywood reading. The text is neither a

Interdisciplinary Study

Theme Link

The story of Frankenstein's scientific discovery and its disastrous results has been interpreted wrongly by Hollywood according to Stephen Jay Gould. He maintains that it is not Frankenstein's pride or misuse of science that is at fault in the Frankenstein story, but rather his failure to take responsibility for his creation and rise above prejudice.

Curricular Connection: Science

Use the information in this interdisciplinary study to explore with students the idea of a creator's responsibilities towards his or her creations. Use examples of other scientific discoveries, such as the atom bomb, to examine a scientist's relationship to his or her discoveries once they are let loose on society.

Terms to Know

ardor (är′dər), an intense or powerful passion.

fastidious (fa stid′ē əs), difficult to please, picky.

aversion (ə vėr′zhən), dislike.

emulate (em′yə lāt), imitate.

predisposition (prē′dis′pə zish′ən), an inclination towards a certain understanding or behavior.

visceral (vis′ər əl), something that is felt physically.

Unit 5 Resource Book
Interdisciplinary Study Guide, page 89

BUILDING ENGLISH PROFICIENCY

ESL LEP ELD SAE LD

Making Personal Connections

Use one or more of the following activities to help students respond to this feature.

Activity Ideas

- Ask students who have seen the 1931 *Frankenstein* to share their recollections and reactions. Alternatively, bring in a videocassette of the film and show a few of its key scenes.
- Gould mentions that *Frankenstein* has had several sequels. Invite students to talk about other film sequels (not necessarily of the horror genre). Ask: Why does Hollywood make sequels? What challenges might the creators of a sequel face?
- Invite students to suggest ideas for new monster movies; note responses on the chalkboard. Ask: Which of these remind you more of the novel *Frankenstein*, and which remind you more of the film *Frankenstein*? How do these suggestions show the influence of earlier monster or horror movies?

Additional Background

Stephen Jay Gould teaches biology, geology, and the history of science at Harvard University. He is the author of numerous books and collections of scientific essays, such as *Dinosaur in a Haystack, Wonderful Life,* and *Time's Arrow, Time's Cycle.*

Research Topics

- The life and work of Stephen Jay Gould
- The making of the atom bomb and the thoughts and feelings of the team of scientists who created it
- Films that depict inventions which ultimately turn against their inventors—such as *Jurassic Park* and *2001: A Space Odyssey*
- Any of the gods or deities pictured on pages 510–511: Greek mythology's Prometheus; Tiki, Maori creator god; the Golem of Jewish legend; Aztec deity Coatlicue

diatribe on the dangers of technology nor a warning about overextended ambition against a natural order. We find no passages about disobeying God—an unlikely subject for Mary Shelley and her free-thinking friends (Percy had been expelled from Oxford in 1811 for publishing a defense of atheism). Victor Frankenstein (I do not know why Hollywood changed him to Henry) is guilty of a great moral failing, as we shall see later, but his crime is not technological transgression against a natural or divine order.

We can find a few passages about the awesome power of science, but these words are not negative. Professor Waldman, a sympathetic character in the book, states, for example:

They [scientists] penetrate into the recesses of nature, and show how she works in her hiding places. They ascend into the heavens; they have discovered how the blood circulates, and the nature of the air we breathe. They have acquired new and almost unlimited powers.

We do learn that ardor without compassion or moral consideration can lead to trouble, but Shelley applies this argument to any endeavor, not especially to scientific discovery (her examples are, in fact, all political). Victor Frankenstein says:

A human being in perfection ought always to preserve a calm and peaceful mind, and never to allow passion or a transitory desire to disturb his tranquillity. I do not think that the pursuit of knowledge is an exception to this rule. If the study to which you apply yourself has a tendency to weaken your affections . . . then that study is certainly unlawful, that is to say, not befitting the human mind. If this rule were always observed . . . Greece had not been enslaved; Caesar would have spared his country; America would have been discovered more gradually; and the empires of Mexico and Peru had not been destroyed.

Victor's own motivations are entirely idealistic: "I thought, that if I could bestow animation upon lifeless matter, I might in process of time (although I now found it impossible) renew life where death had apparently devoted the body to corruption." Finally, as Victor expires in the Arctic, he makes his most forceful statement on the dangers of scientific ambition, but he only berates himself and his own failures, while stating that others might well succeed. Victor says his dying words to the ship's captain who found him on the polar ice:

Farewell, Walton! Seek happiness in tranquillity, and avoid ambition, even if it be only the apparently innocent one of distinguishing yourself in science and discoveries. Yet why do I say this? I have myself been blasted in these hopes, yet another may succeed.

In this scene from the 1935 film* The Bride of Frankenstein, *Elsa Lanchester as Mary Shelley is shown telling her horror story to her husband and Lord Byron.

MINI-LESSON: STUDY SKILLS

Taking Notes

Teach Suggest that students take notes to help clarify and retain the information in Gould's essay. Review the purpose of taking notes and list students' ideas on the board. Remind students that taking notes helps them organize material and understand the meaning of the text they are reading. In addition, notes provide an excellent method of reviewing material at a later time.

Activity Idea Have students practice taking notes on the first page of "The Monster's Human Nature."

- Ask students to read the first page of Gould's essay.
- Individually or in small groups, have students write a one-sentence summary of each of the four paragraphs on the page.
- Compare different students' (or different groups') summaries and discuss the similarities and differences between them.

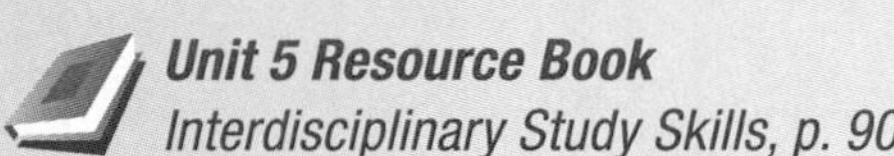

Unit 5 Resource Book
Interdisciplinary Study Skills, p. 90

. . . But Karloff's *Frankenstein* contains an even more serious and equally prominent distortion of a theme that I regard as the primary lesson of Mary Shelley's book—another lamentable example of Hollywood's sense that the American public cannot tolerate even the slightest exercise in intellectual complexity. Why is the monster evil? Shelley provides a nuanced and subtle answer that, to me, sets the central theme of her book. But Hollywood opted for a simplistic solution, so precisely opposite to Shelley's intent that the movie can no longer claim to be telling a moral fable (despite the protestations of the man in front of the curtain, or of Mary Shelley herself in the sequel) and becomes instead, as I suppose the maker intended all along, a pure horror film. . . .

The monster is evil because Henry unwittingly makes him of evil stuff. Later in the film, Henry expresses his puzzlement at the monster's nasty temperament, for he made his creature of the best materials. But Waldman, finally realizing the source of the monster's behavior, tells Henry: "The brain that was stolen from my laboratory was a criminal brain." Henry then counters with one of the cinema's greatest double takes, and finally manages a feeble retort, "Oh well, after all, it's only a piece of dead tissue." "Only evil will come from it," Waldman replies, "you have created a monster and it will destroy you" —true enough, at least until the next sequel. . . .

Karloff's intrinsically evil monster stands condemned by the same biological determinism that has so tragically and falsely restricted the lives of millions who committed no transgression besides membership in a despised race, sex, or social class. . . . Shelley's monster is not evil by inherent constitution. He is born unformed, carrying the predispositions of human nature, but without the specific manifestations that can only be set by upbringing and education. . . . [It is] the cruel rejection of his natural fellow [that] drives him to fury and revenge. (Even as a murderer, the monster remains fastidious and purposive. Victor Frankenstein is the source of his anger, and he only kills the friends and lovers whose deaths will bring Victor the most grief; he does not, like Godzilla or the Blob, rampage through cities.) . . . He becomes evil, of course, because humans reject him so violently and so unjustly. His resulting loneliness becomes unbearable. . . .

But why is the monster so rejected if his feelings incline towards benevolence, and his acts to evident goodness? Shelley tells us that all humans reject and even loathe the monster for a visceral reason of literal superficiality: his truly terrifying ugliness — a reason heartrending in its deep injustice and profound in its biological accuracy and philosophical insight about the meaning of human nature. . . . Frankenstein's creature becomes a monster because he is cruelly ensnared by one of the deepest predispositions of our biological inheritance — our aversion toward seriously malformed individuals. . . .

Frankenstein's monster was a good man in an appallingly ugly body. His countrymen could have been educated to accept him, but the person responsible for that instruction — his creator, Victor Frankenstein — ran away from his foremost duty, and abandoned his creature at first sight. Victor's sin does not lie in misuse of technology or hubris in emulating God; we cannot find these themes in Mary Shelley's account. Victor failed because he followed a predisposition in human nature — visceral disgust at the monster's appearance — and did not undertake the duty of any creator or parent: to teach his own charge and to educate others in acceptance. . . .

Responding

1. Does Mary Shelley's *Frankenstein* present a positive view of science? of scientists? Explain.

2. Do you agree that "Hollywood knows only one theme in making monster movies"? Why or why not?

Interdisciplinary Activity Idea

Students may divide into groups to write a one-act play, short film, or short story about a scientist whose invention or discovery has gotten out of control. Encourage students to use their knowledge of scientific issues and topics to find a suitable story line. Students may want to research possible ideas in their science classes or in the library. Once written, students may act out their plays and read their stories to the class.

Responding

1. Possible response Although Shelley does not clearly present science and scientists in a positive light in *Frankenstein,* her views on science are not clearly negative either. The essential nature of humans and how they put science to use are more central to Shelley's themes.

2. Possible response Monster movies almost always place monsters in the role of the enemy—killing people and destroying cities. This structure works as a narrative device, establishing "the good guys" and "the bad guys." However, if we consider extraterrestrials to be monsters, movies such as *E.T.* and *Star Wars,* with their lovable extraterrestrial creatures, create a different picture.

BUILDING ENGLISH PROFICIENCY

Checking Comprehension

Help students evaluate their understanding of this detailed article. Work with them to complete each of the following sentences in two ways—first with an answer that is true for the 1818 novel *Frankenstein* and then with an answer that is true for the 1931 film *Frankenstein.* (Sample answers are given.)

1. Frankenstein decided to animate dead matter because he wanted ______. *(to help humanity; to be like God)*

2. Frankenstein's monster was evil because ______. *(he was rejected by other people and by his own creator; he was given the brain of a criminal)*

3. The audience for Frankenstein is meant to think that science ______. *(is powerful and has the potential for great things; has limits that people should not try to exceed)*

Interdisciplinary Study

Theme Link

Throughout time, human beings have told stories and made art about the creation of human life. Although all cultures may have creation myths, the specific characteristics of those myths vary across cultures and reflect the beliefs and attitudes of the people who tell them.

Curricular Connection: Multicultural

Use the information in this interdisciplinary study to explore similarities and differences across cultures by examining different myths of creation.

MULTICULTURAL CONNECTION

Invite students to respond to the illustrations by asking if any students can give additional information about the myths and deities pictured.

INTERDISCIPLINARY STUDY

Multicultural Connection

Mary Shelley's *Frankenstein* is a famous example of a theme—the fashioning of a human being—that has been explored throughout the cultures of the world in a wide variety of artistic and literary forms.

The full title of Mary Shelley's novel is **Frankenstein, or the Modern Prometheus.** *According to Greek mythology, Prometheus creates human beings by fashioning them out of clay. Prometheus attempts to aid his creatures by stealing fire from heaven, for which he is punished by the gods. In this detail from a Roman carving, Prometheus is shown animating a human being he has just shaped from clay.*

Creators &

This statue depicts Coatlicue (kō at′lə kü ē), *"the lady of the serpent skirt," a fearsome Aztec deity who is the mother of the gods. Associated equally with life and death, she both creates human beings and devours corpses.*

A synthetic human made from flesh, not machinery, is an android. One movie that features androids is **Blade Runner.** *Technically, Victor Frankenstein's creature is an android.*

MINI-LESSON: VISUAL LITERACY

Analyzing and Responding to Art

Teach Explain to students that pictures like those on pages 510 and 511 often communicate information about other cultures in a more direct and immediate way than words do. Ask students to offer their observations about the figures depicted in the pictures. You may need to ask questions to elicit responses: In what ways do images of gods reflect the culture of the artist? What similarities and differences do you notice among the different pictures?

Activity Ideas

- Divide the class into six groups, assigning one of the pictures to each group.
- Have each group study their assigned picture and make a list of their observations and questions.

  You may list several categories of issues for students to address.
- Production of art (How was the art made?)
- Response to art (What is a viewer's response to the image?)
- Meaning of art (What role do you think art played in the culture that created this artwork?)

According to Chinese mythology, human beings were created from clay by Nu Kwa, a goddess who was half serpent and half woman. She is shown on the right in a rubbing from a Han dynasty stone carving.

Tiki is the creator god of the Maori people of New Zealand. Like Prometheus, he uses clay to make the first human beings.

In Jewish legends of the 1500s, the Golem, a mute creature formed from clay, is given life by a rabbi. In some versions the Golem becomes uncontrollable, forcing the rabbi to destroy his creation.

Creatures

Responding

1. What characteristics are shared by two or more of these creators?
2. Why is Victor Frankenstein a "modern Prometheus"? How does Frankenstein's behavior to his creature differ from that of Prometheus?

Art Study

Excluding the image of the android, all the images pictured on these two pages are related to religion. Across time and cultures, art and religion have been linked, with art approaching the divine, and the divine being represented through art.

Question Using the images on these pages as well as other artwork, explain how artistic depictions of gods often resemble the human form. *(Possible response: In the images on these pages, Tiki and Coatlicue both have human features and adorn themselves similarly to humans of that culture. The Greek gods are usually pictured as human, although often with superhuman characteristics and abilities.)*

Responding

1. Possible response Three of the myths featured involve fashioning humans from clay.The creators (and usually their creations, as well), are capable of both good and evil; Coatlicue is associated equally with life and death; the Golem, who is given life by a rabbi, is destroyed by the rabbi when he becomes uncontrollable; Prometheus is punished for disobeying the gods and bringing fire to the humans.

2. Possible response In the same way that Prometheus created humans out of clay and breathed life into them, Frankenstein makes a human creature come alive. Unlike Frankenstein, though, Prometheus cares for his creations and brings them the gift of fire.

BUILDING ENGLISH PROFICIENCY

Responding to Visual Cues

Use one or more of the following activities to help students grasp the information on this spread.

Activity Ideas

- Have students examine the images and captions. Allow time for students to use their dialogue journals to respond to the images and information.
- Several of the creations are made from clay. Invite students to make a figure out of clay; then have them share how it felt to choose a shape and prepare a satisfactory image.
- Ask pairs or groups of students to choose one of the pictures. Have them improvise either (1) a skit about the creation depicted or (2) paired monologues in which one student describes what it is like to be a creator and the other describes what it is like to be a creature.

Interdisciplinary Study

Theme Link

The concept of the "mad scientist" has been promoted through movies, comics, and science fiction literature. The father of the mad scientist genre can perhaps be found in Mary Shelley's *Frankenstein.*

Curricular Connection: Popular Culture

Use the information in this interdisciplinary study to explore the ways in which popular culture shapes our ideas and understandings of the world around us.

Responding

Possible response Because scientists are responsible for major medical and technological breakthroughs which have improved people's lives, the attitude of the public is generally favorable; as people understand more about the real work of scientists, the image of the mad scientist working on crazy inventions is losing its power.

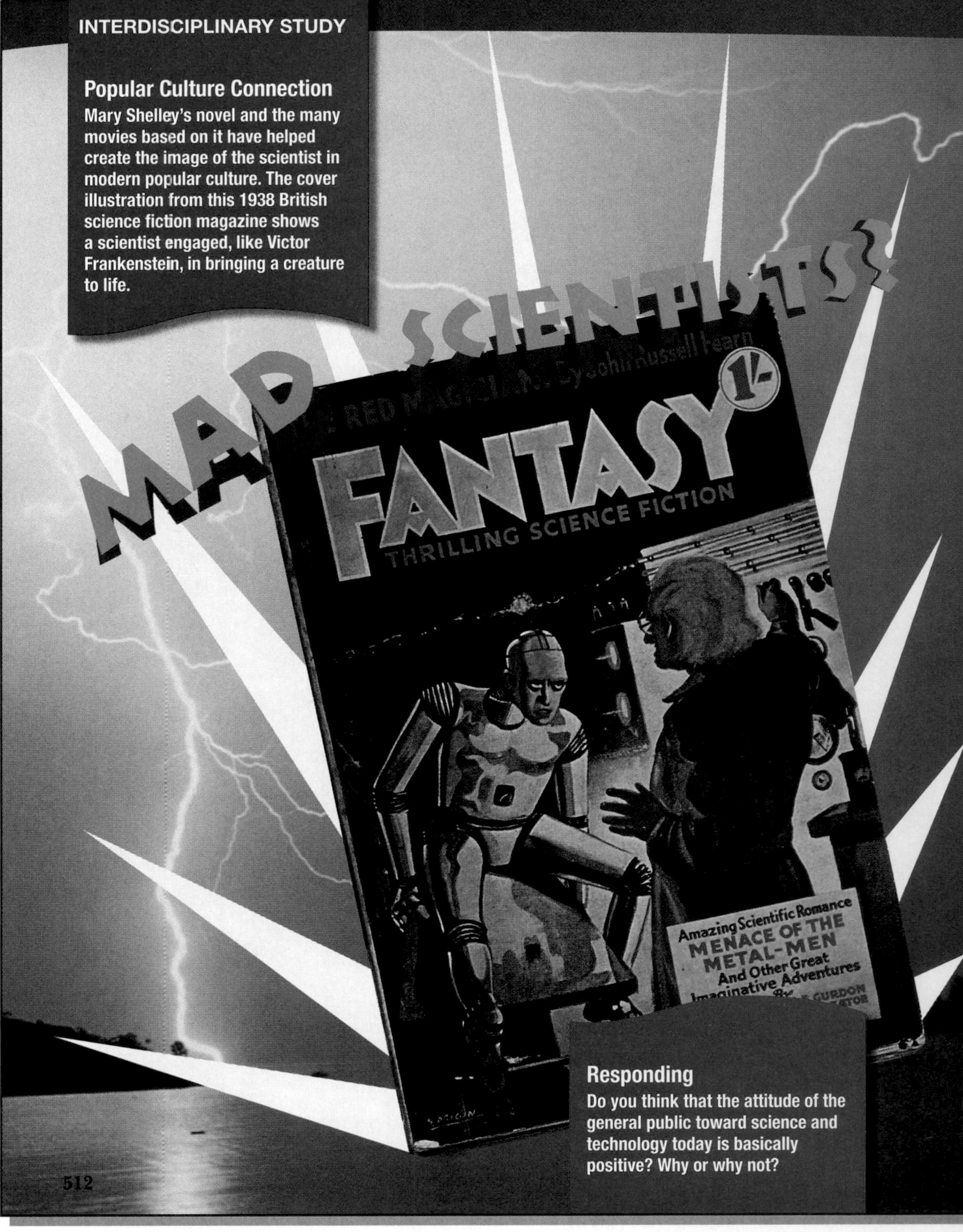

INTERDISCIPLINARY STUDY

Popular Culture Connection
Mary Shelley's novel and the many movies based on it have helped create the image of the scientist in modern popular culture. The cover illustration from this 1938 British science fiction magazine shows a scientist engaged, like Victor Frankenstein, in bringing a creature to life.

Responding
Do you think that the attitude of the general public toward science and technology today is basically positive? Why or why not?

512

MINI-LESSON: VISUAL LITERACY

Recognize Different Purposes for Art

Teach Ask students to study the image on this page. Explain that art has many purposes and that the picture on this magazine cover has a different purpose than the images on the preceding pages. Ask students to compare this image to other illustrations. What idea of scientists does the illustration promote? What does it tell you about the content of the magazine? Why would this image be inappropriate for the cover illustration of Shelley's *Frankenstein?* What is the purpose of this illustration?

Activity Ideas

- Students may create their own cover illustrations for *Frankenstein,* or for a comic book or novel which addresses similar issues.
- Individually or in groups, students may go to the library to find examples of different book jacket illustrations. Students may then write a short statement comparing the different illustrations, their purposes, and the image of the books that they project. In what ways can you judge a book by its cover?

Writing Workshop

My Own Monster

Assignment Using Mary Shelley's *Frankenstein* as a model, narrate a scene for your own horror story featuring a synthetic life form.

WRITER'S BLUEPRINT

Product	A scene for a horror story
Purpose	To explore the theme of exceeding human limits
Audience	People who enjoy suspense
Specs	As the writer of a successful scene, you should:

- ❑ Decide on a point of view—first person ("I") or third person ("He," "She," "It")—and stay with it when you write.
- ❑ Narrate your scene in a sequence of events with a clear beginning, middle, and end.
- ❑ Focus on a synthetic life form.
- ❑ Use dialogue that helps reveal your characters' thoughts and feelings.
- ❑ Convey a strong mood, such as suspense or triumph, through specific sights and sounds.
- ❑ Follow the rules of grammar, usage, spelling, and mechanics. Punctuate dialogue correctly.

OR . . . Rent a video of a favorite horror movie and view it critically. Take notes on the characters, action, and settings. Study how the filmmakers convey mood through lighting, music, color, and camera angles.

STEP 1 PREWRITING

Research favorite horror stories. With a small group, think of the literature you've read and the movies and TV shows you've seen that tell stories like the one you're about to write.

- What are your favorite horror stories?
- What are some favorite scenes, creatures, characters, and settings from these stories? What makes them so memorable?

Writing Workshop

WRITER'S BLUEPRINT

Specs

The Specs in the Writer's Blueprint address these writing and thinking skills:

- point of view
- sequencing
- using dialogue
- developing mood
- using sensory details
- maintaining consistent verb tense

These Specs serve as your lesson objectives, and they form the basis for the **Assessment Criteria Specs** for a superior paper, which appear on the final TE page for this lesson. You might want to read through the *Assessment Criteria Specs* with students when you begin the lesson.

Linking Literature to Writing

Go over with students in detail a short passage from *Frankenstein.* Have students pick out from the passage the details about it that, to them, signal a horror story. Make a list of these details and have students use it to help them with the first prewriting activity.

STEP 1 PREWRITING

Research horror stories

For additional support, see the worksheets referenced below.

Unit 5 Resource Book
Prewriting Worksheets, pp. 91–92

WRITING WORKSHOP OVERVIEW

Product
Narrative writing: A scene for a horror story

Prewriting
Research favorite horror stories—Brainstorm creature characteristics—Try a quickwrite—Plan the scene
Unit 5 Resource Book
Prewriting Worksheets, pp. 91–92

Drafting
As you write
Transparency Collection
Student Models for Writing Workshop 19, 20

Revising
Make a drawing—Ask a partner—Strategy: Strengthening Mood
Unit 5 Resource Book
Revising Worksheet, p. 93

Editing
Ask a partner—Strategy: Maintaining Consistent Verb Tense
Unit 5 Resource Book
Grammar Worksheet p. 94
Grammar Check Test p. 95

Presenting
Read Aloud
Illustrate Text

Looking Back
Self-evaluate—Reflect—For Your Working Portfolio
Unit 5 Resource Book
Assessment Worksheet, p. 96
Transparency Collection
Fine Art Transparency 10

Brainstorm creature characteristics

Some students may want to sketch their creatures.

Try a quickwrite

Students might simply write a series of images or impressions without worrying about structure or complete sentences. Again, students may want to make sketches as part of the process.

Plan the scene

Students might write all the events first on note cards or strips of paper so that they can rearrange them until they are satisfied with the order.

Connections to **Writer's Notebook**

For selection-related prompts, refer to Writer's Notebook.

Connections to **Writer's Resource**

For additional writing prompts, refer to Writer's Resource.

STEP 2 DRAFTING

The Student Models

The **transparencies** referenced below are authentic student models. Review them with the students before they draft. These questions will help:

1. Has each writer created a synthetic life form that is believable enough to be frightening? What would you change about the creature to make it more believable or more terrifying?

2. Focus on mood. What sorts of details could you add to strengthen the mood of each model?

Transparency Collection
Student Models fo Writing Workshop 19, 20

LITERARY SOURCE
"Beautiful—Great God! His yellow skin scarcely covered the work of muscles and arteries beneath; his hair was of a lustrous black, and flowing; his teeth of a pearly whiteness. . . ."
from *Frankenstein* by Mary Shelley

Brainstorm creature characteristics. To help you develop a unique creature, first reread the description of Frankenstein's monster on page 497. See if you can draw the monster, based on Shelley's vivid descriptive language. Then discuss other possible characteristics for a synthetic life form and arrange them in a web like the one shown.

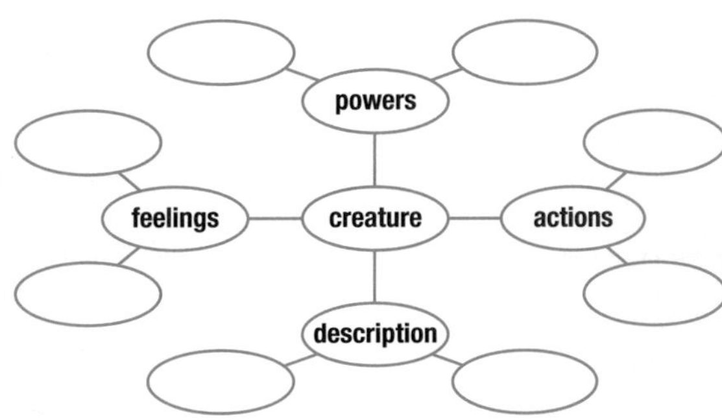

Try a quickwrite. For five or ten minutes, write about your scene. How will it start? How will it end? What will happen in-between? Jot down whatever comes to mind about the plot, characters, and setting.

Plan the scene. Use an organizer like the one shown to plot out your scene from start to finish.

OR . . .
If you're good at drawing, you might make a storyboard instead of an organizer. Draw a picture on a separate piece of paper to represent each event and make notes on the back about action, dialogue, and mood.

Events	Possible Dialogue	Mood	Sights and Sounds to Convey Mood
1. We open in the lab with scientist and assistant as they discover elixir of life.	Scientist: "We shall be gods now, Jamie!" Jamie: "Gods? I wonder."	suspenseful, ominous	—monster's glistening skin —bubbling of greenish liquid —scientist's pounding pulse —clock ticking —dark shadows
2.			

STEP 2 DRAFTING

As you write, keep these tips in mind:

- Begin with dialogue. Have one character ask another character a question that gets things rolling.

MINI-LESSON: DRAFTING

Getting Started

This activity may help students get started drafting. Have them read and respond to the following story starters. After they decide which are more likely to keep them reading, have them discuss why.

> I do not share this story with all whom I meet. I have told to only a few. Now I will tell it to you. The tale I am about to share with you is true. . . .
>
> The incision was not yet healed, and the stitches were visible from a few feet away—obviously not the work of a plastic surgeon. . . .
>
> "No one opens that door," he said firmly. The strained smile told me that he was not really pleased with my presence. . . .
>
> She was sitting at a table when it all began, folding laundry. She folded each sheet precisely and laid it in the basket. She was a tall woman with hair the color of dull sunlight and small, sharp eyes. . . .

- Use a frame-and-flashback structure. Begin in the present as the main character introduces the scene. Write the rest of the scene in past tense as a flashback, and return to the present for a closing comment from the main character.

COMPUTER TIP
If you use frame-and-flashback structure, you might put the present-tense parts of the scene in italics.

STEP 3 REVISING

Make a drawing of your life form and set it aside. When you exchange papers, in the next step, draw each other's "monsters," based on the writer's text. When you return papers and drawings, compare your partner's drawing with your own to see whether your description is vivid enough to help the reader "get the picture."

Ask a partner to look over your draft and comment before you revise.

✔ Have I written a scene for a horror story featuring a synthetic life form of my own design?

✔ Have I narrated the scene from a consistent point of view throughout?

✔ What kind of mood have I created? What are some sights and sounds I could add to strengthen this mood?

Revising Strategy

Strengthening Mood

Mood is important in horror fiction. Notice the details that contribute to the mood of dread and repulsion in the Literary Source at the right. Notice similar details in the second sentence below.

weak mood	I looked carefully around the unfamiliar room for signs that the creature might be there or perhaps somewhere nearby.
strong mood	As my pulse pounded, my terrified eyes peered into the strange room's gloomy shadows for signs of the lurking creature.

Look for ways to strengthen the mood when you revise your scene.

LITERARY SOURCE
"I started from my sleep with horror; a *cold dew* covered my forehead, my *teeth chattered*, and every limb became convulsed: when, by the *dim and yellow light of the moon*, as it forced its way through the window shutters, I beheld the wretch—the *miserable monster* whom I had created."
from *Frankenstein* by Mary Shelley

STEP 3 REVISING

Made a drawing

You might want to remind students to bring colored pencils or markers.

Ask a partner (Peer assessment)

Remind students to offer their peers detailed feedback on specific parts of their compositions rather than vague generalizations.

Revising Strategy: Strengthening Mood

Ask students what words come to mind when they hear the term mood. Discuss the word's connotations when used in the context of creative writing. Have students generate a list of words that would set an appropriate mood for a scene from a horror story.

For additional support, see the worksheet referenced below.

Unit 5 Resource Book
Revising Worksheet, p. 93

Connections to **Writer's Resource**

Refer to the Grammar, Usage, and Mechanics Handbook on Writer's Resource.

BUILDING ENGLISH PROFICIENCY

Analyzing Details

A discussion of details that can lead readers to expect a horror story situation might help students, especially those less familiar with American popular culture, to choose details that will lead the audience for their own work.

1. Have groups of students brainstorm lists of details or events that help an audience guess they are reading or watching a horror story (for example, the lights go out, the doors creak, a cat howls).
2. Make a master list of details on the chalkboard.
3. Ask students to offer reasons why certain details prepare audiences to be frightened.

STEP 4 EDITING

Ask a partner (Peer assessment)

Have students break into groups of five and complete a round robin review session in which each paper is looked over by four students.

Editing Strategy: Maintaining Consistent Verb Tense

Remind students that while verb tenses will vary within any narrative, as when characters in the present tense talk about things that happened in the past, the verbs used to narrate the action during the time the actual scene takes place, whether it be present or past, must be consistent. Point this out in the revised student model.

For additional support, see the mini-lesson at the bottom of this page and the worksheets referenced below.

Unit 5 Resource Book
Grammar Worksheet, p. 94
Grammar Check Test, p. 95

Connections to
Writer's Resource

Refer to the Grammar, Usage, and Mechanics Handbook on Writer's Resource.

STEP 4 EDITING

Ask a partner to review your revised draft before you edit it. When you edit, watch for errors in grammar, usage, spelling, and mechanics. Pay special attention to problems with verb tense.

FOR REFERENCE
For more on consistent verb tense, see the Language and Grammar Handbook at the back of this text.

Editing Strategy

Maintaining Consistent Verb Tense

Shifting verb tenses to go into and out of a flashback is fine, but you don't want to confuse readers by shifting tenses without good reason. Why has the writer of the passage below, who's narrating his scene in past tense, made the revising change?

I threw my arms in the air and roared with joy.

"We've done it, Jamie!" I cried.

"Yes!" he ~~answers~~ *answered* back, "We have."

Notice how the writer of the draft below, who's narrated her scene in present tense, fixed mistakes with inconsistent verb tense.

STUDENT MODEL

The people here don't know that I'm the cause of all this. There are children here. A little boy holds a teddy bear that ~~was~~ *is* missing one eye. A girl holds the hem of her dress and swings it up and down. Some people came here prepared with extra food and changes of clothing. Others simply ran like rabbits down a hole.

"Just think of them up there," ~~said~~ *says* a man. "Running around on our sidewalks, in our buildings."

MINI-LESSON: GRAMMAR

Maintaining Consistent Verb Tense

Have students edit the following paragraph paying close attention to consistent verb tense.

All the while her thoughts are racing far into the night. She wondered where this ride could possibly end and she worried about those left behind. She thinks to herself, but out loud nonetheless, "This road is too icy to be driving on." No one replied.

Unit 5 Resource Book
Grammar Worksheet, p. 94
Grammar Check Test, p. 95

STEP 5 PRESENTING

Here are suggestions for presenting your narrative:

- Read your story to family members and friends in a suitably suspenseful atmosphere, with dark shadows and tense music in the background.
- With your final copy, consider including sketches of characters, floor plans of rooms, maps of settings—whatever you think might make your story more vivid and inviting.

STEP 6 LOOKING BACK

Self-evaluate. How would *you* rate your narrative? Look back at the Writer's Blueprint and evaluate it on each point, from 6 (superior) to 1 (inadequate).

Reflect. Look back at your scene as if someone else had written it and write answers to these questions:

✔ What does the scene tell me about the author's attitude toward exceeding human limits?

✔ On a scale of 1 (dull) to 10 (terrifying), how suspenseful and horrifying was this scene?

✔ Would I like to read more horror stories by this writer? Why?

For Your Working Portfolio Add your finished product and reflection responses to your working portfolio.

STEP 5 PRESENTING

Read Aloud

Before students present their scenes, have them discuss the best atmospheres in which to share scary stories.

Illustrate Text

You might have students look over magazine and newspaper articles and reference books for ideas on how to use illustrations for clairty.

STEP 6 LOOKING BACK

Self-evaluate

The *Assessment Criteria Specs* at the bottom of this page are for a superior paper. You might want to post these in the classroom. Students can then evaluate themselves based on these criteria.

For a complete scoring rubric, use the *Assessment Worksheet* referenced below.

Unit 5 Resource Book
Assessment Worksheet, p. 96

Reflect

After students reflect on paper, ask them to discuss how their thoughts on the subject of human limitations have been affected by this writing project.

To further explore the theme, use the Fine Art Transparency referenced below.

Transparency Collection
Fine Art Writing Prompt 10

ASSESSMENT CRITERIA SPECS

Here are the criteria for a superior paper. A full six-level rubric for this paper appears on the Assessment Worksheet referenced below.

6 Superior The writer of a 6 paper impressively meets these criteria:

- Presents a suspenseful scene focusing on a synthetic life form.
- Grabs the reader's attention from the beginning and holds interest through sustained suspense.
- Maintains consistent point of view as well as consistent verb tense.
- Presents events in a clearly recognizable sequence the reader has no trouble following.
- Conveys a strong mood through vivid sensory details.
- Uses dialogue to reveal the characters' thoughts and feelings as well.
- Makes few, if any, mistakes in grammar, usage, mechanics, and spelling, including the punctuation of dialogue.

Unit 5 Resource Book
Assessment Worksheet, p. 96

Beyond Print

Teaching Objectives

- to learn about the techniques and special effects used in producing horror films
- to plan a scene for a horror film

Curricular Connection: Media Literacy

This article provides the opportunity to make students more aware of how filmmakers use various techniques and effects to create the mood of a film.

Introduce

Invite students to name their favorite horror films and tell what they remember best about each. Encourage them to describe the special effects, music, lighting, makeup worn by the characters, and other techniques that made the movies memorable and horrific. Then ask students to read the lesson. You might return to the discussion afterwards and invite students to discuss how the techniques described were used in the movies they remember.

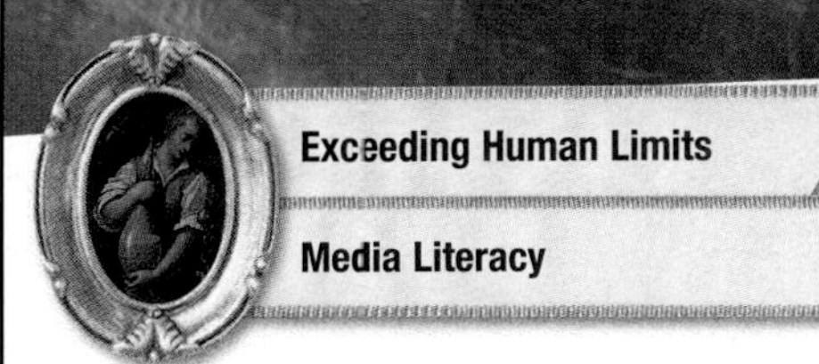

Beyond Print

Looking at Horror Movies

You may or may not find Mary Shelley's original *Frankenstein* a novel of horror today, but almost all of the movies and television programs that have been based on it have emphasized elements of horror. Although Hollywood may be the world's movie capital, England, Germany, France, and other countries have turned out notable horror movies as well. Here are some of the techniques that filmmakers of all countries have found effective.

- **Setting** A spooky setting, such as a drafty castle, an abandoned house, a graveyard at night, always adds a horrific effect. What is the setting in this photograph from the 1931 movie *Frankenstein*?
- **Composition** The closeness of people and objects to the camera lens and their arrangement within the picture frame can create emotional impact. A typical composition might show a monster looming over a helpless victim, but here Igor (an assistant of Dr. Frankenstein's) is shown menacing the creature.
- **Movement** A slow, methodical movement—such as when a killer stalks a victim—helps to build suspense. A lightning fast movement—such as when a killer suddenly strikes—helps create shock.
- **Editing** Film editing is the process of cutting images apart and rearranging them with other images. In one scene, for example, you may see a monster attacking, then a closeup of the screaming victim, then the monster's teeth and claws, then the torch the victim has dropped, and so on.
- **Sound** Screams are to be expected in horror films, as well as some non-human noises for the monster to make. Violent music often serves as a background for violent actions, but sometimes dead silence can create an unbearable suspense.
- **Lighting** Darkness and shadows are horrific in themselves, which is why so many scenes take place by moonlight, or with the light of candles or a torch, as is shown here. Note the shadows cast on the stone walls by the flickering torch.

ANOTHER APPROACH

Analyze a Horror Movie

Divide students into teams, and assign each team one of the techniques discussed in the article. Then show a video of a horror movie, such as James Whale's 1931 version of *Frankenstein,* starring Boris Karloff. Or if you prefer something shorter, consider a segment from Rod Serling's *The Twilight Zone* or *Night Gallery.* Then give each team ten minutes to discuss how the assigned technique was used in the film. Have teams share their conclusions with the class.

- **Makeup** Horror movies are renowned for their creative use of lifelike makeup—and now latex masks and body parts—to create frightening creatures. The famous monster makeup worn by Boris Karloff in *Frankenstein* took hours to apply.
- **Special FX** *FX* stands for "effects." Today, technological effects such as morphing (a technique that blends one person or object into another) and computer animation have raised the art to a high level.

Activity Options

1. What is happening in this frame from the movie *Frankenstein?* What do you think will happen next? Draw one frame that shows what might have happened immediately before this composition and another frame that shows what might happen next.
2. Plan a scene for a horror movie based on your writing in My Own Monster (pages 513–517). You might create a storyboard version of the scene you wrote to show setting, camera angles, lighting—and, of course, character makeup. What special effects would heighten the effect of horror in your movie scene?

Activity Options

Activity 1 Urge students to imagine themselves in the role of the director of a horror film. This scene is part of a sequence that must frighten the audience. How does this frame fit the sequence?

Activity 2 Suggest that students first choose events and characters that will be horrific. Then they can use the special effects to enhance the quality of horror that is already built into their plot.

BUILDING ENGLISH PROFICIENCY

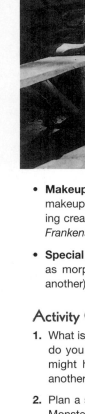

Analyzing Color

Bring in a number of paint chip samples, available in hardware or home supply stores. If possible, get oversized chips, or use multi-colored construction paper. Let students select those colors that they would use to establish a variety of moods. What colors would suggest to them danger? cheer? evil? Can they identify which colors are warm? which are cool?

Unit Wrap-Up

MULTICULTURAL CONNECTION

Emphasize that people's visions and dreams and the way that they decide to spend their lives are influenced by culture, by family and upbringing, and by personal experiences.

Individuality

Possible Response Answers will vary. Use the question to guide a discussion of the complications inherent in making the choice. Emphasize that neither choice is wrong.

Change

Possible Response Answers may vary. Students should explain why they think the change is so important. Encourage them to consider the personal sacrifices they must make in working for change.

Choice

Possible Response Answers will vary. Students should give reasons for their choices of limits. Some students may argue that there are no limits that humans should not attempt to exceed.

Activities

Activity 1 Suggest that students use dotted and solid lines or use different colors to indicate the strength of relationships.

Activity 2 You might allow students to form nominating committees to choose recipients for their awards. Announcement of prizes can be used to stimulate a discussion between groups regarding differences in their choices.

Activity 3 You may wish to set aside a few minutes each week to discuss the human limits highlighted on your bulletin board.

Multicultural Connections

Individuality

Part One: Visions and Dreams Blake, Wordsworth, Coleridge, and Keats, all writers of great individuality, changed the artistic life of England and pointed out further necessary changes.

■ Do you think it's more important for people to work toward realizing their own individuality, their own visions and dreams, or to make the choice to work for change to benefit others?

Change

Part Two: The Outsider The choice to assert your individuality can also make you an outsider; the efforts of Burns, Wollstonecraft, Byron, and Shelley to change the lives of their fellow humans, however, made them part of the greater community.

■ Choose the single most important change that should be made in your culture. Is it important enough for you to work actively for it?

Choice

Part Three: Exceeding Human Limits A person can choose to live among human beings or apart, to work with them or separately, as does Shelley's Victor Frankenstein.

■ Which human limit do you think is the most important one not to exceed? What changes would our culture experience if that limit were broken? What would its effect be on individuality?

Activities

1. Construct a sociogram for your group, in which each person is represented by a circle with a name, and the circles are connected by lines to show relationships. Extend your sociogram to show friends, classmates, and family members.
2. Who are the people working for change in our culture and in other cultures? How successful have they been so far? Create a prize, such as the Nobel Peace Prize, and award it.
3. Compile a bulletin board of newspaper and magazine articles on various human limits—such as genetic engineering—that are currently being tested, if not broken. Keep it up to date.

Independent and Group Projects

Media

Create a Mini-Biography Choose one of the writers in this unit and create a ten-minute audio or video biography, focusing on the life or career of that person or on the lasting impact of his or her work. You will have to do some research to find additional images and, perhaps, writing or quotations. Include music, sound effects, and graphics as appropriate.

Debate

Escape or Reform? The Romantic period was characterized in part by a love of nature, idealization of rural life, and appreciation for wild scenery, untouched by human attempts at "improvement." Were these sentiments an attempt to escape the smoke-filled skies of expanding industrial towns and the wretched poverty of their inhabitants? Or were Romantic writers hoping to stimulate reform? Organize two teams to debate the question of how much influence a writer can hope to have. Team members may have to do some further research on writers and their causes.

Research

On the Go You are organizing a "Romantic Highlights Tour" of England. Prepare a brochure, complete with map, of your destinations. What places will you visit? Will you include a few descriptive paragraphs of each place? Will your tour include hikes? cycling? climbing? lectures? cozy inns or camping out? Will you include in your brochure photos of places or people?

Oral Report

A Novel Experience Two notable English novelists during the Romantic Era were Jane Austen and Sir Walter Scott. With your teacher's help, choose a novel by either of these writers, read it, and review it for the class. As an alternative, watch a videotape of a movie that has been made from one of their novels and review it, concentrating on what you understand to be the Romantic elements of the stories they tell.

UNIT 5 OPTIONS

Media

You may wish to have students work in pairs or small groups to complete this activity.

- Encourage students to create a story-board before creating a video.
- Students might choose to dramatize their biographies by presenting them as dialogues between an interviewer and friends of the writer.

Debate

Direct students to follow standard debate format.

- Establish time limits.
- Students who do not want to participate in the debate might be asked to decide the winner of the debate.

Research

- Have students consider commenting on changes that have occurred since the Romantic Era.
- Online resources and travel agencies may give students access to current travel information and even first-hand descriptions of specific places.

Oral Report

- Students may prepare a checklist of Romantic elements to look for in their books or movies.
- If two or more students choose this activity, you might allow them to present their reviews in a panel discussion.

Unit Test

Unit 5 Resource Book
New Selection
Test 1
Test 2

Glossaries, Handbooks, and Indexes

Glossary of Literary Terms

Words within entries in SMALL CAPITAL LETTERS refer to other entries in the Glossary of Literary Terms.

allegory (al′ə gôr′ē), a NARRATIVE either in VERSE or prose, in which characters, action, and sometimes SETTING represent abstract concepts apart from the literal meaning of the story. The underlying meaning may have moral, social, religious, or political significance, and the characters are often PERSONIFICATIONS of abstract ideas such as charity, hope, greed, or envy. Edmund Spenser used allegory in his long poem, *The Faerie Queene,* which was dedicated to Queen Elizabeth I.

alliteration (ə lit′ə rā′ shən), the REPETITION of consonant sounds at the beginnings of words or within words, particularly in accented syllables. It can be used to reinforce meaning, to unify thought, or simply to produce a musical effect. "Grim and greedy the gruesome monster . . ." *(Beowulf,* page 8) is an example.

allusion (ə lü′zhən), a brief reference to a person, event, or place, real or fictitious, or to a work of art. Auden's "Musée des Beaux Arts" (page 808) alludes to *The Fall of Icarus,* a painting by Bruegel, and to the Greek MYTH that inspired the painting.

analogy (ə nal′ə jē), a comparison made between two objects, situations, or ideas that are somewhat alike but unlike in most respects. Frequently an unfamiliar or complex object or idea will be explained through comparison to a familiar or simpler one. For example, Blake refers to Jesus as the meek and mild "Lamb of God" (page 404).

anapest (an′ə pest), a three-syllable metrical FOOT consisting of two unaccented syllables followed by an accented syllable (⏑ ⏑ ′), as in *interfere.* In the following lines, anapestic feet combine with iambic feet.

> It was in/and about/the Mar-/tinmas time,/
> When the green/leaves were/a falling. . . .
> from "Bonny Barbara Allan"

anastrophe (ə nas′trə fē)
See INVERSION.

antagonist (an tag′ə nist), a character in a story or play who opposes the chief character or PROTAGONIST. In *Beowulf* (page 8) Grendel is an antagonist, as is Satan in Milton's *Paradise Lost* (page 255).

aphorism (af′ə riz′əm), a brief saying embodying a moral, such as Pope's "Know then thyself, presume not God to scan; / The proper study of mankind is Man."

apostrophe (ə pos′trə fē), a figure of speech in which an absent person, an abstract concept, or an inanimate object is directly addressed. "Milton! thou shouldst be living at this hour . . ." from Wordsworth's "London, 1802" is an example of the first; "Death, be not proud . . ." from Donne's Holy Sonnet 10 is an example of the second; and "O sylvan Wye! thou wanderer through the woods . . ." from Wordsworth's "Tintern Abbey" (page 409) is an example of the third.

archetype (är′kə tīp), an image, story pattern, or character type that recurs frequently in literature and evokes strong, often unconscious, associations in the reader. For example, the wicked witch and the enchanted prince are character types widely dispersed throughout folk tales and literature. The story of a hero who undertakes a dangerous quest, as in *Beowulf* (page 8) or *Sir Gawain and the Green Knight* (page 61), is a recurrent story pattern.

assonance (as′n əns), the REPETITION of similar vowel sounds followed by different consonant sounds in stressed syllables or words. It is often used instead of RHYME. In this line from Tennyson's "Ulysses" (page 531), the words *sleep, feed,* and *me* are assonant.

> . . . That hoard, and sleep, and feed, and know
> not me.

autobiography *See* BIOGRAPHY.

ballad, a NARRATIVE song or poem passed on in the oral tradition. It often makes use of REPETITION and DIALOGUE. An example is "Edward" (page 26). If the author of a ballad is unknown, it is called a *folk ballad;* if the author is known, it is called a *literary ballad.*

ballad stanza, a STANZA usually consisting of four alternating lines of iambic TETRAMETER and TRIMETER and rhyming the second and fourth lines.

> The wind sae cauld blew south and north,
> And blew into the floor;
> Quoth our goodman to our goodwife,
> "Gae out and bar the door."
> from "Get Up and Bar the Door" (page 28)

See IAMB.

biography, an account of a person's life. An example is Boswell's *The Life of Samuel Johnson, L L. D.* (page 361). AUTOBIOGRAPHY is the story of all or part of a person's life written by the person who lived it. Brittain's *Testament of Youth* (page 743) is an autobiography.

blank verse, unrhymed iambic PENTAMETER.

I may/assert/Eter-/nal Prov/idence,
And jus/tify/the ways/of God/to men.

Milton, from *Paradise Lost* (page 255)

Macbeth (page 118) and "Ulysses" (page 531) are also written in blank verse.

See IAMB.

cacophony (kə kof′ə nē), a succession of harsh, discordant sounds in either poetry or prose, used to achieve a specific effect. Note the harshness of sound and difficulty of articulation in these lines:

Light thickens, and the crow
Makes wing to the rooky wood. . . .

Shakespeare, from *Macbeth* (page 118)

caesura (si zhůr′ə), a pause in a line of VERSE, usually near the middle. It most often reflects the sense of the line and is frequently greater than a normal pause. It is used to add variety to regular METER and therefore to add emphasis to certain words. A caesura can be indicated by punctuation, the grammatical construction of a sentence, or the placement of lines on a page. For purposes of study, the mark indicating a caesura is two short, vertical lines.

Born but to die, || and reasoning but to err:
Alike in ignorance, || his reason such,
Whether he thinks too little, || or too much . . .

Pope, from *An Essay on Man*

The caesura is a particularly important device in Anglo-Saxon poetry.

caricature (kar′ə kə chůr), exaggeration of prominent features of appearance or character.

carpe diem (kär′pe dē′əm), Latin for "seize the day," or enjoy life's pleasures while you are able. The term is applied to a THEME frequently found in LYRIC poetry, as in Herrick's "To the Virgins, to Make Much of Time" (page 233).

Cavalier poetry, a type of LYRIC poetry of the late Renaissance period, influenced by poet Ben Jonson and the Elizabethan court poets, and consisting mostly of love poems. Supporters of Charles I (1625–1649) were called Cavaliers and included Robert Herrick (page 233).

characterization, the methods an author uses to develop a character in a literary work. A character's physical traits and personality may be described, as are those of John Thomas in Lawrence's "Tickets, Please" (page 758). A character's speech and behavior may be described, as are those of the Beast in "The Courting of Mr. Lyon" (page 933). The thoughts and feelings of a character or the reactions of other characters to an individual may be shown, as in Greene's "A Shocking Accident" (page 926). Any or all of these methods may be used in the same work.

classicism (klas′ə siz′əm), a style of literature characterized by attention to form and influenced by the classical writers of Greece and Rome. Many authors have been influenced by classicism, and it flourished especially during the Age of Reason.

climax, the decisive point in a story or play when the action changes course and begins to resolve itself. In *Macbeth,* the banquet scene in act 3 (page 148) when the ghost of Banquo appears to Macbeth is often regarded as the climax. Not every story or play has this kind of dramatic climax. Sometimes a character may simply resolve a problem in his or her mind. At times there is no resolution of the PLOT; the climax then comes when a character realizes that a resolution is impossible.

See also PLOT.

comedy, a play written primarily to amuse. In addition to arousing laughter, comic writing often appeals to the intellect. Thus the comic mode has often been used to "instruct" the audience about the follies of certain social conventions and human foibles, as in Shaw's *Pygmalion* (page 662). When used in this way, the comedy tends toward SATIRE.

comic relief, an amusing episode in a serious or tragic literary work, especially a drama, that is introduced to relieve tension. The drunken porter's scene in *Macbeth,* act 2, scene 3 is an example of comic relief.

conceit, an elaborate and surprising figure of speech comparing two very dissimilar things. It usually involves intellectual cleverness and ingenuity. In the last three STANZAS of "A Valediction: Forbidding Mourning" (page 227), Donne compares his soul and that of his love to the two legs or branches of a draftsman's compass used to make a circle. The previously unseen likeness as developed by the poet helps us to understand the subject described (the relationship of the lovers' souls) more clearly.

conflict, the struggle between two opposing forces. The four basic kinds of conflict are these: 1. a person against another person or ANTAGONIST, as in *Beowulf* (page 8); 2. a person against nature; 3. a person against society, as in Desai's "Studies in the Park" (page 833); and 4. two elements within a person struggling for mastery, as in Joyce's "Eveline" (page 790).

connotation, the emotional associations surrounding a word, as opposed to the word's literal meaning or DENOTATION. Some connotations are fairly universal, others quite personal. Many of the words in Shakespeare's "Sonnet 18" (page 111) suggest associations that cluster around the idea of summer.

consonance (kon′sə nəns), the repetition of consonant sounds that are preceded by different vowel sounds:

> For*l*orn! the very word is like a be*ll*
> To to*ll* me back from thee to my so*l*e se*l*f!
>
> Keats, from "Ode to a Nightingale" (page 426)

Consonance (also called SLANT RHYME) is an effective device for linking sound, MOOD, and meaning. In the lines above, the *l* sounds reinforce the melancholy mood.

couplet, a pair of rhyming lines with identical METER:

> True wit is Nature to advantage dressed,
> What oft was thought, but ne'er so well expressed.
>
> Pope, from *An Essay on Criticism* (page 325)

dactyl (dak′tl), a three-syllable metrical FOOT consisting of an accented syllable followed by two unaccented syllables (′⏑⏑) as in *settlement.* The following line is basically in dactylic HEXAMETER:

> Loosing his/arms from her/waist he flew/upward, a-/waiting the/sea beast.
>
> Charles Kingsley, from *Andromeda*

denotation the strict, literal meaning of a word.
See also CONNOTATION.

denouement (dā′nü män′), the resolution of the PLOT. The word is derived from a French word meaning "to untie."

dialect, a form of speech characteristic of a particular region or class, differing from the standard language in pronunciation, vocabulary, and grammatical form. Burns's poems (pages 450–452) are written in Scottish dialect. In Shaw's *Pygmalion* (page 662), Eliza Doolittle, as a flower girl, speaks in the cockney dialect characteristic of a certain part of London.

dialogue, conversation between two or more people in a literary work. Dialogue can help develop CHARACTERIZATION of those speaking and those spoken about, create MOOD, advance PLOT, and develop THEME.

diary, a record of daily happenings written by a person for his or her own use. The diarist is moved by a need to record daily routine and confess innermost thoughts. The diary makes up in immediacy and frankness what it lacks in artistic shape and coherence. An example is *The Diary* of Pepys (page 340).
See also JOURNAL.

diction, the author's choice of words and phrases in a literary work. This choice involves both the CONNOTATION and DENOTATION of a word as well as levels of usage. For example, the diction of the characters in Shaw's *Pygmalion* (page 662) indicates their education, background, and social standing.

drama, a literary work in verse or prose, written to be acted, that tells a story through the speech and actions of the characters. A drama may be a TRAGEDY, such as *Macbeth* (page 118), or a COMEDY, such as *Pygmalion* (page 662).

dramatic convention, any of several devices that the audience accepts as reality in a dramatic work. For instance, the audience accepts that an interval between acts may represent hours, days, weeks, months, or years; that a bare stage may be a meadow or an inner room; or that audible dialogue is supposed to represent whispered conversation.

dramatic monologue (mon′l ôg), a LYRIC poem in which the speaker addresses someone whose replies are not recorded. Sometimes the one addressed seems to be present, sometimes not. Examples are Robert Browning's "Porphyria's Lover" (page 539) and "My Last Duchess" (page 542).

elegy (el′ə gē), a solemn, reflective poem, usually about death, or about someone who has died, written in a formal style.

end rhyme, the rhyming of words at the ends of lines of poetry, as in Housman's "Loveliest of Trees" (page 601).

end-stopped line, a line of poetry that contains a complete thought, thus necessitating the use of a semicolon, colon, or period at the end:

> Great lord of all things, yet a prey to all;

Sole judge of truth, in endless error hurled:
The glory, jest, and riddle of the world!
Pope, from *An Essay on Man*

See also RUN-ON LINE.

epic, a long NARRATIVE poem (originally handed down in oral tradition—later a literary form) dealing with great heroes and adventures; having a national, world-wide, or cosmic setting; involving supernatural forces; and written in a deliberately ceremonial STYLE. Examples are *Beowulf* (page 8) and Milton's *Paradise Lost* (page 255).

epigram, any short, witty VERSE or saying, often ending with a wry twist:

'Tis with our judgments as our watches; none
Go just alike, yet each believes his own.
Pope, from *An Essay on Criticism* (page 325)

Compare with MAXIM *and* PROVERB.

epigraph, a motto or quotation at the beginning of a book, poem, or chapter, often indicating the THEME. An example is found at the beginning of Eliot's "The Hollow Men" (page 769).

epiphany (i pif′ə nē), a moment of enlightenment in which the underlying truth, essential nature, or meaning of something is suddenly made clear. Each of James Joyce's stories builds to an epiphany. In "Eveline" (page 790), it is the moment when she realizes she cannot go away with Frank.

epitaph (ep′ə taf), a brief statement commemorating a dead person, often inscribed on a tombstone. Malory's "Day of Destiny" (page 79) concludes with King Arthur's epitaph.

epithet (ep′ə thet), a descriptive expression, usually mentioning a quality or attribute of the person or thing being described. In *Beowulf* (page 8) the epithet *Spear-Danes* is used for the Danes. Often the epithet *Lion-Hearted* is applied to King Richard I (1157–1199).

essay, a brief composition that presents a personal viewpoint. An essay may present a viewpoint through formal analysis and argument, as in Defoe's "The Education of Women" (page 306), or it may be more informal in style, as in Orwell's "Shooting an Elephant" (page 860).

exposition, the beginning of a work of fiction, particularly a play, in which the author sets the amosphere and TONE, explains the SETTING, introduces the characters, and provides the reader with any other information needed in order to understand the PLOT.

extended metaphor, a comparison that is developed at great length, often through a whole work or a great part of it. It is common in poetry but is used in prose as well. Sir Walter Raleigh develops an extended metaphor comparing life to a play in his poem "What Is Our Life?" the first four lines of which appear here:

What is our life? a play of passion;
Our mirth, the music of division,
Our mothers' wombs the tiring-houses be
Where we are dressed for this short comedy.

See also METAPHOR.

fable, a brief TALE in which the characters are often animals, told to point out a moral truth.

falling action, the RESOLUTION of a dramatic PLOT, which takes place after the CLIMAX.

fantasy, a work that takes place in an unreal world, concerns incredible characters, or employs fictional scientific principles, as in "A Mad Tea Party" (page 547).

See also SCIENCE FICTION.

fiction, a type of literature drawn from the imagination of the author that tells about imaginary people and happenings. NOVELS and SHORT STORIES are fiction.

figurative language, language used in a nonliteral way to express a suitable relationship between essentially unlike things in order to furnish new effects or fresh insights. The more common figures of speech are SIMILE, METAPHOR, PERSONIFICATION, HYPERBOLE, and SYNECDOCHE.

flashback, interruption of a NARRATIVE to show an episode that happened before that particular point in the story.

foil, a character whose traits are the opposite of those of another character, and who thus points up the strengths or weaknesses of the other character. Henry Higgins and Liza Doolittle are foils in Shaw's *Pygmalion* (page 662).

folk literature, a type of early literature that was passed orally from generation to generation, and only written down after centuries. The authorship of folk literature is unknown. Folk literature includes MYTHS, FABLES, fairy tales, EPICS, and LEGENDS. Examples are *Beowulf* (page 8) and the Folk Ballads (pages 25–28).

foot, a group of syllables in VERSE usually consisting of one accented syllable and one or more unaccented syllables. A foot may occasionally, for variety, have two accented syllables (a SPONDEE) or two unaccented syllables. In the following lines the feet are separated by slanted lines.

Come live/with me/and be/my Love,
And we/will all/the plea-/sures prove. . . .
Marlowe, from "The Passionate Shepherd to His Love"

The most common line lengths are five feet (PENTAMETER), four feet (TETRAMETER), and three feet (TRIMETER). The lines quoted above are iambic tetrameter.

See also ANAPEST, DACTYL, IAMB *and* TROCHEE.

foreshadowing, a hint given to the reader of what is to come.

frame, a NARRATIVE device presenting a story or group of stories within the frame of a larger narrative. In Chaucer's *The Canterbury Tales* (page 47), the pilgrimage is the frame unifying and providing continuity for the stories told by the pilgrims.

free verse, a type of poetry that differs from conventional VERSE forms in being "free" from a fixed pattern of METER and RHYME, but using RHYTHM and other poetic devices. An example is Eliot's "The Hollow Men" (page 769).

gothic novel, a NOVEL written in a STYLE characterized by mystery, horror, and the supernatural, and usually having a medieval or other period SETTING. An example is Mary Shelly's *Frankenstein* (page 492).

heroic couplet, a pair of rhymed VERSE lines in iambic PENTAMETER:

All human things are subject to decay,
And when fate summons, monarchs must obey.
Dryden, from *Mac Flecknoe*

hexameter (hek sam′ə tər), a metrical line of six feet.

How man-/y weep-/ing eyes/I made/to pine/with woe . . .
Elizabeth I, "When I was Fair and Young"

humor, in literature, writing whose purpose is to amuse or to evoke laughter. Humorous writing can be sympathetic to human nature or satirical. Some forms of humor are IRONY, SATIRE, PARODY, and CARICATURE.

hyperbole (hī pėr′bə lē), a figure of speech involving great exaggeration. The effect may be serious or comic.

If thou be'st born to strange sights,
Things invisible to see,
Ride ten thousand days and nights,
Till age snow white hairs on thee. . . .
Donne, from "Song" (page 226)

iamb (ī′amb), a two-syllable metrical FOOT consisting of an unaccented syllable followed by an accented syllable (⌣ ′), as in *until*. The following line is in iambic PENTAMETER:

For God's/sake, hold/your tongue,/and let/me love. . . .
Donne, from "The Canonization"

idiom, an expression whose meaning cannot be understood from the ordinary meanings of the words in it. For example, "to give a leg up," is to provide someone assistance or encouragement; "to knuckle down" means to apply oneself or work hard.

imagery, the sensory details that provide vividness in a literary work and tend to arouse emotions or feelings in a reader that abstract language does not. Carter's "The Courtship of Mr. Lyon" (page 933) contains many sensory details.

incremental repetition, a form of REPETITION in which successive STANZAS advance the story or reveal a situation by changes in a single phrase or line. Often a question and answer form is used. An example is the ballad "Edward" (page 26).

inference, a reasonable conclusion about the behavior of a character or the meaning of an event, drawn from the limited information presented by the author. In Browning's "My Last Duchess" (page 542), the reader can infer a great deal about the character of the speaker, the Duke, from what he says.

in medias res (in mā′dē äs rās′), Latin for "in the middle of things." In a traditional EPIC the opening scene often begins in the middle of the action. Milton's *Paradise Lost* (page 255) opens with Satan and his angels already defeated and in Hell; later in the poem the story of the battle between Satan and the forces of Heaven, which led to this defeat, is told. This device may be used in any NARRATIVE form.

interior monologue, a technique used by writers to present the STREAM OF CONSCIOUSNESS of a fictional character, either directly by presenting what is passing through the character's mind or indirectly by the author's selection of and comments upon the character's thoughts. Joyce's

"Eveline" (page 790) consists largely of interior monologue.

internal rhyme, the rhyming of words or accented syllables within a line that may or may not have a RHYME at the end as well.

inversion, reversal of the usual order of the parts of a sentence, primarily for emphasis or to achieve a certain RHYTHM or RHYME. In the example that follows, lines 1, 4, and 5 contain inverted order.

In Seville was he born, a pleasant city,
  Famous for oranges and women—he
Who has not seen it will be much to pity,
  So says the proverb—and I quite agree;
Of all the Spanish towns is none more pretty.

Byron, from *Don Juan*

invocation the call on a deity or muse (classical goddess who inspired a poet) for help and inspiration. It is found at the beginning of traditional EPIC poems. In *Paradise Lost* (page 255) Milton invokes the "Heavenly Muse" instead of one of the traditional muses of poetry.

irony, the term used to describe a contrast between what appears to be and what really is. In *verbal irony,* the intended meaning of a statement or work is different from (often the opposite of) what the statement or work literally says, as in Swift's "A Modest Proposal" (page 296). *Understatement,* in which an idea is expressed less emphatically than it might be, is a form of verbal irony often used for humorous or cutting effect. For example, Johnson's remark in his "Letter to Chesterfield" (page 357): "To be so distinguished is an honor which, being very little accustomed to favors from the great, I know not well how to receive." *Irony of situation* refers to an occurrence that is contrary to what is expected or intended, as in Hardy's "Ah, Are You Digging on My Grave?" (page 577). *Dramatic irony* refers to a situation in which events or facts not known to a character on stage or in a fictional work are known to another character and the audience or reader. In Pope's *The Rape of the Lock* (page 314), events known to the sylph Ariel and to the reader are unknown to Belinda.

journal, a formal record of a person's daily experiences. It is less intimate or personal than a DIARY and more chronological than an AUTOBIOGRAPHY.

kenning, a metaphorical compound word used as a poetic device. In *Beowulf* (page 8) there are many examples of kennings: the king is the "ring-giver," the rough sea is the "whale-road," and the calm sea is the "swan-road."

legend, a story handed down from the past, often associated with some period in the history of a people. A legend differs from a MYTH in having some historical truth and often less of the supernatural. Malory's *Morte Darthur* (page 79) is based on legends of King Arthur and the Knights of the Round Table.

literary ballad *See* BALLAD.

lyric, a poem, usually short, that expresses some basic emotion or state of mind. It usually creates a single impression and is highly personal. It may be rhymed or unrhymed. A SONNET is a lyric poem. Other examples of lyrics are Burns's "A Red, Red Rose" (page 452) and most of the shorter poems of the Romantics.

magic realism, a fictional literary work that combines elements of dreams, magic, myths, and fairy tales, along with realistic elements. Carter's "The Courtship of Mr. Lyon" (page 933) can be described as magic realism.

maxim, a brief saying embodying a moral, such as "Look before you leap."

memoir (mem′wär), a form of AUTOBIOGRAPHY that is more concerned with personalities, events, and actions of public importance than with the private life of the writer. Orwell's "Shooting an Elephant" (page 860) is an example of memoir in the form of an essay.

metaphor, a figure of speech that makes a comparison, without *like* or *as,* between two basically unlike things that have something in common. This comparison may be stated (She was a stone) or implied (Her stony silence filled the room). In "Meditation 17" (page 228) Donne compares the individual to a chapter in a book and, later, to a piece of a continent.

See also SIMILE *and* FIGURATIVE LANGUAGE.

metaphysical poetry, poetry exhibiting a highly intellectual style that is witty, subtle, and sometimes fantastic, particularly in the use of CONCEITS. See especially the poems of Donne (pages 226–227).

meter, the pattern of stressed and unstressed syllables in POETRY. *See also* RHYTHM and FOOT.

metonymy a figure of speech in which a specific word naming an object is substituted for another word with which it is closely associated. An example is in Genesis: "In the sweat of thy face shalt thou eat bread." Here, *sweat* is used to represent hard physical labor.

mock epic, a SATIRE using the form and style of an EPIC poem to treat a trivial incident. Pope's *The Rape of the Lock* (page 314) is a mock epic.

monologue *See* SOLILOQUY *and* DRAMATIC MONOLOGUE.

mood, the overall atmosphere or prevailing emotional aura of a work. Coleridge's "Kubla Khan" (page 417) might be described as having a hypnotic, dreamlike mood or atmosphere. *See* TONE for a comparison.

moral, the lesson or inner meaning to be learned from a FABLE, TALE, or other story. The moral of "The Pardoner's Tale" in *The Canterbury Tales* (page 48), as stated by the Pardoner, is "Avarice is the root of all evil."

motif a character, incident, idea, or object that appears over and over in various works or in various parts of the same work. In Shakespeare's SONNETS (pages 111–112) the effect of time is a recurrent motif.

motivation, the process of presenting a convincing cause for the actions of a character in a dramatic or fictional work in order to justify those actions. Motivation usually involves a combination of external events and the character's psychological traits.

myth, a traditional story connected with the religion of a people, usually attempting to account for something in nature. A myth has less historical background than a LEGEND. Milton's *Paradise Lost* (page 255) has mythic elements in its attempts to interpret aspects of the universe.

narrative, a story or account of an event or a series of events. It may be told either in POETRY or in prose, and it may be either fictional or true.

narrative poetry, a poem that tells a story or recounts a series of events. It may be either long or short. EPICS and BALLADS are types of narrative poetry.

narrator, the teller of a story. The teller may be a character in the story, as in Mary Shelley's *Frankenstein* (page 492); an anonymous voice outside the story, as in Greene's "A Shocking Accident" (page 926); or the author, as in Brittain's *Testament of Youth* (page 776). A narrator's attitude toward his or her subject is capable of much variation; it can range from one of indifference to one of extreme conviction and feeling.

See also PERSONA *and* POINT OF VIEW.

naturalism, a literary movement in the late nineteenth and early twentieth century characterized by writing that depicts events as rigidly determined by the forces of heredity and environment. The world described tends to be bleak. There are elements of naturalism in the work of Thomas Hardy.

neoclassicism, writing of a later period that shows the influence of the Greek and Roman classics. The term is often applied to English literature of the eighteenth century.

See also CLASSICISM.

nonfiction, any writing that is not FICTION; any type of prose that deals with real people and happenings. BIOGRAPHY and history are types of nonfiction. An example is the excerpt from Boswell's *The Life of Samuel Johnson, LL. D.* (page 401).

novel, a long work of NARRATIVE prose fiction dealing with characters, situations, and SETTINGS that imitate those of real life. Among the authors in this text who have written novels are Thomas Hardy, Joseph Conrad, James Joyce, Virginia Woolf, H. G. Wells, Anita Desai, Graham Greene, and Angela Carter.

ode, a long LYRIC poem, formal in STYLE and complex in form, often written in commemoration or celebration of a special quality, object, or occasion. Examples are Shelley's "Ode to the West Wind" (page 469) and Keats's "Ode to a Nightingale" (page 426).

onomatopoeia (on′ə mat′ə pē′ə), a word or words used in such a way that the sound imitates the thing spoken of. Some single words in which sound suggests meaning are *hiss, smack, buzz, and hum.* An example in which sound echoes sense throughout the whole phrase is "The murmurous haunt of flies on summer eves," from Keats's "Ode to a Nightingale"(page 426).

parable, a brief fictional work that concretely illustrates an abstract idea or teaches some lesson or truth. It differs from a FABLE in that its characters are generally people rather than animals, and it differs from an ALLEGORY in that its characters do not necessarily represent abstract qualities.

paradox, a statement, often metaphorical, that seems to be self-contradictory but that has valid meaning, as in "The child is father of the Man" from Wordsworth's poem "My Heart Leaps Up" (page 413). Woolf describes a paradoxical woman in "Shakespeare's Sister" (page 814).

parallelism, the use of phrases or sentences that are similar in structure. Churchill's words in his Blood, Toil, Tears, and Sweat speech (page 869) are an example of parallelism: "You ask, What is our aim? I can answer in one word: Victory—victory at all costs, victory in spite of all terror, victory, however long and hard the road may be. . . ."

parody, a humorous imitation of serious writing. It follows the form of the original, but often changes the sense to ridicule the writer's STYLE. Eliot's "The Hollow Men" (page 769) has a parody of the children's rhyme "Here we go round the mulberry bush."

See also SATIRE.

pastoral, a conventional form of LYRIC poetry presenting an idealized picture of rural life.

pentameter (pen tam′ə ter), a metrical line of five feet.

> Shall I/compare/thee to/a sum-/mer's day?
> Thou art/more love-/ly and/more tem-/perate.
> Shakespeare, from Sonnet 18 (page 111)

persona (pər sō′nə), the mask or voice of the author or the author's creation in a particular work. Tennyson is the author of "Ulysses" (page 531), but the persona, in this case the SPEAKER, is Ulysses, through whom Tennyson speaks. In "A Shocking Accident" (page 926), Graham Greene has assumed a voice or persona—detached, witty, ironic—in telling the story.

See also NARRATOR.

personification (pər son′ə fə kā′shən), the representation of abstractions, ideas, animals, or inanimate objects as human beings by endowing them with human qualities. In Shelley's "Ode to the West Wind" (page 469), the Mediterranean is personified:

> Thou who didst waken from his summer dreams
> The blue Mediterranean, where he lay,
> Lulled by the coil of his crystàlline streams. . . .

Personification is one kind of FIGURATIVE LANGUAGE.

play *See* DRAMA.

plot, a series of happenings in a literary work. The term is used to refer to the action as it is organized around a CONFLICT and builds through complication to a CLIMAX followed by a DENOUEMENT or RESOLUTION. (See the plot diagram on page 116.)

poetry, a type of literature that creates an emotional response by the imaginative use of words patterned to produce a desired effect through RHYTHM, sound, and meaning. Poetry may be RHYMED or unrhymed. Among the many forms of poetry are the EPIC, ODE, LYRIC, SONNET, BALLAD, and ELEGY.

point of view, the vantage point from which an author presents the actions and characters of a story. The story may be related by a character (the *first-person* point of view), or the story may be told by a NARRATOR who does not participate in the action (the *third-person* point of view). Further, the third-person narrator may be *omniscient* (om nish′ənt)—able to see into the minds of all characters, as in Lawrence's "Tickets, Please" (page 758). Or the third-person narrator may be *limited*—confined to a single character's perceptions, as in Joyce's "Eveline" (page 790). An author who describes only what can be seen, like a newspaper reporter, is said to use an *objective* or *dramatic* point of view.

prologue, a section preceding the main body of a work and serving as an introduction. An example is the *Prologue to The Canterbury Tales* (page 47).

protagonist (prō tag′ənist), the leading character in a literary work.

See also ANTAGONIST.

proverb, a short, wise saying, often handed down from the past, that expresses a truth or shrewd observation about life. "Haste makes waste" is an example. There are many proverbs in the Bible.

psalm, a song or poem in praise of God. The term is most often applied to the songs or hymns in the Book of Psalms in the Bible. An example is the Twenty-third Psalm on page 272.

pun, a play on words; a humorous use of a word where it can have two different meanings (*pitcher / pitcher*) or two or more words with the same or nearly the same sound but with different meanings (*night / knight*).

quatrain, a verse STANZA of four lines. This stanza may take many forms, according to line lengths and RHYME patterns. Herrick's poem "To the Virgins, to Make Much of Time" (page 233) contains quatrains.

rationalism, a philosophy that emphasizes the role of reason rather than of sensory experience and faith in answering basic questions of human existence. It was most influential during the Age of Reason (1660–1780) and influenced such writers of that period as Swift and Pope.

realism, a way of representing life that emphasizes ordinary people in everyday experiences. The excerpt from Emecheta's *In the Ditch* (page 881) is an example of realism.

refrain, the REPETITION of one or more lines in each STANZA of a poem. The ballad "Edward" (page 26) makes use of refrain.

repetition, a poetic device in which a sound, word, or phrase is repeated for style and emphasis, as in Thomas's "Do Not Go Gentle into That Good Night" (page 823).

resolution, events that follow the climax of a PLOT in which the complications of the plot are resolved.

rhyme, the exact repetition of sounds in at least the final accented syllables of two or more words:

> Hither the heroes and the nymphs *resort,*
> To taste awhile the pleasures of a *court.*
>
> Pope, from *The Rape of the Lock* (page 314)

rhyme scheme, any pattern of end rhyme in a STANZA. For purposes of study, the pattern is labeled as shown below, with the first rhyme and all the words rhyming with it labeled *a,* the second rhyme and all the words rhyming with it labeled *b,* and so on.

> Queen and huntress, chaste and fair, *a*
> Now the sun is laid to sleep, *b*
> Seated in thy silver chair *a*
> State in wonted manner keep; *b*
> Hesperus entreats thy light, *c*
> Goddess excellently bright. *c*
>
> Jonson, from "To Cynthia"

rhythm, the arrangement of stressed and unstressed sounds into patterns in speech or writing. Rhythm, or METER, may be regular, or it may vary within a line or work. The four most common meters are IAMB (◡ ′), TROCHEE (′ ◡), ANAPEST (◡ ◡ ′), and DACTYL (′ ◡ ◡).

rising action, the part of a dramatic PLOT that leads up to the CLIMAX. In rising action, the complication caused by the CONFLICT of opposing forces is developed.

romance, a long NARRATIVE in poetry or prose that originated in the medieval period. Its main elements are adventure, love, and magic. There are elements of the romance in the excerpts from *Morte Darthur* (page 79) and *Sir Gawain and the Green Knight* (page 61).

romanticism, a type of literature that, unlike REALISM, tends to portray the uncommon. The material selected tends to deal with extraordinary people in unusual settings having unusual experiences. In romantic literature there is often a stress on the past and an emphasis on nature. Examples are Coleridge's "Kubla Khan" (page 417) and Mary Shelley's *Frankenstein* (page 492). There are many other examples in Unit 5.

run-on line, a line in which the thought continues beyond the end of the poetic line. For example, there should be no pause after *thine* in the first line that follows:

> For sure our souls were near allied, and thine
> Cast in the same poetic mold with mine.
>
> Dryden, from "To the Memory of Mr. Oldham"

satire, the technique that employs wit to ridicule a subject, usually some social institution or human foible, with the intention of inspiring reform. IRONY and sarcasm are often used in writing satire, and PARODY is closely related. Swift's "A Modest Proposal" (page 296), and Shaw's *Pygmalion* (page 662) provide examples of satire.

scansion (skan′shən), the result of *scanning,* or marking off lines of POETRY into feet and indicating the stressed and unstressed syllables.

See RHYTHM *and* FOOT.

science fiction, a fictional literary work that uses scientific and technological facts and hypotheses as a basis for stories about such subjects as extraterrestrial beings, adventures in the future or on other planets, and travel through time. Wells's "The Star" (page 612) is science fiction.

sermon, a written version of a speech on some aspect of religion, morality, conduct, or the like, meant to be delivered in a church. Donne wrote many sermons.

setting, the time (both time of day and period in history) and place in which the action of a NARRA-

TIVE occurs. The setting may be suggested through DIALOGUE and action, or it may be described by the NARRATOR or one of the characters. Setting contributes strongly to the MOOD, atmosphere, and plausibility of a work. For example, the setting of Conrad's "The Lagoon" (page 586) contributes greatly to the atmosphere of the story.

short story, a short prose NARRATIVE that is carefully crafted and usually tightly constructed. The short story form developed in the 1800s.

simile (sim′ə lē), a figure of speech involving a direct comparison, using *like* or *as,* between two basically unlike things that have something in common.

> And so I dare to hope,
> Though changed, no doubt, from what I was when first
> I came among these hills, when like a roe
> I bounded o'er the mountains. . . .
>
> Wordsworth, from "Lines Composed a Few Miles Above Tintern Abbey" (page 409)

In this example the narrator compares himself when a young man to a small, agile deer.

slant rhyme (also called CONSONANCE), rhyme in which the vowel sounds are not quite identical, as in the first and third lines that follow:

> And I untightened next the *tress*
> About her neck; her cheek once more
> Blushed bright beneath my burning *kiss* . . .
>
> Browning, from "Porphyria's Lover" (page 539)

soliloquy (sə lil′ə kwē), a DRAMATIC CONVENTION that allows a character alone on stage to speak his or her thoughts aloud. If someone else is on stage but cannot hear the character's words, the soliloquy becomes an *aside.*

Compare with DRAMATIC MONOLOGUE.

sonnet, a LYRIC poem with a traditional form of fourteen iambic PENTAMETER lines. Sonnets fall into two groups, according to their RHYME SCHEMES. The *Italian* or *Petrarchan* sonnet, named after the Italian poet Petrarch, is usually rhymed *abbaabba cdecde* (with variations permitted in the *cdecde* rhyme scheme). It forms basically a two-part poem of eight lines *(octave)* and six lines *(sestet)* respectively. These two parts are played off against each other in a great variety of ways. The *English* or *Shakespearean* sonnet is usually rhymed *abab cdcd efef gg,* presenting a four-part structure in which an idea or theme is developed in three QUATRAINS and then brought to a conclusion in the COUPLET.

sound devices, the choice and arrangement of words to please the ear and suit meaning. RHYME, RHYTHM, ASSONANCE, CONSONANCE, ONOMATOPOEIA, and ALLITERATION are examples of sound devices.

speaker, the person or PERSONA who is speaking in a poem, as in Elizabeth Barrett Browning's "Sonnet 43" (page 539).

spondee, a metrical FOOT of two accented syllables (′′), as in *pipe dream.* It serves occasionally as a substitute to vary the meter, as in the last foot of the second line that follows:

> The sedge/has with-/ered from/the lake
> And no/birds sing!
>
> Keats, from "La Belle Dame Sans Merci" (page 423)

sprung rhythm, a metrical form in which the accented or stressed syllables are *scanned* without regard to the number of unstressed syllables in a FOOT. A foot may have from one to four syllables, with the accent always on the first syllable. The term was invented and the technique developed by Gerard Manley Hopkins. The following line is scanned according to Hopkins's theory:

> And for all/this,/nature is/never/spent. . . .
>
> Hopkins, from "God's Grandeur"

The first foot has three syllables, the second foot one, the third foot three, the fourth foot two, and the fifth foot one, with the accent on the first syllable of each foot.

stage directions, directions given by the author of a play to indicate the action, costumes, SETTING, arrangement of the stage, and so on. For examples of stage directions, see Shaw's *Pygmalion* (page 662), where they are printed in italic type.

stanza, a group of lines that are set off and form a division in a poem, sometimes linked with other stanzas by RHYME.

stereotype (ster′ē ə tīp′), a conventional character, PLOT, or SETTING that possesses little or no individuality but that may be used for a purpose. Such situations, characters, or settings are usually predictable. Orwell, in "Shooting an Elephant" (page 860), depicts the Burmese somewhat stereotypically.

stream of consciousness, the recording or recreation of a character's flow of thought. Raw images, perceptions, and memories come and go in seemingly random, but actually controlled, fashion, much as they do in people's minds. James Joyce and Virginia Woolf often depicted stream of consciousness in their writings.

style, the distinctive handling of language by an author. It involves the specific choices made with regard to DICTION, syntax, FIGURATIVE LANGUAGE, and so on. For a comparison of two different styles, see Coleridge's "Kubla Khan" (page 417) and Pope's *The Rape of the Lock* (page 314).

symbol, something relatively concrete, such as an object, action, character, or scene, that signifies something relatively abstract, such as a concept or idea. In Yeats's "Sailing to Byzantium" (page 608), the city of Byzantium is a symbol for the unity of all aspects of life—religious, aesthetic, practical, and intellectual.

synecdoche (si nek′də kē), a figure of speech in which a part stands for the whole, as in "hired *hands.*" *Hands* (the part) stands for the whole (those who do manual labor; those who work with their hands). The term also refers to a figurative expression in which the whole stands for a part, as in "call the *law.*" *Law* (the whole) represents the police (a part of the whole system of law).

tale, a simple prose or verse NARRATIVE, either true or fictitious, such as those told by Chaucer's pilgrims in *The Canterbury Tales* (page 47).

terza rima (ter′tsä rē′mä), a VERSE form with a three-line STANZA rhyming *aba bcb cdc,* and so on.

> O wild West Wind, thou breath of Autumn's being,
> Thou, from whose unseen presence the leaves
> dead
> Are driven, like ghosts from an enchanter fleeing,
>
> Yellow, and black, and pale, and hectic red,
> Pestilence-stricken multitudes: O thou,
> Who chariotest to their dark wintry bed. . . .
>
> Shelley, from"Ode to the West Wind" (page 469)

tetrameter (te tram′ə ter), a metrical line of four feet.

> Had we/but world/enough/and time . . . .
>
> Marvell, "To His Coy Mistress" (page 234)

theme, the underlying meaning of a literary work. A theme may be directly stated but more often is implied. The topic of Wilfred Owen's poem "Disabled" (page 739) is stated in the title. The theme concerns the poignant thoughts of a veteran and the bitter waste of a life once full of promise.

tone, the author's attitude, either stated or implied, toward his or her subject matter and toward the audience. Swift's tone in "A Modest Proposal" (page 296) is ironic. He pretends to be setting forth serious suggestions for alleviating the poverty of the Irish, all the while knowing that his proposal will shock even the most hardened politician or clergyman.

tragedy, dramatic or NARRATIVE writing in which the main character suffers disaster after a serious and significant struggle, but faces his or her downfall in such a way as to attain heroic stature. Shakespeare's *Macbeth* (page 118) is a tragedy.

trimeter (trim′ə ter), a metrical line of three feet.

> Down to/a sun-/less sea.
>
> Coleridge, from "Kubla Khan" (page 417)

trochee (trō′kē) (′‿), a metrical FOOT made up of one accented syllable followed by an unaccented syllable, as in *answer:*

> Double,/double,/toil and/trouble;
> Fire/burn and/caldron/bubble.
>
> Shakespeare, from *Macbeth* (page 118)

verse, in its most general sense, a synonym for POETRY. *Verse* may also be used to refer to poetry carefully composed as to RHYTHM and RHYME XSCHEME, but of inferior literary value.

villanelle (vil′ə nel′), a poetic form normally consisting of five three-line STANZAS and a final QUATRAIN, rhyming *aba aba aba aba aba abaa,* and with lines 1 and 3 repeating alternately as REFRAINS throughout. An example is Thomas's "Do Not Go Gentle into That Good Night" (page 823).

Glossary of Vocabulary Words

a	hat	ī	ice	ü	rule	ə { a in about
ā	age	o	hot	ch	child	e in taken
ä	far	ō	open	ng	long	i in pencil
â	care	ô	order, all	sh	she	o in lemon
e	let	oi	oil	th	thin	u in circus
ē	equal	ou	out	ᴛʜ	then	
ė	term	u	cup	zh	measure	
i	it	u̇	put			

A

abashed (ə basht′), *adj.* ashamed.

abate (ə bāt′), *v.* decrease; reduce.

abject (ab′jekt), *adj.* miserable.

abjure (ab ju̇r′), *v.* take back.

abode (ə bōd′), *n.* place of residence; house or home.

absolution (ab′sə lü′shən), *n.* a declaration that frees a person from guilt or punishment for sin.

abstemious (ab stē′mē əs), *adj.* moderate.

abysmal (ə biz′məl), *adj.* bottomless.

adversary (ad′vər ser′ē), *n.* opponent; enemy.

affliction (ə flik′shən), *n.* pain; misery.

agape (ə gāp′), *adj.* openmouthed with wonder.

agog (ə gog′), *adj.* full of expectation or excitement; eager.

amenable (ə mē′nə bəl), *adj.* responsive; agreeable.

anarchy (an′ər kē), *n.* absence of a system of government and law.

anomaly (ə nom′ə lē), *n.* something deviating from the rule; something abnormal.

anonymity (an′ə nim′ə tē), *n.* condition of being unknown.

apparition (ap′ə rish′ən), *n.* something strange, remarkable, or unexpected.

appease (ə pēz′), *v.* put an end to.

apprehension (ap′ri hen′shən), *n.* expectation of misfortune; dread of impending danger.

arbitrate (är′bə trāt), *v.* decide a dispute.

ardent (ärd′nt), *adj.* enthusiastic; passionate.

arduous (är′jü əs), *adj.* difficult.

artifice (är′tə fis), *n.* skillful construction.

asperity (a sper′ə tē), *n.* harshness.

aspire (ə spīr′), *v.* rise high.

asunder (ə sun′dər), *adv.* in pieces or separate parts.

audacious (ô dā′shəs), *adj.* bold.

augment (ôg ment′), *v.* increase.

avarice (av′ər is), *n.* greed for wealth.

avenge (ə venj′), *v.* revenge.

averted (ə vėr′tid), *adj.* turned away.

avouch (ə vouch′), *v.* affirm.

B

baldric (bôl′drik), *n.* a belt hung from one shoulder to the opposite side of the body, to support the wearer's sword.

baleful (bāl′fəl), *adj.* destructive.

bane (bān), *n.* destruction.

beguile (bi gīl′), *v.* trick.

benign (bi nīn′), *adj.* gracious; gentle.

bewitch (bi wich′), *v.* charm; fascinate.

blackguard (blag′ärd), *n.* scoundrel.

boon (bün), *n.* favor.

booty (bü′tē), *n.* money, especially seized illegally; gains; winnings.

bower (bou′ər), *n.* shelter.

brandish (bran′dish), *v.* wave or shake threateningly.

breach (brēch), *n.* break or gap.

brevity (brev′ə tē), *n.* shortness in time, speech, or writing; conciseness.

brougham (brüm), *n.* a closed carriage or automobile, having an outside seat for the driver.

bruit (brüt), *v.* announce by a great noise.

buoyancy (boi′ən sē), *n.* tendency to be hopeful and cheerful.

C

cadence (kād′ns), *n.* rhythm.

calumnious (kə lum′nē əs), *adj.* slanderous.

cant (kant), *n.* insincere talk.

casement (kās′mənt), *n.* window.

catapult (kat′ə pult), *n.* slingshot.

cataract (kat′ə rakt′), *n.* waterfall.

cauldron (kôl′drən), *n.* large kettle.

censure (sen′shər), *v.* criticize.

centrifugal (sen trif′yə gəl), *adj.* moving away from a center.

certitude (sėr′tə tyüd), *n.* certainty; sureness.

chasten (chā′sn), *v.* discipline.

cherub (cher′əb), *n.* an angel in the form of a child with wings.

chid (chid), past tense of **chide** (chīd), *v.* scold.

cistern (sis′tərn), *n.* reservoir for holding water.

clad (klad), *adj.* clothed.

clamorous (klam′ər əs), *adj.* noisy.

clemency (klem′ən sē), *n.* mercy or leniency.

combustible (kəm bus′tə bəl), *adj.* easily burned.

comely (kum′lē), *adj.* attractive.

commendation (kom′ən dā′shən), *n.* praise.

commiserate (kə miz′ə rāt), *v.* pity; sympathize with.

compass (kum′pəs), *v.* plot; scheme.

complaisant (kəm plā′snt), *adj.* gracious; courteous.

constitutional (kon′stə tü′shə nəl), *n.* walk or other exercise taken for one's health.

contend (kən tend′), *v.* fight; struggle.

contravention (kon′trə ven′shən), *n.* conflict; opposition.

conviction (kən vik′shən), *n.* firm belief.

copse (kops), *n.* thicket of small bushes or shrubs.

corporeal (kôr pôr′ē əl), *adj.* of or for the body.

coveted (kuv′ə tid), *adj.* strongly desired.

crypt (kript), *n.* burial vault.

D

daft (daft), *adj.* without sense or reason; silly.

darkling (därk′ling), *adv.* in the dark.

dauntless (dônt′lis), *adj.* brave.

decorum (di kôr′əm), *n.* proper behavior.

delineate (di lin′ē āt), *v.* describe in words; portray.

deluge (del′yüj), *n.* downpour; a heavy fall, as of rain.

demean (di mēn′), *v.* lower in dignity; degrade.

demeanor (di mē′nər), *n.* behavior.

deprecate (dep′rə kāt), *v.* express strong disapproval of; belittle.

desolation (des′ə lā′shən), *n.* sad loneliness.

despondency (di spon′dən sē), *n.* discouragement.

despotic (des pot′ik), *adj.* having unlimited power.

deterrent (di tėr′ənt), *n.* something that discourages or hinders.

devastating (dev′ə stā′ting), *adj.* very destructive.

diffident (dif′ə dənt), *adj.* lacking in self-confidence; shy.

diminutive (də min′yə tiv), *adj.* very small.

dire (dīr), *adj.* dreadful.

dirge (dėrj), *n.* funeral song.

disburse (dis pėrs′), *v.* pay out.

discreet (dis krēt′), *adj.* careful and sensible; proper.

disdain (dis dān′), *v.* scorn.

disparage (dis par′ij), *v.* speak slightingly of; belittle.

dissipate (dis′ə pāt), *v.* spread in different directions; scatter.

dissuade (di swād′), *v.* persuade not to do something.

dolorous (dol′ər əs), *adj.* sorrowful.

doughty (dou′tē), *adj.* brave.

drear (drir), *adj.* gloomy; sad; sorrowful.

dudgeon (duj′ən), *n.* feeling of anger or resentment.

E

ecstatic (ek stat′ik), *adj.* full of joy.

effrontery (ə frun′tər ē), *n.* shameless boldness.

embark (em bärk′), *v.* begin an undertaking; set out; start.

enmity (en′mə tē), *n.* hatred.

enthrall (en thrôl′), *v.* hold captive.

entice (en tīs′), *v.* tempt.

entreat (en trēt′), *v.* beg.

epicure (ep′ə kyu̇r), *n.* lover of luxury.

epithet (ep′ə thet), *n.* descriptive expression.

erratic (ə rat′ik), *adj.* irregular.

erring (ėr′ing), *adj.* wandering; straying.

essay (es′ā), *n.* trial.

esteem (e stēm′), *n.* high regard.

exhortation (eg′zôr tā′shən), *n.* strong urging to do something.

exotic (eg zot′ik), *adj.* from a foreign country; not native; fascinating or interesting because strange or different.

expedient (ek spē′dē ənt), *n.* method of bringing about desired results.

exquisitely (ek′skwi zit lē), *adv.* beautifully; admirably.

extrinsic (ek strin′sik), *adj.* external.

F

factitious (fak tish′əs), *adj.* artificial.

fallacy (fal′ə sē), *n.* false idea.

fidelity (fə del′ə tē), *n.* faithfulness.

flout (flout), *v.* treat with scorn or contempt.

folly (fol′ē), *n.* a being foolish; lack of sense.

forlorn (fôr lôrn′), *adj.* abandoned; desolate.

G

gallant (gal′ənt), *adj.* noble in spirit or in conduct.

genial (jē′nyəl), *adj.* cheerful and friendly; kindly.

genteel (jen tēl′), *adj.* polite; well-bred.

ghastly (gast′lē), *adj.* very bad. *[informal]*

gibbet (jib′it), *n.* gallows, a structure for hanging criminals.

glaze (glāz), *n.* smooth, glossy coating.

gloam (glōm), *n.* gloaming; twilight.

gravity (grav′ə tē), *n.* seriousness.

grievous (grē′vəs), *adj.* causing great pain or suffering; severe.

grope (grōp), *v.* search blindly.

grot (grot), *n.* grotto; a cave or cavern. *[archaic]*

grovel (gruv′əl), *v.* crawl humbly on the ground.

guile (gīl), *n.* deceit.

H

harbinger (här′bən jər), *n.* forerunner.

hauberk (hȯ′bərk), *n.* a flexible coat of armor made of small loops of chain linked together.

hemlock (hem′lok), *n.* a poison.

herbivore (hėr′bə vôr), *n.* any of a large group of animals that feed chiefly on plants.

hirsute (hėr′süt), *adj.* hairy.

homage (hom′ij), *n.* dutiful respect.

I

imbibe (im bīb′), *v.* drink in; absorb.

imminent (im′ə nənt), *adj.* about to happen.

immortal (i môr′tl), *adj.* living forever.

impartiality (im′pär shē al′ə tē), *n.* fairness.

impecunious (im′pi kyü′nē əs), *adj.* having little or no money.

impenetrable (im pen′ə trə bəl), *adj.* unable to be passed through.

imperialism (im pir′ē ə liz′əm), *n.* policy of extending the rule or authority of one country over other countries and colonies.

impertinent (im pėrt′n ənt), *adj.* rudely bold.

impetuous (im pech′ü əs), *adj.* rash; hasty.

impotence (im′pə təns), *n.* condition of helplessness.

impropriety (im′prə prī′ə tē), *n.* improper conduct.

impudent (im′pyə dənt), *adj.* very rude.

incipient (in sip′ē ənt), *adj.* just beginning; in an early stage.

incoherent (in′kō hir′ənt), *adj.* confused; having no logical connection of ideas.

incomprehensible (in′kom pri hen′sə bəl), *adj.* impossible to understand.

incongruous (in kong′grü əs), *adj.* out of place; inconsistent.

incorporeal (in′kôr pôr′ē əl), *adj.* not made of any material substance; spiritual.

incorrigible (in kôr′ə jə bəl), *adj.* too firmly fixed in bad ways to be changed.

indignant (in dig′nənt), *adj.* angry at something unjust.

indolent (in′dl ənt), *adj.* lazy.

inexpedient (in′ik spē′dē ənt), *adj.* unwise.

inexplicable (in′ik splik′ə bəl), *adj.* mysterious; unable to be explained.

infamous (in′fə məs), *adj.* disgraceful.

infinite (in′fə nit), *adj.* endless.

ingenious (in jē′nyəs), *adj.* cleverly planned.

inglorious (in glôr′ē əs), *adj.* shameful; disgraceful.

inquisitive (in kwiz′ə tiv), *adj.* curious; prying.

insinuate (in sin′yü āt), *v.* act or speak to gain favor in an indirect way.

insolence (in′sə ləns), *n.* bold rudeness.

interfuse (in′tər fyüz′), *v.* blend; mix.

intrinsically (in trin′sik lē), *adv.* essentially; belonging to a thing by its very nature.

irrepressible (ir′i pres′ə bəl), *adj.* uncontrollable.

J

jovial (jō′vē əl), *adj.* cheerful.

judicious (jü dish′əs), *adj.* wise.

L

lamentable (lam′ən tə bəl), *adj.* sorrowful.

languish (lang′guish), *v.* become weak or worn out.

languor (lang′gər), *n.* lack of energy; weariness.

lassitude (las′ə tüd), *n.* lack of energy; weariness.

laudable (lô′də bəl), *adj.* praiseworthy.

lavish (lav′ish), *v.* give or spend freely.

leonine (lē′ə nīn), *adj.* of or like a lion.

liege (lēj), *adj.* honorable; having a right to respect and service.

lissomely (lis′əm lē), *adv.* limberly; supplely.

listless (list′lis), *adj.* seeming too tired to care about anything.

loath (lōth), *adj.* reluctant.

luminous (lü′mə nəs), *adj.* shining; bright.

M

magnanimous (mag nan′ə məs), *adj.* generous in forgiving.

malevolence (mə lev′ə ləns), *n.* ill will.

malicious (mə lish′əs), *adj.* evil.

manifest (man′ə fest), *adj.* plain; clear.

mead (mēd), *n.* meadow.

mendacity (men das′ə tē), *n.* untruthfulness; lie.

mettle (met′l), *n.* courage.

mien (mēn), *n.* manner of holding the head and body; way of acting and looking.

minion (min′yən), *n.* favorite; darling.

N

negligent (neg′lə jənt), *adj.* careless.

nocturnal (nok tėr′nl), *adj.* nighttime.

O

obdurate (ob′dər it), *adj.* stubborn.

oblivious (ə bliv′ē əs), *adj.* unmindful; forgetful.

odious (ō′dē əs), *adj.* hateful; offensive.

officiously (ə fish′əs lē), *adv.* too readily offering services or advice; meddling.

ominous (om′ə nəs), *adj.* unfavorable; threatening.

oppressor (ə pres′ər), *n.* person who is cruel or unjust.

ostentation (os′ten tā′shən), *n.* showing off.

P

pacify (pas′ə fī), *v.* quiet down.

palpable (pal′pə bəl), *adj.* definite.

paltry (pôl′trē), *adj.* worthless.

pandemonium (pan′də mō′nē əm), *n.* wild uproar; lawlessness.

parasite (par′ə sīt), *n.* person who lives on others without making any useful or fitting returns.

parsimony (pär′sə mō′nē), *n.* stinginess.

peerless (pir′lis), *adj.* without equal; matchless.

peremptory (pə remp′tər ē), *adj.* decisive; dictatorial.

perennial (pə ren′ē əl), *adj.* lasting for a very long time; enduring.

perfunctorily (pər fungk′tər i lē), *adv.* mechanically; indifferently.

pernicious (pər nish′əs), *adj.* harmful.

perplexity (pər plek′sə tē), *n.* confusion.

pestilence (pes′tl əns), *n.* epidemic disease.

petrol (pet′rəl), *n.* gasoline. *[British]*

petulant (pech′ə lənt), *adj.* likely to have little fits of bad temper.

piety (pī′ə tē), *n.* reverence for God.

pique (pēk), *n.* anger; wounded pride.

plaintive (plān′tiv), *adj.* mournful.

plinth (plinth), *n.* the lower, square part of the base of a column.

plunder (plun′dər), *v.* steal by force, especially during war.

ply (plī), *v.* supply with in a pressing manner.

precipitous (pri sip′ə təs), *adj.* very steep.

prerogative (pri rog′ə tiv), *n.* right or privilege that nobody else has.

presumptuous (pri zump′chü əs), *adj.* too bold; forward.

pristine (pris′tēn′), *adj.* original.

procrastinate (prō kras′tə nāt), *v.* put things off until later; delay.

prodigious (prə dij′əs), *adj.* huge.

promontory (prom′ən tôr′ē), *n.* a high point of land extending from the coast into the water.

propitiate (prə pish′ē āt), *v.* win the favor of.

propriety (prə prī′ə tē), *n.* proper behavior.

prosaically (prō zā′ik lē), *adv.* in an ordinary way.

prostrate (pros′trāt), *adj.* overcome; helpless.

protracted (prō trak′tid), *adj.* drawn out; prolonged.

provocation (prov′ə kā′shən), *n.* something that stirs up or irritates.

prowess (prou′is), *n.* bravery; daring.

prudent (prüd′nt), *adj.* sensible; discreet.

publican (pub′lə kən), *n.* tavern keeper.

purgatory (pėr′gə tôr′ē), *n.* any condition of temporary suffering.

R

ragout (ra gü′), *n.* a highly seasoned meat stew.

raiment (rā′mənt), *n.* clothing.

recompense (rek′əm pens), *n.* reward.

recourse (rē′kôrs), *n.* appeal for help or protection.

recreant (rek′rē ənt), *n.* coward.

redcoat (red′kōt′), *n.* a British soldier.

reluctantly (ri luk′tənt lē), *adv.* slowly and unwillingly.

remonstrance (ri mon′strəns), *n.* protest; complaint.

rendezvous (rän′də vü), *n.* secret meeting place.

renown (ri noun′), *n.* fame.

replenish (ri plen′ish), *v.* refill.

repudiate (ri pyü′dē āt), *v.* reject.

requiem (rek′wē əm), *n.* musical service or hymn for the dead.

requite (ri kwīt′), *v.* repay.

resolute (rez′ə lüt), *adj.* determined.

restraint (ri strānt′), *n.* limit; restriction.

reticent (ret′ə sənt), *adj.* reserved; quiet.

revelation (rev′ə lā′shən), *n.* disclosure of divine truth.

revelry (rev′əl rē), *n.* noisy partying.

ricochet (rik′ə shā′), *v.* move with a bounce or jump.

robust (rōbust′), *adj.* strong and healthy; sturdy.

S

salutary (sal′yə ter′ē), *adj.* beneficial.

sanctify (sangk′tə fī), *v.* make holy.

scruple (skrü′pəl), *n.* doubt.

sensibility (sen′sə bil′ə tē), *n.* tendency to be hurt or offended too easily.

sepulcher (sep′əl kər), *n.* tomb.

servile (sėr′vəl), *adj.* slavelike.

sidle (sī′dl), *v.* move sideways.

simultaneously (sī′məl tā′nē əs lē), *adv.* at the same time.

sinister (sin′ə stər), *adj.* threatening.

slay (slā), *v.* **slew, slain, slaying.** kill with violence.

slovenly (sluv′ən lē), *adj.* untidy.

smite (smīt), *v.* **smote, smitten** or **smote, smiting.** hit; give a hard blow to.

sordid (sôr′did), *adj.* filthy.

spate (spāt), *n.* a sudden flood.

specious (spē′shəs), *adj.* apparently good, but not really so.

specter (spek′tər), *n.* ghost.

stagnant (stag′nənt), *adj.* still; not flowing.

staid (stād), *adj.* having a settled, quiet character; sober; sedate.

stealthy (stel′thē), *adj.* secret.

steed (stēd), *n.* horse.

strew (strü), *v.* scatter or sprinkle.

stupent (stüp′nt), *adj.* dumfounded; amazed.

subdue (səb dü′), *v.* conquer.

subjective (səb jek′tiv), *adj.* existing in the mind.

subjugate (sub′jə gāt), *v.* subdue; conquer.

suborn (sə bôrn′), *v.* hire or bribe.

superfluous (sů pėr′flü əs), *adj.* needless; unnecessary.

supine (sü pīn′), *adj.* lazily inactive; listless.

suppurating (sup′yə rā′ting), *adj.* oozing.

surmise (sər mīz′), *n.* guesswork.

swoon (swün), *n., v.* faint.

sylvan (sil′vən), *adj.* of or flowing through woods.

symmetry (sim′ə trē), *n.* pleasing proportions between the parts of a whole; harmony.

T

tarry (tar′ē), *v.* delay.

taut (tôt), *adj.* tense.

tempestuous (tem pes′chü əs), *adj.* stormy; violent.

terrestrial (tə res′trē əl), *adj.* earthly.

thrall (thrôl), *n.* bondage; condition of being under some power or influence.

thwart (thwôrt), *v.* prevent from doing something.

tirade (tī′rād), *n.* long, scolding speech.

toll (tōl), *v.* ring.

tranquillity (trang kwil′ə tē), *n.* peacefulness.

transgress (trans gres′), *v.* sin against.

transitory (tran′sə tôr′ē), *adj.* passing soon or quickly.

transpire (tran spīr′), *v.* breathe out.

tread (tred), *v.* **trod, trodden** or **trod, treading.** set the foot down; walk; step.

tremulous (trem′yə ləs), *adj.* quivering.

trepidation (trep′ə dā′shən), *n.* fear; fright.

tumult (tü′mult), *n.* commotion.

turbid (tėr′bid), *adj.* confused; disordered.

tyranny (tir′ə nē), *n.* cruel or unjust use of power.

U

unabashed (un′ə basht′), *adj.* not ashamed or embarrassed.

unguent (ung′gwənt), *n.* ointment; salve; cream.

unprecedented (un pres′ə den′tid), *adj.* never done before; never known before.

upbraid (up brād′), *v.* find fault with.

V

vagrant (vā′grənt), *adj.* wandering.

valiant (val′yənt), *adj.* courageous.

vanquish (vang′kwish), *v.* defeat.

vehement (vē′ə mənt), *adj.* forceful.

verdurous (vėr′jər əs), *adj.* green and fresh.

verity (ver′ə tē), *n.* truth.

vie (vī), *v.* compete.

vile (vīl), *adj.* very bad.

vindicate (vin′də kāt), *v.* uphold; justify.

vindictive (vin dik′tiv), *adj.* bearing a grudge; wanting revenge.

vintner (vint′nər), *n.* wine merchant.

W

wantonness (won′tən nis), *n.* lack of restraint.

wrath (rath), *n.* great anger.

writhe (rīᴛʜ), *v.* twist and turn; suffer mentally.

wrought (rôt), *v.* a past tense and a past participle of **work.** *[archaic]*

Z

zealous (zel′əs), *adj.* enthusiastic.

zephyr (zef′ər), *n.* mild breeze; gentle wind.

Language and Grammar Handbook

Skill-building worksheets can be found in the *Reading, Writing and Grammar SkillBook,* referenced in the blue tabs throughout this handbook.

When your teacher returns papers, are you sometimes confused by comments such as "Incorrect subject-verb agreement" or "Unclear antecedent"? This Handbook will help you respond to such comments as you edit your writing and also provide answers to questions that arise about language during peer- and self-evaluation.

The Handbook is alphabetically arranged, with each entry explaining a certain term or concept. For example, if you can't remember when to use *good* or *well* look up the entry **good, well** and you'll find an explanation of when to use each word and a sentence using each word.

p. 203

A

active and passive voice A verb is said to be in the active voice when its subject is the doer of the action, and in the passive voice when its subject is the receiver of the action. A passive verb is a form of the verb *be* plus the past participle of the verb: *is* prepared, *had been* prepared, *will be* prepared, and so on.

active: The coach *prepared* the team for the playoffs.
passive: The team *was prepared* for the playoffs by the coach.

Active verbs are more natural, direct, and forceful than passive verbs. Passive verbs are useful and effective, however, when the doer of the action is unknown or unimportant, or to emphasize the receiver of the action:

- The soul *is placed* in the body like a rough diamond. . . .
  from "The Education of Women" by Daniel Defoe
- In Moulmein, in Lower Burma, I *was hated* by large numbers of people . . . .
  from "Shooting an Elephant" by George Orwell

p. 159
p. 211

adjective Adjectives are modifiers that describe nouns and pronouns and make their meaning more exact. Adjectives tell *what kind, which one,* or *how many.*

What kind:	*red* car	*denim* jacket	*fast* food
Which one:	*that* video	*this* computer	*those* families
How many:	*six* weeks	*several* papers	*many* years

p. 159
p. 211

adverb Adverbs modify verbs, adjectives, or other adverbs. They tell *how, when,* or *where* about verbs.

How:	quickly	fearfully	courageously
When:	soon	now	tomorrow
Where:	there	near	here

See also **comparative forms of adjectives and adverbs.**

agreement

p. 205

1. Subject-verb agreement. When the subject and verb of a sentence are both singular or both plural, they agree in number. This is called subject-verb agreement.

	Singular	**Plural**
1st person	I drive	we drive
2nd person	you drive	you drive
3rd person	he/she/it/drives	they drive

Some verbs, like *to be,* have irregular forms.

Present tense Singular	**Present tense Plural**	**Past tense Singular**	**Past tense Plural**
I am	we are	I was	we were
you are	you are	you were	you were
he/she/it is	they are	he/she/it was	they were

a. Most compound subjects joined by *and* or *both . . . and* are plural and are followed by plural verbs.

s s v

Both Tomas and Matt were standing in the cafeteria line.

b. A compound subject joined by *or, either. . . or,* or *neither . . . nor* is followed by a verb that agrees in number with the closer subject.

s s v

Neither Margarita nor her sisters attend that school.

s s v

Neither her sisters nor Margarita attends that school.

Problems arise when it isn't obvious what the subject is. The following rules should help you with some of the most troublesome situations:

c. Phrases or clauses coming between the subject and the verb do not affect the subject-verb agreement.

s v

- The appointment of the other Ministers usually takes a little longer. . .
  from "Wartime Speeches" by Winston Churchill

s v

- Some persons of a desponding spirit are in great concern about that vast number of poor people who are aged, diseased, or maimed. . . .
  from *A Modest Proposal* by Jonathan Swift

p. 209

d. Singular verbs are used with singular indefinite pronouns—*each, every, either, neither, anyone, anybody, one, everyone, everybody, someone, somebody, nobody, no one.*

s v
Neither of us was on time.

s v
Everyone attends the free film on Monday.

e. Plural indefinite pronouns take plural verbs. They are *both, few, many,* and *several.*

s v
Both of the bands travel frequently.

p. 187

f. The indefinite pronouns *all, any, more, most, none,* and *some* may take a singular or plural verb, depending on their meaning in a sentence.

Singular	**Plural**
Most of the van *is* filled.	*Most* of the buses *were* full.
All of the snow *has* melted	*All* of the clouds *have* vanished.

p. 207

g. The verb agrees with the subject regardless of the number of the predicate complement (after a form of a linking verb).

s v
Her greatest delight was her flowers.

s v
Flowers were her greatest delight.

h. Unusual word order does not affect agreement; the verb generally agrees with the subject, whether the subject follows or precedes it.

v s
◆ . . . between the layers of cotton-wool were little brass figures . . . .
from "The Lumber-Room" by Saki

i. Be especially careful of sentences beginning with *There;* be sure the verb agrees with the subject.

v s
◆ There are only two people in the car.
from "Tickets, Please" by D. H. Lawrence

2. Pronoun-antecedent agreement. An antecedent is a word, clause, or phrase to which a pronoun refers. The pronoun agrees with its antecedent in person, number, and gender.

antec. pron.
José must let me know when he is free.

antec. pron.
My cousins didn't know it, but their car was in the shop.

b. Singular pronouns are generally used to refer to the indefinite pronouns *one, anyone, each, either, neither, everybody, everyone, somebody, someone, nobody,* and *no one.*

antec. pron.
Did anyone misplace her notes?

antec. pron.
Everybody was told to bring his lunch.

The second sentence poses problems. It is clearly plural in meaning, and *everybody* may not refer to men only. To avoid the latter problem, you could write "Everybody was told to bring his or her lunch." This solution is clumsy and wordy, though. Sometimes it is best to revise: "*Students* were told to bring *their* lunches."

all right *All right* is used both as an adjective and as an adverb. The spelling *alright* is not accepted in either formal or informal writing.

ambiguity An ambiguous sentence is one that has two or more possible meanings. The most common causes of ambiguity are these:

1. Unclear pronoun reference

Ambiguous: He told his Dad that *he* missed the plane.

Since it is not clear who missed the plane, the sentence should be revised.

Clear: "I missed the plane, Dad," he said.
Clear: "You missed the plane, Dad," he said.

2. Misplaced modifiers. Misplaced modifiers, because of their position in a sentence, do not clearly modify the word they are intended to modify. They are also often a source of humor that the writer does not intend.

Ambiguous: The queen left the palace leaning on her husband.
Clear: Leaning on her husband, the queen left the palace.
Clear: The queen, leaning on her husband, left the palace.

3. Incomplete comparisons

Ambiguous: Maria likes pizza as much as Kim.
Clear: Maria likes pizza as much as Kim does.

amount, number *Amount* is used to refer to nouns which name things that can be measured or weighed: large amount of sand, small amount of gold. *Number* is used in referring to nouns which name things that can be counted: large number of rocks, small number of coins.

NOTE: An apostrophe is not used in forming other plurals or in the possessive form of personal pronouns: "The tickets are theirs."

p. 247

apostrophe (') An apostrophe is used in possessive words, both singular and plural, and in contractions. It is also used to form the plurals of letters and numbers.

women's hockey	Marta's boots	won't
P's and Q's	11's and 12's	weren't

It may be used to indicate places in words in which the speaker does not pronounce certain sounds.

◆ I went into a public-'ouse to get a pint o' beer,
The publican 'e up an' sez, "We serve no red-coats here."
from "Tommy" by Rudyard Kipling

p. 171

appositive Apposition means, literally, a "putting beside." An appositive is a noun or phrase that follows a noun and identifies or explains it more fully. It is usually set off by commas or dashes.

◆ The glorious lamp of heaven, the sun,/The higher he's a-getting. . . .
from "To the Virgins, to Make Much of Time" by Robert Herrick

If, however, the appositive is used to specify a particular person or thing, it is not set off.

◆ . . . I was in Mrs. Prothero's garden . . . with her son Jim.
from *A Child's Christmas in Wales* by Dylan Thomas

awkward writing A general term (abbreviated *awk*) sometimes used in theme correcting to indicate such faults as inappropriate word choice, unnecessary repetition, clumsy phrasing, confusing word order, or any other weakness or expression that makes reading difficult and obscures meaning.

Many writers have found that reading their first drafts aloud helps them detect clumsy or unclear phrasing in their work. Once identified, awkward construction can almost always be improved by rethinking and rewording.

bad, badly In formal English and in writing, *bad* (the adjective) is used to modify a noun or pronoun and is used after a linking verb. *Badly* (the adverb) modifies a verb.

She felt *bad* about forgetting to write to her dad. [adjective used with linking verb *felt*]

He limped *badly* after his fall. [adverb modifying the verb *limped*]

HINT: To check yourself, mentally eliminate the first term. You would never say "between *we*," you would say "between *us*," *us* being the objective form of the pronoun *we*.

between you and me After prepositions such as *between*, use the objective form of the personal pronouns: between you and *me*, between you and *her*, between you and *him*, between you and us, between you and *them*.

The contest will be between you and *us*.

◆ . . . those were the terms of the covenant made between *us* in Arthur's hall. . . .
from "Sir Gawain and the Green Knight"

p. 236

capitalization

1. Capitalize all proper nouns and adjectives.

Britain	Wales	Edward
British	Welsh	Edwardian

NOTE: If an article or possessive pronoun comes before a family title, the title is not capitalized: "My dad took us to Wrigley Field." "An aunt arrived from Sioux City."

2. Capitalize people's names and titles.

Mister Fell	Dr. Johnson	Bishop Carr
Ms. Anita Patel	Mother	Uncle John
Senator Rodriguez	Prince Henry	Justice O'Connor

3. Capitalize the names of races, languages, religions, revered persons, deities, and religious bodies, buildings, and writings. Also capitalize any adjectives made from these names.

Indo-European	Islam	Beth Emet Synagogue
Hindu	God	Church of England
Buddha	French	the Bible

NOTE: Do not capitalize directions of the compass or adjectives that indicate direction: "Is Trafalgar Square north or south of here?" "There is a mild wind from the southwest."

4. Capitalize geographical names (except for articles and prepositions) and any adjectives made from these names.

Canterbury	the Lake District	Stratford-on-Avon
the Thames River	North Sea	Irish stew
Loch Lomond	Yorkshire	Sherwood Forest

NOTE: Such terms as *avenue, bridge, square, street* are capitalized when part of a specific name: *Shaftesbury Avenue, Golden Gate Bridge, Times Square, Sutter Street.*

5. Capitalize the names of structures, public places, organizations, and bodies in the universe.

Windsor Castle	the Senate	Scotland Yard
Parliament	the Capitol	the Milky Way
Saturn	Stonehenge	Labour Party

6. Capitalize the names of historical events, times, and documents.

Battle of Hastings	Wars of the Roses	Domesday Book
Magna Carta	the Age of Reason	Gun Powder Plot

7. Capitalize the names of months, days, holidays, and time abbreviations. The seasons are not capitalized.

November	Tuesday	B.C.
Thanksgiving	A. M.	summer

NOTE: Some modern poets do not begin each line with a capital letter.

8. Capitalize the first words in sentences, lines of poetry, and direct quotations.

◆ On either side the river lie
Long fields of barley and of rye. . . .
from "The Lady of Shalott" by Alfred, Lord Tennyson

9. Capitalize certain parts of letters, outlines, and the first, last, and all other important words in titles.

Dear Mr. O'Brien,
Sincerely yours,

I. Mary Queen of Scots
  A. Early Life
    1. Parents
    2. Cousin
  B. Adult Life

Our Mutual Friend (book)
The Times (newspaper)
Macbeth (play)
Masterpiece Theatre (TV series)
"A Shocking Accident" (short story)
The Gondoliers (operetta)
"Born in America" (song)
Time (magazine)
"Ode to a Nightingale" (poem)
The Return of the Jedi (movie)

See also **Italics.**

p. 157

clause A clause is a group of words that has a subject and a verb. A clause is independent when it can stand alone and make sense. A dependent clause has a subject and a verb, but when it stands alone it is incomplete, and the reader is left wondering about the meaning.

Independent Clause	**Dependent Clause**
Jane Austen (s) wrote (v) *Pride and Prejudice.*	Because Jane Austen (s) wrote (v) *Pride and Prejudice.*

collective nouns A collective noun is one that though singular in form names a group of people or things: *committee, mob, team, class.* When a collective noun means the group taken as a whole, use a singular verb and pronoun. When individual members of a group are meant, use a plural verb and pronoun.

The class should bring *its* petition to the study hall at noon.

The committee *were* still in disgreement about *their* purpose.

p. 243
p. 247

colon (:) A colon is often used to explain or clarify what has preceded it.

◆ Ernest, however, never played: he was too grown up.
from "Eveline" by James Joyce

A colon is also used after phrases that introduce a list or quotation.

◆ "There were the Useful Presents: engulfing mufflers of the old coach days, and mittens made for giant sloths; zebra scarfs of a substance like silky gum. . . .
from *A Child's Christmas in Wales* by Dylan Thomas

p. 239
p. 247

comma (,) Commas are used to show a pause or separation between words and word groups in sentences and to avoid confusion in sentences.

1. Use a comma between items in a series. Words, phrases, and clauses in a series are separated by commas:

NOTE: If the items in a series are all separated by a word like *and,* no comma is necessary: Dolphins and whales and seals were the main attractions.

◆ The sun with its specks of planets, its dust of planetoids, and its impalpable comets, swims in a vacant immensity that almost defeats the imagination.
from "The Star" by H. G. Wells

2. Use a comma after certain introductory words and groups of words such as clauses and prepositional phrases of five words or more.

◆ With his towel round his waist, Ajayi strode back to the bedroom, ...
from "The Truly Married Woman" by Abioseh Nicol

3. Use a comma to set off nouns in direct address. The name or title by which persons (or animals) are addressed is called a noun of direct address.

◆ "Mr. Ajayi, these gentlemen have enquired for you," the chief clark said formally.
from "The Truly Married Woman" by Abioseh Nicol

4. Use commas to set off interrupting elements and appositives. Any phrase or clause that interrupts the flow of a sentence is often set off by commas. Parenthetical expressions like *of course, after all, to be sure, on the other hand, I suppose,* and *as you know;* and words like *yes, no, oh,* and *well* are all set off by commas.

◆ The white man, turning his back upon the setting sun, looked along the empty and broad expanse of the sea-reach.
from "The Lagoon" by Joseph Conrad

◆ "After all, why shouldn't you come back with me?"
from "A Cup of Tea" by Katherine Mansfield

NOTE: No comma is used when the connecting words are *so that:*

5. Use a comma before a coordinating conjunction *(and, but, for, or, nor, yet, so)* in a compound sentence.

◆ They were all amazed at his color, for they saw that he was bright green all over. . . . The hood of the mantle was the same . . . and he had thrown it back off his hair so that it lay on his shoulders.
from "Sir Gawain and the Green Knight"

6. Use a comma after a dependent clause that begins a sentence. Do not use a comma before a dependent clause that follows the independent clause.

◆ Though his imagination might incline him to a belief of the marvelous and mysterious, his vigorous reason examined the evidence with jealousy.
from *The Life of Samuel Johnson, LL.D* by James Boswell

◆ Those were the days of darkness that followed the star and the heat.
from "The Star" by H. G. Wells

comma splice *See* **run-on.**

p. 214

comparative forms of adjectives and adverbs To show a greater degree of the quality or characteristic named by an adjective or adverb, *-er* or *-est* is added to the word or *more* or *most* is put before it.

Positive: Ramon is *tall.*

Comparative: Ramon is *taller* than Bill.

Superlative: Ramon is the *tallest* person in the class.

More and *most* are generally used with longer adjectives and adverbs, and with all adverbs ending in *-ly.*

Positive: The video was *disturbing.*

Comparative: The second video was *more disturbing* than the first.

Superlative: That video was the *most disturbing* one I have seen.

See also **modifiers.**

p. 233

conjunction A conjunction is a word that links one part of a sentence to another. It can join words, phrases, or entire sentences. Coordinating conjunctions *(and, but, for, yet, or, nor, so)* connect words, phrases, and clauses of equal value. Subordinating conjunctions *(after, because, so that, unless, while,* and so on) connect dependent, or subordinate, clauses with main clauses.

Coordinating: He arrived early, *yet* he left late.

Subordinating: Marta spoke first *because* she had to leave.

D

dangling modifiers A modifier that has no word in a sentence which it can logically modify is said to be dangling.

Dangling: *Born in Ireland in 1950,* Ian Murphy's books have been translated into many languages. [The books weren't born in 1950.]

Revised: The books of Ian Murphy, who was born in Ireland in 1950, have been translated into many languages.

Dangling: *Having driven the same route for several years,* the landscape was familiar. [Who was familiar with the landscape?]

Revised: *Having driven the same route for several years,* I was familiar with the landscape.

p. 247

dash (—) A dash is used to indicate a sudden break or change of thought in a sentence:

◆ For brave Macbeth—well he deserves that name— . . .
Like valor's minion carved out his passage . . . .
from *Macbeth* by William Shakespeare

dialogue Dialogue is often used to enliven many types of writing. Notice the punctuation, capitalization, and paragraphing of the following passage.

◆ But he was standing in the middle of the room, saying, "A fine Christmas!" and smacking at the smoke with a slipper.
"Call the fire brigade," cried Mrs. Prothero as she beat the gong.
"They won't be there," said Mr. Prothero, "it's Christmas."
from *A Child's Christmas in Wales* by Dylan Thomas

See also **quotation marks.**

direct address *See* **comma 3.**

ellipsis (. . .) An ellipsis is used to indicate that words (or sentences or paragraphs) have been omitted. An ellipsis consists of three dots, but if the omitted portion would have completed the sentence, a fourth dot is added for the period.

◆ . . . Our labor must be to pervert that end,
And out of good still to find means of evil. . . .
from *Paradise Lost* by John Milton

etc. Etc. is the abbreviation for the Latin *et cetera,* meaning "and others." It is usually read *and so forth* or pronounced (et set′ər ə). It is acceptable in reference and business usage but out of place in most other writing.

p. 247

exclamation point (!) An exclamation mark is used at the end of an exclamatory sentence——one that shows excitement or strong emotion. Exclamation points can also be used with strong interjections.

fragment *See* **sentence fragment.**

p. 224

gerund A verb form ending in *-ing* that is used as a noun.

◆ By the pricking of my thumbs,
Something wicked this way comes.
from *Macbeth* by William Shakespeare

HINT: When you are referring to health, use *well* if the meaning is "not ill." "I am quite well, thank you." If the meaning is "pleasant" or "in good spirits," use *good.* "I feel good today."

good, well *Good* is used as an adjective to modify a noun or pronoun. Do not use it to modify a verb. *Well* is usually used as an adverb to modify a verb.

◆ "Don't you see what a *good* thing it was that you met me?"
from "A Cup of Tea" by Katherine Mansfield

◆ "Sit down, Jerome," Mr. Wordsworth said. "All going *well* with the trigonometry?"
from "A Shocking Accident" by Graham Greene

H

hopefully This is often used to mean "it is hoped" or "I hope," as in the following sentence, "*Hopefully,* I may be pardoned." However, in formal writing, avoid this usage.

however Words like *however, moreover, nevertheless, therefore, consequently,* etc. (known as conjunctive adverbs) require special punctuation. If the word comes within a clause, it is generally set off by commas:

◆ He, however, kept his face closed and averted from them all.
from "Tickets, Please" by D. H. Lawrence

If the conjunctive adverb separates two independent clauses, a semicolon is used preceding the word. If it begins a sentence, a comma is used after it:

◆ Therefore, I repeat, let no man talk to me of these . . . .
from "A Modest Proposal" by Jonathan Swift

p. 227

infinitive The infinitive is the simple form of the verb, usually preceded by *to.* Infinitives are used as nouns, adjectives, or adverbs. In the following lines, each infinitive acts as a noun phrase:

◆ Good nature and good sense must ever join;
To error is human, *to forgive* divine.
from *An Essay on Criticism* by Alexander Pope

p. 235

interjection An interjection is a word or phrase used to express strong emotion.

◆ Ring the alarum-bell. Murder and treason!
Banquo and Donalbain! Malcolm! awake!
from *Macbeth* by William Shakespeare

italics Italic type is used to indicate titles of whole works such as books, magazines, newspapers, plays, films, and so on. It is also used to indicate foreign words and phrases or to emphasize a word.

◆ And pictureless books in which small boys, though warned with quotations not to, *would* skate on Farmer Giles' pond. . . .
from *A Child's Christmas in Wales* by Dylan Thomas

See also **Capitalization 9** for titles that are italicized.

NOTE: In formal English the correct way to respond to a question such as, "Who's there?" is "It is I." This sounds too formal in some situations, however. While it is not correct to say, "It's them," "It's him," "it's us," or "it's her"—"It's me" is generally accepted as standard usage.

its, it's *Its* is the possessive form of the personal pronoun *it; it's* is the contraction meaning "it is."

p. 197

lay, lie This verb pair presents problems because, in addition to the similarity between the words, the past tense of *lie* is *lay.* The verb to *lay* means "to put or place something somewhere." The verb *to lie* means "to rest" or "to be at rest."

Present	Past	Past Participle	Present Participle
lay	laid	(has) laid	(is) laying
lie	lay	(has) lain	(is) lying

Notice how the verbs are used in the following sentences:

NOTE: *Lied* refers only to not telling the truth: "The jury was convinced that the defendent lied."

◆ Hark! I *laid* [placed] their daggers ready; He could not miss 'em.
from *Macbeth* by William Shakespeare

◆ Here let them *lie* [rest] / Till famine and the ague eat them up.
from *Macbeth* by William Shakespeare

media *Media* is the plural of *medium.* Many people use a singular verb when referring to the mass media. In formal writing it is best to use a plural verb.

All the media *are* focused on the national election.

misplaced modifier *See* **ambiguity.**

p. 218

modifier A modifier is a word or group of words that restrict, limit, or make more exact the meaning of other words. The modifiers of nouns and pronouns are usually adjectives, participles, adjective phrases, and adjective clauses. The modifiers of verbs, adjectives, and adverbs are adverbs, adverb phrases, and adverb clauses. In the following example, the italicized words modify the words in boldface type.

Besides, the *invariable* **squabble** for money on *Saturday* **nights** had begun **to weary** her *unspeakably.*
from "Eveline" by James Joyce

HINT: When trying to decide which pronoun to use, remember that you would not say, "Myself is going to the game." You would use *I.* Use *I* with a compound subject, too.

myself (and **himself, herself,** and so on) A reflexive pronoun reflects the action of the verb back to the subject. An intensive pronoun adds emphasis to the noun or pronoun just named.

◆ "I'm going to study outside. Even the street is quieter," I screeched and threw *myself* past them. . . . [reflexive]
from "Studies in the Park" by Anita Desai

◆ THE DAUGHTER. It's too tiresome. Do you expect us to go and get one *ourselves?* [intensive]
from *Pygmalion* by Bernard Shaw

Be careful not to use *myself* and the other reflexive and intensive pronouns when you simply need to use the personal pronoun *I* or its objective form *me.*

Incorrect: Ismail told Stephanie and *myself* a good story.

Correct: Ismail told Stephanie and *me* a good story.

p. 161
p. 173

N

noun A noun is a word that names a person, place, thing, or idea. Most nouns are made plural by adding *-s* or *-es* to the singular. When you are unsure about a plural form, check a dictionary.

P

parallel construction Items in a sentence that are of equal importance should be expressed in parallel (or similar) forms. These can take the form of noun phrases, verb phrases, infinitive phrases, and prepositional phrases:

◆ . . . it has been delayed till I am indifferent, and cannot enjoy it; till I am solitary, and cannot impart it; till I am known, and do not want it.
from "Letter to Chesterfield" by Samuel Johnson

◆ . . . we shall fight in France, we shall fight on the seas, we shall fight with growing confidence and growing strength in the air, . . . we shall fight in the fields and in the streets, we shall fight in the hills. . . .
from "Wartime Speeches" by Winston Churchill

parentheses ( ) Parentheses are used to enclose words that interrupt or add explanation to a sentence. They are also used to enclose references to page numbers, chapters, or dates. Punctuation marks that belong to the sentence come after the parentheses, not before.

◆ Those who are more thrifty (as I must confess the times require) may flay the carcass . . . .
from *A Modest Proposal* by Jonathan Swift

p. 222

participle A participle is a verb form used in forming various tenses of verbs. The present participle ends in *-ing: growing.* The past participle usually ends in *-ed, -t, -d, -en,* or *-n: scared, wept, said, risen, grown.* Participles are also used as adjectives, modifying nouns and pronouns.

◆ . . . when the sky darkened towards evening, an unearthly, *reflected* pallor remained. . . . [*Reflected* modifies the noun *pallor.*]
from "The Courtship of Mr. Lyon" by Angela Carter

plagiarism Using the words, ideas, or expressions of others as if they were your own is called plagiarism. Plagiarism problems usually grow from the following circumstances: 1. copying a passage from a source without giving credit; 2. paraphrasing a source so closely that only a few words or phrases are changed; 3. using someone else's ideas without giving credit. In a short paper credit is usually given directly in the text. In a longer piece of writing, you will need to footnote your sources.

p. 175
p. 178

possessive case The possessive case is formed in various ways. For singular nouns and indefinite pronouns, add an apostrophe and *-s:*

my *brother's* car   *no one's* notebook   *everybody's* children

For plural nouns ending in an *-s,* add only an apostrophe:

the *doctors'* offices   the *babies'* shoes   the *teachers'* rooms

If the plural is irregular and does not end in *-s,* add an apostrophe and then an *-s: women's* clothing.

NOTE: Apostrophes are not used with personal pronouns such as *his, hers,* or *ours* to show possession.

p. 231

prepositions Prepositions are words such as *about, between, during, from, in, of, over, under, until,* and *with* that show the relationship between a noun or pronoun and some other word in a sentence.

prepositional phrase Prepositional phrases are groups of words that begin with a preposition and end with a noun or pronoun (the object of the preposition). These phrases act as modifiers.

◆ There was a table set out under a tree in front of the house. . . .

from "A Mad Tea Party" by Lewis Carroll

p. 180
p. 183

pronoun A pronoun is a word used instead of a noun to designate a person or object. Subject pronouns are used as subjects of sentences. Object pronouns can be used as direct objects, indirect objects, or objects of prepositions.

HINT: When you are uncertain about whether to use a subject pronoun or an object pronoun, take out the first pronoun to test the sentence. (You wouldn't say "Me played yesterday" or "Tom asked I to stay.")

When a pronoun is used as the subject, it is in the nominative case. When a pronoun is used as an object, it is in the objective case.

Subject Pronouns	**Object Pronouns**
Singular: I; you; he, she, it	me; you; him, her, it
Plural: we; you; they	us; you; them
He and *I* played yesterday	Tom asked *her* and *me* to stay.

See also **ambiguity.**

p. 245
p. 247

quotation marks (" ") Quotation marks enclose a speaker's words. They are also used to enclose some titles. When you use someone's words in your writing, use the following rules:

1. Enclose all quoted words within quotation marks.

   Matthew Arnold wrote, "And we are here as on a darkling plain."

2. Introductory and explanatory expressions *(he said, I replied)* are set off by a comma, or if they interrupt a sentence, by two commas.

3. Periods and commas are always put inside quotation marks. Semicolons are put outside quotation marks.

   "I've read several of his poems," he said, "and liked them."

4. A question mark or exclamation point is put inside the quotation mark if it applies only to the quoted matter, outside if it applies to the complete sentence that contains the quotation.

   Didn't Matthew Arnold write "Dover Beach"?

5. When both the sentence and the quotation ending the sentence are questions or exclamations, only one mark is used—inside the quotation marks.

   Who wrote "Ah, Are You Digging On My Grave?"

6. A long quoted passage is often presented without quotation marks and indented instead, sometimes in smaller type.

See also **dialogue.**

R

real, really *Real* is used as an adjective, and *really* is used as an adverb.

> We couldn't tell the *real* picture from the fake one.
>
> The concert was *really* great. [not "real great"]

run-on sentence A run-on sentence occurs when there is only a comma (known as a comma splice) or no punctuation between two independent clauses. Separate the clauses into two complete sentences, join them with a semicolon, or use a comma and a coordinating conjunction.

> **Run on:** The student received her schedule, then she went home.
> **Correct:** The student received her schedule. Then she went home.
> **Correct:** The student received her schedule; then she went home.
> **Correct:** The student received her schedule, and then she went home.

Often, in narrative writing, authors purposely choose to use run-ons for effect, such as in the following passage:

> ◆ There was no mistake about it, Annie liked John Thomas a good deal.
> from "Tickets, Please" by D. H. Lawrence

See also **stringy sentences.**

p. 243
p. 247

semicolon (;) Use this punctuation mark to separate the two parts of a compound sentence when they are not joined by a comma and a conjunction.

> ◆ No man is an island, entire of itself; every man is a piece of the continent, a part of the main.
> from Meditation 17 by John Donne

NOTE: While some words or word groups are not complete sentences with a subject and a verb, they are complete in thought and are known as "minor-type sentences." Notice their use in the quoted passage.

p. 149
p. 229

sentence fragment A fragment often occurs when one sentence is finished, but another thought occurs to the writer and that thought is written and punctuated as a complete sentence.

> **Fragment:** I loved the movie. Especially when Hamlet stages the play.
> **Correct:** I loved the movie, especially when Hamlet stages the play.

> ◆ The bell rings. Voices clash, clatter, and break. The tin-and-bottle man? The neighbors? The police? The Help-the-Blind Man? Thieves and burglars?
> from "Studies in the Park" by Anita Desai

stringy sentences A stringy sentence is one in which several independent clauses are strung together with *and.* Correct a stringy sentence by breaking it into individual sentences or changing some of the independent clauses into subordinate clauses or phrases.

Stringy: Saturday morning I have to take my brother to his music lesson and pick up some dry cleaning and then I'm supposed to let Mom have the car so she can shop and I guess I'll have to walk or hitch a ride to football practice.

Correct: Saturday morning I have to take my brother to his music lesson and pick up some dry cleaning. Since I'm supposed to let Mom have the car so she can shop, I guess I'll have to walk or hitch a ride to football practice.

T

titles *See* **capitalization 2** and **9.**

V

p. 189
p. 193
p. 199

verb A verb is a word that tells about an action or a state of being. The form or tense of the verb tells whether the action occurred in the past, the present, or the future.

p. 191

verb tense Verb tenses indicate action in the past, present, future, and so on. Use the same tense to show two or more actions that occur at the same time.

Incorrect: She *brought* [past] two videos and some popcorn. Then she *talks* [present] all through the movies.

Correct: She *brought* [past] two videos and some popcorn. Then she *talked* [past] all through the movies.

When the verb in the main clause is in the present tense, the verb in the subordinate clause is in whatever tense expresses the meaning intended.

Mr. Washington *thinks* that the dinner *was* a success.

voice *See* **active and passive voice.**

W

p. 185

who, whom Use *who* as the subject of a sentence or clause:

Who is the author of this short story?

Use *whom* as a direct object or as the object of a preposition:

◆ So, thanks to all at once and to each one,
Whom we invite to see us crowned at Scone.
from *Macbeth* by William Shakespeare

◆ Any man's death diminishes me, because I am involved in mankind; and therefore never send to know for *whom* the bell tolls . . . .
from Meditation 17 by John Donne

who's, whose *Who's* is a contraction meaning "who is"; *whose* is a possessive.

After talking to everyone, decide *who's* planning to go.

◆ A knave *whose* practice it is to invite the unwary to game . . . .
from *Dictionary of the English Language* by Samuel Johnson

NOTE: In the example from "Shooting an Elephant," notice the last clause, "if I had been alone." In *if*-clauses and wishes pertaining to the past, the verb to use is *had,* not *would have.*

would of This expression is often used mistakenly because it sounds like *would've,* the contraction for *would have.* In formal writing, write out *would have,* and you won't be confused:

◆ For at that moment, with the crowd watching me, I was not afraid in the ordinary sense, as I *would have* been if I *had* been alone.
from "Shooting an Elephant" by George Orwell

your, you're *Your* is the possessive form of the personal pronoun *you; you're* is a contraction meaning "you are."

◆ Commend to me *your* fair and gracious lady. . . .
from "Sir Gawain and the Green Knight"

Even though it's late, I hope *you're* going with me.

Index of Skills

Grammar, Usage, Mechanics, and Spelling

Interdisciplinary Connections

Literary, Genres, Terms, and Techniques

Media and Technology

Multicultural Awareness and Appreciation

Reading/Thinking Strategies

Speaking, Listening, and Viewing

Vocabulary and Study Skills

Writing Forms, Modes, and Processes

Index of Fine Arts & Artists

Index of Authors and Titles

U

V

W

Y

Acknowledgments

continued from page iv

■

599–601 "Loveliest of Trees," "When I Was One-and-Twenty," and "To An Athlete Dying Young" from *The Collected Poems Of A. E. Housman.* Copyright 1939, 1940 by Henry Holt and Co., Inc. Copyright © 1967 by Robert F. Symons. Reprinted by permission of Henry Holt and Co., Inc. and The Society of Authors as the literary representative of the Estate of A. E. Housman. **607** "The Second Coming" by W.B. Yeats from *The Poems Of W.B. Yeats: A New Edition,* edited by Richard J. Finneran. Copyright 1924 by Macmillan Publishing Company, renewed 1952 by Bertha Georgie Yeats. Reprinted with permission of Simon & Schuster, Inc. **608** "Sailing to Byzantium" by W.B. Yeats from *The Poems Of W.B. Yeats: A New Edition,* edited by Richard J. Finneran. Copyright 1928 by Macmillan Publishing Company, renewed © 1956 by Georgie Yeats. Reprinted with permission of Simon & Schuster, Inc. **612** "The Star" by H. G. Wells. Reprinted by permission of A. P. Watt on behalf of the Literary Executors of the Estate of H. G. Wells. **631** "Counting the Years" from *Time,* Fall 1992. Copyright © 1992 by Time Inc. Reprinted by permission. **648** "Stanley Meets Mutesa" by James D. Rubadiri. Reprinted by permission. **649** "England, My England" by William Ernest Henley. Reprinted by permission. **650** "England Your England" by George Orwell. Reprinted by permission. **654** From *The Crack in the Teacup* by Marina Warner. Reprinted by permission. **718** The Upper Class by Marina Warner. **718** Excerpts from *Britain—Twentieth Century: The Story of Social Conditions* by Mary Cathcart Borer. Reprinted by permission. **721** "Burlington Bertie from Bow" by William Hargreaves. Reprinted by permission. **743** From *Testament Of Youth* by Vera Brittain. Copyright 1933 by Vera Brittain. Reprinted by permission of Virago Press and Victor Gollancz Limited. **758** "Tickets, Please" from *Complete Short Stories Of D.H. Lawrence* by D. H. Lawrence. Copyright 1922 by Thomas Seltzer, Inc., renewal copyright 1950 by Frieda Lawrence. Used by permission of Viking Penguin, a division of Penguin Books USA Inc. **769** "The Hollow Men" by T.S. Eliot from *Collected Poems 1909-1962.* Copyright © 1936 by Harcourt Brace & Company; copyright © 1964, 1963 by T.S. Eliot. Reprinted by permission of the publisher and Faber and Faber Limited. **773** "The Horror at Ypres" from *Chemical And Biological Warfare* by L. B. Taylor, Jr. and C. L. Taylor. Copyright © 1985 by L. B. Taylor, Jr. and C. L. Taylor. Reprinted by permission of Franklin Watts. **775** "The Boneyard" from *The Great War And Modern Memory* by Paul Fussell, pp. 69-71. Reprinted by permission. **790** "Eveline" from *Dubliners* by James Joyce. Copyright 1916 by B.W. Heubsch. Definitive text copyright © 1967 by the Estate of James Joyce. Used by permission of Viking Penguin, a division of Penguin Books USA Inc. **797** "A Cup of Tea" from *The Short Stories Of Katherine Mansfield* by Katherine Mansfield. Copyright 1923 by Alfred A. Knopf Inc. and renewed 1951 by John Middleton Murry. Reprinted by permission of Alfred A. Knopf Inc. **806–808** "The Unknown Citizen" and "Musée des Beaux Arts" by W.H. Auden from *W.H. Auden: Collected Poems.* Copyright 1940 and renewed © 1968 by W.H. Auden. Reprinted by permission of Random House, Inc. and Faber and Faber Limited. **810** "Who's Who" by W.H. Auden from *W.H. Auden: Collected Poems.* Copyright 1937 and renewed © 1965 by W.H. Auden. Reprinted by permission of Random House, Inc. and Faber and Faber Limited. **814** "Shakespeare's Sister" from *A Room Of One's Own* by Virginia Woolf. Copyright 1929 by Harcourt Brace & Company and renewed 1957 by Leonard Woolf. Reprinted by permission of Harcourt Brace & Company and The Society of Authors as the literary representative of the Estate of Virginia Woolf. **823** Dylan Thomas, "Do Not Go Gentle into That Good Night." Reprinted by permission. **824** Dylan Thomas, *A Child's Christmas In Wales.* Copyright 1954 by New Directions Publishing Corporation and David Higham Associates Limited. **833** "Studies in the Park" from *Games At Twilight* by Anita Desai. Copyright © 1978 by Anita Desai. Reproduced by permission of the author c/o Rogers, Coleridge & White Ltd., 20 Powis Mews, London W11 1JN. **860** "Shooting an Elephant" by George Orwell from *Shooting an Elephant and Other Essays.* Copyright 1950 by Sonia Brownell Orwell; renewed © 1978 by Sonia Pitt-Rivers. Reprinted by permission of Harcourt Brace & Company, the estate of the late Sonia Brownell Orwell and Martin Secker & Warburg Ltd **876** "Homage To a Government" from *High Windows* by Philip Larkin. Reprinted by permission. **877** "Two Poems on the Passing of an Empire" from *Collected Poems 1948-1984* by Derek Walcott. Reprinted by permission. **881** "Qualifying for the Mansions" and "Drifting to the Mansions" from *In The Ditch* by Buchi Emecheta. Copyright © 1972 by Buchi Emecheta. Reprinted by permission of the author. **907** "Eve To Her Daughters" from *Collected Poems* by Judith Wright. Reprinted by permission. **910–911** "The Frog Prince" and "Not Waving but Drowning" by Stevie Smith from *The Collected Poems of Stevie Smith.* Copyright © 1972 by Stevie Smith. Reprinted by permission of New Directions Publishing Corporation and James MacGibbon. **912** "The Explorers" by Margaret Atwood. Reprinted by permission. **916** "The Truly Married Woman" from *The Truly Married Woman And Other Stories* by Abioseh Nicol. Copyright ©1965 by Oxford University Press. Reprinted by permission of David Higham Associates Limited. **926** Graham Greene, "A Shocking Accident." Reprinted by permission. **933** Angela Carter, "The Courtship of Mr. Lyon." Reprinted by permission. **943** "Some Biomythology" from *The Lives of a Cell* by Lewis Thomas. Reprinted by permission. **956** From *The Theater of the Absurd* by Martin Esslin. Reprinted by permission. **957** "Nicely Nicely Clive" from *In His Own Write* by John Lennon. Reprinted by permission. **959**

From *The Crack In The Teacup* by Marina Warner. Reprinted by permission. **961** "The Dead Parrot Sketch" from *Monty Python's Flying Circus.* Reprinted by permission. **963** From *The Perils of Invisibility* by W.S. Gilbert. Reprinted by permission. **964** "Glory" by Lewis Carroll. Reprinted by permision.

Illustrations

Unless otherwise acknowledged, all photographs are the property of Scott, Foresman and Company. Page abbreviations are as follows: (t)top, (c)center, (b)bottom, (l)left, (r)right.

Front cover & frontispiece page ii Dante Gabriel Rossetti, "The Beloved"/Tate Gallery, London/Bridgeman Art Library, London/Superstock, Inc. **vii** William Morris and Edward Burne-Jones, "The Arming of the Knights," Birmingham Museums and Art Gallery **x** Private Collection **xii** Gerard ter Borch II, "The Suitor's Visit," (detail), c. 1658, Andrew W. Mellon Collection, © 1995 Board of Trustees, National Gallery of Art, Washington **xiv** "View of Broad Quay, Bristol," anonymous, British School, c.1735, City of Bristol Museum and Art Gallery **xxi** David Hockney, "Mr. and Mrs. Clark and Percy," 1970-1971. Acrylic, 84" x 120". © David Hockney/Tate Gallery, London/Art Resource **xxviii** "The Terrible Twins" by P. J. Crook, 1989. Courtesy Montpelier Sandelson, London **xxxvi–1** William Morris and Edward Burne-Jones, "The Arming of the Knights," (detail)/Birmingham Museums and Art Gallery **1, 42, 44, 88, 95,100(icon)** M805fol.48/The Pierpont Morgan Library/ Art Resource **2(t)** Copyright British Museum **2(bl)** Superstock, Inc. **2(br)** Erich Lessing/Art Resource **3(t)** Colchester and Essex Museum **3(bl)** Universitetets Oldsaksamling, Oslo **3(br)** Copyright British Museum **8, 13, 16–17, 21** Werner Forman/Art Resource, NY **27** Bibliothèque Nationale, Paris **31** Scala/Art Resource **32** Michael Holford **33(t)** Copyright British Museum **33(bl)** Koninklijk Instituut voor de Tropen, Amsterdam **33(br)** Hirmer Fotoarchiv, Munich **34(t)** Sonia Halliday **34(cl,cr,br)** Photofest **34(bl)** Foto Marburg/Art Resource **42(l)** Giraudon/Art Resource **42(r), 43(l)** British Library **43(c)** Reverend K. Wilkinson Riddle **43(r)** Erich Lessing/Art Resource **45** Bodleian Library, Oxford **46** British Library **51** Museum of London **53** M630fol.12/The Pierpont Morgan Library/Art Resource **54** Copyright British Museum **56** The Huntington Library, San Marino, California **61** Bridgeman/Art Resource **69** British Library **74** M805fol.48/The Pierpont Morgan Library/ Art Resource **77** E. Hugo **80** Lambeth Palace Library **84** Museo de Arte de Ponce **88** P. Kent **89** The Metropolitan Museum of Art, The Cloisters Collection, Munsey Fund, 1932 (32.130.3a) **90(t)** Bridgeman/Art Resource **90–91** Birmingham Museums and Art Gallery **90(b)** New York Public Library **91(t)** Art Resource **91(b)** Kobal Collection **92** New York Public Library **93** Illustrations by N. C. Wyeth, from *The Boy's King Arthur* by Sidney Lanier are used with the permission of Charles Scribner's Sons, copyright renewed 1945 N. C. Wyeth **101** Richard C. Allen/The Carson Collection **102** Bridgeman/Art Resource **103(t)** Bibliothèque Nationale, Paris **103(b)** M630fol.12, The Pierpont Morgan Library/Art Resource **104–105** Private Collection **106–107** title art, Janice Clark **106(t)** Scala/Art Resource **106(b)** National Portrait Gallery, London **107(t)** Armillary sphere & telescope, Ancient Art & Architecture Collection/Ronald Sheridan Photo-Library; Books, Erich Lessing/Art Resource; da Vinci Self-Portrait, Scala/Art Resource; Sheet music, Folger Shakespeare Library; Lute, The Granger Collection **109** National Portrait Gallery, London **110, 119** Victoria & Albert Museum, London/Art Resource **128** Tate Gallery, London/Art Resource **146(t)** Copyright British Museum **147** Scale drawing by Irwin Smith from *Shakespeare's Globe Playhouse: A Modern Reconstruction in Text and Scale Drawings* by Irwin Smith. Charles Scribner's Sons, New York, 1956. Hand colored by Cheryl Kucharzak **155** Kunsthaus Zurich, © 1995, Copyright by Kunsthaus Zurich. All rights reserved. **165, 179** From the Art Collection of the Folger Shakespeare Library **192–193, 194–195** bloody backrounds, Diane Cole **192, 193** Copyright British Museum **194** Photofest **195** UPI/Corbis-Bettmann **196** Courtesy Diane Bray **205(t)** Victoria & Albert Museum, London/Art Resource **205(b)** Tate Gallery, London/Art Resource **209** Art Resource **210** Laing Art Gallery, Newcastle upon Tyne (Tyne and Wear Museums) **215(tl)** Bridgeman/Art Resource **215(tr)** Courtesy Anthony Green. R. A. c/o The Piccadilly Gallery, London, W1X 1PF **215(b)** © National Trust Photographic Library **217** Kenwood House, Hampstead/Bridgeman Art Library, London/Superstock, Inc. **220–221** Gerard ter Borch II, "The Suitor's Visit" (detail), c. 1658, Andrew W. Mellon Collection, © 1995 Board of Trustees, National Gallery of Art, Washington **222–223** ARXIU MAS **225** National Portrait Gallery, London **228** Staatliche Kunstsammlungen, Dresden. Photo: Sachische Landesbibliothek, Dresden **232(t)** Copyright British Museum **232(b)** Granger Collection **235** Courtesy Lord Sackville, Photo: Lime Tree Studios **239** UPI/Corbis-Bettmann **240(t)** Gamma-Liaison **240(b)** Gamma-Liaison **242–243** UPI/Corbis-Bettmann **244** Diltz/Gamma-Liaison **250–251(t&b)** Scala/Art Resource **250–251(c)** Bridgeman/Art Resource **253** National Portrait Gallery, London **257** Courtesy of the Fogg Art Museum, Harvard University Art Museums, Gift of W. A. White **263** Copyright British Museum **263(background)** Superstock, Inc. **268** Scala/Art Resource **276** Worcester Art Museum, Worcester, MA/Superstock, Inc. **276–277(background)** Superstock, Inc. **277** Everett Collection, Inc. **278(t)** M945fol.168v/The Pierpont Morgan Library/Art Resource **278(b)** Victoria & Albert Museum, London/Art Resource **279(tl)** Tate Gallery, London/E. T. Archives, London/Superstock, Inc. **279(b)** Museo del Prado, Madrid, Spain/A. K. G., Berlin/Superstock, Inc. **288(t)** Courtesy Lord Sackville, Photo: Lime Tree Studios **288(b)** Copyright British Museum **289** Scala/Art Resource **290–291** "View of Broad Quay, Bristol" (detail), anonymous, British School, c.1735, City of Bristol Museum and Art Gallery

291, 292, 294, 328, 331, 335(icon) T. H. Shepherd, "Arthur's Club House, St. James's Street," (detail)/Superstock, Inc. **295** National Portrait Gallery, London **297** Tate Gallery, London/Art Resource **304** Copyright British Museum **305** National Portrait Gallery, London **307** Winslow Homer, "Blackboard," Gift (Partial and Promised) of Jo Ann and Julian Ganz, Jr., in Honor of the 50th Anniversary of the National Gallery of Art, © 1995 Board of Trustees, National Gallery of Art, Washington **313** Bodleian Library, University of Oxford **328(b)** Central Broadcasting **329(tr&b)** Tribune Media Services **330** Jack Higgins **336(t)** National Portrait Gallery, London/Superstock, Inc. **336(c)** Granger Collection **336(b), 337(all)** National Portrait Gallery, London/Superstock, Inc. **339** Corbis-Bettmann Archive **341** Yale Center for British Art, Paul Mellon Collection **343, 349** Pepys Library, by permission of the Master and Fellows, Magdalene College, Cambridge **350, 352–353** National Portrait Gallery, London **360** Scottish National Portrait Gallery, photo by Tom Scott **362, 370(t)** Copyright British Museum **370(b)** Bibliothèque Nationale, Paris **371** Scala/Art Resource **372(t)** Giraudon/Art Resource **372(c)** Erich Lessing/Art Resource **372–373(background)** FPG International Corp. **373(t)** © 1997 Andy Warhol Foundation for the Visual Arts/ARS, New York **373(l)** Library of Congress **381(t)** Tate Gallery, London/Art Resource **381(b)** National Portrait Gallery, London **386–387(t), 390** Museum of London **386–387(b)** Bridgeman/Art Resource **391(t)** The Minneapolis Institute of Arts **391(b)** Associated Newspapers Limited **397, 398, 400, 431, 438, 444(icon)** Dante Gabriel Rossetti, "Reverie" (detail), Christie's, London/Superstock, Inc. **397, 446, 448, 475, 481, 487(icon)** Edvard Munch, "Self-Portrait in Weimar," (detail)/Munch Museum, Oslo, Norway/Lerner Fine Art/Superstock, Inc. **397, 488, 490, 507, 513, 518(icon)** Giovanni Stradano, "Alchemist Laboratory" (detail), Palazzo Vecchio, Florence, Italy/E. T. Archives, London/Superstock, Inc. **396–397** John Constable, "The Hay Wain," 1821 (detail) Reproduced by courtesy of the Trustees, The National Gallery, London **398(t)** Victoria & Albert Museum, London/Art Resource **398–399** Superstock, Inc. **399(tl&tr)** Copyright British Museum **399(b)** Tate Gallery, London/Art Resource **401** National Portrait Gallery, London **403** The Metropolitan Museum of Art, The Elisha Whittelsey Collection, The Elisha Whittelsey Fund, 1967 (67.809.16) **407** Copyright British Museum **408** National Portrait Gallery, London **411** National Railway Museum/Science & Society Picture Library **416** National Portrait Gallery, London **419** Courtesy of the Arthur M. Sackler Museum, Harvard University Art Museums, Loan from Private Collection **422** National Portrait Gallery, London **424** Bridgeman/Art Resource **431** Honolulu Academy of Arts **432** Staatliche Museen Preussischer Kulturbesitz, Antikenmuseum, Berlin **433** National Museum of American History/Smithsonian Institution **434 & 435(all)** Allan Hobson/SS/Photo Researchers **436** Detroit Institute of Arts, Michigan/A.K.G., Berlin/Superstock, Inc. **445** Yale Center for British Art, Paul Mellon Collection **446–447(t)** Copyright British Museum **446(c)** Mansell Collection **446(b)** Bulloz **447(c)** Trustees of the Wedgwood Museum, Barlaston, Staffordshire, England **447(b)** Library of Congress **449** National Portrait Gallery, London **451** Bridgeman/Art Resource **455** Corbis-Bettmann Archive **456** Plate 66 from *Mrs. Hurst Dancing*, text by Gordon Mingay, Watercolors by Diana Sperling. © Victor Gollancz Ltd. 1981 **462** Granger Collection **465** Tate Gallery, London/Art Resource **468** Corbis-Bettmann Archive **472** Bequest of Mrs. Martin Brimmer, Courtesy, Museum of Fine Arts, Boston **475, 476(l)** Corbis-Bettmann Archive **476(r), 478(l)** Granger Collection **477(l)** National Portrait Gallery, London **477(r)** UPI/Corbis-Bettmann **478(r), 479(r)** Sophia Smith Collection, Smith College **479(l)** League of Women Voters of Japan **480** Courtesy Tanya Wallace **488–489(E)(b)** Mansell Collection **489(B)(t)** Museo del Prado, Madrid, Spain/Jack Novak/Superstock, Inc. **489(C)(tc)** Walker Art Gallery, Liverpool **489(F)(cl)** Smithsonian Institution **491** Bodleian Library, University of Oxford **492– 493** diorama, Diane Cole **493** Bridgeman/Art Resource **499** Everett Collection, Inc. Hand-colored by Cheryl Kucharzak **503** Scala/Art Resource **507(background)** FPG International Corp. **507** British Library **508–509(background)** FPG International Corp. **508** Museum of Modern Art, Film Stills Archive **510(t)** Alinari/Art Resource **510(bl)** Boltin Picture Library **510(br)** Everett Collection, Inc. **511(bl)** Copyright British Museum **511(br)** Everett Collection, Inc. **512(background)** Michael Orton/Tony Stone Images **512** From *A Pictorial History Of Science Fiction* by David Kyle. Copyright © The Hamlyn Publishing Group Limited, 1976 **519** Museum of Modern Art, Film Stills Archive **520(t)** Bridgeman/Art Resource **520(b)** Everett Collection, Inc. Hand-colored by Cheryl Kucharzak **521** Bridgeman/Art Resource **523, 524, 526, 559, 564, 569(icon)** Illustration by John Tenniel for *Alice's Adventures in Wonderland* **523, 570, 572, 629, 634, 639(icon)** Ernst Ludwig Kirchner, "Bildnis des Dichters Frank" (detail), Christie's London/Superstock, Inc. **523–524** George Williams Joy, "The Bayswater Omnibus," 1895 (detail)/Museum of London **524(t), 524(b), 525(b)** Hulton Deutsch Collection Ltd. **524(c)** International Museum of Photography/George Eastman House **525(t)** Mansell Collection **527** National Portrait Gallery, London **528** Bridgeman/Art Resource **533** The Saint Louis Art Museum, Bequest of Morton D. May **538(t&b)** National Portrait Gallery, London **541** Erich Lessing/Art Resource **546** Library of Congress **547** Everett Collection, Inc. **554** Corbis-Bettmann Archive **555** High Museum of Art, Atlanta, Georgia; purchase with funds from the Friends of Art 36.20 **560** Brown Brothers **562(tl)** Hulton Deutsch Collection Ltd. **562(tr)** Edwin H. Colbert **562(cr,cl,b)** Mansell Collection **563** Hulton Deutsch Collection Ltd. **570(t)** National Gallery of Canada, Ottawa. Gift of the Massey Collection of English Painting, 1946 **570(tc)** From *Punch*, December 10, 1892, Hand-colored by Cheryl Kucharzak **570(bc)** Newberry Library, Chicago **570(b)** Museum of London **571** Mansell Collection. Hand-colored by Cheryl Kucharzak **573** National Portrait Gallery, London **575**

Tate Gallery, London/Art Resource **580** National Portrait Gallery, London **581** Tate Gallery, London/Art Resource **585** Drawing by Walter Tiffle **586, 593** North Wind Picture Archives **600** Granger Collection **602** National Portrait Gallery, London **606** By courtesy of the Victoria & Albert Museum, London **611** UPI/Corbis-Bettmann **612** Vasily Kandinsky, "Several Circles No. 323," 1926. The Solomon R. Guggenheim Museum, New York, Photograph by David Heald, © The Solomon R.Guggenheim Foundation, New York (FN41.283) **623** National Portrait Gallery, London **628** Richard C. Allen/Carson Collection **639** From *A Pictorial History Of Science Fiction* by David Kyle. Copyright © The Hamlyn Publishing Group Limited, 1976 **641(t),** Everett Collection **641(b)** Erich Lessing/Art Resource **642** Vasily Kandinsky, "Several Circles No. 323," 1926. The Solomon R. Guggenheim Museum, New York, Photograph by David Heald, © The Solomon R.Guggenheim Foundation, New York (FN41.283) **644–645** Mansell Collection **646** Hand-colored by Cheryl Kucharzak **650–651** Oriental and India Office Collections/British Library, Photo 154 f.31d neg. B6140 **653** Robert Opie Collection **655** National Army Museum, London, **657, 658, 660, 717, 723, 728(icon)** Courtesy Bassano Studios, London **657, 730, 732, 773, 778, 784(icon)** Imperial War Museum, London **657, 786, 788, 843, 846, 851(icon)** Amedeo Modigliani, "Jeanne Hebuterne au Foulard" (detail), Christie's, London/Superstock, Inc. **656–657** Charles Ginner, "Piccadilly Circus," 1912 (detail), Tate Gallery, London/Art Resource **658–659** diorama, Diane Cole **658 & 659 (A,B,C,F,G,I & 658–659(background)** Hulton Deutsch Collection Ltd. **658(D)** Museum of London **658(E)** Mary Evans Picture Library **659(H)** Copyright British Museum **661** National Portrait Gallery, London **662(r)** Kobal Collection **662(l)** Museum of Modern Art, Film Stills Archive **667, 670, 678, 690–691** Martha Swope/© Time, Inc. **696(l)** Angus McBean **696(r)** Zoe Dominic **697(l)** Mark Douet **697(r)** Photofest **705, 713** Martha Swope/Time, Inc. **717(t), 720(t&b)** Hulton Deutsch Collection Ltd. **717(b)** International Museum of Photography/George Eastman House **721** Everett Collection, Inc. **722** Photofest **728, 729** Robert Opie Collection **730(t)** National Archives **730(c)** Imperial War Museum, London **730(b) & 731(inset)** From the copy in the Bowman Gray Collection, University of North Carolina at Chapel Hill **731(t)** Imperial War Museum, London **734(t)** Culver Pictures Inc. **734(c)** Fitzwilliam Museum, University of Cambridge **734(b)** Culver Pictures Inc. **736** Imperial War Museum, London **742, 746, 751** Vera Brittain Archive/Mills Memorial Library/McMaster University, Hamilton, Ontario, Canada **757** Corbis-Bettmann Archive **758** From the copy in the Bowman Gray Collection, University of North Carolina at Chapel Hill **768** AP/Wide World **774, 776** Imperial War Museum, London **784** ABC News photo **786–787** Tate Gallery, London/Art Resource **787(br)** Corbis-Bettmann Archive **789** National Portrait Gallery, London **791** Plymouth City Museums & Art Gallery **796** Courtesy of Alfred Knopf **797** Collection of Dr. John Boreske/Vose Galleries of Boston **805** UPI/Corbis-Bettmann **807** ©1996 C. Hercovici, Brussels/Artists Rights Society (ARS), New York/Giraudon/Art Resource **808–809** Musee Royaux des Beaux-Arts de Belgique, Brussels **813** Courtesy of Harcourt, Brace **814** Victoria & Albert Museum, London/Art Resource **822** National Portrait Gallery, London **824** Bridgeman/Art Resource **837** Gallery, Vishva-Bharati University, Santiniketan, India **842** UPI/Corbis-Bettmann **843(l&r), 844(tl,tr,b), 845(tl)** Tate Gallery, London/Art Resource **845(tr)** National Art Gallery of New Zealand **845(b)** Bridgeman/Art Resource **852(t)** Martha Swope, © Time, Inc. **852(b)** Plymouth City Museums & Art Gallery **853** Imperial War Museum, London **854–855** David Hockney, "Mr. and Mrs. Clark and Percy" (detail), 1970-1971. Acrylic, 84" x 120". © David Hockney. Tate Gallery, London/Art Resource **855, 856, 858, 891, 896, 901(icon)** Superstock, Inc. **855, 902, 904, 943, 947, 952(icon)** Pablo Picasso, "Buste D'Homme au Chapeau," (detail) ©1997 Succession Picasso/Artists Rights Society (ARS), New York/Superstock, Inc. **856(t&b)** UPI/Corbis-Bettmann **856(c)** AFP/Corbis-Bettmann **857(tl&tr)** UPI/Corbis-Bettmann **857(b)** S. Ferry/Gamma-Liaison **859** AP/Wide World **860** Popperfoto **868** Brian Seed/Life Magazine, Time, Inc. **869** National Maritime Museum, London **875(t)** Rogers RBO/Camera Press/Globe Photos, Inc. **875(b)** Evan Richman/Reuters/Corbis-Bettmann **876** Diana Walker/Gamma-Liaison **880** George Braziller **881** The Brooklyn Museum, 82.65.2250, Collection of Charles and Lucille Plotz **890** The Seattle Art Museum, Gift of Katherine White and the Boeing Company, Photo: Paul Macapia **891** Corbis-Bettmann Archive **892** AP/Wide World **893(t)** Ian Berry/Magnum Photos **893(b)** Dick Arthur/*Honolulu Advertiser*, HI/Rothco **894** Courtesy Dr. Edward Brynn **902(A)** Spooner/ Gamma-Liaison **902(B)** Joe Taver/Gamma-Liaison **902(D)** Alistair Berg/Spooner/Gamma-Liaison **902(E)** Karim Daher/Gamma-Liaison **902(icon)** Superstock, Inc. **903(C)** Reuters/Corbis-Bettmann **903(F)** Katie Arkell/Gamma-Liaison **903(G)** Alistair Berg/Spooner/Gamma-Liaison **903(H)** Jacob Sutton/Gamma-Liaison **906(c)** National Portrait Gallery, London **906(b)** Laurence Acland **909** Ken Joudrey **915** New York Times/NYT Pictures **916–917** The Jean Pigozzi Collection, C. A. A. C., Ltd. **925** Corbis-Bettmann Archive **927** Portal Gallery, London **932** © Tara Heinemann 1984 **933** Everett Collection, Inc. **953** The Brooklyn Museum, 82.65.2250, Collection of Charles and Lucille Plotz **954(t)** Diana Walker/Gamma-Liaison **954(b)** Portal Gallery, London **959** Bibliothèque Nationale, Paris **960, 965** Portal Gallery, London **964** Granger Collection

Handlettering by Eliza Schulte.

Electronic Illustrations by Bruce Burdick, Steven Kiecker, Nikki Limper, and Gwen Plogman.

Custom Literature Database

The *ScottForesman Custom Literature Database* is a collection of over 1400 literary selections. Over 200 titles in the database have lessons to support students as they read. Eight indices—Title, Author, Genre, Subject, Nationality, Literary Themes, Anthology Correlations, and Lessons for Selected Titles—help you navigate through the database, allowing you to search for, view, and print the exact selection you want. The Anthology Correlations index lets you identify titles in the database correlated to *ScottForesman Literature and Integrated Studies.*

Address to the Apostles from Bible, Matthew, 10:5–42*
African Proverbs
"Aladdin, or The Wonderful Lamp" from *A Thousand and One Nights*
"Ali Baba and the Forty Thieves" from *A Thousand and One Nights*
Anglo-Saxon Riddles
Apocalyptic Utterances from Bible, Matthew 24:4–25:46
Articles of Confederation
Babylonian Law from *The Hammurabi Code*
Battle of Brunanburh, The
"Battle of Otterbourne, The"
Bhagavad Gita
Bible, Acts of the Apostles
Bible, Corinthians 1:13
Bible, Genesis 1–3
Bible, John
Bible, Luke 10:25–37*
Bible, Mark
Bible, Psalm 1
Bible, Psalm 8
Bible, Psalm 23 in Six Translations
Bible, Psalm 24
Bible, Psalm 91
Bible, Psalm 100*
Bible, Psalm 137
Bible, Ruth*
"Birth of Hatshepsut, The"
Birth of Jesus, The from Bible, Matthew 1:18–4:17
"Bonnie George Campbell"
"Bonny Barbara Allan"
Book of Jonah, The from The Hebrew Bible
"Brahman, the Tiger and the Six Judges, The"*
Brown v. *Board of Education of Topeka**
"Caedmon's Hymn"
Chinese Exclusion Act*
Civil Rights Act of 1964*
"Clementine"
Code of Manu, The
Constitution of the Confederate States of America, The
Constitution of the United States
Death of Jesus, The from Bible, Matthew 26:14–28:20
"Deep River"
"Demon Lover, The"
"Descent of Ishtar into the Underworld, The"
Dred Scott v. *Sandford*
"Egyptian Love Song"
"Emergence Song"
"Enchanted Horse, The" from *A Thousand and One Nights*
Everyman
"Experiences of a Chinese Immigrant" from *The Independent**
"Follow the Drinking Gourd"*
"Get Up and Bar the Door"
Gibbons v. *Ogden*
"Go Down, Moses"*
Hammurabi Code, The
"How Thoutii Took the Town of Joppa"
"Joshua Fit de Battle ob Jericho"
Kingdom of Heaven Parables from Bible, Matthew 13:1–52
Laws, The from Bible, Exodus 19:1–23:33
"Little Old Sod Shanty on the Claim, The"
"Lord Randal"
Magna Carta
Marbury v. *Madison*
"May Colvin"*
Mayflower Compact, The
NAACP v. *Alabama*
"Old Chisholm Trail, The"
On Humility and Forgiveness from Bible, Matthew 18:1–35
Parables from Bible, Luke*
"Pat Works on the Railway"
"Peasant and the Workman, The"
Plessy v. *Ferguson*
Preamble to the Constitution of the Knights of Labor
Prince Shotuku's Constitution
Resolution of the Stamp Act Congress
"Scheherazade" from *A Thousand and One Nights*
"Seafarer, The"
Second Shepherd's Play, The
Seneca Falls Declaration of Sentiments and Resolutions, The
Sermon on the Mount from Bible, Matthew 5:1–7:27
"Seven Voyages of Sindbad the Sailor, The" from *A Thousand and One Nights**
"Shenandoah"
"Shipwrecked Sailor, The"
*Sir Gawain and the Green Knight**
"Sir Patrick Spens"*
Song of Creation
"Story of Rhampsinites, The"
"Story of the Fisherman, The" from *A Thousand and One Nights*
"Sumer is icumen in"
Sura LXXV—The Resurrection from *The Koran*
Sura LXXVI—Man from T
"Swing Low, Sweet Chariot
"Three Ravens, The"
Treaty of Peace with Great Brita
Trustees of Dartmouth College v. *Woodward*
"Twa Corbies, The"
Virginia Bill of Rights
Vishnu Purana
Volstead Act, The
"Wanderer, The"
"Western Wind"
"Wife of Usher's Well, The"

Adams, Henry
Education of Henry Adams, The, Chapter XXV, "The Dynamo and the Virgin"
"Prayer to the Virgin of Chartres"

Addison, Joseph
"Artifices in Tragedy" from *The Spectator*
"Party Patches" from *The Spectator*
"Sir Roger at Church" from *The Spectator*
"Westminster Abbey" from *The Spectator*
"Will Wimble" from *The Spectator**
"Wit: True, False, and Mixed"

Aelfric, Abbot
"Colloquy on the Occupations, A"

Aesop
"Crow and the Pitcher, The"
"Fox and the Crow, The"
"Fox and the Grapes, The"

---

*This selection includes background information, a study guide, and comprehension and critical thinking questions in a lesson on the disc.

ustom Literature Database

Hound and the Hare, The"
Mice and the Weasels, The"
"North Wind and the Sun, The

Alcaeus
"Drinking Son
"Summer"
"Winte

May
ey of Humiliation" from
*Women**
l Sketches
-Fashioned Thanksgiving, An"*
awandah, Fourth Spinning Wheel Story"

Alighieri, Dante
Divine Comedy, The, " The Inferno," Canto I
Divine Comedy, The, "The Inferno," Canto III
Divine Comedy, The, "The Inferno," Canto XXXIV

Alline, Henry
"The Conduct of Most Sailors"

Anacreon
"Beauty"
"Combat, The"
"Cup, The"
"Love"

Andersen, Hans Christian
"Emperor's New Clothes, The"*
"Little Mermaid, The"
"Red Shoes, The"
"Snow Queen, The"
"Steadfast Tin Soldier, The"
"Swineherd, The"
"Thumbelina"
"Tinder-Box, The"
"Ugly Duckling, The"*

Anderson, Sherwood
"Discovery of a Father"*
"Stolen Day"

Anonymous
Independent, The
"My mind to me a kingdom is"
"There is a Lady Sweet and Kind"

Anthony, Susan B.
On Woman's Right to Suffrage*
"Political Economy of Women"

Antin, Mary
"Immigrant Goes to School, An" from *The Promised Land**

Aristotle
Poetics, The

Arnold, Matthew
"Isolation, To Marguerite"
"Last Word, The"
"Requiescat"
"Scholar-Gipsy, The"
"Self-Dependence"
"Thyrsis"

Aspinwall, Alicia
"Upsidedownians, The"

Aulnoy, Comtesse d'
"White Cat, The"
"Yellow Dwarf, The"

Aupaumut, Hendrick
A Short Narration of My Last Journey to the Western Contry

Babur
*Babur-nama**

Bacon, Francis
"Of Studies"
"Of Truth"

Bambara, Toni Cade
"Blues Ain't No Mockin Bird"*
"Happy Birthday"*

Barbour, Ralph Henry
"Brewster's Debut"

Beach, Lewis
Clod, The*

Bede
Ecclesiastical History of the English People, The, Book II, Chapters 9–13*
Ecclesiastical History of the English People, The, Book IV, Chapter 24

Behn, Aphra
"Lady's Looking Glass, The"
"Love in Fantastic Triumph Sat from Abdelazar"
Oroonoko

Bellamy, Edward
*Looking Back**

Belloc, Hilaire
"Lion, The"
"Yak, The"

Benét, Stephen Vincent
"By the Waters of Babylon"

Benet, William Rose
"Skater of Ghost Lake, The"

Bennet, John
"Fritz the Master Fiddler"

Bierce, Ambrose
"Occurrence at Owl Creek Bridge, An"

Blackwell, Alice Stone
Indifference of Women, The*

Blake, William
"And did those feet" from *Milton*
"Chimney Sweeper, The" from *Songs of Experience*
"Chimney Sweeper, The," from *Songs of Innocence*
"Divine Image, The" from *Songs of Innocence*
"Holy Thursday" from *Songs of Experience*
"Holy Thursday" from *Songs of Innocence*
"Human Abstract, The" from *Songs of Experience*
"Infant Joy"
"Infant Sorrow"
Introduction ("Hear the voice of the Bard") from *Songs of Experience*
Introduction ("Piping down the valleys") from *Songs of Innocence*
"Lamb, The" from *Songs of Innocence*
"Nurse's Song" from *Songs of Experience*
"Poison Tree, A"
"Proverbs of Hell" from *The Marriage of Heaven and Hell*
"Sick Rose, The"
Song ("How sweet I roamed")
"Tyger, The" from *Songs of Experience*

Bleecker, Ann Eliza
"On the Immensity of Creation"

Boas, Franz
"Raven's Adventures"
"Sedna, Mistress of the Underworld"

Boswell, James
Life of Samuel Johnson, LL.D, The
London Journal, 1762–1763

Bradstreet, Anne
"Contemplations"
"Prologue, The"
"To My Dear and Loving Husband"
"Upon the Burning of Our House, July 10th, 1666"

Brontë, Emily
"No coward soul is mine"
"Remembrance"
Song ("The linnet in the rocky dells")

Brooke, Rupert
"Peace"*

Brooks, Gwendolyn
"Pete at the Zoo"

Brothers Grimm
"Bremen Town Musicians, The"*
"Elves and the Shoemaker, The"
"Fisherman and His Wife, The"
"Frog Prince, The"
"Gallant Tailor, The"
"Hansel and Grethel"
"Juniper Tree, The"
"Rapunzel"
"Rumpelstiltskin"*
"Sleeping Beauty, The"
"Snow-white"
"Twelve Dancing Princesses, The"

Brown, Dee
"Katlian and the Iron People"*

Brown, John
Last Speech

Browning, Elizabeth Barrett
Sonnet 1 ("I thought once how Theocritus had sung") from *Sonnets from the Portuguese*
Sonnet 14 ("If thou must love me, let it be for naught") from *Sonnets from the Portuguese*
Sonnet 26 ("I lived with visions for my company") from *Sonnets from the Portuguese*

*This selection includes background information, a study guide, and comprehension and critical thinking questions in a lesson on the disc.

iopin, Kate
'air of Silk Stockings, A"*

Christie, Agatha
"Third-Floor Flat, The"*

Churchill, Winston
Blood, Sweat, and Tears
Dunkirk
Iron Curtain Has Descended, An*
Their Finest Hour

Clay, Henry
On the Compromise of 1850

Clough, Arthur Hugh
"Epi-Strauss-um"
"Latest Decalogue, The"
"Say not the struggle nought availeth"

Cobb, Frank I. and Walter Lippmann
Interpretation of President Wilson's Fourteen Points

Coleridge, Samuel Taylor
Biographia Literaria
"Christabel"
"Eolian Harp, The"
"Frost at Midnight"
"Kubla Khan"
"Rime of the Ancient Mariner, The"
"This Lime-Tree Bower My Prison"

Colum, Padraic
"Aegir's Feast: How Thor Triumphed"
"Baldur's Doom"
"Building of the Wall, The"
"Children of Loki, The"
"Dwarf's Hoard, and the Curse That It Brought"
"How Brock Brought Judgement on Loki"
"How Freya Gained Her Necklace and How Her Loved One Was Lost to Her"
"How Thor and Loki Be-Fooled Thrym the Giant"
"Iduna and Her Apples: How Loki Put the Gods in Danger"
"Odin Goes to Mimir's Well; His Sacrifice for Wisdom"
"Sif's Golden Hair: How Loki Wrought Mischief in Asgard"
"Sigurd's Youth" from *The Children of Odin*
"Thor and Loki in the Giants' City"
"Twilight of the Gods, The"
"Valkyrie, The"

Conrad, Joseph
Secret Sharer, The
*Youth**

Crane, Stephen
"Bride Comes to Yellow Sky, The"
"Do not weep, maiden, for war is kind"
"Episode of War, An"
"I met a seer"
"Man saw a ball of gold in the sky, A"
"Mystery of Heroism, A"
"Open Boat, The"*
Red Badge of Courage, The
"Think as I Think"

Crevecoeur, Michel-Guillaume Jean de
Letters from an American Farmer

Curtin, Jeremiah, and Hewitt, J. N. B.
"Woman Who Fell from the Sky, The"

Curtis, Natalie
"Creation"
"Deathless One and the Wind, The"
"Morning Star and the Evening Star, The"
"Origin of Corn and Pemmican, The"
"Stories of Wak-Chung-Kaka, the Foolish One"
"Story of Gomoidema Pokoma-Kiaka, The"
"Story of the First Mother, The"
"Story of Wakiash and the First Totem-Pole, The"*
"Vision of the Earth-Maker, A"*

Davis, Jefferson
Inaugural Address of Jefferson Davis
Last Message to the People of the Confederacy
Message to Congress

Davis, Richard H.
"Midsummer Pirates"

de la Mare, Walter
"All But Blind"
"All That's Past"
"Cake and Sack"
"Dwelling Place, The"
"Flight, The"
"Listeners, The"*
"Nobody Knows"
"Silver"
"Song of the Mad Prince, The"
"Tartary"
"Up and Down"

De Quincey, Thomas
"On the Knocking at the Gate in *Macbeth*"
"Poetry of Pope, The"

Defoe, Daniel
Essay Upon Projects, An
Journal of the Plague Year, A

Dekker, Thomas
"Lullaby"

Delgado, Reverend Father Fray Carlos
Report Made By Reverend Father Fray Carlos Delgado

Dickens, Charles
David Copperfield
"Signalman, The"*

Dickinson, Emily
"Alter! When the Hills do"
"Apparently with no surprise"
"Because I could not stop for death"
"Bustle in a House, The"
" 'Faith' Is a fine invention"
" 'Hope' is the thing with feathers"
"I felt a Funeral, in my Brain"
"I heard a Fly buzz – when I died"
"I like to see it lap the Miles"
"I taste a liquor never brewed"
"I Years had been from Home"
"I'll tell you how the Sun rose"
"If you were coming in the Fall"
"Morns are meeker than they were, The"
"Much Madness is divinest Sense"
"Narrow Fellow in the grass, A"*
"Of all the Souls that stand create"
"Some keep the Sabbath going to Church"
"Success is counted sweetest"*
"Surgeons must be very careful"
"There's a certain Slant of light"
"This is my letter to the World"
"To make a prairie it takes a clover"
"Triumph – may be of several kinds"*

Dixon, Roland B.
"Creation, The"
"Theft of Fire, The"

Donne, John
"Bait, The"
"Ecstacy, The"
"Flea, The"
"Indifferent, The"
Meditation 17 from *Devotions*
"On His Mistress"
Song ("Go and catch a falling star")
Sonnet 4 ("At the round earth's imagined corners, blow") from *Holy Sonnets**
Sonnet 6 ("This is my play's last scene; here heavens appoint") from *Holy Sonnets*
Sonnet 10 ("Death, be not proud, though some have called thee") from *Holy Sonnets**
Sonnet 14 ("Batter my heart, three-personed God; for You") from *Holy Sonnets*
"Sun Rising, The"
"Valediction: Forbidding Mourning, A"
"Woman's Constancy"

Dorsey, George and Kroeber, Alfred L.
"Star Husband, The"

Douglass, Frederick
*Life and Times of Frederick Douglass, The**
Meaning of July Fourth for the Negro, The*
Narrative of the Life of Frederick Douglass, The
Oration in Memory of Abraham Lincoln

Dowson, Ernest
"Cynara"
"They are not long"

Doyle, Sir Arthur Conan
"Adventure of the Blue Carbuncle, The"*
*Hound of the Baskervilles, The**
"Man with the Twisted Lip, The"*
"Musgrave Ritual, The"
"Redheaded League, The"
"Silver Blaze"

Dryden, John
Absalom and Achitophel
Essay of Dramatic Poesy, An
"I Feed a Flame Within"
Mac Flecknoe
Preface to *Fables Ancient and Modern, The*
"Song for St. Cecilia's Day, A"
"Song Sung by Venus in Honor of Britannia"
"To the Memory of Mr. Oldham"

DuBois, W. E. B.
Behold the Land
Crisis, The
"Of the Meaning of Progress" from *The Souls of Black Folk*
"Of the Sorrow Songs" from *The Souls of Black Folk*

Dunbar, Paul Laurence
"Booker T. Washington"*
"Douglass"*
"Keep A-Pluggin' Away"*
"Life's Tragedy"*
"Love's Apotheosis"*
"We Wear the Mask"

Duncan, Sara Jeannette
Saunterings

Eastman, Charles
*From the Deep Woods to Civilization**

Edwards, Jonathan
Personal Narrative
"Sarah Pierrepont"
"Sinners in the Hands of an Angry God"

Eisenhower, Dwight
Atoms for Peace

Eliot, George
"Lifted Veil, The"*

Elizabeth I
"When I was fair and young"

Emerson, Ralph Waldo
"American Scholar, The"
"Brahma"
"Concord Hymn"
"Days"
"Each and All"
"Experience"
"Fable"
Journals
"Maxims"
"Nature"
"Rhodora, The"
"Self-Reliance"
"Snowstorm, The"

Emmett, Daniel
"Dixie"*

Euripides
*Medea**

Fitzgerald, Edward
Rubáiyát of Omar Khayyám, The

Forster, E. M.
"Celestial Omnibus, The"

Franklin, Benjamin
Autobiography of Benjamin Frankin, The, Franklin's Childhood
Autobiography of Benjamin Franklin, The, Seeking Moral Perfection
"Dialogue Between Franklin and the Gout"
"Edict by the King of Prussia, An"
"Ephemera, The"
Letter of November 21, 1783
"Receipt to Make a New England Funeral Elegy, A"
Speech at the Constitutional Convention
"Way to Wealth, The"
"Whistle, The"
"Witch Trial at Mount Holly, A"*

Freeman, Mary E. Wilkins
"New England Nun, A"*

Freneau, Philip
"Indian Burying-Ground, The"
"On the Memorable Victory"
"To a Caty-Did"
"Wild Honeysuckle, The"

Frost, Robert
"Death of the Hired Man, The"*
"It Bids Pretty Fair"
"Oven Bird, The"
"Pasture, The"
"Road Not Taken, The"
"Runaway, The"
"Time to Talk, A"
"Wood-Pile, The"

Fuller, Margaret
"Woman in the Nineteenth Century"

Garrison, William Lloyd
"Liberator, The"
On the Death of John Brown

Gascoigne, George
"Lullaby of a Lover"

Gilbert, W. S.
"Aesthete, The"
"Englishman, The" from *H. M. S. Pinafore*
"Let the Punishment Fit the Crime" from *The Mikado*
"Policeman's Lot, The"
"They'll None of 'Em Be Missed"

Gissing, George
"Scrupulous Father, The"*

Goddard, Pliny Earle
"Creation, The"

Goldsmith, Oliver
She Stoops to Conquer, Act One
She Stoops to Conquer, Act Two
She Stoops to Conquer, Act Three
She Stoops to Conquer, Act Four
She Stoops To Conquer, Act Five

Gray, Thomas
"Bard, The"
"Elegy Written in a Country Churchyard"*
"Ode on a Distant Prospect of Eton College"
"Sonnet on the Death of Richard West"

Gregory, Lady Augusta
"Boy Deeds of Cuchulain"
*Spreading the News**

Greville, Fulke, Lord Brooke
"Chorus Sacerdotum"
"Of His Cynthia"
"You Little Stars"

Haines, Alice Calhoun
"Tenderhearted Dragon, A"

Hale, Edward Everett
"Man Without a Country, The"*

Hale, Lucretia P.
"Mrs. Peterkin's Tea-party"
"Peterkins Celebrate the Fourth of July, The"

Hancock, H. Irving
"Rip Van WInkle Man-O'-War, The"

Hardy, Thomas
"Afterwards"
"Ah, are you digging on my grave?"
"Beeny Cliff"
"Channel Firing"
"Convergence of the Twain, The"
"Darkling Thrush, The"
"Epitaph on a Pessimist"
"Hap"*
"In Tenebris"
"In Time of 'The Breaking of Nations' "*
"Man He Killed, The"
"Neutral Tones"
*Our Exploits at West Poley**
"Three Strangers, The"
"Walk, The"
"When I Set Out for Lyonesse"
"Withered Arm, The"

Harper, Ellen Watkins
Colored People in America, The
On the Twenty-Fourth Anniversary of the American Anti-Slavery Society

Harris, Joel Chandler
"Creature with No Claws, The"
"Wonderful Tar-Baby Story, The"

---

*This selection includes background information, a study guide, and comprehension and critical thinking questions in a lesson on the disc.

ustom Literature Database

arte, Bret
'Baby Sylvester"
"Brown of Calaveras"
"Iliad of Sandy Bar, The"
"Luck of Roaring Camp, The"
"Miggles"
"Outcasts of Poker Flat, The"*
"Plain Language from Truthful James"
"Tennessee's Partner"

Hawthorne, Nathaniel
"Birthmark, The"
"Dr. Heidegger's Experiment"
"Drowne's Wooden Image"
"Golden Touch, The"*
"Maypole of Merry Mount, The"
"Minister's Black Veil, The"*
"My Kinsman, Major Molineaux"
Notebooks, The
"Rappacinni's Daughter"
"Young Goodman Brown"*

Hayford, J. E. Casely
"As in a Glass Darkly" from *Ethiopia Unbound*
"Black Man's Burden, The" from *Ethiopia Unbound*
"Gold Coast Native Institutions"
"Saving the Wind" from *Ethiopia Unbound*

Hayne, Paul Hamilton
"Aspects of the Pines"

Hazlitt, William
"Macbeth"
My First Acquaintance with Poets
"On Going a Journey"

Heine, Heinrich
"Loreley, The"*

Henley, William Ernest
"Invictus"

Henry, Patrick
Speech in the Virginia Convention, March 23, 1775

Herbert, George
"Altar, The"
"Avarice"
"Bitter-Sweet"
"Collar, The"
"Easter Wings"*
"Love (III)"
"Man"
"Pulley, The"
"Redemption"
"Virtue"*

Heredia y Heredia, Jose Maria
"Ode to Niagara"

Herrick, Robert
"Argument of His Book, The" from *Hesperides*
"Corinna's Going A-Maying"
"Ode for Ben Jonson, An"
"To the Virgins, to Make Much of Time"
"Upon Julia's Clothes"

Hobbes, Thomas
Leviathan, Part I, Chapters 13–15

Holmes, Oliver Wendell
"Ballad of the Oysterman, The"
"Chambered Nautilus, The"
"Last Leaf, The"
"My Last Walk with the Schoolmistress"
"Old Ironsides"

Hoover, Herbert
Philosophy of Rugged Individualism, The

Hopkins, Gerard Manley
"Carrion Comfort"*
"Felix Randal"
"God's Grandeur"
"Habit of Perfection, The"
"No worst, there is none"*
"Pied Beauty"
"Spring and Fall"
"Thou Art Indeed Just, Lord"
"Windhover, The"

Horace
"Ad Leuconeon"
"Death of Cleopatra, The"
"Golden Mean, The"
"Ship of State, The"

Housman, A. E.
"Loveliest of trees, the cherry now"
"Night is freezing fast, The"
"Oh, when I was in love with you"
"On moonlit heath and lonesome bark"
"To an Athlete Dying Young"
"White in the moon the long road lies"

Howard, Henry, Earl of Surrey
"Alas, So All Things Now Do Hold Their Peace"
"Love, that doth reign and live within in my thought"
"Lover's Vow, A"

Howe, Julia Ward
"Battle Hymn of the Republic, The"*

Howells, William Dean
"Christmas Every Day"*
"Editha"

Hudson, W. H.
Idle Days in Patagonia, The, Chapter XII*

Hughes, Rupert
"Latest News About the Three Wishes, The"

Hunt, James Henry Leigh
"Abou Ben Adhem and the Angel"

Huxley, Thomas Henry
"Method of Scientific Investigation, The"

Irving, Washington
"Early Life in Manhattan" from *A History of New York*
"Legend of Sleepy Hollow, The"*
"Rip Van Winkle"
Tour on the Prairies, A

Jackson, Andrew
Second Inaugural Address

Jacobs, Harriet Ann
Incidents in the Life of a Slave Girl, Chapter I*

Jacobs, Joseph
"Dick Whittington and His Cat"*
"Jack and the Beanstalk"
"Jack the Giant-Killer"

Jacobs, W. W.
*Monkey's Paw, The**

James, Henry
"Four Meetings"
"Middle Years, The"
"Real Thing, The"

James, William
"On a Certain Blindness in Human Beings"

Jefferson, Thomas
Declaration of Independence, The
Jefferson's First Inaugural Address
Virginia Statute of Religious Liberty

Jewett, Sarah Orne
"Courting of Sister Wisby, The"
"Hiltons' Holiday, The"
"Miss Tempy's Watchers"
"Native of Winby, A"*
"White Heron, A"

Johnson, Andrew
Johnson's Proclamation of Amnesty

Johnson, James Weldon
Autobiography of an Ex-Colored Man, The, Chapters 1–2*
Autobiography of an Ex-Colored Man, The, Chapters 3–4*

Johnson, Lyndon
Speech at Johns Hopkins University

Johnson, Pauline
"Corn Husker, The"
"Silhouette"

Johnson, Samuel
Dictionary of the English Language
*Life of Milton, The**
London
"On Choosing Friends" from *the Rambler* No. 160
"On Fiction" from *the Rambler* No. 4
"On Forgiveness" from *the Rambler* No. 185
"On Self-Indulgence" from *the Rambler* No. 155
"On Spring" from *the Rambler* No. 5
"On the Death of Dr. Robert Levet"
"On the Tyranny of Parents" from *the Rambler* No. 148
Preface to Shakespeare, The

Jonson, Ben
"Elegy, An"
"Ode to Himself, An"
"On My First Daughter"
"On My First Son"
"Song: To Celia"
"Still to Be Neat"

---

*This selection includes background information, a study guide, and comprehension and critical thinking questions in a lesson on the disc.

Custom Literature Database

Major, Charles
"Big Bear, The"

Malory, Sir Thomas
"Arthur Marries Gwynevere"
Morte d'Arthur, Le, Book 21, Chapters 5–7

Marlowe, Christopher
"Passionate Shepherd to His Love, The"*
Tragical History of Doctor Faustus, The, Act One
Tragical History of Doctor Faustus, The, Act Two
Tragical History of Doctor Faustus, The, Act Three
Tragical History of Doctor Faustus, The, Act Four
Tragical History of Doctor Faustus, The, Act Five

Marshall, George C.
Marshal Plan, The

Marvell, Andrew
"Bermudas"
"Dialogue Between the Soul and Body, A"
"Garden, The"
"Picture of Little T. C. in a Prospect of Flowers, The"

Masefield, John
"Cargoes"*
"Sea-Fever"*

Masters, Edgar Lee
"Cooney Potter"
"Dow Kritt"
"Hortense Robbins"
"Mrs. Kessler"
"Samuel Gardner"

Mather, Cotton
*Wonders of the Invisible World, The**

Maupassant, Guy de
"Boule de Suif" (Ball of Fat)
"Devil, The"
"Diamond Necklace, The"
"Horla, The"
"Piece of String, The"*
"Two Friends"*

McCrae, John
"In Flanders Fields"*

McNeil, Everett
"King of the Golden Woods, The"

Melville, Herman
"Art"
"Bartleby the Scrivener"
"Maldive Shark, The"
"Portent, The"
"Shiloh"

Meredith, George
"Lucifer in Starlight"

Mill, John Stuart
Autobiography of John Stuart Mill, The
On Liberty
"Black Hero of the Ranges, The"*

Milton, John
"Il Penseroso"
"L'Allegro"
"Lycidas"
"On Shakespeare"
"On the Late Massacre in Piedmont"
Paradise Lost, Book VI
Paradise Lost, Book IX*
Paradise Lost, Book XII
"When I consider how my light is spent"

Monroe, James
Monroe Doctrine, The

Montagu, Lady Mary Wortley
"Answer to a Love-Letter in Verse, An"
"Lady's Resolve, The"
"On The Death of Mrs. Bowes"

Moore, Milcah Martha
"Female Patriots, The"

Moore, Thomas
"Harp that once through Tara's halls, The"
"Minstrel Boy, The"

More, Hannah
"Slavery, a Poem"

Morris, William
"Apology, An" from *The Earthly Paradise*
"Defence of Guenevere, The"*
"Haystack in the Floods, The"
"Love Is Enough"

Morton, Sarah Wentworth
"African Chief, The"

Nashe, Thomas
"Autumn"
"Litany in Time of Plague, A"

Nesbit, E.
"Beautiful As the Day"
"Jungle, The"
"Plush Usurper, The"*
"Pride of Perks, The" from *The Railway Children**

Newman, John Henry Cardinal
"Lead, Kindly Light"

Nightingale, Florence
Cassandra

Northup, Solomon
"Christmas on the Plantation" from *Twelve Years a Slave*
"Picking Cotton" from *Twelve Years a Slave*

O. Henry (William Sidney Porter)
"After Twenty Years"
"Cop and the Anthem, The"*
"Furnished Room, The"
"Hearts and Hands"*
"Man Higher Up, The"*
"Ransom of Red Chief, The"*
"Retrieved Reformation, A"*
"Unfinished Story, An"

Owen, Wilfred
"Anthem for Doomed Youth"*
"Strange Meeting"

Ozaki, Yei Theodora
"Momotaro, or the Story of the Son of a Peach"
"Story of Urashima Taro, the Fisher Lad, The"*
"Tongue-Cut Sparrow, The"

Paine, Thomas
American Crisis, The
Common Sense

Palou, Francisco
Life of Junípero Serra

Parris, Robert
"Refusal to Pay Taxes, A" from *The Liberator*

Peacock, Thomas Love
"War Song of Dinas Vawr, The"

Pepys, Samuel
Diary, The

Perrault, Charles
"Bluebeard"
"Cinderella"
"Little Red Ridinghood"
"Puss in Boots"

Plato
Apology
Crito
Phaedo

Po Chu-i
"After Passing the Examination"
"Chu Ch'en Village"*
"Escorting Candidates to the Examination Hall"
"Golden Bells"*
"In Early Summer Lodging in a Temple to Enjoy the Moonlight"
"Old Man with the Broken Arm, The"
"On Board Ship: Reading Yu Chen's Poems"
"Prisoner, The"
"Remembering Golden Bells"*
"Watching the Reapers"

Poe, Edgar Allan
"Annabel Lee"
"Bells, The"
"Cask of Amontillado, The"
"Eldorado"
"Fall of the House of Usher, The"*
"Hop-Frog"
"Israfel"
"Ligeia"
"Masque of the Red Death, The"
"Oval Portrait, The"
"Philosophy of Composition, The"
Poetic Principle, The
"Purloined Letter, The"*
"Tell-Tale Heart, The"
"To Helen"*
"Ulalume"
"William Wilson"

Pope, Alexander
"Eloisa to Abelard"
"Epistle to Dr. Arbuthnot"
"Epistle to Miss Blount"
"Essay on Criticism, An"
Essay on Man, An
"Rape of the Lock, The"

Pyle, Howard
"Enchanted Island, The"
"Epilogue" from *The Merry Adventures of Robin Hood*
"Good Gifts and a Fool's Folly"*
"King Richard Cometh to Sherwood Forest" from *The Merry Adventures of Robin Hood*
"King Stork"
"Prologue" from *The Merry Adventures of Robin Hood*
"Robin Hood and Allan a Dale" from *The Merry Adventures of Robin Hood*
"Robin Hood and Guy of Gisbourne" from *The Merry Adventures of Robin Hood*
"Robin Hood Seeketh the Curtal Friar" from *The Merry Adventures of Robin Hood*
"Robin Hood Turns Butcher" from *The Merry Adventures of Robin Hood*
"Shooting-Match at Nottingham Town, The" from *The Merry Adventures of Robin Hood*
"Story of Sir Gawaine, The" from *The Story of King Arthur and His Knights*
"Winning of a Queen, The" from *The Story of King Arthur and His Knights*
"Winning of a Sword, The" from *The Story of King Arthur and His Knights*
"Winning of Kinghood, The" from *The Story of King Arthur and His Knights*

Quintero, Serafin and Joaquin Alvarez
*Sunny Morning, A**

Raleigh, Sir Walter
"Even Such Is Time"
"Nature, that washed her hands in milk"
"Nymph's Reply to the Shepherd, The"
"Sir Walter Raleigh to His Son"
"To Queen Elizabeth"
"What Is Our Life"

Rand, Silas
"Bird Whose Wings Made the Wind, The"
"Glooscap"

Ransome, Arthur
"Baba Yaga"
"Fire-bird, the Horse of Power and the Princess Vasilissa, The"
"Fool of the World and the Flying Ship, The"

Richards, Laura E.
"Chop-Chin and the Golden Dragon"

Riley, James Whitcomb
"When the frost is on the punkin"

Robinson, Edward Arlington
"Luke Havergal"
"Miniver Cheevy"*
"Mr. Flood's Party"

Roosevelt, Franklin Delano
First Inaugural Address
Four Freedoms Speech
Japanese Relocation Order*

Roosevelt, Franklin Delano and Churchill, Winston S.
Atlantic Charter, The

Roosevelt, Theodore
Roosevelt Corollary to the Monroe Doctrine, The

Rossetti, Christina
"Birthday, A"*
"Goblin Market"
"Sleeping at last"
Song ("When I am dead, my dearest")
"Up-Hill"

Rossetti, Dante Gabriel
"Blessed Damozel, The"
"Eden Bower"
"Sestina (after Dante)"
"Silent Noon"
"Woodspurge, The"

Ruskin, John
Modern Painters
Praeterita

Ryan, Abram Joseph
"Conquered Banner, The"

Sa'di
"Old Man, The" from *Tales from the Gulistan*
"Padshah and the Hermit, The" from *Tales from the Gulistan*
"Padshah and the Slave, The" from *Tales from the Gulistan*
"Solitary Dervish, The" from *Tales from the Gulistan*
"Son of a Rich Man and The Dervish Boy, The" from *Tales from the Gulistan*
"Thief and the Pious Man, The" from *Tales from the Gulistan*

Saki (H. H. Munro)
"Esme"
"Laura"
"Mrs. Packletide's Tiger"
"Sredni Vashtar"
"Tobermory"

Sandburg, Carl
"Chicago"*
"Fog"

Sappho
"Bride, A"*
"Forgotten"
"Garlands"
"Hesperus the Bringer"
"Hymn to Aphrodite"*
"Love's Distraction"
"Ode to Anactoria"

Sarmiento, Domingo Faustino
"Portrait of Facundo, A" from *Life in the Argentine Republic in the Days of the Tyrants*

Sassoon, Siegfried
"Glory of Women"
"Rear Guard, The"
"They"

Scott, Sir Walter
"My Native Land"
"Proud Maisie"*
"Soldier, Rest! Thy Warfare O'er"

Service, Robert W.
"Shooting of Dan McGrew, The"

Seward, William H.
Irrepressible Conflict, An

Shakespeare, William
"All the world's a stage" from *As You Like It**
"Blow, blow thou winter wind!" from *As You Like It*
"Fear no more the heat o' the sun" from *Cymbeline*
Hamlet, Prince of Denmark, Act One
Hamlet, Prince of Denmark, Act Two
Hamlet, Prince of Denmark, Act Three
Hamlet, Prince of Denmark, Act Four
Hamlet, Prince of Denmark, Act Five
King Lear, Act One
King Lear, Act Two
King Lear, Act Three
King Lear, Act Four
King Lear, Act Five
Midsummer Night's Dream, A, Act One
Midsummer Night's Dream, A, Act Two
Midsummer Night's Dream, A, Act Three
Midsummer Night's Dream, A, Act Four
Midsummer Night's Dream, A, Act Five
Much Ado About Nothing, Act One
Much Ado About Nothing, Act Two
Much Ado About Nothing, Act Three
Much Ado About Nothing, Act Four

---

*This selection includes background information, a study guide, and comprehension and critical thinking questions in a lesson on the disc.

Custom Literature Database

Much Ado About Nothing, Act Five
"O Mistress Mine" from *Twelfth Night*
Othello, the Moor of Venice, Act One
Othello, the Moor of Venice, Act Two
Othello, the Moor of Venice, Act Three
Othello, the Moor of Venice, Act Four
Othello, the Moor of Venice, Act Five
"Sigh No More" from *Much Ado About Nothing*
Sonnet 1 ("From fairest creatures we desire increase")
Sonnet 3 ("Look in thy glass, and tell the face thou viewest")
Sonnet 8 ("Music to hear, why hear'st thou music sadly?")
Sonnet 12 ("When I do count the clock that tells the time")
Sonnet 15 ("When I consider everything that grows")
Sonnet 18 ("Shall I compare thee to a summer's day?")
Sonnet 22 ("My glass shall not persuade me I am old")
Sonnet 23 ("As an unperfect actor on the stage")
Sonnet 27 ("Weary with toil, I haste me to my bed")
Sonnet 29 ("When, in disgrace with fortune and men's eyes")
Sonnet 30 ("When to the sessions of sweet silent thought")*
Sonnet 33 ("Full many a glorious morning have I seen")
Sonnet 46 ("Mine eye and heart are at mortal war")
Sonnet 47 ("Betwixt mine eye and heart a league is took")
Sonnet 49 ("Against that time, if ever that time come")
Sonnet 51 ("Thus can my love excuse the slow offense")
Sonnet 54 ("O, how much more doth beauty beauteous seem")
Sonnet 55 ("Not marble nor the gilded monuments")*
Sonnet 56 ("Sweet love, renew thy force!")
Sonnet 62 ("Sin of self-love possesseth all mine eye")
Sonnet 64 ("When I have seen by Time's fell hand defaced")
Sonnet 65 ("Since brass, nor stone, nor earth, nor boundless sea")
Sonnet 71 ("No longer mourn for me when I am dead")
Sonnet 73 ("That time of year though mayst in me behold")
Sonnet 76 ("Why is my verse so barren of new pride?")
Sonnet 80 ("O, how faint when I of you do write")
Sonnet 87 ("Farewell! Thou art too dear for my possessing")
Sonnet 92 ("But do thy worst to steal thyself away")
Sonnet 93 ("So shall I live, supposing thou art true")
Sonnet 94 ("They that have power to hurt and will do none")
Sonnet 97 ("How like a winter hath my absence been")
Sonnet 98 ("From you have I been absent in the spring")
Sonnet 104 ("To me, fair friend, you never can be old")
Sonnet 106 ("When in the chronicle of wasted time")
Sonnet 107 ("Not mine own fears nor the prophetic soul")
Sonnet 109 ("O, never say that I was false of heart")
Sonnet 110 ("Alas, 'tis true, I have gone here and there")
Sonnet 113 ("Since I left you, mine eye is in my mind")
Sonnet 115 ("Those lines that I before have writ do lie")
Sonnet 116 ("Let me not to the marriage of true minds")
Sonnet 120 ("That you were once unkind befriends me now")
Sonnet 128 ("How oft, when thou, my music, music play'st")
Sonnet 129 ("Th' expense of spirit in a waste of shame")
Sonnet 132 ("Thine eyes I love, and they, as pitying me")
Sonnet 138 ("When my love swears that she is made of truth")
Sonnet 140 ("Be wise as thou art cruel")
Sonnet 144 ("Two loves I have, of comfort and despair")
Sonnet 146 ("Poor soul, the center of my sinful earth")
Sonnet 147 ("My love is as a fever, longing still")
Taming of the Shrew, The, Act One
Taming of the Shrew, The, Act Two
Taming of the Shrew, The, Act Three
Taming of the Shrew, The, Act Four
Taming of the Shrew, The, Act Five
Tempest, The, Act One
Tempest, The, Act Two
Tempest, The, Act Three
Tempest, The, Act Four
Tempest, The, Act Five
"Under the Greenwood Tree" from *As You Like It*
"Who Is Silvia?" from *Two Gentlemen of Verona*
"Winter" from *Love's Labour's Lost*

Shaw, Bernard
Epilogue from *Pygmalion*

Shelley, Mary
Frankenstein

Shelley, Percy Bysshe
"Cloud, The"
Defence of Poetry, A
"Dirge, A"
"England in 1819"
"Hymn of Pan"
"Lines: 'When the lamp is shattered' "
"Song to the Men of England"
"To a Skylark"*
"To Jane: The Invitation"
"To—" ("Music, When Soft Voices Die")
"To Wordsworth"

Sheridan, Richard Brinsley
School for Scandal, The, Act One
School for Scandal, The, Act Two
School for Scandal, The, Act Three
School for Scandal, The, Act Four
School for Scandal, The, Act Five

Sidney, Sir Philip
"My true love hath my heart" from *The Arcadia*
"Oft Have I Mused"
Sonnet 31 ("With how sad steps, Oh Moon, thou climb'st the skies") from *Astrophel and Stella*
Sonnet 39 ("Come sleep! O sleep the certain knot of peace") from *Astrophel and Stella*
Sonnet 41 ("Having this day my horse, my hand, my lance") from *Astrophel and Stella*
"Thou Blind Man's Mark"

Skinner, Alanson, and Slaterlee, John V.
"Manabozho"

Smith, John
Description of New England, A
Generall Historie of Virginia, New England, and the Summer Isles, The

Sophocles
Antigone
Electra
Oedipus at Colonus
Oedipus the King

Southey, Robert
"Cataract of Lodore, The"
"Old Man's Comforts, The"*
" 'You are old, Father William' "*

Spenser, Edmund
"Epithalamion"
Faerie Queene, The, from Canto I
Sonnet 1 ("Happy ye leaves when as those lilly hands") from *Amoretti*
Sonnet 26 ("Sweet is the rose, but grows upon a briar") from *Amoretti*
Sonnet 30 ("My love is like to ice, and I to fire") from *Amoretti*
Sonnet 34 ("Like a ship, that through the ocean wide") from *Amoretti*
Sonnet 54 ("Of this worlds theatre in which we stay") from *Amoretti*
Sonnet 67 ("Lyke as a huntsman after weary chase") from *Amoretti*
Sonnet 75 ("One day I wrote her name upon the strand") from *Amoretti*
Sonnet 79 ("Men call you fayre, and you doe credit it") from *Amoretti*

Stansbury, Joseph
"Ode for the Year 1776"

*This selection includes background information, a study guide, and comprehension and critical thinking questions in a lesson on the disc.

Custom Literature Database

Wheatley, Phillis
Letter to Rev. Occum
"To His Excellency General Washington"
"To S. M., A Young African Painter on Seeing His Works"
"To the Right Honourable William, Earl of Dartmouth"

Whitman, Walt
"A Child's Amaze"
"As Toilsome I Wander'd Virginia's Woods"
"Beat! Beat! Drums!"*
"Beautiful Women"
"Bivouac on a Mountain Side"
"Cavalry Crossing a Ford"
"Crossing Brooklyn Ferry"*
"For You O Democracy"*
"I saw in Louisiana a live-oak growing"
"Joy, Shipmate, Joy!"
"Noiseless patient spider, A"
"On the Beach at Night"
"On the Beach at Night Alone"
"Passage to India"
"Sight in Camp in the Daybreak Gray and Dim, A"
"Song of Myself," 1,16,17,24
"Song of Myself," 3
"Sparkles from the Wheel"
"We Two Boys Together Clinging"
"When I heard the learn'd astronomer"
"When Lilacs Last in the Dooryard Bloomed"*

Whittier, John Greenleaf
"Barbara Frietchie"*
"Hampton Beach"
"Ichabod"
"Kansas Emigrants, The"
"Telling the Bees"

Wiesel, Elie
Acceptance Speech for the Nobel Peace Prize

Wilde, Oscar
"Ballad of Reading Gaol, The"*
"Birthday of the Infanta, The"
"Canterville Ghost, The"
"De Profundis"
"Few Maxims for the Instruction of the Over-Educated, A"
"Grave of Shelley, The"
"Happy Prince, The"
Importance of Being Earnest, The, Act One*
Importance of Being Earnest, The, Act Two
Importance of Being Earnest, The, Act Three
"Phrases and Philosophies for the Use of the Young"
"Prison Reform" from the *Daily Chronicle*
"Symphony in Yellow"

Wilson, Woodrow
First Inaugural Address
Peace Without Victory

Wordsworth, William
"Composed upon Westminster Bridge"*
"Elegiac Stanzas"
"Expostualtion and Reply"
"I travelled among unknown men"
"I Wandered Lonely as a Cloud"
"It is a beauteous evening, calm and free"*
"Lines Written in Early Spring"
"London, 1802"
"Lucy Gray"
"Michael"
"Nuns fret not at their convent's narrow room"
"Ode: Intimations of Immortality from Recollections of Early Childhood"*
Preface to *Lyrical Ballads*
Prelude, The, Book 1
"Resolution and Independence"
"She Dwelt Among the Untrodden Ways"
"slumber did my spirit seal, A"
"Solitary Reaper, The"
"Strange fits of passion have I known"
"Three Years She Grew"
"To a Skylark"

Wyatt, Sir Thomas
"Divers Doth Use"
"He is not dead that sometime hath a fall"
"My lute awake!"
"They Flee from Me"
"Varium et Mutabile"
"Whoso List to Hunt"

Zimmermann, Arthur
Zimmerman Note, The

*This selection includes background information, a study guide, and comprehension and critical thinking questions in a lesson on the disc.